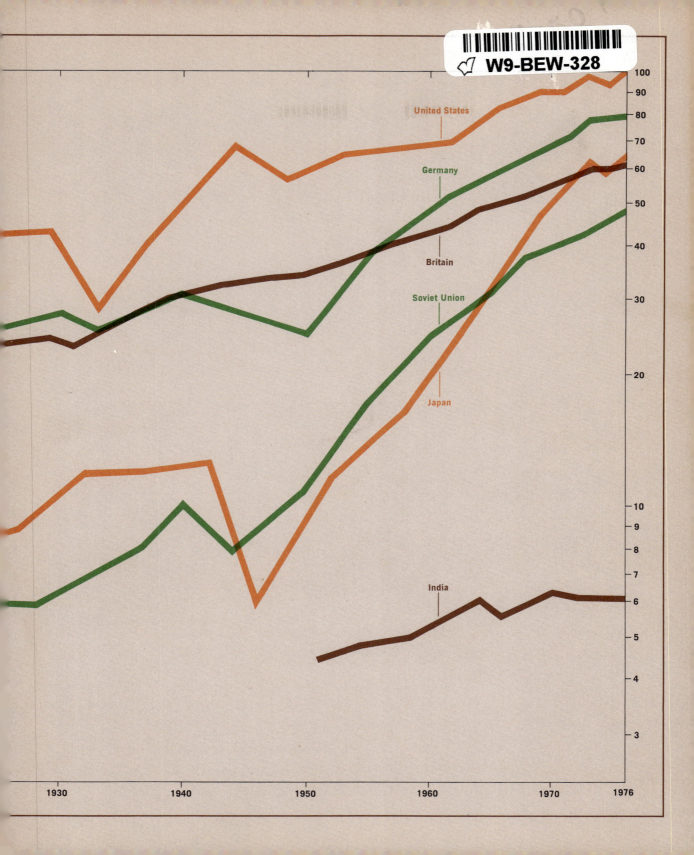

# ECONOMICS

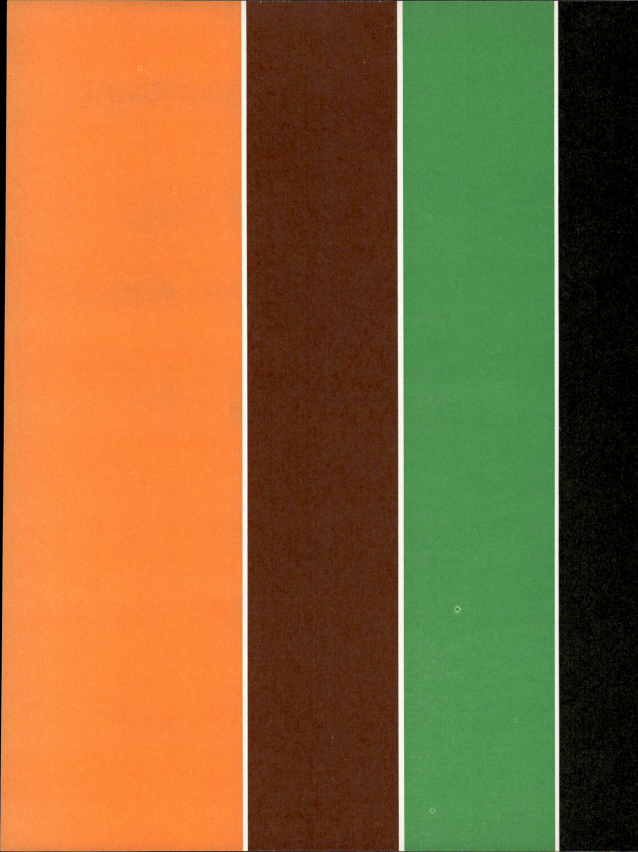

# ECONOMICS

**TENTH EDITION**

## PAUL A. SAMUELSON

**Institute Professor**
**Massachusetts Institute of Technology**

with the assistance
in statistical updating of

## PETER TEMIN

**Professor of Economics**
**Massachusetts Institute of Technology**

## McGRAW-HILL BOOK COMPANY

New York  St. Louis  San Francisco  Auckland  Düsseldorf  Johannesburg  Kuala Lumpur  London
Mexico  Montreal  New Delhi  Panama  Paris  São Paulo  Singapore  Sydney  Tokyo  Toronto

## ECONOMICS

234567890  VHVH  7832109876


**Library of Congress Cataloging in Publication Data**

Samuelson, Paul Anthony, date
    Economics.

    Includes index.
    1.  Economics.  I.  Temin, Peter.  II.  Title.
HB171.5.S25    1976        330       75-42942
ISBN 0-07-054590-1


This book was set in Laurel by York Graphic Services, Inc.
The editors were J. S. Dietrich, Marjorie Singer,
Edwin Hanson, and Earle Resnick;
the designer was J. E. O'Connor;
the production supervisor was Joe Campanella.
New drawings were done by Eric G. Hieber Associates Inc.
Von Hoffmann Press, Inc., was printer and binder.

*For Marion*

# PREFACE

This is an introduction to economics, written for a half-year or full-year course in economics. The book is directed primarily toward readers who, for the most part, will never be going on to further formal study in economics. This present tenth or jubilee edition represents a thoroughgoing revision—with new emphasis on stagflation, energy economics, and environmental constraints. With the help of an eminent economic historian, my colleague Peter Temin, I have tried to redo the economic statistics to bring them current with the last quarter of the century.

Economics is an important subject. Economics can also be an exciting subject. How could it be otherwise, when it deals with the great issues of unemployment and inflation, poverty and wealth, and possible exhaustion of material growth? Dry-as-dust principles take on a new luster under the touch of relevance. For we have in political economy not a finished, embalmed corpus of conventional wisdom—but rather materials for the great debate on revolution, liberty, efficiency, and the endless quest for the good society.

*Why study political economy?*

Political economy is not an easy subject, not hammock reading for a lazy summer afternoon. But millions of readers—literally millions—have proved that they could learn the fundamentals of economics from this book. Some have studied it in English; many have read it in one of the numerous translations into other languages. A surprising number have learned economics by reading the book on their own or in continuing-education programs.

This textbook has been carefully designed so that it can be used both for freshman beginners taken from a cross section of the undergraduate population as well as for elite scholars in the stiffest honors courses. The text is carefully—nay, even cunningly—prepared so that each reader can go as far with it as he cares to go.

*How to study economics*

Experience shows that an economics text has to be read with care. Each chapter is carefully planned. Each has a comprehensive summary. The diagrams and tables are defined so that each also tells its own story. With every new edition there has come new knowledge on how to utilize color most functionally—with key concepts flagged here in orange at each chapter's end, with basic principles set out in green type, and with the diagrams' crucial points made to stand out for emphasis.

This functional design is one reason why a modern text can teach, in the same time, far more than we dared cover in the past. And economies of large-scale production make all this possible. (Although the type is set by the modern computer, the pages of the book are as intricately laid out as in an illuminated medieval manuscript—and with the author having to work with four distinct layers of film.)

*Divide and conquer*

No author can tell you how best to read a textbook. Obviously, this is not like a novel or detective story, not something designed for hit-and-run reading. The first time you read a chapter, turn its pages for perspective. Then read and underline, not stopping to overcome every difficulty. You will be pleasantly surprised to find that the final summaries and checklists of key concepts will help synthesize your understanding. And on review and rereading—giving independent attention to the self-contained story of the figures and tables—your understanding will deepen.

*Study Guide*

I should call to your attention the *Study Guide,* which Professor Romney Robinson has prepared to go along with this edition and which is cited later. Even if your instructor does not assign it, you may find it a great time-saver in the end.

*Programmed instruction*

Or for self-instruction in the analytical core of macroeconomics and microeconomics, you might want to get hold of *Economics: An Introductory Program,* which has been prepared by Professor Edward Foster to go along with the book.

*Optional matter*

You will discover that harder or less important material—they are not always the same!—have been put in appendixes, or often in footnotes. And in this edition I have carried forward the experiment of giving some final "Questions for Discussion" that are marked as "extra-credit problems," which enable the more highly trained student to pursue on his own some of the fascinating further developments of the subject. If you are in a fast, brief course, don't be put off by this carefully planned layering of more difficult material: Experience has proved that this gives the more intensive course meat to bite into, without really inconveniencing those who work with the severest time limitations. And to the bright honors student, may I say: Don't be put off by the use of color and the attempt to state matters plainly. This book is as challenging as you may care to make it. (Several who are now prominent economists have written to say that they used parts of it at every stage of their pilgrimage to the Ph.D.)

The following paragraphs are worth quoting from the *Instructor's Manual* to alert teachers who have been using earlier editions of the textbook to the main changes in coverage, organization, and topics of the tenth edition.

The last half of Part Two on Macroeconomics has been completely rewritten—particularly Chapters 17 and 19. The new chapters reflect the press of new events since 1973 and the changing theoretical conceptions that accompany it. We are now more used to living in an inflationary world, and our economic thinking must be geared to reflect this adjustment.

Chapter 21 on agriculture has been revised to stress the current problem of agriculture—scarcity—which is the opposite of the traditional "agricultural problem."

Part Five has been completely redone, since the international monetary system has been entirely revised in the last few years. The current edition reflects recent changes in exchange rates, changes in the status of gold, and changes in the way exchange rates are expected to adjust to changes in the environment. Of course, the problems stemming from the transfer of wealth to the OPEC countries are given prominence.

In Part Six, Chapters 39, 40, and 41 have been redone to reflect the impact of the current economic crisis on the distribution of income, and on the attempts to clean up the environment in an era of energy scarcity. The debates on limits to growth moved to a new stage. Also, the "new microeconomics" is emphasized with its ambitious attempts to bring into the domain of political economy such problems as (1) the economics of time, (2) marriage and parentage decisions in terms of utility maximization under feasibility constraints, (3) human capital as dependent on education and training, (4) even crime and punishment, no-fault insurance, and use of civil suits for torts as a mode of resource allocation.

The continuing problem of worldwide stagflation is given the new emphasis it deserves.

As one reckons generations in a family, this book is only one-generation old. As one reckons generations in the rapid turnover of college classes, time moves faster. Indeed, although to a superficial observer one edition may look much like its predecessor, a careful comparison will reveal that there is as great a difference between this edition and the original edition as there was between that edition and the earlier nineteenth-century texts of Marshall and Mill! One must be acute to see the small hand of the clock move; but, over time, it does mark off profound epochs.

**To the instructor**

Since almost half the classes using this book are one-semester courses, I append to the Table of Contents a suggested one-semester outline. And in the *Instructor's Manual* further suggestions are given for flexible adaptation.

*Which order?*

Forty per cent of the teachers using this book prefer to teach microeconomics before macroeconomics. A good case can be made for either ordering, and experimental programs show each to have advantages. This text has been carefully designed for either program. The instructor who wishes to deal first with microeconomics can skip from Part One to Part Three, knowing that the exposition and cross references have been tailored with his needs in mind. Because college courses in economics are taught both by large-lecture and small-section methods, we have used MIT classrooms as a laboratory, at certain hours lecturing to a large group and at others confining classes to 25 students. A good text must be prepared with both needs in mind.

I have not hesitated to segregate some of the material into appendixes. Often this involves slightly more difficult topics, with which briefer courses can easily dispense. Sometimes, as in the case of the discussion of the stock market in Chapter 4's Appendix or the presentation of cases on supply and demand in Chapter 20's Appendix, the material is not more difficult, but is such as can be conveniently skipped. Occasionally a teacher has written me questioning the advisability of this use of the appendixes. My answer is a pragmatic one based on experimentation: Because courses differ in their time span and emphasis, it is incumbent upon an author to give signals as to which sections are organically necessary and which are dispensable. (For example, in this edition I have retained a brief treatment of classical Marxism—variable capital, surplus value, and all that. The fact that it is put at the end of Chapter 42's Appendix will not inconvenience the reader eager for a terse account of this important subject; but this arrangement will be deemed a blessing by those instructors who lack the time for such a topic.)

*Auxiliary teaching aids*
*Robinson Study Guide*

To go with this tenth edition, a completely revised *Study Guide* has been prepared by Professor Romney Robinson. Both as assigned by instructors and bought independently by students for self-study, the *Study Guide* has proved to be an impressive success. Available to go with this text (or for that matter with any similar text), is *Economics: An Introductory Program* by Professor Edward Foster of the University of Minnesota. This program, now revised, covers the analytical core of macroeconomics and microeconomics. It can be assigned to the student, thereby freeing the instructor to lecture in class on other material; or students may wish, at their own option, to consolidate

*Foster Program*

their understanding by working through the program. Successful trial tests of the Foster program earlier at MIT and with Professor Dennis R. Weidenaar's Purdue students, have been corroborated by experience.

*Readings in Economics* edited by me are available to go with the text. In its seventh incarnation, generous selection from the great names of the past—Smith, Keynes, Ricardo, Marx—and the titans of the present age—Galbraith, Tobin, Friedman, Hayek, Sweezy, Solow, Burns, Kindleberger, Nader, Heilbroner—a broad spectrum of opinions is put before the student in a format convenient for assignment along with the text.

Reference may be made to the *Instructor's Manual* for information about further teaching aids (such as McGraw-Hill's set of overhead transparencies). Also available to instructors is a *Test Bank* of over 1,000 graded and matched multiple-choice questions that are taken from the *Instructor's Manual* and appear on perforated pages convenient for reproducing quizzes in small or large numbers.

Again I am a hopeless bankrupt when it comes to indebtedness. My greatest debt is to Professor Peter Temin of MIT. His skillful updating of the statistical data is testimonial to his secure mastery of economic history; his patience with a stubborn author is testimony to his generous tolerance. My MIT colleagues have helped in innumerable ways, and I must make special mention of Professors E. Cary Brown, Richard Eckaus, Paul MacAvoy (particularly in regard to educating me in modern antitrust), Lester Thurow, Duncan Foley, and Robert Solow, and also my earlier collaborators on the *Readings*, Robert L. Bishop of MIT, President John R. Coleman of Haverford, and Felicity Skidmore of the Institute for Research on Poverty (University of Wisconsin).

In earlier editions I carried a growing list of economists from other colleges who have left their mark on this work, but alas that list has grown beyond limits. In connection with the present edition I have received particular help from the following professors—but, since I have not always been able to make the changes they suggested, none of them should be blamed for my errors and omissions: Professors Charles A. Berry of the University of Cincinnati, Dale A. Berry of Drake University, John P. Connelly of Corning Community College, Paul H. Kipps of Madison College, Philip A. Klein of Pennsylvania State University, Eugene R. Lebrenz of the College of DuPage, W. Lyons of Franklin and Marshall College, Schuyler Royal of Crafton Hills College, Paul Wonnacott of the University of Maryland, and Reuben Zubrow of the University of Colorado.

Also, serving as an "invisible college," have been the numerous students who constantly write to me with criticisms that help to make each edition less imperfect than its predecessor. They are too numerous to list, but their blessed influence is built into each chapter and Part.

*Staff*

Kate Crowley and Vicki Elms have in this, as in so many other matters, been of inestimable help to me. And Marjorie Singer of McGraw-Hill made a thousand tasks easier.

*Skoal!*

My envy goes out to the reader, setting out to explore the exciting world of economics for the first time. That is a thrill which, alas, no one can experience twice.

To you who are about to begin, may I only say, *bon appetit!*

Paul A. Samuelson

# CONTENTS

# PART 3   THE COMPOSITION AND PRICING OF NATIONAL OUTPUT

## PART 5  INTERNATIONAL TRADE AND FINANCE

# SUGGESTED OUTLINE FOR A ONE-SEMESTER COURSE

Core chapters in green numerals.

Chapters with orange numerals for courses with macroeconomic emphasis.
Chapters with brown numerals for courses with microeconomic emphasis.
Chapters with black numerals for courses with policy emphasis. For courses with institutional emphasis,
    Chapters 6 through 9 and 29, dealing with business, labor, and government finance could be included.

# 1

## BASIC ECONOMIC CONCEPTS AND NATIONAL INCOME

When the Harvard Business School was founded more than half a century ago, President A. Lawrence Lowell described business as "the oldest of the arts, the newest of the professions." Almost the same words can be used to describe political economy: the oldest of the arts, the newest of the sciences—indeed the queen of the social sciences.

As a scholarly discipline, economics is just two centuries old. Adam Smith published his pathbreaking book *The Wealth of Nations* in 1776, a year notable also for the Declaration of Independence. And the nearness of timing is no coincidence: Political freedom from the tyranny of monarchy was closely related to emancipation of free-market pricing from the interfering hand of state regulation.

Adam Smith, of course, represented only a beginning. In more than a century and a half that elapsed from the appearance of *The Wealth of Nations* to the publication of John Maynard Keynes' *The General Theory of Employment, Interest and Money* (1936), economics—or political economy, as it is more traditionally called—has gone through many stages of development. Almost at the halfway point, there appeared the massive critique of capitalism by Karl Marx: *Das Kapital* (1867, followed by two posthumous volumes). A billion people, some third of the world's population, view *Das Kapital* as economic truth.

And yet, without the disciplined study of economic science, how can anyone form a reasoned opinion about the merits or lack of merits in the classical, traditional economics? Or about the achievements of the so-called "New Economics" that has evolved since 1929? Or about problems yet unsolved by mainstream economics?

## FOR WHOM THE BELL TOLLS

Few study economics merely to judge the merits in the grand debates concerning historic capitalism, the modern mixed economy, or the collectivist economic systems of the East. We study economics to answer many, diverse questions. Here are some common ones.

1

**Poverty, development, and affluence**   America is a prosperous nation. We have grown more prosperous over a long period, and our present affluence is an outgrowth from the lower standard of productivity prevailing in past generations. Look at the front flyleaf: Contrast the Western world's affluence with the poverty of India, whose growth curve barely shows on the chart; and note the success story of Japan in its bare century of contact with the modern world. All over the world, men have become preoccupied with economic development.

How can preindustrial economies, teeming with masses of people and poorly endowed with natural resources, break through the vicious circle of poverty and backwardness?

How can policies be formulated and programs be promulgated that will speed the pace of *economic growth and development?*

In the affluent West, "Zero Population Growth" and "Zero Economic Growth" are new goals set by concerned people who are alarmed at the exhaustion of the globe's irreplaceable resources and at deterioration of environmental ecological balance.

How can a modern economy manage—if it should want to—to raise the *quality* of its economic life and forgo mere *quantitative* growth, and do so without bringing on itself a great depression with mass unemployment?

Undoubtedly, this new interest in development and humane growth has made economics an exciting and vital subject in the capitals of the world, and on Main Street as well as Wall Street.

**Personal stake in economics**   An even more immediate reason for studying economics is that it deals with many of the matters that will most concern each one of us:

What kinds of jobs are available? What do they pay? How much in the way of goods will a dollar of wages buy now, and how much in a time of galloping inflation?

What are the chances that a time will come when a trained man won't be able to get work? Are the black days of the depressed 1930s ever likely to return?

Will automation and scientific discovery make man obsolete? How can one make a killing in the stock market? Or best run a business?

Economics is relevant to these diverse questions. But, as will be seen, they are not the prime target of an introductory course.

**Economics for the citizen**   Beyond personal family matters, economics deals even more importantly with decisions each citizen must face. Here are a dozen vital problems:

Will the government tax me to help unemployed miners, or are there other things it can do to help mitigate the problem of unemployment?

Should I vote to build a new school and a road now, or vote to put this aside until business slackens and cement prices come down and jobs are needed? Should I vote to keep married women out of public employment, so there will be more jobs for men?

What about antitrust legislation that purports to fight monopolies?

If you are a humanitarian, deeply concerned to improve the lot of the poor, the disadvantaged black, and the aged, will legislating a good, stiff, high minimum wage serve to help or hinder the good cause for which you fight?

Why not "fair-shares" rationing?

What consequences will follow if the federal budget is not balanced in every year? Is it true, as Moscow no longer claims, that American prosperity is dependent on cold-war military expenditures? If "peace breaks out," are we in for a recession? Can the government wash its hands of the matter, knowing that we can rely on the spontaneous forces of private markets to convert the swords of war into the plowshares of peace?

Is old-fashioned poverty from niggardliness of nature extinct?

And what about "poverty midst plenty" as in the post-1929 Great Depression, when factories lay idle and people couldn't find jobs? Has this given way to the modern pockets of poverty in the ghetto and rural slums?

As Adam Smith said, security is even more important for a nation than opulence. Survival itself can depend on economics.

Can a modern nation afford expensive military expenditures (as, for example, in Vietnam or NATO)? Is it true, as ex-President Hoover once warned, that "inflation is worse than Stalin"?

## WHAT ECONOMICS IS

Beginners often want a short definition of economics; and in response to this demand, there is no shortage of supply. Here are a few such definitions:

1. Economics, or political economy, is the study of those activities which, with or without money, involve exchange transactions among people.

2. Economics is the study of how people choose to use scarce or limited productive resources (land, labor, capital goods such as machinery, technical knowledge) to produce various commodities (such as wheat, beef, overcoats, yachts; concerts, roads, bombers) and distribute them to various members of society for their consumption.

3. Economics is the study of people in their ordinary business of life, earning and enjoying a living.

4. Economics is the study of how human beings go about the business of organizing its consumption and production activities.

5. Economics is the study of wealth.

6. Economics is the study of how to improve society.

The list is a good one. Yet a scholar can extend it many times over. It is always hard to compress into a few lines an exact description of a subject, one that will differentiate its boundaries from those of other disciplines and convey to the beginner all the things it is. Economics certainly does involve all the elements stressed in these various definitions—and all those implied in the larger list that could be compiled.

Economists today agree on a general definition something like the following:

**Economics is the study of how people and society end up *choosing*, with or without the use of money, to employ *scarce* productive resources that could have alternative uses, to produce various commodities and distribute them for consumption, now or in the future, among various persons and groups in society. It analyzes the costs and benefits of improving patterns of resource allocation.**

## QUALITY OF ECONOMIC LIFE

An introduction can serve as a preview. Even before studying economics, everyone will have heard of the *Gross National Product*. This, as Chapter 10 will discuss, purports to measure the total of all goods and services produced each year in a nation. Although measured in money, it can tell us much about real goods and services—food, clothing, penicillin, and so forth.

But these days many critics of political economy have come forth. They deplore materialistic concentration on the *quantity* of economic goods. In the striking words of a young radical: "Don't speak to me of Gross National Product, GNP. To me GNP stands for Gross National Pollution."

What are we to think? Must modern economics make a fetish of *quantity* at the expense of *quality* of life? Or can we correct the official statistician's measure of Gross National Product so that it becomes more of a measure of Net Economic Welfare? That is, can we supplement GNP by a more meaningful measure NEW?

Figure 1-1 shows as the orange curve the traditional measure of GNP per capita. From 1929 to 1976, this more than doubled. But during that same period in which we were getting more necessities and gadgets, we were also having to commute to work over more crowded roads and having to spend more to offset the growing pollution in the air.

Therefore, two economists from Yale, William Nordhaus and James Tobin, believing that economic welfare is too important to leave either to statisticians or noneconomists, have tried to correct traditional GNP numbers to allow for disamenities of modern urban living, for enhanced leisure now enjoyed by the citizenry, for household work by wives that is ignored by the GNP statistician, and for various other adjustments.

The brown curve in Fig. 1-1 shows that the resulting measure of per capita Net Economic Welfare, NEW for short, has grown since 1929. But it has clearly not grown as much as GNP itself has grown.

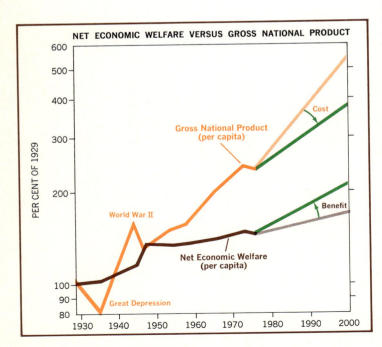

**FIG. 1-1**

**We must compute Net Economic Welfare to gauge quality of economic life**

The upper orange curve shows real Gross National Product per capita (i.e., U.S. goods and services corrected for inflationary changes in the purchasing power of the dollar and changes in population). The lower brown curve shows Net Economic Welfare (NEW for short). This adjusts the conventional measure of GNP to allow for pollution costs, disamenities of modern urban living, leisure, etc.

Now look at the projections of future GNP and NEW shown by the shaded straight lines between 1976 and 2000. These show what might happen if we don't do anything about pollution. But if people really wish to improve the quality of life —and not just talk about doing so—we must adopt public and private policies that sacrifice some ordinary GNP growth to get more NEW growth. Note the stepped-up green line of NEW and the lowered green line of GNP. (Source: Adapted from Fig. 10-4.)

**Trading off quantity to get better quality**   There is something more shown by the figure. Economics cannot stand content merely to *describe* the truths of life. Political economy finds itself called on to help public opinion do something toward improving manifest evils. Look therefore at the green curves of growth from the mid-1970s to the end of the century. These show how the electorate, if it really wishes to, can hope to *improve* the quality of economic life.

As conservative people love to repeat, "There is no such thing as a free lunch in this vale of tears." To get the *benefit* of higher NEW, what *cost* must we pay? Higher taxes and dearer electricity will be necessary if we are to fight pollution and urban blight. Hence, we'll all have to make the sacrifice of registering *slower* growth in ordinary GNP. (Raising the green NEW line means lowering the green GNP line. So it is not a case of pretending to be getting something for nothing.) Thus, *political economy shows people how, if they really wish to, they can trade off quantity of goods for quality of life.*

There is no need to explain these matters in this preview. It will be the task of Part Six to ensure that modern political economy responds to the new age's concern for ecology and the quality of human living.

## LIGHT AND FRUIT

This discussion has illustrated an important truth: Every national issue mentioned requires economic understanding to make progress in dealing with it. A person who has never made a systematic study of economics is handicapped in even thinking about national issues; he is like a deaf man trying to appreciate a symphony: give him a hearing aid, and he may still lack talent, but at least he has a fighting chance of sensing what music really is. The head of state[1] must be constantly making vital decisions that involve economics. But of course he need not *himself* be a professional student of economics; he need only be an intelligent "consumer" of the (often conflicting) economic information being given him.

Of course most students do not expect to *specialize* in economics. Most will study it for only a term or two, and this book is intended to give an overview of the whole subject. One's view of the world can never be quite the same after even a single semester of economics.

C. P. Snow, scientist and novelist, once called for an end to the separation of "the two cultures." Economics is part of both these cultures, a subject that can combine the attractive features of both the humanities and the sciences. For two centuries, educated men have found in political economy the human interest of life itself, while at the same time economic principles display some of the logical beauty of Euclid's geometry. To appreciate the charms of quantum physics, sophisticated mathematical

---

[1] As an example, Winston Churchill was a great man—a leader without peer, an orator, a gifted writer, and a shrewd judge of the Hitlerian threat while most around him slept. Yet all his life, Churchill was a babe in the woods when it came to economics. In 1925, as Chancellor of the Exchequer, he put England back on the gold standard at the pre-1914 parity of $4.87 for the British pound. (Chapter 33 will explain what this means.) Experts at the time warned against such folly, and history has recorded that England never quite recovered from her stagnation of the 1920s.

techniques must first be mastered; but to sense the aesthetic structure of economic analysis requires only a feeling for logic and a capacity for wonderment that such mental constructs really do have a life-and-death significance for billions of men all over the world. Of course, mere beauty is not enough.

We do not study economics for its own sake, but for the light it sheds.

## THE QUEEN OF THE SOCIAL SCIENCES

Economics borders on other important academic disciplines. *Sociology, political science, psychology,* and *anthropology* are all social sciences whose studies overlap those of economics. Here is just one example.

In impoverished India cows are sacred animals and, numbering millions, walk through the streets foraging for food. While a naïve economist might regard these herds as a prime source for protein supplements to an already-inadequate diet, the more profound scholar will take the psychology of custom into account when analyzing Indian economic development.

Economics also draws heavily on the study of *history*.

Was it a coincidence that prices rose for centuries in Spain and Europe after Columbus discovered America with all its silver and gold? Why did the age of the steamship and railroad help Iowa farmers, hurt farmers of Vermont and Oxfordshire, and help slum dwellers of London? Was the institution of slavery dying economically of its own weight before the Civil War?

To the interpretation of recorded history, *analytical* tools must be brought for the reason that facts never "tell their own story." Yet this need for theorizing does not deny the old Chinese proverb, "One peek is worth thousand finesses." Facts count.

Among the numerous other subjects relating to economics, the study of *statistics* is of special importance. Governments and businesses issue vast amounts of numerical information. Most of what we know about the actual shapes of the various curves to be seen in turning over the pages of this book has to come from a careful statistical analysis of recorded information. The mathematical methods of probability and statistics find many of their most important applications in the realm of economics.

Although every introductory textbook must contain geometrical diagrams, knowledge of *mathematics* itself is needed only for the higher reaches of economic theory. Logical reasoning is the key to success in the mastery of basic economic principles, and shrewd weighing of empirical evidence is the key to success in applications to description and policy.

**Nobel prize in economics**   Since the turn of the century, Nobel prizes have been given annually in physics, chemistry, medicine and physiology, literature, and peace. As if to commemorate the coming of age of political economy as a science, a new Nobel prize in economics was instituted in 1969.

The first award went jointly to Professors Ragnar Frisch of Norway and Jan Tinbergen of the Netherlands. Both men have been pioneers in the statistical, theoretical, and mathematical advances of the modern generation. Yet each has also been passionately concerned with economic policy, within his own country and for the world at large. In honoring these men of genius, the Swedish Academy of Science could not have more fittingly summarized the nature of economic scholarship. May their successors live up to their example!

## ECONOMIC DESCRIPTION AND ANALYSIS

It is the first task of modern political economy to *describe*, to *analyze*, to *explain*, and to *correlate* the behavior of production, unemployment, prices, and similar phenomena. To be significant, descriptions must be more than a series of disconnected narratives. They must be fitted into a systematic pattern—i.e., constitute true analysis.

Because of the complexity of human and social behavior, we cannot hope to attain the precision of the physical sciences. We cannot perform the controlled experiments of the chemist or biologist. Like the astronomer, we must be content largely to "observe." But economic events and statistical data observed are, alas, not so well behaved and orderly as the paths of heavenly satellites. Fortunately, our answers need not be accurate to several decimal places; on the contrary, if the right general *direction* of cause and effect can be determined, we shall have made a tremendous step forward.

## ECONOMIC POLICY AND REFORM

This brings us to the important problem of economic policy. Ultimately, understanding should aid in *control and improvement*. How can the vagaries of the business cycle be diminished? How can economic progress and efficiency be furthered? How can adequate standards of living be made more widely available? How can the world avoid ecological disaster?

At each point of analysis we shall seek to shed light on these policy problems. To succeed we must make an effort to cultivate an objective and detached ability to see things as they *are*, regardless of our likes or dislikes. The fact must be faced that economic issues are close to everybody emotionally. Blood pressures rise, voices become shrill whenever deep-seated beliefs and prejudices are involved, and some of these prejudices are thinly veiled rationalizations of special economic interests.

**Wishful thinking versus reasoned opinion differences**   We know that a doctor passionately interested in stamping out disease must first train himself to observe things as they are. His bacteriology cannot be different from that of a mad scientist out to destroy mankind. "Where it is a duty to worship the sun, the laws of heat will be poorly understood." Wishful thinking is bad thinking and leads to little wish fulfillment.

"Beauty is in the eye of the beholder" is an aphorism reminding us that judgments of better or worse involve *subjective* valuations. But this does not deny that one person's nose may be *objectively* shorter than another's. Similarly, there are elements of valid reality in a given economic situation, however hard it may be to recognize and isolate them. There is not one theory of economics for Republicans and one for Democrats, one for workers and one for employers, one for the Russians and still another for the Chinese. On many basic principles concerning prices and employment, most—not all!—economists are in fairly close agreement.

This statement does not mean that economists agree closely in the *policy* field. Economist A may be for full employment at any cost. Economist B may not consider it of as vital importance as price stability. Basic questions concerning right and wrong goals to be pursued cannot be settled by mere science as such. They belong in the realm of ethics and "value judgments." The citizenry must ultimately decide such issues. What the expert can do is point out the feasible alternatives and the true costs that may be involved in the different decisions. But still the mind must render to the heart that which is the heart's domain. For, as Pascal said, the heart has reasons that reason will never know.

And, peculiarly in the social sciences, we must realize that we are subjects—even victims—of our preconceptions, prejudices, sentiments, and sordid interests.[2]

**The ultimate payoff**   The quotation that appears at the beginning of Chapter 42, you will find, reads as follows:

Up 'til now philosophers have only interpreted the world in various ways. The point, though, is to *change* it!

These words of the twenty-six-year-old Karl Marx were chosen for his gravestone in London's Highgate cemetery. But they could serve as the motto on the shields of all the great masters of political economy. For, out of the scores of greatest economists in world history, at most two (and with them, it was something of a pose) were not primarily concerned with "doing good."

## METHODOLOGY OF ECONOMICS: BRIEF PREVIEW

No one can understand a complicated subject such as chemistry without long and careful study. This is an advantage and a disadvantage. The man on the street or behind a newspaper desk cannot possibly consider himself a final authority on such a subject—which is all to the good. On the other hand, the new student of chemistry has to become familiar with all the basic concepts for the first time—which necessarily takes a good deal of effort.

From childhood days on, everyone knows *something* about economics. This acquaintance is both helpful and deceptive: helpful, because much knowledge can be taken for granted; deceptive, because it is natural and human to accept superficially plausible views. A little knowledge may be dangerous. On close examination, common sense may prove to be really nonsense.

A union leader who has successfully negotiated several labor contracts may feel that he is an expert on the economics of wages. A businessman who has "met a payroll" may feel that his views on price control are final. A banker who can balance his books may conclude that he knows all there is to know about the creation of money.

Each individual naturally tends to judge an economic event by its immediate effect upon himself. A worker thrown out of employment in the buggy industry cannot be expected to reflect that new jobs may have been created in the automobile industry; but we, as students of economics, must be prepared to investigate whether this is really so, and the degree to which it is so.

In an introductory survey, the economist is interested in the workings of the economy *as a whole* rather than in the viewpoint of any one group. Social and national policies rather than individual policy are his goals. Too often, "everybody's business is nobody's business." It is just as well, therefore, to reiterate at the beginning that an elementary course in economics does not pretend to teach one how to run a business or bank; or

---

[2] Which questions we ask, and from what perspective we photograph the "objective reality"—these are themselves at bottom subjective in nature.

how to spend money wisely; or how to get rich quick from the stock market. Yet this is not to deny that general economics can provide a useful background for many such activities.

Certainly, the economist must know a good deal about how businessmen, consumers, and investors behave and think. This does not mean that those individuals must use the *same language and methods* in approaching their decisions as economists find useful in describing their behavior—any more than the planets need know that they are following the elliptical paths traced by the astronomer. Just as many of us have been "speaking prose" all our lives without knowing it, so too would many businessmen be surprised to learn that their behavior is capable of systematic economic analysis. Such lack of awareness is not necessarily to be deprecated. It does not help a baseball pitcher to know the laws of aerodynamics; and if we become self-conscious about how to button our shirts, we may find that harder to do.

**Theory versus practice**    The economic world is extremely complicated. As we noted, it is usually not possible to make economic observations under the controlled experimental conditions characteristic of scientific laboratories. A physiologist who wishes to determine the effects of penicillin on pneumonia may be able to "hold other things equal" by using two test groups that differ only in the fact that they do and do not get penicillin injections. The economist is less fortunately situated. If he wishes to determine the effect of a gasoline tax on fuel consumption, he may be vexed by the fact that, in the same year when the tax was imposed, pipelines were first introduced. Nevertheless, he must try—if only mentally—to isolate the effects of the tax, "other things being equal." Otherwise, he will understand the economic effects *neither of taxation nor of transportation improvements, nor of both together.*

**The post hoc fallacy**    The difficulty of analyzing causes when controlled experimentation is impossible is well illustrated by the confusion of the savage medicine man who thinks that both witchcraft and a little arsenic are necessary to kill his enemy, or that only after he has put on a green robe in spring will the trees do the same.[3] As a result of this limitation (and, alas, many others), our quantitative economic knowledge is far from complete. This doesn't mean that we do not have great amounts of accurate statistical knowledge available. We do. Reams of census data, market information, and financial statistics are collected by governments, trade associations, and businesses.

Even if we had more and better data, it would still be necessary—as in every science—to *simplify,* to *abstract* from the infinite mass of detail. No mind can comprehend a bundle of unrelated facts. All analysis involves abstraction. It is always necessary to *idealize,* to omit detail, to set up simple hypotheses and patterns by which the facts can be related, to set up the right questions before going out to look at the world. Every theory, whether in the physical or biological or social sciences, distorts reality in that it oversimplifies. But if it is good theory, what is omitted is outweighed by the beam of illumination and understanding thrown over the diverse empirical data.

Properly understood, therefore, theory and observation, deduction and induction,

---

[3] In logic, the *post hoc, ergo propter hoc* fallacy (after this, therefore necessarily because of this).

will not be in conflict. The test of a theory's validity is its usefulness in illuminating observed reality. Its logical elegance and finespun beauty are irrelevant. Consequently, when a student says, "That's all right in theory but not in practice," he really means, "That's not all right in the relevant theory," or else he is talking nonsense.

**The tyranny of words**   Especially in the social sciences, we must watch out for the "tyranny of words." The world is complicated enough without introducing further confusions and ambiguities as (*a*) two different names are unknowingly being used for the same thing or (*b*) the same word is applied to two different things.

Jones may call Robinson a liar for holding that the cause of depression is oversaving, saying, "Underconsumption is really the cause." Schwartz may enter the argument, asserting, "You are both wrong. The real trouble is underinvestment." They may go on arguing; but if they really stopped to analyze their language, they might find that there were no substantive differences in their opinions about the facts and that only a verbal confusion was involved.

Similarly, words may be treacherous because we do not react in a neutral manner to them. Thus a man who approves of a government program to speed growth will call it a program of "sensible planning," while an unsympathetic opponent will describe the same activity as "totalitarian, bureaucratic regimentation." Who can object to the former, and who could condone the latter? Yet they may refer to the same thing. One does not have to be an expert in *semantics*—the study of language and its meaning—to realize that scientific discussion requires us to avoid such emotional terminology wherever possible.

**Social versus physical science?**   Some distortions of thinking from emotion and prejudice are so blatant as to be clearly recognizable. But at a deeper level, one can ask:

Since economics deals with man and not with inanimate objects, and since the scientist is himself necessarily a man, can there be any hope of an *objective* science of economics? Can the methods of the physical sciences—observation and quantitative measurements, mathematical model building—ever work in the study of human affairs?

No simple answer can be given to this profound question. In a sense, precisely because we are ourselves men, we have an advantage over the natural scientist. He cannot usefully say, "Suppose I were an $H_2O$ molecule; what might I do in such a situation?" The social scientist often, knowingly or unknowingly, employs useful introspective acts of *empathy*.

Still a problem remains. Experienced scholars would put it this way:

Slavish imitation of the physical sciences is a mistake in the study of humans and society. Yet there is no substitute for patient *attendance to the empirical facts* of life, and no substitute for *systematic reasoning* about them. As in the case of modern biology, great advances have resulted from mathematical scientific methods, despite the earlier warnings against imitating the physical sciences. Let experience tell the final story. And let no one be impressed by mere elegance of technique.

**Exactitude and subjectivity**   But recall again this important point. Even in the so-called exact physical sciences, how we *perceive* the observed facts depends on the theoretical spectacles we wear. The light that hits a newborn baby's eyes forms no pattern: the

**FIG. 1-2**

**Facts may tell a different story to scientific observers who wear different theoretical spectacles**

If you look at problems of depression unemployment through pre-Keynesian glasses, you may think it is due to forces that government tax and expenditure policies cannot change. In (a), is this a picture of a leftward-looking bird? Or is it a rightward-looking antelope (or rabbit)? In the presence of (b)'s *field of birds,* most people think it a bird. But next to the footnote's *field of antelopes,* most will see it as an antelope. (Source: N. R. Hanson, *Patterns of Discovery,* Cambridge University Press, London, 1961.)

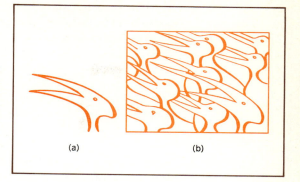

(a)                    (b)

baby *sees,* but it does not *perceive.* Modern historians of science have learned the same lesson from gestalt psychology: post-Newtonians perceived the "same facts" differently from pre-Newtonians. To a degree, we are all prisoners of our theoretical preconceptions. It is not so much discordant fact that kills off an old false theory as the final emergence of a new theory.

That is why science belongs to the young. The old know too many things that are just not so. To illustrate this, we do not have to consider a soft science like economics, where we take for granted that our uncles will think, "What was good enough for Calvin Coolidge ought to be good enough for you." Let us listen to Nobel laureate Max Planck, the physicist renowned for his discovery of the revolutionary quantum theory. In his *Scientific Autobiography,* Planck reports what he observed in the development of physics:

This experience gave me also an opportunity to learn a fact—a remarkable one in my opinion: A new scientific truth does not triumph by convincing its opponents and making them see the light, but rather because its opponents eventually die, and a new generation grows up that is familiar with it.

Just as Galileo, Newton, Einstein, and Planck revolutionized perceptions in physics, so did Smith, Marx, Marshall, Keynes—indeed, all the names that appear on the family tree of economics shown on the back flyleaf of this book—transform economic understanding.

Figure 1-2, taken from a philosophic study of physics, illustrates the irreducible subjective element in *any* science. Does the picture show a bird looking to the left? Or an antelope (or rabbit) looking to the right? It is not an optical illusion to say it is one rather than the other. Each is admissible.[4] So it is with scientific facts and

---

[4]Contrast your gestalt perception of Fig. 1-2's image with its appearance when placed next to this field of antelopes.

The bird-antelope ambiguity cannot be dismissed as an optical "illusion": it is unlike the accompanying two lines, which are really the same length even though most people wrongly infer the lower line to be the longer. What Fig. 1-2 portrays is an objectively reproducible shape that looks subjectively different depending on the context in which it appears. Thus, once we see the forelegs of the beast, we are "right" to perceive it as an antelope.

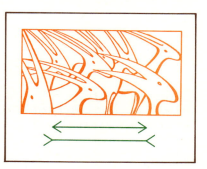

theories in general. When you adopt a new systematic model of economic principles, you comprehend reality in a new and different way. We do not have to be students of physics or gestalt psychology to realize how literally these words apply to the contrasts between new and old economics, or between Western-world and communist economics. So let us be forewarned.

**Probability of errors: normal or not**   There is another important difference between an exact science like physics and a less exact science like political economy. Our laws may hold only "on the average," with considerable dispersion of exceptions around that average.

Figure 1-3 gives a preview of a vital statistical relationship whereby consumption spending by families can be related to the dollar incomes people have. Note that the observation points do not fall exactly on the line, as they might in chemistry or astronomy. Still, we do see a pattern that is stable in a probability sense—the same sense in which a life-insurance company can *count on* a stable proportion of deaths in a sample of 100,000 policyholders of a given age (even though any one man's living or dying cannot be foretold).

And note a further important point: The chance deviations around the expected values will form an especially simple frequency pattern called the "normal curve of error." The normal curve is symmetric and bell-shaped; this is because the addition of *many independent* errors

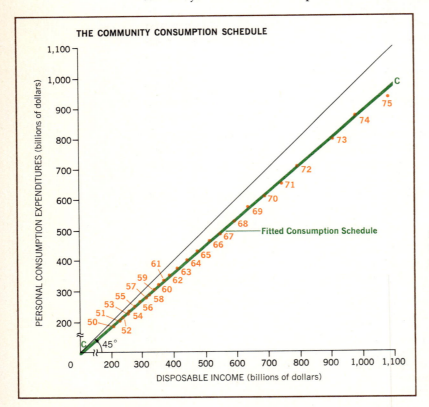

**FIG. 1-3**

**Economic laws are probability laws, not exact relationships**
Observed points of consumption spending fall near to the fitted green line. Thus, the orange point for 1974 is so near the *CC* line that it could have been predicted quite accurately from that line even before the year was over. This regularity between dollar income and spending is typical of regularities in economics. (Source: Fig. 11-4.)

FIG. 1-4
**Abnormal as well as normal patterns of probabilities occur in economics**
Although behavior on the average is predictable in economics, there are exceptions and deviations around the average. The brown curve depicts the well-behaved case in which the deviations follow the symmetric bell-shaped "normal curve of error." The orange curve of abnormal error, which is skewed off to the right, has relatively more extreme deviations than does the normal curve. Where this occurs in the social sciences, we cannot guarantee laws of average behavior with quite so much accuracy. (Source: Fig. 5-5, where normal distribution of abilities is contrasted with asymmetric distribution of dollar incomes and great income spread.)

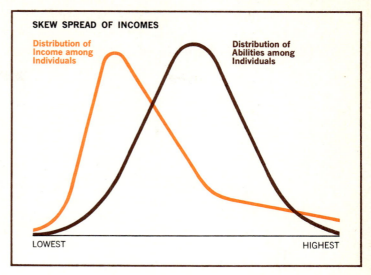

**SKEW SPREAD OF INCOMES**

Distribution of Income among Individuals

Distribution of Abilities among Individuals

LOWEST                                  HIGHEST

tends to give a resultant error which (through probable cancellation) is more likely to be small than large. When this normal distribution appears in economics, it resembles distributions from gambling dice, genetics, or surveying measurements.[5]

In economics, "normality" may not always prevail. Figure 1-4 reproduces a later diagram, Fig. 5-5, showing how abnormally spread out people's incomes are in comparison with the allegedly "normal" distribution of their abilities (IQs, verbal or mathematical aptitudes, etc.). The orange curve of distribution of incomes is asymmetric: unlike the brown symmetric normal curve, it has a long tail skewed to the right. This reflects the fact that, although there are some multimillionaires with incomes equal to hundreds of times the average income, no one can be that many dollars *below* the average. Such asymmetric, superextended distributions, alas, appear often in economics. One says "alas" because where such abnormal probability laws occur, they do not lead to the same *precision of average behavior* that the natural sciences can often count on.

Despite the approximative character of economic laws, economics is a field blessed with many important regularities and valid principles.

[5] Gambling houses in Nevada and Monte Carlo know very well from experience that repeated coin tossing (or dice throwing) will generate a sequence with the following two properties: (a) If we write down 1 for heads and 0 for tails, a random series of tossing will give sequences—such as 0, 1, 1, 0, 1, 0, 1, 0, 0, 0, 1, 0—which eventually average out close to $\frac{1}{2}$ by the famous "law of large numbers." (b) For a long enough sequence of random tosses of a symmetric coin, the fraction of heads appearing will approach a normal-error dispersion around the expected value of $\frac{1}{2}$. This "central limit law" (of approach to a bell-shaped normal distribution) enables mathematicians like De Moivre, Laplace, Gauss, and R. A. Fisher to predict with great accuracy how often deviations will tend to occur, the expected size of the absolute errors halving when the sequence quadruples in length. [Thus, when the number of customers of a firm doubles, it needs only 1.4 (or $\sqrt{2}$) times the amount of inventory.] Many economic distributions, however, like that of income, may have tails too dispersed to be subject to this normal distribution.

## THE WHOLE AND THE PART: THE "FALLACY OF COMPOSITION"

A good final warning in economics is this: Things are often not what at first they seem. The following true statements provide examples:

1. If all farmers work hard and nature cooperates in producing a bumper crop, total farm income may *fall*, and probably will.

2. *One* man may solve his own unemployment problem by great ingenuity in hunting a job or by a willingness to work for less; but *all* cannot necessarily solve their job problems in this way.

3. Higher prices *for one industry* may benefit its firms; but if the prices of *everything* bought and sold increased in the same proportion, *no one* would be better off.

4. It may pay the United States to *reduce* tariffs charged on goods imported, even if *other* countries refuse to lower their tariff barriers.

5. It may pay a firm to take on some business at much *less than full costs*.

6. *Attempts* of individuals to save more in depression *may lessen the total* of the community's savings.

7. What is prudent behavior for an *individual* may at times be folly for a *nation*.

Note this. Each of the above statements is true. But each is outwardly paradoxical. In the course of this book, the seeming paradoxes will be resolved. There are no magic formulas or hidden tricks. It is typical of economics that anything which is really correct must seem perfectly reasonable once the argument is carefully developed.

At this point it is just as well to note that many of the above paradoxes hinge upon a single confusion or fallacy. It is called by logicians the "fallacy of composition." In books on logic, this is defined as follows:

**Fallacy of composition: a fallacy in which what is true of a part is, on that account alone, alleged to be also necessarily true of the whole.**

Very definitely, in the field of economics, it turns out that what seems to be true for individuals is not always true for society as a whole; and conversely, what seems to be true for all may be quite false for any one individual. For everybody to stand on tiptoe to watch a parade does no good, even though one person may gain a better view by so doing. Countless similar economic examples can be given. You might amuse yourself by checking over these seven examples to see which are probably related to the fallacy of composition. Or better still, find some new ones.

We have come to the end of our introductory survey. Perhaps the best answer to the question, Why study economics? is a famous one given by Lord Keynes. The final lines of his 1936 classic, *The General Theory of Employment, Interest and Money*, consist of a famous passage:

. . . the ideas of economists and political philosophers, both when they are right and when they are wrong, are more powerful than is commonly understood. Indeed the world is ruled by little else. Practical men, who believe themselves to be quite exempt from any intellectual influences, are usually the slaves of some defunct economist. Madmen in authority, who hear voices in the air, are distilling their frenzy from some academic scribbler of a few years back. I am sure that the power of vested interests is vastly exaggerated compared with the gradual encroachment of ideas. Not, indeed, immediately, but after a certain interval; for in the field of economic and political philosophy there are not many who are influenced by new theories after they are twenty-five or thirty years of age, so that the ideas which civil servants and politicians and even agitators apply to current events are not likely to be the newest. But, soon or late, it is ideas, not vested interests, which are dangerous for good or evil.

## SUMMARY

1   Economics, both a science and an art, is studied for a variety of reasons: to understand problems facing the citizen and family; to help governments in both underdeveloped and advanced nations promote mankind-fulfilling growth, while avoiding depression and inflation; to analyze fascinating patterns of social behavior; to alter the inequalities in the distribution of income and opportunity.

2   Among many definitions, the leading one today defines economics thus: How do we choose to use scarce productive resources with alternative uses, to better meet prescribed ends—what goods to produce, how, and for whom, now or later?

3   Overlapping with other social or behavioral sciences—psychology, sociology, history—economics uses the deductive methods of logic and geometry, and inductive methods of statistical and empirical inference. Because it cannot employ controlled experiments of the physicist, it raises basic problems of methodology: subjective elements of introspection and value judgment; semantic issues of ambiguous and emotional meanings; probability laws of large numbers, both of normal-error and skewed type; fallacies of reasoning and fallacies of inference.

## CONCEPTS FOR REVIEW

political economy as distinct from
   other disciplines
analysis and policy
practice and theory
wishful thinking, semantics
exactitude and probability
normal and skewed errors

subjectivity and theorizing
valuations and so-called "facts"
tyranny of words
controlled experiment
fallacy of composition
*post hoc* fallacy
definition of political economy

## QUESTIONS FOR DISCUSSION

1   Would a major depression like that of the 1930s, or a peacetime inflation, affect you (*a*) seriously, (*b*) moderately, or (*c*) not at all?

2   Discuss the emotional content of the following words: regimentation, planning, usury, monopolist, gambling, speculation, American way of life, free enterprise, cartels, thrift, hoarding, military-industrial complex.

3   Give examples of the fallacy of composition and of the *post hoc, ergo propter hoc* fallacy. Is the former involved in the debate over cigarettes and longevity? (Why not?) Is the latter involved in this debate? (Why so?)

4   Can you fit into the brief definition of economics many of this chapter's problems?

5    In Fig. 1-3, is income the cause and consumption the effect? Or vice versa? To answer this, economic study is needed. Similarly, does the fact that smoking and cancer are related prove that smoking causes cancer? Is low IQ among the poor genetically caused? How could you form a reasoned judgment?

6    "GNP should be corrected for the fact that Los Angeles smog sends up my dry-cleaning bills and asthma-prescription charges. Also, when affluence cuts our work week from 45 hours per week to 40 hours per week, that may cut down GNP but surely it should raise Net Economic Welfare (NEW). Also, NEW excludes the defense expenditure that occurs in GNP, since citizens of a country are not improved in welfare when these go up—however necessary or unnecessary they may be in this vale of tears. Same goes for expenditure on burglar alarms and watchdogs." Do you not agree?

7    "If society could get an extra 1 per cent annual growth in NEW by the sacrifice of half our ordinary GNP growth rate—say, by our spending more money on conservation and taxing General Motors and the users of electric power for atmospheric pollution they create—this would be a great bargain." Evaluate.

8    Could a scientist believe in "changing the world," and yet not necessarily agree with a Marxian program for thoroughgoing revolution by force? How would different people draw the line? How would you, *before* your first course in economics?

## A PREVIEW

Here in Part One we deal with the fundamental tools needed to analyze the basic facts and institutions of modern economic life, culminating this survey in the unifying concept of national income.

In Part Two we analyze the causes of prosperity and depression: how the processes of saving and investment interact to determine the level of prices, income, and employment; and how public monetary and fiscal policies strive to stabilize business activity at a healthy level of progressive growth.

Part Three is concerned with the forces of competition and monopoly, which act through supply and demand to help determine—efficiently or inefficiently—the composition of the national income, in terms of both goods and services produced and their prices. (Unlike Part Two's "macroeconomics," this is "microeconomics.")

Part Four treats distribution of income: determination of wages, rent, interest, and profits—pricing of factors of production.

Part Five discusses international trade in both its monetary and real aspects.

Part Six deals with our most basic contemporary economic problems: growth analysis and development for low-income countries; the quality of life, protecting the environment against pollution and urban blight; racial and sexual discriminations; energy shortages and exhaustion of natural resources in an overcrowded world; mitigation of poverty and economic inequality; prescribing for "stagflation"—rising price levels in the face of mass unemployment; new and old winds of doctrine in political economy, mainstream and Marxian; comparisons of alternative economic systems—communism, capitalism, and the evolving mixed economy.

At the foundations of any community there will always be found a few universal economic conditions. Certain background problems are as crucial today as they were in the days of Homer and Caesar, and they will continue to be relevant in the brave new world of the future.

In Section A of this chapter we see that every society must meet a certain trio of *basic problems of economic organization*. Then Section B shows that technological *knowledge*, together with limited amounts of *land, labor,* and *capital,* defines the available choices between goods and services open to a community and that these *production possibilities* are subject to change and to the law of diminishing returns. Section C develops the point that the basis of any economy is its *population,* or *human element*.

We leave to Chapter 3 those important economic features characteristic of our own mixed economy—a system of private and public enterprise intertwined.

## A. PROBLEMS OF ECONOMIC ORGANIZATION

Any society, whether it consists of a totally collectivized communistic state, a tribe of South Sea Islanders, a capitalistic industrial nation, a Swiss Family Robinson, a Robinson Crusoe—or, one might almost add, a colony of bees—must somehow confront three fundamental and interdependent economic problems.

1. WHAT commodities shall be produced and in what quantities? That is, how much and which of alternative goods and services shall be produced? Food or clothing? Much food and little clothing, or vice versa? Bread and butter today, or bread and grape plantings today with bread, butter, and jam next year?

2. How shall goods be produced? That is, by whom and with what resources and in what technological manner are they to be produced? Who hunts, who fishes? Electricity from steam or waterfall or atoms? Large- or small-scale production?

# 2

# CENTRAL PROBLEMS OF EVERY ECONOMIC SOCIETY

To get land's fruit
in quantity
Takes jolts of labour
ever more,
Hence food will grow like
one, two, three, . . .
While numbers grow like
one, two, four, . . .
ANONYMOUS
*Song of Malthus: A Ballad
on Diminishing Returns*

3. FOR WHOM shall goods be produced? That is, who is to enjoy and get the benefit of the goods and services provided? Or, to put the same thing in another way, how is the total of national product to be *distributed*[1] among different individuals and families? A few rich and many poor? Or most people in modest comfort?

These three problems are fundamental and common to all economies, but different economic systems try to solve them differently.

**Custom, instinct, command, or the market**    In a primitive civilization, custom may rule every facet of behavior. WHAT, HOW, and FOR WHOM may be decided by reference to *traditional* ways of doing things. To members of another culture, the practices followed may seem bizarre and unreasonable; the members of the tribe or clan may themselves be so familiar with existing practices as to be surprised, and perhaps offended, if asked the reason for their behavior. Thus, the Kwakiutl Indians consider it desirable not to accumulate wealth but to give it away in the *potlatch*—a roisterous celebration. This deviation from acquisitive behavior toward taking turns at favor giving will not surprise anthropologists; their studies show that what is correct behavior in one culture is often the greatest crime in another.

In the bee colony, all such problems, even those involving an elaborate cooperative division of labor, are solved automatically by means of so-called "biological instincts." (Fair enough as a description, but not much of an "explanation.")

At the other extreme, we can imagine an omnipotent benevolent or malevolent dictator who by arbitrary decree and command decides WHAT, HOW, and FOR WHOM. Or we might imagine economic organization by command, but with commands drawn up by democratic vote or by delegated legislative authorities.

As is developed at length in Chapter 3, the WHAT, HOW, and FOR WHOM questions in a so-called "capitalist free enterprise economy" are determined primarily[2] by a system of prices (of markets, of profits and losses).

## THE LAW OF SCARCITY

WHAT to produce, HOW, and FOR WHOM would not be problems if resources were *un*limited. If an *infinite* amount of every good could be produced, or if human wants were *fully* satisfied, it would not then matter if too much of any particular good were produced. Nor would it then matter if labor and materials were combined unwisely. Since everyone could have as much as he pleased, it would not matter how goods and incomes were distributed among different individuals and families.

There would then be no *economic goods*, i.e., no goods that are relatively *scarce;* and there would hardly be any need for a study of economics or "economizing." All goods would be *free goods,* the way pure air used to be.

[1] WARNING: Usually, when an economist is talking about "distribution," he means the distribution *of incomes*—the principles which determine labor's wage, land's rent, capital's interest, and the whole FOR WHOM process. The man on the street usually means by distribution, wholesaling and retailing—how goods once produced get distributed into the hands of the consumer. We shall avoid this last confusing usage.
[2] There never was a 100 per cent purely automatic enterprise system, although Victorian England came close. Certainly in present-day systems, the government has an important role in modifying the workings of the price system. This is what is meant by saying we live in a "mixed economy."

In the world as it is, even children learn in growing up that "both" is not an admissible answer to a choice of "Which one?" Compared with backward nations or previous centuries, modern industrial societies seem very wealthy indeed. But higher production levels seem to bring in their train higher consumption standards.

People feel that they want and "need" indoor plumbing, central heating, refrigerators, penicillin, education, movies, radios, records, television, green lawns, books, autos, travel, sports and concerts, music, chic clothes, and so forth. The biological scientist tells them that they can be well nourished on a thin porridge for a few cents a day,[3] but that leaves them as cold as the information that the chemicals in their bodies are worth only a couple of dollars. Anyone who has kept a family budget knows that the necessities of life—the absolute musts—have little to do with the minimum *physiological* needs of food, clothing, and shelter.

In *The Affluent Society*, J. Kenneth Galbraith[4] has eloquently pointed out that Americans today have for the most part gone beyond the level of physiological necessity; that often the consumer flits from one purchase to another in response to pressures of fashion and advertising. Without challenging Galbraith's thesis that the time has come to spend more on public needs and less on private needs, one may properly point out that our total product would have to become many times higher than its present level if the average American were to become able to live at the level of a moderately well-off doctor, lawyer, professor, or advertising man—to say nothing of the living standards of the really well-to-do.

Whether or not people would be "genuinely" happier spending twice as much as now, observation suggests that folks in the suburbs now act *as if* they want more income to spend. They take on extra work; they resist tax increases; they end up saving much the same fraction of their incomes as in 1900; and middle-class mothers seem to work harder than their mothers did. Even if the national income were divided up equally between every man, woman, and child—an extreme case—there would be only about $90 per week to go around.

Therefore, while political economy recognizes the important germ of truth in the notion that America has become an affluent society, economics must still contend with *scarcity* as a basic fact of life. Abroad, this is even more the case.

## B. THE TECHNOLOGICAL CHOICES OPEN TO ANY SOCIETY

### SOCIETY'S PRODUCTION-POSSIBILITY FRONTIER

We have discussed the basic economic fact that *limitation* of the total resources capable of producing different commodities necessitates a choice between relatively scarce commodities. This can be illustrated quantitatively by simple arithmetic examples and

---

[3]A study suggests that standard requirements of adult nutrition could be bought in 1976 for about $125 per year. But what a diet this implies: kidneys, cabbage, beans, buckwheat flour, and not much else! Cf. George J. Stigler, "The Cost of Subsistence," *Journal of Farm Economics*, May, 1945, pp. 303–314. This paper achieved fame as a forerunner of an important mathematical technique of economics and national defense called "linear programming." Victor E. Smith of Michigan State University in the same journal (May, 1959, pp. 272–283) reported that a family of three could get a "palatable diet" for about 50 cents per person per day, perhaps a dollar in the 1970s.

[4]John Kenneth Galbraith, *The Affluent Society* (Houghton Mifflin, Boston, 1958).

geometrical diagrams. Diagrams and graphs are indispensable visual aids in many aspects of economics. A little care at the beginning in understanding them will be rewarded manyfold later on.

Consider an economy with only so many people, so much technical knowledge, so many factories and tools, and so much land, water power, and natural resources. In deciding WHAT shall be produced and How, the economy must really decide just how these resources are to be allocated among the thousands of different possible commodities. How much land should go into wheat growing? Or into pasturage? How many factories are to produce knives? How much skilled labor for machine shops?

These problems are complicated even to discuss, much less solve. Therefore we must simplify. So let us assume that only two economic goods (or classes of economic goods) are to be produced. For dramatic purposes, we can choose the pair Adolf Hitler ranted about—guns and butter. These two commodities are commonly used to illustrate the problem of choosing between civilian and war goods, but the same analysis applies to *any* choice of goods. Thus the more resources the government uses to build *public* roads, the less will be left to produce *private* houses; the more the public chooses to consume of *food,* the less it can consume of *clothing;* the more society decides to *consume today,* the less can be its production of *machines and capital goods* to turn out more consumption goods for the *next year or decade.*

### Numerical example

But let us stick to the example of guns and butter and begin to study Fig. 2-1. Now, suppose that *all* resources are thrown into the production of civilian goods (butter). There will still be a *maximum* amount of butter that can be produced per year. (The exact amount depends upon the quantitative and qualitative resources of the economy in question and the technological efficiency with which they are used.) Suppose 5 million pounds of butter is the maximum amount that can be produced with the existing technology and resources.

At the other extreme, imagine that 100 per cent of society's resources had been devoted instead to the production of guns. Only some maximum number of guns could then be produced: 15 (thousand) guns of a certain description can perhaps be produced if we are really willing to produce no butter.

These are two extreme possibilities; in between there are still others. If we are willing to give up *some* butter, we can have *some* guns. If we are willing to give up still more butter, we can have still more guns. A schedule of a number of possibilities is given in Fig. 2-1's table, F being the extreme where all butter and no guns are produced, and A being the opposite extreme where all resources go into guns. In between, at E, D, C, and B, butter is being given up increasingly in return for more guns. Butter is "transformed" into guns, not physically, but by diverting resources from one use to the other.

### Graphical production-possibility frontier

It is even more illuminating to represent this same "production-possibility schedule" graphically in Fig. 2-1, by measuring butter along the horizontal axis and guns along the vertical.

The reader should now be able to go directly from the numerical table to the diagram: for *F,* by counting over 5 butter units to the right and going up 0 gun units;

| ALTERNATE PRODUCTION POSSIBILITIES | | |
| --- | --- | --- |
| POSSI- BILITIES | BUTTER (millions of pounds) | GUNS (thou- sands) |
| A | 0 | 15 |
| B | 1 | 14 |
| C | 2 | 12 |
| D | 3 | 9 |
| E | 4 | 5 |
| F | 5 | 0 |

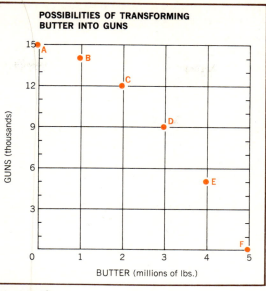

POSSIBILITIES OF TRANSFORMING BUTTER INTO GUNS

**FIG. 2-1**

**Full employment of scarce resources implies guns-butter tradeoff**

As we go from A to B . . . to F, we are transferring resources from the gun industry to the butter industry. The cost of getting extra butter can be reckoned (along the tradeoff relation) as the extra guns we are forced to sacrifice.

On the diagram, the orange point A is plotted by going up 15 and over 0. Similarly each orange point is a careful plot of the table's pair of numbers. (Can you guess where the number midway between B and C might approximately fall? Read off *its* butter-guns numbers.)

for E, by going 4 butter units to the right and going up 5 gun units; and finally, for A, by going over 0 butter units and up 15 gun units.

We may fill in all intermediate positions with new orange dots, even those involving fractions of a million pounds or fractions of a thousand guns—as in the orange so-called "production-possibility frontier" shown in Fig. 2-2 on the next page.

The curve that we now have represents this fundamental fact:

**A full-employment economy must always in producing one good be giving up something of another.** *Substitution* **is the law of life in a full-employment economy. The** *production-possibility frontier* **depicts society's menu of choices.**

**Unemployment and inefficiency**   But what if there had been widespread unemployment of resources: idle men, idle land, idle factories? We have already warned that our economic laws may then be quite different. This is one such instance.

With unemployment, we are not on the production-possibility frontier at all, but rather, somewhere *inside* it. Thus, U in Fig. 2-2 represents a point *inside* the *p-p frontier* where society is producing only 2 (million) pounds of butter and 6 (thousand) guns. If resources are idle, by putting them to work we can have more butter *and* more guns. We can move from U to D and thereby get *more* butter *and more* guns.

This throws important light on the different experience in World War II of three countries: the United States, Germany, and Russia. After 1940, how was the United States able to become the "arsenal of democracy" and to enjoy civilian living standards higher than ever before?

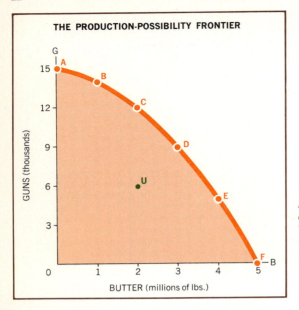

THE PRODUCTION-POSSIBILITY FRONTIER

**FIG. 2-2**

**A smooth curve fills in the plotted points
of the numerical production possibilities**
This frontier shows the menu of choice along which society can choose to substitute guns for butter, assuming a given state of technology and a given total of resources. Any point *inside* the curve, such as *U,* indicates that resources are not being fully employed in the best-known way. (Source: Fig. 2-1's numerical data.)

Largely by taking up the slack of unemployment. On the other hand, Hitler's war effort began in 1933, long before any formal declaration. It stemmed from a period of unemployment acute enough to win him the votes to get into power peacefully. Almost all the extra output made possible by utilizing previously unemployed workers and plants was siphoned into German war goods rather than into higher civilian consumption. Still a third case is that of the wartime Soviet Union. The Russians had little unemployment before the war and were already on their rather low production-possibility frontier. They had no choice but to substitute war goods for civilian goods—with consequent privation.

Business-cycle unemployment is not the only way of being inside the *p-p frontier.* If an economy is inefficiently organized, it may also be well short of the frontier—as in the defeated Germany of 1947 when the whole price system had broken down; or in China of 1960 when the ideological drive for a "great leap forward" resulted in ousting of experts and a short-lived attempt to make steel by backyard furnaces; or in an economy riddled with monopoly and subject to arbitrary decrees by inept bureaucrats. (We shall analyze all this later and find that even a normal mixed economy has monopolistic imperfections that keep it inside its true potential frontier.)

### SOME USES OF THE PRODUCTION-POSSIBILITY FRONTIER

This concept, represented as a simple curve, can help introduce many of the most basic concepts in economics. For example, Fig. 2-2 illustrates the basic definition of economics given in Chapter 1, namely, the problem of *choosing* among *scarce* or limited resources ("means" capable of *alternative* uses), in order to achieve best *goals* ("ends"). Land, labor, and capital can be used to produce guns or butter along the frontier curve in Fig. 2-2. Where does the society choose to end up? Southeastward in the diagram, with much of civilian goods? Or northwestward, with much of defense goods? Economics is a *quantitative* subject: choice is not a qualitative matter of "either-or," but rather of *how many* of each good and just where we draw the line of final decision.

The production-possibility frontier provides a rigorous definition of scarcity.

*Definition:* **"Economic scarcity" refers to the basic fact of life that there exists only a finite amount of human and nonhuman resources, which the best technical knowledge is capable of using to produce only a *limited* maximum amount of each and every good, as shown by the *p-p frontier.* And thus far, nowhere on the globe is the supply of goods so plentiful or the tastes so limited that the *average family* can have more than enough of everything it might fancy.**

The production-possibility schedule can also help make clear the three basic problems of economic life: WHAT, HOW, and FOR WHOM.

WHAT goods are produced and consumed can be depicted by the point that gets chosen on the *p-p frontier.*

How goods are to be produced involves an efficient choice of methods and proper assignment of different amounts and kinds of limited resources to the various industries.

What would happen if the men well fitted for machine-tooling of guns ended up on farms while at the same time land well fitted for butter ended up being used for gun manufacture? We would be *inside* the *p-p frontier,* not on it. Or what if government regulations made the land most suitable for corn be used for wheat production, and the land most suitable for wheat be used for corn? We would end up with less of both corn and wheat, inside the production-possibility frontier on a diagram whose axes were labeled corn and wheat. Being inside the frontier is, as we have already seen, a crime of *economic* inefficiency; but it need not involve any *engineering* inefficiency, since, on the wrongly allocated land, production might still be following the latest methods known to science.[5]

FOR WHOM goods are to be produced cannot be discerned from the *p-p* diagram alone. Sometimes, though, you can make a guess from it: if you find a society on its *p-p frontier* with many yachts and few compact cars, you are justified in suspecting that it enjoys considerable inequality of income and wealth among persons.

### PICTURES IN AN EXHIBITION

The graphs of Figs. 2-3 to 2-7 on the following pages are meant to be self-explanatory. They show that the production-possibility frontier can illustrate many familiar, but basic, economic processes. Later chapters will deal with each of these in depth, and it is necessary here only to comprehend the common-sense ideas involved.

Figure 2-3 illustrates how a society consumes much food when it is poor but shifts toward comforts and luxuries as it develops—a topic to be met in Chapter 11.

---

[5] More difficult is the notion that the economy should often prefer scientifically *less* efficient methods over methods that are allegedly technically more efficient. EXAMPLE: Physics texts teach that converting heat to motion at 2500°C is intrinsically more efficient than converting it at 1200°C. Yet, if metals that can stand the higher temperature are scarce and dear, it is *economically* better for the engineer and businessman to use the thermodynamically less efficient method!

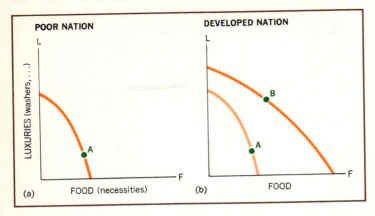

**FIG. 2-3**

**Economic development and progress shifts *p-p frontier* outward**

**(a)**   Before development, the nation is so poor it must devote almost all its resources to food, enjoying few comforts.

**(b)**   After development, it goes from *A* to *B*, expanding its food consumption very little compared with its increased consumption of nonnecessities. (Note that it can now have more than before of all goods if it so wishes.)

Figure 2-4 illustrates how the electorate must choose between private goods bought at a price and public goods paid for largely by taxes, a topic to be met in Chapter 8.

Figure 2-5 illustrates how an economy chooses between (*a*) current consumption goods and (*b*) capital goods (machines, etc.) that make possible more of *both* goods (consumption and capital) in the future. Much of Parts Two, Four, and Six will deal with this basic saving and investment problem.

Figure 2-6 shows how Economy B, blessed by scientific and engineering discoveries, might surpass A, which was showing more thrift and investing for the future, but with less progressive technology. Part Six on growth will develop this theme.

Finally, Fig. 2-7, will prepare us for the next topic, the law of diminishing returns.

## THE LAW OF DIMINISHING RETURNS

Figure 2-7 will alert us to a famous technological economic relationship, the so-called "law of diminishing returns." This law states the relation—*not* between two goods (such as guns and butter), but—between an *input* of production (such as labor) and the output that it helps produce (such as butter or, in the classical examples, corn).

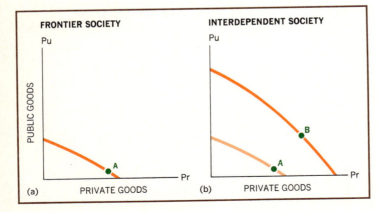

**FIG. 2-4**

**With prosperity comes greater emphasis on public rather than private goods**

**(a)**   The first economy is poor and dispersed, as in Daniel Boone's frontier days: the proportion of resources going to government's public sector is low.

**(b)**   The second economy is more prosperous and chooses to spend more of its higher income on governmental services (roads, defense, research, education); in dense urban life, it has no choice but to spend on traffic lights, police, antipollution programs, and city planning.

**FIG. 2-5**

**Capital formation for future consumption forces sacrifice of current consumption**

**(a)** Three countries start out even. Country 1 does no saving for the future at $A_1$ (merely replacing machines). Country 2 abstains modestly from consumption at $A_2$. Country 3, by private sacrifice or vote, is at $A_3$, investing much and sacrificing much of current consumption.

**(b)** In the next years, Country 3 has forged ahead of 2, which has moved ahead of 1. Possessing more machines for labor to work with, Country 3 now has more of *both* goods.

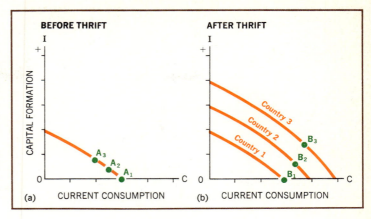

More specifically, the law of diminishing returns refers to the diminishing amount of *extra output* that we get when we successively add *equal extra* units of a *varying input* to a *fixed* amount of some *other input*. (Note the emphasized words.)

Here is an example to illustrate the law of diminishing returns. We make the following controlled experiment: Given a fixed amount of land, say, 100 acres, we shall first add no labor at all. We note that with zero labor input there is no corn output. So, in Table 2-1 on page 27, we record zero product when labor is zero.

Now we make a second related experiment. We add 1 extra unit of labor to the same fixed amount of land. How much output do we now get? Pure reason cannot tell us: we must look to the facts of the experiment. When we do, let's say we observe that we now have produced positive output of corn equal to 2,000 units (bushels or whatever units you choose for corn). We now summarize the result of this second experiment: Adding 1 extra unit of labor to 100 of fixed land gives us extra output of 2,000 units.

To observe the law of diminishing returns, we must make a third controlled experi-

**FIG. 2-6**

**Technical invention can more than match productivity gain from thrift alone**

**(a)** Country A, on the left, is thrifty and advances by accumulating capital goods.

**(b)** Country B advances even more from 1980 to 1990 because it spends more on science and technical research. From 1990 to 2000 it grows faster still by using both methods: technical progress *and* much capital formation.

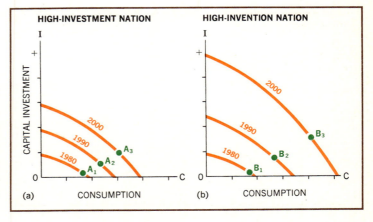

ment. We still hold land fixed. Once more we vary the labor input and make sure to add *again exactly the same extra unit of labor as before;* i.e., we now go from 1 unit of labor to 2 units of labor to match our earlier going from 0 labor to 1 labor. We breathlessly await the outcome of the experiment in terms of extra corn produced.

Shall we now have a total of 4,000 units of corn, which would, as before, represent exactly 2,000 extra units of output produced by the extra unit of the varying labor? Or shall we find *diminishing* returns, with the new extra unit of input adding less than the 2,000 extra units of output which was previously added?

If the law of diminishing returns does in fact hold, our experiment can have but one result. The second extra labor unit will add *less extra output* than did the first. Adding still a third extra unit of labor will, if diminishing returns holds, result in *still lower* extra output. And so forth. Table 2-1 gives numerical values to illustrate exactly what diminishing returns means.

The law of diminishing returns is an important, often-observed economic and technical regularity. But it is not universally valid. Often it will hold only *after* you have added a considerable number of equal doses of the varying factor. Beyond that point, we say the law of diminishing returns has set in. (Before such a point, the varying

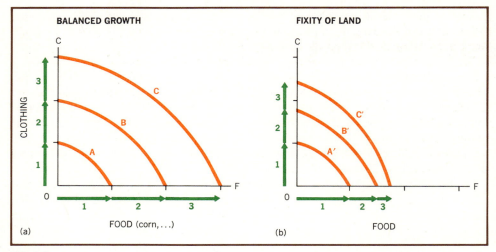

**FIG. 2-7**

**Diminishing returns means outputs on fixed land cannot keep pace with population**

**(a)**   We begin initially at the lower curve A on the left. But population now doubles and is able to spread over double the previous land, leaving each county and state in the same land-labor balance as before. Hence the new curve B depicts exactly twice the scale of food and clothing production. Finally, let labor and land both rise again by the same extra amount as between A and B. We end up at C, gaining fully as much of extra products as we did before from the same *balanced* additions of labor and land. Note that the green arrows 1, 2, and 3 on each axis show no diminishing length.

**(b)**   We begin at the same lower curve A, repeated on the right. Now *land is held constant* while population doubles. Each laborer has *less* land to work with than under balanced growth. Hence, the B' curve is below the B curve of Fig. 2-7(a). Finally, add another equal increment of labor, still holding land constant. The new *extra* product is even lower, as shown by the diminishing lengths of the green arrows 1, 2, and 3, depicting extra outputs. We'll soon understand the reasons for all this, after the "law of diminishing returns" is mastered.

**LAW OF DIMINISHING RETURNS**

| MAN-YEARS OF LABOR | TOTAL PRODUCT (bushels) | EXTRA OUTPUT ADDED BY ADDITIONAL UNIT OF LABOR |
|---|---|---|
| 0 | 0 | |
| | | 2,000 |
| 1 | 2,000 | |
| | | 1,000 |
| 2 | 3,000 | |
| | | 500 |
| 3 | 3,500 | |
| | | — |
| 4 | 3,800 | |
| | | 100 |
| 5 | 3,900 | |

**TABLE 2-1**
**Diminishing returns is a fundamental law of economics and technology**
Law of diminishing returns refers to successively lower extra outputs (e.g., of corn) gained from adding equal increments of a variable input (e.g., labor) to a constant amount of a fixed input (e.g., 100 acres of land). (Pencil in the extra output of the fourth laborer.)

factors might be yielding *increasing* extra returns, since until then we might find that adding extra varying inputs to a fixed input leads to increasing rather than diminishing extra outputs; but, *ultimately*, decreasing returns can be expected to prevail.)

Why is the law of diminishing returns plausible? Frequently we feel that by adding land and labor together—no input being fixed and all being varied in the same balanced proportion so that the whole *scale* of operations is getting larger—then output should also increase proportionately and extra outputs need not diminish. For why should the extra outputs diminish if each of the inputs always has as much of the other inputs to work with?

In short, *balanced* scale changes may often be expected to leave inputs and outputs in the same ratios. [Look at Fig. 2-7(a) to verify this.]

On the other hand, when we do hold one input or group of inputs constant and vary the remaining inputs, we see that the varying inputs have *less and less of the fixed inputs to work with*. Consequently, we are not too surprised that such extra varying inputs begin to add less and less extra product.

In effect, the fixed factor of production (land) is decreasing in proportion to the variable input (labor). As we crowd the land more and more, we may still get some extra corn by intensive cultivation of the soil; but the amount of extra corn per unit of extra labor will become less and less. We shall see in Part Four that the real wage paid to workers depends upon the extra output a last man adds for his employer. Diminishing returns reveals that living standards in crowded China or India are low because of this basic technical truth, and not *merely* because land happens to be owned by the state or by private landlords.

In conclusion, we may summarize as follows:

*The law of diminishing returns:* An increase in some inputs relative to other fixed inputs will, in a given state of technology, cause total output to increase; *but after a point the extra output resulting from the same additions of extra inputs is likely to become less and less.* This falling off of extra returns is a consequence of the fact that the new "doses" of the varying resources have less and less of the fixed resources to work with.

## ECONOMIES OF SCALE AND MASS PRODUCTION: AN IMPORTANT COUNTERFORCE

Before leaving this section we should digress to take note of a phenomenon that is different from our controlled variation of one thing at a time.

Suppose we merely increase "*scale* of operations," i.e., increase *all* the factors at the same time in the same degree. In many industrial processes, when you double *all* inputs, you may find that your output is more than doubled; this phenomenon is called "*increasing* returns to *scale*."

Our previous law of diminishing returns always refers to cases where *some* factors were varied *while some remained fixed*. Hence, this case of increasing returns to scale is not a direct refutation of the law of diminishing returns.

Increasing returns to scale, or so-called "economies of mass production," are often associated with one of the following advances: (1) the use of nonhuman and nonanimal power sources (water and wind power, steam, electricity, turbines and internal-combustion engines, internal nuclear energy); (2) the use of automatic self-adjusting mechanisms (lathes, jigs, servomechanisms); (3) the use of standardized, interchangeable parts; (4) the breakdown of complex processes into simple repetitive operations; (5) the specialization of function and division of labor; and many other technological factors as well. The auto-production assembly line and historical development of textile spinning and weaving exemplify these diverse factors.

Upon thought, it will be evident that *each of these economies or savings comes into full play only when a large enough number of units is being produced to make it worth while to set up a fairly elaborate productive organization*. If only a few guns are to be produced, they might just as well be produced by hand; but if resources are available to produce many

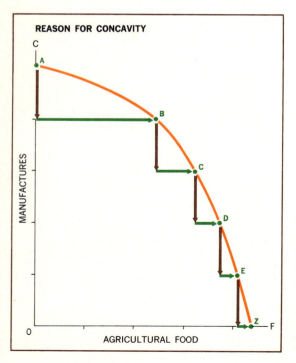

**REASON FOR CONCAVITY**

MANUFACTURES

AGRICULTURAL FOOD

**FIG. 2-8**

**Land scarcity for food, plus diminishing returns, entails increasing (relative) costs**

In going from *A* to *B*, *B* to *C*, *C* to *D*, *D* to *E*, and *E* to *Z*, we have to give up equal amounts of Manufactures as we transfer *equal* labor amounts out of the manufacturing industry. Note the equal vertical brown arrows below *A*, below *B*, . . . , etc. But, as equal units of varying labor are added to fixed agricultural land, diminishing returns yields less and less of extra food—as measured by the shorter and shorter green horizontal arrows. This accounts for the curve's bending concavely, or for the law of increasing relative costs.

thousands, it will pay to make certain elaborate initial preparations that need not be repeated when still more units are to be produced. In such cases, where mere scale matters much, the tendency for land fixity to force diminishing extra returns to labor could be thwarted for a long time by an increase in the total labor scale involved.[6]

Economies of scale are very important in explaining why so many of the goods we buy are produced by large companies, as Karl Marx emphasized a century ago. We shall see that they are important in helping explain "the division of labor" and pattern of "specialization." They raise questions to which we shall return again and again in later chapters—as, for example, monopoly.

## LAW OF INCREASING (RELATIVE) COSTS

We are now in a position to indicate why the production-possibility frontier has been drawn as a bowed-out (concave from below) curve in all our diagrams. If the *p-p frontier* were a straight line, the relative costs of getting some extra guns in terms of sacrificed butter would always be the same. Economists call this a case of "constant (relative) costs." But actually it is more common in life to meet the *law of increasing (relative) costs*.

*Definition:* The "law of increasing (relative) costs" prevails when in order to get equal extra amounts of one good, society must sacrifice ever-increasing amounts *of the other good*. A bowed-out or concave curvature of the production-possibility frontier depicts the law of increasing (relative) costs—as shown by the fact that when we want more Farm Goods, their (relative) cost rises in terms of sacrificed Manufactures.

Why is this reasonable?[7] We'll see that the law of increasing (relative) costs is related to, but definitely not the same thing as, the law of diminishing returns. We'll see that, along with the law of diminishing returns, economists must be able to assume that guns and butter use the factors of production, such as labor and land, *in different proportions or intensities* if we are to deduce this law of (increasing) relative costs.

To derive the law of increasing (relative) costs, let us use an oversimplified example. In Fig. 2-8, suppose that Manufactures (guns) require *labor alone* and negligible land. But suppose that Agricultural Food (butter) requires, along with labor, fertile *land that has grown scarce enough to have become private property*. Now we have the two ingredients needed to explain the law of increasing (relative) costs shown in the *p-p frontier:* The two industries do use land and labor in different proportions; so transferring varying amounts of labor onto fixed agricultural land will turn out to bring into play the law of diminishing returns. Let us see exactly how.

Begin by using all labor to produce Manufactures, at *A* in Fig. 2-8. Now sacrifice equal amounts of Manufactures to get more Agriculture, going to *B* and *C*. How is this transformation

---

[6]Accordingly, it might come about that, unlike our earlier simplified picture, we should have to pay 2 butter units for our first gun unit; but to get still another gun unit we should have to pay only 1 butter unit because of the efficiency of mass production. This would be a case of *decreasing,* rather than increasing, extra-costs-for-one-good-in-terms-of-another. When increasing returns to scale predominate, advanced treatises show that you have to redraw Fig. 2-2 to be "bowed in" (convex from below) rather than "bowed out" (concave from below), at least near each axis.

[7]The remainder of this section may be skipped without loss of continuity.

accomplished? By transferring *equal amounts of labor* away from Manufactures (since no land is used there at all). But note that these equal amounts of transferred labor are now applied to a *fixed* total of agricultural land. As equal amounts of varying labor are applied to a fixed land factor, each has less and less acres to work with and hence adds less and less of extra Agriculture product. We see then why each new Agriculture is procured at higher and higher costs in terms of sacrificed Manufactures.[8]

## C. THE UNDERLYING POPULATION BASIS OF ANY ECONOMY: PAST AND FUTURE POPULATION TRENDS

Now that we have studied the law of diminishing returns, let us put it to work in this last part of the chapter to underline the crucial importance of population growth relative to fixed resources.

### THE MALTHUSIAN THEORY OF POPULATION

The law of diminishing returns has an important and interesting application in the field of population. Around 1800, Thomas Robert Malthus, a young English clergyman, used to argue at breakfast against his father's perfectionist view that the human race was getting ever better. Finally the younger Malthus became so agitated that he wrote a book, his *Essay on the Principle of Population* (1798), which was an instantaneous best-seller. Going through several editions, for a century the book influenced the thinking of people all over the world (including Charles Darwin, the expositor of the doctrine of biological evolution). It is still a living influence today. Malthus' views depend directly on the law of diminishing returns, and continue to have relevance.

Malthus first took the observation of Benjamin Franklin that, in the American colonies where resources were abundant, population tended to double every 25 years or so. Malthus postulated, therefore, *a universal tendency for population—unless checked by food supply—to grow at a geometric progression.* Now, anyone with imagination knows how fast geometric progressions grow—how soon 1, 2, 4, 8, 16, 32, 64, 128, 256, 512, 1,024, . . . , becomes so large that there is not space in the world for all the people to stand.[9]

---

[8] The common sense of this law of increasing (relative) costs does not depend upon one of the goods using labor alone. It depends only on having the two goods—call them guns and butter—differing in the proportions of factors they require. Thus, note that the first few guns can be produced in part with the kind of resources that are no good for butter anyway. If more guns are wanted, we must use resources that are valuable for butter production; and if we insist upon having all guns, we must be prepared to take farmers and farmlands, which are very efficient in the production of butter, and transform them to the production of guns even though they can produce only very little in this sphere. Thus, increasing (relative) cost is to be expected in such a case. (Even if resources could be divided into two uniform classes, such as homogeneous land and homogeneous labor, increasing costs would still result from the fact that guns and butter do not require the same proportion of these resources—butter taking more land, and guns requiring relatively more labor—as in the example above. An Extra-credit problem, for geometry-inclined readers, returns to this problem at end of Chapter 27's Appendix.)

[9] At 6 per cent compound interest, money doubles in value every 12 years. It has been estimated

All this left members of the "perfectionist school," such as the elder Malthus and William Godwin, unimpressed. So at this point Malthus in effect unleashed the devil of the law of diminishing returns.

**As population doubles and redoubles, it is exactly as if the globe were halving in size, until finally it has shrunk so much that food and subsistence fall below the level necessary for life. Because of the law of diminishing returns, food tends *not* to keep up with the geometric-progression rate of growth of population.**

Mind you, Malthus did not say that population *would* increase at these rates. This was only its *tendency* if unchecked. He considered it an important part of his argument to show that, in all places in all times, checks do operate to hold population down. In his first edition, he put emphasis on *positive* checks that act to increase the death rate: pestilence, famine, and war. Later, he backed down from this gloomy doctrine and held out hope for the human race through *preventive* checks operating on the birth rate. Although the birth-control movement is called neo-Malthusianism, clergyman Malthus advocated only *moral restraint* with prudential postponement of early marriages until a family could be supported. In fact, he preached that the struggle for existence was an illustration of the wisdom of Nature, keeping poor people from getting soft and lazy.

This important application of diminishing returns illustrates the profound effects a simple theory can have. Malthus' ideas had widespread repercussions. His book was used to support a stern revision of the English poor laws, whereby destitution was considered a result of laziness and unemployment a state to be made as uncomfortable as possible. His opinions also bolstered the argument that trade-unions could not improve the welfare of workers, since any increase in their wages would only cause workers to reproduce until there was again barely subsistence enough for all. Even in the 1970s, the computer makes headlines when it spells out the "limits of growth" by a more elaborate simulation of Malthus' geometric and arithmetic progressions.[10]

**False prophecies of Malthus**    Despite the statistics covering many countries incorporated in his later editions, it is today recognized that his views were oversimplifications. In his discussion of diminishing returns, Malthus never fully anticipated the miracles of the Industrial Revolution. In the next century, technological innovation *shifted* production-possibility frontiers rapidly *outward* and made possible better standards of living for more people, even though at the same time medical advances were prolonging human life and further lessening the positive checks to population. Nor did he anticipate that after 1870 in most Western nations family *fertility* as measured

---

that the $24 received by the Indians for Manhattan Island would, if deposited at compound interest, be today worth as much as all real property on the island. At 6 per cent, Sir Francis Drake's plunder of Spanish gold would today equal Britain's wealth, as Keynes pointed out. See Question 8 for the exact definition of a geometric progression and its relation to compound interest.

[10]See the study, *The Limits to Growth* (Universe Books, New York, 1972), prepared at MIT for the Club of Rome by Dennis Meadows and other disciples of Jay Forrester, the inventor of the computer's ceramic memory device and philosopher of industrial, urban, and world dynamics. Excerpts from this study appear in Paul A. Samuelson, *Readings in Economics* (McGraw-Hill, New York, 1973, 7th ed.).

by actual number of children would begin to fall far short of family *fecundity*, or biological reproductive capacity.

Nevertheless, the germs of truth in his doctrines are still important for understanding the population behavior of India, Haiti, China, and other parts of the globe where the balance of numbers and food supply is a vital factor.

Table 2-2 shows how much world population has increased. This increase was made possible mainly through the declining death rate, resulting from scientific advances in medicine and from the improved living standards made possible by the Industrial Revolution. Life expectancy of a Western baby has doubled since 1800 to over 70 years at present, and standards of living far exceed those of any previous century.

Even more dramatic has been the reduction of death rates in low-income regions. Ceylon offers the dramatic case where control of mosquitoes by DDT greatly reduced malaria, cutting the death rate by 34 per cent in a single year! In India alone, one of the fruits of modern science has been a great increase in average life expectancy. In the last 20 years India's population grew by at least 120 million, an amount greater than the combined populations of France and England!

Professor Kingsley Davis of California, an expert on population, has warned against the facile belief that it is primarily hunger (or even malnutrition) that makes life so short in poor societies. Disease is important as an independent factor: If inexpensive science greatly lengthens life without greatly increasing productivity and greatly changing preindustrial attitudes, the fears of Malthus take on a new relevance.

## CONTROLLING POPULATION GROWTH

As we shall see in Part Six, much of the world is in a state of underdevelopment and poverty. If the birth rate were to continue at the high levels typical of the past—when you had to have six or more children in order to ensure that there would be a surviving child to carry on your line—population numbers would explode, and the law of diminishing returns would vitiate the gains from technical progress. Little wonder then that, wherever religious and ethical attitudes permit, there is beginning to be an active birth-control or family-planning movement.

As fewer children die before adulthood, people all over the world seem eager to

| POPULATION OF THE WORLD (in millions) | | | | |
|---|---|---|---|---|
| | 1800 | 1940 | 1970 | 1985 (estimate) |
| Europe (including all of U.S.S.R.) | 188 | 572 | 705 | 802 |
| North, South, and Central America | 29 | 277 | 511 | 715 |
| Asia, Africa, and Oceania | 702 | 1,396 | 2,416 | 3,416 |
| World | 919 | 2,245 | 3,632 | 4,933 |

**TABLE 2-2**

**World population quadrupled since 1800**
Even with birth rates falling generally, population of the less developed world will grow relative to the developed world: instead of having twice the population of the developed regions as now, a century from now the presently undeveloped countries will have six times as many people! (Source: UNESCO.)

limit unwanted births. Slowly but surely there has been increased use of the loop, the Pill, and other chemical and mechanical devices; there have been changes in mental attitudes, particularly where women are able to control fertility, so that even methods based on rhythm are applied more effectively; sterilization—male vasectomy, tube tying, etc.—often follows on attainment of desired family size. The older practices of infanticide and infant exposure, relied on in the past by so many cultures, have given way to legal and illegal abortions. Ethical debate accelerates over celibacy and chastity, the right to life of the embryo and foetus, women's liberation and the cult of masculinity ("machismo"). Yet it remains the sober truth that *the globe's population is growing more rapidly right now than ever before in the history of the world!*

## DECLINE AND RISE OF BIRTH RATES

At the end of World War I, people still feared the Malthusian curse of overpopulation. Books then had such alarming titles as *The World Faces Overpopulation* and *Standing Room Only!* But just as these books were coming off the presses, Western Europe and the United States were undergoing a profound revolution in population. This was understood only a generation later. The pendulum then swung to the other extreme; best sellers had flashy titles like *The Twilight of Parenthood* and *England without People*.

Since 1870—even earlier in France—birth rates began to drop in most countries of Western European civilization. After World War I, and especially after the Great Depression of the 1930s, the drop became precipitous.

Before World War II, there was reason for the population expert to despair for the future of the population of Western nations. Nor did the problem appear to be directly economic. Everyone knew that the rich had fewer children than the poor. Before 1940, Harvard and Vassar students were not reproducing themselves. Nor were Iowa State and Oberlin students, nor high school graduates and urban groups generally.[11]

**War and postwar upswing in fertility**   Just then something remarkable happened to jar the expert. Nobody yet knows quite how to explain it fully. During and after World War II the pattern of fertility began steadily to climb, reaching new heights.

Some of the reasons were, of course, obvious. With the war came prosperity, and the backlog of depression-deferred marriages began to melt. The Draft also had something to do with the increase in marriages. The number of single people shrank; and the age of (first) marriage fell sharply, so that more girls would marry at eighteen than at any other age, with half married by shortly after twenty, and with half the men married by age twenty-three!

[11] Most authorities believe birth rates are to be explained by social rather than biological factors. Physiologists now dispute the notion that modern women and men are less fecund than their hungry ancestors. Thus, the French Canadians, who long had high birth rates, once came from just those rural regions of France with lowest rates. Second-generation Italian and Jewish city dwellers show greatly reduced rates, as do Black Americans who move from the South to the North. Some of the highest net reproduction rates are among the white people in Appalachia.

With many more new marriages, it was only natural to expect the birth rate to leap upward. But more than that, couples stepped up the rate at which they had children. In the 1950s third and fourth children became very fashionable among the middle classes, a dramatic reversion from the pre-World War II situation.

A glance at a college faculty—young, old, and middle-aged—would show the changing trends in this regard: the associate professors of 1960 had already had more children than retired professors. Paradoxically, poorer nations such as Japan and Greece, which used to have high birth rates, had begun to restrict family size more than the rich nations.

## NET REPRODUCTION RATES AND REPLACEMENT RATES

The crude ratio of total births to total population can be misleading. Thus, from 1928 to 1940, when American and European populations had really begun to fail to reproduce themselves, crude birth rates fell only slowly and disguised this fact. Why? For the reason that, in those years, there were so many women of childbearing age in consequence of the large families of *their* mothers' fertile 1900 generation.

How can we correct for these temporary ups and downs in the age structure of the population? Demographers do so by concentrating on "age-specific fertility." That is, they ask: How many births occur to 100 women of age 15–20, age 20–25, . . . , age 40–45? How many total births will 1,000 newly born female babies give rise to throughout their lives? Only if this generation's 1,000 women leave behind them more than 1,000 girl babies (who in turn do the same, . . .) will the population hold its own in the long run.[12]

Bringing in both the sexes, what is the *replacement rate* of the number of children the average couple must have if the population is to replace itself in the long run? Since there are 1.06 male births to 1.0 female, even if no female died before the end of child-bearing age, the (gross) replacement rate would be 2.06 children per couple. Allowing for such early deaths, we work out the magic "replacement rate" to be 2.11 children per couple. That means fewer third, fourth, and fifth children per family than in the 1950s or in the olden days.

Table 2-3 shows that the richer countries of Western Europe had pre-World War II net reproduction rates (NRR) far below unity. Then, from 1940 to 1960, they had rates *far above* the critical level of unity. After 1960, NRRs fell everywhere.

## TURN OF THE TIDE?

America has experienced a steady fall in the birth rate since 1957. Significant for the longer-run trend is the fact that the fertility and net reproduction rates have been dropping among married women *of every age*.

---

[12]Demographers define the "net reproduction rate" (NRR) as "the *average* number of girl babies that will be born to a representative newly born girl in her lifetime." Thus, if 1,000 **girls** born in 1976 will, by A.D. 2020, have produced 1,600 girl babies, the NRR = 1,600/1,000 = 1.6; and were such a fertility rate to be maintained indefinitely, population would ultimately be growing at the rate of 60 per cent per "generation," i.e., about every 25 years, the average age of a mother when giving birth. (Can you explain exactly what NRR = 0.7 or = 1.0 means, showing why 1.0 is the watershed between ultimate decay and growth?)

NET REPRODUCTION RATES FOR VARIOUS COUNTRIES

| United States | | | Netherlands | 1.15 | 1935–39 |
|---|---|---|---|---|---|
| Total | 0.98 | 1930–40 | | 1.29 | 1968 |
| | 1.72 | 1960 | Australia | 0.98 | 1935–39 |
| | 0.88 | 1974 | | 1.42 | 1971 |
| White | 0.96 | 1935–40 | | | |
| | 1.66 | 1960 | Israel | | |
| | 1.16 | 1965 | Total | 1.78 | 1968 |
| Nonwhite | 1.14 | 1935–40 | Jews | 1.57 | 1963 |
| | 2.04 | 1960 | Japan | 1.49 | 1935–39 |
| | 1.45 | 1968 | | 1.05 | 1967 |
| United Kingdom | 0.78 | 1935–39 | India | 1.25 | 1931 |
| | 1.13 | 1971 | | 1.31 | 1941 |
| France | 0.87 | 1935–37 | Soviet Union | 1.72 | 1926 |
| | 1.25 | 1967 | | 1.54 | 1938 |
| Sweden | 0.78 | 1935–39 | | 1.14 | 1965 |
| | 0.92 | 1972 | | 1.11 | 1968–69 |
| Germany | | | Taiwan | 2.68 | 1955–59 |
| Total | 0.71 | 1933 | | 1.72 | 1971 |
| West | 0.98 | 1970 | Mauritius | 2.30 | 1955–59 |
| Belgium | 0.90 | 1939 | | 1.98 | 1968 |
| | 1.09 | 1968 | | | |

TABLE 2-3

**Net reproduction rates, which correct for age distributions, are falling everywhere**
An NRR (net reproduction rate) permanently greater than 1 means ultimate population growth. An NRR less than 1 means ultimate population decline. Note the drop in NRRs, both for white and nonwhite in U.S. Note similar drops toward 1 in the U.S.S.R., Japan, and Western Europe generally. Even less developed countries are finally beginning to show some declines. (Source: Office of Population Research, Princeton University; author.)

Note in Table 2-3 the dramatic decline in the NRRs below unity in the U.S.A., Sweden, and Germany. A similar story is told everywhere. Within the United States, fertility rates among blacks have fallen along with those of whites. If the decline in Catholic fertility continues to outpace that of non-Catholics, the historical differential will soon have vanished. National surveys on the number of children that women say they *want* are ceasing to receive as answers, "About 3, on the average." In the 1970s the reported number is dropping sharply below 2.

**Economics and sociology**   No doubt economic factors are involved here. Professor Richard Easterlin of the University of Pennsylvania has put forth an interesting hypothesis. He speculates that a young married couple will be less eager to have many children if their current income is falling far below that which their own families had a few years earlier. He points out that in the 1950s, when young people were scarce and their incomes relatively high, they hastened to have many children. In the early 1970s, when the vast crop of war babies has been coming onto the labor market and bidding down incomes, the comparison is less favorable. In Easterlin's view, this helps to explain the decline in NRR.

Women's liberation and new patterns of social psychology reinforce these economic factors. Mothers with infants are beginning to stay in the labor market. Demands for day-care centers will undoubtedly accelerate. The Census reports a clear pattern: In those regions where income opportunities for women are most favorable, the birth rate has dropped most. Thus, economics and sociology are mutually reinforcing.

**Shape of the future**   Figure 2-9 shows that in the future there will be a declining fraction of the population who are dependent children, and a rising fraction of the population who are in the dependent old-age group. Overall, the burden will be lighter than before on those in the middle working-age groups.

From the military-manpower viewpoint, time may be working against the countries of Western Europe. Note in Table 2-4's estimates of future populations of nations the low numbers for Sweden and the United Kingdom; and note the high numbers for the U.S.S.R. and the United States, which have only recently had drops in their net reproduction rates.

**Zero Population Growth**   As we shall see repeatedly, in Part Six and elsewhere, there is now a strong movement for Zero Population Growth (ZPG). Even if, for the advanced countries like the United States, there is little likelihood of famine and lagging food supplies in the next half-century, what about the long, long run? What about the amenities of life—elbow room and open spaces? What about pollution and ecology? What about the ethics of those in the advanced world, who, just because they reached affluence first, have been getting more than their fair share of the depletable natural resources of the world—rich copper, iron, and oil deposits?

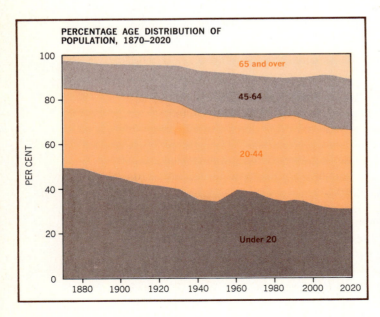

**FIG. 2-9**

**Population is aging with fewer young and more elderly in years ahead**

Declining birth rate means fewer dependent children. But modern medicine means more dependents to be supported in their old age. Fortunately, the fraction of the population in the working ages is rising. (Source: U.S. Bureau of the Census.)

| ESTIMATED FUTURE POPULATION OF DIFFERENT COUNTRIES IN 1985 (in millions) | | | | |
|---|---|---|---|---|
| | ANNUAL GROWTH (% per year) | 1970 | 1980 | 1985 |
| United States | 1.3 | 205 | 226 | 240 |
| United Kingdom | 0.6 | 55.7 | 59.5 | 61.8 |
| France | 0.8 | 50.8 | 55.3 | 57.6 |
| Soviet Union | 1.0 | 243 | 271 | 287 |
| Sweden | 0.7 | 8.0 | 8.6 | 8.8 |
| Italy | 0.8 | 53.7 | 57.9 | 60.0 |
| Japan | 1.2 | 103 | 116 | 121 |

**TABLE 2-4**
**Nation sizes will look different in the future**
Any differences in growth rate accumulate into significant changes. Note how the United States and the Soviet Union grow relative to Western Europe. (Source: United Nations.)

Slowdown in growth of numbers could not alone alleviate the crisis in ecology. *At least two-thirds of the problem stems from our burgeoning per capita standard of life.* Just so that more people can have more fast cars and more comfortable home environments summer and winter, the globe is ravaged by strip mining, oil spills into the ocean, and threats of nuclear radioactivity from power generation.

Moreover, to stop population growth in its tracks now, it would not suffice to bring the NRR down to 1. To accomplish no growth in numbers, the current generation would have to drop its average family size down to one child per family, not merely reduce it from three to two. So the problem will long remain: How can we improve the quality of life for our still-growing (albeit more slowly growing) population?

**Economic issues in population trends**   We have seen that limited growth in population is vital for the underdeveloped world because of the ancient curse of Malthusian diminishing returns. We shall see in later chapters that for the advanced nations, there may be an optimum population size, not too large and not too small, but where scale is just large enough to permit an optimal division of labor.

Can a nation afford *not* to grow? If living in and having large families are deemed pleasures, stabilizing the population will involve some inevitable psychic costs. But what if the alternative is eventually standing room only?

Consider another problem. It was not so long ago that people said, "Babies are good for the diaper and baby-food industry. Young people are needed if we are to have jobs in the beer, record, and ice cream industries. In a growing population, the need to provide durable goods for the population creates a favorable balance of investment in relation to saving and avoids mass unemployment. In short, a capitalistic society cannot afford not to have GNP growth, lest grass grow in the streets."

We shall see, when we come to master Part Two's analysis of the post-Keynesian mixed economy, that society today—perhaps for the first time!—*can afford not to grow* in numbers if that is what most pleases the people. Just as there is no need to dig holes and fill them up just to make jobs, so there is no longer need to go through the motions of filling up the countryside with people just in order to keep the wheels of industry humming nicely.

# SUMMARY

## A. PROBLEMS OF ECONOMIC ORGANIZATION

1  Every economy must somehow solve the three fundamental economic problems: WHAT kinds and quantities shall be produced of all possible goods and services; How economic resources shall be used in producing these goods; and FOR WHOM the goods shall be produced, i.e., the distribution of income among different individuals and classes.

2  Societies meet these problems in different ways—by custom, instinct, command, and in our mixed economy, largely by a system of price and markets.

3  The basic problems are important because of the fundamental fact of all economic life: With limited resources and technology, standards of living are limited. Economic goods are *scarce* rather than free; society must choose and ration among them, because not all needs and desires can be fulfilled.

## B. THE TECHNOLOGICAL CHOICES OPEN TO ANY SOCIETY

4  With given resources and technology, the production choices open to a nation between two such goods as butter and guns can be summarized in the *production-possibility frontier*. This indicates the way one good can be transformed into another by transferring resources from its production to that of the other.

5  Production-possibility frontiers can illustrate many basic economic processes: how we use relatively *less* resources for food *necessities* as we develop; how we choose between *private* market goods and *public* governmental goods; choose between *current consumption* and *capital goods* that enhance *future* capacity to produce. The *p-p frontier* pictures *technical progress* and paves the way for diminishing returns.

6  The *law of diminishing returns* asserts that, after a point, as we add more and more equal doses of a variable input (such as labor) to a fixed input (such as land), the amount of extra product will fall off. This law is really a matter of proportions: the varying input has less and less of the fixed input to work with.

7  *Economies of mass production* or *of scale* are often described as "increasing returns to scale." The word "scale" is a warning that *all* inputs are being varied simultaneously, with none held fixed as in the law of diminishing returns. Many processes do pass through an initial stage of increasing returns to scale.

8  In accordance with the *law of increasing-relative costs*, to get equal extra amounts of one good you must incur the sacrifice of ever larger amounts of other goods. This is shown by a bowed-out (concave from below) *p-p frontier*. Only if the two industries used all productive factors in the same proportion would you be able to avoid encountering the law of diminishing returns as you transfer relatively more of a varying factor onto another relatively fixed factor.

## C. THE UNDERLYING POPULATION BASIS OF ANY ECONOMY: PAST AND FUTURE POPULATION TRENDS

9   Malthus' theory of population rests on the law of diminishing returns. He thought that a population, if unchecked, would tend to grow in *geometric* rate, doubling every generation or so. But each member of the growing population would have less natural resources and land to work with. Therefore, because of diminishing returns, income would have a tendency to fall so low as to lead to a stable population at a subsistence level of starvation and pestilence.

10   For a century and a half after Malthus, populations grew by leaps and bounds everywhere. Numbers grew primarily because death rates fell sharply as a result of improved medical and public health technology; yet technological progress in industry more than offset the law of diminishing returns.

11   After 1870 birth rates began to fall. Prior to World War II, advanced nations had net reproduction rates below 1 and faced depopulation. After 1939, the middle classes swung temporarily back toward a larger-family pattern. But in recent years, there has been a general swing of the tide back toward a small family size and lowered birth rate. Zero Population Growth (ZPG) is a movement that the modern economy can afford if it wants to.

## CONCEPTS FOR REVIEW

| | |
|---|---|
| economic and free goods | increasing returns to scale |
| substitution and law of scarcity | law of increasing (relative) costs |
| production-possibility frontier | of one good for another |
| law of diminishing returns | Malthusian population theory |
| total versus extra product | age distribution of population |
| productive factors or inputs | net reproduction rate (NRR), ZPG |

## QUESTIONS FOR DISCUSSION

1   Without looking at the next chapter, can you anticipate how a price system through supply and demand solves the three problems of *economic* organization?

2   Explain what economists mean by *scarcity*, by *free goods*, by *inefficiency*.

3   Draw society's *p-p frontier* if scientific inventions increased the productivity of given resources in butter production only, and not in guns.

4   If land were increased in a number of steps and labor held constant, would the law of diminishing returns hold? Illustrate and tell why this would happen.

5   Describe and contrast (*a*) the law of diminishing returns; (*b*) the phenomenon of increasing returns to scale. How about (*c*) the law of increasing (relative) costs?

6   How many children were there in your great-grandparents' family? In your parents' family? How many do you think there will be in your own family?

**7**  "Population pressure doesn't cause war, as is commonly believed. Careful study suggests cause and effect are just the reverse. Nations that want to expand try to persuade their citizens to grow in numbers so the nation will be militarily strong and will have a pretext for expansion." Discuss.

**8**  "A *geometric progression* is a sequence of terms $[g_1, g_2, \ldots, g_t, g_{t+1}, \ldots]$ in which each term is *the same multiple* of its predecessor, $g_2/g_1 = g_3/g_2 = \cdots = g_{t+1}/g_t = \beta$. If $\beta = 1 + i > 1$, the terms grow like compound interest. An *arithmetic progression* is a sequence $[a_1, a_2, a_3, \ldots, a_t, a_{t+1}, \ldots]$ in which the *difference* between each term and its predecessor is the same constant: $a_2 - a_1 = a_3 - a_2 = \cdots = a_{t+1} - a_t = \alpha$." (Malthus gratuitously assumed food to grow in an arithmetic progression.) Give examples of each. Satisfy yourself that any geometric progression must *eventually* surpass any arithmetic progression.

**9**  *Extra-credit problem* for those mathematically inclined: We can illustrate the "linear programming" technique referred to in footnote 3 on Stigler's least-cost-diet problem. Suppose each unit of milk, beans, and meat has respectively (1, 8, 2) calories and (4, 2, 1) vitamins. Suppose each unit of the 3 goods costs ($1, $2, $3) respectively. Suppose you must buy at least 120 calorie units per month and 180 vitamin units. Can you show by experiment that the least cost is $60 per month, with meat not being bought at all, and with milk at 40 and beans at 10 units? Mathematically, the linear programmer writes this as

$$\text{Minimize } Z = \$1X_1 + \$2X_2 + \$3X_3$$
$$\text{subject to } 1X_1 + 8X_2 + 2X_3 \geqq 120$$
$$4X_1 + 2X_2 + 1X_3 \geqq 180$$
$$X_1 \geqq 0, X_2 \geqq 0, X_3 \geqq 0$$

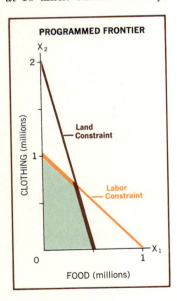

**PROGRAMMED FRONTIER**

$X_2$

Land Constraint

Labor Constraint

CLOTHING (millions)

FOOD (millions)

$X_1$

A similar linear programming problem will define a *p-p frontier* like that shown here. Suppose food and clothing each take 1 unit of labor. But food, being land-intensive, takes 4 acres of land, while clothing takes only 1 acre. If society has 1 (million) men and 2 (million) acres, the frontier is defined by

$$1X_1 + 1X_2 \leqq 1$$
$$4X_1 + 1X_2 \leqq 2$$
$$X_1 \geq 0, X_2 \geq 0$$

the first giving the heavy orange part and the second the heavy brown part.

Every individual endeavors to employ his capital so that its produce may be of greatest value. He generally neither intends to promote the public interest, nor knows how much he is promoting it. He intends only his own security, only his own gain. And he is in this led by an INVISIBLE HAND to promote an end which was no part of his intention. By pursuing his own interest he frequently promotes that of society more effectually than when he really intends to promote it. ADAM SMITH
*The Wealth of Nations* (1776)

## THE MIXED ECONOMY

Most of our attention will be devoted to the special features of economic life found in twentieth-century industrial nations (with the exception of the communist countries). In most of these countries there was a trend in the past few centuries toward less and less direct governmental control of economic activity; gradually, feudal and preindustrial conditions were replaced by greater emphasis on what is loosely called "free private enterprise," or "competitive private-property capitalism."

Long before this trend had approached a condition of full laissez faire (i.e., of complete governmental noninterference with business), the tide began to turn the other way. Since late in the nineteenth century, in almost all the countries under consideration, there has been a steady increase in the economic functions of government.

**Ours is a "mixed economy" in which both public and private institutions exercise economic control.**

Section A of this chapter shows how our mixed economy tackles the three problems of economic organization that must be met by any society. Section B describes some fundamental characteristics of the present economic order.

## A. HOW A FREE ENTERPRISE SYSTEM SOLVES THE BASIC ECONOMIC PROBLEMS

In a system of free private enterprise, no individual or organization is *consciously* concerned with the triad of economic problems set forth in Chapter 2: WHAT, HOW, and FOR WHOM. This fact is really remarkable.

To paraphrase a famous economic example, let us consider the city of New York. Without a constant flow of goods in and out of the city, it would be on the verge of starvation within a week. A variety of the right kinds and amounts of food is required. From the surrounding counties, from 50 states, and from the far corners of the world, goods have been traveling for days and months with New York as their destination.

How is it that 12 million people are able to sleep easily at night, without living in mortal terror of a breakdown in the elaborate economic processes upon which the city's existence depends? For all this is undertaken *without coercion or centralized direction* by any conscious body!

Everyone notices how much the government does to control economic activity—tariff legislation, pure-food laws, utility and railroad regulation, minimum-wage laws, fair-labor-practice acts, social security, price ceilings and floors, public works, national defense, national and local taxation, police protection and judicial redress, zoning ordinances, municipal water or gas works, and so forth. What goes unnoted is how much of economic life proceeds *without* government intervention.

Hundreds of thousands of commodities are produced by millions of people more or less of their own volition and without central direction or master plan.

## NOT CHAOS BUT ECONOMIC ORDER

This functioning alone is convincing proof that a competitive system of markets and prices—whatever else it may be, however imperfectly it may function—is not a system of chaos and anarchy. There is in it a certain order and orderliness. It works.

A competitive system is an elaborate mechanism for unconscious coordination through a system of prices and markets, a communication device for pooling the knowledge and actions of millions of diverse individuals. Without a central intelligence, it solves one of the most complex problems imaginable, involving thousands of unknown variables and relations. Nobody designed it. It just evolved, and like human nature, it is changing; but it does meet the first test of any social organization—it can survive.

A dramatic example of the importance of a pricing system is Germany after World War II. In 1946–1947 production and consumption had dropped to a low level. Neither bombing damage nor postwar reparation payments could account for this breakdown. *Paralysis of the price mechanism* was clearly to blame: Money was worthless; factories closed down for lack of materials; trains could not run for lack of coal; coal could not be mined because miners were hungry; miners were hungry because peasants would not sell food for money and no industrial goods were available to give them in return. Prices were legally fixed, but little could be bought at such prices; a black market characterized by barter or fantastically high prices existed. Then in 1948 a "miracle" happened. A thoroughgoing currency reform set the price mechanism back into effective operation. Immediately production and consumption soared; again the WHAT, HOW, and FOR WHOM were being resolved by markets and prices.

The fact to emphasize is that such so-called miracles are going on all around us all the time—if only we look around and alert ourselves to the everyday functioning of the market. A revolutionist out to destroy the capitalistic system could ask nothing better than a great inflation or deflation that would paralyze the price mechanism.[1]

[1] In the 1970s, governments in the Soviet Union and Eastern European countries are rediscovering some virtues of a pricing system.

## THE INVISIBLE HAND AND "PERFECT COMPETITION"

Students of economics have to avoid the error of thinking that a price mechanism must work chaotically if it is not controlled by somebody. Having learned this lesson, they must not go to the other extreme and become enamored of the beauty of a pricing mechanism, regarding it as perfection itself, the essence of providential harmony, and beyond the touch of human hands.

Adam Smith, whose *The Wealth of Nations* (1776) is the germinal book of modern economics or political economy, was thrilled by the recognition of an order in the economic system. Smith proclaimed the principle of the "Invisible Hand"; every individual, in pursuing only his own selfish good, was led, as if by an invisible hand, to achieve the best good for all, so that any interference with free competition by government was almost certain to be injurious. (See this chapter's initial quotation.)

Undoubtedly this was a valuable insight. But, on reflection and after two centuries of experience, we must recognize some of the realistic limitations on this doctrine. The virtues claimed for free enterprise are fully realized only when the complete checks and balances of "perfect competition" are present.

Perfect competition is defined by the economist as a technical term: "Perfect competition" exists only in the case where no farmer, businessman, or laborer is a big enough part of the total market to have any personal influence on market price. On the other hand, when his grain, merchandise, or labor is large enough in size to produce appreciable depressing or elevating effects on market prices, some degree of monopolistic imperfection has set in, and the virtues of the Invisible Hand must be that much discounted.

Actually, much of the praise of perfect competition is beside the point. As discussed earlier, ours is a mixed system of government and private enterprise; as will be discussed later, it is also *a mixed system of monopoly and competition.* A cynic might say of perfect competition what Bernard Shaw said of Christianity: The only trouble with it is that it has never been tried.

Historians quarrel over whether there ever was a golden age of free competition. And certainly, competition is not now perfect in the economist's sense. We do not even know whether, because of the fundamental nature of large-scale production and technology, consumers' tastes, and business organization, effective competition is becoming less or more intense. (More on this in Chapter 6.)

In any case, society need not accept as inevitable any trend toward big business, mergers, trusts, and cartels such as began to swell in the 1890s. The challenge is to work out laws and customs that help to improve the working of our less-than-perfect competitive system. The polar cases—laissez faire and totalitarian dictatorship of production—dramatize economic principles. Yet the relevant choice for policy is not a decision between such extremes, but rather the degree to which public policy should do *less* or *more* to modify the operation of particular private economic activities.


## THE PRICE SYSTEM

Just how does the unconscious automatic price mechanism operate? The bare outlines of a *competitive* profit-and-loss system are simple to describe.

*Everything has a price*—each commodity and each service. Even the different kinds of human labor have prices, namely, wage rates. Everybody receives money for what he sells, and uses this money to buy what he wishes.

If more is wanted of any good—say, shoes—a flood of new orders will be given for it. This will cause its price to rise and more to be produced.

On the other hand, what if more of a commodity—such as tea—becomes available than people want to buy at the last-quoted market price? Then its price will be marked down by competition. At the lower price people will drink more tea, and producers will no longer produce quite so much. Thus, equilibrium of supply and demand will be restored (as the next chapter and Part Three will show).

What is true of the markets for consumers' goods is also true of markets for *factors of production* such as labor, land, and capital inputs. If welders rather than glassblowers are needed, job opportunities will be more favorable in the welding field. The price of welders, their hourly wage, will tend to rise, while that of glassblowers will tend to fall. Other things being equal, this will cause a shift into the desired occupation. Likewise, an acre of land will go into sugar cultivation if sugar producers bid the most for its use. In the same way, machine-tool production will be determined by supply and demand.

**The general-equilibrium system**    In other words, we have a vast system of trial and error, of successive approximation to an *equilibrium system of prices and production*. We shall see later that the matching of supply and demand and of prices and costs helps solve our three problems simultaneously. Here are the bare outlines of competitive equilibrium.

1. WHAT things will be produced is determined by the *dollar votes* of consumers—not every 2 or 4 years at the polls, but every day in their decisions to purchase this item and not that. Of course, the money that they pay into business cash registers ultimately provides the payrolls, rents, and dividends that consumers receive in weekly income. Thus the circle is a complete one.

2. How things are produced is determined by the competition of different producers. The method that is cheapest at any one time, because of both physical efficiency and cost efficiency, will displace a more costly method.

The only way for producers to meet price competition and maximize profits is to keep costs at a minimum by adopting the most efficient methods. For example, synthetic rubber will be made from oil rather than alcohol if the price of the one is in a certain relation to the price of the other; or electric power will be generated by steam rather than nuclear power if the price of coal is below some critical level. The large, tractor-operated farm will displace the family-size farm if this leads to lower costs of production.

*International example:* Bob Jones farms *extensively*, with much American land relative to each hour of labor; Pierre Reny farms *intensively*, using much labor to each hectare of French land. Who orders these sensible How decisions, which properly adjust to the fact that France is more densely populated than America? Congress? The National Assembly? The UN? Of course not. The price system is society's signaling device. Like a master who gives carrots and kicks to coax his donkey forward, the pricing system deals out profits and losses to get WHAT, How, and FOR WHOM decided.

3. For Whom things are produced is determined by supply and demand in the markets for productive services: by wage rates, land rents, interest rates, and profits, all of which go to make up everybody's income—relative to everyone else and relative to the whole. (Of course, the character of the resulting distribution of income is highly dependent upon the *initial* distribution of property ownership, upon acquired or inherited abilities, educational opportunities, and presence or absence of racial and sex discriminations.)

Note this: Consumer votes do not by themselves determine What goods are produced. Demand has to meet with a supply of goods; so business cost and supply decisions, along with consumer demand, do help to determine What. Just as a broker may help arrange a match between buyer and seller, the auctioneer in the commodity market acts as the go-between who reconciles the consumer votes and business supplies that impinge on the market. (The next chapter explains how.) The profit seeker is society's agent to determine How, seeking least factor-costs for producing each good and being punished by ruthless competition if he fails to use best methods.

## A PICTURE OF PRICES AND MARKETS

To amplify this highly simplified explanation, turn to Fig. 3-1, on page 46. It gives a bird's-eye view of the way market pricing reconciles public demand and supply with business supply and demand. Note that markets serve as the connecting device between the public and business. Fifteen minutes of poring over this diagram may be worth an hour of disconnected musing about economic pricing. (In Chapters 10 and 32, similar circular-flow diagrams will appear, namely, Fig. 10-1 and Fig. 32-1.)

A competitive system is impersonal but not completely so. The consuming families face business enterprises on two fronts, with only prices in between. One front is the widely dispersed one, the retail market on which consumers buy thousands of small items from a score of different retail establishments: grocery, drug, and department stores; movie theaters; gasoline stations; and from electric-power companies, public post offices, landlords, railroad lines, and insurance companies.

On the other front—the market for labor and other productive services—relations are not always so peaceful. To the family breadwinner his wage is not simply another price; it is the difference between luxury and comfort, between comfort and privation. The laborer may feel inferior to the large corporation in bargaining power, and he may turn to collective bargaining through trade-unions. By doing this, he may at times be helping to restore competition, while at other times he may be causing conditions to deviate still further from perfect competition, as later chapters will discuss.

## ETHICAL ASPECTS OF INCOME DISTRIBUTION

The above portrait of competition tending toward ideal efficiency, toward being on the production-possibility frontier and not inside it, is a highly oversimplified one. But even if the system worked as perfectly as described above—which all know is not the case—many would not consider it ideal.

In the first place, goods go where there are the most votes or dollars. John D.

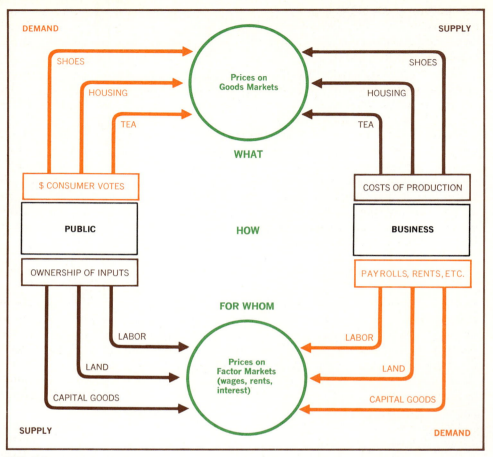

**FIG. 3-1**

**The competitive price system uses supply-demand markets to solve the basic economic problems—WHAT, HOW, and FOR WHOM**

All demand relations are shown in orange; all the supply relations, in brown. See how consumer-dollar votes of demand interact in the upper goods markets with business cost-supply decisions, thus helping determine WHAT is produced. And how business demand for inputs or productive factors meets the public's supply of labor and other inputs in the lower factor markets to help determine wage, rent, and interest income—i.e., FOR WHOM goods are produced. Business competition to buy factor inputs and sell goods most cheaply determines HOW goods are to be produced. (WARNING: All parts of the diagram interact together. WHAT depends on the lower part, just as FOR WHOM depends on the upper part—carpenter wages depend on housing demand, and demand for yachts depends on oil-land royalties.)

Rockefeller's dog may receive the milk that a poor child needs to avoid rickets. Why? Because supply and demand are working badly? Quite possibly badly *from ethical viewpoints,* but not from the standpoint of what the market mechanism is alone geared to accomplish. Functionally, auction markets are doing what they are designed to do—putting goods in the hands of those who can pay the most, who have the most money votes. Defenders and critics of the price mechanism should recognize this fact.[2] And when a democratic society does not like the distribution of dollar votes under laissez faire, it uses redistributive taxation to rectify the situation.

There is another feature of even an ideal market system. Suppose the invention of automatic machines should cause the competitive price of labor to fall greatly, thereby reducing incomes of the poor. Would all ethical observers regard that as necessarily right or ideal? Certainly not.

Should the fact that a man inherited 500 square miles of rangeland, for which oil companies offer a million dollars per year, necessarily justify so large an income?

These questions are discussed repeatedly in Congress. Whether incomes should be completely determined by a competitive struggle—the survival of the survivors—is an ethical question that goes beyond the mere mechanics of economics. In the modern mixed economy, the electorate insists on providing minimum standards when the market fails to do so. Economics teaches how interventions can be accomplished at least costs in terms of inefficiency.

## IMPERFECTIONS OF COMPETITION

As we said earlier, one drawback to the picture of the price system as described above is the fact that, in the real world, competition is nowhere near "perfect." Firms do not know when consumer tastes will change; therefore they may *overproduce* in one field and *underproduce* in another. By the time they are ready to learn from experience, the situation may have changed again. Also, in a competitive system many producers simply do not know the methods of other producers, and costs do not fall to a minimum. In the competitive struggle, one can sometimes succeed as much by *keeping knowledge scarce* as by keeping production high.

The most serious deviation from perfect competition comes from *monopoly elements*. These—as we shall see later on—may result in wrong pricing, creation of distorted patterns of demand by repetitive advertising, incorrect and wasteful resource allocation, and monopoly profits. We shall be reminded again and again how strict is the economist's definition of a "perfect competitor." The mere presence of a few rivals is not enough for perfect competition.

**Monopoly elements**   The economic definition of "imperfect competitor" is *anyone who buys or sells a good in large enough quantities to be able to affect the price of that good*. To some degree that means almost all businessmen, except possibly the millions of farmers who individually produce a negligible fraction of the total crop. All economic life is a blend of competitive and monopoly elements. Imperfect (monopolistic) competition is the prevailing mode, not perfect competition. A good approximation of perfect competition may be the most society can strive for.

Of course, as we shall later see, a businessman cannot set his prices completely as

[2] Cecil Woodham-Smith, *The Great Hunger: Ireland 1845–9* (Harper & Row, New York, 1963), relates the unbelievable details of how a laissez faire Victorian government let millions of Irish children, women, and men literally starve in the great famine when a fungus destroyed the potato crop.

he pleases and still make profits. He must take into account the prices of goods that are substitutes for his own. Even if he produces a trademarked coal with unique properties, he must reckon with prices charged for other coals, oil, gas, and insulation.

Businessmen, farmers, and workers both like and dislike competition. We all like it when it enables us to expand our market, but we label it as "chiseling," "unfair," or "ruinous" when the knife cuts the other way. The worker whose livelihood depends on how the market prices his labor may be the first to howl when competition threatens to depress wages. Farm groups, aware of what competition can do to agricultural prices, bring pressure on the state to restrict production and thereby raise prices.

In the idealized model of an efficiently acting competitive market mechanism, consumers are supposed to be well informed. They recognize low quality and avoid it; they never buy drugs that turn out to be poisonous or ineffective. Most important, their "desires" are supposed to represent genuine "wants" and "needs" and "tastes." But in actual life, as Galbraith never tires of pointing out, business firms spend much money on advertising to *shape*—and, some insist, *distort*—consumer demands. We are terrorized into buying deodorants; from childhood on, we are conditioned to desire what business wants to sell.

The sequence "consumer demand→corporate price and production" is often inverted to become "corporate advertising→consumer demand→high price and profit."

Some of the basic factors responsible for monopoly-creating bigness in business may be *inherent in the economies of large-scale production*. This is especially true in a dynamic world of technological change. Competition by numerous producers would simply not be efficient in many fields and could not last. Trademarks, patents, and advertising are often responsible for still other market imperfections. It would be humanly impossible, therefore, to attempt to create *perfect* competition by law. The problem is one of achieving reasonably effective "workable competition."

We shall proceed later to a more microscopic examination of supply and demand. After that discussion we shall be in a position to appraise the workings of the price system more judiciously. A competitive system is one way of organizing an economy, *but not the only way*. Admiration should not inhibit reform. Still, it is of interest that some socialists plan to continue to use a price mechanism as part of their new society. A price system is not perfect, but neither are its alternatives.

## ECONOMIC ROLE OF GOVERNMENT

It was said earlier that ours is not a pure price economy but a *mixed economy* in which elements of government control are intermingled with market elements in organizing production and consumption. The economic role of government is now so important that two chapters in Part One are devoted to it. An outline of its influence can be briefly indicated here.

**Welfare minima**   Democracies are not satisfied with the answers to What, How, and For Whom given by a completely unrestrained market system. Such a system, as already said, might dictate that some people starve from lack of income while others get inadequate or excessive incomes.

Therefore the citizenry through their government step in with expenditure to supplement the real or money incomes of some individuals. Thus, governments provide hospital beds for citizens, and monthly allowances for the needy in times of unemployment or old age. Minimum standards of life are widespread modern goals.

**Public services and taxes**  More than this, government provides certain indispensable *public* services without which community life would be unthinkable and which by their nature cannot appropriately be left to private enterprises. Government came into existence once people realized, "Everybody's business is nobody's business." Obvious examples are the maintenance of national defense and of internal law and order, and the administration of justice and of contracts.[3]

By and large, in its expenditure of money, government is behaving exactly like any other large spender. By *casting sufficient votes in the form of dollar bids* in certain directions, it causes resources to flow there. The price system then takes over and performs much as if these were private rather than public needs.

Actually, most government expenditure is paid for out of taxes collected. It is here that an important element of *coercion* enters. It is true that the citizenry as a whole imposes the tax burden upon itself; also, each citizen is sharing in the collective benefits of government. But there is not the same close connection between benefits and tax payments as holds when the individual citizen puts a dime into a gum machine or makes an ordinary purchase. I need not smoke Winstons or buy nylon carpeting or choose fried eggs, but I must pay my share of the taxes used to finance the various activities of government.

**Legal commands**  Moreover, a second important form of coercion is involved in the universal custom of passing governmental laws: thou shalt not sell false weight, thou shalt not employ child labor, thou shalt not burn houses, thou shalt not pour out smoke from thy factory chimney, thou shalt not sell or smoke opium, thou shalt not charge more than the ceiling price for food, and so forth. This set of rules gives the framework within which private enterprise functions; it also modifies the direction of that functioning. Together with government expenditure and taxation, *the commands of government* supplement the price system in determining the economic fate of the nation.

It would be fruitless to debate whether public enterprise or private enterprise is the more important—as fruitless as to debate heredity versus environment. Without either, our economic world would be an entirely different one.

Finally, as we shall see in Parts Two and Six, it is part of the government's function to help stabilize acute and chronic cycles of unemployment and inflation and to help achieve and maintain healthy economic growth.

## B. CAPITAL, DIVISION OF LABOR, AND MONEY

There are three further important features of modern economic society:

1. Modern advanced industrial technology rests upon the use of vast amounts of *capital:* elaborate machinery, large-scale factories and plants, stores and stocks of

---

[3]Here is a typical example of government service: lighthouses. These save lives and cargoes; but lighthouse keepers cannot reach out to collect fees from ships. So we have here a divergence between *private* and *social* advantage. Philosophers and statesmen have always recognized the necessary role of government in such cases of "external-economy divergence between private and social advantage." Much more on this subject will come in Chapter 8, Chapter 24, and elsewhere.

finished and unfinished materials. "Capitalism" got its name because this capital, or "wealth," is primarily the *private* property of somebody—the capitalist.

2. The present-day economic system is characterized by an almost incredibly elaborate degree of *specialization* and intricate *division of labor*.

3. Ours is a system that makes extensive use of *money*. The flow of money is the lifeblood of our system. It also provides the measuring rod of values.

All these features are interrelated, each with the other and all with the price mechanism described in Section A of this chapter.

Thus we shall see that, without the great facility for trade and exchange which money provides, an elaborate division of labor would be impossible. Money and capital become related through credit activities of the banking system and through the organized capital markets where securities can be transformed into money by sale or vice versa. Of course, the relationship between the price mechanism and money is immediate and obvious.

### CAPITAL AND TIME

No one has trouble seeing that production of economic goods can result from use of such inputs as labor and land (including in the latter term natural resources generally). These are often called "*primary* factors of production," for the reason that neither land nor (these days) labor is regarded as a result of the economic process, but instead exists primarily by virtue of physical and biological rather than economic factors.[4]

Capital, which is the word often used to refer to capital goods generally, is a different kind of production factor. A capital good differs from the primary factors in that it is *an input which is itself the output of the economy.*

Capital goods, then, represent *produced* goods that can be used as factor inputs for further production, whereas labor and land are primary factor inputs not usefully thought of as being themselves produced by the economic system.

Part Four will show that, just as wages and rent are the factor-prices of primary labor and land, the 4 or 6 or 10 per cent interest rate per annum can, in a more subtle way, be regarded by the apologists for capitalism, as the factor-price that rations and rewards society's scarce supply of various capital goods and investment projects.

Because an interest rate is a percentage per unit of time (per year or month or decade), it calls our attention to another way of looking at capital—a way that stresses its special relationship with time. Let us survey this important economic role of capital.

If men had to work with their hands on barren soil, productivity and consumption would be very low indeed. Thus, when an anthropologist asked of mourning tribesmen,

---

[4] Some qualifications will be evident. Land can sometimes be made by drainage or filling in; this is true of much of Chicago's lake front and Boston's Back Bay. Natural resources such as minerals are laid down by nature, but it may take much economic effort to locate, use, and process them. Therefore, they come to have some of the properties of capital goods. Even if one abandons in the Western world a Malthusian theory of population, whereby people seem to be given a cost of production not unlike that of machines, one realizes that the process of education involves *investing in people*, thereby making them more productive factors of production. When you see a medical-school graduate, you are in a certain sense looking at an expensive chunk of capital.

"Who died?" they replied, "What is death? We have lost the needle!" Over a long time advanced economies have amassed a vast stock of equipment, plant and housing, inventories, and drained land.

Men learned very early that the simple, direct methods of production can be improved upon by using *time-consuming indirect methods.*

We who are inside the economic system are not conscious of *how roundabout* productive processes have become. An outside observer would be struck with the fact that almost no one in our system seems to be producing *finished* goods. Almost everyone is seen to do work of a preparatory nature, with final consumption a distant future goal. The farmer spends his time in fattening hogs, the truck driver in carrying them toward market, and the packer in advancing them further toward the last stage of consumption. A steel worker prepares pig iron, part of which will become a hammer to build a house; another bit will become part of a pig-iron furnace; which in turn will prepare pig iron to be used in making further hammers and more pig-iron furnaces; and so forth, on and on.

## THE NEED TO FORGO PRESENT CONSUMPTION

The fact that it takes time to get things started and synchronized is important. It explains why society does not automatically replace all direct processes by more productive indirect ones, and all indirect processes by still more indirect processes. The advantage in doing so is balanced by the initial disadvantage of having *to forgo present consumption goods* by diverting resources from current production to uses that will bear fruit only after some time.

To the extent that people are willing to save—to abstain from present consumption and wait for future consumption—to that extent, society can devote resources to new capital formation.[5] And to the extent that people are unconcerned about the future, they may at any time try to "dissave"—to snatch present pleasures at the expense of the future. How? By diverting resources, away from the endless task of *replacing and maintaining* capital, and to the job of producing extra present consumption goods. (Turn back to Fig. 2-5, page 25, to review the process of forgoing current consumption in favor of capital formation that adds to future production possibilities.)

We may summarize as follows:

Economic activity is future-oriented. By the same token, current economic consumption is largely the consequence of past efforts. In progressive societies a fraction of current consumption is sacrificed to production of net capital formation in order to increase future production.

## CAPITAL AND PRIVATE PROPERTY

Physical capital goods are important in any economy because they help to increase productivity. This is as true of Soviet communism as it is of our own system. But there is one important difference. By and large, it is private individuals who own the tools of production in a mixed economy.

[5] We shall see later, in Chapter 13, that, *sometimes* in our modern economy, the more people try to save, the less capital goods are produced; and paradoxically, the more people spend *on consumption,* the greater is the incentive for businessmen to build new factories and equipment.

What is the exception in our system—government ownership of the means of production—is the rule in a socialized state where productive property is collectively owned. The returns from such real capital goods accrue to the government, not to individuals directly. The government then decides how such income is to be distributed among individuals. The communist government also decides how rapidly resources are to be invested in new capital formation: the government decides by how much *present* consumption should be curtailed in order to add to the total of factories, equipment, and productive stocks of goods if *future* output is to rise.

In our system individual capitalists earn interest, dividends, and profits, or rents and royalties on the capital goods that they supply. Every patch of land and every bit of equipment has a deed, or "title of ownership" that is supposed to belong to somebody directly—or if it belongs to a corporation, then indirectly to the individual stockholders who own the corporation. Moreover, each kind of capital good has a money market value; hence each claim or title to ownership of a capital good also has a market value. A share of common stock of IBM is quoted at a certain price, an AT&T bond at its price; a mortgage on a house is valued at some amount; the deed to a house is appraised by the real-estate market at some price; and so forth.

It should be pointed out that the government does own a good deal of the national real capital, e.g., Hoover Dam and submarines. In addition, its agencies, such as the Federal Housing Administration (FHA) and the Small Business Administration (SBA), are important sources of capital loans for home owners and private business.

Also, we note that the *legal property rights of an individual are relative and limited.* Society determines how much of "his" property a man may bequeath to his heirs and how much must go in inheritance and estate taxes to the government. Society determines how much the owners of public-utility companies—such as electric and gas firms—can earn and how they must run their business.

Even a man's home is not his castle. He must obey zoning laws and, if necessary, make way for a railroad or slum-clearance project. Interestingly enough, most of society's economic income *cannot* be capitalized into private property. Since slavery was abolished, human earning power is forbidden by law to be capitalized. A man is not even free to sell himself: he must *rent* himself at a wage.

## SPECIALIZATION, EXCHANGE, AND DIVISION OF LABOR

Turn now to the second characteristic feature of the present-day economy. The economies of mass production upon which modern standards of living are based would not be possible if production took place in self-sufficient farm households or regions.

*Specialization* of function permits each person and region to use to best advantage any peculiar differences in skill and resources. Even in a primitive economy men learn that, rather than have everyone do everything in a mediocre way, it is better to start a *division of labor*—better for fat men to do the fishing, lean men the hunting, and smart men to make the medicine, each exchanging his goods for the goods he needs.

Besides resting on interpersonal differences in ability, specialization accentuates and creates differences. Hunting makes a man thin and good at stalking prey; a region with no resources especially adapted to weaving may, through experience, still develop skills that give it advantages in weaving.

Finally, specialization may pay, even with no natural or acquired differences in skills: often in this way alone can a large enough volume of activity be reached to realize all the economies of large-scale production mentioned in Chapter 2. Two *identical* Indian twins might find it better for one to make all bows, the other all arrows—even if they had to draw lots to see which would make which—because only in this way could each be making enough to warrant introducing improved techniques.

To illustrate the increased productivity of specialization, Adam Smith provided the classical example of pinmaking. One man could at best make a few dozen imperfect pins per day. But when a small group of men are subdivided with respect to function so that each performs simple repetitive operations, they can turn out hundreds of thousands of perfect pins per day.[6]

Moreover, the simplification of function made possible by specialization lends itself to mechanization and the use of labor-saving capital. At the same time, specialization avoids the wasteful duplication of tools that would be necessary if every man had to be a jack-of-all-trades; and it also saves time lost in going from one job to another. The modern conveyor system of automobile assembly illustrates the efficiency of specialization. Today automation is the watchword.

## SPECIALIZATION AND ALIENATION

Despite the efficiency of specialization, it may also have the effect of making work tedious and without purpose. Extreme specialization means that a worker does but one single thing: Charlie Chaplin's classic movie *Modern Times*, in which the worker spends his whole lifetime accomplishing nothing more than the turning of bolt 999 on the remorseless assembly line, points up the problem. Specialization, too often, breeds half men—anemic clerks, brutish stokers. No wonder that men and women, as their real incomes rise in modern society, so often find themselves at the same time becoming socially "alienated."

The young Karl Marx, while still in his neo-Hegelian stage and before he had studied

---

[6] Smith recognized that specialization and division of labor were limited by the extent of the market, i.e., by the volume of goods that can be sold. Smith would have approved of the European Common Market, which aims to lower the internal tariff barriers to trade and create a market big enough to support fruitful mass production and specialization.

The following passage describing the extent of specialization in meat slaughtering is often quoted: "It would be difficult to find another industry where division of labor has been so ingeniously and microscopically worked out. The animal has been surveyed and laid off like a map; and the men have been classified in over thirty specialties and twenty rates of pay, from 16 cents to 50 cents an hour. The 50-cent man is restricted to using the knife on the most delicate parts of the hide (floorman) or to using the ax in splitting the backbone (splitter); and, wherever a less skilled man can be slipped in at 18 cents, $18\frac{1}{2}$ cents, 20 cents, 21 cents, $22\frac{1}{2}$ cents, 24 cents, and so on, a place is made for him, and an occupation mapped out. In working on the hide alone there are nine positions, at eight different rates of pay. A 20-cent man pulls off the tail, a $22\frac{1}{2}$-cent man pounds off another part where good leather is not found, and the knife of the 40-cent man cuts a different texture and has a different 'feel' from that of the 50-cent man. Skill has become specialized to fit the anatomy. . . .

"The division of labor grew with the industry, following the introduction of the refrigerator car and the marketing of dressed beef . . . . Before the market was widened by these revolutionizing inventions, the killing gangs were small, since only the local demands were supplied." J. R. Commons, *Quarterly Journal of Economics*, vol. XIX, 1904, pp. 3, 6.

political economy, prophetically discerned the inhumane (and inhuman!) alienation involved in modern industry. Although his emphasis changed in maturity, Marx never completely lost sight of alienation. In his culminating *magnum opus, Das Kapital* (*Capital*), he wrote that in the better society of the future, industry in modern society is compelled

. . . under penalty of death, to replace the detail-worker of today, crippled by the life-long repetition of one and the same trivial operation, and thus reduced to the mere fragment of a man, by the fully developed individual, fit for a variety of labours, ready to face any change in production, and to whom the different social functions he performs, are but so many modes of giving free scope to his own natural and acquired powers.[7]

Out of self-interest, personnel officers in large corporations are learning that a loosening up of the elaborate division of labor may be profitable. It apparently is not good for GM to run itself like an ant-heap. Nor, for that matter, is the best way to run an army necessarily the best way to run an industry. Volvo and Saab in Sweden are experimenting with work teams who follow the job rather than stand at one point in the assembly line like cogs in a machine. Secretarial pools give way to personal assistantships, not because a pool is inefficient, but because in the affluent modern age you can't keep people happy working in an impersonal pool. If the boss, like a superior officer in the army, is always right and must never be talked back to, he may find he will never be told that the corporate ship is springing leaks and sinking. Participatory democracy may be a luxury that only an affluent society can afford; but in that affluent society, where the old patterns of subordination and domination in an inflexible hierarchy may no longer wash, the canny corporation may find that it can no longer afford the luxury of unyielding refusals of alienated workers' demands for greater autonomy and job fulfillment.

## SPECIALIZATION AND INTERDEPENDENCE

Specialization and division of labor involve one further serious problem—*interdependence*. A single-celled low form of life, such as the amoeba, may not be particularly good at doing anything, but it can live alone and like it. In higher animals such as man, every cell will die if once the heart cells fail. When all goes well, extreme specialization of cells is very efficient—but at the cost of extreme interdependence.

In modern economic society this process is carried to the $n$th degree. No one man makes the smallest fraction of the commodities that he consumes. In medieval times the artisan made one article and exchanged it for many others. Today a worker produces not even a single good; he may make only shoe tongues or, as we've seen, simply turn bolt 999 on the Ford assembly line. Such may be his whole life work. In exchange for doing this, he will receive an income adequate to buy goods from all over the world.

---

[7] Karl Marx, *Capital*, vol. 1 (1867). More than a century later, a slowdown strike by young GM workers in Lordstown, Ohio, protesting speed-up on the monotonous Chevrolet conveyor-belt assembly line, gives point to Marx's prophecy (even if their high wage rates make a mockery of any simple Law of Immiseration and Pauperization of Wage Labor).

Thus, specialization involves complete mutual dependence. A bank in Austria fails, and the natives in Fiji, who carry water in empty Standard Oil cans and clothe their infants in Pillsbury flour bags, lose their livelihood—yes, and may even starve. In the backwash of a strike or war, a breakdown in transportation and the economic fabric of exchange reveals how perilously modern economic life depends upon exchange.

Would we, if we could, turn the clock back to a simpler and poorer life? Or can we keep the advantages of division of labor by finding policies that prevent breakdown?

## THE USE OF MONEY

Along with capital and specialization, money is a third aspect of modern economic life. Without the use of money, our present division of labor and exchange would be impossible. To be sure, as we'll see in Chapter 15's full-fledged discussion of money, we could imagine a state of *barter*, where one kind of merchandise is traded directly for another. In primitive cultures, it is not uncommon for food to be traded for weapons; or for aid in the building of a house to be exchanged for aid in clearing a field. Even in the most advanced industrial economies, if we strip exchange down to its barest essentials and peel off the obscuring layer of money, we find that trade between individuals or nations largely boils down to barter—transforming one good into another by exchange rather than by physical transmutation.

Money is a means, not an end in itself. But the King Midas fable, in which that miser forgets about the goods gold can buy and prays that everything he touches (even his fairest young daughter) be turned to gold, reminds us that means may themselves become perverted into ends. And it is no fairy tale that, once a society has become dependent on the mechanism of money, there can be a breakdown of exchange.

Under barter, if I am hungry and you are naked, I can always sew your clothes while you bake my bread. But after 1929, in the richest capitalistic country in all history, the banks failed; money was hoarded; people went hungry while other people went in rags.

The whole of Part Two of this book will deal with the problems of macroeconomics that are rooted in society's dependence on a money economy.

## SUMMARY

### A. HOW A FREE ENTERPRISE SYSTEM SOLVES THE BASIC ECONOMIC PROBLEMS

1   The price mechanism, working through supply and demand in competitive markets, operates to answer the three fundamental problems of economic organization in our mixed private enterprise system. The system is far from perfect, but it is one way to solve the WHAT, HOW, and FOR WHOM.

2   The dollar votes of people affect prices of goods; these prices serve as guides for the amounts of the different goods to be produced. When people demand more of a good, a competitive businessman can make a profit by expanding

production of that good. Under perfect competition, he must find the cheapest method of production, using labor, land, and other factors that are relatively cheap and economizing on the use of relatively expensive factors; otherwise, he will incur losses and be eliminated.

At the same time that the WHAT and How problems are being resolved by prices, so is the problem of FOR WHOM. The distribution of income is determined by competitive bidding up or down of factor-prices—wages of each kind of labor, rents of land, royalties of books, and various returns to capital. Anyone possessing fertile land or widely admired crooning ability will be supplied with many dollar votes for his use in the markets for consumer goods. Anyone without property or education and with skills, color, and sex that the market cares little about will receive a low annual income.

3   Our economy is mixed in two senses: Governments modify private initiative; monopolistic elements condition the working of perfect competition.

## B. CAPITAL, DIVISION OF LABOR, AND MONEY

4   Capital goods—produced inputs such as machinery, housing, and inventories of goods in process—add much to a nation's output. *Roundabout,* time-consuming methods take time to get started; hence, adding to the stock of capital goods requires a temporary sacrifice of present consumption. The interest rate serves to ration and to coax.

5   Under the mixed economy, capital goods are largely owned as private property; the incomes they produce go to their owners and to taxes. Under communism, the state owns capital goods. In no system are private-property rights unlimited.

6   Specialization and division of labor characterize modern economies. This raises productivity, but at the cost of interdependence and alienation.

7   Elaborate systems of present-day exchange go beyond barter to the use of money. But now money, which is only a means toward the end of acquiring goods, can become a fetish of its own. And later chapters will show how, at the macro-economic level, in the absence of modern fiscal and monetary policy, the world could be plunged into deep depression—"poverty midst plenty"—or, at other times, into galloping inflation.

## CONCEPTS FOR REVIEW

mixed economy
demand-and-supply markets for
    goods and for factors of
    production
profit seeking, cost minimizing

price "rationing"
perfect and imperfect competition
roundaboutness of production
abstinence and waiting, forgoing
dissaving by failure to maintain

specialization, interdependence
division of labor, exchange
use of money

possible misbehavior of a
money economy
inconvenience of barter

## QUESTIONS FOR DISCUSSION

1   During World War II, did we let consumers' dollar demand determine their sugar consumption? Why not? Why recourse to rationing?

2   Could supply and demand work out to give salesmen with a "gift of gab" twice the income of skilled scientists? At other times, could it give surgeons about the same income as accountants and plumbers? Five times that of butchers?

3   Do you think an "instinct of craftsmanship" and a "sense of social responsibility" could replace the "profit motive"? Read the chapter head's Invisible Hand quotation. What do you think Smith is trying to say there? And here: "I have never known much good done by those who affected to trade for the public good."

4   List a number of cases where the government modifies the working of an automatic price system. For example: pure food and drug laws; minimum wages; farm supports; rent and interest ceilings.

5   List cases where monopoly elements intervene. How can business by advertising shape, as well as respond to, consumer demands and wants?

6   If it should not be able to borrow abroad, what must China do if it wishes to become an efficient, industrialized nation in the next few generations?

7   "Lincoln freed the slaves. With one pen stroke he destroyed much of the capital the South had been able to accumulate over the years." Comment.

8   Marx pointed out that, under barter, the natural sequence is "clothing-food-clothing-food . . ."; more generally, "commodity-commodity-commodity- . . . ," or "C-C-C." In a natural money economy, the sequence becomes "commodity-money-commodity- . . ." or "C-M-C- . . . ." (EXPLANATION: I sell my cloth for the money I'll use to buy your bread.) But, Marx points out, when capitalism becomes perverted, people want to pile up money for its own sake and not for the commodities it can buy; money's sole purpose then is to use commodities to beget more money in the perverse sequence: "M-C-M . . . ." Discuss.

# 4

## SUPPLY AND DEMAND: THE BARE ELEMENTS

You can make even a parrot into a learned political economist—all he must learn are the two words "supply" and "demand."
ANONYMOUS

Every short statement about economics is misleading (with the possible exception of my present one).
ALFRED MARSHALL

Chapters 2 and 3 introduced the three basic problems every economy must face:

1. WHAT shall be produced of the great variety of possible goods and services, and in precisely what quantities?

2. How shall society combine its different productive factors—land, labor, and so forth—to produce each good?

3. FOR WHOM shall goods be produced—that is, how shall the national product be distributed among the different people with their different labor skills and ownerships of land and capital goods?

Chapter 2 showed that a variety of systems can be thought of to solve these three problems. WHAT, HOW, and FOR WHOM might be determined by custom, instinct, or by collective command. But Chapter 3 indicated that the modern mixed economy relies primarily on none of these to solve its basic problems. Instead, it relies on a system of markets and prices.

The consumer, so it is said, is the king. Or rather, with every man a king, each is a voter who uses his money as votes to get the things done that he wants done. His votes must compete with other men's votes; and the people with the most votes end up with the most influence on what gets produced and on where those goods go.

Now our task is to see just how this spending of money votes—this system of "consumer sovereignty"—takes place under the checks and balances of economic competition.

### THE MARKET MECHANISM

Let us take an example. You wake up this morning with an urge for a new pair of shoes. You would not think of saying, "I'll go down to the city hall and vote for the mayor most likely to give me a new pair of shoes. Of course, I mean a new pair of size 9, soft-leather, dark brown shoes."

Or, to take an actual case from history, suppose men begin to get prosperous enough to afford meat every day and do not have to fill up on potatoes. How does their desire to substitute meat for potatoes get translated into action? What politician do they tell? What orders does he in turn give to farmers to move from Maine to Texas? How much extra rent does he decide will be needed to bribe landlords to transfer land from potato production to cattle grazing? And how does he ensure that people get what they want of pork and lamb as well as beef? And who is to get the choice cuts?

Why belabor the obvious? Everyone knows it never works itself out that way at all. What happens is this. Consumers begin to buy fewer potatoes and more meat. *That raises the price of meat and cuts the price of potatoes.* So there soon results losses to the potato growers and gains to the ranchers. Ranch labor finds it can hold out for higher wages, and many a potato digger quits his job for a better-paying job elsewhere. In time, the higher meat prices coax out larger productions of beef, pork, and lamb. And the different parts of the cow—its horns, hide, liver, kidneys, choice tenderloin, and tough ribs—get auctioned off for what each part will bring.

To show that it is not some important government bureaucrat or businessman who sets relative prices, see what actually happened when science discovered that liver was good for anemia. Kidneys, for reasons somewhat obscure, were previously dearer than liver. In fact, according to the records, you could hardly give liver away before this discovery. Now go to the butcher shop: price liver; and, if you can find any, also price kidneys. A veritable revolution has taken place; the price of liver has risen greatly relative to the price of kidneys, so as to *ration* the limited supply of liver among the eager demanders for it—all through the *impersonal* workings of supply and demand.

**A system of prices**  Similar revolutions are taking place in the economic marketplace all the time. As people's desires and needs change, as engineering methods change, as supplies of natural resources and other productive factors change, the marketplace registers changes in the prices and the quantities sold of commodities and productive services—of tea, sugar, and beef; of land, labor, and machines. There exists a *system of prices*, a concept that is far from obvious.

The purpose of this chapter is to show how supply and demand work themselves out in the competitive market *for one particular good.* We shall define a demand curve and then a supply curve. Finally, we shall see how the market price reaches its competitive equilibrium where these two curves intersect—where the forces of demand and supply are just in balance.

## THE DEMAND SCHEDULE

Let us start with demand. It is commonly observed: The quantity of a good that people will buy at any one time depends on price; the *higher* the price charged for an article, the *less* the quantity of it people will be willing to buy; and, other things being equal, the lower its market price, the more units of it will be demanded.

Thus there exists at any one time a definite relation between the market price of a good (such as wheat) and the quantity demanded of that good. This relationship between price and quantity bought is called the "demand schedule," or "demand curve."

| DEMAND SCHEDULE FOR WHEAT | | |
|---|---|---|
| | (1) <br><br> PRICE <br> ($ per bu.) <br> $P$ | (2) <br> QUANTITY DE- <br> MANDED (million <br> bu. per month) <br> $Q$ |
| A | $5 | 9 |
| B | 4 | 10 |
| C | 3 | 12 |
| D | 2 | 15 |
| E | 1 | 20 |

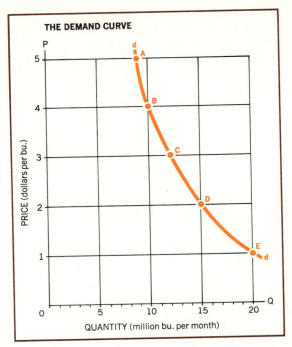

THE DEMAND CURVE

**FIG. 4-1**
**A downward-sloping demand curve relates quantity to price**
At each market price, there will be at any time a definite quantity of wheat that people will want to demand. At a lower price, the quantity demanded will go up—as more people substitute it for other goods and feel they can afford to gratify their less important wants for wheat. Compare table's $Q$ and $P$ at A, B, C, D, E.

In the figure, prices are measured on the vertical axis and quantities demanded on the horizontal axis. Each pair of $Q$, $P$ numbers from the table is plotted here as a point, and a smooth curve passed through the points gives us the demand curve.

The fact that $dd$ goes downward and to the right illustrates the very important "law of downward-sloping demand."

The table of Fig. 4-1 gives an example of a hypothetical demand schedule. At any price, such as $5 per bushel, there is a definite quantity of wheat that will be demanded by all the consumers in the market—in this case 9 (million) bushels per month. At a lower price, such as $4, the quantity bought is even greater, being 10 (million) units. At lower $P$ of $3, quantity demanded is even greater still—namely 12 (million). By lowering $P$ enough, we could coax out sales of more than 20 (million) units. From Fig. 4-1's table we can determine the *quantity demanded at any price*, by comparing Column (2) with Column (1).

## THE DEMAND CURVE

The numerical data can be given a graphic interpretation also. The vertical scale in Fig. 4-1 represents the various alternative prices of wheat, measured in dollars per bushel. The horizontal scale measures the quantity of wheat (in terms of bushels) that will be demanded per month.

A city corner is located as soon as we know its street and avenue; a ship's position is located as soon as we know its latitude and longitude. Similarly, to plot a point on this diagram, we must have two coordinate numbers: a price and a quantity. For our first point *A*, corresponding to $5 and 9 million bushels, we move upward 5 units and then over to the right 9 units. An orange dot marks the spot *A*. To get the next dot, at *B*, we go up only 4 units and over to the right 10 units. The last dot is shown by *E*. Through the dots we draw a smooth orange curve, marked *dd*.

This picturization of the demand schedule is called the "demand curve." Note that quantity and price are *inversely* related, *Q* going up when *P* goes down. The curve slopes downward, going from northwest to southeast. This important property is given a name: the *law of downward-sloping demand.* This law is true of practically all commodities: wheat, electric razors, cotton, Kellogg's cornflakes, and theater tickets.

*The law of downward-sloping demand:* **When the price of a good is raised (at the same time that all other things are held constant), less of it is demanded. Or, what is the same thing: If a greater quantity of a good is put on the market, then—other things being equal—it can be sold only at a lower price.**

## REASONS FOR THE LAW OF DOWNWARD-SLOPING DEMAND

This law is in accordance with common sense and has been known in at least a vague way since the beginning of recorded history. The reasons for it are not hard to identify. When the price of wheat is sky-high, only rich men will be able to afford it; the poor will have to make do with coarse rye bread, just as they still must do in poorer lands. When the price is still high but not quite so high as before, persons of moderate means who also happen to have an especially great liking for white bread will now be coaxed into buying some wheat.

Thus a first reason for the validity of the law of downward-sloping demand comes from the fact that *lowering prices brings in new buyers.*

Not quite so obvious is a second, equally important, reason for the law's validity; namely, each reduction of price may coax out some *extra purchases by each of the good's consumers;* and—what is the same thing—a rise in price may cause any of us to buy less. Why does my quantity demanded tend to fall as price rises? For two main reasons. When the price of a good rises, I naturally try to *substitute* other goods for it (for example, rye for wheat or tea for coffee). Also, when a price goes up, I find myself really poorer than I was before; and I will naturally cut down on my consumption of most normal goods when I feel poorer and have less real *income.*

Here are further examples of cases where I buy more of a good as it becomes more plentiful and its price drops. When water is very dear, I demand only enough of it to drink. Then when its price drops, I buy some to wash with. At still lower prices, I resort to still other uses; finally, when it is really very cheap, I water flowers and use it lavishly for any possible purpose. (Note once again that someone poorer than I will probably begin to use water to wash his car only at a lower price than that at which I buy water for that purpose. Since market demand is the sum of all different people's demands, what does this mean? It means that even after *my* quantity demanded stops expanding very much with price decreases, the *total* bought in the market may still expand as new uses for new people come into effect.)

To confirm your understanding of the demand concept, imagine that there is an increase in demand for wheat brought about by a boom in people's incomes or by a great rise in the market price of competing corn, or simply by a change in people's tastes in favor of wheat. Show that this *shifts* the whole demand curve in Fig. 4-1 rightward, and hence upward; pencil in such a new orange curve and label it *d'd'* to distinguish it from the old *dd* curve. Note that such an increase in demand means that more will now be bought at each price—as can be verified by carefully reading off points from the new curve and filling in a new Q column for Fig. 4-1's table.

## THE SUPPLY SCHEDULE

Let us now turn from demand to supply. The demand schedule related market prices and the amounts *consumers* wish to buy. How is the "supply schedule" defined?

By the *supply schedule,* or *curve,* is meant the relation between market prices and the amounts of the good that *producers* are willing to supply.

The table of Fig. 4-2 illustrates the supply schedule for wheat, and the diagram plots it as a supply curve. Unlike the falling demand curve, the *ss* supply curve for wheat *normally rises upward* and to the right, from southwest to northeast.

At a higher price of wheat, farmers will take acres out of corn cultivation and put them into wheat. In addition, each farmer can now afford the cost of more fertilizer, more labor, more machinery, and can now even afford to grow extra wheat on poorer land. All this tends to increase output at the higher prices offered.

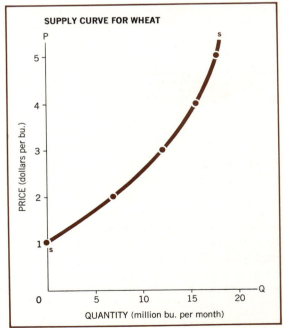

| | (1) POSSIBLE PRICES ($ per bu.) P | (2) QUANTITY SELLERS WILL SUPPLY (million bu. per month) Q |
|---|---|---|
| A | $5 | 18 |
| B | 4 | 16 |
| C | 3 | 12 |
| D | 2 | 7 |
| E | 1 | 0 |

**FIG. 4-2**
**The supply curve relates price to the quantity produced**
The table lists, for each price, the quantity that producers will want to bring to market. The diagram plots the (P, Q) pair of numbers taken from the table as the indicated brown points. A smooth curve passed through these points gives the brown upward-sloping supply curve, ss.

As will be seen in Part Three, our old friend the law of diminishing returns provides one strong reason why the supply curve would slope upward. If society wants more wine, then more and more labor will have to be added to the same limited hill sites suitable for producing wine grapes. Even if this industry is too small to affect the general wage rate, each new man will—according to the law of diminishing returns— be adding less and less extra product; and hence the necessary cost to coax out additional product will have to rise. (Cost and returns are opposite sides of the same coin, as will be shown later.[1])

How shall we depict an increase in supply? An increase in supply means an increase in the amounts that will be supplied *at each different price*. Now if you pencil the new supply curve into Fig. 4-2, you will see that it has shifted *rightward;* but for an upward-sloping supply curve, this change means the new *s's'* curve will have shifted rightward and *downward* (not rightward and upward as in the case of a shifted downward-sloping demand curve). To verify that *s's'* does depict an increase in supply, fill in a new column in the table by reading off points from your new diagram carefully.

### EQUILIBRIUM OF SUPPLY AND DEMAND

Let us now combine our analysis of demand and supply to see how competitive market price is determined. This is done in Fig. 4-3's table (page 64). Thus far, we have been considering all prices as possible. We have said, "If price is so and so, $Q$ sales will be so and so; if $P$ is such and such, $Q$ will be such and such; and so forth." But to which level will price *actually* go? And how much will then be produced and consumed? The supply schedule alone cannot tell us. Neither can the demand schedule alone.

Let us do what an auctioneer would do, i.e., proceed by trial and error. Can situation $A$ in the table, with wheat selling for $5 per bushel, prevail for any period of time? The answer is a clear "No." At $5, the producers will be supplying 18 (million) bushels to the market every month [Column (3)]. But the amount demanded by consumers will be only 9 (million) bushels per month [Column (2)]. *As stocks of wheat pile up, competitive sellers will cut the price a little.* Thus, as Column (4) shows, price will tend to fall downward. But it will not fall indefinitely to zero.

To understand this better, let us try the point $E$ with price of only $1 per bushel. Can that price persist? Again, obviously not—for a comparison of Columns (2) and (3) shows that consumption will exceed production *at that price*. Storehouses will begin to empty, *disappointed demanders who can't get wheat will tend to bid up the too-low price.* This upward pressure on $P$ is shown by Column (4)'s rising arrow.

We could go on to try other prices, but by now the answer is obvious:

The equilibrium price, i.e., the only price that can last, is that at which the amount *willingly* supplied and amount *willingly* demanded are equal. Competitive equilibrium must be *at the intersection point* of supply and demand curves.

[1] Although exceptions to the law of downward-sloping demand are few enough to be unimportant in practice, Part Three gives an interesting exception to the upward-sloping supply curve. Thus, suppose that a family farmer produces wheat and its price rises so much as to give him a much higher income. With wheat so lucrative, he is at first tempted to *substitute* some of his leisure time to produce more. But won't there reasonably come a time when he feels comfortably enough off at his *higher income* to be able to afford to take things easier, work less, and supply less $Q$?

SUPPLY AND DEMAND SCHEDULES FOR WHEAT

|   | (1) POSSIBLE PRICES ($ per bu.) | (2) QUANTITY DEMANDED (million bu. per month) | (3) QUANTITY SUPPLIED (million bu. per month) | (4) PRESSURE ON PRICE |
|---|---|---|---|---|
| A | $5 | 9 | 18 | Downward |
| B | 4 | 10 | 16 | Downward |
| C | 3 | 12 | 12 | Neutral |
| D | 2 | 15 | 7 | Upward |
| E | 1 | 20 | 0 | Upward |

**FIG. 4-3**
**Equilibrium price is at the intersection point where supply and demand match**
Only at the equilibrium price of $3, shown in the green third row, will the amount supplied just match the amount demanded.

In the diagram, at the *C* equilibrium intersection (shown by the green dot), the amount supplied just matches the amount demanded. At any lower *P*, the excess amount demanded will force *P* back up; and at any *P* higher than the equilibrium, *P* will be forced back down to it.

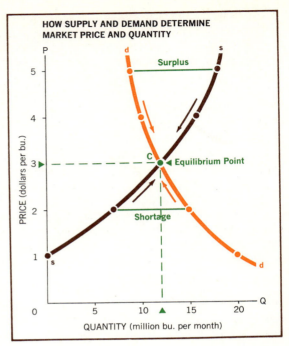

HOW SUPPLY AND DEMAND DETERMINE MARKET PRICE AND QUANTITY

Only at *C*, with a price of $3, will the amount demanded by consumers, 12 (million) bushels per month, exactly equal the amount supplied by producers, 12 (million). Price is at equilibrium, just as an olive at the bottom of a cocktail glass is at equilibrium, because there is no tendency for it to rise or fall. (Of course, this stationary price may not be reached at once. There may have to be an initial period of trial and error, of oscillation around the right level, before price finally settles down in balance.)

Figure 4-3's diagram shows the same equilibrium in pictorial form. The supply and demand curves, superimposed on the same diagram, cross at only one intersection point. This emphasized green point *C* represents the equilibrium price and quantity.

At a higher price, the green bar shows the *excess* of amount supplied over amount demanded. The arrows point downward to show the direction in which price will move because of the competition of excess *sellers*. At a price lower than the $3 equilibrium price, the green bar shows that amount demanded exceeds amount supplied. Consequently, the eager bidding of excess *buyers* requires us to point the arrow indicators upward to show the pressure that they are exerting on price. Only at the point *C* will there be a balancing of forces and a stationary maintainable price.

Such is the essence of the doctrine of supply and demand.

## EFFECT OF A SHIFT IN SUPPLY OR DEMAND

Now we can put the supply-and-demand apparatus to work. Gregory King, an English writer of the seventeenth century, noticed that when the harvest was bad, food rose in price; and when it was plentiful, farmers got a lower price. Let us try to explain this common-sense fact by what happens in our diagrams.

Figure 4-4(a) shows how a spell of bad weather *reduces* the amount that farmers will supply at each and every market price and thereby raises the equilibrium point E. The ss curve has shifted to the left and has become s's'. The demand curve has not changed. Where does the new supply curve s's' intersect dd? Plainly at E', the new equilibrium price where demand and the new reduced supply have again come into balance. Naturally, P has risen. And because of the law of downward-sloping demand, Q has gone down.

Suppose the supply curve, because of good weather and cheaper fertilizers, had *increased*, instead. Draw in a new green equilibrium E'' with lower P and higher Q.

Our apparatus will help us also analyze the effect of an increase in demand. Suppose that rising family incomes make everyone want more wheat. Then at each unchanged P, greater Q will now be demanded. The demand curve will shift rightward to d'd'. Figure 4-4(b) shows the resulting travel up the supply curve as enhanced demand raises competitive price (to the E' intersection).

## TWO STUMBLING BLOCKS

It is well to pause here to consider two minor sources of possible confusion concerning supply and demand. These have puzzled students of economics in all generations. The first point deals with the important fact that in drawing up a demand schedule or

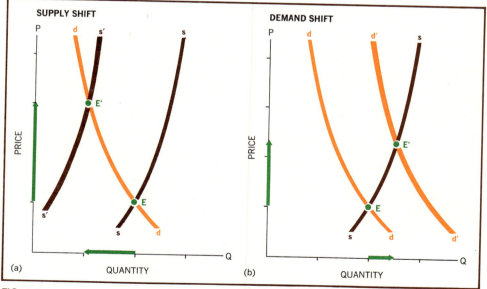

**FIG. 4-4**

**When either supply or demand curve shifts, equilibrium price changes**
**(a)** If supply shifts leftward for any reason, the equilibrium-price intersection will travel up the demand curve, giving higher P and lower Q.
**(b)** If demand increases, the equilibrium will travel up the supply curve.

curve, one always insists that "other things must be equal." The second deals with the exact sense in which demand and supply are equal in equilibrium.

**"Other things equal"**   To draw up a demand schedule for wheat, we vary its price and observe what would happen to its quantity bought *at any one period of time in which no other factors are allowed to change so as to becloud our experiment.*

Specifically, this means that, as we change wheat's *P*, we must not at the same time change family income or the price of a competing product such as corn or anything else that would tend to *shift* the demand schedule for wheat. Why? Because, like any scientist who wants to isolate the effects of one causal factor, we must try to vary only *one* thing at a time. True enough, in economics we cannot perform controlled experiments in a laboratory, and we can rarely hold other things constant in making statistical observations of economic magnitudes. This limitation on our ability to experiment empirically in economics makes it all the more important *to be clear in our logical thinking,* so that we may hope to recognize and evaluate important *tendencies*—such as the effect of *P* on *Q* demanded—when *other* tendencies are likely to be impinging on the situation at the same time.

The case of demand shift back in Fig. 4-4(b) can illustrate this common fallacy based upon a failure to respect the rule. Other things must be held equal in defining a demand curve. Suppose that the supply curve shifts little or not at all. But suppose the demand curve shifts up to *d'd'* in good times when jobs are plentiful and people have the incomes to buy more wheat; and suppose in the more depressed phase of the business cycle, demand always shifts down to *dd*. Now take a piece of graph paper and plot what would actually be recorded in the statistics of the wheat market.

In boom times, you would record the equilibrium point shown at green *E'*, and in bad times, the equilibrium point *E*. Take a ruler and join the green points *E* and *E'* in Fig. 4-4(b). The fallacy to be avoided like the plague is expressed as follows: "I have disproved the law of downward-sloping demand; for note that when *P* was high, so too was *Q*—as shown by *E'*. And when *P* was lowered, instead of that change increasing *Q*, it actually lowered *Q*—as shown by *E*. My straight line joining *E* and *E'* represents an upward-sloping, not a downward-sloping, demand curve; so I have refuted a basic economic law."

Being alerted beforehand, one detects the fallacy in this argument. For at the same time that *P* went up, other things were *not* held constant; rather, income was also raised. The tendency for a rise in *P* to choke off purchases was more than masked by the countertendency of rising income to raise purchases. Instead of testing our economic law by moving *along* the demand curve, the beginner has measured changes that result from the *shift* of the demand curve.

Why is this bad scientific method? Because it leads to absurd results such as this: "On the basis of my revolutionary refutation of the law of downward-sloping demand, I confidently predict that, in the years when the harvest is especially big, wheat will sell for a higher rather than a lower price." Not only will such reasoning lead to absurd predictions that would lose fortunes for a speculator or a miller, but it also fails to recognize other important economic relationships—such as the fact that, when family incomes go up, demand curves for goods such as wheat tend to shift rightward.

**Meaning of equilibrium**    The second stumbling block is a more subtle one, less likely to arise but not so easy to dispel. It is suggested by the following.

"How can you say that the equality of supply and demand determines a particular equilibrium price? For, after all, *the amount one man sells is precisely what another man buys.* The quantity bought must always equal the quantity sold, no matter what the price; for that matter, whether or not the market is in equilibrium, a statistician who records the $Q$ bought and the $Q$ sold will always find these necessarily identical, each being a different aspect of exactly the same transaction."

The answer to this must be phrased something like this:

You are quite right that measured $Q$ bought and measured $Q$ sold must be identical as recorded by a statistician. But the important question is this: At which $P$ will the amount that consumers are *willing to go on buying* be just matched by the amount that producers are *willing to go on selling?* At such a price, where there is equality between the *scheduled* amounts that suppliers and demanders want to go on buying and selling, and only at such an equilibrium $P$, will there be no tendency for price to rise or fall.

At any other price, such as the case where $P$ is above the intersection of supply and demand, it is a trivial fact that whatever goods change hands will show a statistical identity of measured amount bought and sold. But this measured identity does not in the least deny that suppliers are eager at so high a price to sell more than demanders will continue to buy; and that this excess of *scheduled supply* over *scheduled demand* will put downward pressure on price until it has finally reached that equilibrium level where the two curves intersect.

At that equilibrium intersection, and there alone, will everybody be happy: the auctioneer, the suppliers, the demanders—as well as the patient statistician, who always reports an identity between the measured amounts bought and sold.[2]

## WHAT SUPPLY AND DEMAND ACCOMPLISHED: GENERAL EQUILIBRIUM

Having seen how supply and demand work, let us take stock of what has been accomplished. The scarce goods of society have been rationed out among the possible users of them. Who did the rationing: a board? a committee? No. The auctioneering mechanism of competitive market price did the rationing. It was a case of "rationing by the purse."

For Whom goods are destined was *partially* determined by who was willing to pay for them. If you had the money votes, you got the wheat. If you did not, you went without. Or if you had the money votes, but preferred not to spend them on wheat, you did without. The most important needs or desires for goods—if backed by cash!— got fulfilled.

The What question was being *partially* answered at the same time. The rise in market price was the signal to coax out a higher supply of wheat—the signal for other scarce resources to move into the wheat-production industry from alternative uses.

Even the How question was being *partially* decided in the background. For with wheat prices now high, farmers could afford expensive tractors and fertilizers and could bring poorer soils into use.

[2] A similar question of "measured identity" versus "scheduled intersection" can arise in the saving-investment discussion of income determination in Chapter 12.

Why the word "partially" in this description of how the competitive market helped solve the three problems? Because this wheat market is but one market of many. What is happening in the corn and rye markets also counts; and what is happening in the market for fertilizer, men, and tractors obviously matters much.

**We must note that the pricing problem is one that involves *interdependent markets*, not just the "partial equilibrium" of a single market.**[3]

There are, so to speak, auctioneers operating simultaneously in the many different markets—wheat, rye, corn, fertilizer, and land; labor, wool, cotton, mutton, and rayon; bonds, stocks, personal loans, and foreign exchange in the form of English pounds or German marks. Each ends up at the equilibrium intersection point of his supply and demand schedules—wheat, rye, corn, fertilizer prices, and land rent; labor wage, wool, cotton, mutton, and rayon prices; bond price and its interest yield, stock prices and dividend yield, interest charges on personal loans, an exchange rate of $2.43 per pound or $3\frac{1}{8}$ marks to the dollar.

No market is an island unto itself: when wool $P$ rises (because, say, of sheep disease abroad), it pulls up the $P$s of domestic labor, fertilizer, and land needed for expanded domestic wool output; and it raises the $P$s of rival goods like cotton that some demanders will now turn to; and it might well lower the $P$ of wool spinners and of suit-company stock shares, since the latter must now pay more for their raw materials and must bid less eagerly for spinning labor.

The new "general-equilibrium set of interdependent prices" adjusts to the new situation. The price system meets the problem posed by the basic definition of economics: the study of (1) how *scarce means with alternative uses*—limited land and labor that can be switched from one industry to another—are allocated, and of (2) how to *achieve ends or goals*—as prescribed by the tastes for wool, nylon, food, and housing of sovereign consumers, possessed of factors of production that give them money-income votes for the marketplace. Each separate market, with its supply and demand curves, is doing its bit toward creating the general-equilibrium set of prices, which in a mixed economy largely resolves the basic economic problems of WHAT, HOW, and FOR WHOM.

## PERFECTION AND IMPERFECTIONS OF COMPETITION

Our curves of supply and demand strictly apply only to a *perfectly competitive* market where some kind of *standardized* commodity such as wheat is being auctioned by an organized exchange that registers transactions of *numerous* buyers and sellers.

[3] The alert reader will not have to be reminded that the competitive market gives goods to those with money votes and does so efficiently. But the distribution of the money votes depends on how much you can sell your labor and property for in competitive and imperfectly competitive factor markets, and it is affected in an important way by (1) how lucky you are, (2) how lucky your parents and in-laws were, and (3) the advantages and disadvantages of your genetic and acquired skills and aptitudes. If a student writes on a final exam, "FOR WHOM is decided (in part) by how people decide to use their money votes," he is not wrong. Indeed, he gets possibly 50 per cent credit. However, he will not get the other 50 per cent unless he adds, "The basic problem of FOR WHOM is the process by which the money votes *themselves* get determined, which is primarily not by supply and demand in a single good's market, but by supply and demand in the labor, land, and other interdependent factor markets of Part Four; and factor supplies depend much on distribution of ownership."

The Board of Trade in Chicago is one such example, and the cotton exchanges in New York or Liverpool are others. The New York Stock Exchange, while it does not auction goods and commodities or productive services rendered by factors of production, does provide a market where shares of common stocks such as those of General Motors and Royal Dutch Petroleum are auctioned at each moment of the working day. Many corporate bonds are also bought and sold in its bond division.

The economists' curves of supply and demand are important ways of *idealizing* the behavior of such markets. The curves do not pretend to give an accurate microscopic description of what is going on during each changing moment in such a marketplace, as various brokers mill around on the trading floor while frantically giving hand and voice signals to the specialist who serves as auctioneer for each grain or company stock. Nonetheless, the tools of supply and demand do summarize the important average relationships resulting over a period of time from such organized trading.

As far as these fundamental tools of supply and demand are concerned, it matters little what kind of exchange the goods are traded on: whether hand signals or slips of paper or modern computers are used; whether the auction is of the familiar kind, where the auctioneer calls out a *minimum* starting price and accepts higher and higher bids until only one high bidder is left to get the Renoir painting in question; or, alternatively, whether there is a "Dutch auction," where the price *starts high* instead of low and moves downward at stated time intervals until an eager buyer, fearing that someone else will get in the bid first, finally gives the first bid and gets the merchandise; or, as a third alternative, whether the auctioneer asks for written bids and offers in order to be able to make up a table or chart like those of Fig. 4-3 and find the equilibrium intersection at one fell swoop, in effect by solving two simultaneous equations.

Indeed, the market need not have a single auctioneer: all the bidding may well take place by telephone calls, as in the case of the market for United States government bonds, which is a much more nearly perfect one than the corporate bond market on the floor of the New York Stock Exchange. The same can be true of stocks listed on the so-called "over-the-counter market," a market which is conducted throughout the country completely by telephone and by computer listing of price-quotation lists of different brokers. (As an example, an important stock such as Bank of America, which is listed on this market, may actually behave more nearly like our competitive model than some stock *inactively* traded on the floor of the Stock Exchange.)

**Perfection of competition as a limiting pole**   Needless to say, the requirements for absolutely perfect competition are as hard to meet as the requirements for a perfectly frictionless pendulum in physics. We can approach closer and closer to perfection, but can never quite reach it. Yet this fact need not do serious damage to the usefulness of our employing the idealized concept. Actually, it matters little to the economic scientist that different grades of wheat will call for slight variations from the quoted market prices. Nor does it matter in the case of standardized cotton goods, so-called "gray goods," that they are sold and bought in an informal way by many competing firms: so long as there are *numerous* buyers and sellers on each side, *well informed* about quality and about each other's prices and having no reason to discriminate in favor of one merchant rather than another and no reason to expect that variations in their *own* bids and offers

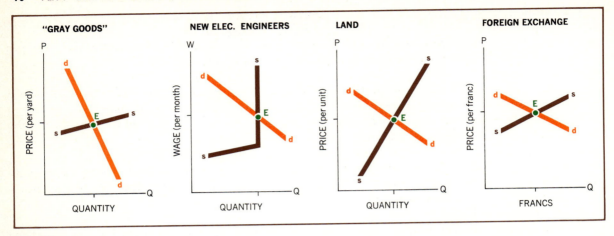

**FIG. 4-5**
**Supply-and-demand tools have many applications: to goods, acres of land, laborers, exchange rates**
Economists often use straight-lined *dd* or *ss* schedules purely for simplicity. Can you interpret the four cases?

will have an *appreciable effect* upon the prevailing market price—so long as all this is true, the behavior of price and quantity can be expected to be much like that predicted by our supply and demand curves.

The various diagrams in Fig. 4-5 illustrate how the tools of supply and demand might be used to give a good approximate description of various economic situations other than that of a staple commodity such as wheat: there is pictured a competitive market for cotton gray goods; for a factor of production such as newly graduating electrical engineers, whose price is represented by a wage per month; for a bond or capital asset such as a corner lot of land; and finally, as will be explained later in the discussion of international trade in Part Five, a foreign exchange market in which the dollar price of a French franc, a German mark, or a single unit of any other foreign currency is determined by the bids of those who need foreign currency and by the offers of those who want to sell such currencies to get American dollars.[4]

To be sure, not all today's markets are anywhere near to being perfectly competitive in the economist's sense. We shall see later, in Part Three, that elements of monopoly power or of market imperfection may enter in, and these imperfections will require us to modify the competitive model. After we have learned how to handle such cases, we shall recognize that the world is a blend of competition and imperfections—which means that the competitive analysis, properly qualified, is still an indispensable tool for interpreting reality.

[4]Question 11 at the end of this chapter reproduces from a newspaper its financial reports for a single day, showing what might have been the market price quotations for grains, bonds, common stocks, and foreign exchange. After studying economics, one is in a better position to understand the basic forces underlying these price quotations; but only experience and study can make one reasonably expert at the hazardous game of forecasting. The stock market is met in this Appendix; Chapter 21's Appendix treats the economics of speculation in organized commodity markets.

## SUMMARY

1   A basic problem of economics is how the mechanism of market pricing grapples with the triad of problems WHAT, HOW, and FOR WHOM.

2   By the *demand schedule* we mean a table showing the different quantities of a good that people will—at any time and with other things held equal—want to buy at each different price. This relationship, when plotted on a diagram, is the *demand curve, dd.*

3   With negligible exceptions, the higher the price the lower will be the quantity demanded, and vice versa. Almost all commodities obey this "law of *downward-sloping demand.*"

4   The *supply curve* or *schedule* gives the relations between the prices and the quantities of a good that producers will—other things equal—be willing to sell. Most usually, supply curves rise *upward* and to the right: diminishing returns implies that higher $P$ is needed to coax out higher-cost extra $Q$ along *ss.*

5   Market equilibrium can take place only at a price where the quantities supplied and demanded are *equal*. At any price higher than the equilibrium intersection of the supply and demand curves, the quantity that producers will want to go on supplying will exceed the quantity that consumers will want to go on demanding; downward pressure on price will result as some of the excess sellers undermine the going price. Similarly, the reader can show why a price lower than the equilibrium price will meet irresistible upward pressure from bids of excess buyers.

6   Competitive pricing *rations out* the limited supply of goods to those with desire or need backed by money votes. Along with helping to decide FOR WHOM, it signals changes in WHAT shall be produced and in HOW goods shall be produced. But any one market only "partially" helps solve the WHAT, HOW, and FOR WHOM because of its interdependence with other commodity and factor markets in setting "the general-equilibrium system of prices."

7   Organized trading markets exist for a number of staple commodities such as wheat; they may also exist for some common stocks, bonds, and other financial items. There are still other markets that behave much like an auction market, even if there is no formal auctioneering procedure: so long as there are numerous well-informed suppliers and demanders, each *too unimportant to have by himself an appreciable effect upon the price* of the standardized good in question—so long as such conditions prevail, the tools of supply and demand will give an adequate approximation of the behavior of such markets. Yet, as will be seen later, a good deal of modern economic reality departs from the strict competitive model of the economist, and economics must find tools applicable to monopoly and imperfect competition.

## CONCEPTS FOR REVIEW

demand schedule or curve, *dd*
law of downward-sloping demand
supply schedule or curve, *ss*
diminishing returns and rising *ss*
equilibrium intersection
shifts of curves

movements along a curve
how supply and demand in one
    market "partially" solves
    WHAT, HOW, and FOR WHOM
general-equilibrium prices
imperfectly competitive situations

## QUESTIONS FOR DISCUSSION

1   Although we'd all like to escape the hardship implied by higher price, show that rising market prices do perform some useful functions in time of scarcity. Show how such hardships work themselves out in a different kind of economy.

2   Define carefully what is meant by a demand schedule or curve. State the law of downward-sloping demand—that there is some kind of *inverse* relation between *P* and *Q*, the latter going down when the former goes up.

3   Define the concept of a supply schedule or curve. Show that an increase in supply means a rightward and downward *shift* of the supply curve. Contrast this with the rightward and *upward* shift implied by an increase in demand. Why the difference? Treat cases of decrease.

4   What factors might increase the demand for wheat? The supply? What would cheap mechanical pickers do to cotton prices? To farm wages?

5   Spell out arguments to show that competitive price must settle down at the equilibrium intersection of supply and demand. Use too high or too low *P*.

6   "An increase (or decrease) in supply will lower (or raise) price. An increase (decrease) in demand will generally raise (lower) price. While we can predict that an increase in demand accompanied by a decrease in supply will be followed by a rise in price, we cannot guess without further information what will happen if we *simultaneously* increase demand and *increase* supply." Verify. Puzzle out this use of parentheses, common in economics, for alternative cases.

7   "A simultaneous increase of demand and decrease of supply, as in question 6 above, is statistically impossible. Demand and supply are identically the same thing." Comment in terms of the section "Two Stumbling Blocks."

8   Give the pros and cons, in peace and war, of a draft, lottery, or high-wage army. Who gets "taxed"? Contrast sale of blood with voluntary donations.

9   "If there is only one seller or only a few very large sellers, monopoly and imperfect competition theory will need to be considered rather than the tools of competitive supply and demand. If products are far from being standardized, then each brand-name seller may well have *a degree of control over his price* not enjoyed by the perfect competitor as defined by the economist." Verify.

10 *Extra-credit problem* (only for those who know some mathematics): The demand curve is a functional relation between $Q$ and $P$, namely, $Q = f(P)$. Downward-sloping demand means $Q$ falls as $P$ rises, or in terms of calculus that $df(P)/dP < 0$. Other variables, such as income $(X_1)$ or price of rye $(X_2)$, are being held constant, etc.; hence $f(P)$ is short for $f(P; X_1, X_2, \ldots)$, and a change in any $X_i$ shifts the demand curve. Similarly, denote the supply functional relationship between $Q$ and $P$ by $Q = s(P)$, with $ds(P)/dP > 0$. Then, equilibrium intersection price, $P^*$, is the root of the equation $f(P) = s(P)$. [For $f(P) = 9 - P$ and $s(P) = 2P$, verify that $P^* = 3$ and $Q^* = 6$. Graph these intersecting straight-line schedules.]

11 Try to puzzle out what the following newspaper reports mean.

**WHEAT**

| | Open | High | Low | Close | Change | Season's High | Season's Low |
|---|---|---|---|---|---|---|---|
| July . . . | 332 | 335 | 330 | 331½–332 | +1 to 1½ | 509 | 324½ |
| Sept. . . . | 340 | 341½ | 336½ | 338 | +1¾ | 513 | 331½ |
| Dec. . . . | 349 | 352 | 347 | 348½–349 | +1½ to 2 | 523 | 340 |
| Mar. '76 . | 356 | 358½ | 353½ | 356 | +3 | 392½ | 349 |

**CORN**

| | Open | High | Low | Close | Change | Season's High | Season's Low |
|---|---|---|---|---|---|---|---|
| July . . . | 283 | 287½ | 283 | 285½–286 | +3¾ to 4¼ | 411 | 254¾ |
| Sept. . . . | 275 | 278¾ | 274½ | 277¼–½ | +4¾ to 5 | 388½ | 246¼ |
| Dec. . . . | 260 | 261¾ | 259 | 260½–261 | +4 to 4½ | 355 | 234 |
| Mar. '76 . | 266 | 266¾ | 264¾ | 206 | +3¾ | 358 | 239 |
| May . . . | 268¾ | 269¼ | 268¾ | 269¼ | +3¾ | 283 | 262½ |

| 1975 HIGH | 1975 LOW | STOCKS AND DIV. IN DOLLARS | SLS 100s | HIGH | LOW | LAST | NET CHANGE |
|---|---|---|---|---|---|---|---|
| 72½ | 46½ | Abb. Lab 1.44 | 140 | 71⅞ | 69¼ | 71½ | +¾ |
| 45¾ | 33¼ | ACF Ind 2.60 | 56 | 40⅛ | 39⅝ | 39¾ | −½ |
| 10⅜ | 7 | Acme Clv .50 | 57 | 9 | 8⅜ | 9 | +¾ |
| 3⅞ | 1¾ | Adm Dg .04e | 15 | 3¼ | 3¼ | 3¼ | −¼ |
| 10¼ | 7¾ | Adm Ex .77e | 32 | 9⅞ | 9½ | 9½ | . . . |

**TREASURY BONDS**

| Rates | Maturities | | Bid | Asked | Yield |
|---|---|---|---|---|---|
| 6¼s, | 1976 | Nov. . . . . . . . . . | 98.28 | 99.0 | 6.95 |
| 6s, | 1977 | Feb. . . . . . . . . . | 97.26 | 97.30 | 7.23 |
| 9s, | 1977 | May . . . . . . . . . | 102.30 | 103.6 | 7.26 |
| 7¾s, | 1977 | Aug. . . . . . . . . . | 100.25 | 101.1 | 7.25 |
| 6¼s, | 1978 | Feb. . . . . . . . . . | 96.24 | 97.0 | 7.46 |
| 7⅛s, | 1978 | May . . . . . . . . . | 98.20 | 98.28 | 7.54 |
| 6s, | 1978 | Nov. . . . . . . . . . | 95.0 | 95.8 | 7.56 |
| 7⅞s, | 1979 | May . . . . . . . . . | 100.13 | 100.21 | 7.68 |
| 6¼s, | 1979 | Aug. . . . . . . . . . | 94.28 | 95.4 | 7.61 |
| 6⅞s, | 1980 | May . . . . . . . . . | 96.12 | 96.20 | 7.70 |
| 9s, | 1980 | Aug. . . . . . . . . . | 104.26 | 105.2 | 7.81 |
| 7¾s, | 1981 | Nov. . . . . . . . . . | 99.0 | 99.8 | 7.90 |

| | FRIDAY | THURSDAY | WEEK AGO | YEAR AGO |
|---|---|---|---|---|
| STERLING | | | | |
| Spot . . . . . . | 2.3520 | 2.3595 | 2.3760 | 2.4180 |
| 90 days . . . . . | 2.3190 | 2.3235 | 2.3480 | 2.3838 |
| GERMANY | | | | |
| Spot . . . . . . | 41.93 | 42.20 | 41.97 | 40.65 |
| 90 days . . . . . | 42.18 | 42.45 | 42.27 | 40.95 |
| INDIA | | | | |
| Spot . . . . . . | 12.60 | 12.65 | 12.70 | 12.75 |
| JAPAN | | | | |
| Spot . . . . . . | 0.3450 | 0.3418 | 0.3429 | 0.3580 |

## APPENDIX: Stock-market Fluctuations

To the public the most dramatic example of a competitive market is in Wall Street, where supply and demand bid up and bid down the prices of common stocks each second. A man makes a fortune one year; another year he is ruined.

The New York Stock Exchange lists more than a thousand securities. It started as a private club with rules on its members, but these days it will cost you a quarter of a million dollars to buy a seat. The American Stock Exchange began as the Curb: it was literally a case where brokers met *on the street* to buy and sell, giving hand signals to the clerks hanging out the windows to record the transactions; and only in this century did it move indoors.

Every large financial center has its stock exchange. Important ones are in London, Paris, Tokyo, Frankfurt, Toronto, Montreal, and Zurich. Within the United States there are such regional markets as the Pacific Coast, Midwest, Boston, and PBW exchanges. They deal in stocks of local and smaller companies, and to tell the truth much of their reason for existing would disappear if the New York Exchange were to lose its monopoly privileges and have its facilities thrown open more evenhandedly to all.[1]

[1]From 1968 to 1975, pressure by the Antitrust Division and SEC caused the Exchange to eliminate its minimum commission rates, and to outlaw "give-ups" (i.e., rebates or fee-splitting).

## PEOPLE'S CAPITALISM

The New York Stock Exchange for many years tried to sell the notion of "people's capitalism," in which everyone owns stock and therefore will vote to take account of the interests of property. Few would oppose the notion of a wider and more equal distribution of wealth, but it is a bit of a confidence trick to entice union workers—or their wives—into owning a few shares of a mutual fund so that at the polls they will go easy on corporation tax rates—when, in fact, their own well-being is trivially affected by what happens to the few shares they own in comparison with even a 1 per cent change in wage rates or pension benefits.

In any case, only about 35 million out of more than 200 million Americans own any appreciable amount of stocks, and that is a generous estimate. Indirectly, now that private and public pension funds are beginning to invest in equities (i.e., in common stocks), low-income people are beginning to get some protection of their savings against inflation, a privilege that up until recently was enjoyed mostly by the affluent.

## THE GREAT CRASH

One traumatic event long kept the general populace fearful to venture into stock ownership—memory of the 1929 panic and crash in Wall Street, which ushered in the long and painful Hoover depression.

In the United States, during the fabulous stock-market boom of the "roaring twenties," Pullman porters, housewives, college students between classes—all bought and sold stocks. Most purchases in this wild "bull" market were "on margin"; i.e., the buyer of $10,000 worth of stocks had to put up only $2,500 or less in cash and borrowed the difference, pledging his newly bought stocks. What matter that he had to pay his broker 6, 10, or 15 per cent per year on his borrowing when in one day Auburn Motors or Bethlehem Steel might jump 10 per cent in value!

The most wonderful thing about a bull market is that it creates its own hopes. If people buy because they think stocks will rise, their act of buying sends up the price of stocks. This causes people to buy still further, and sends the dizzy dance off on another round. But, unlike a game of cards or dice, no one loses what the winners gain. Everybody gets a prize! Of course, the prizes are all on paper and would disappear if everyone tried to cash them in. But why should anyone wish to sell such lucrative securities?

When the whole world is mad, 'tis folly to be sane. Suppose one were so wise or so naïve as to believe that the public-utilities holding companies were paper pyramids on cardboard foundations; or that Florida dream real-estate developments were midway between pine thicket and swamp; or that private foreign loans to South America and Europe were being frittered away in roads to nowhere or on non-revenue-producing public swimming pools? What could such a social misfit do?

He would soon learn the first rule of property values: "A thing is worth what people *think* it is worth." But to be successful, this has to be applied in connection with the second rule, which is as hard to follow in practice as belling the cat or catching birds by putting salt on their tails: "Don't be the sucker left holding the bag."

When the black October crash of 1929 came, everyone was caught, the big-league professionals and the piddling amateurs—Andrew Mellon, John D. Rockefeller, the engineer in the White House, and the economics professor from Yale. The bottom fell out of the market. Brokers had to sell out the "margin" accounts of investors who could no longer pony up extra funds to cover the depleted value of their collateral,[2] sending the market down still further. Even those who did not buy on margin lost one-third of their capital by the end of the year, and five-sixths by 1932!

The bull market was over. The bear market had taken its place. And, as the former had lived on its dreams, so the latter was consumed by its own nightmares. Billions of dollars of security values were wiped out every month, taking with them not only the capital of gamblers out for speculative gains, but also the widow's mite supposedly invested for steady income. A "blue chip" stock like United States Steel fell from a 1929 high of 261 to a 1932 low of 21! Less respectable securities (Studebaker, for example) dropped off the board completely, becoming worthless. Even though President Hoover and his administration were friendly toward business, in vain did they try to restore confidence by predicting "Prosperity

[2]Frederick Lewis Allen's amusing and informative chronicle of the 1920s, *Only Yesterday* (Harper & Row, New York, 1931), gives a detailed account of the role of the stock-market boom in American life. See also John Kenneth Galbraith, *The Great Crash, 1929* (Houghton Mifflin, Boston, 1955).

is just around the corner" and "Stocks are excellent buys at their present levels."

Finally, after the great banking crisis of 1933, the stock market began to follow general business recovery. Figure 4-6, on the next page, shows historical movements of stock-market values. Although stocks were bullish in 1936–1937 and again during World War II, it was not until the mid-fifties that they returned to anything like the peak levels of 1929. The boom in glamor growth stocks, which ended in the mid-1962, mid-1966, and 1969 collapses, was replaced by a succession of sharp rises and falls.

## FAVORABLE ODDS

Actual historical experience has shown that, even in the face of the great crash, over a lifetime one would have done better in risky common stocks than in safe gilt-edge bonds or savings accounts.

Alfred Cowles III, founder of Yale's Cowles Foundation for Economic Research, showed in the 1930s that equity holders did better than bondholders for most of the years between 1870 and World War II. A Merrill Foundation research study at the University of Chicago Business School found that this had become even more true in the 1925–1960 years.

In an age of inflationary price creep and growth of the mixed economy, you could throw a dart at the financial page to select your portfolio of stocks at *random* and, on the average, come out substantially ahead of your "prudent" brother who stayed invested in government bonds and savings deposits!

Again, Fig. 4-6's chart of the 30 Dow-Jones "blue chip" industrial stocks illustrates these facts. But the same story would be told by the more comprehensive 500-stock Standard & Poor's Averages or by the New York Stock Exchange Comprehensive Average, which shows how you would have done if you had spread your money proportionately over *every* dollar's worth of every security listed on the exchange.

## THE CULT OF EQUITIES

People, of course, go from one extreme to another. After shunning the stock market for many years, by the 1960s they began to think that you couldn't lose in it. As a result, they bid up common-stock prices to the point where their dividend yields are scarcely 3 per cent, whereas good bonds yield 7 or more per cent. Why this inverted structure where bonds are allegedly safer yet yield more?

Obviously, investors—most of whom are in fairly high tax brackets—are shooting for lightly taxed capital gains rather than dividends.

Experience with the markets abroad shows that all good things come to an end. Once American share prices have been bid high enough, there is plenty of room for steep declines, and investing in common stock has ceased to be the one-way street it seemed to be from 1942 to 1970.[3]

## OUTGUESSING THE MARKET?

To the age-old question, "Does the market follow business activity or business activity the market?" no simple answer can be given.

It is reasonably clear that business activity, national income, and corporate earnings determine stock prices and not vice versa; and also that the psychological effects of market movements no longer have primary importance. But still the market can occasionally *anticipate* changes in national income and total purchasing power. It then appears to be leading them when really it is following what it thinks they will be doing later.

**How to invest**   There are no simply stated, foolproof rules for making money out of the stock market. Anyone who can accurately predict the future course of business activity will prosper; but there is no such person. At least four main classes of investors and speculators can be distinguished:

1. The group who simply *buy and hold*. Because the national economy has a long-term upward trend, they fare reasonably well over the long run. They might do a little better if they followed the statistical advice of investment services as to how to switch to companies of more favorable growth prospects. Surprisingly, though, representative studies show that the best mutual funds, investment counselors, and institutional money managers rarely do much

---

[3]How high is high enough? No sorcerer can tell for sure. But economic science warns: "Once 'the percentage ratio of share earnings to price plus reasonable estimate of annual percentage growth in earnings that is maintainable comes to exceed the safe interest rate on bonds,' fasten your seat belt and hold on to your hat!"

better over the long run than the Dow-Jones average of 30 industrial stocks.

The effect of this holding group is neither to stabilize nor to destabilize prices; to the extent that they freeze shares off the market and limit the number of tradings, they tend to make the market "thinner." In a thin market there are so few transactions that the attempt to buy a few hundred shares of a stock may send its price up a few points because of the absence of ready sellers around the ruling market price. A simultaneous attempt to sell may depress the price several points.

2. At the other extreme are the hour-to-hour *ticker watchers*, to be seen in every brokerage office. Generally speaking, they buy and sell, sell and buy. Usually, they make money only for their brokers.

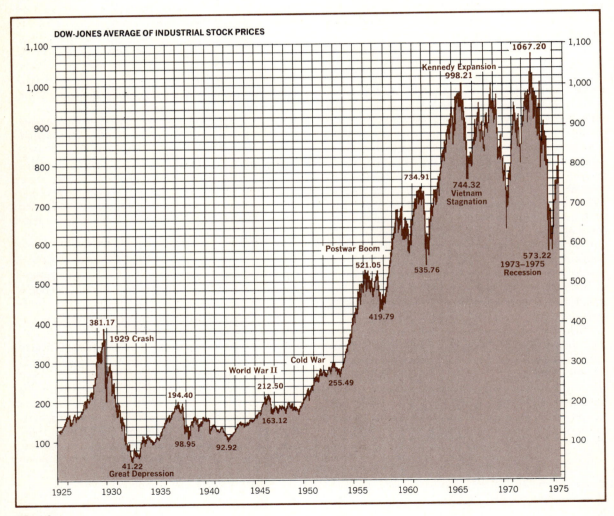

**FIG. 4-6**

**The only sure thing about stock prices is that they will fluctuate**

As money national income rises, from output and price-level growth, trend in common-stock prices is upward. But note the severe oscillations. (Source: Dow-Jones & Co., Inc.)

The existence of this trader group has the effect of making the market less thin. Because of this group, any investor can expect to be able to liquidate his market holdings at any time at some price, although not at a price predictable in advance or that he would like. Still, even this restricted "liquidity" enhances the attractiveness of securities traded on organized exchanges over and above the unlisted issues of smaller companies that are bought and sold by brokers over the counter. So it is argued.

3. In between are those *speculators who play intermediate swings* of many months or years. The least successful of these are the amateurs whose entrance into the market at the top when it is too late is supposed to be the signal for the "smart money" to leave. The most successful speculators are those who are able to avoid the extremes of enthusiasm of the mob and to discern underlying company, industry, and GNP conditions. This does not mean that they buy simply because a stock looks low and sell when it looks high. On the contrary, they buy when stocks look as if they will continue to rise. When a drop seems imminent, they sell short or, more conservatively, they simply go into cash or high-grade bonds. (It takes cool nerves to sell short, because on the whole the market is overoptimistic; and, also, your potential loss is unlimited. But if a single individual does it cleverly, he may succeed in avoiding the losses of a bear market.)

The behavior of such speculators is often destabilizing to prices. They "pile on" to a price rise and send it further; they similarly *accentuate* a decline.

Thus, in the 1960s certain so-called "performance" mutual investment funds became prominent. They would buy electronic or airline glamor stocks just before these became glamorous. Then, as people saw them buying, the public would be attracted to the same stocks. After the prices of these had been bid up, the performance funds would sell out to the public at a nice profit, moving on to new fields to conquer. The evident perils in all this are well illustrated by a modern Wall Street story.

A broker phones me, telling me to buy XYZ at $2 a share. I buy 100 shares. He phones to say: "XYZ has risen to $3, better buy a couple of hundred more." I do. He calls again: "Better buy 300 at $5." Again I do; but when next he calls I finally refuse to buy and ask to sell. "What, sell XYZ?" he says, "Sell it *to whom?*" (*In joco veritas.*)

4. Finally, there are individuals who study special situations. From public or inside sources, they learn in advance of changes in the fortunes of particular companies: of rumored bankruptcies; of special stock dividends, split-ups, or mergers; of likely earnings and dividend announcements. When combined with the successful characteristics of the third group, members of this group—such as the elder statesman of two wars, Bernard Baruch—make the largest profit from the market. Since World War II, some alert operators have been able to run $1,000 up to $10 million or more—at the same time keeping profits in the form of less heavily taxed capital gains.

But the would-be investor must take to heart Baruch's caution:

If you are ready to give up everything else—to study the whole history and background of the market and all the principal companies whose stocks are on the board as carefully as a medical student studies anatomy—if you can do all that, and, in addition, you have the cool nerves of a great gambler, the sixth sense of a kind of clairvoyant, and the courage of a lion, you have a ghost of a chance.

## SCIENCE OF STOCKS

Buying common stocks is an art, not a science. No one can draw the line between risky speculation and safe investment. But an art or a craft, being science in a still-primitive state, has its general rules of behavior. Here are a few gleaned from scientific study of this unscientific field.

1. You can't compile a good track record by *consulting the stars*. Don't laugh. Financial services have become rich—their clients haven't, though—by selling astrological advice, and one man made a fortune purporting to interpret the signals being given in the comic strips!

2. Hunches work out to nothing in the long run.

3. The best brains in Wall Street scarcely do as well as the averages (Standard & Poor's, etc.). At first this seems surprising. They have all the money needed for any kind of research and digging. But remember, they are all competing with each other; and if there is a bargain for one man to see, it is also there for another; and hence it will *already* have been wiped out of existence by competitive bids.

4. Chartists claim to see in plots of stock prices "resistance levels," "gaps," "head-and-shoulder for-

mations," "flags," "pennants," "channels"—all of which are supposed to improve your odds of guessing right. Knowing investors say: "The chartists generally end up with holes in their shoes. So forget it."

5. Are there then no good tricks? Alas, few indeed. Because inflation and growth push the country ahead, a random investment will probably show capital gains in the long run. Not much more can be said.

Statisticians have demonstrated that the day-to-day changes in stock prices are very much like a "random-walk"—like the brownian motion you see in a microscope due to the chance impacts of invisible and unpredictable atoms on just-visible huge molecules or colloidal particles. Wall Street doesn't believe this random-walk theory, but the Ph.D's in the business schools laugh at their disbelief. (Computer calculations show that the "gun-slinging performers" do better than the averager in rising bull markets; they pay for this by doing worse in falling bear markets. Why? Because the performance-happy money managers tend to buy stocks that are volatile in both directions—highly leveraged Chrysler versus General Motors, Memorex versus IBM or stodgy AT&T.)

6. To have unusual performance, you must be able to predict increases in the per share earnings of companies *before* the marketplace in general is aware of them. *After* is too late. For each stock tends to sell at a certain "price-earnings multiple,"—e.g., stagnant and cyclical U.S. Steel at 12/1, glamorous IBM at 40/1. And if you are correct in foretelling an unanticipated rise in earnings, the market will probably mark up the stock price once those earnings become visible. (As a kicker, if you are early in recognizing an area of glamorous earnings growth, you may find the market putting higher and higher price-earnings multiples on your holdings—and after that

has happened, it is a good time to get out. Describing this "greater fool theory," in which you hope to unload on some other sucker is easier than for all to practice it successfully.)

7. The above strategy of anticipating changes in earnings is easy to state, but practically impossible to put into practice even if you have a vast research staff and inside management contacts. Hence, unless you like the fun of investing your own money—and are willing to pay something for that fun in the form of bad performance—most amateurs would be well advised to buy shares in some mutual fund. A mutual fund buys 30 to 100 stocks deemed best by professional money managers and gives you your prorated share in them. If the market goes up, your mutual fund shares will probably go up; but it works both ways. (WARNING: Most mutual funds are sold by salesmen who get a fat commission for doing so—usually an 8 per cent "load" skimmed off your principal. Through the mail you can buy no-load funds involving *no* sales commission at all, and which experience shows do about the same on the *average* as the heavy-load funds. How do the no-loads manage this? Simply by paying the same management fees to money managers but cutting out the selling expenses—the equivalent in finance of the "discount retail store" that quotes low prices for cash-and-carry. You can recognize no-loads on the financial pages by *equality* of bid and asked.)

For an amusing, but well-informed, account of the modern stock market, the reader might refer to *The Money Game* (Random House, New York, 1967) by "Adam Smith," or to Smith's *Supermoney* (Random House, New York, 1972); or to Burton G. Malkiel, *A Random Walk Down Wall Street* (Norton, New York, 1973).

## CONCEPTS FOR REVIEW

New York and other exchanges
common stocks or equities
great crash

dividend versus bond yield
Dow-Jones Stock Index
equities and inflation protection

price-earnings multiple
random-walk versus chartism
mutual funds: load and no-load

Everyone realizes the importance of income. The expression "Clothes make the man" would be more nearly right if it were "Income makes the man." That is to say, if you can know but one fact about a man, knowledge of his income will probably reveal most about him. Then you can roughly guess his political opinions, his tastes and education, his age, and even his life expectancy. Furthermore, unless a family has a steady stream of money coming in every week, month, and year—even though it has saintly endurance—that family is ill. Not only its materialistic activities but its nonmaterialistic activities, the things that convert existence into living, must suffer: education, travel, recreation, and charity, to say nothing of food, warmth, and shelter.

It is a commonplace to state that the American standard of living and level of family income are among the highest in the world. But few people realize just how small the average American income really is, or how great is the range between the highest and the lowest incomes.

This chapter gives some basic facts about incomes and wealth, here and abroad. America has been described by Galbraith as "the affluent society." And the mixed economies of Western Europe are following hot on our heels. Yet pockets of poverty remain: and as we shall see, this kind of poverty is new in history and different from that found in most other parts of the earth. (More on poverty will come in Chapter 40, and more on the search for a more egalitarian society, in Chapter 42.)

## THE DECLINE OF POVERTY

It is now well over a century since Karl Marx and Friedrich Engels in 1848 issued the *Communist Manifesto* containing the lines: "Workers of the world unite! You have nothing to lose but your chains." While some of Marx's predictions about the future of industrial capitalism were proved correct in the intervening years, one prediction about

# 5

# INCOMES AND LIVING STANDARDS

F. SCOTT FITZGERALD:
You know, Ernest, the rich are different from us.
ERNEST HEMINGWAY:
Yes, I know. They have more money than we do.

79

the laws of motion of capitalist development, entertained by many Marxians, has proved to be quite wrong. The assertion that *the rich will become richer and the poor will become poorer*[1] cannot be sustained by careful historical and statistical research. In Europe and America, there has definitely been a steady, long-term improvement in minimum standards of living, whether measured by food, clothing, housing, or length of life. This fact about mixed economies is clear from statistics soon to be given.

**From bad to less bad**   It used to be fashionable for economic historians to dwell on the evils of the Industrial Revolution and the poverty-ridden condition of the masses in the disease-producing cities. In point of fact, no Dickens novel did full justice to the dismal conditions of child labor, length of the working day, and conditions of safety and sanitation in early nineteenth-century factories. A workweek of 84 hours was the prevailing rule, with time out at the bench for breakfast and sometimes supper. A good deal of work could be got out of a six-year-old child; and if a man lost two fingers in a machine, he still had eight left.

However true their lurid picture of industrial factory towns, the earlier historians seem to have erred in thinking that conditions were clearly worse than in the pre-industrial era. The earlier "putting-out," or domestic, system, in which wool or yarn was provided to workers for them to spin or weave in their homes, brought the worst conditions of the sweatshop into the home. The whole family was figuratively forced to run on the treadmill.

Furthermore, poverty is never so obvious in the country as in the industrial cities, where it forces itself on the observer. The idyllic picture of the healthful, happy countryside peopled by stout yeomen and happy peasantry is a mirage in most parts of the world. Even today, New York's Hell's Kitchen or Harlem, Boston's South or North End, "behind the Yards" in Chicago or its black belt hardly overshadow the poverty and squalor of our rural problem areas: the Tobacco Road of the deep South, hillbilly regions of the Appalachian Plateau, dust bowls, and ghost mining towns. More people are at this moment starving in rural Appalachia than in urban slums.

Modern historians therefore emphasize that the conditions of the industrial present, inadequate as they may seem, are nevertheless great improvements in living standards over the previous periods of commercial enterprise and agrarian feudalism.[2]

[1] "The modern labourer, on the contrary, instead of rising with the progress of industry, sinks deeper and deeper below the condition of his own class. He becomes a pauper, and pauperism develops more rapidly than population and wealth." K. Marx and Friedrich Engels, *The Communist Manifesto* (1848), widely reprinted in economic anthologies, as for example, P. A. Samuelson, *Readings in Economics* (McGraw-Hill, New York, 1973), 7th ed. Also "[along with the centralization of capitalists, technological change, and capital accumulation] grows the mass of misery, oppression, slavery, degradation, exploitation . . . the revolt of the working class. . . . The monopoly of capital becomes a fetter upon the mode of production. . . . Centralisation of the means of production and socialisation of labour at last reach a point where they become incompatible with their capitalist integument. This integument is burst asunder. The knell of capitalist private property sounds. The expropriators are expropriated." Karl Marx, *Capital*, vol. I (1867), chap. XXXII. Marxologists still dispute whether the immiserization and pauperization of the labor classes was meant literally, or only in terms of relative shares of labor and property, or even only in terms of growing worker discontent and alienation.

[2] "The bourgeoisie, during its rule of scarce one hundred years, has created more massive and more colossal productive forces than have all preceding generations together. Subjection of nature's forces to man, machinery, application of chemistry to industry and agriculture, steam-navigation, railways,

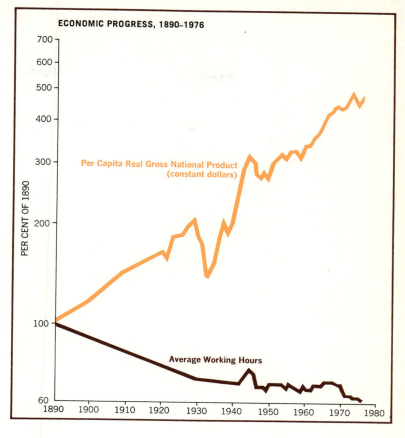

**ECONOMIC PROGRESS, 1890–1976**

**FIG. 5-1**
**Higher productivity gives us more output and chance for more leisure**
Technological improvements, better capital goods, and more highly trained labor have raised production faster than the growth of population. NOTE: This is a "ratio," or "semilog," chart; the vertical scale is arranged so that equal vertical distances depict equal percentage rather than equal absolute changes. EXAMPLE: Verify that 400 is as far above 200 as 200 is above 100. (Source: U.S. Department of Commerce, Bureau of Labor Statistics.)

## TWO WORLDS?

Most of Asia and Africa are even today at lower levels of living than were the Western countries before the Industrial Revolution. Figure 5-1 shows how fortunate the United States growth in output has been.

A great economic statistician, Simon Kuznets of Harvard, has recently shown that the leading Western nations have for decades been averaging rapid rates of growth of output per head. Examine the front-leaf charts to see just how fast countries have grown.

What about the progress of the poorer countries? We lack data to give firm answers. Professor Kuznets has made shrewd guesses and inclines to the view that their productivity growth has been lagging behind. He makes the important observation:[3]

electric telegraphs, clearing of whole continents for cultivation, canalisation of rivers, whole populations conjured out of the ground—what earlier century had even a presentiment that such productive forces slumbered in the lap of social labour?" K. Marx and F. Engels, *The Communist Manifesto* (1848).
[3] Simon Kuznets, "Quantitative Aspects of the Economic Growth of Nations: I," *Economic Development and Cultural Change*, vol. V, 1956, p. 25. From 1950 to 1973, there have been some success stories: Brazil, Thailand, Taiwan, Korea, Mexico, for example, have made remarkable sprints of progress. Leaf forward to Fig. 38-2 to see the divergence between the advanced and poor nations.

| PER CAPITA GNPs, 1976 | | | |
| --- | --- | --- | --- |
| United States | $7,750 | Soviet Union | $3,700 |
| Canada | 7,500 | Hungary | 3,100 |
| Sweden | 7,100 | Portugal | 2,100 |
| Denmark | 6,600 | Brazil | 1,550 |
| France | 6,400 | Turkey | 1,350 |
| West Germany | 6,200 | South Korea | 1,050 |
| Japan | 4,900 | Egypt | 750 |
| United Kingdom | 4,750 | India | 475 |
| Israel | 4,600 | China | 350–500 |
| Italy | 4,000 | Kenya | 400 |

TABLE 5-1

**Spread of real incomes is wide, America's lead is narrowing**

All estimates have been converted into 1976 U.S. dollars at exchange rates designed to reflect *actual purchasing powers;* but all estimates should be regarded as rough approximations, particularly in countries at drastically different stages of development. (Sources: I. Kravis et al., *System of International Comparisons of Gross National Product and Purchasing Power* (1975); R. Summers and S. Ahmad at Econometrics Society, December 1974 Meetings; extrapolations by author.)

. . . the presently developed countries were already in advance of the "rest of the world" when modern industrialization began—and the latter only increased the disparity.

Table 5-1 shows the wide international spreads of income per head. Note the 16-fold ratio of American to Indian incomes!

In the United States itself, the South has much lower incomes than the Northeast and the West Coast. States such as Mississippi have scarcely attained per capita incomes equal to those reached in Pennsylvania and New York back in 1925 or those found in France today.

But it is interesting to note that the regional differentials in income are gradually narrowing and changing. The South and West grow faster than the average; and older regions, such as the Middle Atlantic states and New England, are reverting toward the average.

## DISTRIBUTION OF INCOME IN THE UNITED STATES

A poll of students will show that they are not very sure what their own family incomes really are. Usually it turns out they have a slightly exaggerated notion of their fathers' earnings. An astonishing number of wives—most particularly in the *upper*-income brackets—have no close notion of their husbands' paychecks. In addition, there are some people so inept at keeping records and with such variable earnings that they do not themselves know how much they make. Even where income is known within the family, there is a quite natural reticence to reveal it to outsiders; thus, investigators who made a survey of the birth-control habits of native white Protestants of Indianapolis often found it harder to get financial data than intimate personal information.

In the absence of statistical knowledge, it is understandable that one should form an impression of the American standard of living from the full-page magazine advertisements portraying a jolly American family in an air-conditioned mansion, with a Mercedes, a station wagon, a motor launch, and all the other good things that go to make up comfortable living. Actually, of course, this sort of life is still beyond the grasp of 90 per cent of the American public and even beyond most families from which the select group of college students comes.

**The sober truth**  In the mid-1970s, at the height of American prosperity, the per capita income in the United States is about $130 per week. Such an average figure is derived by pretending that all the income in the United States is divided equally among every man, woman, and child. Of course, income is distributed far from equally; and there is no guarantee that an attempt to divide it equally would leave the total unchanged.

If the members of a classroom, or of the whole country, write down their family incomes on cards, these cards may be sorted into different income classes; i.e., some cards will go into the $0-to-$2,499 class, some into the $2,500-to-$4,999 class, and so forth. In this way we get the *statistical frequency* distribution of income. At one extreme will be the very poor, who have drawn a blank in life; at the other, the very rich. The vast majority fall in between.

Table 5-2 summarizes recent statistics on this subject. Column (1) gives the *income class interval*. Column (2) shows the percentage of families in each income class. Column (3) shows the percentage of the total of all income that goes to the people in the given income class. Columns (4) and (5) are computed from (2) and (3), respectively. Column (4) shows what percentage of the total number of families belongs to each income class *or below*. Column (5) shows what percentage of total income goes to the people who belong in the given income class or have still lower incomes.

This table shows it would be a great mistake to think that the poor and the rich are equally distributed around the middle. The Biblical statement, "For the poor ye

| DISTRIBUTION OF INCOMES OF AMERICAN FAMILIES, 1973 | | | | |
|---|---|---|---|---|
| (1) | (2) | (3) | (4) | (5) |
| INCOME CLASS | PERCENTAGE OF ALL FAMILIES IN THIS CLASS | PERCENTAGE OF TOTAL INCOME RECEIVED BY FAMILIES IN THIS CLASS | PERCENTAGE OF FAMILIES IN THIS CLASS AND LOWER ONES | PERCENTAGE OF INCOME RECEIVED BY THIS CLASS AND LOWER ONES |
| Under $ 2,500 | 4 | 1 (−) | 4 | 1 (−) |
| $ 2,500–  4,999 | 11 | 1 | 15 | 1 |
| 5,000–  7,499 | 11 | 5 | 26 | 6 |
| 7,500–  9,999 | 13 | 7 | 39 | 13 |
| 10,000– 12,499 | 13 | 11 | 52 | 24 |
| 12,500– 14,999 | 13 | 13 | 65 | 37 |
| 15,000– 24,999 | 26 | 38 | 91 | 75 |
| 25,000 and up | 9 | 25 | 100 | 100 |
| Total | 100 | 100 | | |

**TABLE 5-2**

**Income pyramid shows great inequality of incomes**

Half of these families and individuals are below the median income of $12,051. The average (or arithmetic mean) income each would get if all income was distributed exactly equally is $13,622. More families have incomes around the modal $11,500 level than around any other income. (Source: U.S. Department of Commerce. To update these numbers to the late 1970s, increase all money incomes by about one-third.)

have always with you," gives no inkling of their vast numbers. Abraham Lincoln pointed up this fact picturesquely in his statement, "The Lord prefers common people. . . . He made so many of them."

A glance at the income distribution in the United States shows how pointed is the income pyramid and how broad its base. "There's always room at the top" is certainly true; this is so because it is hard to get there, not because it is easy. If we made an income pyramid out of a child's blocks, with each layer portraying $1,000 of income, the peak would be far higher than the Eiffel Tower, but most of us would be within a yard of the ground.

The middle, or "median," income class (which divides the upper from the lower half of the families) corresponds to a modest income—only about $12,051 in the 1973 table. The median income falls short of the average (or "arithmetic mean") income of $13,622.[4] This is primarily because the distribution of incomes is always a skewed one, with a long tail of incomes stretching out above the mean.

## HOW TO MEASURE INEQUALITY AMONG INCOME CLASSES

How great is the spread of incomes, and how shall we measure the degree of inequality of income distribution?

From Table 5-2, we can estimate that roughly half of all Americans fall in the middle-income range of $7,200 to $18,000. This means that one-fourth fall below $7,200, and an approximately equal number have incomes above $18,000. Of course, the fact that there are the same number of individuals and families in the above-$18,000 group as in the below-$7,200 group does not mean that they each receive the same percentage of the total income. Actually, the lowest fourth of the people receives in total income less than a fifth of the total income received by the highest fourth (as Fig. 5-2 will show).

This suggests how to go about the task of getting a numerical measure of the degree of inequality of income distribution. We can ask, What per cent *of all income* goes to the lowest 10 per cent *of the population?* What to the lowest 20 per cent? The lowest 50 per cent? The lowest 95 per cent? And so forth. Such data can be derived from Columns (4) and (5) back in Table 5-2.

If incomes were absolutely uniformly distributed, the lowest 20 per cent of the population (which in this case would mean *any* 20 per cent) would receive exactly 20 per cent of the total income; the lowest 80 per cent would receive 80 per cent of the income; and the highest 20 per cent would also get only 20 per cent of the income.

In fact, as the first two columns in Fig. 5-2's table show, the lowest 20 per cent of the families get only 6 per cent of the total income, while the most affluent 20 per cent of the families get 41 per cent. The second 20 per cent get only 12 per cent of income, the third 20 per cent only 17 per cent; but the fourth 20 per cent get 24 per cent; and the upper 5 per cent of the very rich get no less than 14 per cent—more than the bottom third of the population get all together!

---

[4]Single individuals, not in families, of course have a lower mean income: $5,708 rather than $13,622. Combining both groups, the weighted mean income is $11,651.

**INEQUALITY TABLE**

| FAMILY INCOME BY RANK | PER CENT SHARE OF 1973 INCOME | CUMULATIVE PERCENTAGE OF PEOPLE | CUMULATIVE PERCENTAGE OF INCOME | | |
|---|---|---|---|---|---|
| | | | ABSOLUTE EQUALITY | ABSOLUTE INEQUALITY | ACTUAL 1973 |
| | | 0 | 0 | 0 | 0 |
| Lowest fifth | 6 | 20 | 20 | 0 | 6 |
| Second fifth | 12 | 40 | 40 | 0 | 18 |
| Third fifth | 17 | 60 | 60 | 0 | 35 |
| Fourth fifth | 24 | 80 | 80 | 0 | 59 |
| Highest fifth* | 41 | 100 | 100 | 100 | 100 |

*Top 5 per cent receive 14 per cent of total income.

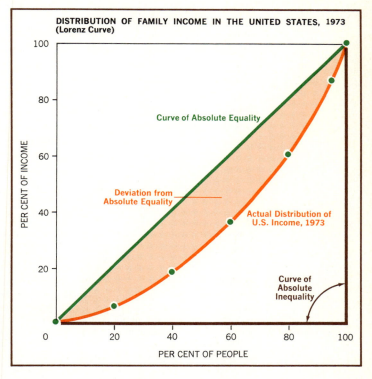

DISTRIBUTION OF FAMILY INCOME IN THE UNITED STATES, 1973
(Lorenz Curve)

**FIG. 5-2**
**Lorenz curve measures degree of inequality between opposite limits**
By plotting from the table's final orange column, we see that the actual distribution-of-income orange curve lies between the two extremes of absolute equality and absolute inequality. The shaded area of this Lorenz chart (as a percentage of half the square's area) measures relative inequality of income. (How would the curve have looked back in the roaring 1920s when inequality was greater? In a 1984 welfare state that narrows income differences?)

In order to plot the degree of inequality on a so-called Lorenz curve, examine the colored columns of Figure 5-2's table, whose cumulative percentages contrast the patterns of (*a*) absolute equality, (*b*) absolute inequality, and (*c*) actual 1973 American inequality.

Absolute equality is depicted by the green column numbers. When plotted, these become the green equality diagonal of Fig. 5-2's Lorenz diagram.

At the other extreme, we have the hypothetical case of absolute *inequality,* where everybody (say, 99 out of 100 people) has no income, except for *one* person, who has *all* the income. This is shown in the brown column of the table. Why those numbers? Because the lowest 0, 20, 80, and 99 people have no income at all. But the lowest 100 do include the last man; and all the people, of course, have all the income. The lowest curve on the Lorenz diagram—the brown, right-angled line—represents this limiting case of absolute inequality.

Any actual income distribution, such as that of 1973, must fall between these extremes. The orange column presents the data derived from the first two columns in a form suitable for plotting as the orange Lorenz curve in the figure. This actual Lorenz curve is given in Fig. 5-2 by the indicated intermediate orange curve, with the shaded area indicating the deviation from absolute equality, and hence giving us a measure of the degree of *inequality* of income distribution.[5] (Since we shall meet Lorenz curves often, Fig. 5-2 repays careful study.)

## TRENDS OF INEQUALITY

What is happening to the degree of inequality of incomes in modern nations? Is it getting greater, as pessimists feared? By calculating Lorenz and other curves, scholars find that inequality is definitely less in America than it was back in 1929, but little different today from 1945. A glance at Fig. 5-3(b) will show that the United Kingdom and the United States have rather similar degrees of inequality of incomes, the major difference apparently not being attributable so much to differences in social philosophy as to the fact that there is a large fraction of subsistence farmers and also of low-paid nonwhite workers in the American economy.

Which country today has the greatest equality? No one knows how to compare the inequality in the Soviet Union[6] or China with that in mixed economies. If we

---

[5] There are still other ways of measuring the degree of inequality of income. One of the most interesting of these we can mention but not discuss in detail here. The Italian-born Swiss professor of economics Vilfredo Pareto was often called, with somewhat questionable accuracy, the ideological precursor of fascism. By using a certain logarithmic chart called the "Pareto chart," he found that the "upper tail" of the income data of many different countries and many different times fell along straight lines of almost the same slopes. He came to believe this to be a fundamental natural law. According to Pareto's Law, *there is an inevitable tendency for income to be distributed in the same way—regardless of social and political institutions and regardless of taxation.* In the past 75 years, more careful studies have refuted the universality of Pareto's Law, as well as its inevitability. Thus, in Great Britain, in the period just after World War II, income taxation had gone so far as to leave only 70 people with incomes of more than $24,000 after taxes were paid! As we'll see, progressive income taxation somewhat reduces the Lorenz curve's inequality; on the other hand, if we correct for exclusion of capital gains from the definition of income, the share of the top 5 per cent goes from 14 to 18 per cent of income. More on all this in Chapter 40's discussion of inequality.

[6] A very careful study of wage inequalities in Russia's communistic economy, Abram Bergson, *The Structure of Soviet Wages* (Harvard University Press, Cambridge, Mass., 1944), showed inequalities and dispersions between the best-paid and the poorest-paid workers surprisingly like those of our own society. Shostakovich, other top Soviet musicians, and top scientists probably make more there than do Copland, Teller, and similar persons in America. The inequality of political privilege among Soviet bureaucrats, military officers, Communist party members, and the Soviet public at large is not susceptible to precise numerical measurement. *Employment* incomes in mixed economies like Australia and Sweden were found in a 1965 study to be slightly more equal than in Poland.

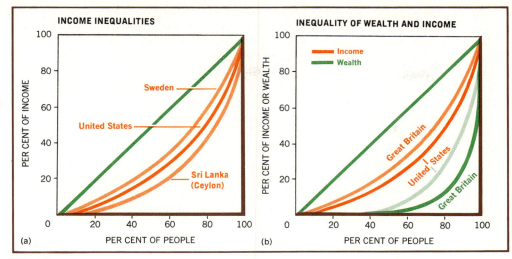

**FIG. 5-3**

**Inequality differs in different societies, and is greater for wealth than for income**

**(a)**   Advanced economies show less inequality of income distribution than do preindustrial economies. Contrary to dire predictions of scientific socialists that the rich get richer and the poor get poorer under capitalism, the mixed economy shows greater equality.

**(b)**   Holdings of wealth tend to be more concentrated than do incomes earned annually. The United States and the United Kingdom have rather similar equality of incomes; but British wealth is much more concentrated than American. Socialist countries like China and the Soviet Union would have much less private concentration of wealth.

confine ourselves to the noncommunist world, it has been suggested that Israel may lead the list. Sweden and other mixed economies have low inequality, as the comparison in Fig. 5-3(a) suggests.

Before industrialization, was there a golden age of greater equality of distribution? Fragmentary historical data suggest otherwise. Have developed societies generally greater inequality than underdeveloped nations? Casual tourist observation often suggests the reverse; the extremes of poverty and wealth *appear* greater in poor countries than in industrialized ones. The limited statistics available do confirm this view; thus, the Lorenz curve for a country like Ceylon in Fig. 5-3(a) or of India (in later Fig. 38-1) will show greater inequality than will such a curve for the United States, the United Kingdom, or Sweden. (The Lorenz curve for Black Americans shows slightly *more* inequality than does the curve for whites.)

## DISTRIBUTION OF WEALTH

A Lorenz curve of distribution of *wealth* ownership shows considerably more inequality than does a curve of *income* distribution. Figure 5-3(b) shows how great is the difference between the wealth and income curves. Whereas the United Kingdom and the United States have similar inequality of *incomes,* note that the United Kingdom has much greater inequality of *wealth* than does the United States. In part this is because certain peers and tycoons in Britain own tremendous concentrations of land and other property. But study of the data shows that much of the difference comes from the fact that many Americans of quite modest incomes do have positive net worth (i.e., assets minus liabilities), whereas this is less common among the lower-income British. The top 10 per cent of our wealthy get almost a third of the American total income, and own more than half the total wealth. While the bottom 10 per cent owe more than they own, the top 1 per cent own 25 per cent of the mid-1970s' U.S. wealth.

Turn back to Fig. 3-1 on p. 46. It shows that the For Whom problem is determined by (1) the price that people can get for the factors they supply—land, labor, machinery, and general capital goods, and (2) the amounts of these factors that they start out with. If labor could be ignored, the distribution of incomes would tend to be that determined by the distribution of wealth: at the same interest return, twice the wealth yields twice the income. Hence, property incomes show great Lorenz inequality.

The earnings from work—wages, salaries, earnings of unincorporated entrepreneurs—are evidently less unequally distributed. But of course they are not uniform, as the following sections show.

## INCOME DIFFERENCES AMONG OCCUPATIONS

What single profession seems to make the most money? In recent years it has without question been the doctors. They have forged well ahead of lawyers. Physicians have mean earnings of over $60,000 and median earnings of about $50,000; lawyers have mean and median earnings of $30,000 and $25,000.[7] Why these high doctor earnings? Primarily because the costs of training doctors are so high and the capacities of our medical schools are so low; as a result, we train not very many more doctors than we did in 1910, even though the demand has greatly increased—particularly as a result of Blue Cross and various governmental health programs. Medical societies (like the AMA) are also accused of helping to keep doctors' incomes up by various devices, including, ironically, the insistence on high quality standards.

Dentists, engineers, and schoolteachers are estimated to have median incomes of about $30,000, $20,000, and $11,500, respectively. College teachers as a class have a median salary of about $16,000 for a 9-month academic year ($18,000 if they also teach summer school, but only half have this opportunity). Full professors at the largest universities get about twice these amounts; professors of physics and engineering average higher incomes than do professors of Greek and botany; supply and demand seem to decree that it is economics professors who average the highest salaries of all. While teachers' salaries have been improving recently, it is ministers who are the lowest paid of all professionals. Their median salary is still significantly below $10,000 (only about half that of a master plumber!). And even with special perquisites, the figure is unbelievably low.

Do incomes increase with age? Yes, but only if you are a white male! And even then, not in the lowest-paid manual jobs. For such work, a man is at his best in his early twenties; after that he goes downhill. In the professions and in business executive jobs, earnings do increase with age: doctors and lawyers reach their prime after fifty;

---

[7]Top New York law firms bill their giant corporate clients at a $100 *per hour* rate for work done.

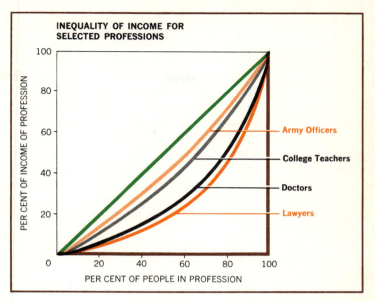

**INEQUALITY OF INCOME FOR SELECTED PROFESSIONS**

PER CENT OF INCOME OF PROFESSION

PER CENT OF PEOPLE IN PROFESSION

Army Officers
College Teachers
Doctors
Lawyers

**FIG. 5-4**

**Lawyers, doctors show more inequality than salaried professors, officers**

Prizes for lucky few are highest in corporate law. Why would the curve for *salaried* doctors and lawyers fall in the middle of the four curves shown? Why would you expect dentists to have a curve just above doctors? How might the curve for speculators in common stocks look? (Source: G. J. Stigler, National Bureau of Economic Research, New York, 1956.)

both can hope to work beyond the normal retirement ages. A junior executive with a good M.B.A. business degree will begin training at $1,500 a month; if he is very successful, he may retire as chairman of the board, earning, say, $150,000 a year and with stock bonuses and retirement provisions.[8]

On the other hand, many corporations and institutions have been fixing inflexible retirement age of sixty-five. With improvements in life expectancies, this poses a problem of long years of wasteful and unhappy retirement. The ultimate solution seems to be along these lines: Let each man taper off slowly rather than abruptly, with other factors besides chronological age being decisive.

Figure 5-4 shows how professions differ in *inequality* of earnings.

## IS COLLEGE WORTH WHILE?

How do education and training affect lifetime income? Are they worth their cost? The evidence answers, Yes. Men who never finish eight grades of school earn around $10,000 annually; college graduates do about twice as well. Unemployment among school dropouts exceeds that of graduates by a growing margin.

Even if you have to borrow at 8 per cent interest, put off years of gainful employment, live away from home, and pay for food and books, your lifetime earnings in the professions that are open only to college graduates will probably turn out to be more than compensatory. (Good grades help: A *Time* study showed, in its own argot,

[8] Salaries of top officers do increase with the size of the firm, but by no means in strict proportion. Statistics suggest that the head of Corporation A, twice the size of Company B, will *not* get twice the salary that the head of B gets, but only about 30 per cent more. The highest paid corporate executive, Harold Geneen of ITT, earns close to $800,000 a year.

that "greasy grinds" end up with slightly higher pay than do "big men on campus"; both outearn the anonymous face in the college crowd.)[9]

Money is not everything—better to be uneducated, poor, and happy than to be well-off and miserable? The Governmental Commission on Mental Illness and Health reported a 1960 survey of how people with different education compared mentally. Were college graduates worried and depressed in comparison with those of little schooling? Surprisingly, the answer was, Definitely not. College graduates reported greater happiness and less mental illness. True, they were more introspective; but coupled with this went a greater sense of well-being and satisfaction. Their perspectives were broader and aspiration levels higher; and when they worried, their worries tended to be over genuine, rather than imagined, troubles. Only 38 per cent of high school graduates say they are "very happy" in their marriage, as against 60 per cent for college graduates. Only 70 per cent of high school graduates say their job is "enjoyable," as against no less than 89 per cent for college graduates.

## DIFFERENCES IN ABILITY AND INCOMES

In Part Four we shall study in detail the economic principles underlying the distribution of income. Our common sense enables us to anticipate part of its analysis and suggests that one factor helping to explain differences in income must be *differences in people*.

These easy-to-exaggerate differences may be physical, mental, or temperamental. They may be associated with biological inheritance; or as we are increasingly becoming aware, with social and economic environment.

These personal differences provide us with only part of the answer to the puzzle of income dispersion. Physical traits (such as height or hip girth) and measured mental traits (such as intelligence quotient or tone perception) appear to be *not* so different among people as are the differences in income distribution. Often, the scientist who measures individual traits finds that they are "normally" distributed, with most people in the middle and fewer people at each end, as represented by the brown bell-shaped curve of Fig. 5-5. (If their IQ scores depart from the normal distribution, psychologists will even *rescale* them so as to force agreement!) Incomes—even those from work, but especially those from property ownership—are distributed *skewly*, as shown by the orange curve with a very long tail off in the direction of highest-paid individuals.

Actually, there is nothing particularly sacred about the so-called "normal curve." If *heights* of cubes (not people) are normally distributed, then their *volumes* will be skewed off to the right. Moreover, careful examination of census data on incomes suggests that *each kind of wage income* may tend to approximate to a bell-shaped distribution curve of modest asymmetry. But when we add together the distributions of earnings for women as well as men, for property owners as well as workers, for

---

[9]Those who graduate from college in 1976 will earn, between ages 18 and 64, about $650,000, while those of their generation who only graduate from high school will earn about $450,000. Those who only finish elementary school will earn but $320,000. Going on to do graduate work will add less than 8 per cent to the 4-year graduate's lifetime earnings. Black college graduates until recently earned less than white high school graduates. Full-time female workers with the A.B. do no better than white male high school graduates!

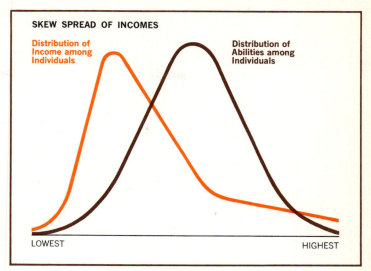

**SKEW SPREAD OF INCOMES**

Distribution of
Income among
Individuals

Distribution of
Abilities among
Individuals

LOWEST                                          HIGHEST

**FIG. 5-5**
**Abilities seem more normally distributed
than incomes are distributed**
Heights, intelligence quotients, and many
measured human traits seem to follow a
so-called "normal" bell-shaped statistical
distribution. Incomes seem to be more
skewed, highest incomes being more than
a hundred times the lowest (as in orange
curve).

lucky speculators, and other diverse groups, the great "skewness" of the whole distribution does emerge. Moreover, if we follow each wage earner over a period of years, a pattern of dispersion will emerge, one of the important factors causing differences among individuals being the different degrees of unemployment they suffer.

Perhaps a warning is in order at this point against jumping to the conclusion that there is something *necessary* and *inevitable* about this dispersion of income. Within the framework of the mixed economy, fundamental changes in education have already made changes in inequality. Moreover, as no one knows better than the man at the top, our system of progressive income taxation has already greatly changed the relative take-home and—what is more important—the "keep-at-home" of the high- and low-paid. Simon Kuznets has verified that lifetime incomes are less unequal than those of any one year. Thus, many with low incomes for a year like 1976 are retired people who did not always have such low incomes, or those with the bad luck to be recently unemployed. Further, the modern system of welfare transfers is recognized as an improvement by observers who remember the bad old days of laissez faire when countless people literally starved while no one even noticed.

## ECONOMIC STRATIFICATION AND OPPORTUNITY

America was always considered the land of opportunity, where anyone with ability might get ahead in the world. The success legend of Horatio Alger, Jr.'s "poor but proud" hero who worked his way to the top and married the boss's daughter has no doubt been overdrawn. (Few black, or even Catholic, go-getters went to the altar with those Alger heiresses.) But the notion of an open society did have elements of truth as compared with the situation in older countries, where an aristocratic tradition lingered and where free schooling beyond the primary grades was late in being established.

| OCCUPATION OF FATHER | PERSONS LISTED IN Who's Who, 1912 (per cent) | AMERICAN MILLIONAIRES, LIVING IN 1925 (per cent) | AMERICAN BUSINESS LEADERS, 1928 (per cent) | AMERICAN BUSINESS LEADERS, 1952 (per cent) | AMERICAN BUSINESS LEADERS UNDER 50, 1952 (per cent) |
|---|---|---|---|---|---|
| Businessman | 35.3 | 75.0 | 60.0 | 61.8 | 67.8 |
| Professional man | 34.3 | 10.5 | 13.4 | 13.5 | 14.8 |
| Farmer | 23.4 | 7.3 | 12.4 | 12.7 | 11.1 |
| Laborer | 6.7 | 1.6 | 12.5 | 7.8 | 2.5 |
| Other | 0.3 | 5.6 | 1.7 | 4.2 | 3.8 |
| Total | 100.0 | 100.0 | 100.0 | 100.0 | 100.0 |

**SOCIAL ORIGIN OF SUCCESSFUL LEADERS IN AMERICA**

**TABLE 5-3**

**Anyone can climb the ladder of success, but it helps to start high**
Though laborers far outnumber businessmen in the population at large, most successful businessmen had a businessman father. What trends do you see in this table? How would you explain them? (Sources: F. W. Taussig and C. S. Joslyn, *American Business Leaders*, Macmillan, New York, 1932; *Fortune*.)

For example, the "old school tie" and, more important, the Oxford accent were until recently almost indispensable to political and social advancement in Britain; even with the free scholarship system, too few members of the lower or middle class could jump this hurdle. In this country, few people even recognize a "prep school" accent, and variations in speech are largely geographical rather than social.

Moreover, ours has been rather a materialistic civilization in which success is interpreted in business terms. Because "money talks," it is easier for outsiders to break into the upper crust than it would be in a culture that puts greater emphasis upon tradition. The *nouveaux riches* of one generation, such as the Vanderbilts a century ago, become the social arbiters of the next.

**Recruitment of the elite** Nevertheless, careful questionnaire investigation of the social origins of successful businessmen, namely, the directors and officers of corporations, turns up some surprising facts. The typical American business executive does not come off a farm or out of a workingman's home. More likely his father was also a businessman or possibly in one of the professions. Table 5-3 summarizes some typical research studies made by Taussig and Joslyn and others.

Does this mean that American economic society is hardening along caste lines?[10]

[10] A generation ago, most scholars inclined toward the view that it was becoming increasingly difficult to go from the bottom to the top. Now they are not so sure. Recent careful studies of the origins of business leaders back *before* 1900 suggest that the present may compare favorably with the good old days, which were not so good after all. Increasingly, as organizations become bigger, the elements of nepotism and personal favoritism seem to become less important, and the increasing emphasis upon civil-servant-like quasi-objective tests of performance (and conformity!) suggests greater mobility among the elite. Aristocrats complain that we are becoming a "meritocracy." (A recent study by Mabel Newcomer for the *Scientific American* supplied the following corroboration of the above view:

Taussig and Joslyn were not sure. They pointed out that two diametrically opposite explanations are possible:

(1) There has long been social mobility in America: all the cream rose to the top some time ago, leaving naturally less gifted people at the bottom. (2) There are strong, and perhaps growing, barriers to circulation between the economic classes.

Taussig and Joslyn inclined rather to the first view, believing that "you can't keep a good man down." Most sociologists would disagree, particularly if one is crass enough to inquire about the absence of women, blacks, Chicanos, Indians, or even southern Europeans among these elites. They would emphasize the thousand and one subtle psychological, social, economic, and educational disadvantages of the children of less fortunate families from the cradle on; that equal ability is not always able to give rise to equal achievement.[11]

Whichever view is right, the implications for policy are the same. Human beings are a nation's most important form of social capital—a high-yielding form, moreover, in which we have invested too little in the past. Talent, wherever it may be, is worth seeking out and nurturing. And certainly when it comes to Chapter 39's analysis of racial discrimination, no one will argue that nonwhites have enjoyed equality of opportunity.

## DEFINITION OF POVERTY

In the 1960s America dropped the complacent notion that it had already become an affluent society with no more economic problems. The last act of President Kennedy, before his tragic 1963 assassination, was to map out a war against poverty. But no one realized how vast the task would be. Prior to Chapter 40's extended discussion, here is a brief outline of the fight against poverty.

The Economic Opportunity Act (1964), proposed by Kennedy, established the Office of Economic Opportunity (OEO) under R. Sargent Shriver. The OEO, building upon earlier work by the Ford Foundation, set up Community Action Agencies to coordinate

---

"Only 10.5 per cent of the current generation of big business executives . . . [are] sons of wealthy families . . . [in] 1950 the corresponding figure was 36.1 per cent, and at the turn of the century, 45.6 per cent.")

The arithmetic of "transition probabilities" can be made to yield the following results. Divide society into two classes, so that I am either a $U$ in the Upper class or a *non-U* in the Lower. If a child's chance to move out of his parents' class is as great as to stay in, then $\frac{1}{2}$ the children, grandchildren, great-grandchildren, and descendants generally of a $U$ parent will be $U$s. But if there is social stratification so that a child has only $\frac{1}{4}$ chance of moving into a class different from his parents, $\frac{3}{4} (= \frac{1}{2} + \frac{1}{4})$ of the children of $U$s will be $U$s. However, it can be deduced that only $\frac{5}{8} (= \frac{1}{2} + \frac{1}{8})$ of grandchildren of $U$s will be $U$s; and only $\frac{9}{16} (= \frac{1}{2} + \frac{1}{16})$ of their great-grandchildren. Evidently, the chance of remote descendants of $U$s being also $U$s goes ultimately down to $\frac{1}{2}$, with 50 per cent of the excess above the $\frac{1}{2}$ equality level being wiped out at each new generation. Hope for the *non-U*s means despair for the $U$s only if a fair race is deemed a tragedy. For more on transition probabilities, see W. Feller, *An Introduction to Probability*, vol. I (Wiley, New York, 1968).

[11] The famous Coleman Report on education discovered in the 1960s that no amount of compensatory spending on education seemed to do much to narrow the differentials in performance already present among six-year-olds entering school for the first time. This suggests the need to improve environments at even the youngest ages.

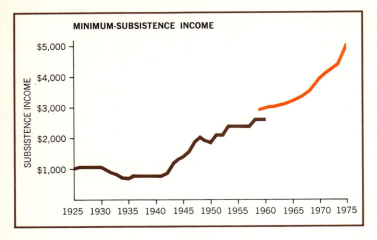

**MINIMUM-SUBSISTENCE INCOME**

SUBSISTENCE INCOME

$5,000
$4,000
$3,000
$2,000
$1,000

1925 1930 1935 1940 1945 1950 1955 1960 1965 1970 1975

**FIG. 5-6**

**Society raises poverty-demarcating line as the economy progresses**

The brown curve shows how the social-service worker's minimum-income welfare budget for a family of four has risen with economic growth. The cost-of-subsistence budget, $5,050 in 1976, is shown in orange, and is in close agreement with the welfare budget.

Even after allowing for cyclical price-level changes, society's estimate of "minimum-subsistence" income moves up in prosperity, down in recession. World War II and postwar high employment much reduced the percentage of population living in poverty; but since 1945 our standards have risen as fast as our incomes; the challenge remains to reduce numbers in poverty further and raise earning abilities. (Sources: Oscar Ornati, New School of Social Research; U.S. Bureau of the Census; updating by author.)

federal, state, and local programs in cities. The Neighborhood Youth Corps, Job Corps, and Work Experience Programs were started by OEO to furnish job training in schools and camps and to provide literacy programs for adults. VISTA, the domestic Peace Corps, was initiated, and project Head Start was begun to help underprivileged preschool children break the vicious circle of environmentally inherited poverty. Both President Nixon and unsuccessful presidential candidate George McGovern favored income maintenance programs, and President Ford introduced a small payment to low-income families in the 1975 tax cut.

Let us see how large the group is that is stuck below an adequate income level, and just which minorities are likely to be in this group.

Economists have tried to calculate "minimum-subsistence" incomes in two different ways: First, they have taken over from social-service welfare workers carefully calculated budgets purporting to measure the cost of a minimum-subsistence income. Second, as a check, OEO economists have noted that poor families generally spend about one-third of their income on food; and hence from calculations by the Department of Agriculture of the cost of a subsistence food budget in different places, they can, by multiplying by 3, get estimates of needed minimum-subsistence income.

The two methods agree fairly well, and Fig. 5-6 shows how the cost of such a minimum-subsistence budget for a family of four[12] has risen in half a century. It is to be stressed that most of the rise comes because, *as the nation as a whole gets more prosperous, the definition of minimum requirements is raised.* What Americans consider

---

[12] Statistical budgetary data throw light on the age-old question, Can two live as cheaply as one? According to the Bureau of Labor Statistics, the answer is, No. Even if one person works in the home, it costs a married couple about $\frac{100}{70}$ times what it costs a single person to live, on the average. There are advantages, however; and this amount is still less than it costs two to live singly. Each child in the family adds to the cost of living. Thus, if it costs $70 to live alone and $100 to live with a wife, it costs about $130 with one child, $160 with two, and so forth, for each extra child.

poverty would be regarded as affluence in Asia, and most families behind the Iron Curtain would be deemed poor if our budget requirements were extrapolated to them.

What do these standards come to? In 1976, the cost of the "subsistence" budget might be about $5,050 for a family of four, and includes only the bare necessities: no movies, little meat, no dental care, no newspapers, little clothing, and so forth. A "minimum-comfort" budget, hardly luxurious, costs about twice as much, and allows for adequate diet, occasional recreation, some tobacco and books, but not much else.

## THE POSITION OF MINORITIES

No discussion of the inequality of incomes would be complete without mention of the position of economic minorities. In a real sense this is the concern of everyone, because everyone belongs to some minority, even the Smiths, or for that matter, the Lodges and the Cabots. What are the characteristics of the people who live in families with less than minimum-subsistence income?

Table 5-4 shows at a glance the relative economic position of the white and black population. Almost one-third of the black population has less than minimum-subsistence income! The United States population is only 11 per cent black, but the poor are 30 per cent black. Other groups with high poverty incidence are farmers (with 20 per cent in poverty, twice the ratio for nonfarmers), the aged, children, and Southerners. Consider the odds against an aged black in the rural South.

Many of the poor are untrained, stuck in economically stagnant areas, isolated in

**TABLE 5-4**

**Blacks and also women have less income, more unemployment, than white males**
Because of less education and racial discrimination, blacks receive fewer good jobs. The resulting lower income makes them less able to afford a good education. The incidence of unemployment compounds the inequality and shows that minorities have a particular interest in full-employment programs. Education is not a cure-all. A black college graduate earns only about the same in a lifetime as does a white high school graduate! Full-time female workers earn only about 60 per cent of what full-time male workers do—a median of $7,596 as against $12,595 in 1973. (Source: U.S. Bureau of the Census; U.S. Bureau of Labor Statistics.)

| DISCRIMINATION AND INEQUALITY OF OPPORTUNITY, 1973 | WHITE | BLACK |
|---|---|---|
| **Income** | | |
| Median income of families | $12,595 | $7,596 |
| Per cent of persons in poverty | 9.9 | 26.6 |
| Per cent of families with incomes of $10,000 or more | 63.9 | 35.0 |
| **Education** | | |
| Median years of school completed by men 25 years or older | 12.3 | 10.6 |
| Per cent of persons 25–29 years old who have completed high school | 75.5 | 64.7 |
| Per cent of persons 25–34 years old who are college graduates | 19.0 | 8.3 |
| **Unemployment rates** (per cent) | | |
| Adult men | 2.9 | 5.9 |
| Adult women | 4.3 | 8.5 |
| Teenagers | 12.6 | 31.4 |

city ghettos, and so forth. Yet many are also active job seekers in the urban labor markets. Surveys show that female-headed households, or those headed by an unemployed male, are most likely to be poor, and there are relatively more fatherless black families than white. As Chapter 39 will discuss, there are signs that nonwhite incomes are growing a bit faster than white, suggesting that legal efforts do make a difference.

Experienced observers used to insist that outright sexual discrimination, in the sense of paying men higher rates for the *same* kind and volume of work, is not a common practice. Similarly, it has often been asserted that racial discrimination in the sense of unequal pay for the *same* work is not common.

How can we reconcile these statements with the economic inequalities which every sophisticated person knows prevail between the sexes and races, as shown in Table 5-4? The answer to the paradox lies partly in the fact that discrimination usually takes the more effective form of *not admitting women to the same jobs as men and barring blacks from skilled labor, executive, and sales positions.*

Undoubtedly this explains much of the story. However, other competent observers maintain that women and blacks on exactly the same job *do* often receive less pay. Some women school teachers still get lower pay than men. In a large electrical-goods plant, job-evaluation experts privately divide all factory work into two parts: women's jobs and men's jobs. The lowest pay of the men begins about where the women's highest pay leaves off; yet both management and the union will admit, off the record, that in many borderline jobs the productivity of women is greater than that of men.

Now, it cannot be denied that there are physical and temperamental differences between men and women; for example, a woman could not win the heavyweight wrestling championship or set a record for the 100-yard dash. Still, the female sex is the stronger sex in the sense of life expectancy and also, perhaps, in being capable of sustained, painstaking effort. It is equally obvious that there are differences of skin color and hair texture between white, black, and yellow peoples, but there is no logical way to infer how much of observed differences in achievement is due to inequality of opportunity.

**Reducing discrimination** Whatever one's views are about the biological and environmental differences between the races and sexes—and the views of the scientists who have studied the question most are quite different from those of the man on the street—it is absolutely clear to any observer that there are numerous good jobs which either sex or any race can do equally well and are prevented from so doing. This is shown by the experience of wartime and boom, when the usual discriminatory barriers were lowered.

Similarly, the older worker in ordinary times finds himself at a disadvantage in our society. A man may be thrown on the scrap heap by the age of fifty when many of his best years are still ahead. It is not true that an older worker is the first to be fired; usually his experience or seniority helps to protect him. But once he is fired, it is much harder for him to become reemployed. Paradoxically, the humanitarian measures adopted by corporations to aid older workers—such as retirement pension schemes—

are one reason for corporations' refusing to hire older men, since it then becomes more expensive to hire them.

From the horror of World War II, a few salutary lessons were learned. Women, blacks, Puerto Ricans, Mexican-Americans, Indians, and older workers showed that they were capable of holding down better jobs and earning more money than was thought possible before the war. The experience of the federal and state Fair Employment Practices Commissions has not been that prejudice can be legislated away overnight, but that steady improvement is possible if the people really want it. Nor can all the blame be placed upon bigoted employers. Organized labor must incur some of the onus for racial discrimination, particularly in the building trades.

The Civil Rights Act (1964) set up the Equal Employment Opportunities Commission, which has been making steady progress in lessening discrimination— discrimination against women and discrimination against nonwhites. Although poverty has not disappeared, young black men now appear to be getting jobs on the same footing as equivalent white men. In Chapter 39, we shall use the tools of economics to analyze racial and sexual discrimination—both to understand it better and to learn how to do more about this social pathology.

## CONCLUSION

Sargent Shriver, when he headed the OEO, prophesied that by 1976, just 200 years after the Declaration of Independence, poverty could be finally terminated in the United States. Of course, the millennium will not arrive in 1976 or on any other date. New times define new challenges. Ideas that seem impractical now will be taken as a matter of course by posterity.

Some experts in the field have put the challenge bluntly:[13]

The U.S. has arrived at the point where poverty could be abolished easily and simply by a stroke of the pen. To raise every individual and family in the nation now below a subsistence income to the subsistence level would cost about $25 billion a year. This is less than 2 per cent of the gross national product. It is less than 10 per cent of tax revenues. It is about one-fifth of the cost of national defense.

Chapter 40 will return to the problem of poverty and inequality.

[13]J. N. Morgan, M. H. David, W. J. Cohen, and H. E. Brazer, *Income and Welfare in the United States* (McGraw-Hill, New York, 1962), pp. 3–4.

## SUMMARY

1  Factual studies of the American distribution of income show that median incomes are lower than popularly believed. Even though incomes today are higher than in any other country or time, they are still not high in comparison with common notions as to what represents comfortable modern living.

2  The view that the poor are becoming poorer in modern industrial nations will not stand up under careful factual examination. Since the Industrial Revolution,

average standards of life in Western Europe and America seem definitely to have been showing a rising long-term trend, tending to outstrip most underdeveloped nations. Even within the United States, the regional differentials in living standards are very great; there is a trend, though, toward narrowing the old differentials between North and South.

3    The Lorenz diagram is a convenient device for measuring the spreads or inequalities of income distribution. It shows what percentage of total income goes to the poorest 1 per cent of the population, to the poorest 10 per cent, to the poorest 95 per cent, and so forth. The modern distribution of American income appears to be less unequal than in 1929 or than that in less developed countries, but it still shows a considerable measure of inequality and little change in recent decades. The distribution of income seems much more skewed than mental and physical human traits which have a more normal spread.

4    Minority groups—such as the aged, women, nonwhites, and various ethnic groups—pose important economic challenges for a democracy. At the borders between economics and sociology, we run into interesting questions concerning the "circulation of the elite." Such popular clichés as "shirt sleeves to shirt sleeves in three generations" appear to have but a partial basis in fact. There is a strong positive correlation between income and social status of a person's parents and grandparents and his own, but the exact direction of causation is hard to establish.

5    Within the affluent society, the public war against poverty needs to go on unceasingly. As each rampart is slowly conquered, higher standards of performance must be set by society for itself. The vicious circle by which poverty is environmentally inherited has to be broken if the antipoverty war is to claim victories.

## CONCEPTS FOR REVIEW

trends of income distribution
per capita incomes by nations
mean, median incomes
Lorenz curve of income and
    wealth
professional incomes' spread

education and human capital
normal and skew distributions
social stratification
minimum budget
war against poverty
racial and sexual discrimination

## QUESTIONS FOR DISCUSSION

1    Let each member of the class write down on a slip of paper an estimate of his own family's income. From these, draw up a frequency table showing the distribution of incomes. What is the median income? The mean or average income?

2    How much do you think it takes for a childless married couple to live comfortably in your community? How would the money be spent?

**3**   Were your parents better off than their parents? What could this suggest with respect to the disadvantages of capitalism versus the modern mixed economy?

**4**   Formulate some of your own ethical beliefs concerning how unequal incomes should be for people of different abilities and needs. How do you justify these beliefs? Would a nineteenth-century American agree? A Russian today? A Chinese? A Fiji Islander? What is the relevance of a Bureau of Labor Statistics report that those in the under-$3,000-income class give 4 per cent of their income to church and charity, while those in the over-$10,000 class give 3 per cent?

**5**   Compare the front-endpaper charts with Table 5-1. Note how Japan has come up. What about Britain? The U.S.S.R.? The United States and Germany?

**6**   What are your views on the Food Stamp program which channels surplus farm products to the poor? Contrast with cash aids.

**7**   How does the fact that different cities and regions have different costs of living affect comparisons of real incomes? Thus, in Anchorage (Alaska) and Honolulu, living is a third to a quarter more expensive than in the average city. Boston, New York, and San Francisco are also expensive places. Austin, Atlanta, and Dallas run 10 per cent below average. Small towns run 10 to 20 per cent below big cities. Although a teacher, secretary, or mechanic in Amsterdam earns less than half the comparable Chicago salaries, most living costs (other than services and rents!) run only about 25 per cent less.

**8**   *Extra-credit problem:* Instead of using the Lorenz curve to measure inequality, why not calculate the "average absolute income difference between *every pair* of families" in society? Such a standardized so-called "Gini coefficient" turns out to be *identical* to the Lorenz measure. Pareto used still a different measure of inequality. He discovered that the upper tail of the distribution became a straight line with negative slope if he used logarithm scales to plot (1) log of percentage of families with income above each income level against (2) log of that income level. When inequality rises, the "average income of those richer than you" becomes a larger constant multiple of your income; but by "Pareto's Law" it has to be the same (new) *common* multiple no matter how rich you become. (Obviously, when you get to Rockefeller or whoever is the richest man in the world, Pareto's Law must finally fail. It also fails at incomes lower than the mode.)

# 6

# BUSINESS ORGANIZATION AND INCOME

The business of America is business.
CALVIN COOLIDGE

Business, labor, and government form the chief institutions of an economy. The chapters that immediately follow deal with the last two institutions; this chapter focuses on the first, business.

To understand our business civilization, we must first understand the organization and functioning of business enterprise. The first part of this chapter leads up to the analysis of the modern corporation, primarily by an extensive case study; the last half deals with the financial structure of corporations, particularly the modern large-scale, or "giant," corporation. The Appendix presents a brief introduction to the fundamentals of accounting. Without some comprehension of accounting, there can be no deep understanding of the economics of enterprise.

The "new industrial state"—to use the name John Kenneth Galbraith has coined for the organization of our large corporate bureaucracy—is something new in the history of mankind. If the corporate structure is not to control man, society must see that it stays subject to control.

## BIG, SMALL, AND INFINITESIMAL BUSINESS

There are 8 million American business units in the 1970s. The majority of these enterprises are very small-scale units owned by a single person. Most businesses are here today and gone tomorrow, the average life expectancy of a business being only half-a-dozen years. Some will terminate in bankruptcy; many more will be voluntarily brought to a close with sighs of regret for dashed hopes and an expensive lesson learned; others will come to a joyous end when their owner lands a good job.

Faster than old businesses die, new ones are born. The present population of business concerns grew up as a result of the cumulative excess of business births over business deaths during previous years. As an economy grows, we can expect a steady excess of business births over deaths.

100

By number, the tiny, self-owned "individual proprietorship" is overwhelmingly the dominant form of business. But in dollar value, political and economic power, payrolls, and employment, some few hundred "giant corporations" occupy a strategically dominant position.

**Tiny business**    Let us glance briefly at the role in our economy of "infinitesimal businesses." There are more than 200,000 grocery-store owners in the United States, all trying to make a living. There are nearly a quarter of a million automobile service stations; more than 40,000 drugstores; and so it goes.

Some of these ventures are highly successful; but it is still true to say that most do not earn for their owners much more than they could get with less effort and risk by working for somebody else. Thus, chain stores do about 60 per cent of all the grocery business, the rest being divided among the independents. Most of these independents consist of the so-called "Ma and Pa" stores, doing less than $200 of business every day. These are often started by people who have only a few thousand dollars of initial capital—less than half the amount necessary for an adequate grocery store to do the volume of business necessary if the owner is to earn even minimum wages for his effort. Such small-scale efforts are doomed from their very beginning. When the owners' initial capital is used up, they are finished. They illustrate why one-third to one-half of all retail businesses are discontinued within 3 years. (In these days of brave talk about "black capitalism," it is sobering to read in Chapter 39 that most Negro businesses are small and of low profitability, being confined chiefly to a protected market of service needs for blacks—as e.g., restaurants, undertaking, hairdressing, etc.)

Of course, business fields differ in the amount of capital required. To build a modern service station costs more than $120,000, but to lease one from an oil company brings the initial capital down to around $10,000. Occupations with a high "rate of turnover of inventory"—such as vegetable stores—obviously require less initial capital than drugstores, hardware stores, or jewelry stores, where many items of stock will stay on the shelves for 3 to 5 years and where the average "turnover ratio" of annual sales to stock of inventory may be a good deal less than one.

Aside from the capital necessary to open a business, there is the tremendous amount of personal effort required. Self-employed farmers work from 55 to 60 hours per week during the peak summer months. Similarly, it has been estimated that the people who are their own bosses put in more hours per week than wage earners. Who, on his Sunday jaunt to the shore or mountains, has not pitied some self-employed drudge, whose own efforts and those of all his family hardly suffice to let him break even?

Still, people will always want to start out on their own. *Theirs* may be the successful venture. Even if they never do succeed in earning more than a few thousand a year, there is something attractive about being able to make your own plans and do the variety of tasks that a small enterprise or franchise operation calls for.

## THE SINGLE PROPRIETORSHIP

We gain insight into the principal forms of business organization—(a) the single proprietorship, (b) partnership, and (c) corporation—by following the history of one business venture as it grows from a small beginning into a good-sized corporation.

Let us suppose you decide to start a business to produce toothpaste. You may have hit upon a good preparation in your chemistry class; or perhaps you simply looked up an old formula in the *Encyclopedia Britannica*. To be a single proprietor you need not get anybody's permission; you simply wake up one morning and say, "Today, I am in business!" And you are.

You can hire as few or as many people as you wish, borrow whatever capital you can. At the end of the month, whatever is left over as profits—after all costs have been met!—is yours to do with as you like. And there is nothing to stop you from going to the cash register at any time, taking out $800 if you can find it there, and giving it to your wife to buy a fur coat or Chippendale chair. (Of course, as an individual you must pay personal income taxes on all earnings.)

The *losses* of the business are all yours, too. If your sales fail to cover the costs you have incurred, your creditors can ask you to dig deeper into your personal assets: the bonds set aside for Junior's education, the old farmstead, and the rest. In legal terms, an individual proprietor has "unlimited liability" for all debts contracted by the business. All his property with the exception of a small minimum, is legally attachable to meet those debts.

## BUSINESS GROWTH AND THE NEED FOR SHORT-TERM CAPITAL

Suppose the business is prospering tremendously—perhaps because your low price has induced a supermarket chain to place a large order for tubes of paste to be marketed under its name. You are now making more money than you expected to; but you find yourself harder pressed for cash than ever before. Why? Because you are not *paid in advance* for your sales, whereas you must pay your workers and suppliers promptly on receipt of their services. For the moment, you are putting out money and getting nothing for it, i.e., nothing except the certainty of future payment on the sales orders which you have booked, nothing but a miscellaneous batch of "goods in process"—unfinished toothpaste, empty tubing, and so forth.

To some extent, the stringency of cash can be relieved by your not paying for supplies until the end of the month or even later. However, there is a limit to how far your suppliers will let you run up bills. Also, letting your so-called "accounts payable liabilities" pile up is an expensive way of raising capital, because goods are often billed at 2 per cent discount if paid within 30 days. When you do not take advantage of such discounts, you are, in effect, paying a very high interest rate—up to 24 per cent per year!

Where is such a single proprietor to borrow? A personal finance company will probably charge you something like 3 per cent per month or 40 per cent per year for a small personal loan; and even it will prefer to lend to a man with a steady wage that can be legally "attached" or "garnisheed" in case of nonpayment. If you own a home without a mortgage, a loan at 7 to 9 per cent might be raised upon it. To borrow in this way is clearly to risk your family's future well-being; but probably, if you are hopeful of your business future, you may go ahead and assume the risk.

Why can't the local banker be called upon for a commercial loan at 6 or 7 per cent? Ordinarily, a commercial bank will not provide "venture capital" for an unproven enterprise. The bank's vice-president looks at your checking balance and finds it has always been near the vanishing point; this is natural, since as fast as payments have come in, you have had to write checks to stave off the ever-insistent claims of your creditors. Ordinarily, the bank likes to make 3-month loans to be used for peak-season needs and to be canceled during the rest of the year. It is idle to pretend that 3 months from now your growing business will be more liquid than now. At that time you will be applying for continuous renewal of the loan; you know it, and the banker knows it.

Even if the bank were emancipated from the older prejudice against "term loans" of some years' duration, it could not conscientiously provide capital to a business like yours. To the banker you are only one of numerous would-be entrepreneurs; and most, he knows, are destined for failure even in the best of times, and almost all would be wiped out if a serious recession should come along. For the bank actually to protect the sums entrusted to it by its depositors, it would have to charge you an extra risk premium of 10 per cent or more,[1] in addition to, say, 7 per cent interest. Otherwise, gains from successful ventures would not offset losses of the unsuccessful.

There is one possibility of your getting a loan from the bank, particularly if you are a member of a minority group. The Small Business Administration (SBA) might join with the bank to make you a loan, thus coaxing the banker to make it. Or there might be a Small Business Investment Company, set up for tax advantages, that will lend you venture capital in return for eventual partial ownership. In some states, there are development commissions which have limited funds to help bring a business to town or keep it there.

Despite your makeshift attempts to raise capital, the business is still suffering from growing pains. You have exhausted all possibilities of raising further loan capital. Perhaps the time has come to look for a partner.

## THE PARTNERSHIP

Any two or more people can get together and form a partnership. Each agrees to provide some fraction of the work and capital, to share some percentage of the profits, and of course to share the losses or debts. A purely oral agreement will do; but it is more businesslike and makes for less misunderstanding if you have a lawyer draw up some sort of formal partnership agreement.

In the case of the toothpaste business, suppose your brother-in-law is given a part ownership in the business in return for putting up $40,000 capital. Like you, he is to work for the company, for, say, $10,000 per year as compared with your $12,000. You are to receive two-thirds of all profits or losses, computed after the partnership withdrawals are treated as costs; and he is to get one-third.

Your partner has put up $40,000 in cash. What have you brought into the venture?

---

[1] Another alternative has been used extensively in Germany but not in the United States or Britain: German banks buy part ownership in business and share in the profits. Such participation in ownership inevitably leads to management responsibilities by the banks and often to monopoly control of business by banking interests. For this reason, and others, such activity is legally forbidden to our banks, which are rarely sources of venture capital.

You have, of course, some unfinished barrels of toothpaste to contribute, along with some uncollected accounts receivable for goods already delivered. This doesn't seem much.

Actually, what you bring to the partnership is an intangible but valuable asset: the profitable sales orders and the know-how, or what is called "good will." In short, you are bringing with you a *potential profit-earning power* over all costs and drawings of, say, $15,000 a year. You are letting your partner have a $10,000-a-year job—which we shall assume is perhaps equal to what he can get elsewhere—and, in addition, for $40,000, he is purchasing a one-third slice of $15,000 every year.

To get this much per year from bond investments would cost him much more than $40,000. He would have to buy $100,000 worth of 5 per cent government bonds to get such a return, or $70,000 worth of $7\frac{1}{7}$ per cent private bonds. Aside from the risk element, your partner is getting a good buy for his $40,000, since he will annually collect some $12\frac{1}{2}$ per cent on his investment. So your two-thirds share is justified by the good will that you supply.[2]

## "THIS IS THE WAY WE GROW"

And your business continues to prosper and grow. Each year, both partners agree to take out of the business only their stipulated drawings (which are like wages) and about a fifth of their share of profits, plowing the rest of the profits back into the business. Why do you decide to take out any profits from the business at all? Because you need the cash to pay your federal personal income taxes, which are levied not only on your salaries but also *upon your respective shares of the partnership's earnings.*

Why does a business like this grow? Here are some possible reasons: (1) Your toothpaste sales have risen as a result of your trade name's becoming advertised and better known and as a result of your sending out more salesmen. (2) As more toothpaste is produced, economies of large-scale production are realized so that you are able to cut your price. (3) A new factor of growth results from "vertical integration." You decide to buy a chemical factory to produce your own raw materials, and you also become your own wholesaler, thus operating three stages rather than only one "stage of production." (4) The company also grows by "horizontal integration": you take advantage of a profitable opportunity to buy out a number of competitors who produce similar toothpastes. (5) New "complementary products" such as soap and lipstick are added. You feel that bringing in the new lines under the same roof will help to spread the overhead expenses, and your salesmen feel that they might just as well get many orders as few when making a call. (6) You might even become a baby "conglomerate," growing by adding *unrelated* activities to your business (e.g., machine tools, car repairing, fortune-telling). (7) Finally, your business may grow just because you are producing a better toothpaste.

## NEW NEEDS AND SOURCES FOR CAPITAL

Once again, the enterprise finds itself in a paradox: The more successful it is and the faster it grows, the harder up it is for capital. The $40,000 of new "equity capital"

[2]Good will and capitalized earning power are discussed in the accounting Appendix to this chapter.

brought into the business did not stay long in the form of cash. It was quickly transformed into circulating assets such as goods in process and office supplies. In part, it went to pay off the most pressing liabilities.

The remainder was used as a down payment on a factory building and equipment. The difference between the down payment and the purchase price of the factory was secured by a mortgage loan on the property. The mortgage money was advanced by a nearby life-insurance company and was to be amortized or paid off in installments over a period of 20 years, along with $7\frac{1}{2}$ per cent interest per year on the actual principal still unpaid at any time. In case the loan should not be paid, the holder of the mortgage of course has the right to foreclose the mortgage, i.e., to take over the ownership of the building and sell it for what it will bring. Since the down payment on the factory came to about one-fourth of its price, since this price was a bargain price to begin with, and since each year the insurance company will be getting back part of its principal, the risk it takes is not very great.

Despite the continuous plowing of profits back into the business, growth still leaves you needing more capital. But now, having established your reputation, so to speak, new avenues of borrowing are open to you. Your banker will be glad to lend you money to tide you over the busy pre-Christmas period. A company, such as the Commercial Credit Corporation, will lend you money on the basis of your safe, but as yet uncollected, "accounts receivable" (i.e., sums owed you for goods already sold).

Suppose, when all is said and done, you need still more capital than you can raise by any kind of borrowing. The painful necessity arises of getting more "equity" capital by letting some new people share in the profits (and losses) of the business. (As a matter of fact, even if you could still find some institutions to borrow from, it would be unwise to do so. You have already superimposed too many liabilities and fixed charges on a narrow equity base. As long as things go well, it would be nice to earn $12\frac{1}{2}$ per cent profit on capital that costs you only 7 or 8. But if losses should occur, they will fall all the more heavily on you, the two partners, who are the residual owners.)

## DISADVANTAGES OF THE PARTNERSHIP FORM

One possibility of getting more ownership capital is to admit new partners. There is no limit to the number you can admit; there have been partnerships in the brokerage and banking fields involving more than 100 people. However, every time a new partner is admitted, or one dies or resigns, a whole new partnership must be formed.[3]

[3] More weighty is the real disadvantage stemming from the fact that a partnership can be dissolved whenever any party finds the existing arrangement unsatisfactory and wishes to withdraw. The law of partnerships also makes it impossible for any partner to sell his share to a new party without the consent of his partners; if agreement cannot be secured, the partnership may have to be wound up.

The reader may recall that the novelist William Dean Howells has his famous title character Silas Lapham, a rising, self-made paint tycoon, present his partner with the ultimatum: "You buy me out or I'll buy you out." Silas' two excuses, that his were the real brains and energy responsible for the success of the business and that the proffered price exceeded his partner's original investment, were cleverly seen through by Mrs. Lapham. She pointed out that, without the partner's money at the critical time, the business could never have succeeded and that Silas' offer to sell was premised upon the knowledge that his partner was not in a position to buy the whole of the business.

As the number of partners increases, there comes to the fore a factor that has been soft-pedaled in our discussion up to now. Each partner is *liable without limit* to the full extent of his personal fortune for all debts contracted by the partnership. If he owns 1 per cent of the partnership and the business fails, then he will be called upon to foot 1 per cent of the bills and the other partners will be assessed their 99 per cent. But suppose they cannot pay any part of their assessment? Then the 1 per cent partner may be called upon to pay *for all*, even if it means selling his fine etchings or auctioning the family home.

This feature of *unlimited liability* reveals why partnerships tend to be confined to small, personal enterprises. According to the doctrine of "mutual agency" involved in the law of partnerships, each partner has broad powers to act as agent to commit the whole partnership. When it becomes a question of placing their personal fortunes in jeopardy, people are reluctant to put their capital into complex ventures over which they can exercise little control.

This explains why agriculture and retail trade are the only sectors of our economy where more than half of the business done is done by single proprietors and partnerships. In the field of investment banking, concerns like J. P. Morgan & Company used to advertise proudly "not incorporated" so that their creditors could have extra assurance. But even these concerns have converted themselves into corporate entities.

Comparatively recently, the giant brokerage concern Merrill Lynch, Pierce, Fenner & Smith incorporated itself. For a long time it had many major partners and scores of junior partners, illustrating that the barriers to running a large enterprise put up by the partnership form are not insuperable. Still, giant partnerships are now rare.

**Unlimited liability and the red tape needed to ensure continuity are the main drawbacks to the partnership form.**


## THE CORPORATION

At this point, therefore—or even long before—you will probably decide to form a corporation rather than a partnership. Usually you will incorporate in the state in which you live and operate. However, you may prefer to establish token headquarters in some state, like Delaware or New Jersey, with especially easy rules.

Centuries ago, corporation charters were awarded by governments very rarely and only by *special acts* of the king and legislature. Parliament or Congress would graciously permit a public-utility enterprise or railroad to form a corporation to do specific things and perform specific functions. The East India Company was such a privileged corporation. The early railroads here and abroad often had to spend as much money in getting a charter through the legislature as in preparing their roadbeds. Gradually, within the past century, this procedure began to seem unfair, and it became the practice to pass general incorporation laws granting almost anyone the privilege of forming a corporation for almost any purpose, without having to get a special vote of approval from the state legislature or from Congress.

Today, for a small fee a lawyer will draw up the necessary papers and will write into the corporate charter almost as wide powers and purposes as you could wish. Automatically, the state will grant the charter.

Let us see how the incorporating procedure works in the case of your toothpaste company. You decide to issue 20,000 shares of common stock in the corporation: 6,600 going to you; 3,300 to your partner; 100 to your wife; and the other 10,000 to be sold to outside interests. Although each share is to have an initial stated value of $10, your lawyer has advised you, for convenience, to make them no-par shares.

The 10,000 shares to be sold to the public are to be marketed through a local *investment banking* firm. These firms are simply merchandisers of securities; and as with any merchant, their profit comes from the difference between their buying and selling prices. Because yours is such a small business, they must drive a hard bargain, especially since they can claim that the costs of selling the securities are likely to be high. Thus the investment brokers may offer you $10 per share and plan to resell at a price of $12.50 per share. Had you been a large company, you might have held out for as much as $12.25—or even $12.40—out of the $12.50 selling price, because of the eager competitive bidding of the different investment banking syndicates.

For a large company the investment banker would probably have agreed to *underwrite* the new issue of 10,000 shares. This means that he would have guaranteed the purchase of the full 10,000 shares at a set price. If the market then refused to buy all these shares from the investment banker at his announced price, he, not you, would have to absorb the loss. But he probably regards you as too small and untried a business to justify his assuming the risk of underwriting. So he takes your issue on a "best effort" basis; and if he cannot sell all the shares, you end up raising less capital. (Also, as a "sweetener," he may insist upon being given warrants—which we shall see are options to buy stock later at a specified price.)

**Corporation structure**    Fortunately, all goes well, and he pays you $100,000 in cash for the securities sold. Unlike the case of the partnership, you need not concern yourself with the people to whom he has sold the shares or with the fact that they may resell their shares. The names of the owners of the shares are registered with the company or its bank agent, in case they get lost and so that you will know where to send the dividend checks or the announcements of stockholders' meetings.

Ordinarily, each share gives its owner one vote. Shares in the corporate earnings are also in direct proportion to the number of shares owned. Those with 1,000 shares get 1,000 votes and correspondingly higher dividends.

The outside owners of 10,000 shares have paid in $100,000 cash to the company. What have you and your partner paid in? Obviously not cash, but rather a sizable amount of earning assets: plant, equipment, goods in process, and perhaps good will, which is, as already seen, the capitalized value of the presumed "excess earning power" of the business, resulting from its trademarks, patents, know-how, and so forth.

Back in the old days before 1929, you and your investment banker might have evaluated the good will as liberally as you wished, possibly giving yourself 20,000 rather than 10,000 shares. This practice has been called "watering the stock." Today, you would have to submit any sizable new issue to the Securities and Exchange Commission (SEC), a regulatory agency set up as part of the New Deal in 1934. It would have to satisfy itself that there are no misleading claims before permitting the new flotation. However, it does not pretend to pass judgment on, or attest to, the value of the stock. *Caveat emptor*—let the buyer beware—still prevails as a doctrine!

## ADVANTAGES AND DISADVANTAGES OF THE CORPORATE FORM

**Private advantage**   The corporation has solved most of the problems that bothered you about the partnership. It is an almost perfect device for the raising of large sums of capital. Of first importance, every stockholder now has *limited liability*. After paying $12.50 per share, the investor need not worry about his personal estate's being in jeopardy. If worse comes to worst and the business goes bankrupt, the most each investor can lose is his original $12.50 per share. He can't be assessed further.

Of secondary importance is the fact that the corporation is a fictitious legal person created by the state. It exists not by "natural right" but only at the pleasure of the state. The corporation, as distinct from its owners, can be sued in court and can sue. Any officer of the company, unlike any partner, is strictly limited in his legal ability to act as agent for the other owners and to commit them financially. Also, the corporation may have "perpetual succession" or existence, regardless of how many times the shares of stock change hands by sale or bequest and regardless of whether there are 10,000 different stockholders.

No group of shareholders can force any other group to sell or retain their holdings, and only a majority vote rather than unanimity is needed to reach usual business decisions. Normally, the stockholders will be too many to meet for every decision; they will prefer to elect a board of directors consisting of a dozen or so members to represent them between annual meetings, in much the same way that democratic electorates select legislative representatives to act for them. As we shall see, the problem of keeping large corporations "truly democratic" is a hard one.

You will face one disadvantage to incorporation that has become increasingly serious in recent years. *The federal government taxes corporate income*. Thus, during World War II, a profitable corporation might have had to pay as much as 80 per cent of its income to the government in excess-profit taxation; the Korean conflict also brought an excess-profit tax. In normal times, sizable corporations must pay almost half of each dollar of income. (This is *in addition* to the personal income tax that owners pay on dividends they get.)

The corporate tax is a rather high price for a small business to pay for limited liability and greater ease of raising capital. Yet there are also tax *advantages* offered by the corporate form. There is a loophole in our present law: *undistributed* corporate profits escape *personal* income taxes; only paid-out dividends are so taxed. A rich man who is taxed about 70 cents of every dollar of personal income can say, "Why pay such rates on partnership earnings? Let's incorporate, pay the lower corporate tax, keep dividends low, and reduce our taxes."[4]

Another loophole used to avoid the disadvantages of double taxation under the corporate form is where the owners of a closely held corporation vote most of its earnings to themselves and their relatives in the form of high salaries, pensions, and

---

[4]To some degree he is only putting off the evil day. For unless his lawyer can work out a lightly taxed "capital-gains deal," his dividends will be taxable *later* when he receives them. But in any case the *delay* in tax payment is worth money to him. Under new tax revisions, many people can win either way: they are given the option of being taxed as partnerships or as corporations. Recent innovations like Keogh plan retirement funds for self-employed individuals have made incorporation relatively less attractive for doctors and lawyers.

perquisites. The Treasury Department tries to check up on avoidance of taxes by such padding of expenses; but it is always hard to know whether a given in-law is worth $25,000 a year, or whether a trip to a Bermuda convention is truly a business rather than a personal expense.

**Social advantage**  When Prime Minister Gladstone was shown electricity on a visit to Michael Faraday's laboratory, he asked, "What is the use of electricity?" Faraday gave the ironic reply, "I suppose some day, Sir, you may come to put a tax on it." Surely the advantage of the corporate form *to society* is not merely that the state can tax it.

**Large-scale production is technically efficient, and a large corporation is an advantageous way for investors to *pool the irreducible risks* of business life. Without limited liability and the corporation, society could simply not reap the benefit that comes when large supplies of capital can be attracted to competing corporations that produce a variety of complementary products, that pool risks, and that best utilize the economies of sizable research units and managerial know-how.**

This is the economic rationale of the legal fiction called the corporation.

## HOW A CORPORATION CAN RAISE CAPITAL

Let us suppose your corporation continues to grow as a result of vertical, horizontal, or conglomerate combinations, new products, economies of mass production, advertising promotion, and so forth. Besides borrowing on promissory notes or mortgages, buying on credit, and relying on earnings not paid out in dividends, what new forms of financing are now available to you?

**Bonds**  First, you may issue bonds. These are nothing but special kinds of promissory notes, nicely printed on gilt paper, issued in $1,000 or other denominations to be readily marketable for resale. A bond is a security promising to pay a certain number of dollars in interest every 6 months for a number of years until it matures. At that time the borrowing company promises to pay off the principal of the bond at its face value. (Often the company has the right to call in the bond a few years before its maturity date by paying the bondholders some previously agreed-upon price.)

Ordinarily, payments for interest and principal must be made on time, regardless of whether the company has been making earnings or not. Otherwise the company is in default of its obligations and can be taken to court like any debtor.[5]

**Common stocks**  Issuing bonds and issuing common stocks are opposite methods of financing. The common stockholder is providing "equity" capital. He shares in profits and in control of business decisions, but he must also share in losses. His is a more risky venture, because he can never receive any dividends until the fixed charges owed

---

[5] Income bonds, whose interest is payable only if there are large enough earnings, are rather rare. Mortgage bonds, secured by property, are sometimes issued. Convertible bonds, which can be exchanged for a stated number of common shares, are a popular hybrid, as will be seen.

to the bondholder are paid off. The bondholder gets a limited but steadier income. Unless the corporation is bankrupt or in danger of being so, the bondholder ordinarily has no legal control over the decisions of the business; but a wise management will take care to stay on good terms with all sources of future capital.

**Preferred stocks**    Between bonds and common stocks are so-called "preferred stocks." These pay *at most* a stated dividend—say, a stipulated 5 per cent of the face value per share—no matter how profitable the business becomes. The preferred stockholder is more likely to get his dividend even when profit is low than is the common stockholder, because legally he stands next in line after the bondholder and before the common stockholder. The latter gets no dividends if the preferred stock fails to receive its full dividend.

Often "cumulative" preferred stock is issued. This means that, if for four years of hard times there has not been enough in the way of earnings to pay any of the 5 per cent dividends on the preferred stock, when good times come back again the "cumulated" $20 (= 4 × $5) of unpaid preferred stock dividends must be made good before the common stockholders can begin to receive any dividends. Often, too, preferred stock is "callable" and "convertible." The first term means that at some previously stated value, say $103 per share, the company can buy back its outstanding preferred stock. The second term refers to the right given the preferred stockholder of converting each share into shares of common stock at some stipulated ratio.[6]

**Hybrid convertibles**    After decades of price inflation, investors have become wary of putting their funds in bonds which merely repay the principal in dollars that have deteriorated in purchasing power. To tempt them back into bonds, corporations have increasingly had to resort to *convertible bonds*. Thus Standard Oil of Indiana has sold $1,000 bonds that pay 5 per cent interest and come due in 1996. These could be sold at so low an interest rate only because each bond is made to be convertible at the owner's will into 20 shares of S.O. (Ind.) common stock. The investor can, so to speak, have his cake and eat it too. If prices stay steady, he has a nice safe bond. If inflation or anything else sends S.O.'s stock far upward, he can convert and protect the real purchasing power of his principal.

Similarly, we today often meet *convertible preferred stock* (as in the case of American Express pfd., which is convertible into one share of common in addition to paying an annual dividend of $1.50).

Finally, some companies issue *warrants*, which are options to buy the common at some stated exercise price until some future date: thus there is a B. F. Goodrich warrant, good until 1979, which permits me to buy a share of its common by paying $30.00 of exercise price. Such warrants are very volatile, often moving in a "leveraged" way in comparison with the common; hence, you can make a lot on them if you are right, but you can also lose your shirt.

---

[6] Also, some preferred stocks are made more attractive by being "participating." This means that, once profit exceeds some agreed-upon figure, they share with the common stockholder in further profits. But this form is rare. When one corporation owns stock in another, it pays tax on only 15 per cent of the dividends; this explains why corporations are important holders of preferred stocks.

## ADVANTAGES OF DIFFERENT SECURITIES

From the standpoint of the investor, bonds, preferred stocks, and common stock usually form a sequence of increasing risk and decreasing security—balanced by an increased chance of making high earnings or capital gains. Today, a "gilt-edge" bond may yield about 6 or 8 per cent, a good preferred stock about the same. Because common stocks may rise in value and give capital gains, they now often have a spread of dividend yields that begins even *lower* than bonds: some "growth stocks" like IBM yield in dividends much, much less than the safest government bonds. To test his understanding of these three forms of securities, the reader should make sure that he understands why common stocks tend to be better investments in time of sudden inflation than the other two.

It would be a mistake to leave the reader with the impression that bonds are perfectly safe investments. On the contrary, during depressions many companies went bankrupt and defaulted on their bonds, paying off only a few cents on the dollar. The basic risk in all corporate investment is a possible loss of earning power, which will greatly reduce the value of its assets. Often a company will undergo reorganization in which the stockholders may be squeezed out completely; the courts may appoint a "receiver" or trustee to run the business, and the bondholders may be given bonds (or even stocks!) equal only to some fraction of their original investments. Moreover, certain bond-holders may have prior claims over holders of other bonds. Many investors in railroad securities have learned of these possibilities the hard way.

From the corporation's view, bond debt creates limited but inflexible fixed charges. These may be embarrassing in bad times. Preferred stock is slightly better with respect to flexibility; equity capital, best of all.[7]

## THE GIANT CORPORATION

While one should not infer that all corporations go through these stages, we have now carried our successful toothpaste enterprise far enough up the ladder of success. The rest of this chapter will be concerned with the economic position and power of the very large modern corporation and the problems that it creates for the American economy. It is these which play the dominant role in today's economy.

A list of the 200 largest nonfinancial corporations reads like an honor roll of American business, almost every name being a familiar household word. Among the industrial companies will be United States Steel, Bethlehem Steel, and the Aluminum Company of America; Exxon (S.O. of N.J.), Standard Oil of California, Gulf, Texaco; Eastman Kodak, Polaroid; RCA, CBS; IT&T; General Motors, Chrysler, and Ford; Swift and Armour meat packing; American (Tobacco) Brands (Pall Mall) and R. J. Reynolds (Camels); The Great Atlantic & Pacific Tea Company, Sears, Montgomery Ward (Marcor), F. W. Woolworth, and J. C. Penney; Procter & Gamble, Lever Brothers; IBM, Xerox, Boeing; and many others.

Among the railroads are such remnants as Penn Central, Southern Pacific, and Union

---

[7]Interest charges can also be deducted for tax purposes from the corporation earnings. There is an incentive, therefore, other things being equal, to use debt rather than stock financing.

Pacific. The public-utility list is headed by AT&T. If we go on to add the largest financial organizations, we bring in such giants as the Bank of America (California), First National City Bank (New York), the Chase Manhattan Bank, the Continental Illinois National Bank (Chicago), and the First National Bank of Boston; Prudential Life, Metropolitan Life, Aetna Life & Casualty, etc. Altogether there are now over 300 companies with assets above the billion-dollar mark! Multinational corporations add to the list such names as Unilever, Royal-Dutch Shell, N. V. Phillips, Siemens A. G., SKF, SONY, and many others.

The tremendous concentration of economic power involved in giant corporations may be gauged from the following facts: The largest 100 nonfinancial corporations own over 45 per cent of the total assets of that group; the 50 largest banks own over 40 per cent of all banking assets. The 50 largest insurance companies own over 83 per cent of all life-insurance assets. The largest 200 corporations hold more than one-fourth of income-producing national wealth. They employ 1 out of every 8 workers. The 500 largest United States industrial corporations have more than half the sales in manufacturing and mining and get more than 70 per cent of the profits. Half-a-dozen industrial corporations each handle more money than any one of our 50 states does.

The power of large corporations did not grow overnight. After 1900 their percentage importance gradually rose. In the 1920s local public utilities were gathered together into vast regional networks, in itself a move toward greater technological efficiency. As the country grew mightily in the recovery from the Great Depression and in World War II, the largest corporations grew too.

In the 1960s there was a speed-up in the merger movement, particularly in connection with take-overs by "conglomerates," which brought under one roof scores of companies belonging to quite unrelated industries. The giants meet on diverse battlefields: Du Pont and Exxon compete in petrochemicals and still once again in insecticides and fertilizers. Who are the rivals of a conglomerate like Litton Industries? Typewriter producers like IBM? Shipbuilders like General Dynamics? Hotel chains like IT&T's Sheraton? Or literally four score different industries?

Large size breeds success, and success breeds further success. But there are also economic and political barriers to largeness. The statistical evidence on profits suggests that profits increase with size but that the very biggest firms in an industry sometimes seem to show a slight dropping off of relative profits compared with the next to the largest.[8] Statistics suggest that, relatively, the giants have probably lost a little ground since 1900, when the "trust movement" had not yet run afoul of the Sherman Antitrust Act (1890). And just as a hotel may be always full—but with different people—so do we find the list of biggest corporations to be a changing one, but at a very slow rate.

## DIVORCE OF OWNERSHIP AND CONTROL IN THE LARGE CORPORATION

Let us examine the internal workings of one of these giant corporations. *The most striking feature is the diversification of ownership among thousands and thousands*

---

[8] A larger percentage of small firms than of large firms falls in the class of firms making losses.

*of small stockholders.* In the 1970s, more than 3 million different people have shares in AT&T. To be sure, half these people have less than 15 shares each; one-quarter of the shares are held in blocks of less than 100 shares; and no single owner has as much as 1 per cent of the total. The Stock Exchange has a goal of "people's capitalism," in which the masses have appreciable ownership of society's capital. While more than 35 million people do own some common stocks, still less than 1 in 10 gets an appreciable return from such ownership.

In a pathbreaking study,[9] Berle and Means pointed out that this wide diversification of stockholding has resulted in a *separation of ownership and control*. Recent studies show that in the typical giant corporation, all management together—officers and directors—holds only about 3 per cent of the outstanding common stock. The largest single minority ownership groups typically hold only about a fifth of all voting stock. Such a small fraction has been deemed more than enough to maintain "working control."[10]

## LEADERSHIP AND CONTROL OF THE LARGE CORPORATION

The problem of keeping a large corporation truly democratic is a difficult one. Until recent years, a few dozen stockholders would turn up for the annual meeting. More recently, many hundreds have been attending some meetings.

Decisions at the annual meeting are really settled by use of "proxies." Each stockholder is asked to mail in a proxy permitting the management to exercise his votes. Some do not reply; but enough usually do to establish a quorum and a comfortable plurality for management. The SEC has tried to improve the democratic structure of corporations by insisting that motions to be decided at the annual meeting be indicated on the proxy statement so that stockholders can indicate their preferences; also, rival groups must be permitted mailing access to the stockholders, and so forth.

Prior to recent years, most managements could be said to be self-perpetuating. Whether the corporation runs well or poorly, whether the managers work efficiently or not, the typical small stockholder can do little about it. He can rubber-stamp acts or vent his feelings by not voting. In any case management goes undisturbed.

Recently there has been some change. Thanks to the SEC rules, some challenging minority groups have attempted—and successfully attempted!—to oust the in-group and put themselves in as new managers. Thus, the late Robert Young ran a tremendous campaign—using all the devices of modern publicity—to oust the New York Central railroad officers. And he did succeed in winning majority support. Similar takeover battles have taken place in connection with United Fruit and Montgomery Ward. These

---

[9] A. A. Berle, Jr., and Gardner C. Means, *The Modern Corporation and Private Property* (Commerce Clearing House, New York, 1932). See R. A. Gordon, *Business Leadership in the Large Corporation* (Brookings Institution, Washington, 1945), chap. II. R. J. Larner, in a 1966 *American Economic Review* study, has shown that the Berle-Means thesis on separation of ownership and control was even truer in the 1960s than in 1929: whereas 6 of the 200 largest corporations were privately owned (80 per cent or more of stock) in 1929, in 1963 there were none; and 84.5 per cent of the firms had no group of stockholders owning as much as 10 per cent!

[10] You can even pyramid control by owning one-fifth of a million-dollar company, which owns one-fifth of a 5-million-dollar company, and so forth. Such a pyramid of so-called "holding companies" can give control over billions to small ownership at the base.

days, if a corporation sits sluggishly on a chunk of liquid assets and disappoints earning expectations of its shareholders, it is vulnerable to a takeover bid by one of the hungry conglomerates, even if these are not run by Yale gentlemen and Episcopalian deacons.

In a sense, therefore, we can hope that democratic control of corporations by stock owners has increased. But competent observers still insist that, barring blatant incompetence, management can often count on remaining in office; and often the proxy battle is fought to determine which minority group shall control.[11]

## A MANAGERIAL REVOLUTION IN THE NEW INDUSTRIAL STATE?

Who makes corporate decisions? Primarily, the increasingly important class of *professional managers*—what Galbraith calls the "technostructure." The old-time captain of industry, for all his creativeness and ability to calculate the risks necessary to build up a great enterprise, often had something of the buccaneer in his makeup and "the-public-be-damned" attitude. In company after company, the original founder has been replaced by a new type of executive, usually having a different surname. He is less likely to be a self-made man than a graduate of Harvard Business School; he will probably have acquired special training and management skills. The new professional executive is more adept at public relations and in the handling of people. He is necessarily more the "bureaucrat," often interested as much in preserving the status quo as in taking risks.

Typically, the dominant man will be the president of the corporation. As he begins to feel his years, he may be made chairman of the board of directors, and together with a small executive or steering committee of the board of directors, advises and approves the actions of the president and his many vice-presidents.

The exact role of the board of directors varies from company to company and from group to group. Some directors are simply well-known men selected to give prestige. Others are insiders with special knowledge who take an active part in determining policy. On the whole, it would be going too far to say that most boards of directors act simply as rubber stamps to approve the decisions already taken by the officers of the company. But it is true that, so long as management possesses the confidence of the board, that body will usually not actively intervene to dictate specific policies. This is the same administrative procedure usually followed by the board of trustees of a philanthropic foundation or college, and is not too unlike the parliamentary system of ministerial responsibility in Great Britain and elsewhere.

**Conflicts of interest**    Generally speaking, there will be no clash of goals between the management and stockholders. Both will be interested in maximizing the profits of the firm—to wit, the growth in earnings and market price per share. But in two important situations there may be a divergence of interests, not infrequently settled

---

[11] A dissatisfied stockholder is told he can always sell his shares (at the low price they've fallen to!) and buy into another company. If enough stockholders do so, the company will find it hard ever to raise capital by selling a new issue; the fall in its share prices may depress the value of "stock options" issued to company executives as a tax-loophole bonus and could galvanize other stockholders into a proxy revolt. These days, managements are not free to do whatever they can get away with.

in favor of management. First, insiders may vote themselves and friends or relatives large salaries, expense accounts, bonuses, retirement pensions, and stock options at the stockholders' expense.[12]

A second conflict of interest may arise in connection with undistributed profits. The managers of every organization have an understandable tendency to try to make it grow and perpetuate itself. The psychological reasons are subtle and by no means always selfish. In some cases when profits are plowed back into a company, there is reason to suspect that the same capital could better be invested by the stockholders elsewhere or spent upon consumption. Indeed, the case occasionally arises when a company would be well advised to wind itself up and pay back its capital. But a cynic can doubt that management is likely to vote itself out of existence and out of jobs.

**Galbraith's semiautonomous corporate monarchs**   Thorstein Veblen, radical son of the Midwest soil at the turn of the century, had looked forward to a time when engineers would run the price system. John Kenneth Galbraith has in our time become the philosopher of the new industrial state. In his words:[13]

. . . the influence of the technostructure of the mature firm extends to *shaping the demand* for its particular product or range of products. . . . [emphasis added]

Paralleling these changes, partly as a result and partly as a cause, has been a profound shift in the locus of economic and political power. The financier and the union leader are dwindling influences in the society. They are honored more for their past eminence than for their present power. The technostructure exercises much less direct political power than did the antecedent entrepreneur. But that is because it has far more influence as an arm of the bureaucracy and in its influence on the larger climate of belief. The scientific, technical, organizational and planning needs of the technostructure have brought into being a large educational and scientific estate.

## THE EVIL OF MONOPOLY

In view of all the above facts, it is not surprising to find that most important American industries are characterized by a few large corporations whose share of the output of that particular industry is vastly greater than their numerical importance would warrant. Figure 6-1, on the next page, gives some large American industries and depicts their degree of concentration by showing the relative proportion of total industry shipments controlled by the first four dominant corporations and by the next four.

In Part Three we shall analyze some of the problems raised by monopoly and imperfect competition. Particularly since the 1890 Sherman Antitrust Act, there has been great concern over the breaking down of free competitive markets under the

---

[12]Other conflicts can involve outright cheating: executives may take bribes, throw business to their own private companies, or violate SEC rules by using inside knowledge and spreading false rumors to make market profits on the company's stock. A president of Chrysler had to resign when it was discovered he had secret ownership in a supplying firm. An insurance executive came under fire for joining privately in a tax deal with a company the insurance company had dealings with. Such cases are rare, but not rare enough.

[13]John Kenneth Galbraith, *The New Industrial State* (Houghton Mifflin, Boston, 1967), p. 320.

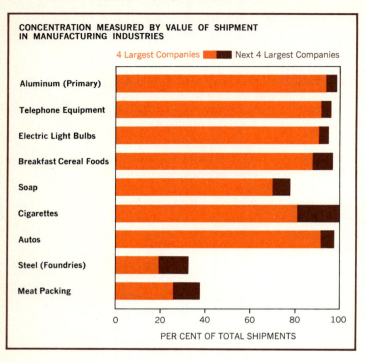

**CONCENTRATION MEASURED BY VALUE OF SHIPMENT IN MANUFACTURING INDUSTRIES**

**FIG. 6-1**

**Numerous industries are dominated by a very few sellers: "oligopolies"**

In aluminum, autos, steel, and many other industries, a few firms get most of the business. This is in contrast to the notion of perfect competition among innumerable small sellers (e.g., farmers), each too small to affect the market price. As in Part Two, economists call this "oligopoly." Concentration was probably greater in 1900 and 1929; but will competition from imports check the growing trend of concentration in the last quarter of the century? (Source: U.S. Bureau of the Census, 1967.)

encroachment of large-scale enterprise. In recent years, officials of General Electric, Westinghouse, and other electric suppliers were even sent to jail for colluding on monopoly price setting.

From an economic point of view it does not much matter which of the following monopolistic devices causes price to be too high:

(1) Mergers of competing firms, (2) cooperative "pools" or "cartel agreements," (3) so-called "trusts" (involving selected "trustees" who "coordinate" pricing policy), (4) interlocking directorates, (5) "holding-company" control, (6) tacit collusion and trade-association action, (7) government "fair price" legislation (Robinson-Patman Act, etc.) and government-sponsored "commodity agreements" (wheat, rubber, cotton, etc.).

Too high a price, wastage of resources,[14] and creation of monopoly profits are economic evils, however brought about and whatever the legal technicalities of the matter. This we shall study in Part Three, but a brief preview can be presented here.

## THE CURSE OF BIGNESS?

Is bigness itself a bad thing? Undoubtedly there is much popular hostility toward large corporations. Even if they could do so, General Motors or United States Steel would be most reluctant to swallow up competitors until they accounted for, say, nine-tenths

[14]Undertakers provide a case in point: People generally, including poor people, pay in some regions an average of $1,100 per complete funeral! But so many undertaking establishments come into existence that—as in New York—each handles only about one funeral per week.

of their respective industries. They would fear the effect on public opinion. Is this antagonism toward big business directed toward bigness itself? Or against the alleged evils of monopoly that are often supposed to be associated with bigness?

**How to tame the beast**   What should public policy be toward a "benevolent, well-behaving, efficient" giant corporation? The so-called "A & P" case provides an example. This chain of food stores was noted for its low prices. Yet the Department of Justice prosecuted it under the antitrust acts. Leaving aside certain minor irregularities that the company may have engaged in, the basic issue was clearly posed: Shall it be a crime to grow large as a result of efficiency and continued maintenance of low, competitive prices? The federal courts at times seemed almost to answer, Yes. Fortunately, as Chapter 26 shows, this trend is abating.

Another example shows that policy problems are not easy. In the mid-fifties there was a rash of mergers; e.g., in the auto industry Nash combined with Hudson to form American Motors. Often there was a "tax angle" to the merger; but in some cases, firms merged in order to try to become more efficient, as, for example, to be able to compete better with General Motors and Ford. Do such mergers—even though they undoubtedly increase the size of the merged units—really *reduce* competition rather than increase it? (Was the Attorney General wrong in forbidding a merger between Bethlehem and Youngstown steel companies? Should the ICC have let the C & O railroad merge with the B & O? Not easy questions to answer.)

To produce an atomic bomb, the government turned to the Du Pont Company and gave it a cost-plus-one-dollar contract. The scientific know-how of General Electric and Western Electric is invaluable for peace as well as war. In the eulogistic words of Schumpeter, a world-famous economist who died in 1950:[15]

The modern standard of life of the masses evolved during the period of relatively unfettered "big business." If we list the items that enter the modern workman's budget and from 1899 on observe the course of their prices not in terms of money but in terms of the hours of labor that will buy them—i.e., each year's money prices divided by each year's hourly wage rates, we cannot fail to be struck by the rate of the advance which, considering the spectacular improvement in qualities, seems to have been greater and not smaller than it ever was before. . . .

Nor is this all. As soon as we go into details and inquire into the individual items in which progress was most conspicuous, the trail leads not to the doors of those firms that work under conditions of comparatively free competition but precisely to the doors of the large concerns—which, as in the case of agricultural machinery, also account for much of the progress in the competitive sector—and a shocking suspicion dawns upon us that big business may have had more to do with creating that standard of life than keeping it down.

---

[15] J. A. Schumpeter, *Capitalism, Socialism and Democracy* (Harper, New York, 1942). Whatever the merits of the Schumpeter thesis, it is still true that there have been great productivity changes in competitive agriculture; that many basic inventions come from independent persons or small companies; and that there is no evidence of an upswing in inventiveness during the turn-of-the-century decades of increased monopoly concentration. Reference will be made later to Galbraith's doctrine of "countervailing power" in *American Capitalism* (Houghton Mifflin, Boston, 1952). It is there argued that big units do characterize American life, but that "big labor" checks big business, and vice versa; that big Sears and A & P check their big suppliers, and so a kind of a tolerable equilibrium is achieved, albeit not one of a competitive type. Part Three studies E. H. Chamberlin's imperfect competition.

### BUSINESS IN THE DOGHOUSE

As this title suggests, the public these days does not act as if it shares Schumpeter's favorable opinion of the functioning of large-scale business enterprise. Public opinion polls held in 1975 reported that only 23 per cent of the population had a great deal of confidence in business; 15 per cent had hardly any confidence in business. Women were even more disapproving than men; 74 per cent of the population thought big business less concerned with people than small business. Each spring it becomes increasingly difficult for business recruiters to interview graduating seniors at the elite colleges and universities and entice them onto the bottom rung of the executive ladder. (To give perspective, along with the recent drop in prestige of business has gone a drop in the prestige of the Supreme Court, the scientific community, and the government generally.)

The handwriting is on the wall for all to see. There is no feasible way of choosing between small-scale competitors and large quasi-monopolistic corporations. But without doubt big business is under the surveillance of public opinion. Can ways be found to improve the social and economic performance of large corporate aggregates, and keep the tremendously creative abilities of the modern large-scale corporation working toward the public good?

The so-called "military-industrial complex" must not be allowed to call the tune. In a system of true voter and consumer sovereignty, it must dance to the music the people prescribe.

We shall study the problem of maintenance of "effective and workable competition" after Part Three's analysis of prices and cost under perfect and imperfect competition.

## SUMMARY

1   The present population of American businesses has grown up as a result of a cumulative excess of business births over business deaths. The great majority of businesses consist of infinitesimal single proprietorships, largely in retail and service establishments. Their turnover is rapid.

2   One should understand how an enterprise grows, its needs and avenues for short-term or long-term capital, and the advantages and disadvantages of the corporate form over the single proprietorship and partnership.

3   One should also be acquainted with the fundamental legal rights involved in the corporation and with the general features of bonds and of preferred and common stocks.

4   Problems created by the separation of ownership and control and by the concentration of economic wealth and monopoly power in the modern giant corporation deserve serious study. (Part Three will discuss imperfect competition and antitrust policies.)

Accounting is a great help to the understanding of economics, and its fundamental principles are presented briefly in the Appendix to this chapter.

# CONCEPTS FOR REVIEW

single proprietorship
partnership
corporation
unlimited and limited liability
investment underwriting
Securities and Exchange Commission (SEC), SBA
corporate, personal income tax
bonds; common, preferred stocks; convertible hybrids

good-will earning power
proxy, minority control
director, executive, technostructure
forms of monopoly control
conglomerate mergers, collusion
conflicts of interest
evils of monopoly
possible dynamic advantages of size
Galbraithian new industrial state
military-industrial complex

# QUESTIONS FOR DISCUSSION

1  Imagine you are starting a business of your own. Write its case history.

2  Compare the advantages and disadvantages of (*a*) the single proprietorship, (*b*) the partnership, and (*c*) the corporate form of business organization.

3  List ways of raising capital for small, medium, and large businesses.

4  What are the advantages and disadvantages of different securities?

5  Discuss the structure of modern corporations. The "military-industrial complex."

6  What is meant by calling ours the age of the "Managerial or Bureaucratic Revolution"? Does this apply outside government?

7  Give examples of conflict of interest between stockholders and management. Of coincident interests. Of problems of democratic control.

8  Defend "bigness as such." Attack it. What evils might accompany it?

9  What are the economic evils of monopoly? Give examples.

10  "Galbraith thinks of the giant corporations as *absolute* monarchs. Actually, they are *constitutional* monarchs who 'reign only so long as they don't rule.' Ford could not force Edsels on the public; RCA lost hundreds of millions in computers; all the dollars in Madison Avenue could not turn Lever Bros.' Swan Soap into a rival to Ivory, or keep Ajax and Dial from growing out of nowhere." Appraise.

11  "When a slide-rule expert from MIT gets too big for his breeches as a member of the Ford 'Technostructure,' it is he who goes, not Henry Ford 2d." Debate.

12  The "cooperative," a business organization "owned" by its own consumers or workers, represents an interesting hybrid form. It is particularly important in Yugoslavia, where workers' cooperatives have great autonomy. In the United

States, 22 million people belong to credit unions, almost 7 million to electric cooperatives, 7 million to farm cooperatives, 1.8 million to consumer and student cooperatives, half a million to housing cooperatives, and a quarter-million to health cooperatives. Evaluate the movement.

# APPENDIX: Elements of Accounting

In this "age of accounts," some literacy in accounting has become a prime necessity.

## THE BALANCE SHEET

We begin with the two fundamental accounting statements: the Balance Sheet and the Statement of Profit and Loss (or the so-called "Income Statement").

The Balance Sheet is presented in a report, usually annually. It represents an instantaneous "still picture" of the condition of the enterprise on some particular day, usually the last day of the year. (Unlike a movie camera that records the "flow" over time of water in and out of the bathtub, the Balance Sheet gives a picture of the "stock" of water now in the tub.)

Corresponding to the dollar value of every *asset*—tangible or intangible—there must necessarily be an exactly equal total amount of *claims or ownership*. The value of a $40,000 house is exactly matched by somebody's claim to its ownership consisting, say, of $25,000 owed a creditor and $15,000 owned by its owner.

This is the fundamental identity underlying every Balance Sheet:

**Value of assets = value of total claims or ownership**
**= value of liabilities (owed)**
**+ value of proprietorship (owned)**

that is,

**Assets = Liabilities + Net Worth**

Or, what is the same thing, by definition of owner's equity,

**Net Worth (owner's equity) = Assets − Liabilities**

Let us illustrate this by considering a simple Balance Sheet, as shown in Table 6-1; on the left, this lists Assets, and on the right, Liabilities and Net Worth for a new company—say, the Apex Toothpaste firm—whose operations have just begun.

A blank space has been deliberately left next to the Common Stock Net Worth item because you should realize that the only correct entry compatible with our fundamental Balance-Sheet truism is $200,000. A Balance Sheet must always balance—because Net Worth, i.e., ownership of the "residual claimants," always adjusts itself to make a balance.

To illustrate this, suppose a thief steals all the cash, and a fire burns up one-half the inventory. The accountant will learn of this sad news without turning a hair as far as bookkeeping is concerned. "Total Assets are down $60,000 all told; Liabilities remain unchanged. This means that total Net Worth has decreased by $60,000, and I have no choice but to write its total down from the previous $250,000 to only $190,000." Such is his way of keeping score.

A number of interesting facts are revealed by even this simple Balance Sheet. First, it is often customary to divide up Assets according to whether they will be convertible into cash by normal operations within a year or the normal accounting cycle, the first category being called Current Assets, and the second, Fixed Assets. The Liabilities can also be subdivided into Current and Long-term Liabilities, depending upon whether they come due in less than a year.

Here is something to be emphasized about a Balance Sheet: Although its two sides must balance *in total,* no single item on one side is matched by an item on the other side. Thus, Bonds do not correspond in value to the Equipment or Buildings, nor do Capital items correspond to Cash. The only correct statement about a Balance Sheet is that creditors have a general claim of a definite value against the enterprise, and owners have a residual claim against the rest.

Most of the specific items listed are more or less

**BALANCE SHEET OF APEX TOOTHPASTE, INC., (DECEMBER 31, 1978)**

| ASSETS | | | LIABILITIES AND NET WORTH | | |
|---|---|---|---|---|---|
| | | | *Liabilities* | | |
| **Current Assets:** | | | **Current Liabilities:** | | |
| Cash | | $ 20,000 | Accounts Payable | | $ 20,000 |
| Inventory | | 80,000 | Notes Payable | | 30,000 |
| **Fixed Assets:** | | | **Long-term Liabilities:** | | |
| Equipment | | 130,000 | SBA Note | | 50,000 |
| Buildings | | 170,000 | Bonds Payable | | 50,000 |
| | | | *Net Worth* | | |
| | | | **Capital:** | | |
| | | | Preferred Stock | | 50,000 |
| | | | Common Stock | | . . . . . . |
| Total | | $400,000 | Total | | $400,000 |

TABLE 6-1

self-explanatory. Cash consists of coins, currency, and money on deposit in the bank. Cash is the only asset whose value is exact rather than an estimate. All other valuations involve some arbitrary assumptions, albeit careful assumptions: The convention understood by accountants is that assets are valued at their costs, but this is not to deny that firms may make mistakes or turn out to be very lucky. Moreover, all accounting reports are made relative to the actual intended purpose or use of the asset in question. If a business is a going concern and not in the process of liquidation, the accountant will be careful not to value doubtful assets at the low figure they would bring at a forced sale; he, rather, will value them at their cost to the company in its normal operation.

Inventory, consisting, in the case of our toothpaste company, of sugar, chemicals, tubing, raw materials, and other goods in process, can be valued in many different ways. Some conservative companies use original cost of the inventories or present market value, whichever is known to be lower. Especially difficult problems arise when the costs of materials vary from month to month. Should we figure the chemical cost of the toothpaste at the original cost of the ingredients actually used, which of course were bought some time ago when prices were different? Or should we figure, as our cost, the price that must *now* be paid for the chemicals to replace those

being used up? An elementary discussion cannot go into these two possible methods of inventory valuation.[1] Obviously, it will make a great difference in stated profits during a time of inflation or deflation which of these two methods is used. It also will make a difference in income taxes. Therefore the government is compelled to say, "Use whichever method you wish, but having made up your mind, stick to it on this item." So much for inventories.

If we assume that the Equipment and Buildings items were bought just at the end of 1978, the date of the Balance Sheet, then their Balance-Sheet values will be listed equal to their purchase price. This follows a fundamental accounting rule or convention: "At time of purchase a thing is presumed worth what the enterprise pays for it." However, as we shall see in connection with the Income Statement and the next year's Balance Sheet, hard problems are involved in deciding how exactly to evaluate equipment and buildings that have depreciated through use and age.

On the Liabilities side, Accounts Payable are, as their name implies, the sums owed for goods bought and charged. Notes Payable are promissory notes owed to the banks or to a finance company. The SBA Note listed under the Long-term Liabilities is a 5-year

[1] Accounting texts refer to them as "First-in-first-out" (FIFO) and "Last-in-first-out" (LIFO), and analyze them in detail.

loan advanced by, or guaranteed by, the federal Small Business Administration. The Bonds Payable are a long-term loan, floated at a 6 per cent coupon rate, and not due for 15 years. (NOTE: What appears as a Liability to this company must show up as an Asset to someone else; thus the creditors who own these bonds will carry them as left-hand-side Assets, "Bonds Receivable.")

Turning now to Net Worth items, we find that 500 shares of $100, 4 per cent, cumulative (nonparticipating) preferred stock have been issued; and 20,000 shares of no-par common stock issued at $10 each.

This completes our first glance at a simple Balance Sheet.

## THE STATEMENT OF PROFIT AND LOSS, OR INCOME STATEMENT

Now let time march on. During the following months, the firm is profitably engaged in producing and selling toothpaste. To show its *flow* of income over the 12 months of the year, we must turn to its Income Statement, or—as many companies prefer to call it—the Statement of Profit and Loss, Table 6-2.

This is a statement which reports the following: (1) Apex's revenues from sales in 1979, (2) the expenses to be charged against those sales, and (3) the profit remaining after expenses have been deducted. That is,

### Total Profit = Total Revenue − Total Costs

(the fundamental identity of the Income Statement).

You will understand it better if at first you disregard the figures in the Manufacturing Cost of Goods Sold section (the indented figures) and look only at those in the right-hand column. Sales were $240,000; and the total Manufacturing Cost of Goods Sold came to $170,000. After deducting another $14,000 for Selling and Administrative Costs, $56,000 remained in Net Operating Profit. A total of $6,000 + $17,500 in inter-

---

**INCOME STATEMENT OF APEX TOOTHPASTE, INC., (JANUARY 1, 1979, TO DECEMBER 31, 1979)**

| | | |
|---|---:|---:|
| **Net Sales** (after all discounts and rebates) | | $240,000 |
| **Less:** Manufacturing Cost of Goods Sold: | | |
| Materials | $ 50,000 | |
| Labor Cost | 100,000 | |
| Depreciation Charges | 20,000 | |
| Miscellaneous Operating Cost | 5,000 | |
| Total Manufacturing Cost | $175,000 | |
| Add: Beginning Inventory | 80,000 | |
| | $255,000 | |
| Deduct: Closing Inventory | 85,000 | |
| Equals: Manufacturing Cost *of Goods Sold* | $170,000 | 170,000 |
| Gross Profit (or Gross Margin) | | $ 70,000 |
| **Less:** Selling and Administrative Costs | | 14,000 |
| Net Operating Profit | | $ 56,000 |
| **Less:** Fixed Interest Charges and State and Local Taxes | | 6,000 |
| Net Earnings before Income Taxes | | $ 50,000 |
| **Less:** Corporation Income Taxes | | 17,500 |
| **Net Earnings after Taxes** | | **$ 32,500** |
| **Less:** Dividends on Preferred Stock | | 2,000 |
| Net Profits of Common Stockholders | | $ 30,500 |
| **Less:** Dividends Paid on Common Stock | | 10,500 |
| Addition to Earnings Retained in the Business | | $ 20,000 |

**TABLE 6-2**

est and taxes had to be paid out of this, leaving $32,500 in Net Earnings after Taxes (or Profit). Dividends of $2,000 on the preferred and $10,500 on the common were paid, leaving $20,000 of Addition to Earnings Retained in the Business.

Now turn to the indented Manufacturing Cost of Goods Sold section, which lists the costs incurred in this part of the business. The firm's outlays for materials, labor, and miscellaneous expenses are listed, together with an item for Depreciation. (Depreciation is worth a section to itself, and we shall consider it soon.) The sum of these four items ($175,000) is the Total Manufacturing Cost. Then follows what may seem a puzzling adjustment. The value of the inventory on January 1 is added, and that of the year-end inventory is deducted. The result, which differs from Manufacturing Cost by $5,000, is the Manufacturing Cost *of Goods Sold*. What is the difference between these terms, and why this inventory adjustment?

Apex began the year with inventory of $80,000 in raw materials and finished goods. During the year, it built up inventories by an extra $5,000. In this case, it would be false to attribute all the manufacturing cost to *the goods actually sold*. Some of these costs are really attributable to goods to be sold *in the future*. To neglect this fact would be to overstate the Manufacturing Cost of Goods Sold in this year; it would mean subtracting too much from this year's Net Sales and understating this year's Profits.

If there had been no change in inventory, then all would be simple: Manufacturing Cost and Manufacturing Cost of Goods Sold would be identical.

On the other hand, what if we had had less inventory on hand at the year's end than at the beginning? Clearly, we would be fooling ourselves if we did not recognize that the cost of the goods we have sold this year ought really to be *greater* than the money we have paid out to labor and other firms. We would have neglected the cost element of used-up and unreplaced inventory.

Summary: To reach a valid figure for Manufacturing Cost of Goods Sold, we must adjust the Manufacturing Cost figure thus:

If the Closing Inventory shows an increase over the Beginning Inventory, deduct that increase; if the Closing Inventory has decreased, add that decrease.

Instead of subtracting $5,000 directly from the $175,000 total manufacturing expense, the accountant does it in two steps. Rather than working with the difference between the two, he first adds the total Beginning Inventory, then subtracts the Closing Inventory. This procedure has the advantage of being standardized; it is the same whether inventory is up or down, whereas a single change-in-inventory figure would in some cases be a subtraction, in others an addition. And this method also reveals the change in inventory relative to the size of the total.

Note that items in Table 6-2 differ from Table 6-1's Balance-Sheet items. Remember income items refer to *flows* over time: moving-picture action. Balance-Sheet items refer to *stocks* at an instant of time: still pictures.

## DEPRECIATION

At first, one may wonder why any Depreciation Charges have been made for 1979. The buildings and equipment were newly bought at the beginning of the year, and surely they will not have worn out already. (It will, of course, be necessary to spend money on men to maintain the equipment and keep the factories painted: but such wages are already included in Labor Cost or Miscellaneous Operating Cost and are not included in Depreciation Charges.)

Here is where the farseeing wisdom of the accountant comes to the fore. He points out that not a cent may have to be spent upon replacement of equipment for 10 years, at which time all the machines may *suddenly* have to be bought anew. It would be nonsense to charge nothing to depreciation for 9 years and fool yourself into thinking you are making a nice profit and then suddenly in the tenth year have to charge off all the value of the machines at once and think you have incurred a great loss in that year.

Actually, he points out, the equipment is *being used up all the time*. A truer, undistorted picture of net income or profit will be reached if the costs of the equipment are spread more evenly over its lifetime. The value of equipment declines as a result of age and use; it depreciates from its price as new to its final scrap value. In recognition of this, the accountant depreciates the value of fixed capital items by some *gradual* formula. Of the various proposed methods, here are two widely used ones.

The first is called "straight-line depreciation." Suppose that you have a truck whose cost new is $10,100 and whose economic life is 10 years; after this, its physical life may continue but its economic life will be over, because of its unreliability and high maintenance costs. Suppose that its scrap value at the end of 10 years is $100. According to the straight-line method, you will each year recognize that one-tenth of the life of the machine has been used up, and will figure in as Depreciation expense for the year one-tenth of the lifetime decline in its total value of $10,000 (new price minus scrap value). Thus, $1,000 will be entered in Depreciation Charges every year.

A second method of more rapid early depreciation has become fashionable, especially since tax laws now permit generous use of it. Instead of writing off a new asset steadily by the straight-line method, firms can use the "declining-balance method," or—what is somewhat similar in its generosity toward fast early depreciation—the "sum-of-the-years-digits" method. Only the first will be described in this brief treatment.

Disregarding scrap value as negligible, consider the 10-year $10,000 truck. Instead of taking one-tenth its value for depreciation in the first year, the tax law lets you charge off, under the declining-balance method, twice that amount, or $2 \times 10$ per cent = 20 per cent in its first year. So you get a much larger deduction for tax purposes. Evidently you cannot go on charging off that amount for each year of life, since that would leave you with zero value by the halfway point, at the end of 5 years. What the declining-balance method does is to let you take off 20 per cent of *remaining* value or balance each year. In the second year, then, you take off 20 per cent of the $8,000 of remaining value, or $1,600. In the third year, you take off 20 per cent of what is left, namely, of $6,400. So the process goes. It can be calculated that by the time the asset has reached half the length of its useful life, you have been permitted to write off for tax purposes almost two-thirds its value—rather than one-half, as under the straight-line method. It is later in life that the declining-balance method begins to be less generous in order to compensate for its early generosity.[2]

**Depreciation and profits**    Although depreciation is usually figured by some apparently exact formula,

[2]Still a third method, called the "service-unit-method," or "unit-of-production method," can be mentioned only briefly here. According to this, we should estimate the number of miles, loads, or service units that the truck will perform in its life. Thus, if the truck goes a million miles in 10 years and its loss of value during that time is $10,000, then each mile used up represents about 1 cent.

every accountant knows that the estimates are really very rough, being subject to large and unpredictable errors and involving arbitrary corrections and assumptions. He comforts himself with two thoughts: (1) A rough method of depreciation, like an imperfect watch, is often better than none at all. (2) Mistakes in depreciation will ultimately "come out in the wash."

Let us see why a mistake in depreciation ultimately tends to correct itself for a given investment. Suppose that the truck lasts 15 years rather than the predicted 10. We have then been overstating our depreciation *expenses* during the first 10 years. But in the eleventh and later years there will be *no* depreciation charged on the truck at all, since it has already been written down to its scrap value by the end of the tenth year. Our profits in these later years tend, therefore, to be overstated by about as much as they were understated in the earlier years. After 15 years, everything is much the same after all. That is, except for taxes. Different methods of depreciation result in a different apparent distribution of earnings over time, and therefore in a different pattern over time of income taxes. A businessman prefers a method of depreciation that will make his income average out more steady over time, so as to keep his effective tax rate as low as possible and permit him to cancel off losses against profits; he also likes a fast method (such as the declining balance) that *puts off* the evil day of taxes as far as possible.

In a growing firm, this result does not hold true for the firm's investment as a whole. At any moment of time, a firm is depreciating investments made more recently with accelerated depreciation than it would with a slower rate. If the firm is growing, recent investments will be larger than older investments, and accelerated depreciation consequently will increase the total amount of depreciation allowed. This gain, unlike the change for a single truck, is never corrected as long as growth continues.

This explains why so many corporations took advantage of the government's past emergency offers to let them amortize (or depreciate) their defense plants and equipment over 5 years. They were glad to be able, by charging high depreciation expenses, to reduce their stated profits during the defense emergency when their profits were enormous. They much preferred to take advantage of this "accelerated depreciation" plan so as to shift their profits from those emergency years to later years when it was hoped that corporation tax rates would be lower.

The Treasury will not let a corporation manipulate its Depreciation Charges to avoid taxes. The company may select *any reasonable* method for the depreciable item; once having chosen, it is to stick to it.

Many people are today worried about the harmful effects of taxation on "venture capital." They argue, we shall get more investment in new tools and create more jobs if the Treasury is more liberal in letting companies depreciate their equipment rapidly, thereby saving on taxes and enjoying the same advantages that European countries bestow on our competitors.

In the 1960s the Kennedy administration introduced an "investment tax credit," which actually gave a subsidy to firms that invest in new equipment. This tax credit could be turned on and off to stabilize investment. Thus, Nixon had it repealed in the Vietnam inflation, had it restored in the 1971 stagnation, and considered reducing it in the 1973 boom. It was raised in the recession of 1975.

## THE RELATION BETWEEN THE INCOME STATEMENT AND THE BALANCE SHEET

Now we must relate the description by the Income Statement of what has happened during the year to the Balance Sheets at the beginning and end of the year. Table 6-3 on page 126 shows the Balance Sheet of our toothpaste corporation at the end of its first year of operation. It has prospered.

Net Worth, the difference between Total Assets and Total Liabilities, has increased between the beginning and end of the accounting period by $20,000—from $250,000 to $270,000. This amount, as seen by comparing Balance Sheets, just equals the profits *available* to the common stockholders but not paid out to them in dividends, or, as we saw at the bottom of the Income Statement, just equal to $30,500 minus $10,500, or $20,000 of undistributed profits.

Some Net Worth item has recognizably risen by $20,000. It would clearly never do to increase the Preferred Stock Capital Account, because such stockholders are not the residual claimants to the profits of the corporation and no new stock has been sold. Conceivably, one could add the $20,000 to the Common Stock Capital Account. However, this is not done. Instead, the Common Stock Capital Account is left at its original par or issued value.

**Retained Earnings**   It is more informative to create a new account called Earnings Retained in the Business or Retained Earnings[3]—to show how much of the increase in "book value" or Net Worth has resulted from accumulated undistributed earnings plowed back through the years.

In many ways, Earnings Retained in the Business can be misleading. It sounds like something extra or unnecessary, or too often like a spare chunk of cash which the company's workers or stockholders might hope to stage a raid against. Actually, Earnings Retained in the Business is decidedly not an Assets account, much less a pool of liquid cash. It simply indicates a part of the ownership—over and above Liabilities to creditors and original subscribed capital ownership—in the polyglot Assets of the corporation. A glance at Table 6-3 shows us that the $20,000 of Earnings Retained in the Business is not matched by an equivalent amount of cash on the Assets side.

We must once more warn against trying to link *specific* items on the Balance Sheets. Only the final *totals* correspond. It is not even possible to say exactly how the $20,000, plowed back into the business as Retained Earnings, was used. An addition to Retained Earnings must be associated with an increase in Assets and/or a decrease in Liabilities—that is all we can say.

It would be an equal mistake to think that the profits of a corporation accrue in the form of cash, so that on the last day of the year, just before the board of directors decided upon its dividend rate, there was some $30,500 of cash on hand, available either for the stockholders or to be reinvested in the business. In the case of our Apex Toothpaste company, the very handsome profit earned was largely embodied in the form of new, noncash Assets and lowered Liabilities; not very much more than $10,500 could have been paid out as cash dividends without forcing serious financial decisions—decisions such as to borrow more, to grow more slowly, to sell off some of the equipment and inventory at a loss, or to operate with a ludicrously low cash balance.

## SUMMARY OF ELEMENTARY ACCOUNTING RELATIONS

Before taking a last look at the new complexities introduced in the 1979 Balance Sheet over that of 1978, we may briefly summarize the relationship between Balance Sheets and Income Statements:

1. The Balance Sheet indicates an instantaneous financial picture: it is like a measure of the stock of water in a bathtub or lake.

2. The Income Statement shows the flow of sales, cost, and revenue over the year or accounting period: it measures the flow of water in and out of the lake, measures the progress of the firm over the year.

[3] Sometimes this is called "Surplus" or "Earned Surplus," but these terms are increasingly frowned on as being misleading.

**BALANCE SHEET OF APEX TOOTHPASTE, INC., (DECEMBER 31, 1979)**

| ASSETS | | | LIABILITIES AND NET WORTH | |
|---|---|---|---|---|
| | | | **Liabilities** | |
| **Current Assets:** | | | **Current Liabilities:** | |
| Cash | | $ 17,000 | Accounts Payable | $ 10,000 |
| Inventory | | 85,000 | Notes Payable | 17,000 |
| **Sinking Fund to Retire Debt:** | | 5,000 | Taxes Payable | 21,000 |
| (U.S. government bonds) | | | **Long-term Liabilities:** | |
| **Fixed Assets:** | | | SBA Note | 50,000 |
| Equipment | $130,000 | | Bonds Payable | 50,000 |
| Less: Allowance for Depreciation | 15,000 | | | |
| | | 115,000 | | |
| Buildings | $170,000 | | **Net Worth** | |
| Less: Allowance for Depreciation | 5,000 | | **Capital Stock:** | |
| | | 165,000 | Preferred Stock | 50,000 |
| | | | Common Stock | 200,000 |
| **Intangible Assets:** | | | **Earnings Retained in the Business:** | 20,000 |
| Patents | | 10,000 | | |
| Good Will | | 21,000 | | |
| Total | | $418,000 | Total | $418,000 |

**TABLE 6-3**

3. The change in total Net Worth between the beginning and end of the period—as shown by comparing the new and old Balance Sheets—is also to be understood from an examination of the changes in Retained Earnings as appended at the end of Table 6-2's Income Statement: the change in the lake's level over the year we can relate to the flows during this year. (If new common stock is sold, that will be revealed by comparing the two Balance Sheets.)

There do remain, however, certain changes in the Balance-Sheet items from their previous levels in the earlier period to which the intervening Income Statement gives no clue. A closer look at the December 31, 1979, Balance Sheet will therefore prove instructive, although enough has been said already to introduce the reader to the fundamentals of accounting.

## DEPRECIATION ALLOWANCES AND FUNDS

The new Balance Sheet looks much like the old for the most part; but some new items are present for the first time. The last of these new items, Earnings Retained in the Business, we have already explained. Among the Liabilities there is a new item, called Taxes Payable, of $21,000. It is not hard to understand. The taxes that the corporation will have to pay the government are as much short-term Liabilities as the Accounts Payable or Notes Payable.

Let us turn to the Assets side for new items.[4] The first stranger, entitled "Sinking Fund to Retire Debt," is listed midway between the Current and Fixed Assets. It is an asset consisting of, say, 6 per cent government bonds which are to be held for the purpose of ultimately paying off the bonds you issued to raise the money to buy your machines. The nature of this Sinking Fund is understandable; it is simply a pool of liquid Assets set aside for a specific future purpose.

[4]Neither this Balance Sheet nor the previous one contains a frequently met Current Assets item, Prepaid Expenses. Often an enterprise will pay its rent or buy some supplies a number of months in advance. Properly, the enterprise is regarded as possessing on its Balance Sheet an equivalent asset.

**Allowance for depreciation**  Turning to the Fixed Assets, we find ourselves in for a surprise. From our previous discussion of the Depreciation Charges of the Income Statement, we should have expected the Buildings and Equipment items to total $280,000. Why? Because at the beginning of the year they added up to $300,000, because no new equipment was bought during the year, and because the Income Statement told us that $20,000 of depreciation was charged during the period as part of the necessary costs of production.

Why, then, are these Fixed Assets carried on the new Balance Sheet at the old $130,000 and $170,000 figures? Looking more closely, we see that they really are not. From the $130,000 nominal Equipment valuation, there is subtracted a $15,000 Allowance for Depreciation, so that really only $115,000 is carried net for Equipment. Similarly, from the $170,000 original value of the Buildings, there is subtracted a $5,000 Allowance for Depreciation. Our faith in the accountant's wisdom is restored; but we may ask why he goes through this roundabout procedure of stating "two" as "four minus two" instead of simply as "two."

Actually, he has his good reasons. An honest accountant knows his depreciation estimate is only the roughest of estimates. Were he simply to estimate and put down the final figure of $115,000 for Equipment, the public would not know how much reliance to place upon the figure. So he puts down $130,000 of original value, which is firmly rooted in the solid fact of original cost; and he then carefully isolates his own calculated Allowance for Depreciation. Then the public is in a better position to evaluate the reliability of the final $115,000 figure. The roundabout procedure does no harm, and may do good.

Now we know the precise meaning of Allowances for Depreciation. They are not sums of money; they are not sinking funds of liquid Assets that can be spent on replacement. They are *subtractions from purposely overstated Assets figures*. Thus, the Allowance for Depreciation of Buildings of $5,000 is an explicit correction of the original value of Buildings, which would be an overstatement of its value left. This correction is made to keep Assets and Net Worth from both being artificially inflated.

It must be made, regardless of whether at the same time any money is or is not being set aside into sinking funds. Note that there is no sinking fund to retire debt incurred to acquire buildings, and that the Sinking Fund is here only one-third as large as the estimated Allowance for Depreciation of Equipment. As a matter of fact, American businesses rarely set aside any considerable sums of money in sinking funds. This is because liquid gilt-edge bonds earn at most only a few per cent interest, whereas capital invested in the firm's own activities usually brings in much more.

## INTANGIBLE ASSETS

Only one further new category of Assets can still be found on the December 31, 1979, Balance Sheet. To illustrate that an asset need not be a tangible commodity, a piece of equipment, or a sum of money, a patent has been introduced into the picture. Suppose it is a patent on a profitable new chemical process, giving us exclusive production rights for 17 years.

Such a patent is obviously worth money. Of course, as 5, 10, 12, and 16 years pass, the patent will be coming near to the end of its 17-year life and will be declining in value. Therefore, some amortization formula will be applied to it much as if it were a truck.

**Good Will and monopoly earning power**  So much for Patents as an illustration of an intangible asset. Let us suppose that, at the same time we bought the patent, we also took over a rival toothpaste company. This horizontal combination will presumably add to our monopoly position and earning power. Therefore we were willing to buy the company for more than its trifling Assets—which happened to consist solely of a little inventory—were worth. Perhaps part of the purchase price went as profits to those who promoted this little monopolistic merger.

An example of the capitalization of earning power is J. P. Morgan's formation of the giant United States Steel Corporation at the turn of the century. He bought out the Andrew Carnegie steel plants and combined them with half-a-dozen other holdings. But in economics, as in atomic physics, the whole is equal to more than the sum of its parts.

After Morgan had put the pieces together, he found himself with $130 million extra capital value!

Who was hurt by this transaction? Certainly not Carnegie or Morgan. Even the people who bought the stock had no right to complain that it had been "watered," since for many years they got more than a fair return on their investments. To have sold them the stock for its actual book value (without water) would be (1) to make them a free gift of the enlarged profits of the concern, and (2) to give them the privilege of reselling the stock at the higher price that its earning power could earn for it in a competitive stock market. (Of course the consumer was not given the full benefit in lower steel prices of the efficiencies achieved by merger; but in terms of standards prevailing at the time, the merger wasn't illegal or necessarily unethical.)

Accounting conventions, however, are not concerned with such matters of public policy and political economy as whether the consumer will or will not now pay higher prices. The careful accountant will tell our toothpaste company or J. P. Morgan the same thing: "If you paid a certain sum of money for a concern, it must presumably be worth that much to you. If its Net Worth and book value don't show this worth, we must recognize it by 'Good Will.'"

The intangible asset Good Will is thus the difference between what a company pays in buying out another company and the book value it gets in identifiable Assets.

## ACCOUNTING ABUSES

In economics and finance, nothing can be measured with the great accuracy of the physical sciences. But approximate measurement will suffice, so long as the method of measurement remains roughly the same over time.

Nowhere is this better illustrated than in accounting. When auditors certify that a company has prepared its accounting reports properly, they are not really able to swear that all measurements are 100 per cent accurate. But *it is valuable for anyone who is contemplating buying the stock of the company to know that the usual methods of accounting have been adhered to.* For example, when the company reports a rise of 10 per cent in earnings per share over the previous year, then, even though there may be some uncertainty in the exact figures for each year, the direction of improvement should be not at all in doubt.

Unfortunately, in the 1960s and 1970s certain abuses crept into the accounting used by some of the "conglomerates." Here are a few examples that

the accounting profession is belatedly engaged in correcting.

1. Manipulation of the way the assets taken over by the conglomerate are treated—good-will adjustments and selling off low-book-value assets at a claimed profit—have been used to permit the conglomerate *to report rising per share earnings every year even though actual operating earnings fell.*

2. Conglomerates will issue many securities that are *convertible* into common stock—convertible bonds, convertible preferred stock, warrant options to buy new common at low prices, stock options for executives and underwriters. These really are potential common stock which, in many cases, are sure to become actual common stock. Hence, accounting committees insist that we restate the earnings per share to allow for this *dilution*—and then what looks like a rising profile of earnings per share may actually be a dismally falling one.

3. Sometimes a small conglomerate will take over a larger corporation that is cash-rich, using in the end the money of the company swallowed to do so. Even where this is not illegal or unethical, it may be possible only because the old accounting book values of the absorbed firm carried its assets *concealed by undervaluations.*

4. Sometimes conglomerates give the appearance of becoming more profitably efficient in their operations than their predecessor companies, when actually all the improvements in per share earnings have resulted merely from taking advantage of tax loopholes—such as changing convertible preferred stocks into convertible bonds so that their dividend return will now appear in the form of interest, which is deductible under the law from corporation income subject to taxes. There may be nothing illegal or even unethical about this razzle-dazzle, but the alert investor will have to learn how to discern that this is all that is taking place and that further improvement is not possible.

The accounting profession and government agencies are working to reform some of these abuses. But, again: *caveat emptor*—let the buyer beware—must still prevail.

## CONCLUSION

Finally, some interesting relations between economics and accounting can be briefly mentioned. (1) All

Balance Sheets depend on valuation of Assets, which is one of the basic questions of the capital and interest theory discussed in Part Four. (2) National-income statistics depend on the accounting data of sales, cost, etc., as Chapter 10 shows. (3) We shall see in later discussion of how firms set price that accounting cost data play a role in price determination.

Business accounts deal with *money* magnitudes; economics tries to probe deeper to the underlying *real* magnitudes. Especially in periods of great inflation or deflation, the conventions of ordinary accounting may give strange results.

One example is the problem of changing price levels and depreciation. Suppose prices are rising. If I sell my goods for enough to cover labor and other costs and also to cover depreciation, you might think I am breaking even. What would the tax collector say who figures my depreciation on the basis of the past low prices originally paid for my tools and plant? He, too, would say I am breaking even. But, in fact, I can be said to have been selling my goods at a *real* loss; for when my machines and buildings have worn out, I shall not have enough money to *reproduce them* at the new, higher price level. The same is true of a merchant who sells off inventory at less than replacement cost.

So we must beware of fictitious money overstatements of real profits during rising prices and of fictitious understatements of profits during falling prices. (Later, in national-income statistics, you will note that profits are "adjusted" for inventory revaluations.)

## SUMMARY TO APPENDIX

Instead of a lengthy recapitulation, here is a check list of accounting concepts that you should understand:

1 The fundamental Balance-Sheet relationship between Assets, Liabilities, and Net Worth, and the breakdown of each of these into Current and Fixed Assets, Current and Long-term Liabilities, Capital, and Earnings Retained in the Business.

2 The character of the Income Statement (or Profit-and-Loss Statement) and the relationship between undistributed profit and Retained Earnings changes on the new Balance Sheet.

3 The whole problem of Depreciation, both in its income-statement aspect as a necessary expense, which need not be an expenditure, and in its balance-sheet treatment as a deduction from a purposely overstated asset; also the logic of the principal depreciation methods. Although any errors in calculating depreciation tend to cancel out eventually, recent tax concessions that allow rapid depreciation do improve the cash position of corporations.

4 Intangible Assets like Patents and Good Will, Sinking Funds, and other general items.

## CONCEPTS FOR REVIEW

Balance-Sheet identity
Income-Statement identity
Assets, Liabilities, and Net Worth
Current versus Fixed Assets
Dividends, Retained Earnings
Manufacturing Cost of Goods Sold

Manufacturing Cost, inventory change
Depreciation (as expense and allowance)
   straight-line or faster depreciation
Intangible Assets—Patents, Good Will
Accounting conventions and
   price levels

# QUESTIONS FOR DISCUSSION

1   Describe the Balance Sheet's right-hand side. Its left-hand side. What items must match from the "fundamental identity"?

2   You are a banker deciding whether to lend money to the toothpaste company. Why be especially interested in current items?

3   Write out a list of many different Assets. Give the nature of each in a few lines. Do the same for Liabilities.

4   Is an Income Statement a "still picture" at an instant of time? Why not?

5   A company has $10 million of net sales, $9 million of costs of all kinds (including taxes, etc.), and rents its equipment. Its inventory doesn't change in the year. It has no preferred stock. It pays no dividends. Draw up its simplified 1979 Income Statement.

6   The same company as in question 5 owes no money, having been completely equity-financed years ago. Fill in the year-end Balance Sheet below.

| ASSETS | | | LIABILITIES AND NET WORTH | | |
|---|---|---|---|---|---|
| **1978** | **1979** | | | **1978** | **1979** |
| | | | Liabilities | 0 | 0 |
| | | | Net Worth | $50 million | . . . . . . . . . |
| Total | $50 million | . . . . . . . . . | Total | . . . . . . . . . | . . . . . . . . . |

7   Redo problems 5 and 6, making the following changes: In addition to the other expenses, its buildings depreciate by $2 million; also its inventory has fallen off by $3 million. Draw up an Income Statement showing its loss, and adjust its 1979 Balance Sheet accordingly.

8   Describe two methods of calculating Depreciation, and explain tax advantages.

9   Guess how much you would pay for a business that is sure of yielding a net profit of $15,000 per year with little risk of principal. Suppose its Total Assets exclusive of Good Will were valued at $100,000. What would you guess for Good Will?

10   Why would use of the word "Surplus" rather than "Retained Earnings" encourage the fallacy of thinking that this represents a hunk of cash that the shareowners or union negotiators might hope to tap?

Nearly everybody is at some time in the labor force. Almost a third of our waking hours are spent on the job. Earnings from work—wages, salaries, and unincorporated earnings—constitute fully four-fifths of the total of national income. It is no wonder that the late Sumner Slichter of Harvard said—with pardonable exaggeration—that ours is a *laboristic* rather than a capitalistic society.

This chapter surveys the important role of labor unions in American life, paving the way for the more detailed discussion of wage determination in Part Four.

## WHO BELONGS TO UNIONS?

More than 22 million Americans belong to a union. Almost one-fourth of the nonagricultural working force is thus made up of union members. If we excluded white-collar workers, foremen, and executives, the proportion would be higher still. In certain important industries, such as rail and other transportation, basic steel, autos, mining, and clothing, practically all eligible workers belong to unions. Few large firms escape being organized by unions.

Figure 7-1, on the next page, shows the growth of union membership since 1900: the slow, steady advance up to World War I; the upsurge during that war and immediately thereafter; and the rather sharp decline and leveling off during the 1920s. It shows the explosive acquisition of new members during the New Deal recovery years following the Great Depression; the continued rapid growth during World War II; the relative stagnation until the mid-1960s; the slow, but steady, growth since then.

To what unions do workers belong? Here are the seven largest, with approximate size of membership in the early 1970s: the Teamsters (TCWH), 2,000,000; the United Auto Workers (UAW), 1,500,000; the United Steel Workers (USA), 1,400,000; the Electrical Workers International Brotherhood (IBEW), 975,000; the Machinists (IAM),

MR. HENNESSEY:
But these open-shop min say they're f'r unions.
MR. DOOLEY:
Shure, if properly conducted. No strikes, no rules, no contracts, no scales, hardly iny wages an' dam few mimbers.
FINLEY PETER DUNNE

**MEMBERSHIP IN LABOR UNIONS**

**FIG. 7-1**
**Union membership still grows, but slower than labor force**
Of nonfarm workers, about 27 per cent now belong to unions—as against but 11 per cent in 1933 and 31 per cent in 1960. Since there is a decline in relative importance of production workers in manufacturing, mining, and transport—the groups most prone to join unions—organized labor is no longer in a stage of vibrant growth. Waiting upon greater female liberation and class consciousness among white-collar workers and Southern workers, union organizing faces hard problems. (Source: U.S. Department of Labor, updated by author.)

875,000; the Carpenters (CJA), 850,000; the Retail Clerks International Association (RCIA), 650,000.

Except for two, they all belong to the merged American Federation of Labor and Congress of Industrial Organizations, i.e., the AFL-CIO. The Teamsters, under their former leader James R. Hoffa, were expelled from the federation because of corruption. The late Walter Reuther more recently pulled the Auto Workers out of the AFL-CIO. Also, the United Mine Workers (UMW), under John L. Lewis and later leaders, have been in and out of the AFL and the CIO. (The UMW reminds us that unions cannot only grow; they can also die away, as their industry dies. The Railway Brotherhoods tell the same story of decline.)

Statistics of membership understate the influence of unions. Many nonunion people are covered by union agreements on wages, hours, and working conditions. If you took a solemn oath never to join a union or work under a union agreement, you would have to give up all hope of being a factory worker in many sectors of manufacturing industries. *In every single manufacturing industry,* at least 20 per cent of all wage earners are under union agreements—even if they are not actually union members. You would have to give up a career in mining; in construction; in transportation. Where could you go? You could better avoid unions on the farm, in finance, and in trade. Or go South: attempts to organize workers have met strong resistance there. Fully two-thirds of all union members now live in 10 industrial states.

Within government itself is the new frontier for unionization: policemen, clerks, and even atomic-energy workers; white-collar, as well as blue-collar. Besides outright trade-unions, there are many organizations of professional people—like the American Medical Association (AMA), to which some 210,000 doctors belong, the National

Education Association (NEA), to which 1,700,000 teachers belong, and the American Bar Association, to which two-thirds of the 300,000 lawyers belong. These are important forces lobbying for higher incomes and specified working conditions. You would be naïve to think that the AMA, the NEA and the ABA are not important influences on the interplay of supply and demand, even though economic betterment is not primary in their written constitutions.

## NATIONAL AND LOCAL UNIONS

There are three layers in the structure of American unions: (1) the *local* union, (2) the *national* union,[1] and (3) the *federation* of national unions.

To a member, the *local* is the front line of unionism. He joins the local in his plant or town. He pays his dues to it. Usually, the local union signs the collective bargaining agreement determining his wages and work conditions.

But the local is only a single chapter or lodge of the national union. Thus, a linotypist in Chicago belongs to the local union located there, but this is one of hundreds of local chapters of the International Typographical Union, whose headquarters is in Colorado Springs. Part of the local dues—one-half or less, usually—goes to the national union; the bylaws and practice of the local cannot transcend the broad policies laid down at the national level. The president and other officers of the local are probably local workers; but the important office of business agent is a full-time job, the salary for which is often paid by the national union. The trend is increasing for the national unions to lend a hand in collective bargaining by the local.

Altogether, there are about 200 autonomous national unions. We have seen that seven of these have more than half a million members. More than half the national unions have between 10,000 and 200,000 members each; and a quarter of the national unions have fewer than 5,000 members each.

The number of local union chapters or lodges exceeds 76,000. Some have as few as a dozen men. A few giant locals cover thousands of men. For example, the Ford local of the UAW in Detroit is the largest of all. It alone has more than 30,000 members! The vast majority of locals number from 50 to 1,000 workers.

## NATIONAL UNIONS AND THE FEDERATION

The AFL-CIO is a loose federation made up primarily of national unions as members. It is dependent upon these member national unions for financial support. Like the Big Five nations on the Security Council of the United Nations, the national unions have insisted upon their "sovereignty" and right of veto and their right to "exclusive jurisdiction" over workers in their area. Most of the headaches and fights come from such jurisdictional disputes.

The public thinks of the federation as being the most important part of the labor movement; but it is not. It acts as spokesman for labor; yet its own power is strictly

---

[1] Many unions have Canadian chapters and more than a million Canadian workers are included in these "international unions."

limited. Thus Paul Jennings wields more real power as head of the International Brotherhood of Electrical Workers than he does as vice-president of the AFL-CIO. Former Teamsters' bosses Beck and Hoffa had more to fear from government action than they did from criticisms of their financial peccadilloes by the AFL-CIO. As a federation the AFL-CIO strongly disapproves of union discrimination against blacks, but it has no power short of expulsion to act against those member unions which still follow restrictive practices. Twenty-five years ago, when the United Electrical Workers and 10 other left-wing unions were expelled for being Communist-infiltrated, this was considered a precedent-breaking action.

The AFL-CIO has been politically quite active, working to elect candidates favorable to labor. Nominally nonpartisan, organized labor has usually supported Democratic candidates; but there have been some notable exceptions (as when the AFL-CIO president, George Meany, refused to support George McGovern). And a few labor leaders do generally support Republican Presidential candidates.

Figure 7-2 gives an organization chart for the AFL-CIO. The state and city federations shown thereon lobby at these levels of government and cooperate in producing TV programs, parades, and election or strike solidarity. The chart also shows a few local unions that attach directly to the federation rather than to any national union. Usually, these locals are in new fields just being organized or in fields that fall between the jurisdiction of the constituent national unions. The departments usually are coordinating bodies made up of unions in similar areas, such as the building trades.

## THE URGE TO UNIONIZE

Aside from the medieval guilds to which craftsmen and their apprentices belonged, how did present-day unions first begin? Why were men tempted to join such organizations? What are their general functions?

In past centuries wages were low everywhere. Productivity was then low, so that no way of dividing the social pie could have given the average man an adequate slice. But workers often felt that they were at the particular mercy of the boss; they felt poor, uninformed, and helpless to hold out economically against the employer, with

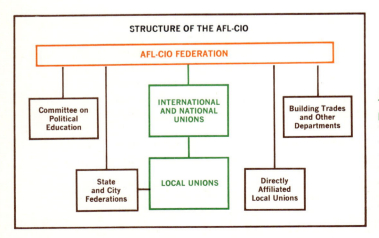

**FIG. 7-2**
**The main split in American labor healed after AFL-CIO merger**
The local unions and their nationals wield the primary power. The federation at the top is primarily concerned with public relations and other lobbying activities. No small committee can speak for all unions in nationwide wage bargaining—in contrast to Scandinavia and some other European countries.

his greater staying power in any conflict. Shops were organized on dictatorial principles, and orders were passed down from on high; the worker was but a cog in the machine, a dehumanized robot. Such was the worker's image of the situation as revealed in historical records.

Men gradually discovered that in numbers there is strength. One hundred men acting in concert seemed to have more bargaining power than all had by acting separately. Workers began to meet in taverns and chapels. They formed fraternal societies for mutual contacts, entertainment, and discussion. Gradually such early unions began to offer mutual death benefits and various other forms of insurance, and promoted self-education. They also began to propose *standard wage rates* that members were to insist upon getting paid.

Naturally, employers fought back. They, too, learned that strength came from formal cooperation, in which each employer backed up the other and refused to hire men on the "blacklist" of known labor agitators. Not unexpectedly, employers invoked the powers of the law against labor conspiracies and group actions. Later they hired gunmen and spies to fight unions.[2]

**"Business unionism"**   This then is the background of the modern American union. In contrast to the labor movements in many foreign countries that have politically waged the class struggle for major reform, American unions exist primarily for *economic* betterment: to try to get higher wages, shorter hours, more vacations, easier work rules, fringe benefits such as pensions and health insurance, democratic rights for men on the job, and so forth.

While economic goals are the major preoccupation and reason for the existence of unions today, unions do also perform purely social functions. Union members bowl together. Through their union they join in campaigns for blood donations, charity, and civic uplift. Just as a person belongs to his lodge, his church, the American Legion, and his boat club, so may he feel the necessity of union affiliation. (This is not to deny that a co-worker down the line may never do more than pay his union dues; or that still another worker, whose wage is also determined by collective bargaining, may detest the whole idea of organized labor.)

## BRIEF HISTORY OF THE AMERICAN LABOR MOVEMENT

Although American labor was late in becoming organized, the beginnings go back well into pre-Civil War times. Local craft unions of highly skilled, strategically placed workers (printers and others) were the first to be formed; and periodically, in boom times or in times of industrial unrest, these would combine in city and national federations for political and reform ends. But not until the 1880s, when the AFL was formed, did the American labor movement assume its characteristic present-day form.

**The Knights of Labor**   In the last third of the nineteenth century, out of the populist revolt against "big interests," the Knights of Labor emerged. At first it was a secret

[2] The chief weapons used by employers to fight unions have been (1) discriminatory discharge of union members, (2) the blacklist, (3) the lockout, (4) the "yellow-dog" contract (requiring agreement in advance not to join a union), (5) the labor spy, (6) the strikebreaker and armed guards, and (7) the "company union." Also, employers have used court injunctions to fight unions.

society which all but "lawyers, bankers, gamblers or liquor dealers, and Pinkerton detectives" could join. Later, secrecy was dropped; and by 1886, the high-water mark, the Knights had some 700,000 members. The Knights represented an attempt to form *one great labor union* to speak for all labor. But it was a heterogeneous collection, throwing together "craft unions" of workers with one skill, "industrial unions" of *all* workers in a given plant or industry, and mixed assemblies of any who cared to join.

The Knights were much interested in political reform and agitation. Some officials were more interested in "uplift" and radical political changes than in day-to-day increases in hourly wages. After a few unsuccessful strikes, the Knights declined in membership as rapidly as they had grown. America did not seem susceptible to such a political labor movement, and the organization of the Knights of Labor was too loose to give it any staying power.[3]

**The American Federation of Labor**   In 1881, and formally in 1886, the present-day labor movement took its form in the birth of the American Federation of Labor. For almost half a century, until his death in 1924, Samuel Gompers dominated this organization and gave the movement its characteristic pattern. Though early interested in socialistic uplift movements, he soon realized that no movement opposed to capitalism would flourish on American soil.

Gompers' main principles were simple:

1. As said, he insisted on "business unionism," aiming at day-to-day higher wages and better working conditions rather than engaging in the class struggle to alter the form of society. Labor was to get more and still more by evolution, not by violent revolution.

2. He committed the AFL to the principle of *federalism,* with each national union having autonomous sovereignty and "exclusive jurisdiction" over its craft specialty. This meant that the AFL would not tolerate "dual unionism": two unions could not try to organize the same workers; and a group of workers could not break away from a recognized national union.

3. Finally, he insisted on *voluntarism,* with the government not to interfere in collective bargaining. In politics he favored rewarding labor's friends and punishing its enemies, but he would not commit labor to any one political party.

Thus, the AFL was a polar opposite of the Knights of Labor in almost every respect. As the Knights dwindled in importance, the AFL grew. As the AFL-CIO, it has continued to grow. One might say that the philosophy of the AFL turned out to be the dominant philosophy of the American labor movement.

**The unfavorable 1920s**   After World War I, the AFL had about 5 million members and seemed to be riding high; but during the 1920s, labor met determined opposition from the National Association of Manufacturers (NAM) and other business groups. The

---

[3] Again, around the time of World War I, the IWW (Industrial Workers of the World, or "Wobblies") tried to organize the whole working class for the overthrow of capitalism. It had limited success in its efforts to organize unskilled migratory workers, loggers, and metal-mine workers. It had greater success in inducing panic in Wilson's Attorney General Palmer, who in 1920 threw suspected radicals in jail in defiance of civil liberties. But, until its recent rebirth, the IWW disappeared.

"open shop" was declared to be the "American plan." Moreover, the 1920s was a "new era" of eternal prosperity. As John J. Raskob, GM executive and Democratic party leader, said, anyone can easily get rich by saving $15 a week and investing it in the stock market. (He added that not only was it possible for people to become rich—it was their *duty* to become rich as well.) Also, the 1920s was one of those rare high-employment periods when prices were not rising; so discontent over the cost of living was not operating to encourage unionization.

**Recovery and the formation of the CIO**   By the depths of the Depression, the AFL had fallen to less than 3 million members. But with recovery, a new era for unionism was in the offing. The Depression had soured the American public on many of the slogans of the 1920s and had excited class antagonisms. Even before Roosevelt's New Deal, the electorate and the courts began to modify their opposition toward unions.

But within the AFL itself, the old insistence on the exclusive jurisdiction of national unions stood in the way of organization of the great mass-production industries. For example, before Judge Gary of United States Steel crushed the great 1919 steel strike, an unwieldy committee of some two-score craft unions was set up to conduct the strike. To this day the Carpenters' and Machinists' unions have never been able to settle some of their differences.

Astute observers in 1933 saw the handwriting on the wall: *Industrial* unions (rather than purely *craft* unions) were to play an important part in the future. John L. Lewis of the UMW, Sidney Hillman of the Amalgamated Clothing Workers Union, and other leaders formed in 1935 the Congress of Industrial Organizations (CIO), with Lewis as president. Helped by new government attitudes, legislation (especially the Wagner Act of 1935), and court decisions, a whirlwind campaign followed; in it the important mass-production industries, such as automobiles, steel, rubber, and oil, were organized, despite the bitter opposition of the principal companies in these industries.

By this time the AFL had learned the important lesson of industrial unionism. It, too, began to organize workers on an industrial basis; but its craft unions remained dominant.

**Unions in the 1970s**   Labor's dream of a united movement was finally realized when the AFL-CIO was formed. The union movement seems now to have settled down, with few new industries left to be organized. A new breed of man seems to be moving to the top. Back in the days when unions were being born and were fighting for their lives, colorful men such as John L. Lewis, Philip Murray, and Dan Tobin were the leaders. The new men who are replacing them are often men with gifts as *administrators*. With millions of members and literally hundreds of millions of dollars in their welfare funds, the unions are in need of men who can administer and who can deal persuasively with Congress, management, and the public.

A new frontier for unionization still exists in the fields of agriculture (as, e.g., the Mexican-American and other farm workers whom Cesar Chavez and the Teamsters have begun to organize) and white-collar workers. Public sector workers and teachers also are on the march toward organization.

## COMMUNISM AND CORRUPTION IN UNIONS

Boring in by Communists used to be something of a problem for the union movement. Thus, in the 1920s David Dubinsky led a successful effort to purge the communist influence from his union, the International Ladies' Garment Workers. During the 1930s the Communists attempted to influence policy in many unions. Although usually forming only a tiny percentage of membership, they exercised an influence beyond their numbers because they acted as a unit, using Machiavellian tactics to achieve their goals. They provided zealous labor organizers, and Lewis himself in his factional disputes for a time tolerated their help. In the United Electrical Workers (until 1949, CIO), the National Maritime, and the longshoremen's unions, the struggles between the "Commies" and anti-Communists were especially severe; and in the International Fur and Leather Workers (CIO), Communists did get control.

After 1949 there was a showdown. In addition to expelling the UEW and half-a-dozen other unions, the CIO expelled Harry Bridges' West Coast longshoremen's union as a Communist-infiltrated union. Later, laws against Communists became stiffer and stiffer, until the Supreme Court intervened. Except in a dozen or so unions, the Communists never attained any considerable power. Theirs was almost entirely a minority influence resting on their cleverness in strategy and in identifying themselves with popular labor causes. Whatever one may think of the economic wisdom of its policies, American labor is red-white-and-blue, not red—often too chauvinistic from the viewpoint of liberal intellectuals.

**Corruption**   Gangsterism has had a minor role in the union movement. Following the repeal of prohibition, corrupt gunmen did work their way into some urban unions (e.g., the longshoremen around New York). Such union officials were more ready to sell out labor than to fight in labor's interests. Labor had some success in cleaning its own house; but the use of violence to keep in power the old guard in the UMW shows that the record for lawfulness is by no means yet a perfect one.

One trouble spot does remain: fraud and mismanagement of the sizable union funds are not yet completely at an end. Teamster Dave Beck got rich speculating with union funds, and other misuses of union welfare funds have been turned up by congressional investigating committees. "Jimmy" Hoffa, Beck's successor, long successfully defied the AFL-CIO, congressional committees, court-appointed monitors, and minorities in the Teamsters Union. Because Teamster members believed that "Jimmy delivers the goods for us," Hoffa remained in control even after courts had found him guilty.[4]

## HOW DEMOCRATIC ARE UNIONS?

In Chapter 6 we discussed the problems involved in democratic control by stockholders of corporation management. Similar problems arise in connection with unions. It is

[4]Stirred by public revelations of graft, Congress overcame labor opposition and passed the Labor-Management Reporting and Disclosure (Landrum-Griffin) Act (1959). Among other things, this requires filing of union financial reports, limits union loans to officials to $2,000, and prohibits nonwage payments by employers to union representatives. The Act also provides a "Bill of Rights" for union members, which guards against rigged elections and summary disciplining of members by the union.

true that union officials are elected to office and all union members are given equal votes. But officers once elected often stay in power for a considerable time, and between annual conventions the union is usually run by a small executive board. Charismatic leaders like John L. Lewis have on the whole been popular with members; but if a member disagreed with their policies, he'd probably not get very far.

The average union member does not participate very actively in policy formation. However, according to the late Sumner Slichter, who must still be regarded as one of the most astute writers on the American labor movement:[5]

This does not mean the rank and file lack influence. Their influence is great, but influence is not participation. If democracy simply means strong rank and file influence, most unions are democratic. The typical situation in a union is similar to that found in most organizations, churches and clubs of all sorts. There is a minority which is sufficiently interested in the affairs of the organization to attend business meetings and to participate actively in discussing problems. In the case of unions this minority usually asks the officers to press for stiff demands—stiffer than employers would be willing to grant without a long fight, stiff enough to force many employers out of business. In order to avoid trouble, the great majority of the union would settle for much less than the active minority demand.

Quite naturally the professional leader feels on the spot. If he disappoints the active minority too deeply, his leadership will be challenged. If he gets the inactive majority into too much trouble, he may provoke revolt also. He compromises, as, of course, he must. Usually he is more interested in placating the active minority than the inactive majority because he knows that the support or opposition of the active members is more important than the support or opposition of the inactive members. The record shows that union officials lose their jobs, not for being too radical for the majority, but for being too conservative for the minority.

## HOW COLLECTIVE BARGAINING WORKS

Let us examine how collective bargaining is carried on.[6] Consider a production-line worker in a factory that has just been organized. An AFL-CIO union has petitioned the National Labor Relations Board (NLRB) for an election to determine the exclusive bargaining agent in this plant. The worker marks a secret ballot in favor of the union, and it wins more votes than an existing so-called "company union" which has no outside affiliations and which management prefers to deal with. The NLRB then certifies the new union as the collective bargaining agent for the plant, limiting any other union from negotiating directly with management.

A day is set for the new union representatives to meet with representatives of management at the bargaining table. Seated at the table will probably be a vice-president in charge of industrial relations; with him will be attorneys from a law firm that specializes in the labor field. On the union side will be the local business agent of the union and a small committee of union officers, and handling the negotiations will be an expert from union headquarters. He may be neither a lawyer nor a professional economist, but the economic research staff of the union helps him prepare an extensive brief backing up the union's demands.

[5]S. H. Slichter, *The Challenge of Industrial Relations* (Cornell, Ithaca, N.Y., 1947), p. 111.
[6]Chapter 29 includes a more analytical discussion of the collective bargaining process.

**The stakes**  Hourly wage rates are not the only issue in bargaining. In addition, the union may ask for a dues "checkoff" (whereby union dues are automatically deducted from the payroll of union members). The union may bargain for a "union shop," requiring all employees to become union members *within 30 days after employment*. Pension and health-insurance demands may be discussed at the bargaining table. In many industries where piece rates prevail, the structure of rates is an important subject for negotiation; the exact work load—how many looms each man will attend, and similar matters—may be discussed, and the general problem of how rapidly techno-logical improvements shall be adopted will enter into the final contract. The seniority rights of workers and a grievance procedure for handling cases of discharge—these and many other problems will come into the collective bargaining.

Indeed, management has become worried over the inroads that union bargainers have been trying to make in what it regards as its prerogatives. Many employers claim they can no longer run their business the way they feel is best. They find it hard to hire whom they will, fire for just cause, determine work methods, and decide on the order in which people will be laid off. They feel that every new decision occasions a committee meeting; and time that could better be spent on production must be devoted to labor relations. They claim the worker acts as if he has a *right* to any job he has held for some time. Such critics complain that many unions oppose incentive wage schemes, insist upon rigid seniority, discourage efficient work methods, and seriously limit the autonomy of management. A recent casebook on collective bargaining devotes more space to issues arising from workers' rights in jobs than to any other subject.

But at last the contract, covering many pages of fine print, is signed. Everything is set down in black and white, including provisions for grievances that arise during the life of the contract; often, too, there are provisions for the *arbitration* of issues that arise under it, each side agreeing in advance to accept the decision of an impartial outside arbitrator. The usual life of a contract is one or more years, with provisions made for reopening negotiations for a new contract under specified conditions.

Collective bargaining is a complicated business—a matter of give and take. Many business leaders have learned to agree with the statement by Cyrus S. Ching,[7] formerly vice-president of United States Rubber Company (Uniroyal) and subsequently head of Federal Mediation and Conciliation:

Where we are dealing with organized labor, we are going to get about the type of leadership that we are ourselves.

And many businessmen recognize the grain of realism in the statement by Philip Murray, who long headed the CIO:[8]

Employers generally get the kind of labor relations they ask for. If the unions indulge in "excesses," then the employer as a rule has no one but himself to blame for it. For instance, if he engages the services of labor espionage agencies such as the Railway Audit, Pinkerton's or others, if he stocks up his plant with tear gas, hand grenades, sub-machine guns, blackjacks, rifles, and other implements of war, if he hires high-priced Wall Street lawyers to harass the

[7]Cyrus S. Ching, "Problems in Collective Bargaining," *Journal of Business*, 1938, part 2, p. 40.
[8]P. Murray and M. L. Cooke, *Organized Labor and Production* (Harper, New York, 1940), pp. 259–260.

union before the Labor Board and in the courts, if he distributes to his foremen anti-union literature and lets it be known to them that any harm they can do to the union would be forgiven by him, if he contributes to anti-labor organizations such as the notorious Johnstown Citizens' Committee, if he quibbles over words, if he refuses to consent to an election or to sign a contract when he knows the union has a majority, if after a contract has been forced from him he delays and hampers the settlements of grievances, if he continues to discriminate against union members, then labor will answer in kind and nine out of ten businessmen, viewing it from afar, will say, "Ah, another excess."

**Peaceful coexistence**   No one should get a false impression that all management has been antiunion. Violence makes the headlines, while patient cooperation goes unnoticed. In most industries there has long been a successful pattern of fruitful cooperation between labor and management. To highlight this fact, the National Planning Association has published studies describing cases of successful labor relations. These reports describe "how historically hostile groups can co-exist on a basis of reasonable equality of position in the enterprise, and at the same time be participants in a common endeavor from which both seek security, opportunity, and sustenance." [9]

Thus, the West Coast pulp and paper industry, whose leading member is the Crown Zellerbach Corporation, has had more than 40 years of healthy labor relations. The Nashua Corporation has maintained relations with no less than seven AFL unions for 40 years without strikes. And the Hickey-Freeman Company, a men's-clothing manufacturer, has dealt with unions for 58 years without a strike; for 43 years no grievance ever went as far as arbitration.

These are not cases where peace has been maintained because the management or the union was soft. Hard bargaining on both sides is likely to accompany a good management-labor relationship; apathy on both sides or one-sided dominance postpones solutions and ultimately leads to breakdowns. In healthy cases, each side has a respect for the rights of the other. The two sides are not in love, but they are compatible. [10]

## ROLE OF GOVERNMENT IN COLLECTIVE BARGAINING

Although unions are relatively free in this country in comparison with their control in collectivist countries, government has played an important role in their historic development. Two hundred years ago, when labor first tried to organize in England and America, the common-law doctrines against "conspiracy in restraint of trade" were used against their members. Well into this century, unions and their members were convicted by courts, assessed for damages, and harassed by various injunctive procedures. Repeatedly the Supreme Court struck down acts designed to improve work

---

[9] *Fundamentals of Labor Peace*, Case Study 14 (National Planning Association, Washington, 1953).
[10] The great Du Pont chemical company provides a not uncommon pattern of coexistence. Some of its many plants, usually the older ones, belong to the great national unions. More belong to "company unions," i.e., local unions that are not affiliated with any units not working for Du Pont. Most of the plants belong to no union. Yet, if you examine the course of wage rates from 1945 to 1973 in the three different kinds of plants, you will find almost the same pattern of steady increase. Why, then, the effort by managements to keep out unions? Apparently, the greater flexibility of management prerogatives is deemed something worth fighting hard for.

conditions for women and children and other reform legislation on hours and wages.

In 1890, the Sherman Antitrust Act made monopolistic restraints of trade illegal. It did not mention labor unions; but in the next 20 years the Sherman Act was used increasingly by the courts to curb the activities of unions. If a union struck for ends that a judge thought undesirable, he might rule against it. And many traditional means used by unions were declared illegal even if in pursuit of a legitimate end.

Finally the AFL was forced into the political arena; and in 1914, labor was successful in getting the Clayton Antitrust Act passed. Although hailed as "labor's Magna Carta" and designed to remove labor from prosecution under the Sherman Act, this act did not end legislative and judicial opposition to the labor movement.

**Prolabor laws**    After 1930 the pendulum swung toward support of union bargaining.

Particular landmarks of legislation involved the Railway Labor Act (1926), which accepted the basic premise of collective bargaining; the Norris–La Guardia Act (1932), which virtually wiped out injunctive interference of the federal courts in labor disputes; the Walsh-Healey Act (1935), which provided that minimum wage standards be required on all government contracts; and the Fair Labor Standards Act (1938), which set a minimum wage ($2.30 in 1976) for most nonfarm workers engaged in interstate commerce, barred child labor, and called for time-and-a-half pay for hours in excess of 40 per week.

The biggest landmark of all was the National Labor Relations (Wagner) Act (1935). Its Section 7 stated bluntly:

Employees shall have the right to self-organization, to form, join, or assist labor organizations, to bargain collectively through representatives of their own choosing, and to engage in concerted activities, for the purpose of collective bargaining or other mutual aid or protection.

Moreover, it set up the National Labor Relations Board (NLRB) to make sure that employers do not engage in "unfair labor practices" against labor.[11] The NLRB also goes into plants and holds elections to see what organization is to be regarded as the collective bargaining representative for all the workers. It can, and does, issue "cease and desist orders" against employers, enforceable by the courts after appeal; and it often makes employers reinstate, with back pay, employees unjustly discharged.

Without such favorable governmental attitudes, it is doubtful that the union movement could have grown to its present status.

**Antiunion trends**    After World War II the electorate became fed up with strikes and rising prices. Labor was no longer considered the underdog; and people felt that the Wagner Act had been one-sided, favoring labor and putting all the penalties upon the employer. Congress passed the Labor-Management Relations (Taft-Hartley) Act

---

[11]The term "unfair labor practices" as used in the Wagner Act refers to employers' activities that interfere with employees' rights to self-organization. Examples of such employer practices are (1) firing men for joining a union, (2) refusing to hire men sympathetic to unions, (3) threatening to close an establishment if employees join a union, (4) interfering with or dominating the administration of a union, or (5) refusing to bargain with the employees' designated representatives. NOTE: Workers always had various rights to organize, but legislation of the 1930s explicitly encouraged and expanded those rights.

(1947). This is a *two-edged* labor relations law that—unlike the Wagner Act—prescribes standards of conduct for unions as well as employers. The hand of the worker who does not want to join a union is also strengthened, and so are rights of a member within the union as against the officers. Among its principal features are the following:

Strikes which "imperil the national health or safety" may be suspended by an 80-day court injunction requested by the Attorney General. Unions must give 60-day notice before any strike.

Unfair union labor practices are defined, and unions' behavior limited. Unions can be sued and held responsible for acts of their agents. The "closed shop," which requires all employees to be union members, is limited, and states are given a free hand to pass stronger laws. Secondary boycotts and jurisdictional strikes are made illegal. Political activity and financial contributions by unions are restricted; the free-speech rights of the employer are reaffirmed and strengthened.

Britain's conservative government has learned in the 1970s how similar legislation to control unions serves to provoke strikes and exacerbate the class struggle. "Right-to-work" referendums, aiming to make it easier for a worker to refuse to join a union, still divide the American electorate politically.

## CURRENT BARGAINING PROBLEMS

The key issues facing America and other nations in the 1970s are these:

1. Organized labor tries to improve its money wage rates, in the vain hope that this will not induce a commensurate rise in prices; hence this leaves *real wages* little or no better off. Because the strike is labor's ultimate bargaining weapon, and the right to refuse a wage increase even though this brings on a strike is the employer's ultimate weapon, work stoppages provide the major headlines in labor relations.

2. In an age of rapid technical change and much talk of "automation," union men are often more concerned about pension "fringe benefits" and *job security* than about mere money wage gains. What good is a raise in pay for a job that no longer exists?

3. Modern mixed economies seem to be subject to a new disease—a tendency for anything like an approach to full employment to lead to "creeping inflation."

**Strikes**  The power to strike is central in present-day collective bargaining. Contrary to common impressions, this power is, as shown in Fig. 7-3, used sparingly: the number of days lost from work on account of the common cold is by far greater than that from all work conflicts.

Chapter 29, which discusses wage determination in detail, points out that without the right to strike, a union's powers to bargain would, for better or worse, be substantially altered. Time and again concessions have been wrung out of an employer only by the realistic threat of forcing upon him the heavy financial losses involved in a prolonged shutdown. And, of course, workers also suffer grievous financial losses and demoralization from a long shutdown. Yet many a time employers have successfully refused union demands by a determined willingness to "take" a painful strike.

When strikes involve key industries (such as steel) or key functions (such as the railroads or the docks) or take place on a nationwide scale in an important sector

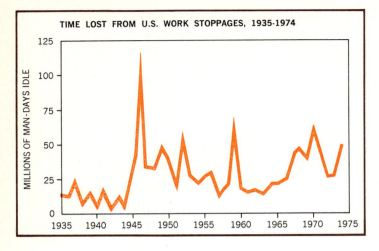

TIME LOST FROM U.S. WORK STOPPAGES, 1935-1974

**FIG. 7-3**

**Work stoppages reached their peak just after World War II**
While time lost from strikes is measured in millions of man-days, as a per cent of total labor days worked, it never has reached $1\frac{1}{2}$ per cent and has averaged less than $\frac{1}{2}$ per cent. In a typical recent year, Switzerland, West Germany, and Japan have had many fewer strikes than the U.S. and Canada; Italy and Iceland have had even more strikes than we have. (Source: U.S. Department of Labor.)

like autos, at this point the public interest becomes overriding. Two men are not free to engage in a fight if that does harm to other people. Just as the rights of private property and of personal freedoms are not absolute and must be reconciled when they come into conflict with the rights of others and of the public generally, so too must the rights of "free collective bargaining" be subject to limitation and coordination with social necessities.

These are not academic questions. In 1919 Governor Calvin Coolidge said in connection with the Boston police strike, "There is no right to strike against the public safety, by anybody, anywhere, any time." But 1976 is not 1919.

In fact, the government will not today let a crippling strike long persist. Again and again, presidents have been forced to use Taft-Hartley injunction procedures or other devices to suspend strikes in crucial areas.[12] In the future, unionization among government and quasi-public workers—teachers, air controllers, firefighters, defense and atomic-energy employees—is bound to make the problem of avoiding pivotal work stoppages more acute.

In one effort to reduce conflicts that can lead to strikes, unions have pressed for wages to be indexed to the cost of living.

**Productivity restraints**   Unions become especially concerned when new techniques threaten the job security of their members. The word "sabotage" was coined when laborers threw their wooden shoes (*sabots*) into the works of the new machines brought in by the Industrial Revolution to replace workers. "Featherbedding" refers to any

[12] Some experts in labor relations claim that, if anything, the state seems prone to interfere too quickly in urging compulsory arbitration proposals: A rail strike, which might reduce the national product by 25 per cent, has to be distinguished from a newspaper strike that hampers the dissemination of news and advertising or from an auto strike that puts off new-car purchases and sends ripples of reduced spending throughout the system. The case of railroads is much more fraught with public interest than the others, serious as they may seem to be.

rules imposed on employers merely for the purpose of keeping up the demand for workers: use of small shovels, limitation on number of bricks laid per day, requirement that use of music recordings be accompanied by a stand-by orchestra that does nothing but draw pay, requirement of a fireman (i.e., coal shoveler) on a diesel engine under the pretense that he is needed for safety reasons. Entrenched unions have power to enforce uneconomical makeshifts. The railroads have been a flagrant example. As Chapter 29 will show, there are limits on how much unions can raise wages, but their powers are particularly great in keeping wages up within dying industries.

**Wage-cost creeps**   Later (in Chapter 41) we shall be discussing the problems involved in inflation. Few modern countries have been able for long to enjoy simultaneously (a) reasonably full employment and (b) reasonably stable price levels. Part of the difficulty will be found to arise in the realm of monetary and fiscal policy. Part may come from a tendency for wage rates to be sticky against downward adjustments, but to be prone to rise in excess of productivity improvements even before full employment is approached.

## SUMMARY

1   Labor unions occupy an important but not expanding role in the American economy, in terms of both membership and influence. Their present structure is in three layers: (a) local unions, (b) national unions, and (c) federation of unions (AFL-CIO), the first two being the most important.

2   By the 1880s, the typical American pattern of federated, nonpolitical, gradualistic business unionism had been established. Since 1933, the CIO and finally the AFL have modified the pattern in the direction of *industrial* unionization of whole mass-production industries rather than rely solely upon *craft unionization* of skilled workers.

3   After a union has been recognized by an NLRB election as the exclusive bargaining agent, management and labor representatives meet together to negotiate a contract fixing wage rates, work conditions, productivity standards, degree of union recognition, seniority rights, and grievance procedures.

4   Right up until the middle 1930s there was bitter opposition to unions. But finally, the pendulum of government swung to support of collective bargaining, and since the Wagner Act (1935), most manufacturing industries have become unionized. The result has been less violence, but still vigorous collective bargaining between the opposing groups. After 1947 Congress felt it had become one-sided in favor of labor and passed the Taft-Hartley Act to correct the balance. Strike threats in crucial industries always invoke governmental action.

5   Aside from strikes and featherbedding, a major post-World War II problem has been the relation of wage increases to the price level. If patterns of "successive

rounds of general wage increases" are established that go far beyond the 3 to $3\frac{1}{2}$ per cent yearly rise in productivity, the price level is almost sure to rise in an inflationary manner and "cost-push" inflation will remain a serious problem—as we shall see in Part Two and Chapter 41.

## CONCEPTS FOR REVIEW

| | |
|---|---|
| national and local unions | craft versus industrial unions |
| AFL-CIO federation | strike, lockout, work stoppage |
| UAW, UMW, NLRB | union corruption, communism |
| collective bargaining | Wagner, Taft-Hartley Acts |
| business versus revolutionary | featherbedding, automation |
|    unionism | wage-cost push on prices |

## QUESTIONS FOR DISCUSSION

1   Describe the structure of America's organized labor. Describe the layers of the union movement. Which are the largest unions in your locality?

2   Historically, American unions have followed principles associated with Gompers. What are these? How have they been modified since 1933? Why has European labor been more active in politics along the lines of European socialism?

3   Describe the swing of the pendulum in the attitude of legislatures and courts toward organized labor before and after the Wagner Act.

4   Should policemen have the right to strike? Postmen? Milkmen? Everyone? Why might one expect in the latter 1970s that the new frontier for union organizing might be among civil service employees in federal, state, and local government?

Government plays an increasing role in the modern mixed economy. This is reflected in (*a*) the quantitative growth of government expenditure, (*b*) redistribution of income by the state, and (*c*) direct regulation of economic life. So in this chapter we survey government expenditure. In the next chapter we survey government taxation and local and state finance. Part Two will study how government fiscal policy helps achieve full employment and fight inflation. Part Six analyzes the war against poverty and inequality, against urban and environmental blight, against racial and sexual discrimination.

## THE GROWTH OF GOVERNMENT EXPENDITURE

Before World War I, federal, state, and local government expenditure amounted to little more than one-twelfth of our whole national income. During World War II, it became necessary for the government to consume about half of the nation's greatly expanded total output. In this century, the cost of all government in the United States rose from a minute $3 billion spent in 1913 to over $400 billion per year in the late 1970s.

For more than a century, national income and production have been rising. At the same time, in almost all countries and cultures, the trend of governmental expenditure has been rising even faster. Each period of emergency—each war, each depression, each epoch of enhanced concern over poverty and inequality—expands the activity of government. After such a period is over, expenditures never seem to go back to previous levels.

Nor is the end in sight. Government expenditure receded from its World War II peak, but it did not drop to the prewar levels of less than $10 billion, levels which used to be considered alarmingly high. In the years ahead, regardless of which political party holds office, the upward trend seems likely to continue.

Figure 8-1, on the next page, shows the historical trend of total government expenditure and federal debt relative to the growth of

# 8

# ECONOMIC ROLE OF GOVERNMENT: EXPENDITURE, REGULATION, FINANCE

Democracy is the recurrent suspicion that more than half the people are right more than half the time.
E. B. WHITE

147

**GOVERNMENT EXPENDITURES, GROSS NATIONAL PRODUCT, AND NATIONAL DEBT, 1900-1976**

BILLIONS OF DOLLARS

Gross National Product

Total Annual Government Expenditure

National Debt

**FIG. 8-1**

**Total government spending has risen with century's rise in GNP** Government expenditures include federal, state, and local expenditures. In this ratio or semilog chart, the parallel brown and orange curves show that, since 1950, GNP and government expenditure have grown together. Public debt grows less rapidly than GNP. (Sources: U.S. Departments of Commerce and Treasury.)

gross national product. And Table 8-1 points up the fact that rich countries tend, relatively, to spend more on government than do poor countries.

Note that mixed economies, such as Sweden, France, and (supposedly laissez faire) Germany spend relatively most on government. And these happen to be the kinds of nations which have shown the greatest growth and progress in recent decades. Contrary to the "law" enunciated by Australia's Colin Clark—that taking more than 25 per cent of GNP is a guarantee of quick disaster—the modern welfare state has been both humane and solvent.[1]

## THE GROWTH OF GOVERNMENT CONTROLS AND REGULATION

The increase in collective expenditure is only part of the story. Besides larger direct participation by government in national production, there has been a vast expansion in its laws, regulations, and executive fiats governing economic affairs.

Perhaps nineteenth-century America came as close as any economy ever has to that state of laissez faire which Carlyle called "anarchy plus the constable." The result was a century of rapid material progress and an environment of individual freedom. There were also periodic business crises, wasteful exhaustion of irreplaceable natural resources, racial and sexual discrimination, extremes of poverty and wealth, corruption

---

[1]When account is taken of high per capita incomes in the United States, our government share is a modest one. Still, we raise a larger fraction from personal income taxes than does a country like France. Studying the pattern among scores of countries reveals that share of government tends to be least at low income per capita and where foreign trade—which is an easy object to tax in poor nations—is relatively unimportant. Exceptions remain, e.g., the low portion for the Caribbean countries compared with those of South America.

| TAXES AS PERCENTAGES OF GROSS NATIONAL PRODUCT, 1976 | | | |
|---|---|---|---|
| DEVELOPED COUNTRIES | RECENT AVERAGE TAX (per cent) | LESS DEVELOPED COUNTRIES | RECENT AVERAGE TAX (per cent) |
| Sweden | 43 | Spain | 21 |
| France | 38 | Jamaica | 17 |
| West Germany | 35 | Colombia | 16 |
| United Kingdom | 35 | India | 15 |
| Canada | 32 | Philippines | 11 |
| United States | 32 | Nigeria | $9\frac{1}{2}$ |
| Switzerland | 23 | Mexico | 7 |
| Japan | 21 | Afghanistan | 6 |

**TABLE 8-1**

Government's share of national product is biggest in wealthy, developed lands
Governments of poor, less developed countries show a tendency to tax and spend less, relative to national product, than advanced countries. With affluence come greater interdependence and less need to spend on private necessities. (Sources: IMF, United Nations, author's updating.)

of government by vested interest groups, and at times the supplanting of self-regulating competition by monopoly.

No longer does modern man seem to act as if he believed "That government governs best which governs least." Gradually, and in the face of continuing opposition, the methods of Alexander Hamilton were applied to the objectives of Thomas Jefferson. The constitutional powers of government were interpreted broadly and used to "secure the public interest" and to "police" the economic system. Utilities and railroads were brought under state regulation; after 1887, the ICC (Interstate Commerce Commission) was set up to regulate rail traffic across state boundaries. The Sherman Antitrust Act and other laws were invoked after 1890 against monopolistic combinations in "restraint of trade." Regulation of banking became thoroughgoing: after 1913, the Federal Reserve System was set up to serve as a central bank, controlling member commercial banks; and since 1933 most bank deposits have been insured by the Federal Deposit Insurance Corporation (FDIC). The FPC (Federal Power Commission) and FCC (Federal Communications Commission) regulate power and broadcasting.

Pure food and drug acts were passed following the revelations of the muckraking era of the early 1900s. Loan sharks came under regulation in many states. The abuses of high finance before and after 1929 gave rise to ever more stringent regulation of financial markets by the Securities and Exchange Commission (SEC) and other bodies.

**Political evolution**  With the passage of time, the radical doctrines of one era became the accepted and even reactionary beliefs of a later era. State and federal legislation was expanded to include minimum-wage laws; compulsory workmen's accident compensation insurance, compulsory unemployment insurance, old-age pensions, public subsidy for medical care; maximum-hour laws for children, women, and men; regulation of factory conditions, compulsory collective bargaining, and fair-labor-relations acts. Private property is never wholly private, free enterprise never wholly free.

To understand the trend toward greater governmental authority one must maintain a sense of historical perspective. Each new step generated strong political feelings on both sides. Thus the "square deal" doctrines of the Republican Theodore Roosevelt, which today would cause no fluttering of pulses, were once considered dangerously radical. Our Republic cannot, and would not if it could, turn the clock back to the conditions of the nineteenth century as represented by Henry Ford's Greenfield Village and McGuffey's *Reader*. Still, it would be wrong to think these historical processes inevitable—to join Omar Khayyám in his mournful chant:

The Moving Finger writes; and having writ,
Moves on: nor all your Piety nor Wit
Shall lure it back to cancel half a Line,
Nor all your Tears wash out a word of it.

A democracy generally gets—in the end—the kind of government it deserves.

Unfortunately, not until long after the event will history tell us—and perhaps not then—whether or not a given expansion of governmental authority was a good or bad policy;[2] whether it deserves the approval of all who are genuinely interested in conserving and improving the good elements in the system. And in politics as elsewhere, it is only too true that the road to hell is paved with good intentions.

But past history does seem to suggest this: Unyielding conservatism defeats its own purpose. Iron without "give" will break suddenly under strain; flexible steel will bend. Brittle economic systems without the flexibility to accommodate themselves in an evolutionary manner to accumulating tensions and social changes—however strong such systems may appear in the short run—are in the greatest peril of extinction, as science and technology constantly change the natural lines of economic life. If a system is to continue to function well, social institutions and beliefs must be able to adjust themselves to these changes. And without a sense of historical perspective, neither radicals nor conservatives nor middle-of-the-roaders can effectively advance their own true long-run interests.

Before applying economic analysis to the nature of governmental activity, we must get a broad picture of what that activity now is.

## FEDERAL, STATE, AND LOCAL FUNCTIONS

Each American is faced with three levels of government: federal, state, and local. It will surprise most people to learn that, of the three, the states have always been the least important with respect to government expenditure. This is still true even though the years after World War II have seen strong expansion at the state level.

Prior to World War I, local government was by far the most important of the three. The federal government did little more than pay for national defense, meet pensions and interest on past wars, finance a few public works, and pay salaries of judges, congressmen, and other government officials. Most of its tax collections came from liquor and tobacco excises and tariff duties levied on imports. Life was simple. Local governments performed most functions and depended primarily on property taxes for their finance.

In Fig. 8-2, we see how the picture has changed since World War I. Though nondefense federal spending grows relatively less than the total of state and local, the federal government is still ahead in total expenditure.

---

[2] For a discussion on the proper scope of government, see a Swarthmore College debate between George J. Stigler and the author in P. A. Samuelson, *Readings in Economics* (McGraw-Hill, New York, 1973), 7th ed.

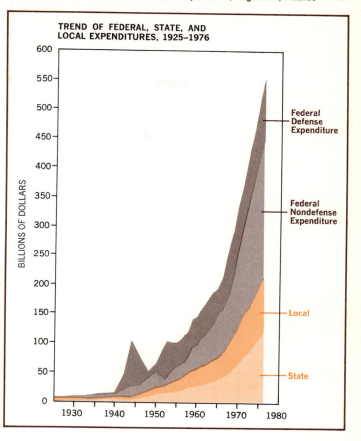

**TREND OF FEDERAL, STATE, AND LOCAL EXPENDITURES, 1925–1976**

Federal Defense Expenditure

Federal Nondefense Expenditure

Local

State

**FIG. 8-2**

Local and state welfare needs grow fastest in normal peacetime years

Federal expenditure rose sharply in the Great Depression, and even more during World War II. Rising standards of humanitarian welfare now more than offset declining defense needs. In particular, local and state expenditures on schools, sewers, roads, and welfare assistance to the poor show the steepest civilian trends. (Sources: U.S. Bureau of the Census, U.S. Department of Commerce.)

## FEDERAL EXPENDITURE

The United States government is the biggest business on earth. It buys more typewriters and more cement, meets a bigger payroll, and handles more money than any other organization anywhere. (The U.S.S.R., regarded as one unit, might provide an exception.) The numbers involved in federal finance are astronomical: not millions or hundreds of millions, but billions (i.e., thousands of millions). Such magnitudes convey little meaning to the human mind. They may have more meaning if we remember that each billion dollars amounts to about $5 per American man, woman, and child. A current federal annual budget of about $300 billion would be equivalent, then, to about $1,500 per capita—about 3 months of the average annual American income.

Table 8-2 on the next page gives the estimated importance of different categories of federal expenditure in the fiscal year 1976, i.e., from July 1, 1975, to June 30, 1976.

In the main, the first five items represent the costs of past and future wars. Together they account for almost half of all federal expenditure, as well as for much of the increase in federal expenditure over prewar levels. Naturally, these are estimates—subject to change when international tension changes.

| FEDERAL EXPENDITURE IN FISCAL 1976 | ESTIMATE (billions of dollars) | PERCENTAGE OF TOTAL |
|---|---|---|
| 1. National security | $ 94.0 | 25.3 |
| 2. Veterans benefits and services | 15.6 | 4.2 |
| 3. Interest on public debt | 36.0 | 9.7 |
| 4. International affairs and finance | 6.3 | 1.7 |
| 5. Space research and technology | 4.6 | 1.3 |
| 6. Natural resources and environment | 10.0 | 2.7 |
| 7. Agriculture and agricultural resources | 1.8 | .5 |
| 8. Health, labor, welfare, and education | 161.4 | 43.5 |
| 9. Commerce, transportation, and housing | 19.6 | 5.3 |
| 10. Revenue sharing | 7.2 | 1.9 |
| 11. Energy tax equalization payments | 7.0 | 1.9 |
| 12. General government and other | 7.5 | 2.0 |
| | | 100.0 |
| Intragovernment deductions (interest and pension payments to trust funds) | −21.7 | |
| Total expenditure | $349.3 | |

**TABLE 8-2**

**Much federal spending is for past wars, more and more for humanitarian needs**
The first five items take about one-half of total expenditure. But revenue sharing and welfare items 7, 8, and 9 now grow fastest. (Source: U.S. Office of Management and Budget; data includes expenditures of $92.3 billion from social security and retirement trust funds and $3.7 billion from the highway and air trust funds.)

Much of the sixth item goes to the support of conservation programs, control of water and air pollution, etc. The other items are largely self-explanatory, representing aid to the farmer; welfare aid to the needy, aged, and handicapped under the Poverty Program, Medicare, the Family Assistance Program, and other programs; expenditure on labor, education, and health; and revenue-sharing aids from the federal government to states and localities. The final category includes costs of running Congress and the courts, as well as general expenses of the executive branch of the government.

## THE CHANGING FUNCTIONS OF GOVERNMENT

The last quarter of a century has witnessed great political changes. How great have been the economic changes? How great have been the departures from the traditional capitalistic system? We can tackle these questions by considering government activity under five headings:

**Direct controls**   As noted, there has been an increase in the amount of government *control*. Much of this regulation can hardly be dignified by the title of "planning," and market prices still run most activities. Economic analysis of government interventions deserves detailed discussion and will be met in later chapters.

**Social consumption of public goods**   As we have also seen, the increase in government expenditure means that as a nation we are consuming more of our national product *socially* rather than individually through private money purchases. Rather than pay to ride on the public roads as we do to ride on railroads, we pay for such valuable services by taxes.

Note that socially consumed goods and services are *largely produced by private enterprise*. The government pays for a hospital or typewriter, but these are produced by private industry. And so it is with most government expenditure on productive goods—the arsenals of the armed services being notable exceptions. This is not what the original socialists meant by socialism—i.e., government ownership and operation of factories and land.[3]

**Stabilizing fiscal and monetary policy**  As will be seen in Parts Two and Six, an important function performed by modern governments involves the control of runaway price inflation and the prevention of chronic unemployment and stagnant growth. Two principal weapons are used: monetary and fiscal policy.

A central bank—which is a bank for bankers and which is given the power to issue currency—either is directly in the executive branch of government or, more commonly, is a public not-for-profit organization ultimately responsible to the legislature. We shall study how our version of it, the Federal Reserve Banks and Board, exercises *money and credit policies* designed for high production and price stability.

Since the beginning of recorded history, governments have had constitutional authority over money. But only in the last 40 years has it become generally recognized that *fiscal policy of government*—variations in public expenditure and tax totals, which create a surplus or deficit rather than a balanced budget—has profound effects on unemployment, total production, money and real incomes, and the level of prices.

Bad fiscal policy can make the business cycle worse. Stabilizing fiscal policy can moderate the ups and downs of business. Now that governments are large, claiming to have no fiscal policy is like claiming to be dead: left to themselves, budgets will definitely not balance; a policy of trying to balance the budget in every month, year, decade, or over the whole business cycle involves deliberate (and rash!) social choice.

Later chapters will study monetary and fiscal policy in depth.

**Government production**  There has been little expansion in this direction in recent decades. Historically, our government has performed certain direct productive operations, and not others. The post office was long a function of government (but even the postal service has been spun off to a quasi-public autonomous unit), while private management has operated telegraph service and railway express. Airports, but not railway terminal facilities, are usually governmentally owned. Municipalities now often provide water, sometimes gas and electric utilities, but rarely telephone service. (Abroad, telegraph, telephones, and railroads are typically publicly operated; here, Amtrak gives some federal subsidy to languishing interurban passenger trains, but even communication satellites are run by private corporations.)

The reasons for drawing the line at one place rather than another are partly historical and are to some degree changing; but, economically, the distinction is not completely arbitrary. Thus, the courts have held that, in the special case of "public utilities affected

---

[3]See the discussion of socialism, communism, and fascism in the final chapter of this book.

with public interest," there is limited possibility of effective competition among many independent producers, so they must be *publicly regulated or owned;* but one would not expect the production of soap or perfume to be a natural candidate for governmental operation.

Whatever the merits of the arguments on each side, it is well to examine the facts to see how much government ownership of production has been introduced these last 45 years. Under the New Deal, there was but one direction in which such expansion took place, namely, the power field. (EXAMPLES: Tennessee Valley Authority, Bonneville Dam in the Northwest, Hoover Dam in the Southwest, rural electrification, and so forth.) Unlike Canada, or Sweden, or Britain, we have never had national ownership of coal mines, steel mills, airlines, or radio and television broadcasting.

If words are used in their traditional meanings, it is not incorrect to call TVA "creeping socialism." The fact to note is how little of that sort of thing has, for better or worse, taken place in recent years.[4]

The atomic-energy program was a post-New Deal development: It shows how poorly traditional "black-and-white" words and concepts are adapted to describe the gray territory of modern life. When the government pays General Electric a negligible fixed fee to start and run a vast nuclear industry, is this private or public enterprise? Private, in that the workers are GE employees and not civil servants. But the government puts up all the money, and certainly audits all major decisions. So the whole development of the atomic and hydrogen bombs could by some be called "galloping socialism." (For peacetime atomic energy and safety, the government is relinquishing some of its monopoly. But decisions about secrecy, about fusionable and fissile materials, about patents, will keep nuclear energy subject to public supervision.)

Finally, we should recognize that *there has been a considerable rise in the federal payroll and in the number of government employees.* Many of the latter are in the Washington executive offices, in regional laboratories, in the armed services, and so forth. Even if they are not producing private goods and services in competition with private industry, such resources are being directly used by the government, with government as employer.

**Welfare expenditures**   Now we turn to an activity of government that has expanded tremendously since 1929 and that will continue to loom large in the decades ahead, namely, *government welfare expenditure,* which transfers purchasing power to the needy or worthy without regard to their providing a current service in return. Payments are made to veterans, old people, the handicapped, pensioned workers, needy families, and the unemployed. These "transfer expenditures" deserve further discussion. Because of them the modern mixed economy is sometimes called the "welfare state."

## TRANSFERS AND TAXES IN THE WELFARE STATE

A government check received by a veteran or needy family head differs economically from that received by a postal clerk or by a man who produces typewriters. It is

---

[4]It is noteworthy that the war plants built by the government were, almost without exception, sold to private industry or shut down after the war. Government research organizations and contracts do, however, finance much of our research and development (R&D) efforts.

important to understand why, because our later discussion of national income will involve this same distinction between items that are "transfers" and items that are directly parts of GNP or of national income.

We shall see later that governmental payments to a soldier and stenographer or to a missile and typewriter producer are counted as parts of national income and GNP. Why? Because they do cover services rendered, they do use up resources and production, and they do provide collective direct or indirect consumption to the citizens of the United States. Whether they are financed by taxes or by any other means, the government uses its dollars to provide services for citizens' use. Such dollars are as much part of national income as the dollars used by a railroad company to provide transportation services for its customers.

A blind widow's pension is something else again. Socially, it may be one of our most desirable expenditures, but nevertheless it is not part of GNP or national income. Why? Because the widow does not render any concurrent services to the government or its citizens in exchange for the pension. She does not provide any labor, land, or capital. The pension does increase her purchasing power, does permit her to live more adequately and to buy goods and services from other individuals. These goods and services *that she buys* are part of the GNP; but they are *attributable* to the people and private factories that have produced them, not to her.

**Minimum standards**    Transfer expenditures have grown greatly in recent years. They grew partly as a result of the Depression, which made relief expenditures necessary, but they grew mostly because new minimum standards of health, nutrition, and security have been set by the collective conscience of the American people. Society now rules that children shall not have rickets because of the bad luck or weakness of their parents, that poor people shall not die young because of insufficient money for operations and needed care, that the old shall be able to live out their years with some minimum of income. President Nixon's unsuccessful proposal for automatic payments to all families with low enough income (a version of the so-called "negative income tax") reflects this new, but not yet widely held, view; Candidate McGovern had to back down on such proposals in his 1972 campaign; President Ford's tax cut in 1975 provided payments to poor families with children for the first time.

Are welfare expenditures anticapitalistic? We shall later see that, "on the first round," these expenditures do not directly consume goods and services; but by swelling the purchasing power of their recipients, they do create orders and jobs for free private enterprise "on the second round." The thing to note is that *the production induced by this process is both privately produced and privately consumed.*

Unless these expenditures are financed by new money creation or by bond borrowing, larger taxes will have to be levied on the public; and it is for this reason that they are usually called "transfer expenditures." Often the more fortunate citizens are paying for consumption of the less fortunate; and doubtless within reasonable limits, most people feel that this is proper and vote for the programs.

In connection with welfare programs of the government, mention should be also made of the fact that various *redistributions* of income among citizens are accomplished *by the form in which the government allocates the burden of the taxes it levies* on different groups and classes. The next chapter shows that there is a tendency in modern states for the well-to-do to be taxed absolutely and relatively more heavily than those below the median income level.

Thus, suppose there were no program of direct governmental transfers. But suppose the government made the very rich pay all the taxes for national defense and most of the taxes for civilian programs. Is it not evident, then, that it would be altering the inequality in the distribution of the after-tax disposable incomes that different classes have to spend on bread, cars, and anything else?

*Along with transfer programs, one must include in the activities of the modern welfare state any redistributions of income it brings about by the way it differentiates in its tax system between the various income classes.*

For the rest of this chapter, we can try to use some of the tools of economic analysis to understand the nature of the various governmental programs already surveyed.

## GRAPHICAL ANALYSIS OF GOVERNMENT ACTIVITY

The production-possibility concept of Chapter 2, particularly Fig. 2-4, on page 24, gives insight into the nature of government activity. Figure 8-3(a) indicates how society can choose between (1) *private* goods (bread, shoes, gum, haircuts), which families buy

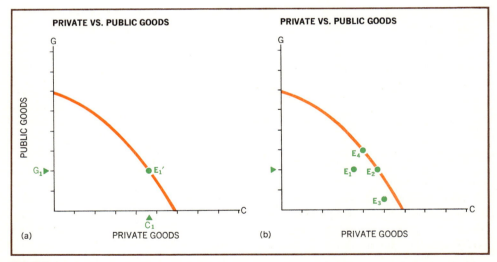

**FIG. 8-3**
Cutting the scope of government is not the same thing as cutting out waste
**(a)** Along society's *p-p frontier* that allows choice between private and public expenditure on goods and services, democratic voting decides on a point like $E_1'$.
**(b)** Cutting out waste and increasing governmental efficiency take society from $E_1$, inside the *p-p frontier*, out to it. This permits the previous level of government to be reached at $E_2$ with less sacrifice of private goods. (Cutting down on scope without change in efficiency would mean, however, moving inside the frontier down to $E_3$.) At $E_4$ the populace has decided to allocate the new affluence that efficiency has brought among new extra goods of both private and government types.

voluntarily out of their after-tax incomes at prices set by markets, and (2) *public* goods (battleships, roads and bridges, services of policemen and civil servants, judges and prison guards, weather forecasts), which we consume collectively and which involve government expenditure (financed by taxes, deficit borrowing, printing of money).

What determines the actual $E_1'$ position, which shows about a fourth of the total product being devoted to *public* goods and the rest to *private?* It is *legislative decision* that puts $E_1'$ where it is and also determines the exact composition of the social expenditure as divided between the three levels of government.

What about the composition of the private sector at the point $E_1'$? On reflection, one realizes that it does indeed depend on governmental decision making, but only in the following respects: (1) Welfare transfers by government help to determine the distribution of spendable incomes of people in the private community, money which they can spend voluntarily for different goods in the market. (2) Tax legislation by our representatives decides how to allocate the tax burden among different individuals and classes; such decisions impinge in a similar way on the allocation, in the background, of income distribution and $E_1'$'s private goods among persons.

Aside from these transfer and tax influences, the private consumption of goods is determined primarily by *voluntary market decisions of individuals*—as they decide to buy white rather than rye bread, beef rather than pork, boats rather than autos, and Scotties rather than Kleenex.

Suppose international tension ended, thereby permitting us to cut down greatly on defense expenditure and on taxes, leaving people with more money to spend individually. Provided the economic system were made to run smoothly without significant unemployment, you should be able to show that the point $E_1'$ would then move down the *p-p frontier* in Fig. 8-3(a), toward more private and less social spending.

Suppose the electorate agrees with Galbraith's *The Affluent Society* and decides it would prefer to enjoy less private consumption of cars and more social consumption of public goods like roads and hospitals. Can you show the northwestward climb of $E_1'$ on the frontier?

## WASTE IN GOVERNMENT AND SCOPE

Our diagram helps to disentangle a common confusion. Government expenditure can be reduced in two quite different ways: First, the people can succeed in making their public activities more *efficient*. They can abolish graft and waste and insist on better planning of programs and on more efficient administration. This is sometimes called "cutting out fat without cutting muscle."

Second, people can change the *scope* of government, reducing public expenditure by having the government drop many of the functions it performs. The government can build fewer roads, provide less weather information, cease to do research, abandon conservation activities, and so forth.

Figure 8-3(b) helps keep the problem of efficiency in government distinct from the problem of scope of government. Its move from $E_1$ out to $E_2$ on the *p-p frontier* shows the result of a successful program of increasing the *efficiency* of government activity: we can now get the same quantity of government goods and services for less sacrifice of resources from the private economy. If the electorate wants to leave the scope of government unchanged, the new $E_2$ point will be due right of old point $E_1$, with same $G_1$ level of social consumption but with private goods now increased as shown.[5]

As an alternative to the above case, suppose people succeed in reducing government expenditure solely by cutting down on the *scope* of government activity. Then there will have been no change in efficiency. Inside the frontier, the nation moves down and to the right to $E_3$.

Consider still another alternative. Suppose everyone favors efficiency and we do succeed in getting out to the *p-p frontier*. But now suppose the electorate decides it will use its greater affluence for *both* private and additional social wants. If it decides to spend its extra real income on something from both categories, then it will move up and to the right—northeast to the point marked $E_4$.[6]

## SOCIAL AND PRIVATE WANTS: EXTREME LAISSEZ FAIRE

Let us return from graphs to the basic issues. *Why is governmental use of goods and services ever required at all?* What light can economic analysis throw on this?

In the first place, suppose all goods could be produced efficiently by perfectly competitive enterprise at any scale of operations. And suppose that all goods were like loaves of bread, the total of which can be definitely divided up into separate consumptions of different individuals, so that the more I consume out of the total, the less you consume. And suppose that there were neither altruism toward other people nor envy of them. And suppose that each person had equal initial access to human and natural resources, had equal opportunity in every sense, and could carry on his activities independently of others, much as in frontier days.

If *all* these idealized conditions were met, would there be any need whatsoever for a mixed economy? Why should there be any government functions at all? Indeed, why speak of "a society" at all, since the world could then be regarded as an array of independent atoms with absolutely no organic connections among them? Clearly, such a case of zero government is at one extreme pole.

Yet even in this case, if there were to be a division of labor between people and regions, and if a pricing system such as that described in Chapters 3 and 4 and in Part Three were to work, the need would soon grow for government courts and policemen to ensure honesty, fulfillment of contract, nonfraudulent and nonviolent behavior, freedom from theft and external aggression, and guarantee of the legislated

[5] This might have come about in the background in something like the following way: The savings in efficiency permits tax reduction large enough to give people the extra income sufficient to use up all the resources released by government.

[6] Recall Colin Clark's alleged law that no government can tax and spend more than 25 per cent of the national income without creating disaster. If there were an absolute real limit, the transformation curves would have a corner at the limit, moving off horizontally to the left of it. There appears to be no evidence of any such discontinuity. The possibility that inflation might be the consequence of going northwest of some critical $E$ point is a quite different argument; after study of Part Two, one can appraise such an allegation. (Figure 40-2 will discuss the fact that as society taxes to transfer from private to social consumption, some distortions of incentives and efficiency are likely to result; in *changing the division* of the pie, you may *alter its size*. This constitutes one of the genuine costs of government, and sensible electorates will want to give it due weight in deciding whether this should lower or should expand government's proper scope.)

rights of property. This would be laissez faire with minimal government—and a good system it might be if the ideal conditions presupposed for it were truly present.

## SOCIAL WANTS IN REAL LIFE

Each and every one of the idealized conditions enumerated above is lacking in some degree in real life as mankind has always known it. Abilities, opportunities, and ownership of property exhibit disparities, depending on biological and social history. It is a fact that many kinds of production can take place most efficiently only in units too large for "perfect competition" as defined exactly by the economist; and many other imperfections mar the simplicity of the scenario. All this forms the subject of analysis throughout this book—analysis designed to provide perspective for the important compromises that a free society must make. But here, in a chapter on public expenditure, we shall concentrate on the factors that call for governmental activity.

**Merit wants**   Why do we let people generally decide what shoes they will buy with their own money, but not what heroin or LSD? Evidently, just as we believe that children of six years of age are to be second-guessed in their buying decisions, we also paternalistically overrule some private adult decisions. Usually, this is done sparingly and only with great hesitation: an adult in good mental health is generally assumed to be free to make the best decision on *his* own wants, needs, and desires.

Before Rousseau, children were treated as if they were little adults (as old paintings will reveal). Since Freud, we realize that as adults we are still only grown-up children—still imperfect beings subject to error, regret, and myopia.

Thus, children's allowances are given in Canada to the mother rather than the father, in the hope that more of it will be spent on milk rather than beer. Again, why do we give the needy below-cost or free hospital services, rather than give them cash to spend either on operations or on TV sets, as they wish?

Clearly, all economies—free, mixed, or controlled—have some sector of what Harvard's Richard Musgrave calls "merit wants." To promote merit wants, government does in a degree exercise paternalism (or, for that matter, maternalism)—taxing cigarettes, forbidding dangerous drugs, subsidizing health care and old-age retirement provision.

Milton Friedman and Beatrice Webb will naturally differ on the optimal degree of such activities—the former advocating freedom of an addict to (quietly!) commit slow suicide, the latter telling families how they should allocate their basic consumption. But there never has been an economy in which merit wants are either completely absent or completely dominant.

**Public goods**   Let us consider national defense as an example *par excellence* of public goods. Nothing is more vital to a threatened society than its security. But national defense, regarded as a commodity, differs completely from the case of a private commodity like bread. Ten loaves of bread can be divided up in many ways among individuals in a group; but national defense has to be provided *more or less automatically for all*. Many individuals will appreciate it, much as they appreciate quantities of bread; but even among them, some would be more willing to give up more bread, if necessary, for a given level of defense than others would. Some, who are pacifists, will aver that defense expenditure does not interest them particularly; while still others may actually experience pain from this public good and would require much bread to bribe them into voluntarily voting for national defense.

Could market laissez faire, with no political voting and no coercion, give the group the national defense desired by the majority? Evidently not. If I knew that I was going to benefit anyway from the defense you had paid for, why should I come into the marketplace and exercise a dollar demand for it? Patriotism would of course motivate me; but it would show itself in the way that my neighbors and I *vote on election day* and in the way we acquiesce to the coercive fiats legislated by our responsive government, rather than *in our day-to-day private purchasing*.

To be sure, the example of national defense is a dramatic and extreme case. But when you think of the night policeman, the presiding judge, the appropriation for a park concert, or the damming of a river upstream to prevent floods downstream—indeed, when you think of government acts in general—you find the common element:

The benefits from a public or social good, unlike those from a purely private good, are seen to involve *external consumption effects* on more than one individual. By contrast, if a good can be subdivided so that each part can be *competitively* sold separately to a different individual, with no external effects on others in the group, it isn't a likely candidate for governmental activity.

In Parts Three and Six, much more will be said about external effects: so-called "external *dis*economies," such as the smoke from my factory chimney which contaminates the air for all; and "external *e*conomies," such as the advantage your fruit trees get from the straying bees I raise to help pollinate my own fruit trees. It is enough here to give examples of government activities justifiable because of external effects.

Take our earlier case of a lighthouse to warn against rocks.[7] Its beam helps everyone in sight. A businessman would not build it for a profit, since he cannot claim a price from each user without great difficulty. This certainly is the kind of activity that government would naturally undertake. It would meet Abraham Lincoln's test: "The legitimate object of government is 'to do for the people what needs to be done, but which they can not, by individual effort, do at all, or do so well, for themselves.'"

Or take the case of government provision of research on corn farming. No one competitive farmer is large enough to do it; and he also knows he cannot retain the monetary advantage

---

[7] The analysis of this section owes much to the nineteenth-century analysis of the Scandinavian Knut Wicksell and other economists and to the important treatise by Richard A. Musgrave, *The Theory of Public Finance* (McGraw-Hill, New York, 1959). In the lighthouse example, one thing should be noticed: The fact that the lighthouse operators cannot easily appropriate a fee, in the form of a purchase price from those it benefits, certainly helps to make it a suitable social or public good. But even if the operators could claim a toll from every nearby user, that fact would not necessarily make it socially optimal for this service to be provided like a private good at a market-determined individual price. Why not? Because it costs society *zero extra cost* to let one extra ship use the service; hence any ships discouraged from those waters by the requirement to pay a positive price will represent a social economic loss—even if the price charged to all is no more than enough to pay the long-run expenses of the lighthouse. If the lighthouse is socially worth building and operating—and it need not be—a more advanced treatise can show how this social good is worth being made optimally available to all. Parts Three and Four go deeper into all this (particularly in Fig. 32-2).

of the research financed by him. Nevertheless, there is great benefit to the group and to society from learning about and adopting any improvements that might be uncovered by research on farming. As a result of these considerations, because of a clear *externality* in the use of knowledge, no prudent private firm can be expected to invest its scarce dollars up to the point of best advantage to the group as a whole.

Therefore governmental activity in this area of research, whether in its own laboratories or by commissioning of private or university research, may well be a desirable act of representative democracy. (Where a government project, like an atomic pile, involves external *dis*economies, policy makers will have to take them into account.)

This concludes our brief economic analysis of the nature of government activity. In Part Three, the discussion will go beyond the question of government finance and will develop the economic principles that determine when a government might prudently intervene in laissez faire to restrain monopoly, regulate it where it is inevitable, and use tax or subsidies to offset distorting external diseconomies and economies. The next chapter will discuss public finance as it relates to the tax systems of the federal, state, and local governments and will discuss expenditures of the states and localities and their coordination with the federal government.

## SUMMARY

1   The economic role of government has been a generally expanding one. More and more activities in our complex, interdependent society have been coming under direct regulation and control.

2   A larger fraction of the total output here and abroad has been going to collective consumption of *public* rather than *private* goods.

3   An increasing part of the national income is being "transferred" by taxation and government *welfare* expenditure from the relatively rich to the relatively poor. There has been in America, however, no trend toward state ownership of industry and of society's means of production; and as yet, little detailed "planning."

4   Since World War I, federal expenditure has far outstripped local and state expenditure. During the Depression of the 1930s, expenditures on relief, public works, and similar matters expanded the federal budget. But the post-World War II budget remains many times prewar levels because of increased defense and space outlays, interest on the public debt, aid to veterans—and because of new humanitarian standards.

5   The production-possibility frontier of Chapter 2 can help distinguish between democratic voting to determine the level of *public goods* and day-to-day family spending decisions to determine the level of *private goods*. The *p-p frontier* can also help us distinguish between reducing government expenditure by (*a*) reducing governmental waste or (*b*) reducing governmental scope of activity.

6    Economic analysis of private goods consumable solely by individuals points up
     the contrast with *social public* goods which involve "external-consumption effects"
     on more than one individual in the group. National defense, research, law en-
     forcement, conservation, lighthouse operation, hospital and school operation, and
     similar activities must pass the test of involving such "external effects" if they
     are to be easily justifiable as government activities. Or they must be defended in
     terms of paternalistic "merit wants."

## CONCEPTS FOR REVIEW

GNP level and government
  spending
public debt and budget
laissez faire versus controls
fiscal policy

welfare state, socialism
transfer expenditures
private versus public goods
paternalistic merit wants
efficiency and scope

## QUESTIONS FOR DISCUSSION

1    Name things which government does now that it did not do in the past.

2    Between now and 1980, how would you expect the government's share in the
     national income to develop? Why? What factors affect your answer?

3    How much does the increasing economic cost of government reflect decreasing
     efficiency? How would you go about making a scientific study of this?

4    "The radical doctrines of three decades ago are the conservative doctrines of
     today." Is this ever true? Always true? Give favorable cases and exceptions.

5    "Government expenditure on goods and services represents public goods in
     considerable degree *produced* by market-operated private enterprise." Appraise.

6    "To bring back the federal budget to earlier levels, defense and veterans' programs
     will have to be the main items cut." Discuss.

7    Define transfer payments, redistributive taxes, and welfare programs.

8    Evaluate critically the statement on the proper role of government attributed
     to Abraham Lincoln, page 160's small print extract. Could believers in big
     government as well as believers in small government both appeal to it?

9    What is a paternalistic merit want? Give examples you would favor; examples
     you would oppose. Comment on the following: "Even if you do not agree with
     me that every adult should be free to kill himself with heroin if he wants to and
     won't harm others in doing so, you should agree with me that it would be better
     to give people heroin at a penny an ounce (or its true minimum cost if legal)—so
     that crazed, incurable addicts will not rob and kill honest, peaceful folk."

Discussion of public finance continues in this chapter with an analysis of taxation in general. Then the chapter surveys the federal tax system, expenditure and taxation at the state and local levels, and the interrelations among the different branches of government. Finally comes the problem of tax incidence—upon whom does the burden of each tax ultimately fall? How does the tax burden on rich and poor compare with the benefits they each receive from public expenditures?

## ECONOMIC NATURE OF TAXATION

**Financing real expenditures**  The state (i.e., the government) needs money to pay its bills. It gets the dollars to pay for its expenditures primarily from taxes. However, what the state really needs to build a battleship or run a lighthouse is not so much money as *real economic resources:* steel and watchmen—in short, the use of society's scarce supplies of labor, land, and capital goods.

In deciding how to tax themselves, therefore, the people are really deciding how resources needed for social wants shall be taken from all the various families and from the enterprises they own and be made available for public goods and services.

**Altering distribution of incomes**  The state also spends on *welfare transfers,* which go to particular individuals in the community for them to spend on *their* private needs and wants. Again, money is a veil that cloaks the *redistribution* of command over real goods and services which results from action by the state to tax some and give to others.

Recall also that, even if there were no direct welfare transfers, the tax system is altering the distribution of incomes that results from laissez faire. In deciding who shall be made to pay for the resources spent on social goods and services, the electorate can vote taxes that will fall heavily on the rich rather than on the poor; on the energetic

**163**

9

ECONOMIC
ROLE OF
GOVERNMENT:
FEDERAL
TAXATION
AND LOCAL
FINANCE

The power to tax . . . is not only the power to destroy but also the power to keep alive.
UNITED STATES
SUPREME COURT

rather than on the weak; on the owners of tangible resources, such as land and property, rather than on the owners of labor power.

**Thus, taxation and transfers help determine the distribution of private incomes.**

In the distant past, taxes were levied by those in power against those out of power, purely in terms of expediency. A nobleman at Louis XIV's court might go scot-free, while a merchant in Lyons or a peasant in Normandy was sorely burdened. When scholars tried to form more rational guides to taxation, what principles finally emerged?

**Benefit versus sacrifice principles**    Of the many principles concerning optimal taxation, two major groups can be distinguished:

1. There is the general notion that different people should be taxed in proportion to the "benefit" they can be expected to receive from public activity.

2. There is the general principle that people should be taxed in such a way as to lead to a desirable pattern of "sacrifice"; or what is much the same thing, that taxation should be arranged to accomplish whatever the good society regards as the proper and equitable *redistribution* of market-determined incomes.[1]

Such general principles are important; but they do not avoid difficult decisions with respect to just what is the desirable structure of taxes.

For instance, consider benefit taxation. If you and I were *exactly* alike, then the benefit we receive from the armed services, the public roads, and general governmental services would be the same; so we ought to pay equal taxes. Similarly, take redistributional taxation. If we were exactly alike, then the amount of sacrifice we each ought to make would again be equal. No one, then, will quarrel with the *dictum:*

**Those who are essentially equals should be taxed equally.**

This notion of equal treatment of equals was important in the past and still is. If Man A and Man B are alike in every respect except that A has red hair, that is presumably not a legitimate reason for taxing them differently—any more than, in a rule of law, the fact that A is a friend of the Prime Minister or the President should relieve him from taxation. As we shall see, the existence of loopholes in tax laws shows how necessary it is not to forget the above dictum.

However, a corollary to this dictum *once again raises* all the hard problems:

**If equals are to be taxed equally, then there is a presumption that *unequals are to be taxed unequally*.**

On the basis of neither the general-benefit criteria nor the optimal-sacrifice criteria does this corollary by itself resolve society's policy issues.

Imagine that Man A and Man B are alike in every respect except that B has ten times the property and income of A. Does that mean that B should pay the same *absolute* tax dollars for police protection as A? Or that he should pay the same

---

[1] Economists, who think the utilities of different persons can be added together to form a total social utility, speak of taxing to produce maximum total utility, or to produce some specified pattern of utility sacrifice. Thus, if each extra dollar brings less and less satisfaction to a man, and if the rich and poor are alike in their capacity to enjoy satisfaction, a dollar taxed away from a millionaire and given to a median-income person is supposed to add more to total utility than it subtracts. See Chapter 22 and also Fig. 21-7 for more on this so-called "law of diminishing utility."

*percentage* of his income as tax to defray police expense? Or that opulent B, inasmuch as the police have greater need to spend their time in protecting the property of the well-to-do, will not have paid his fair share of police expense unless he pays a *larger fraction of his income* in taxes?

The general philosophy of benefit or sacrifice taxation similarly leaves unanswered the question of the best tax formula. It is one thing to say that the rich have greater "ability" to pay taxes than the poor, that their "sacrifice" is less when they pay a dollar of taxes than when the poor pay a dollar. This still leaves open the question: *How much* differently should unequals in income be taxed? What do we really mean by "equity?"

## PRAGMATIC COMPROMISES IN TAXATION

How have modern mixed societies tended to resolve these difficult philosophical questions? Democracies have generally adopted pragmatic solutions that will please neither the enthusiasts in favor of benefit notions nor the enthusiasts in favor of thoroughgoing redistributional-sacrifice notions. Modern tax systems are, in fact, an uneasy compromise.

Where various public services at the local and national levels are peculiarly for the benefit of recognizable groups, and where those groups have no special claim for favorable or unfavorable treatment by virtue of their average incomes or other characteristics, modern governments generally rely on taxes of the benefit type. Thus, local roads are usually paid for by local residents; taxes collected on gasoline may on the whole be devoted more specifically to roads than to schools or libraries; etc.

**Progressive and regressive taxation**   On the other hand, considerable reliance has been placed on *graduated income taxes*. A man with $20,000 of income is taxed more than a man with $10,000 of income. Not only does the higher-income man pay larger income tax, but he in fact pays a progressively *higher fraction* of his income. This "progressive graduation" of the rate of tax is in contrast to a strictly "proportional tax" that makes each man always pay exactly the *same proportion* of his income, and in even greater contrast to a so-called "regressive" tax, which takes a larger fraction from low incomes than it does from high.

*Definition:* A tax is called *proportional, progressive,* or *regressive* depending upon whether it takes from high-income people the *same* fraction of income, a *larger* fraction of income, or a *smaller* fraction of income than it takes from low-income people.

The words "progressive" and "regressive" can be misleading. They are technical terms relating to proportions that taxes bear to different incomes. They have to be appraised on their merits, and it would be wrong to read into the word "progressive" emotional overtones of being up-to-date or particularly right-minded.

A personal income tax that is graduated to take more and more out of each extra dollar of income is progressive. While many taxes on sales of goods will be seen to be regressive, the reader should realize that a tax on fine wine, which only the rich can afford, might well be progressive. Even a tax that is strictly proportional to size of estate left at death could be progressive, since the man with twice the income tends on the average to have and bequeath more than twice the wealth.

**Direct and indirect taxes**    Aside from their degree of progressivity, taxes can also be classified under the headings *direct* or *indirect*.

*Indirect taxes* are usually defined as taxes that are levied *against goods and services* and thus only indirectly on people. Examples: excises, or sales taxes; cigarette taxes; tariff duties on imports; turnover taxes, which are levied every time a farmer sells wheat to a miller and a miller sells flour to a baker and on all transactions at any stage of production; value-added taxes, which tax only the costs added at each stage.

*Direct taxes* are levied directly on people (e.g., income, inheritance, poll taxes).

When certain minimum income is exempt from tax, that is an element of progressivity. When there is a "negative income tax" at very low levels—as in President Ford's 1975 low-income tax credit, which automatically pays out money to very poor families with children—that is even more redistributively progressive.

There are, of course, many borderline cases that do not fall neatly into one category or the other. We generally associate direct and progressive taxes together; indirect and regressive (or proportional) taxes together. But there are many exceptions to such a rule: a poll tax of $2 per head is a direct tax, but a highly regressive tax in that it takes a larger fraction of income from the poor than from the rich; as mentioned, an indirect tax on yacht gasoline or rare brandy might well be progressive.

Modern tax systems are, to repeat, a compromise. They give some weight to benefit notions; some weight to sacrifice and redistribution notions; and, one may add, some weight to expediency and politics—and to the economic fact of life that increasing certain taxes, however favorable it looks to an ardent redistributionist, would at the same time be expected to do some harm to people's incentives and to the efficiency of society's use of resources.

## FEDERAL TAXATION

The great variety of present federal taxes is indicated by Table 9-1. Of these, the first two, personal income taxes and death (estate) and gift taxes, bear down "progressively" more on people with higher incomes.

Payroll and sales taxes are relatively "regressive" in that they take a larger fraction of the poor man's income than they do of the rich man's.

The corporation tax is intermediate in its effects. In one way, it is progressive, since most dollars available for dividends accrue to people of more than median income. (Although it is true that many poor widows and orphans own some shares of stock, still the total that they own is not a large fraction of all stock shares.) But to the extent that corporations can pass the tax on to the consumer in higher prices, a tax on business profits may well end up being regressive or proportional.

A brief glance at the various taxes will be helpful.

**Sales and excise taxes**    In order of regressiveness, these would probably come first, and there has long been controversy over them. As far as *federal* finance is concerned, no *general* sales tax has been passed, but there are excise taxes on cigarettes, liquors, travel, and certain other items.

**Social security, payroll, and employment taxes**    Virtually all industries now come under the Social Security Act. Employees are eligible to receive old-age retirement benefits

| FEDERAL TAX RECEIPTS, FISCAL 1976 | | |
| --- | --- | --- |
| | KIND OF TAX | RECEIPTS (in billions of dollars) |
| **Progressive** | Personal income taxes | | $106.3 |
| | Death and gift taxes | | 4.6 |
| **Intermediate** | Corporation income taxes | | 47.7 |
| **Regressive** | Employment or payroll taxes | | 91.6 |
| | Excise taxes | | 36.4 |
| | Tobacco and liquor | $14.5 | |
| | Customs duties | 4.3 | |
| | Gasoline | 7.0 | |
| | Other manufacturing | 4.1 | |
| | Miscellaneous | 6.5 | |
| | Other taxes and receipts | | 10.9 |
| | Total tax collections | | $297.5 |

**TABLE 9-1**

**Personal and corporate income taxes are main federal revenue sources**

Graduated progressive taxes are now most important for federal government. But attempts to pass federal sales taxes or value-added taxes (VAT) still persist. (Source: U.S. Office of Management and Budget.)

of so much per month, depending upon their previous earnings and not upon any humiliating demonstration of poverty. To help pay for these benefits and for hospital insurance under Medicare, the employee and employer in 1976 each contribute 5.85 per cent of all wage income below $15,300 per year; the limit of taxable income is expected to reach $24,000 before 1985.

Taken by itself, a payroll tax is regressive in its impact upon the poor and middle classes; but when combined with social security benefit payments, the degree of regressiveness is materially less.

**Corporation income taxes**   After a corporation has paid all its expenses and reckoned its annual income, it must pay part of its income to the federal government. In 1976, a small corporation is scheduled to pay 22 cents of each dollar of its net income in taxes; but when its earnings get to be above $25,000 per year, it must pay 48 cents of each extra dollar of earnings.[2]

Some experts oppose taxing corporations on the ground that they are only fictitious legal persons. Besides, they say, the corporate tax becomes a cost that is passed on regressively in the price consumers pay. To the extent that it cannot be passed on, they think it is unfair "double taxation" for the government to tax corporate earnings and also to make the stockholders pay personal income taxes on the dividends received from corporations. They advise: Cut corporate tax rates; or alternatively, give the dividend receiver a more generous tax credit for the taxes his corporation has paid.

In opposition, some experts argue that corporations should be taxed heavily, with the bigger corporations taxed at progressively heavier rates. They believe that, if government must collect large sums of money and if further increases in the personal

---

[2] In wars, this and other countries have had an "excess-profits tax" on corporations in addition to the above ordinary income tax. Thus, in the 1951–1953 Korean emergency period, some corporations were taxed 82 cents of extra dollars earned, keeping but 18 cents.

income tax are not feasible, then a tax on corporations is better than a sales tax. Also, they point out that corporations do not distribute all their earnings to stockholders but retain some to be plowed back into the business. The stockholder may avoid personal income tax on these corporate savings by capital-gains loopholes, as we shall see. According to such critics, a corporation tax will at least partially remedy the tax-loophole inequity.

**Value-added taxes**    Finally, mention should be made of a new tax that has been widely used by the Common Market countries of Europe. The value-added tax, or VAT, as it is called for short, *collects at each stage of production:* thus, for a loaf of bread, VAT is collected at the farmer's wheat stage of production; also at the miller's flour stage of production; at the baker's dough stage; and finally, at the grocer's delivered-loaf stage.

How, then, does it differ from a so-called "turnover tax," widely used in the U.S.S.R. and by Common Market countries before VAT? A turnover tax simply taxes *every* transaction made: wheat, flour, dough, bread. VAT is different because it does not include in the tax on the miller's flour that part of its value which came from the wheat he bought from the farmer. Instead, it taxes him only on the wage and salary cost of milling, and on the interest, rent, royalty, and profit cost of this milling stage of production. (That is, the raw-material costs used from earlier stages are *subtracted* from the miller's selling price in calculating his "value added" and the VAT tax on value added. Table 10-2 in the later chapter on national income will explain all this.)

The Republican administration under Nixon supported the VAT. The Democratic Opposition rejected it as being simply a disguised form of a sales tax on consumption, collected in installments rather than simply at the final source.

## THE PROGRESSIVE PERSONAL INCOME TAX

Spring used to be a most unhappy season, as people had to make a lump-sum payment for taxes on the previous year's income, which had often already been spent. Now April is no longer quite so cruel a month. All through the year employers automatically *withhold* from each paycheck most of what we shall have to pay to the government. This puts us on a pay-as-you-go basis: by the end of the year our income taxes are more or less all paid up.

For some 20 million families with incomes below $10,000 and no appreciable property income, that is all there is to it. They simply turn in their withholding-tax receipts at the year's end; file a simple form; and the Treasury refunds them any excess paid. For still other millions of families, with moderate incomes and not incurring any extraordinary deductible expenses, there is merely a similar short form to fill out.

Those with sizable incomes must fill out a complex form.

How much does a typical person have to pay at each income level? Table 9-2 gives the tax schedule as of 1976. (Rates are always changing, of course.) Column (2) shows about how much is the tax that people would have to pay on each of the incomes listed in Column (1). Note that the tax starts at zero for those with income below $1,500 (actually negatively under the 1975 tax law), and then rises rapidly in relation to income. Indeed, when property income climbs to $10 million, 69.7 per cent will

| FEDERAL INCOME TAX FOR A CHILDLESS COUPLE, 1976 | | | | |
|---|---|---|---|---|
| (1) | (2) | (3) | (4) | (5) |
| NET INCOME BEFORE EXEMPTIONS (but after deductions) | PERSONAL INCOME TAX | AVERAGE TAX RATE, PER CENT (3) = (2) ÷ (1) | MARGINAL TAX RATE (= tax on extra dollar) | DISPOSABLE INCOME AFTER TAXES (5) = (1) − (2) |
| Below $    1,500 | $         0 | 0 | 0 | $     1,500 |
| 2,000 | 70 | 3.5 | 14 | 1,930 |
| 3,000 | 215 | 7.2 | 15 | 2,785 |
| 4,000 | 370 | 9.2 | 16 | 3,630 |
| 5,000 | 535 | 10.7 | 17 | 4,465 |
| 10,000 | 1,490 | 14.9 | 22 | 8,510 |
| 20,000 | 3,960 | 19.8 | 28 | 16,040 |
| 50,000 | 16,310 | 32.6 | 50 | 33,690 |
| 100,000 | 44,280 | 44.3 | 60 | 55,720 |
| 200,000 | 109,945 | 55.0 | 69 | 90,055 |
| 400,000 | 249,930 | 62.5 | 70 | 150,070 |
| 1,000,000 | 669,930 | 67.0 | 70 | 330,070 |
| 10,000,000 | 6,969,930 | 69.7 | 70 | 3,030,070 |

**TABLE 9-2**

**The income-tax schedule climbs progressively as income grows**
Single people would pay up to 20 per cent more; large families less. (Taking the low-income deduction, the couple would begin to pay tax at $2,550. On "earned income" a 50 per cent ceiling applies. Under the 1975 tax law, poor families with children will get from rather than give money to, the government.)

go to the government. Never does the total tax quite reach 70 per cent. (On income from wages and personal effort alone, the highest rate only reaches 50 per cent—much below the 70 per cent rate of the late 1960s or the highest 91 per cent rate of the early 1950s.)

Column (3) shows just how progressive the personal income tax really is. A $20,000-a-year family is made to bear a relatively heavier burden than a $5,000-a-year family—19.8 rather than 10.7 per cent; and a millionaire is made to bear a still heavier relative burden. Column (4) records an interesting fact; namely, the fraction of an *extra* dollar that taxes will take. Note that this begins at 14 per cent and then rises. This so-called "marginal (or extra) tax rate" finally reaches 70 per cent on nonearned income above $200,000.

Column (5) shows the amount of "disposable income left after taxes." Note that it always pays to get more income: even when an heiress moves into a higher tax bracket, the move gives her more income to keep. As Column (4) shows, the government never takes more than 70 cents out of each *extra* dollar. At incomes around $50,000, it begins to take more than half of each *extra* dollar from a couple; a bachelor finds this happens at $32,000. As mentioned, earned income dollars (wage, professional, etc.) pay a maximum 50 per cent.

**Taxation and inequality**   The income tax tends somewhat to reduce the inequality of disposable income. Thus, in Fig. 9-1, the hypothetical effect of progressive taxes on

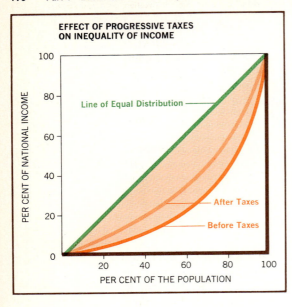

**EFFECT OF PROGRESSIVE TAXES
ON INEQUALITY OF INCOME**

Line of Equal Distribution

After Taxes

Before Taxes

PER CENT OF NATIONAL INCOME

PER CENT OF THE POPULATION

**FIG. 9-1**
**Progressive taxes tend to reduce inequality
of the distribution of after-tax incomes**
The heavy curve represents the unequal distribution of
income before taxes. The lighter curve shows how progressive (or "graduated") taxes create a more equal
distribution of "disposable" income after taxes. The effect
is exaggerated for emphasis. Thus, the top fifth of the
income pyramid still get considerably more than three-
eighths of after-tax income (even more if we count in
capital-gains and tax-exempt incomes).

the inequality of income is indicated in exaggerated form. Note how the area of
inequality on the Lorenz diagram has been reduced; progressive taxation has shifted
the curve somewhat nearer to the 45° line of equality.

**Loopholes and erosion of tax base**   The United States collects a larger fraction of its
taxes from incomes than almost any other country. This is not because our professional
and well-to-do people pay higher rates of tax; they pay generally less than do people
at comparable real income levels in Sweden, Britain, and other welfare states. It is
because our average citizen, who is so much better off, falls in a higher income bracket
that our lower income-tax rates actually are able to produce relatively more revenues.

On paper our tax rates look progressive. But many items in the total income base
escape taxation. First, there are exemptions of $750 per person and various minimum
standard deductions as well. Second, real income in the form of owner-occupied homes
avoids taxation. Third, there is also some illegal tax evasion—cheating by farmers,
doctors, waiters, salesmen with fake expense accounts. The amount of such evasion
can be estimated, and in advanced nations like Great Britain, the United States, and
Sweden, it turns out to be surprisingly small. Fourth, more important than evasion
is legal tax *avoidance,* which is possible because Congress has legislated so many tax
"loopholes" permitting much income to go untaxed or to be taxed at lower levels.

Thus, the single largest tax loophole is the fact that any capital gains I realize on
the sale of an asset at a profit above its original cost is more lightly taxed than is
ordinary income (and there is no capital-gains tax at all if I hold the asset until death!).

**If loopholes were closed and the erosion of the tax base corrected, rates on all income
levels could be cut without revenue loss.**

Here are a few facts. Before the 1969 tax reforms, less than half of all true income was included in the tax base. Those with incomes of over $1 million did not in fact pay an over-all rate of 70 or even 50 per cent: a sample showed they paid an effective rate of 48.2 per cent, which itself was an overstatement if one takes account of many true income items that could be treated as low-taxed capital gains. Eighty-five per cent of all income taxes came from the low-bracket rates of 20 per cent or less: It is not the rich who pay for the bulk of government; they are too few. It is the median-income group who, by their numbers, predominate. Critics often say, "Uncle Sam digs deep into high incomes, but digs with a sieve."

By the 1970s, after voters learned that 155 persons with tax-sheltered incomes of over $200,000 paid not a cent of tax, a taxpayers' revolt threatened. Congress recently curtailed the percentage depletion allowance for oil, but it has only begun to make token moves against capital gains, tax losses claimed by gentlemen farmers, and other forms of tax-sheltered income.

## PROGRESSIVE TAXES, INVESTMENT, AND SPENDING

Often, doubts are raised as to whether high income taxes do not discourage effort and risk taking. So far as effort is concerned, this is not an easy question to answer. For we shall later see that taxation will cause some people to work *harder* in order to make their million. Many doctors, scientists, artists, and businessmen, who enjoy their jobs, and the sense of power or accomplishment that they bring, will work as hard for $30,000 as for $100,000; still others may prefer more leisure to more work, as a result of progressive taxes. The net result is hard to evaluate. We shall return to this problem in Parts Four and Six.

The effects of progressive tax rates on *risky* investment could be quite adverse. In part, the government says to the taxpayer, "Heads I win, tails you lose." But recent reforms have improved the taxpayer's ability to "carry forward" or "carry backward" his losses, and also to spread out an extraordinarily high income by averaging it with the previous 4 years' income, thereby moderating greatly the penalty for erratic earnings from venturesome investment.

Careful studies at the Harvard Business School, cited in Chapter 31, confirm what has just been said—that there are, in fact, sufficient perfectly respectable "loopholes" open to wealthy people so that they may typically pay but 50 per cent tax rates, not the higher rates shown in the table. They take risks and try for lightly taxed capital gains;[3] they invest in tax-exempt municipal bonds; they drill for oil, grow trees, or feed beef cattle—all more lightly taxed.

Opposing any unfavorable effect of progressive taxes on investments, jobs, and national growth, there is an offsetting effect. To the extent that dollars are taken from frugal wealthy people who spend small fractions of their extra dollars, and are not taken from poor ready spenders, progressive taxes may tend to keep spending power at a high level—at too high a level if inflation is threatening. But statistics on how people spend extra dollars, as we shall later see, suggest that this effect on total spending may not be very great.

[3] When we remember the loopholes discussed in this study, which show how the well-to-do can hope to convert heavily taxed income into lightly taxed capital gains from risky ventures, we find that *high tax rates may encourage risk taking by those who seek capital gains* and who know that Uncle Sam finances up to 65 per cent of their deductible costs.

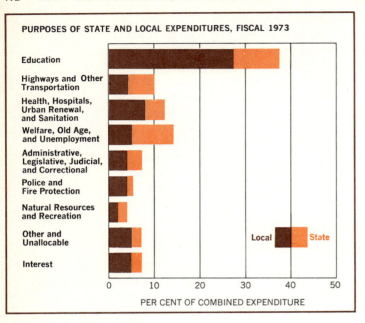

PURPOSES OF STATE AND LOCAL EXPENDITURES, FISCAL 1973

Education

Highways and Other
Transportation

Health, Hospitals,
Urban Renewal,
and Sanitation

Welfare, Old Age,
and Unemployment

Administrative,
Legislative, Judicial,
and Correctional

Police and
Fire Protection

Natural Resources
and Recreation

Other and
Unallocable

Interest

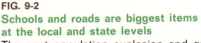

Local    State

0    10    20    30    40    50
PER CENT OF COMBINED EXPENDITURE

**FIG. 9-2**

**Schools and roads are biggest items at the local and state levels**

The past population explosion and growing welfare programs put a strain on local and state finance. Only federal revenue-sharing can meet the gaps. (Source: U.S. Bureau of the Census.)

Economic science can point out these various crosscurrents of progressive taxation. In the end, voters must try to judge the costs and decide on ethical grounds whether they favor a more or less egalitarian society, greater or smaller rewards to provide incentives for initiative.

### STATE AND LOCAL EXPENDITURES

Turn now to public finance other than federal. Although quantitatively the federal government's multi-billion-dollar expenditures exceed those of the states and localities, still these are important in their own right.

To see what the states and localities spend their money on, look at Fig. 9-2. All these items are more or less self-explanatory. Expenditure on schools—historically, mostly by localities—is the biggest single item by far.[4]

### STATE AND LOCAL TAXES

To see the main sources of funds to finance such expenditures, turn to Fig. 9-3 and its table. In terms of the previous discussion of kinds of taxes, the principal taxes of the states and localities are "regressive taxes."

**Property tax**    Note that the property tax still accounts for almost half the total revenues of state and local finance. The diagram and table in Fig. 9-3 show it is mainly the localities that levy property taxes.

The property tax is levied primarily on real estate—land and buildings. Each locality

---

[4] These data represent *net* direct expenditure by state and local governments. Funds transferred by the state to the local governments and spent by them are counted only once, as local expenditure.

sets an annual tax rate. In a large city, $55 on each $1,000 of assessed valuation (5.5 per cent, or 55 mils) might be the rate. If my house has been assessed at $10,000, my tax is $550. However, in many places assessed valuations tend to be but a fraction of true market value. Houses like mine may have a market value of $20,000, but be assessed at half that. My true tax rate is then less than 5.5 per cent. (The average U.S. property-tax payment varies from state to state: in the 1970s, the average in affluent California is five times that in South Carolina.)

In colonial days, a man's total income and wealth may have been connected with real estate; if so, the effect of a tax on such property would have been about the same as a proportional tax on income. Today, when so much of wealth and income is divorced from real estate, the property tax may be regressive relative to income—especially since small properties tend to be assessed relatively higher than large.

The property tax is rather inflexible. Assessments and rates change slowly. In bad times, when real-estate values fall, the property tax is burdensome, giving rise to bankruptcy, mortgage foreclosures, and forced sales. In the zooming contemporary economy, valuations and rates have been edging up. Court cases now pending are likely to create a crisis for the property tax: Affluent districts may have to help equalize school expenditures for poor districts; pressure for new revenue sharing by the federal government therefore mounts.

**Highway-user taxes**    As the name suggests, these revenues come from two primary sources: from a tax on gasoline and from use fees on trucks, autos, and drivers. In many states, more is collected in this way than is spent on roads. The extra revenues are used for schools or old-age pensions or general government purposes, just as some colleges use profits from football games to buy fencing foils or even Greek manuscripts.

Highway and airplane taxes are usually justified on the ground that the taxpayer

| STATE AND LOCAL TAXES AND OTHER REVENUES, FISCAL 1973 (in billions of dollars) | | | |
|---|---|---|---|
| **SOURCE** | | **STATE** | **LOCAL** |
| Taxes | | $ 68.1 | $ 53.0 |
| Property | $ 1.3 | | $44.0 |
| Other | 66.8 | | 9.3 |
| Aid from federal government | | 31.4 | 7.9 |
| Aid from state government | | | 40.0 |
| Fees and misc. | | 30.3 | 28.2 |
| Net total | | $129.8 | $129.1 |

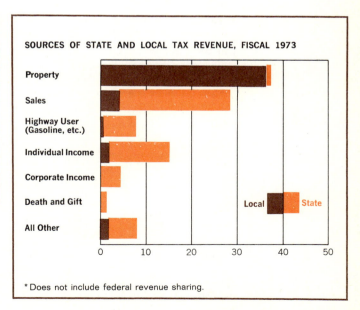

SOURCES OF STATE AND LOCAL TAX REVENUE, FISCAL 1973

Property
Sales
Highway User (Gasoline, etc.)
Individual Income
Corporate Income
Death and Gift
All Other

Local    State

0    10    20    30    40    50

*Does not include federal revenue sharing.

**FIG. 9-3**
**Property and sales taxes still dominate at state and municipal levels**
Most local and state taxes are hard to expand. (Source: U.S. Bureau of the Census.)

is simply paying for his *benefit* from using the roads and airports in much the same way that he pays for a railroad ticket or for his use of water and electricity.

**Sales taxes**   States are getting more and more revenue from general retail sales taxes. Each purchase at the department, drug, or grocery store pays a percentage tax. (Sometimes food and medicines are exempt.) Also, states usually add their own liquor and tobacco excises to the federal excises. (Some cities get into this act.) Most people—including many cigarette smokers and moderate drinkers—feel vaguely that there is something immoral about tobacco and alcohol. They somehow think two birds are being killed with one stone when these are taxed; the state gets revenue, and vice is made more expensive. (Note the element of self-contradiction here.)

The same moral attitude would hardly apply to a 5 per cent tax on everything a consumer buys: shoes, soap, a church candle. Rich and poor are taxed alike on each dollar spent: since the poor are forced to spend a larger fraction of their total dollars, one sees that a sales tax on nonluxuries is a regressive tax, taking a larger fraction of low than of high incomes.

**Payroll and business taxes**   States and localities often charge organizations license fees for their privilege of acting as a corporation, running a tavern, and so forth. Some states tax the net income of a corporation as well, and collect miscellaneous other fees from business enterprises.

In addition, all states have been bribed by the offer of federal aid into collecting a wage tax up to 3.28 per cent of payrolls in most occupations. The proceeds are used to provide "unemployment compensation benefits or insurance" when workers become unemployed.

**Personal income and inheritance taxes**   More than half the states imitate the federal government, but on a much smaller scale, by taxing individuals according to the size of their incomes. Such a method of taxation has already been discussed in connection with federal finance. A few states, such as New Hampshire, do not rely at all on this relatively progressive tax.

Inheritance taxes on individuals who inherit bequests of property upon the death of a relative or friend are self-explanatory. They differ only in minor detail from estate taxes that are levied on the dead giver's estate. Gifts too are taxed, since wealthy people have every incentive to distribute their wealth before death to escape taxation.

Both the federal and the state governments share in estate and inheritance taxes. The federal government tries to act to prevent states such as Florida from advertising to older people, "Come here to die and avoid all inheritance taxes." The federal government gives up part of its revenues to any state that passes an inheritance tax and accepts a state tax receipt as part payment of a citizen's federal estate taxes.

The inheritance and estate tax is called a progressive tax. The poor widow's inheritance usually pays no tax at all because of liberal exemptions, while the rich man's estate pays at a progressive rate. Social reformers attach great importance to death taxes for the purpose of preventing the development of a permanent moneyed caste, living not on its effort and intelligence, but on its property inherited from one generation to the next. Yet, in the 1970s the right to "split income," to make gifts, to set up complex "trusts," to escape capital-gains tax at death, and to bequeath tax-free insurance policies—all these have reduced death-tax collections to a low level. (This is also happening in Great Britain.)

There are other miscellaneous revenues. Some localities sell gas, water, and electricity. Some, especially in Nevada, tax slot machines and racetrack betting. All collect some revenue from assessments on property owners who benefit from specific sewage and road improvements.

### INTERGOVERNMENTAL GRANTS-IN-AID

An important revenue source is the financial aid that states receive from the federal government and that localities receive from the states.

Having access to more revenue sources, the federal government has increasingly been making grants to the states, and in lesser degrees to the localities. These are primarily for highways, public welfare assistance, and education. They help in part to offset the great regional differences in real incomes, as between North and South.

**Federal revenue sharing**    Because local and state needs burgeon while their tax systems are inflexible, recourse is made to the federal tax system that provides the only expansibility in the system. Congress now votes massive grants to the states and localities, some of which are unconditional but some allocated for particular functions. Such revenue sharing has been long followed in Canada and Australia. Undoubtedly this trend will grow.

Similarly, within the states there have been grants-in-aid to the localities—primarily for schools, highways, and public assistance (relief, old-age pensions, and so forth). Only in this way can the poorer parts of each state maintain certain minimum standards of schooling, roads, and living. In this way, well-to-do suburbanites who have fled the city are made to share the burden.

Despite these grants-in-aid, there remain sizable differentials in minimum standards. It still matters where one is born.

### CONCLUSION: THE THORNY PROBLEM OF TAX INCIDENCE

In ending this survey of taxes and other revenues, let us note a few warnings. Even if the electorate has made up its mind about how the tax burden shall be borne by individuals, the following difficult problems remain:

Who ultimately pays a particular tax? Does its burden stay on the person on whom it is first levied? One cannot assume that the person Congress *says* a tax is levied on will end up paying that tax. He may be able to *shift* the tax: shift it "forward" on his customers by raising his price as much as the tax; or shift it "backward" on his suppliers (wage earners, rent and interest receivers) who end up being able to charge him less than they would have done had there been no tax.

Economists therefore say: We must study the final *incidence* of the tax—the way its burden ultimately is borne, the totality of its effects on commodity prices, factor-prices, resource allocations, efforts, and composition of production and consumption. Tax incidence, thus, is no easy problem and requires all the advanced tools of economics to help toward its solution.

EXAMPLE: Does a tax on wheat raise the price to the consumer by as much as itself, so that the incidence is on the consumer? Or does the tax raise the price by half itself or not at all, so that the incidence is partially or wholly on the producers? Does it change oat prices? And does the tax kill off much of wheat production, so that it is having incidence effects beyond those which show up in money prices and wages and even beyond the burdens that you can allocate among the different citizens?

Parts Three and Four will develop some of the important tools that one needs to begin to tackle this thorny problem. Economists are not yet in agreement on final results. Some think the corporate income tax falls mostly on the consumer; some argue it falls mostly on stockholders or capitalists.

Figure 9-4 reports on a valiant statistical attempt to determine how progressive or regressive our over-all tax and expenditure system is. Experts agree that the results of such a study can be only approximate, since no one knows just how a corporate or other tax gets shifted. Even an expert is not a magician capable of making a controlled experiment in which he (a) measures things without taxes, then (b) measures things with taxes, and finally (c) determines tax incidence as the difference between these situations.

Note the regressiveness at the beginning as the poor pay out a disproportionate amount in taxes. Note the lack of any progressive tax around the median-income level. The very affluent do get taxed to help the poor, but the man in the comfortable middle

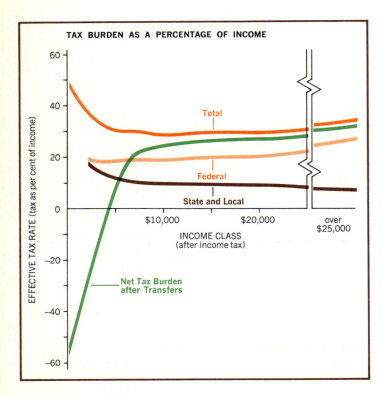

**FIG. 9-4**

**Experts try to answer the key questions: Who pays the taxes? Who gets benefits?** The orange and brown curves show tax burdens; the green curve adjusts these for transfer benefits received by income classes. Note that there is little progression of total tax burden at middle-income levels, as shown by horizontal character of solid orange curve. Fortunately, if non-money income items were included—owner-occupied housing by elderly, farm produce for farm families, etc.—initial regressiveness would be lowered. [Source: R. A. Herriot and H. P. Miller, "The Taxes We Pay (1968)," in the *Conference Board Record* (May, 1971). WARNING: Experts cannot agree on one tax-shifting pattern; so results are only indicative.]

is something of an overlooked man when it comes to tax burden. As the green curve in Fig. 9-4 shows, when we consider which income classes *benefit* from government expenditure, the needy do show a more favorable "net incidence" than the affluent. With a negative income tax and federal revenue sharing, net incidence would be even more progressive.[5]

[5]All Fig. 9-4 data do depend on heroic assumptions that can be questioned. Thus, if we count in nonmoney income items, the orange curve would start only half as high on the left, and the schedule would be less regressive. Further, not all public finance experts would agree on how the property tax is shifted onto renters, or on how the corporate income tax is shifted.

### SUMMARY

1   Taxes give the government the resources it needs for its *public goods*. Taxes also finance *welfare transfer* expenditures that change the distribution of income; and the over-all way taxes are levied affects the final distribution of incomes among people.

2   Notions of "benefits" and "proper sacrifice or redistribution" are two principal theories of taxation. Justice implies taxing equals equally, unequals unequally. Direct and progressively graduated taxes on incomes are in contrast to indirect and regressive excises.

3   About three-fifths of federal revenue comes from personal and corporation income taxes. The rest comes from "regressive taxes" on payrolls and excises. The personal income tax, except for loopholes and erosion of the tax base, is progressive, tending to redistribute income from rich to poor.

4   State and local expenditures have been rising in the modern era: the principal items are education, highways, public welfare, and the ordinary police and safety functions of government.

5   The property tax is the most important source of local revenue. Sales taxes and excises are important for the state. Also states and localities have been spending more than they tax, thereby increasing their debts.

6   The federal government gives large grants to the states, primarily for highways, matching grants-in-aid for social welfare and education. Many advocate further revenue sharing. The states help the localities—primarily in education, highways, and public assistance.

7   The incidence of a tax is its ultimate division of burden, its total effect on prices and other economic magnitudes. Those upon whom a tax is first levied may succeed in shifting part of its burden forward or backward. The tools of Parts Three and Four will help in tackling this difficult problem. Progression in benefits offsets in part the regressive sag of our tax structure at middle-income levels.

## CONCEPTS FOR REVIEW

benefit and sacrifice notions

direct and indirect taxes

progressive, proportional,
    regressive taxes

state and local expenditures

state and local taxes

grants-in-aid, unconditional
    revenue sharing

budget surpluses and deficits

tax incidence and shifting

## QUESTIONS FOR DISCUSSION

1   Make a list of different taxes in order of their progressiveness. What is the importance of each at the federal, state, and local levels?

2   List different state and local expenditure categories in order of quantitative importance. Compare with federal expenditure categories of Chapter 8's Table 8-2.

3   How do you think different government functions should be allocated among the three levels of government? How about revenues and grants-in-aid?

4   Should a citizen in Massachusetts be taxed to help a citizen in Arkansas? To help a citizen in Vermont? In Massachusetts? In Mexico or India?

5   "Since people don't change their smoking habits as a result of taxation, and since the poor smoke, a tax on cigarettes is really no different from a tax on bread." Do you agree? If so, what ought to be done?

6   From Table 9-2, calculate the personal income tax paid by a typical doctor, lawyer, teacher, stenographer, mechanic, and carpenter.

7   Debate VAT pro and con.

8   "More kids and cars mean local expenditure and debt." Evaluate.

9   Should marijuana be made legal and taxed to raise revenue? Should gambling be made legal everywhere, as it is in Nevada, to provide a cheerful source of tax revenues? Should bingo be legalized and taxed? Many foreign countries operate lotteries (like the New Hampshire and New York State sweepstakes). The Russians, instead of paying high interest on government bonds, give prizes to those who draw lucky numbers. Do you approve of such revenue sources? Might they lead to corruption in politics and gangsterism, or will they supplant criminal gambling?

One of the most important concepts in all economics is the national income—or, technically, the gross national product (GNP). This measures the economic performance of the whole economy. Of course, man does not live by bread alone. Nor does society live by GNP alone. But on our way to the state of affluence where material well-being will fall to the second level of significance, we do need a summary measure of aggregate economic performance.

This chapter's discussion of national income can serve as the unifying summary of Part One's introduction to the *basic economic processes and institutions* of modern mixed societies. Alternatively, this analysis of national income, its anatomy and accounting structure, can be regarded as the introduction to the treatment of macro-economics of Part Two—the study of the physiological forces that determine total employment, production, real income, and the price level. The concept of national income is indispensable preparation for tackling the great issues of unemployment, inflation, and growth. In these days, however, there is concern lest mere material growth be at the expense of the quality of life and the ecological environment. Hence, we must break new ground to devise ways of correcting and converting the GNP concept into a better measure of NEW—net economic welfare.

## THE YARDSTICK OF AN ECONOMY'S PERFORMANCE

What is national income? It is the loose name we give to the money measure of the over-all annual flow of goods and services in an economy. Often, instead of it, we use the almost equivalent precise term "national product" or "net national product" (NNP);[1] or the slightly different concept of "gross national product" (GNP).

If you asked an economic historian just what the Great Depression

[1] We shall note later the special, narrow use of the term "national income" in official data.

"The time has come,"
  the Walrus said,
"To talk of many things:
Of shoes—and ships—
  and sealing wax—
Of cabbages—and kings—"
LEWIS CARROLL

Our society can be viewed as a complex machine for transforming high-grade energy, called fuel, into low-grade energy, called waste heat, while extracting the energy required to produce the goods and services we call the GNP.
NATIONAL SCIENCE FOUNDATION

really meant, his best brief answer would be: "From a 1929 NNP of $95.2 billion, there was a drop to a 1933 NNP of $48.6 billion. This halving of the money value of the flow of goods and services in the American economy caused hardship, bank failures, riots, and political turmoil."

In brief, national income or product is the final figure you arrive at when you apply the measuring rod of money to the diverse apples, oranges, and machines that any society produces with its land, labor, and capital resources.

Everyone has heard of GNP, gross national product. To understand it, we will first discuss NNP, net national product. The two will be shown to differ only by the item of depreciation of capital equipment and buildings. So, for the next few sections, we shall be ignoring this complication. We shall speak of NNP, but the reader can treat this as interchangeable with GNP. Later we shall amplify NNP and speak of GNP.

## TWO MEASURES OF NATIONAL PRODUCT: AS GOODS-FLOW OR EARNINGS-FLOW

How do we measure the net national product, NNP? The general idea is simple. Figure 10-1 shows the circular flow of dollar spending in an economy with no government and no accumulation of capital or net saving going on.

Flow-of-product approach    Each year the public consumes goods and services: goods such as apples, oranges, and bread; services such as health care or haircuts. The public

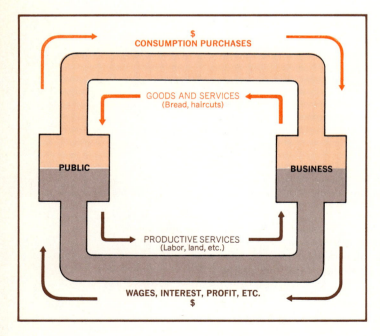

**FIG. 10-1**
**National product is flow of product or, equally, is flow of costs**
In the upper loop, people spend their money on final goods: the total dollar flow of these per year is one measure of net national product, NNP.

The lower loop measures the annual flow of costs of output: the earnings that business pays out in wages, rent, interest, dividends, and accrued profits. With profit properly reckoned as a residual, the two measures of NNP must always be identical. (Same will be true of GNP.)

spends dollars for these consumer goods, as in the upper loop of Fig. 10-1. We add together all the consumption dollars spent for these final goods to arrive at the total of NNP.

Thus, in our simple economy, one can easily calculate national income or product as the sum of the annual flow of final goods and services: (prices of oranges × number of oranges) + (price of apples × number of apples) + ⋯.

Why use market prices as weights in evaluating and summing diverse physical commodities and services? Because, as we shall see in Part Three, market prices are reflectors of the relative desirability of diverse goods and services.

**The *net national product,* or "national income evaluated at market prices," as NNP is technically named, is definable as the total money value of the *flow of final products* of the community.**[2]

**Earnings or income approach**   There is a second, equivalent way to calculate NNP in so simple an economy. Go to the lower loop in Fig. 10-1: What is the total cost of output which business is paying out to the public? It is paying out wages, interest, rents, and profit. Why? Because these factor earnings of land, labor, and capital are the *costs* of production of the flow of product. (NOTE: Here the economist, unlike the accountant, does count profit as a cost or earning item.)

The statistician can measure the annual flow of such factor earnings or income in the lower loop.[3] In this way, he will *again* arrive at the NNP.

**Net national product is also definable, from a second viewpoint, as the total of factor earnings (wages, interest, rents, and accruing profits) that are the *costs of production* of society's final goods.**

Now we have calculated NNP by the upper-loop flow-of-product approach and by the lower-loop earnings-flow approach. Which is greater? Answer: They will be *exactly* the same.

Here is the reason for this identity. Recall that we have included "profit" in the lower loop—along with wages, interest, and rents. What exactly is profit? Profit is what you have left over from the sale of product (your oranges, apples, bread, and haircuts) *after* you have paid the other factor-costs—wages, interest, rents. *So profit automatically is the residual that takes on the size needed to make the lower-loop approach via earnings* exactly *match the upper-loop approach via flow of goods.*

This all reflects the useful device of double-entry which accountants use to keep the two sides of their books in perfect balance.

**To sum up: NNP, or net national product, is measurable as the flow of product; but it is also convenient for the statistician to measure it via the earnings approach in the lower loop. With the proper definition of profit and its inclusion as an economic earning and cost, each approach will yield exactly the same NNP.**

[2] In our first, simplest model, the only final product is private consumption expenditures. But in a moment we shall see that government expenditures on goods and services and private net investment are also to be included.

[3] When we leave our simple model, taxes (and government transfer items) have to be introduced.

An example will show how to go from business accounts to national accounts in the simplest case, without government and investment, and where all final products are produced from land, labor, and capital in 10 million identical, one-stage firms or farms.

| INCOME STATEMENT OF TYPICAL FARM | | | |
|---|---|---|---|
| OUTPUT ATTRIBUTABLE TO FARMING | | EARNINGS | |
| Sales of goods (wheat, apples, etc.) | $1,000 | Costs of production | |
| | | Wages | $  800 |
| | | Rents | 100 |
| | | Interest | 25 |
| | | Profit (residual) | 75 |
| **Total** | **$1,000** | **Total** | **$1,000** |

Adding all the 10 million farms gives the NNP account easily in this trivial case.

| NATIONAL PRODUCT ACCOUNT (in millions!) | | | |
|---|---|---|---|
| UPPER-LOOP FLOW OF PRODUCT | | LOWER-LOOP EARNINGS OR INCOMES | |
| Final output (10 × 1,000) | $10,000 | Wages (10 × 800) | $  8,000 |
| | | Rents (10 × 100) | 1,000 |
| | | Interest (10 × 25) | 250 |
| | | Profit (10 × 75) | 750 |
| **NNP total** | **$10,000** | **NNP total** | **$10,000** |

Note that the definition of profit makes the firm's two sides balance; hence the two NNP approaches must still match after summation.

## REAL VERSUS MONEY NATIONAL PRODUCT: USING A PRICE INDEX TO "DEFLATE"

We saw that NNP uses the measuring rod of money prices in the market to combine diverse apples, oranges, and other goods to a single total figure. But one would hardly choose to measure things with a rubber rather than a wooden yardstick—one that stretched in your hands from day to day.

This is one of the problems economists have to solve when they use money as their measuring rod. Everyone knows that inflations and deflations can send most prices up or down. Or, as the economist puts it, "The value of money does change between years like 1929 and 1933, 1939 and 1978, or 1979 and 1980."

What can be done about this? Economists can repair most of the damage due to the changeability of our measuring rod by using an *index number of prices*.[4] A 1929–1933 comparison will illustrate the process by which one uses a price index number

---

[4]Computing a price index would be easy if all prices were to change by the same percentage. When all *P*s triple, the index rises from 100 to 300; when all halve, it drops to 50. If *P*s increase in different degrees, but all end up between double and triple their base, the index is certainly between 200 and 300. Just where? Evidently we need some kind of *average* of the price changes, each being *weighted* in accordance with its approximate economic *importance*. The official indexes are good

| SAMPLE CALCULATION OF REAL NNP | | |
|---|---|---|
| DATE | (1)<br>MONEY NNP<br>(billions of<br>current<br>dollars) | (2)<br>INDEX<br>NUMBER<br>OF PRICES | (3)<br>REAL NNP<br>(billions of<br>1929 dollars)<br>$(3) = \frac{(1)}{(2)} \times 100$ |
| 1929 | 96 | 100 | $\frac{96}{100} \times 100 = 96$ |
| 1933 | 48 | 75 | $\frac{48}{75} \times 100 = 64$ |

**TABLE 10-1**

**To convert money NNP into real NNP, we deflate by dividing by price index**

Using price index of Column (2), we deflate Column (1) to get real NNP, Column (3). (RIDDLE: Can you show that 1929's real NNP was $72 billion in terms of 1933 prices? HINT: With 1933 as a base, 1929's price index is $133\frac{1}{3}$.) The exact same method of deflation will work for GNP as for NNP.

to "deflate" a "current *money* NNP," converting it into a "*real* NNP in terms of dollars of unchanged 1929 purchasing power."

Table 10-1 gives the actual 1929 and 1933 NNP figures to the close approximations of $96 and $48 billion. It shows a halving of money NNP. But the government estimates that prices of goods and services dropped on the average about 25 per cent in the Depression. Using 1929 as a base of 100, this means the 1933 price index was about 75. So our $48-billion 1933 NNP was really worth somewhat more than half the $96-billion NNP of 1929.

How much more? Table 10-1 divides through by the price index number to "deflate," and shows that "*real NNP*" *fell only to two-thirds the 1929 level:* thus, in terms of dollars of 1929 purchasing power, real NNP fell down to $64 billion. Hence, part of the halving shown by the *money* NNP was due to the optical illusion of the changing price yardstick.

Figure 10-2 on the next page shows in brown the history of *money* NNP (or "nominal" NNP, expressed in the actual dollars and prices that were current in each historical year). Then, for comparison, the *real* NNP (expressed in 1958 dollars) is shown in orange. Note that part of the increase in money NNP is really spurious, being due merely to inflation in the last 40 years of our money yardstick's price units.

### AVOIDING "DOUBLE COUNTING" OF INTERMEDIATE GOODS

Returning to current money figures, we can now show how to handle "intermediate" goods (which are not truly *final* goods) and thus avoid counting anything two, three, or more times.

**Ignoring intermediate goods**  We do want to count bread in NNP, but we must *avoid also counting in the dough that goes to make the bread*. That would indeed be double counting, since the only reason we want the dough is for the final bread. Turn back

---

approximations, but some basic problems remain: getting an accurate sample of prices; allowing for quality improvements; deciding which average to use (arithmetic or geometric mean, median, etc.); defining relative-economic-importance weights, in a statical and in a changing world. Note that the average price change of the goods a poor man buys might be different from the index appropriate for a rich man—because necessities and luxuries may show different rates of inflation.

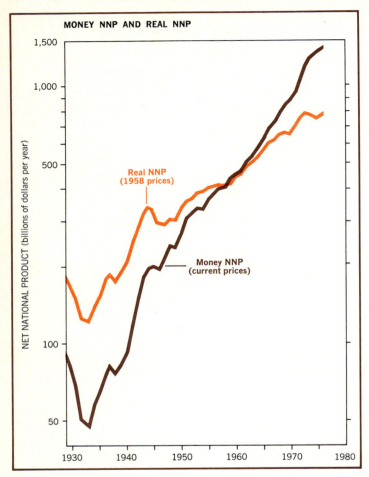

**MONEY NNP AND REAL NNP**

**FIG. 10-2**
**Money NNP grows faster than real NNP because of spurious price inflation**
The rise in money NNP since the Depression and World War II exaggerates the rise in real NNP: because the price index has generally been rising since then, we must use price index to deflate the money NNP in order to arrive at the real NNP trends.

to the two-loop Fig. 10-1. You could find bread (and haircuts) there; but you won't find any dough, flour, or wheat. Where are they? These are so-called "intermediate products" that are produced during all the stages leading up to the final bread product, and they are hidden in the block marked "business." That is as it should be. We don't want intermediate products to be double-counted along with the final product.

**Using "value added" to avoid double counting**   A new statistician who is being trained to make NNP measurements might be puzzled, saying:

I can see that, if you are careful, your upper-loop approach to NNP will avoid including intermediate products. But I'm a little uncertain whether or not you might find yourself in some trouble when you use the lower-loop approach. After all, don't we at the Commerce Department gather income statements from the accounts of firms? Won't we then be picking up what millers pay to farmers, what bakers pay to millers, and what grocers pay to bakers? Won't this result in double counting or even triple and quadruple counting of some items that go through several productive stages?

**TABLE 10-2**

**NNP is the summation of "value added" of all the separate production stages**

To avoid double counting of intermediate products, we carefully calculate value added at each stage, subtracting all the costs of materials and intermediate products not produced in that stage but bought from other business firms. Note that every black intermediate-product item appears both in Column (1) and with opposite sign in Column (2); hence it is canceled out.

| | (1) | | (2) | | (3) VALUE ADDED (wages, profit, etc.) |
| BREAD RECEIPTS, COSTS, AND VALUE ADDED (in cents per loaf) | | | | | |
| STAGE OF PRODUCTION | SALES RECEIPTS | | COST OF INTER-MEDIATE MATE-RIALS OR GOODS | | (3) = (1) − (2) |
| Wheat | 8 | − | 0 | = | 8 |
| Flour | 11 | − | 8 | = | 3 |
| Baked dough | 20 | − | 11 | = | 9 |
| Delivered bread | 30 | − | 20 | = | 10 |
| | 69 | − | 39 | = | 30 (sum of value added) |

This is a legitimate question. Fortunately, we can give it a satisfactory answer. The statistician making lower-loop earnings or factor-cost measurements should always be very careful to use what he calls the "value-added" approach.[5]

The value-added approach refuses to include *all* the expenses shown on each firm's business income statement in the lower-loop factor earnings. Which expenses are excluded? All purchases of materials and services from *other* firms are excluded, because those dollars will get properly counted in NNP from the reports of *other* firms.

EXAMPLE: Apex Co. buys electric power from the Edison Co. This expense on the Apex income statement is *not* included in value added. Why should it be? It is not a wage, interest, rent, or profit payment. In fact, it is not a payment to any Apex productive factor; hence it never shows up at all in Apex's own contribution to the lower loop. It stays inside the business block, where it and all other such expenditures by this firm Apex on intermediate goods are carefully subtracted from the firm's receipts. What is left? Apex's true value added—which is exactly the sum of *its* wage, interest, rent, and profit costs.

Mind you, the electric power was produced by the Edison workers—and by the Edison interest, rent, and profit receivers. So do not fear that this electrical activity will get overlooked by the NNP statistician. It will not. He will pick it up in the lower loop as the value added of the Edison Co. This is as it should be: we want to count each thing once, not twice or three times.

Table 10-2 illustrates by means of the several stages of a loaf of bread how careful adherence to the value-added approach will enable us to subtract the intermediate expenses that show up in the income statements of farmers, millers, bakers, and grocers—ending up with the desired equality between (*a*) net value of final bread and (*b*) the lower-loop factor-costs embodying the sum of the red value-added data of all stages. All this can be summarized as follows:

---

[5] Perhaps recall at this point VAT, the value-added tax of Chapter 9's page 168. Unlike a turnover tax that hits all intermediate goods as many times as they are in exchanged goods—wheat in flour, wheat in dough, wheat in bread (along, of course, with wheat in wheat!)—VAT taxes only each stage's own wage, profit, and other costs (its value added). To accomplish this, it lets firms subtract out the costs they pay for materials from earlier production stages.

*Value-added approach.* To avoid double counting, we take care to include in net national product only final goods, and not the intermediate goods that go to make the final goods. By resolutely sticking to the *value added* at each stage, taking care to subtract expenditures on the intermediate goods bought from other firms, the lower-loop earnings approach properly avoids all double counting and records wages, interest, rent, and profit exactly one time.

Our earlier example with 10 million farmers can now have added to it 10 million second-stage manufacturers, who buy wheat and farm goods and add value to them by processing them into bread and other final products by the use of labor, land, and capital. Alongside the farmer's income statement on page 182 we have the manufacturer's income statement.

| INCOME STATEMENT OF TYPICAL MANUFACTURER | | | |
|---|---|---|---|
| **OUTPUT ATTRIBUTABLE TO MANUFACTURING** | | **EARNINGS** | |
| Sales of goods | $5,000 | Costs or "value added" | |
| Minus goods bought from other | | Wages | $3,500 |
| firms | −1,000 | Rent | 100 |
| | | Interest | 100 |
| | | Profit (residual) | 300 |
| **Total** | **$4,000** | **Total** | **$4,000** |

To get total NNP for society, we can add the bottom items of the left-hand sides of the 10 million farmers *and* 10 million bakers; or to get lower-loop rather than upper-loop NNP, we add all the right-hand items for *all* these 20 million firms.

| NATIONAL PRODUCT ACCOUNT (in millions) | | | |
|---|---|---|---|
| **UPPER-LOOP FLOW OF PRODUCT** | | **LOWER-LOOP EARNINGS OR INCOMES** | |
| Final output (finished bread, etc.) | | Wages (8,000 + 35,000) | $43,000 |
| [50,000 = 10,000 (on farms) | | Rent (1,000 + 1,000) | 2,000 |
| + (50,000 − 10,000) | $50,000 | Interest (250 + 1,000) | 1,250 |
| (in manufacturing)] | | Profit (750 + 3,000) | 3,750 |
| **NNP total** | **$50,000** | **NNP total** | **$50,000** |

## NET INVESTMENT, CAPITAL FORMATION

So far, we have banished all capital growth from our discussion. We talked of people as wanting currently to consume bread, apples, oranges, and haircuts.[6] In real life, however, people often want to devote part of their income to saving and investment. Instead of eating more bread *now*, they will want to build new machines to make it possible to produce more bread for *future* consumption; and they may want to add

---

[6]Indeed, the economic statistician counts in the NNP all consumption items that people want to spend *their* incomes on. He draws the line only at illegal expenditures, e.g., opium consumption or prostitution (but not at alcohol, cigarettes, bubble gum, or legal vices some moralists deplore). During World War II when black-market operations were important, he found it necessary in some countries to supplement his statistics with estimates of black-market money transactions.

to the inventory of bread, dough, flour, and wheat. In short, we must recognize that the final goals of people do include net investment or capital formation, not simply current consumption.

If people are using part of society's production possibilities for capital formation rather than consumption, the economic statistician recognizes that he must include such outputs in his upper-loop flow of NNP. So really, we must modify our original definition to read:

**Net national product is the sum of *all* final products, such as consumption goods and services, and including also *net* investment.**

This net investment (or net capital formation) will include the net additions to our stock of (1) buildings, (2) equipment, and (3) inventories.

WARNING: To economists, investment always means real capital formation—production of added goods in inventories, or production of new plants, houses, and tools. To the layman, investment means merely using money to buy an outstanding share of General Motors stock, to buy a corner lot, to open a savings account. It is important not to confuse these meanings: If I take $1,000 from my safe and now put it in the bank or buy a common stock from a broker, the economist says that neither investment nor saving has gone up from this act alone. Only if some physical capital formation takes place is there investment; only if society consumes less than its income, devoting resources to capital formation, is there saving.

Now the time has come to go from NNP to GNP—to take into account depreciation of capital goods.

## NET INVESTMENT EQUALS GROSS INVESTMENT MINUS DEPRECIATION

How does the economist get accurate figures on net investment?

First he has to make estimates of inventories and of their changes. Harder still is his task of estimating net investment in buildings and equipment.

Why can't he just jot down *all* the buildings built and *all* the machines produced, add them in with his calculated net inventory change, and let it go at that? He does indeed make such a calculation. But the resulting figure is too large—*too gross*. Recognizing this, he gives a new name to the result, namely, "gross investment" rather than "net investment."

Why the word "gross"? The statistician uses this word to emphasize that he has not yet made any *allowances for the using up of capital,* i.e., no allowance for capital *depreciation.* (Recall the accounting appendix of Chapter 6.)

One would not think much of a statistician who estimated the change in human population by ignoring deaths. If he just added up gross births without subtracting a good estimate for deaths, he would get an exaggerated notion of the net change in population. The same holds for economic equipment and buildings: Net change is always gross births (of capital) minus deaths (or capital depreciation).

*Definition:* **Net investment always equals gross investment minus depreciation.**

Table 10-3 on the next page gives typical figures relating net and gross investment. They differ only by depreciation; and fortunately, depreciation is a sluggish item that grows only slowly over a period of a few years. That is why many forecasters, who

| GROSS AND NET INVESTMENT (in billions of dollars) | | | | |
|---|---|---|---|---|
| INVESTMENT COMPONENTS | 1929 | 1933 | 1946 | 1974 |
| New construction | $ 8.9 | $ 1.5 | $14.0 | $ 98.1 |
| Producers' durable equipment | 5.6 | 1.5 | 10.2 | 97.4 |
| Change in business inventories | 1.7 | −1.6 | 6.4 | 13.4 |
| **Gross private domestic investment** | **$16.2** | **$ 1.4** | **$30.6** | **$ 208.9** |
| Allowances for depreciation or capital consumption (also = difference between GNP and NNP) | −7.9 | −7.0 | −9.9 | −119.5 |
| **Net private domestic investment** | **$ 8.3** | **$ −5.6** | **$20.7** | **$ 89.4** |

**TABLE 10-3**

**To go from gross to net investment, we subtract depreciation of capital** Gross births minus deaths equals any population's change. Similarly, net capital formation (or net investment) will equal gross capital formation (gross investment in all new capital goods) minus depreciation allowance for used up capital goods. (Source: U.S. Department of Commerce, which separately calculates data on foreign investment.)

really are interested in net investment, are satisfied to work with the gross investment figures, which are easier to find in the newspapers and official statistics.

## GROSS NATIONAL PRODUCT VERSUS NET NATIONAL PRODUCT

Gross investment can be estimated fairly accurately, involving no difficult depreciation estimate. For this reason governments and the United Nations sensibly decided to calculate a gross national product figure *first* rather than a net national product figure.

Gross national product (GNP) is defined as the sum of final products such as consumption goods and *gross* investment (which is the increase in inventories plus *gross* births or production of buildings and equipment). GNP = NNP + Depreciation.

The official statistics do present NNP data at stated intervals. Generally, though, they concentrate on GNP, for the good reason that depreciation cannot be quickly and accurately measured each quarter. Table 10-3 suggests it will be easy enough to go from GNP to NNP, or vice versa, once we know the total depreciation figure that is to be subtracted or added.[7] Even if the economist is ultimately interested in net measures, he is content to work from day to day with GNP data, knowing that the two concepts do move together closely during any period that is not too long.

## GOVERNMENT EXPENDITURE ON GOODS AND SERVICES

Until now we have ignored government. We have talked about consumers but ignored the biggest consumer of all, namely, the federal, state, and local governments. Somehow NNP and GNP must take into account the billions of dollars of product that a nation collectively consumes or invests. How?

After some debate, the income statisticians of the United States and United Nations decided on using the simplest method of all. To the flow of (1) consumption product

---

[7] Here is a convenient rule of thumb: NNP is usually about ten-elevenths of GNP, depreciation nowadays being about one-eleventh of GNP.

and (2) private investment product, they simply add (3) *all* of government expenditure on goods and services. (Repeatedly in the next few chapters, you will see $C + I + G$, which stands for these three components.)

Here are examples. Along with bread consumption and gross investment in GNP, we include in it government expenditures on roads (i.e., cement and road-builders) and jet bombers. We include government expenditure on the services of jet pilots, judges, policemen, national-income statisticians, firemen, and agricultural chemists. (Although these government expenditures could be conceptually broken down between current collective consumption and collective investment, this would not be easy to do; and in most official statistics, no breakdown is given.)

In short, all the government payroll expenditures on its employees plus the goods (typewriters, roads, and airplanes) it buys from private industry are included in this third great category of flow of product, labeled $G$ and called "government expenditure on goods and services."

Figure 10-3 pictures GNP and its three major components.

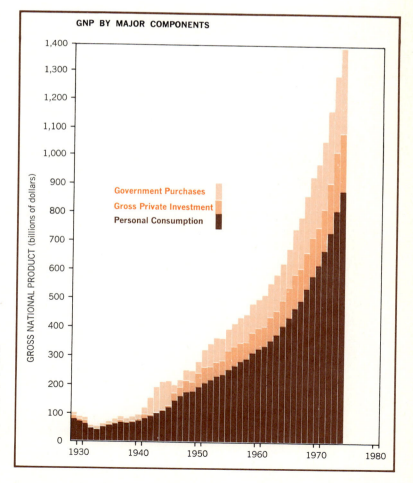

**FIG. 10-3**

**GNP equals $C + I + G$ spending**

Though consumption still dominates GNP, note the World War II and postwar growth in government expenditure and in investment. Actually, in the Great Depression and the war, gross private investment fell short of depreciation (and replacement needs), and net private investment was negative. (Source: U.S. Department of Commerce.)

GNP BY MAJOR COMPONENTS

Government Purchases
Gross Private Investment
Personal Consumption

GROSS NATIONAL PRODUCT (billions of dollars)

**Exclusion of transfer payments**    Does this mean that every dollar the government pays out is included in GNP? Definitely not. If you get an old-age pension from the government, we call that a "transfer payment" and do not treat it as part of GNP. Why not? Because it is not a government expenditure on goods and services of this year. Or if your aunt gets a widow's assistance payment, and your cousin receives welfare aid, those welfare payments are also deemed to be transfer items. The same goes for pensions to the blind, veterans, and other aid recipients. These transfers are not payments for *current* productive services.

Many other government transfer items[8] could be mentioned, but we can conclude with one large item: interest on the public debt. The interest paid on federal bonds was included years ago in GNP, but the fairly universal custom now is for countries to treat this as a transfer item. This is not now included in *G*, on the argument that it is a transfer and not a payment for current goods and services.[9]

Do not think that the Treasury's budget fails to take account of all these government transfer payments. The budget back on page 152 did include these: the government surplus does equal taxes minus the sum of *G and* transfers. But do not confuse the usual budget with national-income accounts, which are related but distinct.

**Treatment of taxes**    In using the flow-of-product approach to compute GNP as $C + I + G$, we would not have to worry about taxes or how government finances itself. Whether the government taxes, issues interest-bearing IOUs, or prints new noninterest IOU greenbacks, the statistician would compute *G* as the value of government expenditure on goods and services (evaluating items at their actual cost to the government, wherever the money came from) and then add in private $C + I$ at actual market prices.

It is all very well to ignore taxes in the upper-loop flow-of-product approach. But what about in the lower-loop earnings or cost approach to GNP? We do indeed have to take account of all taxes down there.

Consider wages, for example. Part of what my employer pays me in wages I have to give to the government in the form of personal income taxes. So these direct taxes do definitely get included in the wage component of the lower loop, and the same holds for direct taxes (personal or corporate) on interest, rent, and profit.

Or take the sales and other indirect taxes that manufacturers and retailers have to pay on a loaf of bread (or on the wheat, flour, and dough stages). Suppose these indirect

[8]The name "transfer payment," as used in Chapter 8 and here, is a little misleading. If the government taxes me to give a relief dole to my unemployed neighbor, that is indisputably a "transfer." But suppose it prints a new green 20-dollar bill to give him, or borrows by selling bonds to make welfare payments. He gets money that is *not* transferred from anybody else. Economists still call the welfare payments transfers, regardless of how they are financed.

[9]How to treat government items in GNP is still somewhat controversial. (*a*) As mentioned, some experts argue that *G* should be broken down into government current *consumption* and into government *net investment* (increase in its buildings, equipment, and inventories), just as private product is so broken up. And a few nations do this. (*b*) Some experts say, too, that part of *G* is really "intermediate" rather than "final" product—much like dough rather than bread—in that it merely contributes to final private product already counted in (e.g., weather information for farmers who help give us our daily bread). But few nations make estimates of how much such double counting may be involved in the *G* figures. Our later discussion of NEW will try to adjust for this.

taxes total 5 cents; and suppose wages, profit, and other value-added items add up to 30 cents in cost to the bread industry. (We do not care how much of this 30 cents goes to direct taxes.) What will the bread sell for in the upper loop? For 30 cents? Of course not. The bread will sell for 35 cents, equal to 30 cents of factor-costs plus 5 cents of indirect taxes.[10]

Hence we definitely do always take account of taxes in the lower-loop cost approach to GNP (and NNP).

Now that the government has been brought into the picture, a final comprehensive definition can be given.

GNP (and NNP) are definable as the sum of three major components: personal *consumption* expenditure on goods and services, plus *government* expenditure on goods and services, plus *investment* expenditure—where it is understood that in GNP, *gross* investment expenditure on all new machines and construction is included, whereas, in NNP, only the *net* investment expenditure is included, there having been subtracted from the gross births of capital goods an appropriate depreciation allowance to take account of deaths, or using up of capital goods.

GNP (and NNP) are each definable, not only as an upper-loop flow of product, but also as a lower-loop total of costs: to factor-costs such as wages, interest, rents, and profit (always carefully excluding double counting of intermediate goods bought from other firms by the value-added technique), there will have to be added all the indirect business taxes that do show up as an expense of producing the flow of products; and in the case of gross national product, there will also be included depreciation expense, whereas the net national product will be less by the amount of this estimated expense.

The two loops of GNP yield identical magnitudes by definition (i.e., by careful adherence to the procedures of double-entry bookkeeping).[11]

## AMERICA'S GNP AND NNP

Armed with an understanding of the concepts involved, we can turn to the actual data in the important Table 10-4 on the next page, a table which merits lengthy study.

**Flow-of-product approach**  Look first at Table 10-4's left side. This gives the upper-loop *flow-of-product* approach to GNP. Distinguishing between domestic and foreign investment, we have four components. Of these, C and G and their obvious subclassifications require little comment. Gross private domestic investment does require one comment. Its $208.9 billion total includes all new business plant and durable equip-

---

[10]This is plainly so by definition of our residual profit and from the fact that residual profit is treated as a cost; but this result says *nothing at all* about whether the tax is passed forward to the consumer or backward to the factors, whose wages and other returns might have been higher had there been no taxes. Chapter 20 analyzes such a "tax incidence" problem of the sort described in Chapter 9.

[11]Statisticians must always work with incomplete reports and must fill in some gaps by estimation. As will be seen in a moment, approximate guesses of the GNP can differ somewhat by what is officially reported as the "statistical discrepancy." Along with the civil servants who are each heads of units called Wages, Interest, and so forth, there is actually a man with the title "Head of the Statistical Discrepancy." If data were perfect, he would be out of a job; but as real life is never so ideal, his task of reconciliation is one of the hardest of all. (In the presentation of the balance of international payments given in Chapter 33, a similar "errors and omissions" item will appear.)

| GROSS NATIONAL PRODUCT, 1974 (in billions of current dollars) | | | | | |
|---|---|---|---|---|---|
| **FLOW-OF-PRODUCT APPROACH** | | | **EARNINGS AND COST APPROACH** | | |
| 1. Personal *consumption* expenditure | | $ 877.0 | Wages and other employee supplements | | $ 855.7 |
| Durable goods | $127.8 | | Net interest | | 61.6 |
| Nondurable goods | 380.1 | | Rent income of persons | | 26.5 |
| Services | 369.1 | | Indirect business taxes and adjustments* | | 135.0 |
| 2. Gross private domestic *investment* (119.5 + 89.4) | | 208.9 | Depreciation | | 119.5 |
| 3. *Government* purchases of goods and services | | 308.8 | Income of unincorporated enterprises (adjusted) | | 93.0 |
| 4. Net *export* of goods and services (139.4 exports −137.4 imports) | | 2.0 | Corporate profits before taxes (adjusted) | | 105.4 |
| | | | Dividends | $ 32.7 | |
| | | | Undistributed profits | 52.5 | |
| | | | Corporate profits taxes | 55.8 | |
| | | | Reported profits (unadj.) | $141.0 | |
| | | | Inventory valuation adjustment | −35.6 | |
| **Gross National Product** | | **$1,396.7** | **Gross National Product** | | **$1,396.7** |
| *Less:* Depreciation (or capital consumption allowance) | | −119.5 | *Less:* Depreciation (or capital consumption allowance) | | −119.5 |
| **Net National Product** | | **$1,277.2** | **Net National Product** | | **$1,277.2** |

**TABLE 10-4**

**Here are the two ways of looking at GNP (and NNP) in actual numbers**
The left side measures flow of product (at market prices). The right side measures flow of costs (factor earnings and depreciation plus indirect taxes). To get NNP, we subtract out from each side the depreciation that is already there in GNP (i.e., in gross investment on the left, and in total costs on the right). (Source: U.S. Department of Commerce. The starred item includes the "statistical discrepancy" and arises from imperfect measurement of upper- and lower-loop data.)

ment; also residential construction; and also increase in inventory of goods. This gross total makes no subtraction allowance for depreciation of capital. Thus, gross investment exceeds the $89.4 billion of net investment by $119.5 billion of depreciation—just as in Table 10-3 on page 188.

The final international item will be discussed further in the Appendix to this chapter and later in Chapter 33. If it were not for complications that arise from government transfer expenditures abroad, the +$2 billion net export of goods and services could be interpreted as our foreign investment, which has to be added to gross domestic investment to arrive at the total of investment. In any case, along with C, G, and domestic I, net exports do represent a fourth component of the flow of product.[12]

[12]EXAMPLE: Of 100 chocolates of GNP, suppose 80 go to C, 10 to G, 6 to domestic I in the form of added inventory, and 4 are exported abroad, with nothing being imported from abroad. Then GNP = 80 + 6 + 10 + (4 − 0) = 100. (If, as in 1972, we imported and consumed more chocolate merchandise than the 4 we exported—say, we imported 7, consuming 87 chocolates in all—we'd have to subtract the "export deficit" of 3 chocolates—giving GNP = 87 + 6 + 10 + (4 − 7) = 100.)

Adding up the four components on the left gives the important total GNP of $1,396.7 billion. This is the harvest we have been working for: the money measure of the American economy's over-all performance for 1974.

Finally, note that if we subtract depreciation from the GNP figure, we get NNP of $1,277.2 billion, which is smaller because it contains net rather than gross investment in its measure of product and thus is reduced by exclusion of depreciation.

**Lower-loop flow-of-cost approach**   Now turn to the right-hand side of the table. Here we have all the *value-added* items plus *taxes* and *depreciation*.

A few explanations are in order. *Wages*[13] and other employee supplements include all take-home pay and fringe benefits, and they also have in them the withheld and other income or payroll taxes that wage earners have to pay.

*Net interest* is a similar item. (Note again, interest on government bonds is not included as part of G or GNP, being treated as a transfer.)

*Rent* income of persons requires only one explanation. It of course includes rents received by landlords. In addition, if you own your own home, you are treated as *paying rent to yourself.* This is a so-called "imputed" item and makes sense if we really want to measure the housing services the American people are enjoying and do not want the estimate to be changed every time a tenant buys the house he has been renting. This imputed item has to be estimated, since no one reports rental receipts on his own home.

*Indirect business taxes,* as we earlier saw, do have to be included in the lower loop if we are to match the upper loop. Any direct taxes on wages, interests, or rents were already included in those items themselves.

Depreciation on capital goods that were used up, $119.5 billion, must appear as an expense in GNP, much like other expenses.

Lastly, turn to *profit.* This should come last because it is the residual determined as what is left over after all other items have been taken into account. There are two kinds of profits: profit of corporations and of unincorporated enterprises, i.e., proprietorships and partnerships. "Income of unincorporated enterprises (adjusted[14])" refers to earnings of partnerships and single-ownership businesses. This includes much farmer and professional income. As we'll see in Parts Three and Four, really a good deal of this is a return to farmers and self-employed people for the labor, capital, and land they provide for their *own* businesses; nonetheless the statisticians count it all as profit.

Finally, "corporate profits before taxes (adjusted)" is shown. Its $105.4 billion includes

---

[13]The late Sir Arthur Bowley of the London School of Economics noted how remarkably constant over almost a century is wages' percentage share of national income. No one is sure why this should be so. (The wages' share does rise at the expense of profit during recession; in recent decades the wages' share has perhaps shown a slight upward creep, as seen in Chapter 37.)

[14]The term "adjusted" refers to an inventory valuation adjustment of the following type: If money prices change *within* the year, our yardstick for measuring profits is faulty. Part of the reported profit is simply a markup (or markdown, if the price level is falling within the year) of inventory. The statistician uses within-the-year price changes to estimate the amount of such overreporting of profits. Actually, in 1974 prices were rising; so there has to be an inventory valuation adjustment of −$35.6 billion that gets subtracted from reported corporate profits of $141.0 billion to give a more meaningful adjusted figure of $105.4 billion. (In 1962, when prices fell, the adjustment was positive and *added* to reported corporate incomes.)

corporate profits *taxes* of $55.8 billion. The remainder then goes to dividends or to undistributed corporate profits, the latter amount of $52.5 billion being what you leave or "plow back" into the business and called "net corporate saving."

Again, on the right side, the flow-of-cost approach gives us the same $1,396.7 billion of GNP, and the same NNP figure of $1,277.2 billion (after subtracting depreciation). The right and left sides do agree.

### THREE RELATED CONCEPTS: DIGRESSION ON DISPOSABLE, PERSONAL, AND NATIONAL INCOMES

Table 10-4 summarized the fundamentals of national-income accounting. For purposes of broad economic description, our task is over. But a businessman, citizen, or statesman who wants to follow carefully what is happening from month to month and quarter to quarter in the American economy or abroad will benefit from a brief digression to define three other concepts that are measured and reported on by the U.S. Department of Commerce and similar official units elsewhere.

*Disposable* income, *personal* income, and (narrowly defined) *national* income are useful rearrangements of the above data.

*Disposable income.* How many dollars per year do private individuals and families have available *to them* to spend? The concept of disposable income tries to answer this question. Broadly speaking, to get disposable income, one subtracts depreciation and all taxes (direct or indirect) from GNP, subtracts all corporate earnings that were not paid out in dividends (i.e., were retained as net corporate savings), and adds in transfer payments of welfare or interest-on-federal-debt type. The result is, so to speak, *what actually gets into the public's hands, to dispose of as we please.*[15]

Disposable income is an important series of data because, as will be seen in Part Two, it is this sum (suitably adjusted to take account of interest on loans that the consumer must pay) that people divide between (*a*) consumption spending and (*b*) net personal saving. Thus, in recent years people have been spending about 94 per cent of disposable income on consumption and interest, with about 6 per cent on net personal saving. It is this *DI* series that will be watched eagerly by a department-store head and a policy maker apprehensive over inflationary pressure or too little consumption spending.

*Personal income.* Unfortunately, *DI* data are available only every 3 months. For those who want up-to-date *monthly* information, the government publishes the series called "personal income." Like *DI*, *PI* removes depreciation and corporate saving from GNP and adds back all transfers and consumer interest. If it excluded *all* taxes, *PI* would be identical with *DI*. Some taxes, however, are hard to estimate in a hurry, on a month-to-month basis. *PI* does eliminate some taxes that can be estimated fairly accurately in the short run: corporate income taxes and certain other payroll taxes; but it does *not* try to estimate the income taxes of people, and thus it does differ slightly from disposable income. If, however, we did have a monthly estimate of *DI*, there is every reason to think that it would change in about the same percentage as *PI* most of the time. Therein lies the principal importance of the personal income concept: it is a quickly available monthly figure that is an excellent substitute for disposable income and is thus an indicator of what is happening to family well-being and spending.

*National income, narrowly defined.* We have followed the common practice and used the term "national income" to refer generally to *all* the concepts of this chapter—GNP, NNP,

---

[15] The spread on pages 200–201 of the Appendix, containing Table 10-5 and Fig. 10-5, could be useful to help you follow these interrelations.

and so forth. Mention should be made of a narrower sense in which the U.S. Department of Commerce defines the term. In the narrow sense, national income, or *NI*, is simply NNP with all indirect business taxes (excises, cigarette stamps, gasoline taxes, and all sales taxes of any kind) taken out. But note that all direct taxes have been left in, as well as corporate income taxes.[16] (Figure 10-5 in the Appendix depicts relations among the different concepts.)

## BEYOND GNP TO NET ECONOMIC WELFARE (NEW)

In the very first chapter, we saw that, these days, there is considerable disenchantment with mere material goods and services, and hence disenchantment with the GNP as a measure of economic welfare. Fortunately, as we saw back in Fig. 1-1 on page 4, modern economists can begin to adjust the GNP numbers in order to get a more meaningful measure of growth in "net economic welfare" (NEW).[17]

**Pluses: example of leisure**   First, in the briefest way, let's see what is wrong with GNP as now measured. Suppose you decide, as you become more affluent, to work fewer hours, to get your psychic satisfactions from *leisure* as well as from goods and services. Then the measured GNP goes down even though welfare goes up. Or, as the Appendix will explain, consider the work women do in the home not for formal pay. The value-added that a master cook imparts to a gourmet family dinner never enters into the goods and services of the GNP—not in the upper-loop nor in the lower-loop.

**Minuses: hidden pollution and ecological costs**   The above understatements and inadequacies of the GNP are easy to understand. More difficult are some overstatements contained in conventional GNP measures. Along with adding in "goods" (e.g., pleasurable air conditioning), GNP should be adjusted so that it subtracts out "bads" (e.g., the pollution of air and water that is involved in generating the power for the air conditioning). Clearly we must adjust for any such "bads" that escape the GNP statistician whenever society is both failing to prevent pollution and failing to make power users pay the full costs of the damage they do.

EXAMPLE: I enjoy 10,000 kilowatt hours of power for air conditioning, paying Edison Co. 1 cent per kilowatt hour. That 1 cent goes for its labor, plant costs, oil-coal-nuclear-hydroelectric fuels. But suppose the company incurs no money costs at all for the damage it does the environment: sulphur from its coal and oil, coal dust, heating of rivers, oil slicks in waters, etc. Did I say "incurs no costs?" I mean, suppose it (and I, the ultimate consumer) gets off scot-free: the costs go on, but they are not faced up to. Suppose they are $\frac{1}{2}$ cent per kilowatt hour. (That is, to restore the environment, which people really think ought just to

---

[16] If NNP can be called "net national product evaluated at market prices," then this version of national income can be called "net national product evaluated, not at market prices, but at the factor-costs (exclusive of indirect taxes) of that output."

[17] My discussion here borrows from the pioneering study, William Nordhaus and James Tobin, "Is Growth Obsolete?" in *Fiftieth Anniversary Colloquium V* (National Bureau of Economic Research, Columbia University Press, New York, 1972). What they call a Measure of Economic Welfare (MEW), I've renamed Net Economic Welfare (NEW). From components of GNP and MEW, I've extrapolated their 1929–1965 estimates to 1976. They summarize on p. 5: "Our adjustments to GNP fall into three general categories: reclassification of GNP expenditures as consumption, investment, and intermediate; imputation for the services of consumer capital, for leisure, and for the product of household work; correction for some of the disamenities of urbanization."

be done, makes true power cost $1\frac{1}{2}$ cents per kilowatt hour.) Then the GNP flow of "goods" must somehow have subtracted from it $50 of pollution "bads" to show the true NEW.

WARNING: NEW differs from GNP when pollution costs go unmet or unnoticed. If society made Edison Co. (and me!) pay the $150 for my "air-cooling plus restoration of ecological balance," real GNP would need no correction. Why not? Because $150 of money GNP, deflated by $1\frac{1}{2}$ cents of price, would yield real GNP of exactly 10,000 kilowatt hours—which is the correct result when no "bads" are allowed to be created along with the "goods."

QUERY: Does this mean, as some noneconomists claim, that "GNP is so stupid a measure that it actually is raised by the fact of pollution—when industry spends more on pollution prevention and control, this raises GNP." No, neither real GNP nor NEW will, when correctly measured, be enhanced by the curse of pollution or other regrettable costs (such as for police against criminals, locks against burglars, defensive fighter planes against offensive bombers and missiles). If science invented a costless way of producing power *without* pollution, less resources would be needed to provide my 10,000 kilowatts of clean power—and hence *more resources* would be available for other good things of life (books, paintings, . . .). MORAL: Properly reckoned, NEW and real GNP would be larger, not smaller, if pollution were nonexistent—and the same money GNP could be deflated by lower prices, to give a higher real GNP.

In summary, when concerned economists like Professors Nordhaus and Tobin calculate net economic welfare, they adjust GNP numbers for such disamenities of modern urbanization that escape costing and notice.

We shall not here enumerate all the various adjustments to go from real per capita GNP (or NNP) to Nordhaus-Tobin NEW. Figure 10-4 tells the main story. It's an historical report on what we've already seen in Fig. 1-1. As there, we see that NEW grows more slowly than GNP. This is more or less inevitable in a densely populated world. And, if you leaf back to page 4, you will recall the point which was made there and which will be developed in Part Six.

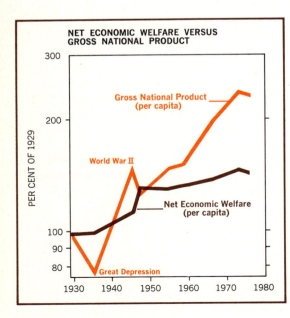

**NET ECONOMIC WELFARE VERSUS GROSS NATIONAL PRODUCT**

Gross National Product (per capita)

World War II

Net Economic Welfare (per capita)

Great Depression

PER CENT OF 1929

**FIG. 10-4**
**Net economic welfare (NEW) grows slower than GNP**
Adjustments for leisure would swell per capita NEW growth beyond per capita GNP growth. But disamenities of modern urbanization (growing pollution, etc.) slow down NEW growth. How much of GNP growth would you be willing to sacrifice to enhance the quality of life and NEW growth? (Source: W. Nordhaus and J. Tobin, "Is Growth Obsolete?" *Fiftieth Anniversary Colloquium V,* National Bureau of Economic Research, Columbia University Press, 1972.)

Public policies can choose to improve economic welfare, NEW—if necessary, at the deliberate sacrifice of mere GNP growth. Political economy must serve mankind's wishes. There is no need for men to be chained to mere material growth unless they wish to be.

This chapter has now given us the tools to chart the progress and health of an economy. It is a culmination of the introductory survey that is the task of Part One. It is a prelude to the subject of Part Two, analysis of *macro*economic forces determining the level, trend, and fluctuations of GNP and of the general level of prices.

## SUMMARY

1   Gross national product, GNP, is definable as a dollar flow of total product for a nation: the sum of consumption plus investment (domestic and foreign) plus government expenditure on goods and services. GNP = $C + I + G$. (NNP is definable in the same way, but investment, $I$, now being interpreted as net, rather than gross, investment.)

2   By use of price index, we can "deflate" money NNP or GNP (in current dollars) to arrive at a more accurate measure of "real NNP or GNP, expressed in dollars of one base-year's purchasing power." Use of such an average price index (of consumer-goods, investment-goods, and government-goods prices) is an approximate way of allowing for the rubber yardstick implied by changing levels of prices.

3   Because of the way we define residual profit, we can match the flow-of-product measurement of GNP (or NNP) by the lower-loop flow-of-cost measurement. This uses factor earnings, carefully computing *values added* to eliminate double counting of intermediate products. And after summing up all (before-tax) wage, interest, rent, depreciation, and profit income, it adds to this total all *indirect* tax costs to business. (GNP definitely does *not* include *transfer* items such as receipt of interest on government bonds or receipt of welfare pensions.)

4   Net investment is positive when people are devoting part of society's resources to creating more inventory and more buildings and equipment than are currently being used up in the form of depreciation. Net investment equals gross investment minus depreciation. As depreciation is hard to estimate accurately, the statisticians have more confidence in their measures of gross than of net investment.

5   For the foregoing reason, the official statistics put greater stress on gross national product rather than net. GNP = NNP + Depreciation, always. Since depreciation is sluggish and varies little from one-eleventh of GNP (one-tenth of NNP), we generally expect GNP or NNP to fluctuate in about the same degree.

6   Disposable, personal, and (narrowly defined) national income are three additional official measurements. *NI* is simply NNP with indirect business taxes (gasoline, sales, and other nonincome taxes) removed. *PI* is simply a convenient monthly approximation to movements in *DI* and the other data that are available only on a quarterly basis. Disposable income is what people actually have left—after

all tax payments, corporate saving of undistributed profits, and transfer adjustments have been made—to spend on consumption (and interest on loans) or to save.

7   Gross national product needs to be modified if we are to approximate to a better measure of Net Economic Welfare (NEW). The Nordhaus-Tobin calculation of NEW adds to GNP certain items—such as value of leisure and housewives' services. It also subtracts from GNP unmet costs of pollution, other disamenities of modern urbanization, and still other adjustments. The result still shows a positive growth in NEW, but at a slower rate than in GNP.

More information about national-income accounting is given in the Appendix to this chapter. Also given are some selected figures on the nation's recent economic history: the Federal Reserve Board's production index, which comes out monthly; and data on employment and unemployment. These vital aggregates chart a nation's economic health.

## CONCEPTS FOR REVIEW

GNP in two equivalent views:
   upper-loop product flow
   lower-loop costs
1975 money NNP (or GNP) in
   current dollars, and 1975 real
   NNP (or GNP) in 1958 dollars
intermediate goods, double
   counting, value added
gross investment − depreciation
   = net investment
GNP − depreciation = NNP

$GNP = C + I + G$
government transfers
indirect and direct taxes
net exports of goods and services
dividends, undistributed profits
income of unincorporated
   enterprise
valuation adjustment
*NI, PI,* and *DI*
NEW: leisure, intermediate costs,
   unmet disamenities (pollution)

## QUESTIONS FOR DISCUSSION

1   Compare the two-loop flow of money of Fig. 10-1 with Fig. 3-1 on page 46, which shows the way a pricing system solves society's WHAT, HOW, and FOR WHOM.

2   "You can't add apples and oranges." Show that money lets us do this. Convince a skeptic that *services* do count as well as material goods—that we actually want most goods only for the consumption services they provide us.

3   Making a guess how prices have risen since 1974, test your knowledge of the deflating process by penciling in, on Fig. 10-2, recent money GNP and recent real GNP. How might you deflate for population change? If the United Kingdom has 1980 GNP of £80 billion, and if £1 then buys what $3 will buy, how would you express U.K. GNP in U.S. 1980 dollars?

4   R. Crusoe produces upper-loop product of $1,000. He pays $750 in wages, $125 in interest, and $75 in rent. What *must* his profit be? Calculate NNP in the upper-loop and lower-loop way and show they must agree exactly.

5   On pages 182 and 186, let a 10 per cent value-added tax be levied. Show (omitting millions) that it collects $\frac{1}{10}$ of $50,000, or $5,000, just as a 10 per cent sales tax on final product would. Of this, $\frac{1}{10}$ of $10,000 or $1,000 came from the farm stage. But manufacturers could subtract from their $50,000 of product the $10,000 spent on farm materials; so they pay the other $4,000.

6   "Political economy has finally, after too long a delay, begun to grapple with the quality of economic life. ZEG ("zero economic growth") in GNP terms may mean life-fulfilling development and growth in NEW." Evaluate unsentimentally.

7   To show how depreciation adds on to NNP in GNP, alter the $50,000 example in page 186's table. Add to manufacturers' costs a $5,000 depreciation item for bread ovens used up; also, add to their output and sales the $5,000 value of new ovens produced. Then note that GNP on the left (or flow-of-product upper-loop) is now $50,000 (bread) + $5,000 (ovens). On the right (or cost lower-loop), we have: $50,000 of NNP + $5,000 of depreciation = $55,000 of GNP.

# APPENDIX: The Official National-income Data

## THE OFFICIAL STATISTICS

Figure 10-5 on page 201 summarizes the relations of the different United States government statistics on national income or product. Many find careful study of this summary, together with Table 10-5 on page 200, a great aid to understanding.

Table 10-6 on page 203, along with national-income data, gives the other principal aggregates which business and public officials watch closely.

## A FEW BRAIN TEASERS

Readers often like to worry about fine points. Here are a few sample cases.

1. *Services of a housewife* do not get counted in the GNP, as we've seen. So if a man marries his housekeeper, the reported GNP may go down! Or if a wife arranges with her neighbor for each to clean the other's house in return for $5,000 a year, then the GNP would go up by $10,000—even though correct NEW has not changed.

This item is not omitted for logical reasons, but rather because it is hard to get accurate estimates of the money value of a wife's services. So long as the number of women working at home does not change much in relative importance, the ups and downs of GNP will be about the same whether or not we count in this or similar items such as home-grown vegetables and other do-it-yourself activities.

All this illustrates an important rule of approximate measurement in economics. *Often it does not matter* which definition of measurement you use, so long as you stick to one definition consistently.

2. For many items it is hard to know whether to put them in the *intermediate* or *final* class. EXAMPLES: A painter's ladder is certainly not to be charged as a final consumption item. Like bread dough, it is an intermediate expense item that has already been counted in as part of the homes he helps build.

What about his overalls? His carfare from one job to another? His carfare from home to work? The coffee he buys a prospective customer? The coffee he himself drinks? The ball game he takes a prospective customer to? Would you treat the last differently if he himself likes baseball?

Each of these items can raise an argument. Each has an element of intermediate business expense in it, and each an element of final consumption. The tax collector and the national-income statistician do not always agree on the treatment of these, and we can raise questions about each one's decisions. (EXAMPLE: The tax collector will not let anyone deduct his commuting costs to work *in town;* but out of town he may be able to deduct travel expenses from his taxable income. The ladder is clearly deductible from taxable income and from GNP; but the overalls are not if it can be shown that wearing them saved an ordinary suit's wearing out. So it goes. Close decisions and arbitrary ones.)

3. *Gifts* that are not disguised payments for work done or for goods and services are not included in

**GROSS AND NET NATIONAL PRODUCT, NATIONAL INCOME, PERSONAL INCOME, AND DISPOSABLE INCOME**
(in billions of dollars)

| ITEM | 1929 | 1933 | 1939 | 1945 | 1950 | 1960 | 1965 | 1970 | 1974 |
|---|---|---|---|---|---|---|---|---|---|
| **Gross national product** | 103.1 | 55.6 | 90.5 | 212.0 | 284.8 | 503.8 | 681.2 | 977.1 | 1,396.7 |
| Less: Capital consumption (Depreciation) | 7.9 | 7.0 | 7.3 | 11.3 | 18.3 | 43.4 | 59.6 | 87.3 | 119.5 |
| Equals: **Net national product** | 95.2 | 48.6 | 83.2 | 200.7 | 266.5 | 460.4 | 621.6 | 889.8 | 1,277.2 |
| Less: Indirect business taxes | 7.0 | 7.1 | 9.4 | 15.5 | 23.3 | 45.2 | 62.6 | 93.5 | 126.9 |
| Business transfer payments | 0.6 | 0.7 | 0.5 | 0.5 | 0.8 | 1.9 | 2.6 | 4.0 | 5.2 |
| Statistical discrepancy | 0.7 | 0.6 | 1.3 | 4.0 | 1.5 | −1.0 | −1.6 | −6.4 | 0.0 |
| Plus: Subsidies less current surplus of government enterprises | −0.1 | 0.0 | 0.5 | 0.8 | 0.2 | 0.2 | 1.0 | 1.7 | −2.9 |
| Equals: **National income** | 86.8 | 40.3 | 72.6 | 181.5 | 241.1 | 414.5 | 559.0 | 800.5 | 1,142.2 |
| Less: Corporate profits and inventory valuation adjustment | 10.5 | −1.2 | 6.3 | 19.2 | 37.7 | 49.9 | 74.2 | 69.2 | 105.4 |
| Contributions for social insurance | 0.2 | 0.3 | 2.1 | 6.1 | 6.9 | 20.7 | 29.2 | 57.7 | 101.5 |
| Excess of wage accruals over disbursements | 0.0 | 0.0 | 0.0 | 0.0 | 0.0 | 0.0 | 0.0 | 0.0 | −0.5 |
| Plus: Government transfer payments | 0.9 | 1.5 | 2.5 | 5.6 | 14.3 | 26.6 | 37.1 | 75.1 | 134.6 |
| Net interest paid by government and consumers | 2.5 | 1.6 | 1.9 | 4.2 | 7.2 | 15.1 | 20.6 | 31.0 | 42.3 |
| Dividends | 5.8 | 2.0 | 3.8 | 4.6 | 8.8 | 13.4 | 19.2 | 24.7 | 32.7 |
| Business transfer payments | 0.6 | 0.7 | 0.5 | 0.5 | 0.8 | 1.9 | 2.6 | 4.0 | 5.2 |
| Equals: **Personal income** | 85.9 | 47.0 | 72.8 | 171.1 | 227.6 | 401.0 | 535.1 | 808.3 | 1,150.4 |
| Less: Personal taxes | 2.6 | 1.5 | 2.4 | 20.9 | 20.7 | 51.0 | 66.0 | 116.6 | 170.7 |
| (Federal) | 1.3 | 0.5 | 1.2 | 19.4 | 16.5 | 42.5 | 54.2 | 92.2 | 131.2 |
| (State and local) | 1.4 | 1.0 | 1.2 | 1.5 | 4.2 | 8.5 | 11.8 | 24.4 | 39.5 |
| Equals: **Disposable personal income** | 83.3 | 45.5 | 70.3 | 150.2 | 206.9 | 350.0 | 469.1 | 691.7 | 979.7 |
| Less: Consumer interest payments plus transfers to foreigners | 1.9 | 0.6 | 0.9 | 0.9 | 2 8 | 7.8 | 11.9 | 17.8 | 26.0 |
| Less: Consumption expenditures | 77.2 | 45.8 | 66.8 | 119.7 | 191.0 | 325.2 | 431.5 | 617.6 | 877.0 |
| Equals: **Personal saving** | 4.2 | −.9 | 2.6 | 29.6 | 13.1 | 17.0 | 25.7 | 56.2 | 76.7 |

**TABLE 10-5**
(Source: U.S. Department of Commerce. Note that detail may not add to totals because of rounding.)

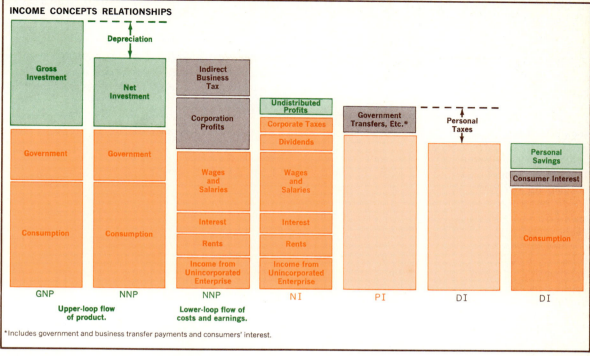

**FIG. 10-5**

GNP. They are like government transfers that we have already discussed. The same goes for the allowance a father gives his son. But what about the fee he pays the son for mowing the lawn? In logic, it should be in GNP, but it rarely is.

4. If I buy an old painting, a corner lot, or a used car from someone else, that transaction is not a final transaction to be put into GNP. He and I have just *exchanged assets:* money for picture. Nothing has been produced.[1] So this is more in the nature of a special kind of transfer.[2] It illustrates an important fact: The total dollar volume of all intermediate transactions greatly exceeds the volume of the final transactions that we call national income or product. The loops of Fig. 10-1 properly include only a minority of the transactions that are taking place within the business and public blocks of that diagram.

[1] If a broker earns a fee for arranging the deal, that fee is counted as part of GNP. Just as some men produce satisfactions in the form of bread, brokers and salesmen produce satisfactions in the form of bringing transactors together.

[2] Do not confuse this kind of transfer with the government transfers we have talked about.

Note, too, that we try not to let *capital gains due to mere nonrecurring price changes* enter into GNP. If Wall Street bids up my Ford stock, I may feel rich and spend more of my *DI.* But that windfall gain is not attributable to current economic activity, and the statistician tries to keep it out. For similar reasons he makes the inventory valuation adjustment in corporate profits.

5. In measuring GNP, we are not interested in consumption and investment goods merely for their money value: *Money is the measuring rod used to give some approximate figure to the underlying "satisfactions" or "benefits" or "psychic income" that comes from goods.* Strictly speaking, then, each time I play a phonograph record, shouldn't that act get into the GNP at its fair market value? In principle, Yes. And if I have put a dime in a juke box, playing that record may in fact get directly into the GNP; but playing it at home won't get it directly into GNP.

Indirectly, this enjoyment of a psychic pleasure does tend to get in the GNP to the extent that I wear out the record by playing it. Hence, as I replace my records, my consumption purchases at the store give a rough money measure of my enjoyments—but only a rough measure.

The statistician admits this, defending his practice by saying that a man's house is his castle and no accountant can enter his abode to measure his actual current consumptions; instead, he settles for treating a thing as consumed when it enters his abode. This all works well enough, except in one case.

More and more, these days, we spend our consumption dollar on durable consumers' goods. (This was seen in the breakdown of consumption into services, durable goods, and nondurable goods in Table 10-4.) Actually, then, in the years that we are building up our home inventories of such durable goods, our true psychic consumption is being overstated by our retail purchases; and vice versa in the years when we run home inventories down.

Some purists say, "In GNP, let's try to estimate actual home consumption of services of durables and put that in $C$, not the mere retail purchases of the year." The Commerce Department thinks this too hard a job to do, but for special purposes economists have tried to make (from gas and mileage records, for example) more accurate estimates of auto consumption than are provided by new car sales.[3]

Fortunately, in the long run, the two methods tend to come to much the same thing, particularly if society is not growing too fast or too unsteadily.

6. Should interest paid by consumers be included in disposable income, $DI$, in consumption expenditure, $C$, and in GNP? Before 1965 the official statistics did include consumer interest in $C$ and GNP. But after 1965 the Commerce Department, with the approval of the United Nations Statistical Office, decided that this was not an item reflecting *current* (as against *past*) production. Hence, by an arguable but reasonable decision, net consumer interest payments (along with personal transfer payments to foreigners, a smaller item) are no longer in $C$ and GNP.

But consumer interest is still in the official Department of Commerce disposable income, $DI$, figures. So, if we want to work with the money income *actually* available to be spent on $C$ or on personal saving, we must first subtract from disposable income "consumer interest (and personal transfer payments to

foreigners)." For 1971 this interest item came to about $17 billion. Thus,

$$DI = C + NPS + \text{consumer interest}$$

where $C$ is the consumption expenditure on current production and NPS is net personal saving. To get an idea of the size of these elements of $DI$, carefully read the bottom four lines of Table 10-5.

## INTERNATIONAL ASPECTS OF INCOME

Here is the place to give a few details on how the figure for net exports was arrived at.

From the beginning we agree to mean by United States GNP the income or product accruing to all "permanent residents" of the United States. This includes American citizens temporarily abroad and also unnaturalized immigrants who live permanently in the United States.

Note that, if an Englishman owns an acre of land in this country, his income therefrom is to be included in the United Kingdom GNP and not in ours. Similarly, if Americans receive dividends from British companies, this is part of the American income and not the British, being treated as payment for a property service that we have exported.

The previous paragraph shows that it is a considerable task to allow for international aspects of income. We must take account of exports, imports, dividends paid in and out of a country, and much more. As we shall see in the discussion of international finance in Part Five, a balance of international payments between the United States and the rest of the world can be drawn up of all such items. There is no need at this point of our GNP discussion to anticipate all the details of this subsequent discussion. We are interested only in the bare logic of the task of finding out the magnitude of net export of goods and services, which is the fourth and final component of GNP.

To get net export of goods and services, we must calculate the surplus of all the goods and services we provide to foreigners over what they provide to us. Thus calculate (a), the total of our exports to them (wheat, shipping, . . .), plus our earnings from factors of production we own abroad (dividends and interest payable to us). Also calculate (b), the total of what we import from them and must pay them for their ownership of productive factors located in this country. The surplus of (a) over (b) represents our net

---

[3] It is interesting that in the case of a house, the most durable consumers' good of all, the officials do actually follow this principle: they do not take expenditures on a house as its $C$, but estimate the house use separately and count it as $C$.

**PRINCIPAL ECONOMIC AGGREGATES** (all income data in billions of current dollars)

| YEAR | GROSS NATIONAL PRODUCT (current prices) | NET NATIONAL PRODUCT | GROSS NATIONAL PRODUCT (1958 prices) | DISPOSABLE INCOME | NET PERSONAL SAVING AS PERCENTAGE OF DISPOSABLE INCOME | GOVERNMENT EXPENDITURE ON GOODS AND SERVICES AS PERCENTAGE OF GNP | FEDERAL RESERVE BOARD INDEX OF INDUSTRIAL PRODUCTION (1967 = 100) | CIVILIAN LABOR FORCE (thousands) | UNEMPLOYMENT AS PERCENTAGE OF CIVILIAN LABOR FORCE |
|---|---|---|---|---|---|---|---|---|---|
| 1929 | 103.1 | 95.2 | 203.6 | 83.3 | 5.0 | 8.2 | 21.6 | 49,180 | 3.2 |
| 1933 | 55.6 | 48.6 | 141.5 | 45.5 | −2.0 | 14.5 | 13.7 | 51,590 | 24.9 |
| 1939 | 90.5 | 83.2 | 209.4 | 70.3 | 3.7 | 14.7 | 21.7 | 55,230 | 17.2 |
| 1940 | 99.7 | 92.2 | 227.2 | 75.7 | 5.1 | 14.1 | 25.4 | 55,640 | 14.6 |
| 1941 | 124.5 | 116.3 | 263.7 | 92.7 | 11.8 | 19.8 | 31.6 | 55,910 | 9.9 |
| 1942 | 157.9 | 148.1 | 297.8 | 116.9 | 23.6 | 37.8 | 36.3 | 56,410 | 4.7 |
| 1944 | 210.1 | 199.1 | 361.3 | 146.3 | 25.5 | 45.8 | 47.4 | 54,630 | 1.2 |
| 1945 | 212.0 | 200.7 | 355.2 | 150.2 | 19.7 | 38.5 | 40.6 | 53,860 | 1.9 |
| 1946 | 208.5 | 198.6 | 312.6 | 160.0 | 9.5 | 12.9 | 35.0 | 57,520 | 3.9 |
| 1948 | 257.6 | 243.0 | 323.7 | 189.1 | 7.1 | 12.2 | 41.0 | 60,621 | 3.8 |
| 1949 | 256.5 | 239.9 | 324.1 | 188.6 | 5.0 | 14.7 | 38.8 | 61,286 | 5.9 |
| 1950 | 284.8 | 266.4 | 355.3 | 206.9 | 6.3 | 13.3 | 44.9 | 62,208 | 5.3 |
| 1951 | 328.4 | 307.2 | 383.4 | 226.6 | 7.6 | 17.9 | 48.7 | 62,017 | 3.3 |
| 1952 | 345.5 | 322.3 | 395.1 | 238.3 | 7.6 | 21.6 | 50.6 | 62,138 | 3.0 |
| 1953 | 364.6 | 338.9 | 412.8 | 252.6 | 7.2 | 22.4 | 54.8 | 63,015 | 2.9 |
| 1954 | 364.8 | 336.8 | 407.0 | 257.4 | 6.4 | 20.4 | 51.9 | 63,643 | 5.5 |
| 1955 | 398.0 | 366.5 | 438.0 | 275.3 | 5.7 | 18.7 | 58.5 | 65,023 | 4.4 |
| 1956 | 419.2 | 385.2 | 446.1 | 293.2 | 7.0 | 18.7 | 61.1 | 66,552 | 4.1 |
| 1957 | 441.1 | 404.0 | 452.5 | 308.5 | 6.7 | 19.5 | 61.9 | 66,929 | 4.3 |
| 1958 | 447.3 | 408.4 | 447.3 | 318.8 | 7.0 | 21.1 | 57.9 | 67,639 | 6.8 |
| 1959 | 483.7 | 442.3 | 475.9 | 337.3 | 5.6 | 22.1 | 64.8 | 68,639 | 5.5 |
| 1960 | 503.8 | 460.3 | 487.7 | 350.0 | 4.9 | 19.8 | 66.2 | 69,628 | 5.5 |
| 1961 | 520.1 | 474.9 | 497.2 | 364.4 | 5.8 | 20.7 | 66.7 | 70,459 | 6.7 |
| 1962 | 560.3 | 510.4 | 529.8 | 385.3 | 5.6 | 20.9 | 72.2 | 70,614 | 5.5 |
| 1963 | 590.5 | 537.9 | 551.0 | 404.6 | 4.9 | 20.7 | 76.5 | 71,833 | 5.7 |
| 1964 | 632.4 | 576.3 | 581.1 | 438.1 | 6.0 | 20.4 | 81.7 | 73,091 | 5.2 |
| 1965 | 684.9 | 625.1 | 617.8 | 473.2 | 6.0 | 20.0 | 89.2 | 74,455 | 4.5 |
| 1966 | 749.9 | 685.9 | 658.1 | 511.9 | 6.3 | 20.9 | 97.9 | 75,770 | 3.8 |
| 1967 | 793.9 | 725.0 | 675.2 | 546.5 | 7.4 | 22.7 | 100.0 | 77,347 | 3.8 |
| 1968 | 864.2 | 789.7 | 706.6 | 591.0 | 6.5 | 23.1 | 105.7 | 78,737 | 3.6 |
| 1969 | 930.3 | 848.7 | 725.6 | 634.4 | 6.0 | 22.6 | 110.7 | 80,734 | 3.5 |
| 1970 | 977.1 | 889.8 | 722.5 | 691.7 | 8.1 | 22.5 | 106.6 | 82,715 | 4.9 |
| 1971 | 1,054.9 | 961.2 | 746.3 | 746.4 | 8.1 | 22.2 | 106.8 | 84,113 | 5.9 |
| 1972 | 1,158.0 | 1,055.1 | 792.5 | 802.5 | 6.6 | 22.1 | 115.2 | 86,542 | 5.6 |
| 1973 | 1,294.9 | 1,184.1 | 839.2 | 903.7 | 8.2 | 21.3 | 125.6 | 88,714 | 4.9 |
| 1974 | 1,396.7 | 1,277.2 | 821.1 | 979.7 | 7.8 | 22.1 | 124.8 | 91,011 | 5.6 |

**TABLE 10-6**

export figure. We shall see that just as domestic investment can provide jobs and expand the economy, so can net exports. Thus, when we write $C + I + G$, we include in $I$ (along with domestic investment) net exports (or foreign investments) as well.

## THE IDENTITY OF MEASURED SAVING AND INVESTMENT

To pave the way for the discussion of intersecting saving and investment schedules in Chapter 12, we can here show that the *national-income statistician defines the saving he measures as exactly the same thing as the investment he measures*. This equality of measured saving and measured investment is an identity of double-entry bookkeeping and holds by definition.

What is the measure of investment? Forgetting government, we know $I$ is the output in the upper loop that is not $C$. What is the measure of saving $S$? Again forgetting government and corporate saving, we know that $S$ is that part of the lower-loop disposable income, or GNP, that is not spent on $C$. To summarize:

$$I = \text{upper-loop GNP minus } C$$
$$S = \text{lower-loop GNP minus } C$$

But the two loops must give the same measure of GNP. So $I \equiv S$: the identity between measured saving and investment.

Our task will be done once we bring the corporation and the government into the picture. Investment is just as before. But now gross saving, $S$, must be split into three different terms: (1) net personal saving, which people do out of their disposable incomes; (2) gross corporate, more accurately, business saving, that part of business incomes which they fail to distribute as dividends, plus depreciation; finally, (3) net government surplus (or "saving"), which represents the algebraic excess of its tax revenues over its expenditure on goods and services *and* on transfers.

Our identity of measured $S$ and $I$ now has to be written in terms of the three components of total $S$.[4]

$$I \equiv \text{NPS} + \text{GCS} + \text{NGS}$$

---

[4] The eager reader can test his grasp of this fundamental identity (which must hold at all times whether or not an economy is in equilibrium or is galloping to or from an equilibrium) by going back to the discussion (page 194 and Table 10-6) of how disposable income is defined in terms of GNP — taxes — GCS + transfers + consumer interest, and how NPS = DI − C − cons. interest. These relations combined with the $C + I + G$ breakdown of GNP can be used to give an algebraic demonstration of our identity.

Thus, from the definition of *DI*,

$$\text{GNP} \equiv (DI - \text{cons. interest}) + \text{GCS} + Tx - Tr$$

Adding and subtracting $G$ and splitting up ($DI$ − cons. interest) gives

$$\text{GNP} \equiv C + [\text{NPS} + \text{GCS} + (Tx - Tr - G)] + G$$
$$\equiv C + [\text{NPS} + \text{GCS} + (\text{NGS})] + G$$

But recall the upper-loop definition

$$\text{GNP} \equiv C + [I] + G$$

So we do indeed verify the saving-investment identity

$$[I] \equiv [\text{NPS} + \text{GCS} + \text{NGS}]$$

# 2

## DETERMINATION OF NATIONAL INCOME AND ITS FLUCTUATIONS

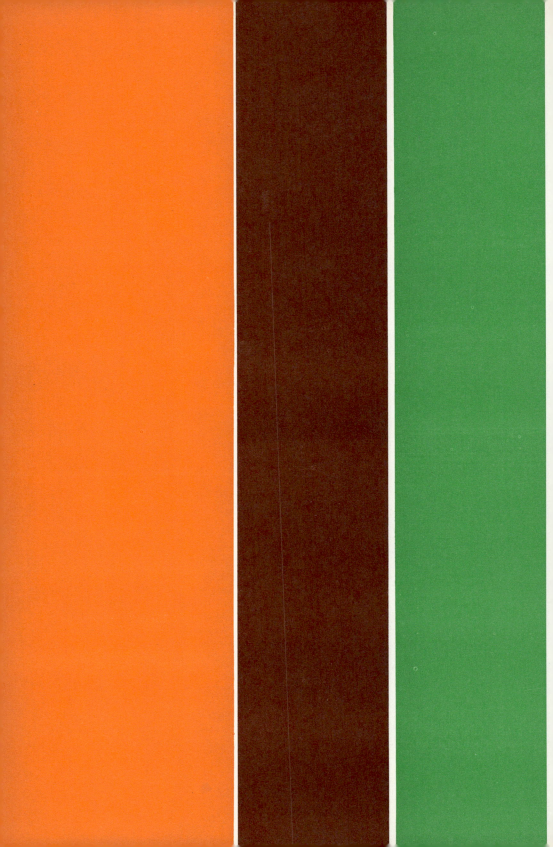

# 11

# SAVING, CONSUMPTION, AND INVESTMENT

I am now a Keynesian.
RICHARD NIXON

We are all Keynesians now.
MILTON FRIEDMAN

In Part One the groundwork was laid for an understanding of the concept of national income. Now we can go beyond the anatomy of the problem to its physiology. What causes national income to rise? To fall? Why is GNP what it is at any time, rather than something larger or smaller? What causes too little total spending—recession and depression? What causes too much total spending—inflationary rises in the index of prices? Part Two analyzes these basic problems of "macroeconomics," which is defined as the study of the aggregate performance of the whole GNP and of the general price level.

This chapter provides an introduction to what is called the "modern theory of income analysis." The principal stress is upon the *level of total spending as determined by the interplay of the monetary forces of saving and investment.*

Although much of this analysis is due to an English economist, John Maynard Keynes (later made Lord Keynes, before his death in 1946), today the broad fundamentals of modern macroeconomics are increasingly accepted by most economists including, it is important to notice, many who do not share Keynes' particular policy views and who differ on technical details of analysis.[1] Because political economy is a dynamic science, post-Keynesian analysis represents an evolution and development beyond the breakthroughs of 40 years ago.

In recent years 90 per cent of American economists have stopped being "Keynesian economists" or "anti-Keynesian economists." Modern economists are "post-Keynesians," keen to render obsolete any theories that cannot meet the test of experience. Thus, in the 1970s,

[1] Keynes himself was a many-sided genius who won eminence in the fields of mathematics, philosophy, and literature. In addition, he found time to run a large insurance company, to advise the British Treasury, to help govern the Bank of England, to edit a world-famous economic journal, to collect modern art and rare books, and to sponsor ballet and drama. He was also an economist who knew how to make money by shrewd speculation, both for himself and for King's College, Cambridge. His 1936 book, *The General Theory of Employment, Interest and Money,* created the greatest stir in economic thinking of the century and will live as a classic.

post-Keynesians accord an importance to the role of money in the process of income determination that would have surprised the first disciples of Keynes (but which would not at all have surprised that brilliant virtuoso of finance). Even Marxian economists, who at first resented Keynesian economics literally as a "mere palliative" to the ills of capitalism, have come to recognize its explanatory powers.

## THE CLEAVAGE BETWEEN SAVING AND INVESTMENT MOTIVATIONS

The most important single fact about saving and investment activities is that in our industrial society they are generally done *by different people* and done *for different reasons*.

This was not always so. And even today, when a farmer devotes his time to draining a field instead of to planting and harvesting a crop, he is saving and at the same time investing. He is "saving" because he is abstaining from *present* consumption in order to provide for larger consumption in the *future*—the amount of his saving being measured by the difference between his net real income and his consumption. But he is also "investing"; i.e., he is undertaking net capital formation, improving the productive capacity of his farm. Not only are saving and investment the same things for a self-sufficient farmer, but his reasons for undertaking them are the same. He abstains from present consumption (saves) only because he wants to drain the field (to invest). If there were no investment opportunity whatsoever, it would never occur to him to save; nor would there be any way to save for the future, should he be so foolish as to wish to.

In our modern economy, net capital formation or investment is largely carried on by business enterprises, especially corporations. When a corporation or a small business has great investment opportunities, its owners will be tempted to plow back much of its earnings into the business. To an important degree, therefore, some business saving does still get motivated directly by business investment.

Nevertheless, saving is *primarily* done by an entirely different group: by individuals, by families, by households. An individual may wish to save for a great variety of reasons: to provide for his old age or for a future expenditure (a vacation or an automobile). Or he may feel insecure and wish to guard against a rainy day. Or he may wish to leave an estate to his children or to his children's children. Or he may be an eighty-year-old miser with no heirs who enjoys the act of accumulating for its own sake. Or he may already have signed himself up to a savings program because an insurance salesman was persuasive. Or he may desire the power that greater wealth brings. Or thrift may simply be a habit, almost a conditioned reflex, whose origin he does not himself know.

**Whatever the individual's motivation to save, it often has little to do with the investment opportunities of society and business.**

This truth is obscured by the fact that in everyday language "investment" does not always have the same meaning as in economics. We have defined "net investment," or capital formation, to be the net increase in the community's real capital (equipment, buildings, inventories). But the plain man speaks of "investing" when he buys a piece of land, an old security, or any title to property. For economists these are clearly *transfer* items. What one man is buying, someone else is selling. There is net investment only when *additional real capital* is created.

In short, even if there are no *real* investment opportunities that seem profitable, an individual may still *wish* to nonconsume—to save. He can always buy an existing security asset; he can accumulate, or *try* to accumulate, cash.

## THE VARIABILITY OF INVESTMENT

Thus, we are left with our proposition: Saving and investing are often desired by different individuals and for independent reasons. While it is families who primarily decide to save, net capital formation takes place largely in business enterprise.

The amount of investment itself is *highly variable* from year to year and decade to decade. This capricious, volatile behavior is understandable when we come to realize that profitable investment opportunities depend on *new* discoveries, *new* products, *new* territories and frontiers, *new* resources, *new* population, *higher* production and income. Note the emphasis on "new" and on "higher."

Investment depends largely on the *dynamic* and relatively unpredictable elements of *growth* in the system, and importantly on elements outside the economic system itself: technology, politics, optimistic and pessimistic expectations, "confidence," governmental tax and expenditure, changes in the supply of money, legislative policies, and much else.

**The extreme variability of investment is the next important fact to be emphasized.**

The independence of forces operating on saving and on investment is like the independence of forces operating on Chapter 4's supply and demand schedules. While recognizing this independence, we should also recognize two qualifications.

(*a*) Often at the corporate level, decisions to invest are closely related to the funds that corporations are able to save out of their earnings and that need not be paid out in dividends; (*b*) at all times, but particularly in times of tight money and high interest rates, how much entrepreneurs can indulge their desire to invest in new, profitable opportunities will depend on how much finance is made available to them by people's saving.

Just as the independent forces operating on supply and demand are resolved by what happens to market prices, we shall see that saving and investment decisions, in their turn, are resolved by what happens to the level of income and employment and to interest rates.

We shall see that an industrial system such as ours can do many wonderful things. It can mobilize men, tools, and know-how to respond to any given demand for goods. Over time it can improve upon its own response. But there is one thing it can't do.

**Unless proper macroeconomic policies are pursued, a laissez faire economy cannot guarantee that there will be exactly the required amount of investment to ensure full employment: not too little so as to cause unemployment, nor too much so as to cause inflation. As far as total investment or money-spending power is concerned, the laissez faire system is without a good thermostat.**

For decades there might tend to be too little investment, leading to deflation, losses, excess capacity, unemployment, and destitution. For other years or decades, there might tend to be too much investment, leading to periods of chronic inflation—unless proper public policies in the fiscal (i.e., tax and expenditure) and monetary (i.e., Federal Reserve central bank) fields are followed.

Nor is there an Invisible Hand guaranteeing that the good years will by themselves equal the bad; nor guaranteeing that scientists will discover just in the nick of time precisely enough new products and processes to keep the system on an even keel. From 1855 to 1875 railroads were built all over the world. In the next two decades nothing quite took the place of this activity. The automobile and public utilities produced a similar revolution in the 1920s. In the 1930s plastics and radio had no comparable effect on total net investment. In the years immediately following World War II, much of the time we were plagued by too much investment spending relative to the resources released by those acts of renouncing consumption which economists call "saving." Then in the Eisenhower years of the 1950s, America experienced sluggish growth, with increasing unemployment. Aided by Kennedy fiscal activism, the years of the 1960s were years of unusual growth. As the 1970s developed, the Vietnam era left its inflationary heritage.

Thus we see that the instabilities are not all on the downward side. Economic history is, alas, a history of inflations. Anyone who comes of age today has seen prices almost double in his own brief lifetime. Unless proper policies are followed, he can look forward to gyrating prices for the rest of his life.

While a realist must recognize that an economy like ours of 1929 or of the 1970s will not *by itself* maintain stability of prices and full employment, critics should still recognize that there are certain elements in a pricing economy that can work toward stability if given a chance to operate and if helped by vigorous public stabilizing actions. The money supply cannot be left to chance. As we shall see later, *the structure of interest rates*—which determines how costly and hard it is to get credit for investing activities—can be helped by Federal Reserve monetary policy to play a *stabilizing* role in moderating investment fluctuations. Also, to a considerable extent the frictions that keep various prices inflexible and sticky in a modern mixed economy can be offset by public fiscal actions.

This, then, is one of our most important economic lessons.

**Where the stimulus to investment is concerned, the system is somewhat in the lap of the gods. We may be lucky or unlucky; and one of the few things you can say about luck is, "It's going to change." Fortunately, things need not be left to luck. We shall see that sensible monetary and fiscal policies can be followed that greatly enhance the stability and productive growth of the mixed economy. We shall also encounter some stubborn unsolved problems in our struggle to reconcile full employment and reasonable price-level stability.**

The next chapters will show how investment and saving determine the equilibrium level of national income. First, we must understand the important budgetary patterns, reflecting how people consume and save at different income levels.

## BUDGETARY EXPENDITURE PATTERNS

No two families spend their money in exactly the same way. Yet statistics do show that there is a predictable regularity—on the average—in the way people allocate their expenditures on food, clothing, and other major items. Literally thousands of

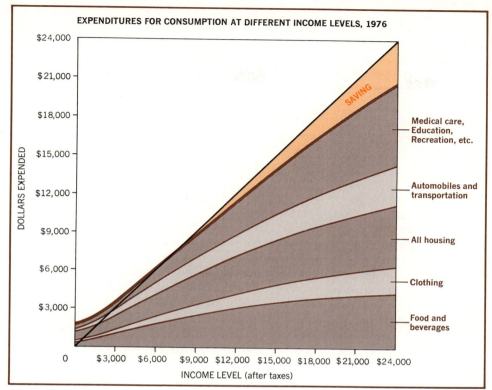

FIG. 11-1

**Family budget expenditures show regular income patterns**
Careful sampling of urban families verifies the importance of income as a determinant of consumption expenditure. Notice the drop in food as a percentage of higher incomes. Note also the rise in saving, from below zero at low incomes to substantial positive levels. (Source: U.S. Departments of Labor and Agriculture; updated to 1976 prices by author.)

budgetary investigations have been made of the ways that people at different levels of income spend their money; and there is remarkable agreement on the general, qualitative patterns of behavior.[2] What are they? Figure 11-1 tells the story.

Poor families must, of course, spend their incomes largely on the necessities of life: food, shelter, and, in lesser degree, clothing. As income increases, expenditure on many food items goes up. People eat more and eat better. They shift away from cheap, bulky carbohydrates to more expensive meats and proteins—and to milk, fruit, vegetables, and labor-saving processed foods.

There are, however, limits to the amount of extra money that people will spend on food when their incomes rise. Consequently, *the percentage importance of food expenditure declines as income increases.* (Actually, there are a few cheap, but filling,

---

[2] Figure 11-1's behavior patterns are called "Engel's Laws," after the nineteenth-century Prussian statistician Ernst Engel (not to be confused with Karl Marx's friend Friedrich Engels). The average behavior of consumption expenditure does change fairly regularly with income; but averages do not tell the whole story. Within each income class, there is considerable spread around the average.

| PROPENSITY OF FAMILIES TO SAVE AND CONSUME | | |
| --- | --- | --- |
| (1)<br>DISPOSABLE<br>INCOME<br>AFTER TAXES | (2)<br>NET SAVING (+)<br>OR DISSAVING (−) | (3)<br><br>CONSUMPTION |
| $ 6,000 | $ −170 | $ 6,170 |
| 7,000 | −110 | 7,110 |
| 8,000 | 0 | 8,000 |
| 9,000 | +150 | 8,850 |
| 10,000 | +400 | 9,600 |
| 11,000 | +760 | 10,240 |
| 12,000 | +1,170 | 10,830 |
| 13,000 | +1,640 | 11,360 |

**TABLE 11-1**
**Most saving is done by families with incomes considerably above the average**
The break-even point at which people cease to dissave and begin to do positive saving is here shown at $8,000. How much of each extra dollar do people around this income level devote to extra consumption? How much to extra saving? (Answer: About 85 cents and 15 cents, respectively.)

items such as potatoes or sausage whose consumption decreases absolutely with income increase. These are called "inferior goods" in Part Three.)

After you get out of the very poorest income class, your proportion of income spent on shelter is pretty constant for a wide range. This is expressed in a familiar rule of thumb: One week's salary should cover one month's expenditure on rent and house utilities. The other rule of thumb—that you should pay about 2 years' income for a house—has a hollow ring these days.

Expenditure on clothing, recreation, and automobiles increases *more than proportionately to after-tax income*, until high incomes are reached. Of course, luxury items, by definition, increase in greater proportion than income; and in many ways, as we shall soon see, saving is the greatest luxury of all, especially at very high incomes.

## THE PROPENSITY TO SAVE AND THE PROPENSITY TO CONSUME

An important use of after-tax income is saving for the future rather than consuming now. This saving facet is what interests us most. It is a matter of common observation that rich men save more than poor men, not only in absolute amounts but also in percentage amounts. The very poor are unable to save at all. Instead they "dissave," i.e., spend more every year than they earn, the difference being covered by going into debt or using up previously accumulated savings. Thus, income is a prime determinant of saving, as shown in Table 11-1.[3]

This table gives data on saving and consumption indicative of *family patterns* in the early 1970s, the so-called "propensity to consume" and "propensity to save." Column (2) shows the net saving that accompanies each level of disposable income. The "break-even point," where the family neither saves nor dissaves, instead consuming

---

[3] These cross-section data do not depict long-run behavior of each family when its income moves from a *permanent* low level to a *permanent* high level. Transitorily, saving rises much; but as people get accustomed to higher "permanent income," consumption rises and saving becomes more moderate. Surprising as it may seem, statistics show that people with $15,000 of *permanent* income save about the same fraction of their income as do people with $10,000 of *permanent* income. (NOTE: In this and later chapters, consumer interest, mentioned in Chapter 10's Appendix, is ignored.)

all its income, falls at $8,000. Below this, as at $7,000 or $6,000, it actually consumes more than its income; it dissaves (see the −$110 and −$170 items). Above $8,000 it begins to do positive saving (see the +$150 item).

Column (3) shows the consumption pattern of each income level—the so-called "propensity to consume." Since each dollar of income is divided between the part consumed and the remaining part saved, Columns (3) and (2) are not independent: they must always exactly add up to Column (1). (Check that they do.)

Economic analysis is interested not simply in the total figures of saving and consumption, but in the *extra* saving and consumption that each *extra* dollar of income brings. Thus, as income goes from $8,000 to $9,000, the extra $1,000 of income is divided between $850 of extra consumption and $150 of extra saving—split up 85 and 15 per cent, so to speak. (Where did these numbers come from? You get them from $8,850 minus $8,000 and from $150 minus $0. And verify that the division between consumption and saving of extra dollars beyond $9,000 is, respectively, 75 and 25 per cent, then 64 and 36 per cent. . . . Does it seem reasonable to you that richer people will consume a little less of each extra income dollar than will poorer?[4])

Family propensity-to-save and propensity-to-consume patterns have been rather stable. (Workers, however, have generally seemed to save less than the self-employed.)

To understand how saving and investment determine the level of national income and employment, we must continue to study in detail (1) the propensity-to-save schedule, relating saving and income, and its twin brother (2) the propensity-to-consume schedule, relating consumption and income.

## THE PROPENSITY-TO-CONSUME SCHEDULE IN DETAIL

Table 11-2, on the next page, rearranges these same data in more convenient form. First, verify its similarity to Table 11-1. Then, disregard its Columns (3) to (5) and concentrate on how consumption expenditure goes up at each higher level of income.

This same consumption-income relation can be shown even more vividly in diagrammatic form. In Fig. 11-2, the total of consumption expenditure in Column (2) is plotted against family disposable income of Column (1); through the resulting circles *A, B, C, D, E, F,* and *G,* a smooth curve has been drawn.

This relation between consumption and income is called the *consumption schedule,* or *propensity-to-consume schedule,* or often simply the *propensity to consume.* It is a basic, important concept whose general properties we must study.

It will help you to understand its properties if, first, you look at the 45° line also shown in Fig. 11-2. Inasmuch as the vertical axis of consumption has been drawn to the same scale as the horizontal axis of income, any point lying on the 45° helping line has the following simple property: Its indicated consumption expenditure—measured by the vertical distance of the point from the horizontal axis—is *exactly*

---

[4]Students at first find it hard to understand that even when family income is below the break-even point and saving is negative, nonetheless each *extra* income dollar goes partly into positive extra saving and partly into positive extra consumption. To convince yourself, compare row 2 of Table 11-1 with row 1. Adding $1,000 to $6,000 of income gives $7,000. This extra income makes consumption go from $6,170 to $7,110, a gain of $940, with $60 of extra saving.

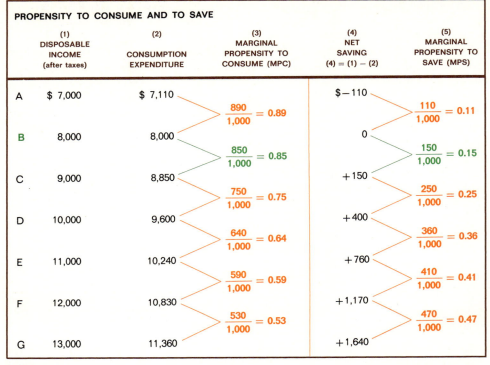

| PROPENSITY TO CONSUME AND TO SAVE | | | | |
|---|---|---|---|---|
| (1)<br>DISPOSABLE<br>INCOME<br>(after taxes) | (2)<br>CONSUMPTION<br>EXPENDITURE | (3)<br>MARGINAL<br>PROPENSITY TO<br>CONSUME (MPC) | (4)<br>NET<br>SAVING<br>(4) = (1) − (2) | (5)<br>MARGINAL<br>PROPENSITY TO<br>SAVE (MPS) |
| A $ 7,000 | $ 7,110 | | $−110 | |
| | | $\frac{890}{1,000} = 0.89$ | | $\frac{110}{1,000} = 0.11$ |
| B 8,000 | 8,000 | | 0 | |
| | | $\frac{850}{1,000} = 0.85$ | | $\frac{150}{1,000} = 0.15$ |
| C 9,000 | 8,850 | | +150 | |
| | | $\frac{750}{1,000} = 0.75$ | | $\frac{250}{1,000} = 0.25$ |
| D 10,000 | 9,600 | | +400 | |
| | | $\frac{640}{1,000} = 0.64$ | | $\frac{360}{1,000} = 0.36$ |
| E 11,000 | 10,240 | | +760 | |
| | | $\frac{590}{1,000} = 0.59$ | | $\frac{410}{1,000} = 0.41$ |
| F 12,000 | 10,830 | | +1,170 | |
| | | $\frac{530}{1,000} = 0.53$ | | $\frac{470}{1,000} = 0.47$ |
| G 13,000 | 11,360 | | +1,640 | |

**TABLE 11-2**
**Numerical table shows consumption and saving schedules and marginal propensities**
Each dollar of income that is not consumed is saved. And each dollar of income goes into extra consumption or extra saving—giving important concepts we need: marginal propensity to consume and to save, MPC and MPS. (NOTE: $890 = $8,000 − $7,110. How about $850?)

*equal to 100 per cent* of its indicated level of disposable income—measured by the horizontal distance of the point from the vertical axis. (Use your eye to verify that any point *not* on the 45° line cannot possibly be equidistant from the two axes.)

**The "break-even" point** The 45° line will tell us right away, therefore, whether consumption spending is equal to, greater than, or less than the level of income. The point on the consumption schedule where it intersects the 45° line shows us the level of disposable income at which families just break even. This break-even point is at *B*; here, consumption expenditure is exactly equal to disposable income; the family is borrowing nothing and on balance saving nothing.

Similarly, *anywhere else* on the propensity-to-consume curve, the family cannot be just breaking even. To the right of point *B*, the curve lies below the 45° line; the long brown arrow in Fig. 11-2 shows that the vertical distance (consumption expenditure) is less than the horizontal distance (disposable income). If the family is not spending all its income, then it must be saving the remainder. The 45° line tells us more than that; it enables us to find *how much* the family is saving. Net saving is

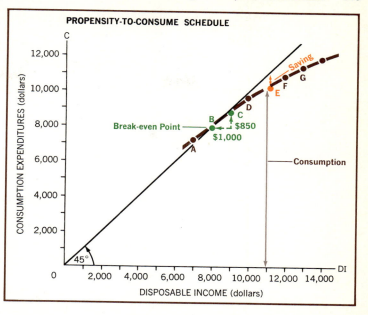

**FIG. 11-2**

**A curve plots the consumption schedule** The curve through *A*, *B*, *C*, . . . is the consumption schedule, or the propensity to consume. Its slope at any point, measured by forming a little triangle and relating altitude to base, is the MPC, the marginal propensity to consume. The 45° line helps locate the break-even point and helps our eye measure net saving. Can you see how? (Source: Table 11-2 and extrapolation beyond *G*.)

measured by the distance from the propensity-to-consume curve up to the 45° line, as shown by the appropriate saving arrow in orange.

Similarly, to the left of point *B*, our 45° helping line tells us that the family is for the moment somehow spending more than the income it receives. The excess of consumption over income is its "net dissaving" and is measured by the vertical distance between the two curves. To review:

**When the propensity-to-consume schedule lies above the 45° line, the family is dissaving. Where the two curves meet, the family is just breaking even. Where the propensity to consume lies below the 45° line, the family is performing net positive saving. And the amount of dissaving or saving is always measured by the distance between the two curves.**

**The "propensity-to-save schedule"** This means that we can easily derive from the consumption schedule in Fig. 11-2 a new schedule: the propensity to save, or as it is sometimes called, the "saving schedule."

Graphically, this is shown in Fig. 11-3. Again we show disposable income on the

**FIG. 11-3**

**The saving schedule is the mirror twin of the consumption schedule** This saving schedule comes from subtracting consumption from income. (Graphically, we vertically subtracted the consumption schedule from the 45° helping line.) Note that the break-even point *B* is at the same $8,000 level as in Fig. 11-2.

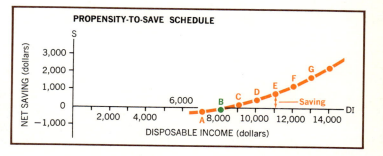

horizontal axis; vertically, we now show what the family *does not* spend; i.e., we show its net saving, whether negative or positive in amount.

This propensity-to-save curve comes directly from Fig. 11-2. It is simply the distance between the 45° line and the propensity-to-consume schedule. At a point such as *A* in Fig. 11-2, the fact that the family's savings were negative was indicated by the propensity-to-consume schedule lying above the helping line. Figure 11-3 shows this fact of negative saving directly, and similarly for the positive saving that begins when family income pushes past point *B*.

## THE MARGINAL PROPENSITY TO CONSUME

In the next chapter, we shall be attaching much importance to the *extra* amount that people will want to spend on consumption if given an *extra* dollar of income. Economists are so interested in this concept that they have given it a special name, the "marginal propensity to consume," or MPC. (The word "marginal" is used by the economist to mean "extra"; thus, marginal cost will later be defined as extra cost of producing an extra unit of product; marginal utility as extra utility; marginal revenue as extra revenue; and so forth.)

Column (3) back in Table 11-2 shows how we compute the marginal propensity to consume. From *B* to *C*, income rises by $1,000, going from $8,000 to $9,000. By how much does consumption rise? Consumption grows from $8,000 to $8,850, or by $850. The extra consumption is therefore .85 of the extra income, as we saw earlier. Out of each extra dollar of income, 85 cents goes to consumption and 15 cents goes to saving. We therefore can say that the marginal propensity to consume, or MPC, is .85 between *B* and *C*, which agrees with Column (3) of Table 11-2.

You can easily compute MPC between other income levels. In Table 11-2, MPC begins at .89 for poor people and finally falls to .53 at higher incomes.

**Marginal propensity to consume as geometrical slope**    Now we know how to compute MPC numerically. What is its geometric meaning? It is a numerical measure of the steepness of slope of the consumption schedule.[5] Look again at Fig. 11-2. Near points *B* and *C* a little triangle is drawn. As we move to the right from *B* by $1,000, in order to stay on the schedule, we must go up by $850; this gives a numerical slope of $850/$1,000, or .85.

NOTE: If higher incomes have a lower MPC, the family consumption schedule will look slightly bowed (convex from above, concave from below.)

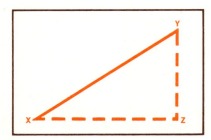

[5] By the numerical slope of the line *XY*, we always mean the numerical ratio of the length *ZY* to the length *XZ*.

See the accompanying drawing. If *XY* were a curve, we could find the slope at any point on it (1) by placing a ruler tangent to it, and (2) by applying the procedure for this triangle to that tangential line.

If the line is the consumption schedule, its slope is the MPC, i.e., is the *marginal* propensity to consume. We'll see that if the line is the saving schedule, its slope will be defined as the MPS, i.e., is the *marginal* propensity to save.

## THE MARGINAL PROPENSITY TO SAVE

Along with the marginal propensity to consume goes a mirror-twin concept, the "marginal propensity to save," or MPS. This is defined as *the fraction of each extra dollar that goes to saving instead of to consumption.*

Why are MPC and MPS related like mirror twins? Since each extra dollar of income must be divided between extra consumption and extra saving, it is obvious that if MPC is .85, then MPS must be .15. (What would MPS be if MPC were .6? Or .99?) A comparison of Columns (3) and (5) of Table 11-2 confirms our common-sense feeling that at any income level, MPC and MPS must always add up to exactly 1, no more and no less.[6]

## BRIEF REVIEW OF DEFINITIONS

For the record, let us jot down the main definitions now learned:

**1. The propensity-to-consume schedule (or consumption schedule) relates in a table or a curve the level of consumption to the level of income.**

**2. The propensity-to-save schedule (or saving schedule) relates saving to income. Since what is saved is the same thing as what is nonconsumed, saving and consumption schedules are mirror twins in the sense that**

$$\text{Saving} + \text{consumption} = \text{disposable income}$$

**3. The "break-even point" is the income level where net saving is zero. Below it, there is dissaving, or negative saving; above it, positive net saving. Graphically, the break-even point is where the 45° helping line intersects the consumption schedule, or where the saving schedule intersects the horizontal axis.**

**4. The marginal propensity to consume (MPC) is the amount of *extra* consumption generated by an *extra* dollar of income. Graphically, it is given by the slope of the consumption schedule—a steep slope meaning a high MPC and a flat one meaning a low MPC.**

**5. The marginal propensity to save (MPS) is the *extra* saving generated by an *extra* dollar of income, or the slope of the saving schedule. Because the part of each dollar that is not consumed is necessarily saved, MPS = 1 − MPC always. Hence, higher income that lowers MPC must raise MPS, implying a concave (from below) consumption schedule and a convex saving schedule.**

## THE COMMUNITY'S OVERALL CONSUMPTION SCHEDULE

So far we have been talking about the budget consumption patterns shown by typical families at varying income levels. To study what determines *a nation's* income, we are interested in a propensity-to-consume schedule slightly different from the family-

---

[6]You can also verify from Fig. 11-3 that the numerical steepness of slope of the propensity-to-save schedule is the geometric expression of MPS. This shows: The saving schedule will always have the opposite curvature to that of the consumption schedule; as MPC falls, MPS must rise. And since every extra dollar divides up between positive extra consumption and extra saving, it follows that neither the consumption nor the saving schedule *anywhere* has a slope as steep as the 45° line, which by definition has a slope of 1. Remember, we are here discussing *marginal* propensities. Thus, at point *A*, the family is spending more than its income; but that does not alter the fact that, at *A*, its *marginal* propensity to consume out of *extra* income is less than 1. (These family data show more exaggerated curvature than would seem realistic in the 1970s for *permanent* income levels.)

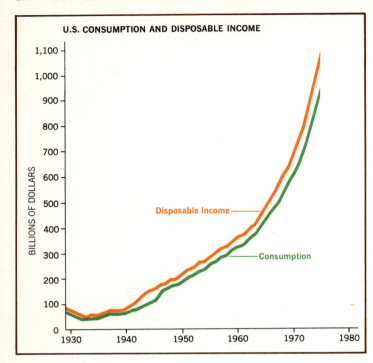

**U.S. CONSUMPTION AND DISPOSABLE INCOME**

**FIG. 11-4**
**Community's consumption spending has moved with national income**
An important determinant of fluctuations in consumption expenditure has been fluctuations in income to spend. Good forecasts of consumption come from income data. Can you see how great saving became during World War II's goods shortage and rationing? (Source: U.S. Department of Commerce.)

budget schedule. We want the "community propensity-to-consume schedule," relating total consumption to total "disposable (after-tax) income." This is because we are interested in how the total of *all* consumption spending in the United States changes as the total of our spendable income rises.

While aggregate income is not the only factor determining aggregate consumption, common sense and statistical experience tell us that it is one of the most important factors. Look at Fig. 11-4 to see how closely consumption seems to follow yearly disposable income; the only exceptional period is that of World War II, when goods were scarce and rationed and people were urged to save.

Figure 11-5 shows this relationship between consumption and disposable income in the form of a "scatter diagram" for the years 1929 up until 1975. Each dot marks the magnitude for each year. The resulting scatter of points shows no particular curvature; so a straight-line consumption schedule was drawn in. The actual data fall near, but not exactly on, the "fitted" consumption schedule,[7] reminding us that economics is not, like physics, an exact science. A good rule of thumb is this: Out of each dollar of disposable income, just over 90 cents goes for consumption; most of the remaining 10 cents goes for saving (except for about 2 cents for consumer interest).

[7] So that no reader may think there is great accuracy in this line, let it be mentioned that it was fitted by stretching a black thread from the lower corner through all the data (excepting those for World War II) at what appeared a reasonable position. As in the case of supply and demand curves in Chapter 4 and Part Three, it will be convenient to go back and forth between drawing propensity-to-consume schedules as curved lines or more simply as straight lines when doing so does no gross violence to the actual facts.

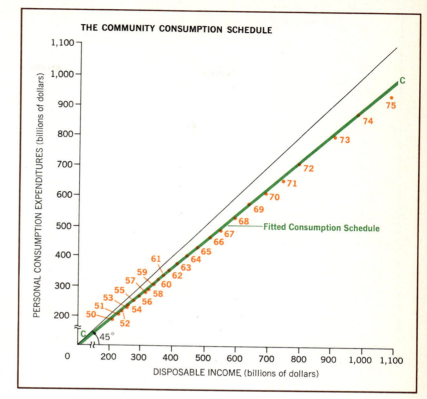

**FIG. 11-5**

A statistical consumption schedule fits data quite closely

A straight line has been passed through the scatter of orange data points. Can you verify that the MPC slope of the fitted line is close to .90? (Source: Fig. 11-4.)

## QUALIFICATIONS

We are now prepared for the theory of income determination. We have introduced the crucially important concepts of consumption and saving schedules that will be used in the next chapter. But warnings are in order. The community consumption schedule must be in some sense an aggregation of the family schedules. Yet even if we knew that the family schedules were perfectly reliable, we should still have to know something about the *distribution of incomes* before we could get the new points of total consumption of the national schedule. Thus, when a national-income rise is associated with the distribution of extra income that is *typical* for such a rise, we shall be moving upward on our unshifted community consumption schedule CC.

Aside from the distribution of income, there is a second factor that must be taken into account in any attempt to relate the family and national patterns. Suppose my income were to go from $15,000 to $50,000 a year. Would I spend and save my money in the same way that the budget studies showed $50,000-a-year people spend their money? Not necessarily. Especially at the beginning, I would be a *nouveau riche* and have different patterns of behavior.[8]

[8] Modern theoretical and statistical researches by Professors James S. Duesenberry, Milton Friedman, and Franco Modigliani suggest strongly that if people were generally to get a prescribed percentage increase in their incomes that was permanent, they would probably add more to their long-run consumption expenditure than would be indicated by budget studies recorded for a single year such as 1950 or 1975. This warning, which appeared earlier in footnote 3, is worth repeating.

A third reason why it is difficult to go from the family to the national consumption schedule is suggested by the expression "keeping up with the Joneses." Back in 1920, if your family had $2,000 worth of purchasing power, you would have been quite well-off and above the break-even point of zero saving. But today many people have incomes above that level. Because man is a social animal, what he regards as "necessary comforts of life" depends on what he sees others consuming. So today, with $2,000 of income, you would be desperately poor and unable to make ends meet. This fact that one man's consumption depends upon the incomes and consumption of others means that we cannot expect the final community pattern to be the simple sum of the separate family patterns. It also means that we must expect the consumption schedule to be shifting upward each decade as living standards rise. Hence, in Fig. 11-5, one would be foolish to push the line back to the income of 1900 or forward to 1999. It is a succinct description of history, rather than a strict law of nature.[9]

Chapter 10 showed that the national-income accounts *always measure* an identity between saving and investment. The present chapter showed that the *motives* and *desires* behind saving and investment are generally quite distinct—which certainly raises the suspicion that the total flow of dollar spending is not guaranteed to proceed at exactly the same rate year in and year out. The hard facts of history confirm this suspicion: at times the economy experienced overexuberant demand and inflation; at times—and they used to be of considerable duration—it experienced considerable unemployment and excess capacity; in the absence of determined public programs of fiscal and monetary controls, only at rare times have economies enjoyed full employment and steady price levels.

The next two chapters investigate how the forces of saving and investment interact to produce an equilibrium level of national income, which can be at high or low employment and which can be conducive to price stability or to price inflation.

[9] The community consumption schedule will shift as prices change and total population grows. So, instead of working with simple, total dollar $C$, statisticians may correct it for Price and Population, by working with doubly deflated $C$/(Price × Population); likewise, they may replace $DI$ by its doubly deflated $DI$/(Price × Population), to get *per capita real* income.

## SUMMARY

1  Motivations making people want to engage in saving and to engage in investing are different. History shows there is no automatic tendency for the same number of dollars to get spent always at the same rate. Hence, our modern mixed economy would be subject to inflationary and depression swings if proper public fiscal and monetary policies did not act to help stabilize the economy and reinforce its spontaneous internal mechanisms that strive to achieve stability.

2  Income is one of the most important determinants of consumption (food, clothing, all items together) and of saving. The propensity to consume is the schedule relating total consumption to total income. Because any dollar of income is either saved or consumed, the propensity-to-save schedule is the other side or mirror twin of the propensity-to-consume picture. The characteristics of the consumption and saving schedules are summarized on page 215.

**3** We could aggregate the family consumption schedules to get the community propensity-to-consume schedule, (*a*) if we knew the distribution of income for each level of disposable income; (*b*) if families always stuck to the same consumption-income patterns in the short run and the long; (*c*) if we could forget the fact that one man's consumption is influenced by the income levels of his neighbors; and (*d*) if price levels, population, corporate saving, and taxes could be neglected. So we must allow for these qualifications.

## CONCEPTS FOR REVIEW

family motives for saving
business motives for investing
volatile investment decisions
consumption and saving
    schedules
propensity to consume or to save
MPC and MPS
MPC + MPS = 1

break-even point and 45° line
after-tax, or disposable, income
permanent versus transitory
    income
community consumption schedule
    versus family schedule
shifts of *CC* with price, time,
    income distribution, etc.

## QUESTIONS FOR DISCUSSION

**1** Summarize familiar budget patterns: food, clothing, luxuries, saving.

**2** What are some of the reasons why people save? What are some of the forms in which they keep their assets?

**3** Exactly how were the MPC and MPS in Table 11-2 computed? Illustrate between *A* and *B*. Explain why it must always be true that MPC + MPS = 1.

**4** I consume *all* my income. Draw my consumption and saving schedules.

**5** Do you think the break-even point is the same in New York as in Mississippi? What do you think is the current break-even point in your community? List a number of ways a person can incur negative net saving for a while.

**6** "Along the consumption schedule, income changes more (absolutely) than consumption does." Why? Show that this is even more true on the saving schedule.

**7** Contrast the meaning of the second of this chapter's opening quotations with the following 1966 letter to the editor of *Time Magazine* by Professor Milton Friedman of the University of Chicago.

Sir: You quote me [Dec. 31] as saying: "We are all Keynesians now." The quotation is correct, but taken out of context. As best I can recall it, the context was: "In one sense, we are all Keynesians now; in another, nobody is any longer a Keynesian."

**8** *Extra-credit problem:* Suppose this equation for *CC* holds: $C = 200 + \frac{2}{3} DI$. Now calculate the MPC as $dC/d(DI) = \frac{2}{3}$. From the identity $S + C \equiv DI$, verify the formula for the *SS* schedule: $S = -200 + \frac{1}{3} DI$. From this calculate MPS as $dS/d(DI)$ and verify that it does equal $1 - \text{MPC} = 1 - \frac{2}{3} = \frac{1}{3}$.

# 12

## INCOME DETERMINATION: THE SIMPLE MULTIPLIER THEORY

Given the propensity to consume and the rate of new investment, there will be only one level of employment consistent with equilibrium.

J. M. KEYNES (1936)

Economists are agreed that an important factor in causing income and employment to fluctuate is fluctuation in investment. Whether we are to face a situation of inflationary bidding up of prices or are to live in a frigid state of mass unemployment can depend, as will be seen, upon the level of investment.

This chapter and the next one outline the modern theory of income determination. Because the problems are so important and because the analysis is so useful, the present chapter stresses the fundamentals: how saving and investment interact to determine the equilibrium level of national income (or GNP) at full employment, below full employment, or in over-full-employment inflationary conditions; and, what we shall see is exactly the same thing, how consumption and investment schedules combine to determine that equilibrium level of GNP. Also we shall analyze how each dollar change in investment leads to more than a dollar—i.e., to a "multiplier"—change in GNP.

Once the tools of this chapter are mastered, we are ready to understand the next chapter's analysis of inflation and deflation, of how government expenditure and government tax policy can alter the income equilibrium, and of the paradox that sometimes when a nation *tries* to save more, it ends up only undermining the actual investment accomplished.

### USING THE CONSUMPTION AND SAVING SCHEDULES

The preceding chapter gave a simplified picture of the propensity-to-consume and the propensity-to-save schedules for the community. As we've already discussed, the consumption and saving schedules are drawn up on the basis of our knowledge of the thriftiness of different families, the distribution of incomes among families, and so forth.

Initially we shall here make the further simplifying assumptions that there are no taxes, undistributed corporate profits, depreciation, transfers, or government expenditure of any kind to worry about; hence, we do not have to concern ourselves yet with any distinction between gross national product and disposable income, and therefore we can legitimately use the word "income" to refer to either or both of these concepts. Also, we shall initially neglect any changes in the price level.

Figure 12-1 shows the community propensities to consume and save. Each point on its consumption schedule shows how much the community will *want to continue to consume* at that level of disposable income. Each point on the saving schedule shows how much it will *want to continue to save* at that income level. Recall that the two schedules are closely related: since $C + S =$ income always, the $CC$ and $SS$ curves are mirror twins that will add up always to the 45° line.

## HOW INCOME IS DETERMINED AT THE LEVEL WHERE SAVING AND INVESTMENT SCHEDULES INTERSECT

We have seen that saving and investment are dependent on quite different factors: Saving tends to depend in a "passive" way upon income, while volatile investment often depends upon various nonincome factors (dynamic growth, technical invention, interest rates, money supply, and so forth).

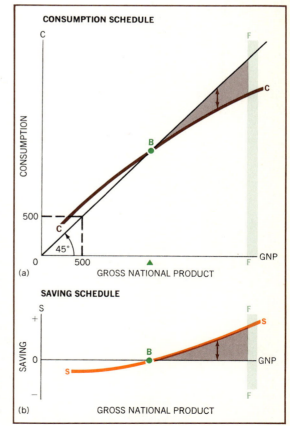

**FIG. 12-1**

**Society's national income determines its levels of consumption and saving**

$CC$ is the propensity-to-consume schedule for the community, and $SS$ is the propensity-to-save schedule for the community.

Recall that these are closely related in a mirror-twin fashion: the break-even point $B$ is shown on the upper diagram where $CC$ intersects the 45° line and on the lower diagram where $SS$ intersects the horizontal axis. Can you explain why the vertically aligned arrows *must* be equal? (The curvature is slightly exaggerated here to help identify the two schedules. The two points marked 500 should help emphasize the important property of the 45° line: it depicts a vertical distance equal to exactly 100 per cent of the horizontal distance.)

The shaded area $FF$ depicts the full-employment GNP. Above this critical level we know real product cannot increase, and beyond it we could no longer adhere to our simplifying assumption of ignoring price-level changes. (Source: Table 11-2, Fig. 11-4, and Fig. 11-5.)

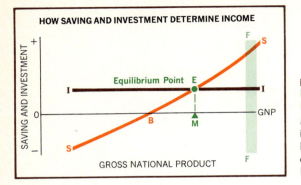

FIG. 12-2
**Equilibrium determination of national income is shown by intersection of saving and investment schedules**
*E* marks the spot where investment and saving curves intersect. Equilibrium is at intersection of *SS* and *II* curves because at no other level of GNP could the desired saving of families continually match the desired investment of business.

For simplicity, first suppose investment opportunities are such that investment would be exactly $60 billion per year regardless of the level of GNP. This means that, if we now draw a schedule of investment against GNP, it will have to be a *horizontal* line—always the same distance above the horizontal axis. Observe Fig. 12-2 where this investment schedule is labeled *II* to distinguish it from the *SS* saving schedule. (Note that *II* does *not* mean Roman numeral two.)

The saving and investment schedules intersect at *E*, which corresponds to a level of GNP equal to the distance from 0 to *M* as shown by the green pointer.

*This intersection of the saving and investment schedules is the equilibrium toward which national income will gravitate.* Under our assumed conditions, no other level of income can perpetuate itself.

The remaining pages of this chapter are devoted to the single task of explaining and interpreting this important truth.

**Stability of the equilibrium**    Let us see why the equilibrium income must eventually be at *E*, the point of intersection between the investment and saving schedules. We consider three cases.

The first case is that in which the system is *at E* itself, where the *II* schedule of what business firms *want* to invest and keep investing just intersects the *SS* schedule of what families *want* to save. Consequently, everyone will be content to go on doing just what he has been doing. Firms will not find inventories piling up on their shelves, nor will they find sales so brisk as to force them to produce more goods. So production, employment, and income spending will remain the same. GNP in this first case does truly stay at the point *E;* and we can rightly call that "equilibrium."

The second case is where the system is *first* at a GNP *higher* than at *E*, so that it begins east of *E*, at an income level where the *SS* schedule is higher than the *II* schedule. Why can't the system stay there indefinitely? Because at such an income level, families are saving—are refraining from spending on consumption—*more* than business firms will be *willing to go on investing*. Firms will thus find they have too few customers and that their inventories are piling up against their wishes, and they will not want to go on being forced into such undesired inventory investment. What can they do about it? They can certainly cut back production and lay off workers.

This moves GNP gradually downward, or westward in Fig. 12-2. Where does the system stop being in disequilibrium? Only when it gets back to $E$, the equilibrium intersection point. There the longer-run tendency to change has disappeared.

The third case should be mastered by the reader. Show that if GNP were *below* its equilibrium level, strong forces would be set up to move it eastward back to $E$. (Hint: At any GNP level where families' *intended* saving falls short of business firms' *intended* investment, the result is consumption of more goods than are being currently produced. What does this mean? It means that business will find itself having to sell inventory off its shelves faster than its production line is producing such goods. Once businessmen notice that they are being forced into less investment, i.e., into more *involuntary* inventory *disinvestment* than the $II$ curve shows they want, what will they do? They will then expand production and hire new men. This will complete the demonstration that the system does move back eastward until it gets to $E$.)

All three cases then lead to the same summary:

**The only equilibrium of GNP is at $E$, where the saving and investment schedules intersect. At any other point, the *desired* saving of families will not match the *desired* investment of business, and this discrepancy will cause businessmen to change their production and employment levels in such a way as to return the system to the equilibrium intersection.**

Before we go on, a warning is in order. An equilibrium level like $E$ is a point where the system tends to stay. But there is nothing necessarily *optimal* about every equilibrium point. Note the shading's vertical boundary at $FF$ in Fig. 12-2 that depicts full-employment income. Note the fact that the $E$ equilibrium shown is at a level of GNP *lower* than that corresponding to $FF$'s full employment.

During a great depression, a capitalistic system may be firmly stuck at a point of very great unemployment. It is then at the $E$ given by its low $II$ schedule. No one would make the mistake of thinking that such a deep-unemployment equilibrium point is in any sense a good thing. Instead, the government would intervene in the economic system with monetary and fiscal policies to shift the curves until a new equilibrium point $E'$ was attained at a desirable level—as the next chapter explains.

## INCOME DETERMINATION BY CONSUMPTION AND INVESTMENT

There is a second way of showing how income is determined, other than by the intersection of the saving and investment schedules. The final result is exactly the same, but our understanding and confidence in the theory of income determination will be increased if we work through this second approach.

This second approach is called the consumption-plus-investment rather than the saving-investment approach. The $C + I$ approach[1] takes advantage of the mirror-twins property of the saving and consumption schedules. Thus it must always lead to exactly the same equilibrium income as does the saving-and-investment approach. This is shown by the fact that if you lined up Fig. 12-3 vertically under Fig. 12-2, you'd always find that in both charts, $E$ marks exactly the same GNP equilibrium.

---

[1] When government is brought into the picture, $C + I$ will soon become $C + I + G$. (Note: Since depreciation is being provisionally ignored, we can regard "investment" as being "net investment" or "gross investment" interchangeably.)

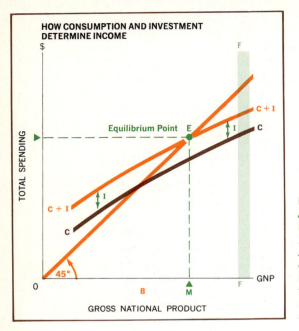

**HOW CONSUMPTION AND INVESTMENT DETERMINE INCOME**

**FIG. 12-3**

**Alternatively, equilibrium GNP level can be shown by intersection of C + I schedule with 45° line**

Adding *II* to *CC* gives the *C + I* curve of total spending. At *E*, where it intersects the 45° line, we get the same equilibrium as in the saving-and-investment diagram. (Note the similarities between this figure and Fig. 12-2: the investment added to *CC* is the same as *II* of Fig. 12-2; *B* and *F* each come at the same place on the two diagrams, *and so must the E intersection*.)

The *C + I* approach of Fig. 12-3 has the advantage of concentrating on *total spending:* spending for consumption goods plus spending for investment goods. The *C + I* approach vertically adds the *II* schedule of business' *desired* investment to the *CC* consumption schedule of families' *desired* consumption spending.

Only where these two *desired* amounts of spending add up to equality with the value of GNP being produced will there be equilibrium.

With what must the combined *C + I* schedule intersect to depict this equilibrium? Figure 12-3 introduces a 45° line to provide our looked-for intersection point. The 45° line, we have seen, has the useful property that it lays out in the vertical direction a distance always exactly equal to the income shown on the horizontal axis. So the 45° line is admirably designed to depict the total expense that firms are incurring for the productive factors required to produce national output, and which they must be getting back if they are to feel safe to continue hiring the same number of men and producing the same level of GNP.[2]

We can summarize the *C + I* method of income determination thus:

---

[2] As the intermediate texts put it: If the system is not at this intersection, there will be *unintended* inventory investment or disinvestment and/or *unforeseen windfall* profits or losses. As a result, there cannot be equilibrium; but rather, a chain of new decisions will be set up to expand or contract output, and possibly to raise or lower prices. So the system will move in disequilibrium until it ends up at the intersection point of equilibrium. Those same intermediate texts point out that *measured* S and *measured* I stay *identical* even during the worst disequilibrium, by virtue of some people's experiencing unintended losses or gains and/or experiencing unintended investment or saving. (Remember that economists include profit in expense and recall Chapter 10's final Appendix remarks on $S \equiv I$.)

INCOME DETERMINATION BY SAVING AND INVESTMENT (in billions of dollars)

| (1) LEVELS OF GNP AND DI | (2) SCHEDULED CONSUMPTION | (3) SCHEDULED, PLANNED, OR MAINTAINABLE SAVING (3) = (1) − (2) | (4) SCHEDULED, PLANNED, OR MAINTAINABLE INVESTMENT | (5) EXPENSE INCURRABLE BY BUSINESS TO PRODUCE GNP (5) = (1) | (6) SCHEDULED SPENDING THAT WOULD PERMANENTLY COME BACK TO BUSINESSES (6) = (2) + (4) | (7) RESULTING TENDENCY OF INCOME |
|---|---|---|---|---|---|---|
| $2,200 | $1,800 | $400 | $200 | $2,200 > | $2,000 | Contraction |
| 1,900 | 1,600 | 300 | 200 | 1,900 > | 1,800 | Contraction |
| 1,600 | 1,400 | 200 | 200 | 1,600 = | 1,600 | Equilibrium |
| 1,300 | 1,200 | 100 | 200 | 1,300 < | 1,400 | Expansion |
| 1,000 | 1,000 | 0 | 200 | 1,000 < | 1,200 | Expansion |
| 700 | 800 | −100 | 200 | 700 < | 1,000 | Expansion |

TABLE 12-1

**The tendency for income to go to its equilibrium level is shown by arithmetic table**
The green row depicts the equilibrium GNP level, where the $200 billion that businessmen will be *willing to continue to* invest is just matched by families' *intended and maintainable* saving. (In higher rows, firms will be forced into unintended inventory investment and will respond by cutting production and GNP back to equilibrium. Interpret the lower rows' tendency toward expansion of GNP toward equilibrium.)

**The equilibrium level of national income is at the intersection of the C + I schedule of desired total spending with the 45° line depicting value of total output.**[3] **This equilibrium E corresponds exactly to the saving-and-investment equilibrium because of the mirror-twins relation between the consumption and the saving schedules.**

We shall see in the next chapter that the C + I approach has great advantages in helping to analyze government expenditure and fiscal policy. It easily turns itself into an exactly similar C + I + G approach.

## ARITHMETIC DEMONSTRATION OF INCOME DETERMINATION: A DIGRESSION FOR A THIRD RESTATEMENT

A thoughtful reader may still want to know more about *why* the equilibrium level of income will have to be at the intersection of the saving and investment schedules. What forces will push income to that level and no other?

An arithmetic example may help verify this important matter. Table 12-1 shows an especially simple pattern of the propensity to save against income. The break-even level of income where the nation is too poor to do any net saving on balance is assumed to be $1,000 billion. Each change of income of $300 billion is assumed to lead to a $100-billion change in saving and a $200-billion change in consumption; in other

[3] Some writers like to call the C + I curve an aggregate *demand* curve, and the 45°-line curve an aggregate *supply* curve. Then, using Chapter 4's language, they say: The equilibrium level of income is where the aggregate demand and supply curves intersect.

words, MPC is for simplicity here assumed to be constant and exactly equal to $\frac{2}{3}$, with $MPS = \frac{1}{3}$. For this reason, the saving propensity schedule SS in Fig. 12-4 takes on the especially simple form of a perfectly straight line.

What shall we assume about investment? For simplicity, let us suppose again that the only level of investment that can be voluntarily maintained indefinitely is exactly $200 billion, as shown in Column (4) of Table 12-1.

Now, Columns (5) and (6) are the crucial ones. Column (5) shows how much total expense business firms undergo at each level of national production for wages, interest, rent, *and* profit. This is the GNP of Column (1) copied once again into Column (5), because our repeated discussions in Chapter 10 showed that upper- and lower-loop measurements must be the same.

Column (6), on the other hand, shows what business firms would in fact be *getting back* in the long run in the form of scheduled or voluntary consumption spending plus scheduled or voluntary investment. (It's really Fig. 12-3's orange $C + I$ schedule.)

When business firms as a whole are temporarily producing a high total product, higher than the sum of what consumers will buy and what business as a whole wants to be investing in equipment and inventory accumulation, businesses will find themselves forced involuntarily to pile up inventory of unsalable goods. At the same time, their total sales revenue will be so low as to be putting disagreeable downward pressure on their profit position. With scheduled SS above $II$, therefore, they will want to contract their operations, and GNP will tend to fall. (Contrariwise, when $II > SS$ and inventories are being involuntarily depleted and profit margins improving, they will increase their employment, and production and GNP will rise.)

When business firms as a whole are temporarily producing at an expense greater than what they can recover, they will want to contract their operations, and GNP tends to fall. When they are getting back more than their current expense for production, they increase their production and GNP rises.

Only when level of scheduled saving in Column (3) exactly equals scheduled investment in Column (4) will business firms stay continually in aggregative equilibrium. Their sales will there be just enough to justify continuing their current level of aggregate output. GNP will neither expand nor contract.

This same story is shown in Fig. 12-4. GNP can be read in either of two ways: on the horizontal axis or (from the nature of a 45° line) as the equivalent vertical distance from that axis up to the helping 45° line. The line SS represents the saving schedule; the line $II$ represents the scheduled level of investment that can be maintained over time. Consumption can also be seen in the figure. Since income not saved is consumed, consumption is always the vertical distance from the saving schedule to the 45° line.

Now we can use Fig. 12-4 to confirm what has just been shown by the arithmetic of Table 12-1. No level of income can *long persist* if it is higher than the equilibrium level given by the *scheduled* saving and investment intersection at $1,600 billion. To the right of the intersection point $E$, the expense incurred by businesses would exceed the *amount received back* by businesses in the form of maintainable consumption plus maintainable investment.

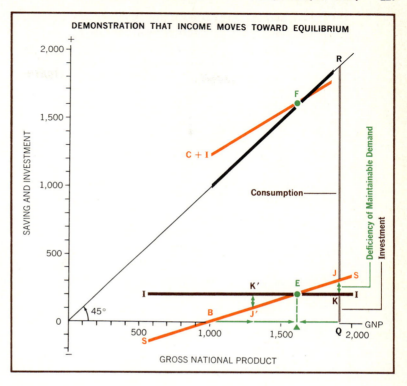

DEMONSTRATION THAT INCOME MOVES TOWARD EQUILIBRIUM

**FIG. 12-4**

**Graph reinforces table's story of tendencies restoring equilibrium**

Only at *E* is there no gap between *scheduled* saving and investment. A gap like that shown at *JK* will soon cause firms to cut their production, which explains the westward green arrow pushing GNP back to *E*'s equilibrium level.

Show that the opposite gap at *J'K'* will mean that firms find their sales so great as to deplete their inventories; interpret the eastward green arrows showing that firms expand production to push GNP back to *E*.

Graphically, this is shown by the following: The amount continuously paid out by business is the whole distance up to the 45° line, i.e., from *Q* to *R;* but the amount that would continuously be received back by business would be only the sum of voluntary investment *QK* and consumption *JR*. There is a gap of *JK*.

Businesses face a real dilemma. For a while they could keep their prices high and let unsold goods pile up on their shelves, but that would not represent an equilibrium situation and could not persist. Or for a while they could lower prices on their goods and sell below needed cost with less profits; but that, too, could not last.

Thus, it is completely clear that income cannot *permanently* be maintained higher than the equilibrium level—*the level where the amount of saving that people want to do is matched by the amount of investment businessmen are willing to maintain.* A persistent gap of the *JK* type must, through attempts to cut down losses and excessive inventories, result in a contraction of employment and gross national product back toward the equilibrium point, where there is no gap. Therefore the green arrow near *Q* points leftward back toward the equilibrium level.

A similar argument shows why income will tend to raise from any place to the left of the equilibrium-intersection level. Indicate on the diagram the relation between business expense and what business can permanently receive back. Show that there will be a favorable gap (as at *J'K'*): Businesses either will be selling so much as to be depleting inventories on their shelves or will be temporarily raising their prices and earning extra profits. In either case, they will be tempted to expand their employment and production. And when they do, the result will be a rise in income back toward the equilibrium-intersection level.[4] Thus ends our digression.

### THE "MULTIPLIER"

Now that we have seen how the intersection of saving and investment determines the level of national income, we realize that an increase in investment will increase the level of income and employment. Thus, an investment boom may bring a nation out of a deep or mild depression—by having a higher $II$ schedule cut the $SS$ schedule at a higher equilibrium level for GNP.

**An increase in private investment will cause income and employment to expand; a decrease in investment will cause them to contract.**

This is not a very surprising result. After all, we have learned that investment is one part of gross national product; when one of the parts increases in value, we should naturally expect the whole to increase in value. That is only part of the story. Our theory of income determination gives us a much more striking result.

**Modern income analysis shows that an increase in investment will increase national income by a *multiplied* amount—by an amount greater than itself! Investment spending—like any independent shifts in governmental, foreign, or family spending—is high-powered, double-duty spending, so to speak.**

**This amplified effect of investment[5] on income is called the "multiplier" doctrine; the word "multiplier" itself is used for *the numerical coefficient showing how much above unity is the increase in income resulting from each increase in investment.***

Some examples will make this terminology clear. Let there be an increase of investment of $100 billion. If this causes an increase of income of $300 billion, then the multiplier is 3. If, instead, the resulting increase in income were $400 billion, then the multiplier would be 4.

*Definition:* **The multiplier is the number by which the change in investment must be multiplied in order to present us with the resulting change in income.**

---

[4]The recorded income statistics never show the gap depicted by $JK$ and by Column (6) minus Column (5). Why not? Because these are gaps in people's *scheduled* quantities. They show levels that cannot continue to persist. On the other hand, the *measurable* statistics of saving and investment are definitionally equal no matter what income is doing: thus, when inventory is *involuntarily* piling up, the Commerce Department statistician cares not that its identity of investment and saving is the result of *unintended* investment. Why should it? It need never go beyond the anatomy of the problem. But we—interested in dynamic physiology of income determination—are vitally interested in schedules. (NOTE: In the last few pages, words such as "voluntary," "scheduled," and "maintainable" were repeated and stressed. This was done to call attention to the difference between a magnitude permanently persisting as a schedule, and the actual amounts measured after the fact in any disturbed short run. In the supply and demand schedules of Part Three, the same problem will recur; Chapter 4 showed that the wheat bought is *always* numerically identical with the wheat sold, but only at *equilibrium* market price do the *scheduled* amounts intersect.)

[5]Our later analysis will show that the multiplier can apply to government and other shifts in spending; but in this chapter we stick to the simplifying assumption of shifts up and down of a horizontal investment schedule, leaving the government out of the picture and not letting the $CC$ schedule shift and thereby itself initiate amplified multiplier effects.

No proof has yet been presented to show that the multiplier will be greater than 1. But by using ordinary common sense one can see why, when I hire unemployed resources to build a $1,000 garage, there will be a *secondary* expansion of national income and production, over and above my *primary* investment. Here is why.

My carpenters and lumber producers will get an extra $1,000 of income. But that is not the end of the story. If they all have a marginal propensity to consume of $\frac{2}{3}$, they will now spend $666.67 on new consumption goods. The producers of these goods will now have an extra income of $666.67. If their MPC is also $\frac{2}{3}$, they in turn will spend $444.44, or $\frac{2}{3}$ of $666.67 (or $\frac{2}{3}$ of $\frac{2}{3}$ of $1,000). So the process will go on, with each new round of spending being $\frac{2}{3}$ of the previous round.

Thus a whole endless chain of secondary consumption responding is set up by my primary $1,000 of investment spending. But, although an endless chain, it is a dwindling chain. And in toto it adds up to a finite amount. By either grade school arithmetic, in which we add the successive numbers until the decimals become insignificant, or by high school geometric progression,[6] we get

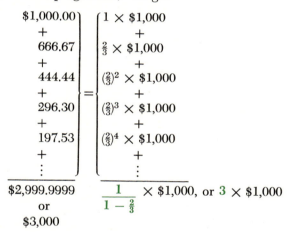

$$\left.\begin{array}{c} \$1,000.00 \\ + \\ 666.67 \\ + \\ 444.44 \\ + \\ 296.30 \\ + \\ 197.53 \\ + \\ \vdots \end{array}\right\} = \left\{\begin{array}{c} 1 \times \$1,000 \\ + \\ \frac{2}{3} \times \$1,000 \\ + \\ (\frac{2}{3})^2 \times \$1,000 \\ + \\ (\frac{2}{3})^3 \times \$1,000 \\ + \\ (\frac{2}{3})^4 \times \$1,000 \\ + \\ \vdots \end{array}\right.$$

$$\begin{array}{cc} \$2,999.9999 & \dfrac{1}{1-\frac{2}{3}} \times \$1,000, \text{ or } 3 \times \$1,000 \\ \text{or} & \\ \$3,000 & \end{array}$$

This shows that, with an MPC of $\frac{2}{3}$, the multiplier is 3, consisting of the 1 of primary investment plus 2 extra of secondary consumption responding.

The same arithmetic would give a multiplier of 4 if the MPC were $\frac{3}{4}$, for the reason that $1 + \frac{3}{4} + (\frac{3}{4})^2 + (\frac{3}{4})^3 + \cdots$ finally adds up to 4. If the MPC were $\frac{1}{2}$, the multiplier would be 2. The size of the multiplier thus depends upon how large the MPC is; or it can be expressed in terms of the twin concept, the MPS. If the MPS were $\frac{1}{4}$, the MPC would be $\frac{3}{4}$, and the multiplier would be 4. If the MPS were $\frac{1}{3}$, the multiplier would be 3. If the MPS were $1/X$, the multiplier would be $X$.

[6] High school algebra says the formula for an infinite geometric progression is

$$1 + r + r^2 + r^3 + \cdots + r^n + \cdots = \frac{1}{1-r}$$

as long as the MPC, $r$, is less than 1 in absolute value. If the MPC were changing along a curved schedule, in the multiplier formula we should have to use an MPC at an income level somewhere between the old and new levels. Footnote 7 in the next chapter handles a nonhorizontal $II$ case.

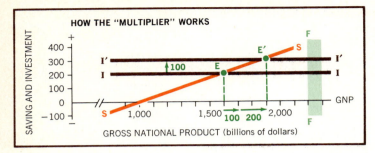

**FIG. 12-5**
**Each dollar of investment is shown as "multiplied" into 3 dollars of income**
New investment shifts $II$ up to $I'I'$. $E'$ gives the new equilibrium income, with income increasing 3 for each 1 increase in investment. (NOTE: The broken horizontal green arrow is 3 times the length of the vertical green arrow of investment shift, and is broken to show 2 *secondary* consumption respending for each 1 *primary* investment.)

By this time it is plain that the simple multiplier is always the upside-down, or "reciprocal," of the marginal propensity to save. Our simple multiplier formula is

$$\text{Change in income} = \frac{1}{\text{MPS}} \times \text{change in investment}$$

$$= \frac{1}{1 - \text{MPC}} \times \text{change in investment}$$

In other words, the greater the extra consumption respending, the greater the multiplier. The greater the MPS "leakage" into extra saving at each round of spending, the smaller the final multiplier.

## GRAPHICAL PICTURE OF THE MULTIPLIER

Up to this point, we have discussed the multiplier in terms of common sense and arithmetic. Will our saving-investment analysis of income give us the same result? The answer must of course be, Yes.

Suppose, as back in Table 12-1 (page 225), the MPS is $\frac{1}{3}$ and a new series of inventions comes along and gives rise to an extra $100 billion of continuing investment opportunities, over and above our previous $200 billion. Then the increase in investment should raise equilibrium GNP from $1,600 billion to what? To $1,900 billion if the multiplier is indeed correctly given as 3 by our previous analysis.

A look at Fig. 12-5 can confirm this. Our old investment schedule $II$ is shifted upward by $100 billion to the new level $I'I'$. The new intersection point is $E'$. And lo, the increase in income is exactly 3 times as much as the increase in investment. This is because an MPS of only $\frac{1}{3}$ means a relatively flat SS saving schedule. As the green arrows show, the horizontal income distance is 3 times as great as the "primary" vertical saving-investment distance, the excess being the secondary "consumption respending."

In short, income must rise enough to bring out a volume of voluntary saving equal to the new investment. With an MPS of $\frac{1}{3}$, income has to rise by how much in order to bring out $100 billion of new saving to match exactly the new investment? Only one answer is possible. By exactly $300 billion,[7] verifying our multiplier arithmetic.

---

[7] Alter Table 12-1 on page 225 to verify this answer. In Column (4), we now put in $300 billion instead of $200 billion of investment. The new equilibrium level of income now shifts one row up from the green equilibrium row. The multiplier can also work downward; thus a decline of $1 billion in investment spending will induce an endless chain of negative items, leading ultimately to a $3-billion *reduction* in equilibrium income. (Check by cutting $I$ from 200 to 100 in Table 12-1.)

## THE SIMPLIFIED THEORY OF INCOME DETERMINATION RESTATED

Figure 12-6 pulls together in a simplified way the main elements of income determination. Without saving and investment, there would be a circular flow of break-even income between business and the public: above, business pays out wages, interest, rents, and profits to the public in return for the services of labor and property; and below, the public pays consumption dollars to business in return for goods and services.

Realistically, we must recognize that the public will wish to save some of its income, as shown at the spigot Z. Hence, businesses cannot expect their consumption sales to be as large as the total of wages, interest, rents, and profits. Why not? Because dollars saved do not come back *as consumption sales*.

Some monetary cranks think this saving necessarily entails unemployment and depression. Such a view is simply incorrect. If there happen to be sufficiently profitable investment opportunities, business firms will be paying out wages, interest, and other costs *in part for new investment goods* rather than 100 per cent for consumption goods. Hence, to continue to be happy, business needs to receive back in consumption sales only *part* of the total income paid out to the public—only that part which involves the cost of current consumption goods. The *saving* that the public wants to make will do no harm to national income so long as it is not greater than what business can profitably continue to be *investing*.

In Fig. 12-6, investment is shown being pumped into the income stream at A. The handle of the pump is being moved by (1) technological invention, (2) population growth, (3) other dynamic factors that affect the profitability of investment, (4) newly printed money given to investors at low, low interest rates; and so forth.

When the investment pump is going at a rapid, steady pace, GNP is high and is at its maintainable equilibrium rate where scheduled saving at Z exactly balances scheduled investment at A.

This demonstrates that the pessimistic monetary cranks who think, "Saving is always disastrous," are plain wrong. But there is also a second misconception: Some go to

**FIG. 12-6**

**It is dynamic investment that pumps national income up and down**
Technological change, interest-rate and money change, population growth, and other dynamic factors keep the investment pump handle going. Income rises and falls with changes in investment, its maintainable equilibrium level being realized only when *intended* saving at Z continues to match *intended* investment at A.

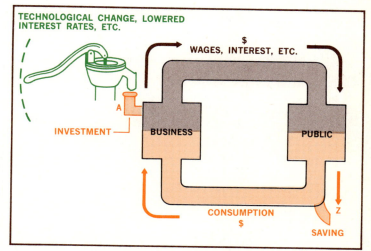

the opposite extreme and insist, "Saving and investment can never [even in our modern mixed economy with all its frictions and rigidities!] cause income to be too high or too low." They make the fatal error of automatically, and without regard to monetary policy and fiscal policy, connecting the pipe at Z with the pipe at A.

Many books have been written on this subject of equilibrium income determination, and it is only in the last few decades that economists have learned how to separate the truth and falsity of both extremes. The next 100-odd pages will deal with this important question in its relation to income, banking, and business-cycle policy. More specifically, the next chapter will discuss fiscal policy's effect on "inflationary or deflationary gaps" and the effects of changes in the propensity to save. Later, we shall integrate the effects of monetary policy with income determination.

## SUMMARY

1  The motives that make people want to save are often different from those that make businesses want to invest. Investment tends to depend on such autonomous elements as *new* population, *new* territory, *new* inventions, *new* tastes, and other *growth* elements; or on how tight or loose monetary policy is; and so forth. Consumption and saving tend to behave in accordance with passive schedules plotted against national income.

2  People's wishes to save and the willingness of business to invest are brought into line with each other by means of changes in income. The equilibrium level of national income must be at the *intersection* of the saving and investment schedules SS and II, or what is exactly the same thing, at the *intersection* of the consumption-plus-investment schedule C + I with the 45° line.

3  If incomes were temporarily above the equilibrium level, business would find itself unable to sell all it was producing at prices that fully covered required costs of production. For a short time inventories might pile up *involuntarily* and sales at a loss or untenable profit margin might take place, but eventually employment and production would be cut back toward the equilibrium level. The only equilibrium path of income that can be maintained is at the income level where families will voluntarily continue to save exactly as much as business will voluntarily continue to invest.

4  To sum up for the simplified case of this chapter: Investment calls the tune; investment causes income to rise or fall until *voluntary, scheduled* saving has adjusted itself to the level of *maintainable* investment.

Investment (and any autonomous schedule shift) has a multiplier effect on income. When investment changes, there is an equal *primary* change in national income. But as these primary income receivers in the capital-goods industries get more earned income, they set into motion a whole chain of additional *secondary* consumption spending and employment.

If people always spend about $\frac{2}{3}$ of each extra dollar of income upon consumption, the total of the multiplier chain will be

$$1 + \tfrac{2}{3} + (\tfrac{2}{3})^2 + \cdots = \frac{1}{1 - \tfrac{2}{3}} = 3$$

The multiplier works *up*ward or *down*ward, amplifying either increases or decreases in investment. The simplest multiplier is numerically equal to the reciprocal of the MPS; this is because it always takes *more* than a dollar's change in income level to bring forth a dollar's change in maintained level of saving.

## CONCEPTS FOR REVIEW

consumption schedule *CC*
saving schedule *SS*
45° helping line
break-even point
*C* + *I* schedule
equivalent intersection of *SS*
    and *II*, or *C* + *I* and
    45° line
equilibrium intersection and
    forces moving GNP

intended maintainable saving and
    investment versus measurable
    identity of saving and
    investment
multiplier impact of primary *I*
    and secondary *C* spending

$$\text{multiplier} = \frac{1}{1 - \text{MPC}} = \frac{1}{\text{MPS}}$$

$$= 1 + (\text{MPC}) + (\text{MPC})^2 + \cdots$$

## QUESTIONS FOR DISCUSSION

1  Can you recall from the last chapter how the *CC* and *SS* schedules are in a mirror-twins relationship, with MPC + MPS = 1 always? Why does the break-even point come at the same level of income (which will be on the horizontal axis in the lower part of Fig. 12-1 and on the 45° line in the upper part)?

2  If investment were always zero, show that equilibrium would take place at the break-even point. (HINT: Income must fall to the low permanent level at which the amount that people would want to go on saving was zero—namely the break-even point.)

3  The saving-and-investment and the 45° line (or *C* + *I*) diagram are two different ways of showing how national income is determined. Describe each. Show their equivalence.

4  Reconstruct Table 12-1 assuming that net investment is equal to (*a*) $300 billion (*b*) $400 billion. What is the resulting difference in national income? Is this greater or smaller than the change in *I*? Why? When *I* drops 100 (or by 1) below $200, how much must GNP drop?

5  Describe briefly (*a*) the common sense, (*b*) arithmetic, and (*c*) geometry of the multiplier. What are the multipliers when MPC = .9? .8? .5? When MPS = .1? .8?

6  Work out the explosive chain of spending and responding when MPC = 2. Explain the economics of the arithmetic of the divergent infinite geometric series.

7  Let *Y* be GNP in billions of dollars. If $C = a + bY = 300 + \frac{2}{3}Y$ and $I = \bar{I} = 200$, solve $Y = C + I = (300 + \frac{2}{3}Y) + 200$ to get $Y^* = 500/(1 - \frac{2}{3}) = 1,500$. Increase $\bar{I}$ by 1 and verify that $Y^*$ goes up by 3. What is the multiplier? Why?

# 13

## INCOME DETERMINATION: FISCAL POLICY, INFLATION, AND THRIFTINESS

The only good budget is a balanced budget.
ADAM SMITH
OF GLASGOW (1776)

The only good rule is that the budget should never be balanced— except for an instant when a surplus to curb inflation is being altered to a deficit to fight deflation.
WARREN SMITH
OF ANN ARBOR (1965)

Chapter 12 set forth the essentials of the modern theory of income determination. Here we must go on to discuss a number of important applications and qualifications.

How do changes in thriftiness—rises in the propensity to save and falls in the propensity to consume—affect the level of national income? What paradoxes lurk there?

How does the theory of income determination analyze inflation and deflation—the so-called "inflationary" or "deflationary gaps."

Finally, and most important for human welfare, what are the effects on output, employment, and price stability of government fiscal policy—of public expenditure, of public taxation, of budget deficits and surpluses?

### THE WASTEFUL "PRODUCTION GAP"

There is little need to emphasize the importance of the problem of income determination. In World War II and the Vietnam years, our economy was plagued by problems connected with *too high* a general money demand, with price increases, and with shortages.

In the Eisenhower years, 1953–1961, the American economy suffered from a worsening trend in unemployment and an insufficiency of total money demand. Figure 13–1 shows how the economy, spurred on by the massive tax cut of 1964, finally moved back toward the full-employment growth path in the middle 1960s. It also shows how the attempt by the Nixon administration to combat the inherited Vietnam inflation resulted in the 1969–1971 era of contrived stagnation, and the 1973–1975 recession.

Memories are short, and there is danger that we shall forget the tremendous costs that were associated with the mass unemployment of the Great Depression. It is scarcely an exaggeration to say that the economic costs of that depression were of the same general magnitude as the *costs of all the economic resources used up in World War II itself.*

234

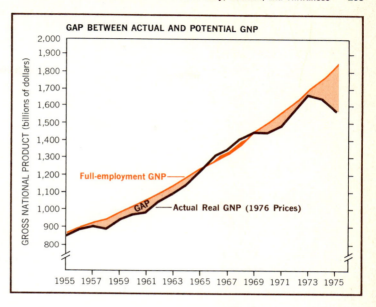

**FIG. 13-1**

**Cost of sluggish growth to living standards rivals cost of war itself**

The shaded orange area shows the gap between what we actually produced in recent years and what our economic system was capable of producing at reasonably high employment and capacity utilization. Public policy aims to reduce this "gap" between potential full-employment GNP and actual realized GNP. (Source: U.S. Bureau of the Census, *Business Conditions Digest*.)

Figure 13-1 reminds us that the American economy, because of failure to maintain full-employment growth, has lost hundreds of billions of dollars worth of goods and services in recent decades. It reminds us that nations have been subject to three kinds of poverty:

1. Ancient poverty due to famine and inadequate production potential

2. Unnecessary poverty in the midst of plenty, poverty due only to bad purchasing-power behavior of the system

3. Poverty due to uneven and bad distribution of an affluent total GNP

Long ago, for the advanced West, unavoidable poverty was conquered by the triumphs of technology. But only with the development of modern income analysis has "poverty midst plenty"—like that of 1929–1939—been rendered obsolete. Here in Part Two, we learn how and why.

Then in Part Six we can grapple with the third kind of poverty, which does still remain as a challenge.

## HOW THRIFTINESS OR SHIFTS IN THE *CC* SCHEDULE AFFECT INCOME

We have seen that investment affects incomes. Let us now consider changes in thriftiness. By an increase in thriftiness we mean a shift in the *SS* saving schedule upward. Won't the new *S'S'* schedule intersect an unchanged *II* schedule in a *new* equilibrium *E'*? And with a new lower GNP?

The answers to these questions are, Yes and yes. Figure 13-2, on the next page, shows that an upward shift in the saving schedule—and, what is the same thing, an equivalent downward shift in the consumption schedule—will tend in the absence of any change in the investment schedule to *lower equilibrium* GNP.

Common sense tells us why. If people consume less out of their incomes and if business will not willingly invest more, sales will fall and production must soon be cut. Cut how far? Cut until so much national income has been destroyed as to make people feel poor enough that they will finally end up not trying to save more than business will go on investing.

Perhaps this point seems obvious. But Fig. 13-2 tells us something more surprising. It shows that a $1 upward shift in the saving schedule will kill off $3 of income! Contrariwise, a $1 downward shift in the saving schedule, which means a $1 upward shift in the consumption schedule, will produce a similar multiplier $3 increase in income. (Figure 13-2's horizontal green arrow is 3 times the vertical green arrow.)

*In short, just as investment spending is "high-powered spending" with multiplier effects on income, consumption spending that represents a genuine shift in the propensity-to-consume-and-save schedules will also be "high-powered"!*

We shall meet many examples of this. Thus, the last part of the chapter will show how reducing taxes can increase consumption and thereby expand income by more than that consumption shift. Or, for a second example, take the case of a famous Harvard economics professor of a past generation, Frank W. Taussig. During the Great Depression he went on the radio to urge everyone to save less, to spend more on consumption. What did he have in mind? That was before the modern theory of income determination was known, but he presumably meant that such spending would on the first round give jobs and incomes to people; that their respending on consumption would create second-round jobs and income; and that it would continue thus in a multiplier chain.

A last example will arise in connection with the next section's so-called "paradox of thrift." This preliminary summary paves the way for it.

*If scheduled investment holds constant, an upward shift in the saving schedule—which means an equal downward shift in the consumption schedule—will kill off national income in a multiplier way until income falls low enough to bring people's new desired saving again into equality with investment opportunities.*

*Thus an attempt to save may not lead to more saving, but instead may then simply reduce national income.*

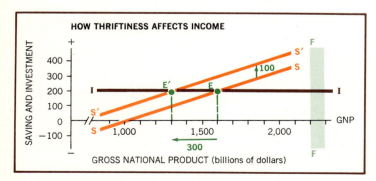

**HOW THRIFTINESS AFFECTS INCOME**

GROSS NATIONAL PRODUCT (billions of dollars)

**FIG. 13-2**
**Saving-and-investment diagram shows how thriftiness can kill off income**
A desire to consume less at every income level will shift the saving schedule upward. With *II* unchanged, equilibrium drops to the *E'* intersection. Why? Because income has to fall—and fall, note, in a *multiplier* way—until people feel poor enough to again want to save what the system can invest.

**FIG. 13-3**

**Higher income induces more investment** Now we drop the assumption of a horizontal *II* schedule. Now *II* slopes upward, showing intended investment less than $200 billion at low GNP and more than $200 billion at high GNP. Equilibrium is still at *E*, where *SS* intersects *II* from below.

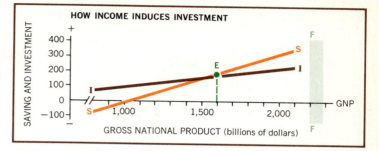

HOW INCOME INDUCES INVESTMENT

## INDUCED INVESTMENT

Until now we have always treated investment as an autonomous element, quite independent of national income. All our investment schedules have been drawn as horizontal lines, their level being always the same regardless of GNP. This simplification can now be relaxed.

Any practical businessman will tell you that he is more likely to add to his plant or equipment if his sales are high relative to his plant capacity. In the short run (before businessmen have had time to adjust their capital stock to a changed plateau of income), it is reasonable for us to redraw the *II* schedule in Fig. 13-3 as a rising curve. *An increase in employment and national product may* induce *a higher level of investment.*

As before, the equilibrium level of (maintainable) national income is given by the intersection of the investment and saving schedules, or by *E* in Fig. 13-3. So long as the *SS* curve always cuts the *II* curve from below, businessmen's action must finally bring the economy back to the equilibrium level shown here at *E*.[1]

Induced investment means that anything which increases national income is likely to be good for the capital-goods industries; anything hurting national income is likely to be bad for them.[2]

## THE PARADOX OF THRIFT

Induced investment throws new light on the age-old question of thrift versus consumption. It shows this:

**An increased desire to consume—which is another way of looking at a decreased desire to save—is likely to boost business sales and increase investment. On the other hand, a decreased desire to consume—i.e., an increase in thriftiness—is likely to reduce inflationary**

[1]If the two curves crossed in the opposite way with *II* steeper than *SS*, the little arrows back in Fig. 12-4, page 227, would point out instead of in and we should have unstable equilibrium; then the economy would rush away—in either direction—from the intersection neighborhood. A physical analogy may help: An egg on its side is in "stable equilibrium"; given a slight disturbance, it returns to equilibrium. An egg on its tip is in "unstable equilibrium"; a light touch topples it.

[2]Note that induced investment makes the multiplier bigger; in addition to a secondary chain of induced *consumption* spending, there will be a reinforcing chain of secondary *induced investment* spending. See the final formula in footnote 7 of this chapter.

*pressure in times of booming incomes; but in time of depression, it could make the depression worse and reduce the amount of actual net capital formation in the community. High consumption and high investment are then hand in hand rather than opposed to each other.*

This surprising result is sometimes called the "paradox of thrift." It is a paradox because most of us used to be taught that thrift is *always* a good thing. Ben Franklin's *Poor Richard's Almanac* never tired of preaching the doctrine of saving. And now along comes a new generation of financial experts who seem to say that the old virtues may be modern sins in depressed times.

**Paradox resolved**   Let us for the moment leave our cherished beliefs aside and try to disentangle the paradox in a dispassionate, scientific manner. Two considerations will help to clarify the whole matter.

The first is this. In economics, remember, we must always be on guard against the logical fallacy of composition. That is to say, what is good for each person separately need *not* thereby always be good for all; under some circumstances, private prudence may be social folly. Specifically, this means that the *attempt* of each and every person to increase his saving may—under the conditions to be described—result in a reduction in *actual* saving by all the people. Note the italicized words "attempt" and "actual"; between them, in our imperfect mixed economy, there may be a world of difference when people find themselves thrown out of jobs and with lowered incomes.

The second clue to the paradox of thrift lies in the question of whether or not national income is at a depressed level. If we were at full employment and always remained there, then obviously the more of our national product we devoted to current consumption, the less would be available for capital formation. If output could be assumed to be always at its maximum, then the old-fashioned doctrine of thrift would be absolutely correct—correct, be it noted, from both the individual and the social standpoints. In primitive agricultural communities, such as the American colonies of Franklin's day, there was some truth in Franklin's prescription. The same was true during World Wars I and II, and during periods of boom and inflation: if people then become more thrifty, less consumption means more investment.

But, according to statistical records, full employment and inflationary demand conditions have occurred only at intervals in our nation's history. Much of the time under laissez faire there were some wasting of resources, some unemployment, and some insufficiency of demand, investment, and purchasing power. When such is the case, everything can go into reverse. What once was a social virtue may then become a social vice. What is true for the individual—that extra thriftiness means increased saving and wealth—may then become completely untrue for the community as a whole.

Under conditions of unemployment, the *attempt to save* may result in *less*, not more, saving. The individual who saves cuts down on his consumption. He passes on less purchasing power than before; therefore, someone else's income is reduced, for one man's outgo is another man's income. If one man succeeds in saving more, maybe it is because someone else is forced to dissave. If one man succeeds in hoarding more money, someone else must do without.

**FIG. 13-4**
**An attempt to save more can well result in less actual saving and investment**
The shift of SS upward to S'S' depresses income; and the drop of income kills off some investment, moving us southwest along the sloping *II* schedule. (If the system were straining at the full-employment level of *F*, the effect of increased thriftiness would be beneficial to *I* as against *C*.)

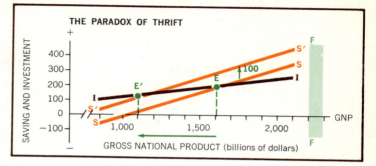

**High C inducing high *I*** Thus, when there is stubborn unemployment, consumption and investment can be complementary, not competitive. What helps one helps the other. The attempt to cut down on consumption (to save) then only results in a reduction of income—until everyone feels poor enough no longer to try to save more than can be invested. Moreover, at lower levels of income, less, and not more, capital goods will be needed. Therefore *investment will actually be less*. (As will be seen again and again, with prudent macroeconomic policies by government, our system will be restored to proper operation and the paradox of thrift robbed of its applicability.)

Let us clinch our common sense understanding of this paradox by combining Figs. 13-2 and 13-3 into Fig. 13-4. An increase in thriftiness or the desire to save will shift the SS curve upward to S'S'. Note that the new intersection *E'* is now at a lower level of income. Because of induced *disinvestment*, the drop in income does also mean lower investment. Thus both income and investment have actually decreased! The attempt to save more in depression times has resulted in less actual saving.

If true, this is an important lesson. It will never again be a satisfactory measure to urge men in time of depression to tighten their belts, to save more in order to restore prosperity. The result will all too likely be the reverse—a worsening of the vicious deflationary spiral. At such a time, many of the usual arguments go into reverse. An economic lobbyist of the capital-goods industries would, if he has their selfish interests at heart, advocate less thriftiness in depressed times, so that the consumption schedule will be pushed upward, and so that attempts to save—which then really lead only to decreases in income—will be discouraged. For only then will investment and sales of heavy capital goods flourish.[3]

Later, we shall see just how fiscal and monetary policies can rid the paradox of thrift of its terrors.

[3]We have seen that this line of argument does not apply in conditions of full employment. It also requires some slight modifications to allow for the fact that thriftiness, by lowering income, may also lower interest rates and (as we shall see) thereby promote investment, or it may depress wages and prices and thereby increase the real purchasing power of people's money holdings enough to destroy their initial thriftiness. These qualifications are discussed later; in a mixed economy, with wage and price levels sticky and inflexible, they seem rather unimportant considerations during deep depression.

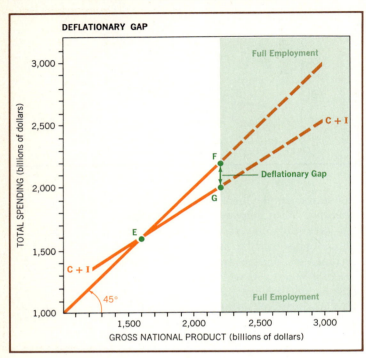

**DEFLATIONARY GAP**

**FIG. 13-5**

**When $C + I$ spending at full employment is less than full-employment GNP level, a "deflationary gap" arises**
The deflationary gap is always measured at the full-employment GNP level. It is the vertical distance there between the 45° line and the $C + I$ schedule, that is, $FG$. Such a deflationary gap will depress income in a multiplied way. (Later, after government is introduced, we'll relabel $C + I$ as $C + I + G$.)

## THE DEFLATIONARY GAP

The multiplier is a two-edged sword. It will cut for you or against you. It will amplify new investment, as we have seen. But it will also amplify negatively any *de*crease in investment. Thus, if investment opportunities drop by $100 billion in our earlier examples, then national income will have to fall by 3 times as much—by $300 billion. If net investment drops away to zero, income will have to fall to the break-even point where the community is made poor enough to stop all net saving.

This reminds us once again that there may be nothing particularly good about what we have called the equilibrium level of national income. If investment is low, the equilibrium level of income will involve much unemployment and waste of national resources. The only level of national income that we are entitled to regard as a desirable goal is that near to full employment; but we shall end up at such a level of high employment only if investment opportunities happen to match full-employment saving.

Unless this full-employment saving is "offset" by private investment (or by public policies), the nation cannot continue to enjoy full employment. There is then said to be a "deflationary gap," its size being measured by the deficiency of investment scheduled at full employment compared with full-employment saving.

We can picture the deflationary gap on a consumption-plus-investment graph, Fig. 13-5. Suppose that $2,200 billion represents the full-employment income. Suppose that,

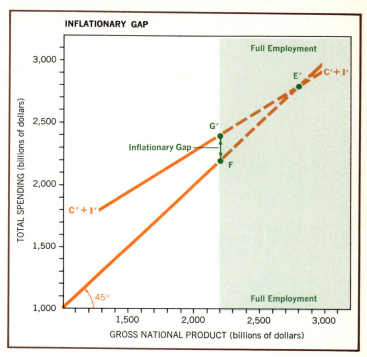

**FIG. 13-6**

**When C + I spending at full employment is greater than full-employment GNP level, an "inflationary gap" arises**
*FG'* measures the inflationary gap. People are trying to buy more than can be produced, and thereby they are inflating the price level. (With all prices changing and no longer ignorable, the spending schedules are likely to shift upward; so it would be a mistake to regard *E'* as an actually attainable equilibrium level of *real* income.)

at this income level *F*, the scheduled total of *C + I* adds up to only $2,000 billion, as shown at *G. This leaves a $200-billion deflationary gap between G and F.* Since obviously we cannot then remain at full employment, what will happen? Will income drop by only $200 billion? Clearly not. It must drop by some greater multiple of the original deflationary gap. If each dollar of reduced income results in a cut of $\frac{2}{3}$ in consumption spending, income will have to fall until it has dropped 3 times as much as the original deflationary gap (see point *E* in Fig. 13-5).[4]

## THE PROCESS OF PRICE INFLATION

Instead of a deflationary gap, we may have an *inflationary gap.* If scheduled investment tends to be greater than full-employment saving, then more goods will be demanded of business than it can produce, and prices will begin to rise. Figure 13-6 shows how we measure the inflationary gap as a vertical distance: The new *C' + I'* curve lies

[4] What can be done about this? If we continue to leave the government out of the picture, we must pray for either an increase in investment or an increase in consumption. By how much must the level of investment or of the consumption schedule shift upward if full employment is to be restored? By the full $600 billion of lost income? No. Because of the multiplier, to wipe out a deflationary gap, the *C + I* schedule need shift upward only by the amount of the gap *itself*, not by any multiple of the gap. (In a saving-investment diagram like Fig. 13-3, you measure the deflationary gap by the vertical distance between the *SS* and *II* schedules at the full-employment income *FF*.)

*above* the 45° line at the full-employment level by the distance *FG′*, giving us an inflationary gap of $200 billion.

> **If full-employment saving falls short of scheduled investment at full employment, there is said to be an "inflationary gap," its size being measured by the excess of the *C + I* schedule above the 45° line's full-employment level (which is the same thing as the excess of full-employment scheduled *II* over *SS*).**

Now what will result from the $200-billion gap? Can production rise by $600 billion to give a new equilibrium at *E′*? Plainly not. Everyone is already fully employed, and factories are producing at their practical capacity points. The region to the right of the vertical full-employment line through *F* is a never-never land. It shows us what we should like to be able to produce, but not what we are actually able to produce. Although an inflationary gap is the opposite of a deflationary gap, its effects upon employment and production are of a slightly different qualitative nature. A deflationary gap can move production leftward, down to 90 or even 70 per cent of a full-employment level; but an inflationary gap can't possibly move employment rightward to 150 per cent of full or maximum employment. The economic system cannot move in *real terms* very far to the right in the full-employment shaded area.

**Demand-pull inflation**   The excess in purchasing power can result only in *price increases*. (*a*) Too much money spending in comparison with (*b*) the limited supply of goods that can be produced at full employment, results in (*c*) bidding up of prices and ultimately of wages too. (Reread this definition of demand-pull inflation.) *Money* GNP will rise because of "paper" price-tag changes, but *real* GNP cannot go above its maximum full-employment level. Unfortunately, the upward movement of prices will continue for as long as there remains an inflationary gap,[5] i.e., until we are lucky enough for investment or consumption demand exuberance to diminish, smart enough as a nation to adopt corrective fiscal and monetary policies that will wipe out the inflationary gap, or until there just isn't enough of a money supply to permit such excessive *II* or *C + I* schedules.

Far from being "depression economics," modern income analysis has many of its most important applications in connection with the process of inflation and what can be done about it. During and after World War II, the concept of the inflationary gap was indispensable in indicating the quantitative magnitude of taxation needed to keep decontrolled prices from rising; and without understanding the rudiments of income analysis, one cannot follow the important economic issues discussed in Congress and the press concerning the need for anti-inflationary tax surcharges.[6]

---

[5]The process does not end with higher prices. The new higher price level will not equilibrate total supply and demand once and for all. On the contrary, since the higher prices received by businesses become in turn somebody's income—that of worker or property owner—demand again tends to shift upward and prices will continue to rise until taxes sop up the excess spending or until the money supply puts limits on demand. Attempts of labor to secure higher wages as compensation for the soaring cost of living may only cause the inflationary spiral to zoom at a dizzier speed. (Lord Keynes formulated this theory of inflation in 1939. Chapters 15 and 18 integrate it with monetary analysis.)

[6]See Chapter 41, which includes, along with this chapter's kind of "excess-demand," or "demand-pull," inflation, the possibility of "creeping cost-push inflationary tendencies."

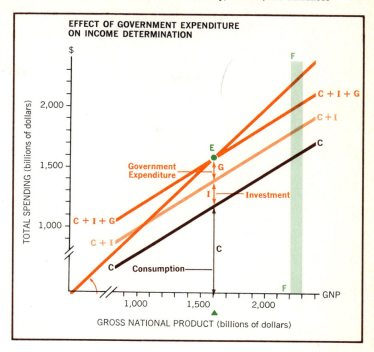

**FIG. 13-7**

**Government expenditure adds on just like investment in determining the equilibrium GNP**

On top of consumption spending and investment spending, we now add government spending on goods and services. This gives us the $C + I + G$ schedule. At $E$, where this intersects the 45° line, we find equilibrium. (What if $G$ increases or decreases? Can you show the multiplied changes in income?)

## FISCAL POLICY IN INCOME DETERMINATION: EXPENDITURE

When there is a large inflationary or deflationary gap, the government is called upon to do something about the price rise or the widespread unemployment. Tax and government expenditure policies—the general name for which is "fiscal policy"—will change the equilibrium level of income. So we must now, for the first time, explicitly introduce government fiscal policy into the picture to see exactly how income determination is affected. As you might guess, we now consider a $C + I + G$ spending schedule to show the equilibrium that results when government is in the picture.

It will simplify our task if in the beginning we analyze the effects of government expenditure with taxes held constant. When taxes come into the picture, we can no longer ignore the distinction between disposable income and gross national product. But with the tax revenue first held constant, they will differ always by the same amount; and taking account of such taxes, we can still plot the $CC$ consumption schedule against GNP rather than against $DI$.

In Chapter 10 we learned that gross national product consists of three, rather than two, parts; namely,

GNP = Consumption expenditure + private Investment expenditure
    + Government expenditure on goods and services
    = $C + I + G$

Therefore, on our 45°-line diagram in Fig. 13-7, we must now superimpose upon the consumption schedule not only private investment but also government expenditure $G$. This is because public road building is economically no different from private railroad building, and collective consumption expenditure involved in maintaining a free public library has the same effect upon jobs as private consumption expenditure for movies or rental libraries.

We end up with the three-layered $C + I + G$ schedule showing the amount of total spending forthcoming at each level of GNP. We now must go to the intersection with the 45° line to read off the equilibrium level of national product. At this equilibrium GNP level, the total the nation wants to spend on all goods is just equal in value to the full costs of production of these goods.

Figure 13-7 shows that government expenditure, taken by itself and disregarding taxes, has a multiplier effect upon income just like that of private investment. The reason is, of course, that a chain of *respending* is set in motion by the road-builders, librarians, and other people who receive primary income from the government.[7]

To show the effects of an extra $100 billion of $G$, shift $C + I + G$ in Fig. 13-7 up to a new drawn-in $C + I + G'$ and show that the new $E'$ will record a multiplier response of GNP to the new government spending.

## TAXATION AND SHIFTS OF CONSUMPTION SCHEDULE

Now let us turn to the depressing effects of taxes on the equilibrium GNP level. Without graphs, our common sense tells us what must happen when the government (*a*) takes away more from us in taxes while (*b*) at the same time holding its expenditure constant. Extra taxes will mean we have lower real disposable incomes, and lower disposable incomes mean we shall cut down on our consumption spending. Obviously, if investment and government expenditure remain the same, a reduction in consumption spending will then reduce gross national product and employment; or if we already are having an inflationary gap, the new taxes will help close the gap and wipe out excessive inflationary price increases.

Our graphs can confirm this reasoning: $I + G$ is unchanged, but now the increase in taxes, $T$, will lower disposable income, thereby lowering consumption and shifting the consumption schedule *downward;* so, the $C + I + G$ schedule shifts downward. Pencil a new, lower $C' + I + G$ schedule in Fig. 13-7 to confirm that its new intersection with the 45° line must definitely be at a *lower* equilibrium level of GNP.

Figure 13-8 shows and explains how tax receipts shift the $CC$ schedule downward. With $CC$ down, $C + I + G$ in Fig. 13-7 is down, and equilibrium GNP must drop.

---

[7]Our saving-investment diagram will give the same answer as the 45°-line diagram. The increase in government expenditure means an equivalent increase in the government deficit if taxes do not increase. Net saving must always equal private investment + government deficit. Therefore we add the deficit on top of the $II$ curve and get our new, greater equilibrium level of national income at the intersection with the $SS$ curve. In more advanced discussions, we could employ Fig. 13-7 to show how induced investment or government expenditure (i.e., induced by a changed level of income) will enter into the multiplier. The final change in income resulting from a unit upward shift in the $C + I + G$ schedule will always turn out to be $1/(1 - K)$, where $K$ is the slope of the $C + I + G$ schedule, and might be called the "marginal propensity to spend (inclusive of induced $C$, $I$, and $G$ effects)."

**FIG. 13-8**

**Higher tax will cut disposable income and shift CC schedule (to right and) down**

Each dollar of tax lowers the *CC* schedule. Why? Because *CC* is shifted to the right by the amount of the tax. (EXAMPLE: First, GNP = $1,300 at *U* with zero tax; *DI* = $1,300 also, *CC* shows consumption at *U* of $1,100. Now introduce tax of $300; GNP must equal $1,300 + 300 = $1,600 if *DI* is to remain $1,300 and consumption $1,100 there. So *UV* arrow shows *CC* is shifted rightward by exact amount of the tax to *C'C'*.) A rightward *CC* shift means a downward *CC* shift. But the downward shift is only two-thirds of the rightward shift if *CC*'s slope of MPC = $\frac{2}{3}$. (Verify that $WV = \frac{2}{3}UV$.)

With *CC* lowered, so will *C* + *I* + *G* in Fig. 13-7 be lowered. Show the drop in income there that would be caused by such a tax increase.

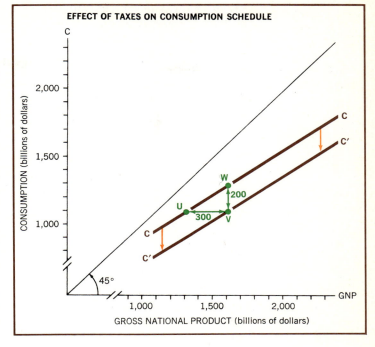

EFFECT OF TAXES ON CONSUMPTION SCHEDULE

REMARK: Now we know something that common sense did not immediately tell us. To offset a $200-billion upward shift in *I* + *G*, we must increase tax collections by *more* than $200 billion. Figure 13-8 shows needed taxes as $300 billion when MPC = $\frac{2}{3}$, if *CC* is to be lowered by $200 billion. This means that (*a*) when increased government spending on a Vietnam war is added to a full-employment economy with a balanced budget, then (*b*) taxes will probably have to be increased by *more than enough to balance the budget* if we are determined to avoid an inflationary gap.[8]

In connection with the massive Kennedy-Johnson tax cut of 1964, a reduction in tax rates served to *raise* the equilibrium level of national income. We can easily see this by reversing Fig. 13-8's analysis, thereby explaining how tax reductions help to fight a depressed economy. Each dollar of tax reduction leads, through an upward and leftward shift in *CC*, to an increase in people's disposable income by a dollar and to almost a dollar increase in initial consumption spending.

**Hence, dollars of permanent tax reduction are almost as powerful a weapon against mass unemployment as are increases in dollars of government expenditure.**

---

[8]Advanced treatises call this phenomenon the "balanced-budget multiplier theorem." This very useful, but highly simplified, doctrine says: A *balanced* rise in *G* and *T* will raise GNP by just that amount; a balanced cut of $1 in *G* and *T* will cut GNP by $1. So it is not merely the budget deficit, *G* − *T*, that has GNP effects. The absolute size of the budget matters too.

Because tax potency is slightly less than expenditure potency, such a program may involve a larger budget deficit than an expenditure program would; but it also means that there is expansion of the private (rather than government) sector of the economic system. Both the United States and Japan used this tax-cut mechanism in recent decades to increase their employment and income levels, a remarkable example of modern fiscal policy at work. And the 10 per cent tax surcharge of 1969 was an attempt to close an inflationary gap by raising tax rates.

## QUALIFICATIONS TO SAVING AND INVESTMENT ANALYSIS

The theory of income determination sketched in the last two chapters is a powerful tool.[9] It helps us to understand the ups and downs of the business cycle. It helps us to understand how foreign lending (which is one part of total investment) affects domestic employment and income. It helps us to understand how governmental fiscal policy can be used to fight inflation and unemployment. All these topics are developed in later chapters.

But it would be a mistake to think that an economist can be made out of a parrot simply by teaching him the magic words "saving" and "investment." Behind the scenes of these schedules a great deal is taking place.

It should be noted that an increase in the public's holding of government bonds and other wealth may shift the consumption schedule upward. Increases in the community's supply of money and other liquid assets will shift the *CC* and other schedules. Or rising living standards (resulting from advertising and the invention of new products) may shift the consumption schedule up, just as it has in the past.

In short, it is an oversimplification to regard investment as always an autonomous factor, and consumption as always a passive factor depending upon income. True, this is a fruitful oversimplification. But, as we have already seen, some of net investment may be "induced" by income changes in the short run; and we shall soon see that changes in interest costs, availability of credit, and stock of money can alter the swings in investment and total spending. Furthermore, consumption also will sometimes shift autonomously even though income has remained constant. And the reader can verify, by experimenting with the saving-investment and the 45°-line diagrams, the truth of our earlier assertion that such shifts in the *CC* or *SS* schedules do have multiplier effects upon national income—*exactly* like the multiplier effects of changes in *I* and *G*.

After the survey of our business-cycle history in the next chapter, the succeeding chapters will discuss money and banking, to show how changes in the supply of money, credit, and interest rates cause spending schedules and their intersections to shift.

[9]Advanced discussions show that corporate saving can be handled graphically much like taxes.

## SUMMARY

1  Unlike ancient poverty due to famine in a preindustrial society or modern poverty due to uneven income distribution, the laissez faire economy used to suffer from "poverty midst plenty"—characterized by the "production gaps" between what full-employment operations could produce and what actual saving-investment intersections were causing to be produced. Now we study how fiscal policy can do something about improving macroeconomic equilibrium.

**2**  The *attempt* to save more is quite different from the achievement of increased saving for society as a whole. The "paradox of thrift" shows that an increase in thriftiness may reduce already depressed income and, *through induced effects on investment,* may actually result in *less* investment. Only when employment remains full or unchanged are consumption and investment necessarily competing. Only then are private virtues always social virtues.

The moral is not for each individual to squander his money during a depression, trying to be patriotic. Instead, by proper national policies, we must re-create a high-employment environment in which private virtues are no longer social follies.

**3**  In short, we must avoid both *inflationary and deflationary gaps,* so that full-employment saving and investment just match without demand-pull inflation. We measure the size of the deflationary or inflationary gap as (*a*) the vertical discrepancy at full-employment income between the saving and investment schedules, or what is exactly the same thing, as (*b*) the vertical distance between the $C + I$ (or $C + I + G$ when government is in the picture) schedule and the 45° line.

**4**  An increase in government expenditure—taken by itself with taxes and investment unchanged—has expansionary effects on national product much like those of investment. The schedule of $C + I + G$ shifts upward to a higher equilibrium intersection with the 45° line.

**5**  An increase in taxes—taken by itself with investment and government expenditure unchanged—depresses the equilibrium level of national product. The schedule of consumption plotted against GNP is shifted downward and rightward by taxes; but since extra dollars go partly into saving, the dollar drop in consumption will not be quite so great as the dollars of new taxes. Therefore, to combat a given inflationary or deflationary gap, we may require an even larger change in taxation.

**6**  The art of economics consists in recognizing both the core of truth in the simple theory of income determination and also its needed qualifications. In later chapters, we shall see how the money supply and interest rates may also cause shifts in the schedules that determine levels of national income.

We leave to the final chapters of Part Two the analysis of government monetary and fiscal policy. In the intervening chapters we turn to an analysis of the wild dance of the business cycle, to the analysis of money, banking, and interest policy.

## CONCEPTS FOR REVIEW

"production gap"
poverty midst plenty
multiplier effects on income of
    consumption or saving shifts
induced investment
paradox of thrift
inflationary, deflationary gaps

cumulative demand-pull inflation
underemployment equilibrium
$C + I + G$ schedule
fiscal policy (expenditure and taxes)
$G$ effect on equilibrium
tax effect on $CC$ and equilibrium
qualifications to the analysis

## QUESTIONS FOR DISCUSSION

1   Just what is meant by "poverty midst plenty"? Illustrate by the United States, 1932 or 1970. Contrast with India, 1976.

2   "Even if the government spends billions on 'wasteful' cold-war armaments, during a depression this action helps create jobs and several billions of new useful production." Discuss critically.

3   Give arguments for and against thriftiness. Contrast carefully (a) the individual and the community viewpoint, and (b) conditions of boom and depression.

4   Describe effects upon income of (a) government expenditure and (b) taxes.

5   "The purpose of fiscal policy is to wipe out inflationary or deflationary gaps. If $C + I + G$ is too high, we have an inflationary gap; and we raise taxes to shift the new $C' + I' + G'$ schedule downward, thereby wiping out the inflationary gap." Explain. Show how (a) a decrease in tax rates or (b) new government expenditures fight a deflationary gap.

6   Analyze the economics of the 1975 debates on a needed tax cut.

7   If cold-war military expenditure could be ended, how might we preserve full employment? Explain your alternative programs in terms of shifts of the $C + I + G$ schedule.

8   Let $GNP = Y$, $DI = Y_d = Y - \bar{T}$. Let $\bar{I} = 100$, and $C = 200 + \frac{2}{3} Y_d$. When $\bar{G} = 0 = \bar{T}$, $\bar{I} = 100$, we use formula $Y = 200 + \frac{2}{3} (Y - \bar{T}) + \bar{I} + \bar{G}$ to solve for $Y^* = 900$. Likewise, verify the values in the following quadruplets of values for $(\bar{I}; \bar{G}; \bar{T}: Y^*)$: (101;0;0: 903), (100;1;0: 903), (100;0;1: 898), (100;1;1: 901).

9   *Extra-credit problem:* If $II$ rises with income instead of being horizontal, we must amplify the multiplier formula, $1/MPS = 1/(1 - MPC)$, to the form $1/(MPS - MPI)$. In Figs. 13-3 and 13-4, $MPI = \frac{2}{15}$. Show that the old multiplier of $3 = 1/(\frac{1}{3})$ now becomes $5 = 1/(\frac{1}{3} - \frac{2}{15}) = 1/(\frac{3}{15}) = 1/(\frac{1}{5})$. Solve $Y = C + I = (A + \frac{2}{3}Y) + (B + \frac{2}{15}Y)$ for $Y^* = 5(A + B)$, where a shift in the $CC$ schedule is a shift in $A$, and a shift in $II$ is a shift in $B$.

We have examined the economic forces operating to determine the level of national income—the balance of saving and investment. We now turn to the related problems of how the level of national income has fluctuated, and how economists try to forecast the future. Any serious science should try to test bold theoretical formulation against a careful description of the empirical facts of life.

## 14

## BUSINESS CYCLES AND FORECASTING

The fault, dear Brutus, is not in our stars— but in ourselves, . . . WILLIAM SHAKESPEARE

### PROSPERITY AND DEPRESSION

Business conditions rarely stand still. Prosperity may be followed by a panic or a crash. Economic expansion gives way to recession. National income, employment, and production fall. Prices and profits decline, and men are thrown out of work. Eventually the bottom is reached, and recovery begins. The recovery may be slow or fast. It may be incomplete, or it may be so strong as to lead to a new boom. The new prosperity may represent a long, sustained plateau of brisk demand, plentiful jobs, and increased living standards. Or it may represent a quick, inflationary flaring up of prices and speculation, to be followed by another disastrous slump.

Such, in brief, is the so-called "business cycle" that has characterized the industrialized nations of the world for the last century and a half at least—ever since an elaborate, interdependent *money economy* began to replace a relatively self-sufficient precommercial society.

No two business cycles are quite the same. Yet they have much in common. Though not identical twins, they are recognizable as belonging to the same family. No exact formula, such as might apply to the motions of the moon or of a simple pendulum, can be used to predict the timing of future (or past) business cycles. Rather, in their rough appearance and irregularities, business cycles more closely resemble the fluctuations of disease epidemics, of the weather, or of a sick child's temperature.

From these introductory remarks, it will be clear that business fluctuations are simply one further aspect of the economic problem of achieving and maintaining high levels of employment, production, and progressive growth along with reasonable price stability.

## MEASURING THE BUSINESS CYCLE

Figure 14-1 shows how the economic system was plagued with the uncertainties of the business cycle throughout our history as a nation, although fortunately rarely with as sustained and costly a slump as the post-1929 Great Depression. With surprisingly few variations, the same pattern of cyclical fluctuations was repeated until World War II in England, Germany, and most other foreign nations. But it is a strange fact that the United States, supposedly one of the youngest and most vigorous of nations, always tended to have greater average amounts of unemployment, and to have greater variation in unemployment than most other countries. Not only was this true in 1933, when our percentage of unemployment rivaled even that of Germany—with 1 in every 4 out of work completely!—but relatively higher American levels of unemployment appear to have been the case for almost as far back as we have any records or indications. In the last 30 years we have generally avoided deep unemployment, but still our rates look bad in comparison with those abroad.

Figure 14-2 shows on page 252 a great variety of economic "time series," shown together for comparison. Note the pervasive common pulse of the business cycle: the recessions of 1948–1949, 1953–1954, 1957–1958, 1960–1961, 1969–1970, 1973–1975

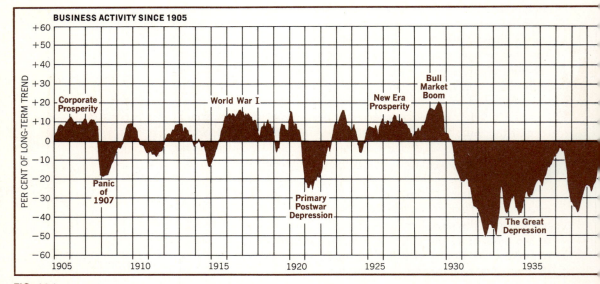

**FIG. 14-1**
(Source: Cleveland Trust Co.; author's updating.)

are shown as shaded areas. These fluctuations show up in production, unemployment, incomes, and even such particular series as stock-market prices and building. Moreover, if data had been included on such noneconomic matters as marriages, births, suicides, and malnutrition, we could have seen the heavy hand of the business cycle in them too. Even political elections follow the business cycle: in slumps, the ins go out. Thus, the 1960 Eisenhower recession helped elect President Kennedy, just as the Hoover depression of the 1930s helped elect Franklin Roosevelt.

Let us first stick to the facts and statistics of the business cycle. Later, we can attempt to devise hypotheses and explanatory theories to account for the facts.

## STATISTICAL CORRECTION FOR SEASONAL VARIATION AND FOR TRENDS

First, of course, we must remove from our statistical data irrelevant, disturbing factors such as *seasonal* patterns, and also certain so-called *long-term* "trends." If Sears' sales go up from November to December, 1973, we cannot conclude from this that the 1973 recession shown in Fig. 14–2 does not exist. Retail trade goes up every Christmas, just as Cape Cod hotels tend to be crowded in summer. The statistician attempts to remove the "seasonal influence" by carefully studying previous yearly patterns. If he finds that every December tends to involve about 150 per cent as much business as the average month of the year, and every January only 90 per cent, then he will take the actual raw monthly data and divide all the December figures by 1.5, all the January figures by 0.9, and so forth for each month. After this has been done, the statistician will end up with a time series of monthly department-store sales which have been "seasonally adjusted." These will show what we expected all along, that business was

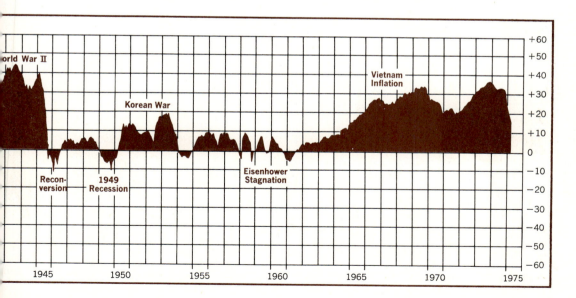

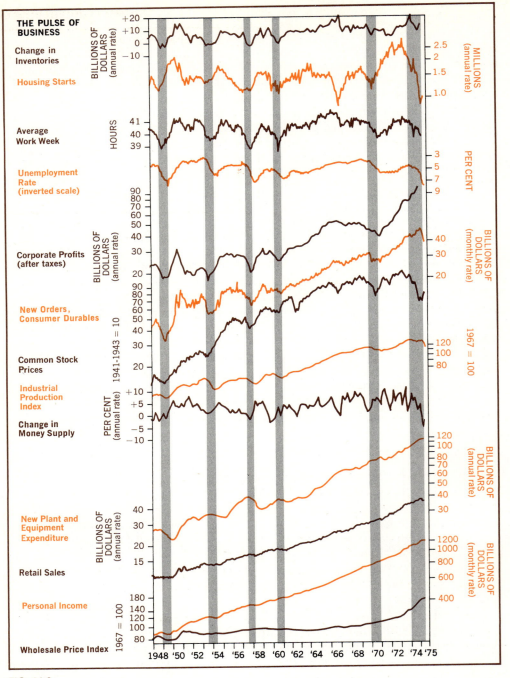

**FIG. 14-2**

**Most economic activities show a common cyclical pulse**

The shaded stretches show years of recession, in contrast to the unshaded periods of expansion. The top curves tend to represent volatile investment items. The bottom curves show less volatile elements that are more like consumption. Similar charts for mixed economies abroad would show the same kind of cycles. (Source: U.S. Bureau of the Census, *Business Conditions Digest*.)

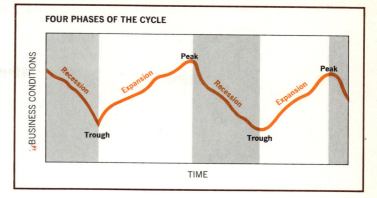

FOUR PHASES OF THE CYCLE

**FIG. 14-3**

**A cycle, like the year, has its seasons**
Expansion follows recession, with turning points in between. The National Bureau of Economic Research has dated these phases for America's history and for many other countries. Not every peak reaches "prosperity" in the sense of low unemployment. Nor does every threatened recession materialize. In the age after Keynes, the common, synchronous international business cycle has finally been broken up.

really still declining throughout the late months of 1973, because December's improvement was less than the seasonal norm.

Another kind of problem arises when we examine the fluctuations through time of such a rapidly growing time series as electric-power production or personal income. (This last can be seen at the bottom of Fig. 14-2.) Such a growing series did not decline in any recent recession. But the recession is evident there, nevertheless. It rears its ugly head in the form of a *slowing down of the rate of growth* of the time series as compared with its normal or long-term "secular trend."

If we draw a smooth trend line or curve, either by eye or by some statistical formula, through the strongly growing components of GNP, we discover the business cycle in the twistings of the data above and below the trend line. If we measure the vertical deviations from the trend line and plot them on a separate diagram, we get a reasonably clear picture of the business cycle.[1] Let us take a look at it.

## THE FOUR PHASES OF THE TRADITIONAL CYCLE

Early writers on the business cycle, possessing little quantitative information, tended to attach disproportionate attention to *panics* and *crises* such as the collapse of the South Sea Bubble in 1720, the panic of 1837, the Jay Cooke panic of 1873, the Cleveland panic of 1893, the "rich man's panic" of 1904, and, of course, the cataclysmic stock-market crash of "black Tuesday," October 29, 1929. Later writers began to speak of two phases of business: prosperity and depression, or boom and slump, with "peaks" and "troughs" marking the turning points in between. Today, it is recognized that not every period of improving business need take us all the way to full employment and true prosperity.

Figure 14-3 shows the successive phases of the business cycle. Each phase passes into the next. Each is characterized by different economic conditions: for example, during expansion we find that employment, production, prices, money, wages, interest rates, and profits are usually rising, with the reverse true in recession. Each phase requires special explanatory principles. But let us continue with more facts before attempting analysis and theorizing.

[1] See any standard textbook on statistics for these technical procedures. However, cautious judgment must be exercised in using the mechanical tools of statistics. A beginner, carelessly "eliminating a trend," if not careful, may throw out the baby along with the bath water.

**Length of cycle**    How long have the traditional economic cycles been? This depends upon how many minor cycles you wish to count. Most observers have no trouble in agreeing on the major cycles, which were about 8 to 10 years in length. Everyone agrees that the late 1920s represent a period of prosperity and the early 1930s one of depression, and similarly with other past major business cycles. Not all economists, however, attach importance to the shorter minor cycles seen in economic charts.

Harvard's illustrious Alvin Hansen gave the following summary to pre-World War II economic history:[2]

The American experience indicates that the major business cycle has had an average duration of a little over eight years. Thus, from 1795 to 1937 there were seventeen cycles of an average duration of 8.35 years. . . .

Since one to two minor peaks regularly occur between the major peaks, it is clear that the minor cycle is something less than half the duration of the major cycle. In the one hundred and thirty-year period 1807 to 1937 there were thirty-seven minor cycles with an average duration of 3.51 years.

. . . It appears that the building cycle averages somewhere between seventeen and eighteen years in length, or almost twice the length of the major business cycle. . . .

. . . American experience indicates that with a high degree of regularity every other major business boom coincides roughly with a boom in building construction, while the succeeding major cycle recovery is forced to buck up against a building slump . . . the depressions which have fallen in the interval of the construction downswing are typically deep and long. And the succeeding recovery is held back and retarded by the unfavorable depressional influence from the slump in the building industry.

The long swings in building construction and other series, which average anywhere between 15 and 25 years in length, are often called Kuznets cycles, being named for the 1971 Nobel Laureate who first noticed them in 1930.[3] Work by A. F. Burns, S. Kuznets, M. Abramovitz, and other scholars suggests that these pervasive swings have been associated with fluctuations in immigration and natural rates of population growth, in building, and in the rate of growth of the money supply.

In the age after Keynes, the business cycle has not become extinct like the dinosaur. But great depressions have ceased to occur. Even recessions have become shorter-lived and less frequent. And the old common pattern of the same business cycle, occurring at about the same time in all countries, has been made almost obsolete by resolute pursuit of fiscal and monetary policies in mixed economies. Today we can raise our standards and talk of recession as occurring, not merely when activity declines *absolutely*, but as soon as activity grows less than the growth rate of our full-employed

---

[2] Alvin H. Hansen, *Fiscal Policy and Business Cycles* (Norton, New York, 1941), pp. 18–24.

[3] Kuznets cycles should not be confused with alleged *very long waves*, whose complete cycle length is about half a century. Thus, from the end of the Napoleonic Wars in 1815 to the middle of the nineteenth century, prices tended to fall and times tended to be unusually hard, on the average. After the Californian and Australian gold discoveries of around 1850, and as a partial result of the Civil and Crimean Wars, prices tended to rise. A new long cycle of falling prices followed the 1873 depression and lasted until the 1890s, when there was a great increase in gold production following the African and Alaskan gold discoveries. Whether these long waves are simply historical accidents due to chance gold discoveries, inventions, and political wars, it is still too soon to say. The interested reader may be referred to J. A. Schumpeter, *Business Cycles* (McGraw-Hill, New York, 1939), Chaps. 6 and 7, where long cycles are called "Kondratieffs" after their Russian discoverer.

economy. A *growth recession,* defined this way, started about March, 1973, while the recession itself started in November, 1973.

## A FIRST CLUE TO BUSINESS FLUCTUATIONS: CAPITAL FORMATION

Hansen's emphasis on *construction* gives us our first clue to the causation of the business cycle. Certain economic variables always show greater fluctuations than others in the business cycle. Thus, if we plot pig-iron production and cigarette consumption side by side, we hardly notice the business cycle in the latter. But in the pig-iron series there is little else to see but the business cycle. Why? Because cigarettes are nondurable consumers' goods, and in both good and bad times people are going to smoke the same amount. Pig iron, on the other hand, is one of the main ingredients of capital and durable goods of all kinds: plant equipment and durable machinery; industrial and residential construction; automobiles, washers, snowmobiles, and other durable consumers' goods.

Check this by reexamining Fig. 14-2. Note how volatile are the top three investment series in contrast to the two series of retail sales and personal income. Note that production and profit fluctuations coincide with investment fluctuations.

By their nature, durable goods are subject to violently erratic patterns of demand. In bad times, their new purchase can be indefinitely postponed; in a good year, everyone may suddenly decide to stock up on a 10-year supply of the services of durable goods at the same time.

Our first clue to the nature of the business cycle lies, then, in the fact that it is the durable- or capital-goods sectors which show by far the greatest cyclical fluctuations.

Their swings are wide compared with those of the economic time series which represent primarily consumption of services, of nondurables, and the *services of* durable goods. Except for a few short, choppy surface disturbances in such series, the latter tend to follow the general flow of income in a rather passive fashion. Ordinarily, consumption movements seem the effect rather than the cause of the business cycle; in contrast, there is good reason to believe that the movements of *durable* goods represent key causes in a more fundamental sense.

## HOW SAVING AND INVESTMENT SCHEDULES APPLY

It is comforting to find that statistical analysis supports the emphasis in previous chapters on the crucial importance of the capital-investment process. The income-determination theories of the previous chapters do indeed help in understanding economic history. Here are but a few reminders:

1. *Wars* have always been great disrupters of an economy. How do they transmit their economic effects? Plainly, they lead to great swings in the $G$ component of the $C + I + G$ schedule, and this causes even greater swings in the over-all level of production and incomes. Inflationary gaps appear at full-employment GNP, leading to wartime price inflation. The post-1965 Vietnam inflation is a case in point.

2. In minor cycles, it used to be quite common for considerable fluctuations in the rate of *inventory investment* to occur. In the years of expansion, inventory accumulation is at a positive rate as merchants seek to rebuild their stocks and accommodate them to the growing level of sales. When merchants veer from a positive rate of inventory accumulation to a negative rate, the $I$ component in the $C + I + G$ schedule goes down: then the production line is cut back, men are put on fewer average hours per week or are laid off, wages and profits fall, and all this gets registered in a multiplier drop in GNP or in its failure to grow along a normal trend.

3. When there are longer waves in construction and equipment, the $I$ component in the $C + I + G$ schedule causes the whole schedule and its equilibrium to go through slow swings of considerable amplitude.

4. While it is an oversimplification to say that the consumption schedule never shifts over time, S. Kuznets, M. Friedman, F. Modigliani, and R. Goldsmith have made studies indicating the over-all stability of saving behavior relative to income over a long period. Their general finding is that, aside from short-term cycles, the percentage saved out of *permanent* income has been remarkably the same over the last century.

The one situation in which we cannot regard consumption purely as a passive and predictable force comes in those times when consumer demand for autos and other durable goods fluctuates. (For example, the record auto sales of 1971–1972 helped much to accelerate the initially anemic Nixon recovery.) Such *shifts* in the *CC* schedule also contribute to movements in the $C + I + G$ intersections; these shifts, like any other shifts in autonomous factors, involve double-duty multiplier reactions.

## A FEW THEORIES OF THE BUSINESS CYCLE

When it comes to explanations of why the income schedules shift, an industrious student could easily compile a list of separate theories of the business cycle that would run into the dozens.[4] Each theory seems to be quite different; but when we examine them closely and throw out those which obviously contradict the facts or the rules of logic, or which just appear to be conveying an explanation when really they are not saying anything at all—when we do all this, we are left with relatively few different explanations. Most of them differ from one another only in emphasis.

One man believes the cycle to be primarily the result of fluctuations in total net investment, while another prefers to attribute the cycle to fluctuations in the rate of

---

[4]We may mention just a few of the better-known theories: (1) the *monetary* theory—attributes the cycle to the expansion and contraction of bank money and credit (Hawtrey, Friedman, et al.); (2) the *innovation* theory—attributes the cycle to the clustering of important inventions such as the railroad (Schumpeter, Hansen, et al.); (3) the *psychological* theory—treats the cycle as a case of people's infecting each other with pessimistic and optimistic expectations (Pigou, Bagehot, et al.); (4) the *underconsumption* theory—claims too much income goes to wealthy or thrifty people compared with what can be invested (Hobson, Sweezy, Foster and Catchings, et al.); (5) the *overinvestment* theory—claims too much rather than too little investment causes recessions (Hayek, Mises, et al.); (6) the *sunspot-weather-crop* theories (Jevons, H. L. Moore). The interested reader should consult G. Haberler, *Prosperity and Depression* (Harvard University Press, Cambridge, Mass., 1958, 4th ed.), or other business-cycle texts for further information. We can add the newer "political" theory of Poland's Kalecki, which traces recessions to periodic political clamping down on creeping inflation.

technological inventions and innovations, which act on business *through* net investment. These sound like two different theories, and in most advanced textbooks they might be given the names of two different writers, but from our standpoint they are but two different aspects of the same saving-investment process. As we shall see, this does not mean there is perfect agreement among all theories of the cycle or that there are not some important differences in emphasis among different writers.

## EXTERNAL AND INTERNAL FACTORS

To classify the different theories, we may first divide them into the two categories of primarily *external* and primarily *internal* ("exogenous" and "endogenous") theories.

The external theories find the root of the business cycle in the fluctuations of something *outside* the economic system—in sunspots or astrology, in wars, revolutions, and political events, in gold discoveries, rates of growth of population and migrations, discoveries of new lands and resources, in scientific discoveries and technological innovations.

The internal theories look for mechanisms *within* the economic system itself which will give rise to self-generating business cycles, so that every expansion will breed recession and contraction, and every contraction will in turn breed revival and expansion, in a quasi-regular, repeating, never-ending chain.

If you believe in the sunspot theory of the business cycle—and no respectable economists today do—then the distinction between external and internal is rather easy to draw; although even here, when you come to explain how and why disturbances on the surface of the sun give rise to the business cycle, you begin to get involved in the internal nature of the economic system. But at least no one can seriously argue that the direction of causation is in doubt, or that the economic system causes the sunspots to fluctuate, instead of vice versa. However, when it comes to such other external factors as wars and politics, or even births and gold discoveries, there is always some doubt as to whether the economic system does not at least feed back on the so-called "external" factors, thereby making the distinction between external and internal not such a hard-and-fast one.

## PURELY INTERNAL THEORIES

As against the crude external sunspot theory, we may describe some simple examples of possible, crude internal theories.

**"Echo" waves of replacement**   If machinery and other durable goods all had the same length of life (say, 8 or 10 years), then we might (with radical Marx and conservative Taussig) try to explain a business cycle of the same length by this fact. If a boom got started—never mind how—then there would be a bunching of new capital goods all of the same age. A few years later, before these goods had worn out, there would be little need for replacement. This would cause a depression. But after 8 or 10 years all the capital equipment would suddenly wear out and would all have to be replaced, giving rise to an inflationary boom. This in turn would give rise to another complete cycle, with new echoing cycles of depression and boom every decade. Thus, self-generating "replacement waves" provide a purely internal business-cycle theory.

Actually, not all equipment has the same length of life; and identical automobiles produced on the same day will certainly not all be replaced at the same time. Consequently, any bunching of equipment expenditures will tend over time to spread itself out, at most giving rise to weaker and weaker replacement peaks. Twenty-five years after the Civil War, one might have noted a deficit of births because of that conflict; but another generation later and the dip would be hardly noticeable; and today it is just as if there had never been that particular violent disturbance of population.

Replacement waves, therefore, are like the vibrations of a plucked violin string: they tend to dampen down and die away, unless there is a new disturbance.

**Psychological self-generating cycles**   The laws of physics guarantee that friction will lessen any purely autonomous physical fluctuations. In social science, there is no law like the conservation of energy to prevent the creation of purchasing power. Therefore, another example of a self-generating cycle would be the case where people became alternately optimistic and pessimistic, each stage leading as inevitably to the next as the manic stage of disturbed people leads to the depressive stage.

We cannot rule out such an internal theory. Nor can we be satisfied with it as it stands, for it says and explains little.

**Political cycles in economics**   Today it is widely granted that the government, through its monetary and fiscal policies, can cause drastic fluctuations in the $C + I + G$ schedules and levels of over-all demand spending. If it uses these powers wisely, government can be a dampening force in *stabilizing* ups and downs of activity. If it uses these powers foolishly or perversely, it can be itself an *originating* source of cyclical instability.

The greatest bursts of government spending have been associated with war. But such externally caused fluctuations are not what is meant by a political cycle. Rather, let us suppose, and here we are not far from the beliefs of the University of Chicago's Milton Friedman, that you think most of the causes of cyclical instability are to be identified with sporadic changes in the rate of growth of the money supply. And suppose you regard the Federal Reserve Board, which we'll soon see determines the growth of the money supply, as composed of mercurial and imperfect men: from 1929 to 1932 they wantonly kill off much of the supply of money, and there follows inevitably the Great Depression; in 1967, they react from being overly tight on credit and money and become overly loose, thereby creating the post-Vietnam inflation that was completely avoidable in the view of the Chicago School.

Of course, few embrace the crude view that government officials, for the same unexplained reasons that coyotes howl on full-moon nights, wantonly pursue a manic-depressive pattern and thereby create the business cycle. A more sophisticated version of this political theory would argue as follows: "No one can forecast the future, with its many chance elements. And yet everything the government does today in the area of monetary or fiscal policy will continue to have its effects for the next couple of years and in a way that we cannot predict exactly. So," in this view, "governmental fiscal and monetary authorities are like the proverbial drunken sailor: when he is falling to the left, he awkwardly overcompensates and falls to the right; in the attempt to stabilize, he actually destabilizes!'' (Chapter 17 will deal further with monetarism.)

One cannot categorically deny this politicians-will-inevitably-blunder view. Actually, it overlaps with the fundamentally pessimistic theory enunciated by the late Michael Kalecki, a distinguished Polish econometrician who independently anticipated Keynes' *General Theory*. Kalecki's political theory says, in effect:

Keynesian policies can control total money spending. But when they succeed in even approaching full employment, they will also induce "cost-push inflation"—in which wage rates rise and push up prices. The only way governments can check this cost-push inflation is by deliberately engineering a stagnation and slowdown. But populist democracies will not long stand for such patently wasteful and inhuman policies. So again we're off to the races, with another contrived march to full employment and cost-push inflation leading inevitably to another contrived slowdown. In short, the mixed economy will generate a new kind of activistic governmental cycle of stop-go driving of the economy—and this not because of the stupidity of the officials or their advising economists, but because of a fundamental contradiction between full employment and price stability.

We shall be encountering later in Part Two this undoubted dilemma between unemployment and inflation. And in Chapter 41, we shall devote much analysis to it as perhaps the fundamental unsolved problem for the modern mixed economy.

## COMBINING EXTERNAL AND INTERNAL ELEMENTS

Everyone has observed how a window or a tuning fork may be activated into pronounced vibration when a certain note is sounded. Is this vibration externally or internally caused? The answer is, Both. The sounded note is certainly an external cause; but the window or tuning fork responds according to its own internal nature, coming into strong resonance, not with *any* sounded note, but only with one of a *particular definite* pitch. It takes the right kind of trumpets to bring down the walls of Jericho.

Similarly, we may look upon business cycles as not unlike a toy rocking horse that is subjected to occasional outside pushes. The pushes need not be regular; great technical innovations never are. But just as the wooden horse rocks with frequency and amplitude that depend partly on its internal nature (size and weight), so too will the economic system respond to fluctuations in external factors according to its *internal* nature. Both external and internal factors are important in explaining cycles.

Synthesis   Most economists today believe in a combination of external and internal theories. In explaining the major cycles, they place crucial emphasis on fluctuations in *investment* or *capital* goods. Primary causes of these capricious and volatile investment fluctuations are found in such external factors as (1) technological innovation; (2) dynamic growth of population and of territory; and even, in some economists' view, (3) fluctuations in business confidence and "animal spirits." With these external factors, we must combine the internal factors that cause any initial change in investment to be *amplified* in a cumulative, multiplied fashion—as people who are given work in the capital-goods industries respend part of their new income on consumption goods, and as an air of optimism begins to pervade the business community, causing firms to go to the banks and the securities market for new credit accommodation.[5]

Also, it is necessary to point out that the general business situation definitely reacts in turn on investment. If high consumption sales make businessmen optimistic, they are more likely to embark upon venturesome investment programs. Inventions or scientific discoveries may occur independently of the business cycle, but their appreciable economic introduction will most certainly depend on business conditions. When GNP moved up in 1971–1973, it was reasonable to expect that a considerable volume of capital formation (new machines, added inventories, construction) would be induced. Therefore, especially in the short run, investment is in part an *effect* as well as a cause of income movements.

In the longer run, no matter how high a plateau of income is maintained, the stock of capital goods will become adjusted at a higher level and new net investment (over and beyond mere replacement) will drop off to zero unless there is (1) a growth of income, (2) a continuing improvement of technology, or (3) a never-ending reduction in interest rates.

The first of these processes, showing how investment demand may be induced by *growth* of sales and income, has been given a rather high-sounding name—the "acceleration principle." Almost all writers bring it in as one strand in their final business-cycle theories. Let us examine how this internal cyclical mechanism works itself out and interacts with our earlier multiplier analysis and other factors.

### THE ACCELERATION PRINCIPLE

According to this law, society's needed stock of capital, whether inventory or equipment, depends primarily upon the level of income or production. Additions to the stock of capital, or what we customarily call *net* investment, will take place only when income is growing. As a result, a prosperity period may come to an end, not simply because consumption sales have gone down, but merely because sales have *leveled off* at a high level (or have continued to grow, but at a lower rate than previously).

A simplified arithmetical example will make this clear. Imagine a typical textile-manufacturing firm whose stock of capital equipment is always kept equal to about 2 times the value of its yearly sales of cloth.[6] Thus, when its sales have remained at $30 million per year for some time, its balance sheet will show $60 million of capital equipment, consisting of perhaps 20 machines of different ages, with 1 wearing out each year and being replaced. Because replacement just balances depreciation, there

---

[5] With two dice you can manufacture something that looks a little like a business cycle. Record the results of successive tosses—as in the random number sequence 7, 4, 10, 3, 7, 11, 7, 2, 9, 10, . . . Then take five-period moving averages—such as the successive numbers $(7 + 4 + 10 + 3 + 7)/5 = 6\frac{1}{5}, (4 + 10 + 3 + 7 + 11)/5 = 7, . . .$ , etc. A plot of these—7.0, 7.6, 6.0, 7.2, 7.8, . . .— will look not too different from GNP or price fluctuations! EXPLANATION: The random numbers are like exogenous investment shocks; the moving average is like the economic system's (or the wooden horse's) internal smoothing reactions of $C + I + G$ type.

[6] To keep the discussion simple, we use the exaggerated ratio 2/1 and ignore changes in interest rates or degree of utilization of capacity. The reader can include inventory change and plant change along with equipment change in the analysis.

is no *net* investment or saving being done by the corporation. *Gross* investment takes place at the rate of $3 million per year, representing the yearly replacement of 1 machine. (The other $27 million of sales may be assumed to be wages and dividends.) The first phase of Table 14-1 shows this.

Now let us suppose that, in the fourth year, sales rise 50 per cent—from $30 to $45 million. Then the number of machines must also rise 50 per cent, or from 20 to 30 machines. In that fourth year, instead of 1 machine, 11 machines must be bought—10 new ones in addition to the replacement of the worn-out one.

Sales rose 50 per cent. How much has machine production gone up? From 1 machine to 11; or by 1,000 per cent! This *accelerated* effect of a change in consumption or other final items on investment levels gives the acceleration principle its name.

If sales continue to rise in both the fifth and the sixth year by the same $15 million, then we shall continue to have 11 machines (10 + 1) ordered every year.

So far, the acceleration principle has given us no trouble. On the contrary, it has given us a tremendous increase in investment spending as a result of a moderate increase in consumption sales. But now we are riding a tiger.

**According to the acceleration principle, consumption has to continue to keep increasing in order for investment to stand still!**

If consumption should stop growing at so rapid a rate—if it should level off in the seventh year even at the high level of $75 million per year—then net investment will fall away to zero, and gross investment will, for many years, fall back to only

| THE ACCELERATION PRINCIPLE (in millions of dollars) | | | | |
|---|---|---|---|---|
| TIME | YEARLY SALES | STOCK OF CAPITAL | NET INVESTMENT NI | GROSS INVESTMENT (NI + depreciation) |
| **First phase** | | | | |
| First year | $30 | $ 60 | $ 0 | 1 machine at $3 = $3 |
| Second year | 30 | 60 | 0 | 1 machine at $3 = $3 |
| Third year | 30 | 60 | 0 | 1 machine at $3 = $3 |
| **Second phase** | | | | |
| Fourth year | **$45** | $ 90 | **$30** | (10 + 1) machines at $3 = $33 |
| Fifth year | 60 | 120 | 30 | (10 + 1) machines at $3 = $33 |
| Sixth year | 75 | 150 | 30 | (10 + 1) machines at $3 = $33 |
| **Third phase** | | | | |
| Seventh year | **$75** | $150 | **$ 0** | 1 machine at $3 = $3 |
| **Fourth phase (to be filled in by reader)** | | | | |
| Eighth year | $73½ | $147 | −$ 3 | _____machines at $3 = $_____ |

TABLE 14-1

**Acceleration principle links GNP growth rate to level of investment**
Investment fluctuates more than sales: to keep the level of investment from falling, sales must not even falter in their rate of growth.

1 machine (see Table 14-1). In other words, a drop of zero per cent in sales has resulted in a 90 per cent drop in gross investment and a 100 per cent drop in net investment! (See the third phase of Table 14-1.)

The acceleration principle can work in both directions. Should sales now drop below $75 million, gross investment would drop away to nothing for a long time; in fact, the firm might want to disinvest by selling off some of its used machinery. (Fill in the fourth phase with the needed zeros—to signify that nothing is now being replaced.)

It is clear that a recession can set in just because sales have stopped growing so rapidly, even if not dropping absolutely but only leveling off at a high rate.

## INTERACTIONS OF ACCELERATOR AND MULTIPLIER

Needless to say, the curtailment of production in the machine-producing industries will curtail income and spending on food and clothing and will lead to still further "multiplier" changes in spending. This itself might ultimately cause textile sales to stop growing altogether, or even to decline. This in turn will cause a further accelerated drop in net investment.

Thus, we may be in a vicious circle where the acceleration principle and the multiplier interact to produce a cumulative deflationary (or inflationary) spiral.

Our example used machines. Does that mean the acceleration principle is not involved in the inventory "recessions" (such as 1920–1921, 1937–1938, 1948–1949, 1953–1954, 1957–1958, 1960–1961)? Not at all. The same principle—that stocks of capital goods tend to be held in some proportion to sales per unit time—is valuable to help explain short inventory cycles.

This analysis can also explain how a downturn can result from the previous expansion itself. Suppose, in a situation of unemployment, we get income growing again. The rising income induces, via the accelerator, new investment. The new investment induces, via the multiplier, further rises in income. Hence, the rate of growth of output may be "self-warranting."

But how can a system grow forever at 6 or 7 per cent if its labor force grows only at 1 or 2 per cent and workers' productivity grows only at 2 or 3 per cent? It can't. The self-warranting expansion, even if we are lucky enough to get and keep it, must ultimately bump into the full-employment ceiling. Like a tennis ball (and unlike a wad of gum), it is likely to bounce back from the full-employment ceiling into a recession. Why? Because the minute the system stops its fast growth, the accelerator dictates the end of the high investment supporting the boom. Like an airplane that falls once it loses its motion, the economic system plummets downward.

Similar accelerator-multiplier analysis may explain the ultimate end of a recession and the onset of an upturn. When output plummets downward rapidly, the acceleration principle calls for negative investment (or disinvestment) greater than the rate at which machines can wear out. This wear-out rate puts a floor on how fast disinvestment can take place, and hence a floor on how far it (the SS-II intersection) can push the economy below its break-even point.

Bumping along such a basement floor means that eventually firms will work down their capital stock to the level called for by that low level of income; and now the acceleration principle calls for a termination of disinvestment! Our image must shift from gum, ball, and airplane to that of an Olympic diver: once he stops moving downward under the water, he is buoyed back up again. A new cycle can begin and repeat itself.

It is easy to see that, in the acceleration principle, we have a powerful factor making for economic instability. If business sales go up and down, the acceleration principle can intensify their fluctuation. It induces net investment on the upswing, but causes about the same amount of net *disinvestment* on the downswing.

In the long run, if the system is growing because of population increase and technical progress, then the acceleration principle works primarily as a stimulating factor: growing national income causes extensive matching growth of capital, which in turn means brisk investment demand and relatively low unemployment.[7]

## FORECASTING THE FUTURE OF BUSINESS ACTIVITY

Businessmen have to form guesses about the future in making their investment and production decisions. If they thought next year would bring a depression, they might want to reduce inventory now. If, on the contrary, they expected prices to rise greatly several months from now, they might hasten today to buy goods in advance and to add to equipment and plant. Similarly, speculators would like to know the future in order to be able to buy or sell common stocks and make a profit. And more important, policy makers in Washington would like to have a peek at next year's national-income accounts to be able to take remedial fiscal and monetary actions *now*.

Statisticians and economists cannot yet make accurate forecasts. Their guesses occasionally turn out to be quite wrong. Nonetheless, people insist that they do their best. Why? Because lack of any forecast usually itself involves an *implicit* forecast, and noneconomists have an even worse long-run average score at making forecasts than do trained statistical economists.

**Forecasting the economic future**  What methods do the best forecasters use? No simple description can be given, but here are a few of the most common practices.

1. They follow the national-income accounts very closely: GNP every quarter; personal income every month; new construction; equipment spending; the important short-run behavior of inventory change; estimates of coming government expenditures and taxes. They also watch monthly data: price indexes; the Federal Reserve Board index of production; changes in the rate of growth of the money supply; and reports on unemployment and job totals. In addition, they watch many diverse statistics as they become available: department-store sales each week; chain-stores sales (Woolworth, J. C. Penney); mail-order sales (Sears, Ward's) each month; new orders and inventory changes of manufacturing and trade each month.

2. In recent years, the forecaster can study various *surveys* of future events: the

---

[7] The Appendix of Chapter 37 discusses this "warranted growth" further, in connection with so-called "Harrod-Domar models of growth."

McGraw-Hill questionnaire of business intentions to invest, the SEC–Commerce official questionnaires on the same subject, and the Conference Board surveys of capital appropriations provide clues to fixed investment (plant or equipment) intentions. The attitudes reported by purchasing executives are important for inventories. For consumers, random sampling by the University of Michigan Group Survey Center and the U.S. Bureau of the Census gives information on whether or not the consumer is in a buying mood and what his spending intentions are. For businessmen generally, Dun & Bradstreet and *Fortune* take frequent polls of opinions about future and present intentions. In Europe this technique of polling heads of business has also made great progress.

3. Some reinforce these guesses by considering whether most diverse time series—such as those in Fig. 14-2—are going up or down. Are certain so-called "leading-indicator series," such as average hours worked per week, stock prices, construction awards, and new orders, predominantly signaling a turn now?

Men long looked for a statistical series (or group of series) that would manifest a turn a *fixed* number of months *before* business turned generally. Such a "leading indicator" would be invaluable for forecasting purposes; however, no such perfect guide has been found. Geoffrey Moore and Arthur F. Burns, then at the National Bureau of Economic Research, and Julius Shiskin at the Budget Bureau, found that certain series, such as have already been mentioned, can give some help in identifying turning points in advance and in confirming that they have just occurred. Forecasters cannot yet rely on indicators alone, for the reason that (as in 1951, 1962, and 1967) they may give misleading signals; in expansions, the indicators often turn down too many months before the true peak; in recessions, they turn up only a month or two before the upturn—by the time the data become available for smoothing, their main (important!) purpose is to tell us we have indeed already turned the corner. Economists look forward with interest to further improvements in these techniques, and practical forecasters do supplement their GNP estimates with this kind of information. See Fig. 14-4 for some improved efforts in this direction.[8]

4. This is the age of computer forecasting. Thanks to the pioneering work of Holland's Nobel Laureate Jan Tinbergen, today we have dozens of macroeconomic models of the GNP: Lawrence Klein of the Wharton School has produced one of the better known models; the University of Michigan, the U.S. Department of Commerce, and Modigliani's group of FRB-MIT-Penn economists have also produced well-known econometric models. Commercial consulting firms—the econometric unit of the Chase Manhattan Bank, or Harvard's Otto Eckstein with his Data Resources model—provide similar alternatives.

How do computer models operate? Essentially, they try to build up consistent statistical estimates of the components of $C + I + G$, based upon past patterns of experience. Thus Fig. 11-5's fitted $CC$ schedule on page 217 provides an example—a primitive example—of the methodology involved. But nowadays dozens of multiple-correlation equations are typically involved. How successful are these computer models? According to careful audits by the

---

[8]A new series of leading indicators was unveiled by the Department of Commerce in May, 1975. Constructed under the direction of Professor Victor Zarnowitz of the University of Chicago at the National Bureau of Economic Research, the new series is designed to give warning of business cycles in the midst of inflation. It should tell when real GNP is about to decline, even if nominal GNP will continue to rise. (The new series is shown in Fig. 14-4.)

**FIG. 14-4**
**Leading indicators call the turns
of the business cycle—usually!**
The coincidental indicators in the middle turn up and down
in agreement with the peak-trough datings shown in gray
shading. Note that the leading indicators above turn down
about five months before the peaks. (Examine the green
dots that mark the peaks of the leading indicators and
compare with the timing of onset of gray-shaded recessions.) Note that the leaders turn up scarcely two months
before the troughs. (Can you pencil in with black dots
the upper curve's troughs and compare with the shading?)
(Source: U.S. Bureau of the Census, *Business Conditions Digest.*)

National Bureau of Economic Research, they do better than naïve guesses that merely estimate
that tomorrow will be as much above today as today was above yesterday. If judgment is
applied to the computer equations in order to alter their coefficients in accordance with the
most up-to-date qualifying information, computer models do about as well at forecasting as
do the most experienced and rarest economists of great judgment and flair. Even this remark
does not do justice to the computer's contribution: The best practitioners of the art of
judgmental forecasting gladly admit that these days their judgment has fed into it the *results*
of computer analyses. What is to be hoped is that the elements of *art* in economic forecasting—which admittedly are still very important—will increasingly be reduced in importance in comparison with the elements of *science* in such forecasting. But it will be a long
time before the millennium of accurate and noncontroversial forecasts finally arrives.

Aside from forecasting models of the general $C + I + G$ type, in recent years simpler
monetarist models have been employed. These are sometimes referred to as black-box models
in which changes in the money supply over earlier periods are fed in as the principal inputs;
by a complicated process that monetarists say need not be investigated so long as the forecasting method works, one derives, as output from the black boxes, multiple-regression equations
estimates of the money value of GNP.

Perhaps the most successful example of such a monetarist forecasting method has been the
work of the Federal Reserve Bank of St. Louis, which has produced pretty fair estimates of
quarterly changes in GNP on the basis of changes in the money supply over the previous
five quarters (and, but with much reduced weight, changes in government expenditures over
a similar interval). Future research must settle whether simple models that estimate totals
rather than components will perform best, or whether eclectic combinations of $C + I + G$
and monetary models (like the FRB–MIT–Penn model) will be the most useful—useful not
only in crude forecasting, but also estimating policy changes of an optimal type.

Experience shows that economic forecasts are indispensable for public and business
decisions. Economists' forecasts, although not infallible, average out to be more accu-

rate than those of readers of tea leaves, senatorial hunch players, computer robots, or simple extrapolaters of present levels and trends. Although not perfect, economists' GNP forecasts are the best science can produce.

## THE BUSINESS CYCLE TODAY

Announcements of the demise of the business cycle have been somewhat premature. At best its virulence may have been somewhat tamed. Yet the fact that the world-wide business cycle of 1973–75 was the most serious of the whole period since World War II shows that the trade cycle is still very much with us.

A rash of poor harvests all over the world, combined with a four-fold raising of the price charged for oil by the OPEC cartel of producing nations, led in 1973–74 to a world-wide acceleration of price increases. The Nixon and Ford Administrations, and for that matter governments in power throughout the industrialized world, tried to cool down their inflation-threatened economies by macroeconomic fiscal and monetary policies that will be discussed in the next chapters. Thus, "stagflation"—stagnation accompanied by price inflation—gave rise to the 1973–75 recession shown in Fig. 14-2.

To paraphrase Mark Twain's comment on the report of his demise, "It is *premature* to speak of the death of the business cycle." Back in 1929, just before the great stock-market crash, experts spoke of the country as being in a "new era" of perpetual prosperity. The gods take their revenge on those who are too proud.

What can be said scientifically about the outlook for business fluctuations? Most economists would pretty much agree with the following formulation:

Although nothing is impossible in an inexact science like economics, the probability of a great depression—a prolonged, cumulative, and chronic slump like that of the 1930s, the 1890s, or the 1870s—has been reduced to a negligible figure. No one should pay any appreciable insurance premium to be protected against the risk of a total breakdown in our banking system and of massive unemployment in which 25 per cent of the workers can find no jobs.

The reason for virtual disappearance of great depressions is the new attitude of the electorate. By the $C + I + G$ analysis of earlier chapters, and the monetary analysis of chapters yet to come, economic science *knows how* to use monetary and fiscal policy to keep any recessions that break out from snowballing into *lasting* chronic slumps. If Marxians wait for capitalism to collapse in a final crisis, they wait in vain. We have eaten of the Fruit of the Tree of Knowledge and, for better or worse, there is no returning to laissez faire capitalism. The electorate in a mixed economy insists that any political party which is in power—be it Republican or Democratic, the Tory or Labour party—take the expansionary actions that can prevent lasting depressions.

Suppose we grant that great depressions are virtually a thing of the past. Does this mean that we must have perpetual prosperity—that recessions will never happen again, being replaced by what are euphemistically called "rolling readjustments" or mere "pauses"? Most scientists take a more cautious attitude, summarizing thus:

A mixed economy still is subject to occasional *recessions:* investment fluctuations can still occur; changes in government spending can have initially destabilizing effects upon general business activity; attempts to bring inflation under control sometimes result in downturns and slowdowns; foreign events like the OPEC oil boycott and price rise can adversely affect American economic activity.

Nevertheless, now that the tools of income analysis are understood and their use is politically mandatory, the probability of recession in any one year is less in the mixed economy than it used to be. Expansion periods tend to be frequent and longer. Now we must redefine the cycle so that stagnant growth below the trend-potential of growth is to be called recession, even though absolute growth has not vanished.

Before leaving the topic of recessions, let us take warning that the forces of democracy are not so strongly balanced in the direction of controlling creeping inflation—as we shall see in Chapter 41.

## SUMMARY

1   The business cycle is a pulse common to most sectors of economic life and to various countries. Movements in national income, unemployment, production, prices, and profits are not as regular and predictable as the orbits of the planets or the oscillations of a pendulum, and there is no magical method of forecasting the turns of business activity.

2   The phases of expansion, peak, recession, and trough can be separated for analysis and distinguished from seasonal and long-term trends. The resulting pattern of 8- to 10-year major cycles, shorter minor cycles, and longer Kuznets construction cycles has been carefully described by statisticians and historians.

3   To explain the cycle, a first clue is to be found in the greater amplitude of fluctuations of investment or durable-capital-goods formation. Although most economists agree on this fact, they differ in their emphasis upon *external* or *internal* factors. Increasingly, however, the experts are tending toward a *synthesis* of external and internal factors. On the one hand, importance is attached to fluctuations in inventions, in population and territorial growth, and in gold discoveries and political warfare. On the other hand, economists stress too the way that these external changes in investment opportunities are modified by the reactions of the economic system; the credit practices of banks and the monetary policies of the Federal Reserve; waves of optimism and pessimism; replacement cycles; *the multiplier and the acceleration principle,* which bring in dynamic rates of change as well as levels; and politically contrived stop-go cycles in mixed economies that face the painful dilemma of inflation or unemployment.

4   Forecasting is still inexact. Those with the best long-run batting averages follow national-income and related statistics very closely. They rely heavily on surveys of government, consumer, and business intentions. They reinforce their $C + I + G$ and money-supply guesses with studies of leading, coincidental, and lagging indicators. Computer models aim to convert the art of forecasting into a science.

5   The business cycle has been tamed, even if not completely made a thing of the past. Although democratic mixed economies are unlikely to experience old-fashioned, prolonged depressions ever again, recessions and periods of relative stagnation will no doubt still occur even though fiscal and monetary policies can moderate their frequency, intensity, and duration.

## CONCEPTS FOR REVIEW

business-cycle phases, crises
peak, trough, expansion, recession
seasonal and trend corrections
external and internal theories
sunspots, wars, innovations
replacement echoes, political
    cycles

acceleration-multiplier
    interactions
monetarism models
leading, coincidental, and
    lagging indicators
computer forecasting methods
mixed-economy improvements

## QUESTIONS FOR DISCUSSION

1   Describe the history of various business cycles in this country—pre- and post-1939.

2   Describe the different phases of the cycle. In what one are you now?

3   Which theory or theories of the cycle do you like best? Why?

4   "The ups and downs of the business cycle are less important objects of study now than 'unemployment gaps' and trends in real growth and prices." Appraise.

5   Write an explanation of the acceleration principle. Combine it with the multiplier.

6   Why is it important to be able to forecast the future of business activity? Give business and government examples. How would *you* forecast?

7   The concept of the business cycle needs to be redefined in modern times as follows: "Expansion should be defined as years when GNP grows faster than *trend;* recession defined as years when GNP grows slower than *trend.* Then we will again have recession half the time, on the average." Support the merits of this view.

8   Is forecasting a science? An art? How may the computer change the mix of qualitative judgment and quantitative formulas?

9   *Extra-credit problem* on accelerator-multiplier cyclical oscillations: Let consumption today, $C_t$, depend by the multiplier principle on yesterday's disposable income, $Y_{t-1}$, according to the formula $C_t = 100 + \frac{1}{2}Y_{t-1}$. Let investment today, $I_t$, be the growth in the stock of machines since last period: $I_t = K_t - K_{t-1}$. Suppose, by the acceleration principle, $K_t$ is always $\beta = 2$ times consumption sales, $K_t = \beta C_t$. Then, from the identity $Y_t = C_t + I_t$, after some substitutions we get $Y_t = C_t + 2(C_t - C_{t-1}) = 3C_t - 2C_{t-1} = 3(100 + \frac{1}{2}Y_{t-1}) - 2(100 + \frac{1}{2}Y_{t-2}) = 100 + \frac{3}{2}Y_{t-1} - Y_{t-2}$. (*a*) Show that if we start the system at equilibrium with $Y_0 = Y_1 = 200$, $(Y_2, Y_3, \ldots)$ will stay at 200. But show that, if the system is given an upward push from equilibrium so that $Y_1 = Y_0 + 64 = 264$, we get the perpetually oscillating "business cycle" (200, 264, 296, 280, 224, 156, 110, 109, $153\frac{1}{2}$, $221\frac{1}{4}$, $278\frac{3}{8}$, ...). (*b*) If either of the numbers, $\frac{1}{2}$ or $2$, is lowered a little, show that the oscillations of the new "second-order difference equation with constant coefficients" will dampen down and the system will eventually return to the 200 equilibrium. If either is raised a little, say, $\frac{1}{2}$ to $\frac{3}{4}$ and $2$ to $3$, the system's oscillations become bigger and bigger.

Earlier chapters showed how the modern economist finds it convenient to analyze the forces making for expanding or contracting money income in terms of saving and investment schedules—or what is the same thing, in terms of the components of consumption, investment, and government spending. For the most part, except in the inflationary-gap discussion, it was assumed that price levels would not change much until an approach to high employment was reached. Alternatively, it was assumed earlier that all the schedules were expressed in terms of dollars that had already been corrected for changes in the measuring rod of the price level. Thus, until now, a shift in the schedule of consumption-plus-investment-plus-government spending could be thought of as expanding employment and production.

Now we want to focus on changes in the *price levels*. Why do prices rise swiftly in major wars? Why do prices increase millionfolds in galloping inflation when a disorganized nation is printing new green-paper currency by the bale? Why do prices begin to creep upward even *before* an expansion of $C + I + G$ spending restores the system to full or high employment? Why in a modern mixed economy might prices and wages rise even at a time of apparent excess plant capacity and slack labor markets, giving rise to what in later chapters we will call "stagflation"—i.e., stagnation in real growth and job opportunity *along with* price and wage inflation?

These vital, and difficult, questions can be fruitfully approached by the following program. Section A first gives the facts about price-level changes and some of their effects. Then it discusses the concept of barter, the nature of money, and the basic facts about the supply of money, $M$. Section B then analyzes the way $M$ has generally moved in relation to long-term prices. In particular, the important "Quantity Theory of Money," in its crude and sophisticated forms, provides an initial glimpse into the importance of banking and Federal Reserve monetary policies, as discussed in later chapters.

We shall discover that changes in the money supply have an

# 15

## PRICES
## AND MONEY

Only one fellow in ten thousand understands the currency question, and we meet him every day.
KIN HUBBARD

important role in causing the $C + I + G$ spending schedule to shift upward and downward. And we shall see that a new kind of inflation—"cost-push" inflation—has reared its head alongside of conventional "demand-pull" inflation.

## A. PRICES AND THE MONEY SUPPLY

Figure 15-1 shows the historical ups and downs of wholesale prices. Each war is clearly marked by a peak. At first glance there seem to be no general upward or downward trends. But the chart of consumer prices in Fig. 15-2 (page 282) pinpoints the general *upward* trend of prices in this century. The value of the dollar—as measured by what it can buy—has been about cut in half since today's college student was born.

As an omen for the future, note one crucially significant fact: After World War II there was no decline in prices at all comparable with what had followed previous wars. Wages and prices seem to have become *sticky as far as downward movements are concerned;* also, government has become quick to act to stem any depression that begins to get under way. When the Vietnam war accelerated the rate of creeping inflation, the target for government policy was not price stability, for that was considered beyond the realm of feasibility. Instead, the target was to halve the rate of price increase, to bring it from 4 to 6 per cent per year down to 2 to 4 per cent. If prices rise in good times and scarcely fall at all in bad times, what is their indicated long-term direction? The answer is plain.

### INFLATION, DEFLATION, INCOME REDISTRIBUTION AMONG GROUPS

First, some definitions will be useful.

By *inflation* we mean *a time of generally rising prices* for goods and factors of production—rising prices for bread, cars, haircuts; rising wages, rents, etc. By *deflation* we mean a time when most prices and costs are falling.[1]

Neither in inflation nor in deflation do prices all move in the same direction or in exactly the same proportion. As a result of changes in *relative* prices and in total spending, the two processes of inflation and deflation cause definite and characteristic changes in (1) the distribution of income among economic classes, and (2) total output.

*Unforeseen* inflation tends to favor debtors and profit receivers at the expense of creditors and fixed-income receivers. Deflation has the opposite effect.

Suppose you lend $1,000 today and are paid back one year from now. If in the meantime prices have doubled, then your debtor will be paying back only one-half as much real purchasing power as you gave him. If prices were to increase a trillionfold, as they did in the German inflation of 1920–1923, then the wealth of creditors would be completely wiped out. This actually happened to German university endowments and life-insurance assets.

---

[1] "Deflation" sometimes has a secondary meaning too, namely, a *drop in real output and an increase in unemployment* regardless of price behavior. And even our simple definition of inflation as rising prices will occasionally need modifying: thus in 1947 when wartime price controls were removed, prices shot upward. Did stability of prices mean no inflation before then? Hardly. As scarcities of goods increased from 1942 to 1947, we were having "suppressed inflation." The 1947 price rise was primarily a "symptom" of the disease we were *already* experiencing.

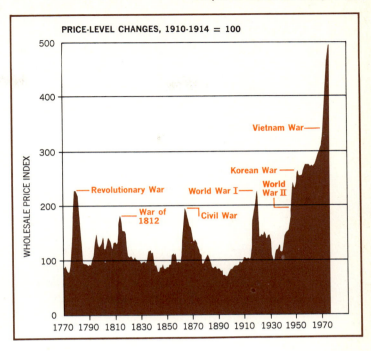

PRICE-LEVEL CHANGES, 1910-1914 = 100

**FIG. 15-1**
Wildest inflations historically come
with periods of war
After each major war in the country's history, there has been slightly less of a price drop. Indeed, after World War II there was no significant drop. For 80 years the general price trend—abroad as well as here—has been biased upward.

After 1939 an American who earned 6 per cent yearly on a mortgage found that, as a result of World War II, he was not even holding his own as far as the *real purchasing power* of the dollar was concerned. United States government savings bonds bought for $75 in 1975 pay off $100 in 1980. But will one hundred 1980 dollars have as much purchasing power as the seventy-five 1975 dollars did at the original time they were lent?

On the other hand, one who invests his money in real estate, common stocks, or sacks of flour makes a great money profit during *unforeseen* inflation. The dollar volume of business sales shoots up. Prices rise between the time businessmen buy and sell their merchandise. Fixed or overhead costs remain the same; other costs rise, but not so fast as prices. For all these reasons profits increase—often more than the cost of living. In periods of great inflation, every reckless fool is a great financier.

In time of deflation, the shoe is on the other foot. Creditors and fixed-income receivers tend to gain at the expense of debtors and profit receivers. If prices fall between the time that a creditor lends money and is repaid, then he gets back more purchasing power than he lent. Between the time that a merchant buys and sells goods, he will have to take a loss.

The schoolteacher who keeps her job finds that her real income has increased. The widow who withstood the temptation to buy common stock during the boom and instead put all her money into gilt-edge government bonds finds herself better off. At the same time, the government finds the real burden of its public debt goes up relative to tax collections and national income. A hoarder who earns no money interest on his mattress cache finds the real value of his wealth increasing every day as prices fall. If prices fall at the rate of 10 per cent per year, he is being rewarded for his antisocial act of hoarding at a 10 per cent rate of interest *in real terms*, while the businessman who is foolish enough to give someone a job may find that he cannot even get back his wage outlay, much less earn a profit.

Modern research suggests that the greatest redistribution of income resulting from inflation is from older to younger people. The dollar put aside for retirement at 70 often shrinks in purchasing power: if prices rise at an average rate of about 5 per cent per year, the real purchasing power of a dollar held for 30 years will halve and halve again in that period.

**Anticipated inflation**   Once an inflation has gone on for a long time and is no longer "unforeseen," an allowance for a price rise will gradually get itself built into the market interest rate. Thus, once we all expect prices to rise at 5 per cent per year, my pension funds invested in bonds and mortgages will tend to pay me 9 per cent rather than 4 per cent. This adjustment of interest rates to chronic inflation has been observed in Brazil, Chile, and indeed in almost all other countries with a long history of rising prices. In the 1970s, one sees a similar inflation pressure in American and European interest rates.

## EFFECTS OF CHANGING PRICES ON OUTPUT AND EMPLOYMENT

Aside from redistributing incomes, inflation may affect the total real income and production of the community.

**An increase in prices is usually associated with high employment. In mild inflation the wheels of industry are initially well lubricated, and output is near capacity. Private investment is brisk, jobs are plentiful. Such has been the historical pattern.**

Thus, many businessmen and union spokesmen, in appraising a little deflation and a little inflation, used to speak of the latter as the lesser of the two evils. The losses to fixed-income groups are usually less than the gains to the rest of the community. Even workers with relatively fixed wages are often better off because of improved employment opportunities and greater take-home pay; a rise in interest rates on new securities may partly make up any losses to creditors; and increases in social security benefits, indexed to adjust for price-level changes, make up losses to the retired.

**In deflation, on the other hand, the growing unemployment of labor and capital causes the community's total well-being to be less; so, in a sense, the gainers get less than the losers lose. As a matter of fact, in deep depression, almost everyone—including the creditor who is left with uncollectible debts—suffers.**

The above remarks show why an increase in consumption or investment spending is thought a good thing in times of unemployment, even if there is some upward pressure on prices. When the economic system is suffering from acute depression, few criticize private or public spending on the ground that this might be inflationary. Actually, most of the increased spending will then go to increase production and create more jobs and more real income.

But the same reasoning shows that once full employment and full plant capacity have been reached, any further increases in spending are likely to be completely wasted in price-tag increases. (Recall Chapter 13's discussion of "inflationary gaps.")

## GALLOPING INFLATION

Slow price increases are one thing. But when each increase in prices becomes the signal for an increase in wages and costs, which again sends prices up still further, we may be in the midst of a malignant, galloping hyperinflation. Nothing good can be said for a rapid rise of prices such as took place in Germany in 1920–1923 and more recently in China and Hungary. Production and even the social order are then disorganized. The total wealth of large groups of the population is wiped out as money becomes worthless. Debtors ruthlessly pursue creditors in order to pay off their obligations in valueless money. Speculators profiteer. Housewives rush to spend their husbands' paychecks before prices rise still further, but in doing so they only bid prices up even faster. As a Southerner said during the Confederate inflation:

We used to go to the stores with money in our pockets and come back with food in our baskets. Now we go with money in baskets and return with food in our pockets. Everything is scarce except money! Prices are chaotic and production disorganized. A meal that used to cost the same amount as an opera ticket now costs twenty times as much. Business is often at a standstill because no one knows how much to charge. (We'll settle after the war, some say.) As a result, everybody tends to hoard "things" and to try to get rid of the "bad" paper money, which drives the "good" metal money out of circulation. A partial return to barter inconvenience is the result.

Aside from hyperinflations of the German 1920–1923 type, we do see in countries like Chile and Brazil a state of chronic inflation—say, at the rate of 20 to 90 per cent per year—that goes on decade after decade. Somehow the people learn to live on such a merry-go-round. They hoard goods; buy houses; never, never lend money at ordinary interest rates; etc. Sometimes, as in Brazil, the economy manages to show real growth; too often, as in Argentina and Chile, growth suffers.

Fortunately, there are few cases of German-type hyperinflation except during war or in the backwash of war and revolution. The primary fear today for a mixed economy like America's is of a steady upward *creep* in prices. Will such a creep inevitably become a trot? A trot become a canter? A canter become a gallop? Few economic experts regard such a development as inevitable. But they still have reason to be concerned with too fast and steady a creep of prices—as we'll soon see.

## GOALS OF LONG-TERM PRICE BEHAVIOR

Ideally, we all want a progressive, full-employment economy in which the excesses of the business cycle are moderated. We want to control the "mad dance of the dollar" as the business cycle passes from boom to crisis and slump. But as far as the *long-run trend* of prices is concerned, there are three possible programs that different economists sponsor as the soundest modern compromise:

1. *Prices—on the average—are to be stable.* As output increases over time because of population increase, capital formation, and technological progress, the total of dollar spending rises. Money wages and real wages also rise as a result of the increase in productivity over time.

2. *Prices are to be gently rising.* As high-employment output increases with productivity and growth, total spending rises even faster than prices. Money wages also

rise steadily; but the increase in real wages is not quite so great, because of the upward trend in the cost of living.

3. *Prices are to be falling steadily.* The total of money wages and property income remains almost constant. But the increase in output resulting from improved technological productivity is passed on to *all* consumers in lower prices. Real wages rise even though money wages may remain constant. Such a fall in prices need not depress business activity unduly, provided that it results from previous reductions in cost.

All three solutions are tolerable if unemployment is kept at a moderate figure. And in some ideal frictionless system, it would not matter much which pattern existed, as long as the trend in prices was foreseeable and all adjustments were made to it. However, economic history and analysis suggest that we do not live in an ideal frictionless system. In a modern mixed economy, high employment is least likely to be maintained under the third possibility of falling price levels.

Most vigorous periods of healthy capitalist development without political unrest came during periods of stable or gently rising prices. Capitalism itself developed during the centuries when Spanish New World silver and gold were raising prices.

We now must examine how the money supply acts, along with fiscal policy and exogenous factors, to help determine the $C + I + G$ intersection of equilibrium GNP—of "nominal" or "money" GNP expressed in current prices.

## BARTER VERSUS THE USE OF MONEY

When W. Stanley Jevons, over a century ago in the first textbook on money, wanted to illustrate the tremendous leap forward made by man when he turned from exchange by barter to the use of money, he could not do better than to quote experiences like the following.

Some years since, Mademoiselle Zélie, a singer of the Théâtre Lyrique at Paris, . . . gave a concert in the Society Islands. In exchange for an air from *Norma* and a few other songs, she was to receive a third part of the receipts. When counted, her share was found to consist of three pigs, twenty-three turkeys, forty-four chickens, five thousand cocoa-nuts, besides considerable quantities of bananas, lemons, and oranges. . . . [I]n Paris . . . this amount of live stock and vegetables might have brought four thousand francs, which would have been good remuneration for five songs. In the Society Islands, however, pieces of money were scarce; and as Mademoiselle could not consume any considerable portion of the receipts herself, it became necessary in the mean time to feed the pigs and poultry with the fruit.

Inconvenient as barter obviously is, it represents a great step forward from a state of self-sufficiency in which every man had to be a jack-of-all-trades and master of none. A great debt of gratitude is owed to the first two ape-men who suddenly perceived that each could be made better off by giving up some of one good in exchange for some of another. Nevertheless, simple barter operates under grave disadvantages. An elaborate division of labor would be unthinkable without the introduction of a great new improvement—the use of money.

In all but the most primitive cultures, men do not directly exchange one good for another. Instead they sell one good for money, and then use money to buy the goods they wish. At first glance this seems to complicate rather than simplify matters, to replace a single transaction by two transactions. Thus, if I have apples and want nuts, would it not be simpler to trade one for the other rather than to sell the apples for money and then use the money to buy nuts?

Actually, the reverse is the case: the two transactions are simpler than one. Ordinarily, there are always people ready to buy apples and always some willing to sell—at a price—nuts; but it would be an unusual *coincidence* to find a person with tastes exactly opposite my own, with an eagerness to sell nuts and buy apples. Such a coincidence would be as unlikely as the chance of flipping a dozen "tails" in a row. (Even if the unusual should happen—as occasionally it must—there is no guarantee that the desires of the two parties with respect to the exact *quantities* and terms of the exchange would coincide.)

To use a classical economic phrase: Instead of there being a double coincidence of wants, there is likely to be a want of coincidence; so that, unless a hungry tailor happens to find an undraped farmer who has both food and a desire for a pair of pants, neither can make a trade.

Money does simplify economic life. But do not suppose that, for society as a whole, a mere increase in the total of money will enable people to consume more than the real products technically producible with existent totals of labor, land, and capital. And, as we've seen, money can misbehave and produce recession and inflation.

## HISTORICAL STAGES OF MONEY

If we were to reconstruct history along hypothetical, logical lines, we should naturally follow the age of barter by the age of commodity money.

**Commodity money**  Historically, a great variety of commodities has served at one time or another as a medium of exchange: cattle (from which come the Latin stem of "pecuniary" and also the words "capital" and "chattel"), tobacco, leather and hides, furs, olive oil, beer or spirits, slaves or wives, copper, iron, gold, silver, rings, diamonds, wampum beads or shells, huge rocks and landmarks, and cigarette butts.

Each of the above has some advantages and disadvantages. Cattle are not divisible into small change; but while it is being hoarded, such "money" is likely to increase by reproduction, giving the lie to the doctrine of Aristotle that "money is barren." Beer does not improve with keeping, although wine may. Olive oil provides a nice liquid currency that is as minutely divisible as one wishes. Iron will rust and is of so little value that one would need a cart instead of a pocketbook. The value of a diamond is not proportional to weight but varies with the square of its weight; if cut into pieces, it loses value.

The yearly additions to (by mining) or subtractions from (by use in teeth, jewelry, and electric relays) the accumulated stock of *precious metals* are small in percentage terms; so their total supplies do not fluctuate much. Silver has luster but tarnishes. Gold keeps its attractive sheen, but unalloyed is soft. Gold's high specific gravity makes detection of counterfeiting and admixture easy; but through most of history, gold's scarcity value has been so great per ounce as to require inordinately minute coins for ordinary purchases. Its main use has been for hoarding.

Most kinds of money tended once to be of some value or use for their own sake. Thus, even wampum had decorative uses, and paper money began as warehouse or mint receipts for so much metal. But the intrinsic usefulness of the money medium is now the least important thing about it.

**Paper money**   The age of commodity money gives way to the age of paper money. The essence of money, its intrinsic nature, is typified by paper currency. *Money, as money rather than a commodity, is wanted not for its own sake but for the things it will buy!* We do not wish to use up money directly, but rather to use it by getting rid of it; even when we choose to use it by holding it, its value comes from the fact that we can spend it *later on*.

Money is an artificial, social convention. If for any reason a substance begins to be used as money, all people will begin to value it, even if they happen to be teetotalers or vegetarians or disbelievers in its intrinsic usefulness. As long as things can be bought and sold for a given substance, people will be content to sell and buy with it. Paradox: money is accepted because it is accepted!

The use of paper currency (dollar bills, fives, tens, . . .) has become widespread because it is convenient as a medium of exchange. Currency is easily carried and stored. By the printing of more or fewer zeros on the face value of the bill, a great or small amount of value can be embodied in a light, transportable medium of little bulk. By the use of decimal points, it can be made as divisible as we wish. By careful engraving, the value of money can be protected from counterfeiting and adulteration. The fact that private individuals cannot create it at will in unlimited amounts keeps it scarce, i.e., an economic, and not a free, good.

Given this limitation in supply, modern currencies have value, i.e., can buy things, independently of any gold, silver, or government backing. The public neither knows nor cares—and need not know or care—whether its currency is in the form of silver certificates, Federal Reserve notes, or copper or silver coin. So long as each form of money can be converted into any other at fixed terms, the best is as good as the worst.

**Bank money**   Finally, along with the age of paper money, there is the age of bank money, or bank checking deposits. Today at least nine-tenths of all transactions, by value if not number, take place by checks. A professor has his salary paid directly into his bank account, after income taxes have already been withheld by his employer. His rent or dentist bills are paid by check; his gasoline and hotel bills, by a credit card. Except for petty sums for lunches and carfare, he needs little cash.

**A moneyless economy in the future?**   In the age of the electronic computer, there is less and less need to carry currency or even to have to depend upon one's checkbook. A credit card serves increasingly for most transactions. Governor George Mitchell of the Federal Reserve Board looked ahead to envision the day when, by telephone or automatic insertion of a noncounterfeitable card into a computer terminal, central memory and data banks will record most transactions. Money as a unit of account will still serve its function; but anything so crude as a poker chip, coin, or bill will be largely dispensed with in favor of records that automatically balance out each person's inpayments and outpayments over a lifetime.

### THREE KINDS OF MONEY: COINS, CURRENCY, BANK DEPOSITS

We may sum up the essence of money briefly:

**Money is the modern medium of exchange and the standard unit in which prices and debts are expressed. By controlling the behavior of money and credit, the government through its Federal Reserve System hopes to affect the balance of saving and investment expenditure—the level of real and money GNP, and hence the rate of price-level inflation.**

By quickening or moderating the growth in the money supply, the Federal Reserve can hope to raise or lower the $C + I + G$ intersections of earlier chapters. Here lies the vital importance of monetary theory and its similarity to fiscal theory.

Let us list the main kinds of money now in daily use: small coins, paper currency, and checking-account bank-deposit money.

Coins   First, there are the *coins* we use for small change: copper pennies, nickel five-cent pieces, and silver-looking dimes, quarters, half dollars, and (in the Far West) dollars. These constitute our small coins. Children think them important; but in total they do not add up to very much—in fact, to less than one-seventh of the community's non-bank cash. Because the metal in coins is worth far *less* than their face value, they are termed "token money."[2] These coins are valued far beyond their metallic worth only because they can be readily converted into other money—20 nickels to the dollar, and so forth. Coins with negligible metallic value are not forced upon us; their quantity is limited by our demand for them to buy gum and newspapers, or to put in various vending machines.

Currency   More significant is the second kind of money: *paper currency*. Most of us know little more about a one- or five-dollar bill than that it is inscribed with the picture of an American statesman, that it bears the signature of a government official, and—most important—each has a numeral showing its face value.

Examine a ten-dollar bill or some other paper bill. You probably find it says "Federal Reserve Note."[3] Also, it announces itself as "legal tender for all debts, public and

---

[2] If a dictator insisted on supplementing the paper currency with coins whose metallic value equaled or came near their face values, he would show what an amateur he was at finance. Thus, as soon as platinum or silver rose enough in price on the auction markets of the world, the dictator would find his coins were being melted down for their metallic content. It is because coins and currency are made of cheap materials that they avoid this fate. Do facts bear out this theory? They do, as the next footnote will show: When the price of silver rose, the government had to stop using silver in dimes and quarters; to keep new coins from being melted down and hoarded, it substituted cheaper cupro-nickel materials.

[3] Some one-dollar bills used to bear the words "Silver Certificate." One who knows American politics and history realizes that these existed only because a few Western senators from mining states could persuade Congress to give silver mining a continuing subsidy by buying up quantities of silver for

private." Until recently it contained the further, and nonsensical, statement that it "is redeemable in *lawful money* at the United States Treasury or at any Federal Reserve Bank." Why italicize "lawful money"? Because for 30 years there was no such thing other than the "legal tender" bills under discussion, namely, Federal Reserve notes and so forth. In short, your old, wrinkled ten-dollar bill is redeemable into a crisp new bill, into 2 fives, or into 10 ones if you prefer! But that is all.[4]

Today, all American currency and coin is essentially "fiat" money. It is money because the government decrees it is money, and because we all accept it. Metallic backing has no real meaning anymore (no longer even serving to limit the total supply of fiat money).

Before 1933, it was common for good little boys and girls to be presented on their birthdays with five- or ten-dollar gold pieces; and gold certificates were often seen in circulation. These certificates were warehouse receipts promising the bearer redemption in gold upon application to the United States Treasury. But in 1933, when Congress raised the buying price of gold from about $21 to $35 an ounce, all gold— except that tied up in wedding rings, dental fillings, and rare coins—was called in. This was done so that holders or hoarders of gold could not make a 67 per cent profit as a result of the devaluation of the dollar. At the same time, all gold certificates were called in. Congress ruled that these certificates were not to be exchanged for gold upon being called in, but simply for ordinary paper dollars.[5] Since 1975, private American citizens can own gold, but the price of gold that ordinary citizens can buy is unrelated to the official price of gold (now nominally $42.22 an ounce, although in fact governments unofficially evaluate it at about five times that official fiction).

From the standpoint of understanding the nature of money, it is perhaps simpler that the citizenry's gold certificates and coins no longer exist. The modern student need not be misled, as were earlier generations of students, by some mystical belief that "gold backing" is what gives money its value. Certainly gold, as such, has little

---

monetary use. Otherwise, silver had absolutely no *monetary* significance; many countries are abandoning it even for small coins, and it is finally losing its hold on the Orient. By 1963, silver for teeth, electronics, and photography rose in price to approach the point where melting dollars and turning in bills for metal became profitable. So Congress dropped the farce of requiring part of our money to be silver certificates. No longer can you demand silver from the government.

Two-dollar bills, long considered to be bad luck, were so-called "United States Notes"—remnants of the greenbacks used to finance the Civil War. After 1966 they ceased to be issued. Some five-dollar bills are also United States Notes. Occasionally you may run into a bill that says "Federal Reserve *Bank* Note" or even a "National Bank Note" containing the name of some nearby national bank; these too are being gradually retired from circulation.

[4] A Cleveland businessman wrote to the Treasury asking for some "lawful money" in return for a ten-dollar bill. He received two polite letters, but no satisfaction. Actually, since 1934 the old distinction between "legal tender" and other money has ceased to have meaning. Since then, if you bring a thousand dollars' worth of pennies in to settle a tax bill or contract, they are as legally acceptable in the federal courts as anything else; earlier a creditor could have insisted on certain specified "legal tender."

[5] As we'll see in Chapter 17, the 12 Federal Reserve Banks still hold gold certificates of a special type, but this is a mere bookkeeping matter.

to do with the problem. Every expert knows that the popular conception "money has more value if it is exchangeable into gold" exactly reverses the true relation. If it were not that gold has some monetary uses, gold's value *as a metal* would be much less than it is today. We should have cheaper inlays and wedding rings, and South African and Russian miners would be poorer.[6]

The sensible reason why a staunch conservative today wants to go back to gold-coin money is not that he thinks gold is needed to give money its value. Rather, he knows that governmental actions can today strongly affect the value of money, and he is convinced that *governments cannot be trusted to refrain from abusing this power;* so he favors taking away from the Congress, the Executive, and the Federal Reserve System their power in these matters and prefers to put his trust in the vicissitudes of mine discoveries rather than in fallible or allegedly corrupt governments.

As we shall see in subsequent chapters and in the international discussions of Part Five, gold still does have a limited role to play in financing international transactions and in international reserves. Therein is found its reduced role in contemporary economics.

**Limitation in the supply of money is the necessary condition if it is to have value. If currency is so unlimited in amount as to become practically a free good, people would have so much of it to spend as to bid up all prices, wages, and income sky-high. That is why constitutional powers over money and banking are never given to private groups but are always vested in government.**

## WHY CHECKABLE DEMAND DEPOSITS ARE CONSIDERED TO BE MONEY

**Demand deposits**    There is also a third category of what economists call money. This involves *bank deposits subject to checking on demand.*

If I have $1,000 in my checking account at the Cambridge Trust Company, that deposit can be regarded as money. Why? For the simple reason that I can pay for purchases with checks drawn on it. The deposit is like any other medium of exchange, and, being payable on demand, it serves as a "standard of value," or "unit of account," in the same sense that $1,000 worth of quarters do; i.e., both the bank deposit and the quarters can be converted into standard money or cash at fixed terms, dollar for dollar.

---

[6]That gold affects prices only through its ability to *limit or to expand the volume of paper money and total spending* was overlooked by foolish European chancellors of the exchequer who, after World War I, tried to stop inflation by *accumulating* new gold reserves through the purchase of gold on the open market with newly *printed* money! Of course, the effect was just the opposite. Only after they had reversed the process and used their gold to buy up and burn outstanding paper money did they enjoy any success. Chapter 33 will discuss the two-tier gold system of international finance: the official-tier, in which gold exchanges between central banks and governments are at the $42-an-ounce rate set by the members of the International Monetary Fund (IMF); and the free-tier, in Zurich, Chicago, and elsewhere, where jewelers, hoarders, and organized crime pay up to $200 an ounce depending upon momentary supply and demand. Also "paper gold"—Special Drawing Rights (SDRs) of the IMF—will be discussed.

| MONEY SUPPLY OF THE UNITED STATES (in billions of dollars) | | | | |
|---|---|---|---|---|
| KINDS OF MONEY | MARCH, 1939 | MARCH, 1946 | MARCH, 1965 | MARCH, 1975 |
| Coin (outside of banks) | $ 0.6 | $ 1.3 | $ 3.1 | $ 7.4 |
| Paper currency (outside of banks): | | | | |
|   Federal Reserve notes | 4.3 | 23.9 | 30.3 | 60.9 |
|   Silver certificates and | | | | |
|     U.S. notes | 1.6 | 2.3 | 1.2 | 0.5 |
|   Other currency (largely in | | | | |
|     process of being retired) | 0.3 | 0.6 | 0.1 | 0.0 |
| | 6.2 | 26.8 | 31.6 | 61.4 |
| Bank money: | | | | |
|   Demand deposits of all banks | | | | |
|     (adjusted to exclude government | | | | |
|     deposits, etc.) | 26.1 | 76.2 | 125.2 | 215.3 |
|     **Total $M_1$** | **$32.9** | **$104.3** | **$159.9** | **$284.1** |
| Time and saving deposits (includes | | | | |
|   mutual savings banks, postal | | | | |
|   savings, savings and loan agencies, | | | | |
|   certificates of deposit) | 30.0 | 59.1 | 132.4 | 430.9 |
|     **Total $M_2$** | **$62.9** | **$163.4** | **$292.3** | **$715.0** |
| U.S. government bonds held by | | | | |
|   individuals and business | | | | |
|   (excluding banks, insurance | | | | |
|   companies, etc.) | 12.0 | 83.2 | 89.1 | 102.4 |
|     Total "near-money" and money | $74.9 | $246.6 | $381.4 | $817.4 |

TABLE 15-1

*M,* the supply of money—deposits plus currency—is a key macroeconomic variable
Coin plus currency plus demand deposits define the narrow money supply, $M_1$. Add time deposits in to get broader $M_2$. Including other liquid assets or "near-moneys" gives still broader concept.

**Possessing the essential properties of money, bank demand deposits might just as well be counted as money, as part of *M*. And they are.**[7]

Actually, as noted, bank money is quantitatively more important than currency because most transactions are made by check. The convenience of checks for mailing, for paying the exact sum of money due, for providing a receipt in the form of the canceled check voucher, for protecting against loss when stolen or misplaced (while unendorsed or, for that matter, endorsed)—all these advantages are obvious and explain the widespread use of bank money.

Table 15-1 shows the quantitative importance of the three components of money: coin, currency, and demand deposits. Their *total* is called $M_1$, money as narrowly defined.

[7]My balance on deposit in the bank is usually called money—not the checks I write.

## TIME DEPOSITS, LIQUID ASSETS, AND OTHER NEAR-MONEY

Along with the total of money narrowly defined, $M_1$, Table 15-1 also shows the total of money broadly defined, $M_2$. Included in this broader definition of money are all kinds of saving and time deposits, whether in commercial banks, mutual savings banks, savings and loan associations, credit unions, etc. Although you cannot write checks on such time deposits, you can usually cash them in on short notice.

Suppose you have $10,000 on demand deposit and your brother has $5,000 on time deposit and $5,000 on demand deposit. Will your saving and consumption schedules be very different ones? At equal incomes, is he likely to save a much larger percentage than you? Probably not; and that is why $M_2$ is important. Time or saving deposits—in commercial banks, mutual savings banks, and federal savings and loan associations—have gained mightily on demand deposits in recent decades, providing all the more reason why we cannot be content with $M_1$ alone.

Because it is difficult to draw a hard-and-fast line at any point in the chain of things that do have a direct bearing on spending, the exact definition of $M$, the money supply, is partly a matter of taste rather than scientific necessity. (Along with $M_1$ and $M_2$, economists have been able to define more than a dozen different money-supply concepts: $M_3$, $M_{1\frac{1}{2}}$, . . . , !)

A century ago, demand deposits would not have been included in $M$. Today, economists would include demand deposits, since even the most stubborn adherent of the old, narrow concept has to admit that the existence of checking accounts does *economize* on the use of currency and thus acts much like an increase in the effective amount of currency. And a growing number of economists argue along the same lines for inclusion of interest-bearing time deposits in the definition of the money supply.[8]

**Definitional problems**    Economists are not all agreed on nomenclature in this field. Many would go so far as to append to $M_1$ and $M_2$ a further category of liquid-wealth items called "near-money."

At the least, they would include in near-money the total of government bonds[9] which anyone could present for redemption or sell for cash in the open market (albeit not at a stable price predictable long in advance). These near-money items have many of the properties of money.

True, you do not pay your monthly expenses directly with government bonds, and so we hesitate to call such an item "money." Still, the fact that you have such an easily cashable asset means that your current spending habits are probably affected in much the same way as they would be if you owned a larger bank deposit instead of the government bonds.

---

[8] Some scholars have even attempted to include government bonds in money, rather than give them zero weight and exclude them; such writers prefer to give them some fractional weight and add them into a total called "effective" money supply, $M_3$. Because data on time deposits in commercial banks are easier to collect than those in S&Ls and mutual savings banks, we shall follow the custom of many scholars and often include only commercial-bank time deposits in our charts of $M_2$.

[9] It would not be illogical to subtract out from people's liquid assets their current liabilities (charge accounts, installment loans, etc.). Along with income, perhaps their resulting "net worth" would be the single most important determinant of their spending.

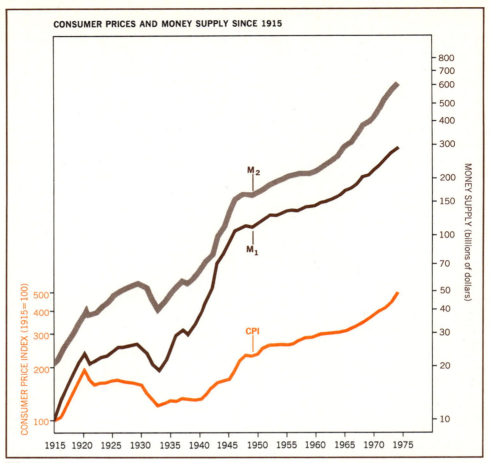

**FIG. 15-2**

**Price level and money supply tend to move together—usually!**
Prices and money do not approximate exact proportionality required by crude Quantity Theory of Money and Prices. As real output grows and grows, $M$ would have to grow just to hold $P$ constant. Because $M$'s rate of turnover, or velocity $V$, has been speeding up since 1945, the money GNP, equal to $PQ$, has been growing faster than $M$.

Table 15-1 shows that all the different kinds of money are now many times greater than before World War II. For the most part, this book will follow the most common practice and define the total money supply thus:

$M$ is the sum of coin and currency in circulation outside the banks, plus checkable demand deposits (after various routine adjustments have been made in this magnitude). Along with this narrow definition of total $M$ (which we may call $M_1$), it is sometimes useful to work with a broader definition (called $M_2$), which includes time and saving deposits in addition to coin, currency, and demand deposits.

See Fig. 15-2 for a picture of the more rapid growth of the broad measure $M_2$ in recent years.

## B. THE DEMAND FOR MONEY AND THE QUANTITY THEORY

What are the functions of money? Here are some just discussed and some new ones:

1. Money is a *medium of exchange* enabling us to transact our national income and product without recourse to hopelessly inefficient barter.

2. Money is the *unit of account* in which we express prices for current transactions and also for future or deferred transactions (such as when I borrow $1,000 today and agree to pay back $1,200 three years from now).

3. Money is a safe *way of holding* at least part of one's *wealth*—safe against the ups and downs inherent in stocks, land, homes, and bonds. When all these are going down in price, the canny hoarder of money is the most successful speculator in the community. (When prices rise, however, many money holders suffer.)

4. Money holding is a necessary *precaution* against having a sudden expense occur or an unexpected delay in a receipt due from someone else. Similarly, it helps one take advantage of a bargain in goods or in securities that might suddenly come up.

All these functions are worth paying for. And we each do incur a cost in holding a coin, a bill, or a demand deposit—namely, the *sacrificed interest and profit yield* that might be obtained from purchase of earning assets.

General Electric works just as hard to keep down its unnecessary cash as it does to keep down its unnecessary steel inventory and wastage. The business manager of a famous cartoonist was aghast to find that he had kept $120,000 idle in a demand deposit, earning no interest for years, and all merely because he never read his mail!

It is clear from the above that there are two main motives for holding money: (1) for the convenience of ordinary *transactions* needed at each level of income; and (2) to fill a prudent *precautionary* need arising from the uncertainties of the safety and the yield from other forms of wealth, and of the uncertainties of timing of expense outpayments and receipt inpayments.

At the turn of the century Alfred Marshall of Cambridge University and Irving Fisher of Yale summarized the factors involved in the demand for money thus:

*Demand for money:* The higher our annual incomes, the more dollars of business we all will want to transact; with various allowances for economies of scale, people hold *M* at any time about in proportion to their *income* rate per year or month. (This *transaction demand* for money will be shifted downward a little at higher interest rates offered on good bonds, savings deposits, and other close money substitutes. At higher interest you will economize on your cash balance, making each dollar turn over more rapidly.)

People also hold *M* as a precautionary store of wealth, not wanting to put all their eggs in the basket of risky assets and wanting to be prepared for bargains or sudden expenses. This *precautionary* (or "asset") *demand* for money will be much affected by factors other than income: total wealth; level of sacrificed interest and profit yields; optimism, pessimism, uncertainty about the future; expected changes in prices of goods and assets (rate of inflation), and interest rates—all the "speculative" elements that any investments depend on.

The elements in the second paragraph of this summary are in Marshall and Fisher, but were not much emphasized until the 1930s, when Keynes and practical bankers noted that transaction demand could not account for massive changes in cash holdings. The pre-1930 discussions emphasized the *M*-and-income link by using the concept of "velocity of circulation of money," and to this we now turn.

### VELOCITY OF CIRCULATION OF MONEY

It is historical fact that as dollar GNP has grown, so has $M$. With $M$ now ten times as large as before World War II, dollar GNP is even more than ten times as large as its earlier figure. Nor is this merely history. If GNP grows from its present level of $1\frac{1}{2}$ trillion to reach, a decade from now, about $3 trillion, the betting odds are that $M$ will be nearly double its present amount then—a fair bet even before we know whether changes in $M$ will be "cause" of changes in GNP or "effect."

Why should there be any connection? $M$ is a *stock* magnitude, something you can measure *at an instant of time* like any other balance-sheet asset. GNP is a *flow* of dollar income *per year*, something that you can measure only from income statements that refer to the passage of time between two dates.

A new concept can be introduced to describe the Fisher-Marshall ratios between two such different magnitudes: it is called the "velocity of circulation of money" per year and is written as $V$.

*Definition of velocity:* **The rate at which the stock of money is turning over per year to consummate income transactions is called the velocity of circulation of money (or more exactly, the *income* velocity, *V*).**

If the stock of money is turning over very slowly, so that its rate of dollar income spending per year is low, $V$ will be low. If people hold less money at each instant of time relative to the rate of GNP flow (price of apples × apples + price of oranges × oranges + . . .), then $V$ will be high.

The size of $V$ will tend to rise with interest rates. Also, $V$ can change over time with changes in financial institutions, habits, attitudes, expectations, computer communications, and relative distributions of $M$ among different kinds of institutions and income classes. These changes in $V$ need not, however, be abrupt, volatile, or completely unpredictable.

**In every case, this formal definition of the velocity of circulation of money holds:**

$$V \equiv \frac{\text{GNP}}{M} \equiv \frac{p_1 q_1 + p_2 q_2 + \cdots}{M} \equiv \frac{\text{sum } pq}{M} \equiv \frac{PQ}{M}$$

**Here *P* stands for the average price level and goes up and down with an index of the price level, while *Q* stands for real (as distinct from current dollar) GNP and has to be computed statistically by the already-mentioned process of "deflating" GNP with a price index.**

Here is a helpful example. Table 15-1 indicates an $M$ in early 1975 of about $285 billion. GNP is shown then at annual rates of about $1,420 billion. So 1,420 per year divided by 285 gives us an income velocity of about 5 per year. This expression means that each unit of money was used for GNP transactions about five times a year; or putting this in an equivalent way, at any one time during the year, people in the economy were holding money that amounted to a bit more than two months' average income.[10]

---

[10]Economists sometimes calculate $V$ for *all* transactions including transfers, intermediate goods, and everything else. From recent statistics of bank checking transactions (or debits), one finds that urban bank deposits outside of New York City turn over 85 times a year, and New York City deposits turn over 340 times a year. Plainly, such over-all velocity figures are far greater than income velocity.

## THE QUANTITY EQUATION OF EXCHANGE: AN IDENTITY

After economists have invented the concept of velocity of circulation of money, they can rearrange its formal definition to get a new identity called the "Quantity Equation of Exchange":

$$MV \equiv PQ$$

This comes merely from shifting $M$ from the denominator of our last definition's right-hand side over to the numerator of the other side. By definition of $V$, the left-hand side in this new equation is equal to GNP, the rate of current national product per year. But the right-hand side, by virtue of what we have already defined $P$ and $Q$ to be, also is definitionally the same thing as GNP.

EXAMPLE: If there were only a single good in the GNP, a trillion baskets of bread selling at a price of \$1 each, then GNP $\equiv PQ =$ \$1 trillion GNP per year; when there is more than one commodity, we sum all such $p \times q$ products; and if all their $q$'s stayed unchanged and all their $p$'s doubled, then the average price level as denoted by $P$ would double, naturally giving us a \$2- rather than \$1-trillion GNP.[11]

All the definitional equations have been written with the three-bar identity symbol rather than with the more common two-bar equality symbol. This is to drive home the fact that they are what logicians call a "tautology"—statements which by themselves tell us nothing about reality but which *would hold true by definition* even if the United States reverted to barter, or if its $M$ halved while its GNP grew tenfold. (Although it is important to remember that the equation of exchange is such a tautology, *it is not legitimate to infer from this fact that it must therefore be useless.* It may, or may not, be a useful way of separating out for individual analysis the factors apt to lead to empirical relations which do best describe actual economic life. Subsequent chapters will show that careful description of income determination by $C + I + G$ schedules and how they are interrelated by changes in banking policy can *also* be expressed in terms of the magnitudes in the Equation of Exchange, and vice versa.)

## THE QUANTITY THEORY OF MONEY AND PRICES: A HYPOTHESIS

**The crude Quantity Theory**   If 1975 $M$ is nine times 1939 $M$, then an adherent of what can be called the "crude Quantity Theory of Money and Prices" would have to predict that the 1975 price level $P$ should be almost exactly nine times 1939 $P$. The fact that prices have only quadrupled in that period would be a refutation of this crude notion that the price level moves in direct proportion to the money supply.

Arithmetically, the crude Quantity Theory might be written as $P = kM$, where $k$ is a positive proportionality constant that depends on units used; thus, if $P$ and $M$ are measured by index numbers which were 100 in the same base year, $k$ could be replaced by 1.0 or omitted. Note

---

[11] Some find the following "explanation" of this necessary equality helpful. Every income transaction involves sales receipts equal to $p \times q$, which leads to the $PQ$ totals on the right. But it is $M$ that is involved in such transactions. How much in a year? The stock $M$ times its average velocity per year. Thus, value of money (that passes hands) equals value (*both* of what has been sold *and* bought), and the two sides must therefore be the same.

that this relation is not intended to be an irrefutable definitional identity, but rather, a useful empirical relationship about $k$'s constancy.

The idea behind the crude Quantity Theory is simple. If the government effects a thousandfold increase in $M$, then one can predict there will be a galloping inflation in which $P$ rises 1,000-fold—or, more cautiously, at least somewhere between 500-fold and 2,000-fold. Crude as this notion is, there is some usefulness to it. Thus, when the head of the German central bank denied that its printing carloads of currency had anything to do with the 1920–1923 trillionfold increase in prices, his statement was nonsensical. If he had said, "I am just a civil servant, forced, by the clamor of the populace in a defeated nation with grave external and internal disorganization, to take part in an upward race between $P$ and $M$"—if he had said this, we could feel sorry for him. But who can deny the elementary fact that a vastly larger bidding of German marks for a limited supply of goods had to send prices expressed in marks skyward?

Money differs basically from ordinary goods like wheat or steel. We want wheaten bread for its own sake, steel for hammers or knives. We want money *only for the work it does in buying us wheat or steel*. If, in 1923, all German prices are a trillion times what they were in 1920, it is natural to want about a trillion times as much $M$ as in 1920. Therein lies the valid core of the crude Quantity Theory. But we must be wary of extrapolating it to real-life cases where all $P$s have not changed in the same balanced proportions.

**Rudimentary as it is, then, the crude Quantity Theory linking $P$ directly to $M$ is useful to describe periods of hyperinflation and various long-term trends in prices, such as those in Spain and elsewhere in Europe after New World treasure was discovered.**

Since galloping inflation can put an intolerable strain on a democratic society, it is well to preach the crude Quantity Theory in season and out of season—not because in its crudest form it is in season very often, but because it is so urgently needed in those disorganized times when its message is in season.

**A sophisticated Quantity Theory**   Few people still subscribe to the crude Quantity Theory. But we should not use its inadequacies to damn the valuable truth that the money supply can have important effects on macroeconomic magnitudes such as investment, employment, production, and prices.

The next few chapters will show how *monetary policy* does have an important influence on the *total of spending*—on the $C + I + G$ intersections of GNP. This analysis can be translated quite easily into the language of $V$ and $M$, even though it was not fashionable to do so a couple of decades back. Since there has been a revival of interest in the quantity theory by a number of competent American economists in recent years, it is worth taking an eclectic approach here and reviewing the fundaments of a sophisticated quantity-theory approach, leaving until later a more extensive reconciliation of the various approaches.

The proof of the pudding is in the eating, and the test of all theories is their correspondence with the facts. Figure 15-2 showed back on page 282 that consumer prices and the supply of money have both generally grown, but by no means in perfect concordance.

Economists such as Chicago's Milton Friedman are not surprised to find $M$ growing sevenfold while $P$ only triples; for they believe that only in time periods when real output remains roughly the same—say, at a high-employment level—can one expect $M$ and $P$ to be directly related. They expect $M$ and GNP (or $PQ$) to be related. This belief is based upon the hypothesis that the velocity of circulation $V$ can be predicted to be reasonably constant, or if not constant, is at least subject to predictable changes.

While it is a fact that GNP has climbed twice as fast as $M$ has since 1939, this rise in velocity has been a gradual one (and perhaps one that might have been expected from the fact that 1939 was still a depressed year and still a time of very low interest rates and abnormally low $V$.)

Historically, one observes that $V$ exhibited a downward trend in the pre-1945 long run, moving down somewhat as real income has grown. The short-run cyclical swings in $V$ are quite the opposite: when production and interest rates have gone up in recovery periods, $V$ has tended also to have a short-run rise; when output has fallen in recessions, $V$ has fallen too. During the recent decades of (*a*) creeping inflation, (*b*) high nominal interest rates, and (*c*) computers, credit cards, and better methods for scheduling inventories of money, $V$ has been generally rising.

A sophisticated Quantity Theorist cannot be accused of believing that $V$ is a fundamental constant of nature. What he does believe is that controlling the behavior of $M$ *will help much* to control GNP, for the reason that the resulting changes in $V$ will be either so small or so predictable as to make one confident that dollar GNP will still move *in the same direction* as $M$. Qualitatively, this is in agreement with almost any modern theory of income determination, and the only possible argument concerns the confidence with which one can predict the quantitative potency of effects on the GNP of changes in $M$ in comparison with other stimuli, such as fiscal policy and external investment swings.[12]

## GOVERNMENTAL CONTROL OF THE SUPPLY OF MONEY

All schools of economics are today agreed that changes in the supply of money are important for macroeconomics. In earlier centuries, it was the happenstance of gold and silver mining discoveries that dictated the chaotic trend of the money supply. Today in all countries, that is a thing of the past.

As we shall see in the next few chapters, it is the government's own central bank—in the United States the Federal Reserve System, abroad the Bank of Japan, the Bank of England, the Bank of Italy, the Banque de France, the German Bundesbank—that determines the rate of growth of a nation's money supply. If it were merely a matter

---

[12] It may be mentioned here that the *crude* Quantity Theory would be correct, if in the following rearrangement of the tautological equation of exchange $P \equiv (V/Q)M$, the expression in parentheses were a strict constant. Thus, if both $V$ and $Q$ changed little, or if their changes were always largely self-canceling, the crude theory would be correct. But once scholars agree that $V$ may change appreciably when the economy goes from a 1929 high-interest prosperity to a 1939 low-interest depression, and that $Q$ may fall from a full-employment 1929 level to a level that is far below full employment in some later year, they realize that a more sophisticated theory of money, production, interest rates, and prices must be studied. A rather crude form of rejection of the significance of $M$ was provided by the Radcliffe Committee Report published in 1959 by the British government. After arguing (correctly) that $PQ$ is affected by over-all "liquidity" and bears no *simple* proportionality to $M$, it incorrectly inferred that induced changes in $V$ are as likely as not to offset fully any contrived changes in $M$. The presumption in *all* modern theories—Keynesian as well as pre-Keynesian!—is that a continued rise in $M$ *will* definitely tend to expand $PQ$. Note the logical fallacy in Radcliffe's argument: "'Money alone matters' is false; *ergo*, 'money doesn't matter.'"

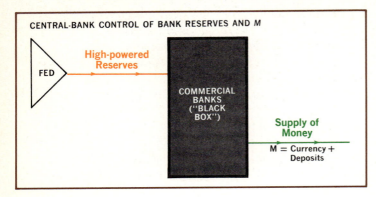

CENTRAL-BANK CONTROL OF BANK RESERVES AND *M*

FED

High-powered Reserves

COMMERCIAL BANKS ("BLACK BOX")

Supply of Money

M = Currency + Deposits

**FIG. 15-3**

**The central bank (the Fed) controls the *M* supply by fixing "reserves" total**

At left the central bank feeds the input of high-powered (reserves) money into the commercial banking system, regarded as a black box (to be examined in the next chapters). The commercial banks produce as amplified output on the right the public's supply of *M*: currency plus deposits. Hence, central responsibility for rate of growth of the money supply rests with government's central bank—in America, the Federal Reserve System (the Fed).

of paper currency, there being no other forms of money, we'd merely have to analyze how the government puts the printing press to work: to help pay for its expenditures or to lend out to private investors.

The next chapter will show that matters are a bit more complicated once we recognize the important role of the private commercial banks in providing the bank-deposit component of the money supply. Figure 15-3 gives a simplified preview of what will be spelled out in Figs. 16-1 and 17-1: (*a*) how the government's central banks determine the supply of the "high-powered money that constitutes the reserves of the commercial banks"; and (*b*) how the *input* of these high-powered reserves into the "black-box" of the member banks of the Federal Reserve System enables the commercial banks to produce as *amplified output* the community's supply of money (currency plus checkable bank deposits, namely $M_1$).

Hence, the modern mixed economy is no longer left at the mercy of the workings of the pump handle of investment as dependent on innovations, business confidence, and population growth. Modern government can modify, control, and offset the exogenous fluctuations in *II* and *CC* schedules by its control over the high-powered money reserves of the commercial banks and by control over its budget deficits and surpluses. The remaining chapters of Part Two show how all this works.

## SUMMARY

### A. PRICES AND THE MONEY SUPPLY

1  It is unrealistic to expect that expansions in investment and other spending will have effects solely on employment and output. Changes in price levels must be expected as well. The effects and causes of a general rise in prices and wages (i.e., inflation) and a general fall in prices (i.e., deflation) are vital.

2  Historically, prices have shown their greatest fluctuations in times of war. But since 1933 the trend in prices seems to have been more of a one-way climb: the absence of a drop in prices following World War II and the Vietnam war is perhaps a sign that modern mixed economies are no longer likely to tolerate lengthy periods of unemployment, soft business conditions, and falling prices.

Creeping "cost-push inflation" is a new disease distinguishable from conventional "demand-pull inflation," in which too much money spending (too much $C + I + G$ or, what is the same, too much $MV$) bids for the limited supply of goods and labor available at full employment and *pulls up* prices and wages.

3 Inflations and deflations are never of the balanced type in which all prices and all wages are anticipated to move by the same percentage, with no one helped and no one hurt by the process. Inflations usually favor debtors, profit seekers, and risk-taking speculators. Unforeseen inflation hurts creditors, fixed-income classes, pensioners, and conservative and timid investors. The old are its prime victims.

4 Aside from redistributional effects of inflation out of a fixed level of production, mild inflations like those found throughout most of capitalism's history have been regarded as being a little more *likely* to keep employment high and business brisk than mild deflations do. But the cause of the inflation and the degree to which it is anticipated may make a difference. And the threat that a mild creep of prices could break into a trot or gallop warns against complacency concerning price rises.

If the processes were *foreseen* and steady, there would not be much difference between three possible long-term patterns that various economists favor: (*a*) steady prices, with money and real wages rising with productivity; (*b*) gently rising prices, with money wages rising even faster than real wages and productivity; (*c*) slowly falling prices, with money wages constant and real wages rising as every consumer's dollar buys more and more goods—a pattern perhaps not feasible in rigid mixed economies.

5 Without exchange, division of labor could not be highly developed. Simple barter is inefficient and tends to be superseded by the use of money. Commodity money is in turn superseded by paper money and bank money. Unlike other economic goods, money is valued because of social convention; *we value money indirectly for what it buys rather than for its direct utility*.

6 In addition to coin, currency, and demand deposits—whose sum is the money supply $M$ (or $M_1$)—there are also very important other liquid-asset items: time or savings deposits (which pay interest and are de facto withdrawable at short notice, and which many economists include in a broad definition of money, $M_2$); and also "near-money" such as government bonds (which anyone can quickly liquidate into cash, at a price that depends on market forces at the time). However defined, $M$ has increased mightily over the decades.

## B. THE DEMAND FOR MONEY AND THE QUANTITY THEORY

7 The demand for money consists of a *transactions* demand importantly related to income, and a *precautionary* (or asset) demand much dependent on interest and profit rates, and on wealth, volatile expectations, risk aversion, and speculative price expectations. (Chapter 18 will relate the demand for $M$ to so-called "liquidity preference.")

8   The (income) velocity of circulation of money is defined as the ratio of dollar GNP flow to the stock of $M$. While $V$ is definitely not a constant, its movements are subject to some regularity and predictability; and from its definition as $V \equiv \dfrac{GNP}{M} \equiv \dfrac{PQ}{M}$, comes the Quantity-Theory-of-Exchange *identity* $MV \equiv PQ$.

9   The crude Quantity Theory of Money and Prices regarded $P$ as almost strictly proportional to $M$. Useful as this view is in hyperinflation and for certain *long-term* trends, few would today uphold it in this crude form. It is generally agreed that action by the government and banks to affect the supply of money, its availability to investor borrowers, and the interest cost of such borrowings can have important effects on the total of *consumption + investment + government* spending, and thus on prices and wage levels. So all schools can agree on the central importance of the next two chapters' analysis of just how the government through its central bank controls the input of "high-powered (reserves) money" that, after being fed into the amplifying black box of the commercial banking system, results in amplified outputs of the community's total supply of money, $M$.

## CONCEPTS FOR REVIEW

inflation, deflation
redistribution and employment
     effects of price-level trends
hyperinflation; chronic and
     creeping inflation
barter, commodity $M$,
     metallic $M$, paper currency,
     bank deposit $M$

"demand-pull" vs. "cost-push"
coin, token money, currency
demand versus time deposits
$M_1$, $M_2$, near-money
Quantity Equation of Exchange,
     $MV \equiv PQ$; $V$ definition
crude Quantity Theory, $P \equiv kM$
high-powered (reserves) money

## QUESTIONS FOR DISCUSSION

1   If sure of inflation ahead, what might you do to protect yourself? List some of the happenings that accompany galloping and mild inflation.

2   If we printed and spent \$100 billion in new greenbacks, what would happen to prices? Is there some truth, then, to the crude Quantity Theory?

3   Show that page 283's Marshall-Fisher-Keynes summary implies nonconstant $V$. In the last 30 years $V$ rose almost every year. Could the fact that a 1976 bond pays 8 per cent as against $3\frac{1}{2}$ per cent in 1945 help explain this rise in $V$?

4   "When real GNP rises by $4\frac{1}{4}$ per cent and the price level by $2\frac{1}{2}$ per cent, $M$ must grow by $6\frac{3}{4}$ per cent if $V$ is constant." Explain.

5   Verify: Money requires only $N$ prices for $N$ goods, as against $N(N-1)/2$ pairs of barter price ratios, a vastly greater number. (E.g., $100 < 9{,}900/2 = 4{,}950$.)

The importance of bank deposits as part of the money supply has been established. This chapter continues with two distinct topics.

First, we examine briefly the important facts and functionings of the banking system, showing how the present-day commercial bank came to keep only "fractional cash reserves" against deposits.

Second, we see how the banking system—once the government's central bank has fed into the member banks as input "high-powered (reserves) money"—is then able to "manufacture" bank deposits, the most important component of our money supply.

## A. NATURE AND FUNCTIONING OF THE MODERN BANKING SYSTEM

Today there are over 14,000 banks in the United States that accept checking deposits. Only about a third of these are national banks, the rest being under state supervision. All national banks are automatically members of the Federal Reserve System, and in addition, most of the larger state institutions are also members. Although this still leaves more than half of all the banks not members of the Federal Reserve System, they are sufficiently small in size so that their deposits are only about one-fifth of the total.[1] Moreover, since 1933, almost all commercial banks, state or national, have their deposits insured by the FDIC (Federal Deposit Insurance Corporation). In 1976, the FDIC insured each deposit up to the sum of $40,000.

Unlike England or Canada, where a few large banks with hundreds of branches are dominant, the United States has tended to rely upon many independent, relatively small, localized units.[2] Until fairly

---

[1] Many state banks that are not full-fledged members nevertheless do belong to the Federal Reserve clearinghouse system for handling checks of other banks.
[2] In California, the Bank of America has numerous branches all over the state, just as the Chase Manhattan Bank has branches all over New York City, and

. . . One rule which woe betides the banker who fails to heed it, . . . Never lend any money to anybody unless they don't need it.
OGDEN NASH

recently, almost anyone could open a bank with relatively limited capital. It is not surprising, therefore, that the American history of bank failures and losses to depositors used to be a grievous one. Indeed, only about one-half the banks in existence in 1915 are still solvent; even in prosperous 1929, even before the Great Depression, no less than 659 banks with estimated total deposits of $200 million failed. Since establishment of the FDIC, a bank failure has become a rare—but not an impossible!—event. When the Franklin National Bank, the 20th largest bank in the country, was declared insolvent in 1974, the FDIC made sure that no depositor lost a cent.

*The primary economic function of commercial banks is to hold demand deposits and to honor checks drawn upon them—in short, to provide us, the economy, with the most important component of the money supply.*

A second important function of commercial banks is to lend money to merchants, homeowners, farmers, and industrialists; and to hold government and municipal bonds.

Banks also perform a variety of other functions in competition with other financial institutions. They usually hold savings or time deposits. Unlike demand deposits, these pay interest; although theoretically withdrawable only after 30 days' notice or more, they are in fact usually withdrawn (by their owners) on demand. (Recall that some economists include saving and time deposits in a broad $M_2$ definition of the money supply.) In this function, the commercial banks are, in parts of the country, competing with the so-called "mutual savings banks," which accept only time deposits; almost anywhere in the country the commercial banks are competing with cooperative building and loan societies and savings and loan associations. In selling money orders or travelers' checks, the banks are competing with the post office, Western Union, and American Express. In handling "trusts" and estates, they overlap with investment counselors and other fiduciaries. Even in lending money to individuals and businessmen, the banks are competing with finance companies and with so-called "factors" who provide corporations with working capital. In buying bonds, mortgages, and securities, they compete with insurance companies and other investors.[3] Large banks even do computing and counseling for firms.

In summary, the commercial banks are by no means our only financial institutions. By definition, however, they are the only organizations able to provide "bank money," i.e., *checkable demand deposits* that are conveniently usable as a medium of exchange. Therein lies their primary economic importance. Their second, related function is that of credit: they help manufacture and transfer short-term credit for businesses and families; they make long-term mortgage loans; and they increasingly provide intermediate-term credit through "term loans" of over a year's duration.

## CREATION OF THE FEDERAL RESERVE SYSTEM

In 1913, the Federal Reserve Act was passed by Congress and signed by President Wilson. It sprang from the panic of 1907, with its alarming epidemic of bank failures. After half a dozen years' agitation and discussion by both parties, the Federal Reserve System was formed—in face of strong banker opposition.

---

just as a few holding companies control many banks in Florida, Minnesota, and Wisconsin. But by and large, the old American distrust of "big finance" has caused us to hamper multiple-branch banking regardless of cost-saving efficiencies and geographical dispersion of risks, to discourage bank mergers, and to limit nonbanking activities of one-bank holding companies.

[3] Massachusetts, Connecticut, and New York savings banks even sell life insurance.

The country was cut into 12 Federal Reserve districts, each with its own Federal Reserve Bank (headquartered in New York, Chicago, San Francisco, Philadelphia, Boston, Cleveland, St. Louis, Kansas City, Atlanta, Richmond, Dallas, and Minneapolis). Their initial capital was subscribed by the commercial bank members of the Federal Reserve System, and so, *nominally*, each Federal Reserve Bank is a corporation owned by the "member banks." All are coordinated by the seven-member Board of Governors of the Federal Reserve System in Washington—the so-called "Federal Reserve Board."

There is also a twelve-man Federal Open Market Committee, with five representatives of the 12 districts as well as the seven-man Board of Governors. This has, with pardonable exaggeration, been called "the most powerful group of private citizens in America," for, as we shall see, the Open Market Committee administers the single most powerful weapon of modern monetary policy—controlling the supply of "high-powered (reserves) money" that underlies the nation's supply of money, *M*. (Glance back at Fig. 15-3 on page 288.)

We can summarize the present-day realities of the Federal Reserve System this way.

**The Federal Reserve Board in Washington, together with the 12 regional Federal Reserve Banks, constitutes our American "central bank." Every modern country has such a central bank, as, for example, the Bank of England, the Banque de France, the Bank of Japan, and the Deutsche Bundesbank of Germany.**

**A central bank is a bank that the government sets up to help handle its transactions, to coordinate and control the commercial banks, and, most important, to help *control the nation's money supply* and credit conditions.**

Although nominally a corporation owned by the commercial banks that are members of the Federal Reserve System, in fact the Federal Reserve (or the "Fed," as it is universally called by the financial press, with no disrespect intended) is a *public* agency. It is directly responsible to Congress; and whenever any conflict arises between its making a profit and the public interest, it acts according to the public interest without question. Its member banks receive fixed and nominal dividends from it; but so profitable is the Fed by virtue of its legal privilege, that its dollars of profit above a certain level go *entirely* to the United States government. The Reserve authorities, meaning by this the regional and Washington officials, never think of its stockholders, the member commercial banks, as dictators of their actions, but instead act as a public body. (So the men on the Federal Open Market Committee are *not* private citizens even though their paychecks do not come from the government.)

Although the President appoints Federal Reserve Governors for 14-year terms and appoints their Chairman, the Board considers its allegiance is primarily to Congress and not to the executive branch. Here is a case where the American practice is different from that of most countries. For example, in Britain, the Bank of England has not only been nationalized, but well understands that it must in the last analysis be subservient to the will of the Cabinet, with a right to protest publicly but a duty to coordinate its policies with those of the Cabinet.

Prior to an "accord" signed in 1951 by the Treasury Department and the Fed, there was considerable pressure by the President and the Treasury on the actions of the Fed. In recent years the Fed has generally (but not always!) cooperated with the President; ultimately, it feels its primary responsibility is to Congress.

| CONSOLIDATED BALANCE SHEET OF ALL MEMBER BANKS, JANUARY 1, 1975 (in billions of dollars) | | | |
|---|---|---|---|
| **ASSETS** | | **LIABILITIES** | |
| Reserves | $ 36.9 | Capital accounts | $ 48.0 |
| Loans and discounts | 429.1 | Demand deposits | 249.4 |
| U.S. government | | Time deposits | 326.8 |
| securities | 38.4 | Other liabilities | 91.1 |
| Other securities | 99.5 | | |
| Other assets | 111.4 | | |
| Total | $715.3 | Total | $715.3 |

**TABLE 16-1**
**Demand deposits are liabilities of banks**
Reserves and demand deposits are the two key items of interest to our later economic analysis. Reserves are this large primarily because of legal requirements and not to provide against possible unexpected withdrawals. (Source: *Federal Reserve Bulletin*.)

## BANKING AS A BUSINESS

Banking is a business much like any other business. The commercial bank is a relatively simple business concern. A bank provides certain services for its customers (depositors and borrowers) and in return receives payments from them in one form or another. It tries to earn a profit for its stock owners.

A member bank's balance sheet shows certain assets, liabilities, and capital ownership. Except for minor rearrangements, the bank's published balance sheet looks much like the balance sheet of any business, and rather simpler than most. The only peculiar feature about the consolidated bank balance sheet shown in Table 16-1 is the fact that such a large portion of its liabilities are payable *on demand;* i.e., they are deposits subject to checking. And the vital reserves on which its deposit liabilities depend are, as we'll see, created and controlled by the central bank.

This fact is intriguing to economists because we choose to call such demand liabilities money; but to the banker it is a familiar condition which has long since been taken for granted. He knows well that, although it would be possible for every depositor suddenly to decide to withdraw all his money from the bank on the same day, the probability of this is quite remote. Each day, as some people withdraw their money, others normally make deposits tending to cancel the withdrawals. In a growing community, new deposits more than offset the withdrawals from an average bank.

This, however, need not be strictly true at any one moment, in any one day, or in any one week. By chance alone the amount of withdrawals might exceed deposits for some period of time—just as a coin may land with heads, rather than tails, turned up for a consecutive number of tosses. For this reason, the banker would voluntarily keep a little cash—but only a little—handy in his vaults and perhaps as a "reserve deposit" at the nearby Federal Reserve Bank.

## HOW BANKS DEVELOPED OUT OF GOLDSMITH ESTABLISHMENTS

All these facts are so much taken for granted by every modern banker that he is hardly aware of them. But it was not always so. According to superficial but useful history, commercial banking began with the ancient goldsmiths, who developed the practice of storing people's gold and valuables for safekeeping. At first such establishments were simply like parcel checkrooms or warehouses. The depositor left his gold for safekeeping, was given a receipt, later presented that receipt, paid a small fee for the safekeeping, and got back his gold.

Quite obviously, however, money is wanted only for what it will buy, not for its own sake. Money has an anonymous quality, making one dollar just as good as another, and one piece of pure gold as good as another. The goldsmiths soon found it more convenient *not* to have to tag the gold belonging to any one individual so as to be able to give to him upon request exactly the same piece of gold that he had left. Instead, the customer was quite willing to accept a receipt for an amount of gold or money *of a given value*, even though it was not the identical particle of matter that he actually left. This "anonymity" is important. Therein lies a significant difference between today's bank and a checkroom or warehouse. If I check my bag at Kennedy Airport and later see someone walking down the street with that same suitcase, I call my lawyer and sue the airline. If I mark my initials on a ten-dollar bill, deposit it in my bank account, and later notice it in the hands of a stranger, I have no grievance against the bank management. They have only agreed to pay me on demand any old $10.

But let us return to the goldsmith establishments, which are supposed to typify the first embryonic commercial banks. What would balance sheets of a typical establishment look like? Perhaps like Table 16-2.

We assume the company has long since dropped its activities as a smith and is principally occupied with storing people's money for safekeeping. Over past time, $1 million has been deposited in its vaults, and this whole sum it holds as a cash asset. To balance this asset, there is a current deposit liability of the same amount. Actually, such a business need have no other assets (except the negligible value of its office space and vaults). But its owners could have—on the side, so to speak—subscribed $50,000 of capital to be lent out at interest or to buy securities like stocks or bonds. On the asset side, this is shown under the heading Loans and Investments; it is balanced on the right-hand side by a like sum in the Capital and Retained Earnings account.

At this primitive stage, the bank would be of no particular interest to the economist. These investment and capital items have nothing to do with the bank's deposits; if all the bank's loans and investments should go sour and become worthless, the loss would fall completely on the stockholders, who have agreed to take that risk in the hope of making a profit. Every depositor could still be paid off in full *out of the 100 per cent cash reserves* held by the bank. The bank would still cover its overhead and

**TABLE 16-2**

**First goldsmith bank held 100 per cent cash reserves against demand deposits** Only 1-to-1 creation of deposits out of new reserves was possible at this primitive stage. There was nothing "high-powered" about reserves in those days.

| BALANCE SHEET OF EARLY BANK | | | |
|---|---|---|---|
| ASSETS | | LIABILITIES AND NET WORTH | |
| Cash reserves | $1,000,000 | Capital and retained earnings | $  50,000 |
| Loans and investments | 50,000 | Demand-deposit liability | 1,000,000 |
| Total | $1,050,000 | Total | $1,050,000 |

clerical expenses by making customers pay storage charges. These would presumably vary with the length of time the customer left his money for safekeeping, the average amount of his money requiring safekeeping, and the number of times the turnover of his account made a clerk wait on him and keep various records.

Economists could ignore such a bank's operations. The bank money[4]—the demand deposits created jointly by the bank's willingness to accept a demand obligation and the customer's willingness to hold a deposit—would *just offset* the amount of ordinary money (currency or coin) placed in the bank's safe and withdrawn from active circulation. The process would be of no more interest than if the public decided to convert dollars into dimes. One says that the banking system has a *neutral* effect on spending and prices—not adding or subtracting from *total M* or its velocity.

## MODERN FRACTIONAL-RESERVE BANKING

Let us return to our early goldsmith-banker to see how modern banks gradually evolved. If he were an alert fellow, he would soon notice that, although his deposits are payable on demand, they are not all withdrawn together. He would soon learn that, although 100 per cent reserves are necessary if the bank is to be liquidated and all depositors are to be paid off in full, such reserves are not at all necessary if his bank is a "going concern." As already seen, new deposits tend to balance withdrawals. Only a little till money, perhaps less than 2 per cent, normally seems needed in the form of cash.[5]

At first he probably thought this discovery too good to be true. Then perhaps he recalled the story of a rival bank whose dishonest clerk ran off with 95 per cent of its cash reserve—which was not discovered for a dozen years. No one ever had occasion to go to the back rooms of the vault because all withdrawals were financed by recently deposited money held in the front vaults.

We can imagine our intelligent banker—at first cautiously—beginning to acquire bonds and other earning assets with some of the cash entrusted to his care. Everything works out all right: depositors are still paid off on demand, and the bank has made some extra earnings. Gradually, the banker no longer feels it is necessary to conceal from his depositors what he is doing. If a depositor complains, the banker retorts, "Your money is safe. If you don't like my way of doing business, you are at liberty to withdraw your funds. Besides, haven't you noticed that the new method of fractional cash reserves has enabled me to *lower my service charges to you?* Also, it has enabled me to give a helping hand to our local businessmen who need more capital to buy

---

[4]The economist would consider the demand deposit as money as soon as the custom grew up for depositors to pay for the goods they bought by giving the storekeeper a little note to the bank saying, "Mr. Goldsmith, pay to the order of Sears, Roebuck $2.99, (signed) John Q. Doe." In other words, as soon as the use and acceptability of checks became customary.

[5]If the bank could pay off its depositors with one of its own checks (or, as in former times, with one of its paper bank notes), it might not have to keep any till money at all. By judiciously limiting the rate at which it was making loans and investments, the bank could ensure that the checks it received from other banks plus cash deposited were just matched by its outpayments. An occasional, temporary outward drain of funds could be met by permitting the bank to pay by check what it owed to other banks for the few hours or days until some part of its asset portfolio could be liquidated or until it contracted its operations so as to get a surplus of inpayments over outpayments.

new tools, buildings, and inventories. Such capital formation benefits consumers because they get better goods for lower prices. It also creates jobs for workers."

Little wonder, therefore, that banks should want to maximize their profits by putting most of the money deposited with them in *earning assets* and keeping only *fractional* cash reserves against deposits.

**Indeed, as long as business confidence remains high and bank managers are judicious in their loans and investments, there is no reason why the bank should keep much more than 2 per cent cash reserves against deposits.**

But what if the banker makes a mistake in his investments? Since nobody's judgment is perfect and all investments involve some element of speculative risk, this is certainly a possibility. To lessen the chance of extreme losses, the banker can try to diversify his investments, not putting all his eggs in one basket. Besides, a conservative bank will have a considerable amount of capital put up by the stockholders. For example, capital stock may have been issued equal to 10 per cent of demand deposits. Then, even if all the bank's assets are in earning investments rather than in nonearning cash, depositors are protected against all capital losses that do not exceed 10 per cent of the bank's investment portfolio. Ordinarily, this will be sufficient, as long as it keeps to high-grade bonds, mortgages, and conservative business loans. (In the 1970s, the Fed has been worrying that large banks have been expanding activities beyond their prudent capital capacities.)

There is one last requirement the bank must meet if we are to give it an A+. The management must watch the general trend in the size of its deposits to make sure that its locality is not becoming a "ghost town" and that it is not losing deposits steadily over time. Were that the case, the bank's investment portfolio would have to be arranged to hold securities and loans that could be gradually liquidated and converted into cash to meet depositors' withdrawals.

**Secondary reserves**   Even if the bank is not a declining business, prudent managers must still protect themselves against a *temporary* surge of withdrawals. To hold cash against such a contingency would be costly, since cash earns no yield. They will usually decide, therefore, to hold as "secondary reserves" in their portfolios some securities that always have a ready market and can be liquidated at short notice.

Short-term government bonds serve this purpose admirably. Called "bills," "notes," or "certificates," they vary little in value and can be liquidated simply by not buying new ones as the old ones come due every 90 days or 12 months. Even long-term government bonds, with 30 years of life before they mature, provide liquidity in the sense that in normal times they can always be transferred[6] to some other buyer at some quoted market price—albeit a varying price. In recent decades, a Federal Funds market has grown up, in which banks with surplus funds can lend on a daily basis to other banks at an interest rate comparable to yields on short-term Treasury bills.

[6]There is a saying, "You can sell government bonds even on Sunday." The important thing is not the *date of maturity* of the bond or loan, but rather how "shiftable" it is to some other investment institution. A 90-day loan to a local merchant, which is nonshiftable, is in this sense less liquid than a 90-year gilt-edge bond traded on a securities exchange.

## LEGAL RESERVE REQUIREMENTS

When we compare a "going and growing" bank with any corporation, the surprising thing is not how little cash reserves the banks keep, but that they keep any at all (in excess of minimal till-money requirements.)

*As long as financial skies are sunny,* we have seen that *the same profit-maximizing logic which compels the abandonment of a system of 100 per cent reserves argues in favor of negligible reserves!*

Yet, if we turn to the facts, we find that a prudent modern bank is expected—and required by law!—to keep a substantial portion of its assets in nonearning cash. About a sixth or seventh of all demand deposits must be kept by banks immobilized in such nonearning reserve form. For the most part, a member bank holds these reserves on deposit with its regional Federal Reserve Bank; but in recent years the Fed has given each member bank the right to count as part of its reserves any cash it finds convenient to hold in its own vaults.

Table 16-3 indicates the level of required reserve ratios. Although they are changed at intervals by the Fed, they are roughly about one-sixth against demand deposits, depending on the category of the member bank. Because one-fifth gives rounder numbers to work our numerical examples with, for the most part we shall refer to 20 per cent reserve ratios, it being understood that such a figure is only for expositional convenience and would have to be lowered a little to correspond with practice in the 1970s (as contrasted to some earlier decades when one-fifth was truly a better approximation than one-sixth and to the 1920s when one-tenth was more accurate).

The many, but unimportant, banks that are not members of the Federal Reserve System do not voluntarily keep such large amounts of nonearning cash reserves. Many experts think *all* banks should be subject to these same legal requirements, and if nonmember banks ever became important in total deposits, Congress might so legislate.

These legal reserve requirements need to be explained since they are so important a mechanism by which the FRB controls bank money.

| LEGAL RESERVE RATIOS FOR FEDERAL RESERVE MEMBER BANKS, MAY 1975 | |
| --- | --- |
| SIZE OF BANK'S DEPOSITS | RESERVE RATIOS REQUIRED, PER CENT |
| Demand deposits | |
| First $ 2 million | $7\frac{1}{2}$ |
| $ 2–$ 10 million | 10 |
| $ 10–$100 million | 12 |
| $100–$400 million | 13 |
| Over $400 million | $16\frac{1}{2}$ |
| Time deposits | |
| Savings deposits, and time | |
| deposits under $5 million | 3 |
| Time deposits over $5 million maturing in | |
| 30–179 days | 6 |
| 180 days and over | 3 |

**TABLE 16-3**

**Fed prescribes reserve requirements**

These required reserve ratios have the purpose of controlling the volume of demand deposits and money supply. Congress gives the FRB the right to vary these rates within broad limits. We'll soon see that raising these ratios will contract *M* supply; lowering legal required ratios will expand *M*.

**Legal reserve requirements too high?**    Many bankers think wistfully about how much they could earn on loans or bonds if they were free to use part of the money they are forced to keep as legal reserves against their own deposits. They argue thus:

Money we are required to keep as legal reserves doesn't earn us one red cent. So why do we have to keep such high legal reserves? One-sixth of our deposits is more than is really needed for safety. After all, our withdrawals never bunch up much; the laws of statistics take care of that. Besides, if we ever needed more, we could sell off some government bills or could turn to the Fed for help or could borrow temporarily from some other bank in the Federal Funds market. We bankers think that legal reserves of as little as 10 per cent—some of us would say 5 per cent!—are all that prudence requires in this age of insured deposits. We smaller banks are therefore quitting the Federal Reserve System in considerable numbers to minimize our need to forego interest income on required reserves. [Economists and the Fed deplore this exodus and favor compulsory reserves on non-member as well as member banks.]

These bankers have a point. Years ago the legal reserve requirements for the member banks were lower: they ranged between 7 and 13 per cent against demand deposits and 3 per cent against time deposits. After the mid-thirties . . . Congress gave the Board the right to raise these ratios considerably, which the Fed did do in a number of gradual steps.

Why did the Board raise the legal requirements? And why did it later ask for authority to raise them further? Because of the belief that such high ratios are needed to assure depositors of being able to withdraw their money when they want to? No.

The main function of legal reserve requirements is *not* that of making deposits safe and liquid, payable on demand. Their vital function is to enable the Federal Reserve authorities to *control* the amount of demand deposits—or bank money—that the member banks can create. By imposing fixed legal reserve requirements, the Fed can *limit* the growth of bank deposits to *its* desired target.

We shall soon learn just how this all works.

## THE GOVERNMENT STANDS BEHIND THE BANKS

Banks are much safer than they used to be before the Depression. If this has little to do with legal reserve requirements, to what is it due?

Banks are safe today because everyone realizes that it is a vital function of government to stand behind them (and behind its Federal Deposit Insurance Corp. set up to protect depositors) should a depression and panicky "run" on the banking system ever recur.

No banking system with fractional reserves—i.e., none which keeps less than 100 per cent of its deposits in cash—can ever turn all its deposits into cash on a moment's notice. So every fractional-reserve system would be a "fair-weather system" if government did not stand ready to back it up. If panic ever came again, Congress, the President, and the Federal Reserve Board would all act, even using their constitutional powers over money to print the money needed to meet a national emergency!

Had this been said and done back in the black days of the early 1930s, history might have been different. Our country might have been spared the epidemic of bank failures[7]

[7] Some 8,000 banks with $5 billion of deposits became insolvent in 1930–1933. To keep all banks from collapse, Franklin Roosevelt's first act as President was to close them by declaring a "bank holiday" until they could be officially reopened with confidence restored.

that destroyed the money supply, creating fear and crisis for the whole capitalistic system. With the American people of both political parties realizing that the government stands behind the banking system, it is highly improbable that a panic could ever get started. Here is a case where being prepared to act heroically probably makes it unnecessary to do so.

### KEEPING EACH BANK SAFE: A FINAL CHECKLIST

Just because the peril of a nationwide bank run has been overcome does not mean that each banker can stop worrying about *his* bank's safety. Numerous reforms have been introduced by government to alleviate the instability of laissez faire banking:

1. *Regulation of bank formation and activity.* For decades, either state or federal authorities have set down conditions under which banks could be formed—the minimum amount of capital they must have, etc. Bank examiners periodically scrutinize bank assets and pass on the bank's solvency, always keeping in mind that an ounce of prevention is worth a pound of cure.

2. *Formation of Federal Reserve System.* The next great step forward was the establishment of a central bank, whose emergency function is to stand as a Rock of Gibraltar in time of panic, to be ready to use the full monetary powers of the government to stem collapse of the banking system. The normal vital function of a central bank is to control money supply and credit conditions.

3. *Government insurance of bank deposits.* Following the bank crisis of 1933, the FDIC was belatedly set up to insure the safety of all bank deposits.[8]

The importance of this measure can hardly be exaggerated. From now on, most banks will be closed by bank examiners and government authorities, not by the panicky behavior of depositors whose fears bring on the very contingency they are most afraid of. A single bank need no longer fear that its reputation is compromised simply by being brought into question. (In the 1970s, the only banks to fail are those involving fraud or gross negligence; their depositors are protected by the FDIC; and their failure no longer sets off a domino collapse of other banks.)

## B. THE CREATION OF BANK DEPOSITS

### CAN BANKS REALLY CREATE MONEY?

We now turn to one of the most interesting aspects of money and credit, the process called "multiple expansion of bank deposits." Most people have heard that in some mysterious manner banks can create money out of thin air, but few really understand how the process works. Few understand that all our money arises out of debt and IOU operations. Actually, there is nothing magical or incomprehensible about the creation of bank deposits. At every step of the way, one can follow what is happening to the banks' accounts. The true explanation of deposit creation is simple. What is hard to grasp are the false explanations that still circulate.

---

[8] In 1976, there were more than 100 million depositors in FDIC banks; the $40,000 limit insured about 98 per cent of all depositors, of whom 99 per cent were *fully* insured.

According to these false explanations, the managers of an ordinary bank are able, by some use of their fountain pens, to lend several dollars for each dollar deposited with them. No wonder practical bankers see red when such power is attributed to them. They only wish they could do so. As every banker knows, he cannot invest money that he doesn't have; and money that he invests in buying a security or making a loan soon leaves his bank.

Bankers, therefore, often go to the opposite extreme, and sometimes argue that the banking system cannot (and does not) create money. "After all," they say, "we can invest only what is left with us. We don't create anything. We only put the community's savings to work." Bankers who argue in this way are wrong. They have become enmeshed in our old friend the fallacy of composition: what is true for each is not thereby true for all.

**The banking system as a whole can do what each small bank cannot do: it *can* expand its loans and investments many times the new reserves of cash created for it, even though each small bank is lending out only a fraction of its deposits.**

Our answer, then, to the basic question is in the affirmative: Yes, the banking system and the public do, between them, create about $5 of bank deposits for each new dollar of reserves that is created for the banks.

Figure 16-1 gives a preview of the process. It enlarges on Fig. 15-3 of page 288. Now we look inside the black box that represents the banking system as a whole: Bank 1, which receives the initial new deposit, is at top; Banks 2, 3, . . . , and all other banks (not shown) are listed below. We shall study how $1 of new reserves, deposited at the left as input into the box, produces $5 of total deposit money, shown at the right. But Bank 1 cannot do this in a single step; as the orange arrows between the banks show, all the banks get involved in the lengthy secondary chain of money

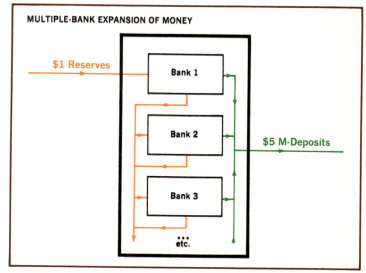

**FIG. 16-1**

**All banks can do what one can't do alone**
For each dollar of new reserves deposited at left into a bank, the system as a whole creates at the diagram's right about $5 of check money. The orange arrows in the box show that Bank 1 cannot do it alone. As we'll see, second, third, and other banks will get their share of the expansion.

| ORIGINAL BANK IN INITIAL POSITION | | | |
| --- | --- | --- | --- |
| **ASSETS** | | **LIABILITIES** | |
| Reserves | + $1,000 | Deposits | + $1,000 |
| Total | + $1,000 | Total | + $1,000 |

**TABLE 16-4(a)**
**Multiple-bank deposit creation is a story with many successive stages: 1st, newly created reserves get deposited in original first-generation bank**
We begin the process of money expansion by having the central bank—the Federal Reserve—provide some new high-powered reserves that constitute the initial deposit.

creation. Though the chain has many links, each is a dwindling fraction and the whole effect does add up to the 5-to-1 total.

Most of the remaining chapter explains this process of money creation.

## HOW DEPOSITS ARE CREATED: THE FIRST-BANK STAGE

We begin with a brand-new input of $1,000 of high-powered (reserves) money brought to a bank. Where it came from is not important. It could have come from someone's having deposited the proceeds received from his selling a government bond to the regional Federal Reserve Bank (which may have paid for it by printing off 20 fifty-dollar bills). We shall see that *in the end* the banking system is going to manufacture $5,000 of new demand deposits out of this, thus taking in $1,000 of one kind of high-powered M and converting it into $5,000 of another kind of M (checkable demand deposits)—for a net gain of $4,000!

**First-bank stage**   Now, if banks were to keep 100 per cent cash-reserve balances, like the old goldsmiths, they could not create any extra money out of a new deposit of $1,000 left with them. The depositor's $1,000 checking deposit would then just match the $1,000 of reserves.

The change in the bank's balance sheet, as far as the new demand deposit is concerned, would be merely as shown in Table 16-4(a).[9]

The bank has not created this deposit *alone*. The original customer had to be willing to make the deposit. Once he took the initiative, the bank was also willing to accept his checking account. Together the bank and the public "created" $1,000 of bank money, or deposit. But there is no multiple expansion yet, no 5 for 1 or anything else. So long as the banks keep 100 per cent reserves, the growth of bank M is just equal to the growth of new reserves created by the Fed.

Suppose, now, that the bank does not have to keep 100 per cent reserves. Suppose that the law requires it to keep only 20 per cent legal reserves. (It can always keep larger reserves if it wishes to; but if there are many outstanding, relatively safe,

[9] For simplicity, all our tables will show only the *changes* in balance-sheet items. To simplify the arithmetic, we use reserve ratios of 20 per cent, which are a little larger than the legal rates of Table 16-3. Hence, wherever an expansion of 5:1 is mentioned, the meticulous reader can choose to think of a 6:1 or 7:1 expansion. If $M_2$ inclusive of saving deposits were studied, the expansion ratio would of course exceed 7:1. (Important reminder: When bankers refer to their loans and investments, by "investments" they mean their holdings of securities. They do not mean what we mean by I in C + I + G, namely, capital formation for the community.)

| IMPOSSIBLE SITUATION FOR SINGLE SMALL BANK | | | |
|---|---|---|---|
| ASSETS | | LIABILITIES | |
| Reserves | +$1,000 | Deposits | +$5,000 |
| Loans and investments | + 4,000 | | |
| Total | +$5,000 | Total | +$5,000 |

TABLE 16-4(b)

2d, Bank can't lend out four times its new deposit

| ORIGINAL BANK IN FINAL POSITION | | | |
|---|---|---|---|
| ASSETS | | LIABILITIES | |
| Reserves | +$ 200 | Deposits | +$1,000 |
| Loans and investments | + 800 | | |
| Total | +$1,000 | Total | +$1,000 |

TABLE 16-4(c)

. . . . only four-fifths of its deposit

interest-yielding government bonds or numerous profitable lending opportunities, the bank will not find it profitable to keep much more reserves than the law requires.)

What can Bank 1 now do? Can *it* expand *its* loans and investments by $4,000 so that the change in *its* balance sheet looks as shown in Table 16-4(b)? The answer is definitely, No. Why not? Total assets equal total liabilities. Cash reserves meet the legal requirement of being 20 per cent of total deposits.

True enough. But how did Bank 1 pay for the investments or earning assets that it bought? Like everyone else, it had to write out checks to those who sold the bond or signed the promissory note. If all such would promise not to cash the bank's check—or what is the same thing, to hold all these moneys frozen on deposit in Bank 1—then, of course, it could buy all it wanted to without losing any cash.

But, in fact, no one will borrow money at 7 or 10 per cent just to hold it all in the bank. The borrower spends the money on labor, on materials, or perhaps on an automobile. The money will *very soon*,[10] therefore, have to be paid out of Bank 1. And if—as is likely—the bank is but one of many banks serving that city, county, state, and country, only a fraction of the sums withdrawn will ever come back to the original bank in another customer's deposit.

This loss of cash by a bank expanding its investments is even more clearly seen if Bank 1 buys a bond rather than making a local loan. When my Boston bank buys a government bond, what are the chances that the man who sells the bond will happen to have an account with it? The likelihood is negligible. Probably he lives in New York City; or Ames, Iowa. So my bank knows it will soon have to pay out *all* the money it places in bonds. A bank cannot "eat its cake and have it, too." The New England bank cannot buy a bond and keep its cash at the same time. Table 16-4(b) gives, therefore, a completely false picture of what an individual bank can do.

Does this mean that Table 16-4(a) tells the end of the story? Must the bank, therefore, behave like the 100 per cent reserve goldsmith-bankers?

Of course not. Although the bank cannot jack its deposits up to five times its cash reserve, it certainly can *reduce its cash* down to one-fifth of its deposits. Nothing is

[10] If the bank made loans of $800 to its own customers, and they kept the proceeds on deposit, then for a brief period it would have deposits of $1,800. But as its borrowers spent their money, and unless the people who got that money were local customers who put the money back on deposit in this original bank, it would soon find itself forced toward the position of Table 16-4(c).

easier. For, as just seen, all it has to do is acquire $800 worth of earning assets—bonds, loans, or mortgages. Soon it will lose practically all this cash as its checks come back for payment. Now its balance sheet is as shown in Table 16-4(c) on page 303.

As far as this first bank is concerned, we are through. Bank 1's legal reserves are just enough to match its deposits. There is nothing more it can do until the public decides to bring in some more money for deposit.

Before leaving the single first bank, note this important fact: It has created money! How? Clearly *it* retains from the initial $1,000 of original new reserves only $200 of cash *M;* and it has added $1,000 of bank-deposit *M* to the public's total. Thus, Bank 1's activity has created a net increase of $800 in money supply.

### CHAIN REPERCUSSIONS ON THE OTHER BANKS

But the banking system as a whole cannot settle down yet. The people who sold the bonds or borrowed from the bank will presumably deposit the proceeds in some other bank or pay them to someone else who will make such a deposit. Our original bank has thus lost $800 *to some other banks* in the system.

**Second-generation banks**    If we lump these other banks all together and call them "second-generation banks" (or Bank 2), their balance sheets now appear as shown in Table 16-4(d). Of course, these banks are scattered all over the country. (Our original bank might even constitute a small part of the second generation as a few of its checks fell into the hands of its own depositors.) To these banks, the dollars deposited are just like any other dollars—*just like our original deposit;* these banks do not know, and do not care, that they are second in a chain of deposits. They do know, and they do care, that they are now holding *too much* nonearning cash. Only one-fifth of $800, or $160, is legally needed against $800 deposits. Therefore they can, and will, use the other four-fifths to acquire $640 worth of loans and investments. Hence, in a few days, their balance sheets will have reached equilibrium as shown in Table 16-4(e).

So much for the second-generation banks. As shown back in Fig. 16-1 by the orange arrows connecting Bank 2 to Bank 1, part of the original reserves end up in these second banks, and they too have created money.

Thus far, the original $1,000 taken out of hand-to-hand circulation and put into

| SECOND-GENERATION BANKS IN INITIAL POSITION | | | |
|---|---|---|---|
| ASSETS | | LIABILITIES | |
| Reserves | +$800 | Deposits | +$800 |
| Total | +$800 | Total | +$800 |

TABLE 16-4(d)

| FINAL POSITION OF SECOND-GENERATION BANKS | | | |
|---|---|---|---|
| ASSETS | | LIABILITIES | |
| Reserves | +$160 | Deposits | +$800 |
| Loans and investments | + 640 | | |
| Total | +$800 | Total | +$800 |

TABLE 16-4(e)

3d, The money lent out soon goes to new banks . . . . . . . which in turn lend out four-fifths of it

| INITIAL POSITION OF THIRD-GENERATION BANKS | | | |
|---|---|---|---|
| ASSETS | | LIABILITIES | |
| Reserves | +___ | Deposits | +___ |
| Loans and investments | 0 | | |
| Total | +___ | Total | +$640 |

**TABLE 16-4(f)**

| FINAL EQUILIBRIUM OF THIRD-GENERATION BANKS | | | |
|---|---|---|---|
| ASSETS | | LIABILITIES | |
| Reserves | +$128 | Deposits | +$640 |
| Loans and investments | + 512 | | |
| Total | +$640 | Total | +$640 |

**TABLE 16-4(g)**

4th, Four-fifths of ⅘ of original reserves go to . . . . . . . . third generation banks, who lend ⅘ of it again

the banking system has given rise to $1,000 (first-generation deposits) plus $800 (second-generation deposits). The total of money has increased, and the end is not yet in sight. Let us continue the story through the infinite, but dwindling, chain of other banks.

**Later-generation banks**    The $640 spent by the second-generation banks in acquiring loans and investments will go to a new set of banks called the "third-generation banks." (Again, on Fig. 16-1, page 301, follow the orange arrow below Bank 2.) The reader should by now be able to fill in their balance sheets as they look initially [see Table 16-4(f)]. Evidently, the third-generation banks will at first have *excess reserves* of an amount equal to four-fifths of $640, or $512. After this has been spent on loans and investments—and only then—the third-generation banks will reach the equilibrium of Table 16-4(g).

The total of bank-deposit $M$ is now $1,000 plus $800 plus $640, or $2,440. This is already almost 2½-to-1 expansion of the original cash deposit. But a fourth generation of banks will clearly end up with four-fifths of $640 in deposits, or $512; the fifth generation with four-fifths of $512, or $409.60; and so on, until finally, by the sixtieth round, we shall have all but a penny of the sum of the infinitely many generations.

**Final system equilibrium**    What will be the final sum: $1,000 + $800 + $640 + $512 + $409.60 + · · ·? If we patiently work out the sum by arithmetic, we shall find that it leads to $4,999.999 · · · and "finally" to $5,000. Table 16-4(h) shows the complete effect of the chain of deposit creation; and we can also get the same answer in two other ways, by common sense and by elementary algebra.[11]

[11] This can be proved by algebra as follows:

$$\$1,000 + \$800 + \$640 + \cdots = \$1,000[1 + \tfrac{4}{5} + (\tfrac{4}{5})^2 + (\tfrac{4}{5})^3 + \cdots]$$
$$= \$1,000 \left( \frac{1}{1 - \tfrac{4}{5}} \right) = \$1,000 \times 5 = \$5,000$$

Just as Chapter 12's multiplier made income rise threefold to generate the one-third of itself equal to the new dollar of $I$, here deposit $M$ must rise fivefold so that 20 per cent of it will match the new dollars of reserves that started the chain. (NOTE: The arithmetic of $M$ expansion is like that of the "Keynes multiplier" of Chapter 12. But don't confuse the two: the amplification here is from the stock of high-powered money reserves to the stock of total $M_1$; it does not refer to the extra income induced by investment.)

**MULTIPLE EXPANSION OF BANK DEPOSITS THROUGH THE BANKING SYSTEM**

| POSITION OF BANK | NEW DEPOSITS | NEW LOANS AND INVESTMENTS | RESERVES |
|---|---|---|---|
| Original banks | $1,000.00 | $ 800.00 | $ 200.00 |
| 2d-generation banks | 800.00 | 640.00 | 160.00 |
| 3d-generation banks | 640.00 | 512.00 | 128.00 |
| 4th-generation banks | 512.00 | 409.60 | 102.40 |
| 5th-generation banks | 409.60 | 327.68 | 81.92 |
| 6th-generation banks | 327.68 | 262.14 | 65.54 |
| 7th-generation banks | 262.14 | 209.72 | 52.42 |
| 8th-generation banks | 209.72 | 167.77 | 41.95 |
| 9th-generation banks | 167.77 | 134.22 | 33.55 |
| 10-th generation banks | 134.22 | 107.37 | 26.85 |
| Sum of first 10 generation banks | $4,463.13 | $3,570.50 | $ 892.63 |
| Sum of remaining generation banks | 536.87 | 429.50 | 107.37 |
| Total for banking system as a whole | $5,000.00 | $4,000.00 | $1,000.00 |

**TABLE 16-4(h)**

**5th, Through this long chain, all banks finally create deposits 5 times reserves**

All banks together do accomplish what no one small bank can—multiple expansion of reserves into M. The final equilibrium is reached when every dollar of original new reserves, wherever it comes to rest in the banking system, supports $5 of demand deposits. (From the seventh generation on, all data have been rounded off to two decimal places. Note that in every generation each *small* bank has "created" new money in the following sense: It ends up with final bank deposit five times *the reserves it finally retains*.)

Common sense tells us the process of deposit creation must come to an end only when no bank *anywhere in the system* has reserves in excess of the 20 per cent reserve ratio to deposits. In all our examples, no cash reserves ever leaked out of the banking system, but simply went from one set of banks to another set of banks. Everyone will be at equilibrium only when a consolidated balance sheet for all the banks together—for the first, second, and hundredth generation—looks as shown in Table 16-4(i). For, if total new deposits were less than $5,000, the 20 per cent ratio would not yet be reached and equilibrium not yet everywhere attained.

If the reader will compare Table 16-4(i) with Table 16-4(b), previously judged "impossible" on page 303, he will see this:

The whole banking system *can* do what no one bank can do by itself. It can expand its deposits to five times the *initial* new reserves deposit. *Bank money has been created 5 out of 1—and all the while each bank has invested and lent only a fraction of what it has received as deposits!*

**CONSOLIDATED BALANCE SHEET SHOWING FINAL POSITION OF ALL BANKS TOGETHER**

| ASSETS | | LIABILITIES | |
|---|---|---|---|
| Reserves | +$1,000 | Deposits | +$5,000 |
| Loans and investments | + 4,000 | | |
| Total | +$5,000 | Total | +$5,000 |

**TABLE 16-4(i)**

**6th, All together end up doing what single one couldn't**

Contrast this with Table 16-4(b)'s impossible feat of one lone, small bank.

| EQUILIBRIUM POSITION OF ORIGINAL BANK LOSING A DEPOSIT | | | |
|---|---|---|---|
| ASSETS | | | LIABILITIES |
| Reserves | −$ 200 | Deposits | −$1,000 |
| Loans and | | | |
| investments | − 800 | | |
| Total | −$1,000 | Total | −$1,000 |

**TABLE 16-5(a)**
**When the Fed kills off reserves, a multiple contraction begins to take place. . . ending in 5-to-1 less M.**

Figure 16-1 on page 301 can be reviewed now with deeper understanding of what actually goes on inside the black box of the member banks.

Who creates the multiple expansion[12] of deposits? Three parties do so jointly: the *public* by always keeping its money in the bank on deposit; the *banks* by keeping only a fraction of their deposits in the form of cash; the *public and private borrowers* who make it possible for the banks to find loans and attractive earning assets to buy with their excess cash. There is also a fourth party, *the central bank* (namely, the Fed), which by its activities determines how much will be the new reserves to come to the banking system.

It is the government's central bank that is the ultimate originator of the money supply, $M$. It will be the task of the next chapters to survey and explain this process.

Before leaving this section, test your knowledge of credit creation by tracing in detail what happens when the regional Federal Reserve Bank permanently kills off $1,000 of reserves by selling a government bond to a widow who withdraws cash from her demand-deposit account to pay for it: (1) Her local bank loses $1,000 of reserves and $1,000 of deposits. But it previously held only 20 per cent cash reserves or $200 against her deposit. Clearly, it must have given up to her some of its legally necessary cash reserves held against its other demand deposits. Show that its total reserves are now below the legal minimum. (2) Therefore it must sell $800 worth of investments or call in that many loans. The first-generation bank will be in equilibrium only when its balance sheet finally looks as shown in a newly constructed Table 16-5(a).

But in selling its securities, our original bank has drained $800 from a second generation of banks; and they in turn, by liquidating securities and loans, drain reserves from a third. And so it goes—until the widow and Fed's withdrawal of $1,000 of reserves from the banking system have produced a chain "killing off" $5,000 worth of deposits throughout the whole system and $4,000 of bank-earning assets. The reader should follow through each stage: hypothetical Table 16-5(b), Table 16-5(c), . . . ; and, in Fig. 16-1, reverse the arrow-flows and introduce minus signs.

---

[12] There is nothing paradoxical in the fact that total bank deposits are several times greater than the amount of paper cash in existence anywhere; the same is true of the total of government bonds and real-estate values. Deposits are something that banks *owe* their customers; cash is *left* in a bank, but it does not *remain* in that bank. Throughout its lifetime a dollar may have been *left* in many banks, just as it may be used over a long period of time to buy hundreds of dollars of merchandise. The one thing to keep firmly in mind is that bank deposits are one of the three forms of modern money and, quantitatively, the most important.

In effect, each small bank creates $1M$ out of $\frac{1}{5}M$, but not $5M$ out of $1M$. (NOTE: Whenever $1 of new reserves produces $5 of new demand-deposit money, the *net* creation of $M$ is only $5 − $1 = $4. So when one writes a 5:1 expansion expression, it means that there is associated with this a 4:1 *net*-creation-of-M expansion.)

You should also be able to show how an initial deposit of $1,000 can result in $10,000 of bank deposits if banks keep only 10 per cent reserve ratios, as they did in the 1920s. And since the reserve ratios of Table 16-3 average below 20 per cent, you might show that 6-to-1 is a more accurate figure than 5-to-1.

### A "MONOPOLY BANK" VERSUS SIMULTANEOUS EXPANSION

In all the above processes, it was assumed that no cash leaked out of the banking system into someone's mattress or into permanent hand-to-hand circulation. The banking system was then in the enviable position of finding that its checks were always deposited somewhere within itself.

This condition being so, it is easy to see that a single "monopoly bank" with many branches, which served the whole nation and represented the consolidated banking system, would be able to do *at once* what we have said each small bank cannot do. Its balance sheet could quickly go to the condition shown in Table 16-4(b) or (i). It could write checks freely to pay for securities or loans, knowing that those who get them would always redeposit their proceeds in the one and only monopoly bank.[13]

In the previous section we saw how the banking system can reach the limits of its expansion through many successive rounds or generations. If we allow half a week for checks to clear at each stage and for decisions to be made, then 5 to 8 weeks might be needed for the process to work itself out through more than a dozen rounds.

As a practical matter, it is not necessary to follow the chain of each dollar deposited through its successive rounds. Here is why. A rise in *initial* reserves will usually affect *almost all the banks at the same time.*[14] They all receive some new deposits at about the same time. They *all* have excess reserves in the first instance, and *all* together make loans or buy securities. When a single small bank, alone by itself, writes checks

---

[13] In countries like England, where there is a "Big Five" group of branch banks, or like Canada, where there are a few large banks, or in states like California, where there are a few great multiple-branch banks—in such cases a bank may be able to lend out more than its legal excess reserves, knowing that part of the money will come back *to itself* in later "generations." However, these so-called "derivative," or "self-returning," deposits are not important for the United States and calling attention to them can confuse beginning students, as it did economists of half a century ago when this process was still novel.

[14] Here in Fig. 16-2 is the story of Fig. 16-1 retold for a monopoly bank or for simultaneous expansion.

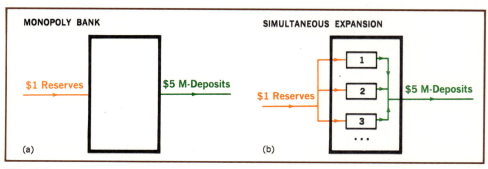

FIG. 16-2

In (a), there is no need for arrows within the box, since there is only one big bank. In (b), the arrows between the banks run in both directions and can be ignored.

to acquire securities, these checks go to other banks and it loses cash. But when *all* write checks simultaneously and in balance, there will tend to be a *cancellation* of new checks deposited and paid out in each bank. No one bank need lose cash reserves.

Hence, without going through the successive generations of the previous section, all banks together can simply and blithely expand their loans and investments—so long as each does not jeopardize its reserve position—until deposits are finally brought into a 5-to-1 relation to reserves. Then the banking system has reached the limit of its ability to create money.

One could follow through the similar process by which all banks *simultaneously* contract money 5-to-1 for each dollar of reserves withdrawn from the banking system, and one could also show how a monopoly bank would contract.

## TWO QUALIFICATIONS TO DEPOSIT CREATION

Finally, two qualifications to the ideal condition must be made. We have shown that $1,000 of new reserves put into a bank can ultimately result in an increase of $5,000 of bank deposits. This assumed that all the new money remained somewhere *in* the banking system, in one bank or another at every stage, and that all banks could keep "loaned up" with no "excess reserves."

**Leakage into hand-to-hand circulation**   It is quite possible, however, and even likely, that, somewhere along the chain of deposit expansion, some individual who receives a check will not leave the proceeds in a bank but will withdraw it into circulation or into hoarding outside the banking system. As a matter of fact, in boom times when bank deposits are expanding, there is usually at the same time an increased need for pennies, dimes, and paper currency.

The effects of such withdrawals on our analysis are simple. When $1,000 stayed in the banking system, $5,000 of new deposits were created. If $100 were to leak into circulation outside the banks and only $900 of new reserves were to remain in the banking system, then the new demand deposits created would be $4,500 ($900 $\times$ 5). *The banking system can always amplify in a 5-to-1 ratio whatever amount of new reserves is permanently left with it.*[15]

We have been concentrating here on checkable demand deposits. But remember that economists include time deposits in the broad $M_2$ definition of the money supply! Recall too that time deposits have legal reserve requirements, albeit (as Table 16-3 shows) lower ratios than do demand deposits. Hence, just as some of our original $1,000 of reserves will leak out of the banks as currency held by the public, so too will some leak into the time-deposit division of the member bank as needed legal reserves for new time deposits. Obviously, the 5-to-1 amplification of demand deposits applies only to that part of the original reserves which does *not* leak out of the demand-deposit division in any shape, form, or manner.

**Possible excess reserves**   Our description of multiple-deposit creation has proceeded on the assumption that the commercial banks stick fairly close to their legal reserve

---

[15] In Figs. 16-1 and 16-2, pencil in holes at the bottom of the black box, with arrows showing that part of the original blue $1 input leaks into currency held by the public.

ratios. But there is no reason why a bank cannot choose to keep an *excess* over the legally required amount of reserves. Thus, suppose the original bank receiving a new $1,000 deposit had been satisfied to hold $800 of it in excess reserves. Then the whole process would have ended right there, with no multiple expansion of deposits. Or if, less absurdly, banks were always to keep 5 per cent excess reserves, on top of the 20 per cent legal requirement, we'd have an expansion chain of deposits $[1 + .75 + (.75)^2 + \cdots]$ rather than $[1 + .8 + (.8)^2 + \cdots]$, with only 4-to-1 instead of 5-to-1 expansion of deposits.

Back in the 1930s excess reserves—i.e., reserves over and above legally required reserves—were substantial, because bankers were then leery of loan opportunities and even of relatively safe government bills that were paying only $\frac{1}{8}$ of 1 per cent interest. Had the Fed then given the banking system $1,000 of new reserves, perhaps half might have gone into excess reserves. Today excess reserves are less important, as most banks find attractive uses in the Federal Funds market even for one-day funds.

In depressed times, the level of excess reserves depends more on the attitudes of banks toward the interest rates they can earn than on their fears that withdrawals will catch them unawares. When short-term interest rates become very low, and a banker finds that keeping an extra million dollars in idle reserves would not much change his earning position, he is not very anxious to get rid of all excess reserves. But as profit opportunities improve and become less uncertain, he turns more aggressive in putting his idle reserves to work earning a yield.

The possibility that the excess reserves of banks can change over time is an important reminder that there is nothing mechanical and completely accurate about using a 5-to-1 or any other *fixed* ratio for money creation.

Accordingly, there is nothing automatic about deposit creation. Four factors are necessary: the banks must somehow receive new reserves; they must be willing to make loans or buy securities rather than hold new excess reserves; someone must be willing to borrow or to sell securities; and the public must choose to leave its money on deposit with the banks, not depleting them of reserves.

## SUMMARY

### A. NATURE AND FUNCTIONING OF THE MODERN BANKING SYSTEM

1    The American banking system consists primarily of relatively small-scale unit banks, chartered by the national government or by the states. Although less than half are members of the Federal Reserve System, member demand deposits include six-sevenths of the total of all deposits.

2    The functions of commercial banks are numerous and overlap with those of such other financial institutions as mutual savings banks, federal savings and loan associations, finance companies, and insurance companies. But in their function of providing demand-deposit $M$, the commercial banks perform a unique and important economic role. Their checkable deposits constitute the single most important component of our money supply or medium of exchange. Also the banks are important sources for credit.

3   The Federal Reserve System (or Fed) consists primarily of (*a*) member banks, (*b*) the 12 regional Federal Reserve Banks, and (*c*) the Board of Governors (or Federal Reserve Board) in Washington. Although nominally corporations owned by the member banks, the Federal Reserve Banks are, in fact, almost branches of the federal government, possessing wide powers and being concerned with the public interest rather than profits. Responsible to Congress, in practice they do not act independently of Treasury and Executive-branch policy. It is the primary responsibility of the Reserve authorities to control the money supply in order to help achieve full employment with stable prices (and backstop the banking system in time of crisis).

4   Modern banks gradually evolved from the old goldsmith establishments in which money and valuables were stored. It finally became general practice to hold far less than 100 per cent reserves against deposits, the rest being put into securities and loans for an interest yield. Fractional-reserve banking had evolved.

5   If the government did not stand ready to use its emergency powers to protect the banking system, an attempt by all depositors at the same time to withdraw their money would ruin any fractional-reserve banking system; but knowing the government is ready to act, people will never put it to the test.

   The member banks are required to keep legal reserves (on deposit with their Reserve Bank or in vault cash) in some proportion to their deposits. These legal reserve requirements are *not* primarily to protect deposits but to permit the Federal Reserve to control the total supply of $M$ and keep credit conditions conducive to proper over-all spending—to proper $C + I + G$ and $MV$ or $PQ$ totals.

## B. THE CREATION OF BANK DEPOSITS

6   If banks kept 100 per cent cash reserves against all deposits, there would be no multiple creation of money when new, high-powered reserves are fed by the central bank into the system. There would be only a 1-to-1 exchange of one kind of money for another kind of money.

7   Modern banks are required to keep legal reserves of only about one-sixth or less of their demand deposits, depending on size of deposits. Consequently, the banking system as a whole—together with public or private borrowers and the depositing public—does create demand-deposit money almost 6-to-1 for each new dollar of reserves created by the Fed and left on deposit somewhere in the system (5-to-1, in our simplified examples).

8   Each small bank is limited in its ability to expand its loans and investments. It cannot lend or invest more than it has received from depositors; it can lend only about four-fifths as much. The system as a whole can expand at once, as each small bank cannot. This can be seen if we examine a monopoly bank in a closed community. The checks written by such a bank always come back to it; therefore

the only restriction upon its ability to expand its investments and deposits (its assets *and* its liabilities in double-entry bookkeeping) is the requirement that it keep one-fifth cash-reserve ratios against deposits. When deposits have expanded until they are five times the new reserves, the monopoly bank is "loaned up" and can create no further deposits until given more reserves.

9   In present-day America, there is no monopoly bank. Nevertheless, the same 5-to-1 expansion of bank deposits takes place. The first individual bank receiving a new $1,000 of deposits spends four-fifths of its newly acquired cash on loans and investments. This gives a second group of banks four-fifths of $1,000 in new deposits. They, in turn, keep one-fifth in cash and spend the other four-fifths for new earning assets; this causes them to lose cash to a third set of banks, whose deposits have gone up by four-fifths of four-fifths of $1,000. Obviously, if we follow through the successive groups of banks in the dwindling, never-ending chain, we find for the system as a whole new deposits of

$$\$1,000 + \$800 + \$640 + \$512 + \cdots = \$1,000 \times [1 + \tfrac{4}{5} + (\tfrac{4}{5})^2 + (\tfrac{4}{5})^3 + \cdots]$$

$$= \$1,000 \left(\frac{1}{1 - \tfrac{4}{5}}\right) = \$1,000 \left(\frac{1}{\tfrac{1}{5}}\right) = \$5,000$$

Only when each $1 of the new reserves retained in the banking system ends up supporting $5 of deposits somewhere in the system will the limits to deposit expansion be reached. Then the system is loaned up; it can create no further deposits until it is given more reserves.

10   In practice, it is not necessary to wait for the successive rounds in the chain of $1,000, $800, $640, . . . , to work themselves out. Usually, many banks tend to get new reserves at about the same time. If all simultaneously expand their loans and investments approximately in balance, their outpayments will tend to cancel each other. Thus, each loses cash; and *all together* can (like a monopoly bank) rather quickly expand their assets and deposits to the 5-to-1 limit.

11   As a minor qualification to the above discussion, we must note that there will be some leakage of the new cash reserves of the banking system into circulation *outside* the banks (and, indeed, some will go abroad) and into the time-deposit division of the banks for their legally needed reserves. Therefore, instead of $5,000 of new demand deposits created, as in the previous examples, we may have something less than that—the difference being due to what is withdrawn from the system. A second qualification results from the fact that a bank may keep *excess reserves* above legally required reserves. While large banks do not hold much excess reserves in prosperous times, others may hold varying amounts of excess reserves, depending upon interest rates and precautionary expectations. So there is nothing automatic about a 5-to-1 or other fixed-gear ratio.

In this chapter we have seen how bank deposits are kept at about five times the legal reserves of the banking system. In Chapter 17 we shall learn how the Federal Reserve Banks make high-powered reserves go up when an expansion of the total money supply is desired. When a contraction of the total supply of money is in order, the Federal Reserve authorities pull the brakes. Instead of pumping new reserves into the banking system, they draw off some of the reserves, and they are then able to reduce the quantity of money, not 1 for 1, but (as just shown) 5 for 1. Thus, within close limits, the Fed can control the rate of growth of the money supply along the pattern it thinks best.

## CONCEPTS FOR REVIEW

national, state, member banks
FDIC-insured banks
Board of Governors, 12 Federal
  Reserve Banks, Fed
bank balance sheet
goldsmiths and 100% reserves
fractional-reserve banking
legal reserve ratio requirements
original high-powered reserves
chain of generations

deposit creation for a monopoly
  bank versus a system of
  many small banks
simultaneous expansion by all
  banks
excess reserves, leakage of
  reserves into public's
  currency or time-deposit
  reserves
ultimate Fed control of $M$

## QUESTIONS FOR DISCUSSION

1  Suppose that all banks kept 100 per cent reserves. How different would they be? What function do legal reserves perform? What are "excess reserves"?

2  Assume a 10 per cent reserve ratio. Trace the process of multiple-bank expansion, duplicating Tables 16-4(a) to (i). Reverse the process.

3  Do bankers create deposits? Who does? If a banker receives a new deposit and new reserves, is he always able to find borrowers? Can he always expand his holdings of government securities?

4  "My bank's books always balance. I merely *pass on* to investors the savings my depositors bring me. Who dares say a banker can create $M$?" Do you dare?

5  "The Fed should create new reserves indefinitely as long as we bankers can find good productive loans to make, because then each new $M$ will be balanced by new product $Q$ and prices won't rise and the community will get a higher real GNP indefinitely." This view was widely supported by the founders of the Fed in 1913. Can you see where the implied *elasticity* of $M$ could be *harmful* in a world of fluctuating $C + I + G$ schedules? (Hint: Banks would expand $M$ in booms and contract $M$ in recessions: inflationary and deflationary gaps worsen.)

6  *Extra-credit problem:* Suppose the public always holds $\frac{1}{21}$ of its $M$ in currency and $\frac{20}{21}$ in demand deposits. Then if banks always keep $\frac{1}{5}$ of reserves against their demand deposits, verify that each $R$ of new reserves gives rise to total $M$ as follows:

$$ M = \frac{1}{\frac{1}{21} + \frac{1}{5}\frac{20}{21}} R = \frac{21}{5} R = 4.2\ R;\ \text{deposits} = \frac{20}{21}\frac{21}{5} R = 4R;\ \text{currency} = .2R $$

# 17

## FEDERAL RESERVE AND CENTRAL BANK MONETARY POLICY

There have been three
great inventions since
the beginning of time:
fire, the wheel,
and central banking.
WILL ROGERS

The Federal Reserve is a central bank, the government's bank for bankers and for itself. Every central bank has one prime function:

*It operates to control the supply of high-powered reserves, and thereby the economy's supply of money and credit. If business is getting worse and jobs are getting scarce, the Federal Reserve Board will try to expand money and credit. But if spending threatens to become excessive, so that prices are rising and there are too many job vacancies, then the Federal Reserve authorities (the Fed) will do all that is possible to step on the brakes and contract money and credit.*

*Monetary policy "leans against the wind" of prevailing deficient or excessive aggregate demand spending, to promote optimal real growth and price-level stability.*

In a nutshell, that is the function of central banking. And all mixed economies rely on such a central bank. In this chapter, we shall survey the weapons that the Federal Reserve uses to expand or contract money and credit.

### HOW MONETARY POLICY WORKS TO CONTROL SPENDING

What is the exact process by which the Reserve authorities affect general spending? Here are five steps:

As shown in Chapter 16, commercial or member banks must have *reserves* to support their assets and deposits. (So important are these "reserves" that we shall capitalize the word for the rest of this chapter.)

1. *The first step of the Fed, therefore, when it wants to put on the monetary brakes, is to act to cut down on the Reserves available to the banks.*

2. *Each dollar contraction in bank Reserves forces about a $5 contraction in total bank money, i.e., in total demand deposits.* (Recall Chapter 16's analysis of multiple-deposit creation.)

3. *The contraction in total money immediately makes credit generally "tight," that is, both dearer and less available.* We shall see that less $M$ will immediately raise interest rates. Just as important, less $M$ will make credit less available to people.

Interest rates will rise for mortgage borrowers (builders and home buyers); for local governments that want to build schools and roads; for businessmen anxious to build plants, buy new equipment, promote new ventures, or add to inventory; for public utilities needing new power stations and wanting to float new common stocks. Higher interest rates will also lower the values of people's wealth assets: bonds, stocks, land, homes, etc.

Reinforcing higher interest cost will be an important *rationing effect* on investment and other components of total $C + I + G$ spending. This contractionary effect comes from the fact of credit's decreased availability. Thus, if you want to build a house, it matters to you that the interest rate has risen from 7 to $9\frac{1}{2}$ per cent. If you are like most families, it matters even more that you may now find it hard to get a mortgage with a low down payment. You may find your banker's manner a shade cooler; and he may discourage you from buying the $45,000 house that you really prefer to the $30,000 one you have been considering. When $M$ is scarce, turndowns on loans become common. (During recent decades, all this happened. Housing starts plummeted for lack of credit in 1966, 1969–1970, and 1973–1974.)

4. *With credit expensive and hard to get and with the wealth of people and firms down, private and public investment will tend to fall.* Why this downward shift in the $I$ and $G$ schedules? Because people's decisions as to whether it is profitable to build a new house or plant, order a new machine, and hold more inventory usually depend upon how they can finance such investment spending.[1] If they have to pay a high interest rate or find it very hard to get loans, they often scale down their investment plans. The same holds for state and local governments. The old road gets patched up and the new school postponed when the town finds it cannot float its bonds at any reasonable interest rate, and citizens learn taxes are going up because it now costs more to borrow.

5. *Finally, the pressure on credit and on investment spending will, through the downward shift in the $I + G$ schedule, have downward effects on income spending, prices, and jobs.* The multiplier analysis of Chapters 12 and 13 showed how such a drop in investment will depress income spending sharply.

If the Fed has been right in its diagnosis of inflationary conditions, the drop in money income will be just what the doctor ordered to help the situation. $M$ contraction will have succeeded in reducing the inflationary gap—in eliminating demand-pull inflation.

Indeed, as a sixth, longer-run effect, the curb on $M$ may *eventually lower* rather than raise interest rates. For suppose that raising interest rates from 6 to 8 per cent does succeed in reducing price inflation permanently from a 6 per cent to a 3 per cent annual rate. Once everyone recognizes that there will no longer be that extra rate of inflation, interest-rate levels can drop from, say, an 8 per cent to a 5 per cent level. No longer will lenders require so

---

[1] Later chapters (particularly Chapter 30) show how higher interest rates tend to depress the market value of wealth items: land, bonds, buildings, equipment. With their total wealth now less and installment credit to buy consumers' durables now hard to get, people's $CC$ schedule will also be shifted down, along with their $II$ schedules and the local $GG$ schedule.

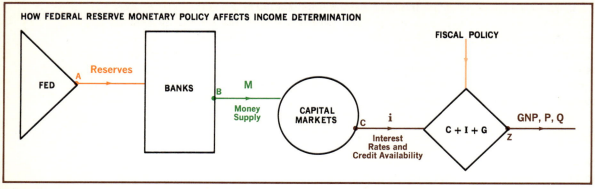

**FIG. 17-1**

**Monetary policy integrates nicely with post-Keynesian $C + I + G$ income determination**

Be sure you understand how the Fed raises high-powered Reserves at left; thereby raising total $M$; which, working through the capital and securities markets, lowers interest rates, $i$, and improves credit availability; leading to upward shifts of $C + I + G$ schedules; and ultimately increasing GNP, real output ($Q$), and price level ($P$). $Q$ cannot grow above its full-employment level. (To warn against thinking monetary policy is the whole story, note fiscal policy input into $C + I + G$ diamond.)

great a premium in the money interest rate to compensate for inflation, and what began as a 6 per cent interest rate could now go to 5 per cent without representing any reduction in the *real* (i.e., corrected-for-inflation) interest rate.

## RECAPITULATION

This five-step sequence—from the Fed's changing the commercial banks' Reserves, to 5-to-1 changes in total $M$, to changes in credit's interest cost and availability, to changes in private and public investment spending, and finally to multiplied changes in money income—is vital. By rereading the italicized parts of the previous section, you can consolidate your understanding of it. Better still, psychologists tell us one learns fastest by participating. The previous section was explained in terms of a time—like 1969—when the Fed wants to *contract* business activity. Tackle the problem of how things proceed when, as in 1971 or 1975, the Fed wants to *expand* business activity.

Suppose you are Chairman Burns of the Fed's Board of Governors at a time when the economy is mildly depressed. Suppose you are called to testify before a congressional committee—as Burns so often is—to explain to an interrogating senator just how your *expansionary* acts would operate. Retrace these detailed steps:

The Fed expands Reserves; member banks then engineer something like a 5-to-1 expansion in demand deposits; increase in society's $M$ is associated with "easier money conditions," i.e., lower interest rates on loans, bonds, and mortgages, and, just as important, more easily available credit to would-be investors and government spenders. There results an increase in $I$, $G$, and even in durable-goods $C$ spending. Finally, there follow multiplier effects of the shift in the $C + I + G$ schedule on income, employment, and possibly price levels.

Figure 17-1 drives home the five-step sequence by adding to the black box of the member banks (as already shown in Fig. 15-3, page 288) the capital markets in which interest rates and credit availability are determined. Then, in turn, from the capital market (shown as a circle) we get the familiar $C + I + G$ link of total spending (shown as the final diamond). Be sure you can follow the steps from the far left (where the Fed initiates changes in Reserves) to the far right (where the money level of GNP, the price level, and the rate of employment are affected by monetary policy).

## BALANCE SHEET OF THE FEDERAL RESERVE BANKS

Now that we have surveyed the process of monetary policy with a telescope, let us study the mechanism in broad detail. We shall not attempt to look at Federal Reserve policy under a microscope, since that is the job of an intermediate course in money and banking; but we do want to get a general idea of *exactly what weapons* the Fed can use to affect bank Reserves.

Look at Table 17-1. This lists the combined balance sheet of the Federal Reserve Banks, the United States government's central bank. The first asset consists mostly of gold certificates, i.e., warehouse receipts from the Treasury to the Fed for official gold. United States government securities make up most of the rest of the assets—the significance of this item will be explained soon. The smaller Discounts, loans, and acceptances item is primarily loans or advances to member banks. (The interest rate the Fed charges banks for such loans, or "discounts," is called the "discount rate," which is usually about the same in all 12 Reserve Districts.)

The right-hand side lists the usual capital accounts: original capital subscribed by the member banks plus retained earnings or accumulated surplus. This would be much greater for so profitable a business were it not for the already-mentioned fact that the Federal Reserve gives *all* its excess profits back to the Treasury. (The Fed's profits

| COMBINED BALANCE SHEET OF 12 FEDERAL RESERVE BANKS, JANUARY 1, 1975 (in billions of dollars) | | | |
|---|---|---|---|
| **ASSETS** | | **LIABILITIES AND NET WORTH** | |
| Gold certificates and other cash | $ 11.9 | Capital accounts | $   1.8 |
| U.S. government securities | 80.5 | Federal Reserve notes | 70.9 |
| Discounts, loans, and acceptances | 1.3 | Deposits: | |
| Miscellaneous other assets | | **Member bank Reserves** | **25.8** |
| (primarily "uncollected | | U.S. Treasury | 3.1 |
| items") | 17.1 | Foreign and other | 1.7 |
| | | Miscellaneous liabilities | 7.5 |
| Total | $110.8 | Total | $110.8 |

**TABLE 17-1**

**Federal Reserve notes and deposits underlie our money supply**

By (*a*) controlling its earning assets (government securities and discounts), the Fed (*b*) controls its liabilities (deposits and Federal Reserve notes), thereby (*c*) controlling the economy's money supply (currency and demand deposits) and affecting GNP.

come from the privilege the government gives it to issue Federal Reserve notes and bank deposits for the member banks at no interest cost; with these it acquires interest-yielding government bonds and loans. Hence, it is only fair that the government take back these privileged profits.)

Federal Reserve notes are the Fed's principal liabilities. These are the dollar, five-dollar, and other bills we carry in our wallets. The Fed is highly privileged to have been granted by Congress this power to issue currency (its "right to counterfeit"!).

Little comment is needed on several of its deposit liabilities: United States government deposits, foreign central bank deposits, and miscellaneous.

Of vital importance, though, are the member banks' Reserve balances kept on deposit with the Federal Reserve Banks and shown as FRB liabilities. Along with small amounts of vault cash, these are the high-powered Reserves we have been talking about. They provide the basis for multiple-deposit creation by the member banks.

We shall see that the Fed, *by altering its holding of government securities and discount assets*, can create changes in the Reserves of the commercial banks—thereby starting off our earlier-mentioned five-step sequence. Later, Fig. 17-3 will show how these important balance-sheet and other items have changed in recent years.

In summary, by varying its government-bond and other assets, the Fed can control the Reserves of the banks, (which, together with the currency held by the public, constitute the important so-called "monetary base") and thereby can control the rate of growth of the total money supply, $M$.

### DISCRETIONARY MONETARY POLICIES BY THE FEDERAL RESERVE: OPEN-MARKET OPERATIONS

To initiate the five-step stabilization sequence, the Federal Reserve has three main weapons, which are, in order of their present importance, (1) open-market operations, (2) discount-rate policy, (3) changes in the *legal reserve ratio requirements* of the member banks. (We shall review its five minor weapons later in the chapter.)

**By selling or buying government bonds in the open market (mostly in New York), the Fed authorities can tighten or loosen member bank Reserves. These so-called "open-market operations" are a central bank's most important stabilizing weapon.**

At monthly intervals, even as you read this book, the Federal Open Market Committee (FOMC) is meeting to decide whether to pump more Reserves into the banking system by buying Treasury bills (i.e., short-term bonds) or longer-term government bonds; or whether to tighten things up a little by selling government securities. It is a never-ending job for this 12-man FOMC.

To see how an open-market operation changes Reserves, let us suppose that the Fed thinks the economic winds are blowing up a little inflation. Its Open Market Committee holds the usual secret meeting. The committeemen say: "Let's sell $1 billion of government bonds from our portfolio to contract Reserves and over-all money and credit." The motion is carried by vote of the seven Washington Governors and five Regional Bank Presidents unanimously, or, say, with one dissenting vote.

| FEDERAL RESERVE ASSETS | | FEDERAL RESERVE LIABILITIES | |
|---|---|---|---|
| U.S. securities | −$1.0 | Member bank Reserves | −$1.0 |
| Total | −$1.0 | Total | −$1.0 |

**TABLE 17-2(a)**
Open-market sale cuts Reserves initially . . . . . . . . . . . .

| MEMBER BANK ASSETS | | MEMBER BANK LIABILITIES | |
|---|---|---|---|
| Reserves | −$1.0 | Demand deposits | −$5.0 |
| Loans and investments | − 4.0 | | |
| Total | −$5.0 | Total | −$5.0 |

**TABLE 17-2(b)**
. . . . . . . . . . . . ultimately cuts deposits 5-to-1

When an open-market sale kills off $1 billion of Reserves, it induces a $5 billion drop in total demand deposits. The member banks must call in loans and sell off their "investments" (i.e., their securities) up to $4 billion.

To whom are the bonds sold? No one knows: to the open market. The dealers in government bonds—the large banks and half-a-dozen large nonbank dealers—will not reveal the names of the buyers. But you can guess that they are primarily insurance companies, commercial banks, big business firms, and the dealers themselves.

The buyer will most likely pay for the bonds by a check to the Fed drawn on his bank account. The Fed will present this check for payment to his member bank. That member bank will *lose* an equivalent amount of its Reserve balances with the Federal Reserve. Table 17-2(a) shows the final effect on the Federal Reserve balance sheet. The open-market sale has cut down on the Fed's assets and liabilities. (It has also initially cut down on member bank Reserves and their demand deposits owed to the bond buyer.)

Actually, this shows only the *initial* potency of open-market sales. In all likelihood the $1 billion sale of government bonds will result in a $5 billion cut in the community's money supply. We've seen why—in Chapter 16.

Reserves go down by $1 billion, and that tends to set off a $5 billion contraction of deposits. Table 17-2(b) shows the member banks' position after Reserves have been extinguished by the open-market operation. In the end, the Fed's open-market sale has put 5-to-1 downward pressure on bank-deposit $M$.

To test your understanding of open-market operations, consider the reverse process. Suppose incomes and jobs are at too low a level. What will the Open Market Committee want to do? Buy government bonds on the open market and thereby create new Reserves for the member banks? Produce thereby a 5-to-1 expansion in $M$, thus making credit cheaper and more easily available to investors, and consequently encouraging an upward shift in $C + I + G$ and a multiplier increase in GNP? Confirm all this. (Locate in Fig. 17-1, page 316, the orange point A at which open-market operations impinge.)

**Open-market targets**   The FOMC meets in private. Only 45 days later will the public and Congress learn what it decided. (Until congressmen put pressure on the Fed in 1975, the delay period used to be 90 days.) The FOMC decides how to instruct the officer in New York who operates the open-market desk as to exactly what should be his targets. Before the 1970s, he used to be given such vague instructions as, "Keep credit conditions and interest rates as tight as they have been." Or "Loosen up on credit a little to help expand GNP." Or, "Lean a bit harder against the winds of inflation."

The result was a great preoccupation with keeping the bond market orderly and keeping interest yields from bouncing around. Alas, the attempts to stabilize interest rates tended, all too often, to destabilize the rate of growth of the money supply as measured by $M_1$, by $M_2$, or by "high-powered" Reserves that provide the monetary base for the banks and the public.

Partly under the proddings of the economists of the Chicago "monetarist school," who attach primary importance to what happens to $M_1$ and $M_2$ growth and not to what happens to interest rates and credit availability, the Fed has altered its methods in the 1970s. Now it usually gives as its primary target, "Aim for such and such growth rate in Reserves, say 6 to 7 per cent annual rate (and what that implies for growth rate of $M_1$ and $M_2$). Only as a secondary target, concern yourself with interest rates, particularly so long as they stay in the interval of, say, $5\frac{1}{2}$ to 6 per cent."

So far so good. In the three or four weeks between meetings of the FOMC, these targets may be approximately realized. What if they are not? Then, after telephone consultation with Washington and the full committee, the open-market desk may find itself paying more attention to the secondary interest-rate target than it would do in normal times.

**Long-term targets**   In the last half of the 1970s a new wrinkle has been added. Often for quarter-year and half-year on end, the FOMC constantly misses its targets. Thus, as the recession worsened in the fall of 1974 and the winter of 1975, $M_1$ never grew anywhere nearly as much as everyone thought proper; the secondary target of reduced interest rates did take place, but the primary target kept eluding the Fed.

Economists criticized. The administration fumed; but the Fed has come to think itself independent of the administration. Finally, the patience of Congress and the public wore thin as unemployment mounted from $5\frac{1}{2}$ per cent in August to 9 per cent by spring. To hold on to its "independence" from day-to-day control by Congress, Chairman Arthur Burns and the Fed agreed to name a long-term target for the money aggregates: Dr. Burns promised that, from March 1975 to March 1976, $M_1$ would grow in the range of 5 to $7\frac{1}{2}$ per cent (unless untoward events suggested otherwise).

Most analysts, nonmonetarist and monetarist, think that some such long-term targeting represents an improvement in the handling of monetary policy.

## DISCOUNT-RATE POLICY: A SECOND WEAPON

The Federal Reserve Banks also make loans to the member banks. These we call "discounts." When its discounts are growing, the banks are borrowing from the Fed, which is thereby helping bank Reserves to grow. When the Fed's discounts are dropping, it is helping bank Reserves to contract.[2]

[2] When the Federal Reserve System was started, it was thought that discount policy would be most important of all. The idea was to have member banks "rediscount" their customers' promissory notes, sending them over to the Reserve Banks in return for new cash. That way, the neighborhood banks would never run out of money to accommodate worthy farm and business borrowers. It did not

Unfortunately, the Fed is not free to pursue a discount policy exactly the way it wants to. It cannot send salesmen out to drum up more discounts whenever it wants to expand them. All it can do is wait for banks to come to it. All it can do is name the "discount rate," which sets its interest charge in each of the 12 Federal Reserve Districts for such discounts or advances to the banks that choose to borrow.

True, it can expect to get more takers by lowering the discount rate; or it can discourage the volume of its discounts by raising the discount rate. But as far as discount policy is concerned, the Fed must play the passive role. It can sit and wait. It can veto. It can make its rate attractive. But it certainly cannot set its amount of *discounts* at precisely the figure it wants. Only in its open-market operations can it take the active role. But do not overlook the power of a veto. A bank knows it must not abuse the privilege of being able to discount; it must not *continually* rely on this source of funds. By being able to say No, the Fed has some power to put contractionary pressure on its discounts.

**Changing the discount rate**    On New York's Wall Street, Chicago's LaSalle Street, and Boston's State Street, everyone keeps careful watch on the discount rate that the Fed charges for its discounts. Thus, on a Thursday when the discount rate is raised, stocks and bonds will usually fall in price. Even London and Paris find their interest rates and investment spending influenced by announced changes in our discount rate.

The discount rate is usually set to *follow* the market. After open-market sales have been forcing interest rates up, banks will more and more try to borrow from the Fed at the not-yet-raised discount rate. To discourage such a growth in its discounts and advances, the Fed will eventually have to raise the discount rate to bring it back into normal alignment with the market or else—as in 1972—step up its distasteful need to ration and discourage use by banks of the discount privilege.

And when the Fed does raise the discount rate, very many in the market will say: "Aha, the Board still thinks the wind is blowing in the inflationary direction." Changes in the discount rate, as well as being *reflections* that follow the tightness of credit, can thus have important reinforcing *causal* effects upon the credit market. The effective interest rates banks charge customers—such as the "prime rate" charged biggest corporate borrowers—may soon get forced up to maintain their usual differential above the discount rate.

These patterns are reversed when the Fed wants easier credit. The discount rate is lowered to reflect the ease *already* apparent in the market, and the announcement of its being lowered usually serves to ease the market *further*. Thus, in August, 1960, when the discount rate was cut from $3\frac{1}{2}$ to 3 per cent, stocks and bonds soared in price. By contrast, the April, 1969, announcement of a discount-rate rise caused bonds

---

work out that way, for two reasons. First and most important, today experts realize that the last thing a healthy economy wants is an *elastic* money supply that will *automatically* expand when business is good and contract when it is bad. That way lies disastrous *reinforcement* of business cycles and inflation. Second, banks find that they prefer to borrow from the Fed on the basis of their numerous government securities rather than on their customers' promissory notes. Since 1935, most borrowing is on government securities, and that is why we now speak of the "discount rate" rather than of the old-fashioned "rediscount rate." (In England, they speak of "bank rate.")

and stocks to plummet downward; now people realized the Fed would keep money tight to fight the Vietnam demand-pull inflation.

**Discount-rate reform**   Few economists like the way discounting now works. When open-market operations tighten the Reserves base by $1 billion, often this induces the banks to *offset* this by going to the discount window for some fraction of $1 billion of new borrowed Reserves. Why countenance such waste motion, which merely makes the needed initial open-market operation bigger?

Banks never quite know how free they really are to use the discount privilege. In 1969, some banks paid more than 13 per cent for funds from the Euro-dollar market[3] and as much as 11 in the Federal Funds market when ostensibly they could still borrow from the Fed at the 6 per cent discount rate. They feared to do so. They feared rebuff or frowns. Most of all, they feared to use up the last-resort avenue they might need more at some later date.

A massive study by the Federal Reserve led to a 1970 proposal to make the right of the member banks to discount (part of the time, but never for *permanent* borrowing) *more automatic*. Of course, to keep banks from making a sure buck by borrowing at a low discount rate and lending at a high market rate, the proposal also contemplated having the discount rate follow market rates more closely than in the past. However, the unsettled conditions in the early 1970s put off the actual introduction of this proposed reform.

## CHANGING RESERVE REQUIREMENTS: A DRASTIC, INFREQUENTLY USED WEAPON

The Federal Reserve Board is given by Congress the limited power to raise or lower the *required legal reserve ratio* that the member banks must keep against their deposits. If the Fed wants to make credit tight very quickly, it can raise the required reserve ratios for the big and little banks to the 22 and 14 per cent statutory limits. (If it wanted credit still tighter, it would have to ask Congress to raise these limits, and to raise the 10 per cent maximum time-deposit requirement.)

If the Fed wants to ease credit conditions, it can do the reverse. It can cut legal reserve ratios, doing this again and again until the banks are down to 10 and 7 per cent. (To go lower than that would require a new act of Congress.) And, as in 1969, the Fed can raise the required reserve ratios behind time deposits.

**Changing reserve requirements is a powerful tool: it is used sparingly—only every few years, not every day as with open-market operations. It could be used more often; but open-market operations can produce about the same effects.**

Exactly how does an increase in required reserve ratios operate to tighten credit? Suppose the banks had built up deposits in a 5-to-1 fashion as a result of the required

---

[3]The "Euro-dollar market" is the name given to the operations outside United States boundaries in which foreign banks and foreign branches of U.S. banks make loan and security transactions denominated not in foreign currencies but in terms of American dollars. The volume of business done in this anonymous market, almost completely free of regulation or control, has soared in recent decades.

| MEMBER BANK ASSETS | | MEMBER BANK LIABILITIES | |
|---|---|---|---|
| Reserves | $ 20 | Demand deposits | $100 |
| Loans and | | | |
| investments | 80 | | |
| Total | $100 | Total | $100 |

| MEMBER BANK ASSETS | | MEMBER BANK LIABILITIES | |
|---|---|---|---|
| Reserves | $20 | Demand deposits | $80 |
| Loans and | | | |
| investments | 60 | | |
| Total | $80 | Total | $80 |

**TABLE 17-3(a)**
Raising reserve ratio leads from 5-to-1 . . . . . . . . . . . . .

**TABLE 17-3(b)**
to final 4-to-1 deposit expansion

ratio having been 20 per cent, with excess reserves being negligible. Now suppose the Fed wants to tighten credit and Congress lets it raise the required ratio to 25 per cent. Even if the Fed does nothing by way of open-market operations or discount policy to change bank Reserves, the member banks now have to contract their loans and investments greatly—and their deposits as well.

Why? Because (as Chapter 16 showed) the bank deposits can now only be in a 4-to-1, not a 5-to-1, ratio. So there must be a drop by one-fifth in all deposits.

This painful cut will start to take place quickly. As soon as the Board signs the new fiat raising requirements to 25 per cent, banks find themselves deficient in Reserves. They will have to sell some bonds and call in some loans. The bond buyers will use up their demand deposits, and the borrowers whose loans are called will use up their demand deposits to pay back such loans. The process ends only after banks have brought down their deposits to 4 rather than 5 times their Reserves.

Table 17-3 shows how their combined balance sheets might look before and after the change. No doubt so great a change in so short a time would result in very high interest rates, in unavailable credit, in great cuts in $I$ (and possibly in local $G$), and in great reductions in GNP and employment. Hence, this powerful weapon of changing reserve requirements is sparingly used.[4] (For review, locate back in Fig. 17-1 the green point $B$, at which the changed legal reserve ratio impinges on the amplification of Reserves into $M$.)

## MINOR WEAPONS: QUALITATIVE VERSUS QUANTITATIVE CONTROLS

The Fed also has used five further minor weapons: (1) "moral suasion," (2) selective controls over "margin requirements" for loans to buy stocks, (3) control over maximum interest rates banks can pay on time deposits, (4) selective credit controls over install-

[4]In 1936–1937 reserve requirements were sharply raised. But at that time banks found loans and bonds so unattractive that they were already holding heavy "excess reserves," i.e., holding more idle cash than the law required. So raising legal requirements did not have the great effects in lowering $M$ or raising interest rates that it would have today. It should also be pointed out that such a sudden squeeze on banks' reserve positions would undoubtedly today cause them to borrow at the "discount window" even at a higher discount rate for some temporary period at least. And today, when reserve requirements are raised, their impact at first is cushioned by offsetting open-market operations.

Late in 1969 the Fed imposed a new 10 per cent reserve requirement against certain Euro-dollar borrowing by the member banks. The requirement was raised to 20 per cent early in 1971 and lowered to 8 per cent in mid-1973.

ment contracts and consumer credit, (5) selective controls over the terms of housing mortgage contracts. (The last two powers Congress has let lapse, but could revive.)

**Moral suasion**    This refers to "jawbone control": the Reserve officials express their displeasure if banks are not doing what is wanted of them. Bankers are called in for heart-to-heart talks. An appeal to community spirit is made. Vague threats concerning future availability of credit may be made, and bank examiners may become especially zealous in going over the books.

Many economists doubt that slaps on the wrist will keep competitive bankers from doing what they want to do. Still, it is a tenable belief that moral suasion does have some significant effects, especially in the short run and especially when banks are heavily reliant on the privilege to "discount" at the Fed. After all, bankers are sensitive to public opinion like anyone else. And they find it only prudent not to get in the bad books of the Federal Reserve (as was demonstrated by extraordinary compliance with the voluntary program of control over foreign bank loans in the 1960s).

**Selective controls: margin requirements**    A selective or qualitative credit control is contrasted with an over-all quantitative credit control that operates merely by affecting over-all bank Reserves and over-all credit tightness. Selective credit controls can be very important in countries that have considerable central planning and supervision by the government of the detailed actions of business. To build a house there, you may need a permit; similarly, to float a new stock or bond issue.

The banks, particularly if, as in England, there are a few great ones, may be called in by the Chancellor of the Exchequer. He may say: "Look here. We want you to favor export industries in making your loans. And favor necessities. And cut back your total loans by 10 per cent before Christmas."

Such selective credit controls can be very powerful indeed. However, in normal peacetime it is the American custom not to rely on these detailed interferences with the pricing process—with one exception. The Federal Reserve is given power to set "margin requirements" that limit how much people can borrow in order to buy and carry listed common and preferred stocks. Thus, I could in 1970 borrow only 20 per cent from my broker but had to put up the other 80 per cent myself. In early 1973, I could borrow 35 per cent.[5]

**Interest-rate ceilings**    When any bank can earn 6 per cent or more on safe short-term government bonds (or even more on riskier loans), it stands to gain when it can owe people demand deposits at a *zero* interest rate. Under competition, free banking would result in banks then bidding up the interest rate paid on demand deposits to a positive level. (That is what used to happen in the 1920s: Our grandfathers often were paid 5 per cent on their *checking* deposits! Or they could often write checks on their savings or time deposits.)

---

[5]Back in the boom market of 1929, there were no rules at all: one could borrow 70, 80, or even 90 per cent of the value of any stock he bought. Little wonder that, once the crash came, brokers began to ask their clients to put up more "margin to cover the declining value of their stocks." Since many clients were already operating on a shoestring, they could not pony up the extra margin. Result: The broker had to sell their stocks; so just when stocks were already weak, the forced selling by low-margin holders added to the avalanche.

But during the Great Depression, Congress made it illegal for banks explicitly to pay interest on checking accounts. This was for two reasons: Banks could earn practically nothing then on safe government bonds, and the industry felt that its earnings would be better if rivals were kept by law from bidding positive interest on demand deposits; aside from this monopolists' cartel reason, many experts jumped to the conclusion that it was *overcompetition* among banks that had given rise to unsound lending practices and which had led to the mass bank runs and failures.

This depression-born stricture against interest on demand deposits stood until the middle and late 1970s. It explains why people and corporations put less and less of their idle funds into demand deposits, kept their checking balances to a minimum and merely replenished them from their savings accounts when they got too low. (And it explains Fig. 15-2's rapid rise in the broadly defined $M_2$ money supply compared with the narrower $M_1$ definition including only deposits payable on demand.)

Finally, Congress restored in 1975 the freedom of the commercial banks to pay interest on their checking deposits beginning at some subsequent date to be named. Permission was also given for the Mutual Savings Bank and the Savings and Loan Association to offer checking rights to their depositers. Undoubtedly, the distinction will be further blurred between $M_1$ and $M_2$.

From the mid-thirties to the late fifties, the Fed also put low ceilings on the interest rates member banks could pay on *time* deposits. As long as competitive ratios to be earned on government bonds remained low, this did not matter much. But when federal savings and loan associations could afford to pay 5 and 6 per cent or higher, people stopped leaving their money in commercial-bank savings accounts. They switched to nonmember banks and to S&Ls; in the case of firms, they switched to the Treasury-bill market. The big New York banks were especially hard hit when their foreign depositors began to withdraw deposits and to buy securities directly themselves.

In recent years, therefore, spurred on by the fear that foreign governments and firms would withdraw their money, the Fed, under so-called "Regulation Q," has raised the rates banks can pay on time deposits (to as much as $5\frac{1}{2}$ to $7\frac{1}{2}$ per cent, depending on length of notice and account size). Critics feared that raising such ceilings would make money tighter. Actually, the reverse happened in 1962–1965, as competitive economic theory predicted it would: the member banks retained more funds than they otherwise would have.

In the tight-money years after 1965, a new problem began to arise. During the 1960s the large New York banks had pioneered a new kind of time deposit—the so-called "certificate of deposit." This was a negotiable instrument that would enable a corporation to deposit $100,000 or $1 million for 180 days (in 1973, say, at $5\frac{1}{4}$ per cent per annum); however, if at the end of a few days the firm should change its mind, it could sell the "C-D" to some other corporation and yet lose little or no interest. What was the result when credit became very tight in order to help calm down the Vietnam-induced inflationary gap? Investors started to withdraw their funds from West Coast savings and loan associations to put them into Eastern C-Ds. A few S&Ls were on the verge of bankruptcy after they began to lose funds in 1966; they now had to pay 6 per cent or more on time deposits, whereas they had obligated themselves to lend money on long-term mortgages that brought in a net yield of less than that!

To Congress it appeared that the competitive scramble for funds led to unwise and risky loans by banks and S&Ls desperate to hold onto their deposits. Therefore, Congress has led the Federal Reserve to use Regulation Q to limit interest rates that banks can pay on *low-denomination* C-Ds. (The poor get soaked!) Inasmuch as the government insures deposits in banks and in S&Ls, it has a burning interest in how competition works out there. But diddling maximum rates to protect S&Ls may not work long. Even if commercial banks are kept by fiat from offering competitive interest rates, depositors can withdraw funds from S&Ls and invest directly in higher-yielding Treasury bills, giving rise to so-called "disintermediation."

Ceilings on deposit interest interfere with the free flow of funds, in and out of housing particularly. Thus most economists urge the abolition of ceilings. A minority argue, "While we have Regulation Q, let's recognize it gives us an extra selective weapon to help achieve the goal of keeping housing from being the prime victim of tight-money programs. Let the S&Ls, which invest primarily in housing, have more generous interest ceilings than the ordinary banks to attract funds for housing. Later, when Fed policy eases generally, reverse this."

**Control over installment terms**    Besides moral suasion and direct controls over margin borrowing and deposit terms, the Federal Reserve for many years had the power to set limits on installment contracts. Thus, in the years of the Korean conflict, the Fed made you put down a minimum amount when you bought cars, furniture, and other goods; and this same so-called "Regulation W" also required you to pay up on your charge accounts before buying more goods on credit. Regulation W seems to have been very effective, and the same has been true of similar regulations in Britain and elsewhere. But it became unpopular, and after the Korean crisis this important emergency power was allowed to lapse.

**Control over mortgage terms**    Congress had long empowered the Federal Reserve to set terms for mortgage down payments and the number of years for amortization of principal. This so-called "Regulation X" gave the Board powerful leverage over the pace of house-construction expenditure. This strong weapon of mortgage control was allowed by Congress to lapse in 1953. The Fed, with its philosophy of over-all quantitative controls rather than selective fiats, was perhaps not too sorry to see this power go; but it soon learned that Nature abhors a vacuum.

If the central bank will not wield these powers, some other body will. Financial intermediaries and governmental housing agencies competitive to the central bank have burgeoned. Thus, much housing is subsidized by the government: the Veterans Administration (VA) guarantees mortgage loans, and so does the Federal Housing Authority (FHA). The Federal National Mortgage Association ("Fannie Mae"), the Government National Mortgage Association ("Ginnie Mae"), and the Federal Home Loan Mortgage Corporation ("Freddie Mac") buy mortgages to make credit for housing more available. The federal S&Ls can borrow from the Federal Home Loan Bank, a government agency which threatens to become practically a second central bank, not always coordinated with the Federal Reserve.[6]

---

[6]These government agencies, which have no connection with the Federal Reserve, have often done what you might expect—they have worked at cross-purposes to the Board. Nowadays, public policy takes special interest in certain sectors of the credit market. It does not seem content to let interest rates find their own level in each market; it seeks to encourage activities such as housing and small business and to discourage others such as stock speculation. Some liberal congressmen have introduced, unsuccessfully, legislation requiring the Fed to ration out credit *qualitatively* by sector and by social purpose—so much to be assured for housing and other worthy activities, rather than "speculative" promotion schemes.

## INTERNATIONAL RESERVES MOVEMENTS

Until now, we have been speaking as if all the movements in total $M$ originate in actions of the Federal Reserve aimed to change bank Reserves in the direction desired by the authorities. There is, however, an *external* force that affects our $M$, namely, movements in and out of the country of international reserves—dollars or gold that come into or leave the country.[7] Such movements in or out of international reserves tend to induce changes in $M$ even when the Fed has done nothing. But it should be realized that the three already-discussed major weapons of Fed monetary policy can enable the authorities to *offset* any such changes in $M$ that are thought to be against the public interest.

Part Five will deal with international trade in detail; here we need only touch upon the banking aspects of international-reserve flows. When American exporters are selling more goods abroad than importers are importing, and consequently foreigners are paying us by shipping Reserves here, we shall see that the deposit of such Reserves in our banking system will give rise to the familiar 5-to-1 expansion process—just as in our earlier examples, where a seller of bonds to the Fed brought new Reserves to deposit in a member bank.

Suppose America is losing Reserves to pay for the excess of her total imports (including government spending abroad on military and foreign aid) over her total exports; there will then be a contraction of the $M$ supply. But, again, the Fed can use its powers to offset any such induced decline in Reserves and $M$.

This completes the discussion of how international reserve movements can themselves affect our money supply. As explained, such international influences on our $M$ *can be offset* by planned Federal Reserve open-market operations acting in the opposite direction. All over the world, central banks have often chosen to offset the influences of international gold movements. In particular, for 25 years after 1933 the United States was in the position of having so much gold that she could determine domestic policy, completely ignoring her international balance of payments and blithely offsetting any international-reserves movements she wanted to.

As we shall see in Part Five, when the Federal Reserve wants to lower interest rates in order to pursue a domestic stabilization policy of expansion, it must now take into account the following fact: If short-term interest rates are lowered here relative to those abroad, many foreigners will want to move their funds to higher-interest-rate markets abroad. There will be a resulting drain of "cool money" from our shores.

## RECENT MONETARY HISTORY

To see changes that have been taking place in recent years, refer to Fig. 17-2, which depicts the important economic variables published monthly by the Fed.

Shown in orange at the bottom is the important high-powered monetary base, *Member Bank Reserves*, provided by the Federal Reserve, in terms of which the banking system and the public determine the other money-supply aggregates. Note that the

---

[7]Official gold is supplemented in the 1970s by "paper gold" in the form of Special Drawing Rights (SDRs) in the International Monetary Fund, as Chapter 36 will discuss.

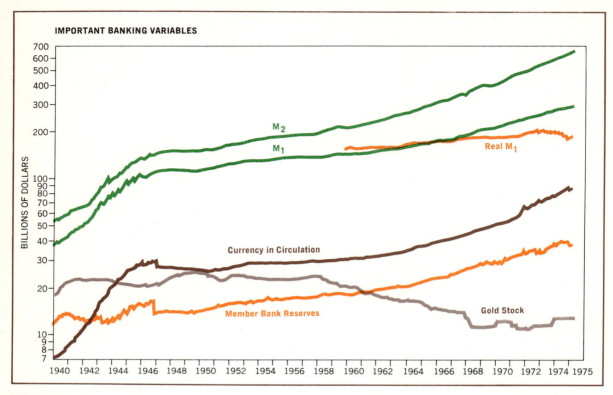

**FIG. 17-2**

**The Fed controls Reserves and total *M*, offsetting international drains**

Currency in circulation and Reserves underlying bank *M* have grown with the economy. The Fed has not let gold and international reserve flows call the tune. Note that the drop in gold during the 1960s was not accompanied by a drop in Reserves! (Source: *Federal Reserve Bulletin*.)

long drop in our gold supply, shown in green, was offset by the Fed's open-market operations so that it would not control the movement and trend of Reserves and of the other major money aggregates.[8]

Note the steady growth in the *currency* that the public has wanted to hold outside the banks, and its dramatic growth in World War II.

Most important, note the growth in $M_1$ (currency and checkable deposits) and the even more rapid recent-year growth in $M_2$ ($M_1$ plus time deposits). These have risen even more rapidly than the Reserves base because of periodic lowerings of legal

---

[8]In the mid-thirties you would have seen a tremendous bulge in excess reserves. Gold flowed here in great amounts; but with banks wary of loans and of further government securities, the result was no multiple expansion—merely a piling up of excess reserves. The Board, nervous always about inflation (even during the slump itself!), feared that these excess reserves might suddenly become the base of deposit expansion. So, as we have seen, they doubled reserve requirements, to bring excess reserves under control. In brisk times, when banks can find attractive earning assets, excess reserves do not become substantial. As the Federal Funds market (in which banks lend to each other) has developed, even the small country banks have cut down on their level of excess reserves.

required-reserve ratios. As price inflation in the 1970s quickened, the Fed also quickened the growth rate of Reserves and of the other money aggregates.

This was both cause and effect: If the rise in prices associated with the OPEC quadrupling of oil prices, with worldwide harvest failures and rising food prices, and with the depreciation of the dollar relative to foreign exchange rates—if these *exogenous* increases in inflation had not been met by the Fed's accommodating step-up in money-supply growth, stagnation would have been the result. But one does not have to be a monetarist to recognize that such accommodating behavior by the Fed to postpone recession served also as a reinforcing *endogenous* cause of the inflation.

To bring out this chicken-egg-chicken dilemma, Fig. 17-2 shows for the 1960s and 1970s the "real money supply," defined as an index number of the ratio of an index of $M_1$ divided by an index of the price level (the GNP deflator). Note how the brown curve of real money supply fell in the 1973–1975 recession, widely regarded as the most serious recession in the post–World War II epoch, the Age after Keynes. Many analysts blamed the Federal Reserve for the virulence and duration of this recession, attributing it to the Fed's concern to end double-digit rates of annual inflation even at the cost of heavy unemployment and prolonged stagnation. Defenders of the Fed claimed that this was the necessary price to keep inflation from accelerating.

Figure 17-3 shows how monetary control affects interest rates and how discount borrowing by the member banks reacts to any credit tightness or looseness engineered by the Fed's open-market operations.

The top panel shows that *excess reserves* have declined as the Federal Funds market was perfected to permit any banks with spare reserves to lend them to other banks short of reserves, at the supply-and-demand-determined *Federal Funds rate* shown in orange in the bottom panel. It also shows how *discounts* tend to rise whenever the Fed puts pressure on interest rates and raises them above the official discount rate that banks must pay for borrowing from the Fed's discount window.

The middle panel shows excess reserves minus discounts: we call this "net free reserves" when this difference is positive, and "net borrowed reserves" when discounts exceed excess reserves. When the Fed is being tight in its monetary and credit policies and interest rates are rising, net free reserves tend to be negative. Notice how net borrowed reserves ease back toward zero in periods when the Fed has shifted from leaning against the wind of expansion to leaning against the wind of recession or stagnation, as in 1967, 1970, and 1975.

The bottom panel of Fig. 17-3 shows how interest rates move up when the Fed is putting on the brakes, and how they move down when it is easing credit and trying to be expansionary. Note that short-term interest rates, so-called *Treasury-bill yields,* are more volatile upward and downward than are the *yields on long-term bonds.* The *Federal Funds* rate is seen to move closely with bill rates.

To see how borrowers and lenders, once they have come to expect and anticipate price inflation, tend to build into the nominal interest rates a premium to allow for inflation, notice how the nominal rates have risen above the *"real interest rate"* since 1960: The brown curve of real interest rate is calculated by subtracting from the nominal long-term interest rate on AAA bonds the annual percentage increase in the Consumer Price Index for the previous five years. Notice how little *real* interest rates have risen in the inflation years of the 1960s and 1970s.

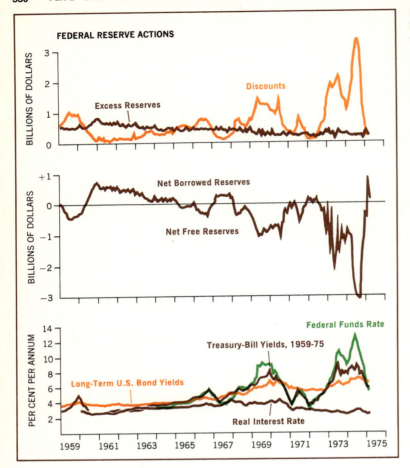

FEDERAL RESERVE ACTIONS

**FIG. 17-3**

**Interest rates and credit tightness follow changes in Reserves**

When discounts exceed excess reserves, net free reserves turn negative (becoming net borrowed reserves). Usually, this means credit is tight and interest rates are high.

When business slackens and the Fed pursues easy-money policies, its open-market purchases give banks new Reserves in order to encourage expansion of $M$ and $C + I + G$. By lowering or raising the discount rate relative to short-term market interest rates (such as Federal Funds or Treasury-bill rates), the Fed can encourage or discourage discounts. (Source: *Federal Reserve Bulletin*.)

## REPORT CARD FOR THE FEDERAL RESERVE: MONETARISM VERSUS THE MAJORITY

How has the Fed been doing? Expert opinion is divided. In the 1920s some thought the Federal Reserve had learned how to tame the business cycle forever. The Great Crash of 1929 and the Great Depression deflated that view, and ever since, most experts think that monetary policy must be *reinforced* by stabilizing fiscal policies.

But there is one important minority dissent to this view. A school called the "monetarists," originating at the University of Chicago and led by the able economist Professor Milton Friedman, believes that essentially everything that can be done to control macroeconomic aggregates—inflationary gaps and epochs of depression and slow growth—has to be done by control of the money supply *alone*. Fiscal policy, Professor Friedman insists, is important in helping to shape how much of the macroeconomic total is in the public sector as against the private sector and in shaping the trend of interest rates and of the consumption share of GNP. But on the basis of his studies of the history of money in the United States and in many other countries, Professor Friedman is convinced that fiscal policy per se has essentially no predictable effect *of any significance* on the prospects for inflation or deflation, for high employment or mass unemployment.

Monetarism represents an extreme view. But since it is proposed by economists with serious scientific interests, it should not be rejected just because it does not involve a mid-ground position. After all, scientific truth *could* turn out to be on one extreme rather than in the middle.

**Monetarism versus the eclectic majority**   The present author, having studied and weighed the evidence in favor of monetarism, has formed the opinion that where it differs from the majority eclectic view of the so-called "post-Keynesian neoclassical synthesis," it is implausible. That synthesis maintains (*a*) that *both* fiscal and monetary policies matter much, (*b*) that the velocity of circulation of money is induced to increase systematically when interest rates rise and make it economical for people to turn over their cash balances more rapidly, and (*c*) that open-market purchases which create new $M$ for the community have their stimulating effects on GNP spending somewhat offset by the reduction in the liquid interest-bearing government bonds now held by the community. Monistic reliance on $M$ growth alone to explain the total of $C + I + G = $ GNP does seem an extreme doctrine.

Thus, I think that the tax cut of 1975 had a stimulating effect on the economy beyond that associated with the Fed's creation of new $M$ to help finance that move. Professor Friedman disagrees. Professor Friedman believes that the tax surcharge of 1968–1969 had no effects on the current rate of inflation that are not attributable to the money-supply behavior of that period. Indeed, to a monetarist, the unprecedentedly long post-Kennedy expansion of the 1960s would have taken place even if the budget had been always in balance at a low level—provided the Fed had made $M$ grow as it actually did during the decade. The majority of the experts do not believe this, arguing that interest rates early in the decade would have been much lower and GNP lower than occurred—because of the difference in the velocity of circulation that would have been induced by increasing money alone.

Economics is not an exact science. We cannot repeat the 1970s under controlled conditions to settle the debate. Therefore, an author should present in his book a framework of analysis that can be shaded in favor of either of these two scientifically proposed models. This text has been written to make this possible.[9] The most important

---

[9]Reference can be made to M. Friedman and A. Schwartz, *A Monetary History of the United States* (Princeton, N.J.: Princeton University Press for the National Bureau of Economic Research, 1963), and to articles pro and con monetarism by M. Friedman, P. A. Samuelson, and Walter Heller in P. A. Samuelson, *Readings in Economics* (McGraw-Hill, New York, 1973, 7th ed.). A list of prominent monetarists would include the following names: Allan Meltzer (Carnegie-Mellon), Karl Brunner (Rochester), Beryl Sprinkel (Harris Trust, Chicago), Leif Olsen (First National City Bank, New York), Leonall Andersen (Federal Reserve Bank of St. Louis), and many foreign economists as well. Some monetarists have proposed that the proof of the pudding is in the eating: which method *predicts* best, the $C + I + G$ method or the MV $\longrightarrow$ GNP method? Among the monetarists, the Federal Reserve Bank of St. Louis seemed to be consistently best in predicting before 1972; but in the 1970s, in comparison with eclectic forecasters, even it was scored as having a high average squared-error-of-prediction of GNP and of $P$. However, few economists in either camp would rest their case on alleged accuracy of short-run predictions.

consideration is that Friedman's researches have joined with the researches of post-Keynesians, such as Yale's James Tobin and MIT's Franco Modigliani, to insist that *money does matter much*, to work out the *channels by which it works*, and to deny the view that some Keynesian followers took after 1939 (and which still prevailed in Britain's 1959 Radcliffe Report) that money does not matter much or at all.

**Leaning against the wind?**   These disputes are not academic. They shape policy. You might guess that a monetarist like Professor Friedman, convinced that money matters exclusively or most, would want to use control over the money supply to fight against the ups and downs of business activity. But you would be wrong. Dr. Friedman insists that *no* "fine tuning" will work: Money matters more than anything else, but even *its* effects are not perfectly predictable, there being always uncertain lags between cause and effect. Reinforcing his skepticism concerning fine tuning is Dr. Friedman's philosophical position that "rules" and not "discretionary authority by men or committees" should prevail. Hence, his sole recommendation for monetary policy is elegantly simple.

**Monetarists tell the Fed to stabilize the growth of the money supply—every year and every month—at some agreed-upon constant rate—say, $5\frac{1}{2}$ per cent per year, or at the least within the range of 5 to 6 per cent. Then, forgetting active fiscal policy and all fine tuning, let the free market take care of the rest—of interest rates, unemployment, price levels.**

In logic, one could be a monetarist—i.e., a believer in the *sole* importance of $M$—without giving up a "lean against the wind" philosophy. Such a monetarist would not want to set a constant-growth-rate-in-$M$ goal; but rather a stabilizing, *counter-cyclical* $M$ policy.

But mere logic cannot settle this issue. If the time lags between $M$ and GNP are long and variable, a well-intentioned countercyclical policy might result in doing more harm than good: thus, the Fed zigs to counter the economy's present zag; but by the time this act takes effect, the economy is on its next zig. While such whipsawing cannot be ruled out, statistical analysis of "automatic control theory in the presence of errors" will show that neither is it inevitable. One must pragmatically relate optimal $M$ policy to the pattern of experience.

**The future**   Economics is an exciting subject because there is always much still to learn. Good-tempered debate on fiscal and monetary policy should gradually identify and perhaps resolve reasoned differences of opinion. It is a tribute to Professor Friedman that new dogmas are being tested before they harden into old orthodoxies.

## SUMMARY

1   The Federal Reserve is a central bank, a bank for bankers. Its duty is to control the monetary base (currency plus bank Reserves) and through control of this "high-powered money" to control the community's supply of money. Its five-step mode of action goes thus: (1) It contracts bank Reserves, which (2) causes multiple contractions in total $M$ deposits, which (3) makes credit expensive (high interest

rates) and hard to get, which (4) depresses private and public investment spending, which (5) puts a multiplied damper on money income and prices. (Fig. 17-1.)

2 The powerful weapons the Fed uses are (*a*) open-market operations, (*b*) discount-rate policy, and (*c*) changes in legal reserve requirements. Minor weapons used at times by central banks are moral suasion and selective controls over time-deposit interest ceilings, margin borrowing, installment sales, and mortgage credit terms.

3 Sales by the Fed of government securities to the open market represent a positive act which reduces its assets and liabilities and which reduces the Reserves of the member banks, and hence their base for deposits. People end up with less *M* and more government bonds. Open-market purchases do the opposite, ultimately expanding *M* at the expense of outstanding bonds. Powerful day-to-day open-market operations should be understood by every student of monetary policy.

4 Outflows of international reserves will reduce Reserves and *M* unless offset by FRB open-market purchases of bonds (as was done in recent years). Inflows have opposite effects until offset. Domestic macroeconomic goals are sometimes constrained by international considerations.

5 The main facts of finance, as shown by the charts of changing Reserves and money supply, are to be understood in terms of this chapter's analysis. The view of monetarists—that the money supply dominates aggregate demand and that it should be set always at a fixed growth rate—challenges the view of the majority's post-Keynesian synthesis—that, while *M* matters much, so also do investment, tax, and government expenditure changes which shift $C + I + G$, and that "leaning against the wind" will improve on automatic *M* rules. All agree, "Money matters."

## CONCEPTS FOR REVIEW

the five-step sequence
high-powered monetary base
availability and cost of credit
Federal Reserve balance sheet
open-market purchases and sales
discount rate, discounts
legal reserve ratio requirements
FOMC Reserves primary target

selective controls: moral suasion,
  interest ceilings, and
  margin requirements
net free reserves (+ or −)
net borrowed reserves (− or +)
offsets to gold movements
monetarism, leaning against the
  wind

## QUESTIONS FOR DISCUSSION

1 In what Federal Reserve District are you? Where is the nearest branch?

2 Trace the effects of a $1 billion open-market purchase; an open-market sale. In terms of Fig. 17-1, pencil in open-market operations and discount borrowing at *A* on the orange Reserves input branch. Pencil in legal reserve ratio changes as the gearing at *B* on the green output-of-*M* branch.

3   Trace the effects of a doubling of reserve requirements; a halving. Which alters bank earnings more: open-market or reserve-requirement action?

4   List weapons of control of the Reserve authorities. How powerful are they to control (a) M, (b) interest rates, (c) prices, (d) employment and unemployment?

5   How might ceilings on time deposits affect housing?

6   "Gold movements affected prices only because we used them as a barometer, signaling us to expand or contract total $M$ supply. Of course, the gold standard was a stupid system; but it was wiser to tie ourselves to such an imperfect system than to trust corrupt legislatures whose tendency is always to print inflationary paper money." Discuss.

7   Discuss the following 1939 FRB statement: "The Federal Reserve System can see to it that banks have enough reserves to make money available to commerce, industry, and agriculture at low rates; but it cannot make the people borrow, and it cannot make the public spend the deposits that result when the banks do make loans and investments."

8   Give both sides of the debates between monetarists and the post-Keynesian majority. How have the events of the 1970s tilted the scientific issues?

9   "The Fed was too expansionary in $M$ (whether in $M_1$ or $M_2$) in the election year of 1972. GNP = $PQ$ grew too much. Since $Q$ reached growth ceilings set by tight labor markets and by bottlenecks of industrial capacity, it was inflation in $P$ that resulted. Aghast at the double-digit rate of annual price inflation (and ignoring the fact that some of it was *exogenously* related to oil and food scarcities), the Fed was so tight in 1973–1974 in controlling the *real-money* supply (i.e., $M/P$) that it brought on the 9 per cent unemployment rates of 1975. From now on, the Fed must be responsible to directives from the Congress on how much 'stag' in 'stagflation' it should create and on how much 'flation' it should tolerate." Comment on this summary statement of the policy debates of recent years. Trace out and spell out just what is meant in each part of the argument.

Chapters 12 and 13 showed how saving and investment schedules intersect to determine the level of national income. And the succeeding chapters have shown how changes in Federal Reserve policy affect the community's stock of money.

This chapter relates the schedules of income determination with those of monetary analysis. Monetary analysis is seen to fit in well with modern theory of income determination. And the stage is set for combined stabilization policy: (1) central bank monetary policies, and (2) government fiscal policies (public expenditure and taxation, with the implied budget deficit or surplus).

It is these macroeconomic programs—fiscal policy and monetary policy—that have to be coordinated to achieve the goals of a progressive economy: one that enjoys reasonable price stability and lives up to its production potentialities.

This chapter shows how stabilization policies work and interact. We leave more detailed study of fiscal-policy issues for the final chapter of Part Two.

## MONEY, LIQUIDITY PREFERENCE, MARGINAL EFFICIENCY, MULTIPLIER

The previous chapters showed that $M$ expansion by the central and commercial banks can shift upward the $C + I + G$ intersection point of Chapter 12. What is the same thing, an increase in $M$ shifts upward the $SS$-$II$ intersection point of Chapter 12, as follows:

When the Fed increases the money supply, $M$, this primarily affects investment, shifting $II$ upward. The Fed's expansion of $M$ bids up bond prices and thus bids down interest rates and makes credit loans more easily available to investors. Now it has become more profitable to undertake new investment projects. In the simplest case, the sequence is this:

$$M \text{ up} \rightarrow i \text{ down} \rightarrow I \text{ up} \rightarrow GNP \text{ up, up}$$

About this time there was a cry . . . for more paper-money. . . . I was on the side of an addition, being persuaded that the first small sum struck in 1723 had done much good, by increasing the trade, employment, and number of inhabitants in the province. . . . The utility of this currency became by time and experience so evident, as never afterwards to be much disputed. . . . Tho' . . . there are limits beyond which the quantity may be hurtful.
BENJAMIN FRANKLIN

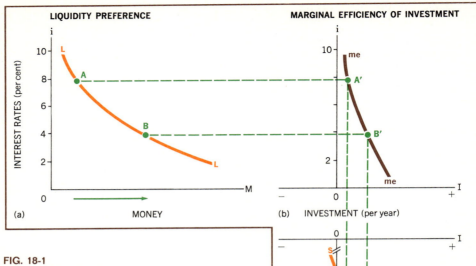

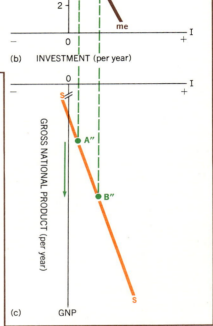

**FIG. 18-1**

**Central bank affects money, thereby affecting investment and GNP**

When the Fed raises M from A to B, that initially lowers interest rates, along the so-called "liquidity-preference" schedule.

The reduced interest rates and increased availability of credit increases investment from A' to B', along the brown so-called "marginal-efficiency-of-investment" schedule of (b).

The higher investment, by the usual multiplier process, raises income from A'' to B''. (Velocity, V, is a bit lower but not enough to keep the new MV and GNP from being larger.)

Can you trace the reverse process by which open-market sales by the Fed will contract M and GNP, and do this by raising interest rates enough to cut down on I?

New graphs can illuminate this; and they can also show the process by which a shift in C + I + G schedules—as, e.g., a change due to a technical investment boom—can shift upward the velocity of circulation (V) in the MV = PQ relation of Chapter 15 and thereby increase GNP even when M itself is unchanged.

Chapter 15 (page 283) showed that the demand for money, along with depending positively on the level of income transactions, also depends inversely on the interest and profit yields that have to be sacrificed in order to have the safety and convenience of holding M. To get the community to hold more M, the Fed must therefore *bid down interest rates enough to make it advantageous for people to economize less on their cash balances and hold more M.* The orange so-called "liquidity-preference schedule" of Fig. 18-1(a) summarizes how an increase in M resulting from monetary policy (open-market purchases, etc.) leads initially to a reduced interest rate—from A's 8 per cent to B's 4 per cent.

Figure 18-1(b) picks up the story to show how reduced interest rates (and what does not show on the graph but is lurking in the background, namely, greater *availability* of credit) make more investment profitable. On Fig. 18-1(b)'s brown so-called "marginal-efficiency-of-investment" schedule, the drop in interest rate induces the rise in investment from A' to B'.

Figure 18-1(c) is merely Chapter 12's saving-investment diagram, page 222, turned on its side to line it up with Fig. 18-1(b)'s investment axis. Note that the interest-rate drop from A to B led to the investment rise from A' to B', and this (through the multiplier) has led to the GNP rise from A'' to B''.

To clinch understanding of this vital sequence, consider the following reverse case where monetary policy is contracting to wipe out an inflationary gap:

**Monetary contraction (open-market sales, increased legal reserve ratios, etc.) bids up interest rates[1] and decreases credit availability. This depresses investment spending, and via the multiplier, depresses income by even more. The basic sequence is now**

**M down → i up → I down → GNP down, down**

Retrace the reverse BA, B'A', and B''A'' sequence in Fig. 18-1 to see how money and income determination interact.

*Depression model.* This reconciliation of the theories of money and of income determination is, of course, oversimplified and needs some qualifications. For example, it does not emphasize what can happen in *severe depression* when the liquidity-preference curve is practically *horizontal* because interest rates are already so low that people are quite indifferent whether they hold M or the near-M government Treasury bills that the Fed wants to swap for M by its open-market purchases. In such a rare, but possible, case, the potency of monetary policy is at least temporarily very low. This is summarized in the aphorism, "The central bank can pull on a string (to curb booms), but it can't *push on a string* (to reverse deep slumps)." Indeed, in such depressed times the profit expectations of businessmen are likely to be so low that they would not employ men and machines on new investment projects even if you let them borrow temporarily at a zero interest rate. In this case, the green marginal-efficiency schedule of Fig. 18-1(b) is practically vertical; and again the chain of monetary action loses potency. (It is these "depression models" which are often, but wrongly, associated with the name of Keynes; and if they were his sole cases, his ideas would be of more limited interest.)

*Classical case.* The opposite "classical" or "monetarist" case, equally extreme, occurs when the liquidity schedule is practically vertical, so that each unit of M is under a strong compulsion to circulate at a constant velocity (with V a hard constant).[2] As most economists interpret the history of the last few centuries, this extreme case is not deemed realistic. They cannot agree with the extreme classical view known as "Say's Law of Conservation of Purchasing Power." The Appendix to this chapter discusses this matter further. It is enough here to characterize Say's Law as alleging:

"There cannot be any such thing as a saving-and-investment problem. What is not consumed is surely destined to be spent on investment goods, without the possibility of any snag."

---

[1]Of course, if this monetary constriction is successful in ending rapid price inflation, interest rates in the longer run will no longer have to include a premium to cover depreciation of the dollar's real purchasing power. So the *initial* rise in interest rates from M restriction may well be reversed *in the end.*

[2]Or where the marginal-efficiency schedule is so horizontal that the slightest reduction in interest rate is enough to wipe out any deflationary gap and the slightest rise in interest is enough to wipe out any inflationary gap. Appendix readers will find more on these polar cases there.

**Qualifications**  Eschewing polar cases, we must notice a point raised by experts in corporate finance. They point out that many firms, particularly large ones, finance their investments *out of retained earnings* and the cash flow generated by their own operations. Many avoid going to the banks or outside markets for borrowings or stock flotations. (EXAMPLE: The giant Du Pont Company did not borrow a cent for more than 50 years, and yet it was an important source of progress in chemicals.)

To the degree that investment depends upon internal funds that are insulated from market fluctuations in interest-rate and credit availability, the potency of monetary policy is just that much less: it then takes greater action by the Fed on $M$ to offset fluctuations in $V$. (One could go on to give other bits of evidence used to play down the importance of monetary policy, as, for example, the fact that when investors are uncertain about the future, small changes in safe-asset interest rates may have little effect upon the high profit rates investors require as inducement to undertake investment; and hence $I$ may be insensitive to Fed policy. Both in 1966 and 1969, the only obvious impact of hard-money policies was on construction—not on business-equipment or inventory spending. And in 1973–1974, housing was hit hard.)

Qualifications are not all in the direction of playing down the importance of $M$. We have noted in passing that credit policy does have some influence on $G$ and $C$ in $C + I + G$. Higher market evaluations of land, plant, and equipment, and of securities generally, will shift $CC$ up. In the long run, if the increase in $M$ comes, let us say, from Fed financing of a new government deficit (and not merely from a swap by the Fed's Open Market Committee of $M$ for near-$M$), the new $M$ *adds directly to people's net worth*, and this does lead them, other things equal, to spend more on $C$, on $I$, and on $G$.[3]

There is another channel by which $M$ changes gain in potency. New $M$ and lower $i$ should raise common-stock prices. Now corporations can float new issues of stock more easily and cheaply. So with cost of capital down, corporations will be induced to expand their investment; again, up goes $C + I + G$ and GNP.

### FISCAL POLICY AND INCOME DETERMINATION

Let us now resurvey fiscal-policy powers of government. Aside from the central bank, the government has another major way of affecting current spending, as we have seen in Chapter 13. As part of its *fiscal policy*, the government can expand its *expenditures*: build useful public roads and schools, hire more civil servants, increase anti-pollution expenditure, do a hundred and one useful (or foolish) things to expand total spending. This could all be shown in a saving-investment diagram like Fig. 18-1(c).

---

[3] Important too is the fact that high interest rates tend to depress stock-market prices; and when people's net worth thereby drops, they cut their $CC$ spending. Some economists used to hope that higher interest rates would stimulate saving and kill consumption; i.e., they hoped an interest rise would shift up the $SS$ schedule in Fig. 18-1(c), thereby reinforcing the effect of a downward shift in $II$. Experience, and the analysis of Chapter 30, suggest that outside the area of installment-financed consumer durables, these effects are probably weak and cannot be much counted on. (WARNING: The $B$ points in Fig. 18-1 are final equilibria only if the Fed now creates just enough further $M$ to satisfy enhanced *income* needs for new transaction balances; otherwise, we repeat the cycle with $LL$ shifted up by the raised GNP level, finding final equilibria somewhere generally north of the midpoint between $A$ and $B$. See the Hicks-Hansen diagrams in the Appendix for a rigorous handling of this transactions-need feedback problem.)

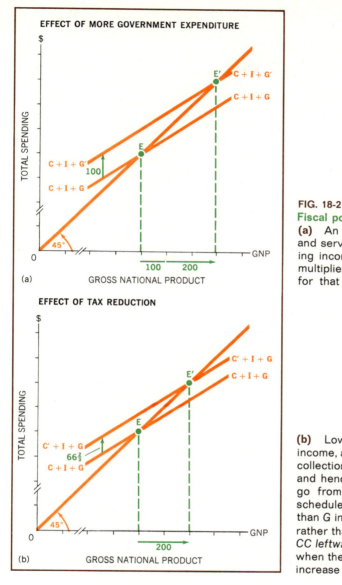

**EFFECT OF MORE GOVERNMENT EXPENDITURE**

(a)

**EFFECT OF TAX REDUCTION**

(b)

**FIG. 18-2**

**Fiscal policy means public expenditure and tax policy**
**(a)** An increase in government expenditures on goods and services will shift $C + I + G$ up to $C + I + G'$, raising income to $E'$. Moreover, there is involved the usual multiplier effect of induced consumption spending (and, for that matter, induced private investment spending).

**(b)** Lowering taxes has similar expansionary effects on income, as was seen after the 1975 Ford tax cut. Lower tax collection gives you more disposable income out of GNP, and hence shifts the consumption schedule upward. We go from $E$ to $E'$ as a result of the new $C' + I + G$ schedule. (Dollar for dollar, tax reduction is a little weaker than $G$ increase. Why? Because some tax rebate is saved rather than used to shift $CC$ up. A tax cut of 100 will shift $CC$ *leftward* that much, but *upward* only by $\frac{2}{3} \times 100 = 66\frac{2}{3}$ when the MPC is $\frac{2}{3}$. Recall Fig. 13-8.) Show that a tax-rate increase shifts $C + I + G$ rightward and lowers $E$.

But better still, we can show it as an *upward shift in the G component* of the $C + I + G$ schedule that was used as an alternative way to show income equilibrium. Figure 18-2(a) recapitulates the demonstration on page 243 of how an expansion of public expenditure $G$ leads to an expansion of income.

The same type of chart[4] can show, in Fig. 18-2(b), the other side of fiscal policy—

[4]The treatment here recapitulates the treatment on page 245 of Chapter 13 and best handles the effects of personal income taxes. For more complicated analysis of indirect and other taxes, also taking account of tax effects on investment, see intermediate texts.

changes in tax collections. To raise GNP, the fiscal authorities cut taxes: a permanent tax cut gives people higher disposable income; and since they have a positive propensity to consume out of extra income, this means they will consume more.

How can we show the increased consumption on Fig. 18-2(b)? We can show the effect of reduced taxes as an *upward shift* of the *CC* schedule, which is plotted against GNP and is a major component of the pictured $C + I + G$ schedule. With taxes lower, we subtract less from each level of GNP to get the corresponding level of disposable income. So, with higher disposable income corresponding to each GNP, we must show higher consumption—hence the *higher CC* and $C + I + G$ curves.

We may summarize the effects of fiscal policy:

**Increased G raises income by raising the GG component of $C + I + G$. Reduced taxes raise the CC component of the $C + I + G$ schedule. Both together—which also means deficit financing or a reduction in the budgetary surplus—result in an even greater upward shift of the $C + I + G$ schedule and of equilibrium income. In the reverse case of contractionary fiscal policy, the final $C + I + G$ schedule shifts downward.**

Here is a good test of one's understanding of the mechanics of fiscal policy:

Show the effect on GNP of the massive 1964 tax cut; and then see what the effect would have been if there had been a matching cut in *G*, as some people then recommended. For such matching changes, expenditure cuts would slightly outweigh tax changes.

**Lessened potency of temporary tax changes**   An important qualification is in order. Suppose, as in 1968, the government introduces a tax rise to combat the Vietnam inflation. But suppose it says that the new tax surcharge is only going to be *temporary*. Then, definitely, the deflationary effects on total GNP spending will be lessened by the fact that everybody expects the tax to apply only for a temporary time. Similarly, a tax rebate, like the one in 1975, is less expansionary than a sustained drop in the tax rate.

Let's review why. Suppose a typical family earns $15,000 a year, pays $2,000 in normal taxes. Its permanent disposable income, what it can count on and plan for, is $13,000. So, for the next many years, it will become adjusted to a living standard appropriate to this presumed level of permanent income.

But now suppose a temporary tax surcharge of $1,000 is passed by Congress. Everyone knows it is to last only one or two years. Should our family now get adjusted to a living standard of only $12,000 of disposable income—cutting down on its consumption, *CC*, spending by the 10 per cent temporary cut in its this year's income? That would go against human nature—and ordinary prudence. Better, surely, for the family to dip a little into the rate at which it normally saves. *Temporary tax-rate changes have less potency than permanent tax-rate changes.*

## BUDGET DEFICITS INTERACT WITH *M* CHANGES

So far, we've been treating monetary policy and fiscal policy as if they take place independently. On one occasion, the Fed acts to change *M*. On another occasion, Congress legislates a budget deficit. How nice to be able to observe these separate controlled experiments and learn experimentally exactly what is the separate potency of fiscal policy and of monetary policy.

But, of course, it doesn't happen that way in real life. Not only do these two separate things tend to happen simultaneously so as to frustrate the economic historian's chance to determine the separate effects of each. Worse than that, or actually better than that from the standpoint of policy, often an act of fiscal deficit spending will be *purposely* combined with an act of central bank money creation. Much more powerful will be the expansionary effect on GNP of a fiscal deficit that is financed by $M$ creation than of one financed by government bond sales to the public. It is no accident that mixed economies deliberately combine the two macroeconomic weapons.

To verify this, contrast the case (*a*) of a deficit or new $G$ expenditure financed by $M$ change, with (*b*) one financed by bond sales. In the last case, start with an initial increase in $C + I + G$ and GNP. With $M$ unchanged, what will happen to interest rates now that GNP has gone up? To get $M$ for their new transactions, people will be selling off some of their bonds, thereby depressing bond prices and raising interest rates. But these higher interest rates will mean, other things being equal, that $I$ now drops a bit. So our initial increase in $C + I + G$, due to new higher $G$, will be later reduced by an induced slight drop in $I$. By contrast, in (*a*) the Fed, to match the deficit, creates the new $M$ needed to keep interest rates from rising and $I$ from falling. So the new $G$ is a complete add-on to the $C + I + G$ schedule.

The same thing can be put in the monetarist language of $MV = PQ$. A fiscal deficit in the form of higher $G$ will push up interest rates if the Fed holds $M$ constant. People will cause $V$, the rate of turnover of their cash balance, to rise a bit now that the interest cost of holding their cash balances has gone up. The higher $V$ with fixed $M$ means higher GNP. But how much more expansionary the same fiscal policy will be if the Fed, aiming to keep interest rates from rising, acts to create new $M$ in $MV = PQ$.[5]

## THE SYNTHESIS AT WORK: TECHNOLOGICAL UNEMPLOYMENT?

To appreciate how modern tools of income and monetary analysis really work, let us here apply them as a case study to one of the great problems of our day.

A notable feature of our time is the development of "automation." Will this "new industrial revolution," in which machinery plays a new role, be a curse or a blessing to mankind? In particular, does it not confront the modern economy with the threat of mass unemployment?

Our tools enable us to give an optimistic answer; but our optimistic answer is quite different from the old-fashioned one, which simply *asserted* that inventions would *necessarily* create new jobs *just as fast* as they killed off old ones. Such a view was based upon an uninformed faith, and it was not persuasive. Sometimes experience accorded with it; sometimes experience went against it. In short, it made the outcome depend merely on *luck*. Our contemporary answer is truly more optimistic.

**What automation is**    The word "automation" was coined in 1947 by Del Harder, vice-president of Ford Motor Company, to apply to "automatic handling of parts

---

[5] In the polar case of the extreme monetarist, $V$ is a hard constant that will not rise even with higher $i$. In such a pole, an increase in $G$ has no effects on GNP, being offset by an equivalent reduction in $C + I$. But there seems no plausible reason to expect people in their inventory decisions on how much $M$ to hold to take no account of the higher interest yields they must now forgo. Only in the most extreme hyperinflation, when people are holding absolutely minimal cash balances and $V$ cannot be speeded up further (even by a doubling of the rate of inflation and melting of the purchasing power of cash held), would we expect this extreme pole to be reached.

between progressive production processes." At about the same time, John Diebold, a management engineer, shortened the word "automatization" into "automation." Diebold stressed the use of control devices that operate by means of "feedback."

Automation has still other meanings. Giant electronic calculators, which are a millionfold faster than hand machines, have simplified data processing and record keeping. One machine does the work of a hundred clerks. Numbers recorded on magnetic tape can make a milling machine or lathe turn out intricate copies of a master pattern. Some modern digital computers can beat a good player at checkers, but none can yet beat a champion. None can yet play a really fine game of chess; at simple games such as ticktacktoe, the machine plays a perfect game.

**Displacement of labor?** Whether one thinks automation is something absolutely new or represents a great postwar quickening of developments already known in principle, all admit it is a force to reckon with. Automation will presumably increase productivity; otherwise it would not be installed. Does this mean it will reduce the total need for labor and create mass unemployment? Back in the depressed 1930s, long before we knew the term "automation," there was much fear of "technological unemployment." Should we again worry that man will become obsolete?

The late Norbert Wiener, MIT mathematician and one-time prodigy, who coined the name "cybernetics" (from the Greek word for "helmsman"), has pronounced on this subject in the following dramatic way:[6]

The industrial revolution has . . . displaced man and the beast as a source of power. . . . The factory of the future . . . will be controlled by something like a modern high-speed computing machine. . . . We can expect an abrupt and final cessation of the demand for the type of factory labor performing repetitive tasks . . . an intermediate transitional period of disastrous confusion. . . . Industry will be flooded with the new tools to the extent that they appear to yield immediate profits, irrespective of what long-time damage they can do. . . . It is perfectly clear that this will produce an unemployment situation, in comparison with which the present recession and even the depression of the thirties will seem a pleasant joke.

**The forward look** Any increase in productivity will indeed, *if output does not increase,* throw men out of work. In the Great Depression men readily believed total product would remain the same, that desired output would fail to grow with the growth of productivity. This view makes you look at unemployment in the following way: "Why did those unemployed workers over there lose their jobs? Which machines displaced them?" And so forth.

Modern students of income determination urge a more fruitful tack. They say:

**Regardless of why those men lost their jobs, why aren't there enough *new* jobs for them? What fiscal and monetary policies are needed to create the new dollar purchasing power necessary for them to be hired anew?**

"Satchel" Paige, the famous baseball player, once advised: "Don't look back, someone may be gaining on you." This is good advice in economics, too. Do not look back to

[6] N. Wiener, *The Human Use of Human Beings* (Houghton Mifflin, Boston, 1950), pp. 180–189.

find what caused past layoffs; look forward to see what you have to do to restore high employment. This is more efficient—and more helpful.

Better still, this approach means you do not have to decide whether the pessimists are right who argue that inventions will kill off more jobs than they create. Why care? *In every case we know that high employment will require monetary and fiscal policies of the correct magnitudes, and—problems of "stagflation" aside!—mixed economies know what needs doing.* Wiener's 1949 prediction of doomsday has come no closer to being reality.

**Graphical restoration of high-employment equilibrium**    To apply this fruitful approach, we can use our consumption + investment + government spending schedule and look for income equilibrium where the $C + I + G$ schedule just intersects the 45° helping line. Figure 18-3 illustrates this.

Suppose that automation makes labor 30 per cent more productive. This means that the same full-employment labor force could produce 30 per cent more real GNP; hence, the $FF$ full-employment line of Fig. 18-3(a) is now shifted rightward 30 per cent to $F'F'$. Let us make quite unfavorable assumptions: (*a*) that government leaves its expenditure $G$ as it was; and that the new machines are so cheap and short-lived that they can be introduced just by using up the depreciation allowances of the wearing-out machines, so that (*b*) investment $I$ is no greater than before; finally, that automation gives people the same things for less but does not whet their appetites for new gadgets, which means that (*c*) the propensity-to-consume schedule (and propensity to save) will be exactly the same as before in terms of disposable income.

In short, we assume the $C + I + G$ schedule has none of its components shifted as a result of automation. Then the schedule must continue to intersect at the same $E$ point as before. Whereas this $E$ point was previously a full-employment equilibrium, with automation it now represents a point of mass unemployment. A large fraction of the populace is now out of work, and many are working only part time. If this were the case, who can doubt that unions and government would agitate to cut the length of the working week and sabotage new methods and machines? And who could blame them?

**Macroeconomics to the rescue**    Even this pessimistic case can be cured by proper therapy. Here is how. Let the Federal Reserve fight this slump by increasing $M$ and making credit much cheaper and much more freely available. (Recall open-market purchases, lowering of reserve requirements, and lowering of discount rates.) What will this do to the $I$ schedule? Push it up. At the same time, let the government cut down on the heavy taxing it was doing in the previous full-employment situation. This will increase people's disposable incomes, will increase their consumption spending, and thus shift upward the $C$ part of the $C + I + G$ schedule. (Maybe $I$ will get further shifted, too.) Without increasing government expenditure directly, we could thus shift the $C + I + G$ schedule far enough upward until the new $C' + I' + G'$ schedule intersects the 45° line at the new full-employment level $E'$. Alternatively, since there are always pressing program needs in the public sector that merit doing when society gets new economic resources, an expansion of $G$ could be used to help shift $C + I + G$ up to the target level.

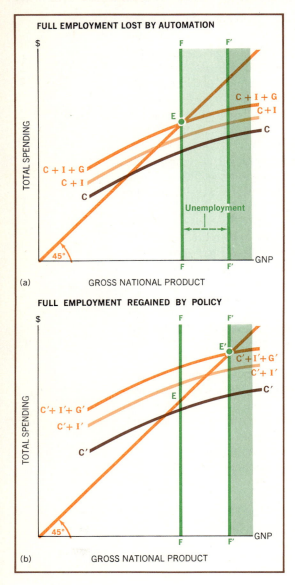

**FIG. 18-3**

**Macroeconomic policies liberate mixed economies from unemployment due to automation or underconsumption**

**(a)** If inventions raise productivity 30 per cent, *FF* of producible full employment shifts 30 per cent rightward to *F'F'*. If *C, I,* and *G* schedules were not to change, the intersection would still be at *E,* but now, alas, with mass unemployment. (Under laissez faire no one can predict what the net final effect of such inventions on the total of *C + I + G* would be. They *might* tempt consumers to less thrift, and investors to more capital formation. But they might instead undermine *C + I + G.*)

**(b)** Regardless of inventions' effect on old spending schedules, expansionary monetary policy can raise *I* by the needed amount. Expansionary fiscal policy can raise *G* to *G';* and can lower taxes, raise disposable incomes, and shift up the consumption schedule to *C'C'.* Full-employment equilibrium will be restored at *E',* where *C' + I' + G'* has been shifted upward the needed amount by macroeconomic policy.

Figure 18-3(b) shows how these upward shifts have restored the full-employment equilibrium. By proper policy we have converted the machine from a curse to a blessing. People now enjoy 30 per cent more output. They are not forced into bread lines. They are not made to work short hours and do not have to take Mondays off because the limited work has to be shared. They do not have to throw their cigarette cases into the works of the new machinery to protect their jobs and take-home pay.

You should be sure you know how to use the same diagram to handle the case where automation or new inventions spontaneously increase investment a great deal and tempt people onto an upward-shifted consumption schedule. You can then show how the desired $E'$ equilibrium could come about spontaneously. Indeed, to test your powers, you should analyze the possible case where automation causes *too great* a burst of investment and consumption spending. You should then show which contractionary monetary and fiscal policy would be needed to wipe out the resulting inflationary gap and to bring the new $C + I + G$ schedule successfully back to the proper intersection.

As a final test, suppose that instead of the problem's being automation, the United States faces high unemployment because Germany and Japan have had miraculous improvements in productivity, and competition of their exports has killed off many American jobs. Can you bring macroeconomics to the rescue?

Of course, higher dollar demand, engineered by fiscal and monetary policy, cannot be expected to provide the same kind of jobs using exactly the same skills and paying exactly the same wage rates. Inevitably there will still be important transitional problems for *particular* workers, firms, and regions. Programs of retraining and of increasing labor mobility and flexibility are vital (as Chapter 41 discusses), along with policies to ensure proper aggregate dollar demand.

## THE NEW MIXED ECONOMY

Critics used to regard the classical principles of economics as out of date. Looking at the long bread lines and the men selling apples on street corners, they said:

Why speak of scarcity? Or efficiency? Or growth? Or fairness? Throw away your tools of supply and demand, your finespun theories of market pricing. Tear up the rule book. We live in a new era in which everything is upside down: attempts to save kill off investment; a hurricane or war is a blessing in that it creates jobs and gives food to the starving unemployed. Capitalism is doomed to collapse in a crisis of underconsumption and overproduction.

What is the modern economist's answer to all this? He says:

You are right to question the classical principles. All principles should be subjected to the closest examination with respect to both logic and factual relevance. The classical arguments were oversimple, and they admittedly did not allow for the facts of nineteenth- and twentieth-century life. Experience since 1932, and careful logical reasoning, suggest that money and aggregate $C + I + G$ spending *will not manage themselves.* A laissez faire system is doomed to wasteful ups and downs of the business cycle and perhaps to long fits of stagnation.

But even among the economists of Eastern Europe there has developed a recognition of the new scientific knowledge about macroeconomic policy.

**Simple capitalism has been replaced virtually everywhere by the mixed economy (a "welfare and managed economy"). Everywhere in the Western world,[7] governments and central banks have shown they can win the battle of the lasting slump if people want them to. They have the weapons of fiscal policy (expenditure and taxes) and of monetary policy (open-market operations, discount-rate policy, legal-reserve-ratio policy) to shift the various schedules that determine GNP and employment. Just as we no longer meekly accept disease, we no longer need accept mass unemployment.**

[7] This, of course, includes Australia and New Zealand; Japan, India, and other Asian nations; Latin America; and the new African states.

Under the managed macroeconomics of the mixed economy, many of the old classical principles of microeconomics will again apply; but now they apply because our macroeconomics has validated their premise of adequate demand—not because the world is lucky enough to have them apply *automatically* and at all times.

This is a brave answer, and essentially—most careful economists would today say—an accurate answer. But let us not be too boastful of our modern conquest of instability. There is no warrant for smugness. Let us add the following qualifications:

The worst consequences of the business cycle, which Chapter 14 showed plagued capitalism from its beginning, are probably a thing of the past; but that does not mean that the cycle is gone. "Fine tuning" is not yet here. We still shall have minor fluctuations, inventory oscillations, and transitions from war to peace and from one kind of boom to another. The difference will be this: The age-old tendencies for the system to fluctuate will still be there, but no longer will the world let them snowball into vast depressions or into demand-pull inflations—no longer will we let our banking system fail and our nation go through the most painful debt deflation and bankruptcy.

We should recognize that all the political pressures in a democracy do work to make a drastic slump unlikely. But can we be so sure that the same pressures will operate to prevent creeping inflation? What about "cost-push inflation" rather than "demand-pull inflation"? And "stagflation"? Chapter 41 will show that the mixed economy is still far from knowing all the important answers to this new dread disease.

The Appendix explores further the analytics of money and of income determination.

## SUMMARY

1   Monetary policy by the central bank is an important way of shifting the saving and investment schedules, or the total schedule of consumption-plus-investment-plus-government-spending.

2   Along the downward-sloping "liquidity-preference schedule," higher $M$ induces a lower interest rate—enough lower to persuade people to hold all the new $M$. Along the downward-sloping "marginal-efficiency-of-investment" schedule, lower interest rates and more available credit make it profitable for new investment projects to get done. Along the familiar saving-investment multiplier-type diagram, the induced increase in $I$ leads to higher production and incomes.[8]

3   Fiscal policy means governmental tax and expenditure policy. It, too, affects income determination by shifting the spending schedules. Higher public expenditure directly raises the $G$ component of the $C + I + G$ schedule and thus raises

---

[8]The Appendix shows that if there is a deep-depression inelasticity of investment response to interest and/or a deep-depression horizontality of $LL$ representing indifference to money holding, the effect of $M$ will fall to nil. In quantity-theory language, then and *only* then will the contrived rise in $M$ be completely negated by a compensating fall in $V$, leaving GNP = $P \times Q$ quite unchanged. Usually the induced drop in interest rates will cause $V$ to decrease, but by not enough to offset the new $M$ in the now-higher $MV$. Only in the other extreme case, that of crude monetarism, will $V$ be a hard constant, responding in no systematic way to $i$, $CC$, $II$, and $GG$ changes. The great neoclassical writers—Marshall, Walras, Wicksell, Pigou, Irving Fisher—never believed in such monetarism.

its equilibrium intersection. Taxes work in reverse: *reduced* tax rates, by shifting the *CC* schedule leftward and upward, push *up* the *C + I + G* schedule; increased tax rates have the opposite, contractionary effect; and in either case, tax changes are, dollar for dollar, a little less potent than changes in government expenditure on goods and services.

**4**  Monetary and fiscal policy interact. A budget deficit financed by new *M* will raise GNP more than one paid for by issue of government bonds. Historically, much of the *M* created by the Fed and other central banks originated in deficit financing.

**5**  The important case of technological invention shows how, by combination of fiscal and monetary policies, a modern economy can ensure the restoration of high-employment equilibrium even in the worst case where automation is reducing the need for men to do any given amount of work and is not bringing in its train any spontaneous expansion of dollar demand elsewhere.

**6**  Modern mixed economies have the fiscal and monetary tools, and the political will to use them, to end chronic slumps and galloping inflations. This makes obsolete the fear of overproduction and underconsumption, and obviates the need to bolster purchasing power by military or imperialistic programs. But it does not solve problems of income inequality or of monopolistic and other imperfections at the microeconomic level. Part Two's successful handling of macroeconomics merely sets the stage for the again-relevant microeconomic problems of Parts Three and Four. But Part Six shows that complacency over cost-push inflation is quite unjustified.

## CONCEPTS FOR REVIEW

**M** down $\rightarrow$ *i* up $\rightarrow$ *I* down $\rightarrow$
    GNP down = *MV* down
shift of *C + I + G:* through
    monetary policy and through
    tax and expenditure changes
leftward *CC* shift from tax cut

liquidity-preference schedule
marginal-efficiency schedule
tax versus expenditure potency
fiscal and monetary interaction
automation and unemployment
macroeconomics of mixed economy

## QUESTIONS FOR DISCUSSION

**1**  Redo Fig. 18-1(a), (b), and (c) to show tight monetary policies. Trace the steps.

**2**  Wipe out a 1980 automation-created deflationary gap by (*a*) fiscal policy alone, (*b*) monetary policy alone, and (*c*) any blend of them. Which path leads to full employment with slowest growth (i.e., least capital formation for the future)?

**3**  "Fiscal and monetary authority should be in one agency, or at least be coordinated. Otherwise, the authorities may conflict, one undoing what the other does." Discuss.

**4**  Use Fig. 18-2 to show that increasing *G* and taxes at the same time tends to have canceling effects on income. Difficult question: Can you follow the intricate reasoning which argues that, dollar for dollar, changes in *G* are a bit more potent than changes in taxes—so that a balanced-budget decrease in $G$ is likely to be a bit deflationary?

5  "The tools that handle automation problems can handle any unemployment that might come from sudden peace and disarmament." Explain.

6  "The worldwide 1973–1975 stagflation shows that the New Economics has not yet solved all our macroeconomic problems." If $P$ rises even when $Q$ falls, show that we indeed face new dilemmas.

7  "To offset underconsumption, capitalism must engage in cold-war spending and imperialism." Show how $C + I + G$ analysis now makes this view archaic.

# APPENDIX: Mechanisms of Monetarism and Income Determination

This is a brief discussion of how money, interest, investment, income, prices, and velocity of circulation are interrelated. Classical views that there can never be unemployment, and depression versions of the Keynesian system, will turn out to be alternative poles of such an analysis. And what most economists would consider to be the most realistic description of how our economy works and what are the potencies of policy weapons will fall somewhere on the continuum between these extreme poles.

The topics will be covered in this order: velocity interrelations; classical and monetarist models; liquidity preference and income determination.

## BEHAVIOR OF VELOCITY

Instead of the chain $M \rightarrow i \rightarrow I \rightarrow$ GNP (or its even further elaboration to take account of wealth-capitalization effects and effects on $G$ and $C$ schedules), some proponents of monetarism prefer to short-circuit the process and use the concept of velocity, $V$. They write

$$M \rightarrow MV \equiv \text{GNP}$$

**This asserts that an increase in $M$, unless offset fully by an induced shift in $V$ of the type that neither they nor the believers in the four-link chain consider likely, will serve to increase dollar GNP with all the implied effects on the product $P \times Q$.[1]**

These different modes of language can formally represent the same facts, just as an account in English or an account in French can be given of any sequence of events. In a sense, therefore, reasonable men will not argue about terminology and semantics.

At a deeper level, however, those who prefer one terminology usually think that certain hypotheses about the real world are more fruitful than others. Thus, those who like to use $MV$ usually have more definite views about the probable behavior of $V$, and its invariance under a wide range of alternative conditions, than do those who like to use the $C + I + G$ and liquidity-preference approach explicitly. While the bulk of economists today incline toward the eclectic view, there is no need to be dogmatic about the matter. If the day ever arrives when the proponents of the velocity approach can prove by their researches that theirs is the more convenient tool, pragmatic scholars will welcome all its help. In any case, post-Keynesians and monetarists both agree that "money matters much."

## CLASSICAL PRICE FLEXIBILITY

More basic than the question of whether to use or not use the terminology of either school is the con-

---

[1] Some proponents think $V$ will stay constant after a sizable change in open-market operations; others do not think this is a necessary assumption. Some, impressed by the empirical fact that in past short-term upswings, rises in $M$ and $V$ have

tended to coincide, choose to extrapolate this *post hoc* experience. Others set up more complicated hypotheses, depending on the environment upon which the open-market operation impinged. Many agree with our later liquidity-preference theory, whose Hicks-Hansen diagrams can be thought of as a theory of velocity—i.e., a theory in which $V$ is an increasing function of the interest rate $i$.

trast between a *frictionless* system in which all market prices are *flexible* and the *realistic* world of a mixed economic system that exists here and elsewhere in the West. Many classical economists thought unemployment to be quite impossible because, in their frictionless models, whatever is not spent in one direction gets automatically spent in another.

**Say's Law**   This view, named for the French writer J. B. Say, has been much debated since 1803 because of its ambiguities. Thus, Say and other classical writers felt that overproduction was impossible by its very nature, since all value relations were relative—shoes being comparable with spoons at some proper relative price; they felt that what a worker saves gets spent as truly on employing men in the machinery trades as what the worker spends on giving work in the food or other consumers' industries; they had at least a vague supposition that the interest rate in a flexible capital market would always find a level at which (full-employment) saving and investment schedules would intersect; they, or their more sophisticated followers, had the notion that, if only the money wage would fall flexibly far enough, it would always bring out job offers for every willing worker. So went the rather vague arguments.

In the years since 1800, there were often short periods of considerable unemployment, and on a few occasions there were longer periods of considerable unemployment or of *under*employment. So economists wanted to go beyond the simpler formulations of Say's Law: to deny some of its implicit presumptions about flexible prices and wages, or to abandon it and work from alternative hypotheses.

Today it is clear that the alternative approaches are capable of being reconciled, so that there is only a difference of degree and realism between them, not a difference of kind. A. C. Pigou of Cambridge University showed, a decade after Keynes' *General Theory*, how his own older, cherished beliefs could be related to what he had first thought were Keynesian heresies. His reconciliation goes thus.

**Pigou effects**   Let there be a certain *M* in the system that consists of coins or of imperishable paper currency. Suppose that initially there is unemployment because the *SS* and *II* schedules intersect to the left of the full-employment level. Suppose interest rates are in equilibrium on every bond and security market,

with auctioneers finding matching supply and demand bids. And just to complete the simplified discussion, suppose there is no central banker or fiscal authority to do anything about the situation.

A sophisticated follower of Say would now assert: "There is just one flaw in this equilibrium. Men who want to work at going wages are not employed. To be fair, whether or not this is realistic, you should also imagine an auctioneer for the labor market. He makes the wage rate expressed in money fall whenever there is excessive labor supply."

Pigou agrees. He lets the wage rate fall. Money wages being an important cost of production, for all the reasons discussed in Parts Three and Four, this drop will result in considerable lowering of all prices. When prices and wages are low enough, what will happen to the *SS* and *II* intersection? Suppose I am a typical man who previously owned an acre of land, a machine, and $100 in cash. (I also may have owed on a mortgage or may have held someone's IOU stated in terms of money; but for the community as a whole, such interpersonal money liabilities and assets have to *cancel* out. Recall also that there are no government bonds in the picture to worry about.)

For dramatic effect, suppose that wages fall to one-thousandth (.001) of their previous level; suppose, although it is unnecessary except for simplicity to stick to exactly the same number, that prices of all things also fall to .001 of their previous levels. This means that my acre of land and machine will fall to .001 of their previous value. Everything falls in value—except one item. My $100 bill is still a $100 bill. But now, in terms of its real purchasing power, I own the equivalent of what was $100,000 before. I am rich!

Will I spend the same amount on consumption and on saving out of *income* levels that are the same as before either in money or in real terms? I will not. I am rich and can consume more before I die.

*At some point, because of the enhanced **real wealth effect** of the increased purchasing power of the hard money in the economic system (induced by a large enough wage and price fall), CC schedules will shift up in real (not money) terms, and SS schedules shift equivalently downward. The new SS and II intersection can thus be moved up to the full-employment level. So, even if there were no favorable effects of the price-level or of interest change on the II curves, by getting money wages and prices far enough down, the condition of "full employment" could theoretically be achieved. QED.*

Pigou thus vindicated abstract classical principles by recourse to this "hard-money effect," which economists today call the "Pigou effect" in his honor.[2] But being a realistic observer of the difficulties of getting wages to move flexibly downward in a mixed capitalistic society, and having lived through eras in which the dynamic process of debt deflation led to bankruptcy, riots, slump, and even revolution, Pigou hastened to point out that he did not recommend such hyperdeflation to cure capitalism's unemployment. He much preferred to accomplish the same thing by increasing dollar $M$; and actually, he adhered to the general notions of Part Two of this book. The fact that he often liked to use the word "velocity" in his Keynes-like theory shows that mere semantic matters are indeed of limited importance.

**Crude Quantity Theory in the classical model**   Recall now the crude Quantity Theory, which held that prices must always be proportional to the amount of money—so that doubling $M$ must exactly double $P$. For many situations in the real world—with its sticky prices, booms, recessions, and thousands of changes always going on to confound the experiment—we saw that the crude Quantity Theory was not a good predicting device. But if we confine our attention to the *perfectly frictionless model* of the classical type used by Pigou and others in the above discussion, we can find an important *nucleus* of truth in the crude Quantity Theory; and we can understand better the reasons why it has a degree of predictive value during galloping inflations and over certain long-enough time intervals.

Recall Pigou's fantastic but happy equilibrium which has made the representative man feel rich enough to save as little as society can invest at full employment. Now suppose his $100 bill had originally been a $10 bill. Do you see that merely by having all prices go down still another nine-tenths, the equilibrium could be *exactly restored*, with every relative

[2] Mention may be made of a non-Pigou, non-1936-Keynes version of full employment originated in 1955 by Professor Nicholas Kaldor of Cambridge. He is widely interpreted to believe that, within broad limits, any drop of exogenous $I$ will induce just enough reduction of the share of income accruing to thrifty profit receivers to produce a *full-employment* (!) intersection of $SS$ and $II$ always. If only it were valid, such a comfortable Say-like view would be important. If only . . . .

price and wage just the same as before and every physical commodity and input the same as before? *Cutting M to one-tenth has cut P to exactly one-tenth* in this classical model.

In this abstract model the crude Quantity Theory has come into its own. In the tautological equation of exchange $MV \equiv PQ$, there has been no slightest reason for the $Q$, $i$, or $V$ to have changed (waiving all dynamic questions of how the system gets into the new equilibrium and "forgets" past price levels). So $P$ does equal $kM$, where $k$ is the ratio $V/Q$, whose numerator and denominator will have been constant in the abstract example, however much they may vary in reality.

This long-period, full-employment, frictionless classical model does have the property that *no* change in interest rates can come from a *balanced* change in $M$. As Ricardo argued, if all prices and wages change in exactly the same proportion, so that what used to be called 4 pence is now 2 pence, then any asset that used to pay 5 per cent per annum in the form of 50 pence on 1,000 pence will now be paying 5 per cent in the form of 25 pence on 500 pence.

It should not be necessary to stress that the real world, as we know it, is a far cry from the abstract model. This is true especially in the short run; in the longer run, to the degree that all price adjustments get made and other disturbances are ruled out, the abstract model fits somewhat better. The art of economics is to know how to blend the elements of absurdity and of relevance of such a model in interpreting living events and policy.

**Permanent public debt**   Even in the extreme classical model, all $P$s would not be proportional to $M$ alone! Interest-bearing public bonds, which correspond to no government capital formation and which no taxpayer rationally expects to have to help retire *in his lifetime*, have effects similar to those of the non-interest IOUs we call $M$. Thus, the Pigou effect from hyperdeflation involves an increase in the real value of such bonds *along with* an increase in the real value of hard-money $M$. Since a rational taxpayer will reckon that he *will* have to help pay taxes to keep up the interest payments (during his lifetime) on the public debt, $1 of such debt will not have the potency to produce as much spending as will $1 of $M$. Even so, believers in a crude Quantity Theory in an extreme classical model *should* reformulate their theory to say:

**Doubling *M* and permanent public debt (*PD*) will, other things equal, double all *P*s and leave all relative *P*s, physical quantities, and interest rates unchanged in the new long-run equilibrium. *Doubling M alone represents a nonneutral change* whose substantive effects are the greater the shorter is taxpayer life expectancy and the higher is the interest rate.[3]**

## LIQUIDITY PREFERENCE AND INCOME

We have seen that the amount of money people will hold depends upon the interest rate and is a declining function of it in the sense that you must contrive lower yields on securities to coax people to be willing to hold more money. Figure 18-1(a) showed this liquidity-preference link between money and interest.

But as already noted, there is a *transactions* motive for holding money along with the *store-of-wealth* or asset reason for holding money. So part of the money held can be said to depend upon the level of income: this so-called "active" component of the money supply is a function of the level of GNP, rising as GNP rises. Indeed, if velocity were a strict constant for *all* money and not just for this idealized active-money component, there would be no room at all for a nonvertical liquidity-preference curve *LL* in Fig. 18-1(a).

This dependence of money on income as well as on interest was not depicted in the important sequence of Fig. 18-1(a), (b), and (c). The chapter's third footnote warned us that the diagram did not take into account the full feedback effect of the transactions demand for money induced by a successful expansion of GNP contrived by an increase in *M*. We can here make good this deficiency, and verify that the chapter's story is essentially correct, even if oversimplified in the telling; now we consider what is known as a Hicks-Hansen diagram, named originally for Sir John Hicks of Oxford[4] and for Alvin Hansen of Harvard, who popularized it.

The brown curve labeled *IS* in Fig. 18-4 recapitu-

lates in a single income-interest-rate diagram the story told by Fig. 18-1 (b) and (c), quite independently of (a). We saw back there on page 336 that, when we change the interest rate, we end up changing the GNP level, as shown here on the brown curve. In Fig. 18-1, this took place in two steps: (1) the marginal-efficiency step of 18-1(b) in which changing interest rate changed investment in the opposite direction; and (2) the old multiplier relation of 18-1(c), inherited from our saving-investment analysis of Chapter 12, in which the change in investment resulted in an amplified change in income in its same direction, owing to primary spending and secondary respending. We call this result of the two steps the *IS* relation, because it shows the resulting correspondence between interest rate and income when scheduled saving and scheduled investment have been kept equal. (Recall this is the definition of maintainable GNP equilibrium.)

The new element in Fig. 18-4 is the orange *LM* schedule. This relationship between the interest rate and the level of income is labeled *LM* because it is the complete liquidity-preference relationship between money and income after we have taken into account *both* the dependence of money holding on interest *and* on income. That is, we have recognized the

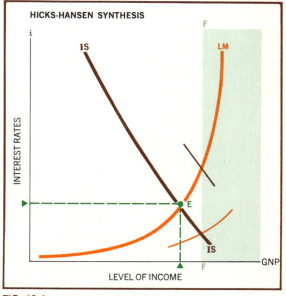

**FIG. 18-4**

[3]WARNING: Doubling *M* and *PD* does not mean you can add *M* + *PD* and treat that magnitude as if *P*s were proportional to it. Rather, it is the case that (2*M*, 2*PD*) implies 2*P*.
[4]Nobel laureate in Economics for 1972, along with Kenneth J. Arrow of Stanford and Harvard.

*transaction* motive for "active money," which depends primarily on income; and also what page 283 called the *precautionary* (or "asset") store-of-wealth motive for holding money, which depends upon the interest rates that investors speculate could be earned on alternative stores of wealth (bonds, stocks, land, real capital goods—earning assets in general). Figure 18-1(a) already reflected this.

It is important to emphasize that the *LM* schedule is drawn up on the proviso that the total amount of *M* is fixed. Why, then, does *LM* slope upward? Because a rightward increase in GNP requires more active *M* for transactions, leaving less *M* for people to hold as a wealth asset. The smaller amount of *M* for wealth holding can only be rationed out at a higher (or northward-moving) interest rate, which is needed to coax people more into securities and *out* of money.

**Now Fig. 18-4 combines the marginal-efficiency-multiplier brown curve *IS* with the orange liquidity-preference curve *LM*, to show their interaction does determine the equilibrium level of GNP and of interest rate for each given total of *M*. E shows the equilibrium intersection. There and only there has the existing amount of money produced just low enough interest rate and just high enough investment to lead to a maintainable level of income: at this indicated GNP and *i* rate, the existing *M* supply just covers the transactions and holding demand for money. QED.**

What if the Fed engineers an *increase* in *M*? What will that do to the *LM* curve? Now with more money to be held at each level of income, the interest rate will have to be bid down. Hence, the *LM* curve clearly shifts downward (and *rightward,* as shown by the new thin orange curve in Fig. 18-4). What about the *IS* curve? In this simplified version, *IS* does not have the money supply in it anywhere; *IS* stays unshifted by an *M* change. The downward shift of *LM* moves the equilibrium GNP upward and the equilibrium interest rate downward (just as, in Chapter 4, page 65, an increase in supply *ss* intersects an unchanged demand curve *dd* in a higher *Q* and lower *P*). Pencil *E'* in on Fig. 18-4.

By contrast to monetary policy, which shifts the *LM* curve, fiscal policy shifts the *IS* curve. How? An increase in government expenditure *G* (just like an increase in any component of a *C + I + G* schedule) will shift the *IS* schedule *rightward* (as in the new thin brown curve). Why? Because it leads to a higher GNP level at the same interest rate. Thus, you can

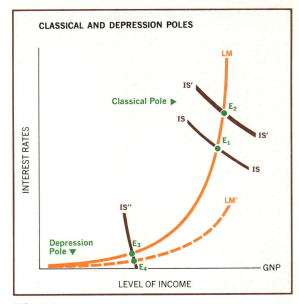

**FIG. 18-5**

show that expansionary fiscal policy leads to a new *E* higher on the unshifted *LM* curve, with equilibrium GNP and *i* both higher. (Test yourself by penciling in on Fig. 18-4 the new higher *E''* intersection.)

**Classical pole**  Figure 18-5 shows at the ends of the *LM* curve the extreme "classical" pole and the extreme "depression" (or so-called "liquidity-trap") pole. Where *LM* turns almost vertical, no shift in the *IS* curve can increase GNP; that is because money's velocity has reached its limit. (Note the near-constancy of GNP at $E_1$ and $E_2$.) At this classical pole, then, fiscal policy would accomplish little unless accompanied by central banking change in the money supply. Few think present-day mixed economies operate in such an extreme classical region.

**Depression pole**  At the other extreme, at vanishingly low interest rates such as prevailed in the late 1930s, the *LM* curve might turn horizontal. If the Fed engineered an increase in *M* by open-market purchases which involved swapping a close-money substitute Treasury bill for *M* itself, the Fed would merely succeed in shifting the *LM* curve rightward, leaving its horizontal part virtually unchanged. At such a liquidity-trap pole, and particularly where extreme inelasticity of the depression marginal-efficiency curve makes *IS* almost vertical, monetary policy is practically impotent to affect GNP.[5] (Note the virtual identity of the $E_3$ and $E_4$ intersections.)

The Hicks-Hansen diagram[6] not only succeeds in synthesizing fiscal and monetary policy, the theory

of income determination, and the theory of money; in addition, it helps synthesize the monetarist and Keynesian theories of macroeconomics by providing a definite and general theory of the velocity of *M*. Thus, the monetarist counterrevolution reduces to debate about the shapes of *LM* and *IS*.

---

[5]Sometimes the "depression model" is called the "Keynesian model," but most authorities agree that this is bad terminology, since Keynes' *General Theory* covered *all* cases and not merely those of the Great Depression.

[6]Not all of the wisdom of post-Keynesian macroeconomics can be neatly depicted on the Hicks-Hansen diagram, which doesn't really do justice to the Pigou effect. Thus, suppose there is a permanent increase in people's net worth from the creation of new money (so-called "outside" money). (Think of gold from California mining discoveries; or think of currency printed by the government to fight last century's Civil War; but don't think of new *M* just created by an open-market operation by the Fed, for the reason that largely offsetting the new *M* in people's net worth will be their loss of near-money bonds sold to the Fed.) It is standard in the Hicks-Hansen diagram, Fig. 18-4, to let this new *M* shift the orange *LM* curve rightward. Agreed. But the Pigou effect

says that this new liquid net worth will *also* raise people's propensity to consume, their *CC* and *C + I + G* schedules. So, to be correct, the change in *M* should *also* shift the brown *IS* schedule rightward and upward, reinforcing the *LM* shift. (See extra-credit problem 5 for numerical *IS* and *LM* curves. There and in Fig. 18-4, the horizontal axis can be thought of as representing *money* GNP, with *P* constant prior to full employment in an oversimplified Keynesian fashion. Or, suppose you are ultraclassical and think prices and wages are flexible downward whenever real GNP is below the full-employment level and out-of-work men bid down the *P* level. Then the axis in Fig. 18-4 can depict *real* GNP; and each drop in the *P* level will shift *LM* rightward until the equilibrium *E* point slides southeastward on *IS* to the level of full employment. Any further increase in *M* will raise *P* proportionately *á la* Quantity Theory, but leave all real points, axes, and curves on the diagram intact.)

## SUMMARY TO APPENDIX

1 The causal interrelations between *M, i, I,* and GNP could also be expressed in *MV* language. So long as one expects any induced changes in *V* to be such as not *fully* to offset the original change in *M*, changing *M* can in one step be described as changing GNP. Semantics alone would be at issue, were it not true that special hypotheses about *V*'s constancy may seem tenable to monetarists who use this concept.

2 In a perfect classical world without frictions and with an inflexible hard-money public-debt base, Pigou proved in the 1940s that a sophisticated version of Say's Law could be asserted. For policy and realistic description, he preferred not to rely on hyper-deflation to produce such "Pigou effects." Pushing such a full-employment model to its logical limits, however, does enable one to reaffirm the crudest Quantity Theory in which *P* is strictly proportionate to *M* and public debt (the degree of the proportion varying only when extraneous *real* changes take place). Hicks-Hansen diagrams synthesize money-income-interest interdependencies, dramatize classical and depression poles, thus providing a Keynesian model of *V* compatible with monetarism.

## CONCEPTS FOR REVIEW

Say's Law and classical models
Pigou effects
crude Quantity Theory
induced changes in *V*
public-debt effects

liquidity preference:
   *M* dependence on both GNP and *i*
   *V* dependence on *i*
Hicks-Hansen *LM* and *IS* intersection
depression and classical poles

## QUESTIONS FOR DISCUSSION

1 Is it reasonable for you to hold relatively less $M$ and have a faster $V$ when $i$ is 9 rather than 1 per cent? When inflation is galloping? Use your reply to criticize crude monetarism.

2 Explain the Pigou-effect mechanism for restoring full employment when wages and prices are perfectly flexible. What is the public debt's role?

3 Show that a rise in $G$ or lowering of taxes will shift brown $IS$ rightward in Fig. 18-4 and will raise GNP at the new $E$. What will $M$ contraction do?

4 Once people can expect price inflation to continue, the same nominal rate of interest, $i$, represents a lower *real* interest rate. So at each unchanged $i$, they will want to invest more and will want to have a higher $V$ for their cash holdings. Therefore, the $LM$ and $IS$ curves will tend to be shifted upward by inflation. Can you see that this will tend to build into the nominal interest-rate structure an inflation premium? If at 1 per cent price inflation long-term bonds yield about 5 per cent, what might you expect them to yield when most people are geared up to expect an inflation rate of 6 per cent per year?

5 *Extra-credit problem:* Intermediate texts can use mathematical symbols to summarize a simple version of this Appendix. Let real saving, $S$, depend on real income, $Q = GNP/P$, namely: $S = S(Q) = .1Q$, say, much as in Fig. 18-1(c). Let real investment, $I$, depend inversely on the interest rate, as in Fig. 18-1(b)'s marginal-efficiency schedule, namely: $I = I(i) = 1/i$, say. In the equation of exchange $MV = PQ$, let velocity, $V$, be an increasing function of the interest rate, namely: $V = V(i) = 4.4i/(1 + i)$, say. Pick units so that full-employment output is $Q_F = 1$ (trillion dollars, perhaps); and suppose that, prior to full employment, prices are constant (as determined by sticky wage-cost levels, etc.), so that by choice of units $P = 1$ until an inflationary gap lifts the price level. Finally, let the money supply, $M$, be set by the Fed at the level $\bar{M}$. Then to determine our two unknowns, $Q$ and $i$, in Fig. 18-4 we have the two equations for the $IS$ and $LM$ schedules

$$S(Q) = I(i) \quad \text{or} \quad .1Q = 1/i \ , \quad \text{marginal efficiency and multiplier: } IS \text{ curve}$$

$$\bar{M} = PQ/V(i) \quad \text{or} \quad \bar{M} = 1Q/[4.4i/(1 + i)] \ , \text{liquidity-preference theory of } V: LM \text{ curve}$$

Solving (by simple substitution or otherwise), we get $Q$ as an increasing function of $\bar{M}$, and $i$ as a decreasing function. After $\bar{M}$ has become so large that full-employment $Q_F$ has been reached, along with its corresponding $i_F$ and $V_F$, we put $Q_F$ in both equations and solve for the price level $P$, with $P$ now simply proportional to $\bar{M}$ (in accordance with the classical Quantity Theory of Money), namely: $P = (V_F/Q_F) \bar{M}$. NOTE: for the suggested special formulas above, substitution gives $i = 10/Q$, $V = 44/(Q + 10)$, $\bar{M} = Q(Q + 10)/44$, a quadratic equation for $Q$ in terms of $\bar{M}$. To get full-employment $Q_F = 1$, evidently, $\bar{M} = \frac{11}{44} = \frac{1}{4}$ (i.e., a quarter of a trillion dollars, with $V_F = 4$ per year, or once every 3 months on the average); and $i_F = 10/Q_F = 10$ per cent per year. For underemployment equilibrium, the quadratic's relevant root is given by $Q = -5 + \sqrt{25 + 44\bar{M}}$. Verify that $\bar{M} = \frac{1}{4}$ does yield $Q = 1$; and, for $\bar{M} > \frac{1}{4}$, $P = (\frac{4}{1})\bar{M} = 4\bar{M}$. If $P$ has classical downward flexibility, replace $P = 1$ by $Q = Q_F = 1$ and solve for $P = 4\bar{M}$ for any $\bar{M}$.

We have seen in earlier chapters that the behavior of saving and investment determines the level of national income and employment. We have seen that investment and other spending often fluctuate widely from year to year. History shows how painful and wasteful the business cycle has been in the past. Today everyone is in agreement that we must continue to succeed in laying to rest the ghost of instability, chronic slump, and snowballing inflation.

The historic Employment Act of 1946 brought the United States up to the other mixed economies in this respect. It set up a Council of Economic Advisers and a Joint Economic Committee to help ensure full employment and healthy growth.

What prescription follows from our economic diagnosis? Earlier chapters have shown that the Federal Reserve System can do much, by way of monetary policy and interest, to moderate instability. To reinforce central bank monetary policy, powerful help is still needed from the weapon of public *fiscal policy* (i.e., governmental tax and expenditure policies, budgetary deficits or surpluses).

## OLD-FASHIONED FINANCE

Forty years ago, the chapter in an economic textbook dealing with public finance read just as it had in Adam Smith's time. From 1776 to 1929 there was little discernible progress. Moreover, the Democratic President Grover Cleveland differed not a bit in his ideology of finance from Republican William McKinley, or for that matter from Calvin Coolidge and Herbert Hoover or Gladstone and Disraeli.

What were the clichés of oldfangled shirt-sleeve economics, the doctrines our grandfathers were taught and preached to us in turn? Here are a few:

1. The budget should be balanced in *every* year (and at a *low* level, with expenditure prudent and purposes strictly limited).

2. The public debt is a burden on the backs of our children and

# 19

# FISCAL POLICY AND FULL EMPLOYMENT WITHOUT INFLATION

The Congress declares that it is the continuing responsibility of the federal government to . . . promote maximum employment, production, and purchasing power. EMPLOYMENT ACT OF 1946

grandchildren (just as though each of us has to carry heavy rocks on our shoulders). All debt is evil; public debt, absolutely evil.

3. Everything that is true of an individual or a family is also true of the government. If a husband and wife spend more than their monthly income, they go bankrupt and misery follows. The same is true for Uncle Sam (or John Bull or Kaiser Wilhelm).

4. In agreement with one of Adam Smith's four fundamental "canons of taxation," a good tax is one that produces *the same revenues in good times as in bad*.

You can extend the list in any club locker room or bar. What is interesting about it is that today no experts agree with it or the reasonings on which it relies. And no nations, even in the heyday of Victorian capitalism, came anywhere near to living up to it; for, fortunately, they could not do so. During each depression and recession, *automatically* budget deficits soared at the same time that the conventional wisdom was deploring the phenomenon. For centuries, in times of distress, local and national governments have had to resort to poorhouse relief, work on the roads, and other public works to relieve the distress. Now political economy has caught up with reality.

As will be seen in this chapter, experienced researchers into the facts and the analytical principles of public finance have today, all over the world, quite different answers to these questions from those of our forefathers. The task for an introductory text is to explain the logic and experience underlying modern doctrines, not indoctrinate the student into any one view. Objective analysis of the issues—both pros and cons—can give each person the materials from which to form his own understanding of the fiscal practices followed by mixed economies all over the world.

## A. SHORT-RUN AND LONG-RUN FISCAL POLICY

By a positive fiscal policy, we mean the process of shaping *taxation* and *public expenditure* in order (*a*) to help dampen down the swings of the business cycle, and (*b*) to contribute toward the maintenance of a growing, high-employment economy free from excessive demand inflation or deflation.

Suppose the economic system in a particular year is threatened with a deflationary gap. Suppose private consumption and investment spending are *too weak* to provide adequate employment. What action then is called for?

The Federal Reserve will use expansionary monetary policy to try to stimulate private investment. To the degree[1] that its actions are not fully adequate, the fiscal authorities would still be faced by a deflationary gap. This is the signal for Congress and the President to introduce tax and public-expenditure policies designed to help reachieve stable full employment.

Fiscal action, but now in reverse, is called for in the case where private investment and consumption decisions threaten the economy with an *inflationary gap*. With prices rising from excessive total spending and employers vying desperately for nonexistent workers, the Fed will initiate contractionary credit programs aimed to reduce the inflationary gap. But if the saving-investment or $C + I + G$ intersections still threaten the economy with a sustained inflationary gap, it is then the clear duty of Congress

[1] How much of the stabilizing load is carried by monetary and how much by fiscal policy depends on public-growth targets and international-payments constraints. Also, the financing of deficits and surpluses itself helps shape the course of money-supply growth.

and the President to initiate higher tax rates and/or lower–public-expenditure programs in the attempt to restore a high-employment equilibrium without inflation.

In summary, fiscal budgetary policies dealing with taxes and public expenditure, in cooperation with stabilizing monetary policies, have for their goal a high-employment and growing economy—but one without demand-pull inflation. The fiscal and monetary authorities "lean against the prevailing economic winds," thereby helping provide a favorable economic environment within which the people can have the widest opportunity for achievement.

## OUR IMPORTANT "BUILT-IN STABILIZERS"

One might get the impression from the above remarks that fiscal policy helps stabilize the economy only so long as government officials are carefully watching trends, are successfully anticipating future developments, and are meeting promptly to take decisive action. Such "discretionary fiscal policies," involving the making and changing of explicit decisions, are important; fortunately, they are only part of the story.

The modern fiscal system has great inherent *automatic stabilizing* properties. All through the day and night, whether or not the President is in the White House, the fiscal system is helping keep our economy stable. If in 1980 a recession gets under way while Congress is out of session, powerful automatic forces will go instantly into action to counteract it before there are any committee meetings or the exercise of special intelligence of any form.

What are these mysterious stabilizers? They are primarily the following:

1. *Automatic changes in tax receipts.* We saw in Chapters 8 and 9 that our federal tax system depends progressively on personal and corporate incomes. What does graduated-income-taxation mean for stability? It means that as soon as income begins to fall off, and even before Congress makes any changes in tax rates, the tax receipts of the government also fall off. (Today, for each $10 billion drop in GNP, total tax receipts drop by about $3\frac{1}{2}$ billion. If ever the negative income tax becomes law, this fraction may become considerably larger.)

Now, reductions in tax receipts are just what the doctor prescribes in case of a dip in income. So our present tax system is a mighty and rapid built-in stabilizer.

NOTE: Taxes stabilize *against upward* as well as downward movements. In times of demand inflation, this is good; but when it impedes healthy growth, we call it "fiscal drag."

A century ago, writers thought that *stability* of tax revenue was a good thing, and they would have looked with disapproval on the present-day tendency for tax receipts to rise and fall with national income. (Recall Adam Smith's canon of prudent taxation!) Today, most economists believe that just the reverse is the truth. Thus, to dampen a boom, a budgetary surplus is desirable. There are two ways to produce such a surplus: by a reduction in government expenditure, yes; but also by an increase in tax receipts. To fight a recession, there are likewise two ways open: raising expenditures, or lowering tax receipts. How lucky we are, therefore, that our present tax system has to some degree "automatic flexibility," with its receipts tending to rise in inflationary times and to fall in times of depression. This is a powerful factor stabilizing the economy and moderating the business cycle.

2. *Unemployment compensation and other welfare transfers.* In the last 40 years we have built up an elaborate system of unemployment compensation. Soon after employees are laid off, they begin to receive payments from the unemployment compensation funds; when they go back to work, the payments cease. Taxes collected to finance unemployment compensation rise when employment is high. During boom years, therefore, the unemployment reserve funds grow and exert stabilizing pressure against too great spending; conversely, during years of slack employment, the reserve funds are used to pay out income to sustain consumption and moderate the decline.

Other welfare programs—such as public-service employment and family relief payments outside the Social Security system—also show an anticyclical automatic behavior of a stabilizing type.

3. *Corporate savings and family savings.* Not all the applause goes to the government. Our private institutions also have built-in stabilizers. Thus, the custom of corporations' maintaining their dividends, even though their incomes change in the short run, does cause their retained earnings to act like a shock absorber or built-in stabilizer.[2] And to the extent that families try to maintain previous living standards and are slow to adjust their living standards upward—to this extent, they too help stabilize. (To the extent that they rush out to spend extra income on down payments or hysterically cut down on consumption when GNP drops, they hinder stability and reinforce cyclical fluctuations.)

Still other stabilizers could be mentioned, but these are the main ones.[3]

## LIMITATIONS OF AUTOMATIC STABILIZERS

Before leaving the subject of automatic stabilizers, we should stress two things. First, the built-in stabilizers are our first line of defense, but are not by themselves sufficient to maintain full stability. Second, reliance on them in preference to discretionary programs raises some philosophical and ethical questions. Let us examine these points.

The automatic tendency for taxes to take away a fraction of each extra dollar of GNP means that the size of the "multiplier" is cut down. Each dollar swing in investment—whether caused by sunspots, inventions, or anything else—will now have its destabilizing effect on the system reduced *but not wiped out completely.* Instead of such disturbances having their effects on GNP multiplied 3 or more times, there will now—because of the automatic stabilizing effect of taxes—be a multiplier effect of only 1.5 or 2 times.[4]

---

[2] To the extent that corporate investment is itself linked to corporate saving, there is less stabilizing.
[3] Many experts advocate increasing the stabilizers by having Congress pass a law making tax *rates* vary *automatically* with changes in various aggregative price and income indices. But Congress so far has not been willing even to vote discretionary power over tax rates to the President, as the Commission on Money and Credit had recommended.
[4] Intermediate texts show that in the simple multiplier formula $1/(1 - MPC)$, we have to cut MPC down to .65 MPC now that .35 of each GNP dollar goes to taxes and only .65 to disposable income. What effect on the multiplier does this attenuation of MPC have? In the case of a multiplier of $3.0 = 1/(1 - \frac{2}{3})$, it cuts the $\frac{2}{3}$ down to .433 and the final multiplier down to only 1.8. (The propensity of corporations to distribute only a fraction of their earnings has similar attenuating effects on the multiplier; but their tendency to let a rise in income induce $I$ and their tendency to increase their $I$ merely because they have some retained profits will work to increase the multiplier.) Transfer expenditures on welfare, which tend to fall when GNP rises, act like taxes to reduce the multiplier.

**In short, a built-in stabilizer acts to *reduce part* of any fluctuation in the economy, but does not wipe out 100 per cent of the disturbance. It leaves the rest of the disturbance as a task for fiscal and monetary discretionary action.**

Philosophically, some reformers dislike the need to have human beings decide policy. They speak of a "government of laws and not of men." They advocate setting up automatic rules and mechanisms that would go into action without ever depending on human decisions. At the present time, an automatic gyropilot can keep an airplane pretty stable while the pilot catches a nap; but when something unusual comes up, the human pilot must still take over. No one has yet found a gadget with all the flexibility of man. Similarly in the social field: we have not yet arrived at a stage where any nation is likely to create for itself a set of constitutional procedures that displace need for discretionary policy formation and responsible human intelligence.

## DISCRETIONARY FISCAL POLICY

The principal weapons of discretionary fiscal policy—programs which involve explicit public decision making—are (1) varying public works and other expenditure programs, (2) varying transfer-expenditure programs, and (3) varying tax rates cyclically.

**Public works**    When governments first began to do something active about depressions, they tended to initiate work on public-investment projects for the unemployed. Often these were hastily devised. In that they aimed primarily to make work for people, they often were inefficient; e.g., road building that used as little machinery as possible to make the work stretch, leaf raking during the Depression by WPA relief workers, trumped-up pork-barrel projects of low utility and lacking careful planning. The extreme case is the mythical program to dig holes and then refill them.

The day is long past when a modern nation will let its economy collapse to the point where its only rescue must come from hastily contrived and wasteful public-works spending. The modern emphasis has, rightly, shifted away from such "make-work" projects. Indeed, where a recession is expected to be a mild and short one, economists today rely much more on monetary policy than on an increase in public works.

Why this shift away from public works as a recession cure? Planners now realize that it takes *a long time* to get a post office started or to put into effect a road-building or slum-clearance program. Plans must be made; blueprints drawn; land acquired by purchase and court condemnation; existing buildings razed; and then new structures and roads constructed. All this may take five or more years; and, at the least, half of this time may elapse before any sizable amount of money will get spent on labor and materials. Suppose the recession turns out to last a year at most, followed by two years of steady advance. Then, just in the third year, when the economy may have gone all the way from too little demand to too much demand, there will suddenly come onto the market the government spending intended to help a recession. Such timing would of course make fiscal policy an aggravator of instability, not a reducer.

The above remarks should not be construed as an argument against public works. Slum clearance, urban rehabilitation, road building, and public construction are deemed by the American people to represent urgent use of their social resources. Therefore, such programs should be pushed hard; but—and this is the point—they should not be pushed hard under the guise of a program designed *merely* to achieve short-run stabilization. They should be carried out for their own sake and over that long period of time which is necessary if they are to be done well and efficiently.

Of course, the case will often arise where the economy is in a recession or pause and where it may be possible to move ahead the date of carrying out a long-term public-expenditure program that Congress has already agreed to anyway. An intelligently planned *shelf* of blueprints for desirable public-works projects, even though some costs would be involved in arranging them ahead of time and keeping them up to date, could much improve fiscal timing. As Secretary of Commerce and President, Herbert Hoover long advocated this, and since 1931 we have had such laws. Likewise, it was logical for President Nixon, during the 1972–1973 inflationary boom, to freeze many new federal construction programs.

**Welfare expenditures**   We saw that existing welfare programs, such as unemployment compensation and old-age retirement payments, do act as automatic stabilizers, rising automatically when incomes fall and needs increase.

In addition to such built-in stabilizers, it is possible for the government to institute various discretionary programs of transfer expenditures that will stabilize further. Thus, the government could refrain from giving some pending veterans' bonus in inflationary times and push forward such disbursements in depressed times. If it intends to lower parity farm payments, Congress might hope to time the change to coincide with a boom period. Most important, in times of prolonged unemployment, the federal government has moderated the decline by aiding the states in prolonging the period for which the jobless can get paid unemployment compensation. It is precisely in times of *sustained* unemployment that the present system is most deficient, and it is in such times that there will be minimal harmful effects on job mobility and incentives from increasing unemployment disbursements and income-maintenance programs.

**Variation of tax rates**   If there is good reason to think that a recession will be brief, a temporary cut in income-tax rates can be one way of keeping disposable incomes from falling and of preventing a decline from snowballing. Under our withholding system, the moment Congress or the executive branch decides the economy needs stimulus through tax reduction, employers can begin to withhold less from salary paychecks. Varying tax rates can be used also to help control an inflationary gap and long-run sluggishness. Thus, in the 1975 slump, Congress and President Ford rebated part of the previous year's taxes, lowered current taxes, and increased the investment tax credit.

Aside from the obvious political difficulty that it takes Congress a long time to debate and act to make tax changes, there is a minor weakness in the case for heavy reliance on discretionary varying of tax rates for stability purposes. An objection to "temporary" suspension of tax rates to counter a recession comes from the political fact of life that in a democracy it may be hard to get tax rates *back up* after the emergency decline is over. Political sentiment to fight unemployment is often easier to mobilize than sentiment to fight inflationary gaps and more-than-full employment. (In long slumps this may be good.) Furthermore, as we've seen in Chapter 17, if people know tax changes are to be *temporary* and will not be altering their permanent incomes much, they may not vary their consumption spending very much. And, alas, states and localities often *perversely* increase their tax rates when stagnation is lowering their tax receipts and increasing their expenditure burden.

### SURPLUS AND DEFICIT FINANCING: STAGNATION, EXHILARATION, AND CONTRIVED GROWTH

So far we have been talking only about ironing out the business cycle. If the business cycle were around some "normal" level, most people would not worry too much so long as the boom-time budgetary surplus were always matched by the depression budgetary deficit. With such regularity, *the budget would be balanced over the business cycle* even though not balanced in every single year or month. There would be no secular trend upward in the public debt, nor downward.

But how can one be sure that the cycle will be so regular? What if America is in for what in 1938 Harvard's Alvin Hansen called "secular stagnation"—that is, a long period of (1) slowing population increase, (2) passing of the frontier's free land, (3) high corporate saving, (4) the vast piling up of capital goods, and (5) a bias toward capital-saving inventions, all of which will imply depressed investment schedules relative to saving schedules? Will not an active fiscal policy designed to wipe out such deflationary gaps then result in running a deficit *most of the time*, leading to chronic growth in the public debt? The modern answer is, "Under these conditions, yes; and over the decades the budget should not necessarily be balanced."

Contrariwise, suppose population is proliferating, new inventions are zooming, and investment is generally excessive relative to full-employment saving. If this threatens to go on most of the time, will not active fiscal policy require a budgetary surplus most of the time? Hence, will not such a condition of "secular exhilaration" lead to a long-term *decline* in the public debt? The modern answer is, "Under these conditions, yes—and a good thing."

In brief, one cannot set in advance the optimal trend of surplus or deficit. A diagram can summarize long-term budget alternatives. Figure 19-1 illustrates three variants of modern fiscal policy, all in contrast to a budget balanced in every single year.

In 19-1(a), we see *simple compensatory finance* designed to iron out the business cycle, with boom surpluses canceling out depression deficits.

In 19-1(b), under secular stagnation, surplus periods are rarer and do not suffice to keep the public debt from having a tendency to grow chronically (along with the growing GNP). (In the last half of the chapter, we study the consequences and true burdens of public-debt growth.)

In 19-1(c), with private $C + I$ spending either spontaneously strong or made strong by expansive Federal Reserve policy, the tendency for the system to run inflationary gaps much of the time is countered by budget surpluses most of the time, with the public debt tending to decline in the long run.

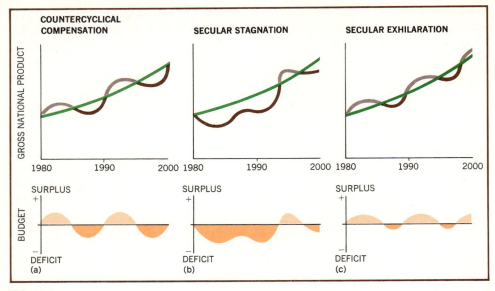

**FIG. 19-1**

**Whether surpluses should balance deficits must depend on circumstances**
In every case the trend line of policy-achieved full-employment output is shown in green.
How the GNP would grow in absence of active fiscal policy is shown in brown. The indicated
budget policy, of successful "leaning against the wind," is shown in orange below. In (*a*),
the light areas of surplus cancel out the dark areas of deficit over the business cycle. In
(*b*)'s case of secular stagnation, the dark deficits prevail over the surpluses and the debt
trends upward. In (*c*), surpluses predominate on the average and debt declines.

In principle, engineering a trend toward full employment with budget surpluses
and easy monetary policy could raise the fraction a society devotes to investment for
the future rather than to current consumption. Under "politics as usual," chronic
deficits can "crowd out" capital formation in favor of consumption—the pattern under
(*b*) rather than under (*c*).

## THE FULL-EMPLOYMENT BUDGET SURPLUS

If it is no longer mandatory to balance the budget in every year, what rule can we
put in its place to keep government spending under some kind of firm discipline?
Modern political economy says that in the last analysis there is no ultimate rule of
fiscal discipline other than that (*a*) *waste and inefficiency are to be avoided, and*
(*b*) *in a democracy, social priorities must guide what fraction of resources goes into
public uses as against private, and must determine just which of the many competing
social programs deserve precedence.* Moreover, these decisions about priorities cannot
be made in absolute terms, but, rather, must take into account the full-employment
needs of the economy and any threatening winds of demand-pull inflation.

The previous paragraph is worth rereading and pondering. No accounting shibboleths or rules of thumb can serve to replace these fundamentals of policy. And yet, people in Congress or on Main Street do yearn for simplifying precepts. One of these, which was proposed in the 1940s by the Committee for Economic Development, a liberal business group, was accepted both by President Kennedy and President Nixon. It says: "Don't balance the budget over each year, or even over each business cycle. Instead, set the budget so that it can be financed by the tax revenues that would be generated from a high-level full-employment economy." It will be helpful to see just what this "full-employment balanced-budget" notion implies.

When, as in 1975, we had 9 per cent unemployment and a sizable gap between our actual output and our full-employment potential, we naturally were running a budget deficit.

But modern economists make a new calculation, asking: "Suppose we were now at high or full employment, say, with only 4 per cent of the labor force unemployed and with firms at their desired 95 per cent of capacity. With all the higher tax revenues that such an increase in GNP would bring, what then would our budget deficit be?"

Figure 19-2 below shows by the orange curve that in the early 1970s there was really a "full-employment budget surplus," even though the green line indicates an actual budget deficit at that time.

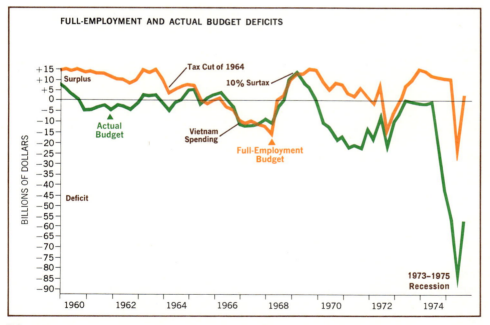

**FIG. 19-2**
**Budget deficit due to lapse from full employment needn't be inflationary or unwise**
The green curve shows the actual budget deficit. The orange curve shows that, on a full-employment basis, the budget was more than balanced from 1969 to 1972 and again in 1974. (Source: Federal Reserve Bank of St. Louis.)

To summarize, the "full-employment budget surplus or deficit" measures what *would* be the budget position *if* the economy were at full employment and the legislated tax and spending structures were in effect. What does this imply over the long run? In an era where growth or inflation would produce extra tax receipts that go beyond desired new programs, tax rates would have to be cut lest a growing full-employment surplus produce "fiscal drag" and keep us from maintaining full employment.

## RECENT FISCAL HISTORY

The first decade after World War II proved to be one of high demand all over the world. The cold war, and in particular, the Korean war, contributed to the buoyancy of output and prices.

During the two Eisenhower terms, concern over inflation led to rather tight fiscal and monetary policies. There were no less than three Eisenhower recessions, those of 1953–1954, 1957–1958, and 1960–1961. Real GNP growth from 1953 to 1960 averaged out to barely $2\frac{1}{2}$ per cent per year, and this at a time when the miracle nations abroad—Western Germany and Japan, Italy, France, and Western Europe generally, were achieving sustained real growth rates several times this amount.

John F. Kennedy came into office on the promise of getting the country moving again. Inheriting the favorable inflationary expectation from his predecessor's investment in austerity, he found conditions favorable to a sustained period of expansion. At first, increased spending provided the stimulus. Before his assassination, the President became persuaded of the virtues of seeking a deliberate deficit and a deliberate tax cut to provide stimulus. At the same time, the Fed was as permissive in its monetary policy as it dared be, given our balance of payment deficit and doctrinaire resolve to try to maintain the dollar exchange rate at its agreed-upon parity rate.

After Lyndon B. Johnson succeeded to the Presidency, he was able to push through the Kennedy tax cut in 1964: it worked about as economists had expected it to. Johnson also promoted the poverty programs of the New Frontier and of his own Great Society. Full employment was achieved, and with tolerable price stability.

In 1965 came Johnson's fateful decision to accelerate the Vietnam war. His memoirs tell us that he purposely disregarded the advice of his economists to raise taxes to pay for the war. The combination of war expenditures and maintained Great Society programs led to three years of demand-pull inflation. The full burden was thrust on Fed monetary contraction, leading to the "money crunch" of 1966 and the mini- or growth-recession of 1966–1967. As usually happens in a modern mixed economy, demand-pull inflation eventually induces cost-push inflation. The union wage rates that had lagged behind nonunion rates in 1965–1968 finally began to run ahead of them.

On taking office in 1969, Richard Nixon first pursued a policy of benign neglect toward private wage and price decision making. Fiscal and monetary tightness led to the recession of 1969–1970 and to the weak recovery of 1970–1971. At this point, with a second-term election only 15 months away, the occasion of an international run on the dollar led Mr. Nixon to tear up his old game plan of gradualism. On August 15, 1971, he suspended gold payments and convertibility of the dollar; promulgated a wage and price freeze; and reduced taxes primarily on business enterprise.

For the next two years expansionary fiscal and monetary policy, coupled with direct wage and price controls, led to overexuberance. By spring of 1973, with the election out of the way, fiscal and monetary tightness contrived a growth recession. The oil boycott in the wake of the October 1973 Mid-East war converted the pause into a full-fledged recession.

And still at the same time, the combination of higher energy prices and bad harvests all over the world for several years running acted to give the United States double-digit annual rates of inflation. This was "stagflation"—growing unemployment and price inflation at the same time, in defiance of the old textbook analytics of simple demand-pull inflation.

The Federal Reserve and the administration knew no other way to fight inflation than to cool off the economy—and, for that matter, no jury of impartial economists could agree on a cure for stagflation that was not as bad as the disease itself. By the fall of 1974, when the unemployment rate began a steep climb from $5\frac{1}{2}$ to 9 per cent of the labor force, economists could say that on the bottom of the current recession was written "Made in Washington." The slowdown was contrived not out of cruelty nor out of ignorance, but for the purpose of decelerating the rate of inflation. Unfortunately, when one plays with avalanches, the consequences can get out of hand. Following the 1974 midterm electoral successes of the opposition party, both the administration and Congress began to shift policy from fighting off inflation to fighting off a replay of the Great Depression of the 1930s.

The revival of the economy by the end of 1975 illustrated that modern fiscal and monetary analysis is indeed applicable. Within the inexactness inevitable in an inexact science like political economy, the chronicles of economic history do seem to substantiate the general validity of modern fiscal and monetary analysis.

We have come a long way from the old-fashioned views of the man in the street. Economic emphasis has been put on the economy's healthy growth without inflation and not on the balancing of the budget. But is this sound economics? Can the economic system *prudently bear the implied burden of the public debt?* To that vital question we turn for the remaining section of this chapter.

## B. THE PUBLIC DEBT AND MODERN FISCAL POLICY

As a result primarily of World War II and the cold wars, the public debt of the federal government is about $620 billion—almost two-thirds of a trillion dollars. What are the various economic problems created by such a debt? Are there any false problems associated with it? What are the important noneconomic factors that must be reckoned with in any discussion of this vital political issue?

In appraising the burdens involved in a public debt, we must carefully avoid the unscientific practice of making up our minds in advance that whatever is true of one small merchant's debt is also necessarily true of the government's debt. Prejudging the problem in this way comes perilously close to the logical fallacy of composition; and instead of permitting us to isolate the true—all too real—burdens of the public debt, it will only confuse the issue.

Modern economists give attention to the debt's true burden and diagnose its problems in a way significantly different from the layperson's approach.

## BURDENS AND BENEFITS OF THE PUBLIC DEBT

The person in the street, if asked to make a list of important economic problems, used to put the size of the public debt near the top of the list. A panel of economic experts, in this country or anywhere else in the Western world, will usually put the debt toward the bottom of any such list of worries, and indeed some will actually include it on the credit side of the ledger as a positive blessing.

Why this difference of opinion? And why is it that in countries like Germany, Britain, Japan, and Holland, statesmen, editors, and the citizenry never even know what their current budgetary deficits (as *we* measure the concept) are? These are interesting *psychological* questions that do not belong primarily in a course on economics. It is our task here to make sure we understand in an objective and dispassionate way the *economic* effects of debts, deficits, and surpluses. The facts agreed on by economic scholars can be briefly summarized in the main body of this chapter. The Appendix will present a survey of the deeper analysis underlying the economics of public debt.

As the Appendix shows,

**The main way that one generation can put a burden on a later generation is by currently using up the nation's stock of capital goods, or by failing to add the usual investment increment to the stock of capital.**

Thus, the bulk of our federal debt came from World War II. The primary burden of that war came fron the need *then* to eat up capital goods without replacing them, in order to maximize our effectiveness against the enemy and shorten the war. (Hence, it was the prohibition against car manufacture or building construction and repair that produced this real burden, and not the happenstance that Congress decided to finance part of the war on a loan-deficit basis rather than on a full tax-as-you-go basis.)

Looking to the future, we can say that (1) *increases in public debt which are incurred in time of full employment* and involve no government capital formation, but *which* (2) *do require that private investment be held down* (by Federal Reserve policy or by inflation itself), do in fact represent a "burden" (future capital and output are less than they would have been). On the other hand, incurring debt when there is no other feasible way to move the $C + I + G$ equilibrium intersection up toward full employment actually represents a *negative* burden on the immediate future to the degree that it induces more current capital formation and consumption than would otherwise take place! (Recall Chapter 13's Paradox of Thrift: less social thrift may sometimes lead to more rather than less capital formation.)

There is a second aspect of the American public debt needing stress. An *external* debt (owed to foreigners), as the Appendix shows in detail, does involve a net subtraction from the goods and services available to the American people, to the degree that we have to send goods abroad to pay interest on that debt.[5] An *internal* debt (owed by the government to its own citizens) is quite a different matter. However, one cannot blithely ignore an internal debt on the ground that "we all owe it to ourselves." There *are* problems involved in an internal debt, even though not those of an external debt.

---

[5] This is like private debt service to Arab oil magnates who have acquired ownership in our assets in return for selling us oil and who later live on earnings from these assets.

**Two internal-debt problems**   First, there are the *transfer* payments of interest that must be made to some people and the taxes that are levied upon all people for this purpose. To the degree that the people involved are different and that the interest receivers are wealthier, more thrifty, or deemed less in need of income, there will be some (admittedly minor) *redistributional* effects to reckon with. But even if the *same* people are taxed to pay on the average the same amounts *they* receive in interest, there will still be the *distorting effects on incentives* that are inescapably present in the case of any tax. (The Appendix shows that taxing Peter to pay Peter interest may make Peter work less hard or harder—and either of these may be a distortion of efficiency and well-being.[6])

Second, because we do not live forever, we tend as individuals to treat the public debt as something of an addition to our net worths (added onto the value of the land, structures, and machinery we own). This feeling of greater wealth may well cause us to consume a bit more and save a bit less. Thus the existence of a large, outstanding public debt may have some long-run influence on interest-rate levels. Some writers fear that channeling investment funds into the purchase of government bonds will raise the rate of interest to private borrowers. Thus, if people want to hold a certain total of assets to provide for their old-age retirement, the existence of government bonds may substitute for ownership of deeds to machinery and buildings.

Alexander Hamilton, the spokesman of the conservative Federalist party, argued otherwise—that the debt could lower interest rates. He felt that, rightly managed and in the right amounts, a public debt would be "a national blessing" because it would provide a secure gilt-edge asset that would give businessmen an income and enable them to trade for smaller profits. Notice, too, the beneficial effects of interest payments to banks, colleges, widows, and other *rentiers*. If there were no public debt, or if interest rates were to fall, (1) charitable institutions would have to be supported by public and private current contributions more than by interest on endowments, (2) social security and annuities would have to take the place of *rentier* interest, and (3) service charges by banks would have to be relied upon instead of public bond interest.

Still other effects are analyzed in the Appendix. But in general, when economists evaluate the magnitude and trend of the public debt, with rare exceptions they agree that its present level does not merit the psychological excitement that used to be accorded it and that occasionally still is. They also agree, however, that *recklessness* concerning deficit spending and debt formation—lack of social priorities and waste in spending—could become an important social evil if it emasculates all public self-discipline, and they point to historical instances of ruinous inflations.

## EFFECTS ON PRIVATE EMOTIONS AND INVESTMENT

Never forget that there is a tremendous amount of emotion involved in people's attitudes toward the debt, and this we must not dismiss lightly. Like sex or religion, the public debt is a subject we all love to discuss. Many people used to predict the end of the world when the debt reached one-hundredth, one-tenth, and one-fifth of

---

[6]But recall, from Table 8-2, debt interest is only one-tenth of the total expenditure budget.

its present level; each year when the dire disaster had not appeared, they renewed their predictions for subsequent years.

Such attitudes may affect private investment. What if private investment is frightened off by government expenditure or by the deficit? This is certainly possible. Businessmen may say, "With that man in the White House spending recklessly, we're going to abandon even the little private investment we had planned." Or a private utility company may curtail investment because it fears the threat of public dam projects. Or when government spending gives people money to buy in retail stores, the effect in time of deep depression may simply be to permit merchants to work off inventory of surplus merchandise; if they don't reorder production goods, the public expenditure has been just neutralized by induced private *disinvestment* (in inventory), and the multiplier chain is stopped dead in its tracks.

On the other hand, there are expansive effects on private investment that are just the opposite of these contractionary repercussions of government finance. When current production is at a low ebb and there is excess plant capacity, no prudent businessman feels like undertaking new capital formation. If the government is able to boost retail sales and the production of consumption goods, then businessmen will have the financial ability and at least some motive to renew equipment and build new plants.[7] Sometimes purely psychological fears about the public debt and deficit could *accentuate* an inflation situation, even one with origins outside the fiscal sphere.

Where there are two such opposing tendencies—expansive and contractionary effects upon private investment—facts rather than rhetoric must be our guide. Although economics does not permit us to make controlled experiments to settle the point conclusively, the bulk of the statistical data seems to suggest that private investment tends on the whole to move sympathetically with the level of national income. The cash register calls the tune.

**Proof of the pudding**    Some congressmen have said, "Deficit financing was tried in the Great Depression and proved to be a failure." MIT's E. Cary Brown studied the fiscal experience of the 1930s to see whether this was true. His careful measurement of the actual statistics of GNP, *G*, and deficits showed that the historical facts agreed remarkably well with multiplier theory: despite the hysterical criticisms of the New Deal deficits as being gigantic, they in fact were what we would consider small today in relationship to the existent deflationary gap—much too small for any scientist to predict that they would restore full employment; but the fiscal actions of the 1930s did, *per dollar*, produce the expansionary effects predicted by multiplier theory. Similar studies have been made of the 1964 and 1975 tax cuts, the 1968 tax increase, and their interactions with Fed monetary policy.

## THE QUANTITATIVE PROBLEM OF THE DEBT

To assess the importance of the present public debt, we must turn to the facts. Do interest payments on it swallow up much of the GNP? How does the total

[7]An example of this was provided by the discussion in Chapter 14 of the acceleration principle relating induced investment to the upward change in sales.

of all interest payments, public and private, compare with past years and with the experience of other countries? What about the future?

To see how the present debt compares with the past and with Britain's debt, look at Table 19-1 on this page. It shows for selected times and places national debts in their relationship to size of gross national product and interest payments. Thus, in 1976 our national debt of about $620 billion represented something more than one-third of our annual $1⅔ trillion GNP (or about 5 months of 1976 GNP), and the debt's interest payments represented less than 3 per cent of national income. Note that England in 1818, 1923, and 1946 had an internal debt estimated at two or three times her GNP, and interest on the debt as a percentage of GNP far exceeded anything that we need look forward to; yet the century before World War I was England's greatest century—greatest in power and material progress. Further, as the table shows, her national debt was not reduced much; but with the steady growth of her GNP, the debt and its charges shrank to almost nothing in relative magnitude!

In the light of these statistics and by careful qualitative analysis, the reader must form his own judgment as to whether the national debt can be rationally regarded

### PUBLIC DEBT AND INTEREST CHARGES RELATIVE TO GROSS NATIONAL PRODUCT

| (1) YEAR | (2) NATIONAL DEBT | (3) INTEREST CHARGES ON NATIONAL DEBT | (4) GNP | (5) SIZE OF DEBT IN YEARS OF GNP (5) = (2) ÷ (4) | (6) INTEREST CHARGES AS A PERCENTAGE OF GNP (6) ÷ 100 = (3) ÷ (4) |
|---|---|---|---|---|---|
| United States (billions): | | | | | |
| 1976 | $621.8* | $36.94 | $1,663.0 | 0.4 | 2.2 |
| 1945 | 278.7 | 3.66 | 213.6 | 1.3 | 1.7 |
| 1939 | 47.6 | 0.95 | 91.1 | 0.5 | 1.0 |
| 1929 | 16.3 | 0.66 | 104.4 | 0.2 | 0.6 |
| 1920 | 24.3 | 1.02 | 88.9 | 0.3 | 1.1 |
| 1916 | 1.2 | 0.02 | 40.3 | 0.0+ | 0.0+ |
| 1868 | 2.6 | 0.13 | 6.8 | 0.4 | 1.9 |
| Britain (billions): | | | | | |
| 1974 | £40.1 | £1.80 | £63.2 | 0.6 | 4.5 |
| 1946 | 23.6 | 0.48 | 8.9 | 2.7 | 5.4 |
| 1923 | 7.7 | 0.33 | 4.0 | 1.9 | 8.2 |
| 1913 | 0.6 | 0.02 | 2.4 | 0.3 | 0.8 |
| 1818 | 0.8 | 0.03 | 0.4 | 2.1 | 7.7 |

*Includes about $250 billion in federal government accounts and the Fed.

**TABLE 19-1**
**Growing debt holds little peril for a dynamically growing economy**
The $40-billion debt that worried people so much in the 1930s looks small against the subsequent rise in our income. (Sources: U.S. Departments of Commerce and Treasury; *Statistical Abstract of United Kingdom*.)

as a problem of the first magnitude in comparison with the problems of national defense, the nuclear bomb, pollution and exhaustible resources, racial tension, unemployment, and stagflation. Whether productivity will continue to rise in the future, whether inequality can be tempered, whether labor and management can learn to bargain collectively without strikes and cost-push inflation—to most informed observers, these seem much more important than the public debt itself.

**Growth in the economy**   In dispassionately analyzing the growth of the debt, there is one error we must avoid: *We must not forget that the real national product of a nation is an ever-growing thing.*

Our population still grows, albeit more slowly. As to the rate of productivity improvement, there is some indication of a slowing down, but not nearly to a halt. Upon this, "stagnationists" and "exhilarationists" both agree. What seemed like a big debt in 1790 would be nothing today. What our children will come to regard as a big debt, our greatgrandchildren will deem relatively unimportant.

This explains why England and France, in the crucially formative years of the capitalistic system and the Industrial Revolution, were able to go on—not only decade after decade, but century after century—with their budgets in balance less than half the time. The historian Lord Macaulay, more than a century ago, said the last word on the debt and growth:

At every stage in the growth of that debt the nation has set up the same cry of anguish and despair. At every stage in the growth of that debt it has been seriously asserted by wise men that bankruptcy and ruin were at hand. Yet still the debt went on growing; and still bankruptcy and ruin were as remote as ever. . . .

The prophets of evil were under a double delusion. They erroneously imagined that there was an exact analogy between the case of an individual who is in debt to another individual and the case of a society which is in debt to a part of itself. . . . They made no allowance for the effect produced by the incessant progress of every experimental science, and by the incessant efforts of every man to get on in life. They saw that the debt grew; and they forgot that other things grew as well. . . .

Figure 19-3 dramatically exemplifies that the growth of our economy and price inflation since 1945 have drastically *reduced* the ratio of United States public debt to gross national product. (This chart, properly, excludes FRB and Treasury holdings; but the point would be the same if these exclusions had not been made.) This fact of growth explains why, in the United States, where money GNP doubles in about a decade, the public debt might increase by another two-thirds of a trillion dollars in that time without its relative percentage burden growing at all.

This would give the wildest believer in government spending an average deficit of tens and tens of billions of dollars per year before he would have to turn to such even more unorthodox financial expedients as printing money or selling interest-free bonds to the Federal Reserve Banks.

Could a nation fanatically addicted to deficit spending pursue such a policy for the rest of our lives and beyond? Study of the mechanics of banking and income determination suggests that the barrier to this would not be financial. The barrier would have

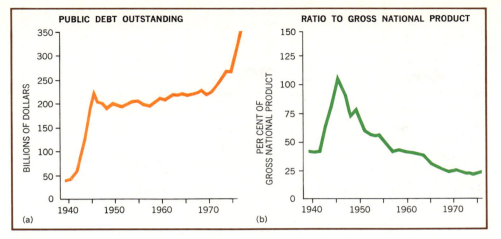

**FIG. 19-3**
**While private debt outpaced GNP, public-debt ratio has been falling steadily**
Most of the federal debt held by the public came from wars. In the last 30 years, its ratio to the growing GNP has declined steadily. (Source: U.S. Treasury. Holdings of bonds by Federal Reserve or government itself are here excluded from the total of federal debt.)

to be political and self-imposed; and the effects of such a policy would depend crucially upon whether it impinges on an economy that is already inflationary or deflationary.

### PRIVATE AND PUBLIC ANALOGIES[8]

Undoubtedly, the major reason for concern about the public debt does not involve sophisticated questions of whether or not it affects the stock of real capital goods. The major concern has to do with the fact that people are uncomfortable at the prospect of anything that may go on growing forever. We all are made uncomfortable by infinity; we are all frightened of the way things grow at compound interest. Some psychologists attribute this to the fact that every child is frightened at the prospect of dying, of *not* living forever. The following case study of the public debt in comparison with the debt of the American Telephone and Telegraph Company adds little to sophisticated analysis of the economics of the matter; but it does bring psychological comfort where it is needed most, to those fearful of ultimate national bankruptcy.

"How can the government go on running up debt? If I or my wife lived beyond our means and ran a debt, we'd soon learn what trouble is." The person speaking has overlooked the fallacy of composition: What is true for each unit may be false for the whole of society.

"Why do conservatives complain about the size of the public debt? Private debt has grown tremendously faster in the postwar period than public debt, and you don't hear complaints about that. All credit involves debt. The pyramid of credit could be called the pyramid of debt. If people are to have liquid assets, other people or institutions must have liabilities—d--t

[8]This section may be skipped by brief courses.

to the squeamish." The speaker here is also trying to use analogies with private finance, but this time to the advantage of a program for large deficits.

Both analogies are in principle suspect. Each contains some element of truth, but every strand of such arguments needs critical testing. Thus, it is true that the total of private debt is about four times the public debt (even when we include state and local public debts). And it is true that private debt has grown much more in the last decades than the public debt, so that the latter has declined as a fraction of all debt. But it is also true that the private assets to back up that private debt have gone up too. And it is true that one could imagine an economy—not ours!—where everything was financed by *equity* issues without fixed debt.

With the warning that no analogy is conclusive, here is an analogy between a private corporation like the American Telephone and Telegraph Company and the United States government.

AT&T has grown all this century. It has floated new debt throughout this century, with never an end to it. If our economy remains healthy, AT&T will undoubtedly have a rising bond debt for the rest of this century. This is prudent finance, not unsound finance. It is prudent to buy that bond debt, but not for the reason that the company has plants and equipment bought from that debt financing and which it could liquidate in a pinch. There is no one to whom AT&T could sell such specialized items in an emergency, since they are good only for the telephone business in which AT&T has complete local monopolies.

Why is never-ending growth in AT&T debt prudent? It is prudent because *the dollar receipts the company can earn from its telephone services are sure to grow along with the population and GNP.* The interest on the debt, and the occasional refunding of the debt, can be paid for out of the revenues from the telephone company's customers. If they all became impoverished, say, by atomic war, AT&T would have to go bankrupt and not repay its debt. But in a growing economy, no going concern proceeds on the assumption that all the people will go bankrupt.

What does the federal government use to pay its debt interest and refundings? Obviously, *it is the taxable capacity of the country's national product that any government can rely on.*

So long as the money GNP grows at 5 or 6 per cent from now until kingdom come, the public debt of the federal government can grow at those rates, ultimately passing one, two, or any number of trillion dollars. No inflation need result if the process takes place in balance. And no bankruptcy or increase in relative tax burden. And no embarrassment to the Secretary of the Treasury. Like life itself, there is no end to the process.

The above analogy is given only for those who feel a psychological need for reassuring analogies and as an antidote to misleading pessimistic analogies. It says nothing about the great harm governments can do if they spend their taxed or borrowed funds rashly and feed fuel to inflationary gaps when such exist. It says nothing about the proper scope and efficiency of government, issues already analyzed in Chapter 8. It says nothing about the proper rate of capital formation and rate of current consumption, or about what should be a nation's growth rate.

## CONCLUSION: MACROECONOMICS OF THE MIXED ECONOMY

The Employment Act of 1946 stated that the government had a responsibility to act to keep employment high and to moderate cyclical instability (and many have suggested that it be amended to mention explicitly a similar government concern for "reasonable stability" of the price level). Even if there were no such legislative proclamations, it is a fact all over the world that the populace of modern mixed economies require their representative governments to pursue economic policies that attempt to keep employment high, growth strong, and prices stable.

Part Two has presented the economic *tools of macroeconomics:* how the various schedules determine levels and movements in incomes and prices; and how monetary and fiscal policies can shift those schedules so as to combat deflationary and inflationary gaps. In Part Six special macroeconomic problems connected with the modern era—cost-push inflation and stagflation versus demand-pull inflation, growth, and so forth—will be discussed in greater detail. The millennium has not yet arrived.

The finding of our macroeconomic analysis rejects both the classical faith that laissez faire must by itself lead to utopian stability and the pre-World War II pessimism that classical microeconomic principles have become inapplicable to the modern world. Instead we end with the reasoned prospect that appropriate monetary and fiscal policies can try to recreate an economic environment which will *validate* the verities of microeconomics—that society must choose among its alternative high-employment production possibilities; that paradoxes of thrift and the fallacies of composition must not be permitted to create cleavages between private and social virtues (or vices).

**By means of appropriately reinforcing monetary and fiscal policies, a mixed economy can avoid the worst excesses of boom and slump. This being understood, the paradoxes that robbed the older classical principles dealing with small-scale "microeconomics" of their relevance and validity now lose much of their sting. The broad cleavage between microeconomics and macroeconomics is closed by active public use of fiscal and monetary policy (save for the unsolved dilemma of stagflation in the mixed economy!).**

With good conscience we can turn to the analysis in Part Three of how the great social aggregates of national income and employment *get determined in their detailed parts* and to Part Four's analysis of *income distribution.*

## SUMMARY

### A. SHORT-RUN AND LONG-RUN FISCAL POLICY

1  When private investment and consumption spending create an inflationary (or deflationary) gap, it is the task of fiscal and monetary policy to offset the gap in the attempt to preserve price stability, high employment, and growth.

2  Fiscal weapons refer to taxation and expenditure policies, to budget surpluses and deficits. In this connection, the modern economy is blessed with important "built-in stabilizers." Requiring no discretionary action, tax receipts change *automatically* when income changes, thereby reducing the size of the multiplier and serving to wipe out part of any disturbance. (The same stabilizing effect is created by unemployment compensation and other welfare transfers that automatically grow as income falls, as well as by the propensity of corporations to pay out in dividends only part of their current earnings.)

3   Because the automatic stabilizers never *fully* offset the instabilities of an economy, scope is left for *discretionary* programs. Public works and other expenditure on goods and services can involve such time lags in getting under way as to make their use to combat short recessions undesirable. Discretionary variations in transfer expenditures and in tax rates—politics aside—have greater short-run flexibility.

4   When men began to drop the notion that the government's budget had to be balanced in every year or month, they first thought that it would be in balance over the business cycle—with the boom-time surpluses just matching the depression deficits. Today, it is realized that only by coincidence would the prosperity years just balance in their intensity the recession years.

  If, as a few believe, we are faced by "secular stagnation," with private saving and investment schedules tending much of the time to produce deflationary gaps, fiscal policy will probably succeed in maintaining stable high employment only by having a *long-term* increase in the public debt. If, as others believe, we are in for "chronic exhilaration," with demand so brisk as to lead much of the time to inflationary gaps, then active fiscal policy will probably mean a bias toward surplus financing and a secular downward trend in the public debt. Perhaps the majority of economists feel there is no need to try to predict what the distant future has in store, being prepared to advocate programs that the developing situation calls for.

5   To get a better measure of changes in discretionary fiscal policy, economists supplement knowledge of the *actual* budget surplus or deficit with the hypothetical "full-employment budget surplus or deficit," which measures what the existing tax and spending structure *would* entail if GNP were at a full-employment level.

## B. THE PUBLIC DEBT AND MODERN FISCAL POLICY

6   The public debt does not burden the shoulders of a nation as if each citizen were made to carry rocks on his back. To the degree that we now follow policies of *reduced capital formation* which will pass on to posterity less capital goods, we can directly affect the production possibilities open to them. To the degree that we borrow *from abroad* for some transitory consumption purposes and pledge posterity to pay back the interest and principal on such external debt, we do place upon that posterity a net burden, which will be a subtraction from what they can later produce. To the degree that we bequeath to posterity an internal debt but no change in capital stock beyond what would anyway have been given them, there may be various *internal transfer effects* as one group in the community receives a larger share of the goods then produced at the expense of another group.

  At any one time there is no "net burden" of such internal transfers quite like the net subtraction involved in the external debt payment; at most there are *transfer effects* between people of different ages then alive and certain effects within each generation's lifetime on how much they will receive of consumption and at what ages. And the process of taxing Peter to pay Paul, or taxing Peter to pay Peter, can have definite costs: these can involve various distortions of production and efficiency, but should not be confused with actually sending goods abroad.

Aside from the above "real" effects, there may also be psychological effects upon the minds of people, and their resulting actions must of course be regarded as real. Moreover, the fact that there are more rather than less bonds being owned by people in the community can be expected to have quite real effects on their stage-of-life propensity to save and consume out of income. Each person regards his government bond as an asset, but the future taxes to service these bonds he does not count in *fully* as a current personal liability, even though all society will have to pay taxes equal to such debt service. (This is not irrational from his viewpoint, since the tax rates he will be subject to have little to do with his personal holding of the debt, as the Appendix discusses.)

This summary point has been written at some length to indicate the complexity of the problem. We see that a debt does have important impacts on the economy, even if they are not primarily those that orators and editors preach about.

7   It is important, also, to keep in perspective the size of the end-of-the-century federal debt in relation to gross national product and interest charges. The growth of the debt must be appraised in terms of the growth of the economy as a whole. Since 1945 the ratio of outstanding public debt to private debt and national product has been substantially declining, a fact few people realize.

## CONCEPTS FOR REVIEW

inflationary and deflationary gap
tax receipts and tax rates
government expenditure on goods
    and transfer expenditures
built-in stabilizers and the
    reduced multiplier
discretionary fiscal programs
the full-employment budget
    surplus
internal versus external debt

present versus future generations
    and bequeathal of real
    capital
debt-income ratios here and
    abroad, today, yesterday,
    and tomorrow
AT&T versus U.S.A.
chronic stagnation, exhilaration,
    and trends in the public debt
Employment Act of 1946

## QUESTIONS FOR DISCUSSION

1   "No nation can avoid having a fiscal policy. With the government such an important part of the present-day economy, it is almost impossible even to define a 'neutral fiscal policy.' It is even harder to give rational reasons for preferring such a policy to an active fiscal program aimed at preventing inflation and deflation." Examine critically.

2    List various "built-in stabilizers." Show how they work in the late 1970s.

3    What phase of the business cycle are you now in? What tax and expenditure policies would seem appropriate? Qualitatively, how would you vary the relative mix of taxes (income-tax rates and exemptions, sales taxes, property taxes) to fight unemployment or inflation?

4    From the early 1870s to the middle 1890s, depressions were deep and prolonged, booms were short-lived and relatively anemic, the price level was declining. What long-run fiscal policy should have been followed in that quarter of a century? Would your answer be the same for the following 20 years leading up to World War I, a period of mild, but chronic, demand-pull inflation?

5    "In the AT&T–debt versus public-debt analogy, it should be noted that along with the private debt went new capital goods—machines, buildings, etc.—which *themselves* enabled growth of real GNP. The same is not true of public-debt growth to finance current public-consumption programs." Verify the element of truth in this.

6    Show briefly why "burden of the debt" is a complicated economic issue.

# APPENDIX: False and Genuine Burdens of the Public Debt

We have seen that the public debt, prorated over the population, is sometimes regarded to be a load on each person's back. According to this same image, when Congress adds a dollar to the debt by running a current deficit of a dollar, that is like just one more rock added to the load our children or grandchildren will already have to carry on their backs.

This image is misleading in two ways. First, it exaggerates the burdens that are truly involved. Second, by giving a mistaken view of the debt burden, it lays itself open to refutation and thereby to the mistaken conclusion that there are, after all, *no* burdens connected with the public debt.

As a preview to a judicious appraisal, see how vulnerable the foregoing "rocks-on-backs" image is.

**Polar case of zero burden**    Suppose all debt came from a past war. That war is over. Suppose *all* families (1) share equally in ideal, nondistorting taxes, (2) hold equal shares of public-debt bonds, (3) all live forever (as individuals or as a cohesive family). With no debt held abroad, then, genuinely we do "all owe it to ourselves."

Then such bonds are genuinely not rocks on our shoulders, or even paperweights. If we unanimously voted to abolish the bonds, there would be no real difference. If an enemy bombed our homes and factories, that would be a genuine personal and national burden. But if an enemy bombed our bond lockboxes out of existence, that would merely save us, in this polar case, the red tape of taxing ourselves to pay each of us back in bond interest just what the extra tax took away.

So goes the argument. Notice how simple the above refutation is. And how clever in taking the wind out of the sails of those who use the oversimplified rock-burden image. Moreover, the refutation is—granted its assumptions—logically rigorous.

Has the refutation proved that the war involved no grievous burden? It has been cunningly silent on that matter. The Devil's Advocate who produced the refutation would, if pressed by a Tireless Truthseeker, have to concede much.

## A DIALOGUE

**Devil's Advocate:**   Yes, the war did involve a grievous economic burden at the time. We had to work hard and long hours. We had to cut wartime consumption to the bone: do with little meat, no cars, no travel, no urban development—make do with few of the things that make life enjoyable rather than merely tolerable.

**Tireless Truthseeker:**   With severe rationing controls, the contemporaneous wartime burden of sacrificed consumption would, according to your view, be much the same even if the war had been financed by pay-as-you-go wartime taxes instead of deficit?

**D.A.:**   Precisely Postwar canceled tax receipts, instead of bonds, would make no difference.

**T.T.:**   But surely, we used up capital goods during the war by not replacing them. The enemy had to be fought with current 1941–1945 goods, not with 1976 goods. By using up capital goods *then,* we could throw more resources into the war effort. And that did put a real burden *on us in the postwar period* since we inherited less capital goods at war's end. In the postwar period we've had to consume less in order to rebuild those capital goods; and we've had to consume less than we could have if 1941–1945 had given us the normal peacetime increase in capital.

**D.A.:**   True. But wartime rationing produced that result. If no wartime deficits and bond indebtedness had been created, that *genuine burden* on the postwar group due to the war would still have taken place.

Let's leave facile debate and sum up.

## SUMMARY OF DEBT BURDENS-BENEFITS

**1. Capital-bequeathed burden**   The principal way one generation puts a burden on itself later or on a later generation is by bequeathing it less real capital than would otherwise have been the case. Any growth of public debt that has this effect—as in the case of full-employment borrowing for current public consumption that has to be offset by contractionary monetary policy which will lower investment—most definitely does involve a genuine "burden."

**2. External-debt burden**   Any public debt that is externally held does involve a current burden on the citizens at home, since in the end they have to send goods abroad corresponding to the interest payments and debt service. (Of course, if the original borrowing from abroad resulted in equivalent fruitful capital goods here, their fruits will cover the external-debt service; so the net effect of such external borrowing, taken as a package, would be favorable to us.)

**3. Transfer effects**   Taxing Peter to pay Paul bond interest, even if they are the same person, is certain to cause some harmful distortions of personal and business decisions. (EXAMPLE: Peter is taxed 10 per cent of his income to pay himself $1,000 of bond interest. He is under the illusion, and rightly so as an individual, that he can work less and cut down on his tax; but if all do so, we have to increase the tax rate. Result: We all end up working less because taxes on each man matched by equal interest payments to him do not economically cancel out!)

Correlated with public-debt operations, but not always in a simple way, are certain transfers that take place between different individuals living at the same time, between the same individual at different periods of life, and between successive generations.

**4. Wealth stimulus to consumption**   The existence of public debt, for reasons already seen, makes the average man feel wealthier. For good or evil, it raises his propensity-to-consume schedule: this may, in a poorly functioning system, be a great thing to reduce unemployment and increase both consumption and investment. But in a system where employment can be counted on to remain full by virtue of price flexibility, luck, or monetary management, the increase in $C$ may be at the expense of $I$ and reinforce the less-capital-bequeathed burden. (In extreme cases, a dollar of public debt might ultimately kill off a dollar of real capital goods!)

**5. Effects on interest and money policy**   A large debt gives the Fed great leverage for massive open-market operations to achieve stabilization—unless, as in 1946–1951, the central bank is pressured by the government to sacrifice the goal of stabilization to the dubious goal of keeping down the interest charges on the public debt. Many experts believe that the existence of a broad market in government securities makes possible extensive open-market operations of a stabilizing type and tends to enhance the effectiveness of monetary policy. Debt management by the

Treasury and the Fed through a proper policy of open-market operations in bonds of all maturities that was properly carried out could enhance the stability of a modern system.

#### 6. How to analyze true debt effects
We must render unto intermediate and advanced texts what is theirs. Suffice it to say here that penetrating analysis requires a theoretical model of some complexity. At the least, it should involve the interplay of three kinds of assets: real capital goods (equipment, plant, etc.); government bonds; supply of money, $M$ (which is the non-interest-bearing, never-maturing "debt" of government). Then we should not ask: "What is the absolute burden of the public debt?" Rather, we ask: "Given the choice of loan-financed deficit over $M$-financed or over laissez faire unemployment, what will the differential effects be?"

The answers will be illuminating.[1]

[1] Two quite different diagnoses can *both* be valid depending upon assumptions!

*Heretical case:* Deep depression spending of $50 billion was the *only* feasible way of reducing 1933–1935 unemploy-

#### 7. Effects on discipline and ideology
It would be a tragedy if people, in giving up their irrational fears of deficit spending, were thereby led to call the sky the limit. Unlimited spending can produce inflation, chaos, and waste.

It is to be hoped that the discipline of rationality can replace the discipline of superstition and misunderstanding. After the shibboleth of a balanced budget has lost its power to limit public spending, the good society will have to replace it by a calculus of cost-and-benefit.

ment; and this debt added to consumption and capital formation then and to the capital stock and GNP potential in 1980.

*Classical case:* Failing to tax to finance the Vietnam war raised our debt and forced the Fed to tighten $M$ and reduce capital formation spending; so this debt is a genuine burden in 1980 in the form of lower real capital then; but by 1990, paying it off by taxing enough to produce a budget surplus, while at the same time employment is kept full by the Fed's loosening $M$ and inducing extraordinary capital formation—that will remove the burden from post-1990 generations at the expense of having put it on the 1980–1990 generation, whose heavy taxes cut down on their consumption in those years.

# 3

# THE COMPOSITION AND PRICING OF NATIONAL OUTPUT

Part One of this book described the modern economic system and discussed the nature of national income. Part Two gave the modern theory of income determination: it showed why and how incomes, job opportunities, and levels of price fluctuate; it showed how money and banking fit in with income analysis; and most significantly, it showed how fiscal and monetary policy can keep the aggregate system working tolerably well. Today such analysis is called *macro*economics.

## PREVIEW

Now Parts Three and Four analyze *micro*economics dealing with the following important questions: What determines the relative prices of *particular* goods? What determines the quantitative breakdown of the national-income aggregates into various goods and services?

In order to understand the *system* of market prices which strikes an equilibrium among people's tastes for different goods and the scarcities of total resources that can produce them, Part Three studies in detail the tools of supply and demand that Chapter 4 introduced briefly.

Part Four follows with a closely related supply-and-demand analysis of what determines the prices of factors of production. Why are wages growing? Why does the share of land rent in the economy move in this way or that? What determines interest? Why have unskilled wages been falling relative to white-collar wages? Are workers being increasingly "exploited" in the sense of receiving an ever-lower share of GNP? Such problems constitute the subject of "distribution of income" in Part Four.

We shall see that the concepts of supply and demand as they are developed further in this chapter are vital tools for mastering the analysis of varied branches of microeconomics. (As a matter of fact, the supply-and-demand tools are indispensable in explaining the international trade problems of Part Five and the current economic issues of Part Six.)

# 20
# DETERMINATION OF PRICE BY SUPPLY AND DEMAND

The end is easily foretold,
When every blessed thing
   you hold
Is made of silver, or of
   gold,
You long for simple
   pewter.

When you have nothing
   else to wear
But cloth of gold and
   satins rare,
For cloth of gold you
   cease to care
Up goes the price of
   shoddy.
GILBERT AND SULLIVAN
*The Gondoliers*

379

## MICROECONOMICS VERSUS MACROECONOMICS?

Macroeconomics deals with the big picture—with the macroaggregates of income, employment, and price levels. But it is not true that microeconomics deals with unimportant details. After all, the big picture is made up of its parts. Mere billions of dollars would be meaningless if they did not correspond to the thousand and one useful goods and services that people really need and want. And who would be impressed by a vast national income if its distribution among human beings was a matter of caprice and pointless inequality?

There is really no opposition between micro- and macroeconomics. Both are vital. You are less than half-educated if you understand one while being ignorant of the other. We cannot even say which comes first: some books begin with one; some with the other. And surveys show that even books like this one, which begin with macroeconomics, are used by 40 per cent of the courses to teach microeconomics first.

Forty years ago our society had such poor mastery over its macroeconomics as to make people naturally give less emphasis to microeconomics. With millions starving because of a slump, who could get excited about whether mutton or pork was in a proper relative-price configuration? Or who thought much about white-collar wage trends relative to unskilled wages, when the unemployed tramped the street in every kind of shirt?

Today we can hope all that is changed. Now that man has gained considerable mastery over many of his macroeconomic problems, the classical problems of microeconomics again claim their fair share of his attention.

## REVIEW OF FUNDAMENTALS OF SUPPLY AND DEMAND

Chapter 3 discussed how a system of pricing and of markets performs the task in any mixed economic system of determining WHAT shall be produced, How goods shall be produced, and FOR WHOM they are to be produced. Then Chapter 4 introduced the basic concepts of supply and demand: their description in terms of schedules of numbers and in terms of intersecting curves. It will be assumed that each reader has this material fresh in his mind, or has gone back to review what was learned earlier, or will stop and take time to master it now.

Our task here is to put the tools of supply and demand to work: to show how they help explain changes in price, in the short run and in the long run; to help predict what effect a tax will have on competitive price; to evaluate various policies that interfere with the laws of supply and demand.

We shall make repeated efforts to see what it is that market pricing is accomplishing in terms of the *efficiency* with which the economy fulfills its basic functions.

All through Part Three new tools of economic analysis will be introduced and the old tools will be gradually developed. But it would be a mistake for any reader to become enamored of tools for their own sake. It is the application of the tools to the richness of modern economic life that makes them exciting. Experience shows that one cannot understand the economic world of the present and the future without having at his command a systematic method of analyzing it. And the testimony of generations of students is that, however far away they later move from formal schooling and examinations, their understanding of the basic economic processes is forever keener, once they have mastered the elementary tools of economic analysis.

**Review**  Glancing back at the supply-and-demand diagram in Fig. 4-3 (page 64), we see how equilibrium $P$ comes at the intersection of competitive $dd$ and $ss$ curves. We note that any departure of $P$ above equilibrium creates an "oversupply" condition leading back to equilibrium, and that any fall in $P$ below equilibrium creates an "excess demand" that bids $P$ back up to restore the equilibrium.

The succeeding diagram, Fig. 4-4(a) on page 65, shows how a shift in supply, such as might be brought about by a bad harvest, will be likely to increase the equilibrium price $P$ and decrease the equilibrium quantity $Q$. The new $E'$ intersection point is found to be higher on the unshifted demand curve—just far enough up to ration consumption down to the depressed harvest level.

This illustrates well that important principle, the law of downward-sloping demand—the fact that the demand curve slopes down toward the southeast, in reflection of the observation that people will buy more at lower prices and buy less at higher ones. Likewise, Fig. 4-4(b) showed how an upward shift of the demand curve leads to a higher equilibrium price. So much for review.

## A. ELASTICITY OF DEMAND AND SUPPLY

Second-graders, it is found, know this: An increase in supply, because of an abundant harvest or for whatever reason, is likely to *depress* price. So it is no surprise that Gregory King, the English writer of the seventeenth century mentioned earlier, should have remarked on this fact. But King also observed a fact perhaps less obvious: his statistical studies convinced him that farmers as a whole receive *less* total revenue when the harvest is good than when it is bad!

This fact, that high agricultural $Q$ tends to be associated with low $P \times Q$, is one that every American president and European chancellor has had to reckon with in facing the farm problem. To understand it and to lay the groundwork for the discussion of farm problems in Chapter 21, we must in this chapter consider and master a new and important economic concept, "elasticity of demand." Henry Ford, and any businessman tempted to *cut* his price in order to sell more goods and make more profit, is also interested in the concept of elasticity. And when a regulatory commission lets a public utility *raise* its prices in order to cut down on losses, the elasticity concept is crucially involved.

### ELASTICITY OF DEMAND

Various goods differ in the *degree* to which the $Q$ bought will respond to changes in each respective $P$. Wheat $Q$ may go up much less than 1 per cent for each 1 per cent cut in wheat $P$; Henry Ford's $Q$ may rise far more than 1 per cent for each 1 per cent reduction in its $P$. In between is the borderline case of a good whose $Q$ just halves when its $P$ doubles—where the percentage changes are just in balance.

Elasticity of demand is a concept devised to distinguish these three cases. Thus, the first case of weak percentage response of wheat $Q$ is put in the category of "inelastic demand." The second case of great percentage response is put in the category of "elastic demand." The borderline case is called "unitary elasticity of demand."

Here is how the economist goes about defining the three cases:

The crucial thing to concentrate on is the *total dollar revenue* that buyers pay to sellers. If consumers buy 5 units at $3 each, what is total revenue? Total revenue is always, by definition, price times quantity, or the $15 product $P \times Q$. By arithmetic multiplication, total revenue can always be calculated for each point in a demand schedule or diagram.

Elasticity of demand is important primarily as *an indicator of how total revenue changes* when a fall in $P$ induces a rise in $Q$ along the demand curve.

*Definition of elasticity of demand:* This is a concept devised to indicate the degree of responsiveness of $Q$ demanded to changes in market $P$. It depends primarily upon *percentage* changes and is independent of the units used to measure $Q$ and $P$. Elasticity ends up qualitatively in one of three alternative categories:

1. When a cut in $P$ raises $Q$ so much as to *increase* total revenue $P \times Q$, we speak of *elastic* demand—or of demand elasticity *greater than unity*. The percentage change in $Q$ exceeds the percentage change in $P$. $E_d > 1$.

2. When a percentage cut in $P$ results in an exactly compensating percentage rise in $Q$ so as to leave total revenue $P \times Q$ exactly *unchanged*, we speak of *unitary elasticity of demand*—or of demand elasticity numerically *equal to unity*. $E_d = 1$.

3. When a percentage cut in $P$ evokes so small a percentage increase in $Q$ as to make total revenue $P \times Q$ fall, we speak of *inelastic* demand—or of demand elasticity that is *less than unity* (but not less than zero). $E_d < 1$.

Figure 20-1 gives a graphic example of the three cases. In each case, $P$ is halved from $A$ to $B$, but it would be just as much in order to have used any small percentage change in $P$. Perhaps at a first glance, it will be easiest to begin with the borderline case of unitary elasticity of demand.

In Fig. 20-1(b), the doubling of $Q$ exactly matches the halving of $P$, with the result that the total revenue collected remains unchanged at $1,000. This can be shown graphically by comparing certain rectangular areas. How? Price and quantity can be

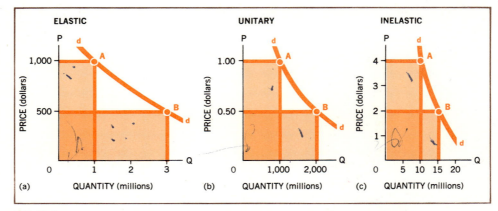

**FIG. 20-1**

**Elasticity of demand comes in three cases, depending on how total revenue moves**
In cutting $P$ from $A$ to $B$, we raise, leave unchanged, or lower the rectangle of total revenue, depending on whether demand is elastic, unitary elastic, or inelastic. That is, elasticity depends on percentage response of $Q$ to each percentage change in $P$.

easily read off the curve at any point; but how do we read off total revenue, which is their arithmetic product $P \times Q$? When we recall that the area of a rectangle is always equal to the product of its base times its altitude, the answer is easy:

Total revenue at any point is always as shown by the area of the rectangle which that point makes with the two axes. (Check that the shaded rectangle at $A$ does have a base equal to $Q$ and an altitude equal to $P$.) Hence, if our eye watches how the area of each point's rectangle changes as we cut price and move down the demand curve, we can know in which of the three categories of elasticity such a movement happens to fall.

Clearly, in the middle diagram, the shaded revenue areas are remaining exactly the same because of offsetting changes in their $Q$ bases and $P$ altitudes; consequently, this is the case neither of elastic nor of inelastic demand, but rather is the borderline case of unitary elasticity of demand.

The reader can now verify that Fig. 20-1(a) does correspond to *elastic* demand, with total revenue going up when $P$ is cut and elasticity hence greater than unity. And Fig. 20-1(c) corresponds to the opposite case of *inelastic* demand, with total revenue falling off when $P$ is cut and elasticity less than unity. [Which diagram represents the Gregory King finding that smaller harvests meant higher total revenues for farmers? Which represents the early belief of Henry Ford that if only he could reduce his car's price, he would meet a great increase in cars sold? Surely, 20-1(c) and 20-1(a), respectively.]

## NUMERICAL MEASUREMENT OF ELASTICITY: A DIGRESSION[1]

The general notion of elastic, inelastic, and unitary elastic as an indicator of the percentage responsiveness of quantity to price and as an indicator of how total revenue behaves is now clear. But some readers will be curious to know how these qualitative cases can be given exact numerical measurement by economists. What does it mean to say that the elasticity of demand is 1.0? 2.3? .5? To answer this question, we give the following definition for a coefficient of demand elasticity, $E_d$, between two different price points on a demand curve:

$$\text{Elasticity coefficient } E_d = \frac{\text{per cent that } Q \text{ has risen}}{\text{per cent cut in } P}$$

Note that the movements along $P$ and $Q$ are in opposite directions because of the law of downward-sloping demand. Note, too, the use of *percentages*, which brings in the nice property that the units of a good or of money—bushels or pecks of wheat, dollars or cents or francs—do not affect elasticity.[2]

[1] In a short course the next two sections may be skipped.

[2] Units will affect the *slope* of the demand diagram, just as the draftsman can make a curve look steep or flat in slope by changing the scale of one of his axes. So the purpose of the next section is to help you avoid confusing *slope* and *elasticity*. As Fig. 20-1(b)'s curve with $E_d = 1$ shows, it is not a straight line with constant slope that corresponds to a curve of constant elasticity, but rather one whose slope varies in order to keep the percentage changes in the same ratio. (Mathematicians call the unitary-elastic curve a ["rectangular"] hyperbola and know that it plots as a straight line on double-log paper.)

Do not get bogged down in numerical details of $E_d$ calculation. Now that you have mastered the general idea of elastic, inelastic, and unitary-elastic demand, you can proceed to numerical examples.

Always there is a slight ambiguity about percentage changes. Suppose a grocer buys bread for 15 cents and sells for 25. Is that the $66\frac{2}{3}$ per cent markup that comes from relating the change of 10 to the lower base 15? Or is it the 40 per cent change that comes from relating 10 to the higher base 25? No one answer can be said to be right, and no one definitely wrong. Fortunately, when it comes to very small percentage changes, as from 100 to 99 or from 100 to 101, the difference between $\frac{1}{100}$ and $\frac{1}{99}$ becomes hardly worth talking about. For small changes, it matters little how you calculate the percentage changes; but for larger ones it may make quite a difference, and no single answer can be declared to be the right one.

What is a good rule to use? As good a rule as any is to relate the price change to neither the higher nor the lower of the two $P$s, but to their average. Thus, is a cut from 101 to 99 a change of $\frac{2}{99}$ or $\frac{2}{101}$? By our convention, it is neither: we call it a change of $\frac{2}{100}$, because the average of 99 and 101 is $(99 + 101)/2 = 200/2 = 100$.

Table 20-1 is self-explanatory: it shows how to calculate $E_d$ for three movements along a *dd* curve. We shall be seeing that most *dd* curves start out *elastic* at high $P$ and end up *inelastic* at low $P$, passing through *unitary elasticity* at an intermediate position where total revenue $P \times Q$ is at its maximum. Table 20-1 illustrates this.

## GRAPHICAL MEASUREMENT OF ELASTICITY: A DIGRESSION

Students tend to make a simple mistake: They often confuse the slope of a curve with its elasticity; they think a steep slope on *dd* must mean inelastic demand, and a flat slope must mean elastic demand. This is not quite true. Why not? Because slope of *dd* depends upon *absolute* change in $P$ and $Q$, whereas elasticity was seen to depend upon *percentage* changes.

The straight line *dd* in Fig. 20-2(a) illustrates the fallacy of confusing slope and elasticity. Everywhere it has the same absolute slope. But toward the top of the line, where (a) $P$ is high and its percentage change low and (b) $Q$ is very low and its

**NUMERICAL CALCULATION OF ELASTICITY COEFFICIENT**

| $Q$ | $\Delta Q$ | $P$ | $-\Delta P$ | $\dfrac{Q_1 + Q_2}{2}$ | $\dfrac{P_1 + P_2}{2}$ | $E_d = \dfrac{\Delta Q}{(Q_1 + Q_2)/2} \div \dfrac{-\Delta P}{(P_1 + P_2)/2}$ |
|---|---|---|---|---|---|---|
| 0 |  | 6 |  |  |  |  |
|  | 10 |  | 2 | 5 | 5 | $\frac{10}{5} \div \frac{2}{5} = 5 > 1$ |
| 10 |  | 4 |  |  |  |  |
|  | 10 |  | 2 | 15 | 3 | $\frac{10}{15} \div \frac{2}{3} = 1$ |
| 20 |  | 2 |  |  |  |  |
|  | 10 |  | 2 | 25 | 1 | $\frac{10}{25} \div \frac{2}{1} = .2 < 1$ |
| 30 |  | 0 |  |  |  |  |

**TABLE 20-1**

**Dividing percentage price cut into percentage quantity rise gives numerical elasticity**
Each $P$ cut, $-\Delta P$, is related to the average $P$, namely, $(P_1 + P_2)/2$; each $Q$ rise, $\Delta Q$, to the average $Q$, namely, $(Q_1 + Q_2)/2$; the resulting ratio gives numerical $E_d$, a measure expressed in percentage (dimensionless) units, not in absolute slope units.

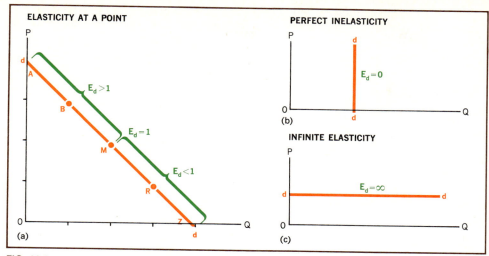

FIG. 20-2

**Absolute slope and percentage elasticity are not the same thing**
All points on $dd$'s straight-line demand in (a) have same absolute slope: but above the midpoint price, demand is elastic; below it, demand is inelastic; at it, demand is unitary elastic. Only in the case of perfectly vertical or perfectly horizontal curves, as in (b) and (c), can you infer inelasticity and elasticity from slope alone.

percentage change therefore almost infinitely great, our numerical formula for $E_d$ results in a very high elasticity.

Thus, above the midpoint $M$ of any straight line, demand is elastic, with $E_d > 1$; at the midpoint, demand is of unitary elasticity, with $E_d = 1$; below the midpoint, demand is inelastic, with $E_d < 1$.[3]

[3]Intermediate books tell how to calculate $E_d$ at any one point on a straight line: $E_d$ equals "the length of the line segment below the point divided by the length of line segment above it." Since $M$ is halfway, the formula there gives $E_d = 1$, unitary elasticity. At $B$, it gives $3/1 = 3.0$; at $R$, $E_d = 1/3 = .33$.

Knowing how to calculate $E_d$ for a straight line enables you to calculate it for any point along a curved $dd$. (1) Draw with a ruler the straight line tangent to the curve at your point (e.g., at $B$ in Fig. 20-3); (2) calculate the $E_d$ for the straight line at that point (e.g., $E_d$ at $B = 3/1$); (3) identify your resulting $E_d$ as the correct elasticity for the $dd$ curve at your chosen point. Question 7, page 401, proves the truth of the geometrical rule for calculating $E_d$.

NOTE: $E_d$ at a point can be shown to be mathematically equivalent to the following limit:

$$-\frac{\Delta Q}{Q} \div \frac{\Delta P}{P} = -\frac{P}{Q}\frac{\Delta Q}{\Delta P} \rightarrow -\frac{P}{Q}\frac{dQ}{dP}$$

as $\Delta P$ goes to zero, taking $\Delta Q$ with it and making it immaterial which of the $P$s and $Q$s or their averages we use to compute percentage changes. Intermediate texts show that, when you plot $dd$ on double-log paper, it becomes correct to identify slope with elasticity—because double-log paper does measure percentage changes. (See footnote 13, p. 402, for more on this.)

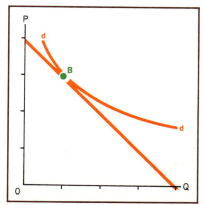

FIG. 20-3

When many people make the same mistake, there is usually a reason. The limiting cases of *completely vertical* and *completely horizontal* demand curves, shown in Fig. 20-2(b) and (c), do validly portray the limiting cases of *completely inelastic* and *infinitely elastic* demands. But do not think that the in-between cases, where most of reality falls, can have their elasticities depicted by slope alone.

Now, we go back to the mainstream of demand and supply.

## ELASTICITY OF SUPPLY

What we did for demand, we can do also for supply. Economists introduce the concept of "elasticity of supply" to give an indication of the percentage increase in the amount of $Q$ supplied in response to a given percentage rise in competitive $P$. (Note that in the case of a *rising* supply curve, we now speak of an *increase* in $P$, rather than of a *decrease*, as in the case of a downward-sloping demand curve.)

If the amount supplied is perfectly fixed, as in the case of perishable fish brought to today's market for sale at whatever price they will fetch, we face the limiting case of perfectly *inelastic*, or vertical, supply. If we have a horizontal supply curve (the "constant-cost case"), so that the slightest cut in $P$ will cause $Q$ to become zero and the slightest rise in $P$ will coax out an indefinitely large supply, we are at the other extreme of *infinitely elastic* supply. Between such extremes, we call supply elastic or inelastic depending upon whether the percentage rise in $Q$ is respectively greater than or less than the percentage rise in $P$ bringing it about.[4]

Supply elasticity is a useful concept but not quite so useful a concept as demand elasticity, for the reason that elasticity of demand has the major additional function of telling us what is happening to total revenue.

There is, however, an important fact that supply elasticity can help describe. A given change in price will tend to have greater and greater effects on amount supplied as we move from the momentary situation to a short-run period of time and on to the long-run period. This means:

**Elasticity of supply tends to be greater in the long run, when all adjustments to the higher price have been made, than in shorter periods of time.**

Let us see why.

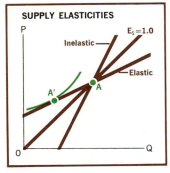

**SUPPLY ELASTICITIES**

Inelastic

$E_s = 1.0$

Elastic

A'    A

**FIG. 20-4**

[4]A numerical coefficient of supply elasticity $E_s$ is defined thus: $E_s = $ (percentage change in $Q$)/(percentage change in $P$). Figure 20-4 shows three straight-line supply curves: at $A$ the line going through the origin has elasticity of exactly 1.0; the steeper curve with intercept on the $Q$ axis is inelastic, with elasticity coefficient less than 1; and the flatter curve is elastic, with elasticity coefficient greater than 1. (If—as we shall see can happen—the supply curve actually bends up backward, elasticity of supply as here defined could actually become negative.) Also, for a supply curve with curvature, one can reckon its elasticity at a point $A'$ by drawing a straight line with a tangential ruler and seeing which curve of Fig. 20-4 it resembles; or, plot it on double-log paper and study its slope at $A'$, in comparison with that of a 45° line. (Verify that supply is elastic at $A'$.)

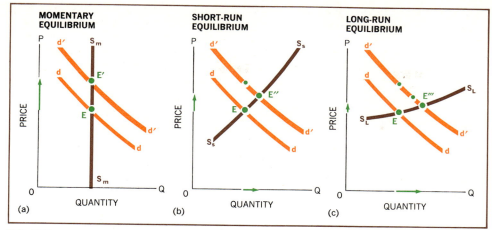

**FIG. 20-5**

**Effect of increase in demand on price varies in Marshall's three time periods**

We distinguish between periods in which supply elements have time to make (a) no adjustments (momentary equilibrium), (b) some adjustments of labor and variable factors (short-run equilibrium), (c) full adjustment of all factors, fixed as well as varying (long-run equilibrium). The longer the time for adjustment, the greater the elasticity of supply response and the less the rise in price.

## MOMENTARY, SHORT-RUN, AND LONG-RUN EQUILIBRIUM

Alfred Marshall, Cambridge's great economist at the turn of the century, helped forge these tools of supply and demand. We can review our understanding of equilibrium and at the same time advance our knowledge if we survey Marshall's important emphasis on the *time element* of the problem.

He distinguishes at least three time periods: (1) *momentary* equilibrium, when the supply is fixed; (2) *short-run* equilibrium, when firms can produce more within given plants; and finally (3) *long-run* equilibrium (or "normal price"), when firms can abandon old plants or build new ones and when new firms can enter the industry or old ones leave it.

Let us imagine that the demand for a perishable good, such as fish that cannot be preserved, increases from *dd* to *d'd'*. With the amount of fish supplied unchanged, the stronger demand will sharply bid up the momentary price of fish. This is shown in Fig. 20-5(a), where the fixed supply curve $s_m s_m$ runs up to the new demand curve *d'd'* to determine the new, sharply higher momentary equilibrium price shown at *E'*. The price has had to rise so much in order to *ration* the limited supply of fish among the now eager demanders.[5]

But with so high a price prevailing in the market, skippers of the fishing boats will be motivated to hire more men and to use more nets. Even if they do not have the time to get new boats built, they will in the short run begin to bring to the market

---

[5] If the short-run stock of goods could be carried over into the future without perishing, the $s_m s_m$ curve would not need to be perfectly vertical. Marshall points out that people might want to reserve some of their supply for the future at low present $P$s, giving the $s_m s_m$ curve some positive slope.

a greater supply of fish than they did at the old momentary equilibrium. Figure 20-5(b) shows the new $s_s s_s$ short-run supply schedule, and shows that it intersects the new demand curve at $E''$, the point of short-run equilibrium. Note that this equilibrium price is a little lower than the momentary $E'$ price. Why? Because of the extra supply of fish induced in the short run by more intensive use of the same number of boats.

Figure 20-5(c) shows the final long-run equilibrium, or "normal," price. The higher prices that long prevailed have coaxed out more shipbuilding and attracted more trained sailors into the industry. Where the long-run supply curve $s_L s_L$ intersects the demand curve $d'd'$ at $E'''$ is the final equilibrium reached after *all* economic conditions (including number of ships and shipyards) have adjusted to the new level of demand.

Note that the long-run equilibrium price is not so high as the short-run equilibrium price, and not nearly so high as the momentary equilibrium price. Yet it is a little bit higher than the price that prevailed previously when demand was lower. Marshall would call this a case of "increasing cost" and would regard it as the normal one to be met in most sizable competitive industries. Why normal? Because when a large industry (which has already achieved the economies of large-scale production) expands, it must coax men, ships, nets, and other productive factors away from other industries by bidding up their prices and thus its own cost. So the long-run supply curve $s_L s_L$ will usually be sloping gently upward as in Fig. 20-5(c). Only if the industry is small compared with the total of all other users of its factors will Marshall's $s_L s_L$ curve in Fig. 20-5(c) be horizontal—which is called the case of "constant cost."[6]

The reader can test his understanding of all the foregoing discussion by now assuming a downward shift in the demand curve back to $dd$. Show what happens in the new momentary run; in the short run; and in the long run. The Appendix to this chapter presents various cases of supply and demand. Chapters 23 and 24 will give in greater detail the factors and processes underlying the various supply curves.

## B. APPLICATIONS AND QUALIFICATIONS OF SUPPLY AND DEMAND

Other things being equal, as economists are fond of saying, there is a unique schedule of supply or demand in any period of time. But other things will not remain equal. The demand for cotton is declining over the years because of reductions in the price of synthetics. The supply schedule of radios is shifting because technological progress permits more to be produced at the same cost. As costs and tastes change, as incomes vary, as the prices of substitute products (coffee in relation to tea) or of cooperating products (sugar in relation to tea) change, our schedules will shift. What will be the effects on consumption, production, and price? That we must now study.

All beginners in the field of economics must beware of a common error. They must take care not to confuse an increase in *demand*—by which is meant a *shift* of the whole curve to the right and upward, as more is now bought at each same price—with an increase in the *quantity demanded* as a result of moving to a lower price *on the same demand curve.* By "demand" is meant the whole demand curve; by "supply" is meant the whole supply curve; by an "increase" in demand or supply is meant a

---

[6] See the cases in the Appendix.

*shift* of the whole curve in question to the right. To indicate a single point on a demand curve, we speak of the "quantity bought" or the "quantity demanded" *at a particular price*. A movement *along* the same curve is "a change in the quantity demanded as a result of a price change." It does not represent any change in the demand schedule. The need for this warning will appear in a moment.

## INCIDENCE OF A TAX

We can illustrate the case of a shift in the entire curve by referring to supply and demand schedules for a good like wheat. Figure 20-6 shows an equilibrium price at E of $3 per bushel before a tax is imposed.

Let us now introduce a new factor, which will disturb this equilibrium. In particular, assume that the government imposes a sales tax on wheat. On each and every sale, the producer is required to pay a tax of $1 per bushel of wheat.

What is the final effect, or what economists call the "incidence," of the tax? Is its burden shifted back completely onto the producer, who must pay it legally in the first instance? Or may it be shifted forward in part to consumers? The answer can be derived only from our supply and demand curves.

There is no reason for the demand curve of the consumers to have changed at all. At $3, consumers will still be willing to buy only 12 (million) bushels; they neither know nor care that the producers must pay a tax.

But the whole supply curve is shifted upward and leftward: leftward because at each market price the producers will now supply less as a result of the tax; upward

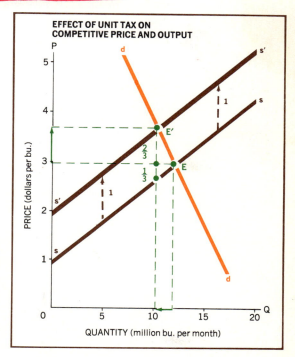

EFFECT OF UNIT TAX ON COMPETITIVE PRICE AND OUTPUT

**FIG. 20-6**
**Wheat tax falls on both consumer and producer**
A $1 tax shifts ss up $1 everywhere to give parallel s's'. This intersects dd in new equilibrium at E', where price to consumer has risen $\frac{2}{3}$ above old E equilibrium and where price to producer has fallen by $\frac{1}{3}$. The green arrows and dots show change in P and Q. (Had dd been very elastic and flat relative to ss, most of the $1 tax would have fallen on the producer. Had ss been completely horizontal, the whole $1 tax would have been shifted forward onto the consumer.)

because, to get the producers to bring any given quantity to market, say, 12 (million) units, we must give them a higher market price than before—$4 rather than $3, which is higher by the exact amount of the $1 tax the producer must pay.

The student should be able to fill in a new supply column, resembling Column (3) of the table with Fig. 4-3, page 64, but with each price raised by $1. Here in Fig. 20-6, the demand curve *dd* is unchanged, but the supply curve *ss* has been shifted up everywhere by $1 to a new vertically *parallel* supply curve *s's'*.

Where will the new equilibrium price be? The answer is found at the intersection of the new demand and supply curves, or at *E'*, where *s's'* and *dd* meet. Because supply has decreased, the price is higher. Also, the amount bought and the amount sold are less. If we read the graph carefully, we find that the new equilibrium price has risen from $3 to about $3⅔. The new equilibrium output, at which purchases and sales are in equilibrium, has fallen from 12 (million) per month to about 10.6 (million) bushels.

Who pays the tax? Well, the wheat farmers do in part, because now they receive only $2⅔ ($3⅔ − $1), rather than $3. But the consumer also shares in the burden, because the price received by the producer has *not* fallen by as much as the tax. To the consumer, the wheat now costs $2⅔ plus the $1 tax, or $3⅔ in all. Because consumers want wheat so badly, they pay ⅔ of the tax, and producers pay ⅓ of the tax.[7]

To check his understanding of the above reasoning, the student should consider the case of an opposite shift in supply. Let the government pay producers a subsidy of $1 per bushel instead of taxing them this amount. Shift *ss* down to the new curve *s''s''*. Where is *E''*, its intersection with *dd*? What is the new price? The new quantity? How much of the benefit goes to the producer? How much to the consumer?

*Summary:* **A sales tax on a good will raise its price most and reduce its quantity least when the demand curve is most *inelastic*. When the supply curve is most inelastic, *Q* and *P* to the consumer will change least, while *P* to the producer falls most.**

**The tax is shifted *forward* onto the consumer when *dd* is very inelastic. It is shifted *backward* onto the producer when *ss* is relatively the more inelastic.**

Only with the apparatus of supply and demand can one analyze the incidence of various different taxes—import tariffs, cigarette and liquor excises, payroll and corporation taxes, etc.

## A COMMON FALLACY

By now the student has mastered supply and demand. Or has he? He knows that a tax will have the effect of raising the price that the consumer will have to pay. Or does he know this? What about the following argument of a kind often seen in the press and heard from the platform:

The effect of a tax on a commodity might seem at first sight to be an advance in price to

---

[7]There is another and equivalent way to handle this tax problem. If the consumer were thought of as paying the tax in the first instance, you could subtract $1 everywhere from his *dd* curve. This new *d'd'* will intersect *ss* at the same new *Q*, and the same $2⅔ and $3⅔ prices will prevail. It goes without saying that all these figures are hypothetical.

the consumer. But an advance in price will diminish the demand. And a reduced demand will send the price down again. Therefore it is not certain, after all, that the tax will really raise the price.

What about it? Will the tax raise the price or not? According to the editor's written word and the senator's oratory, the answer is, No. Evidently, we have here an example of the treachery of words. One of the four sentences in the quotation is false because the word "demand" is being used in the wrong sense. The student has already been warned against confusing a movement *along* an unchanged curve with a shift in the curve. Actually, the correct answer[8] would be more or less as follows:

A tax will raise the price to consumers and lower the price received by producers, the difference going to government. At the higher price a smaller quantity will be bought by consumers. This is as it should be, because producers are also supplying a smaller quantity at the lower price which they receive. Thus the amounts willingly bought and sold balance out where the new *ss* and *dd* schedules intersect, and there will be no further change in price.

## IS THE LAW OF SUPPLY AND DEMAND IMMUTABLE?

Competitive price and quantity are determined by supply and demand. But does not price depend on other factors, such as the amount of money created by the government or whether there is a war going on? Actually, price does depend on many such factors. However, they are not *in addition* to supply and demand, but are included in the numerous forces which determine or *act through* supply and demand. Thus, if government's printing of currency gives everyone a higher income, that will raise demand curves and raise prices. But it is still true that competitive price is determined by supply and demand.

At this point a thoughtful reader might protest. Little has been said about competitive price as being determined by cost of production. Should not this be listed as a third factor in addition to supply and demand? Our answer is stubbornly, No.

**Competitive price is affected by the cost of production only to the extent that such cost affects supply.**

If God sends nutritious manna from heaven without cost but in limited supply, then its price will not be zero but will be given by the intersection of the demand and supply curves. On the other hand, if it would cost $50,000 to print the national anthem on the head of a pin, but there is no demand for such a commodity, it simply will not be produced and would not command $50,000 if it were produced. (What the market price of something nonexistent should be called is left to the reader's pleasure.)

This does not mean that cost of production is unimportant for price determination. Under competition it is especially important. But its importance shows itself *through its effects upon supply.* Businessmen produce for profit. If they cannot get a price high enough to cover their past costs, then they will not like it. Nevertheless, once the crop is in, so to speak, there is not much they can do about it under competition. They have no choice but to minimize their short-term losses. But they will not continue

---

[8]H. D. Henderson, *Supply and Demand* (Cambridge University Press, London, 1922), p. 27, explains this.

*in the future* to supply goods at prices that fail to cover the *extra* costs incurred to produce these goods. Thus supply depends intimately on cost, especially on what Chapter 23 and later chapters will call "extra" or "marginal" cost; and so too must price depend on this.

Moreover, to say that "price *equals* cost" does not in itself tell us which is the cause of which. In many cases where an industry uses a productive factor highly specialized to itself (e.g., baseball players, opera singers, vineyard land), *price determines cost rather than vice versa.* Grain land is dear because the price of grain is high. Apartment buildings sell for much because rents are high. This type of relationship was overlooked by the farmers who petitioned during World War II for a higher milk price "because the price of cows is high." If their request had been granted, they would soon have observed the price of cows chasing the milk price upward.[9]

**Useful categories**   Thus, supply and demand are not ultimate explanations of price. They are simply useful catchall categories for analyzing and describing the multitude of forces, causes, and factors impinging on price. Rather than final answers, supply and demand simply represent initial questions. Our work is not over but just begun.

This should help to debunk the tendency of neophytes to utter sagely, "You can't repeal the law of supply and demand. King Canute knew he could not command the ocean tide to retreat from his throne on the seashore. Likewise, no government can get around, or interfere with, the workings of supply and demand."

It would be better not to have learned any economics than be left with this opinion. Of course the government can affect price. It can do so by affecting supply or demand, or both. In Chapter 21 we shall examine how government programs for restricting farm production can raise price and income by cutting down on supply. Similar programs by government cartels have been pursued all over the world: Brazil has burned coffee to raise its price; Britain during the 1920s tried artificially controlling the price of rubber; sugar and cocoa are still under international control.

These governments have not violated the law of supply and demand. They have worked (not always to good purpose) through the law of supply and demand. The state has no secret economic weapons or tricks. What is true for the state is also true for individuals. Anyone can affect the price of wheat as long as he has sufficient money to throw on the market or wheat to hold off it.

Trade unions often influence wages, or try to, by directly or indirectly affecting the supply of labor. Anyone with a somewhat distinctive commodity may try by advertising to increase the demand for his product and, by restricting supply, to raise price above his extra costs of production. It should be emphasized, however, that as soon as individual producers grow in size and become important enough to affect the price of the things they sell, they then cease to be perfect competitors in the strict sense, and their behavior has to be analyzed in terms of a blend of monopoly and competition, i.e., in terms of imperfect or monopolistic competition as described in Chapters 25 and 26.

---

[9] Where a factor of production is inelastic in supply, as in all these cases mentioned here, its cost is "price-determined" rather than "price-determining" and its return is called a "pure economic rent." For more on this, see Case 3 in the Appendix and Chapter 28.

## PRICES FIXED BY LAW

There is one genuine interference with supply and demand whose effects we must analyze. The government sometimes sets by law a maximum price or a minimum wage. In war or in peace, wage and price controls may be legislated by government—as, for example, in the Nixon Phase I and Phase II programs of the early 1970s. Thus, by 1976, a floor of $2.30, in the form of a minimum hourly wage, is to apply to most workers. These interferences by law are quite different from government actions, previously described, which work *through* supply and demand.

**Price ceilings and rationing**  Consider, say, the market for sugar, which has ordinary curves of supply and demand such as we have repeatedly met in this chapter. Suppose that the government, through an Office of Price Stabilization (OPS), establishes an order prohibiting sugar from rising above 14 cents a pound (retail). Now, because of prosperity or bad crops, let demand be so high and supply so small that the equilibrium price would have been 40 cents a pound if the government had not intervened. This high price would have contributed to "profiteering" in that industry, it would have represented a rather heavy "tax" on the poor who could ill afford it, and it would only have added fuel to an inflationary spiral in the cost of living, with all sorts of inflationary reactions on workers' wage demands. So go the arguments of price fixers.

Therefore the government, through Congress and the OPS, decides to hold the line on prices. It passes a law putting a maximum price on sugar at the old level of 14 cents a pound. The ceiling-price line *CJK* in Fig. 20-7 represents the legal price ceiling. Now what will happen?

At the legal ceiling price, supply and demand do not match. Consumers want

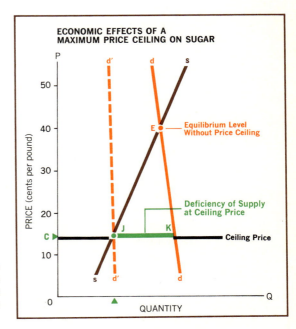

**FIG. 20-7**

**A legal maximum price, without rationing, leaves a gap between demand and supply**

Without a legal price ceiling, price would rise to *E*. At the artificial ceiling price, supply and demand do not balance and some method of rationing, formal or informal, is needed to allocate the short supply and bring the effective demand down to *d'd'*.

thousands of pounds of sugar in excess of what producers are willing to supply. This is shown by the green gap between *J* and *K*. This gap is so large that there will not long be enough sugar on grocers' shelves or in the warehouse to make up the difference. Somebody will have to drink bitter coffee. If it were not for the maximum-price law, this somebody would gladly bid the price up to 30 or 35 cents or more, rather than do without sugar. As in our earlier discussion (Fig. 4-3, page 64), we could have shown this by putting an upward-pointing arrow perpendicular to *JK*. Such an arrow would not stop pointing up till *P* had been bid up to the equilibrium level of 40 cents.

But it is against the law for the consumer to bid a higher price. Even if the consumer should be so unpatriotic, the seller could not legally take the higher price. There follows a period of frustration and shortage—a game of musical chairs in which somebody is left without a seat when the music stops playing. The inadequate supply of sugar must somehow be rationed. At first, this may be done by "first come, first served," with or without limited sales to each customer. Lines form, and much time has to be spent foraging for food. But this is no solution, since somebody must be left at the end of the line when the sugar is gone.

The price mechanism is stymied and blocked. Nonmonetary considerations must determine who is the lucky buyer and who the unlucky one: the warmth of the smile that the customer flashes on the grocer, her previous standing at the store in question, the amount of other things the customer is willing to buy, or the accident of being in the store when the sugar is put on the shelves.

Nobody is happy, least of all the harassed grocer. Were it not for the community's elementary sense of fair play, the situation might soon become intolerable. Patriotism is more effective in motivating people to brief acts of intense heroism than to putting up day after day with an uncomfortable situation. It is no wonder that black markets occasionally develop; the really surprising thing is that they do not occur sooner.

**If for political or social reasons market price is not to be permitted to rise high enough to bring quantity demanded down to the level of quantity supplied, the ultimate solution may require outright allocation or rationing.**

Once rationing is adopted, and people are given tickets dependent on family size, most people heave a sigh of relief, because now sellers need not turn people away and now buyers can count upon getting their fair quota of the limited supplies. Of course, there are always some cranky customers, longer on intuition than brains, who blame their troubles on the mechanism of rationing itself rather than on the shortage. "If only the government could print more ration tickets," they sigh. Such people are like the ignorant ancient kings who used to slay the messengers bringing them bad news. Their complaints need not be taken seriously; they only serve to add spice to the human comedy.

Just how do ration coupons work out in terms of supply and demand? Clearly, the OPS tries to issue just enough of them to lower the demand curve *to d'd', where supply and the new demand balance at the ceiling price.* If too many coupons are issued, demand is still too far to the right and we encounter the old difficulties, but in lesser degree. If too few coupons are issued, stocks of sugar will pile up and *P* will fall below the ceiling price. This is the signal for liberalizing the sugar ration.

One goes to a psychiatric ward to learn to appreciate normal human behavior. So, too, the breakdown of the price mechanism during war, or abnormal times, gives us a new understanding of its efficiency in normal times.

Goods are always scarce, in the sense that there is never enough to give everyone all he wishes. Price itself is always rationing scarce supplies: rising to choke off excessive consumption and in order to expand production; falling to encourage consumption, discourage production, and work off excessive inventories.

**Minimum floors and maximum ceilings**    When there arises any kind of emergency or state of general shortage and inflation, political pressures for wage and price freezes develop. Experience has taught most economists, whether they be liberals or conservatives, that such emergency measures work very well in short emergencies but may create more and more distortions the longer they are in effect. Economists therefore tend to recommend that such direct fiats be reserved for emergency periods and not be squandered on minor peacetime situations.

Nevertheless, as Adam Smith well knew when he protested against the devices of the mercantilist advisers to the earlier kings, most economic systems are plagued by inefficiencies stemming from well-intentioned inexpert interferences with the mechanisms of supply and demand. A few such interferences are shown in Fig. 20-8.

1. *Minimum wage rates*. These often hurt those they are designed to help. What

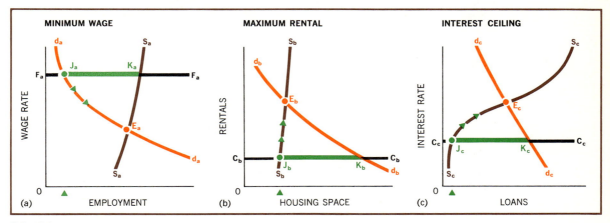

**FIG. 20-8**

**When government by fiat sets maximum or minimum prices, troublesome gaps may arise**

**(a)**   Setting minimum-wage floor at $F_aF_a$, high above free-market equilibrium rate $E_a$, results in forced equilibrium at $J_a$. The too-high floor freezes workers into unemployment from $J_a$ to $K_a$. Lowering the minimum wage will move us down along $dd$, as shown by green arrows, increasing employment. (If $dd$ is elastic, total wage payrolls rise though hourly rate falls!)

**(b)**   Setting maximum rental ceiling at $C_bC_b$, far below free-market equilibrium at $E_b$, causes fringe of unsatisfied renters between forced equilibrium at $J_b$ and $K_b$. Raising the ceiling rate moves the system up $s_bs_b$, as shown by green arrows: new construction provides more living space, and old quarters are used more efficiently.

**(c)**   Setting maximum interest rates at $C_cC_c$, far below free-market equilibrium rate $E_c$, results in drying up of available funds. Desperate borrowers at $J_cK_c$ turn to loan sharks. Raising interest ceiling moves system toward more loans, as shown by green arrows on $s_cs_c$.

good does it do a black youth to know that an employer must pay him $2.00 per hour if the fact that he must be paid that amount is what keeps him from getting a job?[10]

2. *Rent and price ceilings.* Everyone hates a landlord and loves a farmer. Even in peacetime, maximum rentals are often fixed by law. These fiats may do short-run good; but they may also do long-run harm. Thus, France had practically no residential construction from 1914 to 1948 because of rent controls. If new construction had been subjected to such controls after World War II, the vigorous boom in French residential building since 1950 would never have taken place. New York City rent controls favored those lucky enough to have found a cheap apartment, but inhibited new private building of low-cost housing. They discouraged economies of space utilization that high rents tend to induce and resulted in literal abandonment of tens of thousands of dwellings each year, just when housing was most needed.

3. *Usury laws.* Interest rates have always been an object of suspicion. No longer is lending at interest a crime, but in most places a maximum rate is set by law. Unfortunately, the ceiling is often far below what would be set by the competitive supply-and-demand market, after account is taken of riskiness and administrative expense connected with small loans. The result? Funds dry up completely.

The cheap money you can't get does you little good. Veterans who tried to get mortgages learned this in the 1950s; college students trying to get tuition loans from the banks learned this in the 1960s and the 1970s. Federal Reserve ceilings on bank-deposit interest (so-called "Regulation Q") periodically cause massive withdrawals (the so-called "disintermediation" of Chapter 17).

## EFFICIENCY OF SUPPLY-DEMAND PRICING AND "EQUITY"

We do not study competitive pricing for the beauty of the subject. Nor for its realism alone, since often monopoly elements spoil the competitive picture. We study it for the light it throws on *efficient* organization of an economy's resources. The pathology of interference with supply and demand helps to bring out the remarkable efficiencies produced by perfect competition when it is able to operate.

Why, then, do politicians and the populace keep interfering with the mechanism? Primarily, because man does not live by efficiency alone. He is interested in the question: Efficiency *for what?* And *for whom?*

Most of these floors and ceilings are set in the name of "equity"—to help some group deemed deserving at the expense of some other group deemed already affluent and amply well-off. Just as Robin Hood "robbed the rich to help the poor," these devices try to create or restore a distribution of real income considered more equitable. Their advocates are willing to pay some price in the form of lower efficiency and higher waste to bring about a "fairer" distribution of income. Economic science cannot pronounce that they are necessarily wrong if they face the cost.

---

[10] See P. A. Samuelson, *Readings in Economics* (McGraw-Hill, New York, 1973, 7th ed.), for arguments by Milton Friedman against minimum-wage legislation, and other appraisals pro and con. See also Chapter 22's Appendix for graphical analysis of economic inefficiency of controls and rationing.

## MONOPOLY INTERFERENCES WITH SUPPLY AND DEMAND

Aside from governmental interferences, there are serious monopolistic interferences with supply and demand. Competitive supply and demand is one way of organizing an economy. It is one way of getting the job done, but of course it is not the only way relied on in actual modern society. Certainly, when one or a few producers can get monopoly control of an industry, they can move the final outcome away from the competitive equilibrium point. As we shall see later, a monopolist can reduce output and make the consumers travel up their demand curves to higher prices.

Is such an interference with supply and demand a "good thing"? If the monopolist were a more worthy soul than the rest of us, or if he were much poorer and had greater need for money, some might rise to defend his act of raising price. Or if he took our money and devoted it to better causes (charity, scientific research) than we should do, some might still defend him as a modern-day Robin Hood.

Chances are, however, that anyone in a position to contrive a monopoly will be at least as well-off as his customers, and there is not much reason to think he would be of finer clay than anyone else. And though Robin Hood may have been all right in his day, in our day we tend to think it is the government that ought to do any subsidizing of worthy causes, not self-appointed monopolists; and we hope government can be more efficient in financing its good causes out of tax revenues than any monopolist could ever be. So what probably needs emphasis is this:

Any *haphazard* interference with competitive supply and demand is likely—save in some exceptional circumstances—to be a bad rather than a good thing.

Thus, a monopolistic interference in Industry A reduces output there needlessly relative to Industry B. The fact that it produces such scarcity is reflected in the higher $P_A/P_B$ ratio it creates, relative to the citizenry's desires for the goods and to their true relative costs as measured along the production-possibility frontier or by undistorted competitive costs. The monopoly may also lead to a bad distribution of income in that it may give too much income to someone who already has as much income as he deserves.

At this point monopoly's *restriction in output* relative to that of competitive industries perhaps needs more stressing than its distortion of the income distribution. For what if we taxed away the monopolist's ill-gotten gains?[11] We should then have rectified the income-distribution distortion of monopoly. But the community would still be left enjoying less of the (monopolized) consumption goods that it really does want in terms of what it really can produce.

Like sin, monopoly is one of those things most people are against. Therefore one need not labor the point that monopoly interferences with supply and demand are probably a bad thing. Still, it is better to have seen analytically why.

---

[11]Or what if many monopolists entered the industry, with all keeping their price too high but with total business so divided up among them that none ends up making any exorbitant monopoly profit? Then the evil effect on the income distribution would not exist, but the resulting wasteful pattern of overcapacity in the industry and too high price could persist until doomsday. More on all this when Chapter 26 treats imperfect competition along the lines of Harvard's late E. H. Chamberlin.

## GOVERNMENT INTERFERENCES WITH SUPPLY AND DEMAND EVALUATED

In conclusion, let us appraise government interferences. Surely the government means well and its interferences are not to be as harshly judged as those of a monopolist?

Well, that all depends. Where the government does know better than people what is really good and evil, its interferences may improve matters. An example might be opium. We do not treat the consumer as a sovereign who can decide how much opium he will spend his money votes on. Where opium is concerned, we adopt a paternalistic attitude, treating the consumer a little the way we treat the insane, minors, and other "incompetents." Society is similarly beginning to move against cigarettes.

But where cerise-colored cars and bubble gum are concerned, we usually are content to let the consumer spend his own dollars in his own way. We recognize that advertising has given us one set of tastes, which may not be intrinsically better than some other set, but in the interests of freedom we do treat the consumer as sovereign.

As we have seen, the matter becomes more complicated if the sellers or the buyers in a market happen to be especially rich, or especially poor, or especially "deserving," or especially "undeserving." For example, imagine an artificial case where 1 million very rich producers sell milk in competitive markets to 50 million very poor people. Some people would then be tempted to approve of any interference that lowered milk price. "That leads to what we call a fairer income distribution," they might say.

Without foisting his ethical judgments on others, the economist can remind us:

**Interfering with the competitive supply-and-demand mechanism is a partially inefficient[12] way of correcting the income distribution. Whatever distribution you want to end up with can often be more efficiently attained by using the tax system to redistribute income than by ad hoc Robin Hood interferences in a single market.**

Indeed, if taxation always could be counted on to keep society's For Whom problem

---

[12]The fact that buyers and sellers are different people who may have different incomes or wealth hides the truth that the competitive equilibrium point has certain allocative efficiency properties in solving the WHAT and How economic problems. So consider a simplified case where I trade only

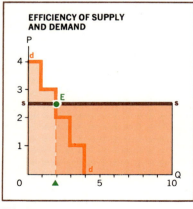

**EFFICIENCY OF SUPPLY AND DEMAND**

FIG. 20-9

with myself. I have 10 hours of leisure worth exactly $2.50 per hour to me. I can produce 1 $Q$ unit with each hour of work or sacrificed leisure. Suppose the first $Q$ unit is worth exactly $4 to me, and successive $Q$ units are worth $3, $2, $1, and $0. Figure 20-9 shows *my* supply and demand for $Q$. Equilibrium is at $E$, where I consume exactly 2 of $Q$. I get $4 + $3 of "satisfaction" from them (as shown by light shading) and 8 times $2.50 from my 8 hours left of leisure (as shown by heavy shading), or $27 of satisfaction in all, as shown by the sum of the areas. You can show that any disturbance which makes me work 1 hour too much, or too little, kills off 50 cents of my satisfaction. Distortion of a second hour kills off $1.50 of satisfaction; each further distortion takes a heavier and heavier toll, as shown by the growing discrepancy between $dd$ and $ss$. (See Figs. 22-4, 26-5, and 32-2 for more on "consumer's surplus," which can be used to demonstrate monopoly harm or price-control inefficiency. Also see Chapter 22 Appendix.)

optimally solved, then perfect competition (were it to prevail!) could be counted on to solve most WHAT and HOW problems efficiently.

Naturally, all this is a controversial area. There is no one answer, and any observer of the modern world can see that nations everywhere do often interfere with the price system. EXAMPLES: Blood for transfusions is not primarily obtained by commercial bidding, but rather through much voluntary effort. (Why?) Doctors often charge rich patients more than poor ones, in part subsidizing the latter from revenues of the former. (Why this private system of taxation?) Milk and other basic foods are often subsidized. And to the degree that our demands reflect merely manipulated fads, engineered by profit-seeking advertisers, the merits of "consumer sovereignty" fade away.

The next chapter will deal with the extensive agricultural aid programs which the government has been following. And later chapters will discuss the effects of monopolistic imperfections of competition once competitive demand has been related to utility and competitive supply has been related to cost.

## SUMMARY

### A. ELASTICITY OF DEMAND AND SUPPLY

1  A basic problem of microeconomics is the mechanism of market pricing: how it grapples with the economy's problems WHAT, HOW, FOR WHOM. The supply and demand curves in Chapter 4 explain what goes on in each competitive market.

2  Elasticity of demand depends on what happens to total revenue as price is cut. Demand is elastic, inelastic, or unitary elastic, according to whether a reduction in price increases, decreases, or does not change total revenue. The numerical coefficient of elasticity of demand is defined as "the percentage increase in quantity divided by the percentage cut in price." Depending upon whether the percentage rise in $Q$ exceeds or falls short of the percentage fall in $P$, we have $E_d > 1$ or $E_d < 1$, with $E_d = 1$ in between. (Elasticity is dimensionless, involving percentages; it is not to be confused with absolute slope, as numerical tables and graphical measurements make clear.)

3  Elasticity of supply measures percentage responsiveness of amount $Q$ supplied by producers when market $P$ is raised by a given percentage.

4  Marshall stressed the time element: (a) *momentary* equilibrium of fixed supply; (b) *short-run* equilibrium with output varying within fixed plants and firms; (c) *long-run* equilibrium of normal price, when numbers of firms and plants, and all conditions, adjust to the new level of demand.

### B. APPLICATIONS AND QUALIFICATIONS OF SUPPLY AND DEMAND

5  The apparatus of supply and demand enables us to analyze the effects of shifts in either curve, or in both simultaneously. Beginners must avoid the pitfall of

confusing the expression "an increase in demand" (i.e., an outward *shift* of the whole demand curve) with "an increase in quantity demanded" as a result of a reduction in price (i.e., a movement *along* an unchanged demand curve).

6   A tax of so many dollars per unit of a good will lead to a new equilibrium intersection: its burden will be shifted forward to consumers rather than backward to the producers to the degree that the demand is inelastic relative to the supply.

7   A thousand forces affect price; but in a free competitive market they do so only by acting *through* supply and demand. For example, cost of production affects competitive price only through affecting supply, not otherwise.

8   Although the government usually affects price by *operating* on either supply or demand, occasionally it sets maximum ceilings or minimum floors that *interfere* with the workings of competitive markets. Then supply and demand need not be equal; some producer or consumer may *wish* to sell or buy more than he is able to at the legal price. Distortions and inefficiencies result. Unless the discrepancies are parceled out by legislation (rationing; etc.), disorder and black markets may result.

9   Haphazard, arbitrary interferences with supply and demand will often be harmful. Monopoly interference provides an obvious case, and here the evil is not so much that the distribution of income is distorted as that society has to put up unnecessarily with reduced relative output of a good that it really wants and really can afford.

Even in cases where government is interfering with supply and demand for the purpose of achieving some desired distribution of income or some other social goal, there may be hidden costs in the use of so *inefficient* a device—and often the same goal would be accomplished better by use of the tax system and preservation of the efficiency of market pricing.

## CONCEPTS FOR REVIEW

microeconomics, macroeconomics
total revenue, $P \times Q$
elastic, inelastic, unitary elastic
$E_d = \% \, Q$ rise $\div \% \, P$ cut
elasticity of supply
Marshall's three time periods
demand versus amount demanded
shift versus movement along a
    curve
government actions to influence
    supply and demand curves

cost of production, supply, and
    price
incidence of a tax
    forward shifting on to
        consumers
    backward shifting on to
        producers
rationing and price fixing
    maximum-price ceilings
    maximum-interest ceilings
    minimum-wage floors

monopoly reduction of relative
   outputs versus monopoly
   distortion of income
   distribution

possible efficiencies sacrificed
   when government interferes
   with supply and demand to
   achieve a worthy goal

## QUESTIONS FOR DISCUSSION

1   What factors might increase the demand for wheat? The supply?

2   Which do you think has the most inelastic demand: perfume, salt, penicillin, cigarettes, ice cream, chocolate ice cream, Sealtest chocolate ice cream? Why?

3   When demand is elastic (inelastic, or unitary), what will a rise in $P$ do to total revenue? What will higher $Q$ do in the three cases?

4   "$P$ drops by 1 per cent, causing $Q$ to rise by 2 per cent. Demand is therefore *elastic*, with $E_d > 1$." If you change 2 to $\frac{1}{2}$ in this passage, what two other changes will be required?

5   Explain Marshall's three time periods, their equilibria, the slope of $s_L s_L$.

6   Examine the diagram below, which shows demand and supply curves for wheat for different years. Identify green historical intersection points. Fill in the columns at the right showing the price and quantity of wheat for each of the four years. (Note how hard it would be to estimate demand or supply curves from a plot of green intersections.)

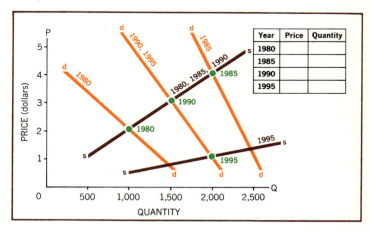

7   As an extra-credit problem for those who like simple geometry and algebra, try to justify the $E$ rule given in footnote 3 (page 385) for a straight line. In the

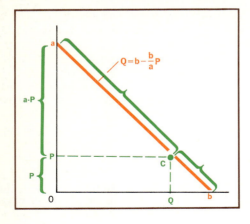

triangle below, the *dd* has the equation $Q = b - (b/a)P$, where $b$ is the $Q$ intercept and $a$ the $P$ intercept, and the absolute inverted slope of *dd* is $-(dQ/dP) = -(\Delta Q/\Delta P) = b/a$. Now apply the formula $E_d = -(dQ/dP)(P/Q)$ to get $E_d = (b/a)\{P/[b - (b/a)P]\} = P/(a - P)$ —the ratio of the lower vertical bracket to the upper. Can you show, by the property of similar triangles, that $E_d = P/(a - P) = bC/aC$, equals "the length of the straight line below the point divided by its length above the point," as stated in footnote 3?[13]

[13] Those who tackled the mathematical question 10 of Chapter 4, page 73, can calculate $E_d$ from the demand function $Q = f(P)$. Define

$$E_d = \lim_{\Delta P \to 0} - \frac{\Delta Q}{\Delta P} \frac{(P_1 + P_2)/2}{(Q_1 + Q_2)/2} = - \frac{dQ}{dP} \frac{P}{Q} = - \frac{P\{df(P)/dP\}}{f(P)}$$

For $f(P) = b - (b/a)P$, calculate $E_d = P/(a - P)$. Show $E_d$ to be respectively 1, 2, $\frac{1}{3}$, $k$ for $f(P)$ successively $c/P$, $c/P^2$, $c/P^{1/3}$, $c/P^k$. Taking logarithms (to any base) of the last expression, verify $\log Q = \log c - k \log P$ does give $E_d \equiv k$. [HINT: $(dQ/Q) \div (dP/P) = d \log Q/d \log P \equiv -k$.]

# APPENDIX: Cases on Supply and Demand[1]

**PROPOSITION 1: (a) As a general rule an increase in demand—supply being constant—will raise price.**

**(b) Probably also, but less certainly, increased demand will increase the quantity bought and sold. A decrease in demand has opposite effects.**

**PROPOSITION 2: An increase in supply, demand being constant, will almost certainly lower price and increase the quantity bought and sold. A decrease in supply has opposite effects.**

These two important propositions summarize the *qualitative* effects of shifts in supply and demand. But the exact *quantitative* degree of change in price and quantity depends upon the specific shapes of the curves in each instance. Here, then, are a number of possible cost and supply situations.

[1] Many may prefer to study this Appendix after Chapter 23 or 24.

**Case 1. Constant cost**  Imagine a manufactured item, like pencils, whose production can be easily expanded by merely duplicating factories, machinery, and labor. To produce 100,000 pencils per day simply requires us to do the same thing as when we were manufacturing 1,000 per day, but on a hundredfold scale. In this case the supply curve *ss* in Fig. 20-10 is a horizontal line at the constant level of unit costs. A rise in demand will shift the new intersection point $E'$ to the right, raising $Q$ but leaving $P$ the same.

**Case 2. Increasing costs and diminishing returns**  Suppose an industry like wine-grape growing requires a certain kind of soil and location (sunny hillsides, etc.). Such sites are limited in number. The annual output of wine can be increased to some extent by adding more labor and fertilizer to each acre of land and by bidding away some hill sites from other uses. But as

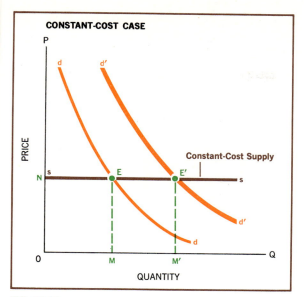

**CONSTANT-COST CASE**

FIG. 20-10

their jobs even at low pay. Once a bridge is built, it must earn "what the traffic will bear" regardless of past sunk costs.

In all such cases the supply curve goes *vertically* up and down, at least in the relevant region. In Fig. 20-12 on the next page, a higher price cannot elicit an increase in *Q;* nor is the higher price necessary to bring out the existing *Q,* for even at lower prices the same amount will still be forthcoming. Because it is price-*determined* rather than price-*determining,* the return to such a factor of production is called a "pure economic rent," or "surplus," which need not be paid to call out the required supply.

If demand now shifts upward, the whole effect is to raise price. Quantity is unchanged. And the rise in price exactly equals the upward shift in demand. (More on this in Chapter 28's section on rents and costs.)

Likewise, if a tax is placed upon the commodity, its whole effect is to reduce the price received by the supplier by exactly the amount of the tax. The tax is shifted back completely to the supplier, who absorbs it all out of his economic rent or surplus. The consumer buys exactly as much of the good or service as before and at no extra cost.

**Case 4. A backward-bending supply curve**  Early explorers often noted that, when you raised the wages

we saw in Chapter 2, the law of diminishing returns will begin to operate if variable factors of production, like labor and fertilizer, are added to fixed amounts of a factor like land. Why is that? Because each new *variable addition* of labor and fertilizer has a *smaller proportion* of land to work with. By the same token, each fixed unit of land has more labor and fertilizer cooperating with it. Therefore land's productivity and earnings are higher. The result: Getting extra amounts of wine sends total costs up more than proportionately. Therefore the cost per unit of wine is rising. The supply curve travels upward from southwest to northeast because at lower market prices, less will be supplied. At higher prices, more will be supplied.

Figure 20-11 shows the rising supply curve *ss.* What will be the effect on price of an increase in demand? Effect on quantity?

**Case 3. Completely fixed or inelastic supply and economic rent**  Some goods or productive factors are completely fixed in amount, regardless of price.

Thus there is only one *Mona Lisa* by Leonardo. Nature's original endowment of the "natural and indestructible" qualities of land can also often be taken as fixed in amount. Raising the price offered for land cannot create more than four corners at State and Madison in Chicago. High-paid artists and businessmen who love their work would continue to work at

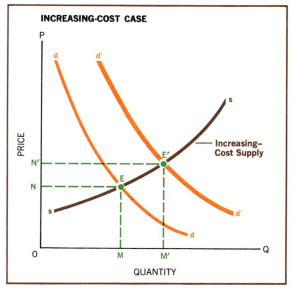

**INCREASING-COST CASE**

FIG. 20-11

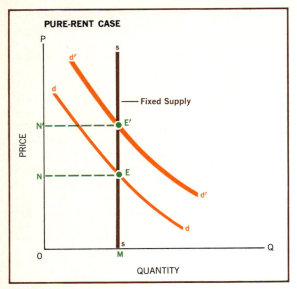

**PURE-RENT CASE**

**FIG. 20-12**

increase in demand raises price. But what about the often-observed case where an increase in demand is followed by economies of mass production and decreasing costs?

A good theory must make room for all the facts. So we must frankly admit that our first proposition may break down and have exceptions. Of course, we can save some face by pointing out that many of the important reductions in cost following an increase in demand really represent *permanent downward shifts* in the supply curve rather than downward movements *along* a falling supply curve.

Illustrate this by the case where the government increases its demand for radar. The first few sets built must be constructed in the laboratory by experimental methods. They are tailor-made and very expensive per unit. But the know-how gained in the process makes possible the production of further sets for much less per unit. Even if demand went back again to its previous level, price would not return up to its previous level. In traveling along the arrow *EE'* marked with a question mark in Fig. 20-14, we are not moving reversibly along the supply curve. Instead, the supply

of natives, you received *less* rather than more labor. If wages were doubled, instead of working 6 days a week for their minimum of subsistence, the natives might go fishing for 3 days. The same has been observed among so-called "civilized" people. As improved technology raises real wages, people feel that they ought to take part of their higher earnings in the form of more leisure, less work. (In Chapter 22, the discussion of the marginal utility theory, or of "income- and substitution-effects," will explain why a supply curve might bend backward.)

Figure 20-13 shows such a supply curve of labor. At first it rises as higher wages coax out more labor, but beyond the point *T*, higher wages induce *more leisure* and *less work*. An increase in demand does increase the price of labor in agreement with Proposition 1(a). But note how lucky we were to have added the words "but less certainly" in 1(b)! For the increase in demand has *decreased* the quantity of labor.

A partial verification of such a possibility is found in the fact that a decrease in demand for farm products during a depression often causes farmers to work harder in order to restore their incomes. The result: More rather than less is produced in response to a decrease in demand.

**Case 5. A possible exception: decreasing cost**   Our examples have agreed with Proposition 1(a), that an

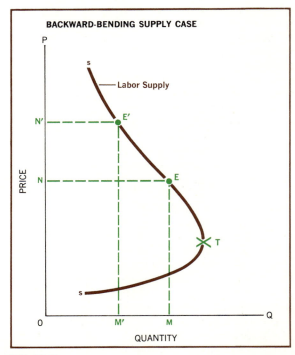

**BACKWARD-BENDING SUPPLY CASE**

**FIG. 20-13**

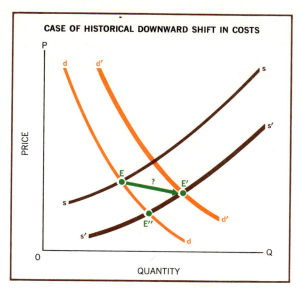

**CASE OF HISTORICAL DOWNWARD SHIFT IN COSTS**

FIG. 20-14

incentive to expand his production through and beyond the decreasing-cost stage.[2] (Later chapters analyze the imperfect competition that results when a few firms have decreasing cost and hence expand to capture much of the market.)

**Case 6. Shifts in supply** All the above discussion, with the exception of part of Case 5, dealt with a shift in demand and no shift in supply. To analyze Proposition 2, we must now shift supply, keeping demand constant. This is done in Fig. 20-15.

If the law of downward-sloping demand is valid,[3] then increased supply must send us *down* the demand curve, decreasing price and increasing quantity. The student may verify, by drawing diagrams or by comparing automobiles and wheat, the following quantitative corollaries of Proposition 2:

**(a) An increased supply will decrease price most when demand is inelastic.**
**(b) An increased supply will increase quantity least when demand is inelastic.**

What are common-sense reasons for these? Illustrate with elastic autos and inelastic wheat.

**Case 7. Dynamic cobweb** There is a famous economic case which shows that tools of supply and demand are not restricted to handling static and unchanging situations, but can also be used fruitfully to analyze dynamic situations of change. (The time-pressed reader may skip the next sections.)

Suppose that a competitive crop—let us take the conventional example of hogs for pork production—is auctioned off in the market in the usual way so as to

curve has shifted *irreversibly* downward from old *ss* to new *s's'*, so that even when demand is back again at *dd*, the price is now lower at *E''* than it was originally.

The case discussed here really does not come under the heading of Proposition 1, but under Proposition 2 dealing with shifts in supply. The final result agrees with the latter's conclusion that an increase in supply will lower price and increase quantity. (Compare *E* and *E''* in Fig. 20-14.) But the present case is still an unusual one because the shift of supply has been *induced* by a shift in demand.

In economic history, there have been important cases of reduced cost over time as a result of technological progress partly induced by the expansion of a mass market. Goods are constantly being improved in quality and cheapened in price.

What about the case of genuine *reversible* economies of large-scale production—cases where going back to small-scale production does send costs up again? The alert modern economist will not deny its importance; but he will suspect that some monopolistic imperfection of competition is present. He will point out that in a competitive industry each firm would have *already* expanded its output to where the *extra* cost of producing a unit of output has begun to turn up. This would be because each competitive producer has no fear of spoiling his own market and has every

[2] There remains the possibility to be mentioned in Chapter 24: the case of an $s_L s_L$ curve that is downward-sloping because of Marshallian *external* economies.
[3] In Chapter 22 we shall meet the legitimate exception to the law of downward-sloping demand in the case of the Irish peasants who might be forced by higher potato $P$ to consume *more* of such necessities. Another exception is provided by items such as diamonds or chic hats, which are valuable, not for their intrinsic qualities so much as for their "snob appeal" and expensiveness, and which may therefore fall off in demand if their price is cut. What appears to be another exception is the case in which a short-run rise in $P$ may make people expect future $P$ to be still higher, thus causing them to buy more rather than less now and thereby leading to unstabilizing speculation; but this is more properly to be interpreted as a case where the whole demand curve is dynamically shifting, rather than as a northeast move along *dd*.

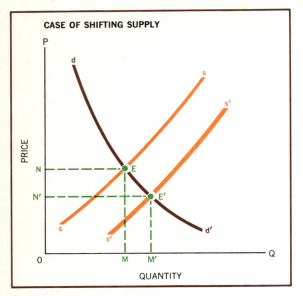

CASE OF SHIFTING SUPPLY

FIG. 20-15

supply curve and produce in the second period at the point marked $F_2$. We can see that this amount of $Q$ is above the equilibrium $Q^*$. What will it sell for in the competitive market? We run down to the demand curve and see that $P_2$ will have to fall to the level shown at $E_2$. But we are not yet in final equilibrium. At this low price, farmers will plan to cut down tomorrow's production by going leftward to their $ss$ curve, ending up at $F_3$. From there we move upward to the $dd$ curve, to find the $P_3$ given at the $E_3$ point.

And thus it goes on and on. First $Q$ is low and $P$ is high. But high $P$ makes next period's $Q$ high and next period's $P$ low. So—like a man on a tightrope who goes too far on one side, then corrects himself by going too far on the other—market price oscillates in successive periods above and below equilibrium, tracing out a spiderlike cobweb.

What is the final outcome? Figure 20-16 was drawn with the supply curve's slope at $E$ *steeper* than the demand curve's falling slope. So, as can be seen from the diagram, the oscillations finally do dampen and die out: the cobweb winds inward to $E$. We are then back at equilibrium, where we can stay forever. Forever? Well, until the next outside disturbance comes to set off another dying-out oscillation.

fetch the $P$ given by running vertically up from any given $Q$ to the $dd$ demand curve.

But now we want to make the supply side dynamic. Suppose farmers look at today's $P$ and use it to determine the $Q$ they will bring to market in the *next* period: specifically, if today's $P$ is high, they begin to breed many new pigs, to feed and fatten them, and finally to bring them to market some months from now. The farmers do indeed have an $ss$ supply curve, but it acts *with a time lag* and connects the next period's $Q$ with this period's $P$. (It is understood that we define a period as the time involved in producing hogs.)

If the market price were at the intersection of $ss$ and $dd$ in Fig. 20-16, this would represent an unchanging equilibrium in exactly the same way that it did in the nondynamic cases. Today, tomorrow, and in the period after that, the farmers would be on their $ss$ curve producing the amount shown by $E$; and the amount consumers would gladly demand at that $P$ would just match what farmers will gladly supply. As yet, then, no difference.

But suppose that, for some reason, such as hog cholera, the crop initially drops to $Q_1$, which is below the equilibrium amount $Q^*$. We run up to the demand curve to $E_1$ and see that we get the higher $P_1$ corresponding to the reduced crop. But that is not the end of the story. We are not at long-run equilibrium; because how much will the farmers produce tomorrow at this higher $P_1$? They will run over rightward to their

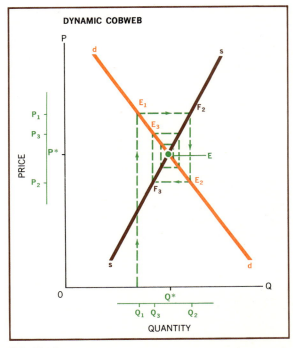

DYNAMIC COBWEB

FIG. 20-16

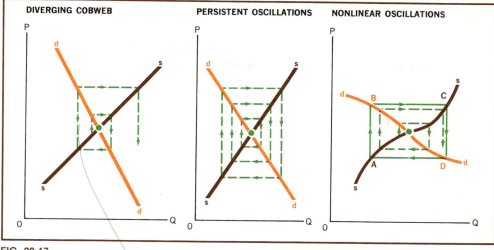

**FIG. 20-17**

Not all equilibrium points are so dynamically stable. Figure 20-17 puts a microscope on the region around *E* in a number of other possible situations. Thus, in its first diagram, *ss* has been made *flatter* than *dd*, and the cobweb diverges outward in an explosive oscillation.

In the middle diagram, the straight lines are of the *same absolute slope* and we get a perfect cobweb: depending upon how severely it is disturbed, the market will oscillate endlessly around equilibrium, getting neither more nor less violent in its swings. (This is like the case of an ideal frictionless pendulum which would repeat its swings forever.)

The final diagram is designed to show that there is no need to stick with straight lines. Because its *ss* is flatter (more "elastic") than *dd* at the equilibrium point, any small disturbance will *at first* send the system into increasing oscillations. But no explosion can go on forever in real life; and the curvature of the schedules finally brings the system to the stable "box," indicated by the letters *ABCD*. Ultimately, then, the system oscillates repeatedly in an every-other-period box and the amplitude or degree of the oscillation will be determined by the curvatures of *dd* and *ss*. After any new disturbance, the system tends to come back to this box from within or without; and even if stationary equilibrium were restored at *E* by accident, the slightest new shock would send the market away from such an unstable equilibrium point. (The thoughtful student may ask at this point: Could prices swing forever in this every-other-period fashion without shrewd speculators beginning to notice the pattern? Would they not then tend to buy at low *P*, store, and resell at high *P*, thus tending to wipe out the price differentials? The Appendix to the next chapter deals with dynamic speculation and suggests that just this might indeed happen.)

There was space here for only the briefest account of this cobweb model. Statistics show that a corn-hog cycle like this has been part of modern history. And our simplified model throws some light on the business-cycle phenomena dealt with in Part Two, where a free enterprise system would tend to fluctuate if not moderated by public policy and equilibrating market mechanisms. Corporations, like pig farmers, can swing from one extreme to the other, thus causing instability.

## CONCEPTS FOR REVIEW

price rise from *dd* increase
probable quantity rise
constant costs, horizontal supply
increasing costs, rising *ss*

inelastic supply, vertical *ss*, rent
backward-rising supply
decreasing costs and monopoly
increased *ss* lowering *P*

dynamic supply and demand cobweb
   lagged supply
   unlagged demand
every-other-period oscillation of *P*

# 21

## SUPPLY AND DEMAND AS APPLIED TO AGRICULTURE

American farm leaders are correct in arguing that our agriculture still must look forward to a definite "surplus" problem. What they tend to overlook, however, is of what our "surplus" consists. Fundamentally America's long-term agricultural problem is not one of "surplus" cotton, wheat or grapefruit. Rather it is one of "surplus" farmers.
WILLIAM H. NICHOLLS

The economist's model of perfect competition, of a homogeneous product produced by many people and auctioned off in a well-organized market, does not fit most of American life at all closely. Therefore, we will have to supplement it later by applying new tools of imperfect, or monopolistic, competition.

There is, however, one great area that does provide a valuable application of the basic tools of supply and demand. Agriculture is an important problem area. It makes the news. It shifts votes. Moreover, our rich food potential is a vital resource in connection with foreign aid to hungry peoples abroad. Without first understanding the basic economic concepts of supply and demand, no one can possibly understand the major policy issues in the field of agriculture—e.g., whether in the decades ahead the Malthusian curse of inadequate food will prevail. This chapter puts these tools to work.

### THE LONG-RUN RELATIVE DECLINE OF AGRICULTURE

Farming was long our largest single industry; but housing, health care, and defense today loom larger. The percentage of people engaged in agriculture has been declining steadily for the last two centuries, and it is no longer true that we are a nation of farmers. Though farmers still swing much political weight, only one in twenty-five Americans lives on a farm today compared with one in four as recently as 1929!

Figure 21-1 shows that farm prices have been generally losing ground to other prices. The parity ratio rose in 1972–73, but this upward movement appears to be—like the wartime rises in the parity ratio—a temporary interruption to the long-run trend.

Why this relative shift away from farming? People seek the higher incomes of the city, shorter hours, and what many seem to regard as the better social life in town; they flee from ancient discriminations. (But, as the analysis of urban and race problems in Chapters 39 and 40 will show, the migrants to the city encounter new problems there.)

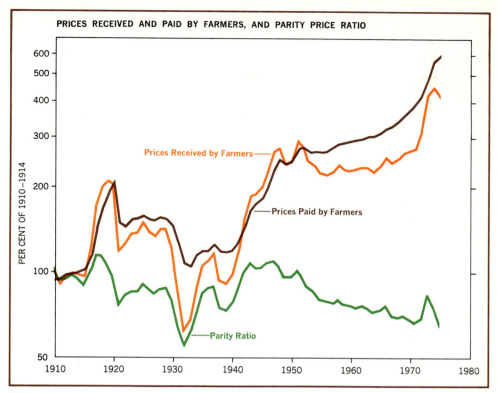

PRICES RECEIVED AND PAID BY FARMERS, AND PARITY PRICE RATIO

FIG. 21-1
**Parity is ratio of prices farmer gets to prices he pays, compared to golden age**
If the change since 1910–1914 in prices farmers receive for their products just matched
the change in the prices they pay for goods, the parity-price ratio curve would be at 100.
Its being recently around 80 shows that prices received by farmers have not risen as much
as have prices they have to pay. (Source: U.S. Department of Agriculture)

**Differential birth rates**   In a way, this out-migration from the countryside is lucky. For,
as we saw in Chapter 2, birth rates are higher in rural areas than in cities. If it were
not for this migration, cities might grow smaller and smaller; the rural share of total
population would grow larger and larger. What does the law of diminishing returns
tell us such an eventuality would mean? It would mean a great reduction in the
productivity of each man-hour spent on the farm. The land would become crowded
with many people, each producing little and each unable to buy many of the comforts
of life with his produce.

Does this sound far-fetched? It is a true picture of about two-thirds of the globe.
In Asia especially, standards of living are pitifully poor. With three out of every four
persons engaged in producing the food necessary for life, only one out of four can
be producing the bare comforts of life. Contrast this with the United States, where
each producer is efficient enough today to feed 50 other people and feed them well.

**Technological change and patterns of taste**    Besides the differential in birth rates, there are two other reasons why agriculture is a problem area.

*Technological progress* has been greatly reducing the number of people needed to produce any given total of food and fiber. Use of the tractor, the combine, the cotton picker, irrigation, fertilizer, selective breeding of hybrid corn and livestock, and numerous other examples come to mind.

Coupled with the improvement in labor-saving technique is the unshakable fact that, *as we get richer, we do not want to expand our food consumption by as much as we want to expand our consumption of city products.* This has been shown by almost every statistical investigation of income elasticities here and abroad. Hence,

Birth rates, tastes, and technology dictate that agriculture must go on exporting people to industry.

## AGRICULTURE'S LONG-RUN DECLINE: GRAPHICAL ANALYSIS

One single diagram is more useful in explaining the sagging trend of farm prices than libraries of orations and editorials.

In Fig. 21-2 let the point $E$ represent the initial equilibrium of supply and demand at some earlier period. Now see what happens to these curves as the years go by. We

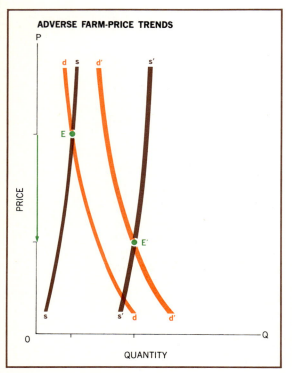

**ADVERSE FARM-PRICE TRENDS**

**FIG. 21-2**
**One diagram goes far to explain the farm problem**
As the years go by, the increase in demand for farm products generated by population and income growth tends to be less than the vast increase in supply generated by technological productivity improvements. Thus free prices fall. With both schedules highly inelastic, prices fall hard; farm incomes deteriorate. And small shifts in inelastic curves generate large price fluctuations.

know that *dd* will shift rightward as population grows and as higher real incomes make people want to consume more food at the same price; but we've seen that basic foods are the kinds of necessities which do not increase in the family budget at all proportionately to increases in real income, and we realize that United States population no longer grows at the prodigious percentage rates of the nineteenth century. So the rightward demand shift to *d'd'* is of modest amount.

What about supply? Though many make the mistake of thinking of farming as a backward business, statistical records show that productivity in American agriculture has increased at a pace even faster than productivity in industry. So each new improvement helps to shift the *ss* curve a great deal to the right.

What, then, must be happening to the new equilibrium *E'* that would prevail in the market if the government did not intervene? Certainly a shift in supply that outstrips the shift in demand must lead to a *downward trend of market prices* (relative, of course, to the general price level, so that effects of over-all inflation are disregarded). Naturally, this declining price trend means financial pressure and hardship on those farmers and rural workers whose efficiency has not undergone tremendous increase; and it means that there will be considerable pressure for people to leave the countryside for jobs in industry. It also means that consumers are paying lower prices for the raw-material component of their foods[1] and that the economy is reallocating its resources toward the things that are *now* most demanded in our growing society.

And, as we know, it means strong political pressures for government aid to agriculture.

## SHORT-RUN INSTABILITY IN AGRICULTURE

Farming is an up-and-down industry. Corn, wheat, beef, pork, and other farm products are sold in highly competitive markets whose prices change yearly, daily, hourly, and by the minute. The farmer swings at the very end of our seesawing economy. Good times bring him great percentage increases in income, and depressions cause his cash income to drop away to very little.

If we look closely at farm statistics, we note a surprising fact:

Farm *incomes* fluctuate between boom and bust to a greater degree than nonfarm incomes, but farm *production* is remarkably more stable than industrial production. Stability of farm output contrasts with instability of farm prices!

Even the weather, which is a great threat to stability of income in *any one* farm region, does not cause sizable fluctuations in *total* farm crops over the whole nation. During the last quarter-century, industrial production had an average year-to-year variation of about 8 per cent, while agricultural production had less than 3 per cent.

---

[1] Even though the price the farmer gets for the food he sells will fall, the retail price need not fall so much—or may even rise. Why? Agricultural experts claim this is not so much because railroads, packers, and supermarkets extort an undue share of the food dollar as that we consumers today want our food more and more fabricated (e.g., frozen, cut, cleaned, cooked, minutely packaged, premixed for baking, and so forth) and that greater technological progress may be taking place in producing raw food than in processing and marketing it. In the 1970s the farmer gets less than one-third of the retail food dollar, as compared with about one-half in earlier years of high farm prices.

No wonder the farmer feels he is at the mercy of a fluctuating market. His supply curves are relatively inelastic for at least two reasons: (*a*) When *P* is low, his own effort to increase output may intensify, as he desperately tries to maintain family income; (*b*) many of his costs go on anyway, whether he produces much or little, and he can save but little extra cost by cutting his *Q*.

Figure 21-1 showed that fluctuations in the prices received by farmers are greater than the fluctuations in the prices of the things they must buy. In the Great Depression days of the 1930s, prices received by farmers dropped about twice as far as did prices elsewhere. In 1972 and 1973, farm prices rose dramatically due to a temporary fall in supply which was due in turn to short harvests at a time when stocks were low.

## GOVERNMENT AID TO AGRICULTURE

Agriculture may be the unlucky stepchild of nature, but it is often the favored foster child of government. From the beginning of time, the public seems always to have hated a landlord and loved a farmer. So there is fairly widespread support among the electorate at large for aid to the farmer, despite the fact that the voting strength of the farm bloc itself has shrunk considerably.

Prior to 1929, the principal government aid to agriculture came through our *public land policy* aimed at getting acreage into the hands of settlers, and through the elaborate *practical and scientific* aids to improved agricultural methods and conservation. The work done in agricultural experiment stations, at the so-called "state land-grant colleges" (Michigan State, Iowa State, etc.), is well known; and in every farm district, the government-paid county agent provides an important source of help toward efficient farming.

After 1929, especially under Roosevelt's New Deal, a new era of direct aid to farmers began. The government stepped in to "interfere with the natural laws of supply and demand" to try to increase the stability and level of farm incomes. Both political parties have pledged themselves to a continuation of such activities; the powerful Farm Bureau Federation, the Grange, and the Farmers' Union maintain close contact with Washington to make sure Congress knows farmers' wishes.

**The parity concept**   The years 1909 to 1914 are often looked back upon as the golden age of agriculture. So, over the years, there has been increasing political pressure to have the government somehow guarantee to the farmer prices as relatively favorable as then prevailed. This is the root notion of "parity"—the simple feeling that if a bushel of wheat or farm goods sold for enough in 1909–1914 to buy a certain market basket of city goods and services, then in the 1970s it should still be able to buy the equivalent of that same market basket.

Parity, as shown back in Fig. 21-1, perhaps sounds simple; and perhaps rather fair—especially since we all like farmers and their votes. Why, then, the fight over it?

Deeper analysis shows that, as demand and supply change over a long period of time, the attempt to peg price at an arbitrary high level results in an avalanche of surplus farm goods. (Show the gap between the *s's'* and *d'd'* of Fig. 21-2 at prices kept higher than $E'$; and show how that gap will grow over time.) The dollar costs of aid become astronomical. The distortions of production become cumulatively greater and greater. Thus, the government storage bins are often bursting, and even the mothball fleet of abandoned warships has had to be used for grain storage.

The reason for this farm surplus, we have already seen. More rapid technical progress on the farm than in town means that an hour of rural labor now produces many more bushels of food than it did in 1909–1914; and if an hour of city labor does not now produce relatively as many more market baskets of industrial goods, why should these city and farm items still swap at the same "parity" terms?[2] In short, the *real costs of production have gone down immensely* since then; so pegging prices at the old levels calls forth a supply much larger than will be bought in the market at the parity prices. For the efficient farmers, parity maintenance may mean incomes running into six figures. For the marginal farmer, it may mean a pittance. And it keeps some inefficient farmers from going to higher-productivity occupations.

Farmers boast of their independence; and when they come to the government for help—as they most certainly do—they claim they do not want a handout, but rather that they want to "earn" their subsidies. But actually, in some of the years following World War II, more than half of what the farmers collected in the market place for certain crops—such as peanuts, sorghum grain, and others—resulted from government aid programs!

## FORMS OF GOVERNMENT AID

What are the economic mechanisms by which government can help, or seem to help, the farmer? They are principally five in number:

1. Outright *gift* or relief payments, given to needy farmers who have established their need and misery (e.g., the negative income tax, social security retirement payments)

2. Programs by the government that aim to *increase the demand* for farm products or *cut their real cost* of production

3. *Crop-limitation* programs (such as acreage allotments or crop quotas to each farm) that aim to cut down on supply and raise price

4. *Purchase-loan storage* programs to support farm prices

5. Finally, *purchase-and-resale differential subsidy* plans

**Gifts and relief**   There is nothing complicated about outright gifts or transfer payments, which might well be adjoined to our Social Security system or be part of Chapter 40's negative income tax. The organized farm pressure groups do not particularly want such aids, even though in strictest economic logic they are the most defensible of all: If our Republic wants to alleviate the burden on farmers (or the poor anyplace!) and

---

[2]Even if productivity were to grow at about the same rate in the two areas from now on, it would still be necessary to have some differential in earnings on and off the farm in order to coax the socially desirable shift of labor to production of those goods and services which expand in people's demand more rapidly than do food and fiber.

provide minimum standards, outright grants will help to clarify what is involved and what it costs, thereby enabling the electorate to decide in a rational way what it wants.

Less than a fifth of our farms correspond to the public image of a "family farm" earning a decent living. Most farms by number are poverty enterprises. A thousand of our largest farms produce more than do our 2 million smallest! As it is now, farm subsidies trickle down only in small fractions to those in greatest need: the Southern sharecroppers who live in credit peonage, the less fortunate tenant farmers, owners of small marginal farms, and paid farm laborers.

**Demand promotion and research**    Little need be said about attempts by the Department of Agriculture to find new chemical uses of farm products or to send out circulars telling people to improve their diets. (The Department may also get Congress to provide funds to finance cheap school lunches, food stamps for the hungry, and other demand-raising programs.) Such activity goes a long way back in our history, as does government aid to land-grant colleges' experimental work to increase farm productivity. Not only will the Agriculture Department send a farmer a pamphlet on baking an angel-food cake or running a Halloween party; it will also send a county agent to teach the farmer good conservation methods, how to keep records, and how best to till his soil. Some observers think it odd that while one branch of the government is trying to get the farmer to produce less, another branch is trying to improve his productivity.

Probably the most important promotion of demand for farm products has come from Public Law 480 (the Agriculture and Trade Redevelopment and Assistance Act, 1954). This permits underdeveloped countries like India, Pakistan, and Egypt to buy our wheat and other grains. But they do not have to pay dollars for these goods; at worst they can pay the United States government in their own currencies (rupees, pounds, etc.). These "counterpart funds" are of limited usefulness to our government, although some of this local currency may be utilized for exchange fellowships and propaganda purposes. (Both Russia and China have been sold wheat at low prices in the 1970s.)

Of course, our farmers get paid for their grain in American dollars that come from the budget and, indirectly, from the general taxpayer. In effect, the government is subsidizing agriculture by shifting the *dd* curve for food upward and to the right; then it proceeds to "dump" these goods abroad where they are much needed, as part of our foreign-aid program. All this is to the good. But it does raise problems that have already surfaced in the 1970s. The recipients of food provided by foreign aid may well become dependent on such aid, and this may put off the day when those countries bring their population growth to more sustainable rates. Also, now that U.S. support prices no longer leave us with overhanging inventories of foodstuffs, humanitarian programs that respond quickly to worldwide harvest failures tend to bid up prices just at those times when American voters are already finding their patience taxed by what appear to be uncomfortable increases in living costs. This understandably cools off some aid support.

Although it will shrink in size, American agriculture will continue to play an important role in helping feed the world. As we shall see in Part Five's discussion of international trade, America does enjoy what is called a "comparative advantage" in the production of food and fiber on highly mechanized large-scale farms.

## ECONOMICS OF THREE MAIN AID PROGRAMS

To understand the final three programs listed on page 413, our economic tools of supply and demand are absolutely necessary. Let us see how each case works.

**Case 1. Crop restriction**   If farmers produce a smaller total $Q$, they will each receive a higher $P$. Because the demand for farm products is generally *in*elastic, limiting total $Q$ will actually *raise* the total revenues received by farmers—as Chapter 20 showed.

Of course, the consumers will be hurt by scarcity of goods and by higher prices, just as they would be if flood or drought created a scarcity of foodstuffs. In deliberately restricting farm $Q$, society is deliberately shifting economic resources away from places that produce the extra goods which people's dollar votes in the marketplace show they really want. Either those resources go into idleness, as occurs with land no longer cultivated, or they may go into secondary uses for which they are ill-fitted and which involve producing items that people do not much want. (A silver lining is provided by the fact that *soil conservation and flood control* may be achieved if land gets a rest or is put into forests and pasture.) Figure 21-3 tells its own story, which can be summarized on the next page.

**FIG. 21-3**

**A cut in farm supply raises price and total revenue**
Before government intervenes, the ss' supply curve intersects the inelastic dd' curve at the low price shown at E. As an individual competitor, each farmer has no motive to do anything to improve the situation. But if all together can get government to put monopolistic limits on their total $Q$, they can benefit.

When production controls cut supply from ss' to SS', $P$ rises to E'. Because demand is inelastic, total gross farm income is thereby increased. (Recall that $P \times Q$ revenues at E and E' are measured, respectively, by the 0sEA and 0SE'B rectangular areas. Let your eye confirm that the gain in E' height over E outweighs the rectangle's loss in width; with elastic demand, the reverse would have been true.)

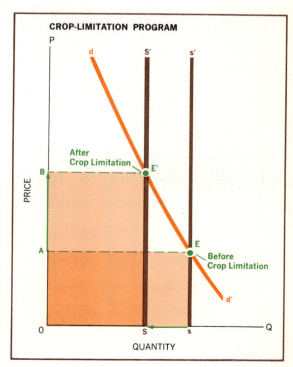

CROP-LIMITATION PROGRAM

If the demand for farm products is inelastic rather than elastic, then a program of enforced crop reduction will result in higher total receipts to the farmer. And since he also saves a little on total costs when he produces less, his net revenue goes up by even more than his total receipts do.

Does the situation described above mean that this form of farm aid is bad? Not necessarily, since noneconomic ethical and political issues are also involved. But it does suggest that each bit of benefit to some farmers is being bought at a greater sacrifice to the rest of the community than is economically and technically necessary. It does suggest that society look around for *more efficient* methods.

**Case 2. Parity price through loan support or government purchase**   This case is a little harder. Now government guarantees the farmer a price higher than would have prevailed in the market. This "price floor" is shown by the line *BB'* in Fig. 21-4. At so high a price, consumers will not buy all the crop supplied. Consumers will be on the demand curve at *C*. But farmers are supplying the full amount shown by *F*. If government does nothing, price must fall to *E*, which is below the parity price.

So what does the government have to do? By outright purchase or through some kind of loan red tape, it must acquire the unsold portion between *C* and *F*, marked with an arrow. This will go into storage, or be dumped abroad (as part of foreign aid, perhaps), or be left to rot. What, then, has the final result been?

The government has increased the price received by the farmer from *E* to *F*. But unlike the setup in the previous case, the farmers can now sell as much as they want to; so the increased price is gravy to them, representing a clear increase in their

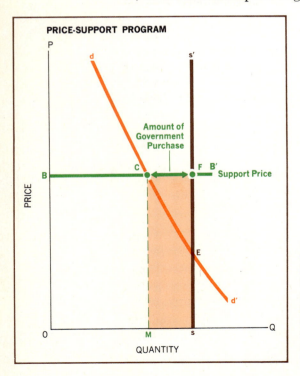

**PRICE-SUPPORT PROGRAM**

**FIG. 21-4**

**Government purchases support price by acquiring unsold surplus**

Price is kept at the indicated floor or support price *BB'* (near or at parity) by the government's stepping in and acquiring for storage unsellable surplus shown by *CF*. The shaded area shows the total cost to the government of raising market price from *E* to *F*. Note that domestic consumers pay the higher price and get no current benefit from the *CF* part of the crop.

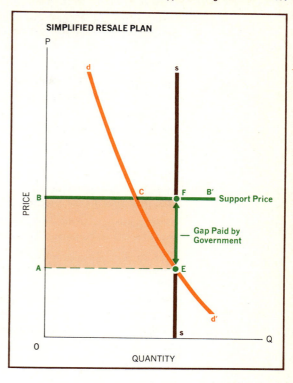

SIMPLIFIED RESALE PLAN

**FIG. 21-5**

**In price-differential system, the government pays farmers the gap between low consumers' price and supported producers' price**
Price to consumer is permitted to fall to competitive *E* level. Government then makes up, by direct payments to farmers of *EF* per bushel, the difference between the low market price and the desired support price. Farmers end up with total price return shown at *F*. The shaded area shows the cost to government of the direct payments involved in such a two-price system.

incomes. The consumers are now paying a higher price and buying less; to them Case 2 is just as bad as Case 1.[3] Who, then, is footing the bill for the extra income now received by the farmers? Obviously, the government: The public Treasury is having to shell out an amount of dollars equal to the part of the crop it must buy times the full market price. (In terms of area, the Treasury's expense is shown by the shaded area *MCFs*. Can you explain why?)

**To guarantee a price higher than the free market would dictate, government must purchase the gap between supply and demand at the support price, storing the difference or dumping it abroad.**

**Case 3. Subsidized producer-consumer price differential**    This is the hardest case of all. It involves paying an artificially high price to farmers, but reselling food to consumers at whatever low price the market will set.

Here the farmer is again guaranteed the *BB'* parity price, just as in Case 2. But Fig. 21-5 shows the new fact that food, instead of being left to rot in storage, is to be resold to the public for current consumption at whatever market price it will bring.

How is the farmer to receive the parity price if market price proves to be below that figure? The Department of Agriculture *simply writes him a check for the difference.* In effect, then, it is much as though the government had bought the crop at the parity

---

[3]Such *Q* as is being produced is presumably being produced *efficiently*. In this case, unlike Case 1, society is not *inside* its production-possibility frontier. It is merely too far southeast on Fig. 2-4's *p-p frontier,* producing more food than spontaneous dollar votes call for. Case 1 led to the opposite.

price—as in the loan support of Case 2—but had then sold it on the open market for whatever price it would bring.

Every bit produced, as shown by the *ss'* supply curve, will now go to the consumer. Consumption will end up at the original point *E*. Why? Because the "law of supply and demand" tells us that, for consumers to buy the full crop, price must fall to the point where the demand curve intersects the market supply.

But producers are promised the parity price for their entire crop. So the price they are to receive is indicated by *F* (just as in Case 2). Who pays the difference? The government—by sending each primary producer a check, whose amount per bushel is shown in Fig. 21-5 by the vertical arrow *EF*. How much does this cost the government? This cost is indicated by the shaded area *AEFB*, which shows that the government must pay the difference between the producer's and the consumer's price *on each and every unit produced!*

**Direct payments to farmers, equal to shortfall of market price below support price, result in low price to consumer and high consumption and avoid storage of rotting surpluses.**

From the standpoint of political economy, a plan which brings price to the consumer more nearly down to the social cost of producing food would have much to be said for it—even if it should happen to result in costing the Treasury more. If farmers are to get the same income in one way or the other, the important thing to us consumers is, not so much how we divide our payments between market purchases and taxes, as that food be produced and consumed up to the point where marginal utilities and costs are more nearly in balance[4]—as the next chapters will demonstrate.

## ISSUES IN DOMESTIC FARM AID

In the early New Deal days, the emphasis was on crop reduction. Acreage was cut, but technical progress and intensive cultivation often kept *Q* from declining. Later, the emphasis shifted from Case 1 to price supports through purchase or loan. These Case 2 programs became colossally expensive as rightward shifts of the supply curves made the free-equilibrium price fall further and further below 100 per cent or 80 per cent of parity. Government warehouses bulged (except during war and cold-war periods, when the surplus turned out to be a godsend). As we've seen, grain rotted;[5] as the cost of storing became great, Case 3 programs of subsidy grew.

Government, with the backing of the associations of larger commercial farmers, has in recent decades favored lowering price supports below parity and closer toward free-market levels. But to avoid too precipitous a fall in farm prices, government has relied on a mixture of crop reduction, loan support, and direct subsidies.

---

[4] Inelasticity of demand means that more is collected from consumers when food is left to rot rather than sold to consumers for the low *P* it will fetch: so the differential-price plan may cost the government a bit more. However, the benefit to consumers of more and better food may be socially worth the extra cost. (If *ss'* were drawn more realistically so as to be somewhat upward-sloping, we should have the evil of slightly too much *Q* being coaxed out by the too high government subsidy; consumers would be getting too much farm *Q* at a price to them below true social costs of resources used.) Footnote readers can refer to page 398 for a graph of the argument that uninterfered-with pricing has a property of being "efficient," even if not necessarily "equitable."

[5] Admittedly, we give some of the surplus to our poor, through school lunch, food stamp, and other programs. And, as already seen, we shipped food and fiber abroad under Public Law 480. So all was not waste.

Still, these policies would involve more reliance on market forces in determining food and fiber prices. As prices fell, consumers generally would be able to afford more food, and especially more of the expensive protein foods such as milk and meat. The United States would be better able to export the food and fiber she is well suited to produce. Commercial farmers would feel pressure on them to become more efficient, and many of the remaining family farmers would find their incomes so low in agriculture as to speed them into industry or into part-time jobs off the farm. The really poor farmers would receive welfare aids under such a program.

Looked at properly, America's real farm problem is that of rural poverty. Real incomes on the farm and in small towns average below those elsewhere. Five million rural people fall below the poverty line in 1976. Although only one-twentieth of the populace are rural, one-fifth of the impoverished live in the country. Many are black; some are Indians; some are of Mexican descent; most, by absolute (but not relative!) number, are white. Silently, invisibly, they lead miserable lives in Appalachia, along the Mexican border, in the Deep South, in the Ozarks, in the upper Great Lakes regions (and, in Canada, in the Maritime Provinces and Quebec).

Solutions for them will not come from the mechanisms of supply and demand. The solutions must come—as Chapter 40 shows—from transfer-payment programs, from education subsidies, from relocation and retraining, and from family-planning clinics. The mixed economy, and not laissez faire,[6] must provide the solutions.

## WORLD FOOD SCARCITY AHEAD?

So far in the 1970s there has occurred a rash of crop failures in Asia, Soviet Russia, and North America, with food prices soaring everywhere. As Part Six will discuss, the Club of Rome and other futurologists worried about exhaustible resources and the deteriorating environment are asking:

Is the Malthus curse of diminishing returns to haunt us as the century ends? Will food prices be rising relative to manufacturing prices and wages, both in the affluent and the less-developed world? Is the five-fold increase in oil prices, as engineered by the Persian Gulf cartel (the so-called OPEC oligopoly that is organized to raise oil prices for the exporting countries), an indication of the wave of the future for food, too?

No simple and exact answer can be given. Here are a few of the relevant arguments:

1. As countries like Japan become more affluent, they turn to meat, which is an expensive way of getting their proteins in comparison with soybeans. This bids up prices.

2. Population is still not under control in large parts of the world.

3. Increasingly, to produce food takes more and more energy: energy for irrigation; for running farm equipment; for manufacturing fertilizer and insecticides. Exhaustion of oil and mineral resources means dearer than ever food.

---

[6] All this will remain for a long time a political issue. No one will begrudge the farmer his desire to be free from wildly fluctuating prices. In the Appendix we shall see how private speculators on an organized exchange are supposed in traditional economic theory to be able to iron out any *foreseeable* fluctuations. The question remains whether, gifts aside, we can expect the government to make better forecasts of the uncertain future than private speculative markets can, and whether we can expect the government, through its storage program, to be better than private markets in stabilizing prices.

4. Maybe even the weather is getting colder as we move into a new ice age. Some geographers fear that the jet winds in the first part of this century were unusually favorable to agriculture in the Sahara and Indian-peninsula regions; that is now over.

Against these pessimistic considerations are the following:

1. Agricultural production has been subject to as much, nay according to the experts even more, technological progress than has manufacturing production or services. There is no deceleration in this technological revolution in sight. New grains—short-stalk wheat and rice, new higher-protein corn—are said to be now in the testing stage.

2. Professors Theodore Schultz and Gale Johnson of the University of Chicago, respected farm economists, claim that *land-saving invention* (which lets one acre do the work of three or more) has been going on for centuries now. They say it still goes on.

3. Weather experts are divided. Some fear the globe is warming up, from carbon dioxide greenhouse effects and from the release of industrial energy. For every "freezer" there is a futurologist who is a "boiler." Both may be wrong as the weather oscillates.

4. Gradually, as societies become less poor and as their children live to survive as adults, people do begin to have families of one, or two, or three children instead of families of four, five and even more.

Where the evidence is still so uncertain, caution in conclusions seems indicated.

## SUMMARY

1   Although the rural birth rate is higher than the urban, a persistent cityward migration means that the percentage of the population engaged in agriculture is declining. Improvements in agricultural techniques mean that supply increases greatly and that the same total of food can be produced with fewer workers; also, as incomes increase, the increase in demand for food is less than proportionate.

So free-equilibrium prices for agriculture tend to fall. Farm income tends to be both low and unstable; as a result, government has adopted a variety of programs to support farm-product prices and maintain farm incomes.

2   Pegging prices at any ancient parity formula, despite its superficial plausibility and fairness, utterly disregards basic changes in demand and real costs of production. As time passes, such a parity will produce prices differing sharply from "natural competitive" levels here and abroad. The result: huge surpluses, with the wrong goods being produced and with growing distortions of efficiency. If we had frozen resource use at the 1800 or 1850 or 1929 rural-urban proportions, poverty would have been perpetuated.

3   Aid programs involving direct gifts or promotion of demand and of cost research require no deep economic analysis. But the tools of supply and demand are needed to understand the three aid programs:

(a) crop limitation by acreage or other allotments

(b) government price support by purchase-loan storage programs

(c) resale to consumers at competitive market prices of food bought at a pegged price, with the government footing the bill for the differential

Hybrids of all three are frequently legislated. The resulting programs are colossally expensive, economically inefficient, and satisfactory to no groups.

4   The long-run solution must involve maintenance of prosperity outside agriculture, so that people can continue to move to the lines of highest productivity and so that demand for agriculture will be optimally high. But mere prosperity in industry is not enough. The 1920s show that the city and town can prosper while the economic position of the rural regions deteriorates.

In the long run, resources have to be helped to move out of low-efficiency rural uses and into more productive uses. That means a continuation of the trend toward fewer but more efficient farmers, and a need for short-run aids to speed the reconversion and to ease its human burdens. It also means flexible pricing practices that permit efficient American farms to help feed the world. And, as Chapters 39 and 40 show, the rural exodus creates urban problems elsewhere.

The real problem of agriculture is seen to be that of poverty. The creative energies of the mixed economy are needed to devise transfers for the poor anywhere.

5   World affluence and Malthusian diminishing returns would tend to raise food prices during the next half-century. But land-saving innovation in agriculture and continued technological progress may serve to keep future prices of food and fiber low—particularly if population planning occurs.

## CONCEPTS FOR REVIEW

inelastic farm demand and supply

farm technology, declining income
   fraction spent on food

free-farm-price trends

parity, 1909–1914 golden age

Public Law 480 food exports

$Q$ limitation

$P$ support or loan

direct payments with different
   consumer $P$ and producer $P$

pros and cons of free farm prices

long- and short-run solutions

rural poverty and welfare aid

pros and cons of future food prices

## QUESTIONS FOR DISCUSSION

1   Contrast long-term and cyclical patterns of agriculture and industry.

2   Describe government indirect and direct farm aids. Explain "parity."

3   Why might limiting a farm's acreage in one crop not reduce the total of it much? How would it affect noncontrolled crops? Fertilizer demand?

4   Debate the merit of taking a dollar from the 19 in 20 employed outside farming and giving it to the 1 in farming. Distinguish ways of giving him the dollar.

5   What does Professor Dudley Johnson of the University of Washington mean here? "Major premise: Society should help poor people. Minor premise (of doubtful validity as stated): Farmers are poor people. (Dubious) Conclusion: Therefore society should help farmers. Actually, if society is to subsidize individuals, it should not be done on the basis of their occupations, but because they are *poor*—i.e., aid on an *income* basis."

6   Why might the negative income tax help the farm problem?

7   Weigh the pros and cons of future food scarcity or plenty.

## APPENDIX: Economics of Speculation, Risk, and Insurance

Here we apply the tools of supply and demand to analyze price relations across space and time and the important problems involved in risk, speculation, and gambling. We deal not only with the purchase and sale of actual commodities such as corn or cocoa, but also with the purchase and sale of something more mysterious—of bits of paper.

These bits of paper are called "commodity futures": they are contracts that brokers deal with on organized commodity exchanges like the Chicago Board of Trade or the New York Cocoa Exchange. You and I may buy or sell such commodity futures even though we have never seen any *real* corn or cocoa. As speculators in such futures, the last thing in the world we should want to happen would be for a truck to roll up to our door seeking to deliver honest-to-goodness corn or cocoa.

Yet, as we shall see, even though speculators never touch the real thing, they may under certain conditions be helping to even out the consumption of the crop between harvest times and to carry over the proper amounts of food and fiber between seasons.

In his autobiography, the elder statesman Bernard Baruch said that 10 years after he heard Professor George B. Newcomb lecture on supply and demand at CCNY, he had made more than a million dollars from speculation—implying that those lectures might have had something to do with it. Certainly, this Appendix is not designed to make you rich, and if you skip it, your knowledge of the rest of the book will not suffer. But speculation is a fascinating topic and can serve as an example of important applications of supply and demand. Inevitably, it is a complicated subject which no introduction can pretend to treat completely.

### GEOGRAPHICAL PRICE PATTERNS

In a well-organized competitive market, there tends to be at any one time and place a single prevailing price. This is due to the action of professional speculators or "arbitragers" who keep their ear to the market and, as soon as they learn of any price differences, buy at the cheaper price and sell at the dearer price, thereby making a profit for themselves—at the same time tending to equalize the price.[1]

Two markets at a considerable distance from each other may have different prices. Wheat in Chicago may sell for a few cents more per bushel than identical wheat in Kansas City, because of shipping, insurance, and interest charges involved in transportation. If ever the price in Chicago should rise by more than the few cents of shipping costs, speculators will buy in Kansas City and ship to Chicago, thereby bringing the price up in Kansas City and down in Chicago to the normal maximum differential.

Nobody legislates these patterns. They follow from supply and demand.

### SPECULATION AND PRICE BEHAVIOR OVER TIME

In an ideal competitive market there tends to be a definite pattern of prices *over time* just as there is over space. But the difficulties of predicting the future

[1] On the floor of the Chicago Board of Trade, the important market for grain, some hundred important "pit scalpers," or dealers, are said to make all their profits on price changes within each day, closing out all their transactions every night and sleeping peacefully until the next day. Specialists on the floor of the Stock Exchange are meant to play a similar role.

make this pattern a less perfect one: we have an equilibrium that is constantly being disturbed but is always in the process of re-forming itself—rather like the ocean's surface under the play of the winds.

**Stabilizing seasonal patterns** Consider the simplest case of a grain, like corn, that is harvested at one period of the year. This crop must be made to last all the year if privation is to be avoided. Since no one passes a law regulating the storage of grain, how is this desirable state of affairs brought about? Through the attempts of speculators to make a profit.

A well-informed speculator who is a specialist in this grain realizes that if all the grain is thrown on the market in the autumn, it will fetch a very low price because of the glutting of the market. On the other hand, months later, with almost no grain coming on the market, price will tend to skyrocket.

The above description tells what would tend to happen were it *not* for the action of speculators. Speculators realize that by (1) purchasing some of the autumn crop while it is cheap, (2) withholding it in storage, and (3) selling it later when the price has risen, they can make a profit. This they do. But in doing so, they increase the autumn demand for grain and raise its autumn price; and they increase the spring supply of grain and lower its spring price. At the same time that they are equalizing the price over the year, they are also equalizing the supply coming on the market in each month—which is as it should be.

Moreover, if there is brisk competition among speculators, none will make an excessive profit over the costs that he incurs (including, of course, the wages necessary to keep him in this line of activity). The speculator himself may never touch a kernel of corn or a bag of cocoa, nor need he know anything about storage, warehouses, or delivery. He merely buys and sells bits of paper. But the effect is exactly as described.

Now there is one and only one monthly price pattern that will result in neither profits nor losses. A little thought will show that it will not be a pattern of constant prices. Rather, the ideal price pattern will involve lowest prices in the autumn glut, and then gradually rising prices until the peak is reached just before the new corn comes in. The price must rise from month to month to compensate for the storage and interest costs of carrying the crop in storage—in exactly the same way that the price must rise over space from one mile to the next to compensate for short''[3] for future delivery, tending to depress current prices, raise present consumption, and reduce carry-over of stocks.

### Spreading of risks

Aside from their influence toward stabilizing prices, speculators have another important function. By being willing to take risks on their own shoulders, they enable others to avoid risk.

For example, a warehouse owner must carry large inventories of grain in the course of his business. If the price of grain goes up, he makes a windfall capital gain; if down, he incurs a windfall loss. But let us suppose that he is content to earn his living by storing grain and wishes to forgo all risk taking. This he can do by a process called "hedging." This complicated procedure is rather like a man who bets on Army to win the Army-Navy game and then washes out this transaction, or covers it, by placing an equal bet on the Navy. Whichever side wins, he comes out the same, his left hand winning what his right hand loses.

To get a notion of how the complicated process of hedging works out, here is a highly simplified example. Suppose I am buying and storing corn in the late fall. I am a specialist in running a warehouse and wish to stick to my job rather than become involved in the risky business of taking speculative bets as to whether the price of corn will change between now and next spring, when I expect to stop storing corn and to sell it. In effect, I should really like to sell it now for an agreed-upon price that will compensate me for my storage expenses between now and later delivery time (amounting, let's say, to 9 cents per bushel). If a

---

[3] There is nothing mysterious about selling short. I simply put in an order to my broker in which I agree, in return for a certain price *now*, to deliver *at some later date* an amount of grain. Usually, at the time of putting in the order, I do not have the grain on hand. But I can legally fulfill my contract by later "covering," i.e., buying the grain and making delivery. If I later have to pay a higher price in covering than I now receive when selling short, then I take a loss. But if I have guessed right and prices do fall in the intervening period, then I "buy in" for less than I have sold and make a profit.

Selling short in the stock market works out similarly, except that I am free to cover and make future delivery of the stock at any time I please. Meanwhile, the man who has bought the stock receives his stock shares. How? As a result of the fact that my broker, obligingly, lends me the stock certificates to make delivery. Later, when I cover, I buy in some stock and turn over the certificates to my obliging broker.

speculative market exists, that is precisely what I can do by the device of hedging.

How do I hedge? For each 5,000 bushels of corn I buy in November to put into storage until next May, let us suppose I have to pay $1.00 a bushel to local Illinois farmers. I look up the price quoted today, November 30, on the Chicago Board of Trade for next May corn futures and see that this quotation is $1.09. I realize that this 9-cent excess over today's price will give me a fair return for my expenses of storage and that is why I am glad to store. I now hedge by *selling* a 5,000-bushel May corn-future contract. (The brokerage commission on this "short-sale" transaction will be less than $\frac{1}{2}$ cent per bushel; my broker will require that I put up less than 10 cents per bushel as "margin" to ensure that I fulfill my contractual obligation, and he neither knows nor cares whether I actually have some physical corn with which to make later delivery.)

Now I am hedged. I happen to own 5,000 bushels of physical corn in storage. I also have sold 5,000 bushels of May corn futures.

What will happen if slack corn demand and a tremendous winter wheat and oats crop cause the price of corn to fall to 90 cents by next May?

My brother, who owns a warehouse and bought corn in the fall as I did *but did not hedge,* will now lose 10 cents per bushel. Indeed, he is worse off than that, because he is also out the 9 cents that it costs him to keep his warehouse going (watchmen's pay, and so forth). So he has really lost 19 cents per bushel in toto.

What about me, the cagy hedger? I do lose 10 cents a bushel *on my physical corn* because of the unforeseen change in price. But when, as May arrives, I look in the paper for the Board of Trade quotation on my May future, I am relieved to see that it has fallen from $1.09 all the way down to 90 cents—at which price I buy in, or "cover," my futures. Thus, *on short sale of my futures* I have gained 19 cents, or exactly as much as I (like my brother) have lost (inclusive of warehouse costs) on the sale of physical corn. *The hedge has protected me from all price fluctuations:* my left futures pocket has gained what my right physical-corn pocket lost. I'm left with my 9-cent costs well covered. The speculator who made my hedge possible took the price risks off my shoulders.[4]

---

[4] To check your understanding, work through the case where a war scare sends up the price of physical corn in the May

To the extent that speculators forecast accurately, they provide a definite social service. To the extent that they forecast badly, they tend to aggravate the variability of prices. Were it not for the detailed statistical information provided by the Department of Agriculture and private agencies, the traders of the Chicago Board of Trade would find themselves at the mercy of every idle rumor, hope, and fear. For speculation is often a mass contagion, like the inexplicable dancing crazes that swept medieval villages, the Dutch tulip mania that sent the price of a single bulb higher than that of a house, the South Sea Bubble in which companies sold stock at fabulous prices for enterprises which would "later be revealed."

## GAMBLING AND DIMINISHING MARGINAL UTILITY[5]

The defenders of speculation resent the charge that it represents simply another form of gambling, like betting on the horse races or buying a lottery ticket. They emphasize that an uncertain world necessarily involves risk and that someone must bear risks. They claim that the knowledge and the venturesomeness of the speculator are chained to a *socially useful purpose,* thereby reducing fluctuations and risks to others. (We have just seen that this is not always the case and that speculation may indeed be destabilizing; yet, no one can deny all validity to the above claims.)

Why is gambling considered such a bad thing? Part of the reason, perhaps the most important part, lies

in the field of morals, ethics, and religion; upon these the economist as such is not qualified to pass final judgment. There is, however, a substantial economic case to be made against gambling.

First, it involves simply *sterile transfers of money or goods* between individuals, creating no new money or goods.[6] Although it creates no output, gambling does nevertheless absorb time and resources. When pursued beyond the limits of recreation, where the main purpose after all is to "kill" time, gambling subtracts from the national income.

The second economic disadvantage of gambling is the fact that it tends to promote *inequality* and *instability of incomes.* People who sit down to the gaming table with the same amount of money go away with widely different amounts. A gambler (and his family) must expect to be on the top of the world one day, and when luck changes—which is the only predictable thing about it—he may almost starve.

**Law of diminishing marginal utility and chance**   But why is inequality of income over time and between persons considered such a bad thing? One answer is to be found in the widely held belief that the gain in utility achieved by an *extra* $1,000 of income is not so great as the loss in utility of forgoing $1,000 of income. Where that is the case, a bet at fair odds involves an economic loss: the *money* you stand to win balances the money you may lose; but the *satisfaction* you stand to win is *less* than the satisfaction you stand to lose.

Similarly, if it could be assumed that individuals are all "roughly the same" and are ethically comparable, so that their utilities can be added, then the dollars gained by the rich do not create so much "social

---

market to, say, $1.19. Now my unhedged brother, in addition to his 9-cent return as a warehouseman, makes an additional windfall risk profit of 10 cents per bushel. What about me? On my physical corn which I bought at $1.00 and sell for $1.19, I gain; but I lose 10 cents on having to buy in my May futures at 10 cents more than I sold it for. So I end up making my 9-cent warehouse return and no more—regardless of what can happen to corn price fluctuations.

Actual hedging of millers, farmers, and storers can become more complicated. Also, it could happen that, in order to coax out speculators, the quotation in November of the May future would on the average have to sell for a little less than the $1.09 such physical corn can be expected to sell for in May; this means that the risk-bearing speculators require a premium for the insurancelike risk taking they are providing—a premium (called "normal backwardation") that, like any cost, must be borne by producers and ultimate consumers.

[5]Some of this material leans on (and illustrates!) the later discussion of marginal utility, beginning on page 433.

[6]Actually, in all professional gambling arrangements, the participants lose out on balance. The leakage comes from the fact that the odds are always rigged in favor of the "house," so that even an "honest" house will win in the long run. Moderate gambling among friends may be considered a form of consumption or recreation activity whose cost to the group as a whole is zero. Oddly, some people who do not trust their ability to save do use steady purchase of lottery tickets as a way to cut down on current consumption and put themselves in the position of occasionally accumulating larger sums of money. In some past and present societies, the enhancement of inequality of income distribution by gambling may have made a roundabout contribution to social thrift and capital formation.

welfare" or total utility as the dollars lost by the poor. This has been used not only as a criticism of gambling, but as a positive argument in favor of "progressive" or steeply graduated taxation aimed at lowering the inequality of the distribution of income. (The issue of incentives must also enter into forming any decision on policy, since discussions elsewhere show that redistributing the national pie may lessen its total.)

Just as Malthus saw the law of diminishing returns as underlying his theory of population, so is the "law of diminishing marginal utility" used by many economists to condemn professional gambling. According to utility theory (discussed in the next chapter), as money income increases, each new dollar adds something to utility, but less and less. Similarly, each extra unit of any good that can be bought with money contributes less and less satisfaction or utility. When we get as much of a good as we wish (e.g., air), it becomes a "free good" because still further units add nothing new to our utility.[7]

### WHY IDEAL STABILIZATION BY SPECULATORS IS OPTIMAL

We can now use the tools of marginal utility to show how ideal speculation would maximize total utility over time. Suppose every consumer has a utility schedule that holds for each year independently of any other year. Now suppose that in the first of two years there were a big crop—say, 3 units per person—and in the second a small crop of only 1 unit per person. If this crop deficiency could be foreseen, how should the

consumption of the two-year 4-unit total be spread over the two years?

If we agree, for simplicity, to neglect all storage, interest, and insurance charges and all questions of utility commensurability over time, we can prove this:

**Total utility for the two years together will be maximized only if consumption is equal in each year.**

Why is uniform consumption better than any other division of the available total? Because of the law of diminishing marginal utility. Here is the reasoning: "Suppose I consume more in the first year than in the second. My last unit's marginal utility in the first year will be low, and then in the second it will be high. So if I carry some crop from the first to the second year, I shall be switching from low to high marginal utilities—and that will maximize my total utility."

But is not that exactly what the following ideal speculation pattern would accomplish? Yes, it is.

If speculators can neglect interest, storage, and insurance charges and happen to forecast accurately next year's low crop, what will they do? They will figure it pays to carry goods over from this year's low price resulting from the high crop, hoping instead to sell at next year's scarcity price. But as each speculator subtracts from this year's supply and adds to next year's, what must finally happen? Equilibrium can be reached only when the two prices have been *equalized!* Then there will be no further incentive to carry over more crop.[8] (Of course, a small payment for the speculator's effort might have to be included—but we have agreed to waive all costs just to keep the example simple.)

Do not for a moment get the impression that real

---

[7] The astute reader will note (*a*) that economics proves that those subject to diminishing marginal utility should not gamble and should insure, but that a man with *increasing* marginal utility will maximize his expected utility by gambling (and, as we'll soon see, by noninsuring); and (*b*) that any economist who uses observations on a person's reaction to situations involving probabilities as his test of how marginal utility varies for that person may end up with the following circular reasoning: Those who gamble should gamble; those who insure should insure. So the case for prohibiting gambling must rest on extraneous ethical or religious grounds; or must be withdrawn; or must be based on the notion that society knows better than individuals what is truly good for them; or must be based on the notion that we are all imperfect beings who wish in the long run that we were not free to yield to short-run temptations. Some political economists feel that moderate gambling might be converted into socially useful channels.

[8] A graph can illuminate this argument. If utility could be measured in dollars, with each dollar always denoting the same marginal utility, the demand curves would look just like the marginal utility schedule on page 434. The two curves of Fig. 21-7 show what would happen if there were no carryover—with price first determined at $A_1$, where $s_1s_1$ intersects $dd$, and second at $A_2$, where the lower supply $s_2s_2$ intersects $dd$. Total utility of the orange shaded areas would add up only to $(4 + 3 + 2) + 4$, or $13 per head. But with optimal carryover to the second year of 1 unit by speculators, $P$s and $Q$s will be equalized at $E_1$ and $E_2$, and now the total utility of the shaded areas will add up to $(4 + 3) + (4 + 3)$, or $14 per head. (Show that the gain in utility of $1 is measured by the dark block, which represents the excess of the second unit's marginal utility over that of the third: hence, one can show that equality of marginal utilities is optimal.)

flesh-and-blood speculators can guess the future infallibly. They often make mistakes and often are prey to rumors and mass enthusiasms. So the process is not as ideal as here pictured. Still, to the degree that speculators can intelligently foresee the future—and those who have a terrible batting average may get eliminated fast as their capital is lost—they (and for that matter, *farsighted* government agencies, too) may help to provide a useful stabilizing function.

## ECONOMICS OF INSURANCE

We are now in a position to see why insurance, which appears to be just another form of gambling, actually has exactly opposite effects. For the same reasons that gambling is bad, insurance is economically advantageous. Whereas gambling creates risks, insurance helps to lessen and spread risks.

In buying fire insurance on his house, the owner seems to be betting with the insurance company that his house will burn down. If it does not—and the odds are heavily in favor of its not burning—the owner forfeits the small premium charge. If it does burn down, the company must reimburse the owner to the tune of the agreed-upon loss. (For the obvious reason of removing temptation from hard-up home owners who like fire engines and excitement, the face value of the policy tends to be something less than the money value of the property insured.)

What is true of fire insurance is equally true of life, accident, automobile, or any other kind of insurance. Actually, at the famous Lloyd's of London, which is a place for insurance brokers to come together, you can arrange to insure a ball team or vacationer against rain, dancers against infantile paralysis, *and* a hotel keeper against a damage suit from the widow of a man killed in a fight with another man who bought a drink in the hotel's cocktail lounge; and you can get numerous other bizarre policies. But by the common law, Lloyd's may refuse to bet $10,000 with me that it will not snow on Christmas, since I do not have an "insurable interest" of that amount and the bet would be unenforceable in the courts. However, a ski-resort owner, who stands to lose that much if it does not snow, would have such an insurable interest and could certainly buy such a policy. Economic theory shows that the difference between these two cases is that insuring the resort owner *stabilizes* income while insuring me *destabilizes* it.

The insurance company is not gambling, because what is unpredictable and subject to chance *for the individual* is highly predictable and uniform *in the mass*. Whether John C. Smith, age twenty and in good health, will live for 30 more years is a matter of chance, but the famous *law of large numbers* guarantees that out of 100,000-odd twenty-year-olds in good health, only a definite proportion will still be alive at the end of such a period. The life-insurance company can easily set a premium at which it will not lose money. Hence, the company certainly is not gambling.

What about the buyer of insurance? Is he gambling? The reverse can be shown to be true: The man who does not insure his house is doing the gambling. He is risking the whole value of his house against the small premium saved. If his house does not burn down in any year, the noninsurer has won his bet; if it does,

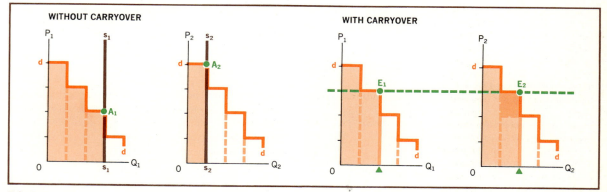

**FIG. 21-7**
The orange areas measure total utility enjoyed each year. Carrying one unit to the second year equalizes Q and also P, and increases total utility by amount of dark block. (Footnote 9 suggests other applications.)

as occasionally must happen, he loses his bet and incurs a tremendous penalty.

At this point, a sporting man will say, "So what? Of course, a man gambles when he doesn't buy insurance. But the odds on such a bet are not unfavorable. In fact, they are favorable, because we know that the insurance company is not in business for its health. It must keep records, support insurance salesmen, and so forth. All this costs money and must be 'loaded' onto the insurance premium, detracting from the perfect mathematical odds of the buyer and making the odds for the nonbuyer better."

To which a rational man will reply: "When I am among friends, I don't mind a small game of chance for relaxation even at slightly unfavorable odds. But when a big bet is involved, even if the odds are favorable, then I pass. I insure my house because I hardly miss the premium each year; but if it burned down without being covered, I'd feel the loss an awful lot. When I insure, my living standards over time and my income remain the same, come what may. When I don't insure, I may be up for a while, but I risk going way down."

Obviously, the law of diminishing marginal utility—which makes the satisfaction from wins less important than the privation from losses—is one way of justifying the above reasoning.[9] *This law of diminishing marginal utility tells us that a steady income, equitably divided among individuals instead of arbitrarily apportioned between the lucky and unlucky people whose house did or did not burn down, is economically advantageous.* (Also, when a family chooses to buy hospital and medical insurance, it may express the belief that this will be relatively painless, forced "saving against a rainy day." This self-imposed "compulsory-saving" feature is another benefit of insurance.)

Quite a few nations and several of the states—New York, New Jersey, New Hampshire, Massachusetts—have been helping pay for government and relieving the tax burden by introducing official lotteries and

[9] Figure 21-7 of footnote 8 can show all this. Change the titles "Without Carryover" and "With Carryover" to "Without Insurance" and "With Insurance" to see the gain in utility from insuring. To prove the loss from gambling, relabel the left-hand figure "After Gambling" and the right-hand one "Before Gambling." To illustrate that equal incomes maximize the sum of ("social") utility of two ethically commensurable persons, relabel Fig. 21-7 once again to read "Before Redistribution" and "After Redistribution."

even off-track betting. The cynical notion here is that one might as well channel private vices to the public good. Also, there is the realistic consideration that law enforcement to rule out illegal gambling may be quite imperfect: legal gambling may be a way of checking organized crime.

## WHAT CAN BE INSURED

Undoubtedly, insurance is a highly important way of spreading risks. Why, then, can we not insure ourselves against *all* the risks of life? The answer lies in the indisputable fact that certain definite mathematical conditions are necessary before sufficiently exact actuarial probabilities can be determined.

First, we must have a *large number of events*. Only then will a pooling of risks and a "cancellation" and "averaging of extremes" be possible. The bank at Monte Carlo knows there is safety in numbers. The lucky streak of an Arabian prince one night will be canceled by his next night's losings or by the losings of a fake Balkan countess. Once in a blue moon someone may "break the bank"; but in a few more lunar cycles the "house" will more than break even. Large numbers alone are not enough. No prudent fire-insurance company would confine itself to the island of Manhattan even though there are thousands of buildings there. *The uncertain events must be relatively independent.* Each throw of the dice, each chance of loss by fire, should stand relatively by itself. Obviously, a great fire like that of Chicago in 1871 or of the San Francisco earthquake would subject all the buildings in the same locality to the same risk. The company would be making a bet on *one* event, not on thousands of independent events. Instead, it must diversify its risks. Private companies cannot, without government aid, bear the risks of nuclear-war insurance. Nor is it possible to buy unemployment insurance from a private company. Depressions are great plagues which hit all sections and all classes at one and the same time, with a probability that cannot be computed in advance with any precision. Therefore only the government, whose business it is to take losses, can assume the responsibility of providing unemployment compensation.

There will probably always remain numerous risks of personal and business life. No one can insure the success of a new shop, a new mousetrap, or a hopeful opera singer. Without error there cannot be trial; and without trial there cannot be progress.

## SUMMARY TO APPENDIX

1 The intelligent profit-seeking action of speculators and arbitragers tends to create certain definite *equilibrium patterns of price over space and time*. To the extent that speculators moderate price and consumption instability, they perform a socially useful purpose. To the extent that they provide a market and permit others to hedge against risk, they perform a further useful function.

    But to the extent that speculators pile onto price changes and cause great fluctuations in stock and commodity prices, and in foreign-exchange rates, they do social damage.

2 The economic principle of diminishing marginal utility is one way of showing why consumption and price stability is good, and why gambling is economically unsound and insurance is sound. There are fundamental differences among what can be insured by private rather than social agencies and what can scarcely be insured at all.

## CONCEPTS FOR REVIEW

spatial *P* equality but for transport costs

ideal seasonal price pattern

hedging, speculation, and short sale

law of diminishing marginal utility

consumption stability versus instability

gambling versus insurance

insurable and uninsurable risks

social versus private insurance

## QUESTIONS FOR DISCUSSION

1 How does ideal speculation work to stabilize seasonal prices? To spread risks?

2 "Insurance reduces total risk; gambling increases the total. Therefore the former is good and the latter is bad." Explain.

3 "I love the thrill of gambling, or risking all on the turn of a card. What do I care for odds or economic principles?" Can economic science pass judgment on such a person?

4 Can you reverse the reasoning on the desirability of gambling and insurance so that it will apply to two individuals with increasing rather than decreasing marginal utility of income?

5 If $1 of gain is worth less than $1 of loss, show that people will prefer to hold a portfolio of *diversified* securities.

6 List some important differences between private and social insurance.

7 *Extra-credit problem* (for students of statistics): Suppose each of four cab companies faces accidents "normally distributed," with a standard deviation, $\sigma_i = \$3,000$, around a mean loss of $50,000. Let them now pool risks through mutual reinsurance. Show that this gives a total mean loss of $200,000 [or still $50,000 for each one's fair share; but now total variance is only $4 \times (\$3,000)^2$, or $\sigma^2 = 4\sigma_i^2 = 36,000,000 = (6,000)^2$]. So each ends up with a standard deviation of only $1,500 = $6,000/4—halving the risk through quadrupling the size! Can you use the same reasoning to see the following? (*a*) Diversifying your wealth into *four* independent stocks, each with the same mean return and same (independent!) variability, will *halve* the expected variability of your portfolio. (*b*) Pooling the independent peak-load demand of two utility systems will reduce the need to have twice the stand-by capacity.

# 22

## THE THEORY OF DEMAND AND UTILITY

In a competitive market, price is determined by the schedules of supply and demand. But what principles of economics lie behind the demand schedules? What principles behind the supply schedules?

In this chapter we shall investigate briefly the economic principles of *total utility* and *marginal utility* that underlie the market demand schedule. Subsequent chapters will survey the cost concepts that underlie the competitive supply schedule and the behavior of monopolists.

### SUMMING INDIVIDUAL DEMANDS TO GET MARKET DEMAND

The demand curve for a good such as tea is arrived at for the whole market by summing up the amounts of tea that will be demanded by each consumer. Each consumer has a demand curve along which the quantity demanded can be plotted against the price of tea. It generally *slopes downward* and to the right, declining from northwest to southeast. If all consumers were exactly alike in their demands and there were 1 million consumers, then we could think of the market demand curve as a millionfold enlargement of each consumer's demand curve.

But people are not all exactly alike. Some have high incomes; some low. Some greatly desire tea; others prefer coffee or concerts. What must we do to the demand schedules or curves of each consumer to arrive at the total market *DD* curve?

All we have to do is calculate the sum total of what *all* the different consumers will consume at any given price; we then plot that total amount as a point on the market demand curve. Or if we like, we may set the total down in a demand table like that first seen in Chapter 4.

*Summary:* We sum individual demands at each price to end up with the market demand curve. (Figure 22-1 adds *dd* curves "horizontally.")

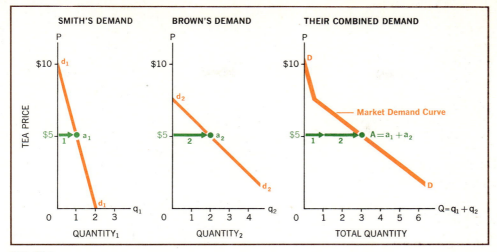

**FIG. 22-1**
**To get market demand, we add all consumers' demand curves**
At each price, such as $5, we *horizontally* add quantities demanded by each man to get market quantity demanded.

## DEMAND SHIFTS FROM INCOME AND OTHER CHANGES

Factors other than changes in the price of tea can change the quantity demanded of tea. We know from budget studies, from historical experience, and from thinking about our own behavior that an increase in money income is a factor that will normally tend to increase the amount we are willing to buy of any good. Goods that are necessities tend to be less responsive to income changes, and goods that are luxuries tend to be more responsive; a very few abnormal goods, called "inferior" goods, may actually go down in quantity bought when we get enough income to be able to afford to replace them in the budget by other goods. (Hamburger, bologna, soup bones and offal, potatoes, lard, and oleomargarine might be examples of inferior goods, but the species is so rare that we can usually neglect it in our discussions.)

Let us now show what all this means in terms of the demand curve. This curve is, of course, simply the graphical picture of the response of quantity bought of a good to the change in its *own* price. But quantity bought may change also as a result of changes in the *prices of other goods* or as a result of a change in the consumer's *income*. The demand curve is drawn on the assumption that these other things do not change. But what if they do? Then the whole demand curve will *shift* to the right or to the left.

Figure 22-2 on page 432 shows such changes. Given his certain income and established prices for all other goods, we can draw the consumer's demand for tea, *dd*. First, assume price and quantity are at the point *A*. Suppose now that his income rises. Even though the price of tea is unchanged, he will in all probability buy more tea than before; hence the demand curve will have shifted to the right, say, to *d'd'*, with *A'* indicating his new total purchase of tea. If his income should fall, then we

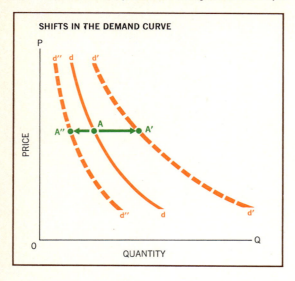

**SHIFTS IN THE DEMAND CURVE**

**FIG. 22-2**
**Demand curve shifts with change in income,
or with change in another good's price**
With higher income, you'll want to buy more of a good,
thus shifting *dd* to *d'd'*. (Explain why; and why lowering
income will shift *dd* to *d''d''*.) Similarly, a rise in price
of coffee, which is a substitute for tea, might shift tea's
*dd* out to *d'd'*. (What would a cut in coffee price do? Can
you explain why a great rise in price of lemon, a complementary good used with tea, might shift *dd* leftward to
*d''d''*?)

may expect a reduction in quantity bought—there *must* be a reduction if income falls
far enough. This downward shift we illustrate by *d''d''* and by *A''*.

Income is only one of many factors that the position of the demand curve depends
on. An increased taste or fashion for tea would also shift the demand to the right,
and a decreased taste would have the opposite effect. Advertisers seek to shift the
*dd* curve. Even if each person consumed the same amount of a good, a growth in
population would have the effect of increasing the total market demand for a product.
If people think that a boom is about to get under way, they may increase their
purchases now in order to beat the gun.[1] Still other factors operate all the time to
shift demand.

## CROSS RELATIONS OF DEMAND

Everyone knows that raising the price of tea will decrease the amount demanded of
tea. We have seen that it will also affect the amounts demanded of *other* commodities.
For example, a higher price for tea will *lower* the demand for a commodity such as
lemon; i.e., it will shift the whole demand schedule of lemon downward. But it will
also *raise* the amount demanded of coffee. Probably it will have little or no effect
on the demand curve for salt.

We say, therefore, that tea and coffee are rival, or competing, products, or *substitutes*. Tea and lemon, on the other hand, are cooperating, or complementary,

---

[1]In fact, when I see in today's paper that the price of tea is going up, I may rush out to buy more:
this may seem superficially to be an exception to the law of downward-sloping demand, but (as
discussed on page 435, footnote 3) it can be reconciled with that law when we realize that I am
buying more because of the *rising* price of tea and because I want to be able to buy less of it tomorrow
when its price will have stabilized at a high level. Despite this *dynamic* effect of *changing* prices,
it remains true that at a steady high price for tea, I shall consume less than at a steady low price.

commodities—so-called *complements*. In-between pairs such as tea and salt are said to represent *independent* commodities. The reader should classify such pairs as beef and pork, turkey and cranberry sauce, automobiles and gasoline, truck and railroad freight, oil and coal.

Besides showing effects of income changes, Fig. 22-2 also illustrates the effect of any changed prices of other goods. A fall in the price of coffee may well cause our consumer to buy less tea; the demand curve shifts to, say, *d″d″*. But what if the price of lemon were to fall? The resulting change on this *dd* may not be very large. But if there is any change, it will be in the direction of *increased* tea purchases—a rightward shift of *dd*. Why this difference in response? Because coffee is a rival, a *substitute* product for tea; lemon is a *complementary* commodity to tea.

## THE LAW OF DIMINISHING MARGINAL UTILITY

Return to the law of downward-sloping demand, which is so basic a law that we have to investigate the economic principles operating in the background to justify and explain it. A century ago economists hit upon the fundamental notion of "marginal utility," and it was from this analysis that they felt able for the first time to derive the demand curve and explain its properties. There is space here only to sketch the basic notions underlying such theories, leaving refinements and developments to specialized treatises on advanced economic theory.

As a customer you will buy a good because you feel it gives you satisfaction or "utility." A first unit of a good gives you a certain amount of psychological utility. Now imagine consuming a second unit. Your total utility goes up because the second unit of the good gives you some additional utility. What about adding a third and fourth unit of the same good?

A century ago economists proclaimed an important law that sounds like the law of diminishing returns; but instead of referring to the extra output added by successive doses of an input (as in Table 2-1 on p. 27), this is a law about the behavior of psychological utility as you add more and more of a good. It can be described by words, by a table of numbers, and by two curves.

*The law of diminishing marginal utility.* **As you consume more of the same good, your *total* (psychological) utility increases. However, let us use the term marginal utility to refer to "the extra utility added by one extra last unit of a good." Then, with successive new units of the good, your total utility will grow at a slower and slower rate because of a fundamental tendency for your psychological ability to appreciate more of the good to become less keen. This fact, that the increments in total utility fall off, economists describe as follows:**

**As the amount consumed of a good increases, the *marginal utility* of the good (or the extra utility added by its last unit) tends to decrease.**

Column (2) of the table with Fig. 22-3 on page 434 shows that *total utility* enjoyed increases as $Q$ grows, but at a decreasing rate. Column (3) measures *marginal utility* as the increment of total utility resulting when one last unit of the good is added; the fact that marginal utilities in the table are declining exemplifies the law of diminishing marginal utility.

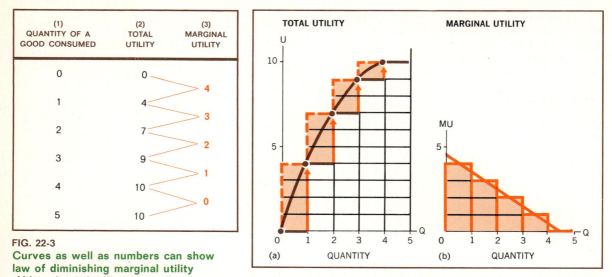

| (1)<br>QUANTITY OF A<br>GOOD CONSUMED | (2)<br>TOTAL<br>UTILITY | (3)<br>MARGINAL<br>UTILITY |
|:---:|:---:|:---:|
| 0 | 0 | |
| | | 4 |
| 1 | 4 | |
| | | 3 |
| 2 | 7 | |
| | | 2 |
| 3 | 9 | |
| | | 1 |
| 4 | 10 | |
| | | 0 |
| 5 | 10 | |

**FIG. 22-3**

**Curves as well as numbers can show law of diminishing marginal utility**

Although *total utility* rises with consumption, the table shows it rises at a decreasing rate. This means that marginal utility—the extra utility added by each last extra unit of the good—will be decreasing. From this psychological fact, earlier economists prepared their demonstration of the law of downward-sloping demand. (Note similarity to Chapter 2's law of diminishing returns.)

The orange blocks show the extra utility added by each new unit. The fact that total utility increases at a decreasing rate is shown on the right by the declining steps of marginal utility. If we make our units smaller and smaller, the steps in total utility are smoothed out and total utility becomes the smooth brown curve. Now *smoothed marginal utility is shown in* (b) *by the orange downward-falling smooth curve, and* marginal utility becomes indistinguishable from the *slope* of the smooth curve of (a).[2]

Figure 22-3(a) pictures how total utility increases, but at a decreasing rate. Figure 22-3(b) depicts marginal utilities—increments of utility (not the total of utility itself). Whether we work with sizable units of the good and measure utilities by blocks and steps, or whether we smooth the drawings by use of the brown and orange curves to reflect continuously divisible units, the law of diminishing marginal utility means that the relations in Fig. 22-3(b) must slope downward and—what is exactly the same thing—that the total utility relations in Fig. 22-3(a) must look concave (from below), reflecting total utility's growth becoming less and less.

The validity of the law of diminishing marginal utility seemed probable to economists of an earlier generation as they looked into their own minds for their own psychological reactions to extra consumption. These findings of *introspection* seemed strengthened when they learned about numerous laboratory experiments by psychologists of the 1850s.

[2]NOTE: It will be found that the sum of all the marginal utilities in Column (3) of the table with Fig. 22-3, if reckoned above some point, must equal the amount of total utility in Column (2) at that point. [Thus, 4 + 3 + 2 does give us the 9 shown in Column (2). What does 4 + 3 give?] In terms of Fig. 22-3(b), the area under the marginal utility curve, as measured by blocks or by the area under the smooth curve, must add up to equality with the numerical height of the total utility curve shown in (a)—it being understood that we make our comparison at a specified quantity level. All this portrays the fact that total utility is the sum of all the marginal (or extra) utilities added from the beginning.

Suppose you blindfold a man and ask him to hold out his hand, palm up. Now place a weight on his palm; he certainly will notice it. As you add more units of weight, he notices their addition too. But after his palm is carrying a good deal of weight, you can add just as big a weight as you did in the beginning, and yet this time he will reply that he is not conscious of any addition. In other words, the greater the *total* weight he is already carrying, the *less* will be the effect of an extra or *marginal* unit of weight.

When earlier economists learned that perception of sound, light, and other sensations seemed to show a similar *Weber-Fechner* law of decreasing marginal effect, this—rightly or wrongly—gave them even greater confidence in the economic law of diminishing marginal utility.[3]

## EQUILIBRIUM CONDITION: EQUAL MARGINAL UTILITIES PER DOLLAR FOR EVERY GOOD

What is the fundamental equilibrium condition that has to be satisfied if a consumer is spending his income on the variously priced goods so as to make himself truly best off in terms of utility or well-being? Certainly he would not expect that the last egg he is buying brings him exactly the same marginal utility as the last lamb chop he is buying. For lamb chops cost much more apiece than eggs. On reflection, it would seem more reasonable that he should keep buying a good which costs twice as much per unit as another until it ends up in his equilibrium bringing him just twice as much in marginal utility.

In short, if he has arranged his consumption so that every single good is bringing him marginal utility just exactly *proportional* to its price, then he would be assured that he could not better himself by departing from such an equilibrium. This fundamental condition can now be stated: A consumer with a fixed income and facing given market prices of goods can come into his equilibrium of maximum satisfaction or utility only when he acts thus.

*Law of equal marginal utilities per dollar.* Each good—such as sugar—is demanded up to the point where the marginal utility per dollar (or penny) spent on it is exactly the same as the marginal utility of a dollar (or penny) spent on any other good—such as salt.

Why must this law hold? If any one good gave more marginal utility per dollar, the consumer would gain by taking money away from other goods and spending more on that good—up to the point where the law of diminishing marginal utility brought its marginal utility per dollar down to equality. If any good gave less marginal utility

---

[3]The modern generation, however, has found that the exact way in which one measures utility is not particularly important to explain the price-quantity demand curve. Some economists would still use introspection. Others would want to observe whether you had to give a man 2:1 odds to get him to wager on the toss of a fair coin the loss of a new hat against the winning of a second new hat; and they would conclude from this that the marginal utility of the second hat decreases to half the marginal utility of the first hat. Such economists thus hope to measure his marginal utility "behavioristically" rather than introspectively. Probably the majority of economists in advanced graduate theory today would feel that what counts for consumer demand theory is whether certain situations have *more* total utility than others. These economists would not care to look for any numerical measure of utility beyond such "greater or less than" comparison; they would use the "indifference curves" of the Appendix to this chapter. By any of these methods, the general properties of the market demand curve can be securely established. (NOTE: Demand theory never needs to make *interpersonal* comparisons of utility that involve adding or comparing utilities of *different* minds.)

per dollar than the common level, the consumer would buy less of it until the marginal utility of the last dollar spent on it had risen back to the common level.[4]

This fundamental condition of consumer equilibrium can be written in terms of the marginal utilities and prices of the different goods as follows:

$$\frac{MU \text{ Good 1}}{P_1} = \frac{MU \text{ Good 2}}{P_2} = \frac{MU \text{ Good 3}}{P_3} = \cdots = \text{common } MU \text{ per \$ of income}$$

The logical meaning of this condition rather than the rote memorizing of a formula is, of course, what matters.

Nor need all this apply just to spending money. Suppose you have only a certain number of hours to spend on study for examinations. If you are so uncreative as to seek merely to maximize your grade average, how should you allocate your time? By spending equal hours on each course? Not necessarily. You have to shift from history to chemistry, from German to economics, until you are getting *the same marginal grade advantage from the last minute spent in each alternative use.*[5] The same marginal rule can show you how to allocate your time on a pleasant weekend. Our marginal equilibrium condition is not merely a law of economics; it is a law of logic itself.

A final remark may be in order at this point. A consumer is not expected to be a wizard at numbers or graphs, nor need he be, to approximate the demand behavior of this chapter. He can even make most of his decisions unconsciously or out of habit. As long as he is fairly *consistent* in his tastes and actions, all he has to do to make the present analysis relevant is to avoid repeating those mistakes which he found in the past failed to give him the goods and services he most wanted and to avoid making wild and unpredictable changes in his buying behavior. If enough people act in this way, our scientific theory will provide a tolerable approximation to the facts.

## SUBSTITUTION- AND INCOME-EFFECTS: A DIGRESSION

The concept of marginal utility has lent credence to the fundamental law of downward-sloping demand. A different way of looking at the demand's sloping downward makes no mention of marginal utility explicitly; but it does lead rigorously to the desired result, and does provide an interesting insight into the factors that tend to make the elasticity of response of quantity to price very great or very little.

**Substitution-effect**   The first factor explaining diminishing consumption when price rises is an obvious one. If the price of tea goes up while other prices do not, then

---

[4] At a few places in economics the indivisibility of units is important and cannot be glossed over. Thus, Cadillacs do not come like peas, and their indivisibility may matter. Suppose I buy one but definitely not two Cadillacs. Then the marginal utility of the first car is enough larger than the marginal utility of the same number of dollars spent elsewhere to induce me to buy this first unit. The marginal utility that the second Cadillac would bring is enough less to ensure I do *not* buy it. When indivisibility matters, our equality rule for equilibrium can be restated as an inequality rule. NOTE: As mentioned, the validity of the equilibrium condition can be made quite independent of how, or whether, we measure utility *numerically*. Only relative marginal utilities matter.

[5] This does not mean that you study to get the same 89 grade in all classes. Your average may be maximized with grades of 93, 92, 90, and 81, but with each marginal hour of study adding one-tenth of a grade point to any subject.

tea has become relatively dearer. It pays, therefore, to *substitute* other goods for tea in order to maintain one's standard of living most cheaply.

Thus tea becomes a relatively dearer source of stimulation than before, and less of it will be bought and more of coffee or cocoa. Similarly, a rise in price of movies relative to stage plays may cause the consumer to seek less of his amusement in the dearer direction.

The consumer is doing here only what every businessman does when rises in the price of one productive factor cause him to adjust his production methods so as to substitute cheap inputs for the dear inputs. By this process of substitution, he is able to produce the same output at least total cost. Similarly do consumers buy satisfaction at least cost.

**Income-effect**   In the second place, when your money income is fixed, being forced to buy a good at a higher price is just like having a decrease in your *real* income or purchasing power, particularly if you have been buying a great deal of the raised commodity. With a lower real income, you will now want to buy less tea. Thus, unless a good is an "inferior" good like bologna or margarine, the income-effect will *reinforce* the substitution-effect in making the demand curve downward-sloping.[6]

Of course, the quantitative importance of each of these effects varies with the good in question and with the consumer. Under some circumstances the resulting demand curve is very *elastic:* as where the consumer has been spending a good deal on the commodity and where ready substitutes are available—for example, a drunkard's demand for one brand of gin. But if a commodity, such as salt, involves only a small fraction of the consumer's budget, is not easily replaceable by other items, and is needed in small amounts to complement more important items, then demand will tend to be *inelastic.*

## THE PARADOX OF VALUE

The preceding theories help to explain a famous question that troubled Adam Smith in *The Wealth of Nations.* He asked, How is it that water, which is so very useful that life is impossible without it, has such a low price—while diamonds, which are quite unnecessary, have such a high price?

Today even a beginning student can give a correct answer to this problem. "That's simply explained," he can write on an examination. "The supply and demand curves for water are such that they intersect at a very low price, while the supply and demand

---

[6]Income- and substitution-effects not only explain the downward slope of demand but also explain a possible, albeit extremely rare, exception to that law. When the 1845 Irish famine greatly raised the price of potatoes, families who consumed a lot of potatoes merely because they were too poor to consume much meat might have ended up consuming *more* rather than less of the high-*P* potatoes. Why? Because now they had to spend so much on potatoes, the necessary of life, as to make it quite impossible to afford any meat at all, and hence were forced to become even more dependent than before on potatoes. In brief, the substitution-effect was here overcome by the perverse income-effect applicable to a peculiar "inferior" good, such as the potato, which tends to *decrease* in the poor man's budget when incomes *rise.* This *curiosum* is attributed to Sir Robert Giffen, a Victorian economist. (Note: In the case of ordinary inferior goods on which we spend little money, the perverse income-effects will not outweigh the substitution-effects and produce the odd Giffen case.)

curves for diamonds are such that they intersect at a high price." (Today he could add that water is no longer all that cheap.)

This is not an incorrect answer. Adam Smith could not have given it because supply and demand curves as descriptive tools had not yet been invented, and were not to be for 75 years or more. But after he had mastered the new lingo, old Adam Smith would naturally ask the question, "But *why* do supply and demand for water intersect at such a low price?"

The answer is by now easy to phrase. It consists of two parts:

Diamonds are very *scarce*, the cost of getting *extra* ones is high; and water is relatively *abundant*, with its cost low in many areas of the world. This first part would have seemed reasonable to even the classical economists of more than a century ago, who would probably have let it go at that, and would not have known how to reconcile these facts about *cost* with the equally valid fact that the world's water is more *useful* than the world's supply of diamonds. In fact, Adam Smith never did quite resolve the paradox. He was content simply to point out that the "value in use" of a good—its total contribution to economic welfare—is not the same thing as its "value in exchange"—the total money value or revenue for which it will sell. Smith had not arrived at the point where he knew how to distinguish *marginal* utility from *total* utility!

Today, we should add to the above cost considerations a second truth:

The *total* utility of water does not determine its price or demand. Only the relative marginal utility and cost of the *last* little bit of water determine its price. Why? Because people are free to buy or not buy that last little bit. If water is priced higher than its marginal utility, then that last unit cannot be sold. Therefore the price must fall until it reaches exactly the level of usefulness of the last little bit, no more and no less. Moreover, because every unit of water is exactly like any other unit and because there is only one price in a competitive market, *every unit must sell for what the last least useful unit sells for*. (As one student put the matter: The theory of economic value is easy to understand if you just remember that the tail wags the dog: concentrate on *marginal* and not on *total* utility.)

**Paradox resolved: The more there is of a commodity, the less the relative desirability of its *last* little unit becomes, even though its *total* usefulness grows as we get more of the commodity. So, it is obvious why a large amount of water has a low price. Or why air is actually a free good despite its vast usefulness. The many *later* units pull down the market value of *all* units.**

## CONSUMER'S SURPLUS

The foregoing discussion emphasizes that the accounting system which records the "total economic value" or revenue of a good (price × quantity) differs from the measurement necessary to record "total welfare." The total economic value of air is zero; its contribution to welfare, very great.[7] Similarly, if we increase the quantity produced of a good, we increase the community's welfare; but if it is a good like wheat, whose demand is inelastic, we do at the same time destroy some economic value.

---

[7]Or, as Adam Smith would say, its value in use is very great; its value in exchange, negligible.

Thus, there is always a sort of gap between total utility and total market value. This gap is in the nature of a *surplus,* which the consumer gets because he "receives more than he pays for."

Nor does he benefit at the expense of the seller. In a swap, one party does not lose what the other gains. Unlike energy, which cannot be created or destroyed, the well-being of all participants is increased by trade.

It is easy to see how this consumer's surplus arises. Each unit of a good that the consumer buys costs him only as much as the last unit is worth. But by our fundamental law of diminishing marginal utility, the *earlier* units are worth *more* to him than the last. Thus, he enjoys a surplus on each of these earlier units. When trade stops benefiting him and giving him further surplus, he stops buying.

As final clinching evidence that the consumer always receives a surplus, we cite the fact that a ruthless seller can present the consumer with an ultimatum—what is called an "all-or-none" offer: "Either you pay me an extra amount of money for the whole block of the good that you are consuming, or go without all the units, from first to last. Take it or leave it!" The consumer will surely be willing to pay extra rather than do altogether without the good of this discriminating monopolist.

How is the concept of consumer's surplus used? It is sometimes needed to help make correct social decisions. Suppose a new branch road would cost your town $100,000. Being free to all, it is expected to bring in no dollar revenues, and all the utility it gives to each user will represent his consumer's surplus. (To avoid extraneous interpersonal difficulties, let us assume there are 1,000 users all exactly alike in income and in their benefit from the road, and all equally worthy.) If each such similar man enjoys $100 (the road's *per capita* cost) or more of consumer's surplus from the road, they should all vote to build the road. If the consumer's surplus of each is less than $100, it is uneconomical for them to tax themselves for this public project.[8]

Many ingenious ways have been suggested for measuring consumer's surplus, but they are of no particular significance here.[9] The important thing is to see how lucky the citizens of modern efficient communities really are. The *privilege of being able to buy a vast array of goods at low prices cannot be overestimated.*

[8]See Fig. 32-2 for a diagram illustrating this all-or-nothing social decision.

[9]In the special case where money provides a firm measuring rod of utility, consumer's surplus is easily measured and depicted. In Fig. 22-4, when the consumer buys $OM$ sugar at $ON$ price for each, he pays the total revenue indicated by the dark rectangular area $OMEN$; but that much sugar gives him total utility (expressed in money) which is the whole area $OMER$; the light triangular area $NER$ left over is his consumer's surplus, and it obviously will be greater the lower the price becomes.

This geometrical concept is useful in illustrating how taxes, farm quotas, and monopolistic interferences create social inefficiency and loss.

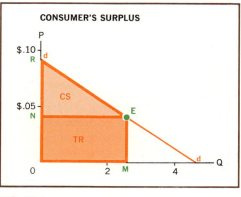

FIG. 22-4

This is a humbling thought. If ever a person becomes arrogantly proud of *his* economic productivity and *his* level of real earnings, let him pause and reflect. If he were transported with all his skills and energies intact to a primitive desert island, how much would his money earnings buy? Indeed, without capital machinery, without rich resources, without other labor, and above all without the technological knowledge which each generation inherits from society's past, how much could *he* produce? It is only too clear that all of us reap the benefits of an economic world we never made. As L. T. Hobhouse said:

> The organizer of industry who thinks that he has "made" himself and his business has found a whole social system ready to his hand in skilled workers, machinery, a market, peace and order—a vast apparatus and a pervasive atmosphere, the joint creation of millions of men and scores of generations. Take away the whole social factor and we have not Robinson Crusoe, with his salvage from the wreck and his acquired knowledge, but the naked savage living on roots, berries, and vermin.

## SUMMARY

1  The market demand curve for all consumers is derived by adding *horizontally* the separate demand curves of each consumer. A demand curve can shift for many reasons. For example, a rise in income will normally shift *dd* rightward, thus increasing demand; a rise in the price of a *substitute good* (coffee for tea, and so forth) will also create such an upward shift in demand; a rise in the price of a *complementary good* (such as lemon in its relation to tea) will represent a cross effect that shifts the *dd* curve downward and leftward. Still other factors— changing tastes, population, or expectations—can increase or decrease demand.

2  The concepts of total and marginal utility were introduced to explain the law of downward-sloping demand. The fact that *total utility* rises with each new marginal addition of a good but at a decreasing rate of growth can be expressed in a technical way. With equal additions to a good's quantity, its *marginal utility* (which is the increment of utility coming from adding a last extra unit of quantity) tends to decrease.

3  To get the most utility, the consumer must achieve a fundamental marginal condition for demand equilibrium: A consumer has not maximized his well-being until he has succeeded in *making equal the respective marginal utilities per dollar spent on each and every good*. (BEWARE: The marginal utility of a $25-per-ounce bottle of perfume is not equal to the marginal utility of a 10-cent glass of cola; but their marginal utilities divided by price per unit—that is, their marginal utilities per last dollar, $MU/P$—are all to be equalized in optimizing equilibrium.)

   This is a fundamental rule of logic that transcends demand theory: If you want to allocate any limited resource among competing uses, whenever the marginal advantage in one use happens to be greater than in another, you can benefit by transferring from the low-marginal-advantage use to the high—until a final equilibrium is reached at which all have become equal.

4 Without using the marginal utility concept explicitly, we can gain new insight into the factors making for downward-sloping demand by analyzing the effect of a price rise into (*a*) its *substitution-effect* component and (*b*) its *income-effect* component. When *P* for a good rises, you tend to maintain the same level of well-being by *substituting* other goods for the good that has just become dearer. Reinforcing this decrease in a good's *Q* that arises out of substitution is the income-effect: Since you ordinarily buy less of the good in question when your family income is lower, the rise in its price—which has produced a *drop in your real income* or purchasing power—thus induces a further cut in consumption as the result of your now having a lower real income.

5 Adam Smith's paradox of value—that a commodity important for welfare may sell for less in the market than one less important—is clarified by the distinction between the concept of marginal and total utility. The scarcity of a good, as determined by its cost (i.e., supply conditions), interacts with the market demand for the good as determined by the usefulness of its *marginal* unit (not the usefulness of the *total* stock of the good).

6 The fact that market price is determined by marginal rather than total utility is dramatized by the concept of *consumer's surplus*. Since we pay in the market the same price for each unit that the marginal unit is worth to us, we reap a consumer's surplus on all the previous units. This consumer's surplus reflects the benefit we gain from being able to buy at low prices, rather than being confronted by a ruthless monopolist who insists we pay him for the whole of our consumption just what that total is worth to us. However difficult it may be to quantify consumer's surplus, advanced treatises show it is a concept relevant for many social decisions—such as deciding when the community should incur the heavy initial expenses of a road or bridge.

Without reading the Appendix, we can go from the utility background of demand to the next chapter's cost background of supply.

## CONCEPTS FOR REVIEW

market versus individual demand

demand shifts from income and other changes

substitute, complementary, and independent goods

income-effect and substitution-effect

law of diminishing marginal utility

equating marginal utility of last dollar spent on each good, $MU_1/P_1 = MU_2/P_2$

value in use versus value in exchange

paradox of marginal versus total utility

consumer's surplus

## QUESTIONS FOR DISCUSSION

**1**  As you add horizontally the demands of more and more people, the aggregate market curve begins to look flatter and flatter on the same scale. Show that this merely reflects the fact that the same cut in price induces more new sales from many buyers than from few. (NOTE: Elasticity need not change. Guess why. HINT: $E$ is dimensionless, unaffected by scale changes.)

**2**  List several goods in order of their responsiveness to higher income.

**3**  Which of the following goods do you think could be classified as *complementary, substitute,* and *independent* goods: beef, ketchup, lamb, mint sauce, cigarettes, gum, pork, butter, paperbacks, taxis, and oleomargarine? Illustrate the resulting shift in the demand curve for one good when price of another good goes up. How would a change in income affect the demand curve for butter? The demand curve for oleomargarine?

**4**  Explain the difference between marginal and total utility. State the law of diminishing marginal utility. Be sure you understand what it means in terms of numbers and diagrams.

**5**  Why is it nonsensical to say, "In equilibrium, the marginal utilities of all goods must be exactly equal"? Reword to give a correct statement and explain.

**6**  If you wanted to avoid using the marginal utility concept, show that you still can justify the law of downward-sloping demand by reasoning that involves (*a*) substitution-effect and (*b*) income-effect.

**7**  How much would you be willing to pay rather than give up *all* movies? How much do you spend on movies? Estimate roughly your consumer's surplus.

**8**  *Extra credit problem:* Your utility function for food, $q_1$, and clothing, $q_2$, is given by the logarithmic function of Weber-Fechner and Bernoulli, namely, $U = \frac{2}{3}\log q_1 + \frac{1}{3}\log q_2$. You can calculate your marginal utilities of the goods by taking the derivative of the $U$ function with respect to each $q_i$: we use the rule for differentiating the natural logarithm, namely $d\log q_i/dq_i = 1/q_i$, showing that as you consume double of any good, its *marginal* utility halves (which is not to deny that its total utility does rise, but less than doubles). Hence, we get for food and clothing marginal utilities: $MU_1 = \frac{2}{3}/q_1$, $MU_2 = \frac{1}{3}/q_2$. To maximize $U$ subject to the budget restriction: income (per week) $= I = P_1q_1 + P_2q_2 =$ expenditure on the goods, we invoke our maximizing rule of equal-$MU_i$-per-dollar:

$$MU_1/P_1 = MU_2/P_2 \qquad \text{or} \qquad \tfrac{2}{3}/P_1q_1 = \tfrac{1}{3}/P_2q_2$$

This says, "Food expenditure, $P_1q_1$, must be twice clothing expenditure; or we spend two-thirds our income on food and one-third on clothing." Hence, final demand functions are, $q_1^* = \frac{2}{3}I/P_1$, $q_2^* = \frac{1}{3}I/P_2$. EXAMPLE: for $I = \$12$, $P_1 = \$1$, $P_2 = \$2$, we get $q_1^* = 8$, $q_2^* = 2$. Can you verify all this by solving the budget equation for $q_1 = (I/P_1) - (P_2/P_1)q_2 = 12 - 2q_2$; substituting into $U$ to get $U = \frac{2}{3}\log(12 - 2q_2) + \frac{1}{3}\log q_2 = f(q_2)$; then finding the maximum of $f(q_2)$ by differentiating it with respect to $q_2$ and equating to zero, namely, $f'(q_2) = 0 = -(\frac{2}{3})2/(12 - 2q_2) + \frac{1}{3}/q_2$, which can be solved for $q_2^* = (\frac{1}{4})(12 - 2q_2^*) = 3/(\frac{3}{2}) = 2$. Then $q_1^* = 12 - 2q_2^* = 8$. QED.

# APPENDIX: Geometrical Analysis of Consumer Equilibrium

It is instructive to show graphically, and without using the language of numerical utility, exactly what the consumer's equilibrium position looks like.

## THE INDIFFERENCE CURVE

We start out by considering a consumer who buys only two commodities, say, food and clothing, at definite quoted prices. We suppose the consumer can tell us whether (1) he prefers a given combination or batch of the two goods, say, 3 units of food and 2 of clothing, to some second combination or batch, say, 2 units of food and 3 of clothing, or (2) he is "indifferent" as between the two combinations.

Let us suppose that, actually, these two batches happen to be equally good in the eyes of our consumer—that he is indifferent as to which of them he receives. Let us go on to list in Fig. 22-5's table some of the other combinations of goods between which he is likewise indifferent.

Figure 22-5 shows these combinations diagrammatically. We measure units of clothing upon one axis and units of food upon the other. Each of our four combinations or batches, A, B, C, D, is represented by its point. But these four are by no means the only combinations that would leave our consumer just indifferent as between them. Another batch, such as

1½ units of food and 4 of clothing, might be ranked as equal to any of A, B, C, or D above, and there are many others not shown.

The curved contour of Fig. 22-5, linking up the four points, is an "indifference curve." *Every* point thereon represents a different combination of the two goods; and the indifference curve is so drawn that, if our consumer were given his choice between any two points on it, he would not know which one to choose. All would be equally desirable to him, and he would be indifferent as to which batch he received.

It should be noted that this indifference curve is of convex curvature viewed from below. As we move downward and to the right along the curve—a movement which implies increasing the quantity of food and reducing that of clothing—the slope of the curve becomes more nearly horizontal. The curve is drawn so because this illustrates a property which seems most often to hold true in real life and which we may call the "law of substitution":

The scarcer a good, the greater its relative *substitution* value; its marginal utility rises relative to the marginal utility of the good that has become plentiful.

For example, the consumer who is at position A in the

| INDIFFERENCE COMBINATIONS | | |
|---|---|---|
| | FOOD | CLOTHING |
| A | 1 | 6 |
| B | 2 | 3 |
| C | 3 | 2 |
| D | 4 | 1½ |

**FIG. 22-5**
Getting more of one good compensates for giving up something of the other. The consumer likes situation A exactly as well as B, C, or D.

The food-clothing combinations that yield equal satisfaction can be plotted as a smooth "indifference curve" (or so-called "equal-utility contour"). This is convex (from below) in accord with the law of substitution, which says: As you get more of a good, its "substitution ratio," or "indifference slope," diminishes.

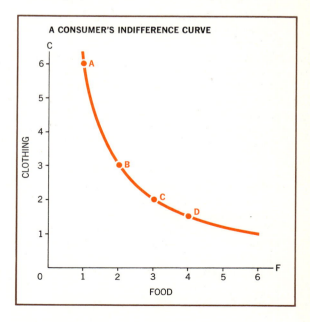

A CONSUMER'S INDIFFERENCE CURVE

table with Fig. 22-5 is willing to give up 3 units of clothing in order to get a second unit of food; thus, at A, he would swap 3 of his 6 clothing units in exchange for 1 extra food unit. But when he has moved to B, he would sacrifice only 1 of his remaining clothing supply in order to obtain a third food unit—a 1-for-1 swap. For a fourth unit of food, he would sacrifice only $\frac{1}{2}$ unit from his dwindling supply of clothing.

If we join the points A and B of Fig. 22-5, we find that the slope of the resulting line (neglecting its negative sign) has a value of 3. Join B and C, and the slope is 1; join C and D, and the slope is $\frac{1}{2}$. These figures—3, 1, $\frac{1}{2}$—are simply the "swapping terms" that we noted just above.

But to move from A to B is to move a considerable distance along the curve. What about the swapping terms for smaller movements? If the consumer is at A and we consider a movement to the intermediate position (not shown in the table) of $1\frac{1}{2}$ food and 4 clothing, the swapping ratio would be 4. And it is clear that, as the movement along the curve grows smaller, then the closer the swapping terms come to the actual slope of the indifference curve.[1]

*So the slope of the indifference curve is the measure of the goods' relative marginal utilities, or of the terms on which—for very small changes—the consumer would be willing to exchange a little of his supply of one good in return for a little more of the other.*

And an indifference curve which is convex in the manner of Fig. 22-5 conforms to the law of substitution earlier noted. As the consumer's food goes up—and his clothing goes down—food must become relatively cheaper and cheaper in order for him to be persuaded to take a little extra food in exchange for a little sacrifice of clothing. The precise shape and slope of an indifference curve will, of course, vary from one consumer to the next; but for this introductory dis-

[1] By the arithmetic slope of the indifference curve, we mean this: To find the slope of the curve at, say, point B, take a ruler and place it so that it is just tangent to the curve at B—it touches the curve, but does not cross it either above or below B. Mark the points at which the ruler's edge crosses the two axes. The slope is the ratio of the distance cut off on the vertical axis to the distance cut off on the horizontal axis; e.g., at B, the slope is 6/4, or $1\frac{1}{2}$. Intermediate texts refer to the slope of the indifference curve at any point as the "substitution ratio," or "the marginal rate of substitution," or the "*relative* marginal utility ratio" at that point.

cussion, it seems reasonable to assume that the general convex shape as shown in Fig. 22-5 is typical.

## THE INDIFFERENCE MAP

Our previous table is one of an infinite number of possible tables. We could have started with a still higher level of satisfaction or indifference and listed some of the different combinations that belonged to it in the mind of our consumer. One such table might have begun with 2 food and 7 clothing; another with 3 food, 7 clothing. Each table could be portrayed graphically; each has its corresponding curve.

Figure 22-6 shows four such curves; the old curve of Fig. 22-5 is now labeled $U_3$. This figure is analogous to a geographical contour map. A person who walks along the path indicated by a particular height contour on such a map will find that he is neither climbing nor descending; similarly, the consumer who moves from one position to another along a single indifference curve enjoys neither increasing nor decreasing satisfaction from the change in the flow of goods he is getting. Of course, only a few of the

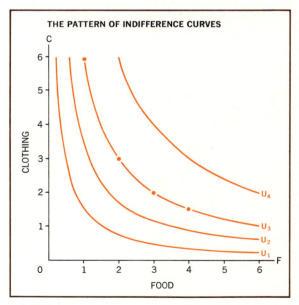

**FIG. 22-6**

The curves labeled $U_1$, $U_2$, $U_3$, and $U_4$ represent indifference curves, or equal-utility contours. (Why is it better to be on a farther-out indifference curve?)

| ALTERNATIVE CONSUMPTION POSSIBILITIES | | |
|---|---|---|
| | FOOD | CLOTHING |
| **M** | 4 | 0 |
| | 3 | $1\frac{1}{2}$ |
| | 2 | 3 |
| | 1 | $4\frac{1}{2}$ |
| **N** | 0 | 6 |

**FIG. 22-7**
The budget limit on expenditures can be indicated by a numerical table. The costs of these budgets (reckoned as $1.50F + $1C) all add up to $6 income.

The budget constraint plots on a diagram as a straight-line tradeoff, whose absolute slope equals the $P_F/P_C$ ratio. *NM* is the consumer's budget line. When he spends just $6 daily, with food and clothing prices $1.50 and $1, he can choose any point on this line. (Why is its slope $1.50/$1 = 3/2?)

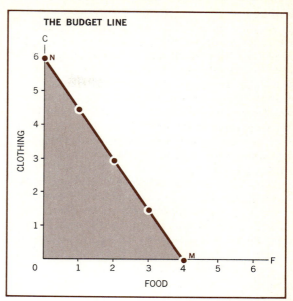

THE BUDGET LINE

possible indifference curves or equal-utility contours are shown in Fig. 22-6.

Note that, as we increase both goods and hence move in a northeasterly direction across this "map," we are crossing successive indifference curves; we are reaching higher and higher levels of satisfaction. Unless the consumer is satiated, he would be enjoying increasing satisfaction from receiving increased quantities of *both* goods. Hence, curve $U_3$ stands for a higher level of satisfaction than $U_2$; $U_4$, for a higher level of satisfaction than $U_3$; etc.

## BUDGET (OR CONSUMPTION-POSSIBILITY) LINE

Now let us set the consumer's indifference map aside for a moment and give him a fixed income. He has, say, $6 per day to spend, and he is confronted with fixed prices for each food and clothing unit—$1.50 for food, $1 for clothing. It is clear that he could spend his money on any one of a variety of alternative combinations of food and clothing. At one extreme, he could buy 4 food units and no clothing; at the other, 6 clothing units and no food. The table with Fig 22-7 illustrates some of the possible ways in which his $6 could be allocated.

Figure 22-7 shows these five possible positions on a diagram with axes similar to those of Figs. 22-5 and 22-6. Each position is indicated by a small brown dot, and it will be noted that they all lie on a straight line, which is labeled *NM*. Moreover, any other attainable point, such as $3\frac{1}{3}$ food units and 1 clothing unit, would lie upon *NM*. The straight line *NM* sums up all the possible positions that our consumer could occupy in spending his $6 of budget income.[2]

The slope of *NM* (neglecting its sign) is 3/2, which is necessarily the ratio of food price to clothing price; and the common sense of line *NM* is clear enough. Given these prices, every time our consumer gives up $1\frac{1}{2}$ clothing units (thereby dropping down $1\frac{1}{2}$ vertical units on the diagram), he can gain 1 unit of food (i.e., move east 1 horizontal unit). Or what is the same thing, he can exchange 3 clothing units for 2 food units. We can call *NM* the consumer's "budget" (or "consumption-possibility") line.

---

[2] This is so because, if we designate quantities of food and clothing bought as $F$ and $C$, respectively, total expenditure on food must be $1\frac{1}{2}F$ and total expenditure on clothing, $1C$. If daily income and expenditure is $6, the following equation must hold: $6 = $1\frac{1}{2}F + $1C$. This is a simple linear equation, the equation of the budget line *NM*. NOTE:

Arithmetic slope of $NM = $1\frac{1}{2} \div $1$

$\qquad$ = price of food ÷ price of clothing

## THE EQUILIBRIUM POSITION OF TANGENCY

Now we are ready to put our two parts together. The axes of Fig. 22-7 were the same as those of Figs. 22-5 and 22-6. We can superimpose the brown budget line NM upon the consumer's indifference map, as in Fig. 22-8. He is free to move anywhere along NM. Positions to the right and above NM are barred to him unless he has more than $6 of income to spend; and positions to the left and below NM are unimportant, since we assume that he will want to spend the full $6.

Where will the consumer move? Obviously, to that point which yields the greatest satisfaction; or, in other words, to the highest available indifference curve, which in this case must be at the green point B. At B, the budget line just touches—but does not cross—the

indifference curve $U_3$. At this point of tangency—of the budget line to an indifference contour—is found the highest utility contour he can reach.[3]

Geometrically, the consumer is at equilibrium where the slope of his budget line is exactly equal to the slope of his indifference curve. And as already noted, the slope of the budget line is the price ratio of food to clothing.

**We may say, then, that optimal equilibrium is attained when the consumer's *substitution* ratio (or slope of relative marginal utilities) is just equal to the ratio of food price to clothing price.[4]**

## CHANGES IN INCOME AND PRICE

Our understanding of the process will be furthered by considering the effects of (a) a change in money income and (b) a change in the price of one of the two goods.

**Income change**   Assume, first, that the consumer's daily income is halved, the two prices remaining unchanged. We could prepare another table, similar to Fig. 22-7's table, showing the consumption possibilities that are now open to him. Plotting these points on a diagram such as Fig. 22-9, we should find that the new budget line occupies the position N'M' in Fig. 22-9. The line has made a *parallel* shift inward.[5] The consumer is now free to move only along this new budget line. Again he will move to the highest attainable indifference curve, or to the point B'. A similar tangency condition for optimal equilibrium again applies. The green curve through B'B depicts the Engel's curve of consumption changes with income.[6]

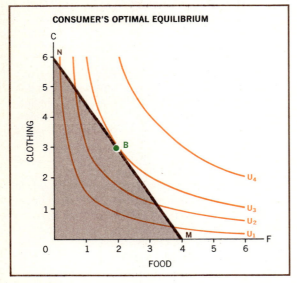

**CONSUMER'S OPTIMAL EQUILIBRIUM**

**FIG. 22-8**
Now we combine the budget line and indifference contours on one diagram. At B the consumer reaches highest indifference curve attainable with his fixed income. B represents tangency of budget line with highest indifference curve. (Why? If slopes were unequal, NM would *intersect* a U contour and he could cross over onto higher satisfaction levels.) At tangency point B, substitution ratio equals price ratio $P_F/P_C$. This means that all goods' marginal utilities are proportional to their prices, with marginal utility of the last dollar spent on every good being equalized—as demonstrated in the chapter's main text.

[3] At any point on NM other than B, NM is crossing indifference curves. And as long as the consumer can keep crossing indifference curves, he can keep moving to higher ones.
[4] The substitution ratio, or slope of the indifference curve, can be shown to be nothing but the ratio of the marginal utility of food to the marginal utility of clothing. So our tangency condition is just another way of stating that a good's price and its marginal utility must be proportional in equilibrium—the consumer there getting the same marginal utility from his last penny spent on food as from his last penny spent on clothing (in agreement with page 436).
[5] The equation of the new brown N'M' budget line is now $3 = $1\frac{1}{2}F + $1C$.
[6] Recall the important budgetary income-expenditure patterns of Fig. 11-1, page 210.

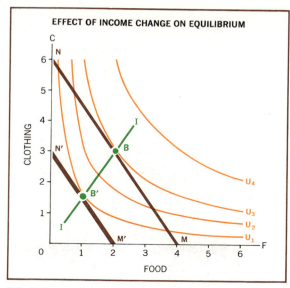

**FIG. 22-9**

An income change shifts the budget line in a parallel way. Thus, halving income to $3 shifts *NM* to *N'M'*, moving equilibrium to *B'*. (Show what doubling income to $12 would do to equilibrium. Guess where the new tangency point would approximately come.)

**Single-price change**   Now return our consumer to his previous daily income of $6, but assume that the price of food rises from $1.50 to $3. Again we must examine the change in the budget line. This time we find that it has pivoted on the point *N* and is now *NM''*,[7] as in Fig. 22-10.

The common sense of such a shift is clear. Since the price of clothing is unchanged, the point *N* is just as available as it was before. But since the price of food has risen, point *M*, which meant 4 food units had been purchasable, is no longer attainable. With food costing $3 per unit, only 2 units can now be bought with a daily income of $6. So the new budget line must very definitely still pass through *N*, but it must pivot around *N* and pass through *M''*, which is below *M*. (The new line has a slope of 3/1. Why?)

Equilibrium is now at *B''*; we have a new tangency situation in that equilibrium. Higher food price has definitely reduced food consumption; higher $P_F$ may change clothing consumption in either direction. (The

[7] The budget equation of *NM''* is now $6 = $3F + $1C.

*dd* demand curves of this chapter were derivable by plotting the $P_F$, $Q_F$ data that you should be able to read off from the green curve passing through *B* and *B''*.)

To clinch understanding, the interested reader can work out the cases of an increase in income and a fall in the price of clothing or food. (In a diagram like those of Figs. 22-9 or 22-10, he can connect all the tangency points generated by income changes to get the Engel's budgetary patterns of Chapter 11.)

**Balanced-price changes**   Suppose *all* prices exactly *double*. Then it is easy to see that this is exactly like a *halving* of income. Hence Fig. 22-9's halving of *NM* to get *N'M'* will handle this case. This illustrates an important property of consumer demand.

**Changing all prices and income in exactly the same proportion leaves equilibrium quantities demanded quite unchanged.**

This provides the germ of truth underlying the Quantity Theory of Money and Prices (of Chapter 15 and Chapter 18 Appendix).

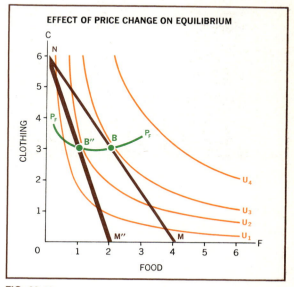

**FIG. 22-10**

A rise in the price of food makes the budget line pivot on *N*, rotating from *NM* to *NM''*. New tangency equilibrium is at *B''*, with less food and either more or less clothing. (Can you handle a change in $P_C$?)

## SUMMARY TO APPENDIX

1 An "indifference curve" or "equal-utility contour" depicts the points of equally desirable consumption. The indifference contour is usually drawn convex from below, in accordance with the empirical law of diminishing relative marginal utilities (or of substitution ratios).

2 If a consumer has a fixed money income, all of which he spends, and is confronted with market prices of two goods, the budget (or consumption-possibility) line upon which he is free to move is a straight line. The steepness of the line's slope will depend on the ratio of the two market prices; how far out it lies will depend on the size of his income.

3 The consumer will move along this budget line until he reaches the highest indifference curve attainable. At this point, the budget line will touch, but not cross, an indifference curve. Hence, equilibrium is at the point of *tangency*, where the *slope of the budget line* (the ratio of the prices) exactly equals the *slope of the indifference curve* (the substitution ratio or relative-marginal-utility ratio of the two goods). This provides an additional proof that marginal utilities are made to be proportional to prices.

4 A fall in income will move the budget line parallel inward, usually causing less of both goods to be bought. A change in the price of one good alone will, other things being equal, cause the budget line to pivot so as to change its slope. In any case, whatever change has occurred, a new equilibrium point of highest satisfaction will be reached. It is at a new point of tangency, where the marginal utility per dollar has become equal in every use. By comparing the new and old equilibrium points, we trace out the usual *dd* demand curve and income pattern.

## CONCEPTS FOR REVIEW

indifference curves or contours
slope or substitution ratio
budget or consumption-possibility
  line, *NM*
convexity and law of diminishing
  relative marginal utilities

optimal tangency equilibrium:
  $P_F/P_C$ = substitution ratio
  $= MU_F/MU_C$
parallel and pivoted shifts of *NM*
  and new tangency equilibrium
  after income or price changes

## QUESTIONS FOR DISCUSSION

1 Explain why one, and only one indifference curve will go through any point on an indifference map: i.e., why two such curves never cross.

2 If the consumer is at a point on his budget line where it *crosses* an indifference curve, explain why he cannot have reached equilibrium. How will he still want to keep moving?

3 Can *you* generate food's ordinary *dd* demand curve from Fig. 22-10? To get the demand for clothing, show that *NM* must now pivot around *M* rather than around *N*.

4   Give Robinson Crusoe (or Utopia) a production-possibility curve between food and clothing like the curve of Fig. 2-8. Give him the indifference curves like those of this Appendix. Can you depict the basic equilibrium of any economy from the resulting tangency and interpret its price aspects? (Peek ahead to page 459, footnote 9, for the answer.)

5   If the indifference contours were concave instead of being convex, show that the law of diminishing relative marginal utilities would be negated. And then note that a tangency point would be a point of minimum total satisfaction rather than a point of maximum satisfaction.

6   In Fig. 22-8, label the indifference contours with the utility numbers 1, 2, 3, 4. Show that any other four numbers would give the same demand equilibrium, provided only that they are in the same more-or-less relationship. Infer from this that only "ordinal utility" rather than "numerically measurable" utility is needed for demand economics.

7   *Extra credit problem:* Can you explain how a consumer's-surplus diagram can illustrate the deadweight harm, or economic inefficiency, that any sales tax must entail? The figure below is much like Fig. 20-9 on page 398 and Fig. 22-4 on page 439. Each new unit of good bought will add more and more utility, as shown by the area under the *dd* curve and as measured in terms of the unchanging units of utility from leisure forgone, reckoned at $2.50 for each of the 10 hours of the day. Now suppose the government needs to raise $5 (or 2 hours) per person for its army or roads. The most efficient tax would be for it simply to take $5 as a lump-sum tax from the man, as shown by the rectangle marked $5 at the southeast of the diagram, subtracted from his leisure. But suppose, instead, we put a sales tax of $1.00 per unit on this good he buys. With the supply curve shifted upward as from s to s', the new equilibrium will be shifted up from E to E', as shown by the rectangle sAE's'. The government will collect exactly its needed $5 of taxes (explain!). But the consumer has cut back sharply his consumption of this good, and now the utility benefit of this good in excess of its forgone utility leisure—its "consumer's surplus"—has gone from being the triangle sEd to being the smaller triangle s'E'd. The tax rectangle sAE's' is an *unavoidable* loss, for the government cannot get its resources for the army without depriving us citizens of labor-leisure resources. But what about the little, green-shaded triangle AEE'? That is the avoidable, or deadweight, loss of consumer's surplus that results from using a sales tax with its distorting of equilibrium away from true social costs and human utility.

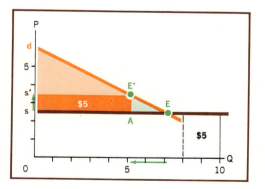

**8**   Geometry buffs can interpret the accompanying diagrams to show how the efficiency of rationing can be improved on. Before war, Man 2 at brown $B_2$ is richer than Man 1 at orange $B_1$. With food scarce in wartime, men are rationed to $R_1$ and $R_2$ points of food consumption. But the men have unequal substitution slopes there (as shown by

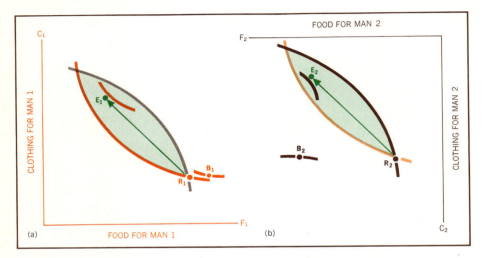

(a)   FOOD FOR MAN 1          (b)

light comparison curve of the other chap). Hence, shaded areas show how *both* can be made better off if the rich man can buy some of the poor man's food ration. They trade on parallel green arrows, ending at green $E$ points (of equal slopes!) where no further mutually beneficial moves are possible. Can you show that prerationing equilibrium of pure competition at $B_1$ and $B_2$ was "efficient" in the sense that *both* could *not* be made better off? HINT: Slope at $B_1$ equals slope at $B_2$ because of common tangency to common market-price ratio. NOTE: Final efficient $E$ situation might also have been reached by a heavy money tax on the rich, with scarce goods being auctioned off to all men at common $E_i$ price ratio. (*Reference:* Question 4 of Chapter 27's Appendix uses a similar geometric technique of "box diagram" useful for more advanced "welfare economics," and you might later reread the two together.)

The previous chapter looked behind the market demand curve for its base in terms of the marginal utilities of individuals. It showed how the demand curves of the different individuals in the marketplace can be summed to form the aggregate market demand schedule.

In this chapter we look behind the supply curve of the industry to find its base in the costs of the different competitive firms. A new concept—that of "marginal" or "extra" cost—is seen to be crucial.

We are interested in competitive supply not merely as a descriptive device. Here in this chapter, we are also interested in showing that the marginal cost concept has a crucially important role to play in allocating for any society its resources in the most efficient manner. (We leave to the following chapter a detailed view of the different kinds of costs that are important in economics.)

## SUMMING ALL FIRM SUPPLY CURVES TO GET MARKET SUPPLY

Figure 22-1 showed how we add horizontally all individual demand curves to get the aggregate market demand curve. The same horizontal addition now applies to supply.

Suppose we are dealing with a competitive market for fish. How much of this commodity will be brought to market at each different level of market price? Firm A will bring so much to market at a particular price; Firm B will bring so much at this same price; Firm C will bring the amount shown on its supply curve; and so it goes. The total $Q$ that will be brought to market at a given market $P$ will be the sum of all the $q$s which firms will want to supply at that price. And similarly at any other price.

*Summary:* To get the aggregate SS supply curve for a good, we must add horizontally the ss supply curves of the independent producers of that good.

# 23
## COMPETITIVE SUPPLY

Cost of production would have no effect on competitive price if it could have none on supply.
JOHN STUART MILL

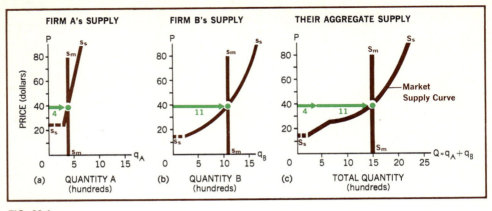

**FIG. 23-1**

**To get market supply curve, we add all firms' supply curves**

At each price, such as $40, we horizontally add quantities supplied by each firm to get total market supply. This applies to any number of firms. If there were 1,000 identical firms, the market supply curve could be made to look just like the supply curve of each firm by a careful, thousandfold change of horizontal scale in the third diagram; if no horizontal scale change is made, aggregate supply must look flatter than each firm's.

This is illustrated for two firms by Fig. 23-1. Recalling that the firms' momentary-run supply curves are defined as the inelastic supplies in a time period so short that no variability in output is possible, we can say:

To get the *industry's* vertical momentary supply curve $S_m S_m$, add horizontally, at the same *P, all firms'* vertical momentary supply curves.

Now recall from Chapter 20 (page 387) that Marshall's "intermediate" or "short run" is defined as that period of time in which the firm is stuck with certain fixed commitments, but in which some variable factors of production can be altered so as to produce more output along the various firms' supply curves:

Again, to get the industry's *short-run* supply curve $S_s S_s$, add horizontally, at the same *P,* the *short-run* supply curves of the fixed number of firms existing in that short run.

Our problem is to see how a firm's supply curve is determinable from its costs.

## DEFINITION OF MARGINAL COST NUMERICALLY AND GRAPHICALLY

Basic to industry supply is Marginal (or extra) Cost. Table 23-1 shows how we go about calculating Marginal Cost: By subtracting the $16,000 total cost of producing $q^* = 400$ units from the $16,040.05 total cost of producing $q = 401$, we find $MC = \$40.05$ for producing 1 more unit beyond $q^*$; to produce 1 less unit involves a difference, $MC = \$39.95$, or $\$16,000 - 15,960.05$. So at $q^*$ itself we may, by disregarding or averaging over the trifling differences caused by the trifling lumpiness of units, estimate $MC = \$40$.

**TABLE 23-1**

**Marginal (or extra) cost can be shown numerically by subtraction of successive items**

The difference in total dollar cost from producing an extra unit is found by subtracting adjacent items of total dollar cost in Column (2). At $q^* = 400$, $MC = \$40$ to a high degree of approximation (as shown by the light-brown average of $MC$ data).

| CALCULATION OF MARGINAL COST | | |
| --- | --- | --- |
| (1)<br>QUANTITY<br>PRODUCED<br>$q$ | (2)<br>TOTAL<br>COST<br>$TC$ | (3)<br>MARGINAL<br>COST<br>$MC$ |
| 399 | $15,960.05 | |
| | | $39.95 |
| 400 | 16,000.00 | 40.00 |
| | | 40.05 |
| 401 | 16,040.05 | |

*Definition:* Marginal Cost at any output level $q$ is the extra cost of producing one extra unit more (or less);[1] it comes from subtracting total dollar costs of adjacent outputs.

Just as we can calculate $MC$ for $q^* = 400$, we can calculate it for any and every $q$. Table 23-1 had put a microscope on cost behavior around 400 and 401 units. To see the big picture,[2] let us stand off and see how the Marginal Cost curve behaves at *all* levels of output. On the next page Fig. 23-2 and its table show that Marginal Cost is related to Total Cost in the same way that Fig. 22-3, page 434, related Marginal Utility to Total Utility. From Fig. 23-2(b), you will see this:

$MC$ tends to be U-shaped: ultimately it is rising, even though there may be an initial phase in which $MC$ is falling.

Why can you expect Marginal Cost to be ultimately a rising curve? This takes us back to the law of diminishing returns of Chapter 2, pages 24 to 27. Behind the dollar costs of the firm lies the production relationship between the firm's output and the labor and other inputs it hires. This will be discussed in depth in Chapter 27, but here we can indicate the general logic of the situation.

Suppose some factor is held fixed in the short run we are considering: it could be fixed land, or, in manufacturing, it could be fixed plant capacity. Suppose that we get our varying amounts of $q$ by hiring varying amounts of some input such as labor. If we can always buy labor at the same wage per unit, the only reason our marginal or extra cost of getting more $q$ should rise would be because the extra product added by each successive unit of labor is going down. Hence, if we do get diminishing returns to the varying labor factor, we shall certainly get increasing Marginal Cost.

Costs and productivity returns are merely opposite sides of the same relationship.

---

[1] WARNING: $MC$ is usually not the same as average cost per unit, which we get by dividing total cost by number of units produced: $MC$ is extra cost, or incremental cost, or differential cost; or, as we have seen from the use of the word "marginal" in connection with *extra* utility, the appropriate name is indeed Marginal Cost.

[2] Figure 23-2 and the accompanying table measure $q$ in units of hundreds; hence, $q = 300, 399, 400, 401, 500$ in Table 23-1 would show in Fig. 23-2 as $q = 3, 3.99, 4, 4.01, 5$, etc.

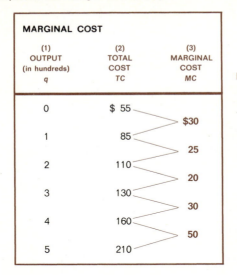

**MARGINAL COST**

| (1)<br>OUTPUT<br>(in hundreds)<br>q | (2)<br>TOTAL<br>COST<br>TC | (3)<br>MARGINAL<br>COST<br>MC |
|---|---|---|
| 0 | $ 55 | |
| | | $30 |
| 1 | 85 | |
| | | 25 |
| 2 | 110 | |
| | | 20 |
| 3 | 130 | |
| | | 30 |
| 4 | 160 | |
| | | 50 |
| 5 | 210 | |

**FIG. 23-2**

**Marginal Cost is to Total Cost exactly as Marginal Utility is to Total Utility**
To find the *MC* of producing the fifth unit, we subtract $160 from $210 to get $50. This table can be compared with the Marginal Utility table of Fig. 22-3 on page 434. (Source: Table 23-1 but with *q* measured in hundredfold coarser units.)

In (a) a smooth curve has been drawn through the points of *TC*. In (b) a smooth *MC* curve has been drawn through the steps of extra cost. Ultimately *MC* is rising (because of diminishing returns), but it may at first fall, giving the curve a U-shaped contour.

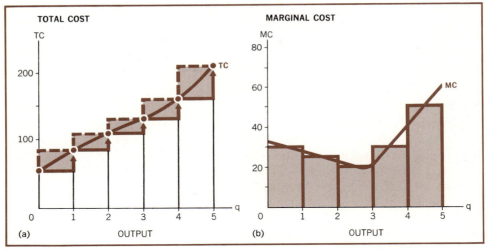

Why does *MC* often decline *at first*, as shown in Fig. 23-2(b)? Recall that the law of diminishing returns tends *ultimately* to hold: at the beginning, it might be negated by a strong tendency toward *increasing* returns, owing to the economies of large-scale production associated with indivisibility of the process and chances to introduce more elaborate division of labor as scale expands. If at first we have strong *increasing* returns, we must at first have *declining*, rather than increasing, Marginal Cost.[3]

---

[3] Later we shall examine the behavior of Marginal Cost in the long run. Suppose we consider so extended a period of time that nothing can be regarded as fixed. Old plants can wear out and be replaced. New plants can be designed and built. Old land obligations can expire. New land contracts can be made. And so forth. In the long run, as a small firm, we may be able to buy *all* the factors of production in balance at unchanged prices. Now what will happen to long-run costs, particularly long-run *MC*, if the firm has no fixed factors and can enjoy "constant returns to scale"? (This is

We can summarize the relationship between the productivity laws of returns and the laws of Marginal Cost:

*A tendency for varying factors to show diminishing returns when applied to fixed factors implies a tendency for MC to be rising. If at first there is increasing returns, there is at first declining MC—but ultimately diminishing returns and increasing MC.*

## HOW TO DETERMINE MAXIMUM-PROFIT COMPETITIVE SUPPLY BY *MC*

It is evident that costs are vital determinants of how much a firm will be willing to supply. It would supply nothing if market $P$ were too low to cover its out-of-pocket expenses, and would supply much if $P$ were very high. To decide how much to supply at each market $P$, the firm will want to know the *extra* or *marginal* cost to it of each extra unit of $q$. Thus, consider Firm A back in Fig. 23-1, which was shown supplying 4 (hundred) units at a market price of $40 per unit. Why does $q = 4.00$ and not 4.01 or 3.99?

At first you might be tempted to reply: "Firm A has no choice but $q = 4$ because that is all it can sell at $40—no more, no less." What is wrong with such an answer? It overlooks the fact that this is a model of *perfect competition.*

*Definition: A perfect-competitor is too small and unimportant to affect the market price. Like a wheat farmer, he is a "price taker" who can sell all he wishes at the ruling market price. In terms of demand elasticity, a perfect-competitor faces a (virtually) horizontal dd demand curve for his product—his elasticity of demand is infinite.*[4]

Granted that a perfect-competitor can sell *any* $q$ he chooses at the going $P$, how does he pick his best $q$ supply response? A perfect-competitor picks the quantity he will supply by referring to his marginal-cost curve, so that $P = MC$. Why?

He will do this because he is interested in maximizing the total profit he can earn. Profit is the difference between the total revenue he receives from selling his output and the total cost incurred in producing that output. He increases his total profit so long as the *extra* revenue brought in from the last unit sold is greater than the *extra* cost which that last unit entailed.

---

defined as a state where there is no reason for diminishing returns to operate, since *all* factors grow in balance, and where all economies of large-scale production have already been realized.) *Answer:* If long-run constant returns to scale holds, then doubling all inputs will exactly double their total dollar costs and will at the same time exactly double total output. Hence, there will be constant Marginal Cost, *MC* being *horizontal* rather than rising or falling. (See page 471 of Chapter 24 for the longest-run "planning" or envelope cost curves.)

[4] Figure 23-3 shows the contrast between the industry demand curve *DD*, relating $P$ to the sum of firm demands $Q = q_1 + q_2 + \cdots$, and the *dd* curve facing any one small competitor. If there are thousands of firms in the industry, the draftsman will have to rescale the horizontal axis and focus a microscope on point $A$ of the industry demand curve, *DD*, in order to show dramatically how this sloped curve will reappear as the horizontal *dd* curve to the lilliputian eye of the firm.

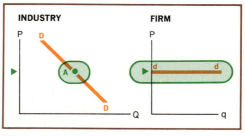

FIG. 23-3

Total profit reaches its peak—is maximized—when there is no longer any extra profit to be earned by selling extra output. The last little unit he produces and sells is just in balance as far as extra revenue and extra cost are concerned. What is that extra revenue? It is price per unit. What is that extra cost? It is marginal cost. QED.

Specifically, back in Fig. 23-1(a), why did you choose to produce quantity $q^* = 4.00$ (or 400 in the old units) at $P = \$40$? Only one answer is correct: Because the 401st unit would involve you in extra (or so-called "marginal") cost of just over $40; and the 399th unit involved you in extra cost of just under $40; so best-profit $q^* = 400$ involves an *extra* or *marginal cost* just exactly equal to price $P$ of $40. (To clinch your understanding, refer back to page 453's Table 23-1 to verify optimality of $q^* = 400$.)

## DERIVING THE FIRM'S SUPPLY CURVE FROM ITS *MC* CURVE

We have now demonstrated that a competitive firm is at its Maximum-profit position when it is definitely producing all units that had *MC* less than *P*, and is definitely not producing further units for which *MC* is definitely greater than *P*. Evidently, its Maximum-profit equilibrium comes when it follows the rule

Price = Marginal Cost   or   P = MC

This means that the firm's supply curve is given by its rising *MC* curve as shown in Fig. 23-4. Thus, at the indicated horizontal $d'd'$ level of $50, the firm will find its Maximum-profit supply response at the intersection point $A$. (To check this, note that the loss of profit from producing a little less than at $A$ is shown by the green-shaded triangle, depicting the surplus of $P$ over $MC$ on the last little units.)

Alternatively, suppose the firm were faced by a horizontal $dd$ at $40. Its Maximum-profit supply response is shown at the intersection point $B$. It happens, as our original cost Table 23-1 shows, that the firm just breaks even there, covering *all* its long-run costs at this point, including both fixed costs and variable costs.

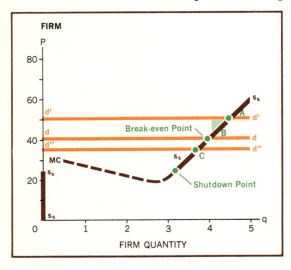

**FIG. 23-4**

**Profit-maximizing firm's supply curve is its rising Marginal Cost curve**

If you can sell all you wish at $P$ given by horizontal $d'd'$, your Maximum-profit equilibrium comes at its intersection with the $MC$ curve at $A$: your Maximum profit is positive; and the green-shaded triangle shows you would lose some profit if you produced less than at $A$, since your extra revenue of $P$ would exceed your extra cost, $MC$.

If $P$ dropped to $d''d''$ level, you maximize profit at $C$: $P = MC$ there minimizes your unavoidable short-run loss. If $P$ falls below Shutdown point, your revenue fails to cover out-of-pocket expenses and you will shut down. If $P$ is at Break-even point $B$, your maximized profit (inclusive of normal return to your labor and capital) is just zero: new firms will not enter, and old ones will not leave.

Or suppose the firm faced $d''d''$. At this price below $40, the firm cannot break even; but it does *minimize its short-term losses* (or maximize its "algebraic" profit) there at the $C$ intersection on the $MC$ curve (as you can show by penciling in a green-shaded triangle like $A$'s).

Thus, the firm's rising $MC$ curve does indeed constitute its competitive supply curve.

## TOTAL COST AND SHORT-RUN SHUTDOWN CONDITIONS[5]

Recall that earlier the "short run" was defined as that period of time in which certain equipment, resources, and commitments of the firms are fixed; but it is a period long enough for the firm to vary its output by hiring more or fewer variable factors of production, such as labor, raw materials, and so forth. It is certainly not a precise period of time which will be the same for all industries. Even within an industry, we can be asking questions about "short-run" periods of different duration. At one ultrashort extreme, so many decisions have already been frozen as to make the resulting Marginal Cost curve practically a vertical and inelastic line. Or at the other extreme, we can permit so much time to pass as to let more and more of the equipment have a chance to wear away or be replaced, thereby making the resulting Marginal Cost curve almost as flat as it will be in the longest run, when *no* fixities are possible except those associated permanently with the management of the firm itself.

Now consider a firm making its short-run decisions. It has a certain "fixed cost": this is defined as the total of costs that will go on anyway because of its fixed commitments that are already frozen in the short run; examples would be bond interest, rentals, overhead salaries, franchise taxes, and so forth. The rest of its "total cost" is called "variable cost": this is defined as the sum of all costs that vary with output; examples are cost of materials, wages for workers on the production line, and so forth. Chapter 24 will discuss all these in detail.

But now consider the firm facing lower and lower $P$. It has the option of producing nothing at all. How much will it then lose? With its revenue zero and all its fixed cost going on anyway, its shutdown loss will exactly equal its fixed cost. When $P$ falls so low as to give it *less revenue than the variable cost it incurs* from producing positive $q$, it will prefer to shut down completely: why should it produce if that means it incurs loss greater than the fixed cost it incurs when shut down? So this rule holds:

*Shutdown point.* At the critically low market price, where the firm just recovers its variable cost by producing, it will be on the verge of shutting down. Below that point, it will produce nothing at all.

Above that $P$, it *will* produce along its short-run Marginal Cost curve. For, at such $MC = P$ points, the firm will be getting something toward covering its fixed cost; and either it will be getting maximized positive profits, or, if $P$ is below the Break-even point, at least the firm will be minimizing its losses (and, in that sense, maximizing its algebraic profit).

The location of the Shutdown point was shown in Fig. 23-4. The $MC$ curve continues down below that point, but it no longer corresponds to an $ss$ supply curve.

---

[5]This section may be skipped in a brief course.

### SYNTHESIS OF MARGINAL COST AND MARGINAL UTILITY

We can summarize what has now been established. Just as Marginal Utility lies behind the demand curve, Marginal Cost lies behind the supply curve. *The supply curve of an industry is seen to be the summed rising MC curves of the firms in that industry.*[6]

Having described market equilibrium, we are now in a position to understand *how important the MC concept is in helping society to organize its production efficiently and responsively.* We can now combine cost and utility, or more precisely Marginal Cost and Marginal Utility.

**Robinson Crusoe**    Begin with the simplest case—that of Robinson Crusoe. A single man, so the story goes, works so many hours picking strawberries. (*a*) Each extra berry brings him *diminished* marginal utility. (*b*) Each extra hour of sweaty labor brings him *increasing marginal disutility.* (*c*) Working with fixed land, each extra minute of work, because of the law of *diminishing returns*, brings fewer and fewer extra berries.

It must follow from these assumptions that Crusoe will work up to the critical equilibrium intersection where a declining marginal-utility-of-berries curve (which looks like both an *MU* and a *dd* curve) intersects with a rising marginal curve of disutility involved in providing the effort needed for additional berries (which is like an *MC* and *ss* curve).

Figure 23-5 gives the Robinson Crusoe welfare equilibrium.[7] The brown *MC* curve is now rising because diminishing returns makes the *MC* of extra strawberries rising; the orange *MU* curve falls because of diminishing *MU*. Welfare is maximized at *E*, where *MU* of berries is in balance with *MC* (measured, remember, in utils of forgone-leisure). The "triangular" orange area *AEB* represents the consumer's (net) surplus, and it is larger at *E* than anywhere else. (The shaded green "triangle" beyond *E* shows the loss of well-being from producing too many berries. You can pencil in a similar orange loss "triangle" to the left of *E* reflecting what you would lose of net consumer's surplus if you did *not* produce the last units.)

**Communal state**    Economics is a science of *society*, not of a single isolated individual. Still, we can keep our story simple if we now apply it to a communal state, where all families are treated exactly alike or where some single benevolent or malevolent dictator provides the utility and disutility magnitudes that are to be maximized.

Figure 23-5 still serves to show optimal welfare for a monistic, communal state, just as it did for the one-man Crusoe world. Now a Planner, using computers or market devices, would want to realize the same *MU* and *MC* equality shown there.

Indeed, both Crusoe and a planning board might achieve the *MU* = *MC* equilibrium

---

[6] The next chapter will discuss the longest-run case in which new firms can come into the industry and old firms leave it.

[7] To keep matters at their simplest, suppose we can ignore the increasing marginal disutility of sweaty labor, measuring all our welfare in fixed "disutils" of labor time; or better, what is the same thing, we consider each hour of forgone-leisure as having a constant marginal utility so that we can arithmetically reckon all utilities and costs in these leisure-labor utils. This important notion of "forgone-*opportunity* cost" will be discussed again in the next chapter.

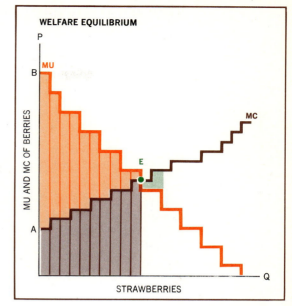

**FIG. 23-5**
**Supply-demand intersection can help solve Planner's welfare optimum of Marginal Utility and Marginal Cost**
Here Robinson Crusoe or a communal-state Planner utilizes apparatus of supply and demand to determine optimal well-being output. Orange *MU* curve intersects brown *MC* curve at *E*. Cost of picking strawberries is given by brown area, measuring "utils" of forgone-leisure. Vertical slabs of orange area under *MU* give excess strawberry utils over utils of cost. Hence orange-shaded area of consumer's net surplus is maximized by producing at *E* intersection (green area to right of *E* showing loss from producing too much).

by introducing a price of strawberries, $P$.[8] Then, by equating $MU = P$ and $MC = P$, they would succeed in achieving their welfare optimum.

**Many goods**  One last complication before considering the real world. Crusoe or a planning board would have to cope with many goods: strawberries versus tea versus cotton gloves, etc. Suppose labor is freely transferable among the different activities—tea, berries, etc. And, to keep the parable simple, suppose that *varying* labor is applied to different grades of *fixed* land, each land being completely specialized to its industry. Clearly, then, each good will have a rising *MC* curve in terms of labor (and hence leisure-utils) applied to it.

What about society's (or Crusoe's) marginal utility from berries, tea, gloves, etc.? For simplicity, suppose each good *independently* has its own total utility and marginal-utility schedules like Fig. 22-3, p. 434. Now comes the vital question. How should Crusoe or the Planner most efficiently allocate labor among different industries to effect the optimal-welfare pattern of berry production, tea production, etc.?

Obviously, to maximize welfare and allocation efficiency we must in each industry[9] get a balance of *MU* and of *MC*. If tea involves twice the *MC* of strawberries, its *P* must be twice as great. These $P_i = MC_i$ equivalences are vital in any society aiming to solve WHAT and HOW efficiently.

[8]This price could be in units-of-utility-of-forgone-leisure. Or, if we defined labor so that $1 equals the wage of 1 unit of work or of forgone-leisure, then strawberry $P$ could be expressed in dollars.
[9]For each new industry, we draw a new diagram like Fig. 23-5, and again maximize the orange area of "consumer's (net) surplus" where $P_i = MC_i$ and $P_i$ reflects *MU* of the *i*th good as determined

By now, the essential point of optimal *MC* pricing should be obvious enough. But in leaving it, please notice that a simple "labor theory of value" will not properly solve the problem. Only if you reckon the full *Marginal Cost* of a good can you get its proper price in terms of labor or of anything else! And setting prices merely proportional to labor used in an industry does not properly adjust for the scarcity of nonlabor inputs.

## EFFICIENT MARKET ALLOCATION OF PRODUCTION

Now forget parables. Forget Robinson Crusoe. Forget a communal state. What about the anarchy of a million small competitors? Can a perfectly competitive market really achieve the same optimal *MC* equilibrium?

**Qualifications**   The answer is, "Yes." Better still, "Yes, maybe." First, you must rule out monopoly: no one expects that an unbridled profiteer will achieve the social optimum. Second, you must not be considering cases where people's demand curves *deviate* from true utility. That is, don't try to apply the theory to heroin production. Or, if you believe that Madison Avenue advertisers have manipulated consumers into demanding worthless gadgets that don't deserve to have the word "utility" applied to them, don't try to apply the theory to that area. If there remains a group of goods and industries—say shoes, beef, housing, etc.—where there are many reasonably informed consumers and many mutually competing producers, then you may hope to achieve efficiency[10] by market pricing along *MC* lines.

**Market synthesis**   Now turn to Fig. 23-7 to see how a competitive system does bring out a balance between utility and cost. On the left, we add horizontally the demand

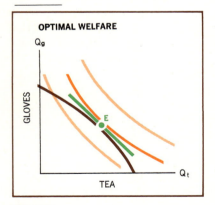

**OPTIMAL WELFARE**

$Q_g$

GLOVES

E

$Q_t$

TEA

**FIG. 23-6**

from consumer *dd* curves. (WARNING: If coffee is not *independent* of tea, you could not draw its diagram *independently* of that of tea. Also, if the transferable inputs in terms of which we measure the $MC_i$ did not satisfy our simplifying axiom of strict constancy of forgone utils, the consumer's-surplus exposition here would have to be made more complicated; advanced economics handles the problem rigorously by the more complex tools of intermediate economic treatises.

Figure 23-6 here uses the methods of the Appendix to Chapter 22 to show the same welfare optimum as did Fig. 23-5. Robinson Crusoe maximizes welfare at *E*, where $MC_{tea}/MC_{gloves}$ (as measured by the brown slope of his *p-p frontier*) and $MU_{tea}/MU_{gloves}$ (as measured by the orange slope of his indifference curves) are each equal to the market $P_{tea}/P_{gloves}$ (as measured by the green slope of the price-line through *E*.)

Verify that *E* does represent the highest well-being possible for this simplified society. The same story holds if the orange contours depict Planner's preference.

[10]If the dollar votes of different consumers represented an "equitable" allocation, so that each person's dollar represented as ethically deserving a pull on the market as any other's, there would be no need to make the following qualification: Efficient production and pricing does not mean that the FOR WHOM problem of society is being properly solved; it only means that the WHAT and HOW problems are being solved in the best way they can be solved consistent with the *existing distribution* of dollar-voting power and of sharing in national wealth and GNP. This qualification is vital.

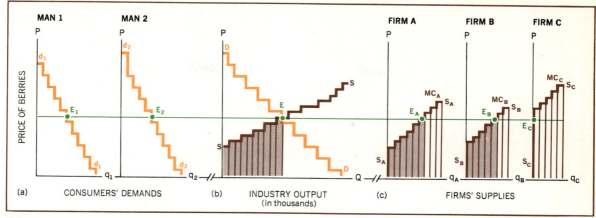

**FIG. 23-7**

**Competitive-industry market integrates consumer demands and producer's minimized costs**

**(a)** Individual demands (as derived from Chapter 22's marginal utility considerations) are shown on the left. If there were 1,000 consumers like Man 1 and 1,000 like Man 2, we would add (horizontally) all their *dd* curves to get industry *DD* curve in the middle.

**(b)** The market brings together all consumer demands and firm supplies to equilibrium at *E*. The horizontal green line shows where each consumer on left and firm on right reaches equilibrium. [NOTE: Brown area under *SS* represents total social cost (e.g., labor-leisure) of *Q*, and this area is at a minimum when all *MCs* are equal.]

**(c)** For each competitive firm, profits are maximized when supply curve is given by rising *MC* curve. Brown area depicts firm's cost of producing. At $MC_A = P = MC_B$, we have Least-cost efficient allocation for industry!

curves for all consumers to get the market *DD* curve in the middle. (Recall Chapter 22, p. 431.) On the right, we add all the separate firms' *MC* curves to get industry *SS* curve in the middle. Note what the equilibrium price at the *E* intersection achieves: It gives people on the left what they are willing to pay for and buy of the good at the *P* reflecting efficient social *MC*. On the right, we see that the equilibrium market price does allocate production most efficiently. (That is, the brown area under *SS* in the middle does represent the minimized sum of brown cost areas on the right![11])

*Summary:* **The ideal competitive market is a device for synthesizing (a) the willingness of people to pay for goods with (b) the actual (minimized) marginal costs of those goods. Without conscious planning, the competitive market does achieve the Robinson Crusoe or the Planning Board most-efficient allocation of resources.**

Although Fig. 23-7 shows only one good, say, wheat, it can be duplicated to show how shoe production gets organized. Remember that labor and other resources are transferable not only between different wheat farms but also between the wheat and the shoe industries. Their respective $MC_i$ reflect these social costs; and without the $P_i = MC_i$ conditions being satisfied, economic allocation would be "inefficient" in the following strong sense: "Unless *all* $P_i = MC_i$, one can reorganize production and make

---

[11]Because dollar-voting power may not have been distributed so as to reflect ruling ethical notions of proper welfare and equity, the area under the market *DD* curve has not been shaded orange: for that would involve "adding" incommensurable utilities of different persons' dollars and an illegitimate leap from consumer's surplus to consumers' surplus. Remember the last footnote's qualification!

*everybody* better off—the poor, the rich,[12] wheat producers, shoe producers, etc.!" Who pays for such an improvement? No one. It comes from cutting out deadweight waste and inefficiency in social allocation!

## FINAL SUMMARY OF EFFICIENCY OF MARGINAL-COST PRICING

A coldly objective scientist, who wanted to know nothing beyond how to describe and analyze competitive supply behavior and who had not the slightest interest in society's welfare, would consider the Marginal Cost concept important. But what about a person who is concerned also with human happiness and with the social efficiency of a pricing system? He would find the equating of price to Marginal Cost even more interesting. Our analysis has demonstrated the following remarkable truth:

**Only when prices of goods are equal to Marginal Costs is the economy squeezing from its scarce resources and limited technical knowledge the *maximum* of outputs. Only when each source of industry output has had its rising *MC* equated to *any* other source's *MC*—as will be the case when each *MC* has been set equal to the common *P*—can the industry be producing its total *Q* at *minimum Total Cost*. Only then will society be out *on* its production-possibility frontier and not *inefficiently inside* the frontier.**

This equal-marginal-cost dictum is as applicable to a communist, socialist, or fascist society as to a capitalistic society. Unless wheat cultivation has been pushed in different parts of the Soviet Union so as to equalize Marginal Costs (including transportation), the Planners there will be failing to achieve the abundance of wheat and other goods that could be theirs with more efficient allocation of resources. (Perhaps it is not surprising to learn from recent debates in their socialist economic journals that they are becoming increasingly aware of this basic fact of logic and economics.)

Because Marginal Cost has this optimality property, it can with some care be used as a yardstick to detect inefficiency in any institutional setup. Thus, if perfectly competitive industries did not exist at all, or if they were rarer even than they are today, one would still derive great benefit from defining and studying the concept of Marginal Cost.

## NONOPTIMALITY OF COMPETITIVE LAISSEZ FAIRE PRICING

But we must not leave the subject of efficient pricing without a warning. We have *not* proved that laissez faire with perfect competition maximizes the greatest good of the greatest number. We have *not* proved that it produces a maximum of social utility. We have *not* proved that it results in the best attainable level of social welfare.

For people are not equally endowed with purchasing power: some are very poor through no fault of their own. Some are very rich, and not necessarily because of any virtue or effort that they or their ancestors have ever performed. So the weighting of dollar votes, which lie behind the individual demand curves on the left of Fig. 23-7, is not necessarily equitable or even tolerable as judged by many ethical systems (various forms of Christianity, Buddhism, "fair shares," etc.). In terms of many ethical systems the social welfare might be improved by redistributive taxation, rather than let the

---

[12]This is the first time we meet explicitly an important concept of intermediate economics, namely "Pareto-optimality." Named after Vilfredo Pareto, an equilibrium is said to be "Pareto-optimal" if (and only if) there is no possible movement from it that could make *everyone* better off.

end result depend upon laissez faire pricing of the property ownership that happens to prevail. All that marginal-cost pricing has been demonstrated to achieve in these discussions is the property of helping to lead to efficiency—efficiency in the sense that there is no "deadweight loss" in the system (i.e., *no possibility of making everybody better off*). When we depart from $P = MC$ pricing, along with any existing inequities of distribution, we compound the inefficiency of deadweight loss. Marginal-cost pricing is part of the recipe for getting the good society; it is not alone a sufficient condition for having achieved it.

This completes our discussion of the relationship between Marginal Cost and industry supply, and of marginal-cost pricing in its relationship to efficient allocation of resources. The next chapter will go more deeply into the nature and variety of concepts of cost. And later chapters will examine the important cases that deviate from perfect competition—such as monopoly or oligopoly or external nuisances on other people.

## SUMMARY

1   In a competitive market, aggregate supply of a group of independent firms comes from adding horizontally their separate supply curves.

2   The short run is defined as that period of time in which some of the firm's productive factors and costs are fixed and some are variable. For a firm, we can define Marginal Cost as its *extra* or incremental cost of producing an *extra* unit of output, and can compute the instantaneous rate of Marginal Cost at each output from a smoothed schedule or graph of costs.

3   Trends of costs and of productivity returns are reverse sides of the same coin: when the law of diminishing returns ultimately holds, the $MC$ curve ultimately rises; when there is an initial stage of increasing returns, $MC$ initially falls; if *all* factors of production could be bought in balance at unchanged prices and output were to then show constant returns to scale, long-run Marginal Costs could be horizontal forever.

4   A perfectly-competitive firm is defined as one which is able to sell all it wants to at the posted market price. To maximize its (algebraic) profit, it will move along its (horizontal) demand curve until it reaches its rising Marginal Cost curve. At this intersection, $MC = P$, and the firm is maximizing its profits (or minimizing its short-run losses). So the industry supply curve from a given number of firms will come from adding horizontally their relevant Marginal Cost curves.

5   Out-of-pocket costs (or avoidable, variable costs) must be taken into consideration in determining a firm's short-run "Shutdown point." Below some critical $P$ the firm will not even be recovering in price revenues the variable cost that could be saved completely if it shut down; so rather than end up losing more than its fixed cost, it will shut down and produce nothing at lower $P$s.

6   Beyond its importance for describing and explaining *competitive supply*, the

concept of Marginal Cost has great importance for *welfare economics*. The problem of How goods are to be produced is being solved most efficiently only if every source of production for a good is being utilized up to the same $MC$ level—an optimal result that is achievable when $P = MC$ everywhere. The problem of WHAT goods are best to be produced and in what amounts is solved in a Robinson Crusoe or Planning world by equating Marginal Utilities and Marginal Costs. Just as $MU$ lies behind $dd$, so does $MC$ lie behind $ss$; the competitive market, despite its surface appearance of anarchy and chaos, does provide one method for achieving economic efficiency. (WARNING: By itself, competitive pricing cannot ensure that the FOR WHOM distribution of dollar-voting power is ethically optimal; taxes and transfers might be needed for that, after which competitive pricing could do the rest of the job.)

## CONCEPTS FOR REVIEW

summing $ss$ curves to get $SS$

Marginal (or extra) Cost

$P = MC$, Maximum-profit condition

identity of firm $ss$ supply curve and rising $MC$ curve

diminishing returns and rising $MC$

Shutdown point

Robinson Crusoe or Planner's welfare optimum at $MU = MC$

market efficiency of $P = MC$

## QUESTIONS FOR DISCUSSION

1 Show that the differences between momentary, short-run, and long-run periods are a matter of degree and not of kind. In reality, there is a continuum of time periods in which there are fewer and fewer factors that are *fixed*. Give reasons why (positive) Marginal Cost might at first fall and later rise.

2 "If a good can be stored, momentary supply will not be vertically inelastic. When $P$ gets very low, producers will *reserve* some product, storing it for future sale at a higher $P$." Justify. Can you show that this makes $S_mS_m$ have a rising slope?

3 Why will you ever supply goods at a loss along a short-run $MC$ curve?

4 "If I can get more than enough to cover my *fixed* costs, I will produce, forgetting my *variable* costs." Show that two words have been exactly reversed here.

5 Appraise this dialogue. *A:* "What does efficiency matter if the wrong people have all the money?" *B:* "Why risk making everybody worse off? Besides, use the tax system for redistribution rather than deviate from competitive pricing at $P = MC$ since such a method of redistribution is inefficient." *A:* "But will the tax system be so used?"

6 *Extra-credit problem:* Utopia can generate power from two generators: the newest one has lower $MC$ at first. Show that only at peak loads will the firm use the older generator, only after the new generator's $MC$ rises above the beginning $MC$ of the older generator. At high loads, it should charge high $P$, equal to the common $MC$s of the two. (HINT: Add the two $MC$ curves horizontally as in Fig. 23-1.)

The previous chapter introduced the definition of marginal cost, a fundamental concept that was seen to lie behind the supply curve of the competitive firm. Here in this chapter we shall go deeper into a variety of different cost concepts.

To understand the Maximum-profit equilibrium of any firm—whether it be the most perfect competitor, the most complete monopolist, or anywhere in the vast terrain of oligopoly and imperfect competition—we need to know how marginal and total costs are related to other cost concepts (such as average, or unit, costs) and to the breakdown between fixed costs and variable costs. Then we shall be ready in Chapter 25 to see how the marginal cost of *any* firm, whether competitive or not, has to be related to a similar concept on the demand side—namely, Chapter 25's *marginal* (or extra) *revenue*—in order to arrive at the Maximum-profit equilibrium of the firm.

## TOTAL COST: FIXED AND VARIABLE

Consider a typical firm that produces the output $q$. At this stage, we do not care whether it is a perfect- or imperfect-competitor. At any one time, it has a certain state of technical knowledge, and it is confronted with the prices of the labor and other inputs it must buy. Now its accountants have been able to calculate what will be *its total dollar costs for producing each different level of q.*

Table 24-1 shows the simplified Total Cost[1] for each different level

---

[1]These data depend upon engineering technology *and* upon the market prices of labor, land, fertilizer, and other factor inputs that the firm needs to produce each output of the good in question. Before its accountants and production men were able to write down the numbers in Table 24-1, they had to make efficiency decisions in *engineering*, ensuring that the physical inputs could not be combined to give more physical output. And what is not so obvious until we have studied production theory in Part Four, the firm must also have made minimizing decisions of an *economic* kind in arriving at its lowest expense for each $q$ produced.

# 24

# ANALYSIS OF COSTS AND LONG-RUN SUPPLY

A class in economics would be a real success if the students gained from it a real understanding of the meaning of cost in all its many aspects.
J. M. CLARK

**VARIOUS COST CONCEPTS**

| (1) QUANTITY $q$ | (2) FIXED COST $FC$ | (3) VARIABLE COST $VC$ | (4) TOTAL COST $TC = FC + VC$ | (5) MARGINAL COST PER UNIT $MC$ | (6) AVERAGE COST PER UNIT $AC = \dfrac{TC}{q}$ | (7) AVERAGE FIXED COST PER UNIT $AFC = \dfrac{FC}{q}$ | (8) AVERAGE VARIABLE COST PER UNIT $AVC = \dfrac{VC}{q}$ |
|---|---|---|---|---|---|---|---|
| 0 | 55 | 0 | 55 | | Infinity | Infinity | |
| | | | | 34 / 30 | | | |
| 1 | 55 | 30 | 85 | | 85 | 55 | 30 |
| | | | | 27 / 25 | | | |
| 2 | 55 | 55 | 110 | | 55 | $27\frac{1}{2}$ | $27\frac{1}{2}$ |
| | | | | 22 / 20 | | | |
| 3 | 55 | 75 | 130 | | $43\frac{1}{3}$ | $18\frac{1}{3}$ | 25 |
| | | | | 21 / 30 | | | |
| 4* | 55 | 105 | 160 | | 40* | $13\frac{3}{4}$ | $26\frac{1}{4}$ |
| | | | | 40 / 50 | | | |
| 5 | 55 | 155 | 210 | | 42 | 11 | —— |
| | | | | 60 / — | | | |
| 6 | 55 | 225 | 280 | | $46\frac{4}{6}$ | $9\frac{1}{6}$ | $37\frac{3}{6}$ |
| | | | | 80 / 90 | | | |
| 7 | 55 | —— | 370 | | $52\frac{6}{7}$ | $7\frac{6}{9}$ | 45 |
| | | | | 100 / 110 | | | |
| 8 | 55 | —— | 480 | | 60 | $6\frac{7}{8}$ | $53\frac{1}{8}$ |
| | | | | 120 / 130 | | | |
| 9 | 55 | 555 | 610 | | $67\frac{7}{9}$ | $6\frac{1}{9}$ | $61\frac{6}{9}$ |
| | | | | 140 / 150 | | | |
| 10 | 55 | 705 | 760 | | 76 | $5\frac{5}{10}$ | $70\frac{5}{10}$ |

* Minimum level of Average Cost.

**TABLE 24-1**

**From schedule of firm's Total Cost, all other costs can be computed**
All the costs can be calculated from Column (4)'s rising $TC$. Columns (5) and (6) are the important ones to concentrate on: incremental Marginal Cost is calculated by subtraction of adjacent rows of $TC$ and shown in orange; the light numbers of smoothed $MC$ come from Fig. 24-1(b). In Column (6) note the point of minimum cost of $40 on the U-shaped $AC$ curve. (Realize why the green $MC$ = green $AC$ at the minimum.)

of output $q$. Columns (1) and (4) are the crucial ones, showing that $TC$ goes up as $q$ goes up. This is natural because it takes more labor and factor inputs to produce more of a good, and these extra factors involve an extra money cost. It costs $110 in all to produce 2 units, $130 to produce 3 units, and so forth.

**Fixed Cost** Columns (2) and (3) break down Total Cost into two components: total Fixed Cost, $FC$; and total Variable Cost, $VC$. Figure 24-1(a) shows the breakdown.

Even when the firm produces zero output, it must honor its short-run commitments (contractual rentals, watchmen's pay) and continue to incur its total Fixed Cost of $55. By definition, $FC$ is the amount of cost that goes on independently of output; so it remains constant at $55 in Column (2). Another name for Fixed Cost is overhead cost.

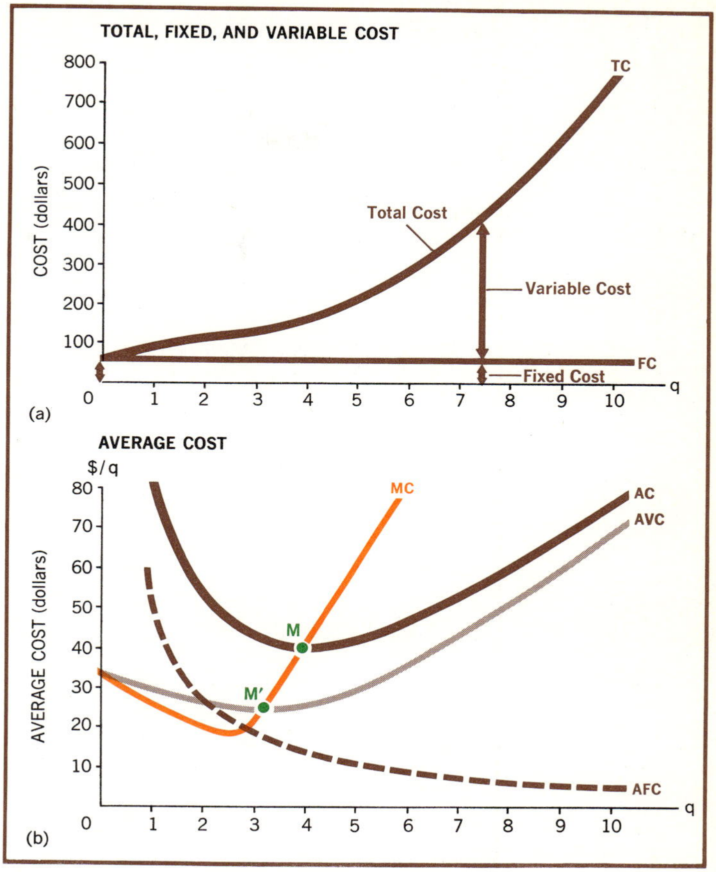

**FIG. 24-1**

**Total Cost curve gives all other curves**

**(a)**  The total Fixed Cost curve is horizontal by definition. Adding on top of it the rising total Variable Cost gives the rising Total Cost curve.

**(b)**  The orange curve of Marginal Cost falls and ultimately rises, as in Chapter 23. *MC* is shown as a smooth curve after the steps of incremental cost are smoothed out; the numbers from the smooth *MC* curve are given in light orange in Column (5) of Table 24-1 (and also correspond to the slope of *TC* curve shown above).

By dividing *TC* by *q*, we can plot Average Cost: *AC* = *TC*/*q*. Similarly, *AFC* comes from *FC*/*q*, and *AVC* comes from *VC*/*q*. At any point, we can add these two brown curves and also get the *AC* curve at that point.

Note that *MC* intersects the U-shaped *AC* at *AC*'s minimum. This is no coincidence. To the left of *M*, *MC* < *AC*, and hence is pulling *AC* down. To the right, *MC* > *AC*, and hence is pulling *AC* up. At the *M* minimum point, *MC* = *AC*; hence *AC* is horizontal there, being neither raised nor lowered by the equivalent *MC*. Also, *MC* cuts the *AVC* curve at its bottom.

**Variable Cost**  Column (3) shows total Variable Cost. By definition, *VC* begins at zero when *q* is zero. It is the part of *TC* that grows with output; indeed, the jump in *TC* between any two outputs is the same as the jump in *VC*. Why? Because *FC* stays constant at $55 throughout and cancels out in any such comparison. (Fill in by subtraction the missing *VC* data of the third column.)

*Definitions:* "Total Cost" represents lowest *aggregate* dollar expense needed to produce each level of output *q*. *TC* rises as *q* rises.

"Fixed Cost" represents the total dollar expense that goes on even when a zero output is produced. It is often called "overhead cost" and usually includes contractual commitments for rental, maintenance, depreciation, overhead salaries and wages, etc. It is a sunk cost that is quite unaffected by any variation in *q*; in the time period for which it is sunk, the only rule is this: Disregard Fixed Cost because *FC* cancels completely out of every decision.

"Variable Cost" represents all items of *TC* except for *FC*—as, for example, raw materials, wages, fuel, etc. Always, by definition,

$$TC = FC + VC$$

Note that *TC* and *VC* always show exactly the same increments of *MC* as *q* changes, because *FC* is a strict constant.

Review carefully how in Fig. 24-1(a) the rising *TC* curve is shown broken down into its constant *FC* and rising *VC* components.

## MARGINAL COST REVIEW

We saw in Chapter 23 how Marginal Cost is defined as the increment of Total Cost that comes from producing an increment of one unit of *q*. (Recall that "marginal," whether applied to utility, cost, or anything else, always means "extra" in economics.)

The orange *MC* numbers in Column (5) of Table 24-1 come from subtracting the adjacent *TC* numbers in Column (4). Thus *MC* is $30 in going from 0 to 1 unit of *q* (i.e., $85 − $55 = $30). *MC* is seen to be $110 − $85 = $25 in going from *q* = 1 to *q* = 2. *MC* is $20 for the third unit of *q*, $30 for the fourth, and thereafter rising steadily until it is shown as $150 in going from *q* = 9 to *q* = 10. (What is *MC* in going from *q* = 5 to *q* = 6? Pencil in your answer in orange.)

Instead of getting *MC* from the *TC* column, we could as easily get the *MC* number by subtracting each *VC* number of Column (4) from the row below it. Why? Because Variable Cost always *grows* exactly like Total Cost, the only difference being that it must—by definition—start out from 0 rather than from the constant *FC* level. (Check that 30 − 0 = 85 − 55, and 55 − 30 = 110 − 85, . . .)

Figure 24-1(a) and (b) show the behavior of Total Cost (in brown) and Marginal Cost (in orange). Note that the *q* axes of the graphs on page 467 are just lined up so that the eye can see the correspondence between *TC* and *MC*.[2]

This example shows *MC* to be U-shaped—at first falling, but ultimately rising. We saw why on page 453. At first there may be great economies in using some or all of the productive factors on a larger scale; and so *MC* at first falls down to a minimum positive number before again rising. If we stick to the short run where some factors of production are fixed, ultimately the old law of diminishing returns will operate to reduce the extra product that comes from adding equal physical and dollar increments

---

[2] As on page 453, we have assumed that units can be made indefinitely small, so that the smoothed-instantaneous *MC* values can be plotted and read off to give the *light* numbers of Table 24-1, Column (5). To help understand the smoothed-instantaneous *MC* at a point *q*, see Fig. 24-2. It helps to clarify the distinction already mentioned between *MC* as an increment of cost for a finite step between two points of *q*, and *MC* as a smoothed-out instantaneous rate depicting the tangential slope at which *TC* is rising at one given *q* point. The distance from *a* to *b* represents one extra unit of output. The distance from *b* to *a'* represents the resulting increase in Total Cost, which is the first and simplest definition of incremental Marginal Cost. The second definition is given by the slope of the Total Cost curve at point *a*—and what mathematicians call $d(TC)/dq$—or what is the same thing numerically, by the distance from *b* to *c* divided by the unit distance *a* to *b*. In the limit, as the size of the extra units becomes small and we reexamine the ratios in the new smaller triangle, the discrepancy between the two definitions becomes relatively negligible. (That is, $ba' \div bc$ approaches 1 as *a'* approaches *a*.)

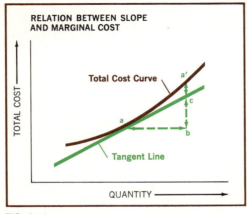

**RELATION BETWEEN SLOPE AND MARGINAL COST**

TOTAL COST

**Total Cost Curve**

a'

c

a

b

**Tangent Line**

QUANTITY

**FIG. 24-2**

of the varying factors onto the fixed factors. So the cost of getting extra product will ultimately become more expensive, and the short-run curve of Marginal Cost will ultimately be rising.

Marginal Cost has many uses. We saw in the last chapter that the rising $MC$ curves of the firms provide us with the rising short-run $ss$ supply curves which we sum horizontally to get the industry's short-run $SS$ supply curve. In the next chapter we shall see that any firm—monopolistic or competitive—will find its Maximum-profit equilibrium by nicely balancing its extra cost against its extra revenue (i.e., by finding an intersection of its Marginal Cost curve and what will be defined as its "Marginal Revenue" curve).

## AVERAGE OR UNIT COST

But first turn back to Column (6) of Table 24-1. This gives Average Cost (per unit), which is simply the Total Cost divided by the number of $q$ units produced.

$$\text{Average Cost} = \frac{\text{Total Cost}}{\text{output}} = \frac{TC}{q} = AC$$

In Column (6), when only 1 unit is produced, Average Cost has to be the same as Total Cost, or $85/1 = $85. But for $q = 2$, $AC = TC/2 = $110/2 = $55, as shown. Note that Average Cost is, at first, falling lower and lower. (We shall see why in a moment.) But $AC$ reaches a minimum of $40 at $q = 4$, and then slowly rises.

Figure 24-1(b) gives a careful plotting of U-shaped $AC$, nicely arranged below the $TC$ it came from. We can now break down Average Cost into its two components, fixed and variable, just as earlier we had the breakdown of $TC$ into $FC$ and $VC$. By dividing each of the last two by $q$, we get Average Fixed Cost, $AFC = FC/q$ of Column (7); and Average Variable Cost, $AVC = VC/q$ of Column (8).

**Average Fixed Cost**   Since total Fixed Cost is a constant, dividing it by $q$ gives in Column (7) a steadily falling Average Fixed Cost curve. The dashed brown $AFC$ curve in Fig. 24-1(b) looks like a unitary demand curve, or hyperbola, that approaches both axes: it drops lower and lower, approaching the horizontal axis as the constant $FC$ gets spread over more and more units. If we allow fractional and zero units of $q$, $AC$ starts infinitely high, as the finite $FC$ is spread over tinier and tinier units of $q$.

**Average Variable Cost**   $AVC$ of Column (8) and Fig. 24-1(b) at first falls and then ultimately rises. We could have predicted this U-shaped behavior of $AVC$ from the U-shaped behavior of $MC$. When $MC$ at first falls, each new $q$ is pulling down the Average Variable Cost calculated over all the items.

**The points of Minimum Average Cost**   Figure 24-1(b) is an important economic diagram. Fix it on your eye's retina. Note particularly the typical U shape of the $AC$ curve.

**The $AC$ curve is always pierced at its minimum point by the rising $MC$ curve.**

This is no coincidence. And now we can explain why this has to be the case. Any average curve is pulled downward when $MC$ is less than $AC$: If the last increment of cost is less than the average of all previous ones, it must pull the average down!

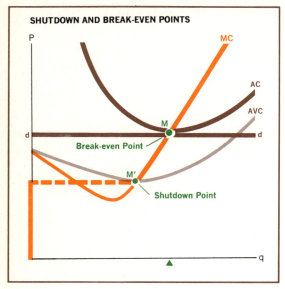

**FIG. 24-3**
**Competitors are in long-run equilibrium where Price equals Minimum Average Cost**
The Break-even point is at *M* where *dd* is tangent to *AC* and *AC* is at its minimum. The short-run Shutdown point is similarly at the bottom of the *AVC* curve, at *M′*.

But when *MC* gets as big as *AC*, *AC* no longer is pulled down; it now turns sideward or level. Then, if *MC* rises above the *AC*, it must of course pull *AC* up. So at the point where rising *MC* = *AC*, and only at that point, shall we find the point of Minimum *AC*.[3]

*Summary:* **So long as Marginal Cost is below Average Cost, it is pulling Average Cost down; when *MC* gets to be just equal to *AC*, *AC* is neither rising nor falling and is at Minimum *AC*; after *MC* is above *AC*, it is pulling *AC* up. Hence:**

**At bottom of U-shaped *AC*, *MC* = *AC* = Minimum *AC***

Likewise, the *MC* curve cuts the *AVC* curve at the bottom of its U, pulling it down before this point because *MC* < *AVC* and pulling it up beyond that point because *MC* > *AVC*.

Now that we know how the *MC* curve intersects the *AC* and *AVC* curves where their U's bottom out, we can describe exactly how the firm's Shutdown and Break-even points of Fig. 23-4, page 456, had been determined. The Break-even point of long-run no-profit competitive equilibrium is seen here in Fig. 24-3 to be at the bottom of the U-shaped *AC* curve, in accordance with

*P* = *MC* = Minimum *AC*, in long-run equilibrium of zero excess-profits

Likewise, the Shutdown point would come at *M′*, once the horizontal *dd* of the firm

---

[3]Here is an explanation of the *MC* and *AC* relationship in terms of college grade averages. With *MC* below *AC*, Average Cost keeps being pulled down by the lowered cost of the final unit—just as one's cumulative grade average is pulled down when one's incremental average in the junior year is less than one's cumulative average up to that time. Only when one's "marginal or current" grade average crosses above or below one's cumulative grade average will the latter reverse its direction.

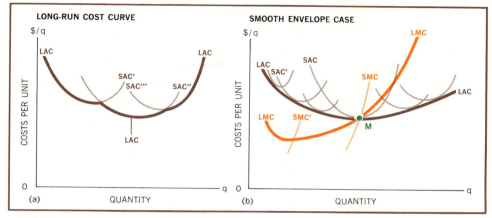

**FIG. 24-4**

**In the long run, a firm can choose its best plant sizes and its lower-envelope curve**
**(a)** *LAC* is the brown "envelope" or lower frontier of the three possible choices of plant.
**(b)** There is now an indefinite number of choices, and we get *LAC* as a smooth brown envelope. In the usual way we derive from brown *LAC* curve its orange marginal curve, *LMC*.

had fallen to a level of $P$ so low as to just cover minimum $AVC$. A price below this level would cause the firm to produce zero output.

## LONG-RUN PLANNING ENVELOPE CURVE[4]

We now have all the technical apparatus of the various cost concepts needed to permit us to tackle the problem of how any firm will find its Maximum-profit equilibrium. But one last technicality is needed to explain how a firm may *in the longest run* be able to have lowest costs through adapting and varying the size of its plant.

Recall that, once the firm has a fixed plant, it has a short-run U-shaped $AC$ curve (call it $SAC$ to emphasize its short-run nature). If the firm builds a larger plant, the new $SAC$ curve must be drawn farther to the right. Now, suppose the firm is still in the planning stage, still quite uncommitted by any fixed obligations. It can write down *all possible* different U-shaped $SAC$ curves, and then choose to select for each prescribed output the $SAC$ that gives it the lowest costs. As $q$ changes permanently, the firm hops to a new $SAC$ curve.

Figure 24-4(a) shows how, in the longest run, the firm selects $SAC'$ for low $q$; for intermediate $q$, it does better to plan to use $SAC''$; for still larger $q$, $SAC'''$ leads to lowest costs. The heavy brown curve of Long-run Average Cost ($LAC$) is composed of the three *lowest* branches. Figure 24-4(b) shows the same lower limit in the case where the firm has choice of infinitely many smooth short-run $AC$ curves ($SAC$, not $AVC$!): now $LAC$ is the U-shaped smooth "lower-envelope" curve; and *its* well-behaved $LMC$ provides the firm's long-run Marginal Cost curve, emerging from the $LAC$ minimum point with a gentler slope than the short-run $SMC$ curve there.

[4]This section may be skipped in brief courses.

## TASKS ACCOMPLISHED AND TASKS YET TO COME

The first half of this chapter is done. The important concepts of cost have been introduced: Total Cost, and its breakdown into total Fixed and total Variable Costs; Marginal Cost; all the different Average Costs (per unit), *AC, AFC,* and *AVC;* the interrelations between marginal and average concepts, including their intersection at the minimum point of the U-shaped average curve; long-run envelope cost, *LAC,* when number of plants and all elements can be adjusted to the level of production.

Since competitive firms must in the longest run realize a price equal to average cost—so that total dollar revenue equals total dollar cost, with no excess-profit—we are now equipped to carry on the analysis of longest-run competitive supply.

## TOTAL COST AND LONG-RUN BREAK-EVEN CONDITIONS

Once I am stuck with certain fixed cost commitments, I will be willing to produce in the short run along my *MC* curve above the Shutdown point—even though I am not earning enough to cover *all* my costs—as the last chapter showed. But only at some higher point on my *MC* curve will I be earning enough to cover *all* the costs that have to be met if I am to stay in business after the short run is over and I have regained my long-run freedom (*a*) to renew my old commitments or (*b*) to move to another industry.

There is, then, a critical "Break-even point" below which *long-run P* cannot remain if I am to stay in this business. If every other firm were exactly like me, the long-run supply would dry up completely below this critical Break-even level which covers all costs of staying in business.

Now let us suppose further that entry into the industry is absolutely free in the long run, so that any number of firms can come into the industry and manage to produce in exactly the same way and at exactly the same costs as the firms already in my industry. Under such conditions of free "replication," it is obvious that long-run *P* cannot remain above this same critical Break-even point at which they all cover their long-run total costs—including in these (1) all labor, materials, equipment, taxes, and other expenses; (2) all wages payable to the identical managers at the level determined competitively by the bidding in all industries for people of such talents and industriousness; and (3) the interest yield that any of them could get on the amounts of capital that they tie up in this industry instead of investing it elsewhere.

Long-run Break-even condition: This comes at a critical *P* where the identical firms just cover their full competitive costs. At lower long-run *P*, firms would leave the industry until *P* had returned to the critical equilibrium level; at higher long-run *P*, new firms would enter the industry, replicating what existing firms are doing and thereby forcing market price back down to the long-run equilibrium *P* where all competitive costs are just covered.[5] Thus, as shown back in page 470's Fig. 24-3,

$P = MC$ = minimum competitive costs, the long-run Break-even equilibrium

[5] If investors tend to be overoptimistic and repeatedly produce an oversupply in the industry so as to create permanent losses on the average, full competitive costs might be defined compatibly with such chronic losses resulting from repeated miscalculations. And, of course, those who own exceptionally good cornland will be garnering as part of their costs juicy rent returns.

Figure 24-5 shows the longest-run supply curve for the industry. If this industry uses general factors, such as labor, that can be attracted from the vast ocean of other uses without affecting the level of wage rates, we get the case of constant costs as shown by the horizontal $S_L S_L$ supply curve.

By contrast, suppose the labor readily attracted from other industries must be applied to fixed factors peculiar to this industry alone—as, for example, rare vineyard land for the wine industry. Then enhanced $DD$ for wine must intersect a rising $S_L S_L'$ long-run supply curve, as shown. Why rising? Recall the law of diminishing returns: varying labor, applied to fixed land, produces smaller and smaller increments of wine product; but each dose of labor costs the same in wages—and, hence, $MC$ of wine rises. This longest-run rising $MC$ means the supply curve must be rising.

It will be noted that in industries where $S_L S_L'$ slopes upward, owners of mines, land, know-how, and any other productive factors peculiar to this industry will earn a higher income (or what will be called "rent") from them as the industry expands.

If you do not like their earning such an extra return, you might take some of this away from them by taxes or other devices. But any special price ceilings placed on them in order to keep them from reaping such a return will definitely interfere with the equality-of-marginal-cost condition that is needed for maximal social efficiency—and such egalitarian legislation should be passed only if no better way of achieving this purpose can be found and the game is deemed worth the candle it will cost.

The relative rise in this industry's $P$ and in its peculiar-factors' prices is a fact, but it also can be termed a desirable fact. Why? Not because the consumers who must pay more for this good are undeserving, nor because owners of the peculiarly scarce productive factors are especially deserving of higher incomes. Then why? Because any expansion of $Q$ ought to be accomplished *efficiently* with least possible sacrifice of other $Q$s: the especially scarce factors have now to be severely rationed and be given more of other factors to work with; this will come about, not by a planning board's edict, but by a rise in the prices of this good and its peculiar factors, which will both signal the news of what must be done for efficiency and actually induce people to make the substitution needed if society is not to be inefficiently inside its *p-p frontier*.

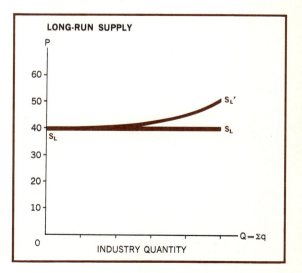

**FIG. 24-5**

Long-run industry supply depends on cost conditions
With entry and exit free and any number of firms able to produce on identical, unchanged cost curves, the long-run $S_L S_L$ curve will be horizontal at each firm's Break-even level. If industry cannot attract all the factors it uses at unchanged factor-prices, the $S_L S_L'$ supply curve will have to slope upward as each firm's cost curves are all shifted upward.

If entry is really free, not only has perfect competition the nice property of ensuring that *each firm* ends up on an efficient curve and at the minimum point on it, but in addition the Invisible Hand ensures that *industry* gets its Q from the proper number of firms as some are squeezed out or attracted in.[6]

## IMPLICIT- AND OPPORTUNITY-COST ELEMENTS: A DIGRESSION

It is important to stress that the "full competitive minimum costs" which have to be just covered by normal price include more than accountants usually include in costs. Economists include a normal return to management services, as determined competitively in all industries; and a normal return to capital, as determined competitively everywhere by industries of equal riskiness. In the above sense we may say that "normal profits" are included in costs and that "excess-profits" are competed away by entry of new firms, and "abnormal losses" are eliminated by long-run exit of firms.

**Implicit-cost elements**   The return to a factor of production is economically important regardless of how it happens to be owned. To the economist, the returns that go to factors of production owned by the firm itself are so important as to deserve a new name: in contrast to wages that are *explicitly* paid to outside labor, we defined the concept of "implicit wages" as the return to the labor provided by the owner himself; and similarly, implicit rent and interest would be the returns to the land and capital provided by the owner himself rather than hired from outside owners.

Through miscalculation, a person may fail to receive his implicit wages in the short run; on the other hand, he may in the short run be getting more than the needed implicit return, the difference being a transient profit that has not yet been competed away. If he owns some special factors of production, like rich ore land, exceptional know-how, or fertile soil, his accounts may show a high return even in the long run; but we realize this is not so much profit as a return to that special factor of production he is lucky enough to own.[7]

**Opportunity-cost elements**   Related to the above discussion is an even broader notion about cost. The man in the street can clearly recognize costs that are actual cash

---

[6]If industry demand is large enough to permit numerous firms, then the optimal quantity each firm should produce is at the bottom of its U. It can be proved that the no-profit no-loss condition of ruthless competition will then achieve the most efficient number of firms to *minimize TC* for the industry's Q. For why force more expensive extra output from an existing number of firms if it can be got cheaper by replication of firms? And why not be sure that each of the identical firms produces neither too much nor too little, instead producing that Break-even q where $P = MC$ and where, likewise, P equals the lowest Average Cost per unit that will keep the firm in business in the long run? (If market demand is not large enough to keep numerous competitors viable, there will arise problems connected with the discreteness of firm sizes that will be depicted in Fig. 25-2.) See question 10 for more on this.

[7]If he happens to own very fertile land and persists in cultivating it by uneconomical methods, he will be paying for his folly or stubbornness by forgoing the high return such land is capable of yielding; in dollars, the land becomes worth more to others than to him, and if he refuses to rent or sell it, he is as surely spending his sustenance to please his own tastes as he would be doing if he sold the land and spent the proceeds on wine, song, or being a country squire. A young person with high IQ and versatile talents who stays in a dull dead-end job or dying industry is similarly squandering his economic potential—but he may be happier that way.

payments; the accountant must go well beyond that. But the economist goes even further. He realizes that some of the most important costs attributable to doing one thing rather than another stem from the *forgone opportunities* that have to be sacrificed in doing this one thing. Thus, Robinson Crusoe pays no money to anyone, but realizes that the cost of picking strawberries can be thought of as the sacrificed amount of raspberries he might otherwise have picked with the same time and effort or the sacrificed amount of forgone-leisure. This sacrifice of doing something else is called "opportunity cost." (Note that opportunity cost would still exist even if he loves to spend that hour in doing both kinds of picking and recognizes not the slightest disutility or sweat in performing that type of work.)

How does all this apply to industry supply and the firm's Break-even costs? In this way: The long-run Break-even level of costs includes, in addition to *explicit* cost outlays, those *implicit* costs accruing to factors that might otherwise be used in alternative ways. If my labor in wheat could have been used in rye or even in some other man's wheat patch, then its value in those uses has to be met[8] or I shall not continue to supply it to my own wheat patch. For these reasons, full competitive cost intimately involves *opportunity cost.* The latter is an important concept, which covers much more territory than does the notion of implicit costs. The prices of labor and other factors that competitive farmers in an industry are forced to pay out explicitly depend importantly on the forgone opportunities for use in other industries or for leisure; and this means that all competitive costs involve opportunity costs in the background.

The terminology of economists is not uniform in this connection, but the concept of opportunity cost is important and we shall run into it again and again.

## DECREASING COSTS AND THE BREAKDOWN OF PERFECT COMPETITION

Economic textbooks of years ago used to supplement the cases of horizontal supply and upward-sloping supply by a third case in which Marginal Costs of the firms were *falling* rather than rising and in which this was thought to create an industry long-run supply curve that sloped gently downward. Actually, if we review our argument of page 456 telling us why a maximizing firm will want to produce where $MC = P$, we see that the argument *fails completely* in the case where the firm's $MC$ curve is a downward-sloping one. For, if you move to the right of a point on a falling $MC$ curve, you find that your additional $P$ per unit is in excess of the now lower $MC$; and so, in the case of decreasing Marginal Cost, the firm will expand its output more and more beyond the $MC$ curve to gain extra profit.

Under decreasing Marginal Cost, the first firm to get a head start will find its *advantage increasing the greater it grows!* As it forces other firms to contract their $q$s, their disadvantage will become aggravated as they are forced to travel back up their falling $MC$ curves.

---

[8]The *best* alternative use is of course the proper one to use in reckoning opportunity cost. If alternatives exist along an infinite and smooth continuum, such opportunity cost will set a tight limit on costs to this industry. If alternatives come in steps, then the next-best alternative may give us only a lower limit on factor-price, leaving a possible area in which it has to be determined by the "rent" analysis of Part Four.

The result must be obvious:

Under persisting decreasing costs for the firms, one or a few of them will so expand their *q*s as to become a significant part of the market for the industry's total *Q*. We shall then end up with one of the following three cases:

1. A single monopolist who dominates the industry

2. A few large sellers who together dominate the industry and who will later be called "oligopolists"

3. Some kind of imperfection of competition that, in either a stable way or a series of intermittent price wars, represents an important departure from the economist's model of "perfect" competition wherein no firm has any control over industry price

As the next section will show, when the firms in this industry all expand together, they could create what are called *external economies* (or *diseconomies*). Thus, a school for fishermen might become feasible only at high industry *Q*; and this training might cause a downward shift of every firm's cost curves as the industry total *Q* rises. The result could be an industry $S_L S_L$ curve that slopes *downward* owing to *external* economies. But this does not deny the fact that ("internally") decreasing cost for a firm destroys perfect competition, as Chapter 25 will discuss further.

### EXTERNAL ECONOMIES AND DISECONOMIES[9]

Our discussion of decreasing costs has shown that it would be wrong to draw a curve of downward-sloping industry supply based upon costs falling *internally* within the firm. There is, however, a possible theoretical case in which the expansion of the industry's *Q* somehow causes each firm's cost curves as plotted against its *q* to *shift downward*. Alfred Marshall deemed this a case of downward-sloping industry supply based upon what he called *external* economies.

An "external economy" is defined as a *favorable effect* on one or more persons that emanates from the action of a different person or firm; it shifts the cost or utility curve of each person it helps, and such an *externally* caused shift should be distinguished from any *internal* movement along the affected individual's own cost curve.

An "external *dis*economy" is defined in the same way, except that it refers to external *harm* that is done to others. The case where expansion of fishing by others in limited waters serves to shift up each boat's cost curves would be an example of an external diseconomy; another case would be one where each man's haste to drill for oil near his neighbors' boundaries lowers the amount of oil ever recovered. Smoke nuisance and water pollution are two familiar other instances.

External economies have a considerable importance in connection with government activities that provide benefits to many individuals (so-called "public goods"). They are important too in connection with growth, where the building of a public road or some kind of "social overhead capital" like a hospital or dam has favorable external repercussions on many families, firms, and industries. The kinds of favorable external economies that are peculiarly associated with expansions along an industry supply curve—our main subject here—are not so easy to find. But here are a few examples.

As fishing *Q* expands, the number of trained fishermen that any firm might find to

---

[9]This section is independent of the rest of the chapter.

hire may go up. Or it may now pay the government, or some profit-seeking monopolist, to build a training school for fishermen, whereas previously such a school could not pay because of its high marginal cost at low scales of operation. A similar case would be one where specialized machinery for the fishing industry was producible by another industry only at decreasing marginal cost. Or if all of us in a neighborhood keep bees, I may find that I gain more wandering bees from your nearby acres when total $Q$ of the honey industry rises; whereas, when total honey $Q$ is small, I find that some of my bees wander uselessly off to neighboring cornland and my neighboring corn-grower has few bees that might in return wander back to me. Or one might conjure up the case where, when I drain my mine of water, I cannot help but make your neighboring mine somewhat drier and thereby confer an external economy on you.

It is easier to find examples of so-called "external diseconomies" resulting from higher industry $Q$. Recall that these are defined as harmful effects upon other people that result from one man's production. Thus, expanding along a supply curve for steel will cause great belching forth of smoke. This external effect is not only a nuisance, it may actually be harmful to good health and costly in terms of needed cleaning bills. Smog in many cities comes from the external diseconomies of each man's auto and factory. The greatest external diseconomy of all results from one country's setting off nuclear bombs and filling the whole atmosphere with radioactive fallout.

One does not need the case of the nuclear bomb to know that, *Wherever there are externalities, a strong case can be made for supplanting complete individualism by some kind of group action:* consumers should be made to pay for the smoke damage that their purchases make inevitable, as would be the case if we supplemented laissez faire by a tax or by coercive ordinances; a conservation subsidy to farmers, so that they will keep trees growing and thereby prevent disastrous floods hundreds of miles downstream, might represent rational social policy; regulations that prevent small-holders from digging oil wells frenziedly at the edge of their neighbors' property would be economically efficient. The reader can think of countless other externalities where sound economics would suggest some limitations on individual freedom in the interest of all.[10]

[10] The late Professor A. C. Pigou, Marshall's prize pupil at Cambridge, was the economist who most emphasized the problem of externalities. There is a clear-cut economic case for a tax (or a subsidy) whenever an external diseconomy (or economy) creates a divergence between private pecuniary Marginal Cost as seen by a firm and true social Marginal Cost. But this truth is quite independent of the supply slope of the industry in question. And Marshall and Pigou erred in thinking that a tax should be put on an industry whose supply curve rises, in the fashion of Fig. 24-5, because some *pecuniary* factor-costs are raised to the firm externally by the expansion of industry $Q$—as Allyn Young pointed out some sixty years ago. We may add, they also erred in thinking an industry should be subsidized if its $SS$ curve slopes down because of pecuniary reductions in its input prices, reductions which shift firms' curves down externally: so long as government assures that such an input is sold at *its* declining $MC$ price, the pecuniary external economy it creates for *our* industry can be safely ignored. Young correctly emphasized that external *technological* economies and diseconomies merit interference. He showed that rent collecting on private property in land succeeds in preventing it from becoming overcrowded by rugged individualists. Similarly, in the case of overcrowded fishing waters, subdividing the sea might somewhat reduce social inefficiencies; but certain government fees and rules of the road might well be devised which would do still better than would ordinary private ownership of the sea's acres.

No more need be said at this point about externalities. They can shift firm cost curves and thereby alter the slope of industry supply curves upward and downward. But even more important is their general role in connection with causing free pricing to be nonoptimal, thereby creating a prima facie case for zoning laws, government controls, effluent taxes and penalties, and alert planning. Again and again we shall be returning to the important subject of externalities.

The main cost concepts, and their relation to supply in the short and the long run, have now been introduced. In the next chapter we can pit cost against revenue to learn how any firm finds its Maximum-profit equilibrium.

## SUMMARY

1   Total Cost can usefully be broken down into its Fixed and Variable Cost components. *FC* cancels out of all decisions relevant to the period for which it is truly fixed.

2   Marginal Cost is the increment of extra Total Cost resulting from one increment of extra $q$. (If our units are divisible, *MC* can be defined as the slope of the smooth *TC* curve at any $q$ point, and this slope will give a close approximation to the extra cost of producing one more small $q$ increment.)

3   Average (total) Cost, *AC*, is the sum of ever-declining Average Fixed Cost and of usually U-shaped Average Variable Cost. *AC* is U-shaped, being intersected at its bottom by the rising *MC* curve. Similarly, *AVC* is cut by *MC* at its bottom.[11]

4   In the long run, when all fixed commitments expire and a firm is free to plan to operate any number of plants, the long-run cost curve *LAC* (and *LTC*) must be the lower-envelope frontier of best choice of plant for each level of output. This frontier will be a smooth envelope, containing at any point a tangential short-run cost curve, if potential plant sizes are smoothly continuous. Usually the long-run curve *LAC*, and its associated marginal curve, will be U-shaped: ultimately it will rise if not all factors of production (including management) are expandable at constant prices; and at very small outputs, indivisibilities in the inputs or the methods of combining them will cause costs initially to fall.

5   An industry's long-run supply curve, $S_L S_L$, must take into account the entry of new firms and exodus of old ones. In the long run, all the commitments of any firm will expire, and it will decide to stay in business only if price at least covers all its long-run costs—whether they be "explicit" out-of-pocket payments to labor, lenders, material suppliers, or landlords; or whether they be "implicit" wages (defined as the "opportunity costs" of its owners' labor which could be employed elsewhere in producing or in leisure) or implicit interest and rent on the property assets owned by the firm (and whose opportunity costs are measured by what they will fetch in other equally risky uses).

[11]See no. 9 in the Questions for Discussion section for useful rules about *AC* and *MC* curves.

6  Under conditions of free entry, where no one firm has any particular advantages of location, skill, or resources specialized to this industry, one can expect in the long run that free entry of would-be competitors will compete away any excess profits earned by existing firms in the industry. So, just as free exit means *P* cannot fall below the Break-even point, free entry means it cannot persist above that point in the long-run equilibrium. Where an industry can expand by replication without pushing up the prices of any factors peculiar to it or used in peculiarly large proportions by it, the resulting long-run supply curve will be horizontal. More likely, any but the smallest industry will generally use some factors of production in large enough amounts to force up their prices slightly. As a result, its long-run supply curve will be sloping upward, at least gently.[12]

7  It is not true that *downward*-sloping Marginal Cost curves of competitive firms can serve as their supply curves—for the very good reason that their profits will be at a minimum along such curves and they will rush away in either direction from such points. As a result, one or a few firms will tend to expand and the remaining firms will tend to contract. Thus lasting decreasing costs that are *internal* to firms implies destruction of perfect competition. So it is wrong to talk of decreasing supply curves in such a case, or of competitive supply at all.

8  There is, however, the possibility that *external economies* could prevail in an industry. In such cases expansion of *industry Q* could *shift* downward the cost curves of *single firms;* and in the complicated adding of the resulting supplies of all firms, the industry supply curve could end up as downward-sloping.

   The concept of external economies or diseconomies is important beyond any such Marshallian application to industry supply. By definition, such externalities involve good and bad economic effects *upon others* resulting from one's own behavior. Since in the search for individual gain and well-being, one person takes into account only private money benefits and costs as seen by him, there will then be a divergence between *social* costs and *pecuniary-private* costs. This means that there is a prima facie case in such instances for group action, by subsidy or public control, to expand situations fraught with external economies; and a similar case to contract, by tax or fiat, activities involving external diseconomies.

## CONCEPTS FOR REVIEW

Total Costs: Fixed and Variable
$TC = FC + VC$
$AC = TC/q = AFC + AVC$
Marginal Cost (incremental and
   smoothed)

Shut-down point at
   $P = MC = $ Min $AVC$
horizontal and rising $S_L S_L$
implicit costs and opportunity
   costs

[12]Or in extreme cases, where the labor it uses actually is supplied by families in reduced amounts when $Q$ expansion bids up the wage, the industry $S_L S_L$ curve could even bend backward toward the northwest, as in Case 4 of the Appendix of Chapter 20.

<table>
<tr><td>long-run envelope of cost, *LAC*<br>and *LMC*</td><td>decreasing costs and breakdown<br>of competition</td></tr>
<tr><td>Break-even point at<br>$P = MC = $ Min *AC*</td><td>external economies, diseconomies,<br>and public policy</td></tr>
</table>

## QUESTIONS FOR DISCUSSION

1  Make a list of cost elements: wages, salaries, fuel, rentals, etc. Divide into Fixed and Variable categories. (Your division will depend on your time periods.)

2  Explain the difference between Marginal Cost and Average Cost. Why should *AVC* always look much like *MC*? Why is *MC* the same when computed from *VC* as from *TC*?

3  To the $55 of Fixed Cost of Table 24-1, add $90 of additional *FC*. Now calculate a whole new table, with the same *VC* as before but new *FC* = $145. What happens to *MC*, *AVC*? To *TC*, *AC*, *AFC*? Can you verify that minimum *AC* is now at $q^* = 5$ with *AC* = $60 = *MC*? (You can check *MC* and *TC* of your table against Chapter 25's Table 25-3.)

4  Explain why *MC* cuts *AC* and *AVC* at the bottom of their U's. Recall, in connection with Chapter 23, that minimum *AVC* can be shown to provide the short-run Shutdown point, and minimum *AC* to provide the long-run Break-even point.

5  Explain how the long-run envelope cost curve is defined as the lower frontier of all short-run curves. Illustrate with (*a*) the case of a few plant sizes, and (*b*) the case of infinitely-continuous plant sizes.

6  Relate the rising *MC* curve to the law of diminishing returns. Contrast the falling part of the curve with that law.

7  Interpret this dialogue. *A*: "How can competitive profits be zero in the long run? Who'll work for nothing?" *B*: "It is only *excess*-profits that are wiped out by competition. Managers get paid for their work; owners get a normal return on their capital in long-run equilibrium—no more and no less."

8  Give examples of external economies. External diseconomies. What public interferences might you possibly suggest? What rights to sue in court?

9  *Extra-credit problem:* With the help of the adjoining diagram, puzzle out the meaning of the following rules. *First rule:* If a Marginal Cost curve is below its associated Average Cost curve, it is pulling the *AC* curve down; if *MC* is above *AC*, it is pulling *AC* up; if *MC* = *AC*, *AC* must be horizontal. *Second rule:* If *AC* is a straight line, as in (a), (b), or (c), *MC* will be a straight line starting from the same vertical intercept point but with twice the slope of *AC*. (NOTE: This tells us how to find the *MC* point above or below the *AC* point on *any* non-straight-line *AC* curve. At a chosen *q* in (d), merely draw the tangent straight line to *AC*; from that line's vertical intercept, draw an *MC* line with twice the

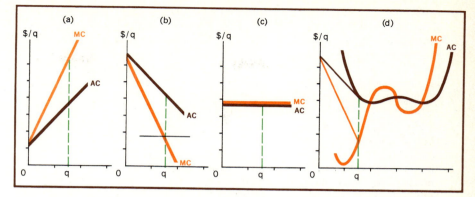

slope; read off from this last line the *MC* value at your chosen *q* level. Of course, you must draw two new straight lines for every different *q* level.) Final query: Note fine black line in (b); label it *dd* for perfect-competitor's demand. Shade in triangle formed between *dd* and *MC* and note that you gain by increasing your *q* indefinitely!

10  *Extra-credit problem:* Can you interpret the diagram below to show that society does get industry *Q* at lowest dollar and resource cost when each of many firms is at bottom of its U-shaped *AC*? First U on left comes with 1 firm. Second U comes with *Q* divided equally between 2 firms (so second U is merely the first with twice the horizontal scale; and similarly for the *n* = 3, 4, . . . U's). Beyond the // break, *n* is large—say, 100 firms. Naturally, industry *Q* is procured at least cost on *heavy lower curve*, with lower and lower green switch points at which it just pays to add one new firm. Then to see how costs *for each typical firm* drop as *Q* and *n* grow, concentrate on the markings on the left side of the first

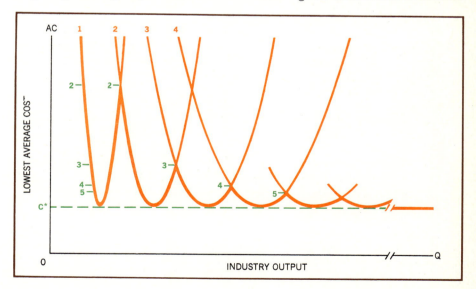

U. With $n = 1$, the sky is the limit. For $n = 2$, the green 2 shows highest that $AC$ can ever be for any firm; for $n = 3$, green 3 gives lower highest $AC$; and green numbers (which are drawn at exact level corresponding to respective switch points) drop to minimum $AC$ when $DD$ is big enough for numerous competitors to survive. So beyond the // break, with many firms, the heavy industry curve looks smoothly horizontal.

11  *Extra-credit problem:* Interpret the accompanying diagrams. (*a*) The first three depict Adam Smith's labor theory of value: each 1 hour's labor catches 1 beaver; each 2 hours' labor catches 1 deer; then long-run supply curves are constant or horizontal; then the production-possibility frontier is a straight line, with relative prices or exchange values set by embodied labor requirements of 2 to 1. (*b*) The second three diagrams depict a case where scarce Ricardian land and diminishing returns (to labor producing corn) destroys the labor theory of value and produces cornland rent. As people demand more corn, the corn industry moves on its rising $MC$ or $S_C S_C$ curve. The rising corn receipts are divided between variable labor costs (the dark brown area under the $MC$ curve) and between competitively bid-up land rent (the light brown area, often called by economists "producers' rent" or "producers' surplus"). By contrast, since haircuts need labor only, $S_h S_h$ is horizontal. Why is the *p-p* frontier for corn and haircuts concave from below?

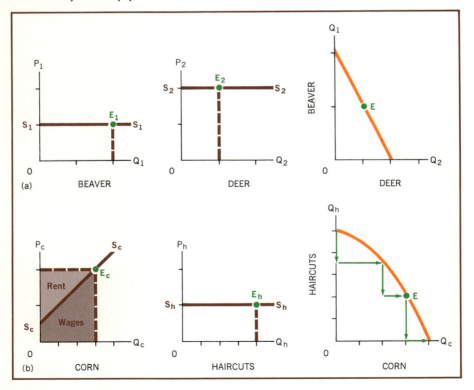

In the last several chapters we have studied the workings of competitive supply and demand in considerable detail. For the most part, we have been studying the case called "perfect competition."

Perfect competition means something very definite to the economist. As we saw, the economist means something *much stronger* by it than the man in the street and the businessman do when they talk of "strong rivalry and keen competition among different business firms and industries."

The special case of perfect competition is very important. But it is only one case, and economists pay it so much attention because of the light it throws on the *efficiency* of resource use. Certainly, it cannot faithfully represent many of the facts about modern industries. The real world—as we know it in America, Europe, or Asia—contains significant *mixtures of monopoly imperfections* along with *elements of competition*. The real world, then, is for the most part to be classified in the realm of "imperfect competition": it is neither perfectly competitive nor perfectly monopolistic.

The remaining chapters of Part Three, therefore, will give us the tools to analyze imperfect as well as perfect competition. They will show what modifications have to be made in any conclusions that were based on an analysis of perfect competition. We shall see that the way a pricing system succeeds in solving the basic problems of WHAT, HOW, and FOR WHOM is affected to an important degree by any elements of monopolistic imperfection that may be involved in numerous modern industries.

Part A of this chapter gives an overview of *patterns of imperfect competition and of real-world market structure*. It also presents a new important tool—the concept of Marginal Revenue. Part B portrays the equilibrium analysis of an idealized monopoly firm, to show how it *achieves maximization of profit by balancing its Marginal Cost and Marginal Revenue*. We then are ready to appraise at the end of this chapter the *inefficiency* inherent in imperfection of competition, and to develop in the Appendix some principles of public regulation.

# 25

# MAXIMUM-PROFIT EQUILIBRIUM: MONOPOLY

Both monopolistic and competitive forces combine in the determination of most prices.
EDWARD H. CHAMBERLIN

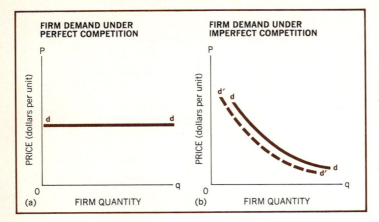

**FIRM DEMAND UNDER PERFECT COMPETITION**

(a)    FIRM QUANTITY

**FIRM DEMAND UNDER IMPERFECT COMPETITION**

(b)    FIRM QUANTITY

**FIG. 25-1**
**Acid test for imperfect competition is downward tilt of firm's demand**
The perfect-competitor firm can sell all it wants to along its horizontal *dd* curve, never depressing market price. But the imperfect-competitor firm will find that its demand curve slopes downward as its increased *q* forces down the *P* it can get. And unless it is a sheltered monopolist, a cut in its rivals' *Ps* will appreciably shift its own *dd* leftward to *d'd'*.

## A. OVERVIEW OF MARKET STRUCTURE, AND THE CONCEPT OF MARGINAL REVENUE

### PERFECT COMPETITION CONTRASTED WITH IMPERFECT COMPETITION

Figure 25-1(a) reminds us that, to an economist, a perfect-competitor is defined as a firm that has no control over price—in the sense that the firm faces an essentially *horizontal dd* curve along which it can sell as much or as little output as it likes.

Remember how strict this definition of perfect competition is. Think of any commodity that comes to mind: razor blades, toothpaste, steel, aluminum, potatoes, wheat, cigarettes, tobacco, nylon, cotton. Which will fit in with our strict definition? Certainly not razor blades or toothpaste or cigarettes. Who ever heard of an auction market for blades, toothpaste, or cigarettes?

Neither aluminum nor steel meets the definition of perfect competition. For a long time there was only one aluminum company, Alcoa (Aluminum Company of America); and even today there are only Alcoa, Reynolds, Kaiser, and one or two others. Contrast this with the case of thousands, if not millions, of cotton and wheat farmers.

What about steel? United States Steel and Bethlehem are the industry giants. Together with Republic Steel, Jones & Laughlin, and the few others that constitute Little Steel, they produce a large fraction of the total market. It is true that one plant's steel output may be much like another's, but it is not true that Bethlehem and Republic are so weak that each could never depress the price of steel by throwing on the market as much as it could comfortably produce.

When you go down the above list, you will find that only potatoes, tobacco, wheat, and cotton come within our strict definition of perfect competition. Nylon must compete with cotton; that is very true. But in the economist's strict sense, nylon is not a product supplied under "perfect competition," nor is each of its few producers a "perfect-competitor" in the economist's sense of the term.[1]

---

[1] Sometimes economists use various synonyms for perfect competition: they often call it "pure competition," in contrast to "impure, or imperfect, or monopolistic competition"; or they occasionally call it "atomistic competition," to convey the notion of numerous small firms which combine like a multitude of tiny atoms to make up the industry. Occasionally, too, an economist will say: "By

## IMPERFECT COMPETITION DEFINED

But suppose the single firm finds itself facing a demand curve which slopes appreciably downward as in Fig. 25-1(b)—which means that when it insists on throwing more on the market, it definitely does depress price along its *dd* curve—then the firm is classified by the economist as an "imperfect competitor."

*Definition:* "Imperfect competition" prevails in an industry or group of industries wherever the individual sellers are imperfect competitors, facing their own *nonhorizontal dd* curves and thereby having some measure of control over price.

This does not mean that a firm has absolute monopoly power over the price it can charge; as we shall see, there are varying degrees of monopolistic imperfection in different imperfectly competitive markets.[2]

Mind you, we are not saying that the owner of an imperfectly competitive firm is of poor character, that he beats his wife, or fails to pay his bills. Nor does the fact that a firm is an imperfect competitor mean that it is not keenly seeking to outsell and outadvertise its rivals. Intense commercial rivalry and "perfect competition" are not at all the same thing; indeed, Farmer Jones, perfect-competitor, will do no advertising at all. Why should he? He can sell all the wheat he can produce without depressing market price. But American Products Co., producer of Pall Mall, Lucky Strikes, and other cigarettes, and an imperfect competitor, will spend much of its energies in trying to outsell Winston, Kent, and other brands, the snuff industry, and even the candy industry.

## COST PATTERNS AND STRUCTURE OF MARKET IMPERFECTION

At the end of Chapter 24 we saw that continuing decreasing cost is incompatible with perfect competition. If every, or even *any*, firm in an industry could always bring down its Marginal and Average Cost in the long run merely by expanding its output $q$, it would soon expand to become an important fraction of the industry. In short, it would expand to become some kind of monopolist, ceasing to be a price taker and now having some measure of control over the price it gets. As soon as it has control over price, it will cease to follow the $P = MC$ rule for profit maximization. Presently we shall see why. And as soon as somebody in the system raises Price above Marginal Cost, a critic is able to find a flaw of inefficiency in the economic organization of society.

---

perfect, I mean really perfect. The wheat market isn't 'perfect competition' unless everyone in it is perfectly *informed* about all the future, there being nowhere any *uncertainty*." However, that is not the sense used here for perfect competition. The price of wheat will fluctuate in a way that no one can now foresee, but as long as *no seller can appreciably influence wheat price*, we shall agree to call the wheat market *perfect*. (Naturally, once you bring government control programs into the wheat picture, as in Chapter 21, you are bringing monopolistic imperfections into this perfect-competition setup.)

[2] The standard book on all this is E. H. Chamberlin, *Theory of Monopolistic Competition* (Harvard University Press, Cambridge, Mass., 1963, 8th ed.). Chamberlin prefers the term "monopolistic competition" for what is here called "imperfect competition," but that may give the impression to the layman that there is something especially nasty, or illegal, in not being a perfect-competitor, which is not Chamberlin's view. Also, confusion can result from the fact that "monopolistic competition" is sometimes used by Chamberlin as a name for Fig. 26-3's special large-group case of symmetric sellers of differentiated products, an ambiguous usage avoided in this book.

Figure 25-2 illustrates some patterns of costs that lead to a breakdown of perfect competition. In Fig. 25-2(a), the firm is shown to have Average and Marginal Costs that fall forever. It displays "increasing returns to scale": as $q$ grows, the firm finds more elaborate ways of specializing its equipment; it organizes its work gangs in larger and more efficient units; it can afford ever-larger boilers and machines, which display greater net efficiency. All this without end. No matter how big is the demand for its product—no matter how far out the industry $DD$ curve happens to lie, the most efficient operating size for this one firm will be greater, and peaceful competitive coexistence of thousands of price takers will be quite impossible.

Perhaps the pattern of unlimited decreasing cost is unrealistic. Perhaps *ultimately* the economies of scale will all have been achieved, and the cost curves will level out or turn up. Figure 25-2(b) shows such a case: the firm's long-run $MC$ and $AC$ curves do finally turn up. But, alas, they do not turn up soon enough to avoid the breakdown of perfect competition. For note where the industry total demand curve $DD$ now lies: it does not provide a big enough market to enable *numerous* firms to coexist at the efficient level of operation called for by the indicated cost curve. We shall still end up in some kind of monopoly or few-seller "oligopoly" situation. (*Oligos* means "few" in Greek.)

In Fig. 25-2(c), the outlook is more favorable for perfect competition. Why? Because the industry $DD$ (even in each local market) is so great compared with the optimum size of each firm, we can hope to replicate the large number of firms needed for truly perfect competition.

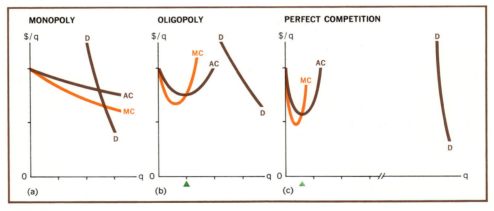

**FIG. 25-2**

**To avoid monopoly or oligopoly, average costs must turn upward soon**

When costs fall indefinitely, as in (a), any one firm can expand to monopolize the industry. In (b), costs eventually turn up, but not soon enough relative to total industry demand $DD$. Coexistence of numerous perfect-competitors is impossible; some kind of few-seller oligopoly is likely. In (c), total industry demand $DD$ is so vast relative to efficient scale of any one seller as to permit viable coexistence of numerous *perfect-competitors*. [What if firms contrive to differentiate their product in (c), fragmenting the market and moving $DD$ far to left, ending in some kind of Chamberlinian imperfect competition—like (b) or (a)?]

There is one encouraging feature of the modern industrial state. Large corporations find it pays them to produce many *different* products, not just the single q shown in these diagrams. Thus, Ford produces trucks, tractors, refrigerators, precision equipment, and not just automobiles. It is a big company—but it is really not big in the refrigerator or tractor or equipment markets. It must compete with G.E., Deere, Litton Industries, Sears, IBM, and other giants in these markets. As far as producing more refrigerators is concerned, its costs will *not* continue to fall, as in Fig. 25-2(a) or (b), until it has a dominant position. Actually, because of the *competition of numerous other conglomerate giants*, Ford's costs relative to each diverse market's demand might look more like that of Fig. 25-2(c). The result is encouraging because it may lead to a tolerable approach to the P and MC equivalences of efficient, perfect competition.

As Adam Smith said, "Specialization is limited by the extent of the market." He meant by this that you often cannot use the most efficient known methods when serving a *small* market. And this provided him with good ammunition for attacking the mercantilistic interferences by governments of his time that served to fragment the DD demands into many smaller DD demands—one for each country or county. He might have gone on to add this:

If you are *still* in the stage where efficient specialization is being limited by the extent of the market, then you are not yet in the state appropriate for perfect competition; instead, not-yet-exhausted economies of scale leave you in some area of imperfect or monopolistic competition. In such a case there is all the more reason for society to promote measures that will extend the market.

One more important point. Suppose we begin in the Fig. 25-2(c) situation where DD is big enough relative to the efficient size of firm operation to permit coexistence of numerous viable competitors. But suppose something arises to fragment the aggregate DD demand into much smaller separate demands for the different firms. Then perfect competition will be dethroned. Since the new DD curve confronting any firm or segment of the market will then be moved far to the left, we are really put back in Fig. 25-2(b) or even 25-2(a).

Such a case arises when restrictive tariffs are used to fragment markets and create a monopolistic situation. "The tariff is the Mother of trusts," is a slogan from American history showing that even the man in the street understands the point. And one of the purposes of the Marshall Plan for reconstructing Europe was to help pave the way for the Common Market, so that DD curves would become large enough relative to efficient production levels to promote vigorous and effective competition.

## DIFFERENTIATION OF PRODUCTS

What is not so obvious is that the DD demand curves for an industry can be *deliberately fragmented* into smaller segments by the profit-seeking activities of firms. This is what the late Edward Chamberlin of Harvard called "differentiation of product."

**Contrived product differentiation**   Each seller tries to make his product a little different from that of any other sellers. He avoids the price competition of classical "perfect competition." Instead, he introduces brand quality competition, precisely because it is a profitable form of imperfect competition.

EXAMPLE: He makes penicillin a little different chemically. He seeks patent protection. He advertises, or sends so-called "detail men" to call on doctors, to make them think his penicillin is different, whether or not it significantly is; or more important, he advertises so that you will attach significance to such differences as are there.

What results when everyone successfully differentiates his product? The result is that the *DD* curves of Fig. 25-2(c)'s model of perfect competition are contracted so far to the left as to become like those of the models of monopoly or oligopoly shown in Fig. 25-2(a) and (b). Fortunately, each firm is not able at will to differentiate its product successfully to any degree that it wishes, even though Galbraithian converts do exaggerate the unilateral power of advertisers.

Chamberlin would agree with much said here. But he would resent the implication that all product differentiation is an artificial, contrived thing whose only purpose is to increase monopoly power and bilk the consumer. Rather, he would insist that people's tastes differ: different people want different degrees of sourness of cider; and even the same person may not want all his units of cider to be of the same sourness. Creating a great variety of differentiated products is often, Chamberlin insists, a genuine catering to basic human wants and needs. Chamberlin does not agree that we would be better off if we all agreed to wear a few basic styles of clothes, each produced in long and efficient factory runs. He would stress that all tastes, including noble tastes for Bach and Rembrandt, are made by society rather than arising from the individual himself. The change of fashion, frivolous though it be, adds zest to life.

In effect, Chamberlin is reemphasizing *the importance of decreasing costs* in making perfect competition *unviable*. He is saying, "Once we replace a homogeneous output $Q$ of the industry (or what is the same thing, the homogeneous output $q$ of a typical firm) by a whole complex of somewhat different $Q_1, Q_2, \ldots$, then the demands will just *not* be big enough to permit you to have many different producers at the bottom of their efficient U-shaped cost curves." Chamberlin is arguing, "You think that as *DD* grows in Fig. 25-2(b), with population or for any other reason, society will move from the imperfect-competition model of (b) to the perfect-competition model of (c). But you are wrong. With the *bigger scale* of *DD* will come a bigger opportunity for making *more*, and more minute, *differentiations of product*."

**Natural product differentiation** Even if we do not agree with Chamberlin's implication that the world is perpetually assigned to the realm of imperfect competition regardless of increases in scale, we must concede that he does have a valid and important point. His general *Weltanschauung*—that the economic world cannot be properly understood in terms of the simple models of perfect competition or complete monopoly, but must be interpreted in terms of a richer theory that involves phenomena not to be described as mere blends of these polar cases—is made more convincing by the following:

**Products are often differentiated by natural as well as man-made causes. Spatial distance itself, and the transport costs associated with it, provides one important example.**

Consider the steel industry. It involves very large-scale production. Yet this is a big country. So you might argue that we can tolerate numerous replications of the most efficient-sized plant. But what follows? The United States does not constitute one single market for steel. Because of transport costs, each region and each part of each region provide us with relevant *DD* curves to compare with the efficient large-scale U of cost. It would be ridiculous to think that even New York City could have the dozens or hundreds of independent integrated steel producers needed for the market model of perfect competition. And if the lobbyists of the steel industry got the import quotas they crave, the departure from competitive *MC* pricing would become even worse.

Similarly with electric-power production. In order to reach minimum Average Cost, one might today want to build a generating plant of more than 2 million kilowatts of capacity. But that efficient size is already much too big for perfect competition to prevail. Any *compact region* that had 10 such competing plants would be plagued with dreadful overcapacity.

We may conclude as follows:

Patterns of returns in which costs still decline relative to the effective size of the market imperil the realism of perfect competition and of *P = MC* efficient social pricing. This problem is accentuated by man-made or natural differentiations of product which lower the effective *DD* levels of demands relative to the bottom of the U levels of efficient production, making competitive coexistence of numerous competing units simply nonviable.

On the other hand, if larger firms produce many, many different kinds of products, each firm may be checked in its monopoly power in any one market by the fact that it meets the competition of *many* other large, conglomerate firms in each separate line.

Let us now survey the principal patterns of imperfections of competition.

## IMPERFECT COMPETITION: MONOPOLY, OLIGOPOLY, AND DIFFERENTIATED PRODUCTS

**Monopoly**   How imperfect can imperfect competition get? The extreme case would be that of a *single* seller with practically complete monopoly power. (He is called a "monopolist," from the Greek word *mono* for "one" and *polist* for "seller.") He is the only one producing in his industry, and there is no industry producing a close substitute for his good. [Back in Fig. 25-1(b) on page 484, a change in another firm's price would shift his *dd* curve negligibly.]

Exclusive monopolies, like public utilities or telephones, are usually regulated by the government; and even they must usually take account of the potential competition of alternative products—oil for coal, or cables for telephones. This shows how relatively unimportant complete monopolies are.

**Oligopoly**   We have seen that this horrible-sounding word means "few sellers." Oligopolists are of two types.

First, an oligopolist may be one of a *few* sellers who produce an *identical* (or almost identical) product. Thus, if A's steel delivered in the New York area is much the same as B's, then the smallest price cut will drive the consumer from A to B. Neither A nor B can be called a monopolist. Yet, if the number of sellers is few, each can have a great effect on market price.

This first kind of oligopoly is thought to be common in a number of our basic industries where *product is fairly homogeneous* and size of enterprise is large—as in the aluminum and nylon industries. Another example would be that of moving freight between New York and Chicago by any of the three or four alternative rail routes.

In the old days when rail rates were unregulated, there would be periodic price wars in which each railroad undercut the other in an attempt to gain more of the business: sometimes it would become cheaper to move freight from New York to Chicago than to move it from New York to Buffalo; and occasionally cheaper to move freight from New York to Buffalo via Chicago, with all the implied wasteful crosshaulage.

The second kind of oligopoly is typified by the case where there are *few* sellers who sell *differentiated* (rather than identical) products. The Big Three in the auto industry are examples: three producers dominate the industry, but the Fords, Chevrolets, and Plymouths that they make are *somewhat differentiated* products. In the cigarette industry, a few large sellers own the numerous brands and types (filter, king-size, and regular) that compete for and get the bulk of the business. In heavy machinery, such companies as General Electric, Westinghouse, Allis-Chalmers, and others illustrate the case of an oligopoly that has few sellers and some differentiation of product.

**Many differentiated sellers**   This is the last in our list of imperfect competitors. Here there are many sellers, but now they do *not* produce *identical* products as in the case of many perfect-competitors. Instead, they produce "differentiated products," i.e., products which differ somewhat in real qualities or which the buyer thinks differ in real qualities. My toothpaste is a little different from yours; and if I raise my price above yours, I may still hope to sell a good deal to those consumers conditioned by my advertising or by past use of my product.

Advertising, brand names, trademarks, patents, and custom may explain why there is product differentiation. Or it may merely be that a given barber shop or grocery store is in a locality near to certain consumers: the fact of this nearness may give it a measure of monopoly power; and yet, if its price gets too high, it will find itself losing trade to more distant competitors. [This time back in Fig. 25-1(b), when your rivals cut their *P*, your *dd* curve shifts leftward and downward *appreciably*.]

All these four categories of market structure overlap. They range in degree from perfect competition to a large number of differentiated sellers, to the two kinds of oligopoly, and finally to the limiting case of monopoly.

## BRIEF SUMMARY OF KINDS OF COMPETITION AND MARKET STRUCTURE

Table 25-1 gives a picture of the various possible categories of imperfect and perfect competition. It merits close study, for we shall later examine each of its cases.

The remainder of this chapter will analyze the principles of profit maximization, concentrating mostly on the limiting case of a complete monopoly. As has been mentioned, few firms in real life enjoy anything like a complete monopoly: usually some other products will be partially substitutable for the ones you sell. If for some unnatural reason you were in a position of practically unchecked monopoly, we can be sure that the modern mixed economy would make you subject to public regulation. The example of public regulation of such utilities as electricity, gas, and telephones comes immediately to mind; and by the end of the chapter we shall be in a position to understand the proper principle of monopoly regulation (as in the Appendix).

| TYPES OF COMPETITION | | | | |
|---|---|---|---|---|
| KIND OF COMPETITION | NUMBER OF PRO- DUCERS AND DEGREE OF PRODUCT DIF- FERENTIATION | PART OF ECONOMY WHERE PREVALENT | DEGREE OF CONTROL OVER PRICE | METHODS OF MARKETING |
| **Perfect competition** | Many producers; identical products | A few agricultural industries | None | Market exchange or auction |
| **Imperfect competition:** Many differ- entiated sellers | Many producers; many real or fancied differences in product | Toothpastes, retail trade; conglom- erates | Some | Advertising and quality rivalry; administered prices |
| Oligopoly | Few producers; little or no difference in product | Steel, aluminum | | |
| | Few producers; some differentiation of products | Autos, machinery | | |
| **Complete monopoly** | Single producer; unique product without close substitutes | A few utilities | Considerable | Promotional and "institutional" public-relations advertising |

TABLE 25-1

**Most industries are imperfectly competitive—a blend of monopoly and competition**

The tools useful to understand Maximum-profit equilibrium for the complete mo- nopoly—namely, Marginal Cost and Marginal Revenue—turn out to be the tools needed to understand Maximum-profit equilibrium in the more realistic cases of oligopoly and various forms of imperfect competition. They lay the groundwork for Chapter 26's antitrust policies of government to prevent and control monopolies.

## PRICE, QUANTITY, AND TOTAL REVENUE

What is the Maximum-profit output $q$ that a monopolist will try to produce in any situation? What is the accompanying Maximum-profit price $P$ that it should charge?

It turns out that old and new *marginal* concepts provide the key to the common-sense trial-and-error procedure of maximizing profit. The final results will agree with com- mon sense, after analysis discloses the good sense in common sense.

As far as costs are concerned, all the tools that we shall need have already been developed in Chapter 24's discussion of costs ($MC$, $AC$, $TC$, and so forth).

Here, therefore, we can begin with the sales revenue side of things. From the firm's demand curve $dd$, we know the relation between $P$ and the $q$ it can sell. Table 25-2

**TOTAL AND MARGINAL REVENUE**

| (1)<br>QUANTITY<br>q | (2)<br>PRICE<br>$P = AR = R/q$ | (3)<br>TOTAL REVENUE<br>$R = P \times q$ | (4)<br>MARGINAL<br>REVENUE<br>MR |
|---|---|---|---|
| 0 | 200 | 0 | +200 |
| | | | +180 |
| 1 | 180 | 180 | +160 |
| | | | +140 |
| 2 | 160 | 320 | +120 |
| | | | +100 |
| 3 | 140 | 420 | +80 |
| | | | — |
| 4 | 120 | 480 | +40 |
| | | | +20 |
| 5 | 100 | 500 | 0 |
| | | | −20 |
| 6 | 80 | 480 | −40 |
| | | | −60 |
| 7 | 60 | — | −80 |
| | | | −100 |
| 8 | 40 | 320 | — |
| | | | −140 |
| 9 | — | 180 | −160 |
| | | | −180 |
| 10 | 0 | 0 | |

**TABLE 25-2**

Marginal Revenue numbers can be derived from demand-schedule P and q data

First, Total Revenue comes from multiplying $P$ times $q$. To get orange Marginal Revenue, we increase $q$ by a unit and calculate the difference in Total Revenue it brings. Note MR is at first positive, but after demand turns inelastic, MR becomes negative. Price never becomes negative, but MR lies below P because of loss owing to the necessity to lower price on previous units if the new unit of q is to get sold. [Light data of instantaneous Marginal Revenue come from smoothed MR curve of Fig. 25-3(a). Page 494 explains the Marginal-Revenue concept in detail.]

indicates this relationship, for a hypothetical firm, in Column (2). And Fig. 25-3(a) depicts, in brown, the *dd* demand curve for this monopolist (who is given, for simplicity, a straight-line demand curve). Column (3) of Table 25-2 shows how to get the firm's Total Revenue by multiplying $P \times q$: thus 0 units bring in $TR = 0$; 1 unit brings in $TR = \$180 \times 1$; 2 units bring in $\$160 \times 2 = \$320$. The general rule is this: $TR = P \times q$.

Total Revenue at first rises with $q$, since the reduction in $P$ needed to sell the extra $q$ is moderate in this first *elastic* range of the demand curve. But when we get to some intermediate point on *dd*, TR reaches its maximum—at $q = 5$, $P = \$100$, and $TR = \$500$. Increasing $q$ beyond this point brings you into *inelastic* demand regions, and now the percentage cut in $P$ needed to sell 1 per cent more $q$ is so much greater than 1 that it cuts down on TR. Figure 25-3(b) shows TR to be dome-shaped, rising from zero to a maximum of $500 and falling back to zero when $P$ has become vanishingly small.

Already Table 25-2 illustrates an important fallacy: "A firm out to maximize its profits will always charge what the 'traffic will bear.' That means charging the highest possible price." This statement is wrong. A profit maximizer may not be an altruist; but that does not mean he is a fool. To charge the highest possible price is to sell *no q* at all and to get no TR at all! Even if we reinterpret this doctrine to mean charging

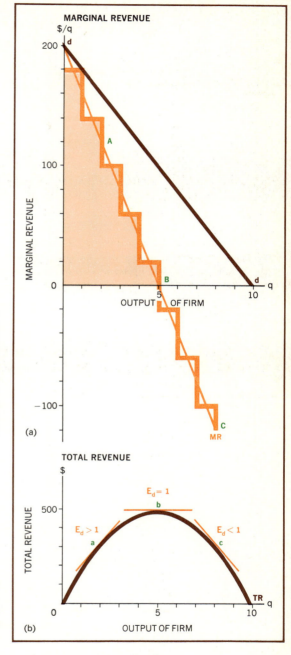

**FIG. 25-3**

**Marginal Revenue curve comes from demand curve**

**(a)**   The orange steps show the increments of Total Revenue from each new unit of output as calculated from Table 25-2 (or from the *TR* of Fig. 25-3(b) below). *MR* falls below *P* from the beginning, actually dropping twice as fast as the straight-line *dd* curve. *MR* becomes negative when *dd* turns inelastic. Smoothing the incremental steps of *MR* gives the orange *MR* curve, which in the case of straight-line *dd* will always have twice as steep a slope as *dd*. [NOTE: These values for smoothed *MR* are the same as the light numbers in column (4) of Table 25-2.]

**(b)**   Total Revenue is dome-shaped, rising from zero (where *q* = 0) to a maximum (where *dd* has unitary elasticity) and then falling back to zero (where *P* = 0). *TR*'s slope gives instantaneous smoothed *MR*, just as jumps in *TR* give steps of incremental *MR*.

the highest price at which anything at all can be sold, it is obvious that selling but one unit even at a high price is not the way to maximize your profit. Even if we neglect (for a moment) all costs, the correct interpretation of charging what the traffic will bear must mean that we find the best *compromise* between a high *P* and a high

$q$ if we are to get the best profit. In Table 25-2, it is at $q = 5$ that $P \times q = TR$ is at a maximum: this is the point where demand elasticity turns into demand inelasticity.

Before proceeding now to introduce the important concept of Marginal Revenue, we can note the fact that the *Price* at which each $q$ is sold could be called *Average Revenue* to distinguish it from Total Revenue. Thus, we get $P \equiv AR$ by dividing $TR$ by $q$ (just as we earlier got $AC$ by dividing $TC$ by $q$). Verify that if Column (3) had been written down *before* Column (2), we could then have filled in Column (2) by division. To test understanding, fill in the blanks of Columns (2) and (3).

### MARGINAL REVENUE AND PRICE

We need a test to determine by how much Total Revenue is gaining or losing as we increase $q$. Marginal Revenue is the convenient concept for this purpose.

*Definition:* "Marginal Revenue" is defined as the increment of Total Revenue (plus or minus) that comes when we increase $q$ by an increment of one unit. MR is plus when demand is still elastic, minus when demand is inelastic, and just crosses zero when demand turns from being elastic to being inelastic. (If units of $q$ are divisible, the orange MR steps of Fig. 25-3(a) can be replaced by a smooth MR curve.)

The orange numbers of Marginal Revenue are shown in Column (4) of Table 25-2; they are calculated by subtracting the $TR$ we get by selling $q$ units from the $TR$ we get by selling $q + 1$ units, the difference being our extra revenue or $MR$. Thus, from $q = 0$ to $q = 1$, we get $MR = \$180 - 0$. From $q = 1$ to $q = 2$, $MR$ is $\$320 - 180 = \$140$.

$MR$ is positive until we arrive at $q = 5$, and negative from then on. That does not mean you are giving goods away at a negative price. Actually, Average Revenue, which is $P$, continues to be positive. It is merely that, in order to sell the sixth unit of $q$, you must reduce the price so much on *all* the units as to end up getting less $TR$—which is what the negative $MR$ is telling you.

This warns us: Do *not* confuse Marginal Revenue with Average Revenue or Price. The table shows they are different. Review Fig. 25-3(a) and note that the plotted orange steps of $MR$ definitely lie below the brown $dd$ curve of $AR$. In fact, $MR$ will have already turned negative when $dd$ is only partway down toward zero.

Let's review why $MR$ is definitely less than $P$ (or $AR$) for the imperfect competitor. True, I sell my last unit of $q$ for $P$. But what did I have to do to coax out that last unit of sale? Clearly, I had to lower my $P$, since I didn't face a perfect-competitor's horizontal $dd$. But in lowering my $P$ for the last new buyer, I also had to *lower* P *for all the previous buyers.* So my extra revenue, my $MR$, is evidently less than $P$ by this loss on previous units from the price drop. QED.

*Summary:* With *dd* demand sloping downward,

$$P > MR \ (= P - \text{loss on all previous } q)$$

In Column (4) of Table 25-2, the light numbers of smoothed $MR$ are also seen to be less than Column (2)'s $P$s.

Only under perfect competition, where the sale of extra units will never depress price, is the loss-in-revenue term zero. Only then will Price and Marginal Revenue be identical. Graphically, a straight-line *MR* curve always has twice the steepness of the *dd* curve. But if *dd* is horizontal, as in perfect competition, so then must *MR* be: thus, a perfect-competitor's *dd* and *MR* coincide as the same horizontal line!

This completes our analysis of Marginal Revenue and equips us for the task of finding Maximum-profit equilibrium of the firm.

## B. MAXIMUM-PROFIT MONOPOLY EQUILIBRIUM: DIVERGENCE OF PRICE AND MARGINAL COST

Now suppose the firm wants to maximize its Total Profit. To do this it must bring in, along with the Total Revenue information it gets from its demand side, the Total Cost information described in Chapter 24.

*Definition:* Total Profit equals Total Revenue minus Total Cost:

$$TP = TR - TC = P \times q - TC$$

To maximize its profit the firm must seek out the equilibrium price and quantity, $P^*$ and $q^*$, that gives it the largest difference, $TR - TC$.

Common sense tells us this Maximum-profit will occur only where the firm's Marginal (or extra) Revenue has just come into balance with its Marginal (or extra) Cost.

We may now bring all our relevant facts together in a supertable, Table 25-3 on the next page. Total Profit is, of course, the column of greatest interest in this table.

What quantity $q^*$ will maximize Total Profit, and at what price? The easiest way to solve this problem is to compute Column (5), Total Profit, which is simply the difference between Total Revenue and Total Cost. This column tells us:

The optimal quantity is 4 units, with a price of $120 per unit. After taking account of Total Cost, we see that no other situation will give us as much profit as the $230 at $q^* = 4$ and $P^* = \$120$.

Another way of arriving at the same result is to compare Marginal Revenue, Column (6), and Marginal Cost, Column (7). (*MR* is computed from the *TR* column, as in Table 25-2. Recall from the previous chapters that *MC* is similarly calculated from *TC*.)

As long as a step toward extra output gives more Marginal Revenue than Marginal Cost, our profit is *increasing* and we continue to produce more output. But whenever Marginal Cost exceeds Marginal Revenue, we *contract* output. Where is equilibrium?

Maximum-profit equilibrium is where Marginal Revenue equals Marginal Cost:

$$MR = MC, \text{ the Maximum-profit point}$$

This second way of finding the optimum point by comparing Marginal Cost and Marginal Revenue is neither better nor worse than the first way of simply examining Total Profits. They are essentially exactly the same method.

### GRAPHICAL DEPICTION OF FIRM'S MAXIMUM-PROFIT POSITION

Figure 25-4 on page 497 shows these procedures. In Fig. 25-4(a), *MC* intersects *MR* at *E*, the Maximum-profit point, where $q^* = 4$. We run up vertically from *E* to the

**SUMMARY OF FIRM'S MAXIMUM PROFIT**

| (1) QUANTITY $q$ | (2) PRICE $P$ | (3) TOTAL REVENUE $TR$ | (4) TOTAL COST $TC$ | (5) TOTAL PROFIT $TP$ | (6) MARGINAL REVENUE $MR$ | (7) MARGINAL COST $MC$ | |
|---|---|---|---|---|---|---|---|
| 0 | 200 | 0 | 145 | −145 | +200 | 34 | |
| | | | | | +180 | 30 | $MR > MC$ |
| 1 | 180 | 180 | 175 | +5 | +160 | 27 | |
| | | | | | +140 | 25 | |
| 2 | 160 | 320 | 200 | +120 | +120 | 22 | |
| | | | | | +100 | 20 | |
| 3 | 140 | 420 | 220 | +200 | +80 | 21 | |
| | | | | | +60 | 30 | |
| 4* | 120 | 480 | 250 | +230 | +40 | 40 | $MR = MC$ |
| | | | | | +20 | 50 | |
| 5 | 100 | 500 | 300 | +200 | 0 | 60 | |
| | | | | | −20 | 70 | |
| 6 | 80 | 480 | 370 | +110 | −40 | 80 | |
| | | | | | −60 | 90 | |
| 7 | 60 | 420 | 460 | −40 | −80 | 100 | |
| | | | | | −100 | 110 | $MR < MC$ |
| 8 | 40 | 320 | 570 | −250 | | | |

\* Maximum-profit equilibrium.

**TABLE 25-3**

**Equating Marginal Cost to Marginal Revenue gives firm's Maximum-profit $q$ and $P$**
Total and Marginal Cost of production are now brought together with Total and Marginal Revenue. The Maximum-profit decision is where $MR = MC$, with $q^* = 4$, $P^* = \$120$, and maximum profit $TP = \$230 = \$120 \times 4 − \$250$. (NOTE: For convenience, the light $MR$ and $MC$ numbers are put in to give the smoothed instantaneous values at each $q$ point itself: disregarding these, we could get the same result.)

$dd$ curve at $G$, where $P = \$120$. The fact that $G$ lies *above* $F$, the point on the $AC$ curve at $q^* = 4$, guarantees a positive profit. [We cannot read directly the amount of Total Profit unless we calculate the area of the shaded rectangle in Fig. 25-4(a).]

The same story is told in Fig. 25-4(b) with total curves. Total Revenue is dome-shaped. Total Cost is ever rising. The vertical difference between them is Total Profit, which begins negative and ends negative. In between, $TP$ is positive, reaching its maximum of \$230 at $q^* = 4$, where the orange slopes of $TR$ and $TC$ are equal and parallel: if these $MR$ and $MC$ slopes were pointing outward in a nonparallel fashion (as at $q = 2$), we should gain a little extra profit by expanding $q$. At $q^* = 4$ things are at their best balance. This is verified by the Total Profit curve, whose orange slope is horizontal at its peak: $TP$'s slope is clearly the difference $MR − MC$, and this slope should definitely have a zero value at the maximum.[3]

[3] Those who know elementary calculus need not use the finite-step definitions of $MR$ and $MC$ as $\Delta TR$ and $\Delta TC$. Instead, they can use the smoothed instantaneous slopes of the $TR$ and $TC$ functions of $q$; i.e., define $MR = d(TR)/dq$ and $MC = d(TC)/dq$, and note that maximizing $TR − TC$ of profit requires finding the $q^*$ root of the equation: $d(\text{profit})/dq = 0 = d(TC)/dq − d(TR)/dq = MR − MC$. QED. (See Extra-credit problem, question 7, on page 502 for more on this.)

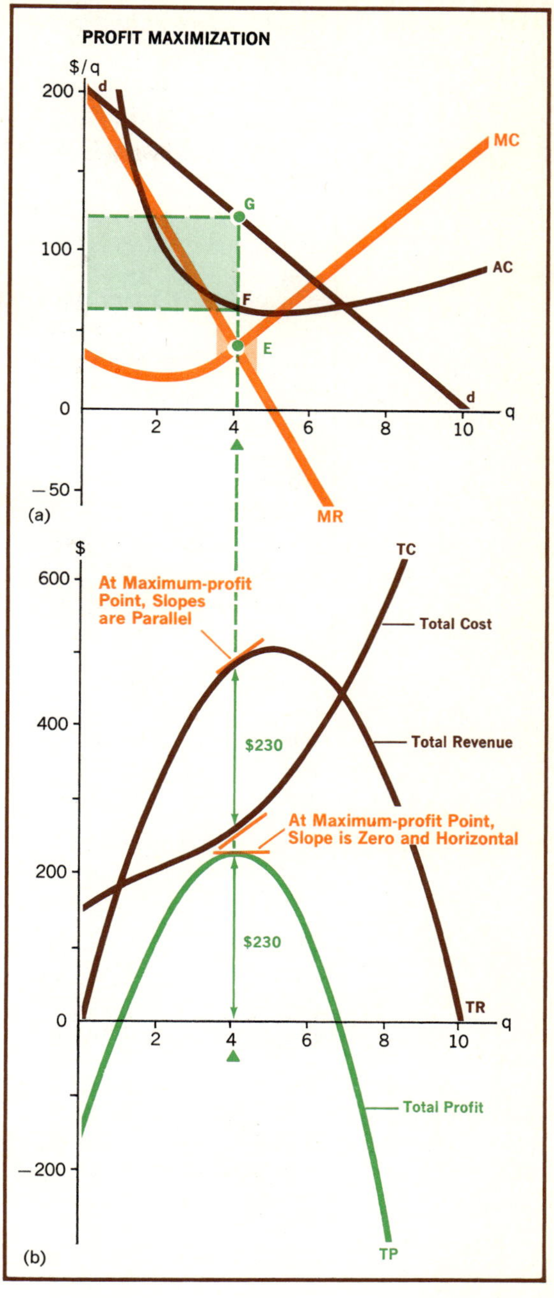

**PROFIT MAXIMIZATION**

**FIG. 25-4**

Graphs of marginal and total curves can show this same maximum-profit equilibrium

**(a)** At *E*, where *MC* intersects *MR*, equilibrium position of Maximum-profit is found. Any move from *E* will lose some profit. Price is at *G* above *E*; and since *P* is above *AC*, the maximized profit is a positive profit. (Can you understand why the shaded green rectangle measures Total Profit? And why the orange triangle of shading on either side of *E* shows the reduction in Total Profit that would come from a departure from *MR* = *MC*—i.e., the greater loss of extra revenue in comparison with extra cost?)

**(b)** This tells the same story of maximizing profit as above, but uses total concepts rather than marginal concepts. Total Profit is given by vertical distance from *TC* up to *TR*. This is at a maximum where the two brown total curves have equal and parallel slopes, *MR* = *MC*. This is necessary if green Total Profit curve is to be at a maximum, with its orange slope horizontal as *MR* cancels out *MC*.

*Summary on excess of P above MC.* For the firm with some monopoly power, maximizing profits by equating Marginal Revenue to Marginal Cost leads to a price that is *above* Marginal Cost. The canny seller *contrives an artificial scarcity of his product* so as not to spoil the price he can get on the earlier premarginal units.

### PERFECT COMPETITION A SPECIAL CASE OF IMPERFECT COMPETITION

This completes our discussion of Marginal Revenue and Marginal Cost as tools to maximize profit. It will add to your confidence in the result if you find that the general $MR = MC$ rule is consistent, when applied to a *perfect-competitor*, with Chapter 23's $P = MC$ rule for a profit-maximizing perfect-competitor. Is it? Yes, indeed. Here is why: For a small perfect-competitor, Marginal Revenue works out to be exactly the same thing as Price. With no need to cut your $P$ to sell an extra unit of $q$, the incremental Marginal Revenue it brings you is precisely the $P$ received for that last unit, with no loss on previous units being subtracted.[4] Hence, $MR = MC$ and $P \equiv MR$ do lead to the special rule for profit maximizing by a perfect-competitor:

$$P = MR = MC \text{ at a perfect-competitor's Maximum-profit point}$$

These tools to show how a rational firm will find its Maximum-profit equilibrium will later apply to firms under monopoly, oligopoly, or anything else.

### BYGONES AND MARGINS

While economic theory doesn't aim to make you necessarily a successful businessman, it does introduce you to some new ways of thinking. Here is one instance.

The economist always stresses the "extra," or "marginal," costs and advantages of any decision. He says:

Let bygones be bygones. Don't look backward. Don't moan about your sunk costs. Look forward. Make a hard-headed calculation of the *extra* costs you'll incur by any decision and weigh these against its *extra* advantages. Cancel out all the good things and bad things *that will go on anyway*, whether you make an affirmative or negative decision on the point under consideration.

This disregarding of bygones is extremely important, and most successful decision-makers practice it intuitively, even if they have not had a formal course in economics. Here is an application of this principle:

The Crown taxes a monopolist a flat sum for his match-monopoly franchise—say $100 per day, no matter what he does. How will this affect the new Maximum-profit $P$ and $q$? If you have grasped the tools of this chapter, you will discover that a flat-sum tax will not shift either the $MR$ or $MC$ curve. If the monopolist successfully maximizes his profits before and after the tax and if nothing else changes and if he stays in business, the *flat-sum tax will have absolutely no effect on price or output*, but will be borne completely by the monopolist! [Can you verify that adding $100 to every $TC$ number in Table 25-3 merely subtracts $100 from every profit in Column (5), leaving you with exactly the same Maximum-profit $q^* = 4$ and $P^* = \$120?$][5]

----

[4] If you redraw Fig. 25-4(a) for a perfect-competitor, make $dd$ horizontal and coinciding with $MR$. Then proceed to find the $MR$ and $MC$ intersection as usual (which gives the old $MC$ supply story of Chapter 23). In this new version, Fig. 25-4(b)'s $TR$ merely becomes a straight line, rising from the origin, but the slopes of $TR$ and $TC$ must still match at the Maximum-profit equilibrium point.
[5] Suppose the King put a flat-sum tax of $230 on Fig. 25-4's monopolist to wipe out all his profit. The new Fig. 25-5 shows the story. $MR$, $MC$, and $dd$ are exactly as before. (Why?) But now $AC$ has been shifted up because of the tax spread over each unit, which adds $230 of new Fixed Cost: only at the price of $G$, where the $dd$ curve is *tangent* to the new $AC$ curve, can the firm break

## HOW IMPERFECTION OF COMPETITION HURTS RESOURCE ALLOCATION

In the next chapter we shall study some of the important cases of imperfect competition—oligopoly and so forth. This will involve us in important public questions that lie in the field of "antitrust policy." As preparation, let us recall again how deviations from perfect competition affect the efficiency with which a free-price system solves the important problems of WHAT, HOW, and FOR WHOM.

Under free pricing, when firms face a sloping demand curve, their Marginal Revenue (and hence Marginal Cost) is below their Price. Then, to the degree that such imperfect competitors intelligently pursue their self-interest, they will *not* be led by Adam Smith's Invisible Hand to perform the acts needed to promote the general interest.

Let us recapitulate how this divergence between Price and Marginal Cost will affect the goodness or badness of the way the economy is organizing its production and distribution. We have already met this complex question, and will do so again.

**Excess-profit of monopoly**  First, the imperfect competitor may be earning more than he would if the government made him compete like a perfect-competitor. If so, is that excess-profit a good or a bad thing? Is he a more worthy man than most? Is he poorer than most and more in need? (And will he use his gains to subsidize the arts, or to pay for vulgar display? Will he use any monopoly profits to sponsor new industrial research? Or only to sponsor research in ways to convince consumers that his product is better than those of others.)

When the man in the street thinks of the monopoly problem, he gives most weight to the excess-profit question—to the way it affects the FOR WHOM problem of distribution.[6]

---

even; everywhere else it makes a loss; maximizing profit by finding $MR = MC$ now means avoiding loss. (But see the next section and the Appendix for a demonstration that taxing away monopoly profit does still leave society with a discrepancy between Marginal Cost and Price or Marginal Utility.)

[6]In Fig. 25-5, the monopolist was stripped of his excess-profit by taxes, but the vertical arrow showing the discrepancy between $P$ (at $G$) and $MC$ (at $E$) shows that monopoly $q$ is still too small and should be expanded as shown by the lower horizontal green arrow.

As the next chapter shows, imperfect competition of many differentiated producers might result in no one's making a profit if there is "free entry" into the Chamberlinian industry in question. Yet $P$ might still stay above $MC$, and so the result might still be tremendous wastage of resources because we have too many corners with too many gas stations, each with too many idle attendants (who in the end are not even well rewarded for being imperfect competitors). To be sure, more gas stations could mean shorter walks for people out of gas, and more consumer convenience generally; but who is to say that

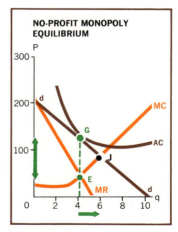

**FIG. 25-5**

the optimal amount of such differentiation-of-product convenience is being provided under any particular regime of imperfect competition?

The moral is this: Imperfect competition can introduce a new evil that was not present either under perfect competition or under perfect monopoly—namely, excessive differentiation of products, but without excess profits being achieved by anyone.

Yet, *even if it has no harmful effect on income distribution by creating excess-profits, monopolistic imperfection can still be shown to represent an important economic evil.*

**Deficient output of monopoly**   To see this, imagine that all money votes are distributed properly, and A is the only imperfect competitor in the system. Everyone else is a perfect-competitor, who keeps his *MC* equal to *P*. Price is the signal that consumers use to indicate how much they value various goods. Costs, and particularly Marginal Cost, are the indicators of how much of society's valuable resources each good's production utilizes: scarce land, sweaty labor, and other resources that could produce other goods. Everywhere else, competitive firms are giving people what they most want by producing right up to the point of $P = MC$, where goods are shown to be worth what they cost. (If you are unsure on this, flip back to page 461's Fig. 23-7 to refresh your understanding.)

But take the imperfect competitor A—the one deviant. What is he doing? A is not forcing people to buy from him. But the fact that A faces a sloping demand curve shows he does have some control over *P*. How is he using that power? Does he produce goods up to the point where their social cost—as measured by his *MC*—is equal to what the last unit of the good is worth to society—as measured by market *P* resulting from consumer money votes? No.

The imperfect competitor is contriving to keep things a little scarce. He is contriving to keep *P* above *MC* because in that way he sets $MR = MC$ and thereby maximizes his profit. So society does not get quite as much of A's good as it really wants in terms of what that good really costs society to produce![7]

Do not think A is a villain. If he did not intelligently try to maximize his firm's long-run profits, he might be displaced by the stockholders or sued. Even if A owned the company and chose to lower *P* to *MC*, he would be shunting money from his wife and kids to the public at large. While there is no law against his being such an altruist, such a Santa Claus, the betting odds are against this. And in any case such an optimal solution to the problem *by chivalry* has nothing to do with Adam Smith's Invisible Hand—which insisted that *self*-interest (not altruism) would perform, under ruthless competition, the miracle of providing for the general interest.

The clue to the Invisible Hand paradox is this: Adam Smith would have to rely on strictly defined "perfect competition" to get his result. As soon as we have imperfect competition in the real world, we have left the Garden of Eden. There then arises the problem of how to minimize the evil and wastes involved in such imperfections of competition. Chapter 26 analyzes the main forms of imperfect or monopolistic competition and surveys the antitrust policies of modern governments. And the brief Appendix to this chapter indicates the *economic* principles that should underlie public regulation of monopoly and imperfect competition and shape antitrust philosophy and law. The monopoly firm must be made to behave socially.

---

[7] As Fig. 20-9, page 398, showed, it is a social inefficiency when monopolists' outputs are too small and competitor's outputs are thereby expanded beyond their optimal amounts. Chapter 23's Fig. 23-7 clinched the point with its comparison of competitive *MC* pricing with a Crusoe-Planner optimum of welfare. (See this chapter's Appendix, pages 503–504, for more on this.)

## SUMMARY

### A. OVERVIEW OF MARKET STRUCTURE AND THE CONCEPT OF MARGINAL REVENUE

1 Most market situations in the real world can be thought of as falling on a line between the limiting poles of perfect competition and complete monopoly. Imperfect competition involves some control by each firm over its own price, by virtue of the fact that there *are not a very large number of rivals* who sell *exactly the same product* as it does. (Note the italicized words.) Important cases are: (*a*) *Oligopoly*—few sellers of similar or differentiated products—and (*b*) *many sellers of differentiated* products.

2 Decreasing-cost tendencies are destructive of perfect competition, since one or a few corporations then kill off the numerous sellers needed for the competitive model. (However, big conglomerates, which produce many products and invade each other's markets, may find themselves constitutional rather than absolute monarchs, unable to dominate their separate markets by exercise of unilateral, unchallenged power.)

3 From the firm's demand curve, we can easily derive its Total Revenue curve. From the schedule or curve of Total Revenue, we can easily derive its Marginal Revenue—the extra revenue resulting from the sale of an extra unit of output. Ordinarily, Marginal Revenue will fall short of Price because of the *loss on all previous units* of output that will result when we are forced to drop our price in order to sell an extra unit of output.

### B. MAXIMUM-PROFIT MONOPOLY EQUILIBRIUM: DIVERGENCE OF PRICE AND MARGINAL COST

4 A firm will find its Maximum-profit position where the last little unit it sells brings in extra revenue just equal to its extra cost. This same $MR = MC$ result can be shown graphically by intersecting $MR = MC$ curves, or by the equality of the slopes of the Total Revenue and Total Cost curves. In any case, *Marginal Revenue = Marginal Cost* must hold at the equilibrium position of Maximum-profit always.

5 Economic reasoning leads to an emphasis upon *marginal* advantages and disadvantages—to a *cancellation of bygones* and factors that go on no matter how you make a decision.

6 Imperfection of competition, by putting Price above Marginal Cost ($P > MC$) for some goods, acts as one extra deterrent to Adam Smith's Invisible Hand, which tried to convert mankind's selfish interest to a best solution of society's WHAT and HOW problems (but, alas, not necessarily to a best solution of the FOR WHOM problem.)

## CONCEPTS FOR REVIEW

perfect versus imperfect competition
decreasing costs and monopolistic
  imperfection
monopoly, oligopoly, product
  differentiation (natural
  or contrived)
rivalry versus perfect competition
$MR = MC$ at Maximum-profit

$MR$ in relation to $P$ (loss on
  previous units)
$MR = P$, $P = MC$, for perfect-
  competitor
bygones versus relevant alternatives
inefficiency of $P > MC$
imperfection of competition and
  Adam Smith's Invisible Hand

## QUESTIONS FOR DISCUSSION

1   List distinguishing features of perfect and imperfect competition. How might you characterize U.S. Steel? Bethlehem Steel? AT&T? A & P? Sears? Farmer Jones?

2   "A corporation charges what the traffic will bear." Explain the error here, and restate correctly in terms of the Marginal-Revenue and Marginal-Cost concepts.

3   What is $MR$'s numerical value when $dd$ has unitary elasticity and $TR$ is constant?

4   Relate $MR$ to $P$, at $q = 4$ or 5 in Tables 25-2, 25-3. Show loss on previous units.

5   Figure 25-4(a) and (b) describe the Maximum-profit equilibrium position. Explain in detail that it really shows two different ways of describing exactly the same fact, namely, that a firm will stop expanding where the extra cost of a further move just balances its extra revenue.

6   Here is a hard question. "If a monopolist is big enough to affect the $P$ for the good he sells, he may also be big enough to affect the price of materials and the labor he buys. (He becomes what is called a 'monopsonist'—or 'single buyer.') In computing $MC$ as it *looks to him*, he will debit against the last unit of $q$ the *rise* in wage forced on all the *previous* units of labor by his need to hire more labor. Private pecuniary $MC$, so computed, is higher than the true $MC$ that society wants $P$ equated to for efficiency."

  Interpret this if you can (but if you cannot, don't worry, as Chapter 29's footnote 4 will return to this.)

7   *Extra-credit problem:* Firm A has $dd$ demand function, $P = 15 - .05q$, and hence $TR = qP = 15q - .05q^2$. Its $TC = q + .02q^2$. Verify: $MR = d(TR)/dq = 15 - .1q$, $MC = d(TC)/dq = 1 + .04q$. So $d(\text{profit})/dq = 0$ at $MR = MC$ or at $15 - .1q = 1 + .04q$ or at $q^* = 100$. Then $P^* = 15 - 5 = \$10 > MC^* = \$5$. Maximum-profit $= \$1,000 - (100 + 200) = \$700$. Can you show that a tax of $\$1$/unit will add $1q$ to $TC$, cutting $q^*$ by $100/14$ units and raising $P$ by $5/14$ units? Were A a perfect-competitor, with horizontal $dd$ at $\$5$, its Maximum-profit on $q^* = 100$ would have been $\$500 - \$300 = \$200$; and now a $\$1$/unit tax would cut competitor's $q^*$ by more than monopolist's—namely, by $100/4 = 25$ units. [HINT: Now maximize $\{5q - (q + .02q^2) - 1q\}$.]

# APPENDIX: Monopoly Regulation and Exploitation; Game Theory

Figure 25-6 repeats a monopoly equilibrium like that of Fig. 25-4(a). The monopolist is seen to be (a) making a profit, as shown by the green-shaded rectangle near G; and (b) charging a P above MC, as shown by the EG discrepancy.

Suppose a public-utility commission is set up to regulate the monopolist. Or suppose the antitrust department of the government threatens to arrest him. If the regulators decide to make him charge a price that will wipe out his excess-profits, they will move him to H, the intersection of his dd and AC curves. Here P = AC, and price covers only normal costs.

How good is this solution? Economically speaking, it probably does represent something of an improvement. First, the owner of the monopoly is presum-

ably no more deserving, or poorer, than the consumers. So there is no reason to let him extort monopoly profits from them to him. By wiping out monopolistic profit, we probably have a more "equitable distribution of income." (WARNING: Value judgments beyond technical economics are involved in such a conclusion.)

Second, the regulators have lowered the discrepancy between Price and Marginal Cost in making the monopolist cut his P from G to H. Why deem this an improvement? Because (equity considerations aside and assuming that dollars truly reflect social utilities and social costs) the expanded q units are worth more to people in Marginal Utility than their extra or Marginal Cost. (PROOF: Between G and H, dd lies *above* the MC curve.)

## IDEALLY REGULATED PRICING

If P = MC is such a good thing, why shouldn't the regulators go all the way and make the monopolist lower P until he is at the intersection point of the dd and MC curves (at J)?

Actually, requiring P = MC *is* the ideal target for optimal efficiency. But with a decreasing-cost situation like this one—and we saw in Fig. 25-2, page 486, that much of monopoly, oligopoly, and other forms of imperfect competition come from decreasing-cost cases—setting P = MC while AC is still falling will involve the firm in a *chronic loss*. (REMEMBER: Falling AC means MC < AC; or P = MC < AC.)

How can society achieve its ideal of P = MC, where the Marginal Utility of output just matches its Marginal Cost at the equilibrium amount? The answer involves a *permanent government subsidy* to the decreasing-cost producer. Where does the subsidy come from? From the general budget (and ideally from taxes collected on a "lump-sum" basis so that people's marginal decisions are not distorted by attempts to minimize taxes.)[1]

What if dd in Fig. 25-6 shifts to intersect MC at J′,

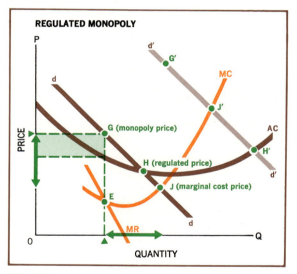

**FIG. 25-6**

Maximum-profit equilibrium for the unregulated monopolist is at G, directly above the intersection of MR and long-run MC, with P above MC and with monopoly profit shown by the shaded rectangle.

Public-utility regulation of the monopoly would set its price down to the H intersection of demand with long-run average cost; this wipes out excess-profit; more important, it brings price down closer to the Marginal Cost level at J, where marginal social costs and benefits are appropriately balanced.

Ideally, P should be forced all the way down to MC at J, with the chronic loss being covered by permanent government (lump-sum) subsidy.

[1] Some qualifications are given in advanced treatises. (1) If lump-sum taxes are not politically feasible, the evil from P > MC must be balanced against the distortion from taxing to provide subsidies. (2) As Fig. 32-2 will show, a decision has to be made whether the money needed to subsidize the J point could not be used better elsewhere, with this q set equal to zero. (3) If the consumers of this good are especially "deserving"—or if this should be a good that society pater-

beyond the bottom of U-shaped *AC*? Then the state should insist on having *P* at the profitable *J'* point, not at the new *H'* Break-even point. But, as with profitable TV channels, the state should auction off licenses or tax away all their excess-profit.

**Helping all**    We can now briefly demonstrate that if $P_1 > MC_1$ in one monopolized industry and $P_i = MC_i$ in *all* other perfectly competitive industries, then it is possible to expand the monopoly $Q_1$ and contract the competitive outputs in such a way as to make *any* (and hence, if we wish, *every*) consumer or worker better off.[2]

Suppose we define units of goods so that monopoly $P_2$ equals competitive $P_2$ (i.e., we could use a dollar's worth of monopolized berries and of competitive wheat as our unit amounts). Since only the monopolist's *P* exceeds *MC*, this means that the ratio of *MC* in monopoly to *MC* in the competitive industries is less than 1. But recall from Chapter 22 that, for each consumer, $MU_1/P_1 = MU_2/P_2$. Hence for any single consumer the ratio of Marginal Utilities is exactly 1, and is thus greater than the ratios of Marginal Costs. This means that the monopoly good is being kept so scarce that it is still yielding more $MU_1$ than its true $MC_1$ cost.

Any one sovereign consumer could command: "Transfer a small amount of labor from competitive industry 2 to monopoly industry 1. This will give you *more* than 1 unit of new $Q_1$ for each lost unit of old $Q_2$, because $MC_1 < MC_2$, (that is, the resources in 1 extra unit of $Q_1$ are less than the resources in 1

extra unit of $Q_2$). Now freeze everyone in the United States, except me, at their old consumption levels. Then they are certainly *as well off as before*. But when you give me more than 1 new $Q_1$ for 1 sacrificed old $Q_2$, I am certainly *now better off* since previously each good has had the *same MU* to me. Hence, any one man like me can be made better off by removing monopoly imperfections without hurting anyone else! QED."

**Monopoly exploitation of labor**    This sagacious consumer might even add: "Actually, dividing up the benefits more widely, you could have made *all* people who consume the two goods better off.

"And furthermore, any worker who now chooses to work an extra, new minute picking berries in the monopolized industry will find that the true amount of new berries he picks is greater than what he could buy at the monopolist's $P_1$ with his last minute's wage—because the monopolist is *marking up* $P_1$ over true Marginal Cost. [NOTE: the same improvement is *not* possible under competition.]

"Hence, the monopoly imperfection is indeed inefficient in the sense that there is seen to exist a way to depart from it and improve any worker's welfare while at the same time not hurting *anyone* else (i.e., have the worker spend an extra minute picking berries and eating them)! QED again."

*Summary:* **Monopolistic deviation from $P = MC$ means "exploitation" of labor (and other transferable resources) in the sense that society's labor is misapplied as between goods and leisure or as between too-scarce monopolized goods in relation to too-plentiful competitive goods.**

We shall have more to say about exploitation in Parts Four and Six. But one warning is in order here. Often monopolies can afford to pay workers *even more* than competitive industries can, sharing a mite of the monopoly swag with the workers. So raising wages in monopoly industries by trade-union action is *not* the way to get rid of *this* kind of exploitation.[3] It is *all* society that is being exploited, and it is a task for antitrust policy to reform the situation.

---

nalistically deems even more worthwhile than the valuations that consumers themselves act on—there may be a case for even greater subsidy. (Reverse the argument if the good is opium or is something bought only by those who already have too large a share of society's income.) (4) Recall Fig. 25-5 (and see Fig. 26-3), where it is shown that a flat-sum tax could wipe out the monopolist's profit but leave you with the socially inefficient $P - MC$ discrepancy. (5) If in *many* other industries $P > MC$, it may not be optimal to bring *P* all the way down to *MC* in this industry *alone*.

[2] In terms of the concept mentioned in Chapter 23's footnote 12, page 462, this is being said: "It is not 'Pareto-optimal' to have $P_i > MC_i$ anywhere: everyone could be made better off by the proper move to $P_i = MC_i$." The Pareto-optimality concept does not come to grips with "interpersonal equities," but it does throw light on the problem of "efficiency."

[3] See footnote 4, on page 588, for union actions that can offset "*monopsonistic* exploitation of labor" by employers who have monopoly-bargaining buying power in the labor, not the *Q*-good, market.

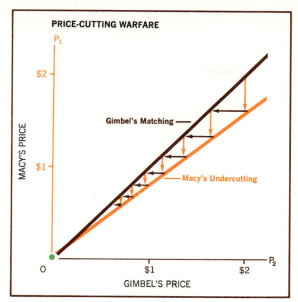

PRICE-CUTTING WARFARE

Gimbel's Matching

Macy's Undercutting

MACY'S PRICE

GIMBEL'S PRICE

**FIG. 25-7**

## ECONOMIC WARFARE AND THE THEORY OF GAMES

Oligopoly sometimes breaks out into intermittent warfare. Vanderbilt and Drew used to cut and recut shipping rates on their parallel railroads. By undercutting competitors' prices, John D. Rockefeller used to drive them to the wall or into mergers. When Boeing and Douglas first brought jet planes to market, each had to wonder how high his rival would set his price, asking, "What do they think we think they will do?"

Such a situation, "where two (or more) *free wills* each choose strategies that will affect both *interdependently*," constitutes the essence of the philosophical problems involved in the theory of games. This theory, which sounds frivolous in its terminology borrowed from chess, bridge, and war, is fraught with significance and was largely developed by John von Neumann (1903–1957), Hungarian-born mathematical genius and one of the three coinventors of the United States hydrogen bomb.

Here we can only sketch the general notions involved in game theory.[4] Figure 25-7 shows a case of

[4]Aside from the classic by von Neumann and Morgenstern cited in next chapter's footnote 3, the reader might study John McDonald, *Strategy in Poker, Business and War* (Norton, New York, 1950).

perpetual price cutting. The New York department store Macy's used to advertise, "We sell for 10 per cent less." But its rival, Gimbel's, advertised, "We will not be undersold." The vertical orange arrows show Macy's (or Orange's) price cuts; the brown horizontal arrows show Gimbel's (or Brown's) responding strategies of matching them.

It is just as if Orange and Brown were playing a chess game: at Orange's turn, he moves north-south; at Brown's turn, he moves east-west. Here the game ends in mutual ruin, at zero price, where 90 per cent of nothing is compatible with equal (zero!) prices.

But finally Macy's gets wise and realizes that when it cuts its $P_1$, the other $P_2$ will not stay constant but will follow it downward. Only if it is shortsighted does it think it can move south; actually, as Brown reacts to match, both move southwestward together toward lower profits for both. If there were but two sellers and no antitrust laws to worry about, the two might collusively raise price to the monopoly level that maximized joint profits and represented $P > MC$.

Our joint-strategy diagram can be replaced by an equivalent two-way table (or "game-payoff matrix"). In Table 25-4, Orange picks his $P_1$ strategy by selecting a row. Brown's $P_2$ strategy involves his choosing a column. Then in each of the four cells A, B, C, D, the orange number represents Orange's profit-payoff

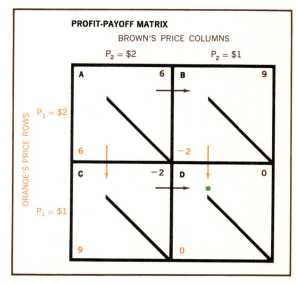

PROFIT-PAYOFF MATRIX

BROWN'S PRICE COLUMNS

$P_2 = \$2$        $P_2 = \$1$

ORANGE'S PRICE ROWS

$P_1 = \$2$

$P_1 = \$1$

A 6   B 9

6   −2

C −2   D 0

9   0

**TABLE 25-4**

at those prices and the brown number gives Brown's profit-payoff. Thus, in Cell A, joint profits of $6 + 6$ (thousand dollars) are maximized at the common monopoly price, $\$2 = P_1 = P_2$. But A is not "stable," in that if Orange knew Brown would really stay in his first column, Orange would gain by cutting $P_1$ down to C, getting the lion's share of the business there with payoff $9 > 6$. But, of course, Brown will now prefer to match Orange's $\$1$ $P_1$, taking us from Cell C to D.

Here at D (whose excess-profits just happen to be minimal), the competitive solution is stable. (That is, 0 is the largest orange number in the *column* Brown has picked, and 0 is the largest brown number in the *row* Orange has picked. Verify this green-dot equilibrium.)

But we must be warned. The competitive solution is not stable as against a "collusive" move from D to A. This might come about by overt agreement or by tacit agreement. (If Orange were reluctant to follow suit, Brown might, in Hitler fashion, blackmail him by threatening mutual ruin through cutting $P$ far below any cost levels.) The only safe guarantee of competition is thus the potential pressure of really numerous sellers.

These game-theoretic considerations show the importance to oligopolists of finding some way to "agree." And they help explain, along with the next chapter's "kinked" demand curve, why oligopoly prices tend to be administered in a "sticky" or rigid way. Were prices to change often, tacit agreements would be hard to identify and enforce.[5]

---

[5] Collusion is less worrisome in the simpler two-person games studied by von Neumann: the "constant-sum" games in which the brown and orange payoffs add up to the *same* constant in *every* cell, as in the accompanying Table 25-5(a) and (b).

In (a), Cell D is a stable solution—representing what is called a "saddlepoint," i.e., a cell which gives maximum

**Prisoner's dilemma and love** Game theory can throw light on one of the great needs of our age—the need for altruism. (In a more sentimental time, love might be the word.)

In the game matrix of Table 25-4, self-interest (in a word, selfishness) was channeled by the mechanism of economic competition to bring the system to Cell D, which happens in this context to be the optimum state. Thus, by a happy accident, so to speak, there does exist a facet of social life—the perfectly competitive market, when that is strictly applicable and viable—where Adam Smith's Invisible Hand does contrive the maximum of well-being out of the motivation of selfishness.

But that is a lucky accident, unlikely to be realized in other social situations. The following model, or fable, called "prisoner's dilemma," illustrates this basic truth in game-theoretic language. Table 25-6 is like Table 25-4, but reinterpret it in terms of prisoner's dilemma so that Orange and Brown are two prisoners who have been caught in a joint crime. The district attorney interviews each separately, saying, "I have enough on both of you to send you to jail for a year. But if you *alone* will confess to the 10-year crime, I'll make a deal with you: You'll get off with a 3-month sentence, while your partner will serve 10 years. But if you *both* confess, you'll both get 5 years."

What should Orange do? Confess and hope to get only a really short sentence? That's better than the year from not confessing. But wait. There is an even

orange numbers in *its* column and *minimum* orange (and hence, maximum brown) numbers in its row.

But in (b), which can be given a penny-matching interpretation (Brown turns up his coin to try to match Orange's winning in A and D and losing in B and C), you will find no such minimax or green-dot stable saddlepoint. (Thus, from A, Orange moves to C; then Brown moves to D; then Orange to B; then Brown back to A; and so we oscillate counterclockwise forever!)

Von Neumann proves this remarkable theorem about (b); namely, each player should introduce *randomized* strategies: thus, if each picks heads or tails with equal and independent probabilities, neither can then gain in *average* payoff by departing from this stable, minimax saddlepoint solution. Using probabilities, every constant-sum matrix has a saddlepoint. (Von Neumann proves many other fascinating theorems. For example, chess is as "trivial" as ticktacktoe. This means that when played "correctly," it must *always* end in the *same* one of the following: a draw, first man wins, second man wins—but what that outcome is for chess with its multiplicity of moves, no one knows, not even the electronic computer.)

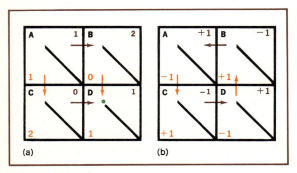

(a)          (b)

**TABLE 25-5**

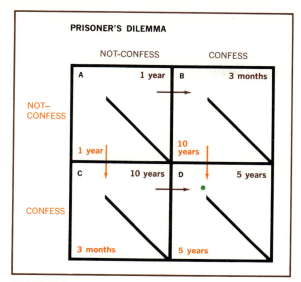

**TABLE 25-6**

better reason for confessing. For suppose Orange doesn't confess and, unknown to him, Brown does confess. Orange stands to get 10 years! Better than *that* is to confess and get no worse than 5 years.

Brown is in the same dilemma: If only he knew what Orange is thinking (or what Orange thinks Brown thinks Orange is thinking . . .).

Note that selfishness leads inevitably to long prison terms—5 years—in Cell D of Table 25-6. Only by altruism—or social agreement (in this case, collusion)—can the best *common* state of the world, Cell A, be realized.

To see the need for altruism—or failing that, for collective decision making—apply Table 25-6 to the air pollution problem. (Replace not-confess by not-pollute, . . . , etc. And assume that when I pollute and you do not desist from polluting, I will be somewhat worse off if I alone decide to desist.) Then the same

logic as in Table 25-6 proves that individual pursuit of self-interest leads to everyone's breathing the same foul and polluted air that shortens life expectancies.

Thus, game theory does point up the need for brotherhood and common rules of the road.

**Power**   Critics of political economy claim, often with some justice, that it has not mastered the analysis of power. General Motors can harass a Ralph Nader by private investigations into his sex life, in the hope of quashing his criticisms. The employer in a one-plant town, like the seigneur during feudalism, may have the power to drive women into prostitution or concubinage if he withholds his job-giving powers. IT&T can use its vast finances to lobby in Washington—to get contracts, or soften antitrust prosecutions.

Von Neumann's theory of games provides some tools for analyzing power. Thus, the impotence of perfect-competitors to raise price above marginal cost is not understandable in terms of Freudian concepts. Or in terms of class-struggle terminology. It is the fact of "constant returns to scale"—*if* that fact prevails, so that what one firm can do can be easily replicated by countless others—that enables us to understand and predict this impotence.

Similarly, the power of a monopolist has to be understood in terms of his patents, or technological secrets, or the increasing-returns nature of his industry that makes giant scale mandatory and frees him from threats of effective competitors.

Beyond the simple two-person games of earlier tables, von Neumann has developed an elaborate theory of *collusions*. (*Trivial example:* Given three sadists, we can assert: Some two will gang up on the third. *More profound example:* Given universal suffrage, the majority will legislate in some degree against the minority of plutocrats—who in turn can be expected to use their financial power to try to limit this redistribution.)

<h1 style="text-align:center;color:#d2691e;">CONCEPTS FOR REVIEW</h1>

| | | |
|---|---|---|
| $P = MC < AC$ regulation | row and column strategy | randomized strategies and |
| improving all when $P_1 > MC_1$ | stable point | necessarily-existent stable |
| economic warfare, $P$ cutting | constant-sum game | saddlepoint or minimax |
| monopoly exploitation of labor | collusion | altruism and love |
| profit-payoff game matrix | prisoner's dilemma | power |

# 26

## IMPERFECT COMPETITION AND ANTITRUST POLICY

The whole logic of private enterprise rests on the fundamental assumption of active competition in free markets. If such a system is to be preserved, it is essential that competition be kept active and markets free.

COMMITTEE ON CARTELS AND MONOPOLY OF THE TWENTIETH CENTURY FUND

Chapter 25 gave us the tools for analyzing the actual markets of the real world. Now we focus on the real world of the modern mixed economy in the last quarter of the twentieth century. We seek answers to questions like the following: How do firms actually go about setting their prices? What is the role of the theoretical tools developed to analyze profit maximization? What are some of the important patterns of imperfect competition? How does Galbraith's "new industrial state" change the conventional wisdom of the past? Part A deals with these subjects.

Part B then takes up the basic problem of the relevance of economics to improving the workings of the system. What are the important issues for public antitrust policy raised by patterns of imperfect competition?

## A. ANALYTICAL PATTERNS OF IMPERFECT COMPETITION

### DO FIRMS MAXIMIZE PROFITS?

To what degree do businessmen actually try to maximize their profits? To what extent do they succeed if they do try to? It is not easy to give precise answers to these questions. Certainly, this much is true:

*If a firm is absolutely reckless in calculating costs and revenues, then the Darwinian law of survival of the fittest will probably eliminate it from the economic scene. Therefore, those firms which do manage to survive cannot be completely oblivious to the maximization of profits.*

But this does not necessarily mean that every oligopolist or monopolist is seeking desperately to squeeze the last ounce of profit from every transaction. As soon as the firm becomes of any considerable size and begins to enjoy some control over price, *it can often afford to relax a little* in its maximizing activities.

508

Moreover, it is probably good business to take the long view and not concentrate on purely immediate gains. Many acts of altruism and apparent generosity can be amply defended in terms of public relations and the maximization of *long-run* profits.

Consider a firm that is maximizing its profits in a fairly sensible manner. Does this mean that it is calculating elaborate geometrical curves of cost and revenue and from them deriving elaborate measures of marginal cost and revenue? Obviously not, as you will soon learn if you inquire about current business practices.

But even if the firm is not itself tackling the problem with conscious awareness of the particular marginal tools of the theoretical economists, *to the extent that it is truly making a pretty fair guess as to where its highest profits are realized,* it will be succeeding in making marginal revenue and marginal cost approximately equal. It does this without curves, just by feeling its way to the optimum by trial and error. And increasingly, managerial economics is becoming a sophisticated art, utilizing giant computers and involving the statistical and mathematical techniques of operational research, linear programming, and probabilistic decision theory.

## MARKUP PRICING

One reason why business is a challenge is the fact that best guesses must be made in terms of incomplete information. It is no small task for a business to make an estimate of the demand curve for its products. Because other things do not remain equal, a firm has no exact way to judge accurately the demand elasticity for its many products. A railroad can only guess whether a cut in fares will bring many more customers.

Many observers claim that modern business firms—even the largest—cannot in real life accurately determine marginal revenue and marginal cost. They cannot determine their optimum price and output with neat exactitude. Yet the day's work must somehow get done. Prices must be set on their products. Here is where average, or unit, cost is often thought to play an important role. The argument goes as follows:

Put yourself in the position of the president of a company producing many products. Prices are partly at your disposal. Your last year's sales are known to you, but your next period's sales can only be guessed even if you leave prices unchanged. Not knowing the extent or elasticity of demand for your products, you are unable to determine marginal revenue. What will you do?

Probably, you call in your accountants and sales managers and ask, "What is our likely volume if we stay on our toes and keep our share of the market?" In answering, the sales force has to guess at the probable level of business activity, consumers' needs and how your advertising can reshape them, results of market surveys, and much else.

After they have made their estimates, you turn to the cost experts and probably ask for the average cost of producing each product in question at those levels of output. There will be plenty of headaches in arriving at any sort of figure. For example, how should the administrative and plant overhead costs be allocated between different products? Or if a given process simultaneously creates joint products like meat and hides, how should the costs be allocated between them? Or if a building will last for many years, how much should be charged against current operations?

Headache or no headache, it is the practice of accountants to come out with some sort of answer as to average costs. Management must now decide by how much to mark up price over the cost figure. Depending upon its estimate of the consumers' reaction and the pricing policy of its competitors, the firm may perhaps decide on a 5, 10, 30, or 110 per cent markup.[1] Whether aware of it or not, the businessman is making some kind of implicit guess about his demand elasticity in setting his markup.

In bad times, when price competition is particularly keen, businessmen may even set prices at less than "full costs" because they realize that fixed expenses will go on whether or not production is at a low level. But price will never be set below average *variable* costs unless the item in question is being used as a "loss leader" to attract other business now and in the future, or unless the firm is willing to incur temporary losses in order to crush a rival and drive him out of business completely.

Investigators of actual business pricing policies have testified that corporations often do follow the above-described practice of quoting administered prices on a "cost and markup" basis, hoping thereby not only to recover their "full cost outlays," but also to make a return on their investments. This theory therefore seems realistic. But it is not very informative. It stops tantalizingly short of telling us *why* the average markup is 40 per cent in one industry and 5 per cent in another; it cannot tell why, before World War II, General Motors in the auto industry was able to earn 30 per cent on the book value of its invested capital while Ford, almost as large, could earn but $\frac{1}{2}$ of 1 per cent. Demand and cost just have to be regarded as lurking in the background of any business case.

Careful reading of the foregoing accounts suggests that it is compatible with the principles outlined in Chapter 25. So long as the percentage markup is subject to the pressures implicit in *MC* and *MR* analysis, markup pricing may hinge on the same conditions as in the simplified theory.

### GALBRAITH'S NEW INDUSTRIAL STATE

Prior to John Kenneth Galbraith's 1958 masterwork, *The Affluent Society*, this versatile giant emphasized in his 1954 *American Capitalism* the notion of "countervailing power." Thus a mammoth corporation like General Electric produces, among many other things, refrigerators. It is, of course, checked somewhat in its market power in selling them by the competition of Westinghouse, Philco, General Motors, and many other selling rivals (particularly in this post-Galbraithian era of proliferating "conglomerates," which merge into one large corporation unrelated activities that cut across scores of industries).

Competition between selling rivals is old-fashioned competition, which may or may not suffice to prevent monopoly. Galbraith's emphasis is on something different.

**Countervailing power**   This is the check upon a giant corporation that comes from the organized competition among *the units it buys from* and among *the units to which it sells*. Countervailing power is the check on GE that comes from its being faced with a giant trade union in the market where it buys its labor; from its being faced

---

[1]General Motors, one of the world's most successful enterprises, has used such markup methods for 50 years. Note that the average costs used prior to markup will for most firms *not already* include a return on the firm's own equity capital.

with a government-led cartel of farmers and miners when it buys its raw materials; from its being faced by powerful chains of retail stores (Sears, Allied Stores, Korvette Discount Stores), consumer cooperatives, and Pentagon purchasing agents to which it must sell, and which use their mass purchasing power to bargain down price and keep profits in check.

Essentially then, *countervailing* power adds, along with the conventional competition of rival sellers, the checks and balances of competition between giant buyers and sellers at every stage in the productive and distributive process.

To the degree that it does prevail, countervailing power will improve the performance of a mixed economy in comparison with the unlimited oligarchy of the giant trusts of 1900. But it does take us a long way from the world of simple laissez faire, and inevitably it puts a great premium on lobbying and participation in politics to influence economic activity. (The whole concept of the "military-industrial complex" takes on a new potential in a world of countervailing power.)

**The technostructure**   In *The New Industrial State* (1967) and *Economics and the Public Purpose* (1973), Galbraith views the large corporation as the strategic economic unit of our time. Having much at stake, the corporation desires *stability*, not adventure or uncertainty. Desiring growth, growth, growth, it embraces rational *planning*. Needing *experts*, it increasingly uses, and *is increasingly taken over by*, a new breed of technicians and professional managers who possess the esoteric skills of science, engineering, and social psychology. Members of this "technostructure" travel between New York and Washington. This year the graduate of Groton (or Bronx Science High), Yale, and the Harvard Business School is merging seven companies; next year he or she is in Washington, helping negotiate an arms treaty with the Russians.

It is Galbraith's contention that all over the world—in Los Angeles or Leningrad, in Peking or Poona—there is a *convergence* toward the same kind of society. On the other side of the international bargaining table, the expert faces someone who is essentially his twin—the graduate of the top Moscow Institute, or the Inspecteur de Finance who led his class at the Ecole Polytechnique or the Ecole Normale Supérieure. In what may be Galbraith's own Walter Mitty dream of glory, the new establishments everywhere are converging to the same pattern—to a "meritocracy" based on expert skills, in short, to a "technostructure."

**Pluses and minuses**   Critically, how are we to evaluate these new ideas? To say they are nonsense would itself be nonsense. To insist that they are not new—that Veblen had prophesied the triumph of the engineers 50 years ago, that Berle and Means had emphasized long ago the separation of ownership and control in the modern corporation, that James Burnham had stressed the role of the bureaucracy, that every tired radical of the 1930s took it for granted that consumer preferences were shaped by advertising efforts and did not well out of the spontaneous nature of man—is beside the point: those who live on in the history of thought and ideas are not those who *first* think of a notion, but rather those who synthesize its various meanings, who package it, and put it across.

Scholarly research is still going on to document quantitatively the merits and demerits of the Galbraithian vision. The findings seem, all over the Western world, to be converging to a balance sheet something like the following.

1. Experts are increasingly in demand. But Galbraith exaggerates the unilateral power that they can exercise. Those who control the plurality of stockholders' votes—themselves usually a minority—still call the tune. The minute the company hits upon hard times and slow growth, the whiz-kid expert is reminded of the layman's definition of the expert—"a bastard from out of town." All this applies, as well, to the Soviet computer expert who gets too big for his breeches, or the Chinese physicist who begins to preach about world peace. The technostructure is put in its place by the men of ultimate power.

2. Large corporations do certainly have the elbow room for unilateral action denied to a small farmer or conventional family enterprise. They can give money to slum clearance. They can relax in their pursuit of profit. They can pursue growth even when it is more that of cancerous than of healthy cells. They can tempt consumers to buy the goods that the corporation would like to sell.

But the large corporation is not an absolute monarch. Ford could not sell Edsels. Lever Brothers could not, with all the wizardry of Madison Avenue, sell Swan soap. Montgomery Ward was gradually dethroned by Sewell Avery's stubborn stupidity. The great RCA lost hundreds of millions in computers and had to abandon the field ignominiously. General Foods lost heavily in franchise food operations. If one minority group of management lets profits languish so that the common-stock holders do not get capital gains, another ring of capitalists will stage a successful "take-over." The new crew may not be gentlemen from Princeton, but this is the mixed economy's way of cutting its losses.

3. Having said all this, the objective scholar must assert that economics will never quite be the same as in the days before the Galbraith trilogy.[2]

### OLIGOPOLY: COMPETITION AMONG THE FEW

Table 25-1, page 491, gave a classification of different forms of market structure. It is important enough to warrant reproducing again here as Table 26-1.

Monopoly (one seller) is a rare case. Duopoly (two sellers) happens occasionally, particularly in geographically distinct markets where a couple of steel makers or a couple of railroads dominate the market. More common still is the case of oligopoly (few sellers). We saw in Chapter 6, page 116, that most large-scale industries are dominated by a few giant firms: In automobiles, the Big Three saturate most of the market; in aircraft, a few big firms dominate; and so it goes in the cigarette, steel, breakfast-food, aluminum, meat-packing, soap, and communications industries.

---

[2]For attacks on Galbraith, both from the left and the right, see P. A. Samuelson, *Readings in Economics* (McGraw-Hill, New York, 1973, 7th ed.). Those who study the modern corporation with the objectivity of an anthropologist studying a new culture testify that the large firm is neither absolute monarch nor slave to impersonal market forces. For every case where it pays some management to overstress growth at the expense of profitability, there is a case where losses are cut on activities that didn't work out. Only those who knew the old-fashioned owner-entrepreneur realize how often he failed to maximize profits in the pre-Berle-Means days, and how more commercially rational are modern corporate cost-minimizers and capital budgeters.

| TYPES OF COMPETITION AND MARKET STRUCTURE | | | | |
|---|---|---|---|---|
| KIND OF COMPETITION | NUMBER OF PRODUCERS AND DEGREE OF PRODUCT DIFFERENTIATION | PART OF ECONOMY WHERE PREVALENT | DEGREE OF CONTROL OVER PRICE | METHODS OF MARKETING |
| **Perfect competition** | Many producers; identical products | A few agricultural industries | None | Market exchange or auction |
| **Imperfect competition:** Many differentiated sellers | Many producers; many real or fancied differences in product | Toothpastes, retail trade; conglomerates | | |
| Oligopoly | Few producers; little or no difference in product | Steel, aluminum | Some | Advertising and quality rivalry; administered prices |
| | Few producers; some differentiation of products | Autos, machinery | | |
| **Complete monopoly** | Single producer; unique product without close substitutes | A few utilities | Considerable | Promotional and "institutional" public-relations advertising |

**TABLE 26-1**
**This is a reminder that most industries fail to be perfectly competitive**
(Source: Table 25-1, page 491.)

An economic theory of oligopoly has been developed to try to account for the facts of *administered* prices (which, by definition, are posted prices that change infrequently), and to account for the prevalence of markup pricing. Let us consider the case of three or four dominant firms. Already we know that the pattern of costs and returns is likely to be such that the *optimal size of efficient production*—at the bottom of the U-shaped long-run *AC* curve (recall page 486 and elsewhere)—*will be very large relative to the total market demand.* That is why the 3 or 4 firms do not become 30 or 40, or 300, or 3,000.

Thus, it probably costs a billion dollars to produce an integrated steel plant. Kaiser Steel is the only integrated producer on the West Coast. If steel could be produced at the scale that wheat is produced, there would be thousands of West Coast steel companies, and Kaiser would have to fear much more competition than it now gets from Japanese imports and shipments from the eastern United States.

Figure 26-1 on the next page shows the large-scale operation of a typical oligopolist. The worst case threatening instability of oligopolistic competition is when different firms produce virtually *identical* or *homogeneous* products. If Firm A's sulfuric acid

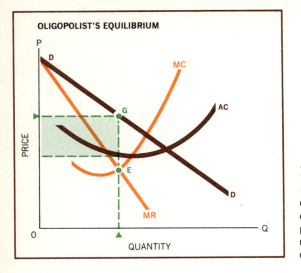

OLIGOPOLIST'S EQUILIBRIUM

**FIG. 26-1**

**Oligopoly means few sellers of identical products or of differentiated products**

After experience with disastrous price wars, each of the few rivals who dominate a given market is almost sure to recognize that price cutting *begets* canceling-out price cutting. So the typical oligopolist will estimate his demand curve *DD* by assuming others will be charging similar prices (and by taking into account the potential entry of new oligopolists). Since he gains little from extreme cutting of *P*, he will settle for sizable markup of *P* over *MC*.

undersells Firm B's by even $1 a cartank, A will get practically all the business. In this case, we oligopolists are practically sure to recognize our "mutual interdepend-ence"[3]—namely, that we must end up charging about the same prices, and that any initial advantage I get in undercutting your price will be lost when you are induced to cut your price in return. That is why the *DD* demand curve shown for Corporation A in Fig. 26-1 is *not* drawn up on the assumption of "other things (including rivals' prices) being held constant"; instead A's *DD* is about as inelastic as the whole industry's *DD*, since it is A's prorated one-third or one-fourth of the shared market.

Where is the Maximum-profit equilibrium for the oligopolist? It is shown in Fig. 26-1 at *E*, the intersection of his *MC* and *MR* curves, with *P* at *G* on *DD* just above *E*. If you turn back to page 497, you'll see that this oligopoly equilibrium looks much like the simple monopoly equilibrium of Fig. 25-4(a).

**Inflexible, administered pricing**   But there is an important difference under oligopoly. A monopolist might be expected to change his price every time his *DD* or *MC* curve shifts, which could be every year, every quarter, every month. We need an economic theory to explain the more inflexible price quotations administered typically by oligopolists. We can deduce a theory of *P* inflexibility from the fact that rivals may

[3] A century of theorizing by economists about what Mind A thinks Mind B will do if *he* thinks A will do such-and-such culminated in J. von Neumann and O. Morgenstern, *The Theory of Games and Economic Behavior* (Princeton University Press, Princeton, N.J., 1953, 3d ed.). This mathematical theory (briefly surveyed in the previous Appendix), while it cannot clear up all the philosophical problems of how two omniscient minds will act against each other in an interdependent world, does offer many incisive insights for political warfare as well as economics. (EXAMPLES: A teacher picks quiz questions *at random* from a book; a watchman makes his rounds at random, not in a discernible pattern. Facing you as a smart rival, I shall work hard to maximize my *most vulnerable* defense, knowing you will find out the weakest link in my chain. I bluff at poker, not simply, as some think, to win a pot with a *weak* hand, but rather to ensure that all players do *not* drop out when I bet high on a good hand.)

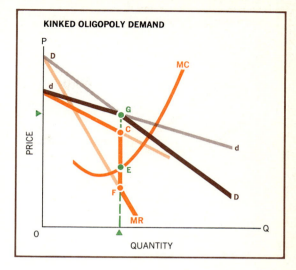

**KINKED OLIGOPOLY DEMAND**

**FIG. 26-2**

**A "kinked" or cornered demand curve can explain rigidity of oligopolists' administered prices**

The *DD* curve through *G* is the demand curve when all sellers move prices *together* and share total market. However, *dd* is the more elastic demand curve when this firm *alone* changes its price and loses sales to its rivals. Below *G*, as others match your price cut, *DD* prevails. Above *G*, when rivals do not match your price increase, *dd* prevails. Geometrically, the different demand curves generate different *MR* curves, with the *FC* vertical discontinuity (or "kink") resulting from the corner at *G*. Considerably shifting *MC* curves will still lead to intersection on *FC*, and hence unchanged oligopoly price and quantity at *G*.

behave one way when you *cut* your price—namely, *matching* your cuts and thwarting your hope for new sales; and they behave another way when you *raise* your *P* above the customary level—namely, holding their prices constant in order to pick up some of your customers. In consequence, you have little motive to change your price in either direction. Instead you "administer" your price in a rigid fashion, particularly since each oligopolist learns from game-theoretic experience that it is easier to agree— tacitly or explicitly—on a common *P* that is fixed rather than on one that is changing from month to month.[4]

Figure 26-2 illustrates the "kinked" or "cornered" demand curve that economists postulate to explain rigid price behavior. The equilibrium price *G* is shown in the diagram at about that viable markup level over costs which the oligopolists think will be best for them in the long run.

But at *G* there is a kink in the effective demand and marginal revenue curves of the oligopolist. Why? Because if he cuts his *P* below *G*, his rivals will follow him, and he moves down the old steep *DD* curve.[5] But what if he *alone* raises his *P* above the tacit customary price at *G*? No rival will follow him, because they all hope to pick up some business at his expense. Most, but not all, of his customers are likely to leave him: hence, for *increases* in *P*, he is on the more elastic *dd* curve that reflects what he would sell when he *alone* changes *P* while all rivals *hold their prices constant* at the customary *G* level.

Geometrically, the corner on the demand curve implies the vertical discontinuity

[4]The remainder of this section may be skipped if desired.

[5]Actually, it would be realistic for them to draw up their *DD* curves allowing for entry of *potential* rivals who might be tempted into the industry if they collude on so high a *P* as to make it profitable for new firms to come in. In consequence, each firm's *DD* might be somewhat more elastic than that for the whole industry, but still more inelastic than the *dd* that results from no change in rival's *P* induced by your change in *P*.

in the *MR* curve marked *FC*.[6] And now we see that the *MC* level for the firm could shift considerably—anywhere between *F* and *C*—without changing the $q^*$ intersection of *MC* and *MR* or the Maximum-profit $P^*$ at *G*.

**A "cornered" or "kinked" demand curve around an administered level of markup price—because *P* cuts are matched and *P* increases are not—can help explain rigidity of oligopoly price compared with both perfect-competition and complete-monopoly flexible price. Also, this rigidity makes tacit agreement more easily possible.**

**Collusion, tacit or explicit**    We see why the antitrust laws should be greatly concerned with the problem of oligopoly collusion. Even where there is some differentiation of products, if there are but two or a few sellers, they may come to realize that their prices are closely *interrelated*. Each will guess, or may soon learn from experience, that when it cuts its price, its rivals tend to meet or to exceed such a price cut. Economic warfare may result, until the few sellers come to realize that they are in the same boat.

Back in the old days before the antitrust laws were important, such oligopolists might have formed a merger, or a tight little cartel or trust. Meeting at celebrated dinners, such as those that Judge Gary of the United States Steel Corporation held decades ago, the sellers would collusively set some kind of monopoly price. A full monopoly price? Sometimes, if they were sure they could keep out newcomers. But, in the more realistic case where the oligopolists had to take account of the fact that setting a high price would tempt new rivals into their field, they would agree on a price higher than the purely competitive one but set with some moderation for fear of attracting new entry.

Today it would be illegal in the United States, and a few other countries, for cartels to set prices collusively and shamelessly in order to maximize their mutual profits. On the other hand, if a few large firms encounter the same problem, experience suggests that they may—without ever meeting, phoning, winking, or corresponding—arrive at a *tacit* mode of behavior that avoids fierce price competition. With or without a price leader, the sellers may be quoting rather similar prices[7]—prices which come nowhere near the level of *MC*, as would have been the case of the perfectly competitive industry discussed in Chapter 23.

The richness of possible outcomes would exhaust a specialized book on the subject. The final equilibrium may end up much or little above the firm's marginal-cost level. If fear of entry is great and if the number of existing sellers is considerable, then the *DD* curve might be quite near to horizontal and give results not too different from perfect competition. But if sellers are few, and if they are large relative to the total demand, not very fearful of new entrants, and keenly conscious of the *mutuality* of their interest, the tacit price pattern may become a very high one relative to long-run or short-run marginal cost.

---

[6] The straight-line *AC* and *MC* curves of p. 481's top diagram can demonstrate this. The flat *dGd* straight line generates the flat *MR* line; the steeper *DGD* line generates the steeper *MR* line; between these *MR* lines comes the vertical "kink," *FC*.

[7] In 1946 the Supreme Court held that cigarette oligopolists could be guilty of price fixing even when there was no overt collusion!

**Also, oligopolists particularly love to shift rivalry and competition into dimensions other than price: into advertising the real or fancied merits of their brands, into changing the wrapping of their product and the size of its replacement parts, into providing quick and reliable service.**

Some of this is undoubtedly valuable; some is definitely wasteful. What is the net balance of advantage over disadvantage? A priori reasoning alone cannot tell us; even study of the facts cannot lead to a conclusive answer completely independent of ethical value judgments.

But what needs emphasizing by the economist is this: Once the rules of perfect competition are left behind, there is no Invisible Hand principle which sets up a presumption that the working out of laissez faire is likely to be in the direction of satisfying wants most efficiently.

## MANY DIFFERENTIATED SELLERS: WASTE UNDER FREE ENTRY

Let us leave few-seller oligopoly and turn to the case of many sellers, but not of a homogeneous single product. This important case is the brainchild of the late E. H. Chamberlin.

In Fig. 26-3, a typical firm is briefly in short-run equilibrium at $G'$. His $d'd'$ is sloped because his product is a little different from anyone else's.

However, we assume that *entry is free* for new firms to produce their own differentiated products on as favorable terms as our typical firm can produce his. Since he and all the other initial sellers are making good profits at the initial $G'$, new firms are tempted into the market. These new entrants cut into his demand and shift his $d'd'$ curve leftward to $dd$ until it just touches (and does not cross above) his $AC$ curve.

Thus, final long-run equilibrium for the typical seller ends up at the *tangency* point $G$—the only point at which the firm can avoid losses. Note that downward-sloping

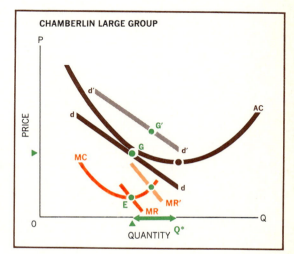

**FIG. 26-3**

**Free entry of numerous imperfect competitors may wipe out profit but still leave waste**
The typical seller's original profitable $d'd'$ curve will be shifted downward and leftward by entry of new rivals. Entry ceases only when each seller has been forced into a long-run, no-profit tangency such as at $G$. Such rivals split up the markets without depressing price to the marginal-cost level as in perfect competition. He and all his rivals end up with $P$ above $MC$; and each producer is on the left-hand declining branch of his long-run $AC$ curve with output less than the particular $Q^*$ which is at the bottom of the U.

*dd* means that tangential *AC* must be falling and that final output is smaller than the $Q^*$ corresponding to the bottom of the U-shaped *AC* curve.[8]

*Chronic excess capacity and waste.* **Free entry into the large group of sellers of differentiated products merely divides up markets, leading to excessive prices at the tangency points of downward-sloping demand curves with still-falling long-run *AC* curves. Minimum-average-cost scale of production is not attained. The imperfect competitors make no monopoly profits, but price does not get lowered to the bottom-of-the-U level.**

**The consumer has to pay for chronic excess-capacity operation of too many sellers, each producing too little. These wastes are different from those of complete monopoly and, of course, different from the efficiency of perfect competition.**

If consumers were willing to sacrifice the differentiation of product, a lower equilibrium *P* would be possible as fewer firms were used more intensively to produce a more standardized output. But laissez faire has no way of deciding how much extra people *ought* to pay in return for the extra variety of products they enjoy in Fig. 26-3.

## B. MODERN ANTITRUST PROBLEMS

### SOME WASTES OF IMPERFECT COMPETITION RECAPITULATED

Before going into the legal, historical, and institutional aspects of antitrust legislation, we ought to remind ourselves what the economic evils are that are associated with various monopolistic and other imperfections of competition.

**Monopoly restrictions**   Recall that it is not the profit a monopoly (or oligopoly, for that matter) exacts that constitutes its greatest evil, but rather its setting too high a price in relation to social marginal-cost pricing. To recall this, imagine our taxing away all the monopolist's profit by imposing on him a franchise tax of the right size.

Clearly, the monopolist would end up with no profit. The state would get that profit,

---

[8]The Chamberlin excess-capacity tangency of Fig. 26-3 should not be confused with the tangency under *perfect* competition shown here in Fig. 26-4. As discussed in earlier chapters, this typical perfect-competitor is one of so many producers of an identical good that he faces a practically horizontal ("infinitely elastic") *dd* curve, even though the industry's very much larger *DD* curve can be much more inelastic. If there is free entry-and-exit of well-informed firms that can replicate the cost conditions of any other firm, long-run equilibrium at *E* will involve no excess of profit over competitive costs (including properly computed implicit- and opportunity-cost returns). Society is getting its total output most efficiently, in recognition of the $P = MC$ condition, both in long- and short-run, as seen in earlier chapters; and it is not forcing out of existing firms any output that could be obtained more cheaply by adding new firms (as page 481's lower diagram showed).

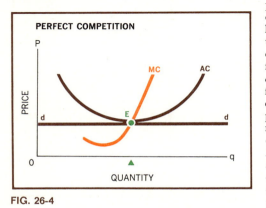

FIG. 26-4

but the monopoly would not lower its $P$ or raise its $Q$. Why not? Because the intersection of $MR$ and $MC$ would be unchanged by a lump-sum franchise tax: since such a tax is a fixed cost that varies not at all with $Q$, it will not affect $MC$; and $MR$ depends only on the demand curve, not on costs or franchise taxes.

So the consumer goes on getting too little of the product and paying too high a price. The state has now become the villainous recipient of monopoly profit and has failed to correct the misallocation of resources.[9]

**The moral: It is the contrived divergence between $P$ and $MC$ that constitutes the true additional burden of monopoly.[10]**

**Overentry and "sick" industries**    Many fields are characterized by an excessive number of firms.[11] Most of these do a small volume of business and remain in the industry only until they have lost their capital. Grocery stores, taverns, undertakers, restaurants, nightclubs, and gasoline stations are typical examples taken from retail trade. But much the same thing is true of the textile trade, the dress trade, the shoe or plastic business, and many others that require little initial capital.

Why don't such unprofitable concerns leave the industry? The answer is, They do. But as fast as they leave, new firms enter the industry, leaving the total number unchanged and even growing. Why do new firms enter the industry in the face of the fact that most existing firms are incurring losses? Apparently, partly out of ignorance and partly out of misplaced hope.

Such chronically overcrowded industries need not be what the economist has called "perfectly competitive"—although in the case of agriculture or "cotton gray goods," they may happen to be approximately so. Having too many firms in a perfectly

---

[9]Figure 20-9, Chapter 23's Robinson Crusoe parable, and Chapter 25's Appendix elaborate on this.

[10]Advanced treatises use the accompanying Fig. 26-5 to approximate the "deadweight loss" due to monopoly. At the competitive ideal $I$, each similar consumer enjoys Marshallian consumer's surplus given by the whole triangular area $NIR$. When monopoly raises $P$ to the Maximum profit point $G$, the consumer loses to the monopolist that part of his consumer's surplus measured by profit rectangle $NEGN'$ and is left only with the consumer's surplus triangle $N'GR$.

What happens to the little triangle $EIG$? It is lost to everybody and represents "deadweight loss." Thus consumers lose more than the monopolist's profit; and even if we took back the $NEGN'$ profit by lump-sum taxation, we would be losing to the devil of inefficiency all the "deadweight-loss triangle" which is *of no benefit whatsoever to anybody*.

[11]Even if, as Chamberlin insists, people may want some of the extra variety of differentiated products that the tangency solution of Fig. 26-3 makes possible, that pattern cannot be ideally efficient. For it can be shown that wherever $P$ exceeds $MC$ anywhere, there definitely exists a new configuration (possibly involving subsidies, as in Chapter 25's Appendix) in which *everyone* can be made better off. This point is alluded to again on next page's footnote 12.

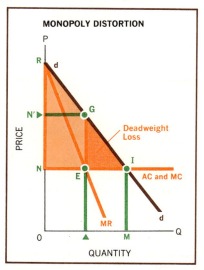

FIG. 26-5

competitive industry is an undesirable condition, involving as it does wastes of resources and losses. But at least in such a *competitive* industry the consumer partly gains, through lower prices, much of what the overoptimistic producers are losing.

Unfortunately, in most chronically overcrowded, sick industries, market competition is quite *imperfect*. Being inefficient producers, the small concerns do not sell very cheaply. Instead of competing on a price basis, they tend to charge fairly high prices and simply to *divide* the business.

The resulting economic situation under this form of free-entry numerous-seller imperfect competition may be worse even than under complete monopoly: not only is price excessive, but, in addition, valuable resources are wasted because each firm has too much idle plant and manpower. The situation is triply bad: producers incur losses, resources are wasted, and the prices charged the consumer are too high; and there is the new element here that the producers incur chronic losses.

Our earlier diagram from Chamberlin, Fig. 26-3 on page 517, showed how imperfect competition may result in wastage of resources, too high price, and yet no long-run profits for the imperfect competitors. Figure 26-3 portrayed such a typical imperfect competitor, say, a local barbershop that can count on some customers' being unwilling to walk a long way to get a haircut. Its original demand $d'd'$ slopes downward; and hence it has been marking up $P$ above $MC$. It is maximizing positive profit and charging more than full unit costs.

But now other barbers see this profit opportunity. They move in. There is now one barbershop for every three blocks rather than every four. What happens to the demand curve for our typical barber? Clearly, entry of new competitors divides up the existing business and causes demand to shift downward and leftward to $dd$, with each barber wasting more time in frustrating idleness. Now at the new maximum-profit point, each barber makes no profit, as can be seen from the fact that the new demand curve just touches the average cost curve tangentially. Marginal cost is equated to new marginal revenue—but this serves only to avoid losses, not to produce a positive profit.

The long-run equilibrium at $G$, which Marshall might shudder to call "normal," very clearly shows that price is higher than the most efficient cost level which prevails at the bottom of the U-shaped average cost curve. The barbershop has excess capacity, with empty chairs much of the time. (Of course, customers have to walk only three blocks now, not four, and may have to wait less time. And that is worth something. But note that they have never, in most cities, really *been given the choice* of a slightly longer walk and haircuts at the lower prices that efficient capacity utilization would make possible.[12])

(If there is lasting overentry of overoptimistic barbers, draw in a $d''d''$ curve still lower than $dd$ and show wasteful social losses and turnover of disappointed entrepreneurs. You can do the same for perfect competition as illustrated in Fig. 26-4.)

---

[12]Repeatedly, in our discussion of pricing "efficiency," we have seen what is proved rigorously in advanced texts: Price in excess of marginal cost leads to a state of "Pareto-nonoptimality," a state from which it would be possible theoretically to make *everybody* better off—barbers, bald people, long-haired people who hate long walks and waits, and everybody else. But do not leap from this to the invalid inference that variety does not matter or that enforcing $P = MC$ everywhere would (in decreasing-cost situations with differentiated products) lead spontaneously to the "ideal" amount of variety. Here is a case where defining an optimum is actually a difficult social task.

**Evils of oligopoly**  Antitrust regulators must be even more aware of the economic effects of oligopoly. Recall the already-mentioned railroad price wars of the past century. Customers shipping goods from Chicago to New York always picked the route that offered even a few-pennies' saving. Thus, each of the three or four trunk lines would intermittently undercut the existing rate schedules, until finally a disastrously low level of rates was reached. At the same time, for short hauls where shippers had no alternative, the railroads would jack up the rates, thus creating an anomalous, discriminatory pattern of charges.[13]

Even without government regulations, in industries characterized by heavy overheads, decreasing costs, and identical products, there is often a realization that competition is ruinous. Therefore, tacitly or explicitly, the firms try to agree on a price that maximizes the long-run profits of all. Secret committees, keeping one eye on the Justice Department lawyers who enforce the Sherman Antitrust Act, may impose penalties on any chiseler in the industry who makes secret price concessions. Occasionally, as new conditions or firms upset the status quo, another price war may break out—to last until each of the belligerents has again learned his lesson and industry morale is restored.

In appraising oligopoly we must note that the desire of corporations to earn a fair return on their *past* investments can at times be at variance with the well-being of the consumer. Too much plant capacity may have been built in the industry in the past; but that is not justification for continuing high prices and scarce output. Competition, which the businessman regards as destructive, cutthroat, and ruinous, may actually be the only way to get the redundant plant capacity into operation or to discourage its maintenance. (Having made the mistake of building the plants, society ought not to add the further error of failing to use them to best advantage.) Losses or subnormal profits is the free enterprise way of discouraging excess capacity, brutal as that may sound.

The steel and other metal industries are examples of this pattern of imperfect competition. How does all this work out these days in practice? In 1954, 1958, 1960, and 1971, we hit a lull. Steel production went down to far below capacity. Some feared this would initiate a wave of price cuts which would reduce steel companies' earnings to the break-even point or below. Did it work out that way? Not quite. The industry discovered it could still make money at levels far below capacity; price morale stayed high in the industry. Even massive competitive steel imports have not forced steel prices down to marginal-cost levels.

In a perfectly competitive industry, when demand shifts leftward, *P* will fall. Profits will decline greatly. Yet competitive *Q* may not fall much at all, being sold for whatever it will fetch. The consumer does benefit from what the producer loses, and in time output will adjust to the new state of demand.

By contrast, under oligopoly, price tends to stay firm, with output taking up the great variation. Plants stand partially idle, and the product is not cheapened in the hope of coaxing out new quantity demanded.

---

[13] We have seen that the Interstate Commerce Commission was established in 1887 to regulate railroad rates and earnings and prevent such unstable price conditions. (Alas, in modern times the ICC too often *protects the railroads,* not the consumers! Too often regulatory commissions, which start as the protector of the consumer, end up aiding his oppressors.)

This downward inflexibility of "administered" (or named) prices, many economists fear, adds to the danger of Chapter 41's creeping inflation. Why? Because if prices and costs rarely ever fall, there is but one way for the price index to go.

## DYNAMIC RESEARCH AND MONOPOLY

All is not evil in any field. Some arguments concerning the *virtues* of imperfect competition can also be made. A common industrial pattern is that of a firm with considerable control over price by virtue of its technological efficiency, its patents, its trademarks, and its slogans. Its "monopoly profits" are plowed back into further research and advertising, so that it is always able to keep abreast or ahead of its rivals. GE, RCA, IBM, and Du Pont are perhaps typical of such companies.

Because research and advertising are expensive and their results cumulative, success tends to breed success, and profits breed more profits. Therefore small business claims it cannot always effectively compete with such firms. In other words, industrial research may be subject to economies of large scale that small businesses can't enjoy.[14] And yet, when John Jewkes traced the source of the more important inventions of the century, he found that less than half came from laboratories of large corporations.

Furthermore, instances of beer, cigarettes, and soap remind us that advertising and research are quite different things. Budweiser beer sales may stay large because a national audience has been persuaded of its merits. Much soap advertising is aimed more to solidify the sales of one brand than to expand total soap use and cleanliness. Yet, in many cases, it will not be easy to decide whether a certain bit of applied industrial research is technical improvement or merely for market improvement.

Reread Schumpeter's eulogy of the dynamic innovational contribution of monopolists (page 117). Weigh this with the claims that many of our best discoveries come from small business, government, lone-wolf inventors, and university researchers. A sensible student realizes this is indeed no black-and-white matter.

While admitting the efficiency and progress of some of the firms described, critics argue that society would be *still* better off if the full advantages of efficiency were passed on to consumers or plowed back into research aimed at technological improvements and not simply at profits; and if fewer dollars were spent on "soap operas" and jingles and more went into fundamental science rather than into patentable gadgets.

Obviously, we are dealing here with moot issues, on which each citizen must form his own judgment. In controlling, how much do we emasculate vigor? Yet, it is axiomatic today that the giants of the new industrial state must be placed under ever-vigilant public scrutiny and surveillance.

## WHAT TO DO ABOUT MONOPOLY IMPERFECTIONS

Is there no hope for limiting monopoly and oligopoly? Yes, there is.

For one thing, if we make sure that *barriers to entry are kept to a minimum,* the

---

[14] Also, large firms are "poolers of risks," being favored by the statistical fact that, when you aggregate independent risks, you cancel out much variation. (In fact, quadruple the size and independent risks of a firm, and you halve its average risk per dollar—as probability books show.)

fear of potential competition and the actuality of that competition may help to keep the oligopoly prices down.

For a second thing, if government antitrust policy bears down hard on the slightest sign of collusion designed to peg prices high and to control supply, the oligopolists may find it harder to equate their marginal revenue and cost at a level far above society's true marginal cost.

For a third thing, some economists—such as George J. Stigler of the University of Chicago—would argue that large firms should be broken up into many small pieces. Stigler thinks the bottom of U-shaped cost curves comes early enough to make this a practical possibility and one that will not sacrifice any appreciable economies of large-scale production. With sellers now numerous, he hopes that competition can become much more like perfect competition than like oligopoly. (Needless to say, Stigler is against any mergers that might reduce numbers still further; and he believes that many of today's giants grew from mergers which had as their goal not *productive efficiency,* but rather monopoly *control over market price.*)

Government regulation and government antitrust laws are the principal weapons a mixed economy uses to improve the workings of the price system. This is plainly a developing and dynamic area. Even the Supreme Court has been gradually changing its mind on the legalities of the issues, as we shall see.

## PUBLIC-UTILITY REGULATION

To show what government can do about monopoly, let us consider in detail a monopoly licensed by the state and under government regulation. Such "public utilities" include gas and light companies, telephone and communication services, railroads and public carriers, and so forth. Since it seems uneconomical to have two local sets of telephone wires, an exclusive franchise is given to a single company. (Why not the same for milk delivery?—which is no easy question.)

But having given the utility company a complete monopoly, the state steps in to protect the consumer by setting maximum rates. Usually this is done by public regulatory commissions, which specify the *maximum prices* that can be charged for each kind of service.

In setting such prices, it has long been customary to pick prices that will try to give the company "a fair return on its capital." Rates such as 7, 8, or 9 per cent are often selected as representing a fair return. (Of course, any "guarantee" of a rate of return raises the problem of *motivating* the utility to keep efficient and cost-conscious.)

It is a complex problem, that of determining the *capital-value* base of the company to which this "fair rate" is to be applied. Three measures of fair capital value have been suggested at times: (1) *original cost* (minus depreciation)—*i.e.,* the sum of all past prudent investments; (2) *current reproduction or replacement cost* (minus depreciation)—or the cost of replacing the company's equipment *at present prices,* corrected for age and condition of the property; and (3) *capitalized market value* of the public utility's securities or assets.

**Advantages and disadvantages of different methods of regulation**   Of these methods, the third is universally recognized to be nonsensical. As was shown in the earlier discussion of good will (Chapter 6), the market value of any income-earning property is given by capitalizing its annual return by the interest rate.[15] For a regulating authority to use capitalized market value as a base for measuring capital would be tantamount to recognizing *any level of earnings,* high or low, as fair. (For example, let the earnings be high—excessively high. The stock market will then pay a lot for them.) Once having been capitalized into a new base, excessively high earnings will appear as only moderate interest returns, and the same is true of excessively low earnings. The method of capitalized earnings begs the question that the authorities must answer!

American courts have therefore vacillated between *original* cost and *reproduction* cost. So long as the general price level does not change, the two are not very different. But over decades when prices may greatly increase, reproduction cost will involve higher rates and earnings than original cost. In periods of declining prices, the reverse discrepancy is to be observed. All in all, reproduction cost leads to a more flexible price structure, giving less weight to the dead hand of past costs.[16]

## OVERVIEW OF ANTITRUST POLICY

Around the turn of the century, America went through a period of widespread trust formation. Big and small companies combined collusively to limit supply and raise price (often putting voting stock of the different firms into a so-called "trust" agreement providing for collective action and profit sharing). Small companies were flagrantly merged into big combines. Price cutters were punished brutally by competitive retaliation. Huge stock-market promotion schemes flourished.

The common law had long forbidden monopolistic conspiracies. And often these doctrines had been used against the youthful trade-union movement. But it was apparent toward the end of the last century that antitrust legislation would be needed if the game of effective competition was to be maintained.

Any history of antitrust policy must take into account (*a*) the history of *legislative acts*—e.g., the Sherman Act (1890), the Clayton Act (1914) and the Federal Trade Commission Act (1914), the Celler-Kefauver Antimerger Act (1950); (*b*) the history of attempted *enforcement of the laws by the Department of Justice*—e.g., inaction

---

[15] The capitalization process is more fully discussed in Chapter 30.

[16] From the standpoint of the advanced discussions of "welfare economics," neither method is ideal, as the last Appendix made clear. Writers in this field have set up a perfectionist formula that would involve pricing of public-utility services at not more than the extra or marginal costs of services. (We have already seen many times why $P = MC$ is "efficient.") However, marginal-cost pricing is a doctrine which, as a practical matter, few economists would endorse all the way. It could lead to excessive returns to the owners if demand was large in comparison with capacity. But with decreasing-cost situations so likely in the public-utility area, it would more likely give *inadequate* returns to original investors. Although the state could then, if it wished, *by a subsidy* secure justice for investors without interfering with desirable output or price, this would represent a wide departure from present practice and be unlikely to come about fully. The great regional power projects such as the TVA and Bonneville Dam are, from one viewpoint, partial approaches toward such a system of pricing. However, the fact that the government can raise capital in larger sums and at lower costs than private industry, and the fact that the same set of dams can simultaneously achieve the ends of national defense, navigation, flood control, and irrigation, make any simple yardstick comparison between private and public operations difficult, if not impossible.

in the 1890s; Theodore Roosevelt's activism; the lull from 1911 when Standard Oil and American Tobacco were broken up until Franklin Roosevelt's late New Deal days when Thurman Arnold became so active in prosecuting cases that wags referred to the Sherman Act as the "Thurman Act;" the increased activism of federal lawyers in the 1960s and 1970s; (c) the history of *federal court decisions*—e.g., the post-1911 period when the Supreme Court followed its 1911 "rule-of-reason" doctrine and refused to break up U.S. Steel; the post-1945 period when the courts in effect reversed themselves and held that the Aluminum Company of America was guilty just by virtue of controlling most of the market, even if it did not engage in particularly predatory practices; and (d) the history of *private actions*—e.g., the increase since 1970 of treble-damage suits against suspected monopolists.

Any survey of the field must also note that some antitrust legislation has acted to *increase* monopolistic imperfection of markets rather than *decrease* it. To protect inefficient businesses from the competition of larger efficient firms, Congress passed the Robinson-Patman (1936) anti-chain-store legislation, and the related Miller-Tydings Act (1937), aiming to enforce "retail price maintenance" agreements.

Legal technicalities rather than economic realities have often been dominant. The *act of monopolizing* has been the target rather than the condition of *existing* monopoly; two firms acting in concert have been hit harder than one giant firm which has continued the same excess of price over marginal cost! Punishment *after* the fact rather than *prevention* of bad market behavior and bad market structure has often been emphasized. And the distinction between bad *market structure* (per se) and bad or unreasonable *market conduct* has often been blunted by the legal mind.

From these perversions of the antitrust philosophy, one can see that the economist's preoccupation with how well the pricing system serves to determine WHAT, HOW, and FOR WHOM is not quite the same thing as the judge's preoccupation with who is a nasty man who has been doing nasty things and with whom.

Yet these criticisms should not blind us to the fact that the antitrust activity of government has been evolving into a stricter pattern. Nor blind us to the fact that without our antitrust acts the imperfection of competition in America would presumably be significantly heightened. When one looks at monopoly and cartel patterns of behavior abroad, in such countries as Germany and Japan, we understand why so many foreign nations have in recent years been imitating the American policies. Indeed, many experts feel that the whole of our antitrust programs adds up to more than the sum of its parts: the system seems to work better than anyone can account for.

The Sherman and Clayton Acts, and most of the antitrust laws have contributed enormously toward improving the degree of competition in our system. All who value social reliance on decentralized markets and economic efficiency should applaud this kind of public intervention, which helps to lessen the imperfections of competition.

## BRIEF HISTORY OF ANTITRUST POLICY

**Sherman Act (1890)**   This made it illegal to "monopolize trade" and outlawed all "combination or conspiracy in restraint of trade." On paper, this act represented a major advance over the previous common-law restrictions on monopolistic conspiracies. But it was adopted with little discussion, indeed without attracting much attention of a favorable or unfavorable nature; and beyond an antipathy toward "monopolizing," there is no evidence that anyone had clear notions as to which actions were to be regarded as legal or illegal.

In the early 1900s, the Republican administrations of Theodore Roosevelt and William Howard Taft witnessed the first surge of activity under the Sherman Act. Thus, the Supreme Court prevented J. P. Morgan and E. H. Harriman from using a holding company to bring about a merger of their Northern Pacific Railroad with Hill's Great Northern. In 1911, the Supreme Court ordered the American Tobacco Company and Standard Oil each to be broken up into a number of separate companies.

In condemning these flagrant monopolies, the Supreme Court enunciated the mentioned "rule of reason": Only *unreasonable* restraints of trade (agreements, mergers, predation, and the like) were to come within the scope of the Sherman Act and to be considered illegal. Thus, although Eastman Kodak and International Harvester were clearly near-monopolies, the court used its "rule of reason" to acquit them of guilt, arguing that they had not engaged in *visible* coercion or attack on rivals to build up their monopoly position.

The "rule-of-reason" doctrine almost emasculated the antitrust program, as shown by the U.S. Steel Case (1920). Although J. P. Morgan had put together this giant by merger, and it did in the beginning enjoy 60 per cent of the market, the court held that mere size per se was no offense. Once again, monopoli*zing* and not monopoly seemed to constitute an offense to the legal mind! Until the 1930s, the antitrust programs hibernated under the probusiness Coolidge and Hoover administrations.

**Clayton Act (1914) and FTC (1914)**    To spell out the vague intent of the Sherman Act and strengthen it, the Clayton Act was passed. It outlawed *price discrimination* to lessen competition and *"tied contracts"* (in which you forced a buyer or seller to deal exclusively with you). It banned *interlocking directorates* designed to lessen competition, and *mergers* for this purpose formed by acquiring common stocks of competitors. The Clayton Act emphasized prevention before the fact as well as punishment after the fact. In contrast to the early common law, which had been used particularly against organized labor, the Clayton Act specifically excluded labor as a commodity in the sense of antitrust. (Today many critics of the monopoly power of labor would like to subject unions to new antitrust legislation; however, many experts in the field argue that this would exacerbate rather than moderate intransigent union behavior.)

Also in 1914 the Federal Trade Commission (FTC) was established. It was to have power to investigate, hold hearings, and issue cease-and-desist orders. But the courts construed away most of its powers. And it was not until a 1938 amendment (Wheeler-Lea) that it acquired its primary present-day function—that of banning false and deceptive advertising.

**New Deal activism**    Congress passes laws, the courts enforce them, but nothing happens unless the Department of Justice brings suit to execute them. Thus President Cleveland's Attorney General disapproved of the Sherman Act after it was passed and refused to prosecute under it. As we have seen, Theodore Roosevelt instituted a more activist phase after the turn of the century; but it was only in the late 1930s, when Franklin Roosevelt put Thurman Arnold in charge of antitrust, that a real burst of prosecutions got under way. Arnold tackled the notoriously backward building industries, glass, cigarettes, cement, and many others.

Today the Department of Justice has hundreds of lawyers in its Antitrust Division, as against the few of Teddy Roosevelt's time. And it needs them: 45 or more cases are prosecuted each year, in contrast to the 2 or 3 of earlier times. Certain classes of cases average $6\frac{1}{2}$ years in duration!

The Aluminum Company Case (1945) represents a culmination of this new activity. Reason and rules had changed since the disastrous U.S. Steel Case. Monopoly and not simply monopoli*zing* was declared illegal. For Alcoa had gained its 90 per cent of the market by subtle and nonpredatory means: building ahead of market demand, keeping its price low enough to forestall competition, etc. For the first time the courts emphasized market *structure* rather than so-called "market *conduct*." In the Cigarette Case (1946), the Supreme Court found the Big Three guilty of *tacit* collusion: recognizing that Camels and Luckies must sell at the same price per pack, Reynolds and American Tobacco did not need to hold secret meetings or telephone conversations; they had only to recognize mutual interdependence and engage in *parallel* action. (Though punishing them as oligopolists, the Court could not tell them how to avoid sin and turn over a new leaf: if one undercut the other's price, that would be predatory oligopoly; if they matched prices, that was tacit oligopoly. Apparently, moderate exercise of monopoly power would be the prescription for a quiet life.)

## MODERN ANTITRUST

In the decades since World War II, the Justice Department and the courts have been increasingly vigorous in their prosecution of the antitrust laws. Thus the Cement Case (1948) abolished the "basing-point" system of quoting prices at any place in a region at a differential, reflecting transport costs, above the price at a given point—like the old "Pittsburgh-plus" pricing of the steel industry. In 1961, the electric equipment industry was found guilty of collusive price agreements. Executives of the largest companies—such as GE and Westinghouse—were held to have met in hotels secretly for that purpose. Although the top men in these companies apparently were unaware of what the vice-presidents just below them were doing, they had put much pressure on them for results. The companies agreed to pay extensive damages to their customers for overcharges; and some of the executives involved spent time in jail on criminal (as against civil) prosecutions initiated by the Eisenhower administration.

**Celler-Kefauver Antimerger Act (1950)**   Because the Clayton Act had only ruled out mergers resulting from acquisition of stock, there was a loophole in the law that permitted mergers via acquisition of assets. In 1950 this loophole was plugged up. Today *horizontal* mergers—as, for example, where one retail chain takes over another retail chain in the same area—are close to being ruled illegal per se. Former Chief Justice Warren actually stated in the Brown Shoe Case (1962) that a merger achieving 5 per cent control might further "the oligopoly Congress sought to avoid." Contrast this with an earlier view of the Court that a 60 to 64 per cent share of the market might be admissible. Indeed, in the Von Grocery Case (1965) a merger of two supermarkets leading to only a $7\frac{1}{2}$ per cent share of the Los Angeles market was disallowed.

Vertical mergers—as, for example, when Reynolds Aluminum tried to expand its fabrication and sale of aluminum wrappings—tend to be frowned on too.

## CONGLOMERATES AND BACKLASH

Conglomerate mergers, where a company in one industry takes on a company in another, unrelated industry, present more difficult cases. In 1957 the Supreme Court ruled that Du Pont unduly dominated General Motors and made Du Pont get rid of its GM stock. In the Phillips-Tidewater Case (1966), the head of the Justice Department started prosecution on the ground that if Phillips Petroleum were refused the merger, it would start hundreds of new gas stations in that area and thereby increase the degree of competition. Similar reasoning was involved in the prosecution by the government of the proposed merger by Bethlehem Steel, which had no plant in the Chicago area, and Youngstown Steel, which did have such a plant. By forcing Bethlehem to build a new plant there, it was hoped that one extra competitor would be established. In the Pabst Case (1966), mere fear of size as such—quite independent of considerations of dominant share of market—was used against mergers by Judge Warren Burger (later Chief Justice of the Supreme Court). Pegged commission rates by the New York Stock Exchange and the Chicago Board of Trade have been successfully attacked by the antitrust division's suits.

Litton Industries, IT&T, and others had been the darlings of Wall Street during the 1960s, each taking over dozens and dozens of smaller firms in unrelated industries. A host of imitators sprang up, of course.

Thus, Ling-Temco-Vought began with an airplane company but soon acquired scores of companies by clever offers of new varieties of Ling securities—preferred stock, convertible preferred, second convertible preferred, convertible bonds, bonds with attached (but detachable) warrant options to buy the common. One had to be an Einstein of finance to calculate the amount of dilution of ownership that would occur if all convertible securities were ultimately to be converted into common stock. (Professor Warren Law of the Harvard Business School admitted the Ling prospectus was beyond him!) Often, little conglomerates would take over giant, cash-rich companies many times their own size, using in the end the cash of the company taken over to pay for the acquisition. Thirty-year-old whiz kids pyramided thousands of dollars into tens of millions almost overnight.

Each new successful acquisition increased total sales and reported per share earnings, thereby enabling the conglomerates to acquire still more companies at lower and lower cash cost. (Often the reported gain in earnings was misleading, being merely the product of imaginative accounting, which ignored potential dilution by conversion, treated once-and-for-all paper gains on security sales as if they were recurring operating earnings, juggled the accounting treatment of good will, and reported as current income items for which payment would be received only in future installments. Franchise and land companies were some of the worst offenders.)

But what, after all, does the airplane business have in common with meat packing? Or typewriters with birth-control pills? Or computer leasing with passenger-bus operations? Good modern management, coupled with adequate finance, can of course help in any line of activity. And the history of the East India and Hudson Bay companies does remind us that in underdeveloped countries the only way to get the efficiencies associated with large-scale corporations may be through conglomerates. (Fancifully, if Harold Geneen has the genius to run scores of unrelated activities under the headship of the notorious International Telephone & Telegraph, could he be the prototype and forerunner of Galbraith's expert-planner under socialism or some equivalent form of organization of the future industrial state?)

By the 1970s the bubble had burst on the conglomerates. It was a chain-letter form of growth which had to grow ever faster in order not to lead to disillusionment and collapse. When even the mighty Litton Industries had a pause in earnings growth, the jig was up for the Lings, Littons, and later imitators. Now "conglomerate" became a dirty word. Conglomerate stocks plummetted. Acquisitions failed. Mergers were blocked by the Justice Department. A scapegoat was needed by Congress and the public: conglomerates provided a convenient target. Bigness as such was held against them, on the *simpliste* theory that the unit with the "deeper pocket" can outbargain and destroy its competitors. There were threats to tax them, or take away from them the usual privilege of having bond interest tax-deductible. Fear of "reciprocity"—the practice of one big business to buy products from its own branches or from those other companies which reciprocate with purchases from it, even at unfavorable market terms—became rampant in the Antitrust Division and in the courts. Nonetheless, Professor Stigler, in a task-force investigation for President Nixon, concluded that reciprocity is quite trivial in economic importance and that much of the hostility to conglomerates is hysterically irrational. Often those seeking take-overs represented "outsiders," self-made newly arrived chaps who hadn't belonged to Yale's Skull and Bones or been vetted by the existing business establishment. Their crudities were thus specially resented. And yet, corporate oligarchies that had grown soft and arrogant under previous minority rule were often goaded into reform by fear of take-over or were replaced by those better able to utilize the corporation's resources.

Take-overs, like bankruptcy, represent one of Nature's methods of eliminating deadwood in the struggle for survival. A more open—and more efficiently responsive—corporate society can result. But, without public surveillance and control, the opposite could also emerge. The Darwinian jungle is not guaranteed to produce a happy ending. Influencing and corrupting governments may be the only thing conglomerates are better at—as is suggested by the IT&T scandals during the Allende Chile takeover and the Nixon administration.

## FUTURE OF ANTITRUST POLICY

In summary, both Republicans and Democrats are spending more and more money on lawyers and investigators to enforce the antitrust laws with ever-increasing vigor. Firms no longer dare to use group practices that used to be standard in American industry. Aside from civil and criminal suits initiated by government, they face the threat of suits for triple damages initiated by aggrieved rivals.

Judges are tougher in their judgments. More and more they weaken the powers that a business firm has to exploit its patents and its market advantages. Even after a case has been decided against a company, it is not off the hook. It may feel forced to enter into "consent decrees" which bind it to follow certain policies, and the judge may for years afterward keep his careful eye on the firm's performance. (The United Shoe Case is a good example, where the company had to agree to sell its machines instead of only renting them. Like a truant schoolboy, it had to keep reporting to the federal judge. In a similar way, the FTC has kept the giant meat packers under surveillance literally for decades.)

The Justice Department recently instituted suits against two giant firms that are products of the electronic age: IBM and AT&T. Both firms are very large, and AT&T is already regulated by the government. Yet they are leaders in industries in which technical progress is rapid and research vital. The government suits appear to be an attack on the Schumpeterian idea that innovation is encouraged by the presence of large firms in the market. Or perhaps the idea is that the short-run loss from monopolistic pricing outweighs the long-run benefit from increased innovation.

Too often the law—as drawn up by Congress, enforced by the Department of Justice, and adjudicated by the courts—regards various vigorous forms of competition that tend to eliminate firms and reduce the discrepancy between price and marginal cost as crimes rather than good deeds. The legal mind is not so much concerned with the distortion of prices, which it has no means of measuring, as it is with methods by which prices are set. Yet economic and legal minds do seem today to be converging.

As to the future evolution of antitrust policy, there are two opposing philosophies. Carl Kaysen, formerly of Harvard and now director of the Institute for Advanced Study in Princeton, together with Donald F. Turner, professor at Harvard Law School and formerly President Johnson's head of the Antitrust Division, believes the test should be whether a firm has "market power per se," stemming from its monopolistic market *structure*. Independently of its *conduct*, Kaysen and Turner would say there is a prima facie case for breaking up such a company. At the opposite pole is the view that an updated "rule of reason" should be applied to every case. If even the biggest monopoly is found to display marvelous Schumpeterian innovation, it should be left undisturbed by antitrust litigation. There is an unresolved conflict here, and all that can be said now is that economists tend to lean toward the market-structure viewpoint.

## FINALE

Our discussion of antitrust has concentrated on United States experience for the very good reason that this country has been a pioneer in such legislation. For many years countries such as Britain, Germany, and Japan, as well as other European nations, appeared to us to take a very lax view of the legality of monopolistic arrangements. After World War II, American occupational authorities in Japan and Germany tried to introduce legislation in those countries to break up their old combines. For a while this seemed to succeed. Then, as those nations began to stand on their own feet, there was some backsliding. However, the Common Market countries have been strengthening their antitrust statutes, and it remains to be seen in what spirit the letter of the regulations will be interpreted. And Britain has belatedly begun to adopt antitrust practices. (Many nations, like the U.S. in the Webb-Pomerene Act, 1918, lighten their antitrust rules for their own exporters; many more exempt them completely. Economists must now resist the movement to exempt firms from antitrust legislation in order to help balance of payments—or for other good causes, such as environmental protection: the Devil of vested interests can quote Scriptures for his purposes.)

While no one would claim that American antitrust legislation and enforcement have been completely logical or have come anywhere near complete success, one has but to look abroad to realize how much worse off our economy might have been were it not for the omnipresent threat of legal prosecution. American enterprise is kept on the defensive and would never dream of adopting the flagrant devices that are all too common in most places.

Professor Richard Caves has compared American antitrust action to traffic laws. Most citizens do not consider breaking the traffic laws mortal sins. And the police tend to act only against the most flagrant offenders—the driver who goes 80 in a school zone. But the fact that the policeman may be there, *ready to make an arrest*, does keep drivers generally more in conformity with the laws of the road. "The guilty flee where no man pursueth." And so, often, do the innocent. To cynics, part of the efficacy of the antitrust laws may even result from their arbitrariness: like the emperor who would take out a general at random and shoot him—"in order to encourage the others"—the antitrust program hangs like the sword of Damocles over every businessman, limiting his temptation to exercise monopoly power.

By laissez faire one does not automatically get perfect competition. To reduce imperfections of competition, a nation must maintain perpetual vigilance.

**Workable competition**  Repeatedly, in Part Three, we have stressed the basic problem of how a pricing system solves society's questions WHAT, HOW, FOR WHOM. This frames the rational goal of antitrust policy.

We cannot expect competition to become everywhere "perfectly perfect," in the strict sense of the economist. But what we must strive for is what the late J. M. Clark years ago called "workable competition." By public and private policies, we can hope to improve the efficiency with which market prices reflect underlying individual needs, desires, and wants against the background of true costs of goods—marginal costs in terms of alternative goods that could be produced and in terms of used-up, scarce productive factors which involve sweat and disutility. Just as concentration in control of share of market was made to decrease from 1900 to mid-century, so by century's end can monopoly imperfections be weakened further. But laissez faire cannot be counted on to do this. Public vigilance and support for antitrust will be required.

Part Four will be concerned with identical problems that arise in connection with the pricing of land, labor, and capital. Again, the function of such pricing in trying to solve society's problems is the focal point of interest.

## SUMMARY

### A. ANALYTICAL PATTERNS OF IMPERFECT COMPETITION

1  Few business firms are able to develop exact curves of cost and revenue. This does not mean that they are oblivious to profit maximization. Through trial and error, they may be doing a tolerably good job of keeping alive as a business entity and of achieving long-run optimum profits.

2   Under imperfect competition, a firm may have to make rough guesses in setting its price. Often it will use some kind of *markup* over an estimate of unit cost. Nonetheless, it is often market conditions that determine how much of a markup any firm can safely count on getting; so in a sense the problem is merely re-posed. Only factual investigations of each market situation can tell what the result is likely to be.

3   In Galbraith's vision of the new industrial state, bureaucrats of the technostructure exercise unilateral power to mold consumer tastes. They may be checked by the "countervailing power" of their large-scale suppliers or customers; and despite Galbraith's prose, even the largest corporations are subject to checks of numerous rival conglomerates, making collusion difficult and despotic rule shortsighted.

4   Various patterns of competition lend themselves to economic analysis: (1) monopoly; (2) oligopoly, in which few sellers compete with similar or differentiated products; (3) Chamberlinian models of many sellers of differentiated products; and (4) the case of perfect competition itself. The kinked demand curve of oligopoly helps to explain its rigid administered pricing around a level that can be agreed upon. The no-profit tangency equilibrium of Chamberlin's large group leaves society with the wastes of excess capacity and overdifferentiated products.

## B. MODERN ANTITRUST PROBLEMS

5   The economic evils of such imperfections transcend the mere matter of monopolistic profits: Entry may cut out excess-profits *without* bringing prices down to marginal costs; overentry of imperfect competitors may waste resources without giving the consumer the benefit of lower prices; monopolistic and oligopolistic pricing above true marginal costs brings distortion of resource allocation (inefficiency and nonresponsiveness) even if the firms involved have their excess-profits taxed or competed away.

6   Against the evils of monopoly and oligopoly must be weighed the possible Schumpeterian *dynamic* efficiencies which they may introduce. A large firm in a protected market may have the wherewithal to develop new inventions and also the assurance that it will not lose to competitors the advantages of its own research efforts. In strongly decreasing-cost industries, there is no hope for viable *perfect* competition, and substitute checks on the powers of few dominating firms have to come from public control.

7   By public regulation of utilities and by various formal and informal antitrust activities of the state, some of the checks and balances that are not automatically enforceable by perfect competition can be achieved by governmental action.

8   The history of American antitrust legislation and enforcement has been an irregular one. Inaction has been followed by vigorous action; and sometimes by various backward steps, including price-maintenance laws which seem to reduce rather

than enhance effective price competition. Although the legal mind of judges and legislators has not always concentrated on what economists consider the key pricing issue—e.g., being excessively concerned with "reciprocity," conglomerates, and bigness as such—evolutionary progress has been made. And many nations abroad are beginning to imitate our methods. After economists realize that perfect competition is not spontaneously attained or enforceable, the problem of defining and approaching "workable competition" becomes paramount. Here is the frontier for economic policy.

## CONCEPTS FOR REVIEW

| | |
|---|---|
| markup pricing, administered $P$ | utility rate regulation |
| Galbraithian countervailing power and technostructure | fair return on original or reproduction cost or on market valuation |
| oligopoly, with or without tacit collusion, kinked demand | Sherman, Clayton, Celler-Kefauver Acts |
| free entry | Antitrust Division and Federal Trade Commission (FTC) |
| no-profit equilibrium of producers of differentiated products | conglomerates |
| evils of imperfect competition | Schumpeterian dynamic advantages |
| | challenge of "workable competition" |

## QUESTIONS FOR DISCUSSION

1  Give examples of behavior by business firms suggesting that they do seek to maximize their profits. Give some apparent exceptions.

2  Suppose you ran an electric company. How could you go about maximizing profits? How would you estimate elasticity of demand? Would an economics textbook be the source for learning how to be successful in this respect?

3  What are meant by markup and administered pricing? Show how these might work.

4  Describe the pattern of imperfect competition in the auto industry, cigarette industry, aluminum industry, mousetrap industry, women's-dress trade, retail grocery trade, barbershop trade, undertaking industry.

5  "The tragedy of monopolistic competition often has nothing to do with excessive profits. Rather, there may be no profits at all, the high price being frittered away in small volume and inefficient production." Discuss.

6  Recapitulate highlights of antitrust activity here and abroad.

7  "It is utopian to try to break up monopolies into even a few effectively competing units, because the basic cause of monopoly is the law of decreasing cost with mass production, and, in any case, a few competitors are not enough to duplicate the pricing patterns of perfect competition." Discuss both parts of this statement.

8 "The A & P Company is not bad just because it is big." Discuss.

9 Eisenhower's Justice Department permitted Hudson and Nash to merge as American Motors, permitted Studebaker and Packard to merge, but forbade the merger of the Bethlehem and Youngstown steel companies. All these decisions were made in the interest of promoting competition. Do you think they are necessarily inconsistent? Give arguments pro and con.

10 "The modern corporation is a good pooler of risks. Other things being equal, the larger the firm, the more it can cancel off one risk against another, the more it can economize on inventory, excess peak-capacity, and taxes, and the more it can spread the indivisible costs of the best-grade research among its many units. Larger size tends to help, and if it emulates the example of General Motors and other efficient decentralizers of decision making, there are almost no penalties from larger size. I conclude that trying to prevent monopolies is a fight against nature." Comment critically.

# 4

## DISTRIBUTION OF INCOME: THE PRICING OF THE PRODUCTIVE FACTORS

In the next few chapters of Part Four we shall be primarily concerned with how factors of production get priced in the marketplace; that is, we shall analyze the determination of (1) *rents* of land and other resources (Chapter 28), (2) *wages* of various kinds of labor (Chapter 29), (3) *interest* rates on capital assets (Chapter 30), and (4) *profit* (Chapter 31), and grand summary (Chapter 32).

Economists call this the problem of "distribution." They do not mean by this term what the man in the street means when he refers to distribution as the marketing of goods and the carrying of goods to the final consumer. Instead, in Part Four distribution deals with the problem of FOR WHOM goods are to be produced. It is pricing of factors of production by supply and demand that is helping determine FOR WHOM. This same factor pricing also operates to solve the problem of HOW society is to produce.

The theory of distribution is still in an unsettled state. Questions still being debated among economists are these: What is the role of *power* relations, as against *market* relations, in determining how large a share of the national income goes to labor? To property? To different classes of labor (skilled, unskilled), and of property owners (landlords, interest-receiving *rentiers,* equity shareowners)? Here in Part Four we shall give the theories of microeconomics all the rope they can use to try to corral the complex trends of factor shares in distribution. Later, in Part Six, we shall meet some alternative models of distribution.

Why are wages some three-quarters of the total national product? To help us understand this, we must study the forces that determine market wage rates, market land rentals, market interest rates. Thus, if technological changes (reflecting, for example, automation) lowered market wage rates relative to the returns to property, the wage share might fall. Because the number of owners of property is so much smaller than the number of owners of labor, the result would be to shift the Lorenz-curve measure of inequality toward greater income

# 27

# THEORY OF PRODUCTION AND MARGINAL-PRODUCTS

Knowledge is the only instrument of production that is not subject to diminishing returns.
J. M. CLARK

inequality. We hope to understand the economic question of distribution primarily by focusing on the markets where factors of production get priced. This analysis seeks to give us insight into optimality equilibria and into "exploitation."

The key to such factor pricing is sought in the economic *theory of production*. So, as a prelude to our general discussion of distribution of income, this chapter investigates the theory of production. It defines the important economic concept of "marginal-product" and relates this to the familiar law of diminishing returns. Finally, the chapter shows that the demand curves for the various factors of production—the demands for labor, land, and so forth—are to be expressed in terms of their marginal-products.

### DEMAND FOR FACTORS A JOINTLY INTERDEPENDENT DEMAND

The basic peculiarity about the demand for inputs stems from this technological fact: Factors usually do not work alone. A shovel by itself is worthless to me if I wish a cellar; a man with his bare hands is equally worthless. Together, the man and shovel can dig my cellar. In other words, the quantity of a good produced depends *jointly* upon all the available inputs.

Sir William Petty put the matter in this striking, seventeenth-century way: Labor is the father of product and land the mother. One cannot say which is more important in producing a baby—a mother or a father. So, too, one cannot in most cases hope to demonstrate how much of the physical product has been *caused* by any one of the different factors *taken by itself*. The different factors *interact* with each other. Usually they reinforce each other's effectiveness, but sometimes they are substitutes for one another and they compete with, rather than complement, each other.

There is an important consequence of this jointness, or interdependence, among the productivities of the different factor inputs, namely: The amount of labor demanded will depend on its wage rate, but the labor demanded will also depend upon the price of machines. The same is true of the demand for machines. By raising miners' wages, John L. Lewis created good business for power tools.

Thus, the demand for each input will depend upon the prices of *all* inputs, not on its own price alone. *Cross elasticities* between different factors are as important as regular "own" elasticities.

It is this interdependence of productivities of land, labor, and capital goods that makes the problem of distribution complex. For suppose we had to distribute at one harvest time the whole aggregate of output constituting the NNP. If land by itself had produced so much, and labor by itself had produced so much, and some third factor had by itself produced the rest, distribution might seem easy indeed. Crude notions of fairness might suggest that each factor share be simply set at what each has alone produced. Ethics aside, under free supply and demand, if the separate factors çould produce goods by themselves, they could jolly well make sure that they got the fruits of their activity; so, with all value judgments disregarded, this would be a good description of the facts.

But reread the above paragraph and underline such words as "*by itself* produced" and "*has alone* produced." They refer to an *independence* of productivities which we know is simply lacking in the real world. If land and labor *together* produce the corn harvest, just how do you unscramble the separate contributions that supply and demand will parcel out to each?[1] A proud American worker might reflect on what *he* would produce and get in India or in 1900 America.

How is the problem of distribution resolved? It gets resolved by the processes of supply and demand, operating in perfectly or imperfectly competitive markets and modified by government laws. A brief analysis of the economic theory of production provides the indispensable key.

## TECHNICAL LAW RELATING OUTPUT TO INPUTS: THE "PRODUCTION FUNCTION"

The theory of production begins with specific engineering or technological information. If you have a certain amount of labor, a certain amount of land, and certain prescribed amounts of other inputs such as machines or raw materials, how much output of a particular good can you get? The answer depends upon the state of technology: if someone makes a new invention or discovers a new industrial process, the obtainable output from given factor inputs will go up. *But, at any time, there will be a maximum obtainable amount of product for any given amounts of factor inputs.*

This technical law relating inputs to output is so important that economists have given it a name. They call it the "production function."

*Definition:* The production function is the technical relationship telling the maximum amount of output capable of being produced by each and every set of specified inputs (or factors of production). It is defined for a given state of technical knowledge.

Here are some examples.

An agricultural engineer lists in a thick book the various combinations of land and labor that will produce various quantities of corn. On one page of the book he lists the alternative combinations of land and labor needed to produce 100 bushels of corn; on another page, the alternative input combinations that will produce 200 bushels of corn; and so forth. Another example of a production function would be the chemical engineer's listing of the various ways of producing gasoline of a given octane rating.

The concept of an "average"—such as the "arithmetic mean" or "geometric mean" of two positive numbers—can help you understand the production function. Recall the *arithmetic mean* of two numbers, such as 8 and 2, is half their sum, or 5. Similarly, we define the *geometric mean* of two positive numbers as the square root of their product. For 8 and 2, we get a geometric mean of "square-root of 16," or 4. (Don't be surprised that the geometric mean

---

[1] Labor leaders used to say, "Without labor there is zero product. So attribute to labor *all* the product." Spokesmen for capital used the same bad logic to produce the opposite result: "Take away all capital goods, and labor scratches a bare pittance from the earth; so practically all the product should go to capital." The trouble with such foolish proposals is that, taken together, they allocate 200 or 300 per cent of the total product to the two or three factors, whereas there is only 100 per cent of the harvest to be allocated. And it makes no sense to say, "There is some truth on both sides; so let us apply the Golden Mean and, by a rule of unreason, give each of the factors the largest equal shares that will use up the available 100 per cent of product." A real-world economy is not a courtroom where nimble legal minds illogically split hairs in order to solve society's problem of FOR WHOM.

is less than the arithmetic mean; it always will be if the numbers are not equal.) Now suppose 1 man on 1 acre of land produces 1 unit of corn output. Suppose statisticians tell us that the production function in this corn industry is "the unweighted geometric mean of the two inputs." Can we then predict how much 1 man will produce on 16 acres of land? Yes, the production function constitutes our needed law or formula. To get the geometric mean of $1 \times 16$, we take the square root of their product to get 4 of corn output as our answer.[2]

There are thousands of different production functions in the American economy: at least one for each of the innumerable firms or productive units. A purpose of this chapter is to show how the firm's production function lies behind its Total Cost curve (discussed in Chapter 24) and to show how this provides the basis for the firm's derived demand for land, labor, capital, fertilizer, and numerous other productive inputs that it goes out into the market to buy.

Thus, the firm is poised between two kinds of markets: (1) the commodity market in which it appears as a supplier, selling its wares along the demand curve *of its customers;* and (2) the markets for factors of production in which it itself appears as a demander, buying inputs so as to minimize its total costs of production and to produce its Maximum-profit output. It is these factor markets which put prices upon the various productive inputs of the community and thus determine the distribution of income (wages, rent, interest, and so forth).

## THE AGGREGATE AMERICAN PRODUCTION FUNCTION

Suppose, first, we put away our microscope and train a telescope on the aggregate magnitudes for American manufacturing of total labor, total capital, and total product. Such magnitudes must be measured with care, involving innumerable index-number problems of correct weighting; yet they are useful in giving a broad description of society. Back in the late twenties, former Senator Paul H. Douglas, then a University of Chicago professor of economics, won an important prize for his pathbreaking statistical measurement of America's production function. Later, MIT's Robert Solow carried these researches a significant step further by showing how technological progress has been improving the productivity of American labor and capital.[3]

What have Douglas and Solow shown? Their statistics suggest that labor is the single most important factor of production in a certain subtle sense. Both labor and capital are needed in production: take away all capital, or alternatively all labor, and you will be left with negligible total product. But they find that a 1 per cent increase in labor seems to increase output about three times as much as would a 1 per cent increase in capital. This largely corresponds with the widely known fact that wages

[2] We'll learn in a moment that it turns out to be more realistic to give labor 3 times the weight of other factor inputs; so the fourth root of $1 \times 1 \times 1 \times 16$ gives us the empirically more correct answer of 2 rather than 4, the augmentation of land not being so important in the case of the weighted geometric mean as in the unweighted case.

[3] P. H. Douglas, *Theory of Wages* (Macmillan, New York, 1934); R. M. Solow, "Technical Change and the Aggregate Production Function," *Review of Economics and Statistics*, vol. 39, 1957, pp. 312–320. Neither study measures land's separate contribution and share. In the 1970s this would probably be only about 5 per cent for the whole economy, and much less for manufacturing alone; but early in the century it was perhaps double that. Further work by E. Denison will be cited in Chapter 37, where modern growth models are discussed.

are about three-fourths of the national product, while one-fourth (which is one-third of wages) is about the share of property incomes.[4]

**Empirical findings**   There are numerous other findings from such studies, many of which have received important corroboration from similar researches by the nonprofit National Bureau of Economic Research. Here are a few.

1. The productivity of both labor and capital together has been increasing throughout this century because of improved technology and skill. The average rate of improvement appears to be between 1 and 2 per cent per year.

2. The amount of capital has been growing at a faster rate than the labor supply because of successful thrift on the part of society as a whole and slower growth in man-hours worked. As a result, each laborer has more capital goods to work with, and hence his productivity wages have tended to rise even faster than the 1 to 2 per cent attributable to technological growth alone.

3. The return per unit of capital might have been expected to encounter diminishing returns because each capital unit now has less labor to cooperate with it. Yet capital's return per unit has in fact remained about the same. Why? Because of the offsetting effect of *technological progress*.

4. Technical improvements by themselves would probably have raised profits on capital had not the diminishing returns to increasing capital per laborer been taking place as an offset. In consequence of these simultaneous offsets, the sharing of the growing social pie has remained not too far from the same three-fourths and one-fourth level—a remarkable fact in view of the growing union movement, the vast structural changes in our economy since 1900, and the widespread notion that "automation" has downgraded the value of human brain power and skills.

Similar statistical measurements all over the globe help to put flesh on the bare bones of the microeconomic theory of production and distribution, and serve as factual tests of the validity of economic principles—principles that Chapter 37 will use for growth theory. But now let us put the production function under a microscope.

## MARGINAL-PRODUCTS DEFINED

In Chapter 2, the law of diminishing returns was defined. Figure 27-1 reproduces the table (shown earlier on page 27) of diminishing *extra product* for varying extra labor units added to fixed land. Back there, we were using the production-function concept without yet knowing the name.

Now we can introduce the economist's name for extra product. Recall that in economic theory the word "extra" is typically replaced by the word "marginal." It is natural, then, to define terms as follows:

*Definition:* The "marginal-product" of a productive factor is the extra product or output

---

[4]That is, their so-called Cobb-Douglas production function is the weighted geometric mean of footnote 2's numerical example. Consistent with the law of diminishing returns, discussed in Chapter 2 and in the next sections of this chapter, a 1 per cent increase in either factor *alone* increases product by *less* than 1 per cent: actually by $\frac{3}{4}$ per cent in the case of labor and by $\frac{1}{4}$ per cent in the case of capital.

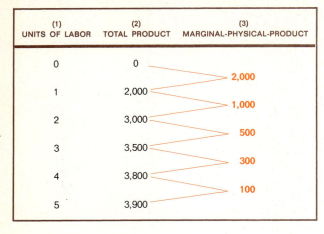

| (1)<br>UNITS OF LABOR | (2)<br>TOTAL PRODUCT | (3)<br>MARGINAL-PHYSICAL-PRODUCT |
|---|---|---|
| 0 | 0 | |
| | | 2,000 |
| 1 | 2,000 | |
| | | 1,000 |
| 2 | 3,000 | |
| | | 500 |
| 3 | 3,500 | |
| | | 300 |
| 4 | 3,800 | |
| | | 100 |
| 5 | 3,900 | |

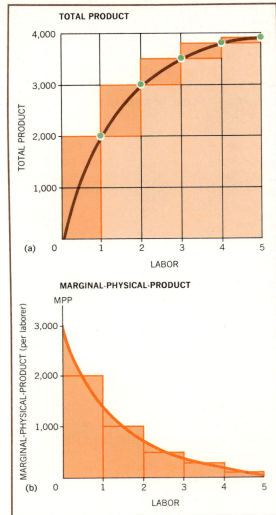

**FIG. 27-1**
Diminishing returns can be stated, numerically and graphically, as diminishing marginal-product

Marginal-physical-product is calculated as difference to total product added by 1 extra unit of input (as when fourth worker adds $300 = 3,800 - 3,500$ units of product). Each new worker adds diminishing marginal-product.

The upper diagram shows that total product increases by smaller and smaller steps as new input units are added.

The lower diagram shows the declining steps of extra- or marginal-product. Smoothing the steps gives the declining curve of smoothed marginal-physical-product. The area in (b) under the marginal-physical-product curve (or of the rectangles) adds up to the total product shown in (a) above. (For example, $2,000 + 1,000 + 500 =$ total product of 3,500 for three men. What gives total product for four, or five, men?)

added by one extra unit of that factor, while other factors are being held constant. Labor's marginal-product is the extra output you get when you add one unit of labor, holding all other inputs constant. Similarly, land's marginal-product is the change in total product resulting from one additional unit of land, with all other inputs held constant—and so forth, for any factor.[5]

Note that the marginal-product of a factor is expressed in *physical* units of product per unit of extra input. So careful economists often speak of "marginal-physical-product" rather than plain marginal-product, particularly when they want to avoid any possible confusion with a later *dollar* concept called "marginal-revenue-product."

[5]Chapter 30 will discuss some inescapable intricacies involved in defining "capital."

## MARGINAL-PHYSICAL-PRODUCTS AND DIMINISHING RETURNS

Column (3) of the table in Fig. 27-1 can now be identified with the term "marginal-physical-product." Note the drop from 2,000 to 100, in accordance with diminishing returns. The same marginal-product is pictured in the lower diagram, which shows the steady drop of labor's marginal-physical-product. This reflects the fact that the upper chart shows *total* product rising in ever-smaller steps as we hold land constant and add equal extra units of labor. The law of diminishing returns, we see, could be renamed the "law of diminishing marginal-physical-product." (For brevity, one skips the word "physical" when no misunderstanding is likely and writes $MP$ for $MPP$.)

What is true for one input is also true for another. We can interchange land and labor, now holding labor constant and varying land. We can make up a new table, showing land's marginal (physical) product in its column. And this would also presumably obey the law of diminishing returns. Why? Because now each of the extra land units would have less and less of the fixed labor factor to work with.

## DISTRIBUTION SOLVED BY MARGINAL-PRODUCTS

Now the riddle of the Sphinx—how to allocate among two (or more) cooperating factors the total product they *jointly* produce—can be solved by use of the marginal-product concept. John Bates Clark, a distinguished Columbia economist, provided a simplified theory of distribution around 1900. It can be applied to competitive price-and-wage determination when there are any number of goods and factor inputs, but it is most easily grasped if we concentrate on one total harvest output—call it corn, or a basket of goods, or $Q$. A production function tells how much $Q$ is produced for each amount of man-hours, $L$, and number of acres of homogeneous land, $A$.

Although diminishing returns applies when one factor is added to the other fixed factor, perfect competition is best maintained when there are "constant returns to scale" when *all* factors are increased simultaneously in the same proportion. (Thus, when Clark doubles land *and* labor, he finds output has just doubled; when he increases $L$ and $A$ together by any equal per cent, $Q$ increases by that same per cent. For if $Q$ were to grow by a greater per cent, there would be long-run decreasing costs for each firm, and the firm that grew largest first could create a monopoly.)

Now Clark reasons as follows. A first man produces great marginal-product because he has so much land to work with. Man 2 adds a large, but slightly less tall, vertical slab of marginal-product. But the two men are alike: they must get exactly the same wage. Which wage? The $MP$ of Man 1? The lower $MP$ of Man 2? The average of these?

Under free competition, where landowners are free to employ as few or many $L$ as they like, the answer is plain:

Landlords will never freely hire that second man if the market wage they must pay him exceeds his marginal-product. So the $dd$ demand curve for labor will ensure that *all* the men who get hired do receive *the lowest marginal-product of the last man.*

What happens to the excess of $MP$ produced by the first man and all the earlier men up to the very last? That stays with the landlord. It is his residual rent. In free competitive markets, no one can take it away from him. Is he "profiteering"? Not in the usual sense of the word. Each landowner is but one of thousands: any acre of his is no better and no worse than the acres of the rest. Just as worker competes with worker for jobs, landowners compete with landowners for workers. There are no conspiracies, no employer associations, and no unions in Clark's competitive world.

Figure 27-2 shows that the marginal-product curve of labor gives the *dd* demand curve of all employers in terms of real wages (in corn, or market baskets of goods, or *Q* units). The population supply gives us *ss*, and the equilibrium wage comes at *E*. The total wage share of labor is given by $W \times L$ (e.g., $W = 5$ and $L = 1$ million, total wages = 5 million); this is shown by the dark orange area of the rectangle at *E*.

We have determined not only the distributive share of labor but also land rent. The indicated light rent triangle simply measures all the "excesses over final marginal-product that the early workers brought and never got paid in wages." Whether fair or unfair, all the men are alike; all landlords are free competitors who can demand or not demand as they like; so it is inevitable under competition that all workers get paid the *MP* of the last worker and, because of diminishing returns, that there be left the residual triangle of rent that goes to the landowners.

This completes the marginal-productivity theory of distribution. Note that labor wages exceed property rents in this example: the wage rectangle of *MP* is about three times as large as the residual rent triangle of property. That is realistic, but it depends on the facts of technology. A new invention that was very "labor-saving" could twist the *dd* curve inward near *E* and make property's triangle swallow up 60 to 80 per cent of the total NNP!

If mass immigration or seven children per family increased *L* so much as to move society down the *dd* curve to a low wage, the rectangle share of labor *might* fall relative to the rent triangle of land. It might, but might not. Here is the explanation:

An increase in *L* along the *dd* curve of *MP must* always raise the *absolute* total of land's

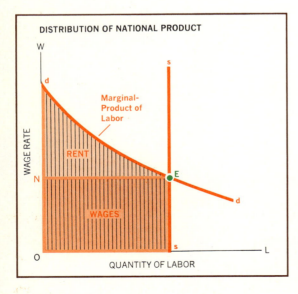

**FIG. 27-2**
**Marginal-product principles determine traditional factor distribution of income**
Total wages is dark rectangle's area: the wage-rate altitude times labor-quantity base. Rent gets what is left over, as shown by the light residual triangle. Total product, the sum of wage-rectangle plus rent-triangle areas, is area under demand curve of society's marginal-product (the sum of all the vertical slabs added by each new worker).

rent triangle. (Try it.) What about the absolute total of labor's rectangle? The elasticity discussion of Chapter 20 reminds us that labor's total wage rectangle will most certainly increase if *dd* has more-than-unitary elasticity, $E_d$. But can labor's rectangle grow *as great* in percentage as land's triangle, or even greater? Although not obvious until you experiment with drawing in *dd* curves, the answer is definite: Yes, the relative share of wage's rectangle can increase and the relative share of land's triangle can decrease if the marginal-product curve slopes downward slowly enough. Senator Douglas' researches, corroborated for England and elsewhere by the late Sir Arthur Bowley, suggest that, despite changing birth rates and technology, labor's relative share remains surprisingly constant over the decades!

**Generalizations**   Before summarizing the marginal-productivity theory of wages, let us appreciate J. B. Clark's advance over such classical economists as David Ricardo, a follower of Adam Smith and a leader of economic thought in the early 1800s. Ricardo would have soon grasped, and agreed with, Clark's Fig. 27-2; it fits in well with Ricardian rent theory. But Clark said more than that. He also proved these remarkable facts:

**You can switch the roles of labor and land. Now hold labor constant. Add successive units of variable land to fixed labor. Calculate each successive acre's marginal-product. Draw a *d'd'* curve showing how many acres labor-owners will demand of land at each rent rate. In the new version of Fig. 27-2 that you draw, find a new *E'* point of equilibrium. Identify land's *rectangle* of rent as determined by *its* MP. Identify labor's *residual* wage triangle. Ricardo would be impressed by the complete symmetry of the factors: that *all* factors can be thought of as having their distributive shares determined simultaneously by their respective interdependent marginal-products.**

That is not all. Instead of labor and land, suppose the only two factors were labor *L* and some versatile capital goods *K*. Suppose a smooth production function relates *Q* to *L* and *K*, with the same general properties as in Fig. 27-2. Then you can redraw Fig. 27-2 and get an identical picture of income distribution between *L* and *K*.[6]

**Summary**   Marginal productivities provide the clue to competitive pricing of factor inputs—of labor or of skilled and unskilled labor, of each grade of land, of capital goods (i.e., rentals for their use), of fertilizer, and of other inputs.

**Profit-maximizing employers in competitive factor markets will have their demand curves for inputs determined by what additions to their product successive units of a factor will bring, i.e., by marginal-products. In the simplified Clark case of a single *Q* output, firms' physical *MP*s are added horizontally—as *dd* and *ss* curves were in Chapters 22 and 23—**

---

[6]That is still not all. Suppose we have three (or more) factors of production: *L*, *A*, and *K*. Again assume that a well-behaved production function gives *Q* output in terms of all three inputs. Again vary *L* alone; calculate its *MP*s. Then vary *K* alone; calculate its *MP*s. Vary *A* alone; calculate land's diminishing *MP*s. Now set up *three* simultaneous, interdependent demand curves of marginal-products. Set up three supply curves for the factors. It will follow that all *Q*, and no more, will get distributed by competition among the three factors according to equality of each factor-price to its marginal-product: $P_L = MP_L$, $P_A = MP_A$, $P_K$ = price charged for use of capital good = $MP_K$. Each unit of any factor gets what its last unit produces of *MP*; the residual surplus, of early units' *MP*s over final *MP*, provides just enough *Q* to pay the other factors their final *MP*s. (Some qualifications of this simple Clark model will occur in the Appendix to this chapter. Note here that monopoly bidding by employers would require alterations in the Clark model, as shown in Fig. 29-7's footnote.)

to get the market demand *dd* for labor or for any other factor. At the level determined by intersection of each *dd* with its factor-supply *ss*, we get

Wage = marginal-product of labor
Rent = marginal-product of land
And so forth for any factor

This distributes 100 per cent of *Q*, no more and no less, among all the factors of production.

### COMPETITIVE EQUILIBRIUM A GOOD THING?

We have now completed a sketch of how the marginal-product theory "distributes" total product between two factors—land and labor—in a simplified world.

We have simply been observing how hard-boiled competition would work itself out under simple conditions. Just as the jungle has its laws without regard to right and wrong, so does the competitive market have its brute facts.

But did you notice one efficient thing that happened? Without a planning board, *society got its food produced in the most efficient way*. How did that happen? Well, efficiency certainly requires that the homogeneous land and labor be everywhere combined for food in exactly the same proportions. (PROOF: Suppose society were using much labor on half its land and little labor on the other half. The law of diminishing returns tells us that the marginal-product of the workers will be less on the dense than on the sparse half. So we can get some extra *Q* by shifting men to the sparse acres with higher *MP*. Maximum output comes when marginal-products are equal on both halves, i.e., when labor and land are combined in the same proportions on both halves. QED.)

Ruthless competition with only the commercially fittest surviving did bring about the desirable equality everywhere of factor proportions and marginal-products. How did it do this? By landlords seeking maximum rents in competition with one another; by workers seeking maximum wages in competition with one another; by market prices being forced to lowest costs of production by inexorable competitive forces. These were the vital processes. (WARNING: A tendency toward "increasing returns to scale" would have killed off perfect competition and have brought in monopoly to spoil the whole story. So would collusions among any of the factors. Note also that if different acres were of different qualities, we would no longer use the same proportion of labor on each; instead, the desirable equality of marginal-products of transferable labor would be achieved by competition's making sure that relatively more laborers get used on the better lands with higher marginal products—a sensible result!)

We shall see again, in Chapter 32, that competitive pricing can help solve efficiently the How problem of any society. We shall see that charging a rent for God-given land is necessary if such scarce land is to be rightly allocated. But notice that we have not proved that the competitive result is "fair" or "equitable": efficiency by itself does not necessarily imply justice in distribution. To this issue we now turn.

### THE CONCEPT OF EXPLOITATION

For two centuries socialist critics of the present order have asserted that labor has the right to the full product of society. What price the efficiency of marginal-product distribution if it gives a sizable fraction of the total product to property owners? This, they assert, represents "exploitation" of labor.

It is naïve to think that if a word exists, there must always then exist some obvious real phenomenon corresponding to it. Thus, if I can say the name of a unicorn, need there be in some jungle somewhere such an animal with a horned horse's head and a goat's beard? Or, if I can think of a perfect God-Being, *ergo* must He exist? Or, if the dictionary contains the word "exploitation," must there surely be some *simple* meaning to the concept that anyone can understand even *before* he has studied economics? To the scholar who studies economics and does research in the field, a naïve approach must be replaced by an attempt to analyze and isolate the meaningful and essential concept of exploitation.

The late Oskar Lange, after spending a sojourn in the United States from 1934 to 1944 as a distinguished professor of both Marxian and non-Marxian economics, returned to his native Poland to become Ambassador to the United Nations and subsequently to serve as Vice-President of Poland and a professor. In his view of that time, what Marx wished to convey by the concept of "exploitation of labor" could be achieved without the trappings of the "labor theory of value" (which seemed to deny that scarce land and time-intensive processes can also contribute to competitive costs and to true social costs). Said Lange in effect, "The fact that people, who don't deserve to own the tools of production which work with labor and which are given their positive marginal-products out of the total product that might otherwise go to labor, receive a substantial fraction of the GNP, is ethically bad. The cure is to see that labor owns the tools of production and nature's gifts of land and other natural resources. Then labor, either in the form of wages or in the form of *its* share of property income, will indeed get all of the national product. Anything else is exploitation even in a prosperous capitalistic system where wages are very high (and much higher than are total incomes in egalitarian socialist societies)."

When we come to discuss land reform and increased education for labor, we shall see how laborers may come themselves to get a larger part of the property income of society. But before leaving the subject of exploitation, note that the Lange version of the concept does not depend upon monopoly or any imperfections of bargaining power between employer and employees.[7] What is involved is a "value judgment" about the distribution of wealth ownership, not an alternative scientific finding.

## MARGINAL-PRODUCT THEORY OF THE SINGLE FIRM[8]

Our main task is done. But there remains the need (1) to tie up these theories of production and distribution with Maximum-profit decisions of the firm; and (2) to show

---

[7] See Fig. 29-7, page 589, for a discussion of a quite different concept of exploitation based on employer monopoly power in the buying of labor (so-called "monopsony"). Still a third concept of exploitation of a factor like labor comes from what Cambridge's Joan Robinson calls "monopoly power of the firm in its product markets." As will be seen in the next sections, such a firm will be paying its factors less than the money value for which their marginal-products actually sell. Instead, the factors get marginal revenue (which is less than price) times their marginal-products. Since the biggest and most monopolistic firms usually are the ones that actually pay the *highest* wages, such Robinsonian exploitation really means merely that monopolists are producing too little of their goods, that society at large is being exploited by this inefficiency, and that workers cannot from their wages buy for themselves the last extra product that an extra hour of work might actually produce.
[8] Brief courses may skip the rest of this chapter without discontinuity.

that the cost curves of Part Three were implicitly based on the marginal-productivity decisions of this chapter.

**Marginal-revenue-product and maximizing profit**   Exactly what does each last worker bring to my firm in cash dollar terms? He brings his marginal-physical-product—that we have seen. But he does not want his wage paid in toothpaste: the market wage is in *dollars*, not $q$ units. And I, the employer, want to maximize dollars of profit.

Under perfect competition, the answer is easy. The physical-marginal-product the worker brings me, $MPP_L$, can all be sold at the market price for my $q$ output, $P_q$, which I as a perfect competitor cannot affect. If his $MPP_L$ is 8 units of $q$ and each sells for $P_q = \$5$, then the dollar value of the last worker to me is \$40 ($= \$5 \times 8$). Generally, then, under perfect competition, each laborer is worth $P_q \times MPP_L$ to the firm: the dollar value of his marginal-products. (For acres of land, this would be $P_q \times MPP_A$.)

But perfect competition is merely one limiting case of imperfect competition. It is the case of a horizontal *dd* schedule for my $q$. In the more common case of imperfect competition, *dd* is somewhat downward-sloping: Chapter 25 taught that the actual marginal revenue I then get from each extra physical $q$ is *less than* market $P_q$ (because of loss on previous units). With $MR_q < P_q$, the laborer's marginal-physical-product of 8 units will *not* each be worth the market $P_q = \$5$ to me. How much, then? If $MR_q = \$3 < \$5 = P_q$, the answer is clear-cut: his final $MPP_L$ is worth to me only $\$3 \times 8 = \$24$.

Generally, then, a firm's demand curve for a factor, such as labor, is given in dollar terms by "marginal revenue of $q$" times "marginal-physical-product of $L$." This important concept is given a name and defined as follows:

*Definition:* **"Marginal-revenue-product" is defined as marginal-physical-product multiplied by the marginal revenue the firm gets for its extra physical goods sold:**

> **Marginal-revenue-product of $L$ = $MR_q \times$ marginal-physical-product of $L$**
> **Marginal-revenue-product of $A$ = $MR_q \times$ marginal-physical-product of $A$**
> **And so forth**

Now we can put the new concept to work.

*Rule:* The firm's demand curve for any factor is given by its curve of marginal-revenue-product for that factor, a curve which declines because of (1) diminishing physical returns and (2) the downward slope of the $MR_q$ curve that usually prevails under imperfect competition.

**In Maximum-profit equilibrium, every firm faced with competitive factor-prices—the money wage, the money rent rate per acre of land, and so forth—will aim to achieve**

> **Marginal-revenue-product of $L$ = price of $L$**
> **Marginal-revenue-product of $A$ = price of $A$**
> **And so forth**

**Maximum-profit equilibrium is attained when every factor is hired until its marginal benefit and costs are equated.**[9]

---

[9] Repeatedly in Part Three, we saw that departures from the conditions of perfect competition led to inefficiencies and to nonoptimal responsiveness to people's dollar-vote desires. It is to be understood here, therefore, that such aberrations will be ruled out *only* in the special case where $P_q = MR_q$ and $P_L = P_q \times MPP_L$, etc. This is actually what happened in the Clark model, where perfect

**Marginal-products and Least-cost** Chapter 24 presented Total Cost data for each firm $q$. How did such minimal $TC$ estimates get made? Marginal-productivity theory can now give the answer. Engineers told the firm it could produce $q = 9$ units with much land and little labor or with little land and much labor. Which is a more efficient choice: $A = 10$ and $L = 2$, or $A = 4$ and $L = 5$? Evidently, that must depend on the wage and rent rates the firm faces. If $P_L = \$5$ per hour and $P_A = \$2$ per acre, 10 acres and 2 hours give lower $TC$ than do 4 acres and 5 hours. [Why? Because ($\$2 \times 10$) + ($\$5 \times 2$) = $\$30 < (\$2 \times 4) + (\$5 \times 5) = \$33$.]

What is the rule to follow to get lowest $TC$? The Least-cost position for producing each $q$ comes from studying the marginal-physical-products of land and of labor. If an acre of land cost $P_A = \$200$, which is 100 times more than an hour of labor's factor-price $P_L = \$2$, no one in his right mind can expect Least-cost to come from achieving equal *physical*-marginal-products of land and labor. Since land costs 100 times as much, it must be made to give us 100 times the $MPP$ of labor.

It is evident that what has to be equalized is the $MPP$ per dollar spent on each factor if $TC$ is to be minimized for producing $q = 9$. (Recall Chapter 22's similar equating of marginal-utilities-per-dollar.)

*Least-cost rule:* **To get the lowest Total Cost at each point on its $TC$ curve, a rational firm will hire factors until it has equalized the marginal-physical-product-per-last-dollar spent on each factor of production.**

$$\frac{\text{Marginal-physical-product of } L}{\text{Price of } L} = \frac{\text{marginal-physical-product of } A}{\text{price of } A} = \ldots, \text{ at Least-cost}$$

An obvious corollary of the above[10] can now be stated.

*Substitution rule:* If the price of one factor, like labor, rises while other factor-prices remain fixed, it will generally pay the firm to produce its same $q$ outputs by substituting for the now-dearer factor more of the remaining factors. (A rise in $P_L$ will thus reduce $MPP_L/P_L$ and cause $L$ to be fired and $A$ hired until equality is restored, thus lowering the amount of needed $L$ and increasing the demand for land acres; a fall in $P_L$ will do the reverse. A rise in $P_A$ alone will, by the same logic, cause labor to be substituted for now dearer land.)

\* \* \* \* \*

**Finale** We have shown that the bird's-eye view of Clark's aggregate distribution is completely compatible with the realistic microeconomic pricing of any number of goods produced by any number of factor inputs. The triad of forces which determines competitive microeconomic distribution and value theory is seen to be (1) technology (the production function), (2) tastes and dollar-vote-power to demand various goods (the ultimate demand curves for goods, from which factor-price demands are derived), and (3) relative factor supplies (as determined by nature's abundance, inherited and acquired abilities, disutilities of different occupations).

The picture is oversimplified but important.

---

competitors produced a homogeneous $Q$ and had no "spoiling of the market problem" to bring $MR_q$ below $P_q$ and distort resource use.

[10]The Least-cost rule involves no mention of marginal revenue, because it applies for *all* $q$ on the $TC$ curve even before the firm's demand curve has been mentioned. The Appendix will relate it to the marginal-revenue-product rule of Maximum-profit where $MR_q = MC$.

## SUMMARY

1  Distribution is concerned with the determination of different people's incomes, or with the basic question of For Whom economic goods are to be produced. To understand what determines labor's and property's share in national product, and to understand forces acting on the degree of equality of income, distribution theory must study the problem of how the different factors of production—land, labor, capital, entrepreneurship and risk taking—get priced in the market. Thus it must study how supply and demand interact to determine all kinds of wages, rents, interest yields, and profits.

2  To understand why the demand curves for the factors of production are what they are, we must investigate the theory of production and cost within each firm. The demand for factor inputs is a *joint demand*—joint because the factors interact in producing final product.

3  The relationship between quantities of available inputs—land, labor, machines, fertilizer—and quantity of output is called the *production function*. By varying one factor in successive small increments, we define its marginal-physical-product. Diminishing returns implies falling *MPP* of any factor if other factors are held fixed. But when *all* inputs increase *in balanced proportion*, the J. B. Clark model of competition presupposes that there will be exactly *constant* returns (i.e., constant returns *to scale*).

4  Competition of numerous self-seeking landowners and labor-owners will ensure that total product gets allocated among the factors by each having its factor-price equal to its marginal-product. That will allocate *exactly* 100 per cent of the product. Any factor, not just labor alone, can be the varying factor: because each unit of it gets paid only the *MP* of the *last* hired, there is enough of a residual surplus left (from the triangle of excess-of-early-over-last-*MP*s) to pay the other factors their exact marginal-products. Hence, Clark's neoclassical theory of distribution, though simplified, is a logically complete picture of idealized competition.

5  Ambitious attempts to measure an aggregate production function for the whole of American manufacturing seem to provide rough corroboration for the theories of production and marginal-products. In this century, technological progress has been shifting the productivities of both labor and capital upward. At the same time, capital has been growing faster than the labor supply, with the following implications: (*a*) the increase of capital per worker has shifted his productivity wages up even faster than technological change would alone; (*b*) the tendency of each unit of capital to encounter diminishing returns has just about been canceled by technological innovations; (*c*) the relative shares of labor and property incomes have remained at about three-quarters and one-quarter despite the vast institutional changes in union organization and in automation of production. (Chapter 37's growth theory will return to this.)

6  When the marginal-products of a factor in different uses are all equal to their common market price, society's resources are being most efficiently allocated. (Any deviation from this equality, whether under centralized planning or under monopoly imperfections interfering with perfect competition, means that we are inside rather than out on Chapter 2's production-possibility frontier.) To socialists, like Poland's Oskar Lange, the efficiency of the marginal-product method of costing factor inputs (to enlarge the size of the social pie) was not an excuse for labor's failing to receive all of the product. If "owners" of scarce land and scarce tools could withhold them from the worker except when they command a fraction of the GNP through their competitive marginal-product prices, then to Lange that represented "exploitation" even if he had no particular need for Marx's labor theory of value (and even if other kinds of exploitation associated with monopoly power of firms in commodity or labor markets were absent or could be assumed to be ignorable).

7  If the firm is given ruling market prices of all factors and is given engineering, technical information about the effects of factor changes on final product, it can simultaneously solve the two problems (a) of substituting the different factors for each other so as to realize the Least-cost combination—at which it has *equalized the marginal-physical-product-per-dollar spent on every factor used*—and (b) of finally determining which of all possible outputs is its Maximum-profit position, where $MR = MC$.

8  An exactly equivalent condition of factor equilibrium is the following: *equality of marginal-revenue-products to factor-prices*. Why must this hold in the Maximum-profit equilibrium? Because any businessman with common sense will stop hiring any factor at the point where what its marginal-physical-product will bring in to his firm in actual dollars of marginal revenue begins to fall short of the market price he must pay to hire as much or little as he wants.

9  Our analysis has shown why, when a factor-price rises, the quantity of it that is demanded will tend to fall. Higher labor price will cause other factors to be substituted for it in producing each output; and higher labor cost probably means that the Maximum-profit output will be at a lower level where $MR$ equals a now higher $MC$.

   What is the same thing, the marginal-revenue-product demand curve for the factor tilts downward because of technical diminishing returns, reinforced by spoiling of the monopolist's market. (This last fact reminds us that monopolists produce too little and hire too few factors.)

   In the next few chapters we shall apply these principles to show how supply and demand operate in the factor markets to determine rents, wages, and other factor-prices.

   The Appendix to this chapter provides a review of the theory of production for those interested in a more geometrical approach.

# CONCEPTS FOR REVIEW

For Whom, How, factor pricing, distribution theory
joint demand
production function
diminishing returns
symmetry of land and labor
marginal-product: *MP* or *MPP*
*MP* rectangle, residual rent triangle
relative constancy of labor and property shares

marginal-physical-product, marginal-revenue-product, and factor-prices
marginal-physical-product-per-last-dollar-spent on each factor equalized at each *q*
monopoly output and misallocated factors
exploitation as too-low competitive returns and as monopoly victimization

# QUESTIONS FOR DISCUSSION

1 What do economists mean by the theory of "distribution"? Is this what the Census means when it discusses retailing?

2 Explain the "production-function concept." Then explain the various marginal-products.

3 Give an outline of Clark's distribution theory, varying land in a new version of Fig. 27-2.

4 Define marginal-revenue-product, distinguishing it from marginal-physical-product. Give a common-sense explanation to show that Maximum-profit is not attained unless each factor-price exactly equals its marginal-revenue-product.

5 Convince a skeptic of the truth of the rule that to reach a Least-cost point you must equalize the marginal-productivity-per-dollar spent on every factor. Show this to be true even when we have not yet decided on the Maximum-profit output.

6 Suppose NNP grows in a mixed economy faster than labor supply in every decade. If, contrary to Karl Marx's predictions, wage share stays about the same fraction of NNP, show that real wage rates must rise.

7 *Extra credit problem:* Let output be $Q$ and inputs be $L$ (for labor) and $A$ (for acres of land). Show that the *arithmetic mean* of $L$ and $A$, namely $Q = \frac{1}{2}L + \frac{1}{2}A$, would not make a good production function because it does not show diminishing marginal-products. (Hint: Each equal increment of $L$ by 1 always increases $Q$ by the same increment of $\frac{1}{2}$.) But the *geometric mean* $Q = \sqrt{LA} = \sqrt{L}\sqrt{A}$ is a good production function with diminishing returns. (Hint: The square roots of $1, 2, 3, \ldots$ are $1, 1.41, 1.73$, which do show decreasing increments of $Q$, namely, $.41, .32, \ldots$. Actually the Appendix's Table 27-1 satisfies this special symmetric case of the so-called "Cobb-Douglas" form, being like $Q = 141\sqrt{LA}$. The general Cobb-Douglas production function is $Q = bL^k C^{1-k}$, with all variables positive.)

# APPENDIX: Graphical Depiction of Production Theory

The production theory of this chapter can be graphically presented. Table 27-1 is a numerical example of a simple production function relating output to two inputs, labor and land. It is in the form of a two-way table, looking like a baseball or mileage schedule.

Along the left-hand side are listed the varying amounts of land, going from 1 unit to 6. Along the bottom are listed amounts of labor, also happening to go from 1 to 6. Output corresponding to each land row and labor column is listed inside the table.

If we are interested in knowing exactly what output there will be when 3 units of land and 2 units of labor are available, we count up 3 units of land and then go over 2 units of labor. The answer is seen to be 346 units of product. Similarly, we find that 3 units of land and 6 of labor will produce 600 units of output.

Thus, for any combination of labor and land, the production function tells us how much product we shall have (using, of course, the best engineering methods known).

## THE LAW OF DIMINISHING MARGINAL-PHYSICAL-PRODUCT

Table 27-1 can nicely illustrate the law of diminishing returns.

First recall that we have given the name "marginal-physical-product of labor" to the extra production resulting from *one* additional unit of labor, land being held constant. At any point in Table 27-1, the marginal-physical-product of labor can be derived by subtracting the given number (representing product at that point) from the number on its right lying in the same row. Thus, when there are 2 units of land and 4 units of labor, the marginal-physical-product of an additional laborer would be 48, or 448 minus 400 in the second row.

By the "marginal-physical-product of land" we mean, of course, the extra product resulting from one additional unit of land, labor being held constant. It involves a comparison of adjacent items in a given column. Thus, when there are 2 units of land and 4 units of labor, the marginal-physical-product of land is shown in the fourth column as 490 − 400, or 90. The reader can compute the marginal-physical-product of labor or land at any point inside the table.

Having defined what we mean by the marginal-physical-product of an input, we are now in a position to restate the law of diminishing returns:

**As we hold a fixed input constant and increase a variable input, the marginal-physical-product of the variable input will decline—at least after a point.**

To illustrate this, hold land constant in Table 27-1 by sticking to a given row, say, that corresponding to land equal to 2 units. Now let labor increase from 1 to 2 units, from 2 to 3 units, and so forth. What happens to product at each step?

As labor goes from 1 to 2 units, product increases from 200 to 282 units, or by 82 units. But the next dose of labor adds only 64 units, or 346 − 282. Diminishing returns has set in. Still further additions of a single unit of labor give us, respectively, only 54 extra units of output, 48 units, and finally 42 units. The reader should check some other row to verify that the law

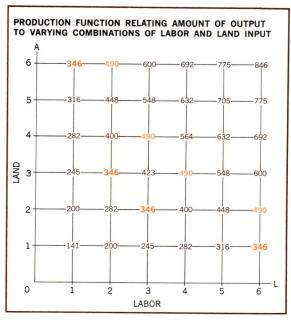

**PRODUCTION FUNCTION RELATING AMOUNT OF OUTPUT TO VARYING COMBINATIONS OF LABOR AND LAND INPUT**

**TABLE 27-1**
When you have 3 land units and 2 labor units available, the engineer tells you your maximum obtainable output is 346 units. Note the different ways to produce 346, and to produce 490.

of diminishing returns holds there too. He should also verify that the same law holds true when labor is held constant and land is added in a number of steps. (Examine the changes in product in any column.)

At this point, it is well to recall the explanation given for diminishing returns. In Chapter 2, it was attributed to the fact that the fixed factor decreases *relative* to the variable factor. Each unit of the variable factor has less and less of the fixed factor to work with. So it is natural that extra product should fall off.

If this explanation is to hold water, there should be no diminishing returns when both factors are increased in proportion. When labor increases from 1 to 2 and land *simultaneously* increases from 1 to 2, we should get the same increase in product as when both increase simultaneously from 2 to 3. This can be verified in Table 27-1.[1] In the first move we go from 141 to 282, and in the second move the product increases from 282 to 423, an equal jump of 141 units.

Also, this explanation of diminishing returns in terms of the *proportions* of the inputs would lead us to expect that increasing land will improve the marginal-physical-product of labor. Again this can be verified from our table: The fifth unit of labor adds 48 units of $Q$ when there are only 2 units of land; but at 3 units of land, a fifth unit of labor adds 58 units of $Q$.

### Apologetics for thrift

This fact, that an increase in tools or land for each worker to work with increases his marginal-product and real wage, forms the basis for what is often derisively referred to as the "filter-down theory of economic progress." Workers are supposed to applaud the thrift of capitalists because the fruits of that thrift in more and better capital goods will cause labor productivity to rise later and cause the competitive marginal-product real wage to be bid up higher then by the spirited bidding of one employer against another.

The germ of truth in this can be admitted at the same time that spokesmen for labor may ask:

"Why give the extra income to the capitalist *for him* to save it and *for him* to get the future interest fruits on his savings? If the state or a workers' cooperative gets the income and saves it, then the workers will not only get the higher real wage later but will also get along the way the extra income that capitalists would otherwise have got."

[1] Not all production functions met in real economic life would have these special properties of so-called "constant returns to scale." Recall Chapter 2's discussion of increasing returns to scale, or economies of mass production.

---

**EQUAL-OUTPUT FACTOR COMBINATIONS**

|   | LABOR $L$ | LAND $A$ | TOTAL COST WHEN $P_L = \$2$ $P_A = \$3$ | TOTAL COST WHEN $P_L = \$2$ $P_A = \$1$ |
|---|---|---|---|---|
| A | 1 | 6 | $20 | —— |
| B | 2 | 3 | 13 | $7 |
| C | 3 | 2 | 12 | —— |
| D | 6 | 1 | 15 | —— |

**TABLE 27-2**

Factors can be substituted for one another to produce the same output. More labor can be substituted for less land to produce 346 units. When $P_L = \$2$ and $P_A = \$3$, calculate total of wage cost plus land cost to verify that their combination gives lowest cost of $12 at C. Show that lowering $P_A$ to $1 causes land to be substituted for labor as it pays to move from C to B.

### LEAST-COST FACTOR COMBINATION FOR A GIVEN OUTPUT

The numerical production function shows that the engineer is not able to tell us definitely how any given output is to be produced. There is more than one way to skin a cat. And there is more than one way to produce any given output. Thus, the orange numbers in Table 27-1 show that the output $q = 346$ can be produced in any one of the ways shown in Table 27-2.[2]

As far as the engineer is concerned, each of these combinations is equally good at producing an output of 346 units. But the accountant, interested in keeping profits of the firm at a maximum and costs at a minimum, knows that only one of these four combinations will give Least-cost. Just which one will depend, of course, on the respective factor-prices.

Let us suppose that the price of labor is $2 and the price of land $3. Then the sum of the labor and land costs in Table 27-2's situation A will be $20 equals $(1 \times \$2) + (6 \times \$3)$. And costs at B, C, and D will be, respectively, $13, $12, $15. At these stated input prices, there is no doubt that C is the best way to produce the given output.

If either of the input prices changes, the equilibrium proportion of the inputs will always change so as to use *less* of the input that proportionately has gone up most in price. This is just like the substitution-effect of Chapter 22's discussion of consumer demand.

[2] You can make a similar table for $q = 490$.

Thus, if labor stays at $2 per unit but land falls to $1 per unit, the new optimal combination will be *B*, where more land is substituted for reduced labor and where total cost is only $7. The reader should verify this by computing the new total expense of all other combinations and seeing that they are higher. (Pencil in missing costs in Table 27-2.)

Exactly the same sort of thing can be done for any other output; as soon as all input prices are known, we can experiment until we have found the Least-cost input combination. (To guarantee your understanding of the principles involved, work out the optimum production decision and cost for output equal to 490 units when price of labor is $4 and price of land is $3. Verify that, of all the light-blue combinations, 3 labor and 4 land units will turn out in that case to produce Least-cost of $24 for *q* = 490.)

## EQUAL-PRODUCT AND EQUAL-COST CONTOURS: LEAST-COST TANGENCY

The common-sense numerical analysis of the way in which a firm will combine inputs to minimize costs can be made more vivid by the use of diagrams. From the production schedule we can draw a picture of the different input combinations that will produce a given output. Figure 27-3 is the exact counterpart of Table 27-2. In it the smooth curve indicates the different combinations of labor and land that yield an output of 346 units. This could be called a "production-indifference curve" by analogy with the con-

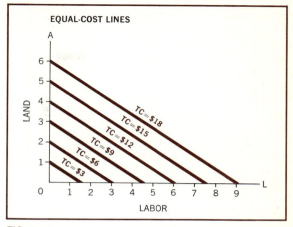

**FIG. 27-4**
Every point on a given line represents the same total cost. The lines are straight because of constant factor-prices, and they all have a numerical slope equal to the ratio of labor price to land price, $2/$3, and hence are parallel.

sumer's indifference curve of the Appendix to Chapter 22. But a more expressive name to call it would be an "equal-product" curve. (You should be able to draw on Fig. 27-3, as a light-orange curve, the corresponding equal-product curve for output equal to 490 by getting the data from Table 27-1. You should realize that an infinite number of such equal-product contour lines could be drawn in, just as a topographical or weather map could be covered with an indefinitely large number of equal-altitude or equal-pressure contour lines.)

Given the price of labor and land, the firm can evaluate the total cost for points *A*, *B*, *C*, and *D* or for any other point on the equal-product curve. Obviously, it will be maximizing its profits only when it has found that optimum point on the equal-product curve at which it reaches Least-cost.

Purely as a graphical trick, the firm might try to save itself much tedious arithmetical computation by evaluating once and for all the total cost of every possible factor combination of land and labor. This is done in Fig. 27-4, where the family of parallel straight lines represents all possible equal-cost curves when the price of labor is $2 and the price of land $3.

To find the total cost for any point we have simply to read off the number appended to the equal-cost line going through that point. The brown lines are all straight and parallel because the firm is assumed to be able to buy all it wishes of either input at constant prices. The lines are somewhat flatter than 45° because

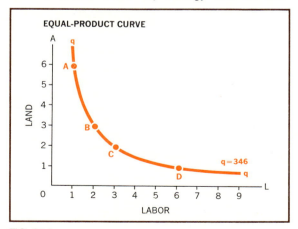

**FIG. 27-3**
All the points on the curve represent the different combinations of land and labor that can be used to produce the same 346 units of output.

the price of labor $P_L$ is somewhat less than the price of land $P_A$. More precisely, we can always say that the arithmetic value of the slope of each equal-cost line must equal the ratio of the price of labor to that of land[3]—in this case 2/3.

It is now easy to recognize the optimum equilibrium input position of the firm at which total costs are minimized for the given output. The single orange equal-product curve has superimposed upon it the family of brown equal-cost lines, as is shown in Fig. 27-5. The firm will always keep moving along the orange convex curve of Fig. 27-5 as long as it is able to cross over to lower cost lines. Its equilibrium will therefore not be at *A*, *B*, or *D*. It will be at *C*, *where the equal-product curve touches (but does not cross) the lowest equal-cost line.* This is, of course, *a point of tangency*, where the slope of the equal-product curve just matches the slope of an equal-cost line and the curves are just kissing.

We already know that the slope of the equal-cost curves is $P_L/P_A$. But what is the slope of the equal-product curve? This slope is a kind of "substitution ratio" between the two factors, and it depends upon the *relative* marginal-physical-products of the two factors of production, namely, $MPP_L/MPP_A$—just as the rate of substitution between two goods along a consumer's indifference curve was earlier shown to equal the ratio of the marginal, or extra, utilities of the two goods (Appendix to Chapter 22).

## LEAST-COST CONDITIONS

Thus, our Least-cost equilibrium can be defined by any of the following equivalent relations:

**1. The ratio of marginal-physical-products of any two inputs must equal the ratio of their factor-prices.**

Substitution ratio, or

$$\frac{\text{Marginal-physical-product of labor}}{\text{Marginal-physical-product of land}} = \frac{\text{price of labor}}{\text{price of land}}$$

**2. The   marginal-physical-product-per-dollar   re-**

---

[3]The careful reader will notice the parallel between the geometry of this section and that of the analysis of consumer equilibrium in the Appendix to Chapter 22. Each equal-cost line indicates all the possible different quantities of labor and of land that the firm might buy for any given cost outlay. Each line is straight since its equation is $TC = \$2L + \$3A$. In the Appendix to Chapter 22, the consumer is buying

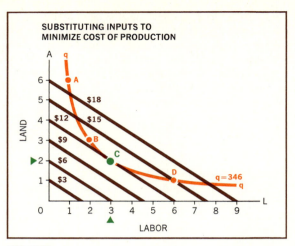

**SUBSTITUTING INPUTS TO MINIMIZE COST OF PRODUCTION**

**FIG. 27-5**

To find Least-cost equilibrium for fixed output of 346, we move along orange curve of alternative factor combinations and strive to be on farthest out parallel line of total cost. Where the equal-product curve touches (but does not cross) the lowest total-cost contour is the Least-cost optimum position. This tangency means that factor-prices and marginal-physical-products (or "substitution ratios") are proportional, with equalized marginal-physical-products-per-dollar.

**ceived from the (last) dollar of expenditure must be the same for every productive factor.**

$$\frac{\text{Marginal-physical-product of } L}{\text{Price of } L}$$
$$= \frac{\text{marginal-physical-product of } A}{\text{price of } A} = \cdots$$

Relation 2 is discussed in detail in the main body of the chapter. (It could also be derived from relation 1 by transposing terms from one numerator to the other denominator, i.e., by "interchanging means and extremes," as in going from $a/b = c/d$ to $a/c = b/d$.)

---

goods, not factor services; otherwise his "budget line" exactly parallels the equal-cost lines we are now discussing. We can explain, similarly, why the slope of an equal-cost line equals the ratio of the two prices involved.

But note this difference: The consumer was assumed to have a fixed budget; hence, he had but one budget line. The firm is not limited to any particular level of costs; so it must consider many equal-cost lines before discovering its Least-cost equilibrium.

But the student should not be satisfied with any such abstract explanation. He should always remember the common-sense economic explanation which shows how a firm will redistribute its expenditure among inputs if any one factor offers a greater return for each last dollar spent on it. Finally, we may state the above Least-cost relations in the following form:

**3. Input prices and their marginal-physical-products must be proportional, the factor of proportionality being marginal cost, MC.[4]**

MC of output × marginal-physical-product of labor
= price of labor

MC of output × marginal-physical-product of land
= price of land

And so on for any number of inputs

The Least-cost relationships 1, 2, and 3 are all equivalent. Each holds at every point along the Total Cost curve, *whatever the output*. They do *not* tell the firm where it should finally produce.

## MARGINAL-REVENUE-PRODUCT CONDITION OF MAXIMUM-PROFIT

But now we add the Maximum-profit condition that $MR = MC$; and we recall the definition of "marginal-revenue-product" as equal to "marginal-physical-product times marginal revenue." Then we can combine the Least-cost relations of item 3 just above and the Maximum-profit relationship to reach our final equilibrium condition:

**Marginal-revenue-product of labor = price of labor**
**Marginal-revenue-product of land = price of land**
**And so on for any number of factors:**

$$MR \times MPP_i = P_i$$

Thus, our graphical analysis has arrived at the same final result as our common-sense reasoning of this chapter—which tells us that we shall stop hiring more of a factor only at the point where the marginal-revenue-product it brings just matches its market price. This is what lies behind the firm's demand curve for a productive factor.

[4]Why are these marginal-physical-products-per-dollar each equal to the reciprocal of marginal cost, or to $1/MC_q$? Because extra output per dollar is nothing but the upside-down of extra dollars per unit of product, which is what we mean by MC.

## FIXITY OF PROPORTIONS

An important qualification must sometimes be made. We have calculated the marginal-physical-product of any one input by (1) holding all the other inputs constant and then (2) increasing the input in question by 1 unit. The resulting increase in physical product was then measured, and that was identified as the factor's marginal-physical-product. But in some technological processes the factor inputs work very intimately together, so that when you increase only one of them, holding the others constant, you get *zero extra product;* and when you decrease one factor alone, you lose the *whole product* produced by both together.

Only when you change both factors *in combination* do you seem to get a nice smooth curve of marginal-physical-product.

**Smoothing discontinuities**    Certainly, such extreme discontinuities can sometimes happen. But perhaps they do not occur quite so often as some critics have claimed. Thus, critics often point out examples where 1 man is always using 1 shovel, or where it seems to take a certain amount of gold to produce a watchband and no amount of labor can substitute for this gold. But actually, in any digging operation, extra shovels[5] must usually be kept on hand; and if shovel prices were very high and wages were low, workers on different shifts might use the same implements so that the shovel requirements could be kept to a minimum; also, we might in time change the size of the shovels or introduce bulldozers, thereby changing the factor proportions. Or in the above case of the gold watchband, there will almost certainly be some waste of metal in the form of shavings and dust; if wages were low enough relative to the price of gold, it would pay to hire more men to produce the same number of watchbands out of less gold—labor being, in effect, a substitute for the use of more gold.

Other arguments and examples could be given in reply to those who stress fixity of factor proportions and discontinuities in substitutability and marginal-products. Nonetheless, in some technical processes, there may not be continuous substitutability between

[5]Probability variations strengthen the case for variability of proportions. Even with 1 machine to 1 operator, the fact that each machine has a probability of breaking down means that 11 machines for 10 men is better—on the average!—than 10 machines.

the various inputs, and so the calculated marginal-physical-products may become erratic and lumpy.

**Fixed-coefficients case** It was once thought that lack of substitutability would spoil the economic theory of production; but that is not always so.

To see the case of fixed-proportions, we would have to replace the smooth orange contour of Figs. 27-3 and 27-5 by an orange, L-shaped, equal-product contour. Regardless of how high or low the positive $P_L/P_A$ ratio is, the Least-cost point of "tangency"—where the orange contour touches but does not cross the minimal brown line of $TC$—comes always at the corner of the L. Hence, the Least-cost condition is even more easily found in the fixed-proportions case. (There now will be *no* substitution when one factor becomes dear relative to another, for the reason that no technical substitutability is possible.)

The derived demand of firms for factors is still well determined, but with the difference that there may be vertical ranges and discontinuities in the factor-input demand curve. In Fig. 27-2, both $ss$ and $dd$ curves being overlappingly vertical can spoil the simple Clark tale of determinate rectangle and residual triangle.

Fortunately, dropping the one-good assumption of Clark and replacing a single $Q$ by many goods $(Q_1, Q_2, \ldots)$ can sometimes restore determinacy of distribution. Let's see why.

## INTERCOMMODITY SUBSTITUTION AND QUALIFICATIONS

It is not hard to show what happens when we drop the simplified case of a single product. As any factor, such as unskilled labor, becomes more plentiful, its marginal-revenue-product and rental will tend to fall. Not only will more of it tend to be substituted for other factors in each line of production, but in addition, *those special goods which happen to use much of this factor in their production* will fall in price more than will other prices generally. This relative price drop will tend to cause consumers to use more of such cheapened goods; in this way the derived demand for the factor will become even more elastic.

Thus, *in addition to intracommodity technical substitutability between factors, there is also intercommodity substitutability resulting from differential price effects*. This suggests how distribution will be determined even when the continuous-substitutability assumptions of the marginal-product theory of production break down. If factors must be used in fixed

proportions, their derived demands are still perfectly well determined. These demands, together with supply relations, help determine all prices. Intercommodity substitutions now become extremely important, as do the supply conditions for the factors.[6]

To understand the different aspects of the problem of distribution is to begin to understand much of the history of the classical and modern theories of dis-

---

[6]An example shows how intercommodity substitutions may be able to determine factor-prices even in the worst case of fixed-proportions, e.g., where 1 unit of land *and* 1 unit of labor are needed to produce 1 unit of wine; and where 1 land *and* 2 labor units are needed to produce 1 of bread. Assume wine sells for $10 per unit, bread for $12. Bread differs from wine by $2 in price and cost; in terms of inputs, it differs by what? By 1 extra unit of labor. Hence wages must be exactly $2 per unit ($= \$12 - \$10$), and land use must be priced at $8 per unit ($= \$10 - \$2$, or $\$12 - 2 \times \$2$). So from commodity prices we can obtain factor-prices—even in this fixed-coefficients case.

You will realize that the prices of wine and bread had also to be determined by supply and demand and will depend in part upon how much income goes to hungry laborers and thirsty landowners and upon the initial supplies of the factors. For example, imagine that we started with a supply of 200 acres of land and 300 laborers, and let us summarize the resulting general equilibrium.

*If* we had started with factors in a 1/1 ratio—say, 200 of each—and *if* we required them to be fully employed, they would *all* have to go into wine production. We could not produce any bread and still keep all our factors employed. Similarly, if our factor totals had been in a 1/2 proportion—say, 200 acres of land, 400 laborers—we should have to produce nothing but bread to preserve full employment.

But we start with a halfway ratio—200/300. Common sense and simple algebra tell us that we must then split our land half and half between the two industries, thereby using up the total of both factors in producing 100 wine units and 100 bread units. The prices of these supplies of goods would then be determined by the interplay of competitive supply and demand for the two goods and for the two factors, and thus we end up at the above equilibrium prices for goods and services. (NOTE: A factor-price can be made zero by some demand and supply patterns, but this "free-factor" possibility is neglected for simplicity. If both goods used both factors in the same ratio in which they are inelastically supplied, we would indeed be in a singular case where equilibrium would be indeterminate.)

Turn to page 460, Fig. 23-6. With fixed coefficients, the brown frontier becomes two straight lines intersecting in a corner point like $E$. The orange indifference-contour slope "tangential" at $E$ to the brown frontier will determine final goods' price ratio; and this price ratio will determine factors' price ratio.

tribution and of competitive pricing. But it does not tell us much about the cases of imperfect competition: (1) where there may be economies of scale that lead to a few firms gaining semimonopoly power, and (2) where consumers may develop a special preference for products that can be produced only by factors owned by a single firm.

As Chapter 31 shows, in these cases the firms may earn "monopoly profits" or "monopoly rents" which the attempted competition of other firms may not take away from them. To "natural scarcity" is then being added artificial "contrived scarcity," brought about by someone's holding in his supply for fear of "spoiling the market."

## SUMMARY TO APPENDIX

1 A production function lists, for each labor row and each land column, the output that is producible. Diminishing returns, to one variable factor applied to a fixed factor, can be shown by calculating the fall-off of marginal-products in any row or column.

2 An equal-product contour, usually drawn to be convex (from below), depicts the alternative input combinations that produce the same level of output. The slope, or substitution ratio, along such an "isoquant" equals relative marginal-products (e.g., $MPP_L/MPP_A$). Contours of equal Total Cost are parallel lines with slopes equal to factor-price ratios ($P_L/P_A$). Least-cost equilibrium comes at tangency point, where equal-product contour touches but does not cross the lowest $TC$ contour. There marginal-products are proportional to factor-prices, with *equalized* marginal-product-per-dollar spent on all factors (e.g., equalized $MPP_i/P_i$).

3 Of all points on $TC$ curve, the Maximum-profit equilibrium comes where $MR = MC$; there each factor has marginal-revenue-product just equal to its price. (That is, the Least-cost condition $P_i = MC \times MPP_i$ becomes at Maximum-profit $P_i = MR \times MPP_i$ as in the main chapter.)

## CONCEPTS FOR REVIEW

convex equal-product contours
parallel equal-*TC* lines
substitution slope $= MPP_L/MPP_A$
$P_L/P_A =$ slope of parallel
    equal-*TC* lines

Least-cost tangency:
   $MPP_L/MPP_A = P_L/P_A$ or
   $MPP_L/P_L = MPP_A/P_A = 1/MC$
Maximum-profit condition,
   $MR \times MPP_L = P_L, \ldots$

## QUESTIONS FOR DISCUSSION

1 Show that raising labor wage while holding land rent constant will steepen the brown equal-cost lines and move tangency point $C$ in Fig. 27-5 northwest toward $B$ with now cheaper input substituted for now dearer one. Should union leaders recognize this?

2 (The remaining questions are not easy and can be skipped by those who have no interest or training in geometry and elementary calculus.) The famous statistical equation of Senator Douglas related $Q$ output to $L$ labor and $C$ capital by the formula $Q = 1.01 \ L^{.75}C^{.25}$. [Ignoring the 1.01 scale factor and identifying marginal-products with partial derivatives, show that labor's relative share is given by $WL/PQ = L(W/P)/Q = L(\partial Q/\partial L)/Q = L(.75L^{.75-1}C^{.25})/L^{.75}C^{.25} = .75$. Show also that capital's share is $C(\partial Q/\partial C)/Q = .25$. Instead suppose $Q = [(3L)^{-1} + C^{-1}]^{-1}$, a weighted *harmonic mean*. Verify that $MPP_C = \partial Q/\partial C = [\frac{1}{3}(C/L) + 1]^{-2}$, and hence the nonlabor share, $C(\partial Q/\partial C)/Q$, *declines* as $C$ increases relative to $L$ as a tedious calculation shows.]

**3** Let $P = P(q)$ be the declining demand curve for a monopolist firm, with $TR = qP(q) = R(q)$. Let its total costs be given by $TC = P_L L + P_A A$. Let its production function be written as $q = q(L,A)$, with marginal-products given by $MPP_L = \partial q/\partial L$, etc. Then Maximum profit requires the maximization of $R - C = R[q(L,A)] - P_L L - P_A A$. Such a maximum requires differentiating partially with respect to each input, giving us by the chain rule for the calculus the equality of marginal-revenue-products to factor prices.

$$\partial\{R[q(L,A)] - P_L L - P_A A\}/\partial L = R'[q] \times \partial q/\partial L - P_L = 0 \qquad \text{QED}$$

and do likewise for the $MR \times MPP_A$ equivalence. In the case of perfect competition, set $P(q) \equiv P$, a constant; then $R[q] \equiv Pq$, $R'[q] \equiv P$, and you derive the equivalence of factor-price and value of its marginal-product. Do it.

**4** As a test of creative free association, use the following geometry to understand an important theorem in modern welfare economics: "Planners or markets are socially efficient, being out on, and not inside, society's production-possibility frontier for butter and guns (or, better, for food and clothing) only if the ratio of labor's marginal-physical-product to land's marginal-physical-product has been equated in every industry—equated to a common wage-rent ratio." HINT: We superimpose (a) and (b) on (c) to get (d). At inefficient point like $D$, lack of tangency leads to green area of waste. At typical efficient frontier point on green $AZ$ curve, orange and brown $MPP$ ratios are equal to common wage-rent as shown by mutual tangency to green price line through $E$. Be sure you relate (e)'s inside point $d$ to the nontangency point $D$ in (d).

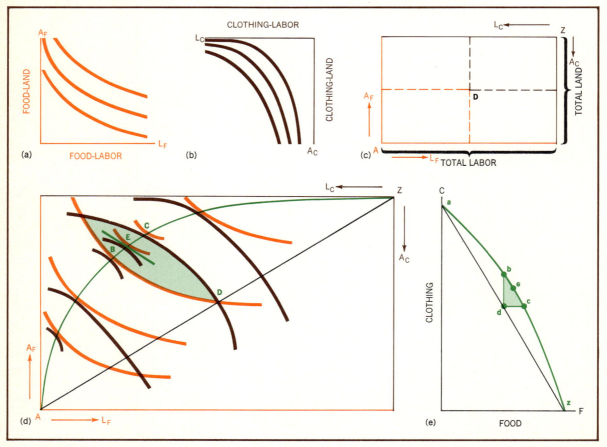

28

PRICING OF
FACTOR
INPUTS:
LAND RENTS
AND OTHER
RESOURCES

Chapter 27 gave an overall view of the microeconomic theory of the distribution of income by means of marginal-products. In this chapter we shall develop the details by which the marginal-product demand curves for factors interact with various supply curves for the factors of production to determine their market prices. Thereby the relative income shares of the owners of the factors of production (the FOR WHOM of laissez faire economics) get determined.

Also in this chapter, as a convenient preparation for the following chapters' discussions of wage, interest, and profit determination, we shall study the special case of rents to land and other natural resources that are in relatively inelastic supply.

## DEMAND FOR FACTORS A DERIVED DEMAND

Begin with some obvious and elementary observations about factor demand.

Why do consumers demand a finished output like a magazine or an overcoat? They do so because of the satisfaction they hope to enjoy from its use. But why does a businessman demand a factor input such as fertilizer or sulfur or unskilled labor? Surely not for the *direct* satisfaction he hopes to get. He wants the productive factors because of the production and revenue that he hopes to secure *indirectly* from those factors.

Satisfactions are in the picture, but at one stage removed. The satisfactions that consumers get from an overcoat help to determine how much a textile company can sell the coat for and how many coats it can sell. Therefore you would be right to insist that consumer demands do *ultimately* determine the firm's demand for inputs. The firm's demand for labor is *derived indirectly* from the consumer demand for its final product.

So economists speak of the demand for productive factors as a "derived demand."

The price of pig,
Is something big;
Because its corn, you'll
    understand,
Is high-priced, too;
Because it grew
Upon the high-priced farm-
    ing land.

If you'd know why
That land is high,
Consider this: its price is big
Because it pays
Thereon to raise
The costly corn, the high-
    priced pig.
H. J. DAVENPORT

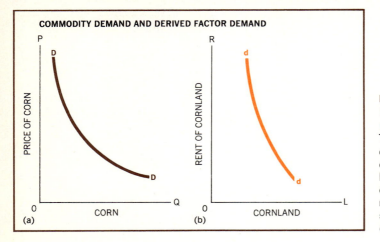

COMMODITY DEMAND AND DERIVED FACTOR DEMAND

(a) PRICE OF CORN — CORN

(b) RENT OF CORNLAND — CORNLAND

**FIG. 28-1**

**Demand for factors is derived from demand for goods they produce**

The orange curve of derived demand for cornland comes from the brown curve of commodity demand for corn. Shift the brown curve up, and up goes the orange curve. (Make the brown commodity curve more inelastic and vertical, and in part the same tends to happen to the orange factor curve.)

*Definition:* Derived demand refers to the fact that, when profit-seeking firms demand a factor of production, they do so because that factor input permits them to produce a good which consumers are willing to pay for now or in the future. The demand for the factor of production is thus derived ultimately from consumers' desires and demands for final goods.

In short, effort involved in making coats or sewing machines is of no interest to society for its own sake; we pay men and machines to sew because of the satisfaction believed to be gained from the finished product. Sometimes the derived demands go through many stages: Wool is wanted to spin yarn; yarn is wanted to weave cloth; cloth is wanted to make coats. All the previous demands are derived from the ultimate consumer demand for the satisfactions to be secured from the finished product.

Figure 28-1 shows how the demand for a given input, such as fertile cornland, must be regarded as derived from the consumers' demand curve for corn. This assumes, of course, that we hold constant the prices of such cooperating inputs as fertilizer, labor, and farm machinery. Chapter 27 showed this: At each land-rent price prevailing in the market place, any small farmer must decide on the Least-cost combination of the various inputs, and he must also decide on the Maximum-profit scale of his output to throw onto the market. Therefore each farmer will want to hire more and more of cornland up to the point where its marginal-revenue-product is equal to its market rental. At that point, the last unit just brings in an amount equal to its extra cost. That is why it is the equilibrium point at which the farmer ceases to demand more or less.[1]

---

[1] We are dealing with a competitive industry in which the single farmer is too small to affect the market price of corn. In such a competitive industry, no one need worry about spoiling the market for the previous units of corn being sold; consequently, marginal revenue and price are the same thing. It follows that marginal-revenue-product will be exactly the same thing as marginal-physical-product times corn price. For such a special perfectly competitive case, economists often use the special name "value of the marginal-product" instead of marginal-revenue-product.

Five principles governing elasticity of this factor demand will perhaps seem reasonable. Demand

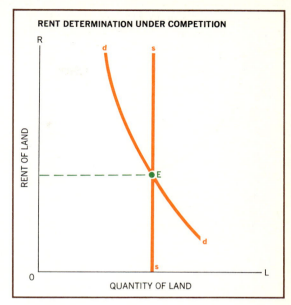

**RENT DETERMINATION UNDER COMPETITION**

FIG. 28-2
**Fixed land must work for what its demanders bid**
Perfect inelasticity of supply characterizes the case of so-called "pure economic rent." We run up ss curve to factor demand curve to determine rent. (Aside from land, we can apply rent considerations to oil and mining properties, 7-foot basketball players, and anything else in inelastic supply.)

## FACTOR-PRICE DETERMINATION BY SUPPLY AND DEMAND

Until now we have worked only with the demand curve for a factor, taking its market price as given to the demanding firms. But obviously it is *all the firms together* that determine the factor's market price which each small firm faces. Let us see how the total demand curve of all firms for the factor, together with its total supply curve, will interact to determine the equilibrium price tending to rule in the marketplace.

Figure 28-2 repeats the total derived demand curve for cornland dd. It was arrived at by adding together the demand curves of all the firms.

Now it is one of the peculiarities of land that, unlike most things, its total supply is relatively fixed by nature and in general cannot be augmented in response to a higher price for it or diminished in response to lower land rentals. (This is not strictly true. Land can sometimes be created by drainage, and the fertility of existing land can be depleted by overcropping.)

Nonetheless, we can accept the complete fixity of land's supply as its characteristic feature. By tradition, we may confine our discussion to the "original and inexhaustible gift of Nature" whose total supply is by definition *completely inelastic*. It was the price or return to such a factor that the classical economists of the last century called "rent."

---

for a factor tends to be the more inelastic (*a*) the more inelastic is the demand for the product; (*b*) the less important is the fraction of total cost of this indispensable factor ("It is important to be unimportant"); (*c*) the less other factors can be technically substituted for this factor; (*d*) the more inelastic are the supplies of other factors; and (*e*) the more inflexible is the administered price at which the firm continues to sell its product. (Skilled electricians meet all the first four requirements: little is spent on them; they are indispensable; other labor, such as carpenters and masons, is inelastically supplied; and the demand for new structures is quite inelastic.)

This differs from ordinary usage in which rent or rental is the money paid for the use over a period of time of anything—of a house, truck, and so forth. (For the rest of Part Four we shall use the word "rent" to refer to the return to a factor whose supply is completely inelastic and "rental" to refer to money paid for the services, over a period of time, of any factor.)

In Fig. 28-2, the supply curve for land $ss$ is made to be completely inelastic because of the fixity of its supply. The demand and supply curves intersect at the equilibrium point $E$. It is toward this factor-price that the rent of land must tend. Why? Because if rent rose above the equilibrium price, the amount of land demanded by all firms would be less than the existing amount that would be supplied; some property owners would be unable to rent their land at all; therefore they would offer their land for less and thus bid down its rent. By similar reasoning, the rent could not long remain below the equilibrium intersection. If it did, you should be able to show how the bidding of unsatisfied firms would force the factor-price back up toward the equilibrium level. Only at a competitive price where total amount demanded of land exactly equals the total supply will there be equilibrium. It is in this sense that supply and demand determine any factor-price.

Note that the man who owns land does not have to be a particularly deserving citizen in order to receive this rent. A virtuous and poor landowner will be given exactly the same rent by competition as will a wealthy wastrel. It is the productivity of the acre of land that is being paid for, and not the personal merits of the landowner.

Even this productivity of the land is not something absolute. For example, what would happen if the price of corn were to fall greatly because people began to desire other goods? Then the derived demand for cornland would shift drastically downward and to the left. What would happen to the rents received by landowners? After a time, rents would have to sink down to a new equilibrium intersection. The land is not less productive in a technical sense than it was before, and the landlords are neither more nor less virtuous than they were before. But factor demand-and-supply intersection has changed.

A factor of production like cornland is said to earn a "pure economic rent" (1) when its total supply is regarded as perfectly inelastic; and (2) when we can assume that the land *has no other uses,* such as in the production of sugar or rye. Adam Smith's great follower in England, David Ricardo, noted in 1815 that the case of such an inelastically supplied factor could be described as follows:

**It is not really true that the price of corn is high because the price of cornland is high. Actually the reverse is more nearly the truth; the price of cornland is high because the price of corn is high! Land's total supply being inelastic, it will always work for whatever is given to it by competition. Thus the value of the land is completely derived from the value of the product, and not vice versa.[2]**

_____

[2] Land is not the only factor whose return may be considered economic rent. For an example where most of an individual's unique wage payment is a "pure rent," see page 581. And in the short run, the supply of a machine or plant may be entirely fixed; thus a hydroelectric plant takes a long time to build, still longer to wear out. The return to any factor in temporarily fixed supply is sometimes called a "quasi rent"—"quasi," because in the long run, its supply need not be fixed. Those farmers who petition for higher milk prices because of higher land and cow prices, without knowing it, illustrate rent and quasi-rent doctrines.

## RENT AND COSTS[3]

Some economists went so far as to say: "Rent does not enter into the cost of production." As a digression, let us see why.

The last section shows that there is a grain of truth in this. But still it is very dangerous terminology. If you were a farmer trying to go into the corn-raising business, you would certainly find that the landlord has to be paid like anybody else. You would certainly include rent in your costs of production; and if you could not pay your rent, you would go out of business.

**Implicit versus explicit returns**   Even if you were a farmer who owned your own land, it would be a mistake to think that rent does not enter into your costs of production. After you had paid all your other bills, including wages to yourself at least as great as what you could earn elsewhere in the market, there would have to be left an amount at least equal to the market rental value of your land. For what if there were not? Then you would soon find that it would be better for you *to rent out your farm on the open market* and hire out your own labor to somebody else.

Sometimes economists call rent paid by a man to himself "implicit" rather than "explicit" rent. Very clearly, implicit rent is as much a part of long-run competitive costs as are any other costs, and the same can be said of the implicit wages or implicit interest earned on any other factors that you could sell rather than use personally. The reader is urged to refer to the discussion of opportunity cost and implicit cost in Chapter 24 (page 474) which bear on this point.

**Relativity of viewpoint**   When some economists claim rent does not enter into society's cost of production, what are they driving at? As already noted, they are saying this.

Since rent is the return to an inelastically supplied factor that would still be supplied to the community even at much lower prices, the direction of causation goes as follows: *The prices of goods really determine land rent—rather than having land rent determine the prices of goods.*

But at this point we must avoid our old enemy "the fallacy of composition." What appears as a cost of production to each and every small firm using a particular kind of land may, as we have seen, be to the whole community merely a derived, price-determined rent expense rather than a price-determining one. More than that, suppose the land is specialized and can be used only for the production of one industry. If a grade of land is inelastically supplied to one industry and has no place else to go, it will always work for whatever it can earn there, then its return will appear to every small firm as a cost like any other. But as scientific observers of the whole industry, we still must recognize that the land return is a price-determined rent and not a price-determining cost.

Now let us move on to an alternative case. Suppose this land can be used for a variety of industries: for corn growing, rye growing, buckwheat growing, cattle grazing, and so forth. Then to each small industry (such as buckwheat growing), land's return will definitely appear as a necessary expense that the consumers of buckwheat will have to pay as cost before they can get their buckwheat. One small industry is just

---

[3] This theoretical digression may be skipped by brief courses.

like any one small firm in this case: although the total of land is *inelastic* in supply for *all* uses, to any *one* small firm or industry it is in completely *elastic* supply.

**To conclude: Whether rent is or is not a price-determining cost depends upon the viewpoint: that of a small firm, small industry, large and even exclusive-user industry, or whole economy. What is a price-determined rent return to a factor which is inelastic in supply to the whole community or dominant industry may, to each firm and to any small industry that is only one of many potential users, appear as a price-determining cost.[4]**

### HENRY GEORGE'S SINGLE-TAX MOVEMENT: TAXING LAND'S SURPLUS

In the last part of the nineteenth century, a western frontier still existed in this country. As more and more people came here from Europe, each acre of land had more and more people to work with. In a sense, therefore, the land became more productive. In any case, its competitive rent value certainly tended to rise. This created handsome profits for some of those who were lucky or farsighted enough to get in on the ground floor and buy land early. As Will Rogers put it, "Land is a good investment. They ain't making no more."

Nor was this true only in agriculture. Men still alive in the Middle West can remember when towns first began. They will tell you how they might have been rich if their fathers had recognized 100 years ago that the corner of State and Madison would eventually become the center of town and grow tremendously in value as a result of the great increase in urban populations. *Urban sites with good locations earn rents in the same sense that fertile areas do.* Many people began to wonder why lucky landowners should be permitted to receive these so-called "unearned land increments."

Henry George, a printer who thought much about economics, crystallized these sentiments in the single-tax movement. This movement had a considerable following a century ago, and there are still some adherents to it; but it is not likely that anyone running on the single-tax ticket will again come so close to being elected mayor of New York City as George did in 1886. Nor is it likely that anyone will soon come along and write so persuasive a bible for the movement as Henry George did in his *Progress and Poverty,* a book which sold millions of copies.

**Taxing land's unearned surplus**   This is not the place to attempt any assessment of the merits and demerits of George's political movement. But one important principle of distribution and taxation can be illustrated by his valid central tenet:

**Pure land rent is in the nature of a "surplus" which can be taxed heavily *without distorting production incentives or efficiency.***

[4] The Davenport verses opening this chapter hint at such a conclusion. To cover cases like this, economists invented the technical expression "opportunity cost." (Again see Chapter 24's discussion.) To each owner of land, using it in his own business is wise only if its marginal-product there will be sure to cover his "opportunity cost," or cost forgone in not selling it in the market for others to use. Similarly, a competitive industry can employ a factor only if its derived worth there at least measures up to the opportunity cost of using it elsewhere. In the terminology of Chapter 2's production-possibility frontier: The cost of guns is the forgone (or opportunity) cost of not producing butter with the same resources; gun cost can be measured in terms of sacrificed butter even if every factor were in inelastic supply, involving no disutility and involving price-determined or "residual" rents that are quite *unnecessary* to elicit the factors' supply and effort.

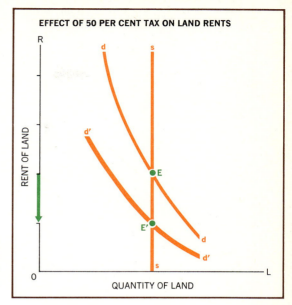

**FIG. 28-3**
**Tax on fixed land is shifted back on landowners, skimming off pure economic rent**
A tax on fixed land leaves rentals paid by users unchanged at E but reduces rent retained by landowners to E'. (What can the landowners do but accept less return?) This provides the rationale for Henry George's single-tax movement.

Let us see why. Suppose that supply and demand create an equilibrium land rent, as in Fig. 28-3 at E. Now what would happen if we were to introduce a 50 per cent tax on all land rents? Mind you, we are not taxing buildings or improvements; for that certainly would affect the volume of construction activity. All we are supposed to be taxing is the yield of the *naturally fixed supply* of agricultural and urban land sites, assuming that this can somehow be identified.

There has been no shift in the total demand curve for land; firms are still willing to pay the same amount as before for the same amount of land. Hence, with land fixed in supply, the market price that they pay must still be at the old intersection E. Why? Because supply to users has not changed and neither has demand. Because at any higher price than before, some land would have to go without any demanders. Hence, competitive rents could not permanently be raised to land users.

Of course, what the farmer pays and what the landlord receives are now two quite different things. As far as the landlords are concerned, once the government steps in to take its cut of 50 per cent, the effect is just the same as if the *net demand to the owners* had shifted down from *dd* to *d'd'*. Landowners' equilibrium return *after taxes* is now only as high as E', or only half as high as E. *The whole of the tax has been shifted backward onto the owners of the factor in inelastic supply!* The landowners will not like this. But under competition there is nothing they can do about it, since they cannot alter the total supply and the land must work for whatever it can get. Half a loaf is better than none, or even than one-fourth of a loaf.

**Ethical issues**   Whether or not it is a fair thing to take away part of the return of those who own land is quite another question. Perhaps many voters will feel that such owners are not less deserving than are investors who have put their money into other things; perhaps many will feel that no one should have the right to benefit from Nature's windfall gifts of oil, minerals, or soil fertility.[5] But these are political questions that must be brought out at the polls. What is relevant is to point out that a similar 50 per cent tax put upon a different factor of production whose total supply is *not* completely inelastic would certainly produce definite effects on the factor-prices charged in a competitive market. To some extent this tax would distort the pattern of production, and it would shift part of the burden *forward* onto the users of the factor and onto consumers. Thus, if the same acre of land were to be taxed differently when used for wheat rather than corn production, this would certainly have distorting effects on the price of wheat relative to that of corn.

Since statistics quoted in the last chapter show pure land rent today is barely 5 per cent of the total GNP, if Henry George were alive today and facing the need of government for more than 25 per cent of GNP, he would perhaps change his movement's name from "the single tax" to "the useful tax on unearned land surplus."

## SUPPLY AND DEMAND FOR ANY FACTOR

The competitive determination of land rent by supply and demand is only one instance of the general analysis applicable to *any* factor of production. How is the rental value per week of a tractor to be determined in a competitive market?

We first sum up the derived demands of all business firms for tractors. (Of course, these derived demands have behind them marginal-revenue-product considerations of the preceding chapter; but this behind-the-scenes relation need not concern the observer of the aggregate market demand for this factor.) Along with the *dd* curve shown in Fig. 28-4, we must also have a supply curve such as *ss*. But there is now no reason why the supply curve should be perfectly vertical. It may now be positively elastic, rising upward toward the northeast. (EXAMPLE: The case of tractor supply, dependent on rising marginal costs of production.) Alternatively, if the factor of production were labor, it might be that people would feel they could afford to work *fewer* hours when wages rise, so that the *ss* curve might eventually bend backward and northwestward from the vertical, rather than rising forward.

In any case, whether the supply curve is vertically inelastic, positively elastic, or negatively elastic, there will be an *ss* curve as in Fig. 28-4.

**Where the derived demand curve for a factor intersects its supply curve, the final equilibrium factor-price will be set. And if the demand curve for the factor shifts up, its market price will tend to rise; on the other hand, if the supply offered of a factor increases, so that the supply curve shifts rightward, then the factor-price will tend to fall.**

In a competitive market economy, therefore, factor-prices and the distribution of income are not determined at random. There are definite forces of supply and demand operating to create high returns to scarce factors that are very useful in producing the things wanted by people with purchasing power. And, of course, any factor's

---

[5] As the Organization of Petroleum Exporting Countries (OPEC) accumulates fantastic wealth from the sale of oil, for example, the question of OPEC's "right" to this wealth may come into question.

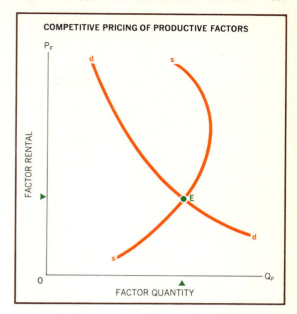

**FIG. 28-4**

**Factor supply and derived demand interact together to determine factor prices and income distribution**

Land's share in national income rises when its rent is bid up. In the same way, skilled and unskilled labor shares are determined, in competitive markets, by interplay of factor supply and demand. The same would hold for any factor of production in the traditional theory.

earnings tend to drop if more of it becomes available, or if other close substitutes for it are found, or if people stop wanting the goods that this factor is best suited to make. Competition gives, and competition takes.

### FACTOR PRICING AND EFFICIENCY: RENT AND FACTOR-PRICES AS DEVICES TO RATION SCARCE RESOURCES

Competitive supply and demand helps determine the For Whom problem of society. Whether or not we like its answer to this distribution question—and in the case of rent, Henry George certainly did not—we have to admit that it does contribute to an *efficient* solution of the How problem for society.

Thus, as a result of supply and demand in markets for goods and for factors, in America where land is plentiful and labor scarce, we find extensive farming. In Asia, where people are plentiful relative to land, we find intensive farming.

Why? Because of government planning? No, not necessarily.

Rather it is the *signaling* of market pricing that results in efficient How. Land has to be auctioned off at a low price here; labor, auctioned off at a high price here. So every farmer, seeking his Least-cost combination lest he go bankrupt, substitutes land for labor here. By contrast, abroad, cheap labor gets substituted for land. (More than that: with labor scarce here, we find that fussy vegetables, which require much care, are priced relatively higher than those which lend themselves to extensive methods. So the resulting high commodity prices tend to make us *substitute the cheaper land-intensive goods* in our diet for the more expensive labor-intensive ones. Abroad the opposite commodity substitutions take place. Hence, the pricing system signals best commodity substitutions as well as best factor substitutions!)

Thus, we see that charging rent has a function—even if you later tax part or all of it away. And we can now appreciate examples showing how troubles in the real world come from the fact that often there is no way to charge the appropriate rents.

*Item:* The sea is free to all. So everyone fishes in it until the fish are all killed off or decimated. If society could somehow charge rents for commercial fishing licenses, we might in the long run all be better off—including fishermen! Refer to the discussion of external diseconomies in Chapter 24, and show that international fishing competition is less efficient than unified—national or international—control.

*Item:* Our roads get very crowded on weekends and during rush hours. We usually cannot charge tolls or rents. If we could, we might coax shoppers and people who are on the margin of indifference to do their driving at some less crowded time.

*Item:* Even if policemen can inspect and make collections from parking meters at a negligible fraction of the cost of the revenue collected by parking meters, it may be socially desirable to keep the tolls of such meters high enough to create a rational use of limited curb space.

Other examples of how charging rent leads to efficient How could be given. But this does not justify the status quo of taxation or of unequal land ownership. That must be attacked or defended in terms of ethical value judgments concerning the proper For Whom resolutions in society.

## CONSERVATION AND LAND TENURE

David Ricardo and Henry George emphasized the original, unaugmentable, and indestructible gift of Nature. Actually, much of the land we use *has* been augmented by man: it has been drained, filled, and fertilized by investment effort quite like that which builds machines and plants. Equally important, Nature's gifts *can* be destroyed. There are now deserts where green acres once flourished. There are used-up mines; deforested timberlands; eroded and depleted topsoils. Part of the rental element in the sale of Minnesota iron ore was a return of capital for this exhaustible resource. More and more we must go abroad for the raw materials to feed our machines.

Charging rents for use of resources may slow down their rate of depletion and serve to ration out such scarce, exhaustible resources. But in a freely competitive system, the self-interest of owners may well lead to the rapid using up of natural resources. The resulting depletion is not merely to the owner, who is left with nothing more to sell or rent. Unsightly and unhealthy slag piles may also be created. There may be short-term and long-term regional unemployment. There may be deforestation that causes floods and soil erosion downstream. All these "external diseconomies" create a presumption toward public concern and toward public regulation or coordination.

**Land-use programs**   As Chapter 40 will discuss, civilization pollutes the atmosphere, rivers, lakes, and even seas. Urbanization and irrigation deplete water reservoirs and depress the level of the water table below ground. Fresh water becomes a vital scarcity, and regions fight over the disposition of scarce water: Colorado versus California; northern versus southern California; Illinois versus Michigan versus Canada. That is one reason why huge dam projects are undertaken publicly—TVA in Tennessee, Bonneville and other projects in the Northwest and Canada, the Aswan Dam on the Nile, the Volta in Ghana—for irrigation, conservation, electric power, and defense.

As we shall see in Chapter 38's discussion of underdeveloped nations, at the village and farm level, inefficient systems of land tenancy may keep society inside its production-possibility frontier and even depress that frontier. Absentee landlords will not put money into the land; tenants on short and uncertain tenure have every incentive to mine the land and to refuse to make needed long-term improvements; credit is lacking for productive investment; and peasants who pay 40 per cent interest to moneylenders in order to tide themselves over until the new harvest alleviates starvation can hardly be expected to make capital investment in the land or even maintain it.

Thus, the choice is not between ideal perfect competition and public regimentation. It is between imperfect laissez faire and imperfect public coordination; between inefficient government fiats and rational democratic programming.

This is why most of the mixed economies put some limits on freedom to use land. They make zoning restrictions and draw up regional and urban plans. They employ the right of eminent domain, in which owners are made to sell their land at publicly determined prices. Parklands, owned by government, are used to create "external economies" and common consumption benefits. In Britain, Italy, France, Sweden, and elsewhere, limitations are put on the windfall capital gains that can be secured by those lucky enough to own farmland where a new city is to be located or those clever enough to speculate successfully on future developments.

## CONCLUSIONS

The same general principles determining land rent also determine the prices of all inputs: capital goods, natural resources, or labor. Thus the rentals of threshing machines or of trucks are determined in essentially the same way. One can even say that wages are the rentals paid for the use of a man's personal services for a day or a week or a year. This may seem a strange use of terms, but on second thought, one recognizes that every agreement to hire labor is really for some limited period of time. By outright purchase, you might avoid ever renting any kind of land. But in our society, labor is one of the few productive factors that cannot legally be bought outright. Labor can only be rented, and the wage rate is really a rental.

The next chapter deals with the peculiar problems of wages and labor markets. Chapter 30 will analyze the problems of capital and interest, which will be seen to be important in determining the supply of durable goods available for rental and use.

## SUMMARY

1   Factor demand curves are derived from commodity demand curves. An upward shift in the latter causes a similar upward shift in the former; and inelasticity in commodity demand makes for inelasticity of derived factor demand.

2   We add up for all the firms their derived demands for a factor in order to get the aggregate demand curve. This, together with the specified supply curve of the factor, can be expected to determine an equilibrium intersection. At the equilibrium market price for the factor of production, the amounts demanded and supplied will be exactly equal—only there will factor-price have no tendency

to change. Anywhere above the equilibrium price, suppliers will tend to undercut the market and to cause price to fall; anywhere below the equilibrium price, shortages will cause demanders to bid the price upward, restoring the equilibrium.

3  The unchangeable quantity of natural land is an interesting special case where the supply curve happens to be perfectly vertical and *inelastic*. In such a so-called "*pure* rent" case, competition will still determine an equilibrium market rental. But in this case, we are faced with a cost element that is more price-*determined* than price-*determining*; the land rent is more the result of the market prices for the finished commodities than their cause. (Yet we must not forget that, to any small firm or to any industry too small to affect appreciably the total demand for land, rent will still seem to enter explicitly or implicitly into the cost of production just like any other expense. To such a small industry, rent reflects the opportunity cost of using land elsewhere and appears to be as much price-determining as any other cost element.)

From the standpoint of the community as a whole, the rent of an inelastically supplied factor will be reckoned in the GNP at its full dollar value, like anything else. But below the veil of money, it still remains true that this factor would be willing to work for less if it had to, and in that sense its return is in the nature of a "surplus" rather than in the nature of a reward necessary to coax out the factor supply. This provides the basis for Henry George's "single-tax" program, proposing to tax the unearned increment of land value—and without any shifting forward of the tax to the consumer or distorting effects on production.

4  Whatever some may feel about the ethical nicety of its answer to the For Whom problem, proper factor pricing does under perfect competition contribute to efficient solution of society's How problem. Indeed, *not charging rents* may cause inefficient overcrowding and bad choice of use in many situations.

Because land utilization is fraught with "neighborhood and externality effects," zoning fiats and public controls on land use are common. Exhaustibility of natural resources, conservation, and distorting forms of land tenure raise special problems of economic analysis for land.

5  The general principles of supply and demand can also be used to explain the competitive price determination of all services other than those of land. The rental of all inputs—including the wages that have to be paid for the use of the services of human beings and the rentals of durable machines—is determined in a competitive system by supply and demand.

## CONCEPTS FOR REVIEW

derived demand
inelastic supply of God-given
    land, pure rent
society's rent as firm's cost

single tax, backward shifting of
    land tax, unearned increment
price-*determined* expense versus
    price-*determining* expense

supply-and-demand equilibrium
factor-price equilibrium
price signaling of efficient factor
    and commodity substitutions

How, For Whom, and rents
resource exhaustibility and
    conservation
land zoning and public policies

## QUESTIONS FOR DISCUSSION

**1** Define the "pure rent" case. Explain the sense in which price of such a factor is "price-*determined*" rather than "price-*determining*." Show that, nonetheless, an increase in supply of the rent-earning factor will depress its return and lower prices of goods that use it much.

**2** What was the Henry George single-tax movement all about? Use a diagram to show the effect of taxing pure rent. Apply this to a ballplayer's inelastic supply.

**3** Discuss why it might avoid confusion if you reserved the word "rent" for the strong case of inelastically supplied factors and used "rentals" for other cases.

**4** *Extra credit problem:* See if you can puzzle out how economists define "producer's surplus (or rent)" in close analogy to Chapter 22's "consumer's surplus (or rent)." The accompanying diagram shows two industries, corn and wine. Each is produced by transferable labor, which must work with cornland or vineyard land, no land being transferable between industries. Each diagram is like Fig. 23-7(b) on page 461. Labor-leisure is assumed to have strictly constant marginal utility in the background: each $S_iS_i'$ curve rises because transferred varying labor encounters diminishing returns on fixed specialized land. Each $D_iD_i'$ curve falls for the usual declining marginal-utility reasons. Note the orange-shaded areas of consumer's surplus, much as in Fig. 22-4, page 439. But now note that the brown-shaded areas can be thought of as representing producer's surplus or rent. Thus, the second diagram shows less-diminishing returns and hence less-rising rent to vineyard land. If vineyard land were superabundant and therefore free, the supply curve there would be horizontal and there would then be only orange consumer's surplus with no brown producer's surplus there at all.

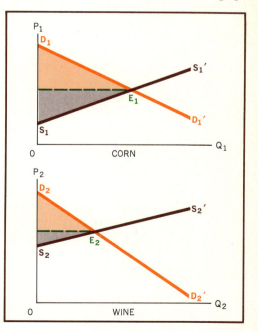

# 29

## COMPETITIVE WAGES AND COLLECTIVE BARGAINING

*The labourer is worthy of his hire.*
*New Testament*

A man is much more than a commodity. Yet it is true that men do rent out their services for a price. This price is the wage rate, and of all prices it is by far the most important. For the vast majority of the population, the wage is the sole determinant of family income. And when we remember that much of the income of farmers, of professional people (such as doctors and lawyers), and of nonincorporated enterprises is in actuality a form of labor income, we realize that wages must constitute 80 per cent of the national income.

What is supposed to determine wage rates under competitive conditions? This is the first problem we shall tackle, in Section A below. Then in Section B, we shall investigate the effects of deviations from competitive conditions. Developing further the problems introduced in Chapter 7, we shall analyze the economics of collective bargaining between trade-unions and employers.

### A. WAGE DETERMINATION UNDER PERFECT COMPETITION

Wage rates differ enormously. The average wage is as hard to define as the average man. An auto executive may earn $700,000 a year at the same time that a clerk earns $9,000 and a farmhand $4,500. In the same factory, a skilled machinist may earn $240 a week, while an unskilled man gets $110. Experienced women may be paid $100 a week at the same time their younger brothers are *starting* at $130. Part of any theory of wages must explain these differentials.

But important as these wage *differences* are, we must not overlook *the general wage level*. Wages of virtually every category of labor are higher than they used to be half a century ago. Wages are higher in the United States than for similar categories of labor in Europe; higher in Sweden than in Italy; higher in northern than in southern Italy; higher in Europe than in Asia; higher in some "subsistence" economies than in others.

Economic analysis must be applied to the understanding of such basic facts.

## REAL WAGE DETERMINATION FOR A SINGLE GRADE

Let us begin by examining the simplified case of wages paid for similar jobs to laborers who are all exactly alike in skill, effort, and every other respect. Then competition will cause their wage rates per hour all to be exactly equal. No employer would pay more for the work of one man than he would pay for his identical twin, and no worker would be able to ask more for his services.

How is this single market wage determined? If we know the supply and demand curves for these laborers—as in Fig. 29-1(a)—then the competitive equilibrium wage must be at $E_a$, the intersection point. If the wage rate were lower than $E_a$, spirited bidding by frustrated employers would restore the equilibrium.

We are interested in *real wages*—in what the wage will buy—and not just in the money wage. Therefore, in our illustrations, we express wages in money units whose purchasing power over goods is held constant at the level of some particular year and place, e.g., in terms of American dollars of 1939 or 1976 purchasing power. By definition, an index of the real wage represents an index of actual money wages deflated (or divided) by an index of the price level. (EXAMPLE: Money wage rates doubled from 1966 to 1976; however, since prices increased about 50 per cent in that period, real wages increased by only one-third; i.e., $200/150 = 1\frac{1}{3}$.)

Imagine that Fig. 29-1(a) represents the state of affairs in America and Fig. 29-1(b) that in Europe. Why are wages so much higher in America than in Europe? Is it because we have unions and they do not? Or because we have passed higher

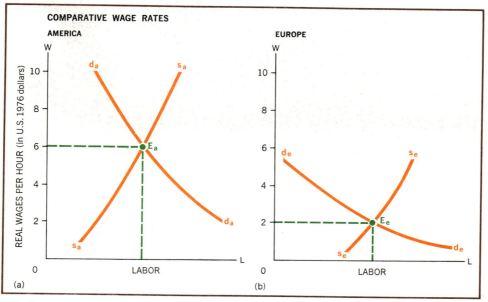

FIG. 29-1

**Favorable resources, skills, management, and technology explain high American wages**
Supply and demand determine a higher competitive wage in America than in Europe. Historically, productivity improvement underlies shift of $d_a d_a$ to its high current level.

minimum-wage laws than they have? Experts doubt that these factors can explain the difference. In any case, such explanations are ruled out in our simplified competitive paradigm.

A true answer would be:

*Supply and demand are such in America, compared with Europe, as to lead to a higher real wage here.*

But *why* are supply and demand such as to lead to high American wages? What lies behind these schedules? Why is labor's productivity (its marginal-product) so high here? Why do competing employers who ruthlessly seek to maximize their profits find themselves, in America, bidding real wages up so high?

### RESOURCES, CAPITAL, AND TECHNOLOGY

In the first place, we recall that the derived demand schedules for labor slope downward. The law of diminishing returns suggests that adding more and more labor to the same American natural resources and land area will tend to diminish labor's marginal productivity and wages. Suppose you let American population increase so as to shift the supply curve $s_a s_a$ far to the right in Fig. 29-1(a). Then the wage might fall eventually to the European level or even lower.

One important explanation of high American wages, therefore, lies in the sphere of economic geography:

*Compared with the size of our working population, we have been generously supplied with land, coal, iron, oil, and water power.*

The per capita supplies of these vital sinews of modern industrial production are less in Europe and still less in many other regions. What resources we do not possess in abundance, we could historically trade for.

But economic geography does not tell the whole story. Two regions may be exactly alike in endowment of natural resources; but if one uses superior managerial and technological methods, its productivity and real wages may be much higher than the other's. (Compare Denmark and Crete; or Hong Kong and Calcutta; or Connecticut and Mississippi.) In part, using superior technological methods involves better know-how, better applied science, better economic laws and customs, better management, more highly skilled and educated people, and better work methods; in part, it involves relative abundance of capital goods—of man-made machinery, fabricated materials, and industrial plants.

Just why America developed a superiority in know-how and capital availability is not well understood by economic historians. Our lead is beginning to narrow, as know-how and capital investment spread abroad. But the truth of this superiority is not in doubt.

### IMMIGRATION AND RESTRICTIONS OF LABOR SUPPLY

This raises the question, Why don't Europeans move from their low-wage area to our higher-wage area? People *did* migrate to this country in great numbers during the three centuries prior to World War I. A few came to seek religious freedom, many because they liked our system of government, but by far the greatest number came to better their economic condition.

After World War I, laws were passed severely limiting immigration. Only a trickle of immigrants has been admitted since then. This is a first example of interference with the free play of competition in the wage market. By keeping labor supply down, immigration policy tends to keep wages high. Let us underline this basic principle:

**Limitation of the supply of any grade of labor relative to all other productive factors can be expected to raise its wage rate; an increase in supply will, other things being equal, tend to depress wage rates.**

The law of diminishing returns makes it easy to understand why trade-unions used to favor restrictions on immigration. The same analysis helps to explain why they have pressed for (1) a shorter and shorter working week, and more days of vacation per year; (2) restrictions on child labor, encouragement of early old-age retirement, and exclusion of women from some areas of labor; and (3) restrictions on degree of effort and speed-ups. The old labor jingle,

Whether you work by the week or the day
The shorter the work the better the pay

expresses the hope that the working class can travel upward on the demand curve for labor.

## THEORY OF THE OPTIMUM POPULATION

At this point we must be careful not to overstate the law of diminishing returns. Working against it, for a range at least, is a counterlaw: *the law of increasing returns to scale*, or of *economies of mass production*.

One of the reasons the United States is so prosperous is that ours is so *large* a free-trade area. Modern technology increasingly requires larger and larger plants: unless you can produce a thousand electric refrigerators per day, you will not realize the full economies of large-scale mass production. Before the Common Market brought trade barriers down in Europe, a small country with a limited domestic market found it difficult to have an efficient domestic industry.

This raises a question: Would the per capita living standard be higher for the United States in the 1970s and 1980s if our population were cut by one-half? If you apply the law of diminishing returns uncritically, the answer is, Yes. But in view of the counterlaw of increasing returns, the answer is in doubt.

This discussion suggests a rather interesting theory of population. Why not have the best of both situations? Why not take advantage of increasing returns per capita as well as of diminishing returns? Specifically, why not aim at letting population grow up to the exact point where increasing returns begin to be outweighed by decreasing returns? This point will give the highest level of real wages or real incomes and is called the "optimum population." Figure 29-2 on the next page illustrates how the optimum is defined at the very top of the productivity curve.[1]

---

[1] Figure 29-2 plots *average* rather than *marginal* product: i.e., total NNP ÷ people.

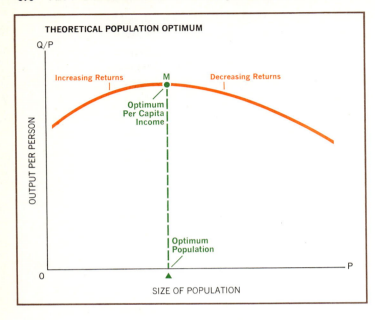

**THEORETICAL POPULATION OPTIMUM**

Q/P

Increasing Returns    M    Decreasing Returns

Optimum
Per Capita
Income

OUTPUT PER PERSON

Optimum
Population

0                                    P

SIZE OF POPULATION

**FIG. 29-2**
**Per capita incomes average out highest at population not too large or small**
At the point where decreasing per capita returns begins, output per person is at its very highest. Unfortunately, economists are unable to estimate just where the optimum is for a modern nation. No doubt many nations in Asia have population density well beyond the optimum. But for the advanced nations, loss of privacy and of an unpolluted environment are probably more important than diminishing returns in terms of food. (WARNING: Since total output does not get divided equally between labor and property owners, any optimum must take into account the distribution of the social pie.)

## THE IRON LAW OF WAGES: MALTHUS AND MARX

In Chapter 2, we encountered the Malthusian theory of population, and we shall meet it again in Part Six. According to this theory, you should draw in on Fig. 29-1(a) a *horizontal* long-run supply curve of labor. This is to be drawn in at the wage level corresponding to the *subsistence standard of living* at which people will just reproduce their numbers. A century and a half ago, economics was called "the dismal science" because many classical economists believed wages tended toward the bare minimum of subsistence. Our survey of rising living standards and growing populations showed how unrealistic for the West is this notion of a bare-minimum, long-run supply curve of labor, and how misleading it would be as a basis for any predictions about the long-term "laws of motion of the capitalistic system."

A quite different version of the gloomy law of wages was provided by Karl Marx. He put great emphasis upon the "reserve army of the unemployed." In effect, employers were supposed to lead their workers to the factory windows and point to the unemployed workers out at the factory gates, eager to work for less. This, Marx thought (or is interpreted by naïve Marxists to have thought), would depress wages to the subsistence level.

Let us try to show this on our diagrams. Figure 29-1(a) is redrawn as Fig. 29-3. Suppose that the wage is pegged at $8 per hour in 1976 prices. Employment is at the level indicated by the point *A*. At this high wage, there would indeed be unemployment, as alleged. The amount of unemployment would be represented by the distance between the labor supplied and demanded *AB*. In our simple, idealized model of competition, such unemployment could certainly be expected to put downward pressure on wages.

But does the basic Marxian conclusion follow? Is there any tendency for real wage rates to fall to a *minimum-subsistence level* such as *mm* in Fig. 29-3? None at all. There is absolutely no reason why, in our simple model, real wage rates should ever fall below the equilibrium level at *E*. In a country well endowed with technology, capital, and natural resources, this competitively determined equilibrium wage might be a very comfortable one indeed. Only in a less fortunate country should we expect it to be anywhere near as low as the minimum of subsistence. Thus we reach an important principle:

If competition in the labor market were really perfect, there would be no necessary tendency in an advanced country for wages to fall to any minimum-subsistence level.

Employers might prefer to pay low wages. But that would not matter. In a competitive market they are unable to set wage rates as they would *like*. As long as employers are numerous and do not act in collusion, their demands for any grade of labor will bid its wage up to the equilibrium level at which the total forthcoming labor supply is absorbed. The workers may aspire to still higher wages, but under competition they do not get what they would *like*, either; as long as they do not act collusively to limit the labor supply, their wishes will not serve to make wages rise above the competitive level.

## LUMP-OF-LABOR FALLACY AND THE THIRTY-HOUR WEEK

It would be wrong to think that diminishing returns alone explains why unions pursue policies to restrict labor and effort. There is a related and still more powerful reason why workers fight for shorter hours. They fear unemployment; they tend to think the

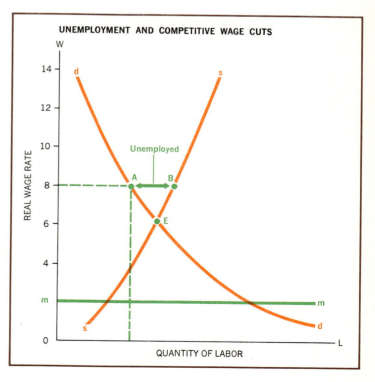

**FIG. 29-3**

Marxians exaggerated power of "reserve army of unemployed" to depress wages
The "reserve army of the unemployed"—as shown by *AB*—is not able to depress real wages to the *mm* "minimum-subsistence" level. It can only depress competitive wages from *A* to *E*. If labor supply became so abundant that *ss* intersected *dd* at *mm*, the wage would be at a minimum level, as in many underdeveloped regions; but institutional or legal changes can do little when marginal productivity remains abysmally low.

*total amount of work to be done is constant* in the short run. So what happens if a foreigner is put to work? Or a woman comes into the labor market? Or an old man refuses to retire? Or a fellow worker works too efficiently? Or a machine replaces a man? Or men work overtime? Each of these looms up as a threat to a worker's job and livelihood.

This attitude, that there is only a fixed amount of work to be done, is sometimes called by economists the "lump-of-labor fallacy." We must give this notion its due. To a particular group of workers, with special skills and status and stuck in one region, the introduction of technological change may represent a real threat. Viewed from their personal standpoint, the lump-of-labor notion may not be so fallacious.

True enough, in a great depression, when there is mass and chronic unemployment, one can understand how workers generally may yield to a lump-of-labor philosophy. But the lump-of-labor argument implies that there is only so much useful remunerative work to be done in any economic system, *and that is indeed a fallacy.*

If proper monetary, fiscal, and pricing policies are being vigorously promulgated, no mixed economy need resign itself to depression unemployment. Though technological unemployment can't be shrugged off lightly, its optimal solution lies in combining expansionary macroeconomic programs (fiscal and monetary policies) with retraining policies that create adequate job opportunities and new skills, rather than in restrictions on production.

There are, of course, still other arguments for or against cutting standard working hours from, say, 40 per week to 30. As our standards of living and productivity rise, it is only natural that we should feel we can afford more leisure. Historically, working hours have been progressively shortened, as we have already seen. Saturday work will no doubt become rarer and rarer in American industry. Probably there will be a trend toward increased vacations with pay—not so much because the vacation will improve workers' productivity as that people get enjoyment from summer and winter vacations. Taking more time off will probably be one of the ways in which we shall choose to enjoy the fruits of technological progress. No doubt, too, our grandchildren will choose to work a still shorter week; but that should reflect choice, not necessity.

Still, at this stage of history would American workers really wish to purchase 10 extra hours of leisure per week if this meant forgoing a sizable fraction of real and money income—say, 20 per cent of what potentially might be earned? The facts do not bear this out. As our economy approached full employment in the 1960s, agitation for the 30-hour week declined. This suggests that the unemployment rather than the leisure argument really carried most weight. Moreover, when a union leader favors a shorter week, he at the same time asks that there be no cut in take-home pay. What worker could be against a free present of more leisure? A few pages later, we shall investigate the degree to which unions can squeeze higher wages out of employers. But there is no doubt that drastic shortening of hours would imply lower real earnings than a full-employment economy is capable of providing at a longer workweek.

**Four-day week**   In the early 1970s, a number of firms began to experiment with a 4-day, 10-hours-per-day workweek. Since this still leaves the total workweek at 40 hours, it shouldn't be confused with a movement toward fewer hours at the same pay.

What are the advantages of this 4-day week? Usually it means the weekend begins on Friday or ends Monday night. It involves one less round trip of commuting. Employed wives and mothers particularly like it, since it gives them better chances to shop. For the employer, it may mean happier workers, and a gimmick to attract more recruits for employment. It also can mean less turnover time. (Two shifts instead of three may become feasible if one is 10 hours.) Better work scheduling may be possible. (A paint factory finds 4 cycles per day 4 days a week is better than 3 cycles 5 days a week. When all phone calls *within* an insurance company are banned from 8 to 9 A.M., efficiency leaps as each person catches up on schedule and planning.)

The 4-day week has disadvantages. That tenth hour can be tiresome—and inefficient. Car pools may be disrupted. Some people dislike leisure around the house.

In summary: The 4-day week is no panacea for labor relations. It will grow (and occasionally be abandoned). Perhaps its big importance is to facilitate the evolution toward a *shorter* workweek. (Only this feature, generally, appeals to the unions.)

## GENERAL SUPPLY CURVE OF LABOR

Return now to the case of competition. What is the supply curve of labor like? How does the wage rate affect population? How does the wage affect people's desire for a longer or shorter average working day? Influence the number of people *not* in the labor force (age of retirement, years of schooling, and women workers)? Will higher wages motivate people to work more effectively or enable them to relax?

These questions show that the supply of labor involves at least four dimensions: (1) population, (2) proportion of the population actually in the labor force, (3) average number of hours worked per week or year by workers, and (4) quality and quantity of effort and skill that workers provide.

These four labor-supply dimensions all depend on sociological as well as economic forces.[2] The third, though, is of particular economic interest.

**"Substitution-effect" versus "income-effect"**  What effect will wage rates have on the number of hours worked per year? We have touched on this earlier. A diagram may help to make the issues clear. Figure 29-4 on the next page shows the supply curve of total hours that a group of people will want to work at each different wage. Note how the supply curve rises at first in a northeasterly direction; then at the critical point *c*, it begins to bend back in a northwesterly direction. How can we explain why higher wages may either *increase* or *decrease* the quantity of labor supplied?

Put yourself in the shoes of a worker who has just been offered higher hourly rates

---

[2] The labor force sometimes tends to grow in recessions: when a husband is thrown out of work, his wife and children may seek jobs. Tending to cancel this is the fact that women and other workers are, under prosperous conditions, attracted into jobs by plentiful employment opportunities. The labor force grew less from 1957 to 1965 than demographers had expected: apparently the high level of unemployment discouraged new entrants. When full employment finally reappeared, new entrants were coaxed back into the labor force. The labor force fell in 1971 and 1975 as unemployment rose, but a larger proportion of the population stayed in the labor force in the early 1970s than in the early 1960s.

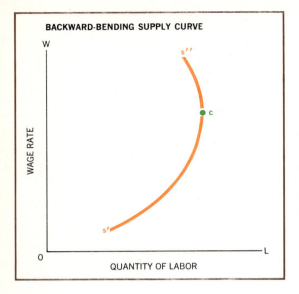

**BACKWARD-BENDING SUPPLY CURVE**

**FIG. 29-4**

**At a high enough wage we can afford more leisure, can afford to work less rather than more**

Above the critical point c, raising the wage rate *reduces amount of labor supplied!* (Income-effect overcomes substitution-effect: at higher income, you feel you can afford more leisure even though each extra hour of leisure is costing you more in forgone wages.)

and is free to choose the number of hours worked. You are torn two different ways: On the one hand, you are tempted to work some extra hours because now *each hour of work is better paid.* Each hour of leisure has become more expensive—hence you are tempted to *substitute* extra work for leisure. But acting against this so-called "substitution-effect" is an opposing "income-effect."[3] With the wage higher, you are, in effect, *a richer man.* Being richer, you will want to buy more clothes, more insurance, better food, more of other consumer goods. But most important for the present problem, *you will tend also to buy more leisure!* Now you can afford to take Saturday off, have a week's vacation in the winter or an extra week in the summer.

Which will be more powerful, the substitution-effect or the income-effect? Or will they just balance each other and cancel each other out—so that the supply curve neither rises forward nor bends backward, but rises perfectly vertically and inelastically? There is no one answer. It depends upon the individual. In Fig. 29-4, from s' to c the substitution-effect outweighed the income-effect. But from c to s'', the income-effect was the more important.

## RENT ELEMENTS IN WAGES OF UNIQUE INDIVIDUALS

Generally, one could expect that, after people receive a comfortable margin over what they consider to be conventionally necessary, further increases in wage will not bring

[3] See Chapter 22 for a discussion of "substitution-effect" and "income-effect" in connection with consumption. The income-effect of a wage increase is defined as its tendency to make you feel richer and able to *afford more* pleasurable leisure. Its substitution-effect is its tendency to make you want to react to the higher price of leisure—higher because of the higher hourly wage you now forgo to get each hour of leisure—by *substituting* for leisure the new goods your higher pay will buy. The two effects of a wage change oppose each other; when the income-effect wins out over the substitution-effect, labor's supply curve bends back. (Recall Fig. 20-13, page 404.)

out further hours of work. This was tested by a tax lawyer who studied his professional and business friends in New York City to learn the effect on them of heavy graduated taxes. Somewhat to his surprise, he discovered that taxes seemed to make them work harder so as to maintain their previous standards of living. Apparently, the short-run income-effect of reduced after-tax wages was more powerful than the substitution-effect. But probably most powerful were their nonmoney drives—desire for achievement and liking for their work. A Harvard Business School study gathered similar evidence, as did a recent study of English accountants and solicitors.

As we shall see in Chapter 31 on profits, the most harmful effects of graduated tax rates on incentives seem to involve risk taking and venture capital rather than any connection with the supply of effort by gifted people.

Most of the high earnings of outstanding people are probably "pure economic rent." Babe Ruth earned $80,000 a year playing baseball, something he liked to do anyway. Outside sports, one doubts he could have counted on earning more than, say, $5,000 a year. Between these limits his supply curve was almost completely *inelastic*, not affected by tax rates; hence economists can term the excess of his income above the alternative wage he could have earned elsewhere *a pure rent*, logically like the rent to nature's fixed supply of land as Chapter 28 discussed.

## EQUALIZING DIFFERENCES IN WAGES

Turn now from the problem of supply of labor in general to the vital problem of *differentials in competitive wages* among different categories of people and jobs. The next few sections discuss why supply and demand curves for different occupations intersect at different wage levels. Supply conditions now become all-important in explaining the tremendous wage differentials observed in everyday life.

When you look more closely at the differences among jobs, some of the observed pay differentials are easily explained.

Jobs may differ in their unpleasantness; hence wages may have to be raised to coax people into the less attractive jobs. Such wage differentials that simply serve to *compensate for the nonmoney differences among jobs* are called "equalizing differences."

Steeplejacks must be paid more than janitors because people do not like the risks of climbing flagpoles. Workers often receive 5 per cent extra pay on the 4 P.M. to 12 P.M. "swing shift" and 10 per cent extra pay for the 12 midnight to 8 A.M. "graveyard shift." For hours beyond 40 per week or for holiday and weekend work, $1\frac{1}{2}$ times the base hourly pay is customary. And when you observe a doctor who earns $50,000 a year, remember that a part of this is an equalizing difference needed to induce people to incur tuition costs and endure the lack of pay during years of training.

Jobs that involve dirt, nerve strain, tiresome responsibility, tedium, low social prestige, irregular employment, seasonal layoff, short working life, and much dull training all tend to be less attractive to people. To recruit workers for such occupations you must raise the pay. On the other hand, jobs that are especially pleasant or attractive find many applicants, and remuneration is bid down. Many qualified people like white-collar jobs, and so clerical wages are often lower than blue-collar pay.

To test whether a given difference in pay is an equalizing one, ask people who are well qualified for both jobs: "Would you take the higher-paying job in preference to the lower?" If they are not eager to make such a choice, then it is fair to conclude that the higher-paid job is not really more attractive when due weight is given to all considerations, nonmonetary and monetary.

### NONEQUALIZING DIFFERENTIALS: DIFFERENCES IN LABOR QUALITY

If all labor were homogeneous, we have seen that every observed competitive wage differential could be explained as an equalizing difference. But turn to the real world. True, some of the observed differentials can be regarded as equalizing. Yet everyone knows that the vast majority of higher-paid jobs are also *more pleasant,* rather than less pleasant. Most wage differentials cannot therefore be of the equalizing type.

Are they perhaps due to the fact that competition is imperfect? No doubt some observed differentials are of this type. Studies show that workers do not have anything like perfect knowledge of job opportunities. Trade-unions or minimum-wage laws or a monopoly by the workers in a particular occupation can also explain part of the existing nonequalizing differentials. If you removed these obstructions due to monopolistic or imperfect competition, enough people would flow into some of the higher-paid jobs to bring pay in these jobs into equality with that prevailing elsewhere. We shall analyze these interferences with competition in a moment. But never forget that many of the observed differentials in wages have little to do with the imperfections of competition; they would still persist if there were no monopoly elements.

Even in a hypothetically perfect auction market, where all the different categories of labor were priced by supply and demand, equilibrium would necessitate tremendous differentials in wages.

This is because of the tremendous *qualitative* differentials among people—traceable to differences in environmental opportunity that go back to early life and to other individual differences—all of which lead to competitive wage differentials.

No one expects the competitive wage of a man to be the same as that of a horse. Then why expect one man to receive the same competitive wage as another man or woman? A zoologist may call us all members of the same *Homo sapiens* species, but any personnel officer who is trying to equalize the marginal-physical-product-per-dollar expended in every direction knows that people vary much in their abilities and contributions to a firm's dollar revenue.

There are almost 100 million people in our labor force. There is no single factor of production called labor; there are thousands of quite different kinds of labor. Yet, if you are hiring men to shovel railroad trains out of a blizzard, it will probably pay you to lump together as one indistinguishable factor of production all adult males of certain ages who appear on the surface to be reasonably healthy, muscular, and sober.

Thus, the labor market groups people into certain general classifications for purposes of wage determination. But even after arbitrary (and often bigoted!) groupings are made, many distinguishable categories of labor remain, with wide dispersion of pay.

## "NONCOMPETING GROUPS IN THE LABOR MARKET"

A century ago, economists began to call these different categories of labor "noncompeting groups in the labor market." Instead of being a single factor of production, labor was recognized to be many different factors. Economists expected that as many different wage rates would result as there were noncompeting groups. Their instinct was sound, but there is some danger of misunderstanding their terminology.

In the first place, we must not think that in a perfectly competitive labor market the so-called "noncompeting groups" would disappear. We should still have different categories of labor—just as in the wheat market we have winter wheat, spring wheat, grade 2 red wheat, etc. Second, no one can doubt that these different groups are in some sense competing with each other. Just as I decide between hiring a horse and a tractor, so must I decide between hiring a very skilled, fast-working, high-paid worker and a lower-paid, less skilled one.

The essential point, then, is this: The different categories compete with each other; yet they are not 100 per cent identical. They are *partial rather than perfect substitutes*.

Workers can to some degree cross over from one category into another. If welders' wages were to become $100,000 a year, I might study the craft and quit being a teacher. Or if I did not, others would. Therefore, even when the wages of the different categories of labor are different, quantitative wage differences are still subject to the laws of supply and demand. "Cross elasticity" of supply becomes very important: The wage you must pay to recruit foundrymen depends on what the nearby auto plant is paying men on the assembly line.

Or take the case of skilled surgeons. They receive high pay in all countries, compared with butchers. Why? Because their work is important? Only in part on this account. Suppose that (1) as many babies were born every year with the capacity necessary for a surgeon as with the capacity necessary for a butcher, (2) we knew how to train surgeons in no time at all, and (3) a surgeon's activities and responsibilities were not regarded as less pleasant or more taxing than those of a butcher. Then do you really think that surgeons would continue to receive higher earnings than butchers? And if you think the sanctity of human life is the key explanation, how do you account for the fact that plastic surgeons are often more highly paid than heart surgeons?

Chapter 39's analysis of the economics of racial and other discrimination will emphasize that many of the differences in "quality" are in the eye of the beholder. If employers think that skin color denotes lower efficiency, or that women are incapable of handling certain jobs, their belief can become a stereotype built into the demand and supply schedules. All categories are dynamic, not static, being changeable by training, custom, and legislation. The economic status quo must be recognized for what it is—something that is there, but also something that people can shape *and change*.

## GENERAL EQUILIBRIUM OF LABOR MARKET

In real life as we know it, distinctions are not absolute. There is some mobility between different jobs; differences in wages will tend gradually over a long period of time to encourage greater and greater mobility; nor is it necessary for all workers to be mobile—a few movers are enough.

| COMPETITIVE WAGE DETERMINATION | |
| --- | --- |
| SITUATION | RESULT |
| 1. People all alike—jobs all alike. | No differentials. |
| 2. People all alike—some jobs differ in disutility. | Equalizing wage differentials. |
| 3. People differ, but each type of labor is in unchangeable supply ("noncompeting groups"). | Wage differentials that are "pure economic rents" or "surpluses." |
| 4. People differ, but there is some mobility between groups ("partially competing groups"; "cross elasticity" important). | General-equilibrium pattern of wage differentials as determined by general demand and supply (includes 1–3 as special cases). |

**TABLE 29-1**
Market wage structure shows great variety of patterns under competition

But there will still remain certain permanent barriers to mobility that depend upon the irreducible differences in biological and social inheritance. Hence, wage differentials will persist even in the long run—unless offset by social policy.

How big will these differentials be? Suppose we made it easy for people to get the education they are fitted for and to travel from one region to another where their skills can be better used. And suppose we provided people with the best possible information about job opportunities and about their personal potentialities. Then differentials would be much reduced. But for such differentials as remain, how exactly are they determined? The answer is provided by supply and demand.

*The market will tend toward that equilibrium pattern of wage differentials at which the total demand for each category of labor exactly matches its competitive supply. Only then will there be general equilibrium with no tendency for further widening or narrowing of wage differentials. Table 29-1 sums up our conclusions.*

## B. IMPERFECTIONS OF THE LABOR MARKET AND COLLECTIVE BARGAINING

Real-world labor markets are far removed from the ideal model of perfect competition. You can grade wheat into neat market categories, but you cannot do that with human beings. No auctioneer allocates workers to the highest bidders. Area studies show that workers often have only the most imperfect knowledge of nearby wage rates.

Wage stickiness  Two tests indicate that the labor market is imperfect. When there is a considerable increase in unemployment—as in depressed 1975—do wage rates drop as they would in a competitive market? History answers, No.

You may be every bit as capable as someone who has a job, and yet there is no way that you can take his job away by underbidding him. Just imagine going to General Motors or any other large corporation when the next depression comes, brandishing your degrees and certificates of IQ and excellence, and offering to work for less than it is paying. Only the naïve think they could get a job that way.

**Wage policy of firms**  The fact that a firm of any size *must* have a wage policy is additional evidence of labor market imperfections. In a perfectly competitive market, a firm need not make decisions on its pay schedules; instead, it would turn to the morning newspaper to learn what its wage policy would *have* to be. Any firm, by raising wages ever so little, could get all the extra help it wanted. If, on the other hand, it cut the competitive wage ever so little, it would find no labor to hire at all.

But just because competition is not 100 per cent perfect does not mean that it must be zero. The world is a blend of (1) competition and (2) some degree of monopoly power over the wage to be paid. A firm that tries to set its wage too low will soon learn this. At first nothing much need happen; but eventually it will find its workers quitting a little more rapidly than would otherwise be the case. Recruitment of new people of the same quality will get harder and harder, and slackening off in the performance and productivity of those who remain on the job will become noticeable.

Availability of labor supply does, therefore, affect the wage you set under realistic conditions of imperfect competition. If you are a very small firm, you may even bargain and haggle with prospective workers so as not to pay more than you have to. But if you are any size at all, you will name a wage for each type of job, then decide how many of the applicants will be taken on; and in terms of the number of applicants who respond, you may alter your wage rate over time. Even in the absence of unions, you will find it a perplexing task to decide on an optimal wage policy.

**Inequality of bargaining power**  One of the reasons given in the past for starting trade-unions was the feeling that unorganized workers, facing financially strong employers, lacked "equality of bargaining power." By union organization it was hoped that a greater equality of bargaining power could be restored. But exactly how one goes about measuring equality or inequality of bargaining power remains a difficult problem.

It is safe to say that prior to the formation of labor unions, the labor market was not a perfectly competitive one in the economist's sense of the term. And after the formation of unions it continues to differ from the perfectly competitive model. Moreover, a number of the features of labor markets usually associated with unions are also present even where there are no unions. Thus, large companies without unions will typically introduce a standard trend-rate of pay and be slow to change it, even though the number of workers locally unemployed might go up or down. In years of labor market slack these firms raise their wage rates as much as unionized trades do, despite the fact that competitive theory might expect them then to be cutting rates. [EXAMPLE: Du Pont raises wages about the same in (1) its nonunion plants as in (2) its few unionized plants and in (3) its few plants with a "company union."]

## FOUR WAYS UNIONS SEEK TO RAISE WAGES

Leaving the oversimplified picture of perfect competition behind, we can use economic theory to analyze how unions operate. How can they raise particular wages?

There are four main methods by which a union might hope to raise wages: (1) Unions can *reduce the supply* of labor. (2) They can use their collective bargaining power to *raise standard wage rates* directly. (3) They can cause the derived demand curve for labor to *shift upward*. (4) Unions can resist exploitation of laborers facing an

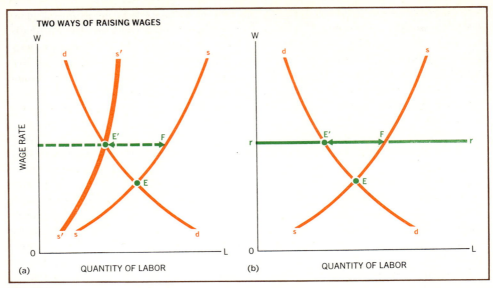

**TWO WAYS OF RAISING WAGES**

**FIG. 29-5**
**To raise pay, unions restrict supply or merely enforce standard wage rate**
Raising the standard wage to *rr* in (b) has exactly the same effect on wages as reducing the effective supply from *ss* to *s's'* in (a); the workers from *E'* to *F* are excluded from employment in either case.

*employer with monopoly bargaining power.* These four devices are much alike and often are reinforcing; but they also display significant differences.

**1. Restriction of labor supply**   We have already seen that a union may restrict the supply of labor in order to travel upward on the derived demand curve for labor. Immigration barriers, maximum-hour legislation, high initiation fees, long apprenticeships, refusal to admit new members into the union or to let nonunion members hold jobs—all these are obvious restrictive devices that have been used in the past.

In addition, there are other, more subtle restrictions on labor supply: explicit union limits on work loads (artificial limits put on number of bricks laid or looms attended, width of paintbrush, stand-by orchestras, "bogus" type, and similar "featherbedding" labor practices) and implicit understandings forcing a slowdown of the working pace.

**2. Raising standard wage rates**   Direct limitations on the labor supply are today no longer so necessary to unions, except to reinforce their ability to secure a high standard wage rate and maintain it. Union leaders have learned this important fact:

**If you can persuade or force employers always to pay a high standard wage—a wage rate that is publicly known and adhered to—then the supply of labor will take care of itself. At the standard rate, employers will hire the number of men they want, and any surplus job applicants will be *automatically excluded* from the labor market.**

Figure 29-5(a) and (b) contrast *direct* restriction of labor supply and *indirect* restriction via a high standard wage. In Fig. 29-5(a), the union cuts down supply from *ss* to *s's'* by insisting on long apprenticeships and high training fees. The wage consequently rises from E to E'. (Test your understanding of this: Explain the effects on doctors' earnings of a policy that reduces the relative number of medical students.)

Alternatively, in Fig. 29-5(b), the union gets all employers to agree to pay wages no lower than the minimum standard rate, as shown by the horizontal line rr. Note that here, too, the equilibrium is at E', where rr intersects the employer's demand curve. The workers from E' to F are as effectively excluded from jobs as if the union had directly limited entry. What now limits supply? It is the lack of job opportunities at the high standard wage rate.

**3. Shifting the derived demand curve upward**  A union may hope to increase wages by any policy that improves the demand for labor. Thus, like the International Ladies' Garment Workers Union, it may study ways of reducing garment prices by improving productivity of labor and management, or it may help the industry advertise its products. *Or* a union may agitate for a tariff to protect its industry, hoping thereby to raise the demand curve for domestic workers. *Or* it may persuade the government to pay higher rates on public contracts and to write make-work featherbedding restrictions into building codes. *Or* it may help the employers in an industry maintain a high monopoly price, with some of the extra profits going into higher wages.

Moreover, if collective bargaining raises wages, and *if increased wages increase the marginal productivity of labor*, then labor will have shifted its own demand curve upward. Figure 29-6 depicts the case in which an increase in the wage from rr to r'r' itself results in an upward *shift* in the demand curve for labor—from dd to d'd'. Note that, at the new equilibrium E', both wage and employment have increased.

In the old days, the standard example of this was the case where workers were being paid so little that they were malnourished and hence inefficient; higher wages might

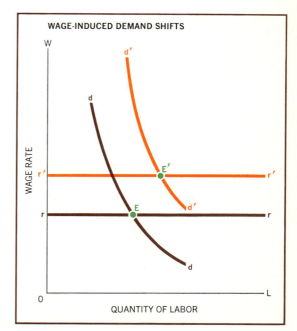

**FIG. 29-6**
**Some union policies seek to shift upward the demand curve for labor**
Raising wages (from rr to r'r'), by making ill-fed workers stronger or resentful ones more energetic, in this case shifts the curve of demand productivity upward (from dd to d'd'), with employment actually increasing (from E to E').

then have made them more efficient and thus resulted in lower rather than higher production costs. Today, in this country, few workers are so physiologically under-nourished. But psychological elements can be as important as physiological. Many an employer has found that too-low wages are bad business even from a hard-boiled, dollars-and-cents standpoint. The quality and contentment of his workers fall off so much that he is losing rather than gaining from the cheeseparing.

It can be argued that high wages have a favorable "shock effect" on the employer's efficiency in using labor. One reason advanced for the high productivity of American industry, even in the nineteenth century when unions were unimportant, was the fact that high farm earnings made it necessary for industry to develop good machine methods in order to be able to pay high wages and still stay in business. Adversity, in the form of a kick in the pants from unions or from fate in general, can at times galvanize businessmen into finding improved methods. How much there is to this shock-effect argument, nobody knows. It has therefore to be used with discretion.

**4. Removing exploitation by monopolist of labor (the "monopsonist")**  Finally, there is the case where unions arise to *offset* monopoly power that employers may have in a labor market that has been far from competitive. Suppose there is a company town: unless you work for the dominant firm, you are unemployed; your alternatives are few or nonexistent; you must take what the employer offers. In this case the employer does not think of himself as too small to affect appreciably the wage he pays; he does not hire factors up to the point where their marginal-revenue-products (as defined in the chapters just preceding) are equal to the wage he pays. Instead, he realizes that hiring an extra worker will raise the wage he must pay to all, and hence he had better not hire that worker unless his marginal-product much *exceeds* the wage.

In this situation (which economists call "monopsony" after the Greek words for the case of a "single buyer," just as "monopoly" means the case of a "single seller"), *organizing a union can result in higher wages without any decline in employment!* Once the employer realizes the union is going to make him pay the standard wage, he will again be a "wage taker" who will hire men up to where their marginal-product fully equals that standard wage.

The lessening of exploitation by union organization is more important in isolated places, like the tin mines of Bolivia or the lumber camps of American history, than it is in an urban economy where people are, in fact, mobile in moving to better job opportunities. There do still, however, remain areas of agriculture where employers hire workers below the market because of the workers' lack of other opportunities or their ignorance of such opportunities as do exist.[4]

**Wage increases and reductions in employment**  If raising wages means simply that you climb up the existing demand curve for labor, then employment will decrease

[4]Intermediate economics texts show that, where an employer was previously possessed of monopsony-buying-power over labor, collective bargaining can—if not pushed to excess—right the balance, leading to both increased wages *and* increased employment. Before unionization, the employer monopsonist who is on his toes will set his equilibrium wage at *mm* in Fig. 29-7. This will be lower than the so-called "competitive wage" at *E*. Why will the monopsonist's equilibrium be at a point

in consequence. This is because demand curves almost always slope downward and to the right.[5]

The amount of unemployment created in a particular occupation by wage increases would depend upon the elasticity of the demand curve for that particular category of labor. We saw in Chapter 28 that a factor demand is a "derived demand," and we discussed (page 560, footnote) some of the conditions that determine how elastic or inelastic the derived demand might be.

## THEORETICAL INDETERMINACY OF COLLECTIVE BARGAINING

Just as unions sometimes realize it would not be to their interest to ask for higher wages, managements sometimes take the view that a wage increase would improve their long-run corporate earnings. But both these views are exceptional. Usually, at any collective-bargaining conference, the workers are pressing for higher wages and fringe benefits than management wishes to pay.

What will be the terms of the final agreement? Unfortunately, this is one important question that no economic theory can answer with precision. The game-theoretic[6] result depends on psychology, politics, and countless intangible and unpredictable factors. As far as the economist is concerned, the final outcome of bilateral monopoly is in principle indeterminate—as indeterminate as the haggling between two millionaires over a fine painting.

Eight main arguments will be appealed to during the bargaining:

1. If the cost of living is rising, the union economist will talk a great deal about the workers' *standard of living;* but if prices are falling, the employer brings this up.

2. If the company and industry have been prosperous, the union will stress *ability to pay;* but if the industry has had low profits, the employer will emphasize this fact.

3. If *productivity* has risen or fallen recently, this will be introduced into the negotiations by one of the interested parties.

---

like $M$? The monopsonist will not want to travel upward from $M$ to $E$ because he realizes that any employment increase beyond $M$ will raise the wages paid to *already hired workers* by more than the extra revenue resulting from hiring the new men. But now let the union raise the wages toward $E$ by collective bargaining; the monopsonist employer now reluctantly travels up the *ss* curve, as shown by the green arrows. Note we do not travel up the marginal-revenue-product curve *dd*. Wages and employment both rise together. (QUERY: Suppose collective bargaining raises the standard wage to a level $r''r''$ that lies *above* $E$. By drawing in the resulting arrows *above* $E$ on *dd*, show that now unemployment will follow. What then will happen to employment? Draw in the resulting green arrows on the demand curve.)

[5] Cases have been noted where short-run demand is virtually completely inelastic.

[6] See Chapter 25's Appendix for rudiments of the theory of games.

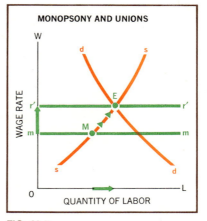

FIG. 29-7

4. If other firms in the same area are paying *going wages* higher or lower than the firm in question, this fact will be brought out.

5. Labor will extol the philosophy of high wages as a means of bolstering *purchasing power* and prosperity; management will emphasize higher-cost aspects of wages.

6. If a *national pattern* of "fourth- or *n*th-round" wage increases of so much per hour has already been set by a few "key bargains" in large industries such as coal, steel, or automobiles, that will have great weight in the deliberations.

7. American workers and employers have grown accustomed to steady money-wage increases. Almost as certainly as spring brings robins, it brings wage increases. So General Motors and many other firms build into their wage agreements a steady upward trend—the so-called "improvement factor." This may mean an average 3 to 4 per cent wage boost each year in addition to any cost-of-living escalator wage clauses.

8. The government may set forth guideposts for wages and prices, and these may be appealed to or be ignored depending on the interests of the bargaining parties. Such guideposts broadly aim to have money wages rise with *national* productivity: then, if prices are lowered in industries of above-average productivity growth and raised in those of below-average growth, the general price level can be stable and customary wage-property shares be preserved. Or controls may supersede guideposts.

Most often, labor and management will arrive at a new yearly contract after some days of negotiation. But sometimes when they get stalled, a government mediator may try to narrow down the few-cents disagreement. Or there may be an understanding that a disinterested "arbitrator" will render a decision, which both parties will accept. Unfortunately, economic theory cannot tell us how such an arbitrator will arrive at his final decision. All the previously mentioned factors will be weighed in his mind, plus the all-important question, What decision is likely to be *acceptable* to both sides?

**Strikes and collective bargaining**   Both sides realize that failure to reach agreement will mean a costly strike. It may sometimes happen that management refuses to go above $6.50 an hour while labor refuses to take less than $6.60. A "work stoppage" will result. Should we call this an "employees' strike" or an "employer's lockout"? Popularly, it will be referred to as a strike. But since each party knows it can end the work stoppage by agreeing to the other party's terms, we could call it either.

Newsmen ask why workers go out on strike just because of a 10-cent disagreement; they point out that it might take two or three years for the workers to recover—at 10 cents an hour—their loss of earnings during the strike. But the workers look at it differently. To them the employer caused the strike by his stubbornness. They point out that the employer will also lose more by the strike than refusing the extra 10 cents would save him in many years.

Actually, a strike is *not* over just the last 10 cents of wage disagreement! The workers believe that the employer would not have been forced from $6 up even to $6.50 except for the threat of a strike, which hangs over the negotiation like a time bomb. To keep the bomb from going off, both sides must agree.

Threats become hollow unless occasionally carried out. Both parties must show that they are truly prepared to incur at some point the costs of a strike. Thus, suppose the employer was deprived, voluntarily or by law, of the right to refuse any wage demand if it would bring on a strike. Would this cost him only 10 cents an hour? Obviously not. There would then be no reason why the union might not hold out for a 90- rather than a 55-cent wage increase. Similarly, if the union could never exercise the right to strike, why should not the employer offer $4 rather than $6?

## QUALIFICATIONS

**Has unionization raised wages?**    The advocates of organized labor claim unions have raised real wages; the critics blame unions for having done just that and for having thereby distorted the efficient use-pattern of resources. Despite this agreement that unions raise real wages, the true facts are not at all clear.

Since 1933, for example, low-paid, nonunionized occupations (such as domestic service and farm work) have shown greater percentage wage increases than unionized trades. In this same period of tremendous organization of labor, there has been a general tendency toward higher wages, but with wage differences remaining about the same in *absolute* terms. This means that *percentage* differentials are diminishing. (For example, suppose you are a unionist earning $6 an hour, and I earn $3 in a nonunion trade. Now we both get a $2 increase; this leaves the absolute differential unchanged; but you no longer get twice my wage; instead you receive $8 to my $5.)

Most other countries also show a lessening of percentage wage differentials in recent decades, a trend in part quite independent of union trends.

It is true that the average wage in unionized industries is about 18 per cent higher than the average wage in nonunionized industries. But that in itself does not prove that unions are responsible for the difference. The industries that are unionized tend also to be those dominated by large rather than small enterprise and by firms which use workers of higher-than-average skills. Even before they were unionized, these same industries paid higher-than-average wages.

Arthur Ross, formerly Commissioner of the Bureau of Labor Statistics, was one of many who studied the change in wage rates since 1933 in union and nonunion industries.[7] He finds that the industries *most recently unionized* do seem to show a slightly greater wage increase since 1933 than do similar industries that have either never been unionized or that had already been unionized prior to 1933. (That is, if we examine Industries A, B, and C, all paying about the same wages in 1933, then A, the recently unionized industry, shows a slightly greater wage increase than B, the never-unionized industry, or C, the industry unionized before 1933.)

One Warning: Such statistics on the differential movements of union and nonunion wages cannot give the whole answer to the question whether unions have raised wages. Labor spokesmen claim that unions also help raise wages *for the unorganized workers*. Thus, a nonunion industry's policy may be to follow any changes in the wage scale hammered out in unionized plants nearby. Also, if an industry raises wages in order

---

[7] A. M. Ross, *Trade Union Wage Policy* (University of California Press, Berkeley, 1948). See L. G. Reynolds and C. H. Taft, *The Evolution of Wage Structure* (Yale University Press, New Haven, Conn., 1956), and H. G. Lewis, *Unionism and Relative Wages in the United States* (University of Chicago Press, Chicago, 1963), for references to confirming later studies by R. A. Lester, A. E. Rees, J. T. Dunlop, and others.

to keep the union out, the union will get no credit for its influence in the figures. On the other hand, suppose the targets for union organizers are profitable, expanding, high-productivity, concentrated industries; then the union may be riding aboard a moving demand curve and be given credit for wage increases that would have occurred even in its absence. Which is cause and which is effect?[8]

**Pitfalls in the concept of a general demand for labor**    A second important warning must be given. It is legitimate to draw up a demand curve of the usual general shape for one *small* labor market: as long as *all other* prices and wages are more or less unaffected, it is indeed true that a higher money wage in one sector is the same as a higher real wage there; it is true also that employment there can be expected to fall off somewhat at the higher wage.

But remember the fallacy of composition. What is true for any *small* sector of the economy need not be true for *the whole aggregate*. If all wage rates rise, it is dangerous to suppose that commodity prices will remain constant. Thus, doubling all money wages *might* well result in a doubling of all prices. Were that the case, the real wage would not be changed at all. And hence, in a diagram such as Fig. 29-1, we should be moving neither upward nor downward on the demand curve. (Turn to Fig. 29-1 and note that the vertical axis represents real wages in dollars of *constant purchasing power*.)

Remember that wages are not simply costs: they also represent *incomes* of most of the population. Therefore the sales revenue of business enterprises is vastly affected by a substantial change in wage levels. Since the demand for labor is a demand derived from the demand for business products, it is clear that any change in general wages must shift the general demand curve for labor. Hence, it is dangerous to argue in terms of an unchanged demand curve for labor.

To illustrate this pitfall, ask the following question: In 1932 or 1975, when there was widespread unemployment, would an all-round cut in money wages have *increased* employment? Or, as claimed by the trade-unionists, would such a decrease in general money wages have decreased "purchasing power" and *decreased* employment?

To the extent that a halving of wages would result in a halving of *all* prices, and of *all* money incomes, and of *all* money spending, the answer must be obvious. Such a completely balanced deflation would neither help nor hurt the unemployment situation.[9] This serves as a warning against accepting the superficial claims of those critics of labor who argue in terms of simple *dd* curves, and of those friends of labor who argue in terms of crude "purchasing power."

---

[8] Study of the 1970 census will suggest that union power can keep wages higher than what they otherwise would have been for male production workers in monopolistically concentrated industries. Many studies also suggest that unions keep wage rates from falling, as they would competitively, in declining high-wage industries such as coal and railroads.

[9] Today most economic theorists believe that the favorable effects during recession of any over-all general wage cut will depend upon how it affects the balance of saving and investment, or total real demand. If (a) lower wages cause prices to drop and (b) people's cash and holdings of government bonds do not drop in proportion, then the increase in people's *real wealth* may have expansionary effects on the real propensity to consume and on employment. But falling prices may aggravate debts and bankruptcy and, by making people pessimistic, may harm investment; consequently, most advanced treatises in economics advocate expanding people's real wealth and real consumption schedule by means of expansionary bank and fiscal policy rather than by deflation. (Chapter 18's Appendix discusses this so-called "Pigou effect" on page 348.)

**Summing up** We may cautiously conclude discussion of the economic effects of unions by quoting in turn from two leading students of labor economics, Princeton's Albert E. Rees and Yale's Lloyd G. Reynolds. According to Rees,[10]

We tend to overemphasize the role of the unions, both in . . . their own industries and . . . the economy as a whole. . . . The other two thirds may have their wages and salaries influenced by what the unions do, but I feel there are very strong independent forces on the demand side that govern their rates of pay. . . . Even in the . . . unionized [one third] there are some very weak . . . unions that have had very little to do with the wages of their members. . . .

In a series of rough guesses, I would say perhaps a third of the trade unions have raised the wages of their members by 15 per cent to 20 per cent above what they might be in a nonunion situation; another third by perhaps 5 per cent to 10 per cent, and the remaining third not at all. . . . The high figures tend to be found, not in periods of inflation, but in periods of prosperity combined with stable prices. . . . In [an inflationary] period like 1946–1948, for example, the union people may even lag behind simply because of the rigidities involved in the collective bargaining process.

And Reynolds states the following conclusions of his researches:

Summing up these diverse consequences of collective bargaining, one can make a strong case that unionism has at any rate not worsened the wage structure. We are inclined to be more venturesome than this, and to say that its net effect has been beneficial. This conclusion will doubtless strike many economists as surprising. . . .

Fears that complete unionization will bring seismic disruption of the wage structure do not seem to be well founded. . . . The countries with the strongest union movements appear to have a wage structure which is more orderly and defensible than the wage structure of countries where unionism has been weak.

In Part Six's Chapter 41 we shall face the important problem, as yet unsolved, of finding an "incomes" or "guidepost" policy to cope with "creeping inflation" and make full employment compatible with reasonably stable price levels.

---

[10] The Rees quotation is from *Wage Inflation* (National Industrial Conference Board, New York, 1957), pp. 27–28; the Reynolds quotation, from Reynolds and Taft, *op. cit.*, pp. 194–195. Cf. the following quote from Sumner Slichter, J. Healy, and E. R. Livernash, *The Impact of Collective Bargaining on Management* (Brookings Institution, Washington, 1960), p. 951: "Collective bargaining seems to have greatly encouraged the development of management. . . . companies that have been relatively successful in union-management relations gave evidence of following wise basic policies, of negotiating balanced general policies, of developing good implementing and procedural arrangements to make policy effective at the operating level, and of having considerable initiative in labor relations administration. The challenge that unions presented to management has, if viewed broadly, created superior and better-balanced management, even though some exceptions must be recognized."

## SUMMARY

### A. WAGE DETERMINATION UNDER PERFECT COMPETITION

1 In perfectly competitive equilibrium, if all men and jobs were exactly alike, there would be no wage differentials. The equilibrium wage rate would be determined by supply and demand. To the extent that Country A has (1) more natural resources per worker than Country B and (2) better productive methods (because of capital availability and technical knowledge), A's competitive wage is likely to be higher than B's.

**2** The law of *diminishing returns* suggests that a reduction of labor relative to natural resources might be expected to raise real wages. While this principle lies back of labor's immigration policy and other restrictions, historical examples of economies of mass production do point to the operation of a countertendency of *increasing returns*. In theory, *"optimum* population" size is at the point where the two countertendencies reach balance of maximum per capita income.

**3** Though Malthusian overpopulation threatens many an underdeveloped country such as India, there is no tendency for population growth in the United States and developed nations to push real wages down to a minimum-subsistence level. Pressure exerted on real wages by the "reserve army of the unemployed" tends to depress wages only to the *equilibrium* level. In the Western world, this equilibrium wage is much above physiological *subsistence* and rises steadily.

**4** Fear of unemployment leads often to acceptance of the "lump-of-labor" fallacy. This belief, that there is only a fixed amount of useful work to be done, may result from experiencing technological unemployment or depression. It lies behind much of the agitation for a 30-hour week and featherbedding work rules. But unemployment calls for macroeconomic policies to furnish adequate job opportunities, not for defeatist restrictionism.

**5** The supply of labor has four dimensions: population size, percentage of people gainfully employed, average number of hours worked, and quality of effort.

**6** As wages rise, there are two opposite effects on the supply of labor: The "substitution-effect" tempts each worker to work longer because of the higher pay for each hour of work; the "income-effect" exerts influence in the opposite direction— in that higher wages mean that workers can now afford more leisure along with more commodities and other good things of life. At *some* critical wage, the supply curve may bend backward. The labor supply of very gifted, unique people is probably quite inelastic; their wages are largely so-called "pure economic rent."

**7** Once we drop the unrealistic assumptions concerning the uniformity of people and jobs, we find substantial wage differentials even in a perfectly competitive labor market. "Equalizing wage differences," which compensate for nonmonetary *differences in disutility* between jobs, explain some of the differentials.

**8** But differences in the *quality* of various grades of labor are probably the most important cause of wage differences. Although it cannot be claimed that labor consists of wholly "noncompeting groups," it is nonetheless true that there are innumerable categories of partially competing groups. When the relative wage of one category rises, there are substantial cross-elasticity effects on labor supply as some people switch to the improved-pay occupation. The final pattern of wages would, in a perfectly competitive labor market, be determined by the general equilibrium of the interrelated schedules of supply and demand. Cf. Table 29-1.

## B. IMPERFECTIONS OF THE LABOR MARKET AND COLLECTIVE BARGAINING

9   Labor markets are not perfectly competitive in real life. With unions or without them, employers usually have some control over wages, but their wage policy must be conditioned by the available supply of labor.

10   Unions affect wages by (*a*) restricting labor supply, (*b*) bargaining for standard rates, (*c*) following policies designed to shift upward the derived demand schedule for labor, and (*d*) countering exploitation of labor by employers with monopoly bargaining power (i.e., by so-called "monopsonists").

11   Relative increases in wages will result in most industries in less employment there. This assumes the union is moving *along* a given demand schedule (i.e., that there are no demand shifts from higher productivity).

12   At the collective-bargaining table the following are some of the determining factors around which argument is likely to center: (*a*) cost and standards of living, (*b*) ability to pay and profits, (*c*) productivity trends, (*d*) "going wages" paid elsewhere in the locality and in the industry, (*e*) the influence of higher wages on purchasing power and on the level of costs, (*f*) the "national pattern" as determined by "key bargains" in important industries, (*g*) continuous increases based upon improvement factors from long-term technical improvements, and (*h*) government guideposts designed to keep increases in money wages in line with *average* productivity increases of the economy, with prices coming down in industries of over-average productivity increase by enough to cancel out price increases in industries of below-average productivity increase. Economic theory can just not tell us what the final wage bargain will be, it being theoretically indeterminate.

13   Usually a compromise settlement will be possible, without government intervention, formal arbitration, or a strike. But the *threat* of strike is ever present and conditions the whole bargaining procedure. In vital industries, however, the interest of the public transcends the individual interests and rights of the disputing parties; consequently, voluntary collective bargaining is subject to government controls whenever damaging work stoppages occur.

14   Historically, the extent to which unions have succeeded in raising wages is in doubt. Since 1933, union membership has greatly increased, but in this same period wage differentials seem to have remained much the same in absolute terms. There seems to have been, here and abroad, a narrowing of percentage wage differentials. While it is true that *recently unionized* industries seem to show slightly greater wage increases since 1933, the quantitative difference is not great and it is not clear which is cause and which effect. Heavily concentrated and expanding industries may have been targets for unionization, and the high wages may have been the result of factors associated with, or causing, unionization, rather than of unionization as such.

15    A final warning is in order: We must beware of the fallacy of composition in ascribing to the *demand curve for labor in general* the shape characteristic of the *demand curve for one small category of labor*. Wages are more than costs; they also constitute much of the income of consumers and react heavily back upon the demand for products of business. A general change in money wage rates can be expected to have important effects on prices. It is even possible that real wages will not change at all. To the extent that a general wage change is balanced by an equivalent percentage change in *all* prices, little substantive effect upon unemployment may result.

## CONCEPTS FOR REVIEW

general equilibrium  
optimum population  
subsistence wage level  
backward-bending supply curve  
income- versus substitution-effect  
rent element in wages  
equalizing and nonequalizing  
    wage differences  

noncompeting groups  
standard wage rate  
monopsonist-firm's exploitation  
elastic, inelastic derived demand  
collective bargaining  
strike, lockout, work stoppage  
percentage and absolute differ-  
    entials under unionization  

## QUESTIONS FOR DISCUSSION

1    Explain narrowing of wage differentials from competition of like people.

2    What factors of technology, economic geography, and legislation help to determine the level of real wages? Show how diminishing returns and countertendencies are linked with the theory of optimum population.

3    Define and contrast "equalizing and nonequalizing differences in wages." Which concept is exemplified by high wages that contained much "pure economic rent"? What about noncompeting groups?

4    Give a list of imperfections in the labor market. Show that not all are related to monopoly power or to trade-union organization.

5    Give three ways unions try to influence wages, as described in this chapter. Contrast the first two, and gauge their importance. Do the same for the third.

6    "Unions can raise real and money wages in a particular industry, but the result will be less employment." Evaluate, utilizing the elasticity of demand for labor.

7    What is the public interest in voluntary collective bargaining?

8    Explain dangers involved in treating the general demand for labor like a particular group's demand. Show that wages are costs *and* sources of demand.

9   "In his 1964 State of the Union message, President Johnson suggested that a penalty might be put on firms that chronically offer overtime work. This is defeatism, and could have been avoided with activist macroeconomic policies (fiscal and monetary)." Evaluate.

10   President Nixon tried in his first year—not very successfully—to keep the government out of collective bargaining. Do you think this is possible in (*a*) a rail strike, (*b*) a steel strike, (*c*) a longshoreman or teamster strike, (*d*) a one-town-newspaper strike, (*e*) an auto strike? Where would you draw the line?

11   *Extra-credit problem:* Just as we must distinguish between marginal cost and average cost, *MC* and *AC*, we must distinguish between marginal product and average product, *MP* and *AP* = *Q/L*. Here Fig. 29-2's optimum population diagram is redrawn to show that *MP* cuts *AP* at its maximum. (HINT: This should remind you of *MC* cutting *AC* at its minimum. When *MP* > *AP*, *MP* pulls up *AP*; when *MP* < *AP*, *MP* pulls down *AP*.) Can you verify that at the optimum population, *M*, labor's marginal-product absorbs 100 per cent of the total product, leaving zero for land rent?

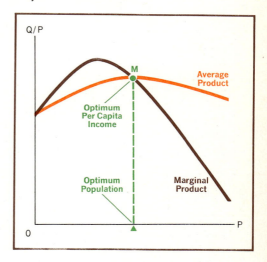

# 30

## INTEREST
## AND CAPITAL

How to have your cake
and eat it too:
Lend it out at interest.
ANONYMOUS

The preceding chapters have sketched the determination of the rents of resources and the wages of labor. Now in this chapter we turn to the third great category of productive factors, capital; and to the determination of its special price, which is called "interest."

Capital theory is one of the most difficult parts of economic theory. For this reason, an introduction cannot hope to grapple with all the important issues. It seems best, therefore, to proceed as follows:

The main part of this chapter summarizes in an uncritical way the traditional key notions involved in capital and interest. Then, at the end, are briefly given some of the key qualifications that ought to be made concerning the oversimplified traditional treatment. For the Appendix and Part Six to come are reserved certain special topics of classical capital theory and its modern qualifications.

### LAND, LABOR, AND CAPITAL

Our traditional account of capital theory begins with a rather arbitrary division of all productive factors into three categories:

1. *Natural resources* provided by Nature in fixed supply, which cannot be augmented or used up. The return of this inelastic factor of *land* is called (pure economic) *rent*.

2. Human *labor* resources, not produced in response to economic conditions, but taken by the economist as determined by social and biological factors. The return of this human factor is called *wages* (which includes the salaries for skilled workers as well as wages for unskilled workers).

In the oversimplified traditional account, factors (1) and (2) are called "primary factors of production"—primary in the sense that their supplies are determined largely outside the economic system itself. To them we must now add an "intermediate" factor.

3. Capital goods, *produced by the economic system itself* to be used as productive inputs for *further* production of goods and serv-

ices. These capital goods, which are both outputs and inputs, can be long- or short-lived. They can be rented out in the competitive market just the way acres of land or hours of labor can be. These rents—or perhaps we might use the term "rentals," to avoid confusion with pure economic rent to land in fixed supply—these rentals of capital goods are traditionally supposed to be determined by the same demand conditions of marginal productivity discussed previously

However, in the traditional capital theory, the return or yield of capital is not taken to be the *rentals* of capital goods. What, then, is it?

The yield of capital is the *interest rate per annum,* which is a pure percentage per unit time—independent of dollar or other value units. Of what is the interest rate 5 per cent per annum the yield? Obviously, it is the yield applied to the *dollar* value of capital goods.[1]

## CAPITALIZATION OF ASSETS

Now we can take a brief look at the important economic process by which capital goods get priced in the market at their "capitalized value." The *interest rate* plays a key role; and when this rate drops from a high down to a low level, we shall see there must result a considerable rise in the capitalized value of machines, bonds, annuities, or any other asset providing a stream of future property revenues.

To see how assets get capitalized, look at the simplest case of a piece of land or an annuity contract that is certain to pay you the *same* number of dollars each year from now until *eternity.* It turns out we can quite easily write down the formula for the present capitalized value $V$ of any *permanent* income stream of $1 per year or $N per year. We ask, "How many dollars left permanently at the market rate of interest $i$ per annum will give us exactly the same return of $1 per year or $N per year?" The answer is summarized in the rule

$$V = \frac{\$N}{i}$$

where $V$ = present capitalized value (often called "present discounted value")

$\$N$ = permanent annual receipts

$i$ = interest rate in decimal terms (e.g., .05, or $\frac{5}{100}$, for 5 per cent)

Thus, if the interest rate will always be 5 per cent, any permanent income will sell for exactly 20 ($= 1 \div \frac{5}{100}$) times its annual income.[2] (To check our formula, realize

---

[1] In taking a census of total capital, we should not add to the 1-million-dollar value of a firm's plant, equipment, and inventory the 1-million-dollar value that its common-stock shares may sell for on Wall Street. That is, we must avoid double counting.

[2] In the Middle Ages, they called this "20 years' purchase" and thus got around the taboo against interest. Show that 4 per cent interest means 25 years' purchase; 6 per cent, $16\frac{2}{3}$ years'. (See the Appendix for discussion of capitalization of nonpermanent income streams.)

NOTE: After land has been capitalized, its rent may appear as *interest* earned on its market value. In principle, *all* the nonwage part of NNP could be reported as interest on the value of property: if selling ourselves into slavery were not illegal, even wages might be reported as interest on the capital value of men! As is also noted in Parts One and Six, investing in human capital by education and training is important: much of the wage of a high-income surgeon can be regarded as interest and return of principal on his father's or wife's investment in his training.

that a principal of $20 at 5 per cent will yield $1 every year; so $20 must be the perpetuity's capitalized value.)

## NET PRODUCTIVITY OF CAPITAL

Now we ask ourselves this question: Why do people ever bother to transform the primary factors of labor and land into intermediate capital goods or into capital? The traditional answer is this: It is taken to be a technological fact of life that you *can get more future consumption product by using indirect or roundabout methods.*

To see this, imagine two islands exactly alike. Each has exactly the same primary factors of labor and land. Island A uses these primary factors *directly* to produce consumption product; she uses no produced capital goods at all. Island B, on the other hand, for a preliminary period sacrifices current consumption; instead, she uses some of her land and labor to produce intermediate capital goods such as plows, shovels, and synthesized chemicals. After this preliminary period of sacrificing current consumption pleasures in the interests of net capital formation, she ends up with a varied stock of capital goods, i.e., with a sizable amount of capital. Now let us measure the amount of consumption product she can go on permanently producing with her land, labor, and constantly replaced capital goods.

Careful measurement of Island B's "roundabout" product shows it to be greater than Island A's "direct" product. Why is it greater? Why does B get *more* than 100 units of future consumption goods for her initial sacrifice of 100 units of present consumption? That is a technological engineering question. To sum up, the economist traditionally takes the following answer as a basic technical fact:

There exist roundabout processes, which take time to get started and completed, that are more productive than direct processes.

From this basic technological fact we can draw an important economic conclusion:

After allowing for all depreciation requirements, capital has a *net productivity* (or real interest yield) that can be expressed in the form of a percentage per annum; and the only reason you do not take further advantage of this opportunity to get more product by roundabout methods is that you would have to cut down on *present* consumption if you are to speed up capital's rate of growth and *future* consumption.

## DEFINITION OF NET PRODUCTIVITY OF A CAPITAL GOOD OR INVESTMENT PROJECT

We need an exact definition of the net productivity of any capital project. We first calculate the original dollar cost of the factors bought to begin each roundabout process. Then we calculate the total receipts that the roundabout methods give. We know very well that the receipts total must add up to *more* than the original cost total, or else there is no net productivity. Having satisfied ourselves that there is indeed a positive net productivity, we need a way of measuring it quantitatively so as to make diverse projects comparable—projects involving apples and oranges, projects involving 50-year bridges and 5-month beer. Our final solution is to look for a measure that is a *percentage per annum.*

We end up defining the net productivity of a capital project thus:

A capital or investment project's net productivity is that annual percentage yield which you could earn by tying up your money in it. What is the same thing, the project's net productivity is that market rate of interest at which it would just pay to undertake it.

EXAMPLE: I buy grape juice for $10, and a year later sell it as wine for $11. If there are no other expenses and no risk or effort to me, my interest yield (or "net productivity") is 10 per cent per annum—equal to $1/$10.[3]

As a community transfers part of its resources away from current consumption and toward capital accumulation, projects with lower and lower net productivity will be undertaken. Thus, a 50-year bridge with a net productivity of, say, 10 per cent will not be worth building if the market rate of interest is 11 per cent. But when the market interest drops to 10 per cent or below, you will build the bridge.

The law of diminishing returns is traditionally invoked as more and more capital goods of all types become available to work with the limited supply of natural resources and land, and with the more slowly growing number of workers. This law implies that society and the private investors will run out of new projects with net productivities as high as the previous ones. And unless offset by technological innovations, this law of diminishing returns would result in interest rates and investment yields falling through time as the community successfully saves. For without such a fall in interest rates, the low-yielding, long-lived projects would not get undertaken.

## A BIRD'S-EYE VIEW OF INTEREST DETERMINATION

We can now define the rate of interest and summarize the forces traditionally supposed to determine its competitive level.

*Definition:* The market rate of interest is that percentage return per year which has to be paid on any safe loan of money, which has to be yielded by any safe bond or other security, and which has to be earned on the value of any capital asset (such as a machine, a hotel building, a patent right) in any competitive market where there are no risks or where all risk factors have already been taken care of by special premium payments to protect against any risks.

Thus, in an ideal capital market, the riskless rate of interest might be set by supply and demand at 6 per cent, just as competitive market forces set the rent of fertile land at $20 an acre per year and the wage of skilled labor at $200 per 40-hour week.

That does not mean that I shall make a small loan at this low an interest rate to an applicant whom I do not know and who has lost three jobs in 6 months' time: I may have to charge him as much as 20 per cent per annum to compensate me for having to investigate him, dun him for collection, and cover the risk premium from

---

[3] Here are two more examples. I plant a pine tree at labor cost of $50 plus 25 years' land rental cost—paid in advance—of $50, or $100 in all. At the end of 25 years the grown tree sells for $430. The net productivity of this capital project is then 330 per cent per quarter-century, which, interest tables tell us, is equivalent to a net productivity of 6 per cent per year. Or I buy a $10,000 truck. For 10 years it earns annual rentals of $5,000, but I pay $3,000 annually for fuel, driver, and maintenance. Its scrap value is zero. What is its net productivity or yield? The same as the annual percentage yield of an annuity of $2,000 per year payable for 10 years and bought for $10,000. Compound interest tables for annuities show this truck's yield to be 15 per cent per year. The tables also show the truck's value will depreciate with age.

default and costly litigation. Nor shall I buy risky mining stock that yields only 6 per cent. At any time, there is a *whole spread of interest rates for ventures of different riskiness,* and this whole spread will move up or down when the pure, riskless rate of interest changes.

What are the changes in supply or demand that could move the pure interest rate up or down? Certainly, if scientists and engineers create new projects for capital investment, with *net productivities* greatly increased from the previous equilibrium, this will tend to bid up the market rate of interest. On the other hand, if people become *less impatient* to consume now rather than in the future, their successful attempt to save—to shift resources from consumption-goods production to formation of capital goods—will bid down the interest rate, as more and more capital accumulation leads to diminishing returns and creates the need to take up capital projects with lower and lower net productivities.

As Yale's great Irving Fisher put the matter a half-century ago:

Supply-and-demand determination of the interest rate means that its level is determined by interaction between (1) people's *impatience* to consume now rather than accumulate more capital goods for future consumption (perhaps in old-age retirement or for that proverbial rainy day); and (2) *investment opportunities* that exist to procure higher or lower net productivities from such capital accumulated.

The market rate of interest traditionally has two functions: it *rations out,* into the uses with highest net productivities, society's *existing scarce supply of capital goods;* and in the long run, it may (or may not[4]) induce people to *sacrifice current consumption and add to the stock of capital.*

## GRAPHICAL DETERMINATION OF INTEREST

Supply-and-demand diagrams can amplify this survey of traditional interest determination. But in the field of capital theory, they become rather complicated. At this point we can greatly simplify the exposition of the traditional theory if we agree to concentrate on the case where all physical capital goods are exactly alike and highly versatile. (Of course, in the real world, they are not all alike; and therefore advanced treatises have to go through a rather lengthy discussion to show how the diversity of capital goods is to be handled.[5])

---

[4] There is evidence that some people save *less*, rather than more, at higher interest rates; and that many people save about the *same* amount regardless of the level of the interest rate; and that some people are induced to consume less only by the promise of higher interest returns. As we saw in the discussion of substitution- versus income-effects, in Chapters 22 and 29, economic principles alone cannot give us a decisive prediction as to whether or when a supply curve will become backward-bending. The bulk of the evidence suggests that the level of interest tends to cancel out of consumption and saving decisions, even though a rise in the rate paid by one savings bank may bring *it* increased business because people will tend to transfer their assets from commercial banks or mutual funds (without their having altered consumption one bit). Some classical economists sought to justify interest as the reward for the pain of abstinence and waiting, just as they justified wages as the reward for sweat and psychic disutility. This gave rise to jests among Continental socialists concerning Baron Rothschild's painful sacrifices!

[5] See the Appendix's Fig. 30-3, page 613, for some further discussion of this problem and of the Irving Fisher analysis.

Figure 30-1 illustrates how the interest rate is determined in traditional capital theory. Curve *dd* shows the demand curve for the stock of capital. Remember how the demand for labor was formed from the marginal productivity curve for labor. Similarly, the demand for capital is a "derived demand"—derived ultimately from the value of extra consumption goods that extra capital makes possible. The demand for capital is its *net productivity curve* (reckoned as a yearly per cent, as we've seen).

**Diminishing returns**   We see the law of diminishing returns applying to capital as well as to other factors. This is shown by the *dd* curve's sloping downward; e.g., at levels where capital is very scarce, there are some very profitable roundabout projects that yield 12 or more per cent per annum. Gradually, through thrift, capital formation takes place and the community finds it has exploited all the 12 per cent projects; with total labor and land fixed, diminishing returns to the varying capital have set in. The community must then invest in 11 and 10 per cent projects as it moves down *dd*.

In Fig. 30-1, capital formation has taken place in the past, bequeathing the existing supply of the stock of capital as given by the vertical supply curve *ss*. The equilibrium rate of interest must in the short run take place at the intersection of the *dd* demand curve and the *ss* short-run supply curve. Why? Because below the equilibrium interest rate, there would exist too many investment projects; above the equilibrium rate, there would be too few; and the community's stock of capital is only big enough to take care of the projects yielding the shown equilibrium interest rate of 8 per cent.

**Short-run equilibrium**   Why is the equilibrium at *E* only a short-run, moving equilibrium? Because 8 per cent is a rather high rate; and even though capital is currently scarce enough to keep us at *E*, people are shown as wanting to go on saving part

**FIG. 30-1**

**Traditional theory determines interest rate by intersecting supply and demand**

Existing supply of capital intersects net productivity schedule to determine a moving equilibrium rate. Continued capital formation shifts *ss* rightward and leads to the indicated fall in interest rate along *dd*. Long-run equilibrium interest rate is at *E'*, where net saving ceases.

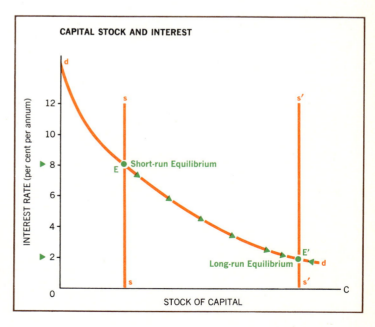

of their income there. This means the community will have capital formation continuously taking place; so, as time passes, the community will be moving southeast on the *dd* curve as shown by the green arrows.

Specifically, (1) we move rightward because the accumulating amount of positive investment and capital formation means that the capital stock, and therefore the short-run supply curve, is being pushed more and more rightward. (In each new short run, the curve will again be vertical but farther to the right.) Now why does the interest rate move downward? (2) It moves downward because the law of diminishing returns tells us—other things such as labor, land, and knowledge of technology remaining unchanged!—that the net productivity of the increased stock of capital goods falls to ever lower percentages.[6]

**Long-term steady-state equilibrium**    The equilibrium at *E* was in the nature of a short-run equilibrium; short-run, in the sense that people were still saving at the interest rate shown there. Capital was still growing, as is shown by the green arrows; we were still moving down the *dd* curve. The interest rate at *E* was just big enough to keep us growing at the rate we were growing. But the interest rate at *E* was not yet low enough to choke off all desire to save, not yet low enough to make the community's average propensity to consume equal to 100 per cent of income.

It is at *E'* that *long-run equilibrium* is finally achieved. Again, the existing stock of capital is being auctioned off in the market for the highest short-run interest rate it can fetch. (You run vertically up the *s's'* supply curve and read off the *E'* interest rate.) But now interest is so low that the net saving is zero; now capital stops growing, and the supply curve no longer shifts rightward. The arrows converge on *E'*: at higher interest, capital would grow through positive saving and investment; at lower interest, it would decline through positive disinvestment and dissaving. So *E'* represents the stable long-run equilibrium that could prevail in the absence of technical change.

## ANCIENT MISCONCEPTIONS ABOUT INTEREST

Before proceeding to criticize and qualify its oversimplifications, we can use the traditional theory of capital and interest to clear up some ancient debates.

**Fairness and inevitability of interest**    Pointing out that money is "barren," Aristotle said it was unfair to charge positive interest for loans. Many sophisticated medieval Schoolmen followed him in this view that interest represents unjustified usury. Indeed, interest was forbidden by canon law throughout the Middle Ages, and many were the dodges to get around these restrictions.

How do we answer this view? First, we could point out what has been shown in

---

[6]The process of accumulating capital goods faster than labor grows is important, and will be called "deepening of capital" in Chapter 37 (in contrast to mere duplication of capital goods to match a growing labor force, called "widening of capital"). The steady-state equilibrium shown at *E'* could, if population were growing at, say, 2 per cent per year, be a moving equilibrium in which capital is being accumulated *in balance* with labor, with no "deepening" but only "widening." See page 614, Appendix, footnote 2.

earlier chapters—that holding a cash balance often does serve a useful function for which people will gladly pay up to a point. But let us meet the issue head on. Let us make the realistic assumption that when I borrow money from you, my purpose is not to hold onto the cash: instead, I use the borrowed cash to buy capital goods; and, as we have seen, these intermediate capital goods are so scarce as to create a net product over and above their replacement cost. Therefore, if I did not pay you interest, I should really be cheating you out of the return that you could get by putting your own money directly into such productive investment projects!

**Consumption loans**    The Biblical utterances against interest and usury clearly refer to loans made for consumption rather than investment purposes. Suppose I, a poor man, borrow from you, a rich man, so that I can eat more today or pay a hospital bill. (*a*) Is it fair that I should have to pay you interest? (*b*) How do such consumption loans affect the short-run and long-run equilibrium interest rates?

The answer to the second question will help answer the first. Consumption lending is today less important than productive-investment lending; therefore productive investment primarily determines the behavior of interest rates.[7]

Now we can treat the fairness question. Are we assuming that there is effective competition in the money market for consumption loans so that no one—rich or poor—can take unfair *monopoly* advantage of anyone else by preventing him from borrowing at the cheapest available terms? If we explicitly assume effective competition *and* that people will not rashly sacrifice their future well-being just to consume more now, then it is hard to see why there is anything more unfair about *loan* transactions between rich and poor than there would be in *other* competitive transactions between rich and poor, e.g., when a rich butcher sells a poor consumer a pound of meat. Of course, the poor man would rather pay nothing for the meat than have to pay a positive price. But, being a scarce good, the meat commands a positive price and one that changes with supply and demand. The same holds for interest. If the existing distribution of income seems unfair to the populace, the field of taxation would seem to offer the best remedies—not random interference with competitive loan or other market transactions.

**Is a zero interest rate possible?**    In a world of perfect certainty, it is hard to see how people could ever save enough to bring the net productivity of capital all the way down to a zero interest rate. As long as there is a single hilly railroad track left, it would pay at a zero rate of interest to make it level. Why? Because in enough years, the savings in fuel would pay for the cost. As long as any increase in time-consuming processes could be counted on to produce any extra product and dollars of revenue, the yield of capital could not be zero. Also, as long as any land or other asset exists with a *sure perpetual net income*—and as long as people are willing to give only a

---

[7] Nonetheless, to the extent that there is a desire to borrow now for present consumption purposes, we can take this into account in Fig. 30-1. If some people want to dissave, their consumption borrowing will make the community less thrifty as a whole than it would otherwise be. So we find the *ss* curve of the stock of capital shifting *more slowly* rightward; and we thereby progress more slowly downward on the *dd* curve from *E* toward *E'*, with interest not falling so fast nor so far.

*finite* amount of money today in exchange for a perpetual flow of income spread over the whole future—we can hardly conceive of the interest rate as falling to zero.[8]

A zero rate of interest is a little like an "absolute zero of temperature" in physics. We can imagine getting closer and closer to it, but we can hardly imagine actually reaching the limiting state of a zero equilibrium rate of interest. Thus, interest is a basic phenomenon unlikely to disappear even in the most ideal economic world.

**Interest under socialism?**    Our economic analysis suggests that thinking is superficial if it concludes that interest is solely a monetary phenomenon of predatory capitalism. Students of planning in a centralized socialistic society have discovered that even such a society must introduce a concept like the interest rate into its plans. Every known society has, since Eden, had some limits on its supply of capital goods. Every society, therefore, has the important task of screening out investment projects, giving first priority to those that are most immediately productive of the things that society wants. Even in Utopia, you simply cannot do everything at once.

How, then, does the screening out among possible projects take place, so that definite priorities can be given? Clearly, there is no alternative but to choose (1) how much of present resources are to be used, and (2) how much of future useful products will be created. To reduce all the alternative patterns into a final single figure is not easy; but something like our earlier calculation of net productivities must be made. Unless you are satisfied to toss a coin or proceed by chance in your collectivist's society, *you have to introduce first those investment projects with the higher net productivity.* After much investment has gone into these in the past and diminishing returns has brought down the yield, you can go on to lower-net-productivity projects.

At some point, therefore, something like the interest rate necessarily comes into being. Recent studies show that the social engineers of the Soviet Union are anxious not to be denounced as capitalistic apologists; yet they need some form of interest rate (or "discount factor," or "payoff period") for making efficient investment calculations. As a result, about a dozen different accounting methods are in vogue there for introducing a thinly disguised interest-rate concept into Soviet planning procedures. But, of course, no person need receive interest income from them.

## SUMMARY OF INTEREST DETERMINATION

We have now seen what determines interest rates over time. If Robinson Crusoe (or a Communist Planner or the average citizen in a free economy) cuts down on current consumption, then capital formation can be high and capital goods can grow in number. The more capital goods there are, the lower their net productivities will tend to be. Why? Because of the good old law of diminishing returns: with population and natural

---

[8] Under realistic conditions of uncertainty, we must qualify the above. Before you have recovered the costs of leveling the roadbed of the railway, airplanes might make railways obsolete—or earthquakes might undo your work. In 1932 people expected and experienced zero or negative returns from most capital projects. That is why investment lagged. Even today, if the profit rate (pure interest rate plus premium to cover risk) were forced down to a low-enough level, business as a whole might be unwilling to undertake an investment level equal to desired full-employment saving. Fiscal budgetary deficits would then be indicated. See Appendix, page 614, for more on floors to returns.

resources unchanged, when you add more and more physical capital goods—or, what is closely related, when you make production more and more roundabout and time-consuming—you will add to total product, but generally at a decreasing rate.

When you have built the bridges, dams, and factories that yield a net productivity of 20 per cent, you have then to go on to investment projects with 19 per cent and still lower net productivities. The market rate of interest that can be earned on investments will thus fall; and this will be the signal for investors to undertake projects previously unprofitable at the earlier higher rates of interest.[9]

Two kinds of thrift are involved. First, people must resist the temptation to eat up some of the capital amassed in the past; they must "abstain" from consuming more than their current incomes, that is, must continue to replace capital and abstain from making net saving become negative. Second, if there is to be positive net capital formation, the community must usually undergo "waiting"—in the sense of giving up consumption goods now in return for more such goods in the future.

All in all, consumption-saving decisions plus the technical net productivity of capital goods are needed to explain behavior of interest rates over time.[10]

## SOME MAJOR QUALIFICATIONS

Now the main task of this chapter is done. But any traditional account of capital theory is in need of some important qualifications. This chapter concludes with only brief mention of the more important ones. The Appendix provides further discussion.

**Technological disturbance**    In real life we cannot hold other things constant while the system proceeds to accumulate capital and travel down the road of diminishing returns. In particular, new inventions and discoveries are constantly being made. Such techno-logical changes will often raise the net productivity and the interest rates to be earned on the community's stock of capital and on its extensions. So, instead of there being a movement down an unchanged schedule, inventions may cause an upward shift of the net-productivity-of-capital schedule.[11] (All this is not a fanciful possibility. Histori-cal studies suggest that, for America and the West generally, the tendency toward falling interest rates via diminishing returns has been just about canceled out by technological progress: though real wage rates have been rising, the real interest return on capital has not been generally falling in this century, as would have been expected from a primitive classical analysis of capital accumulation.)

If technical change came to an end, the rate of interest might again march down

---

[9] What is the same thing, a lowering of the interest rate at which we calculate present discounted values (as indicated on page 615) will raise more and more investment projects above their initial cost—and they will be undertaken to society's advantage.

[10] As we shall see, the government—through its monetary and fiscal policies that favor or retard the rate of capital formation and ensure against the paradox of aborted thrift—is also an important determinant of investment and interest rates. So two economies in which *private* individuals and corporations show the same thrift propensities may develop very differently over a decade or century, depending upon the policies being followed by government.

[11] Some inventions may be "capital-saving" and twist the net productivity relationship downward, often tending to lower interest. (See Chapter 37.) Note that inventions may also destroy some capital by making it obsolete; and changes in consumer tastes can have similar disturbing effects.

toward zero or to the point where no saving took place. But, actually, new inventions are constantly coming along to give interest rates an upward lift. Some economists (such as Schumpeter) have likened the process to a plucked violin string: other things being equal, the string will gradually come to rest as competitive capital formation undermines net yield; but before this can happen, some outside event or invention comes along to pluck it once more and to set it again into motion. (See Chapter 37 and its Appendix for more on this.)

**Uncertainty and expectations**   Our exposition of the traditional capital theory has assumed perfect foresight. This is a serious oversimplification. In real life no one has a crystal ball to read the future: all evaluations of capital and all investment decisions, resting as they do on estimates of future earnings, must necessarily be guesses—accurate guesses based on much thought and information in some cases, wild guesses in other cases, but in every case uncertain guesses. Each day we wake up to learn that our expectations were not quite accurate and have to be revalued; each night we go to bed realizing that the next morning will have some surprises for us.

The next chapter will show how significant uncertainty is for profit theory. Here, in connection with interest theory, we must note an important effect of uncertainty.

Investors' optimism about future yields and risks can change markedly in a very short time; hence all relations are very *shiftable*. They shift with changes in opinion and rumor; changes in population; changes in technology and innovation; etc.[12]

**Shifts in schedules with income**   Even without disturbing outside factors, there is a serious drawback to traditional schedules. Changes in the level of *real income* profoundly *shift* classical saving and investment schedules at each rate of interest. (Only recall our long statistical and theoretical discussions of Part Two dealing with the propensity to consume and to save at different levels of income. Also recall discussions of investment induced by increases in the level of income relative to fixed capacities of capital—or what is closely related, the "acceleration principle" of Chapter 14.)

Shifts of the basic schedules—as, e.g., of *dd* in Fig. 30-1—represent serious weaknesses in the traditional theory. Many classical economists of a century ago were unaware of this problem because they had the comfortable view that chronic unemployment was impossible and income would not fluctuate. They didn't always know why they believed full employment was inevitable. But they did think "supply always creates its own demand: general overproduction is an impossibility."[13]

**Real versus money interest rate**   In Brazil interest rates often exceed 40 per cent a year. During the 1923 German inflation, they were often 1 million per cent per month!

---

[12] To illustrate this subjective volatility, Keynes once characterized the 1929 crash as "a sudden collapse in the [net productivity or] marginal efficiency of capital"—a true, but surface, explanation.
[13] For example, some believed in a miraculous law of conservation of market purchasing power: what was not spent in one direction they said *had* to be spent in another. A more defensible version of the theory claims that, if only wages and prices were never sticky, then flexible decreases in *all* prices and wages would ultimately so increase the real purchasing power of the coin and currency in each man's pocket as to reduce his thriftiness enough to restore full employment. The modern version of this hyperdeflation theory we have associated with A. C. Pigou, who did not recommend it for policy purposes. (See Appendix to Chapter 18 on Say's Law and on Pigou effects.)

Americans who bought government savings bonds almost a decade ago, with a nominal yield of $4\frac{1}{2}$ per cent, can actually buy less today with $100 than with the $75 the bonds cost—entailing a *"real* interest return" of less than zero per cent.

These examples stress the need to define the "real interest rate" as the "money interest rate" minus "the percentage price rise." Thus, if the money rate is 8 per cent for Americans and the annual price rise is 5 per cent, then the true real rate of interest is $8 - 5 = 3$ per cent. So to speak, 100 market baskets of goods lent today gives you next year only 103 (not 108!) market baskets in return.

As people come to anticipate a steady rate of inflation, they build into their interest-rate supply and demand schedules an allowance for the inflation. Thus, in the 1970s, interest rates of 8 and 10 or more per cent became common. High rates? Yes, in money terms. But the calculated real interest rate held pretty steady from 1965 to 1973, and then fell as inflation accelerated.

## PUBLIC AND PRIVATE POLICY IN DETERMINING CAPITAL FORMATION

Concretely, how does the modern macroanalysis of Part Two fit in with the valid elements of the traditional microeconomic theory? Here is its basic contribution:

Fiscal and monetary policies interact with private thrift to determine how fast society builds up its capital.

Consider, for example, a successful pattern of full-employment equilibrium without inflation. Recall that this requires the saving and investment curves of income determination in Chapters 12 and 13 to be intersecting at full employment, with no inflationary gap and no deflationary gap. Two instances are shown here in Fig. 30-2.

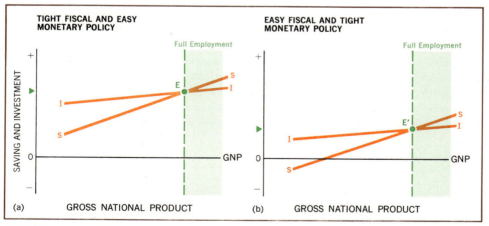

FIG. 30-2

Mix of monetary and fiscal policy determines rate of capital growth
**(a)**  By tight fiscal and easy monetary policies, the first economy is causing full-employment saving and investment to reach equilibrium at *E*, with rapid rate of capital formation.
**(b)**  The second economy uses easy fiscal policy (low taxes and deficits) matched by tight monetary policy to create a low-saving-and-investment (high-consumption) full-employment equilibrium. Note that *E'* is much lower than *E* in investment.

The community's propensity-to-save-out-of-income curve will crucially depend upon budgetary fiscal policy. To see this, suppose tax rates are very high, so that revenues collected at full employment are very high relative to expenditure, the budget being overbalanced. Suppose, too, that the taxes fall most heavily on the relatively thriftless lower-income groups. Then the community's propensity-to-consume schedule will be a low one at every level of national income, including the full-employment level. The amount not consumed (equal to net personal saving plus the government surplus) will then be very great at every level and—what interests us here—SS will be great at the full-employment level of income shown in Fig. 30-2(a).

Will such a depressed consumption level cause unemployment? Not if macroeconomic management[14] is working. Aggressive easing of monetary policy (open-market purchases, lowered reserve requirements, lowered discount rate, and possibly aggressive selective credit programs) will push the community's investment schedule upward. Result: Tight fiscal policy plus very expansionary monetary policy has given us a full-employment income characterized by very high capital formation and relatively low consumption. [See E in Fig. 30-2(a).]

We can work out the opposite mix of tight monetary and easy fiscal policies appropriate for a community that seeks a high-consumption, low-investment, full-employment income, as in Fig. 30-2(b). Looked at together, the two diagrams (a) and (b) show the alternative rates of capital formation in two societies, each characterized by the same degree of private thrift (as measured by family budget studies at each level of disposable income), but with alternative public policies. Note the resulting differences in capital formation, and remember that diminishing returns would be operating to bring down interest more rapidly in the high-investment society unless offset by special technological progress there.

**A sobering public responsibility**   We conclude, then, with two reminders. Macroeconomic management can banish the paradoxical possibility of thrift's becoming abortive and can in this sense validate the classical notions concerning capital formation and productivity. On the other hand, modern societies necessarily are engaging in monetary and fiscal policies—and it is these public policies that to an important degree do shape the resulting pattern of high-employment consumption and investment.

This power over the community's rate of capital formation constitutes an exhilarating—and sobering—responsibility for the voters in any modern democracy.[15]

---

[14] See pages 345–350.

[15] Joan Robinson and Piero Sraffa of Cambridge University have pointed out that there may be no unambiguous way to define the degree of roundaboutness of the production process. They have also cogently pointed out that although labor and land might be characterized under simplifying conditions by "the quantity of labor, and the quantity of land," it is not possible under realistic conditions to reduce a heterogeneous array of different kinds of capital goods—hammers, raw leather, engines of type 99a and of 13d—into a meaningful, quantitative magnitude called "homogeneous capital." Hence, it is false to think that one can speak of the marginal productivity of capital in the same concrete terms that one can hope under suitable conditions to speak of the marginal productivity of labor or of clay land of defined grade. These considerations lead critics to introduce macroeconomic as well as microeconomic elements into a model of income distribution, and also to invoke institutional elements of power—militant trade-union bargaining, etc.—into their models. See the appendixes to this chapter and to Chapters 37 and 42 for some qualifications that this entails for the traditional theory of interest expounded in this main chapter.

## SUMMARY

1   We can apply *primary* factors of production, land and labor, in indirect ways by introducing *intermediate* productive factors called *capital goods*. It is taken as a technological fact that this "roundaboutness" yields a *net productivity* over and above all replacement costs, expressible as an annual interest percentage and subject to the usual law of diminishing returns. (Read again the exact definition of net productivity.)

2   To get the capitalized value of an asset, the interest rate is needed. It is also the device society uses to select investment projects that are most urgent and economical. When interest is high, only projects with highest net productivities can qualify. Gradually, after much past capital formation has invoked the law of diminishing returns, the interest rates will be falling. This provides the signal for introducing capital projects with lower net productivities.

3   Thrift, in the sense of *abstaining* from consuming past capital accumulations and *waiting* for future consumption goods rather than consuming now, interacts with the technical net productivity of capital goods to determine the developing pattern of interest rates and capital formation. Even outside a collectivist world, government monetary and fiscal policies play an important role in this process.

4   Even a planned state which is not run for private profit or gain would have to use some device like an interest rate as a sieve to determine which of the many possible investment projects represent the best use of the resources available today after present consumption needs have been determined. "Come the revolution"—come laissez faire—Nature's law of diminishing returns (of "future consumption goods" in return for "sacrificed present consumption goods") is likely still to be in business.

5   Consumption loans, while they are of minor importance today, do have some influence on the rate at which the community accumulates capital rather than consumes. Like the subjective factors of thrift, abstinence, waiting, foresight, impatience, and so forth, (*a*) personal borrowings do interact with (*b*) the technological fact of opportunity to invest in long-lived projects with a net yield.

  Critics of interest had in mind the occurrence of consumption-loan transactions in highly imperfectly competitive markets where the poor are at the mercy of the rich lender's bargaining power. Today no one would be in favor of usurious overcharges that take advantage of the poor man's inadequate access to competitive loan markets or his desperate neglect of his own future; but economists and philosophers recognize that the net productivity of capital is the technological fact most basic to modern-day interest: when you lend me money, you are giving up the opportunity to invest in land, machines, bonds, and stocks—forgone opportunities of which interest is some kind of measure.

6   Important qualifications of the oversimplified traditional capital theory include the following: Lack of perfect foresight means that the capital net productivity

is very *shiftable* as expectations, technology, and income levels change. Also, a classical theory that ignores deviations from full-employment income does need modification. Finally, to get the real rate of interest, one must subtract from the money rate the anticipated percentage rate of price inflation.

7   A great variety of compensating monetary and fiscal policies can succeed in maintaining reasonably full employment. Stable employment being assumed, Fig. 30-2 gives the needed qualification to the traditional theory; and it reveals that public policy has great responsibility for determining whether the composition of the full-employment national income will be heavily weighted toward investment or toward consumption; this means that the central bank and the legislature between them shape the environment within which private thriftiness provides one part of total social thriftiness.

## CONCEPTS FOR REVIEW

net productivity of capital

indirect, roundabout methods and
    diminishing returns

interest rate per annum

capitalization by $V = \$N/i$

choosing among investment
    projects

zero interest under any ism?

abstinence and waiting

uncertainty and technological
    change

real versus money interest rate

austere fiscal policy and easy
    monetary policy, or opposite

public responsibility for rate of
    capital formation

## QUESTIONS FOR DISCUSSION

1   Give some examples of efficient roundabout processes. Of "produced" or "intermediate" outputs that serve in their turn as inputs.

2   Contrast three "prices" of capital: (*a*) rental of a capital good, (*b*) market price of the capital good, and (*c*) interest yield on the value of the good.

3   Irving Fisher wrote a book with the title *The Theory of Interest*. He gave it the subtitle *As Determined by Impatience to Spend and Opportunities to Invest*. Explain what these mean. Defend the following: "Fisher should have added 'and as affected by government monetary and fiscal policies.'"

4   "The interest rate was simply a bourgeois device for exploitation." Discuss.

5   Protestant, Catholic, and Jewish organizations today issue mortgages to build local places of worship, and they invest surplus funds in bonds, or possibly, as in the case of the Church of England, in equity stocks. How might they ethically distinguish this from "taking usury"?

6   How do innovations and expectations affect traditional interest theory?

**7** Interpret macroeconomic management in a modern mixed economy. Contrast full employment *cum* "tight money" and "easy fiscal policy" with its opposite.

**8** Explain the rule for calculating present discounted value of a perpetual income stream. At 5 per cent, what is the worth of a perpetuity paying $100 per year? Paying $200 per year? Paying $N per year? At 6 or 8 per cent, what is the worth of a perpetuity paying $100 per year? What does doubling of the interest rate do to the capitalized value of a perpetuity—say, a perpetual bond?

# APPENDIX: Theoretical Aspects of Interest

Here, very briefly, can be mentioned some elaborations and qualifications of this chapter's discussion.

## PRODUCTIVITY OR IMPATIENCE?

Some people like to find a single cause for everything, and such people ask: "Is interest caused by the productivity of capital? Or by the fact that savers must be paid for the unpleasant task of 'abstinence' or 'waiting'? Which is more important: opportunity to invest or impatience to spend?"

Our previous argument shows this is a false antithesis. *Both* factors operate to determine the time path of interest: the impatience to spend, or the tendency to prefer the present to the future, limits the growth rate and attained size of capital; and the productivity factor tells us what the interest or net productivity is that can be earned as we have various amounts of diverse capital goods. Just as both blades of a scissors are needed to cut—so that you cannot say that one blade rather than the other is doing the actual

work—both factors, impatience *and* productivity, interact to determine the behavior of interest rates.[1]

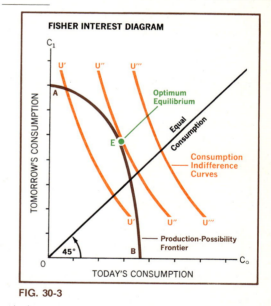

FISHER INTEREST DIAGRAM

$C_1$

$U'$   $U''$   $U'''$

A

Optimum Equilibrium

Equal Consumption

E

Consumption Indifference Curves

TOMORROW'S CONSUMPTION

$U'$   $U''$   $U'''$

Production-Possibility Frontier

45°   B

O   $C_0$

TODAY'S CONSUMPTION

**FIG. 30-3**

[1]Those who have mastered the indifference-curve graphs of the Appendix to Chapter 22 can use Fig. 30-3 to see that positive interest is caused by two factors: (1) a vertical bias of the *AB* production-possibility frontier between present and future consumption goods, and (2) a general vertical bias of the typical consumer's indifference contours between present and future consumption goods. Hence, the tangency-equilibrium at *E* has a slope steeper than 1.0, corresponding to positive interest. The experienced reader will recognize that these can be related to Böhm-Bawerk's three famous causes for interest. His third cause, technological superiority of roundabout processes, and his first cause, the expectation by the typical consumer that his future dollars will have lower marginal utility because his

income will be higher in the future (as a result of technological progress or of the productivity of roundaboutness), relate to factor (1). Böhm's second cause—systematic time preference by consumers for present rather than future goods, for rational reasons of life's uncertainties and brevity or for irrational reasons—relates to (2). [Suppose we were to rule out factor (1) by making *AB* "symmetrical around the 45° line" and rule out factor (2) by making the indifference curves "symmetrical around the 45° line." Having thus ruled out net productivity and time preference, we should find that the equilibrium interest rate must then be zero. Leaving either bias in, or both, leads to positive interest.]

## DETERMINATION OF THE INTEREST RATE

Can our account of interest determination avoid the use of Fig. 30-1's simplifying concept of a stock of homogeneous capital? Yes, in a number of ways, some too complex to discuss in an introductory work. Thus, we may work with various different physical capital goods and processes, being careful never to add their heterogeneous units together, noting that the sum of their capitalized market values does depend (in a virtuously, and not viciously, circular way) on the market interest rate, and never forgetting that it is machines and not hunks of dollars which enter into physical production functions. If the realistic problem of uncertainty about the future and the risks thereby implied could be ignored, advanced treatises can show rigorously how an equilibrium interest-rate pattern can be defined in such a heterogeneous model.

This is clearly not the place for such refinements. But it is desirable to mention that a theory of equilibrium interest rates can be given which avoids the homogeneous-capital assumptions of Fig. 30-1.

The key to a simple approach comes from Fisher's diagram, Fig. 30-3, in footnote 1, which states the following fundamental proposition about the theory of interest:

**Society can exchange present consumption goods for future consumption goods at a tradeoff rate depicted by the rate of interest.**

**Long-run equilibrium**  How long could this accumulation process of sacrificing current consumption go on? Just as Fig. 30-1 suggested, it can go on until the interest rate is zero, or until people want to do no net saving. At the zero rate of interest, if we could ever quite reach this point on the horizon, the plateau of consumption would be as high as is technically possible with the given labor, land, and primary resources. It would be a kind of "golden age."[2]

---

[2] Advanced books show that this golden rule must be modified if primary resources such as labor are *all* growing at 3 or 5 per cent per year. Then the golden age of maximal per capita consumption comes when the interest rate has been brought down also to 3 or 5 per cent: then the young earners in society, who are saving for their old age, are just enough more numerous than the retired earners, who are eating up what they had earlier saved; and then there is just enough net saving and investing to keep all capital goods growing in full proportion to the growth in primary labor. Then we

In real life three or more things keep us from reaching the golden age:

1. People may be so impatient and so conscious of death that at some interest rate like 3 per cent, society won't want to do net saving.

2. Inventions may come along and offset diminishing returns by shifting upward Fig. 30-1's *dd*.

3. There is always riskiness in a dynamic society: long before the pure interest rate reaches zero, the profit-rate-inclusive-of-premium-for-risk may have hit a floor below which investment lags. We must examine this important matter.

## AN UNCERTAINTY FLOOR TO RISKY RETURN?

It may be that under conditions of perfect certainty, persistent thrift can lead to no floor for interest except that of zero. But what about the real world where a measure of uncertainty must always be feared for any actual investment project? Can it not be the case that investors will dislike the task of taking risks on their shoulders? That they will insist on a rate of return on such investments which includes a certain definite, positive percentage premium? Thus, even if the rate of interest to be earned on perfectly safe holdings were forced down to zero, might not people still insist on a 5 per cent after-tax return on a risky investment in a machine or in the purchase of land that produces an uncertain yearly rental?

This floor at 5 per cent, or at some positive level above zero, might be a realistic problem to contend with. And if it were to materialize, some serious problems for full-employment policy might one day arrive. Here is why: Suppose that Federal Reserve expansionary policies lowered the rate of interest on very safe short-term government bonds toward zero; this could be expected to bring the rates of return on risky enterprises down from, say, 12 per cent to 8 per cent. And since at the lower rate many new investment projects would now pay, an upswing in investment spending might result that, through the mechanism of the familiar multiplier process, would lift output, income, and employment.

But suppose all this were not enough to reestablish

---

have an equilibrium, a nice, moving equilibrium with balanced growth (and "widening of capital"). (If land will not grow at all, Malthus reminds us that this Eden must, in absence of inventions, ultimately end with stationary population.)

full employment. Then the Federal Reserve could do more of the same. *But by no amount of expansionary moves could it reduce the safe interest rate below the floor of zero.* And it might well be the case that a zero floor on safe holdings could pull the rates on risky investment down only to their floor of 5 per cent—and no further. Then it would be conceivable that the sticky 5 per cent floor would bar further reduction in rates needed to coax out a pace of job-giving investment that is big enough to restore full employment.

Therefore it is conceivable that an impasse, a kind of Day of Judgment for our mixed system with its inflexible wage and price levels, might arrive when conventional monetary measures to stimulate investment could not restore full employment and let our optimistic "managed money" work itself out smoothly and fully.[3] Fortunately, deficit budgetary policies can come to the rescue!

While this pessimistic possibility may not now be at hand, a prudent society has to keep it in mind. And if that unhappy day should ever approach, more extensive remedial programs (such as investment-

tax-credits and insurance of loan risks or new institutions to provide venture capital) could be explored.

## MARKET CAPITALIZATION OF ASSETS EQUALS PRESENT DISCOUNTED VALUE

Here we can go beyond page 599's simple case of perpetual annuities to the general case. Under conditions of absolute certainty, anyone can borrow or lend as much as he wishes at the single competitive market rate of interest. Every asset must be yielding that same market rate of interest. This equality of yield emerges from the way competitors bid up or bid down the market price of any asset—whether it be a bond, stock, patent, going business, corner lot, or any earning stream of net rentals whatsoever.

What exactly is the formula for the capitalized market value of *any* asset?

Under absolute certainty, every asset will be capitalized *by the price bids of buyers and sellers* in the market place at the *present discounted value* of all its future net receipts. These dollar receipts cannot simply be added up regardless of the date when they are received. The farther off in the future a given dollar receipt is, the less it is worth today. Why?

Because the positive market rate of interest means that all future payments must be *discounted.* A building far off looks tiny because of spatial perspective. The interest rate produces a similar shrinking of time perspective. Even if I knew you would pay $1 to my heirs 999 years from now, I would be foolish to advance you more than a cent today. To see why, let us review the arithmetic of this discounting process.

At 6 per cent interest I can set aside about 94 cents today, and it will grow to $1 within the year. Hence, the *present discounted value* of $1 payable a year from now is today only 94 cents (or, to be exact, $100/1.06 = 94\frac{36}{106}$ cents). The present discounted value of $1 payable in 2 years' time is about 89 cents, or $\$1/(1.06)^2$. Similarly tables of compound interest show how to compute present discounted values.[4]

---

[3]Without risk, the problem of placing my assets is easy. I put all my wealth in Bank A if it offers me $5\frac{3}{4}$ per cent while Bank B offers only 5 per cent. I put all my wealth in building plants or tools if these projects offer more than Bank A's $5\frac{3}{4}$ per cent. So long as I know I can get any safe positive interest return, I hoard no money, keeping only minimal balances for transaction purposes. Without any risks, so long as interest yields remain positive, we'd never run out of investment opportunities and into unemployment problems.

With risk, if I obey the law of diminishing marginal utility of Chapter 22, the Appendix of Chapter 21 showed that I shall avoid gambling and want insurance (since a gain in my wealth will be worth less to me than an equivalent *dollar* loss). Now I refuse to put all my eggs in one basket: I put some money in both banks in case one should fail; I prefer $5,000 in General Motors and $5,000 in General Electric to $10,000 in either one alone; I buy many independent stocks for my portfolio; I particularly buy both ice and coal stocks so as to be hedged against the worst that can happen. For safety's sake I always hold some idle cash even though it pays no interest. When the pure interest rate is below 2 per cent, I may just as soon hoard cash equal to a large fraction of my wealth or just as soon hold less. This is why Part Two's problem of great unemployment can persist: When a low investment schedule intersects the saving schedule at a point of low-employment GNP, and with profit and interest rates already at their bottom, there is relatively little that conventional banking policy can do in such unlucky times. Then we thank Providence for fiscal policy!

[4]The general rule for present discounted values is the following: To figure out the value today of $1 payable $t$ years from now, ask yourself how much must be invested today at compound interest to grow into $1 at the end of $t$ years. Now we know that at 6 per cent compound interest any principal grows in $t$ years proportionally to $(1 + 0.06)^t$. Hence, we need only invert this expression to arrive at the final answer. Therefore the *present discounted value* of $1

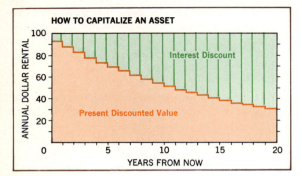

**FIG. 30-4**
The present value of a machine giving net annual rentals of $100 for 20 years (with interest rate prescribed at 6 per cent) is shown by the lower area. The upper area has been discounted away. (Show that raising the interest rate depresses the market price of an asset such as a machine or bond. It does so by enlarging the green discount area subtracted.)

*Computation of PDV:* To arrive at any asset's present discounted value, let each dollar stand on its own feet; evaluate the present worth of each part of the stream of future receipts, giving due allowance for the discounting required by its payment date. Then simply *add together* all these separate discounted values. Thus we have arrived at the asset's capitalized market value, or what is called its "present discounted value." (See the Appendix Summary for the general formula.)

Figure 30-4 shows this graphically for a machine that earns steady net annual rentals of $100 over a 20-year period and has no scrap value at the end. Its present value is not $2,000, but only $1,147. Note how much the later dollar earnings are scaled down or discounted because of our time perspective. The total area remaining *after* discounting (the orange-shaded area) represents the total of the machine's *present discounted value*—its capitalized market value.[5]

──────────

payable *t* years from now is only $1/(1 + 0.06)^t$. What if the interest rate were 8 per cent? Replace 0.06 by 0.08.

[5] Can you now verify our $V = \$N/i$ perpetuity formula? In high school algebra we learn to sum a convergent geometric progression

$$1 + K + K^2 + \cdots = \frac{1}{1 - K}$$

for *K* any fraction less than 1. If you set $K = 1/(1 + i)$ you

**Acting to maximize present discounted value**    Our formula tells us how to write down on our balance sheets the value of any asset once we know how that asset will be used. But note that an asset's future receipts usually depend on our business decisions: Shall we use a truck 8 or 9 years? Overhaul it once a month or once a year? Replace it with a cheap, nondurable truck or an expensive, durable one?

There is one golden rule for giving correct answers to all investment decisions:

**Calculate the present discounted value resulting from each possible decision. Then always act so as to achieve the maximum present discounted value. That way you will have more wealth, to spend whenever and however you like.[6]**

──────────

can with a little work verify our capitalization formula for a permanent income stream: write out *all* the discounted terms

$$\frac{\$N}{1 + i} + \frac{\$N}{(1 + i)^2} + \cdots$$

$$= -\$N + \$N \left\{ 1 + \frac{1}{1 + i} + \left(\frac{1}{1 + i}\right)^2 + \cdots \right\}$$

$$= -\$N + \$N \frac{1}{1 - \frac{1}{1 + i}} = \frac{\$N}{i} \quad \text{[QED]}$$

But note that common-sense economics gives us an equally convincing proof: At interest *i*, $\$N/i$ is the only sum *whose earnings will exactly match the $N per year of income.*

(A FINE POINT: Sometimes you cannot be sure just which of two machines is the more "durable" one that will be brought into use at a lower interest rate. Suppose Machine A yields $100 of output one period from now and $132 of output three periods from now. Let Machine B yield $230 units of output two periods from now, and let it cost the same as A. Which is more durable? More capital-intensive? We can't say. At low rates of interest, present discounted value or *PDV* of A exceeds *PDV* of B, since 100 + 132 > 230. At very high rates of interest, *PDV* of A exceeds *PDV* of B, since the second and third periods' outputs are discounted away to almost nothing. But at intermediate interest rates, between 10 and 20 per cent per period, calculation shows *PDV* of B exceeds *PDV* of A, and B will be chosen. This "reswitching" phenomenon spoils any simple diminishing-returns story, as advanced treatises show.)

[6] This rule shows that business decisions in an ideal capital market would be independent of the decider's *personal* consumption-saving time preference. Why? Because it is always better to be able to sell out now for a larger money sum than for a smaller sum, no matter in what time pattern *you* decide to spend on consumption. In imperfect markets, personal time preference may matter.

## RESWITCHING AND ALL THAT[7]

Traditional capital theory, scholars now recognize, is overly simple. They know that an increase in the money supply will not be neutral in its real-life effect on interest rates. They know that the level of unemployment, and the macroeconomic policies of government,[8] can affect the rate of interest.

But there are more subtle difficulties with the simple notion of (a) a homogeneous stock of measurable capital, and (b) the law of diminishing returns as applied to capital's "set productivity" or "degree of roundaboutness." Briefly, we can indicate some of the important modern critiques.

The classical parable has been challenged in its overly simple claim that people (1) give up current consumption goods ("waiting and abstinence"); (2) transmute them into a greater quantity of some homogeneous stuff called "capital"; (3) then collect the marginal productivity of such capital in the form of interest, in exact analogy to the fact that wage rates and rents are the marginal productivity of labor and land; and (4) experience declining interest rates as more capital accumulates, for the alleged reason that capital is subject to the law of diminishing returns just like any other factor input.

Nonsense, Joan Robinson has pointed out again and again. Throw out the notion that the rich man earns his interest by the sweat of his abstinence in much the same way that the worker earns his wage by the sweat of his brow. There is no abstract quantity of capital to put in an aggregate production function like $Q = 1.01\,L^{.75}K^{.25}$. If abstract $K$ does not exist, how can its marginal product $\partial Q/\partial K$ exist? Or how can we hold "it" constant to compute neoclassical marginal products of labor, $\partial Q/\partial L$?

To dramatize the oversimplicity of the neoclassical parable, critics belonging to this "Anglo-Italian" school—P. Sraffa, L. Pasinetti, N. Kaldor, and Joan Robinson being prominent members—point out cogently that there is no technological way of validat-

ing in the most general case the primitive notion that "lower interest rates involve *more-roundabout* methods of production." An example involving so-called "reswitching" illustrates the point.

**Well-behaved parable** Suppose there are two ways of making 1 unit of sulphuric acid (or standardized wine). Method A requires 7 units of labor 2 periods *before* the final output is produced. Method B requires 5 labor units 3 periods before final output.

"Obviously," says the neoclassical parabolist, "B is more roundabout than A. And actually, only when the interest rate falls below 40 per cent will B be more profitable to use than A. [EXPLANATION: 7/5 = 1.40.] But that is as it should be, since society can't move to the longer pipelines of B until some rich man (or the state) is prepared to sacrifice some present goods for future ones. Also, when many do accomplish this thrift and accumulation of (or 'deepening' of) capital, the lowering of interest rate they accomplish [and the new higher GNP for society!] raises real wages of workers, as we can verify by some elaborate calculations of how final product's cost is now broken down between wages and interest."

These are tall claims. But they are deflated when we alter the numerical example.

**Reswitching example** Suppose, instead of Method B, the only alternative to A were the following Method C. In Method C, you produce 1 unit of product with 2 labor units 3 periods earlier *and* 6 labor units 1 period earlier. Now the critic has his turn.

Which is more roundabout and time-intensive, A or C? As Piero Sraffa pointed out in his classic 1960 book *The Production of Commodities by Means of Commodities* (Cambridge University Press, Cambridge, England), there is no technological way to say which is the more time-intensive.

What can we say? Suppose the interest rate were zero (or very small). Since $7 < 6 + 2$, Method A must be cheaper at very low interest rates. Again, at very high interest rates—say 200 per cent per period—compounding 2 labor units for 3 periods will be much, much worse than 7 for 2 periods. So again, at very high interest rates, Method A will be selected over C by ruthless competition.

But, with the help of compound interest tables (or the quadratic equation of Question 4, page 619, we can ascertain that Method C will be cheaper than A

---

[7] This section may be skipped. Footnote 5's fine point provided an example of reswitching for a durable machine.

[8] See the Hicks-Hansen diagrams in Chapter 18's Appendix. We can be, and stay, at full employment by having contractionary fiscal policy shift the *IS* curve rightward while expansionary central bank policy shifts the *LM* curve rightward. (Can you show how to get a high-consumption, low-investment, full employment by reversing this prescription?)

at all interest rates between 100 per cent per period and 50 per cent! In brief, at low $i$ we encounter reswitching back to the methods used at high $i$. What now of the notion that Baron Rothschild's abstinence is needed to accumulate capital in order to bring down the interest rate and raise workers' real wages!

**In this simple model, use of power by unions or the state, to lower the interest rate from 101 to 0.001 per cent will shift the distribution of income from little going to workers to *almost all* going to them.**

**Evaluation**   The science of political economy has not yet the empirical knowledge to decide whether the real world is nearer to the idealized polar cases represented by (*a*) the neoclassical parable, or (*b*) the simple reswitching paradigm. My own opinion should not be foisted on the beginning reader. But I do owe it to him.

When we consider what greater amounts of plant, equipment, and inventories could do for developing countries like India, Brazil, or South Korea, for planned economies like Russia, China, or North Korea, for advanced economies like Japan, Italy, or the United States, I am led to think that *great gains in the size of the social pie to be divided up in the future can be hoped for from capital accumulation at the expense of present-day consumption*. But this does not mean that private property, unequally distributed, is the only twentieth-century mechanism to bring this about.

In conclusion, the economic concepts that all can agree on, regardless of reswitching, are twofold.

1. Any tradeoff between present and future goods is subject to diminishing returns in the manner of Chapter 2's guns-and-butter concave frontier.

2. The lower is the interest rate (or profit rate—they are the same thing in absence of uncertainty), the higher will be the real wage [in accordance with Fig. 37-2(b)'s factor-price frontier, to come later].

## SUMMARY TO APPENDIX

1   Technical opportunities to invest (to swap present consumption for future consumption goods) interact with people's subjective time preferences (about how much to consume or to add to the accumulated stocks of past capital formation) to determine the interest rate. As in all markets, *both* supply and demand factors interact.

2   Avoiding the highly useful device of homogeneous stock of physical capital, we can still have a complete interest theory along Fisher lines. The interest rate equals terms of trade at which we can get next year's consumption goods for today's—106 chocolates next year for 100 today means a real 6 per cent interest rate per annum.

3   The formula for capitalizing the asset value of a perpetual constant income can be extended when receipts are neither constant nor perpetual. Each dollar payable $t$ years from now is worth only its "present discounted value" of $\$1/(1 + i)^t$. So for *any* net receipt stream $(N_1, N_2, \ldots, N_t, \ldots)$,

$$PDV = \frac{N_1}{(1 + i)} + \frac{N_2}{(1 + i)^2} + \cdots + \frac{N_t}{(1 + i)^t} + \cdots$$

4   Under conditions involving no uncertainty and no technical innovations, if the community insisted on accumulating more and more capital, diminishing returns might finally force capital's net productivity and the interest rate indefinitely down toward zero. Under real-life conditions of great uncertainty, there is the possibility that the floor on risky returns would be considerably higher than the floor of zero return on risk-free loans. So we cannot rule out the pessimistic possibility of a future Day of Judgment, where the authorities would have to supplement the orthodox methods by which the central bank eases interest rates if they are to succeed in coaxing out the volume of job-creating investment needed to keep employment high or full. But that day seems remote.

5  Reswitching examples alert us to the fact that, in the general case, there is no technological criterion of "roundaboutness or time-intensity of capital and the productive process" that can be applied independently of observed lowering of the market rate of interest. In general, one cannot assert that of two societies alike in know-how, A, with a lower interest rate, must have a higher steady-state plateau of real consumption than B, with a higher interest rate. However, the real wage in A must in *all* examples (not involving extraneous joint products) be higher when the interest rate is lower; and, always, as you give up more and more chocolates today, the increments of chocolates tomorrow diminish.

## CONCEPTS FOR REVIEW

abstinence, impatience, waiting
opportunity to invest
present discounted value
interest rate and planning

tradeoff between today's and
    tomorrow's consumption
uncertainty
reswitching versus parables

## QUESTIONS FOR DISCUSSION

1  After the H-bomb was developed, my time preference for present over future consumption increased. After having learned that my uncle will bequeath me a fortune a decade from now, the same happened. Was this rational? Thinking of a lobster dinner tonight, I offer you $6 on Monday for $5 now. Is this irrational?

2  Two communities have the same technological production functions. Why might they show different interest-rate patterns in history?

3  Give reasons why lower interest rates might increase investment demand.

4  *Extra credit problem:* If a doubling of $i$ halves the *PDV* of a perpetuity, can you show that the truck in Fig. 30-4 will *less* than halve in capitalized value? (HINT: The perpetuity has a rectangle that goes on forever, with its orange area getting less and less. The truck lacks this infinite tail off to the right. Now the early year receipts get hardly changed in value at all, since, say, .96 is not much changed when it becomes .92. So the average change in all the truck's orange area is less than that for the perpetuity.) By similar reasoning establish the rule: Interest changes have their biggest effects on *long-term* bonds; their least effects on *short-term* bonds—whose principal will be repaid soon and is therefore hardly affected by any discounting. Also, can you verify the reswitching example's demonstration that only below 50 per cent and above 100 per cent interest will Method A displace Method C? [HINT: $7(1 + i)^2 = 2(1 + i)^3 + 6(1 + i)$ has roots $= i = 0.50$ and $1.00$.]

# 31

## PROFITS AND INCENTIVES

The world will always be governed by self-interest. We should not try to stop this, we should try to make the self-interest of cads a little more coincident with that of decent people.
SAMUEL BUTLER

In addition to wages, interest, and rent, economists often talk about a fourth category of income: profit. Wages are the return to labor; interest is the return to capital; rent is the return to land. What is profit the return to?

The answer that economists give is a complex one. This chapter will show that the word "profits" has many different meanings in everyday usage. From these different possible meanings, the economist, after careful analysis, ends up relating the concept of profit to dynamic innovation and uncertainty-bearing, and to the problems of monopoly, incentives and exploitation.

We shall first discuss the main notions of profit. The usual profit figures bandied about will not check with any of these, as we shall see. Then, along with analyzing the notion of competitive profit as a return to risk bearing and other traditional notions, we shall discuss criticisms of profit as the fruit of monopoly and exploitation.

### REPORTED PROFIT STATISTICS

When a statistician from the United Nations or U.S. Department of Commerce gives newspaper reporters a figure involving profits, what does he usually include?

Certainly he includes *corporation earnings*—whether they are paid out as dividends or retained as undistributed profits. (In some reports he includes, and in some he excludes, corporate profit taxes, and sometimes he "adjusts" corporate profits for changes in evaluation of inventories due to price-level changes. So you must be careful in using published statistics.) He may also give another figure that has the flavor of profits about it, namely, *income of unincorporated enterprises* (farmers, the self-employed, doctors and other professionals, partnerships, and so forth).

We understand how he arrived at such a statistical figure of profits for a corporation or an unincorporated enterprise. From the sales revenue of the firm, he subtracted its costs: cost of materials, wage payments to employees, bond interest, depreciation, expense, land rents, and the rest. What is left goes into the figures as profit.

Polls of public opinion show that people generally exaggerate the size of profits. The majority will answer, "Over 25 per cent," when asked how large corporate profits bulk in the national income; not a few answer, "Over half." The prosaic truth, when we examine official income and tax statistics, is otherwise: Corporate profits after taxes, in the mixed economies of the 1970s, are significantly below 10 per cent of total GNP! (In 1972, a year of fair expansion for the United States, corporate profits after taxes were not quite 5 per cent; before taxes, less than 10 per cent.) Since (because of double counting of bread sales as well as wheat, flour, and dough sales) total sales are a multiple of GNP, profits as a percentage of the corporate sales dollar are only a few per cent; and it is this very low number to which apologists for profits tend to appeal in their campaigns to improve people's attitudes toward profits.

## FIRST VIEW: PROFIT AS "IMPLICIT" FACTOR RETURNS

To the economist, such statistical profits are a hodgepodge of different elements. Obviously, part at least of reported profits is merely the return to the owners of the firm for the factors supplied *by them*. Thus, part may be the return to the personal work provided by the owners of the firm—by the farmer and his family, by the doctor, by the partners, or by corporate executives who also happen to be principal stockholders. Part may be the rent return on self-owned natural resources. Part may be the equivalent of interest on the owner's capital. (Recall Chapter 24's discussion of implicit costs and opportunity costs, page 474.

This shows us the first fact about profit:

Much of what is ordinarily called profit is really nothing but interest, rents, and wages under a different name. *Implicit* interest, *implicit* rent, and *implicit* wages are the names economists give to this part of profit, i.e., to the earnings of *self-used* factors.

## SECOND VIEW: PROFIT AS THE REWARD TO ENTERPRISE AND INNOVATION

Suppose we lived in a dreamworld of perfect competition, where we could read the future perfectly from the palms of our hands and where no innovations were permitted to disturb the settled routine of things. Then, the economist says, there would really be no profits at all!

Here is what he means.

The statistician might still be reporting some profit figures to the press; but we know that, under these ideal equilibrium conditions, the *implicit returns* to the labor and property supplied by owners *would exactly swallow up all the profits reported*. Why? Because owners would hire out their factors on the market if they did not get equal rewards from using them in their own businesses. And because people who previously were hiring out their labor and property services would soon go into business for themselves if they knew they could earn more in that way.

Perfectly free entry of numerous competitors would, in a static world of perfect knowledge, bring price down to cost and squeeze out all profits above and beyond competitive wages, interest, and rent.[1]

We do not live in such a dreamworld. We never shall. In real life somebody must act as boss to decide how a business shall be run. Competition is never "perfectly perfect." Somebody must peer into the future to guess the demand for shoelaces or what will be the price of wheat. And in the world as we know it, there is a chance for a man with a brand-new idea to invent a revolutionary machine or a softer soft drink—to promote a new product or find a way to lower costs on an old one.

Let us call the man who does any of these things an *entrepreneur* or *innovator*. Although it is hard to draw the line, let us distinguish him from the bureaucratic executive or manager who simply keeps an established business running. Many economists—such as the late Joseph Schumpeter, Austrian-born economist who taught at Harvard—do not think of the wages of management as profit: they think of the wages of management as wages—implicit or explicit, and high as they may be in the competitive market for gifted managers. But they think of *profit as the return to innovators or entrepreneurs*.

Today it is easier for us to understand this distinction than it used to be half a century ago. We are all acquainted with huge corporations run by managers who own less than 1 per cent of the common stock. Although these executives run the business, they are paid wages much like anybody else. Management of this type is a skill not different in kind from other skills, such as being able to keep books or supervise production. People who possess this skill are bid for in the marketplace, and like any other factor, they move into those jobs where they will receive the highest wages.

The innovator is different. Though he may not always succeed, he is trying to carry out new activities. He is the man with vision, originality, and daring. He may not be the scientist who invents the new process, but he is the one who successfully introduces it. Maxwell developed the scientific theory of radio waves, Hertz discovered them experimentally, but Marconi and Sarnoff made them commercially profitable. On the other hand, De Forest, who discovered the triode tube, also sought to put his inventions to commercial use; yet he went broke a number of times and on each occasion disappointed the hopes of investors who had put money into his enterprises. Many try; a few succeed.[2]

The dollars earned by the successful innovators are defined by some economists—like Schumpeter—as profit. Usually, these profit earnings are temporary and are soon competed out of existence by rivals and imitators. But as one source of innovational profits is disappearing, another is being born. So these innovational profits will continue to exist.

### THIRD VIEW: RISK, UNCERTAINTY, AND PROFIT

If the future were perfectly certain, there would be no opportunity for a bright young man to come along with a revolutionary innovation; everything would already be

---

[1] If people like running their own business, they may gladly take lower implicit wages. If, by contrast, people dislike having to boss other people and if it is tiring to take responsibility for management decisions, then management wages may have to be higher.

[2] Incidentally, the problem of innovation provides a partial defense of patents. Society deliberately gives a man a monopoly; this contrivance permits him artificially to keep something *partially* scarce. But society hopes the offered bribe of temporary monopoly will encourage the invention and the disclosure of things that would otherwise be 100 per cent scarce.

known. This shows that innovators' profits are closely tied up with risk and uncertainty. Frank Knight, a famous University of Chicago economist of the last 50 years, had an important theory that *all true profit is linked with uncertainty.* Innovators' profits, discussed in the preceding section, represent but one important category of uncertainty-induced profit.

A factual examination of the great fortunes of the past shows a strong element of luck in many of them. Oil discoveries, fortunate patents, marketing and speculative successes are examples of the chance elements in a profit-and-loss system.

In examining any profit figures, we must always keep uncertainty and risk in mind. We saw in earlier chapters that some low-grade risky bonds may appear to be yielding 12 per cent at the same time that high-grade safe bonds yield only 7 per cent. But if the chances are that 1 out of 20 low-grade bond issues will default on their principal in the coming year, then you are fooling yourself if you think that these bonds are a better buy. Actually, the extra 5 per cent may just cover the risk of default.

While people who buy lottery tickets face uncertainty, the promoter of the lottery faces no risk. He knows *he* will come out ahead. Similarly, a large insurance company may rely on mathematical laws of probability to reduce its relative riskiness. Why? Because the different risks tend to be canceled by each other if the numbers are large enough. To the extent that we can eliminate uncertainty by pooling and spreading risks, the problem of profits fails to arise. It arises only for the irreducible minimum of riskiness that remains.

In some years, the total losses may be greater than the total profits. Then risk bearers as a whole have paid out to labor, to capitalists, and to landowners more than those factors would have earned if the future had been certain. In another year, the algebraic total of Knight-defined profits may turn out to be positive—so that the factors of production have then received less than they would have if the future were certain. An important question is this:

Are risk bearers on the whole overly optimistic? As a class, do they lose money and subsidize the other factors of production? Or are risk bearers as a class overly "pessimistic"—as claimed in most economics textbooks—so that profits represent a net positive payment for the service of risk bearing? Many economists think that businessmen on the whole act as if they dislike mere riskiness, and hence they must on the average be paid a positive premium or profit for shouldering risks.

## FOURTH VIEW: PROFIT AS A PREMIUM FOR RISK BEARING

All this means that, for risky industries, long-run costs of production must be high enough to include, along with wage and interest costs, *a positive profit premium* to compensate for aversion to risk and coax out the supply of risk bearing.

EXAMPLE: Wheat involves harvest risks due to weather. Production of synthetic rubber does not. Suppose both involve the same wage costs per unit; suppose both involve the same capital outlay per unit. Suppose capital in rubber pays a sure return of 10 per cent, but in wheat there are even odds that on each dollar invested you double your money or lose half of it. Your average return is then $\frac{1}{2}(2.00) + \frac{1}{2}(.50) = 1.25$, or 25 per cent per year. The 15 per cent premium, over and above the safe 10 per cent interest return, is competitively needed profit; and at the intersection of the long-run *dd* and *ss* schedules of the wheat industry, such profit will be included as a cost that must be covered.

We summarize the notion of profit as the reward of risk bearing thus:

**If people generally act like risk averters, feeling that the marginal utility of the dollars they gain is less than that of the dollars they lose, they will prefer smaller steady incomes to erratic incomes even when those average out to a higher figure. Therefore, *economic activities that involve much uncertainty and risk,* which will fall on the people who engage in them, *will be forced by competitive entry and exit of risk takers to pay,* over the long run, a *positive profit premium to compensate for aversion to risk.* The yield on capital invested in such industries will involve, in addition to pure interest corresponding to safe investments, an extra element corresponding to positive profit.**

Here, actually, we have the economist's traditional view of profit—as a fourth component of competitive price to be added to wages, interest, and rent to compensate for risk bearing.

**Competitive price = wage + interest + rent + profit risk-premium**

## FIFTH VIEW: PROFIT AS A "MONOPOLY RETURN"

Most people are critical if not downright suspicious of profit, regarding it (like oil in gears) as at best a necessary evil. The critic of profits does not have in mind implicit wage earnings, or canceling-out risk-premia in competitive markets. His image of the profiteer is more likely that of a fat man with a penchant for sly arithmetic who somehow exploits the rest of the community. Presumably what critics have in mind is a fifth, quite different meaning of profit: *profit as the earnings of monopoly.*[3]

**"Natural scarcities"**   When we examine the ownership of productive factors, we see that no two factors are quite alike. Your abilities as a worker and those of your neighbor are somewhat different. If we define your precise pattern of abilities as a separate factor of production, then we must admit that you do own and control an appreciable fraction of the total of that unique factor of production—100 per cent, in fact. Or you may be the sole owner of the patent to a particular process, or own the only site where the river narrows down to its most suitable place for a bridge. Or there may be no acre of Iowa land quite like yours.

Let us see how this ties in with imperfect competition. Your neighbors are a little different from you, certainly. But probably they are enough like you that the hourly wage rate for your services would not be appreciably higher even if you *withheld* some from the market. You really do not possess any appreciable monopoly power because the demand for the factor you own is, for practical purposes, infinitely elastic.

The same is true of your acre of good Iowa cornland. If you let half of it stand idle, the price of corn would not be affected; and the derived price for each acre of your land would be unchanged, even though you and your family know that there is really no other farmstead quite like it.

And note this: If the land is sufficiently fertile, you will, of course, be making a fine living off your farm. Perhaps you may even be in the top 2 per cent of the income distribution. Even though competition is perfect, this rent return to the land you own

[3] Brief courses may wish to skip the rest of this chapter.

*cannot* be competed away by rival farmers. Because the Good Lord made only a limited amount of fertile Iowa farmland, it will earn a rent for its owner—regardless of how he originally acquired title to the land. *Competitively determined rents are the results of a natural scarcity.* They yield a "surplus" but not a pure profit.[4]

**"Contrived scarcities"**  It is quite a different matter if the demand for one of your factors of production is negatively inclined rather than infinitely elastic. (Let us review what this means: It means that when you raise your price, you still can sell *some* of your factor; this is the sense in which you have some monopoly control over price.) If you are the sole owner of an important patent, it will pay you to charge a price so as to limit its use. If audiences swoon to your singing as to nobody else's, then you will have to remember that the more you sing, the lower will be the price the customers will pay for your singing. If you own the best site for a bridge, then you must be careful not to sell anyone else the lot next to it; otherwise, he will be able to offer the bridge builders a site nearly as good as yours, and this will limit the dollars you can derive from yours. Thus, part of the rent you earn on Nature's bridge site has a monopoly element in it by virtue of your withholding its use for fear of spoiling your dollar market.

What does all this add up to? It means that, *as soon as there is an appreciable deviation from perfect competition, it will pay you to take account of the fact that you will spoil the market the more you offer of your factor.*

Any profit-maximizing firm takes account of the loss on all previous units resulting when it sells an extra unit of product, and it is its marginal revenue—lower than price because of the loss on previous units—which a prudent firm concentrates on. Again with you as the owner of a factor: you are interested in the *marginal,* or *extra, revenue* that the factor brings you. You will not withhold all the factor from the market—that would bring you in *no* revenue at all. Nor will you provide so much of the factor that it becomes a free good and brings in no revenue. As a quasi-monopolist, or imperfect competitor, what will you do to maximize your return? You will withhold just as much of that service as will bring its marginal revenue down to zero and give you maximum return.[5]

Our principle is this: *Under imperfect competition, it pays people to limit the supply of their factors somewhat.* By definition, natural scarcities are such that nothing can be done about them. But under imperfect competition, we encounter in addition so-called "contrived scarcities."

Hence, the fifth view of profits as a monopoly return is often reformulated in the economics textbooks to read as follows:

**Part of what is called profit is the return to a contrived or artificial scarcity.**

---

[4] If there is great inequality in the distribution of ownership of factors of production, then even under the most perfect competition (where pure profit is zero) there can still result a very rich, possibly idle, minority of plutocrats surrounded by masses of lower-income people. Recall Chapter 27's discussion of exploitation, pages 544–545.

[5] Of course, there may be some discomfort to you in rendering the service, or you may have the opportunity of selling the service in some other market—as in the case where you could use your bridge site to grow corn. In these cases, you will obviously equate marginal revenue to some defined positive marginal *cost* rather than to zero.

This return takes the form of rent, wages, or interest, depending upon the nature of the factor in question and on the contractual relations set up to handle the particular situation. (For example, an investor may buy the bridge-site land at the full capitalized value of its monopoly earning power. To him, the return will seem to be interest.) So monopoly profits are inextricably tied up with wages, interest, and rent.

Wherever contrived scarcities exist, they distort the optimum pattern of resource use. They may also create high earnings for the people involved. But high earnings do not always follow. Thus, under imperfect or monopolistic competition, there may be many taxicabs or grocery stores. Each owner may have a sloping demand curve and may be setting a price in excess of marginal cost. Yet there may be so many imperfect competitors that none of them is earning more than he could get in a perfectly competitive industry. Wiping out the imperfections and illegally contrived scarcities may improve the pattern of production, but still might not have much effect on relative distribution of income (see Chamberlin's Fig. 26-3, page 517).

Progressive redistributive taxing of personal and business income, in order to achieve less inequality in the Lorenz curve of income distribution, may itself have some adverse effects on efficiency of resource allocation. High marginal tax rates could diminish risk taking and effort. Or, because of tax loopholes, there might actually result too much venturesomeness.[6]

### SIXTH VIEW: PROFIT AS MARXIAN SURPLUS VALUE

A final view held for profit is that of Karl Marx. Everything in the national income that does not go to the worker—i.e., all return to property, whether it be in the guise of interest or profit—constitutes surplus value.

As will be seen in Chapter 42, Marxians wish to analyze the deviation of capitalist pricing from the "labor theory of value." In that labor theory of value, all goods would sell at their socially necessary labor costs: food which required 2 hours of direct labor to produce would sell for half that of housing which required 4 hours, and one-third that of clothing which required 6 hours of combined direct and indirect labor. Under the strict labor theory of value, all the GNP would go to labor and none to property. (In Proudhon's colorful phrase: "All property is theft!")

But, pointed out Marx, under capitalism the labor is employed by capitalists. These exploiters pay labor less than the product it produces. In the simplest case of Marx, capitalists mark up each commodity by a constant rate over the wages paid—by the "rate of surplus value."

EXAMPLE: Though food costs 2 hours to produce, the worker works 6 hours to buy it. Then the rate of surplus value is 200 per cent: $(6 - 2)/2 = 2.00$. In effect, of the 12-hour day each man toils, he works 4 hours for himself, 8 hours for the exploiting capitalists.

---

[6]Thus, a movie star borrows from a bank to invest in a new firm; he knows his interest will be paid 70 cents on the dollar by the government through his tax savings; he knows, too, that when the firm rises in value and he sells his shares that he will pay only 35 per cent long-term capital-gains tax. A 1953 Harvard Business School study suggests that the rich men it examined were able to keep their tax rates down to 50 per cent on the average, and that taxes pushed some toward venturesome investment. "Appreciation-minded investors . . . may have been so stimulated by the tax structure to seek out investments offering unusually large capital gains potentialities, such as promising new ventures, as actually to increase the flow of capital to such situations." J. K. Butters, L. E. Thompson, and L. L. Bollinger, *Effects of Taxation: Investment by Individuals* (Harvard Business School, Boston, 1953).

Chapter 27 mentioned that something over three-fourths of the national income goes to wages and salaries, and one-fourth to various property owners in interest, rents, profits, etc. Because Marxians would regard many high executive salaries as having in them elements of profit or surplus value, more than one-fourth of the NNP would be regarded as surplus value. Critics ask:

Are any profits necessary? The world's stock of land and capital goods exists; but why should anyone get an income from owning it? Why shouldn't the state get the income (whether reckoned as marginal-products or by whatever rational planning allocation and costing) and distribute it to the workers (i.e., to everybody) in transfer payments or public goods?

Defenders of profits and property incomes reply:

If you don't keep rewinding the clock of entrepreneurial venturing, the nationalized clock will slow down. Resources don't, in a dynamic world, organize themselves; the inherited stock of capital goods will obsolesce, left to anarchism or bureaucratic planning. The checks and balances of competition, plus democratically voted income distribution by progressive taxation of incomes and wealth and by welfare transfer payments, will outperform the good intentions of government ownership and control of production.

The next chapter and its appendix on socialist pricing will return to this fundamental debate. Value judgments, and not merely scientific appraisals of empirical experiences, must obviously play a crucial role in such discussions.

This survey of the variegated notions on profit reveals an important generalization. *Much of the hostility toward profit is really hostility toward the extremes of inequality in the distribution of money income that comes from unequal factor ownership;* this is distinguishable from hostility toward profit created by imperfections of competition. Chapter 40 will return to the challenge of inequality.

## SUMMARY

1   In traditional microeconomic theory, just as competitive price must cover (*a*) *wage* cost of labor, (*b*) *rent* cost of land, and (*c*) *interest* cost of capital, it must also cover (*d*) *profit*-risk-premium cost of inducing people who are averse to variability of returns (plus and minus around mean values) to bear risk.

2   In popular parlance, profit as reported in national-income statistics is a highly miscellaneous category: it is the total of lumped-together corporate earnings and income of unincorporated enterprise. Economically we must distinguish half a dozen different profit concepts.

3   The special category of *high temporary earnings resulting from innovation* is often termed profit by many economists. Routine management earns wages, they say, but profit may accrue to genuine entrepreneurship.

4   *Uncertainty* is the all-pervading fact of life. It makes innovation possible and also creates positive and negative divergences between what factors expect to earn and what they actually end up earning. Pure luck determines much of the dispersion of incomes under free private enterprise. Knight and other economists define profit and loss as the *unforeseeable discrepancies created by uncertainty.*

5   Profit as an undeserved return to property and as the evil fruit of monopoly is a concept with many facets. (*a*) Even if perfect competition prevailed in all goods and factor markets, many critics would deplore the deviation from the labor theory of value represented by any return to landowners, machine owners, or highly paid executives. (*b*) Or the critic may distinguish between competitive rents to "natural scarcities" and monopolists' returns from "contrived scarcities." (*c*) Profit is sometimes regarded as a taxable surplus; or, in Marxian terminology, surplus value is the ethically unwarranted markup over labor costs that causes the worker to toil part of the day for his own wage subsistence and the rest of the day for his capitalist exploiter.

The next chapter will review microeconomic pricing and distribution of income, showing how, under dynamic conditions, the problem of knowledge and information is tied up with the problem of incentives and efficiency criteria.

## CONCEPTS FOR REVIEW

profit as premium for risk bearing
reported statistics of profits
implicit versus explicit factor
    returns
wages of management
innovation, uncertainty
imperfections of competition,
    monopoly

contrived versus natural scarcity
rent and surplus, incentive
    payments
Marxian surplus value
ethical questions and value
    judgments
hostility to profit as hostility to
    income inequality

## QUESTIONS FOR DISCUSSION

1   Contrast, for a safe industry (salt) and a risky industry (apple growing), the breakdown of $P$ into four symbolic components: $P = w + r + i + x$. What is $x$?

2   "It is misleading to talk about 'a profit system.' Ours is a *profit-and-loss* system. Profits are the carrots held out as an incentive to efficiency, and losses are the kicks that penalize using inefficient methods or devoting resources to uses not desired by spending consumers. This metaphor of carrots and kicks is ancient, but apt." Evaluate.

3   Give cases of innovation; of risk taking. How will taxes affect them? What is meant by perfect competition? By imperfect competition? Can you specify a monopoly profit ("contrived" as against "natural") that all will think bad?

4   Discuss ethical and incentive aspects of taxing so-called "profits" or higher incomes.

5   Define "implicit" factor earnings. Contrast with other profit concepts.

6   We each work 12 hours a day: 8 hours for our own subsistence, 4 hours for the capitalist boss. Verify the rate of surplus value as 50 per cent. (HINT: $4/8 = .50$.)

32

EPILOGUE TO
MICROECONOMIC
PRICING

Truth can never be told
so as to be understood
and not be believed.
WILLIAM BLAKE

Parts Three and Four are now completed. We can now give a bird's-eye review of the broad principles of microeconomics—of *value* and *distribution*.

## SURVEY OF THE INTERDEPENDENT PRICING PROCESS

We have seen:

1. How competitive supply and demand operate in a *single* market, in both the short and long run.

2. How the relative marginal-utility (or indifference) preferences of men lie behind their respective demand curves.

3. How marginal costs lie behind the competitive supply curves.

4. How the technical production function relating output to factor inputs lies behind the total and average cost curves, which have been minimized by the firm's demanding inputs until their *marginal-physical-products are proportional to factor-prices.*

5. How these marginal-physical-products and *marginal-revenue-products,* summed for all firms, provide the "derived demands for the factors."

6. How these derived demands for land, labor, or capital goods interact with their market supplies to determine factor-prices such as rent, wages, rentals, and so forth.

7. How primary resources like labor and land are used to make produced capital goods, which are in turn used in roundabout ways to increase society's final output; how this "net productivity of capital" is reflected in the rate of interest, which, in the absence of technical change, is generally subject to diminishing returns in some analogy to the way that labor and land are subject to that law; and how competitive markets evaluate all assets at their "present discounted values," using interest yields to screen out best investments.

8. Finally, how, along with elements of wage, rent, and interest costs, competitive prices have in them an element of profit as the

**629**

systematic premium needed to coax risk-averting people to invest their shiftable funds into industries with great variability of returns around their predictable mean level of returns.[1]

## SIMULTANEOUS MUTUAL DETERMINATION

Notice how, in the listing of the eight steps above, each follows from the preceding one—from step 1 to step 2 and then step 3, until finally we come to step 8. In the textbook chapters they follow in almost the same order.

But in real life, which comes first? Is there any order and sequence, with prices being determined in single markets on Monday, consumers evaluating preferences on Tuesday, businessmen reckoning costs on Wednesday and marginal-products on Thursday? Obviously not. All these processes are going on at one and the same time.

That is not all. These different processes do not go on independently side by side, each in its own little groove, careful not to get in the way of the other. All the processes of supply and demand, of cost and preference, of factor productivity and demand—all these are really different aspects of one vast, simultaneous, *interdependent* process.

Thus, the supply curve for wheat given in the first chapter of Part Three is itself the resultant of the cost calculations given at the end of Part Three, of the production considerations given early in Part Four, and of the wage and rent and interest determinations given late in Part Four. Actually, you can take any one of the eight steps in the outline and draw arrows connecting it causally *with every other step*.

Figure 32-1 gives a summary picture of the interdependent system which economists call "general equilibrium." Recall the circular-flow diagram on national income (Fig. 10-1, page 180), showing plumbing pipes carrying dollars clockwise from business to families and from families to business. That gave what economists call the "aggregative," or "macroeconomic," picture of the nation's grand economic totals.

Now turn to Fig. 32-1. It also gives the circular flow of dollars. But this time we take a microscopic approach—what economists call the "microeconomic" picture. Now we do not talk about the grand total of factor incomes; instead, we show derived demand by business for skilled labor, unskilled labor, good vineyard land, and every other factor of production. Nor do we speak of total consumption: We specify; we show the consumer's demand for coffee, tea, shoes, or any commodity and service.

Note that in the lower loop we have for each factor *both* a supply and a demand. (QUERY: Which of these schedules comes from business? Which from the public? Match orange and brown colors.) And in the upper loop, you see *both* a business supply and consuming-public demand for each good. (Match colors there.)

Thus, we can give an optimistic answer to the logical purist who poses the em-

---

[1] Pursuit of profits and avoidance of loss is supposed to furnish the motive force behind the whole competitive process. Paradoxically, under static conditions free of uncertainty and innovational change, competitive profits—other than implicit factor returns and wages of management—would tend to zero; but dynamic innovational change creates and recreates Schumpeterian profits that are constantly being eroded by imitation under nonmonopolistic competition. Also irreducible Knightian *uncertainty* constantly throws up a divergence—plus and minus!—between equilibrium returns and actual returns of all the factors. Chapter 31 discussed all this.

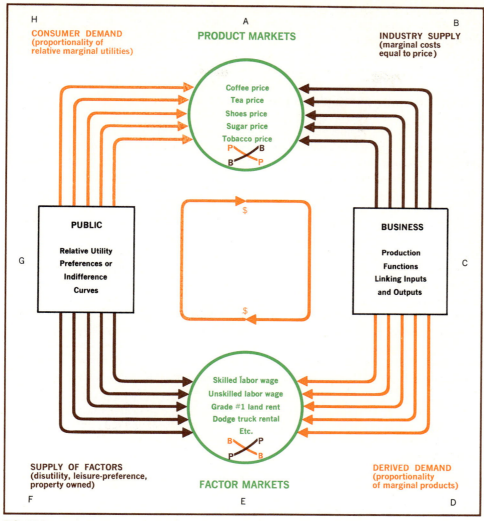

FIG. 32-1

**WHAT, HOW, and FOR WHOM is determined by general-equilibrium pricing**

The clockwise money flow is broken up to show consumer demand meeting industry supply at *A* to determine equilibrium price and quantity of each good. Similarly, derived factor demands of business meet public's supply of factors at *E* to determine equilibrium factor-prices and amounts. (Interpret what is going on behind *B, D, F,* and *H*—and inside *C* and *G*—and compare this with the WHAT, HOW, and FOR WHOM of Fig. 3-1, on page 46.)

barrassing question: "Your economic system isn't determinate until you have found conditions to determine a price *and* a quantity for each output and for each input. Do you have enough simultaneous conditions (or equations) to make your interdependent equilibrium system determinate?"

Fortunately, we can answer: "We do have for each output or input *both a supply and a demand condition*. So we can hope that the system will, by trial and error in the marketplace, finally settle down—if left undisturbed!—to a determinate competitive equilibrium."[2] And we can add: "The final competitive equilibrium is an 'efficient' one. Because prices equal marginal costs, output is being maximized, inputs are being minimized; because prices reflect relative marginal utilities for each consumer, people who like apples are not being given oranges, etc. From so efficient a final point, you can no longer make everyone better off. You can help Joe only by hurting Tom."

Figure 32-1 is the final development of Fig. 3-1, where we first asked how a price system goes about solving WHAT, HOW, and FOR WHOM. Only after mastering the tools of Parts Three and Four can we present this culmination of our original inquiry.

## IMPERFECTIONS OF COMPETITION

This survey proceeded on the basis of some heroically abstract assumptions: no monopolies, no imperfections, no dynamic innovations or unforeseen disturbances, no governmental distortions, and so forth. Figure 32-1, therefore, is like the no-friction model of the physicist; it is not a picture of the real world as we know it when we step outside the library and rub elbows with real, live, breathing people on the street.

Yet, even though every engineer knows he must meet friction, he does find the frictionless model a valuable tool in throwing light on complicated reality. So it is with our ideal competitive model. In the long run, many imperfections turn out to be transient. *The competitive model, therefore, may suggest in its oversimple way some interesting hypotheses that turn out to have a measure of long-run validity!*

EXAMPLE: An invention cuts cost of aluminum; the competitive model says price will fall and pressure will be put on use and price of steel. The sophisticated student of imperfect competition says the real world is not perfectly competitive, so no hard-and-fast conclusion can be drawn. Still, bet with him that the prices will fall *in the long run*—and probably you will win his money. A sure thing? No, but often a good bet.

Even if we agree that the perfect-competition model does give some approximate descriptions of reality, we cannot be satisfied with such crude approximations. Fifty years ago an economics textbook would have had to confine itself to the case of perfect competition, and let it go at that. Thanks to the pioneering work in the theory of imperfect and monopolistic competition over the last generation, economists now have the tools (marginal revenue, etc.) to analyze oligopoly, monopoly, differentiation of products of numerous sellers, collective bargaining, and various intermediate cases. (Recall Chapters 25 and 26.)

We have seen that prices are often inflexibly administered, changing rarely and

---

[2] Léon Walras, a French economist three-quarters of a century ago, is usually credited with the discovery of general equilibrium. But W. S. Jevons of England, C. Menger of Austria, Alfred Marshall and F. Y. Edgeworth of England, J. B. Clark of America, Vilfredo Pareto of Italy, and Knut Wicksell of Sweden all made significant contributions; and, even in Adam Smith, you can hunt out the germ of the idea of general equilibrium. By use of topology and set theory, the system has now been analyzed with rigor, thanks to J. von Neumann, A. Wald, K. J. Arrow, G. Debreu, and others.

subject only to minor, hidden discounts, which is in contrast with the minute-to-minute volatility and year-to-year gyrations of competitive prices. We have seen that two workingmen may work in the same city at different wage rates for comparable work; that interference by a union with wage setting may correct a previous monopsony condition of unequal bargaining, or may increase the departure from the model of perfect competition. We have seen Chamberlinian cases where free entry may squeeze out profits while still leaving price above minimum average costs. We shall see that prejudice under laissez faire may lead to unequal employment opportunity and both social inefficiency and inequity. We have emphasized repeatedly, and shall have reason to emphasize again, that "externalities" distort the system from its efficiency and optimality conditions. (Polluting products do not bear their full social costs. Knowing we cannot appropriate to ourselves all the returns from our inventing, we spend too little under laissez faire on research and development.)

There is no need, therefore, to warn against overemphasis on the elegant model of perfect competition as a close description of economic reality.

## A WORD ON WELFARE ECONOMICS

Even if perfect competition were a poorer descriptive tool than it is, students of economics would still want to study it intensively and master its principles. This is so for a reason unconnected with mere description. The competitive model is extremely important in providing a bench mark to appraise the *efficiency* of an economic system. Russians, Chinese, Indians, as well as Swiss, need to study its analytical principles.

For the most part in science, scholars discuss what *is* and what will be under this or that situation. The task of positive description is kept as free as is humanly possible from the taint of wishful thinking and ethical concern about what ought to be. Why? Because scientists are cold-blooded robots? No, because experience shows that a more accurate job of positive description will be achieved if one *tries* to be objective. (Experience also shows that, try as we may, we humans never succeed in separating completely the objective and subjective aspects of a discipline. Indeed, the very choice of what scientists choose to measure, and the perspective from which they observe and measure it, and the reactions the observer produces in that which is observed—all these make the distinction between *is* and *ought*, between objective and subjective issues, at bottom a matter of degree rather than kind. Recall, for example, Chapter 1's bird-antelope paradox and be warned that Part Six will be much concerned with policy and value judgments.)

The citizenry, unlike the specialist, is in the end most interested in problems of "norms," of what *ought* to be done, of policy rather than mere description. That citizenry is best served by the scientist who can give it the most accurate description of what is relevant, and of what the consequences of different policy actions will be.

Very briefly then, in this epilogue, let us again devote a few lines to implications for economic welfare that have been developed in Parts Three and Four.

**Efficiency optimality**   First, we have seen repeatedly that a regime of perfectly competitive pricing would have certain efficiency properties if conditions were really present for maintaining perfect competition. Adam Smith, in his talk about an Invisible Hand which leads the selfish actions of individuals toward so harmonious a final result, did have some point. Smith never could state or prove exactly what that point was, but modern economics can state this property of ideal competitive pricing:

**Under perfectly perfect competition, where all prices end up equal to all marginal costs, where all factor-prices end up equal to values of marginal-products and all total costs are minimized, where the genuine desires and well-being of individuals are all represented by their marginal utilities as expressed in their dollar voting—*then* the resulting equilibrium has the efficiency property that "you can't make any one man better off without hurting some other man."**

What does this mean exactly? It means that a planner could not come along with a slide rule and find a solution, different from the laissez faire one, which could improve the welfare of everyone.[3]

**Arbitrary distribution of dollar votes**   What does competitive efficiency not mean? It does not mean that actual laissez faire, with the imperfections of competition that will go with it, leads to efficiency or necessarily even to a close approximation to efficiency. And inefficiency aside, it does *not* mean that *the people who are deemed by various religious or ethical observers to be most worthy, most deserving, or most needy will necessarily get their ethically best share of goods and services.*

Laissez faire perfect competition *could* lead to starving cripples; to malnourished children who grow up to produce malnourished children; to perpetuation of Lorenz curves of great inequality of incomes and wealth for generations or forever. Or, if the initial distribution of dollar-wealth votes, genetic abilities, early conditioning, and training happened to be appropriate, perfect competition might lead to a rather egalitarian society characterized by uniformity greater than might please many an aristocratic, ethical tradition. Or more likely, lead to inequality deemed too glaring.

In short, Adam Smith, in the famous passage quoted on page 41, had no right to assert that an Invisible Hand successfully channels individuals who selfishly seek their own interest into promoting the "public interest"—as these last two words might be defined by a variety of prominent ethical and religious notions of what constitutes the welfare of a nation. Smith has proved nothing of this kind, nor has any economist since 1776.

**Redefining the Invisible Hand doctrine**   If Smith were alive today, he would agree with all this; and one ventures the guess, from his biography, that he would probably reword his doctrine pretty much along the following lines.

1. Only if abilities and *dollar-wealth votes were originally distributed in "an ethically optimal" manner*—and kept so distributed by nondistorting, nonmarket interventions— could even perfectly competitive pricing be counted on (*a*) to produce an efficient configuration of production out on society's production-possibility frontier (and not

---

[3]If *A* is the competitive equilibrium, there is no point *B* the planner could devise which could be approved over *A* by a *unanimous* vote. Some would be hurt in going to *B*, some might gain; but the gainers could never find it worthwhile to give big enough bribes to win the losers over to approving the move to *B*. We've already encountered this notion of "Pareto optimality," named after Pareto's work at the turn of the century as elucidated in our time by Abram Bergson of Harvard.

inside it), and (*b*) to give people what they really deem is best for them, in accordance with their dollar votes that now reflect equally significant social utility. But, if laissez faire were abandoned in favor of an ethically proper distribution of wealth and opportunity, then perfect-competition equilibrium could be used as an instrument to attain optimally efficient and equitable organization of society.

2. Admittedly, *the demands of people in the marketplace sometimes do not reflect their true well-beings* as these would be interpreted by even the most tolerant and individualistic of ethical observers. (EXAMPLES: A dope addict's craving for heroin even at the expense of his food or his children's food; a child's desire for a seventh lollipop; a diabetic's craving for sweets; a spendthrift's mortgaging his house for an advertised sports car.) As a pragmatist, were Smith alive today, he would say, "People are entitled to make their own mistakes in many matters, but it is arrogant to think that anyone who is not a minor or a certifiable mental incompetent is in every respect a sovereign will; as men, conscious that we were born not perfect and as inhabitants of a post-Freudian world, *we* shall sparingly and for good cause want (with due process) democratically to place restrictions on *our own* behavior. So again, laissez faire perfect competition would not inevitably be the ideal."

Then, after emphasizing the need for tolerance and the virtues of freedom, Smith might strike a more technical note.

3. Where there are *monopolistic imperfections* that produce deviations from ideal competitive marginal-cost pricing—and in situations of strong increasing returns and decreasing costs, such deviations are practically inevitable—of course there is a prima facie case that laissez faire pricing is not efficient. Public scrutiny, to see whether democratic controls would make the situation better or worse, has to be presumed in such quasi-monopoly situations.

4. Finally, Smith would add that wherever there are "external economies and diseconomies" (such as were analyzed at the end of Chapter 24 and in the discussion of public versus private goods in Chapter 8), there is a prima facie case for study to see whether zoning laws, taxes or subsidies, and government expenditure and regulation should be initiated in some degree. Where the checks and balances of perfect competition are not operative, the Darwinian struggle for existence is not led by an Invisible Hand to any kind of optimum. The creative role of government in economic life is vast and inescapable in an interdependent, crowded world.

## CONCLUSION

The reader is warned that all the above issues of welfare economics can be given varying interpretations and can lead to controversial debate which cannot be presumed to be settleable within positive science. Conservatives may legitimately interpret the above principles in terms of their version of the good society. Middle-of-the-roaders may do the same for theirs. And radicals may call for small or large reforms of the present structure of a mixed economy by giving their interpretation of these principles. That means the reader may do so, too. Economic science arms one for the great debate; it does not preclude that debate or prejudice its conclusions.

The following Appendix gives in greater depth a view of the efficiency aspect of the system of interdependent economic pricing under capitalism or socialism.

# APPENDIX: Review of Commodity and Factor Pricing: General Equilibrium and the Parable of Ideal Welfare Pricing

## PARABLE OF UTOPIAN PRICING

Economists used to be twitted that their books always harp on Robinson Crusoe. True enough: we do find that the economic decisions of a single man furnish a dramatic way of simplifying our basic principles. But these days we have an even more dramatic device for illustrating the fundamental facts of economic life: we use the example of a fully collectivized society. This retains the same simplicity of ultimate decision making, but at the same time it involves the social interactions between people that the Crusoe model lacks. The contrast between such a model and our realistic everyday world is, of course, enormous. And therein lies its value. By examining the logic of such a model, we get new insight into the nature of our own pricing system.

Let us, therefore, examine how our economic analysis of pricing can apply to a completely artificial planned society of the kind never seen in Russia, China, or anywhere else. Call it Utopia or call it Hades. By analyzing pricing in a planned socialist state, we kill two birds with one stone:

1. We get one of the best possible reviews of the working of a perfect *capitalistic* price system.

2. We get an introduction to "welfare economics," the study of what is considered right and wrong about any economic system. This depends, of course, upon ethical points of view, themselves necessarily beyond science. But the economist may help to throw light on how successfully an economic system realizes any suggested ethical *goals*.

## A DILEMMA FOR CENTRALIZED PLANNING

The earlier chapters of this book have shown how a system of market prices operates to solve the basic economic problems of WHAT, HOW, and FOR WHOM. To drive home what all this really means, try a mental experiment. Suppose you were given the job of making the blueprints for a completely planned economic system. How might you begin?

First, let us suppose you are interested in giving people what *they* want, not in telling them what they *ought* to want. Obviously, you cannot give them everything they want: land, labor, capital goods, and technological knowledge are limited in amount. So you must make compromises and choices.

You may say: This is merely a complicated mathematical problem, calling for the use of lots of high-powered, electronic, high-speed calculating machines. But remember that we shall have to deal with the millions of items that are to be found in department stores, with thousands of grades of productive factors, and with numerous individuals and families. The number of unknowns of the mathematical problem will be in the millions, and the number of steps to its solution in the billions of billions. No known set of computing machines can tackle such a problem.

You are stumped. And discouraged. Perhaps you will lower your sights and stop being a perfectionist. Instead of giving people exactly what they think they want, you may decide that there are to be only a few types of, say, shoe styles and sizes, so that the calculation problem will be simplified. Or you may abandon individual freedom of choice and give people goods that *you* find it convenient to give them.

One thing is clear: If centralized planning means that one centralized person or committee must have in mind all the myriad intricacies of detail, then it is an impossible job to do with any efficiency.[1]

So you will naturally begin to experiment with various devices to *decentralize* the job. And quite possibly you will end up by introducing a *pricing* system in many ways like that of capitalism.

How might such a system work?

## PRICING IN A UTOPIAN STATE: CONSUMER-GOOD PRICES

In your new society, the consumer will still have *freedom of choice* and will not have dictated to him the relative amounts of different commodities which he is to "enjoy." As in the capitalist system, each

---

[1] Perhaps Lenin had his tongue in cheek when, just prior to the October Revolution of 1917, he wrote: "The bookkeeping and control necessary for this [production and distribution] have been simplified by capitalism to the utmost, till they become the extraordinarily simple operations of watching, recording, and issuing receipts, within the reach of anybody who can read and write and knows the first four rules of arithmetic." This is as ironic as his later characterization of Communism as "democracy plus electricity," a witty half-truth like the aphorism attributed to him: "Liberty is precious—so precious it must be rationed."

person will receive a sum of money or abstract purchasing power to spend among commodities as he wishes. Thus, vegetarians will not have to eat meat, and those who prefer meat can buy it.

How will relative prices between salmon and ham and any other consumers' goods be set by the socialist state? Generally speaking, prices will be set with the same double purpose as in a capitalist society:

1. Just high enough to ration out the existing supplies of consumer goods, so none are left over and none are short;

2. Just high enough to cover the socially necessary extra costs of producing the goods in question. In technical terms, relative *P*s are to be set equal to relative "marginal utilities" and "marginal costs."

## THE DISTRIBUTION OF INCOME

So far, the process has worked much like the capitalistic system. Almost by definition, however, socialism means a society in which most land and capital goods or nonhuman resources of all kinds are owned collectively by society and not individually by people. In our society, an Astor who owns 500 parcels of New York City land, each of which produces $80,000 of net rents per year, will receive an income of $40 million per year—which may be 10,000 times what a night watchman is able to earn, and 2,000 times what the average skilled engineer can earn. In a society where most property is owned collectively rather than distributed with great inequality among different individuals, an important source of inequality of income would be absent.

Many people profess to hold the ethical and philosophical belief that different individuals' wants and needs are very much alike, and that the present market mechanism works inadequately because the rich are given so many more votes in the control of production than the poor—which makes the market demand for goods a faulty indicator of their true social worth.

Such people with a relatively egalitarian philosophy will welcome a great reduction in the spread of incomes between the lowest 90 per cent of all families and the highest 10 per cent. They may argue that taking away $1,000 from a man with an income of $100,000 and giving it to a man with an income of $5,000 will add to social well-being (by taking dollars from a place deemed low in marginal social utility to a place deemed higher).

After the distribution of income between families has been determined correctly, according to society's fundamental (a-scientific) value judgments, then and only then will it be true that the dollars coming on the market will be valid indicators of the value of goods and services; and only then will they be serving to direct production into the proper channels and goods into the right hands.

Hence, *lump-sum taxes and transfers will be used in Utopia to give ethically proper income distribution.* So goes the argument.

**Social dividends**  How is that which is considered the proper ethical distribution of income to be achieved—aside from by the negative act of wiping out unduly high property owning and the appropriate lump-sum taxing of individuals?

Perfectionists have two answers: (1) in part, by letting people get some of their income in the form of wages; but (2) in part, by having these wages supplemented by receipt of a lump-sum *social dividend payment* or negative income tax. This cash payment in an egalitarian society might involve differences to compensate for numbers of children, age, health, and abilities acquired or inherited.

It is an ethical rather than a scientific question as to just how large, relatively, each person's final income ought to be. As a pure science, economics can concern itself only with the best means of attaining given ends; it cannot prescribe the ends themselves.

Indeed, if someone decided that he preferred a feudal-fascistic kind of society in which all people with little black mustaches were to be given especially high incomes, a pathological economist could set up the pricing rules for him to follow to best achieve his strange design. He would be told to determine his social dividend payments to achieve the required optimal distribution of income, after which each dollar coming on the market could be regarded as correctly representing (that eccentric's) true social values.

The social dividend differs from a wage because it is to be given to every individual *regardless of his own efforts.* That is why it is called a "lump-sum" dividend or transfer.[2] (Any bonus based upon productivity or effort is to be treated as a wage.)

We have not yet seen how wages are to be determined, but before doing so, let us first turn to another important problem.

---

[2] If the state is providing public goods for the people which require greater use of resources than the state owns, most of the social dividends may have to be negative—lump-sum taxes rather than transfers.

## PRICING OF NONHUMAN PRODUCTIVE RESOURCES AND INTERMEDIATE GOODS

What should be the role of land and other nonhuman productive resources as an element of cost in such a utopia?

Some people would say that such nonhuman resources should not enter into cost at all; that only human sweat and skill are the true source of all value; and that any extra charges based upon the cost of land or machinery represent a capitalistic surplus that the owners of property are able to squeeze out of the exploited laboring masses by virtue of the private ownership of the means of production. We have seen that this view is the traditional "labor theory of value" of Karl Marx and John Locke. (Learned scholars dispute just what Marx meant by the "labor theory" and whether he meant it to apply to a socialist economy in the short or long run.)

We need not enter into this dispute. However, it is important to note that, in its simple form, *the labor theory of value will lead to incorrect and inefficient use of both labor and nonlabor resources in even the most perfect socialist society.*

So long as any economic resource is limited in quantity—i.e., *scarce* rather than free—the socialist planners must give it a price and charge a rent for its use. This price need not, as in the case of the Astor millionaire under the capitalistic system, determine any individual's income. It can be a purely bookkeeping or accounting price (or so-called "shadow price") set up by the planners, rather than a market price. But there must be a price put upon the use of every such resource.

Why? First, we must price nonhuman resources to ensure that society is deciding HOW goods shall be produced in the best way, so that we really end up on the true production-possibility frontier of society and not somewhere inside it.[3] It would be absurd to get rid of the capitalistic system with its alleged wastes due to unemployment, and then, by stupid planning, end up far inside society's true production potentialities.

Related to the above point is the second need for all resources to be given a value if correct higher prices are to be charged for those final goods *that use up a great deal of scarce resources.* In other words, for society to find itself in the best choice among all possible positions on the production-possibility frontier, we must price such con-

sumption goods as food and clothing to reflect their true relative (extra or marginal) costs of using up *all* scarce resources. Otherwise, even with incomes equitably distributed, the free choice exerted by consumers on their dollar spending will not truly maximize their own and society's preferences, with *utilities and costs properly balanced at the margin.*

## THE EXAMPLE OF LAND RENT

The foregoing two reasons may be hard to grasp. However, let us try to make the necessity for nonlabor pricing clear by considering a single land example. Suppose there are twins in a farming utopia. What if one were to produce wheat on an acre of good land, and the other were to produce less wheat by the same year's work on an acre of bad land. If they are identical twins, working equally hard, we would certainly have to agree that their wages ought to be the same.

Now, if wages were to be treated as the only cost, in accord with the simple labor theory of value, then the same price could not be charged for the two different outputs of wheat, even though the kernels of wheat were identical. The good-land wheat would have involved lower labor costs and would then have to sell for less than the poor-land wheat.

This, of course, is absurd. A well-wishing social planner might try to get around the dilemma by charging the same price for both, losing money on the poor-land wheat and gaining on the other. Or, what is not quite the same thing, he might say, "To keep the costs of the two wheats the same, let's pay the twin on bad land lower wages; but then let's make the one brother share his wages with the poorer."

Such a solution is not absurd, but it falls short of achieving the desired best results: maximum production and equal pay for equal human effort. In particular, *it fails to shift more labor onto the more productive land.*

The only correct procedure is to put an accounting price or rent tag on each land, with the good land having the higher tag. The prices of both kinds of wheat will be equal, because the land cost ("Ricardian rent") of the good-land wheat will be just enough higher than that of the poor-land wheat to make up the difference.

Most important of all, the socialist production manager must try to minimize the combined labor and land cost of producing each kind of wheat. If he does so according to the marginal-product principles dis-

---

[3] See Question 4 of Chapter 27's Appendix for proof.

cussed in Part Four, he will accomplish something undreamed of by the simple believer in the labor theory of value.

He will find it pays to work the good land more intensively, perhaps with the time of $1\frac{1}{2}$ men, until the extra product there has been lowered by the law of diminishing returns so as to be just equal to the extra product on the poor land. Only by putting a price upon inert, sweatless land are we using it, and sweating, breathing labor, most productively! The price or rent of land rises in order to ration its limited supply among the *best* uses.

Note, too, that the most finicky humanitarian will have nothing to complain of in our solution. By transferring labor from one acre to the other until labor's marginal productivity has been made equal, we get the largest possible total production of wheat.[4]

The two brothers are paid the same wages because they have worked equally hard. But their wages are not high enough to buy all the wheat, since part of the cost of the wheat has come from (bookkeeping) land-rent charges. However, the people through their government own the land equally. The land's return does not go to any property owner but is available to be distributed as a lump-sum social dividend to both brothers according to their ethical deserts.

**By putting a proper accounting price or rent on land, society has more consumption than otherwise!**

If we turn now to the production of more than one consumer good, it will be obvious that their cost prices must be made to reflect the amount of socially limited land and machinery which they each use up. Field crops like wheat require little labor and much land compared with garden crops like tomatoes. If we price each good on the basis of labor costs alone, wheat will sell for too little, and too much land will be forced out of tomato production. All people will be worse off than they need be.

## MARGINAL-COST PRICING

One last point concerning the final determination of a product's cost and price. After the costs of all

necessary factors of production have been added together to arrive at total cost, the planning authorities must set their prices at the marginal cost of production. Or more accurately, the socialist managers of a plant must behave like a perfect competitor: they must *disregard* any influence that their own production might have on market price and must continue to produce extra units up to the point where the last little unit costs just its selling price.

For many industries, such as railroads, where unit costs are constantly falling, setting marginal costs equal to price will imply that *full* average costs are not covered. In a noncapitalistic society the difference would be made up by an (accounting) lump-sum grant from the state; for, if a railroad system is worth building, it is worth being utilized well.[5]

---

[5] The long-run question as to whether to build a railroad in the first place may involve an "all-or-none decision," which cannot be made step by step. In such a case, there must still be a balancing of the extra (or marginal) advantage and extra cost to society of the enterprise. But for such a big step, price is no longer a good indicator of total welfare, since—as we saw in Chapter 22—there is always an element of consumer's surplus in the total amount of goods a person consumes over what he has paid for them.

Figure 32-2 pictures a case where $dd$, which we assume reflects true marginal utilities to society, everywhere lies below decreasing long-run $AC$. So pricing at long-run $MC$ can never recover full long-run social costs. Yet, with the $a$ area clearly larger than the $b$ area, the total-utility area under $dd$ is greater than the total-cost area under $LMC$. So society should produce at $E$, giving a lump-sum subsidy to cover the inevitable loss or somehow getting people to pay

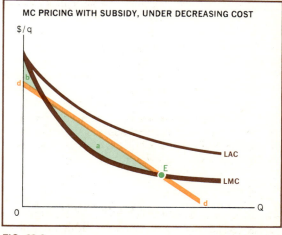

MC PRICING WITH SUBSIDY, UNDER DECREASING COST

FIG. 32-2

---

[4] As earlier discussions of marginal productivity have shown, *total product will be at a maximum only when labor has been transferred from the land where its marginal-product is low to the good land where its marginal-product is high.* Every such transfer must necessarily yield us extra product, until finally no further increases in output can result when the marginal-products have been equalized in the two uses.

## RULES FOR RESOURCE PRICING

Correct social planning requires that all scarce resources, whether human labor or not, be given accounting prices at least. The final costs of consumer goods should include the sum total of *all* extra costs necessary to produce each good, or, in short, should equal *marginal cost*. The demand for consumer goods is really an indirect demand for all productive resources, a demand which can be kept in proper check only by putting appropriate valuations on productive resources.

Otherwise, society's valuable nonhuman—and human!—resources will be incorrectly allocated and the market pricing of finished goods will not lead to maximum consumer's satisfaction. It is to be emphasized that the accounting prices of land and other nonhuman resources need not, in a socialist state, be part of the incomes of anyone. In the language of the visionary critic of private enterprise: no one is "exploited" by having a property owner skim off part of the final product. Instead, the contribution of capital and land to production is given to deserving people in the form of government goods and the algebraic *social dividend*.

## ROLE OF THE INTEREST RATE IN UTOPIA

We have seen that the interest rate has an important function in a capitalistic, socialistic, or any other kind of economic system. Capital goods have a "net productivity." As long as resources can be invested for the present or the future, it will be necessary to make important decisions with respect to capital. Shall we apply present land and labor to the production of a corn crop this year or to apples 15 years from now?

Shall we have grape juice today or wine 10 years hence? Shall we replace a worn-out loom with a new, expensive one which yields its services over 20 years, or buy a cheap one that will last only 14 years?

Every one of these questions can be answered only by using an interest rate to relate future and present economic values. Without such an interest rate, the existing stock of fixed and circulating capital goods cannot be devoted to their best uses; and whatever amount of national income society has decided to invest in capital formation cannot be embodied in the best form without such an interest rate.

**The interest rate acts as a sieve or rationing device: all projects that can yield 10 per cent are undertaken before any projects that yield only 8 per cent.**

It should be added that many economic writers on socialism do not think that the rate of interest should also determine—as it does in our economy, to some degree—the rate at which capital growth is to take place at the expense of current consumption. The decision as to how much should be saved would be determined by the state "in the light of national and social needs," and not by the "haphazard" notions of individuals with respect to the future. But the level of social saving and capital growth once having been determined, the interest rate must be used to allocate scarce "capital supplies" optimally and to determine the priority of alternative projects.[6]

## WAGE RATES AND INCENTIVE PRICING

We must now return to the problem of how the utopian planners would set wage rates, and then we are done. If the amounts of labor of all kinds and of all skills were perfectly fixed, there would be no reason why labor should not be given accounting prices just like any other productive factor. Workers would receive no wages at all. They would then receive all the national income as an enlarged *social dividend*.

However, if heterogeneous people are to be free to choose their own occupations and be given the choice of working a little harder and longer in return for extra consumption goods, then it will be neces-

---

more for their earlier units that yielded great consumer surplus. (EXAMPLES: A railroad line to a country region; a monorail for urban commuters.) If *dd* shifted down enough to make *a* < *b*, the whole project should never be undertaken in the first place, or should not ultimately be replaced. Even if *dd* shifted up a bit, so that part of it lay above *LAC* and price could cover all costs, *P* still should be kept down to *LMC* for efficient pricing. (All this needs qualifications if dollars do not represent true and constant marginal utility and true social costs, as in a world of many monopolies and in making big decisions.) Also, taxing to finance the subsidy may involve some distortions: so we may have to settle for a second-best solution with *P* between *LMC* and *LAC*.

[6]There is no logical reason why individuals who are willing to forgo present for future consumption should not be permitted to do such voluntary extra saving and receive an interest return equal to the net productivity of capital.

sary to set up a system of *actual market wages* at which people can sell their services. These wage rates will be set just high enough to equate demand and supply for labor.

Wages may differ depending upon how the irksomeness of the job affects voluntary labor supplied; and, unlike now, the pleasanter jobs may then be less well paid, and the ditchdiggers or garbage collectors may have to be more highly paid to attract people into these jobs. Piece rates might be used, and a worker with a 20 per cent higher productivity will be receiving higher (pretax and pre-social-dividend) wages. Workers will in every case be offered wages equal to their marginal, or extra, productivity.

Therefore, it is not necessarily true that all incomes will be at a dead level in the utopian society. They will differ somewhat as a result of two distinct factors: (1) society's appraisal of the "needs and worth" of different individuals and families—as reflected primarily in the size of the individuals' lump-sum *social dividends,* and (2) the need for wages to differ to provide incentives and to compensate people for extra disutility and effort. Incomes need not differ, however, because of inequality in the ownership and inheritance of property and genetic talents. Wage rents (like Babe Ruth's) and rents to state-financial training could be heavily lump-sum-taxed, exactly like Henry George's surplus land rents.

## SUMMARY OF UTOPIAN PRICING

1. A utopian system could make use of four different kinds of pricing: (*a*) consumer-good prices, (*b*) wage and incentive rates, (*c*) accounting prices of intermediate goods or produced inputs, and (*d*) final lump-sum dividends (when positive, transfers; when negative, taxes). The first three prices would be determined by supply and demand. Any consumption good would be produced up to the point where the full marginal cost of production (necessary to keep all resources from other uses and from leisure) is just equal to the price.[7]

2. The final distribution of income would be made to correspond to what society regards as the ideal distribution pattern by means of payment of a lump-sum social supplement or dividend to people, depending upon "need, wants, and deservingness," but not—like a wage—on effort or performance. In Utopia, it might be felt that a much more nearly equal distribution of income will be necessary before the dollar votes of consumers can be expected to reflect true social preferences. However, this is an a-scientific, ethical question; and a misanthrope could use the same economic principles to run an *in*egalitarian utopia.

3. None of these processes except the last requires detailed *comprehensive planning by a central agency.* Mathematicians would not have to be called in to solve thousands and thousands of simultaneous equations. Instead, the *decentralized planners* would proceed by successive approximation, by trial and error—setting provisional market and accounting prices and cutting them or raising them, depending upon whether available supplies are piling up or running short.

It would be naïve to think that any actual society would succeed in reaching the ideal equilibrium positions described above. Errors of foresight would inevitably be made. Existing vested interests, anxious to preserve their security in a dynamic world of change, would resist and sabotage such change in the same qualitative fashion as they have done in historical societies. Even where politicians and the electorate do not pay much attention to the incentive mechanisms outlined in the preceding pages, the importance of this discussion is that it teaches us how to appraise the mechanical efficiency of pricing in a *non*socialist society.

## BRIEF HISTORY OF WELFARE PRICING

A brief history of welfare-pricing doctrines may be of interest. From Smith's time at least, men saw beauty in the laissez faire mechanism and inferred that it must have teleological significance in giving efficiency. But they were often uncritical, and often they overlooked the assumption that dollar votes

---

[7] The decentralized managers of industries could generally achieve this by seeking to maximize their net algebraic profits, measured in accounting points or actual dollars, but with *all P*s taken as given parameters. (NOTE: Under cost conditions suitable for viable laissez faire, such behavior is actually policed by competition, but where bureaucrats "play the game of competition," there may be a hard administrative problem to make sure they do act as price-takers.)

were to be distributed in the ethically desired way; and they could not prove what they believed.

Around 1900 Pareto showed that an ideal socialism would have to solve the same equations as competitive capitalism. Around 1920, Ludwig von Mises, perhaps unaware of Pareto's proof, set forth the challenging view that rational economic organization was *logically* impossible in the absence of free markets. Fred Taylor of Michigan, A. P. Lerner of England and California, and Oskar Lange of Poland answered Mises with the view that socialism could conceptually solve the problems of economic organization by a decentralized process of bureaucratic trial and error—"playing the game of competition" and "deliberately planning not to plan."

F. A. Hayek has argued that this answer overlooks the problem of giving *each man the initiative* to better the existing allocation of resources and that only with actual free enterprise do you efficiently utilize the dispersed information which each of us may possess. He points out that it is naïve to think that production and cost functions are known. They and shifting demand functions must be learned and be improved on. Who can police the Lerner-Lange decentralized bureaucrats to motivate them to play this competition game? And who can audit that they truly do, if their self-interest in the form of profits or higher incomes is not involved? (The final chapter will discuss the trends in the communist economies of Eastern Europe (Yugoslavia, the Soviet Union, etc.) toward more reliance on market pricing and profitability calculations.)

## MIXED-ECONOMY WELFARE ECONOMICS

On the basis of the above principles of pricing, we are in a position to see what friendly and unfriendly critics think is wrong in our system, or not necessarily right from various ethical viewpoints. Critics list these deviations from the social optimum:

1. The existing distribution of property, income, education, and economic opportunity is the result of past history and does not necessarily represent an optimum condition according to the ethical philosophies of Christianity, Buddhism, paganism, the American creed, or other ideologies. Defenders of the mixed economy counter with the claim that such deviations from the optimum distribution can be corrected by appropriate tax policies, if that is desired. (There are, though, some costs to be incurred from

such policies because of taxation effects upon incentives, risk taking, effort, and productivity.)

2. The widespread presence of monopoly elements in our system and the limited appearance of perfect competition mean that production is rarely being pushed to the optimum point of equality of marginal cost to price; because the elasticity of demand is not infinite to imperfect competitors, production is pushed only to the point of equality of marginal cost to marginal revenue. Because of the fear of "spoiling the market," monopoly price is then too high and its output is too low relative to competitive outputs.

This is related to a further Chamberlinian evil under imperfect competition when entry of new firms into an industry is very easy. There may then tend to be an inefficient division of production among too many firms; the *P* charged is too high, but, through wasteful use of resources, no one need be making any profits.

3. Remember also the failure of laissez faire pricing to deal properly with "externalities." (For example, the fact that individual firms, in making their decisions, do not take into account some possible effects of their production decisions on *other* firms or industries. In digging his oil well, Pat does not mind that he may be robbing Mike's oil pool; and the same with Mike—with the result that less oil is obtained in the end, and with more cost.) Because of such "external diseconomies or economies," apparent "private marginal costs" do not reflect true "social marginal costs"; and certain lines of activity deserve to be contracted and others to be expanded.[8]

4. Finally, of course, as shown in Part Two, under a laissez faire system, there may be great wastes due to unemployment and the business cycle. Consumers, labor, farmers, and business, together with public fiscal and monetary policy, must be mobilized in a never-ending war against this social scourge—poverty which has no real cause but stems only from an intricately misbehaving monetary society.

---

[8] Compare A. C. Pigou, *Economics of Welfare* (Macmillan, New York, 1932), which stresses externalities.

The paradox that really perfect competition would discourage people from inventing (since they would know their profits would disappear) can be understood in terms of external economies: my pecuniary reward from an invention may be much less than its social value after it has been widely imitated. Governmental activities are needed when "public goods" involve external benefits to more than one person at the same time, as shown in Chapter 8. See, too, Chapter 24's discussion, pp. 476–478.

## SUMMARY TO APPENDIX

1   In a pure, unmixed, competitive society, the economic problems of WHAT shall be produced, HOW, and FOR WHOM are solved in an interdependent manner by the impersonal workings of profit-and-loss markets. Each variable depends upon every other, but all tend to be simultaneously determined at their general-equilibrium values by a process of successive approximations and readjustments.

2   Unless a utopian economy were uninterested in efficiency and economizing, or in freedom of choice of goods and jobs, it would have to institute a system of pricing. However, some prices would be purely accounting or bookkeeping figures; in addition, the final determination of the distribution of income would involve an outright social dividend or tax, in various lump-sum amounts to people, as determined by explicit a-scientific, ethical decision of government and society designed to make dollar votes properly reflective of society's value judgments.

3   From the standpoint of welfare economics, it is seen that any capitalistic system may depart from what is considered a social optimum in three main ways: through improper distribution of income, monopoly and externalities, and unemployment.

## CONCEPTS FOR REVIEW

interdependence, general
    equilibrium
determinate final equilibrium
efficient final equilibrium
labor theory of value versus proper
    pricing of nonhuman resources
interest rate in capitalism and
    socialism
social dividend: lump-sum tax or
    transfer incomes

incentive wages and job choice
accounting prices versus actual
    prices
monopoly restrictions
"external" divergences between
    social and private cost-benefits
information and incentives
welfare economics, ethical
    distribution questions, value
    judgments

## QUESTIONS FOR DISCUSSION

1   Summarize how a pricing system works to solve the three fundamental economic problems. Illustrate their interdependence.

2   Discuss the four kinds of prices in a utopian state.

3   What do you deem to be imperfections in our economic order? Virtues? What defects would plague a collectivist society?

4   "It is a vicious circle, to talk about simultaneous equations determining equilibrium. Suppose that I say, 'My age, $X$, is twice yours, $Y$. Your age, $Y$, is twenty-five years less than mine.' What a swindle: To know $X$, I must first know $Y$; but to know $Y$, I must first know $X$!" Show that the logical circle is a virtuous one, not a vicious one. The only solution to $Y = 2X$ and $X = Y - 25$ is obviously $X^* = 25$ and $Y^* = 50$. So it is with supply and demand determining wheat's $P$ and $Q$. And so it is with general equilibrium.

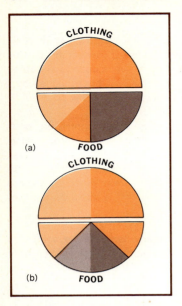

(a)

(b)

**5** *Extra-credit problem* on general equilibrium and welfare pricing: Half the people own no land; half own all the land; all work the same 10-hour day. Everybody spends half his income, whether large or small, on food, and half on clothing. Clothing is produced by labor only; food is produced by a production function involving labor and land, being a constant-share, unweighted geometric mean (or Cobb-Douglas) function—so that half the returns of food go to land and half to labor. Can you verify the following general-equilibrium solution?

The proletariat, or workingclass taken all together, will get only three-eighths of the national income: half of the half GNP that goes to clothing they get for their labor in clothing; but land subtracts off half of the half GNP that goes to food, and of the remaining share for labor, the proletariat get half for *their* labor, i.e., $(\frac{1}{2})(\frac{1}{2}) + (\frac{1}{2})(\frac{1}{2})(\frac{1}{2}) = \frac{3}{8}$, as can be verified from the light-orange area of the accompanying social pie. Now suppose it is deemed ethically just that all people should share alike. By redistributive taxation of all land rent à la Henry George, or by nationalization of land and lump-sum dividends of its equilibrium rent to all, the final distribution of income will be made equal for both classes, as shown by the second social pie's equal light- and dark-shaded areas.

# 5

## INTERNATIONAL TRADE AND FINANCE

In the earlier chapters of this book we took international trade more or less for granted. Here in Part Five we wish to analyze explicitly the interesting economic problems arising as soon as an economy engages in foreign trade.

This chapter and its Appendix deal with the *monetary* mechanisms involved in international trade. Then the next two chapters concentrate on the basic *real* factors which underlie international trade and which are often obscured by the monetary veil that covers all international transactions. These basic real factors are involved in any rational appraisal of the problems raised by tariffs, quotas, and other barriers to the international division of labor. In Chapter 36 all the principles are put to work to help understand the contemporary international economic scene.

International trade is important for a basic reason:

**Foreign trade offers a "consumption-possibility frontier" that can give us more of all goods than can our own domestic production-possibility frontier!**

EXAMPLE: Japan sells us cameras; we sell Australians machine tools; Australians complete the circle selling the Japanese iron ore. *Each of us ends up consuming more than he could produce alone.* The world is out on—and not inside—its true production-possibility frontier. That is the essence of foreign trade. So simple. And yet apparently so hard for congressmen and voters to grasp and remember.

Our task in Part Five is to study the mechanics of international trade and finance: foreign exchange rates; balance of international payments; foreign aid and loans; tariff duties and quotas; the so-called "principle of comparative advantage," which tells what kind of trade will take place, and why it ought to; and finally, the international economic problems of the 1970s—stable versus floating exchange rates, the World Bank and the International Monetary Fund (IMF), free-market gold versus the official tier of monetary gold, Special

# 33

## THE BALANCE OF INTERNATIONAL PAYMENTS

MISS PRISM: Cecily, you will read your Political Economy in my absence. The chapter on the Fall of the Rupee you may omit. It is somewhat too sensational. Even these metallic problems have their melodramatic side.
OSCAR WILDE
*The Importance of Being Earnest*

Drawing Rights (SDRs or "paper gold"), recycling of oil revenues accruing to the Mideast and to other nations in the OPEC cartel (Organization of Petroleum Exporting Countries), foreign aid, and many other vital matters.

These are anything but abstract economic problems. They make the difference between fruitful international exchange and chaos.

## A. MECHANISMS OF FOREIGN EXCHANGE AND TRADE

### FOREIGN EXCHANGE RATES

First, how does trade take place? If I buy oranges from Florida or ammonia from Chicago, I naturally want to pay in dollars. Also, the grower and the ammonia producer expect to be paid in dollars; after all, their expenses and living costs are settled in dollars. Within a country, economic transactions seem simple.

If, however, I wish to buy an English sports car directly, matters are more complicated. I must ultimately pay in British money, or what is called "pounds sterling," rather than in dollars. Similarly, an Englishman must somehow get dollars to an American producer if he wants our merchandise. Most Americans have never seen a British pound note. Certainly they would accept pounds only if they could be sure of converting them into American dollars.

Clearly, therefore, exports and imports of goods between nations with different units of money introduce a new economic factor: *the foreign exchange rate*, giving the price of the foreigner's unit of money in terms of our own.

Thus, the price of a British pound was in the general neighborhood of $2.00 in late 1975. There was also a foreign exchange rate between American money and the currencies of each and every country: 40 cents to the German mark;[1] 23 cents for the French franc; less than $\frac{1}{7}$ cent for an Italian lira; $\frac{1}{3}$ cent for the Japanese yen (or, alternatively, 300 yen to $1).

Given the foreign exchange rate, it is now simple for me to buy my English car. Suppose its quoted price is £4,000 (i.e., 4,000 British pounds). All I have to do is look in the newspaper for the foreign exchange rate for pounds. If this is $2.00 per pound, I simply go to a bank with $8,000 and ask that the money be used to pay the English car exporter. Pay him what? Pounds, of course, the only kind of money he needs.

Whether I use the bank or a broker is of no particular importance. In fact, it is all the same if the English exporter sends me a bill requesting payment in dollars or if he deals with me through an American dealer. In any case, the English exporter ultimately wants pounds, not dollars, and will soon trade the $8,000 for £4,000. (Needless to say, we ignore commission charges and the cost of money orders.)

---

[1] There are also foreign exchange rates between the pound and the German mark. But these rates between other countries need not interest us much, particularly since, in a free competitive market, the pound-mark rate can be simply calculated from the pound-dollar and mark-dollar rate, because sharp-eyed international arbitragers see to it that relative "cross rates" do not get out of line: thus a pound then had to sell for about 5 (= $2.00/$0.40) marks. Of course, these 1975 examples have to be modified when exchange-rate parities change, floating upward or downward.

You should be able to show what a British importer of American grains has to do if he wants to buy, say, a $24,000 shipment from an American exporter. Here pounds must be converted into dollars. Why, when the foreign exchange rate is $2.00 per pound, will this cost him £12,000?

The businessman or tourist does not, as an individual, have to know anything more than this to get his imports or exports transacted. But the true economics of the problem cannot be grasped until we find out *why* the foreign exchange rate is at the level it is. What economic principles determine foreign exchange rates? And underlie their movements?

## STABLE EXCHANGE RATE UNDER THE CLASSICAL GOLD STANDARD

There are four important cases to study:

1. The working of some kind of pure or modified *gold standard*.

2. The case of "clean" *floating foreign exchange rates*, available to all in either country, but fluctuating from day to day according to *market demand and supply* (quite like the case of wheat, which is available to all at a price that fluctuates from day to day, depending upon competitive supply and demand).

3. The case of *controlled* international trade, where each transaction requires a government license and where the foreign exchange rate may be different for different kinds of transactions, being set according to the will of the state.

4. The present-day interim "managed floating" regime still loosely related to official gold and the dollar and with its mixture of (*a*) somewhat stable and pegged rates, and (*b*) exchange rates floating within wide limits.

The gold-standard case has been historically most important. It is also one of the easiest cases to analyze as an introduction.

**Gold bars**   Suppose people everywhere insisted on being paid in bits of pure *gold metal:* weight alone would count, so long as there was a guarantee of its purity. Then buying a car in Britain would merely require payment in gold at a price expressed in ounces of gold; and buying grain in Chicago would involve the same kind of payment. By definition, there would be no foreign-exchange-rate problem.

**Gold coins**   Since slivers and blobs of gold are inconvenient to carry and to assay for purity and for weight, it became customary for the state—in earlier days, the prince—to stamp out in coin form a specified number of ounces of gold carrying the seal of the state to guarantee purity and weight. (The edges were milled to reveal light weight and fraud. Even so, since gold rubs off, merchants weighed the coins.)

With gold coins as the exchange medium, would not foreign trade still be like domestic trade? Yes, essentially. But with some minor differences: If we used ounces and Britain used grams to measure weight, you would merely have to have a table of units' conversion. And the same problem would arise if Queen Victoria chose to make her coins about $\frac{1}{4}$ ounce of gold (the "sovereign") and President McKinley chose to make his $\frac{1}{20}$ ounce of gold (the dollar). In that case, the pound sovereign, being five times as heavy as the dollar, would naturally have an exchange rate of $5 to £1.

Now that is essentially how the pre-1914 gold standard actually worked. Of course, local pride tended to keep us using our coins and the English using theirs. But anyone was free to melt down our coins and have them converted into English coins (at nominal costs). So, except for the trifling costs of melting down, shipping across the ocean, and recoining, *all countries on the gold standard had stable exchange rates whose par values, or parities, were determined by the gold content of their money unit.*

*Minor qualifications.* Gold being quite inconvenient to carry around for spending purposes, inevitably governments issued paper certificates that were pledged to be redeemable in gold metal. People had the right to turn in gold for certificates and certificates for gold, and they often exercised that right. Also, in those days ocean transport was slow and costly: so there were "gold points" around the true mint parities within which band the pound and dollar exchange rates could fluctuate. Thus, if it cost 2 cents to ship $\frac{1}{4}$ ounce of gold either way across the Atlantic Ocean (inclusive of insurance and interest costs), could the exchange rate depart a little from $5? Yes. In New York, the quoted price of a pound could rise to as much as $5.02 before it would pay to get gold bars and ship them to London to be exchanged for pounds; a price higher than $5.02 could not prevail because enough gold would be flowing to keep the price no higher than the upper gold point. It should be evident that the pound could fall below the mint parity of $5 by 2 cents to $4.98. When the exchange rate got down to this lower gold point, it would be cheaper for gold to be shipped from Europe to America. All this actually happened (except that $5 is substituted here for the correct pre-1914 parity of $4.87 to simplify the arithmetic, and the shipping costs are given only approximately). Before 1914, the foreign exchange rate of the pound and dollar stayed essentially stable, varying but a trifle from these weight-determined mint parities until the gold points were touched and gold had to flow in the indicated direction.

**The Hume gold-flow equilibrating mechanism**    Now that the mechanics of the problem are understood, we probe deeper to answer this question:

Under the gold standard, what kept America from buying more goods from England than England bought from us—which, after all, would have required us to keep shipping gold in final payment? Why wouldn't we be drained of all our gold?

This is a good question, and the mercantilist writers, who preceded Adam Smith and his friend the noted philosopher David Hume, gave a plausible but superficial answer. The mercantilists said:

"A country will lose its gold unless the Prince introduces tariffs and quotas to cut down on imports of goods; and unless he gives subsidies to encourage exports; and unless he forbids skilled workmen to take their knowledge abroad and he makes sure all shipping takes place in our own boats, however dear they may be." As an afterthought, almost too obvious to require mention, they said: "Of course, losing gold is a terrible thing for a nation. Don't ask why. Everyone knows it to be one of the worst tragedies that can happen to a nation."

David Hume in 1752, and economists ever since, have given the refutation to this line of reasoning. First, Hume noted that it could not be true that everyone would all the time be losing gold under free trade. Where would it go—into the sea? And he demonstrated that it is no tragedy at all if a country goes permanently from having

10 million ounces of gold to having 5 million, or even 1 million. *If* possessing half the amount of gold means merely that *all* prices are exactly halved, no one in the country is the least bit better or worse off. So, losing half or nine-tenths of a nation's gold is nothing to worry about, Hume pointed out, if the nation merely ends up with an equivalently reduced price and cost level.

Here it is well to recall the crude Quantity Theory of Money and Prices discussed in Chapter 15. David Hume, along with John Locke and earlier writers, was one of the first to enunciate and hold to this theory concerning the proportionality of all prices to the stock of money (in this case, $M$ being gold).[2]

Now comes the second and important part of Hume's classical refutation of mercantilism and defense of free trade. He went on to assert that there is a four-pronged mechanism that tends to keep in equilibrium the international balance of payments of countries on the gold standard. Briefly, the Hume mechanism is this:

Whenever one country imports too much and begins to lose gold, its loss of gold *reduces its price and cost level,* thereby (1) *decreasing its imports* of foreign goods that have become relatively dear, and (2) *increasing exports* of its now-cheapened home-produced goods.

The other country, which has been having a so-called "favorable balance of trade," in which it was sending more goods abroad than it was importing and merely receiving barren gold in exchange, now has (via the Quantity Theory) its price and cost levels of goods *raised*. This is a further reason (3) for its now-expensive *exports to go down* in physical amount, and (4) for its citizens to import *more* of the now-cheap goods of the first country.

**The result of this four-pronged gold-flow price-level mechanism is (normally) to improve the balance of payments of the country losing gold, and worsen that of the country with the favorable balance of trade—until equilibrium in international trade is established at relative prices that keep imports and exports in balance with no net gold flow. The equilibrium is stable and self-correcting, requiring no tariffs and other state interference.**

## FLEXIBLE OR FLOATING EXCHANGE RATES

Having seen how an idealized gold standard works, we turn now to the case where *supply and demand are left free to determine the foreign exchange rate.* In the absence of any tie to gold, the pound might have had an average price of $4.00 or $5.00 in the 1940s, and in this decade an average price of $2.00. Who knows, once floating exchange rates become the rule, perhaps next decade it could be at $1.50 or $3.20.

The forces of supply and demand will determine the outcome. If Americans want to buy so many English goods at an existing $1.90 level and Europeans want so few American goods, then we might be demanding *more pounds* as our needed foreign exchange than they will be wanting to supply us with. What then will happen? If there is no longer a gold standard, one cannot get gold and ship it over in order to keep the foreign exchange rate within narrow gold points around the $1.90 parity.

---

[2] He admitted that the equilibrium predicted by the Quantity Theory would not take place instantaneously; indeed, he was one of the first to recognize that a period of rising $M$ and rising prices, when it was first happening and was not foreseen, would give profits to businessmen by causing their prices to rise more than their costs; he thought this would be good for full employment and capital formation in the short run.

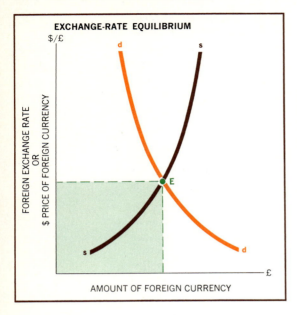

EXCHANGE-RATE EQUILIBRIUM

$/£

FOREIGN EXCHANGE RATE
OR
$ PRICE OF FOREIGN CURRENCY

AMOUNT OF FOREIGN CURRENCY

£

**FIG. 33-1**

**Floating exchange rates are forced flexibly up or down by supply and demand for goods or capital movements** Behind our *dd* is our desire to import British goods, buy British securities, visit the Bard's grave, and so forth. Behind their *ss* supply of pounds to be traded for dollars is their desire for our export goods and other items, and their need to send us earnings on our past capital movements. If the rate were above *E,* there would be an excess of foreign currency that they would want to supply us over what we should want to demand. Such an excess of supply would bid the rate back down to *E,* where the market of foreign currency for dollars is just cleared. (If we doubled our domestic money supply and all prices, purchasing-power-parity doctrine says curves should shift up to twice the scale resulting in exact doubling of *E*'s price, a 100 per cent appreciation of the pound relative to the depreciated dollar.)

Instead, *our urgent demand will bid up the foreign exchange rate.* How far? Just far enough so that, at the new higher price of, say, $2 for the pound, our total demand for foreign exchange will be brought again down into equality with their enhanced supply of foreign exchange.

Two main steps are involved: (1) With the pound rate more expensive, it will cost more to import British bikes; and then our physical demand for them will fall off in the usual fashion. (2) With the dollar now cheaper, our goods will cost less to Europeans, and they will want to demand more of our export goods. (If we look at these two effects from both their viewpoint and our own, we have something like the four-pronged action of Hume. But with certain important differences. Our whole *domestic* wage and cost level need not change, and neither need theirs. The change in foreign exchange rate can *itself* directly bring about enhanced relative dearness and cheapness *of export and import* price levels.)

The familiar curves of supply and demand developed in Chapter 4 and Part Three are applied in Fig. 33-1 to show equilibrium determination of flexible exchange rates.

America's *dd* curve comes from our desire for foreign exchange rate to buy import goods, to make tourist visits, to hire shipping and insurance services, to finance our troops abroad and our foreign-aid grants, to pay the dividends and interest we owe to foreign owners of our securities and property; and also to finance long-term investment abroad by American firms or stock buyers, and short-term investment in foreign near-term bonds or savings accounts.

What is behind foreigners' demand for dollars—which is the *ss* supply curve of the pound-foreign-exchange they offer us? The exactly similar items in their balance of payments: desire to import our export goods, need to pay us dividends, etc.

**At the *dd* and *ss* intersection, the floating foreign exchange rate will get set, having then no tendency to rise or fall from this equilibrium level.**

What will happen if tomorrow we send more troops abroad, travel abroad more, find new bargains in their catalogues and expand our dollar demand for their goods, and are forced by domestic inflation to raise our export-goods prices? Such changes will obviously shift our *dd* upward and rightward and also their *ss* leftward and upward. With what resulting intersection? With a new, higher equilibrium level of the exchange rate; as described above, just enough higher to coax out more American exports and choke off imports from Europe. The exchange rate at which we buy foreign currencies has risen; the dollar's relative value has fallen.

**Purchasing-power parity theory**   A classical economist like Hume would understand all this very well. In fact, he (and Ricardo around 1817 and Sweden's Gustav Cassel around 1917) would seek, as a clue to the equilibrium level of a flexible exchange rate, the relative behavior of its price level.

*Purchasing-power parity.* **Let America and Europe be at equilibrium, say, at $2.00 per £1. Now let America double *all* her prices by domestically inflating her *M*; and let Europe keep her *M* limited enough to produce a steady price level. Then, other things being equal (such as employment remaining full and there being no inventions, crop failures, tariffs, or change in tastes), the new *dd* and *ss* intersection will come at twice the old $2.00 rate, namely, at $4.00 per £1—with the dollar depreciating by as much as its price level rises.**

The reasoning would be classically simple. With all wages and prices here *exactly doubled* (and *M* doubled here to finance them), we can *buy exactly the same* physical imports and *sell exactly the same* physical exports at the new exchange rate that has doubled like everything else. (It is just as if every American old dollar is now called two American dollars.)[3]

Under floating exchange rates, in the longest run it is the *monetary policies* of the different countries that ultimately determine their price levels and exchange rates.

**Depreciation, appreciation, and devaluation**   A doubling of the pound is a halving of the dollar. By definition, the fall in the price of one currency in terms of one or all others is called a "depreciation." A relative rise in the price of a currency in terms of another currency is called an "appreciation." Evidently, the pound has appreciated in our example, and the dollar has undergone a large depreciation.

The term "devaluation" is often confused with the term "depreciation." Devaluation usually is defined to mean a rise in the price of gold relative to the currency in question.

Thus, Roosevelt devalued the dollar in 1933 when he raised the price of gold from $21 an ounce to $35 an ounce. In 1971 when Nixon and the IMF raised gold's official price from $35 to $38, and from $38 to $42.22 in 1973, we say the dollar was devalued. (NOTE: A devaluation may also involve a depreciation. Thus, when the franc kept its previous gold price and the dollar raised its gold price, that meant a depreciation of the dollar relative to the franc; or, what is the same thing, an appreciation of the franc relative to the dollar.)

*Devaluation defined.* **When gold officially goes up in price relative to a currency—as from $38 an ounce to $42.22—we say the currency has been *devalued*.**

---

[3]Cassel and other writers developed the doctrine of purchasing-power parity to predict how much World War I currencies would depreciate when internal inflation sent their price levels up by 100 or more per cent. His long-run predictions worked out better than his short-run, but neither had perfect accuracy. In the real world, unlike the classical model, other things didn't stay equal.

*Depreciation defined.* **When the price of a foreign currency rises relative to a given currency—e.g., when the price of the German mark rose about 25 per cent in the 1970s, from about $0.32 to $0.40 per mark—we say the (domestic) currency has *depreciated,* and that the foreign currency has had a relative *appreciation.***

**If *all* countries *simultaneously* raised the price of gold by 100 or 200 per cent, there would be *no* depreciation or appreciation, but there would be a devaluation.**

**Restoring equilibrium**    When a country chronically runs a balance-of-payments deficit, we say it has pegged its exchange rate at too high a level. Its costs are not competitive. It is said to have an *overvalued* currency.

Consider the country it is trading with. That country must be running a chronic surplus. Its currency is said to be *undervalued.*

How to cure the disequilibrium? Economists say: "Depreciate the overvalued currency. What is exactly the same thing—repeat, *exactly*—appreciate the undervalued currency. That should tend to help restore balance-of-payments equilibrium."

Politically, it seems always harder to get a country to appreciate than to depreciate. Thus, in Germany, which was the nation with the most stubborn international surplus in the last dozen years, vested interests grew up in their swollen export industries. They hated to see the surplus go. (We'll see more on this in Chapter 36.)

## MODIFIED GOLD AND DOLLAR STANDARDS

Now that we have surveyed the idealized cases of a pure gold standard and a completely flexible exchange-rate system, we can describe the international system as it has in fact operated in recent decades, paving the way for Chapter 36's discussion of future modifications that are on the way.

**Evolution of the gold standard**    There is nothing sacred about gold. Silver, platinum, lead, or, for that matter, paper napkins would do, provided they had convenience for exchange, could not be falsified, and were enough limited in supply to keep the price level from soaring. Actually, the old gold standard prevailed in its heyday only for a brief half-century prior to 1914. Before the nineteenth century, England had been more on a silver than on a gold standard, and had stumbled onto the gold standard as a result of market revaluations of the two precious metals without anyone's realizing it. Her great prestige caused France, the United States, and the rising empires of Germany and Japan to adopt the gold standard later.

Even in its brief heyday, several crises caused the gold standard to break down periodically (as, for example, when our Civil War forced us off gold for more than a decade). Moreover, the price level was at the mercy of the happenstance of gold discoveries. If world physical output (GNP) was increasing in the years 1875 to 1895 at the rate of 5 per cent per year, the gold supply would—according to the crude Quantity Theory of Money—have to increase by 5 per cent per year to keep prices stable. But mines, because of the ending of the Californian and Australian gold rushes, were not producing this much gold then; and as a result, price levels were sagging all over the world in the last third of the nineteenth century.

This gave rise to much social unrest. In an ideal world of perfect price and wage flexibility, where the Quantity Theory worked smoothly both down and up, falling prices should not have mattered much. But, as Hume himself insisted, prices and wages tend to be sticky downward; and falling price levels tend to lead to labor unrest, strikes, unemployment, and radical movements generally. Precisely that happened in the United States and other countries during the 1875–1895 era of populism. (Recall Chapter 7's account of the rise of the Knights of Labor.) Since gold seemed to be squeezing prices downward, there was a clamor on the part of farmers and workers for use of silver to supplement gold. This culminated in the historic speech by William Jennings Bryan in favor of "bimetallism" at the 1896 Democratic Convention, where the Boy Orator of the Platte warned against crucifying mankind on a cross of gold.[4]

**Fractional-reserve banking and the gold-exchange standard**   With Germany and Japan going on the gold standard, the deflationary pressure on prices would have been even worse had it not been for new methods of economizing on gold. Modern banks, which hold only fractional reserves, began to develop: the demand-deposit $M$ they created meant that not quite so much gold was needed to keep up with growing total output. Moreover, most of the countries on the gold standard did *not* keep 100 per cent gold reserves to back up the token coins and paper currency they issued. Thus, if the typical country held only one-fourth gold against its paper money, only a quarter as much gold would have to be mined to support the same world price level.

This process of domestic banking evolution to economize on the use of gold is important. For, as we shall see, it foreshadows the modern international development of economizing on and displacing gold by creating so-called "paper gold," i.e., SDRs which are Special Drawing Rights in the International Monetary Fund (IMF).

Another development helped economize on gold. Many countries, particularly small ones (like the Philippines), kept their money exchangeable at fixed rates with respect to gold. But they held little or no gold. Instead, they would hold the money of some big country (like the United States) that was on the gold standard. So long as the small country could stay on such a "gold-exchange standard," the effect would be much like the pure gold standard, but with great economizing on gold.

Fortunately for those who favored the gold standard, the deflationary pressures eased some when gold was discovered in the Klondike and South Africa in the mid-nineties and when the cyanide process greatly increased the output of gold mines. Together

---

[4]Bimetallism would mean that the Treasury would exchange dollars for *either* gold or silver, at some agreed-upon weight ratio, such as 16 ounces of silver to each ounce of gold. Unless all countries agreed on the same 16/1 ratio, there would be a one-way movement of each metal to the place where it was most valued; the place where gold was most valued would be stripped of all its silver and would end on the gold standard; while the place where silver was most valued would end on the silver standard. As a result, with every change in the relative supplies and demands for the two metals, there would be an ensuing fluctuation in the foreign exchange rates between the two countries. [The percentage size of the fluctuation could be only two-sixteenths if their respective bimetallic parities were 16/1 and 18/1. Even if all countries went on the same 16/1 ratio, any tendency for relative (marginal) mining costs to differ from this ratio would result in all of one metal being sold to all the treasuries of the world. For example, if the official parity is 16/1 and the ratio in the market is 20/1 (indicating that 20 ounces of silver is as cheap to produce as 1 ounce of gold), then, by a form of what is known as Gresham's Law—"bad money drives out good"—all silver will be sold to the government and the world is effectively on a single gold standard. Today no one favors "bimetallism" and silver sells like tin or other ordinary goods.]

with the increasing leverage attained by having smaller and smaller fractional-reserve ratios and more and more gold-exchange standards, the increase in mining enabled the world to keep on the gold standard and stave off deflation up until the 1929 crash. But this did involve a strain on international liquidity, and some economic historians actually attribute that slump to an increasing shortage of world liquidity.

**The dollar as key currency**  During the Great Depression of the 1930s, political unrest and fear of Hitler's aggression caused an avalanche of gold to flow into the United States. After World War II people said with some exaggeration that *the world was in fact on a dollar standard*. The American dollar was the "key currency" in terms of which international trade and finance were carried on. Private and governmental reserves were kept largely in the form of dollar balances (i.e., in cash, bank deposits, and liquid short-term dollar securities). Whereas before 1914 the pound had been king, by 1945 the dollar was established as *the* key currency.

EXAMPLE: As Chapter 36 will show, the Bretton Woods Conference of 1944, which set up the International Monetary Fund and the World Bank, defined in its Charter the parities of currencies not simply in terms of gold, but also in terms of dollars (then the equivalent of $\frac{1}{35}$ ounce of gold, now $\frac{1}{42}$). The dollar was the so-called "intervention currency" that governments used in adhering to their official exchange parities.

## DEMISE OF THE GOLD STANDARD AND BRETTON WOODS

In August 1971, President Nixon formally abandoned gold convertibility. No longer does America pay even lip service to the Bretton Woods obligation of making dollars convertible on demand into something other than themselves—into official gold, yen, marks, or any other international reserves at the IMF official exchange-rate parities.

We shall study in Chapter 36 the struggle for a system to replace Bretton Woods and the modified gold standard by some new kind of system. All that needs to be said here is that the world is in a not uncomfortable limbo. We are not on the pre-1914 automatic gold standard with its specie-flow self-correcting mechanism. We are not yet on a "clean" floating exchange-rate system where (as in Fig. 33-1) the parity rate depreciates or appreciates to whatever degree it is bid in order to restore balance-of-payments equilibrium.

**Smithsonian agreement**  In December 1971, at the Smithsonian Institution in Washington, the main IMF nations reached an interim agreement. Here are some of its features.

To correct the decade-old "overvaluation" of the dollar, which had kept our costs and prices so high that we ran chronic deficits of imports over exports, the dollar was depreciated sharply relative to the mark and yen, and more moderately relative to most other European currencies. In the several years since 1971, the Swiss franc and German mark have floated further upward, as in lesser degree have most Common Market currencies; the Italian lira however, and the British pound, in accordance with their greater rates of internal price inflation, have predictably floated downward since 1971.

The two-tier system was retained at Smithsonian. The official gold price was marked up by a token amount, from $35 to $38 an ounce, and again in 1973 to $42.22 an ounce. This was meaningless in any case as no transactions took place at this price. In 1975, the IMF took the final step and abolished the official price of gold completely.

The IMF system of Special Drawing Rights (SDRs) was retained. As Chapter 36 will discuss in more detail, the IMF in effect creates international money when it gives each member an account to draw on up to a specified quota. This is just like the process within a country of my receiving a checking deposit that I can draw on for my excess spending. The value of the unit in the SDR accounts is defined in effect as a market basket of 16 leading currencies— so many dollars, marks, pounds, yen, francs, and so forth. Instead of stating the parity of a currency, or its day-to-day floating value, in so many meaningless ounces of $42.22 official gold, the modern system uses the SDRs as the "paper gold" in terms of which international reserves are to be evaluated. Even the OPEC oil cartel, fearful that the dollar might float downward in value, in 1975 began to quote its monopoly oil price in SDR units.

The world in the post-Smithsonian 1970s finds itself on a (somewhat!) "managed floating" exchange-rate system. Chapter 36 will deal with the current and future problems of international finance.

We have been surveying international trade mechanisms with a telescope in the first part of this chapter. In the remaining sections, we must train a microscope on the balance of payments of a country.

## B. BALANCE OF INTERNATIONAL TRADE AND CAPITAL MOVEMENTS

### THE BALANCE OF INTERNATIONAL PAYMENTS

The time has come to explain exactly what we mean when we speak of a country's "balance of international payments." We mean the statement that takes into account the values of all goods, all gifts and foreign aid, all capital loans (or "IOUs"), all gold and international reserves coming in and going out of a country, and the interconnections among all the items that lie behind Fig. 33-1's curves.

The balance of international payments summarizes these important relations. If you understand it, you have a fairly good grasp of foreign trade.

The U.S. Department of Commerce keeps records and makes official estimates of all international transactions during a year: merchandise exported and imported, money lent abroad or borrowed, gold movements, tourist expenditures, interest and dividends received or paid abroad, shipping services, and so forth. They all go to make up the "balance of international payments"—which is simply a double-entry listing of all items, drawn up so that it must always show a formal over-all net balance.[5]

The balance of international payments is usually listed in three sections:

**I. Current account**

  Private:

    Merchandise (or "trade balance")

    Invisibles:

      Travel (tourists, etc.) and transportation (shipping services, etc.)

---

[5] Smuggling and some innocent items elude the record keepers; so it is necessary to introduce a miscellaneous category of errors and omitted items, as in GNP's "statistical discrepancy."

Income on investments (interest, royalties, dividends, foreign bond earnings)
Other services
Governmental:
Government export of military goods to allies
Government grants, etc.

**II. Capital movements**
Long-term:
Private
Government
Short-term:
Private
Government
**Errors and Omissions, net**

**III. Gold-and-reserve-assets movements (out and in)**

**Balance on current account**   The totality of items under section I is usually referred to as the "balance on current account." This important magnitude summarizes the difference between our total export of goods and services and our total import of them.

In a moment, we shall see how any surplus or deficit balance on current account is "financed"—or, more precisely, is offset—by reserve-and-gold assets or by capital movements under sections III and II. But before doing this, we shall describe briefly I's major current items under the headings Private and Governmental.

Centuries ago, when *merchandise* items predominated, writers concentrated on them alone. If merchandise exports were greater in value than merchandise imports they spoke of a "favorable balance of trade"; if imports exceeded exports, of an "unfavorable balance of trade." This is not a good choice of terms, for we shall see that a so-called "unfavorable" balance of trade may be a fine thing for a country.

In addition to such so-called "visible" merchandise items, we must not forget the important role played these days by the "invisibles." These consist of such items as shipping and insurance services which we provide for foreigners or they provide for us, American tourist expenditures abroad, gifts that immigrants send back home, and most importantly, our earnings from abroad. On reflection, one sees that an invisible item such as an American's expenditure for a drink in Paris has the same effect on the final balance of payments as does his import of French wine to be drunk here at home. And when we provide shipping insurance service, that acts like an export.

**Debits and credits**   A good way to decide how any item should be treated is to ask the following question:

**Is the item like one of our merchandise exports, providing us with more foreign currencies? Such an export-type is called a "credit item" and gives us a supply of foreign money. Or is the item like one of our merchandise imports, causing us to use up our stock of foreign currencies and making it necessary to get more foreign currency? Such an import-type item is called a "debit item" and gives us a demand for foreign money.**

To show how this rule works, ask the following question: How shall we treat interest, royalty, and dividend income on investments received by Americans from abroad?

Clearly, they are credit items like exports, in that they provide us with foreign currencies. The reader can reverse the argument to show that such items which foreigners receive from us must be treated like debit items—like imports, they use up our foreign currencies.

At this point a close look at Table 33-1 will be helpful. It presents official data on the balance of international payments of the United States for 1974. Note its three main divisions into current, capital, and reserve-and-gold items; in addition, it has an item (line 17, in brown for emphasis) to account for statistical errors and omissions. Each row is numbered to make reference easy. Then, after each item has been listed by name in Column (*a*), we list in Column (*b*) the *credits*, i.e., the amounts of those items that are like exports in earning us foreign currencies. Next, in Column (*c*), we list the *debits*, i.e., the amounts of the items that use up foreign currencies because of our need to pay for imports, etc.

Thus, in 1974 our merchandise exports gave us credits of $98,268 million; but our merchandise imports gave us debits of $103,796 million. The *net* difference between credits and debits is in this case −$5,528 million. This "unfavorable balance-of-trade deficit" is shown listed in Column (*d*), of the first row. (Be sure you know why the algebraic sign is shown − rather than +.)

The reader can interpret each line of the invisible items. He will know why the American tendency to travel abroad results in a negative—or net debit—entry under travel and transportation expenditures. He will also know why net earnings from abroad—line 3 of investment income—serve to provide us with foreign currencies and are listed as credits. (Of course, in their balance of payments, foreign countries would think of *our* credit as *their* debit, and of this last item as "making less *dollars* available.")

Table 33-1 shows that as far as the private current items are concerned, the final effect of invisible items was to more than offset line 1's trade deficit.

The whole net credit balance of the first four private rows cannot, however, offset the governmental items of the next three rows. Government military transactions and various foreign-aid grants and payments resulted in the debit balance of −$9,340 million in line 9, more than enough to wipe out the positive private balance and make the final "balance on current account" (line 10) equal to −$3,608 million, a deficit.

In computing the net balance on current account, we have completed the first great block of Table 33-1. How must a nation offset its net balance on current account? Either by reserve-and-gold asset payments (e.g., we could export SDRs or foreign-currency holdings), as in section III of the table, or by net borrowing as in section II. For it is a tautology that, *What you get you must either pay for or owe for.* And this fact of double-entry bookkeeping means that the whole table of the balance of international payments must show a final definitional balance. (Statistical errors and omissions, as in the case of the GNP statistical discrepancy discussed in Chapter 10, must of course be reckoned with if the double-entry bookkeeper is not given all the accurate facts; but this should not affect the *logic* of the perfect balance.)

**Capital movements**    We can now turn to capital movements: (*a*) the long-term and short-term loans *private* citizens make or receive from foreign private citizens (e.g., when General Motors builds an automobile plant abroad or when I buy a French bond

**UNITED STATES BALANCE OF PAYMENTS, 1974 (in millions of dollars)**

| No. | (a) ITEMS | (b) CREDITS | (c) DEBITS | (d) NET CREDITS (+) OR DEBITS (−) | |
|---|---|---|---|---|---|
| **I** | **Current account** | | | | |
| 1 | (Private) merchandise trade balance | $98,268 | $103,796 | − $ 5,528 | |
| | Invisibles: | | | | |
| 2 | Travel and transportation | | | − 2,692 | |
| 3 | Investment income | 26,068 | 15,946 | + 10,122 | |
| 4 | Other services net | | | + 3,830 | |
| **5** | **Balance on private goods and services** | | | | **+$ 5,732** |
| 6 | Military transactions | | | − 2,158 | |
| 7 | Remittances, pensions, and other transfers net | | | − 1,721 | |
| 8 | U.S. government grants (excluding military) | | | − 5,461 | |
| **9** | **Government current balance** | | | | **−$ 9,340** |
| **10** | **Balance on current account** | | | | **−$ 3,608** |
| **II** | **Capital account** | | | | |
| | Long-term loans (−) or borrowing (+) | | | | |
| 11 | Private | | | − 8,437 | |
| 12 | Government | | | + 1,119 | |
| 13 | Net long-term foreign investment | | | | −$ 7,318 |
| **14** | **Basic balance on current account and long-term capital** | | | | **−$10,927** |
| 15 | Nonliquid short-term private capital flows, net | | | − 12,949 | |
| 16 | Allocations of new SDRs to U.S. by IMF | | | + — | |
| **17** | **Errors and omissions, net** | | | + 4,834 | |
| 18 | Short-term capital movements | | | | −$ 8,115 |
| **19** | **Net liquidity balance** | | | | **−$19,043** |
| 20 | Liquid private capital flows (from foreigners to their central banks) | | | | +$10,669 |
| **21** | **Official reserves transactions balance** | | | | **−$ 8,374** |
| **III** | **Net reserve-and-gold asset movements** | | | | |
| 22 | Liabilities to foreign official agencies incurred | | | + 8,481 | |
| 23 | U.S. official-reserve assets net outflow | | | − 107 | |
| 24 | Total | | | | +$ 8,374 |
| 25 | Formal over-all net total | | | | 0 |

**TABLE 33-1**
(Source: Adapted from U.S. Department of Commerce.)

or deposit funds in a Swiss bank, or when Arabs buy New York real estate or treasury short-term bills here); and (*b*) the long-term and short-term *government* loans and credits that take place through various direct or intermediate channels.

It is easy to decide which are credit and which debit items in the capital accounts if you use the following rule: Always think of America as exporting and importing *capital securities*—or, for short, exporting and importing IOUs. Then you can treat these exports and imports like any other exports and imports. When we lend abroad, is it a credit or debit? Obviously, we are importing IOUs—and imports always give rise to debits. Therefore it is a debit.

Similarly, when we are borrowing from abroad on balance, this export of IOUs creates a net credit. If you do not follow this rule, you will find yourself getting confused: when we lend abroad, you will be tempted to think of us as exporting capital abroad and thereby earning a credit. This is wrong: we are then importing IOUs, and these imports are debit *offsets* enabling us to be paid for a surplus of credit exports on current account.

Line 13 shows that in 1974 America was a net long-term foreign lender: we were doing more long-term lending or investing abroad than foreigners were lending or investing here. We were the net importers of long-term IOUs by −$7,318 million.

**Basic deficit**    Now let us depart from a simple consideration of current, capital, and gold items. Let us investigate the concept of America's "basic deficit." Certain short-term capital movements take place to make up for, and offset, our inability to generate enough credit items. (Examples are holdings of treasury bills and bank deposits, or volatile portfolio purchases of our common stocks.) So we exclude such short-term items in order to discover where we really stand on a sustainable longer-term basis.

Line 14 totes up the score of *all* our current transactions and long-term capital movements. So great were current governmental debits and long-term private investment debits as to give America a so-called net "basic deficit": for 1974, a basic deficit of −$10,927 million.

It is somewhat dangerous to speak of a "deficit in the balance of payments," for, as we have just seen, the whole balance of payments must always be in tautologically perfect balance because of the identities and conventions of double-entry bookkeeping. What, then, do newspapers and congressmen mean when they refer to the American deficit in the balance of payments for the years 1958–1973? They probably have reference to something like line 14, the sum of the current-account deficit and the long-term (nonportfolio) investment deficit.

**Short-term capital movements**    Almost completely offsetting our 1974 basic deficit of Line 14 was Line 20's credit item, originating for the most part from the fact that the OPEC oil producers had recently quadrupled the price of oil; being unable in so short a time to spend their avalanche of receipts on enhanced imports for home development or for home consumption, they ended up through their central banks in effect holding U.S. Treasury bills. As Line 22 shows, it was their central banks who primarily had physical ownership of our U.S. Treasury bills. A glance at Lines 15 and 17 shows that, oil aside, U.S. citizens continued to do short-term lending—as when a Milwaukee producer of tractors extended credits to foreign dealers who stocked their equipment. Line 17, Errors and Omissions, showing a positive credit balance of $4,834 million suggests that by 1974 unrecorded money was beginning to return back to the dollar, instead of tending to leak off in massive amounts to Switzerland and elsewhere as in the pre-1971 days when the U.S. currency was so badly overvalued.

**Reserve-and-gold movements**  After the basic deficit is augmented by short-term capital movements, line 19 shows a whopping net liquidity deficit of $19 billion. An offsetting line 20 capital flow of $10⅔ billion of liquid transfers, from foreign holders of dollars to their own central banks, gives finally line 21's official reserves transactions balance, a deficit of $8,374 million.

Finally, block III of the table indicates that we, unavoidably, lost international reserves and incurred liabilities for line 24's $8⅜ billion total. Line 25 shows the purely formal balance of double-entry bookkeeping.

## STAGES OF A COUNTRY'S BALANCE OF PAYMENTS

Historically, the United States has gone through the four stages typical of growth of a young agricultural nation into a well-developed industrialized one. A review of this history is useful to consolidate understanding (but may be skipped in a short course).

1. *Young and growing debtor nation.* From the Revolutionary War until after the Civil War, we imported on current account more than we exported. England and Europe lent us the difference in order to build up our capital structure. We were a typical young and growing debtor nation.

2. *Mature debtor nation.* From about 1873 to 1914, our balance of trade appears to have become favorable. But growth of the dividends and interest that we had to pay abroad on our past borrowing kept our balance on current account more or less in balance. Capital movements were also nearly in balance, our new lending just about canceling our borrowing.

3. *New creditor nation.* In World War I, we expanded our exports tremendously. At first, private American citizens made loans to the warring Allied Powers. After we got into the war, our government lent money to England and France for war equipment and postwar relief needs. We emerged from the war a creditor nation. But our psychological frame of mind had not adjusted itself to our new creditor position. We passed high tariff laws in the 1920s and in 1930. Because we refused to import, foreigners found it difficult to get the dollars to pay us interest and dividends, much less repay principal.

So long as we remained in this third stage of being a new creditor country—so long, that is, as we kept making *new* private foreign loans all through the 1920s—everything momentarily appeared all right on the surface. We could continue to sell more than we were buying, by putting most of it "on the cuff." The rest of the world met our export surplus by sending us gold and by sending us IOUs. As long as Wall Street bankers could interest Main Street investors in foreign bonds, everything seemed rosy. But by 1929 and later, when Americans would no longer lend abroad, the crash finally came. International trade broke down. Debts were defaulted. America, as much as the rest of the world, was to blame.

Japan and West Germany seem to be repeating in the 1970s many of the phases—and errors!—of the United States in the 1920s.

4. *Mature creditor nation.* England reached this stage some years ago, and as in such cases, her merchandise imports exceeded her exports. Before we feel sorry for her because of her so-called "unfavorable" balance of trade, let us note what this really means.

Her citizens were living better because they were able to import much cheap food and in return did not have to part with much in the way of valuable export goods. The English were paying for their import surplus by the interest and dividend receipts they were receiving from past foreign lending.

Fine for the English. But what about the rest of the world? Were they not worse off for having to send exports to England in excess of imports? Not necessarily. Normally, the capital goods that England had previously lent them permitted them to add to their domestic production—to add *more* than had to be paid out to England in interest and dividends. Both parties were better off. Nineteenth-century foreign lending was twice blessed: it blessed him who gave and him who received. Of course, international trade and finance did not always operate quite so smoothly. Some investments proved unwise. Political problems of colonies and nationalism complicated the situation. And the whole process went awry and broke down after World War I.

America has moved into the mature stage, where our earnings from abroad help finance our net imports from abroad and also our aid and security programs. Past capital movements are responsible for these vital investment earnings.

## BASIC SIGNIFICANCE OF INTERNATIONAL CAPITAL MOVEMENTS

Turn now to the nature of capital movements. If political problems of nationalism and domestic problems of unemployment did not enter the picture, the fundamentals of international lending would be easy to understand. We could cut through the fog of money and finance to concentrate on the real aspects in terms of goods and resources.

How does capital grow within a country? By our diverting labor, land, machinery, and other resources away from the production of current consumption goods. Instead, we plant trees, drain rivers, or build new machinery and buildings. All these add to our future income and consumption.

We are postponing present consumption for future consumption—for an even *greater* amount of future consumption. Where does the increase in future consumption come from? As Chapter 30 showed, *capital goods have a "net" productivity*. This constitutes the real aspect of the interest rate.

Different parts of the world have different amounts of resources: labor, minerals, climate, know-how. Were it not for ignorance or political boundaries, no one would push investment in North America down to the point of 5 per cent returns *if elsewhere there still existed 10 per cent opportunities*. Some capital would certainly be invested abroad. This would give foreign labor higher wages, because now the foreign worker has more and better tools to work with. It would increase foreign production. By how much? Not only by enough to pay for the constant replacement of used-up capital goods but, in addition, by enough to pay us an interest or dividend return on our investment. This interest return would take the form of goods and services which we receive from abroad and which add to our standard of living. An all-wise scientist would probably approve of the process.[6] It would make sense to him because capital is going into the regions where its productivity is highest.

---

[6] A qualification is in order. Sometimes a multinational corporation gets ownership of mines or oil wells even though it has brought in few funds net from abroad. Corrupt governments may have permanently given away the nation's resources.

When would we be repaid our principal? So long as we are earning a good return, there is no reason why we should ever wish to have it repaid. However, the once-backward country may finally become rather prosperous. It may wish to pull in its belt as far as consumption is concerned and to use its savings to buy out our ownership in its factories, farms, and mines. But suppose that we are rich, with plenty of savings and with so much capital at home that our rate of interest is low. We might not particularly wish to sell out or be repaid. We might raise the selling price of our farm and factory holdings abroad. In other words, we might be content with a smaller percentage interest return. Thus, there is no necessary reason why a country should ever be paid off for its past lending, unless it has become relatively poorer.

**Economic nationalism**   When nationalism rears its head, matters change. Within the United States, interest and dividends may stream from South to North and West to East until doomsday. A few people may grumble about absentee ownership; but the courts and police are there to see that property rights are respected.

Not so between nations. When a country is poor, it may be anxious to borrow. After it has borrowed, it becomes unhappy to have to pay dividends and interest abroad. It chooses not to remember that its prosperity stemmed in part from its past borrowing. More than an economic burden is involved; politically, countries do not like the principle of absentee ownership by foreigners. They are prone to insist upon getting rid of their international liabilities—paying them off at a fair or an unfair price, or often by outright expropriation of the "imperialistic exploiters" (as in Castro's Cuba).

Economics and politics mix in ways too complicated to resolve. Some say "trade follows the flag." Others say the flag follows trade. Some say the pursuit of economic gain is the primary motive behind the imperialistic search for colonies. Others claim that national power (offensive and defensive) is an end in itself; that economic well-being is sacrificed to this end; and that economic resources are sought for their contribution to military strength (offensive and defensive) rather than for their contribution to economic well-being.

According to this view, without wars and nationalism, anyone could invest and trade anywhere, and sensible people should prefer to live in small countries unhindered by costly military establishments and colonial administration. At the opposite extreme is the view that victory in battle, rather than comfortable living, is the only worthy end in life; that the foreigner is of no importance compared with the fatherland; that he can be stripped of his goods and land, and be made to work for the conquerors.

The world of the last few centuries lies somewhere between these extreme cases.

# SUMMARY

## A. MECHANISMS OF FOREIGN EXCHANGE AND TRADE

1   Buying or selling abroad presupposes a foreign exchange rate between home and foreign currencies. Two countries on a gold standard have a stable foreign exchange rate set by the stable parity prices at which they each buy and sell gold—whether gold bars, coins, or gold-exchange standards are used.

2   Classical economists (such as David Hume) relied on gold movements to alter relative price levels: (*a*) raising exports and (*b*) curbing imports of the deficit country, and (*c*) cutting exports and (*d*) raising imports of the surplus country.

3   Once stable exchange rates under a gold standard are abandoned, flexible foreign rates are set by interaction of supply and demand schedules for foreign exchange. The average level around which the exchange rate floats is determined in the longest run essentially by the amount of money determined by each country's central bank: each one's price level is proportional to its *M;* and then, by "purchasing-power parity" the relative exchange rates find their general level.

4   Gold coin and bullion evolved into gold-exchange standards internationally and fractional-reserve banking domestically. In time the dollar displaced the pound as a key currency. And by the 1970s, the modified-gold-standard regime of Bretton Woods finally broke down.

5   The post-Bretton Woods system of the middle 1970s is de facto a somewhat "managed floating" regime. Relative exchange rates rise and fall depending upon supply and demand for exports and imports; but governments sometimes intervene to limit or amplify movements, so that "clean floating" is less the case than "dirty floating." A two-tiered gold market prevails, with the free gold price set by supply and demand of private corporations and investors. For the official reserves of IMF member nations, Special Drawing Rights (SDRs, or "paper gold") serve to supplement official gold holdings.

## B. BALANCE OF INTERNATIONAL TRADE AND CAPITAL MOVEMENTS

6   The balance of international payments refers to all the transactions that use up foreign exchange or make foreign exchange available to us. It relates the total of our exports of goods and services to our imports. Our exports of goods, services, gold reserves, or IOUs are credit items, making foreign currencies available to us. Our imports of those items are debits, using up foreign currencies.

7   Our net balance on current account comes from adjusting our merchandise trade balance for "invisible" service items and taking into account our unilateral government aid programs. It and net long-term capital movements constitute the "basic deficit" which are offset by short-term capital movements and shipments of reserve-and-gold assets. Even greater is the final Official Settlements Deficit, including as it does short-term capital outflows from the U.S., and transfers by foreign holders of their liquid dollar balances onto their own central banks.

8   As a nation passes from the "young debtor" to the "mature creditor" stage, its payments go through a characteristic sequence of stages, ending up living off earnings from past foreign investments.

9   No problem in international finance is more important than that of understanding the real and the monetary aspects of capital movements in their effect upon the industrial development of nations and nationalistic rivalries.

# CONCEPTS FOR REVIEW

gold standard versus floating
    exchange rate
currency depreciation and
    appreciation vs. devaluation
over- and under-valued currencies
gold-exchange and dollar standard
"managed-floating" system
debits and credits
balance of payments

balance of trade
"favorable balance"
invisibles, government items
America's "basic deficit"
IOUs, capital movements
gold and reserves movements
net foreign investment
historical capital movements
    in politics and economics

# QUESTIONS FOR DISCUSSION

1 Contrast free and stable foreign exchange rates. Explain each.

2 Contrast "managed" or "dirty" floating with "free" or "clean" floating.

3 What is the meaning and sense to the purchasing-power-parity doctrine?

4 Draw up a list of items that belong on the credit side of the balance of international payments and another list of items that belong on the debit side. What is meant by a "favorable balance of trade"? By the balance on current account? By the "basic deficit"? Why the term "invisible items"? What is the difference between short- and long-term capital movements?

5 Construct hypothetical balance sheets for a young debtor country, a mature debtor country, a new creditor country, and a mature creditor country.

6 A mideast nation suddenly discovers huge oil resources. Show how her "balance of trade" and "current balance" suddenly turn favorable. Show how she acquires assets in London or New York as an offset. Later when she uses these assets for internal development, show how her current and capital items reverse their role.

# APPENDIX: Unemployment Aspects of International Trade and Overvaluation

## FOREIGN-TRADE MULTIPLIER

The classical mechanism of Hume depended primarily on relative prices. It seems to have assumed, essentially, that employment is always full: that foreign trade never moved society inside its *p-p frontier* or pushed it outward toward that frontier from an initial underemployment equilibrium.

Yet we saw in Part Two that a laissez faire system is not automatically always at full employment. That condition cannot be guaranteed unless stabilizing monetary and fiscal policy is brought to bear on it (or unless there is more ideal flexibility of wage and price levels than modern mixed economies have.)

What, then, will be the effects of international forces on the $C + I + G$ equilibrium of Part Two?

One can guess that additional exports and foreign investment will have the same expansionary effects on domestic production and employment as will additional domestic investment.

That guess is correct: similar multiplier effects are involved. New exports do have exactly the same multiplier effects on output and prices. They raise incomes directly, but in addition they set up a chain of further spending and responding.

Thus, $1 billion worth of new export orders to New England machine-tool factories will create $1 billion of primary jobs and income. Then workers and owners may respend perhaps two-thirds of their new income on the consumption products of Indiana and California; two-thirds of this extra income is in turn respent. The process finally comes to a halt only when the total adds up to

$$3 = 1 + \tfrac{2}{3} + (\tfrac{2}{3})^2 + \cdots = 1/(1 - \tfrac{2}{3})$$

—i.e., to $1 billion of initial expenditure plus $2 billion of extra secondary consumption expenditure.

**Import leakages**  Besides introducing a multiplier effect of exports, international trade has a second important effect. Our higher American GNP will increase our imports, let us say, by one-twelfth out of every extra dollar. This means that our chain of induced domestic purchasing power will peter out faster than in the above example. At each step, these imports act as "leakages," just like the marginal propensity to save.[1]

Therefore, out of the original $1 billion of income in the export industries, perhaps only $\tfrac{7}{12}$ $(= \tfrac{2}{3} - \tfrac{1}{12})$ rather than $\tfrac{8}{12}$ will be respent on *American* consumption goods (in Indiana, California, and so forth). And so it will go at each stage. The whole multiplier will now add up to only

$$1 + \tfrac{7}{12} + (\tfrac{7}{12})^2 + \cdots$$

or only to

$$1 \div (1 - \tfrac{7}{12}) = 1 \div \tfrac{5}{12} = 2\tfrac{2}{5}$$

instead of to 3. Note that $\tfrac{1}{12}$ of our extra $2\tfrac{2}{5}$ billion of generated income—or $\tfrac{1}{5}$ billion in this case—tends

to go abroad for extra imports. A general rule can be stated.

**Exports raise domestic income, but with a multiplier reduced by our induced imports. So long as some fraction of income at every stage is leaking into domestic saving, a new dollar of exports will raise income, but can never lift it by enough to call forth a full dollar of new imports.[2]**

In conclusion, we may say that variations in income generated by international trade will often go partway to effecting the needed adjustments; but they do not obviate the need for some price or exchange-rate reductions, since a spontaneous increase in demand for our exports can never create a large enough induced expansion of our imports to cancel out all final effects on the balance of payments between us and abroad.

## OVERVALUATION OF A CURRENCY AND UNEMPLOYMENT

Consider two countries. Call them A and E for America and Europe. Although Germany is not identical with Europe, let the respective currencies be called dollars and marks. Let A and E begin in long-run foreign exchange equilibrium with 4 marks to the dollar, or $.25 per mark.

Now let productivity in Europe, even though it begins far below that in America, grow faster than in America. If all money wages and profits grew in E as quickly as productivity, there need be no lasting disturbance to the equilibrium: thus, doubling productivity and money wages and factor payments in E will leave her prices just as they were in relation to A's unchanged prices. The real income level in E has grown relative to that of A, perhaps closing some

---

[1] Applying the foreign-trade multiplier analysis to a small city or country, you will find that secondary multiplier effects upon the workers of that region are almost negligible, since most extra income leaks out to other regions.

[2] Suppose that each extra dollar of income is always split up into the three fractions: $c$ for American consumption goods; $b$ for America's propensity to import goods from abroad; $a$ for the remaining amount going into saving. Then let exports go up by 1 unit. The multiplier tells us that our income will go up by $1/(1 - c) = 1/(b + a)$. Multiplying this extra income by the fraction $b$, we get induced imports of $b/(b + a)$, which is certainly less than our original 1 of new exports—to the extent that the marginal propensity to save $a$ is positive. (If there is any induced domestic investment, it can be thrown in with $c$, and our result will still hold for any "stable" system with positive "leakage" $a$.)

of the gap between them. But so long as Engel's laws imply that A's goods are as much in demand at higher income levels as E's, there need be no disturbance of the equilibrium. A is not yet hurt or helped by E's improved real income.

However, it is more realistic to assume that money wage and other factor-costs do not *at once* grow abroad as fast as productivity does, even though they grow much faster than in relatively stagnant A. Now E's goods are bargains. Even if A has not had domestic wage or other inflation, A's goods are now relatively dear. What is the effect? E's exports expand physically and (probably) in value; A's exports dwindle physically and (probably) in value. If payments were in balance before, now A runs a chronic international deficit.

We can say: Before, at 1 dollar to 4 marks, the dollar was neither undervalued nor overvalued; now at 1 to 4, the dollar is definitely an "overvalued currency," running a chronic deficit and having too high a cost level. This results from the more rapid technical change abroad, which partially closed the gap between foreign technology and ours and lowered their relative costs.

The deficit disequilibrium in A's balance on current account will probably be aggravated by a tendency for A's investors to want to invest in E, where profitability is likely to be very high as a result of (*a*) rapid growth in E; (*b*) rapid technical change in E; (*c*) great opportunity for A firms to profit from applying their know-how in E.

**Effects of overvaluation**  1. If in A we previously had full employment, our loss of export production (and perhaps of domestic production displaced by cheap imports) implies a multiplier drop in employment and real GNP.

2. We cannot use Federal Reserve easy money to stimulate domestic $I$, for fear that low interest yields will drive cool money to seek higher yields in E.

3. If, like Kennedy and Johnson in the 1960s, we use militant fiscal policy, expanding $G$ expenditure and cutting tax rates to expand $C$ and $I$, we can overcome our unemployment; but the resulting increase in GNP will wipe out the drop in our imports from E that had resulted from our income drop (and which has *partially* relieved our international deficit.)

4. If E previously had full employment, she now is threatened with overemployment, with demand-pull and cost-push inflation. If E previously had some

slack, she would be delighted with her good fortune to have become an *undervalued*-currency nation, with the extra GNP and employment thereby implied. If she was previously at full employment, E will now complain bitterly that she is "importing inflation" from profligate A (and vested interests will be growing up in her overswollen export industries—interests which will fight hard politically to resist any later correcting of the undervaluation of E's currency).

5. Actually, now that E is quoting prices low relative to those A is quoting, the disturbed-equilibrium terms of trade—the ratio of our export to import prices—have moved in favor of A. E is, so to speak, throwing away goods to A. Not only is A getting cheap goods—the goal of rational nonmercantilistic nations—but we in A are, for the moment, getting some goods in return simply for our shipping out barren gold or mere dollar IOUs (no wonder the comfortable doctrine of "benign neglect of international disequilibrium" will tempt many people in A).

**Correcting overvaluation**  What can correct the situation? We in A can wait for inflation in E to raise E's prices and end the undervaluation of E's currency. If E's productivity continues to show miracles of growth, the wait may be a long and grueling one.

Or, in premodern times, A could try to deflate her own wage and cost level by 15 or 30 per cent. This seems not very practical in a mixed economy of rather rigid administered prices and wages: blood runs in the streets of nations trying to adjust to an overvalued currency by internal cost deflation.

Or A might pray for a miracle that would increase her productivity. Exhortations to have us all work harder and more skillfully will no doubt be forthcoming in abundance.

Or E might *appreciate* the mark.[3] When the mark has risen from \$.25 to \$.40, German exports will be dear and imports from America cheap. Thus, there may again be equilibrium, with neither currency overvalued.[4] However, let us suppose that for the years

---

[3] Or, what is the same thing, A might *depreciate* the dollar.
[4] If E's improved productivity has occurred across the board in all industries, she will be better off in the new equilibrium and we need not be hurt or helped. (For example, a relative 30 per cent improvement in her productivity and costs relative to ours could be just offset by a 30 per cent appreciation. We import the same German goods at the same dollar costs as before; Germans now can buy 30 per cent more of their domestic goods from an hour's work at home and 30 per

in question, currency appreciation is just not politically feasible.

If A's gold is large enough to meet the chronic drain and E's willingness to take A's IOUs is sufficiently great, the disequilibrium situation may go on for a long time. Perhaps in that time luck will shift the winds of demand in A's favor; or A's productivity might grow; or A may become a more profitable place for investors in either country to place their long-term funds; or the government in A may, reluctantly, cut down on troop and aid expenditures abroad.

A country with an overvalued currency will be under great internal pressure to interfere with free trade. Employers and workers will clamor for protective tariffs and quotas. Congress will consider preventing costly tours abroad, curbing free flow of capital abroad, introducing comprehensive exchange controls, initiating export subsidies, "tying" foreign aid, and requiring purchase of military equipment at home even at prices twice as high. The President will exhort business to moderate profitable investments abroad by a "voluntary" and mandatory capital-investment program, and will introduce so-called "interest equalization taxes" which place perhaps a 15 to 30 per cent tax on long-term investments abroad.

Most chronically overvalued currencies in history have resulted in suspension of freely convertible currencies and in controlled international trade. And once overvaluation of the currency has been handled in this way, there is no easy way of removing the controls: when controls are ended, the international payments deficit reappears. History is replete with cases of premature dashes toward convertibility, ending in fiascoes or return to controls.

---

cent more of imports from us at the 30-per-cent-cheapened dollar.) But suppose, as is more likely, that Germany's productivity is biased to rise more in goods that she had been on the borderline of importing from America. Then there is a presumption that in the new equilibrium, our export prices will fall relative to what we now pay for imports. Europe's progress has hurt us a bit, as we now lose "consumer's surplus" from no longer being able to trade at so "favorable terms of trade."

**The Achilles heel of classicism**   What needs emphasis here is the economics of overvaluation. We shall discover that all the discredited notions of the mercantilists—fear of gold drain, insistence on import curbs and export subsidies, wish to export unemployment abroad, desire to give goods away cheaply rather than dearly, etc.—make some sense in the case of an overvalued currency. The skilled classical and neoclassical arguments of Hume, Smith, and Samuelson no longer carry the day because their major premise of equilibrium currency valuation is explicitly denied. Protectionism becomes rampant.

The next two chapters will elucidate the pro-and-con arguments for tariffs and quotas. It will demonstrate the basic theory of comparative advantage that justifies mutually advantageous geographical division of labor and trade. If prices and wages were everywhere perfectly flexible and/or exchange rates could be counted on to be neither overvalued nor undervalued, the arguments of those chapters would be unanswerable. Here is an example:

Chapter 34 points out that the veil of money and foreign exchange merely covers the true barter nature of trade. It says, "One country cannot undersell the other in *all* goods, but only in those in which it has a comparative advantage, being undersold by the other country in those goods in which that country has a comparative advantage." That is absolutely true in a Ricardian model where the wage ratio between the two countries moves flexibly so that the foreign exchange rate is never *over-* or *under*valued.

But it is still quite obvious that if one country insists on pricing its goods sky-high in money terms (because of sky-high wage rates *or* profit markups), it can certainly price itself out of the market, bringing upon itself an overvalued currency, unemployment, and international deficits. After all, any one of us can do that by insisting on $100,000 per hour; and any region, such as New England, could be undersold by the South in everything if it insisted on prices that cleared no markets. So this can certainly happen internationally as well as intranationally.

## CONCEPTS FOR REVIEW

| | | |
|---|---|---|
| foreign-trade multiplier | overvaluation, undervaluation | importing inflation |
| "leakage" into imports | unemployment and overvaluation | a case for mercantilism? |

# 34

## INTERNATIONAL TRADE AND THE THEORY OF COMPARATIVE ADVANTAGE

The benefit of international trade—a more efficient employment of the productive forces of the world.
J. S. MILL

Again and again we have seen how specialization increases productivity and standards of living. Now we must show exactly how this works out in the field of international trade, going behind the facade of international finance.

Why did the United States specialize a century ago in the production of farm goods and exchange these for the manufacturing output of Europe? Why is she today able to export highly complex mass-produced goods to the far corners of the globe? Why is the agriculture of Australia so different from that of Austria? How great would the costs of complete self-sufficiency be to a modern nation? How do all countries benefit from trade?

The key to such questions, and many more, is provided by the theory of "comparative advantage," or "comparative cost." Developed more than a century ago by David Ricardo, John Stuart Mill, and other followers of Adam Smith, the theory of comparative advantage is a closely reasoned doctrine which, when *properly* stated, is unassailable. With it we can identify gross fallacies in the political propaganda for protective tariffs aimed at limiting imports. With it we can identify the germs of truth that sometimes appear in the heated claims for tariff or quota protection.

### DIVERSITY OF CONDITIONS BETWEEN NATIONAL REGIONS

For simplicity, begin by imagining two countries or continents say, Europe and America, or the tropics and the temperate zone. Each is endowed with certain quantities of natural resources, capital goods, kinds of labor, and technical knowledge or know-how. The first link in the comparative-cost chain of reasoning is the *diversity in conditions of production between different countries.*

Specifically, this means that the production possibilities of the different countries are very different. Although people could try to produce something of every commodity in each and any region, it is obvious that they would not succeed; or if they did succeed, it would only be at a terrific cost. Adam Smith pointed out that, with hothouse procedures and forcing methods, wine grapes could perhaps be grown in Scotland; but the cost in terms of economic resources would be exorbitant, and the resulting product would be scarcely fit to drink.

**Even if by chance two countries can both produce the same commodities, they generally find that it pays for each to specialize its production especially on some goods—and trade for other goods.**

If we consider trade between, say, the temperate zones and the tropics, the foregoing proposition will seem true and trite. Of course, resources near the equator are more productive in the growing of bananas, and northern resources are better designed for wheat growing. Everyone can readily see that in this case specialization and trade will increase the amount of world production of both goods, and also each country's ability to consume both goods.

It is not so immediately obvious, but it is no less true, that

**International trade is mutually profitable even when one of the countries can produce *every commodity* more cheaply (in terms of labor or all resources) than the other country. Can America with $7-an-hour wages benefit from trade with Japan at $3 an hour? Yes, asserts the theory of comparative advantage.**

One country may be *absolutely* more efficient in the production of *every* good than is the other country; and this means the other country has an *absolute* disadvantage in the production of every good. But so long as there are differences in the *relative* efficiencies of producing the different goods in the two countries, we can always be sure that even the poor country has a *comparative* advantage in the production of those commodities in which it is *relatively* most efficient; this same poor country will have a *comparative dis*advantage in those other commodities in which its inefficiency is more than average. Similarly, the rich, efficient country will find that it should specialize in those fields of production where it has a comparative advantage, planning to import those commodities in which it has a comparative disadvantage.

A traditional example used to illustrate this paradox of comparative advantage is the case of the best lawyer in town who is also the best typist in town. Will she not specialize in law and leave typing to a secretary? How can she afford to give up precious time from the legal field, where her comparative advantage is very great, to perform typing activities in which she is efficient but in which she lacks *comparative* advantage? Or look at it from the secretary's point of view. She is less efficient than the lawyer in both activities; but her relative disadvantage compared with the lawyer's is least in typing. Relatively speaking, the secretary has a comparative advantage in typing.

So with countries. Suppose America produces food with one-third the labor that Europe does, and clothing with one-half the labor. Then we shall see that America has comparative advantage in food and comparative disadvantage in clothing—this, despite the fact that America is absolutely most efficient in everything. By the same token, Europe has comparative advantage in clothing.

The key to the concept is in the word "comparative"—which implies that *each and every* country has both definite "advantage" in some goods and definite "disadvantage" in other goods.

## A SIMPLE CASE: EUROPE AND AMERICA

Let us illustrate these fundamental principles of international trade by a simplified example. Consider America and Europe of a century ago, and concentrate on only two commodities, food and clothing. In America, land and natural resources were then very plentiful relative to labor and capital. But in Europe, people and capital were plentiful relative to land.

This contrast is best seen if we look at the *intensive* agriculture of a country such as Belgium. There, in order to get the greatest possible output, small plots of land have to be cultivated assiduously by many people using much fertilizer. Compare this with the extensive agriculture of early America: here one family cultivated many acres, and national product was maximized by each man's "spreading himself thin" over the virtually free land. A Belgian would have thought this wasteful. But in view of the relatively high cost of our labor or capital and the low cost of land, it was prudent.

Of course, if surplus population could all have migrated from Belgium to the United States, the law of diminishing returns implies that real wages here would fall toward equality with rising wages there; and high land rents there would fall toward equality with rising rents here.[1]

But suppose that immigrants from abroad are to be kept out of the United States in order to keep labor scarce here and wages high. From this same selfish point of view, should the United States also impose a protective tariff designed to keep out imports from abroad? Or should it not? To answer this important social question, we must measure carefully the amounts of food and clothing that will be produced and consumed in each country (*a*) if there is no international trade, and (*b*) if free trade, according to comparative advantage, is permitted to follow its own course.

## THE LAW OF COMPARATIVE ADVANTAGE

David Ricardo, stockbroker and self-made millionaire, expert on the theory of land rent and of currency, came up in 1817 with the beautiful proof that international specialization pays for a nation. This is the famous theory of comparative advantage, or, as it is sometimes called, the "theory of comparative cost."

For simplicity, Ricardo worked with only two countries; we shall call them America and Europe, and make the unimportant assumption that they are both about the same size. For simplicity, he worked with only two goods; we shall call them food and clothing. For simplicity, Ricardo chose to measure all costs in terms of hours of labor; we shall do the same, recognizing that more advanced treatises and the Appendix to this chapter give some of the qualifications needed when our simple assumptions are relaxed. The germ of truth in the principle of comparative advantage still remains.

**Uncommon sense**  Using common sense, people will probably agree that trade between America and Europe is likely to be mutually profitable in a first simple case where European labor has greater productivity in one good, and American labor has greater productivity in the other.

---

[1] Actually, this would have tended at the same time to increase *total world production*. Why? Because the transfer of workers from their poor Belgian farms to rich American farms would increase their labor productivity and total world product. Factor mobility shifts the world *p-p frontier* outward.

**TABLE 34-1**

### Comparative advantage depends only on *relative* industry efficiencies and inefficiencies

America has lower labor costs in both food and clothing: our labor productivity is between two and three times Europe's (twice in clothing, thrice in food). Yet it pays both of us to trade: America to export food, in which we have greatest comparative advantage (greatest *relative* efficiency), and to import clothing in which we have comparative *dis*advantage (least relative efficiency). Our comparative disadvantage is Europe's comparative

| AMERICAN AND EUROPEAN LABOR REQUIREMENTS FOR PRODUCTION | | |
|---|---|---|
| PRODUCT | IN AMERICA | IN EUROPE |
| 1 unit food | 1 labor hr. | 3 labor hr. |
| 1 unit clothing | 2 labor hr. | 4 labor hr. |

advantage: she has relatively "least inefficiency" in clothing exports; most "least efficiency" in food, which she'll import. All depends on four labor-cost numbers: particularly on the ratios 1/2 and 3/4: Our 1/2 being less than her 3/4, we export food.

In this case, to produce a unit of food in America requires a smaller number of labor days than is needed in Europe to produce it, while to produce a unit of clothing takes a smaller number of labor days in Europe than in America. The man in the street needs no Ricardo or trained economist to tell him that in such a case, America will probably specialize in food production, exporting some food for Europe's clothing exports.

But Ricardo showed much more than this. He showed that even in a more difficult second case—where American labor (or resources generally) is more productive than Europe's *in both* food *and* clothing—trade is still likely to be mutually advantageous.

Table 34-1 portrays, for this second and general case, the principle of comparative advantage. In America a unit of food costs 1 hour of labor and a unit of clothing costs 2 hours of labor. In Europe the cost is 3 hours of labor for food and 4 hours of labor for clothing. By forming the proper two ratios of these four crucial numbers, Ricardo can prove conclusively that America and Europe will *both* benefit if America specializes in food and exports it for the clothing exports that Europe specializes in.

Before examining this, listen to the European in the street as he says:

*Mon Dieu!* Trade could never be profitable for us with that American colossus. Her efficiency will enable her to undersell us in every line—food and clothing. She is twice as productive as we are in clothing, and three times as productive in food. We need import tariffs and quotas to protect the honest European worker.

Now listen to what is being said here in America by the small-town editor and the congressmen who have not grasped the law of comparative advantage:

The European wage level most assuredly will be far below that of this most prosperous (and productive) nation on earth. If we subject the American workers to the unbridled competition of the European pauper laborers, who subsist on less per day than we do, the real wage of the American worker must drastically fall. A protective tariff against cheap imports is desperately needed to maintain the American standard of living.

What Ricardo shows is that both arguments are wrong.

**In free-trade equilibrium, Europe's real wage rate will be somewhere between one-half and one-third of America's—not low enough for her to undersell us in all goods; and also not high enough for us to undersell her in all goods. But these final free-trade real wage rates will be higher in *each* region than they were in pretrade self-sufficiency—because workers everywhere get the imported goods for fewer hours of labor.**

It follows as a corollary that prohibitive tariffs on either or both sides will reduce real wages in both places. (And we may add this in our day: There are better tools than protective tariffs to make sure that there are plenty of job opportunities in both places—namely, the tools of proper fiscal and central-bank monetary policies, and appropriate flexible exchange-rate policies.) Let's now prove all this.

**Before trade**  We start with a prohibitive tariff that prevented all international trade. Table 34-1 shows the real wage of the American worker for an hour's work as 1 unit of food or $\frac{1}{2}$ unit of clothing. The European worker is even less well off and gets for an hour's labor before trade only $\frac{1}{3}$ unit of food or $\frac{1}{4}$ unit of clothing.

Evidently, under domestic competition in each isolated continent, the price ratios of food and clothing will be different in the two places because of the difference in relative labor cost ratios. In America clothing will be 2 times as dear as food because it takes twice as much labor. In Europe clothing will be only $\frac{4}{3}$ times as dear as food.

**After trade**  Now we repeal the protective tariff and make trade free. The relative prices of clothing and food must now come to a common level, just as the water in two connecting pipes must come to a common intermediate level once you remove the barrier between them. Why?

Competitive merchants buy where things are cheap and will sell where they are dear. With clothing relatively more expensive in America, eager merchants will soon ship clothing from Europe to America. And they ship food from America to the European markets, where food has been relatively dear. Our clothing industry will feel the keen price competition of imports, and if the figures in Table 34-1 do not change, it may lose *all* its workers to its rival U.S. food industry. The opposite will happen in Europe: workers will leave the food industry for the clothing industry, in which Europe has a comparative advantage.[2]

America as a whole has benefited. Like any merchant who will buy electric power from another firm if he cannot produce it as cheaply himself, America has taken advantage of the fact that clothing does cost us less by barter than by production at home. The same goes for Europe's benefit from specializing in clothing and getting her food more cheaply by barter than by domestic production.

*Example of benefit:* Each unit of American labor still gets the 1 unit of food it produces here. But now 1 American food unit trades for *more* than 1/2 unit of clothing. How much more? Certainly not more than the 3/4 ratio set by Europe's costs. The common ratio after trade will be *somewhere between* 1/2 and 3/4. American labor gains in clothing by any degree that it exceeds 1/2. Similarly, European labor gains in bartering clothing for food by any degree that the ratio falls short of 3/4. (See the Appendix for elaborations.)

Granted that Ricardo has proved that both countries have benefited from trade in accordance with comparative advantage, what about the workingman in each place? Table 34-1 can show that his real wages have improved in both places. Now the

---

[2] A 1970 Cornell student, Henry Morgenstern, wrote me the following rule. Write down the relative labor costs from each country's column: 1/2 and 3/4, here. Find the country with the *smallest* fraction: 1/2 here. Its numerator tells us the good it will export: in this case, food is America's export. (Likewise, the denominator of the largest fraction, of 3/4, tells us that Europe exports clothing.)

American worker's day of labor will buy him the same food as before, but he gets *more* imported clothing for a day of labor and can now afford to consume more of *both* goods. Likewise, the European worker can get more of the cheapened imported food for a day of his labor, and inasmuch as he gets the same real wage in clothing, his budget is also better off. It is the expanded *world* production of both goods, which specialization and trade created, that makes it possible for *everyone* to be better off.

**1. *The principle of comparative advantage restated:* Whether or not one of two regions is absolutely more efficient in the production of every good than is the other, if each specializes in the products in which it has a *comparative advantage* (greatest *relative* efficiency), trade will be mutually profitable to both regions. Real wages of productive factors will rise in both places.**

**2. An ill-designed prohibitive tariff or quota, far from helping the protected factor of production, will instead reduce its real wage by making imports expensive and by making the whole world less productive through eliminating the efficiency inherent in the best pattern of specialization and division of labor.**

This simple principle provides the unshakable basis for international trade.[3]

[3] To see this graphically, look at Fig. 34-1(a), which shows America's domestic production-possibility frontier, with its slope depicting a 1/2 food-to-clothing price ratio.

Europe's brown domestic *p-p frontier* in Fig. 34-1(b) has its 3/4 slope. (Since Europe's population happens to be about equal that of America, why is the brown curve this much "smaller" than the orange? Because America has double or more the productivity of Europe.) Ricardo says, "It is the difference in slopes that makes profitable trade possible." How profitable? The limits (as explained

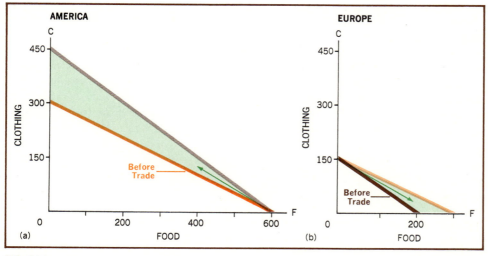

**FIG. 34-1**

in the Appendix) are shown by the green areas between (*a*) each country's domestic curve and (*b*) a line drawn parallel to the other country's curve passed through each point of specialization. Thus the necessarily-parallel intermediate green arrows of free-trade equilibrium, with slopes intermediate between America's 1/2 and Europe's 3/4, show one possible outcome: At post-trade equilibrium with food selling for two-thirds clothing (i.e., at 2/3), America gains by producing food alone and exporting it for clothing: Europe gains by producing clothing and exporting it in exchange for food.

**Free-trade full employment**   Final remark: So long as money wage rates in each country are not forced unreasonably high by union or governmental actions, neither country can, in free-trade equilibrium, be undersold in all goods. Thus, American money wage rates will have to be between 2 and 3 times Europe's (expressed either in dollar terms or pound terms—say, $7 here and $3 there; or £$3\frac{1}{2}$ and £$1\frac{1}{2}$. But take warning: if unions or Congress or Federal Reserve $M$-expansion raised our wages to $9 an hour while European wages stayed at $3, then of course such wage-cost rises will destroy balance-of-payments equilibrium and even throw *all* American workers out of work. Depreciation of the dollar's parity relative to the pound—as in Chapter 33—would be necessary to restore viable money wage levels.

The rest of this chapter is not needed to understand the unshakable basis of interregional trade—principles as valid for Russia-Poland or Russia-China trade as for America-Britain trade.

## OTHER CAUSES OF INTERNATIONAL TRADE

**Decreasing costs**   If economies of mass production are overwhelmingly important, costs may decrease as output expands. This would strengthen the case for international exchange of goods. In fact, decreasing costs are a second great factor—in addition to differences in comparative costs—explaining why specialization and trade are profitable. For, as was discussed in Chapters 3 and 25, large-scale specialization is most fruitful when there is a widely expanded market.

In fact, even if there were no differences in comparative costs between two countries, it might pay for them to toss a coin to decide who was to produce each of two goods subject to increasing returns or decreasing costs. Complete specialization would increase world production of both goods. This may be illustrated by our example in Chapter 3 of the identical Indian twins who, despite their similarity, still find it advantageous to specialize to reap the efficiencies of "mass" production. As we'll see in Chapter 36, the expanded European Common Market hopes to reap the advantages of such an extended division of labor.

Moreover, there is one very practical aspect of international trade to be observed under decreasing cost. Peculiarly under such conditions, perfect competition is likely to break down and be succeeded by monopoly, or imperfect competition. By excluding foreign competition, protective tariffs and quotas consolidate the position of the monopolist. This is recognized in the old slogan, "The tariff is the mother of trusts." Freer international trade is often an efficient way of breaking up monopoly positions.[4]

**Differences in tastes or demand**   Here is a third possible cause for trade. Even if costs were identical in the two countries and were increasing, trade might take place as the result of differences in *tastes*.

Thus, it might pay both Norway and Sweden to produce fish from the sea and meat

---

[4] Still, one must concede that violently decreasing-cost situations might under free trade lead to bigger monopolies; also, that decreasing-cost situations may have in them some of the valid elements of the "infant-industry" argument to be met in the next chapter.

from the land in about the same amounts. But if the Swedes have a relatively great fondness for meat and the Norwegians for fish, then a mutually profitable export of meat from Norway and fish from Sweden would take place. Both parties gain from this trade. The sum total of human happiness is increased, just as it is when Jack Spratt trades fat meat for his wife's lean. Both get some "consumer's surplus" from the swap.[5]

We have now gone beyond the financial facade of international trade to the real fundamentals. Now we can handle the remaining two chapters of Part Five.

## FOREIGN-TRADE SUPPLY-AND-DEMAND CHARTS[6]

The foregoing theory of comparative advantage stripped international trade down to its barter essentials. It said nothing about dollars, pounds, or foreign exchange rates. How does the matter appear to the perfect-competitors in one small food or clothing industry in America? Why does competitive $P$ settle down so that America will export this item of wheat but not that item of cloth? How do the supply and demand curves look in the competitive market for a small clothing item exported by Europe—say, linen cloth? Or for an American export item like wheat?

Figure 34-2 on the next page first takes up the case of wheat, in the case where Europe's unit of money—call it a pound—is worth exactly \$2. Figure 34-2(a) shows the orange American demand and supply curves $d_a d_a$ and $s_a s_a$ for wheat expressed in dollars (which, by a 1/2 scale change, can also be read in pounds). Figure 34-2(b) shows the brown European supply and demand for wheat as $d_e d_e$ and $s_e s_e$ (in pounds, with vertical scales nicely aligned so as to be read in dollars or pounds).

Suppose trade in wheat were prohibited by quotas, tariffs, or sky-high transport costs. Where would *pre-trade* equilibrium be in each nation? Under such an assumption of no trade, equilibrium would be at the separate intersection points $A_a$ and $A_e$: Wheat's price (per bushel) in America would be \$2, or £1; its price in Europe would be \$6, or £3. Both markets are cleared; being forbidden, autarky exports and imports are, of course, zero.

Now open up trade in wheat. If there are zero transport costs, quotas, and tariffs, both markets must have the same price. Why? Because sharp-eyed arbitragers could buy where wheat was cheap and send it for sale where it was dear. With what result? Evidently, $P_e$ would fall and $P_a$ rise until equality was achieved. How much would prices change? The answer must depend on the slopes of each country's $dd$ and $ss$ curves.

**The condition for the free-trade equilibrium is that the new common price should coax out an import demand abroad just equal to our export supply.**

---

[5] Even two individuals with identical amounts of two goods and the same tastes may in rare instances trade. Two sailors, each with a fifth of whiskey and a fifth of gin, might toss a coin to decide which is to have two fifths of gin and which two fifths of whiskey. You can reason out why the same might be true of herring and chocolate, but not of corned beef and cabbage. Such cases of trade are oddities (and can be shown, in more advanced treatises, to result from a reversal of curvature of the convex indifference contours of Chapter 22's Appendix).

[6] The next two sections are quite independent of the rest of this chapter. The next chapters do not require them or this chapter's Appendix.

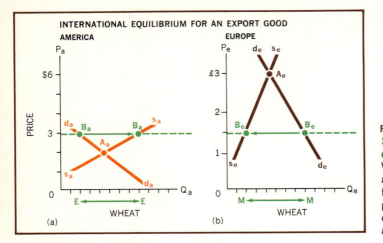

FIG. 34-2
**Supply and demand schedules determine dollar and pound prices of U.S. exports**
With zero trade, American wheat price is at $A_a$, below European price at $A_e$. With free trade, goods flow from low- to high-price place, finally equalizing $P$s at that common level where the green export arrow just matches the green import arrow.

Free-trade equilibrium at the \$3 and £1½ level, where America's export arrow $EE$ or $B_aB_a$ just matches (and opposes in direction) Europe's import arrow $MM$ or $B_eB_e$. No other equilibrium can persist.

Figure 34-3 shows exactly the same phenomenon for the case of an American import: Let us import oil from abroad, primarily from Mideast sheikdoms that for simplicity will be assumed to use the pound as their currency (as they used to do when part of the British Empire and "sterling block"). Who decides that oil will be our import and wheat will be our export? The levels of no-trade equilibria intersections predetermine the decision: Goods flow uphill toward higher prices under free competition! (Because $A_e$ is below $A_a$, the rest of the world exports oil to the United States.)

The reader could draw a new figure for the case where the no-trade $P$s happen to start out equal and where free trade leads to zero trade. This is a rare razor's-edge case of coincidental levels. However, in real life, there are always transport costs that impede trade. Thus, although bricks may seem to be cheaper in America, if the difference between the no-trade equilibrium intersections is less than the substantial *costs of shipping* heavy and bulky bricks, each country will produce its own bricks and there will be neither exports nor imports. Goods try to flow uphill toward higher prices, but transport-cost or tariff impediments can inhibit their flow—resulting in some goods being purely "domestic goods" in both countries.

This supply-and-demand analysis is a simple extension of that given in Chapter 4 (or Part Three). It is useful. But note that we should have to go to Ricardo's deeper analysis of comparative advantage to explain *why* both countries' *dd* and *ss* schedules will be such as to give America a money-cost advantage in exporting this food item. That same analysis of basic comparative advantage is needed to explain why the clothing item, linen, will have *dd* and *ss* intersections, causing Europe to export it.[7]

### EFFECTS OF TARIFFS AND QUOTAS

**Prohibitive tariff**   Figure 34-3 can be used to illustrate the effect of President Ford's

---

[7]Economists explain: These supply and demand curves of Marshall depict only "partial equilibrium." They must be anchored on "general-equilibrium" analysis, of which Ricardo's is a special case.

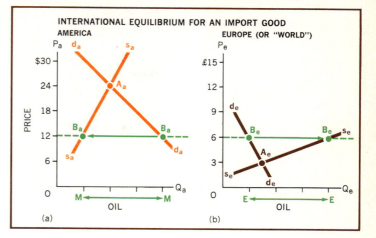

**FIG. 34-3**

**Supply and demand schedules determine dollar and pound prices of U.S. imports**

Lower European *P* at zero or *autarky* trade means linen will be imported from Europe when trade is permitted. Common *P* is where imports and exports match. (Quotas, tariffs, or transport costs will make *P*s unequal.)

1975 tariff (or "customs tax") on the import of oil. If we tax oil imports by more than the difference in prices ($18 ≡ £9 = $24 − $6) shown between the no-trade $A_a$ and $A_e$ intersections, how much oil will be sent here? Absolutely none: the tariff of more than $18 will be a *prohibitive* one, shutting out all imports. Why? Because any importer who tries to buy oil at the lowest world $A_e$ price of $6 (or £3) or more can sell it here for not quite as much as our autarky price, $24 (or £12). But the tariff the importer has to pay would come to *more* than that difference! Hence, such a tariff kills off *all* the advantage of specialization and trade.

A smaller tariff will kill off some (but not all) oil imports, in that sense partially "protecting" our domestic industry.

**Social cost of tariffs**   What happens to our domestic linen industry? The tariff gives it a higher price than under free trade. The effect of a tariff that "protects" against imports is to raise the price to the domestic consumer.[8]

But does not the government collect in tariff receipts about what the consumers now pay in extra prices? Our special example of a prohibitive tariff points up the negative answer that generally applies. Here consumers pay more in price, but the government collects nothing! This needs emphasis, and shows how foolish it is to try to measure a tariff's height and capacity for doing harm by the tax revenue it brings in. Also, any tariff that limits imports will make consumers pay a higher *P* for all *domestically supplied* output, and *none* of this shows up in government revenue.

[8]The price rise need not be as great as the tariff itself; it will be that great only if the industry abroad is so large compared with our use of the product that one or both of their *ss* and *dd* schedules can be treated as virtually horizontal, our imports being too small to move their *P*s appreciably. If instead of behaving oligopolistically the OPEC oil cartel really behaved according to Fig. 34-3's straight-line $d_e d_e$ and $s_e s_e$ schedules, we could compute the effect of a $2 Ford tariff: being 2/18 of the prohibitive $18 tariff, it would cut our oil imports by one-ninth, thereby raising $P_a$ by $12/9, or to $13\frac{1}{3}$ from $12. Under competition the $2 tariff would force down world price to $13\frac{1}{3} − $2 = $11\frac{1}{3}$ or to £5$\frac{2}{3}$; but if the cartel held firm, $P_a$ might rise here by the full $2, to $14, thereby slashing our oil imports by one-sixth rather than one-ninth. With U.S. now importing less oil, some members of the cartel would no longer be able to sell at the $12 world price all that their $s_e s_e$ schedule says they would like to.

The higher $P$ lowers the satisfaction and well-being of consumers. Whom does it benefit? The suppliers of this particular industry do benefit. To the extent oil is a monopoly industry here, the monopolists will benefit and can afford to lobby for tariffs. Some of the benefit will trickle down to their employees and to owners of resources especially fitted for oil production. Even if, as in Fig. 34-3(a), there is perfect competition, the productive factors specialized for the protected industry do stand to get some benefit (higher $P$ for oil, more jobs, higher wage rates, higher economic rents on factors inelastically supplied to that industry).[9] When the wife of one of these specialized employees complained about the high cost of oil and of living generally, resulting from a high-tariff program, her husband could reprimand her: "Stop complaining. *We* get more than *we* give as a result of the tariff. It's *the rest of the community* that experiences the net harm from the cessation of oil imports."

In wheat and other nonprotected industries, wives and husbands can both legitimately complain about this oil tariff. Indeed, let us consider (*a*) the harm done to consumers, (*b*) the revenue collected by government, and (*c*) the benefit received by suppliers. What is the net effect, on the supposition that rich and poor, worthy and unworthy, are equally involved on all sides of the argument? The Appendix shows that the harm of a prohibitive tariff outweighs its gain, in this sense:

**A system of prohibitive tariffs puts a society inefficiently *inside* the consumption-possibility frontier that would be available if the efficiencies of international exchange and division of labor were utilized. This is absolutely true of the world as a whole, and particularly true for a country that cuts off all imports and becomes self-sufficient.[10]**

**Quotas**   The effect of a prohibitive tariff could be achieved by imposing a zero quota on all imports. The prices would find their $A_a$ and $A_e$ levels in both markets as in the no-trade cases already discussed. Consumers here will be hurt; and in the sense described above, they will be hurt more than producers are helped.

Suppose the quota is set, not at zero, but, say, at half the level of free-trade imports. The reader can verify that, in the special case of Fig. 34-3's straight-line curves, the American

[9] Indeed, if $s_a s_a$ were completely vertical, all the money newly extorted from the consumer would be transferred to the producers in extra rent: this would presumably be a switch from not particularly unworthy consumers to not particularly worthy producers. More commonly, though, with $s_a s_a$ having some positive elasticity, the higher $P$ will coax out extra domestic $Q$; this will represent a definite social inefficiency, to the degree that resources are drawn from fields where America has a comparative advantage into protected industries where she has a comparative disadvantage. In the extreme case of a horizontal $s_a s_a$, where factors are indifferent between this and other industries, *all* the tariff's benefits to producers are frittered away in inefficient resource allocation, and not even those in the industry derive a selfish benefit at the expense of the hard-hit consumers.

[10] It is also true, with rare (and unimportant) exceptions, for a country that levies prohibitive tariffs on a subset of its goods. The exceptions apply to a country large enough to affect appreciably the relative prices of the goods it imports. By levying sufficiently small, shrewdly gauged tariffs, it might exploit its monopoly power to "make the foreigner pay" for its tariff. [This is an esoteric point, which could be illustrated by means of utility-disutility areas under the schedules in Fig. 34-3(a). But readers of Chapter 25's discussion of marginal revenue (and the loss taken on all earlier units when an extra unit of $q$ is sold by a monopolist) can understand the point thus: The last little unit of import under free trade brings us zero marginal benefit; that is why it is the last unit. If we impose a tiny tariff to keep it out, we do force a reduction in the $P$ we pay on *all* previous units imported. So we could benefit a little from such a move (unless the $s_e s_e$ and/or $d_e d_e$ curves were horizontal). However, Europe could do the same to our wheat, and when all play this game, there is some presumption that world inefficiencies will make all (or most) worse off.]

$P$ will rise half the distance between the free-trade $B_a$ price and the no-trade $A_a$ price. (In Europe $P$ will fall halfway.) Only at these new respective $P$s of \$18 and £$4\frac{1}{2}$ will the arrow of world oil export match our import arrow. (Verify.)

The quota has produced a price difference between here and abroad. As just said, that equilibrium difference is defined as just large enough to make exports and imports match. (NOTE: A tariff on each unit import of oil, which was exactly equal to this price difference, could have achieved the same equilibrium.[11])

There is thus no essential difference between tariffs and quotas. Except this: A nonprohibitive tariff at least gives revenue to the government, in part offsetting the net harm done to the importing country by the restriction on imports. A quota, on the other hand, puts the profit from the contrived price difference into the pocket of the importer lucky enough to get a quota license. He can afford to wine and dine the officials who give out import licenses; or if they are not already his kinfolk or political cronies, he can afford to bribe them.

This is why economists generally regard tariffs as a lesser evil than quotas. "At the least," they advise, "if you must introduce inefficient restrictive quotas, be sure that the government auctions off the scarce import-quota licenses so that the Treasury gains the swag, and so that bureaucracy is not put under the strain of corruption and exercise of arbitrary power and caprice."

**The harmful effects of a nonprohibitive tariff or quota are of the same type as, but lesser in degree than, those of prohibitive tariffs or quotas. Generally, there is net harm done to the citizenry as it is forced to curb its consumption of the goods it desires most and to channel resources from lines of true comparative advantage to economically inefficient uses. Generally, real wages and average living standards are hurt by tariffs and quotas.**

**Transportation costs**   The economic costs of moving bulky and perishable goods also lessen the extent of profitable regional specialization.

The effects are like those produced by the passage of artificially restrictive tariff legislation. In the case of transportation costs, the evil is unavoidable, whereas protective tariffs or artificial barriers to interregional trade within a nation are squarely the responsibility of man.

This ends two sections of digression on particular markets' price equilibria under trade and tariffs. We now return to our discussion of basic comparative advantage.

## QUALIFICATIONS AND CONCLUSIONS

Of course, comparative advantage holds for *any* two countries and goods, not just for America and Europe and food and clothing. (Ricardo used England and Portugal and cloth and wine in his examples.) The following Appendix shows how the principle of comparative advantage can be generalized to handle any number of goods; and

[11] This gives the clue to how to compute the new equilibrium prices for any tariff rate between the prohibitive and zero levels. In Fig. 34-3, shift the exporting country's whole diagram *upward* by the amount of the tariff (so that its vertical-scale prices now differ from the importing country's vertical scale by the amount of the duty). Then move a horizontal ruler up and down until you have located exactly equal export and import gaps (green arrows) between the respective schedules.

more advanced books show how it can handle any number of countries or regions. Instead of using simple labor cost examples, we could easily measure costs in terms of "doses" of labor, land, and capital goods of fixed-proportions. We can also allow for changing factor proportions and diminishing returns. For all this, see the Appendix.

Perhaps a more serious defect of comparative advantage is its static assumptions. The theory is stated in terms of barter and relative price ratios. It disregards all stickiness of prices and wages, all transitional inflationary and overvaluation gaps, and all balance-of-payments problems. It supposes that when workers go out of one industry, they always go into another more efficient industry—never into chronic unemployment. It ignores sticky money wage rates, set at too high a level to provide viable jobs at home.[12]

No wonder this abstract theory sold at a discount during the Great Depression. Recently its prestige has been coming back. To the extent that we can in the future avoid inflexible exchange rates and wage rates and can count on the successful macroeconomic management, which mobilizes modern theories of monetary and fiscal policy to banish chronic slumps and inflations—to that extent will the old classical theory of comparative advantage retain its vital social relevance.

If theories could win beauty contests, comparative advantage would certainly rate high in that it is an elegantly logical structure. Indeed, one must admit that it is a simplified theory. Yet, for all its oversimplification, the theory of comparative advantage provides a most important glimpse of truth. Political economy has found few more pregnant principles. A nation that neglects comparative advantage may pay a heavy price in terms of living standards and potential growth.

[12] See the Appendix to the previous chapter for a demonstration that overvaluation of a country's currency can undercut these basic classical principles.

## SUMMARY

1   As soon as there are diversities of productivities within a country, specialization and exchange become profitable. The same holds for nations: International exchange is an efficient way for us to (in effect) transform one good into another, more efficient than having to rely solely on domestic production.

2   Without much study of economics, people see that trade is mutually beneficial between the tropics and the temperate zones—or between two countries where one is more efficient in producing one good and the other is more efficient in producing the other good. But it takes the important Ricardian principle of *comparative* advantage to see that trade is no less mutually beneficial between two countries (or, as in the case cited of the lawyer and stenographer, between any two units) even when one of the countries happens to be *absolutely* more efficient in every industry than is the other.

As long as there is a difference in *relative* efficiency, every country must enjoy both a comparative advantage and a comparative *dis*advantage in some goods. There will then be powerful benefits derived from *specializing* in those goods in which there is a comparative advantage, *trading* them for goods in which the other nation has a comparative advantage.

3   The law of comparative advantage not only predicts the geographical pattern of specialization and direction of trade. It also demonstrates that *both* countries are made better off and that the real wages (or, more precisely, returns to the factors of production taken as a whole) are potentially improved by trade and the resulting *enlarged* totals of world production. Quotas and prohibitive tariffs that re-create *autarky* (i.e., national economic self-sufficiency) will hurt real wage and total factor returns—not help them.

4   Decreasing costs (economies of scale) are an important cause of specialization and regional trade. Differences in tastes can also cause trade.

5   Completely-free trade will equalize prices in supply-demand markets for one small good causing the good to be exported from the place with lowest zero-trade price. The equilibrium common $P$ is at the level equating physical exports to physical imports.

6   A tariff or quota, by lowering imports, will cause a rise in domestic $P$ and a fall in foreign $P$. (So long as some imports continue, the competitive $P$s will differ by the amount of the tariff.) The harm done to the domestic economy, from higher $P$ and decreased home consumption and from wastage of resources on goods lacking comparative advantage, will generally exceed the benefit to producers. Transport costs also cut down on trade and well-being.

7   The important law of comparative advantage must be qualified to take into account certain interferences with it. Thus, if exchange-rate parities and money wage rates are rigid in both countries or if fiscal and monetary policies are poorly run in both countries, then the blessing of cheap imports that international specialization gives might be turned into the curse of unemployment. With proper public policies, modern nations can achieve a managed macroeconomics which need not sacrifice the great benefits from trade, but rather can re-create the environment in which the principle of comparative advantage will apply.

## CONCEPTS FOR REVIEW

| | |
|---|---|
| personal and regional diversity and specialization | barter versus domestic production |
| absolute versus comparative efficiencies | international price equilibrium |
| comparative advantage and disadvantage | quota and tariff equilibrium |
| taste differences in trade | prohibitive quotas or tariffs, and lower real wages |
| | sticky money-wage or exchange rates |

## QUESTIONS FOR DISCUSSION

1   "Buying a good cheaper abroad than we can produce it at home is to our advantage." Is this consistent with comparative advantage? Show that it indeed is.

2   Are real wage levels, like water in connecting pipes, brought to the same level by completely free international trade? Why not? Are international prices? Why?

3   What happens if two countries are exactly alike in productivity and efficiency? Explain. Justify the slogan *"Vive la différence!"*

4   Holland's Jan Tinbergen, using modern linear programming to analyze geographical capital-labor supplies and industrial intensities, estimates the following 1970 pattern of true comparative advantage for the world. (*a*) The United States would produce planes, chemicals, drugs, pumps, vacuums, cast iron, telecommunication equipment, soaps, and ceramic products. (*b*) Western Europe would concentrate on autos, textile machineries, alcoholic beverages, batteries, washing machines, animal and vegetable oils. (*c*) Japan would be shipbuilder for the world. (*d*) The less developed countries would produce textiles, shoes, and glass. (*e*) The Soviet Union, to Tinbergen's surprise, would produce computers. Which of these allocations seem most reasonable? Which least reasonable?

5   What if (1,2; 3,4) in Table 34-1 became (1,2; $1\frac{1}{2}$,3) or (1,2; 1,2)? Can you show that all trade is killed off? And that this certainly would be a less happy position for America? (Footnote readers: Redraw Fig. 34-1 with equal *p-p* slopes.)

6   Can a country once have a comparative advantage, say, in steel, and then lose it? What then *will* happen? Should it? If at a future date a cartel might capriciously (perhaps for non-economic, political reasons) cut off our supply of oil imports, might it make sense to use tariffs to lessen oil-import dependence even at some current economic cost?

7   Why might a new continent have a comparative advantage in food?

8   "If some goods continue to be imported after a tariff, the sum of the rise in domestic *P* and the fall in foreign *P* must equal the tariff." Can you show why?

## APPENDIX: Comparative Advantage Amplified and Qualified

Our discussion of comparative advantage has until now followed Ricardo and measured all costs in terms of labor. Modern economists know that the theory is still valid even if you do not want to assume a labor theory of value.

The production-possibility, or transformation, frontier that we used in Chapter 2 to discuss guns and butter is the tool that enables us to dispense with labor units: users of the production-possibility frontier choose to measure the cost of clothing in terms of the food we must sacrifice to get more clothing. (This is sometimes called "opportunity cost.")

The first part of this Appendix follows through in detail an America-Europe food-clothing case, showing the irrelevance of absolute labor costs.

### AMERICA WITHOUT TRADE

In Chapter 2, we saw that every economy has a production-possibility schedule indicating how much

of one commodity, food, can be produced if all resources are diverted to it; also how much of the other commodity, clothing, can be produced if all resources are diverted to its production; and how either good can be transformed into the other.

For simplicity, let us suppose food can always be transformed into units of clothing in America at the *constant ratio* of 10/3. For each 10 units of food sacrificed, we can always get 3 units of clothing. We further assume that when all resources are diverted to food production, America will have altogether 100 (million) units of food.[1]

We may put all this in the form of a schedule, as

---

[1] Note that labor is never mentioned in the following discussion. But if you wanted to relate this discussion to Ricardo's labor treatment, you could merely change the numbers in Table 34-1 from (1,2; 3,4) to (3,10; 8,10), or more generally to (3*a*,10*a*; 8*b*,10*b*), where *a* and *b* are arbitrary positive numbers depending only on units and absolute efficiencies.

| PRODUCTION-POSSIBILITY SCHEDULE OF AMERICA (10/3 CONSTANT-COST RATIO) | | |
|---|---|---|
| | AMERICA | |
| POSSIBILITIES | FOOD (millions of units) | CLOTHING (millions of units) |
| A | 100 | 0 |
| B | 50 | 15 |
| C | 30 | 21 |
| D | 0 | 30 |

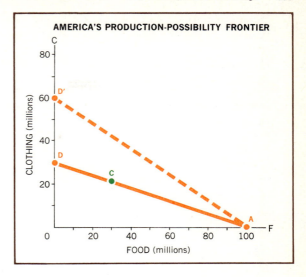

AMERICA'S PRODUCTION-POSSIBILITY FRONTIER

**FIG. 34-4**

The constant-cost line *AD* represents America's domestic production-possibility frontier. The new frontier *AD'* indicates an increased ability to produce clothing and means that America can move northeast from *AD*, enjoying more of *all* goods.

shown in Fig. 34-4's table. Or it may be plotted in Fig. 34-4, just as was done in Chapter 2, Fig. 2-3 (page 24). The solid *AD* is America's production-possibility frontier. This new production-possibility frontier is a straight line, whereas the earlier one was rounded, being concave when looked at from below. The straight-line production-possibility schedule has been introduced in order to keep the argument simple—to relieve the student from having to remember many different cost ratios. As will be seen later, this will not seriously affect the validity of the argument. The few qualifications needed are made later.

So far, we have been talking only about production. However, if the United States is isolated from all trade, what she produces is also what she consumes. Let us suppose, therefore, that the green quantities for *C* in Fig. 34-4's table represent the amounts produced and consumed by America in the absence of trade; or in numbers, America then produces and consumes 30 units of food and 21 units of clothing.

Why was this particular combination decided upon rather than one of the other possibilities? We know from earlier chapters that in a competitive system nobody "decides" upon this, but that the price mechanism, operating through supply and demand for goods and services, determines WHAT shall be produced, HOW, and FOR WHOM. Well, the indicated quantities are the WHAT. Very little need be said here about the HOW, except for the obvious remark that agricultural food production will require more land relative to labor than will more highly fabricated

clothing output. As to the FOR WHOM, we need only remark parenthetically that scarcity of labor in the United States will mean rather high wages for workers, while superabundance of land here will mean low rents (per acre) for landlords.

**Technical progress**  Let's now introduce Europe into the picture. Before we do so, it will pave the way for the later argument to interject a question. What would happen if some American (like Eli Whitney, inventor of the cotton gin, for example) should make a clever invention, allowing each 10 units of food to be transformed into 6 rather than 3 units of clothing? Would America be potentially better off?

The answer is, obviously, Yes. The production-possibility frontier has shifted outward and upward and is now shown by the broken line *AD'* in Fig. 34-4. (Show that America could now go from *C* northeast to a new point *C'* and have *more of both* food and clothing.)

## EUROPE WITHOUT TRADE

We can now do for Europe exactly what was done above for America, but with an important difference. Europe's plentiful endowment of labor relative to land would give her a different cost or transformation ratio between food and clothing.

Figure 34-5 and its table define Europe's straight-line *p-p* frontier. Europe is given a comparative advantage in clothing rather than in food. For her, each

| PRODUCTION-POSSIBILITY SCHEDULE OF EUROPE (10/8 CONSTANT-COST RATIO) | | |
|---|---|---|
| | **EUROPE** | |
| **POSSIBILITIES** | **FOOD** (millions of units) | **CLOTHING** (millions of units) |
| a | 150 | 0 |
| b | 100 | 40 |
| c | 50 | 80 |
| d | 0 | 120 |

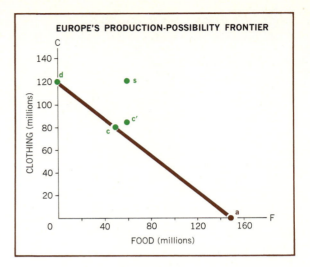

EUROPE'S PRODUCTION-POSSIBILITY FRONTIER

**FIG. 34-5**
Before international trade, Europe is on her domestic production-possibility frontier at c, consuming just what she produces. (Disregard the points c′ and s until later in the chapter.)

10 units of food may be transformable into, say, 8 units of clothing. She gets 5 more than was true of the United States because of her comparative advantage in clothing. However, in terms of food, America gets 10/3, or 3.33 units, for each unit of clothing sacrificed, while Europe's comparative disadvantage in food production gives her only 10/8, or 1.25 units of food, for each sacrificed unit of clothing. *The important thing to concentrate upon is the difference in the two cost ratios: 10/3 for us and 10/8 for Europe.*

We shall still keep the two continents isolated. What is Europe's exact production-possibility schedule? Let us suppose that Europe's population is so large and her land area such that before trade she was at c, producing and consuming 50 units of food and 80 of clothing. This fact, plus the constant-cost ratio 10/8, tells us all we have to know to draw up Europe's complete production-possibility schedule as in the table of Fig. 34-5, and in its *ad* frontier.

## THE OPENING UP OF TRADE

Now, for the first time, let us admit the possibility of trade between the two regions. Food can be bartered for clothing at some *terms of trade,* i.e., at some price ratio.[2] To dramatize the process, let us suppose

[2] Terms of trade (or an exchange ratio) of, say, 10 food for 6 clothing means that clothing is more expensive than food, with the price ratio, (clothing price)/(food price) = 10/6 = 1⅔.

that in mid-ocean there stands an impersonal auctioneer whose business it is to balance supply and demand—offers of clothing and offers of food. He does this by calling out to both countries an exchange rate or price ratio between food and clothing. Until supplies and demands are balanced, he keeps the bidding going. When he finally hits on the equilibrium price level *at which supply and demand balance,* he raps his gavel and says, "Going, going, *gone!*"

Probably, he will suspect in advance that Europe is going to specialize in clothing production, in which she has a comparative advantage, and that she will wish to export part of her clothing production in exchange for food imports. But he has no idea what the final exchange ratio, or terms of trade, between food and clothing will be—whether it will be 10/3, 10/8, 10/5, 10/6, or anything else. For that matter, if the auctioneer is very new at the game or very stupid, he may think that the final equilibrium exchange level, or terms of trade, will be 10/1 or 10/12.

**Limits to final equilibrium**    Actually, neither of these last two can be the final exchange ratio. He would soon learn this from bitter experience. For let him tell America and Europe that they can get all the clothing they want in exchange for food at the rate of only 1 unit of clothing for every 10 units of food. What will America do? By producing at home, she can get 3 units of clothing for each 10 of food.

Clearly, she will not trade food for clothing on those terms; she would rather remain self-sufficient.

That is only half the story. Why should not America go to the other extreme and export clothing in exchange for food imports? Each 1 unit of clothing gets her 10 units of food from the auctioneer. What will 1 unit of clothing get at home in domestic food production? Obviously, from Fig. 34-4 and its accompanying table, only 10/3, or 3.33, units of food. At 10/1, therefore, we should certainly shift all our resources to clothing production; we should export some surplus clothing for food imports.

Now, what about Europe? At home she gets only 10/8, or 1.25, units of food for each unit of clothing. At 10/1, she too will want to trade clothing for food. We see, therefore, what a green hand the auctioneer was. By calling out 10/1, he brings a flood supply of clothing on his head and only demands for food. Since he has no supplies of either good up his sleeve, he must now change his tactics. He must raise the price of food relative to the price of clothing. He had better try the ratio 10/2, or perhaps even 10/9. You are now in a position to reason why neither of them will do: why 10/2 will still induce a tidal wave of clothing and, on the other hand, why 10/9 represents the opposite error, in which there is a tornado of food.

Clearly, *the final exchange ratio cannot be outside the original two-country limits of 10/3 and 10/8!* Anywhere between is a possibility—with America following her comparative advantage and specializing in food, and Europe following her comparative advantage and specializing in clothing.

## EXACT DETERMINATION OF THE FINAL PRICE RATIO

Just where between the domestic cost ratios will the terms of trade settle down? Some Ricardians were foolish enough to say, "Split the difference between the two countries' cost ratios, and pick the 'halfway' point $10/5\frac{1}{2}$ as the equilibrium ratio."[3]

Actually, as John Stuart Mill, the third great classi-

cal economist (after Smith and Ricardo), showed a little later, *the exact final level of the terms of trade between the two cost ratios will depend upon the strength of world supply and demand for each of the two commodities.* If people have an intense desire for food relative to available supplies of food and clothing, the price ratio will settle near the upper limit of 10/8; if clothing is much demanded by both countries, the final price ratio will settle near to 10/3.[4]

Mill did what our auctioneer would have to do. He drew up a schedule showing supply and demand at *every possible price ratio:*[5] how much food Amer-

---

[4] Also, if America were very small relative to Europe, so that its supplies made hardly a dent on the market, then the price ratio might even stay at Europe's 10/8. America would then be specializing in food and importing clothing, but all America's food exports would amount to so little that Europe would still have to produce some food for herself. This is possible only at a price of 10/8. America would in this case get *all* the gains from international trade. It pays to have a large (different!) neighbor.

[5] Chapter 22's indifference curves can be used to summarize each country's tastes for food and clothing. Together with the p-p curves, these could derive the reciprocal demand

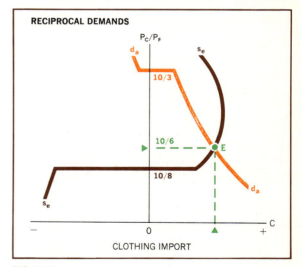

**FIG. 34-6**

---

[3] Or would they have said "halfway" between 10/3 and 10/8, at 110/48, which corresponds to $10/4\frac{4}{11}$? Both are silly. Back in Fig. 34-1 of page 673's footnote 3, there is no sense to saying that the final terms-of-trade parallel green arrows are at *half* the shaded angle. They can be anywhere in the shaded area, depending on supply and demand.

curves of Mill, shown in Fig. 34-6. Unlike ordinary *dd* and *ss* curves, *C* is trading against *F*, not against money; hence, relative prices $P_C/P_F$, rather than money $P_C$, are plotted. (If tastes and incomes vary within a region, group indifference curves must yield to more elaborate analysis.)

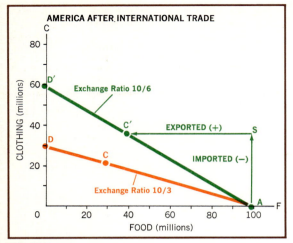

**AMERICA AFTER INTERNATIONAL TRADE**

**FIG. 34-7**

The orange line *AD* represents America's domestic production-possibility curve; the green line *AD'*, her new consumption-possibility curve when she is able to trade freely at the price ratio 10/6 and in consequence has decided to specialize completely in the production of food (at *A*). The green arrows from *S* to *C'* and *A* to *S* show the amounts exported (+) and imported (−) by America. As a result of free trade, she is shown finally ending up at *C'* with more of both goods available than before at *C*.

ica would wish to export and how much food Europe would want to import; and at the same time showing how much clothing Europe would be willing to export at each price ratio in comparison with the amount of clothing America expected to import.

**At one, and (hopefully) only one, intermediate price ratio, exports and imports will balance. At this equilibrium price, exports and imports will "mesh" (or match), quantitatively as well as qualitatively; the auctioneer and Mill will heave a sigh of relief, and trade will continue indefinitely until tastes or technology have changed.**

For our numerical problem, it has been assumed that the equilibrium terms-of-trade ratio is 10/6, a bit "nearer" to Europe's pretrade ratio than to America's.

America concentrates her production completely on food. In Fig. 34-7, America has her production at *A*. But since she can now trade freely at 10/6, America is no longer limited to her old production-possibility frontier. By trading, she can now

move on the green line *AD'* just exactly as if a fruitful invention had been made.

Is America made potentially better off by trade? Indeed she is. Just where she will stop on this green line, which we may call her new *consumption-possibility curve*, depends upon the workings of her internal price system. We assume that this causes her to stop at the point *C'*, where 40 units of food and 36 units of clothing are consumed. The green arrows show America's exports (+) and imports (−).

All this is summarized in America's rows in Table 34-2. This table should be studied carefully. To understand it is to understand comparative advantage.

As a result of specialization and trade, America has become better off; she has more clothing and more food to consume. The same is true of Europe.

What is the black magic by which something seems to have been had for nothing? In Table 34-2, the rows marked World, which represent the sum of the American and European rows, show this:

**World production of both goods has been stepped up by specialization and trade.**

Actually, the sixth row gives the data the auctioneer would be most interested in. He is assured that equilibrium has been reached by two facts shown there: (*a*) World consumption of each product is identical with world production—no more, no less; and (*b*) the amounts that each country exports are just balanced by the amounts that the other country wishes to import. Thus the price ratio 10/6 is the right one.[6]

This completes our explanation of comparative advantage. You might test your full understanding by filling in on Fig. 34-5 for Europe all that has now been filled in for America on Fig. 34-7.

Europe's new consumption-possibility line, made possible by trade, pivots around the green point *d* on

---

[6] To find this equilibrium the auctioneer could have made up a whole book of such tables, each page corresponding to a different price ratio. Typically, only one page is the right one—because at other prices the algebraic total of exports and imports would not cancel out. Thus, at 10/7, America's desire for clothing imports would surpass Europe's willingness to export clothing. The world as a whole would be trying to consume more clothing than had been produced. Since the auctioneer has no inventories to draw upon, he would have to turn the pages toward a higher price for clothing and a lower price for food. On the right page the price ratio would be an equilibrium one: exports would balance imports at the *E* intersection of Fig. 34-6.

| AREA COMPARED | EXCHANGE RATIO OF FOOD FOR CLOTHING $P_C/P_F$ | FOOD PRODUCTION | FOOD CONSUMPTION | FOOD EXPORTS (+) OR IMPORTS (−) | CLOTHING PRODUCTION | CLOTHING CONSUMPTION | CLOTHING EXPORTS (+) OR IMPORTS (−) |
|---|---|---|---|---|---|---|---|
| **SUMMARY SHOWING SPECIALIZATION AND GAIN FROM TRADE ACCORDING TO COMPARATIVE ADVANTAGE** | | | | | | | |
| **Situation before trade** | | | | | | | |
| America | 10/3 | 30 | 30 | 0 | 21 | 21 | 0 |
| Europe | 10/8 | 50 | 50 | 0 | 80 | 80 | 0 |
| World | none | 80 | 80 | 0 | 101 | 101 | 0 |
| **Situation after trade** | | | | | | | |
| America | 10/6 | 100 | 40 | +60 | 0 | 36 | −36 |
| Europe | 10/6 | 0 | 60 | −60 | 120 | 84 | +36 |
| World | 10/6 | 100 | 100 | 0 | 120 | 120 | 0 |
| **Gains from trade** | | | | | | | |
| America | ____ | ____ | +10 | ____ | ____ | +15 | ____ |
| Europe | ____ | ____ | +10 | ____ | ____ | +4 | ____ |
| World | ____ | +20 | +20 | ____ | +19 | +19 | ____ |

**TABLE 34-2**

International trade makes possible larger world production and consumption of all goods. How these net gains are shared between countries depends on competitive supply and demand. (Small regions may benefit most.)

the vertical axis and goes through green c'. Draw in new arrows from d to s and from s to c' representing the amounts exported (+) and imported (−), as was done in Fig. 34-7. Note that Europe's arrows match America's but are opposite in sign and direction. (Why is this quantitative meshing of exports and imports necessary at equilibrium?)

The eager reader could add labor measurements and wage data to the example. But the thing to note is that comparative advantage, not absolute labor advantage, is the all-important condition.

## MANY COMMODITIES

Very briefly, we now show what happens when we remove some of the oversimplifications in the above discussion. The conclusions are not essentially changed, and even changes in details of the discussion are minor.

First note that up to now we've simplified the story by considering only two commodities, food and clothing. Obviously, food stands for many different items (beef, milk, etc.), and likewise, clothing. Moreover, the advantages of exchange are equally great when

we consider the thousands of commodities that can and do enter into international trade.

As is shown in advanced treatises,[7] when there are many commodities producible in two countries at constant costs, they can be arranged in order according to their comparative advantage or cost. For example, the commodities automobiles, flax, perfumes, watches, wheat, and woolens might be arranged in the comparative-advantage sequence shown in Fig. 34-8 at the top of page 688. This means that wheat costs are lowest relative to all other commodities in America; Europe has its greatest comparative advantage in perfumes; its advantage in watches is not quite so great; and so forth.[8]

[7] For example, G. Haberler, *Theory of International Trade* (Macmillan, New York, 1937). Haberler also pioneered the use of *p-p frontiers* in trade theory.

[8] This ordered array of goods might have arisen from the numerical data of Table 34-3 on page 688, presented only for the curiosity of more advanced readers and are not essential for the above discussion. As before, it is not necessary to measure costs in terms of money or labor, but only in terms of the relative commodities into which any good can

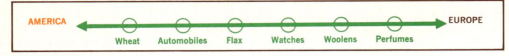

**FIG. 34-8**
(Source for this example of ordering: Table 34-3.)

From the beginning we can be virtually sure of one thing. The introduction of trade will cause America to produce wheat, and Europe perfume. But where will the dividing line fall? Between automobiles and flax? Or will America produce flax and Europe confine herself to watches, woolens, and perfumes? Or will the dividing line fall on one of the commodities rather than between them, so that, say, flax might be produced in both places at once?

You will not be surprised to find that the answer depends upon the comparative strength of international demand for the different goods. If we think of the commodities as beads arranged on a string according to their comparative advantage, the total demand-and-supply situation will determine where the dividing line between American and European production will fall. And an increased demand for

automobiles and wheat, for example, may tend to turn the terms of trade in the direction of America and make us so prosperous that it will no longer pay us to continue to produce our own flax.

## MANY COUNTRIES

So much for the complications introduced by many commodities. What about many countries? Europe and America are not the whole world, and even they include many separate so-called "sovereign nations."

Introducing many countries need not change our analysis. As far as any one country is concerned, all the other nations with whom she trades can be lumped together into one group as "the rest of the

---

be "transformed." Suppose that we chose to measure the costs of every good in both countries in terms of woolens—selected arbitrarily because it comes last alphabetically. Then our data might be arranged alphabetically as in Table 34-3. This means that in America one must give up the production of 1,000 units of woolens to get 1 automobile, while in Europe the cost of 1 automobile is the sacrifice of 3,000 units of wool production. Therefore, the comparative cost of automobiles

| (1)<br><br>GOODS | (2)<br><br>AMERICAN<br>COST<br>RATIO,<br>IN TERMS OF<br>WOOLENS | (3)<br><br>EUROPEAN<br>COST RATIO,<br>IN TERMS<br>OF WOOLENS | (4)<br>COMPARATIVE<br>EUROPEAN<br>COSTS,<br>IN TERMS OF<br>AMERICAN<br>COSTS<br>(4) = (3) ÷ (2) |
|---|---|---|---|
| Automobiles | 1,000 | 3,000 | 3.0 |
| Flax | 0.8 | 1.6 | 2.0 |
| Perfumes | 5.0 | 3.0 | 0.6 |
| Watches | 50 | 75 | 1.5 |
| Wheat | 0.2 | 0.8 | 4.0 |
| Woolens | 1.0 | 1.0 | 1.0 |

**TABLE 34-3**

relative to woolens is in Europe three times that in America, and so forth for the other goods. Now what can we infer? Very obviously, Europe's relative cost advantage is greatest in perfumes and least in wheat; in between, the commodities are arranged as was shown in Fig. 34-8's beads. The fact that the figures in the last column are predominantly greater than 1 in no way reflects on the efficiency of Europe; it merely comes from the accidental fact that we chose woolens, as our common denominator in which to express costs. Had we selected wheat or watches, the opposite would have been the case, and yet none of our results would be any different—except for a "scale factor" (such as converts inches to feet or yards).

TECHNICAL NOTE: Anyone who feels he must bring in labor productivities can write the respective American requirements in labor hours as $A, B, C, \ldots$, and Europe's as $a, b, c, \ldots$. The whole analysis can then be worked out in terms of comparative ratios of the form $A/B, C/B, \ldots$, and $a/b, c/b, \ldots$; to explain trade patterns it is never necessary to compare absolute advantages between countries $A/a, B/b, \ldots$. Of course, if he wants to compare money and real wages, these absolute advantages are necessary: by extending the analysis of Table 34-1, it can be shown that the ratio of European to American real wage must lie between the least and greatest of $A/a, B/b, \ldots$; just where between depends on the working out of reciprocal demands. Likewise, the terms of trade between any two goods, e.g. $\text{price}_a/\text{price}_b$, must lie between $a/b$ and $A/B$.

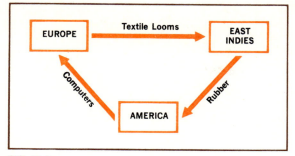

**FIG. 34-9**
Advantages of multilateral trade would be much reduced if bilateral balancing were required.

world." The advantages of trade have no special relationship to state boundaries. The principles already developed apply between groups of countries and, indeed, between regions within the same country. In fact, but for historical accident, they would be just as applicable to trade between our Northern and Southern states as to trade between the United States and Canada.

From the standpoint of pure economic welfare, the slogan "Buy American" is as foolish as "Buy Wisconsin" would be, or "Buy Oshkosh, Wisconsin," or "Buy South Oshkosh, Wisconsin." Part of our great prosperity comes from the fortunate fact that there are no restrictive customs duties within our 50 states.

**Triangular and multilateral trade**  Now with many countries brought into the picture, America may well find it profitable to trade *indirectly* with Europe. America sells Europe much, including finished commodities such as computers. It buys little from Europe; but it does buy rubber and raw materials from the East Indies. They in turn do not usually buy goods from America; however, they do buy textile machinery and other goods from Europe. Thus, we have an advantageous *triangular* trade, as seen in Fig. 34-9. The arrows show the direction of exports.

What would happen if all countries tried to sign bilateral trade agreements, so that America could not and would not buy from the Indies unless they bought an equal amount from us? And suppose the same bilateralism held for every two nations? Clearly, trade would be cut down severely. Imports would balance exports, but at the level of which is the lower. Each region would end worse off.

## INCREASING COSTS

Returning again to two countries and two commodities, we must now drop the assumption that costs are constant. The *p-p frontiers* of Figs. 34-4, 34-5, and 34-7 should have been concave, as they generally were in Chapter 2. It is no longer possible to specify a single cost figure for each country.

On the whole, America is better endowed for food production than Europe; still, after a great amount of American food is produced, the cost of *extra* food will begin to exceed that in Europe. Even after American competition has drastically lowered the price of food relative to clothing, a little of the best land in Europe will be able to hold its own in food production. Similarly, that first little bit of American clothing production which can be achieved at low costs will continue even after international trade has reached an equilibrium level. However, any attempt to expand American clothing production further would entail higher extra costs and competitive losses.

We may summarize the modifications in international trade made necessary by increasing costs:[9]

[9] For the geometrically minded, Fig. 34-10 may be helpful. It shows America's condition before and after trade when increasing costs prevail. The production-possibility frontier is now bowed out. Before international trade, America is

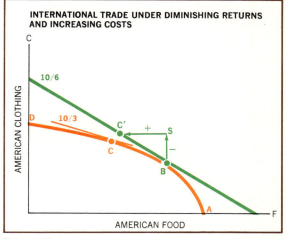

INTERNATIONAL TRADE UNDER DIMINISHING RETURNS AND INCREASING COSTS

**FIG. 34-10**
consuming and producing at C. The domestic price ratio is 10/3, just equal to the ratio of extra costs of getting (at C) a little more clothing for a little sacrificed food. This is shown by the slope of the AD curve at the pre-trade C. Then

As a result of international trade, each country will tend to specialize, as before, in the commodity in which it has the greatest comparative advantage; and it will export some of that commodity in exchange for the other country's surplus exports. But because of increasing relative costs, specialization need not be complete: something of both commodities may still be produced in either country, because even the less favored commodity may have low enough costs to compete when its production is small.

## INTERNATIONAL GOODS MOVEMENTS AS A SUBSTITUTE FOR FACTOR MOVEMENTS

Having acknowledged the law of increasing costs described in Chapter 2 and elsewhere and gone beyond the straight lines of the overly simple labor-only model, we now examine implications of the related law of diminishing returns within each country.

After international trade takes place, resources in Europe flow from food to clothing production. Because clothing requires relatively much labor and little land, the pressure of population on the limited land of Europe is relieved. Land is no longer relatively so dear; rents fall compared with wages. In America the reverse happens after trade: concentration upon food production, in which labor is economized and land heavily utilized, tends to raise rents relative to wages.

In each case, free international movement of goods has effects partly like those following from free inter-national movement of factors of production. Just as migration of labor from Europe to America would relieve the scarcity of labor in America and of land in Europe, so movement of clothing from Europe to America and of food from America to Europe tends to make the superabundant factor in each country less abundant and the scarce factor less scarce.

The person who has most clearly emphasized how commodity trade partially relieves the scarcity in all countries of the less abundant factors of production is the Swedish economist and statesman Ohlin (pronounced O'Lean).[10] He has made this important addition to the classical doctrine of comparative cost:

Free movements of factors between countries will tend to equalize wages and factor-prices.

However, even without any movements of productive factors across national boundaries, a tendency toward equalization of factor-prices often results from free movement of goods in international trade.

It is clear, therefore, that although international trade increases national product in Europe, it may at the same time so reduce the share of particular groups that *they* are made worse off. Thus, the large British landowners who a century ago constituted the backbone of the Conservative party may have been selfish in opposing the famous repeal of the English corn-law tariffs in 1846, but they were not necessarily unintelligent in making their unsuccessful last-ditch fight to retain protective tariffs on imported grains.

---

after trade, when the common price ratio is 10/6, American production shifts to B, toward less clothing but not away from clothing altogether. The new production point B will be reached as a result of competition, because the slope of the curve there—i.e., the ratio of costs of extra clothing for extra food—is 10/6, or just equal to the common international price ratio. Only at B will the value of America's GNP (evaluated at the 10/6 price ratio) be at a maximum.

The green straight line represents the new consumption-possibility curve America can achieve as a result of trade. It is straight and not bent because the auctioneer offers to trade freely, giving America at the 10/6 ratio as much or little clothing for food as she wishes. The final levels of consumption, determined by supply and demand, are shown at C'. As before, the directional arrows indicate exports or imports.

There are still gains from trade; but because of diminishing returns and increasing costs, there is not so much specialization as before, and not quite such large gains. Note that at the equilibrium point, where no further trade is possible, relative (extra, or "marginal") production costs in the two countries are equal, each to the common price ratio 10/6.

[10] Bertil Ohlin, *Interregional and International Trade* (Harvard University Press, Cambridge, Mass., 1933). Ohlin acknowledges inspiration from the earlier eminent Swedish economic historian, Eli Heckscher.

## SUMMARY TO APPENDIX

1   If nature endows two regions unequally with factors of production, the *relative* cost of transforming one commodity into another domestically will probably be different for the two areas. (For example, a land-rich area will have a comparative advantage in food and other land-intensive goods. A labor-rich area's comparative advantage will be in labor-intensive goods.)

2   Under free trade, goods will exchange for each other at a price ratio somewhere *intermediate* between the original domestic cost ratios of the two countries (depending on reciprocal supply and demand).

3   Each country will specialize in the commodity in which it has a comparative advantage and export its surplus of that product for imports from abroad.

4   Each country is made better off by trade and specialization: America can get by trade more units of clothing than when she domestically transforms food into clothing; Europe does better when she trades clothing for food, doing better than when she domestically transforms clothing into food.

5   When there are more than two goods, the same principles of comparative advantage apply. The same is true when there are more than two countries trading, or when we have many factors of production other than labor.

6   Trade is *indirect* production. It is efficient production. Efficient production is always better than inefficient production. (Note that advantages of trade have nothing to do with *relative wage rates*. Under free trade, a country's wage tends to be pulled up to the higher levels of productivity of its export industry, not down to the low-efficiency level of its import industry.)

7   Free migration of productive factors can, without trade, equalize factor-prices. But even without migration of any factors, free movement of goods in trade can work to reduce or sometimes eliminate the differences in factor-prices that result from different geographical factor proportions.

## CONCEPTS FOR REVIEW

straight-line *p-p frontier*
specialization point
terms of trade
pre- and post-trade
equilibria
matching trade arrows

many-good ordered array of
comparative advantages
triangular and multilateral trade
concave frontiers and tangencies
factor-price equalization
by trade

## QUESTIONS FOR DISCUSSION

1   Two countries have same-sloped *p-p frontiers* that are straight lines. Why will there still have to be self-sufficiency even if one greatly exceeds the other in labor productivity all around?

2   Show that I benefit if your *p-p frontier* is as different from mine as possible.

3   Why would you expect land-rich Canada to export wheat to labor-rich China?

4   *Extra-credit problem:* Add to Table 34-3 the information that woolens happen to cost 1 hour's labor in each country. Begin with $2 to £1. With wages $7 an hour here and £3½ there, show that the cost-price of flax will be the same in both countries. Which goods will America produce cheapest? Which goods will Europe? Now let our wage rise relative to theirs (or let the $ appreciate relative to the £). Show that our exports will suffer and our imports will rise.

# 35 PROTECTIVE TARIFFS, QUOTAS, AND FREE TRADE

It would be absurd to try to decide whether God exists or not by counting on one hand all the arguments in the affirmative and on the other hand all the arguments in the negative, and then to award the decision to the side with the greater *number* of points. It is as absurd to evaluate the case for tariff or quota protection by a mere count of unequally important pros and cons.

Indeed, as was shown in the previous chapter, there is essentially only one argument for free or freer trade, but it is an exceedingly powerful one, namely:

**Free trade promotes a mutually profitable regional division of labor, greatly enhances the potential real national product of all nations, and makes possible higher standards of living all over the globe.**

Recall that putting on a tariff duty (i.e., tax) discourages imports and raises prices to the domestic consumer. By killing off the fruitful international division of labor, it "protects" the relatively inefficient domestic producer. Import quotas do the same.

The arguments for high tariff protection against the competition of foreign imports take many different forms. They may be divided into three categories:

1. Those that are definitely economically false: some so obviously and palpably as hardly to merit serious discussion; but some whose falsity can be detected only by subtle and sophisticated economic reasoning.

2. A few that are without validity in a perfectly competitive "classical" static full-employment world, but that do contain some kernels of truth for a sizable nation with some monopoly (or anti-monopoly!) power, or for a nation undergoing economic development and subject to underemployment and an overvalued currency.

3. Certain noneconomic arguments that may make it desirable national policy to sacrifice economic welfare in order to subsidize particular activities admittedly not economically efficient.

## NONECONOMIC GOALS

Let us begin with the last category of arguments, for they are most simply disposed of. If you ever are on a debating team and are given the assignment to defend free trade, you will strengthen your case at the beginning by conceding that economic welfare is not the sole goal of life. Political considerations are also important. Thus, it may be necessary to become partially self-sufficient in certain lines of activity, even at great cost, because of fear of future wars.

An example is the production of oil. If oil reserves and capacity are considered necessary for national defense and if the needed amount of capacity is not able to survive under free trade, the economist cannot assert that national policy should be against protection of this industry. The case for protection is strengthened if oil is controlled by a cartel that may, on some future occasion, cut off supplies to us for power-politics reasons. But even in such strategic cases, the economist can suggest that a *subsidy* to domestic production might be preferable to a tariff. This would bring the domestic price down to the international price instead of raising the price to the consumer up to the domestic cost; also, the subsidy would show clearly what the total costs of national defense are and would better enable the public to decide whether the game is worth the candle. Moreover, a policy of encouraging imports of oil plus a subsidy to exploration and storage might leave us with more oil in the ground at a time of future emergency than would a simple policy of tariff or quota protection.

The question of a national policy to foster the American merchant marine is a similar one. Doubtless the United States does *not* possess a comparative advantage in building or operating a merchant fleet. As soon as American seamen, through trade-unions or on their own, insist upon living conditions and wages remotely resembling those in Detroit factories, then we cannot compete with Greek, Japanese, and Norwegian ships. If we give no weight to America's "glorious seafaring tradition"—a long way back!—and consider purely economic welfare, the correct policy is obvious. If America has a comparative advantage in factory production, let men go to factories where their real productivity is high. American international trade need not suffer by being carried in other countries' ships.

However, if national defense is deemed to make a large merchant marine necessary, that is another matter. Subsidies for building ships may then be justified.

**Security and ways of life**   The problem of deciding how much to spend in peacetime on national defense is a perplexing one, especially since armament races are both *cause* and effect of international disunity. The economist can claim no special competence to advise on this problem. He can point out that selfish economic interests often wrap themselves in the flag and try to justify uneconomic projects in terms of national defense. He can ask suspiciously, "Would an increase in tariffs on Swiss watches be really justified by our defense needs for precision workers? Or is this merely a case of political pressure?" Finally, the economist can also point out that mutually profitable international trade may help to promote international understanding and unity, and that political interferences with trade have in the past provided some of the frictions that led to war and perpetuation of poverty in poor regions.

In conclusion, it is well to point out other noneconomic goals that may deserve consideration. Society may feel that there is some special sanctity about farm life, something worth preserving in the way of life of the "stout agricultural yeoman or happy peasant." (It is to be doubted that people who rhapsodize in this fashion typically come from farms.) Or some may agree with the Soviet generals who think that rural living is worth fostering because the country has a higher birth rate than the cities.

In such cases, subsidies rather than tariffs seem called for. A tariff is simply a rather indirect and clumsy form of subsidy that draws attention away from the problem.

Do not be left with the impression that the political noneconomic arguments are generally favorable to tariffs. They are not. Every congressman knows that America has a tremendous diplomatic interest these days in winning friends and allies. And nothing is so disruptive to our popularity abroad as our reputation for being a high-tariff country. Foreigners are convinced that as soon as they carve a piece of the American market, we will clamp down with quotas or tariffs. We do not deserve that reputation as much as we used to. So it is all the more to our political interest to resist many of the pressures that make for restrictions on international trade.

## GROSSLY FALLACIOUS ARGUMENTS FOR TARIFFS

**Keeping money in the country**    To Abraham Lincoln has been attributed the remark, "I don't know much about the tariff. But I do know that when I buy a coat from England, I have the coat and England has the money. But when I buy a coat in America, I have the coat and America has the money."

There is no evidence that he ever actually said this; but it does represent an age-old fallacy typical of the so-called "mercantilistic" writers of the seventeenth and eighteenth centuries who preceded Adam Smith. They considered a country lucky which *gave away* more goods than it received, because such a "favorable" (!) balance of trade meant that gold would flow into the country to pay for its export surplus.

In this day and age, it should be unnecessary to labor the point that, while an increased amount of money in the hands of one person will make *him* better off, doubling the money in the hands of everybody in a full-employment economy will only serve to raise prices. Unless the single individual is a demented miser like King Midas, the money makes him better off, not for its own sake, but for what it will buy or bid away from other individuals. For society as a whole, once full employment is reached, new money cannot hope to buy any new goods.[1]

**A tariff for higher money wages**    Today it is agreed that extreme protection can raise prices and attract gold or international reserves into one country, if all other countries do not retaliate with tariffs. The tariff may even increase *money* wages; but it will tend to increase the cost of living by *more* than the increase in money wages, so that

---

[1] Of course, our gold might be spent abroad. But this perfectly sensible way of improving welfare by importing was precisely what the mercantilist "bullionists" were arguing against.

*real* wages will fall as labor becomes less productive. It is simply not the case that our general living standards can be raised by protecting every domestic industry threatened by cheaper imports.[2]

One could go on giving examples of protectionist fallacies that a thoughtful person can explode in a minute by subjecting them to analysis. This does not mean that such crude fallacies can be dismissed as unimportant. Actually, they are most important in influencing legislation, the fancier arguments simply being window dressing.

**Tariffs for special-interest groups**  The single most important motivation for protective tariff is obvious to anyone who has watched the "logrolling" in Congress when such legislation is on the floor. Powerful pressure groups and vested interests—both business and labor—know very well that a tariff on their products will help *them*, whatever its effect on total production and consumption. Outright bribery was used in the old days to get the necessary votes; today powerful lobbies exist in Washington to drum up enthusiasm for the good old crockery, watch, or buttonhook industry.

Economically the case for freer trade may be strong, but politically the beneficiaries from protection exert most pressure. Why? Because *freer trade helps everybody a little*, while *protection helps a few people a lot*. Does it matter politically that the bad points of protection outweigh the good? Not if those few who benefit from protection (or who are kept by protection from suffering harm) are politically active in pressing for this cause. It is much harder to organize the masses of consumers and producers to agitate for the even larger gains that they get from an efficient pattern of specialization and trade. If political votes were in exact proportion to *total* economic benefit, every country would selfishly legislate most tariffs out of existence.

## SOME LESS OBVIOUS FALLACIES

**A tariff for revenue**  First, there is the claim that the tariff should be used to raise government tax revenue. Actually, a customs duty on imports is only one form of regressive sales tax, and a rather bad one. A customs duty or tariff is especially bad because it draws economic resources away from their best uses. If the people who advance the revenue argument were sincere, they would advocate a sales tax which would *also* fall on domestic production. But this would provide no protection. (In some less developed countries, about the only tax source administratively feasible is that on imports. So, admittedly, a case for revenue tariffs can be made in such instances.)

To clinch the case in advanced countries against the revenue argument, only re-member that a prohibitively high tariff, which perfectly "protected" us from imports, would collect no revenue at all! Back in 1890, the so-called "billion-dollar Congress" found itself with a surplus of tax revenue over expenditure. Since there was no suitable debt to retire, Congress found the situation embarrassing. It finally met the problem of excessive tariff revenues, not by lowering tariff rates, but by *raising them high* enough to reduce the total of revenue collected.

[2] Recall Chapter 34's discussion of comparative advantage and effects of a tariff.

**Tariffs and the home market**   A second argument, which by itself is on the whole false but whose fallacy is rather difficult to spot, goes as follows: "Farmers should support a tariff for industry because that will gain them a large new home market for their products." Henry Clay, the perennial candidate who turned out to be neither "right" nor "President," used this argument.

Its falsity can be seen from different points of view. First, by cutting down industrial imports we are really at the same time indirectly tending to cut down our farm exports. Thus the farmer is hurt directly. "But," Clay might remonstrate, "what about the extra home market for farm produce?"

Well, what about it? Our detailed example of comparative cost showed that isolation from foreign trade *decreases the total of real GNP*. The total domestic demand for farm products is certainly less at a low level of real GNP than at a high. So unless it can be buttressed by one of the quite different arguments for protection coming later, the slogan "to create a home market" is seen once again to be fallacious.

**Competition from cheap foreign labor**   A third argument for protection has been the most popular of all in American history, because it appealed to the large number of labor votes. According to its usual version, "If we let in goods produced by cheap foreign labor—by Chinese coolies who live on a few cents' worth of rice per day or by low-paid Japanese electronic workers—then the higher standard of living of American workers cannot be maintained." So stated, the argument cannot stand up.

We have seen that trade is mutually profitable even if one country can produce every good more cheaply in terms of resources than the other. The important thing is comparative advantage, not absolute advantage. In the last analysis, trade boils down to two-sided barter. At the current exchange rate, one country cannot indefinitely undersell the other in every line of merchandise.

Earlier we showed that full employment at home need not depend in the long run on foreign trade. If, then, everyone in this country remains fully employed at his most suitable occupation, is it not to *our selfish advantage* for the workers of other countries to be willing to work for very little? To put the matter another way:

The comparative-cost doctrine shows that we benefit most by trading with countries of the Far East or the tropics which have economies *very different* from ours, rather than with countries such as England or Germany which have an industrial economy like our own.[3] Against the pauper-labor argument, there is the clinching fact that the analysis of comparative advantage showed that absolute wage levels had nothing to do with the long-run increase in national income that resulted from trade.

So much from a theoretical point of view. If we turn to the real world, we find the arguments to be even more incorrect. In Europe and in Asia the workers beg for tariffs, saying, "Protect us from the 'unfair competition' of high-paid, efficient American workers who have skill and machinery far better than our own." The rest of the world

---

[3] This argument must be qualified and amplified. Backward countries, so poor that they have little real purchasing power with which to import, at best can export little to us. Most trade today is between industrialized countries. As a backward country advances industrially, it buys more from industrial countries, not less; but perhaps not proportionally more, and perhaps there is *less consumer's surplus from trade* accruing to both parties.

lives in fear of competition from American mass-production industries. The English protectionist claims that an American worker in Bridgeport, Connecticut, who is paid $7 per hour is more than three times as efficient as an English worker who gets paid $3 an hour. This is perhaps an overstatement, but it is close to an important truth.

High American real wages come from high efficiency, not from tariff protection. Such high wages, the *result* of productivity, do not handicap us in competing with foreign workers.

**A tariff to raise wage share**    Thus far we have had nothing but adverse criticism for the "cheap, pauper foreign labor" tariff argument. To be objective—and without objectivity there can be no science—we must admit that it may have the following iota of possible truth. The Ohlin proposition in the Appendix to the preceding chapter suggested that free trade in goods may serve as a partial substitute for immigration of labor into the United States. This implies that labor scarcity in the United States could be alleviated by our international specialization in labor-economizing products and that real wages here might actually fall under conditions of free trade. Real national product would go up, but the relative and absolute share of labor might go down.[4]

Although admitting this as a possibility, most economists believe its grain of truth for a typical country is outweighed by more realistic considerations. No doubt, immobile laborers such as textile workers might be hurt by removing a tariff or quota. But since labor is such an important and flexible factor of production, it seems likely that other laborers would gain from expanded trade more than those hurt would lose. Labor as a whole would presumably share in the increased GNP from trade.

**A tariff for retaliation**    Some people admit that a world of free trade would be preferable to a world of tariffs. But they say that as long as other countries are so foolish or so wicked as to pass restrictive tariff legislation, there is nothing that we can do but follow suit in self-defense.

Actually, however, a tariff is much like an increase in transportation costs. If other countries were foolish enough to let their roads go to ruin, would it pay us to chop holes in ours? The answer is, No. Analogously, if other countries hurt us and themselves by passing tariffs, we should not add to our own hurt by passing a tariff.

To make sure that you grasp the point that our tariff harms *us* as well as the foreigner, you should realize that there are four gains when a trade-agreement program succeeds in getting another country and ourselves to lower tariffs reciprocally. The other country's tariff reduction bestows gains (*a*) on us and (*b*) on them. Our tariff reduction adds two more gains: (*c*) for ourselves and (*d*) for them.

Therefore, the only possible sense in the argument that we should retaliate when a foreign country raises tariffs is that our threat of retaliation may deter them from raising tariffs, and our promise to reduce tariffs may persuade them to reduce theirs. This would justify our passing an occasional tariff as a bluff, but if our bluffs do not work, we should give them up.

[4] A study by W. Leontief of Harvard suggests that in America capital rather than labor is the relatively scarce factor! If correct, this would be an argument for raising real wage share of GNP by *lowering* tariffs. (The preferred explanation for this Leontief Paradox of alleged capital scarcity is that each U.S. worker is technically like three foreign workers, but we lack triple the capital per head.)

Most realistic students of political science infer from historical studies that retaliatory tariffs usually lead other nations to raise theirs still higher and are rarely an effective bargaining weapon for multilateral tariff reduction.

**The "scientific" tariff**    This is one of the most insidious arguments for a tariff; insidious because it often sounds plausible and moderate but, if taken literally, would mean the end to all trade! In its usual form, tariffs should be passed to "equalize the cost of production at home and abroad." Chapter 34 showed all the advantage from trade to rest on *differences* in cost or advantage. If tariffs were passed raising the costs of imports to that of the highest home producer, no goods would come in at all.[5]

There is nothing scientific about such a tariff. It is a grave reflection on the economic literacy of the American people that this least defensible of all protectionist arguments had tremendous political importance in our history.

**Peril-point tariff argument**    According to this congressional argument, America is to keep tariff duties low on an industry. However, if this results in so many imports that the very existence of that domestic industry is threatened, we have reached the so-called "peril point." When that point is reached, we are to increase duties or tighten quotas to keep our domestic industry from disappearing or becoming perilously small.

What about this argument? While it may sound moderate, note that its basic philosophy runs completely counter to the economic theory of comparative advantage. Our nation gains from trade by *specializing*, i.e., *by giving up* certain activities and moving their resources into other industries in which we have a greater comparative advantage. The industries in which we have strong comparative disadvantage should never have come into existence. And suppose an industry (like, say, steel) formerly had a comparative advantage but has lost it—because other industries have had greater technological improvements, because the domestic factors it uses have become more expensive through becoming more valuable elsewhere, or for any other reason. Then this industry *ought* to be imperiled. It ought to be killed off by the competition of our more productive industries.[6]

This sounds ruthless indeed. No industry willingly dies; no region gladly undergoes conversion to new factor uses. In truth, any field that is imperiled is probably already a sick industry with a past history of suffering. So the already weak industry and region feel they are being singled out to carry the burden of progress.

Perhaps the best policy, then, is to introduce tariff reductions gradually, so that vested factors will have time to move; and, as in the 1962 Trade Act, to give federal aid to retain and relocate factors of production. This tends to speed the transition, share the burden among strong and weak, and perhaps lessen effective opposition to the needed reorganization of national production. Fortunately, in a growing economy

---

[5] With nonconstant costs the scientific-tariff formula is indeterminate. A zero tariff may equalize foreign costs with those of our few most efficient producers; an almost prohibitive tariff may equalize with those of our high-cost producers. Where can one scientifically draw the line?

[6] Of course, national-defense and other valid arguments for tariffs might apply; but if they do, it is *those* arguments, and not the peril-point argument, that have to be respected.

the ineffective industries gradually dwindle in importance relative to the dynamic effective ones.

## THE "FOREIGNER-WILL-PAY," OR TERMS-OF-TRADE, ARGUMENT[7]

After dealing with fallacious tariff arguments, we find it refreshing to come now to a possibly valid one—which hopes tariffs will shift the terms of trade against the foreigner. Indeed, it is about the only argument that would be valid even under static competitive conditions, and it goes back 150 years to J.S. Mill. Paradoxically, valid arguments for protection seem to come from free traders, not protectionists!

If we put a tariff on rubber, Mill would argue, that will raise the price here over its price abroad. But with our demand now curtailed, and as we are an important demander of rubber, the price abroad will be bid down. So part of the tariff really falls on the foreigner. (Show that a very small country could not use this argument, since a tiny country cannot budge world prices.)

In summary, a judicious small tariff might improve an important country's terms of trade (defined as the ratio of her export to her import prices).

But here is a warning. *Prohibitive* tariffs, which suit the protectionist who really is against *all* trade, could never be justified by this terms-of-trade argument. Why? Because killing off *all* trade would kill off *all* the advantage you get from shifting the terms of trade in your favor. Economists therefore insist that the "optimal tariff" is one just large enough to improve your terms of trade and small enough to keep physical exchange of imports and exports at your most favorable level.

Most economists think that all this would imply rather small tariff rates for most countries.

## ARGUMENTS FOR PROTECTION UNDER DYNAMIC CONDITIONS

At last we are arriving at a point in the protection versus free-trade debate where those in favor of tariffs can begin to score some weighty points. Three important arguments fall in this category: (*a*) a tariff may help reduce unemployment; (*b*) tariffs may create diversified industries more immune to risk; and (*c*) temporary tariff protection for an "infant industry" with growth potentialities may be desirable.

**Tariffs and unemployment**  Historically, one of the strongest arguments for protection has been the desire to make or preserve jobs. Earlier, we discussed the favorable multiplier effects of exports and foreign investment on jobs and domestic spending, and also the unfavorable "leakage" effects of imports. So a beggar-my-neighbor high-tariff policy might increase employment in the short run before other nations retaliated.

But can we accept such measures as a valid part of our national full-employment program? Is not freer trade much like a scientific discovery of new machinery and

---

[7] The argument is exactly like that of a domestic monopolist who raises his price above marginal cost but does not raise it sky-high, instead stopping where $MR = MC$. Advanced texts sometimes call this optimal tariff a "scientific tariff." But don't confuse this with the cost-equalizing tariffs.

methods? Both represent increases in our *potentially producible* level of real national output; but either *might* in the short run tend to lower our actual *attained* level of output and employment. And yet, there is no need, in either the short or the long run, to tolerate a gap between actual and potentially producible product, for that represents an unnecessary frittering away of the gains from progress.

How, then, do we meet the arguments relating unemployment to too low tariffs? We refute these arguments just as we refute arguments concerning "technological unemployment." We point out the existence of domestic monetary, foreign-exchange-rate, and fiscal policies that can successfully *and efficiently* solve the problem of economic slump. (Recall Part Two's macroeconomics.) If workers displaced by imports can find other jobs in a strong labor market, this protection plea falls down.

"But," it may be argued, "what about the new modern disease of 'stagflation'—too few jobs because full employment seems to be incompatible with stable prices? Doesn't that create a case for tariffs?" On reflection, we see that the answer is, No. The stagflation problems we shall discuss in Part Six are not alleviated by tariff protection in either the short run or long run. Creating inefficient jobs by tariffs creates a worse stagflation problem than does creating efficient jobs by fiscal and monetary stimulus.

A point needs emphasis. Today we include in a rational program the requirement that the foreign exchange rate not be a disequilibrium one. If the dollar parity represents "overvaluation," unemployment may result (as was shown in Chapter 33's Appendix). Of course, a tariff might work a little to offset such an overvaluation. But it is much more efficient—and equitable too—to lower the exchange rate rather than rely on quotas, tariffs, and exchange controls.[8]

**Diversification to reduce terms-of-trade risk**    Comparative advantage might tell a country to specialize completely on one good or a few goods. So she is to put all her eggs in one basket. But then what will happen if the prices of those goods drop? Or if her export prices oscillate? And suppose, as with cartelized oil, that in the future import prices may rise and may fluctuate. A nation will find such variations in her terms of trade very destabilizing to her real income; and she may be left with an industry that has become permanently unprofitable.

To avoid the perils of "monoculture," Latin American economists advise the use of tariffs. Just as an investor will diversify securities to reduce risk rather than keep all his eggs in one basket, so a country is to use tariffs to induce diversification.

This argument certainly deserves careful examination. Note that it assumes private citizens are neglecting to take account of the riskiness in future prices of the industries they put their money and labor skills into. This argument has to assume that the government is better informed than private investors, or at least that the government is more farseeing than private investors in taking account of the future perils of price gyrations. If the future risks are genuine and are foreseen by private investors, those investors will not be misled by temporarily high profits into investing in only a few

---

[8] If money wage rates are generally too high, the dollar may be "overvalued" (as defined in Chapter 33's Appendix). Chapter 36 shows this would preferably call for a new exchange-rate parity rather than for a tariff.

export industries; in truth, such industries will not then have a genuine long-run comparative advantage, and there will be no effective tendency to specialize in them.[9]

At this point a related Latin American argument for tariffs should be mentioned. Dr. Raúl Prebisch, long an adviser to the United Nations, argued that *the long-run terms of trade are always shifting against agricultural products.* So nations that specialize in them are betting on the wrong horse. He argued their governments should instead impose tariffs aimed at building up manufacturing industries whose future terms of trade will be more favorable. (Against this argument is the following: If past and future reductions in food prices are matched by even greater drops in food's real costs, as agriculture undergoes great technological progress, then long-run comparative advantage might still validly tell a nation to specialize in food to improve its real income or at least to minimize its losses. And all the doomsday pronouncements of the Club of Rome argue the reverse of Prebisch; namely, that food, fiber, and minerals are to get scarce and dear in the future!)

This argument is really an argument about what the *future* comparative advantage of the countries in question will be. To the degree that governments are smarter than private investors in discerning trends threatening to the terms of trade, a valid case can be made for interfering with free-market forces. But if government is wrong in its comparative-advantage forecasts, the loss in real income to the nation can become very considerable, and the nation may then find its rate of development slowed down.

**Tariffs for "infant industries"**    Alexander Hamilton, in his famous "Report on Manufactures," raised this argument. It is also associated with the name of a nineteenth-century German economist, Friedrich List, and it has received the cautious blessing of John Stuart Mill, Alfred Marshall, Frank Taussig, and other orthodox economists.

According to this doctrine, there are activities in which a country would really have a comparative advantage, *if only it could get them started.* If confronted with foreign competition, such infant industries are not able to weather the initial period of experimentation and financial stress; but given a breathing space, they can be expected to develop economies of mass production and the technological efficiency typical of many modern processes. Although protection will at first raise prices to the consumer, once the industry grows up it will be so efficient that cost and price will actually have fallen. If the benefit to consumers at that later date would be enough to more than make up for the higher prices during the period of protection, a tariff is justified.

There is certainly something to this, at least as a possibility. Historical studies have turned up some genuine cases of infant industries that grew up to stand on their own feet; but history reveals even more cases of the contrary—of the perpetual infants! Unfortunately for the practical importance of this argument, infant industries cannot

---

[9] Suppose private employers do foresee the risk, but think they can fire workers when export prices drop, thereby throwing the burden of the unemployed workers on the state. Then we face a genuine so-called "external diseconomy," which might justify government intervention in the form of tariffs, quotas, or other programs. Also, recall the limited conditions under which the "foreigner-will-pay" argument has terms-of-trade validity. Followers of Prebisch might also claim that fostering industry will improve labor's share of the social pie more than it reduces the size of that total pie.

swing many votes. It is not they who get protection from Congress, but rather the old vested interests who have never shed their diapers for lo these many years.

**The "young-economy" argument**    Probably the infant-industry argument had more validity for America a century ago than it does today, and it has more validity for present-day undeveloped nations than for those which have already experienced the transition from an agricultural to an industrial way of life. In a sense, such nations are still asleep; they cannot be said to be truly in equilibrium. All over the world, farmers seem to earn less than industrial workers. Consequently, there is everywhere a relative growth of industry and a decline of agriculture. Populations migrate city-ward, but this movement is not rapid enough to achieve an equilibrium of earnings and productivity. A strong case can be made for using moderate protection to acceler-ate these economically desirable long-run trends. Such a defense of protection might better be called a "young-economy," rather than an infant-industry, argument.

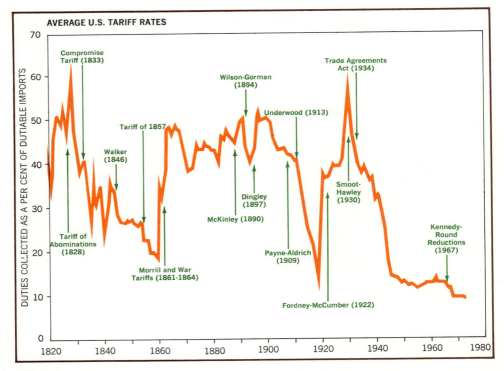

FIG. 35-1

**America was historically a high-tariff nation—but by now duties have come down sharply**
It is cultural lag to think import duties are still higher here than most places abroad. The newest threat comes from import quotas. Textiles, shoes, steel, oil, along with food indus-tries, want competing imports kept out in the mistaken belief that a nation can lift its wages by such a bootstrap operation, rather than depress its real wages by losing the efficiencies of geographical division of labor.

One final word: Please note that the infant-industry or young-economy arguments are not contradictory to the principle of comparative advantage. On the contrary, their validity rests upon the presumption of an induced, dynamic shift of the production-possibility frontier outward and in the direction of a *new* comparative advantage in the lines needing temporary protection.

## CONCLUSION

While this chapter has usually spoken of tariffs, almost everything it has said would apply equally well to any other impediments to trade. Thus, quotas have all the bad effects of tariffs, and often quotas are even more restrictive. An insidious modern development is to use political pressure to get exporters abroad "voluntarily" to place quota limits on their exports to us, as with textile quotas by the Japanese.

Finally, we should mention the so-called "invisible tariff." In many countries—and the United States is no exception—the complicated administration of the customs can be as destructive to trade as the monetary duty that has to be paid.

This completes our discussion of the tariff controversy. No fair-minded reader who takes the trouble to think the matter through can fail to see how shallow are most of the economic arguments for tariff protection. The only serious exception is the infant-industry or young-economy argument.

It is not surprising, therefore, that economists—who are supposed to agree on almost nothing—have been overwhelmingly in favor of the Hull Reciprocal Trade Agreements and GATT (General Agreement on Tariffs and Trade), aimed at lowering trade barriers. Figure 35-1 shows dramatically the fact, too little appreciated at home and abroad, that America has at long last ceased to be a high-tariff nation.

## SUMMARY

1  The case for freer trade rests upon the increased productivity that international specialization, according to the law of comparative advantage, makes possible. Higher world production is made possible, and all countries can have higher standards of living. Trade between countries with different standards of living is especially profitable.

2  Most arguments for tariff protection are simply rationalizations for special benefits to particular pressure groups and do not stand up under analysis.

3  An exception to the law of comparative advantage is provided by the wish to favor certain uneconomical lines of activity for reasons of national defense. Perhaps outright government subsidies would be better in such cases.

4  The only other exception of any practical importance in a full-employment economy is provided by the case of infant industries or young economies that need temporary protection in order to realize their true long-run comparative advantages. To the degree that public planning for development can discern

long-term trends better than the free market can, trade interventions to spur industrialization might turn out to be beneficial.

## CONCEPTS FOR REVIEW

tariff protection, quota
grossly fallacious arguments
higher home market and wage
national-defense arguments
subsidy versus tariff or quota
scientific cost-equalizing

terms-of-trade shifts
unemployment and tariffs
infant industry and young
    economy
GATT and Kennedy Rounds
legal or voluntary quotas

## QUESTIONS FOR DISCUSSION

1  What do you think is the single most favorable argument for a tariff or quota?

2  List fallacious tariff arguments. Weigh pros and cons. (Apply, say, to steel.)

3  Comment critically on the infant-industry and young-economy arguments. What is their relation to comparative advantage?

4  Mention some noneconomic considerations relevant to tariffs.

5  Relate the peril-point and "scientific-tariff" arguments to comparative-advantage theory.

6  Suppose labor productivity grows mightily abroad, and American goods start to be undersold in every line. Suppose that a mixed economy like ours has sticky wage rates. Suppose depreciation of the dollar is not feasible. Show that new tariffs might then be a stopgap measure.

We must now turn to the main international economic problems facing the United States and the rest of the world in the years ahead. How to understand the important facts? Which economic policies to avoid? Which policies to follow?

Economists have achieved more nearly unanimous agreement about the principles of international trade than about any other aspect of their subject. Yet the gulf between the plain man's beliefs about international finance and those of the experts is wider than elsewhere in economics. Fortunately, that gulf has seemed to be narrowing in recent decades. Section A provides a survey of the main historical and contemporary trends in foreign trade. Section B analyzes the breakdown in the international system—pegged exchange rates, America's chronic gold drain, shortage of international liquidity, and other trade problems. Against this background, one can understand the basic reforms in international finance now under way.

## A. MODERN TRENDS AND INSTITUTIONS OF INTERNATIONAL FINANCE

### TRENDS, 1914–1950

**Exports and jobs** When war broke out in 1914, the belligerent nations—particularly England, France, and Russia—increased their imports from the United States. The effect of this could not be analyzed by the tools known at that time to the highest experts; but the multiplier analysis of Part Two can, as the Appendix of Chapter 33 and common sense show, explain what actually happened—a multiplied expansion of GNP. We see here a general principle at work: changes in exports and imports have macroeconomic effects on employment and price levels. During the 1920s, when we were making many foolish private loans to the rest of the world and whooping it up for tariffs, allegedly to "protect the American workers' standard of living," a contributing factor to our buoyant

# 36
# CURRENT INTERNATIONAL ECONOMIC PROBLEMS

Before I built a wall
I'd ask to know
What I was walling in
or walling out . . .
ROBERT FROST

economy was heavy foreign lending. Like domestic investment or government deficit expenditure, the foreign-trade balance was adding to total money spending and jobs.

The hard-boiled businessmen summed it up: "Of course, many of our foreign loans later turned sour, and investors lost their money, but while we were shipping goods abroad, jobs were created. It didn't matter, as far as *current* jobs and prices in the twenties were concerned, whether 10 years later the loans turned out good or bad or whether they represented public or private gifts." Or, as Leon Fraser, who used to be president of J. P. Morgan's First National Bank of New York, put it: "It is better to have lent and lost than never to have lent at all."

**Great Depression and beggar-my-neighbor policies**    After the 1929 stock-market crash, foreign loans became worthless, new foreign lending ceased, and in every country there was much unemployment and unrest. With jobs scarce at home, the political forces of protectionism became rampant. Tariffs were raised, quotas imposed, and in many countries exchange controls were also imposed. Against the advice of almost 100 per cent of the economics profession (who signed a petition to Congress), the Smoot-Hawley (1930) high tariff was passed. Cynics were delighted at the spectacle of a country *trying to collect debts from abroad and at the same time shutting out the import goods that could alone have provided the payment for those debts;* and at the swindle perpetrated on farmers—who were net exporters and not importers, and who were being given *import* tariffs on their export(!) products in exchange for their voting for tariffs on manufactures.

The fallacy of composition was at work. Each country believed that if *it* could develop a favorable balance of trade, *its* employment would increase at the expense of its neighbors; in effect, it would be succeeding in exporting some of its joblessness. But for everybody to run a favorable trade balance simultaneously is a self-contradiction—as impossible as for everybody to be taller than anybody else.

Of course, the attempt to be taller—that is, to generate a favorable surplus of exports over imports—could be predicted to cut down on the fruitful division of labor. And precisely that happened. As much as domestic and total world production declined, the volume of international trade declined still more. The situation reached its height of absurdity when countries would trade with each other only on a *bilateral* basis: A would buy from B only as much as B would buy from A; under Hitler's economic adviser Schacht, Latin American countries were sending staples to Germany in return for aspirin, which was piling up in warehouses.

Today, even schoolchildren ask why people did not insist on deliberate programs of fiscal and monetary expansion. It is only too easy to remake history *after* the fact. But—and this is what concerns us here—one reason a single nation could not introduce expansion at home was the genuine fear that if she increased her GNP while others kept their GNP depressed, her imports would grow in the face of languishing exports. Thus, she would lose gold and, under the gold standard, she would either have to contract again or be forced into devaluation or bankruptcy.

As it happened, by 1931 England was forced off the gold standard along with the Commonwealth and Scandinavia. With the pound depreciated, these countries could afford to push their *internal* expansion; and if you look at the records, you see that Sweden and Britain were already recovering nicely from the Depression when the United States, Germany, and France were experiencing the worst of it. Doubtless, some of the gains to the depreciating countries were at the expense of those who stayed orthodoxly on gold. But most studies suggest that the gain to the expanding countries came *primarily from the freedom depreciation gave them to expand domestically.*

Was old-fashioned virtue rewarded? Not in the 1930s. Belgium clung precariously to the old gold mint parities, even after Roosevelt deliberately devalued the dollar. Political unrest and depression were Belgium's reward—until 1935, when she gave up the struggle and, instead of being smitten by thunderbolts for her apostasy, she immediately registered relief in her production and unemployment statistics. France, having been the wayward inflationist in the 1920s, practically tore herself apart politically by clinging to the old gold parity beyond the middle 1930s.

**War**    The Depression, which hit Germany and the United States especially hard, contributed to Hitler's rise to power. His preparations for war "solved" Germany's mass-unemployment problem and proved—in a tragically unnecessary way—the potency of Keynes-like fiscal and monetary policies. When World War II came, deficits in every country, financed with a new supply of money, engineered vast increases in the $G$ of $C + I + G$. This had the predictable effect of, first, expanding production enough to get rid of unemployment, and, second, swelling total demand so much as to create inflationary gaps and outright inflation. As in World War I, shipments of exports for the warring nations again brought full employment to America.

**The period of "dollar shortage"**    When the war was over, the scarcity of resources remained. Only the United States had not been physically devastated by the war. Elsewhere there was a great need to rebuild, develop, and make up for wartime scarcities. At prevailing exchange rates, the American dollar was vastly "undervalued."

*Undervalued dollar and dollar shortage defined:* **The total demand abroad for American dollars to finance needed imports from us was much greater than the total of dollars our private citizens would want to supply (to pay for trips, imports, direct investments, etc.). If we had not introduced a governmental policy of providing relief and reconstruction aid, of making loans and gifts, no country would have had the needed amount of gold or credit worthiness to finance its international deficit with us. In a free-trade, flexible-exchange world, the price of the dollar would have been bid sky-high.**

Under the conditions of 1945–1950, in the absence of vast American aid programs and tight regulation abroad of imports and capital movements, the *dd* and *ss* schedules of Fig. 33-1, page 650, would have shown a tremendous "dollar gap" at existing foreign exchange rates; this gap could have been closed only by dropping to an equilibrium intersection where the dollar was much, much dearer in terms of foreign currencies— perhaps at $2 per £1 rather than $4, which was then prevailing, and likewise for the needed appreciation of the dollar relative to the mark, franc, and yen.

The previous paragraph defines the technical meaning of the term that used to be heard so widely then, namely, the "dollar shortage," or "dollar gap."

How was the gap handled? Not by immediate postwar depreciations abroad (although later in 1949 Britain and most nations did have to depreciate, the pound dropping from $4 to $2.80). Instead, the so-called "dollar gap" was handled primarily by comprehensive exchange and import controls on the part of the nations with "overvalued currencies" and, as we shall see, by vast American aid and loan programs.

## MARSHALL PLAN, MILITARY AID, AND OTHER PROGRAMS

Table 36-1 shows how sizable the American aid programs have been. After the United Nations Relief and Rehabilitation Administration (UNRRA) had helped meet the immediate postwar emergency needs, we introduced our dramatic Marshall Plan for European recovery. Subsequently, our aid shifted toward grants to the North Atlantic Treaty Organization (NATO) and other military alliances. (Thus, the "Truman Doctrine" brought financial aid to Greece when that country was threatened by communism. Even Yugoslavia has received aid.)

Undoubtedly, the motive for many of these programs was our fear of the spread of communism. Full stomachs may not save a democracy, it was argued, but empty ones can seal its doom. Putting modern guns into the hands of our friends was intended

| UNITED STATES GOVERNMENT POST-WORLD WAR II FOREIGN AID (billions of dollars, fiscal years) | | | | | | |
|---|---|---|---|---|---|---|
| TYPE OF AID | 1945–1950 | 1951–1956 | 1957–1962 | 1963–1968 | 1969–1974 | TOTAL POSTWAR PERIOD |
| **Net nonmilitary grants** | | | | | | |
| Western Europe | 10.9 | 5.4 | 1.0 | 0.0 | 0.1 | 17.4 |
| Asia, Africa, and Near East | 4.6 | 5.0 | 8.3 | 7.6 | 7.6 | 33.1 |
| Rest of world | 1.6 | 0.6 | 1.9 | 1.6 | 5.2 | 10.9 |
| | 17.1 | 11.0 | 11.2 | 9.2 | 12.9 | 61.4 |
| **Net government loans** | | | | | | |
| Western Europe | 8.1 | 0.2 | −2.1 | 0.1 | 3.7 | 10.0 |
| Asia, Africa, and Near East | 0.7 | 0.8 | 2.8 | 8.6 | 10.1 | 23.0 |
| Rest of world | 0.6 | 0.5 | 1.8 | 2.5 | 5.1 | 10.5 |
| | 9.4 | 1.5 | 2.5 | 11.2 | 18.9 | 43.5 |
| **Net military grants** | | | | | | |
| Western Europe | 0.3 | 11.0 | 4.2 | 1.3 | 0.8 | 17.6 |
| Asia, Africa, and Near East | 1.4 | 5.1 | 7.3 | 8.6 | 17.4 | 39.8 |
| Rest of world | 0.1 | 0.6 | 0.6 | 0.3 | 0.5 | 2.1 |
| | 1.8 | 16.7 | 12.1 | 10.2 | 18.7 | 59.5 |
| **Net total, grants and loans** | 28.3 | 29.2 | 25.8 | 30.6 | 50.5 | 164.4 |

**TABLE 36-1**

**Aid goes for relief, recovery, development, and military security**
Although advanced nations are urged to give 1 per cent of their GNPs in aid, few do. U.S. foreign aid has been edging downward, both in absolute amounts and relative to our GNP and aid of other nations. (Source: U.S. Department of Commerce. This excludes IMF and World Bank operations.)

both to help their defense and save American soldiers' lives. Since other advanced nations—such as Britain, Germany, and the Soviet Union—have also given foreign aid, an element of emulation and competition also entered our motivations.

However, a close study of the events leading up to the Marshall Plan and other foreign-aid plans will show that America in the postwar period also had intermittent "do-good" motivations. Call this altruism if you wish, or call it long-run expediency. The fact that the globe holds 15 non-Americans to every American makes our future depend upon a stable international order not overly hostile to Western society. Close study of the facts does not well bear out the hypothesis that we embraced aid programs because that was the only way to prevent a depression at home. On the contrary, we gave most *at times when domestic inflation problems were most pressing;* and one of the costs of aid was aggravation of our concurrent internal scarcities.

**The Point Four program**   Aside from providing substantial material aid, there is one important thing we do for foreign countries that costs us very little, namely, *help them acquire the technical know-how to enable them to increase their levels of productivity and living standards.* This is known as the "Point Four" program because it was first enunciated as the fourth point in the 1949 inaugural address of President Truman.

Fourth, we must embark on a bold new program for making the benefits of our scientific advances and industrial progress available for the improvement and growth of undeveloped areas. . . . I believe that we should make available to peace-loving peoples the benefits of our store of technical knowledge in order to help them realize their aspirations for a better life. . . . We invite other countries to pool their technological resources in this . . . world-wide effort for the achievement of peace, plenty, and freedom.

Besides these government plans, we have been privately exporting our know-how. Many of our largest companies establish branch factories abroad; often the capital is largely raised there, with Americans supplying the technical knowledge.

Some people throw up their hands in horror at the thought of our helping foreign nations to become our industrial competitors. Despite the statistical fact that international trade is largest between developed industrial nations and not between highly developed and backward countries, in terms of selfish long-run economic interest, there is some factual basis for this gloomy view—as the post-Marshall Plan economic revival of Europe and Japan well illustrates. However, in terms of both long-run political interests and altruism, helping others to develop is deemed definitely good policy for the United States, albeit embraced by the electorate in ever-less enthusiastic degree.

## FOREIGN LENDING AND THE BRETTON WOODS SYSTEM

Since the United States is more developed industrially than the rest of the world, there is no doubt that South America, Asia, Africa, Europe, and the U.S.S.R. could use our capital for their industrial development. Such capital could be expected to increase their production by more than enough to pay generous interest and repay the principal.

But private American citizens were long loath to lend. American corporations will build branch plants abroad and will invest in oil or mineral resources. But substantial private lending through Americans' buying risky foreign bonds or stocks greatly diminished after 1929. Yet American citizens do have savings which they would be glad to lend if such capital transactions could be made safe; and our nation could benefit in future standard of living from such foreign lending.

Therefore, the leading nations of the world (except Soviet Russia by her choice) came together at Bretton Woods, New Hampshire in 1944 to form the International Bank for Reconstruction and Development (the World Bank) and its sister institution, the International Monetary Fund (the IMF). As its name implies, the World Bank is formed to provide sound long-term loans for reconstruction and development. (The International Monetary Fund is concerned, as we shall see shortly, with short-term credit and the cooperative management of foreign exchange rates.)

## THE INTERNATIONAL BANK FOR RECONSTRUCTION AND DEVELOPMENT

The World Bank is easy to understand. The lending nations subscribe toward its capital stock in proportion to their economic importance. (The United States quota is about one-third.) The bank can use its capital to make international loans to people or countries whose projects seem economically sound but who cannot get private loans at reasonably low interest rates.

The World Bank's true importance arises from something greater than the loans that it can make out of its own capital. More important is the fact that it can float bonds and use the proceeds to make loans. (It has successfully floated bonds in the United States, Switzerland, Japan, and elsewhere.) The bonds are safe because they are backed by the credit of all the nations (up to their 100 per cent of quotas). Also, the Bank can *insure* loans in return for a small premium; private parties can then put up the money, knowing the Bank's credit is squarely behind the loan.

As a result of such long-term credits, we have seen goods and services flowing out of the advanced nations aimed at international development. If sound, these loans will be repaid in full. If some go sour, the loss will be paid out of the Bank's interest or premium earnings. If still more go sour, the loss will be spread over all the member nations. While the loans are being made, the advanced world is forgoing current resources. When the loans are being "serviced" or repaid, the advanced nations should have an import surplus of useful goods. Production in the borrowing lands should have risen by more than enough to pay interest on the loans; wages and living standards generally should then be *greater*, not less, because of what foreign capital has added to the GNP of the borrowing country.

Has the Bank been a financial success? Decidedly. Especially after Robert McNamara (formerly of Ford Motor and the Pentagon) became its head in the late 1960s, the Bank has stepped up the scale of its activities sharply. An increasing proportion of its financing now goes through the International Development Agency, set up by the Bank to make "soft loans" to nations for education, roads, hospitals, etc.; and through its International Finance Corporation, set up to make loans to foreign development banks for financing private investment projects.[1]

---

[1] Our own Export-Import Bank makes foreign loans that enable an American exporter to sell on credit, for example, machine tools to Brazil or Yugoslavia.

## THE INTERNATIONAL MONETARY FUND

The IMF, like the World Bank, grew out of the 1944 international conferences. It hoped to secure the advantages of the gold standard without its disadvantages; e.g., exchange rates were in the beginning *envisaged to be relatively stable*, but with international cooperation to replace the previous automatic mechanism. Also, countries were to be spared the need to make adjustments by *deflating themselves into drastic unemployment*. And the IMF still hopes to lessen the need for import controls.

Ordinarily, a country pays for its imports by means of its exports or long-term borrowing. Suppose a country, say, England, is in need of short-term credit from the IMF. How exactly does the IMF enable such a debtor country to get hold of dollars? It does this by extending "purchasing rights." It simply lets the British buy with British currency some of the Fund's own holdings of dollars. After the British balance of payments has improved, Britain is expected to buy back with gold or dollars (or, as we'll see, with SDRs or "paper gold") the pounds it has sold to the Fund.

From 1945 until 1971 when the Bretton Woods system broke down forever, the IMF nurtured the illusion that it could keep exchange rates stable most of the time. Only under the extreme pressure of fundamental disequilibria persisting in a country's balance of payments would the IMF expect that country to depreciate its exchange rate. Increasingly in the 1950s and 1960s, the IMF found that pegging of exchange rates could not succeed in a world where costs and demands were changing differentially between regions, and where speculators could safely bet that the currencies which were overvalued would become unpegged.

The IMF and its leading members put up a gallant but hopeless fight to make stable exchange rates work. Indeed they continued to defend the indefensible for years after it became clear that the U.S. dollar, which had been the lynch-pin of the new Bretton Woods system, was becoming progressively overvalued in the 1960s. Germany, Japan, and other countries with undervalued currencies ran chronic payments surpluses, while the U.S. was running chronic and growing payments deficits. Under the Bretton Woods rules, the surplus countries had only two choices: they could appreciate their currencies and thereby get rid of their undervaluation and lose their payments surpluses; or, if appreciation was politically unpopular at home because it would hurt jobs and profits in the swollen export industries, Germany and Japan had no choice but to take in U.S. dollar IOUs in ever-increasing amounts—thereby contributing to an increase in their own domestic money supplies and in their own uncomfortable rates of domestic inflation.

As will be seen, after 1971 the Bretton Woods system of pegged exchange rates broke down permanently and has been replaced by a system of managed floating-exchange rates.

## THE EUROPEAN COMMON MARKET (EEC)

The previous chapters analyzed the economic gains from freer trade. One way of getting trade impediments down is for several countries to form a customs union. Within such a union, tariffs and quotas might be reduced or banished; but they might still persist with respect to external trade. History provides us with many examples. The 50 states of the United States can be thought of as a large customs union. In the 1830s the many independent German states formed a *Zollverein*, or customs union.

One of the most exciting international developments of the century has been the formation of the European Economic Community (EEC)—more usually known as the European Common Market. In 1957 the six nations of Belgium, France, Italy, Luxembourg, the Netherlands, and West Germany signed treaties to create a Common Market. Subject to exceptions, by the mid-1970s each nation is to eliminate tariffs and import quotas on nonfarm goods produced *within* the area;[2] to set up a common tariff against goods from countries outside the Common Market; and to allow free movement of capital and labor. It looks to become the second-largest free-trade area in the world now that Great Britain, Ireland, and Denmark have joined the EEC.[3]

Anxious over the progress of the Common Market, other European nations have formed a free-trade area: e.g., Austria, Norway, Portugal, Sweden, and Switzerland. This loose federation aims eventually at free trade, but its development does not compare in importance with that of the Common Market.

Some economists have worried whether the lowering of tariffs between countries of a bloc is truly a movement toward a more efficient world pattern: "Won't there be a danger that the lower-than-average tariffs between the countries in the union will distort the 'normal' pattern of trade even more than it is already being distorted by separate nations' tariffs? Won't the difference between the ins and the outs be magnified and act as serious distortion?"

Others have replied: "Two wrongs don't make a right. If you can't get rid of trade impediments everywhere, at least get rid of them where you can. Then maybe a few great customs unions can ultimately merge into a worldwide free-trade area."

No definitive answer will cover every case. Perhaps most economists would venture the guess that lowering of tariffs in Europe could have such good effects there on the division of labor as to lead to net benefit for these countries, and ultimately for others.

### FREER MULTILATERAL TRADE: GATT

The Cordell Hull reciprocal-trade program for reducing American and other tariffs has now been with us for more than a third of a century. Contrary to common opinion, our high 1930 tariffs have been cut substantially (in some cases they have been halved and then halved again, as you can see by referring back to Fig. 35-1, page 702). As a result, careful measurement of the degree to which all the nations of the world restrict trade will show that in the mid-1970s, the United States is near the top of the list of "relatively free traders." To be sure, we ought (in our interest as well as in the interest of others) to go on and lower tariffs further, as well as eliminate quotas. Admittedly, foreigners never know when Congress will raise tariffs. Still, those who talk about restrictive American trade policy should study the quantitative facts of the informational lag that was pointed out at the end of the preceding chapter.

All stand to gain if fruitful multilateral trade can be restored. As mentioned before,

---

[2] When France found herself inundated in 1975 by cheap wines from Italy, protests from her own wine industry led her reluctantly to impose restrictions on imports.

[3] The EEC aims ultimately at one Eurocurrency. Thus, in the mid-1970s its members agreed to the so-called "snake within the tunnel." This means they agreed to narrow the bands within which their respective currencies could fluctuate relative to each other to *half* the $2\frac{1}{4}$ per cent range of the original Smithsonian IMF agreement. However, within months Britain and Italy ran into payments difficulty, and as Britain was forced to let the pound float, the scheme broke down.

GATT (the General Agreement on Tariffs and Trade) is a most important development toward international cooperation. The so-called "Kennedy Round" was the sixth round of reciprocal tariff reduction under the auspices of GATT, earlier efforts having taken place after 1947. Still further rounds for the mid-1970s were agreed to by GATT in a 1973 Tokyo conference.

## B. BREAKDOWN AND RECONSTRUCTION OF THE INTERNATIONAL SYSTEM

Now that we have surveyed the post-World War II institutions of international finance, we can face up to the burning issues that confront America and the world.

### FROM DOLLAR SHORTAGE TO DOLLAR GLUT

The Marshall Plan and other aid programs had spectacularly favorable effects on the less-than-most-affluent countries—Japan, Germany, Holland, France, and Italy. Primarily on their own, by a process no one had predicted, they began a miraculous sprint of productivity growth in the 1950s. This miracle persists.

This growth in the *competitiveness* of foreign economies, plus the expensiveness of America's *cold-war programs* (the Korean conflict, the Vietnam war, the NATO alliance, etc.), plus our *civilian foreign-aid programs,* plus the burgeoning outflow of *direct foreign investments by American corporations* facing juicy profitability opportunities abroad—all these factors led to a gradual cessation of the dollar shortage and an actual swing toward a shortage of foreign currencies.

The "dollar shortage" of the 1950s turned into the "dollar glut" (i.e., draining of gold and reserves from America, with chronic balance-of-payments deficits) of the 1960s and early 1970s. Relatively high costs here led inevitably to "overvaluation of the dollar."

At first the drain on our gold supply went unnoticed. But after 1958, one could see a new trend in the making.

Page 714's Fig. 36-1(a) shows how America in the 1960s turned into a deficit nation in her balance of payments. Note that by 1971 the deficit exploded, requiring breaking of the diagram's scale. How was this deficit financed? As Fig. 36-1(b) shows, in part it was financed by our shipping gold abroad. By 1970 our official gold stock had dropped from its peak of $24 billion in 1949 down to about $10 billion—where it has since remained. But in larger part, the international deficit was financed by foreigners accepting our short-term IOUs. Figure 36-1(b) shows how liquid claims on us have grown to vastly exceed our gold holdings. No wonder the dollar had to be devalued in 1971 and allowed to float to find its proper level thereafter.

### REASONS FOR U.S. CHRONIC INTERNATIONAL DEFICIT

Many reasons were given for America's chronic international deficit. Most had an element of truth in them, but we shall see that the crucial cause for the 1955–1971

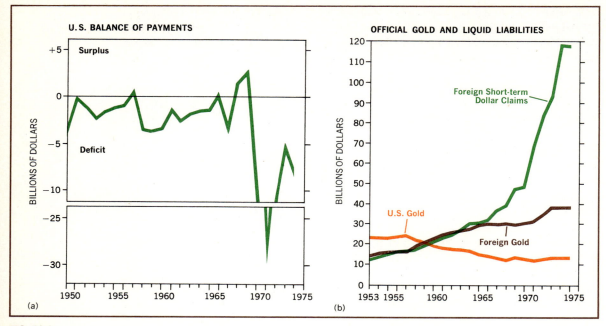

**FIG. 36-1**

**Chronic overvaluation of dollar caused hemorrhage of gold and reserves, soaring balance-of-payments deficit**
By the late 1950s the "dollar shortage" was over. The dollar shifted from currency undervaluation to increasing overvaluation, culminating in the post-1971 floating-exchange rate regime. Note growth of our dollar liabilities abroad, which helped provide the world with much-needed increments of international liquidity. (Source: U.S. Department of Commerce, U.S. Official Settlements Balance. Warning: These gold totals are reckoned at the old "official" gold price, not at the much higher free-market prices of the mid-1970s.)

period is probably to be found in the vast improvement of technical productivity abroad in recent years, compared to our own more modest progress. Below are the causes commonly named for any chronic payments deficit:

**1. Too much inflation here at home**    If a country has more rapid wage increases than its neighbor, and if these are not matched by compensating differentials in worker productivity gains, then it is indeed likely to find itself running a chronic deficit.[4]

Tragically, the post-1965 Vietnam escalation created a price-level escalation that caused acute deterioration of our private current balance of exports over imports. Hence, after 1965, America's basic deficit problems vastly worsened.[5]

**2. Overgenerosity in our aid and military programs**    Until Vietnam, our governmental foreign-aid and military programs had not grown much in relative size; rather, it was

[4]For further analysis, see Chapter 33's Appendix discussion on overvaluation of a currency.
[5]If you plot (a) our declining share of world exports against (b) the post-World War II rise in the ratio of our export prices to those abroad, the result does look a little like a downward-sloping *dd* curve, with the rise in our relative *P* explaining the loss in our relative *Q*.

more the case that, with the growth in private long-term investment, our surplus on current *private* account was no longer large enough to let our aid programs be as generous as they had been previously.[6] After 1965, Vietnam did become an important aggravator of our payments deficit.

**3. Lack of trust in the dollar**   From 1933 to 1955, the dollar was considered everywhere to be a holding even better than gold. It was *the* key international reserve currency. But what happens when people and governments begin to believe that America is in international disequilibrium? And when they become apprehensive that the dollar *might* depreciate relative to marks, francs, or official gold? It is natural enough, under these circumstances, that some governments and private persons should want to hold less dollars, and hold more gold or other strong currencies. This so-called "shift in international liquidity preference" can help explain much of the chronic 1955–1971 gold drain from our shores.

**4. Discriminations abroad against American goods**   While the dollar was in short supply abroad, it was understandable why discriminatory barriers against our exports should have been common in other countries. With the dollar no longer strong, a case could be made that remaining discriminations against American goods be removed or reduced; and some progress has taken place.

**5. The rapid growth of productivity abroad**   From a long-run viewpoint, the fundamental cause of the change in America's international position would seem to be the remarkable speeding up of productivity increase in Western Europe and Japan.

Their production technology is still largely behind ours, but the gap, particularly in the goods which we customarily export and specialize in, has been narrowing.

Even with real wages rising abroad more rapidly than here, productivity improvements abroad enable foreigners to produce for themselves more cheaply than we have been producing for them. Hence they came to outsell us increasingly in third markets, and can even begin to outsell us in our home markets. Auto, steel, and TV imports typify the changing patterns of comparative advantage. We maintain our export shares primarily in farm products and in highest-technology items—aircraft, computers, automatic machine tools.[7]

[6]Even experts often don't realize how high America's surplus on current private account must be if we are to stay in healthy equilibrium with free long-term investment and are to carry out desired government operations abroad. Equilibrium might then require us to expand our exports of goods and services, in comparison with imports, by enough to create a current private surplus of perhaps several billion dollars. It is quite wrong to think that developing such a sizable surplus would do harm to our trading partners. On the contrary, financial equilibrium and equilibrium of comparative advantage require that this be reached; inasmuch as we would then be supplying the rest of the world with the means to finance our enlarged surplus, they are in no genuine sense harmed. The private surplus must be large enough, however large that is, to fit in with overall equilibrium.

[7]A rise in productivity abroad can often increase real wage here by cheapening imports. But (*a*) if it takes the form of improvement in productivity there in goods we have been specializing in, and (*b*) if it reflects the discovery by American corporations that their know-how can be applied to non-American workers, then the whole process could actually slow up the rate of real wage growth here and result in a *loss* of American consumer's surplus from trade. Cf. Chapter 33's Appendix.

**6. High investment abroad by American firms** The miraculous productivity spurt abroad created tremendous profit opportunities for American corporations. In recent decades, instead of wishing to invest in the underdeveloped world, they hastened to build branch factories in Europe (and, when possible, in Japan), where rapid growth seemed sure.

To cut down on this outward flow of private capital investment, the U.S. government all through the late 1960s introduced direct controls on foreign investment—quotas, penalty taxes, etc. Only after the dollar was allowed to float freely and find its own equilibrium level in the 1970s were these inefficient restrictions allowed to lapse.

**7. Quadrupled price of OPEC oil** Most industrial countries, including the U.S., were hard hit by the sharp increase in energy prices after 1973. The LDCs were also put into balance of payment deficit by the new need to pay much more for their necessary oil imports and imports of fertilizers and other goods whose costs depend much on the price of energy. The problem of "recycling" the tens of billions of dollars that each year accrued to the Persian Gulf countries represented a definite threat to world prosperity and to multi-lateral balance-of-payments equilibrium.

Some OPEC countries quickly spent their new revenues on imports designed to accelerate internal development. (Iran is a good example.) But others, such as Saudi Arabia and Kuwait, now took in enormously more than they could sensibly spend in the short run. The only rational alternative was to acquire earning assets of the affluent countries; then as it becomes increasingly feasible to spend increasing amounts on home development and home consumption, the interest and dividends from these nest eggs, as well as the principal, can be gradually used up. In the end, if the process is managed with good planning, the oil that is gone from those regions will have left behind it factories, roads, and improved capital structure able to keep living standards there on a rising trend.

The actual numbers of billions of oil revenues needing recycling turned out in the later 1970s not to be so excessive as had been earlier feared. But there still remains the problem of multi-lateral balancing: Suppose the excess oil revenues from selling to, say, India or Belgium, are wished by the oil exporters to be held in U.S. bonds and stocks or U.K. bonds and stocks and not in Indian or Belgian assets. Will the U.S. be willing to lend to India and Belgium to make this all possible? Or, will Belgium and India be able to develop a favorable trade surplus with the U.S., thereby causing the whole process to balance out on a triangular basis? Clearly international cooperation is important here.

## THERAPY FOR A CHRONIC DEFICIT AND DEPRECIATING CURRENCY

Economists know what are the programs generally needed to reverse a chronic international deficit. These are easy to preach but not so easy to follow.

1. American workers and industry can be urged to *increase domestic technical productivity*. Supports for scientific research and investment can help.

2. American exporters can be urged to *improve selling practices* abroad. Since foreign salesmen are also similarly urged, mere exhortation accomplishes little.

3. We can press for further *reductions in remaining discriminations against the dollar*.

4. We can ask that the prospering nations of the free world take up a *larger share of defense and aid burdens*.

5. We could *keep our economy depressed* at home, eschewing low interest rates needed for expansion and growth, diminishing our demand for imports, and putting pressure on profit margins in export industries and making them hungry to drum up export business.[8] But no mixed economy can face its electorate with contrived slow-downs and survive at the polls.

6. There could be a *further depreciation of the dollar or appreciation of other currencies*. The dollar could float down to a new equilibrium.

**Second-best measures**    Any or all of the above measures are designed to get rid of any overvaluation of the dollar relative to other currencies. But suppose that America foolishly refuses to let her dollar depreciate, thinking she has to live with an over-valued dollar for some time. A host of new, and somewhat distasteful, measures can combat overvaluation.

7. We can *"tie" foreign-aid grants and loans further*, requiring that their proceeds be spent directly in the United States even if our goods cost more. (For example, we tie our military expenditures in the sense that an item must be bought at home even if it costs 50 per cent more than abroad.) This is but one of many piecemeal de-preciations of the dollar that take place when outright depreciation isn't feasible.

8. We can *limit tourism* and cut down on the amount of goods that travelers can bring home free of duty.

9. *Restrictions or tax penalties can be put on foreign investment.* Corporations and banks can be given quotas, or can be taxed on capital outflows.

10. We could revert to *protectionism* generally. Tariffs and quotas will not raise *real* wages, for the reasons seen in the previous chapters, but they can compensate a little for sticky money wages and an overvalued currency. Such a solution will be deplored by all who value the advantages that come from specialization according to comparative advantage and by all who think America's political advantage lies in our living down our old reputation as a bad neighbor.

11. When the medicine agreed to in December, 1971, at the Smithsonian Institu-tion—namely, depreciation of the dollar relative to the yen, mark, and other curren-cies—seemed to be working slowly at best, many followed France's example. Switzer-land, Belgium, and others had a *split* exchange rate: a parity rate for *current* transactions; but with the rate for *capital flows* allowed to float.

12. Finally, to close the list, we could hope that *the surplus countries of Europe and Japan would again experience an acceleration of inflation in their costs and prices.*

## THE NEW SYSTEM OF MANAGED FLOATING EXCHANGE RATES

The automatic gold standard died in 1941, despite attempts between World Wars I and II to revive it. The brave attempt by the Bretton Woods system to work with *stabilized* exchange rates lasted for 25 years and served the world well. But it, too, ultimately

---

[8]To the degree that unemployment at home means low profit opportunities, it might worsen our short-term balance by encouraging more foreign investment (i.e., more debits)!

foundered on the impossibility of pegging exchange rates in a world *where costs and demands are subject to divergent trends; and where electorates in the mixed economy will not be willing to deflate and to contrive stagnation just because balance of payments deficits under a pegged parity rate call for such Pyrrhic therapies.* Nor will modern nations submit to inflation just because fixed exchange rate parities call for that.

When an old system breaks down it does not mean a perfected new system is at hand to be adopted. Conferences after conferences were held in the 1970s by the leading IMF member countries trying to agree on a new system to replace Bretton Woods. On the whole, the French, particularly before General Charles de Gaulle died, tried to insist upon restoration of stable exchange rates—perhaps with an important role for official gold in the reconstructed system. By and large the United States, with the concurrence of several other large powers, resisted going back to a regime of rigidly pegged exchange rates.

**Managed floating**   So no sweeping agreement was possible. De facto, therefore, without anyone planning it exactly that way, the world moved on to a *somewhat managed floating exchange rates system.*

And that system worked not too badly. The quantum of international trade continued to grow in the 1970s, much as under Bretton Woods. Small and large businesses engaged in importing and exporting found that, even in a regime of exchange rates that fluctuated from month to month, they could purchase from banks and from speculators "hedging cover" that enabled them to make plans for deliveries and orders far ahead and to recover their costs and make a profit. There was a cost to all this, to be sure, but it proved not to be a prohibitive cost or even a serious deadweight burden on the fruitful international division of labor.[9]

Chaos and beggar-my-neighbor trade wars by protectionist nations were feared, but did not materialize even though some gigantic shocks were experienced by the international system in the mid-1970s. Experts, realizing how difficult it would have been to

---

[9]To ensure against the risk that the foreign exchange rate for marks will rise 10 per cent between now and the time my import of German dyestuffs arrives, I turn today to the forward market and buy marks 90 days ahead. Who sells them to me? Possibly an American exporter who wants to play safe and know exactly how many dollars he's going to get for the computer he is shipping today to Germany, and for which he will be paid marks in 90 days. But even if export and import transactions in both directions don't balance out, some speculators with sporting blood will sell marks forward hoping to be able to buy them cheaper later. If speculators are overoptimistic, they may end up providing this hedging service even at a loss to themselves; or if risk taking is so irksome as to require a positive premium for hedging, that cost will be added onto the price of international goods and, to a degree, will lessen the volume of and gains from trade. (The analysis of hedging and speculation in a market for corn, as described in the Appendix of Chapter 21, cannot be confidently applied to foreign exchange markets. Speculation in foreign exchange is more in danger of being destabilizing, since there is no natural par of supply and demand set by crop conditions and basic human demands for wheat. Instead, when the dollar is weak, all the speculators will pounce on it and make it weaker; they will force America into depreciation and into internal inflation, and thereby the new proper level for the dollar will be permanently lower, rewarding the speculators for their bear raid. If the authorities resist such raids by keeping a tight rein on the domestic money supply, price level, and GNP level, they are as much restrained by the balance of payments as under a stable exchange standard. So, critics of floating exchange rates ask, Why give up advantages of stable exchange rates if you are going to have, in any case, their disadvantages?)

have found stable exchange rates that would have been correct ones both before and after the 1973 quadrupling of OPEC oil prices, were thankful that flexibility of exchange rates permitted Italy, the U.K., and the U.S. to adjust to these unforeseen events.

The important problems still to be resolved are these:

What role, if any, shall gold have in the international monetary system?

How flexible should exchange rates be? Completely free, or "clean," floating without limits? Or subject to some governmental intervention (so-called "dirty" floating)?

## WHAT ROLE FOR GOLD?

After 1971, nations dropped even the pretense of making currencies convertible into gold. The messy two-tiered system of gold still remains.

**Free tier**  In this unofficial tier, gold is auctioned off every day. Mines from South Africa and Russia, and in lesser degree from Canada and the United States, supply gold to this market. Who buys it, and who holds the stocks of existing free gold?

A part of the demand, probably a small part, comes from jewelers and dentists and from engineering operations that need a non-tarnishing metal. But probably the largest source of demand for holding gold comes from (*a*) Indians, sheikdoms, French peasants, and middle-class people who have always held gold as one form of wealth—either because they distrust paper currencies and government or because they do not care to report their income and wealth transactions; (*b*) footloose refugees, underworld interests, tax evaders, currency-control evaders, and opponents of the modern welfare state who wish to emancipate themselves from its reach; (*c*) honest citizens who are convinced that inflation is coming and that free gold will hold its real value better than any other investment—better than common stocks, bonds, savings accounts, real estate, diamonds, paintings, antiques, and hoarding of commodities; (*d*) shrewd and unshrewd speculators, who do not necessarily believe in any of these things, but who are willing to bet that there are enough people who do believe in them to make it a good (if risky!) speculation to put part of their portfolios into gold. To be included with any or all of the above are (*e*) those who are confident that *ultimately* gold will be restored to a central place in the official monetary systems of the world, and that when this happens a massive increase in the official price of gold will serve to raise the free-market price and make gold a valuable speculative holding.

**Official gold**  In this tier national treasuries and central banks, along with the IMF itself, still continue to hold official gold as part of their international reserves—along with their other reserves of SDRs (i.e., IMF Special Drawing Rights) and their holdings of foreign and domestic currencies that can be bought and sold in the foreign exchange market.

No longer is official gold completely sealed off from the free gold market. Several times nations have sold gold at auction to the free market (as the U.S. government did twice in 1975). After 1975 the fiction of an official gold price of $42.22 per ounce was explicitly dropped by the IMF members. This nominal number had become way out of line with free-market prices of $130 to

$200 an ounce; no transactions between nations were done at so meaningless a price. Instead various loans have been made between countries secured by gold valued at some closer approximations to prevailing market prices.

The 1975 Fall Meetings of the Fund and World Bank agreed to return to the member nations part of the gold they had put into the IMF. Another part was to be used by the Fund *to provide help for the developing nations*. Left for later agreement was the question of whether any member governments will at some future date be free to actually go out and buy gold from private persons in the free-tier gold market.

Those who regard gold as a barbaric relic have not yet realized their desire to eliminate it from any role in the international monetary mechanism. Those who hanker for the disciplines of the automatic gold standard as a substitute for arbitrary and fallible government actions have noted with unhappy impatience that events have not been going their way. Only the future can tell how long the present compromise system will prevail, in which gold still constitutes an important official reserve for nations but in which gold no longer calls the tune in determining domestic money supplies and price levels.

**"Paper gold"**  Accounts between nations are still kept in terms of the Special Drawing Rights as a unit. These units of accounts have no "$" or "£" symbol. There are no green or gilt-edged certificates representing one or so many units of SDRs. What exactly are they then?

The SDR is the official unit of account used between governments, central banks, and the IMF.[10] What it is really is a basket of 16 main currencies of the world, each with a given weight depending upon its importance: the dollar, mark, pound, yen, franc, lira, . . . etc. A basket of 16 currencies is more diversified than is any one, say the dollar or the mark. That is why many private transactions are beginning to be expressed also in SDR units; and why the OPEC countries began to peg their post-1974 oil prices in SDR rather than dollar units.

**Long-term shortage of international liquidity?**  A decade ago experts used to worry that the quantum of international trade was growing at about 10 per cent in nominal terms (6 per cent real and 4 per cent price inflation). They knew that gold production could barely keep the world stock of gold growing at 2 per cent, and that much of this went into the hands of private hoarders. "Where," they would therefore plaintively ask, "will

---

[10] The SDRs were set up by vote of the IMF members, subject to a veto by 15 per cent of the voting quotas. The exact amount newly created per year is determined by the Director General of the IMF, in consultation with the voting members. But the allocation of the new SDRs among the members is determined in proportion to their quotas in the IMF. Thus up to early 1976, $7.7 billion of new SDRs were created, the United States getting $2.8 billion, Canada $447 million, Britain $1.3 billion, West Germany $675 million, France $604 million, India $406 million, Japan $469 million, etc. The less-developed world continues to hope that there will be set up a "link" that will give poorer nations, *on the basis of their need,* more SDRs than their present importance warrants. The mentioned intention of the IMF to sell one-sixth of its gold on the free market for the benefit of the LDCs is a partial response to this hope for a "link".

there be forthcoming a long-term trend of international liquidity needed to keep the system in healthy growth? Won't we be facing the danger, as in 1929, of a world-wide recession brought on by too little international liquidity?"

Now that the world of the 1970s is on flexible exchange rates, the fears for a shortage of international reserves have in a degree evaporated. Discrepancies in balance of payments can now be met by adjusting exchange rates, rather than by having to pay out massive reserves in order to keep rates pegged at some historical parity. Indeed, many experts fear that some of the world-wide inflation of the 1970s has to be attributed to the fact that *nations are generally awash in paper liquidity.*

Once exchange rates are allowed to float, that does not end all problems. There remains the vital question of just how they are to be allowed to float.

## FLEXIBLE EXCHANGE RATES

The post-Smithsonian system that has replaced Bretton Woods continues with its flexible exchange rates and somewhat "dirty" floating exchange rates. By *dirty* floating is meant a regime in which governments do occasionally intervene to support or depress their currencies, not permitting the free forces of supply and demand to let them float up and down without limits. If they intervened so completely as to peg the price of their currency to a fixed parity in terms of gold or some other exchange rate (as for example the dollar), we would in effect be back to stable exchange rates and the gold standard. On the other hand, completely "clean" floating, *without any government stabilization or intervention,* could result in speculative ups and downs of the exchange rates, serving no apparent useful purpose and making the life of exporters and importers a precarious and inefficient business.[11]

[11]Before the debate between stable and flexible exchange rates had been resolved in favor of floating, some economists proposed as an ingenious compromise the following system of "gliding" (or "crawling") bands. Within any year the exchange rate was to be allowed to adjust a little, but no more than some agreed-upon percentage—say 1 or 2 per cent. That way, over a decade, even a significant needed adjustment could be made; but, so it was argued, the speculators would not have a field day so long as the short-term adjustments were so limited. The accompanying Figure 36-2 and its legend should be self-explanatory on the basic logic of the scheme.

**FIG. 36-2**

Instead of fixed parity at $2.00 per £, under this plan the parity can glide downward or upward by 1 or 2 per cent per year, achieving in a decade's time the 11 or 22 per cent needed to adjust for drifting apart of cost levels. Also at any one time the band between upper and lower "points," within which supply and demand can freely operate, is a bit widened.

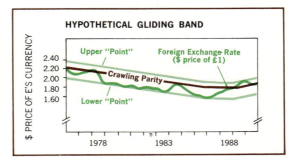

HYPOTHETICAL GLIDING BAND

$ PRICE OF £'S CURRENCY

Upper "Point"    Foreign Exchange Rate ($ price of £1)

Crawling Parity

Lower "Point"

2.40  2.20  2.00  1.80  1.60

1978    1983    1988

**Regional blocs**   Certain countries have wanted to have the stability of fixed exchange rates between themselves, while at the same time having flexibility in exchange parities with the rest of the world. Thus, the Common Market countries of Western Europe share one labor market and have close trade relations. Therefore, they have periodically entered into mutual agreements to intervene in the foreign exchange markets to keep their various exchange rates—the mark and the franc, the lira and the guilder, and so forth—within *narrow* limits of each other.

This arrangement has sometimes been called the "snake." The exchange rates of the whole group can slither up or down relative to the dollar, the yen, the SDR, and the day-to-day free-gold price. But each currency relative to all others in the EEC block must stay within the narrow band that constitutes the snake's diameter.

This has some of the advantages of both worlds: Frenchmen and Germans conveniently transact with each other on quite predictable currency terms; still, at the same time, any fundamental change in world affairs, such as a great increase in prices for the oil that Europe must import, can be adjusted to by having the Common Market exchange rates float flexibly upward or downward.

Regional stable exchange rates also have some of the *disadvantages* of the old regime of pegged exchange rates. Thus, suppose that Italy has more inflation than Germany. The lira will then tend to sink to the snake's belly. The rest of the countries will be called upon to support the lira by buying it. After they have bought a lot, they will begin to wonder whether the printing press of the Bank of Italy will not produce more than they can stomach; and in the end, they will begin to balk—at which point the snake has been blown apart. When incidents like this happen every few years, all the parties become wary that announced stabilizations are in name only and cannot be counted on to succeed.

## FINANCE IN A WORLD OF NATIONALISMS

From considerations like this, one learns to marvel that the 50 states of the U.S. should be able to keep to one dollar currency that allows of no exchange-rate variations between the states. The convenience for commerce is obvious. On the other hand, if Alaska or West Virginia were to become more depressed than the other states, they would not be able to depreciate *their* currencies and thereby lower the costs of their goods and pick up some employment at the expense of the rest of the country. What makes the system work is the fact that workers can migrate to any region in the country that provides best job opportunities and wages; and the fact that we have one Treasury and one Central Bank, the Federal Reserve with its Board of Governors in Washington and its unified control of the money supply for the whole nation.

If ever there should be *one* world government, *one* world central bank, *one* world labor market, then the ambitions intrinsic to the old gold standard with its stable exchange rates could again have some chance of becoming a reality. Such Utopia still seems a long way off. The real miracle is that the evolving system of international finance does seem to work—to accomplish useful trade and permit investment across national boundaries.

# SUMMARY

## A. MODERN TRENDS AND INSTITUTIONS OF INTERNATIONAL FINANCE

1 Expanded exports—as in World Wars I and II—will have multiplier expansionary effects on a country. If previously it had unemployment and excess capacity, the result will be more jobs and output. If previously it had inflationary pressures, the result will be an intensification of them. The beggar-my-neighbor policies of the depressed thirties, by which each nation vainly tries to export its unemployment abroad, are self-defeating.

2 The World Bank, the International Monetary Fund, Marshall Plan and military-aid programs, Point Four, the reciprocal-trade program for tariff reduction and GATT, the European Common Market—all these are important factors in the postwar bid for more rational world trade.

3 The initial aftermath of World War II found the dollar *undervalued,* as others desperately needed our cheaper goods. Thanks to the Marshall Plan, our aid and military programs, the efforts of the World Bank and the International Monetary Fund—and above all to the miracles of productivity growth abroad—the initial undervaluation of the dollar turned gradually into *chronic overvaluation* of the dollar at the Bretton Woods *pegged* exchange-rate parities. After years of gold drain and massive balance-of-payment deficits, the U.S. and the whole world finally in 1971 had to abandon the Bretton Woods makeshift of pegged exchange rates deemed subject to only occasional depreciations and appreciations in serious emergencies.

## B. BREAKDOWN AND RECONSTRUCTION OF THE INTERNATIONAL SYSTEM

4 The 1970s find the world on *somewhat managed floating exchange rates*. How free or "clean" the floating is to be, how "dirty" or government limited, are questions still to be resolved by actual practice. Also still to be worked out is the feasibility of stabilization of exchange rates within regional blocks such as the Common Market.

5 Gold no longer has the official key role that it did under the automatic gold standard. A *free-tier* system prevails for private persons and corporations. But still within the *official tier* of governments and the IMF, gold still constitutes an important international reserve. Only very gradually have Special Drawing Rights of the IMF (SDRs or "paper gold"), come to play a significant role in the monetary system. The SDR unit, a weighted average of 16 principal currencies, is employed in official agreements and transactions; any future shortage of international liquidity, however remote that shortage may seem in a decade of world-wide inflation and floating exchange rates, could be augmented by the creation of more SDR drawing rights; and aid to LDCs might come in part from generous allocations to them of new SDRs, as well as sale for them of some official gold.

## CONCEPTS FOR REVIEW

exports, foreign investment,
  foreign-trade multiplier
World Bank and IMF
Marshall Plan and UNRRA
Point Four and aid programs
Common Market, customs union
dollar shortage to dollar glut and
  chronic deficits
breakdown of Bretton Woods

floating versus stable or pegged
  exchange rates
"clean," "dirty" floating
free gold tier
official gold tier
paper gold (SDRs)
regional currency blocs
  and the "snake"
long-term world liquidity

## QUESTIONS FOR DISCUSSION

1  Describe analytically post-World War II changes in the position of the dollar. Contrast "dollar shortage" and "dollar glut" in terms of dollar "undervaluation" and dollar "overvaluation." Explain this.

2  Contrast and compare the World Bank and Monetary Fund.

3  Draw up a list of what you consider our most important international problems. If you were in Congress, what would you do about them?

4  What effects can one expect from the European Common Market?

5  Describe the extent of our post-World War II aid to the rest of the world. Was this merely "generosity"? Did generosity play any important role?

6  "The Bretton Woods system was an improvement over the automatic gold standard in that it did, eventually, let a country depreciate its currency rather than force it to undergo long-term unemployment in a painful effort to deflate itself and thereby cure the overvaluation of its currency. But its flexibility came *too rarely;* and *too late,* long after speculators could make a killing betting against the weak currency." Explain this.

7  Give highlights of the 1970s two-tier gold system.

8  What do you understand the term "paper gold" to mean?

9  What is "clean" floating? "Dirty" floating? Explain.

10  "Under floating rates, countries A and B each create their desired money supplies, $M_A$ and $M_B$. These, respectively, determine their price levels at $P_A$ and $P_B$. As Chapter 33's purchasing-power-parity doctrine claimed, long-term changes in $P_A/P_B$ determine how much A's currency will depreciate (or appreciate) relative to B's." Can you follow this argument?

# 6

## CURRENT
## ECONOMIC
## PROBLEMS

# 37

# THE THEORY OF GROWTH

. . . When you can measure what you are speaking about, and express it in numbers, you know something about it; when you cannot measure it, when you cannot express it in numbers, your knowledge is of a meager and unsatisfactory kind; it may be the beginning of knowledge, but you have scarcely, in your thoughts, advanced to the stage of science. . . .
LORD KELVIN

In the final section of this book, we can mobilize the tools of economic analysis to show their relevance to the burning issues of our age. To theories of economic growth (Chapter 37). To the processes by which the less developed countries can better their economic well-being (Chapter 38). To the problems of creeping inflation and its tradeoff with unemployment in the advanced economies (Chapter 41).

As old problems get partially solved, new problems are forced onto the social agenda. Chapter 39 faces up to the ancient pestilence of discrimination: racial, ethnic, sexual. Chapter 40 analyzes the quality of economic life: inequality and poverty, urban blight, ecological deterioration; possible future limits on growth set by energy scarcity and exhaustion of natural resources. Chapter 42 discusses new currents in economics and ideology: the old and new left; laissez faire, or libertarianism; mainstream liberalism and its critics; the young and mature Karl Marx. Finally, in Chapter 43, comes economic analysis of alternative economic systems: pure capitalism, the mixed economy, fascism, socialism, and communism.

All the tools of economic analysis developed in this book are needed to throw light on such difficult and important social problems. This chapter will apply the *principles* of economic theory to the process of growth and development, in preparation for the next chapters.[1]

## STAGES OF HISTORY

Napoleon agreed with Voltaire that history is but "a fable agreed upon." It was long the fashion to regard economic development as proceeding according to a timetable. A doctor can guess that a baby at so many weeks will begin to see things, and he can make predictions about when it will walk and talk. Often he may err, but *it is re-*

[1] For a short course, skip this chapter, particularly the theoretical parts of pages 729–738.

725

*markable how predictable the stages of biological growth prove to be.* Scholars used to think economic history could be treated in the same way.

Friedrich List, in his 1841 *National System of Political Economy,* was one of the first to divide economic history into stages. Especially in Germany, this became a popular notion a century ago. A new group of scholars, called the Historical School, came near to saying: "Throw away fancy theories. Grub in the facts. Collect them. Sort and sift them. Let them tell their own story."

The first step for any scientist is indeed to maintain a respect for the facts. But alas, it is not the last step. *The facts never tell their own story.* Truth, like beauty, is oft in the eye of the beholder. No two writers ever seem to be told the same fables of development by the accumulated almanac of facts. Some, and they included Karl Marx (1818–1883), saw in history a one-way evolution:

**Primitive culture** First, there were marauding hunters and self-sufficient tribal families cultivating crops. (Supposedly they still survive in some isolated jungles.)

**Feudalism** Gradually, as elbow room began to be scarce, the primitive economy was succeeded by classical autarchy, which evolved into feudalism. In the Middle Ages, a settled chain of command and exploitation, based largely on land relationships, governed all economic and social life from nobility down to serf.

**Capitalism** Whether or not one thought the Middle Ages idyllic, feudalism in its turn was brought to an end when the periods of the Renaissance and Reformation ushered in the commercial and industrial revolutions. Peasants were alienated from the soil and forced into the cities as a proletariat. Rivers were dammed to harness water, and the invention of the steam engine enabled the energy of wood and coal to replace the energy of beast and man. The Calvinist ethic helped to create business-minded entrepreneurs.

As if in a play, the curtain came down on feudalism and mankind was supposedly ushered onto the stage of bourgeois, middle-class capitalism. (Of course, isolated countries like Russia and Japan were not expected to move from feudalism to capitalism in exactly the same time periods; but when their time came, the process could be expected to be qualitatively similar even if more compressed in duration.)

Self-satisfied historians of the Victorian age, such as Lord Macaulay or Herbert Spencer, saw the evolution of society as an ascent of man toward higher forms. But now that the more or less perfect state of Victorian capitalism had been reached, they thought evolution could have its final rest. All that remained was further progress toward removing tariffs and the few other governmental fiats still interfering with the laissez faire marketplace. Spencer could contemplate with mathematical certainty the withering away of the state and the supremacy of free markets. Invention by science, better education of the masses, and individual initiative could be expected to produce steady gains in living standards in this best of all possible worlds. (In our time, Friedrich Hayek in Austria and Milton Friedman in Chicago look back to the Victorian Whig society as a golden age, to be reattained by democratic dismantling of the welfare state.)

**Socialism and communism**   Having eaten of the fruit of the tree of evolution, why should men think that the play of history has to be written in only three acts? In a country like Germany, not yet imbued with the tradition of individual and business freedom, philosophers thought that capitalism, too, was but a passing stage, to be succeeded in its turn by state socialism or communism, just as capitalism had succeeded dying feudalism. Marx and Engels wrote in *The Communist Manifesto:*

The modern bourgeois society has sprouted from the ruins of feudal society. . . . The modern laborer . . . becomes a pauper. . . . What the bourgeoisie therefore produces . . . are its own grave diggers. Its fall and the victory of the proletariat are equally inevitable.

## FACT AND FICTION

Events rarely agree with fable.[2] Thus, the revolutions in France and Germany that Friedrich Engels and Karl Marx predicted to each other in their letters failed to materialize in the weeks, months, and years as they had confidently projected. And real wages, instead of falling or remaining constant in the decades since Marx's 1867 *Das Kapital,*[3] turn out, on statistical examination, to have been rising dramatically under industrial capitalism. Even the rate of profit stubbornly refused to follow the law of decline predicted for it and instead oscillates and wanders without any strong trend.

It is correct that *around the turn of the century there seemed to be a burgeoning of monopolies in advanced economies.* But it turned out that even the most capitalistic democracy, the United States, could and did produce antitrust legislation to limit this development; and study of the statistics of concentration of market shares among a few big oligopolists suggests that monopolistic concentration is less in the 1970s than it was in 1900 or 1929. (The fact that concentration in 1976 may, nonetheless, be more than in 1950 reminds us that economic history is indeed not a one-way movement.) It is true that the Great Depression of the 1930s was one of the worst the capitalistic system has ever known. But it is also true that a mixed economic system subsequently replaced rugged individualism and laissez faire. The mixed economy introduced fiscal and monetary policies to moderate business cycles and combat chronic slumps. No educated observer of the post-Keynes world can believe in one final depression as capitalism's fate. We live in a world no prophet ever predicted!

**Mid-century miracle?**   What has been the single most surprising economic development of the mid-twentieth century?

Rapid progress under communism? No. Few experts in 1950 expected the Soviet Union, China, and the Eastern European planned economies to do much better or worse than they have since performed.

---

[2] M. I. Rostovtzeff, *Social and Economic History of the Roman Empire* (Oxford University Press, New York, 1926), showed that an elaborate system of international markets and trade in nonluxury goods existed long before the Middle Ages. Compound interest appears on Babylonian cuneiform tablets, and some nations are repeating in the 1970s the worst errors of historic mercantilism. Neither progress nor perpetual oscillation correctly portrays the richness of economic history.

[3] Translated as *Capital,* and ultimately including posthumous Volume II (1885) and Volume III (1894).

Reversion to beneficent laissez faire and free private enterprise? Certainly not that, since except for the usual ebb and flow of political elections, there has been no trend back to the Victorian condition. When a Conservative party, in Britain, Norway, or Australia, ousts a so-called "socialist" regime, most of the apparatus of a mixed economy is retained. When an age of Kennedy gives way to an age of Ford, only marginal changes in the American *Zeitgeist* emerge.[4]

**The single most surprising development of our age was the unpredicted vigor of the modern mixed economy. The miracles of sustained growth in production and living standards have taken place in the second-level countries—Japan, Germany, Italy, France, Scandinavia, Western Europe generally—rather than in the most advanced countries like the United States and Canada or in the less developed countries of Latin America, Africa, and Asia, whose slower rates of growth threaten a widening relative gap.**

Social prophets of our day, such as Schumpeter and Toynbee, to say nothing of Veblen or Spengler years ago, thought of the mixed economy as "capitalism in an oxygen tent." But the growth experience of the third quarter of the twentieth century revealed that a market economy enriched by government planning and macroeconomic control could perform favorably in comparison to past epochs of both capitalist and communist development.

We are thus warned to place limited confidence in the allegedly scientific proofs that one stage in history must inevitably be succeeded by a particular next stage. When Nikita Khrushchev said to an American audience, "We will bury you . . . your grand-children will be communists," he was only repeating what is taught in elementary Russian economics textbooks.

WARNING: Critics of Russia should not make a similar mistake about immutable timetables of development. It involves wishful thinking to argue, as some scholars did for the Eisenhower administration: "True, the U.S.S.R. is now showing a faster percentage rate of growth than the U.S. But wait until she becomes as mature as we; then she'll *have* to slow down!" Right-wing determinism is as poorly founded as left-wing.

This sketch of the development of the mixed economy is all too brief, but it represents a fair summary of the views of historians on this side of what used to be called the Iron Curtain. Since this view of the mixed economy is completely rejected by communist scholars, Voltaire and Napoleon were wrong: Apparently, "History is a fable *not* agreed upon."

Let us turn now to various economic models which can help us to understand history rather than to compress it into neat explanations that only pretend to predict the future with certainty. Our task is to understand the actual development of wages and profits, of labor and capital, and of national product.

## THE "MAGNIFICENT DYNAMICS" OF SMITH AND MALTHUS

In *The Wealth of Nations* (1776), Adam Smith wrote a handbook of economic development. Achievement-oriented, Smith preached the great efficiency that comes from *specialization, division of labor, and exchange*. He stressed the need to *remove* the blundering hand of mercantilistic governments; to cultivate attitudes of honesty, zeal,

---

[4]It was a Republican, not a Democrat, who put in price-wage controls and the 1972 huge deficit.

and thriftiness; *to unleash the competitive profit motive, which would—as if led by an Invisible Hand—achieve the maximum well-being of all.*

**Labor theory of value in a golden age**    Smith had also a theory of dynamic development. He and Malthus began with a hypothetical golden age—"that original state of things, which precedes both the appropriation of land and the accumulation of stock"—when labor alone counted, when land was freely available to all, and before the use of capital had begun. What determined pricing and distribution in this simple and timeless dawn? Answer: The undiluted labor theory of value.

To see this, consider once again Smith's famous case of deer and beaver. Suppose 2 hours of hunting yields 1 deer; or 4 hours yields 1 beaver. Then the competitive price ratio of exchange between deer and beaver will be set by comparative labor time alone: the price of 1 beaver will equal 2 deer. Why 2 deer per beaver? Because the price ratio can be computed in necessary labor time as 4 hours (of sweaty work)/2 hours (of sweaty work).

The determination of price by labor cost alone would apply no matter how many goods there were; and it would be enforced in any primitive market by having hunters shift from one good to the other if ever that other good's price got out of line and offered a profit advantage. It is still true that supply and demand are operating in this golden age; but the situation is so simple that we do not need elaborate *dd* and *ss* curves. The long-run *ss* curves for the different goods are simple horizontal lines at the stated labor costs; so long as there is enough demand to have the goods produced at all, labor costs will be determining of prices.

NOTE: Demand is still there in the background; thus, if it would cost 10 hours to hunt a skunk, and yet nobody received any utility from skunks, skunks would not be hunted and would not be bought and sold at a price of 10 hours, or of 5 deer.

**Population growth**    Now consider Smith-Malthus dynamics. Life is pleasant in the golden age. Babies are born, and the population doubles every 25 years. Since there is plenty of land, people move west and spill over onto more acres. National output exactly doubles as population doubles. Price ratios of deer and beaver remain exactly as before. What about real wages? Real wages still get *all* the national income, there being as yet no subtractions for land rent or interest on capital. What is the real wage per hour? So long as land can expand *proportionally* to the expansion of labor, the law of diminishing returns cannot come into operation. The wage rate per hour remains at one-half deer or at one-fourth beaver, as determined by labor productivity.

That would be the end of the story, until, say, some clever inventor found a new way of doing in 1 hour what used to take 2 hours. This would *raise* the national product per capita. Such a balanced improvement would leave the price ratio of beaver to deer unchanged; but it would double the real wage rate. In the rude dawn of the undiluted labor theory of value, inventions can only raise wages and the pace of balanced expansion.[5]

[5] The graphical production-possibility frontier of Chapter 2 can show all this. For a society with 100 hours of labor, the *p-p frontier* must now be drawn as a straight line going from the intercept on the vertical axis of the 50 deer producible with that much labor to the intercept on the horizontal axis of 25 beaver. The absolute slope of this *p-p frontier* gives the 2/1 ratio prevailing at any point where both goods were being produced and consumed. (The marginal-utility and indifference-curve analysis of Chapter 22 is still needed to tell *where* society ends up on the *p-p frontier*.) Now, a new

**Scarce land and diminishing returns**    Even had golden ages ever existed, they could not have lasted once all land became fully populated. As we saw in Chapter 2, Malthus pointed to a fatal flaw in the happily expanding economy. Once the frontier of virgin land disappears, new laborers begin to crowd onto existing cultivated soils. For the first time, private property in land springs up. Now land is scarce, and a rent is charged to ration it.

Growth does take place in this new classical world of Smith-Malthus following on the golden age. Population still grows, and so does national product. But product can no longer grow proportionally to labor. Why? *Because, with new laborers added to fixed land, each worker now has less land to work with.* Naturally, therefore, the law of diminishing returns (of Chapters 2 and 27) comes into operation. The increasing labor-land and decreasing output-land ratios mean a declining contribution of each last (or marginal) worker to product, and hence declining real wage rates.

As David Ricardo essentially pointed out:

**A conflict of interests arises between classes. More babies mean lower per capita incomes and wage rates; lower wage rates mean higher rent rates per acre of land. Landlords gain as labor loses. This is why Carlyle criticized economics as the "dismal science."**

To understand the brute fact of economic inequality, we have to jettison the simple labor theory of value and study the effects of scarcity in the productive factors that labor needs access to.

**Paradise lost and regained**    How bad can things get? Gloomy Malthus thought, at least in his first edition of 1798, that the end of economic development could be an equilibrium only down at *the minimum level of subsistence.* Above this subsistence wage, population would continue to grow; below it, population would die off; only at this level could there be lasting equilibrium. (Recall Chapter 2's discussion of Malthus.)

Biological fecundity was a fact of nature; diminishing returns was a fact of nature. Only sentimentalists could refuse to face the sad facts of life prevailing once man had left the golden Garden of Eden. It is for precisely these reasons that Adam Smith had earlier said: Lucky is a nation that is growing rapidly, for it has not yet made its sad rendezvous with its destined equilibrium at the minimum of subsistence. Sad is that nation which has reached the stationary equilibrium of the subsistence level, where deaths just cancel out births.

---

doubling of labor productivity in all industries would move the *p-p frontier* outward in a parallel position so as to depict an exact doubling of national product. The interested reader can show that an invention which tripled the productivity of beaver hunting, while only doubling that of deer hunting, would flatten the shifted-out curve, changing the price ratio from 2/1 (equals 4 hours per beaver ÷ 2 hours per deer) to 4/3 (equals $\frac{4}{3}$ hours per beaver ÷ 1 hour per deer). Now the real wage rate has risen, but unequally when computed in terms of the different goods: the real wage has tripled in terms of beaver, but only doubled in terms of deer; lovers of fur coats have gained more than lovers of venison. (NOTE: Suppose laborers are not homogeneous. If women are *everywhere* twice as productive as men, Marx and Ricardo would redefine socially necessary labor units, treating 1 woman as 2 *basic* labor units, etc. But if women are *unequally* superior to men in different jobs—being twice as productive in beaver, thrice as productive in deer, and just as productive in potatoes—the crude labor theory of value breaks down: Now we must know the demand conditions of non-Marxian economics to determine equilibrium prices.) Cf. Chapter 42 for more on Marx.

What did Malthus (and Smith) forget, or at least underestimate? Malthus failed to realize how technical innovation could intervene—not to *repeal* the law of diminishing returns, but to *more than offset* it. He stood at the brink of a new century and failed to anticipate that the succeeding two centuries would show the greatest scientific gains in history—a chastening fact, well to keep in mind as one listens to the voice of the modern computer as it sings out the same Malthusian dirge.

## DETAILED ECONOMIC ANALYSIS OF SMITH-MALTHUS

To understand the world's population problem for the next centuries—and the problems of India, Indonesia, and China in the next two decades—we must master the above classical model, which may have more *future* relevance for the world than it has had for the West since Malthus' time. As a bonus, the same graphical tools will apply when we investigate the role of capital formation as a factor of growth for Germany, Japan, the United States, and the less developed countries of the world.

Table 37-1 and next page's Fig. 37-1 show succinctly how the tendency of population to grow when the wage is above the level of minimum of subsistence will (1) end the golden age of abundant and free land, and (2) lead to an economic growth path that approaches a stationary equilibrium at the minimum of subsistence. Begin with the table.

Table 37-1 shows the decline in wage rate when the fixity of land keeps output from growing as fast as labor. Column (1) shows unchanged land. Column (2) shows growing labor. Column (3) shows the resulting growth in output ($Q$ or GNP), which, because of the fixity of land, is *less* than proportional to labor growth. All the remaining information can be computed from these production-function data alone.

| RELATION OF OUTPUT TO LABOR AND LAND | | | | | |
|---|---|---|---|---|---|
| (1) | (2) | (3) | (4) | (5) | (6) |
| ACRES OF LAND | MAN-DAYS OF LABOR | OUTPUT OF FOOD | WAGE IN FOOD PER DAY | LABOR'S SHARE OF GNP (%) | RENT IN FOOD PER ACRE |
| **A**  1,000 | 500 | 4,000 | 8 | 100 | 0 |
|  | 501 | 4,008 |  |  |  |
| **A'**  1,000 | 1,000 | 8,000 | 8 | 100 | 0 |
|  | 1,001 | 8.008 |  |  |  |
| B  1,000 | 3,000 | 20,000 | 5 | 75 | 5 |
|  | 3,001 | 20,005 |  |  |  |
| E  1,000 | 6,000 | 33,600 | 4.2 | 75 | 8.4 |
|  | 6,001 | 33,604.2 |  |  |  |
| Z  1,000 | 8,000 | 39,000 | 0 | 0 | 39 |
|  | 8,001 | 39,000 |  |  |  |

**TABLE 37-1**

**Diminishing returns from population growth ends golden dawn of development**
Higher labor-land density reduces output per man, lowers marginal-product wage; hence land rent per ever-scarcer acre becomes increasingly positive.

To get the declining wage rate of Column (4), we have to repeat Chapter 27's calculation of what the *last* worker *adds* to total output. (Recall that this is termed the marginal-physical-product of each of the identical workers.) Let us add one worker to 1,000 existing workers at *A'*. Note that output rises from $Q = 8,000$ to $Q = 8,008$ units. This gives extra product per extra worker of 8; so the marginal-product and real wage rate must then be 8 units of output per worker. Check that the extra product and wage later falls to 5.0 at *B*; to 4.2 at *E*; and finally to zero at *Z*, where land is so overcrowded as to be unable to produce any extra output regardless of added labor.

To get the relative share of labor in the gross national product, we multiply the wage rate of each worker by the number of workers. Then we divide this total wage bill, *wL*, by total GNP, *Q*. Note that labor's share in Column (5) soon falls from 100 per cent of GNP to 75 per cent, and ultimately down to 0 per cent. Who gets the remaining share? By our assumption that there is no capital to clutter up the labor-and-land model, all other returns must go for land rent. With total acres unchanged, we simply divide up land's calculated share of total output by the fixed number of acres. Obviously, the rent per acre must therefore *rise* in Column (6) as the wage rate *falls* in Column (4), just as David Ricardo warned.

## GRAPH OF MALTHUSIAN DEVELOPMENT

Figure 37-1 depicts all this. In Fig. 37-1(a), we see the wage rate declining as the law of diminishing returns pushes labor's marginal productivity downward along orange *dd* (which goes through *d*, *A'*, *B*, *E*, and *Z*). What keeps the wage from falling down to zero on this *dd* demand curve for labor? Actually, the wage stops falling where *dd* intersects the green *ss* horizontal supply curve set by the minimum wage at which people can subsist and just barely reproduce their numbers. The Malthusian final equilibrium at *E* is a gloomy one, anything but golden.

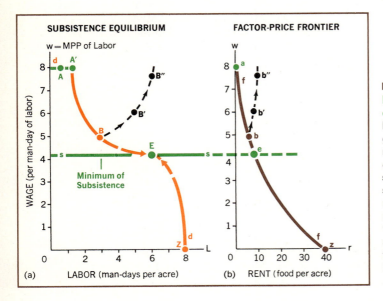

FIG. 37-1
**Numbers grow until Malthusian state of minimum subsistence is reached**
Population growth moves us from the golden age of *A, A',* and *a*—down the di-minishing-returns marginal-product curve *dd* to the Malthusian equilibrium at inter-section with green *ss* supply curve of subsistence wage. The fall in real wage rate from *a* to *b* to *e* implies rising rent rates along the brown "factor-price frontier" *ff*. Because inventions shift *dd* and *ff* upward and rightward, historically the real wage rose from *B* to *B'* to *B''* levels, with rent also rising from *b* to *b'* to *b''*.

Gloomy or not, it does represent a *stable* equilibrium. Test it. Let a plague temporarily reduce numbers, moving us to the left of *E*. Real wages then become high (as they actually did after the Great Plague of 1665), standing at a point on the *dd* curve above *E*. But the system cannot stay there. With wages high enough to cause population to grow, we again move gradually back toward the equilibrium at *E*, as shown by the converging orange arrows. (Note that a temporary growth of population beyond *E*, as from a temporary run of good harvests, soon induces a wage rate so much below subsistence as to kill people off until the arrow moves us up *dd* back to *E*.)

Figure 37-1(b) shows that the rent rate per acre rises as the wage rate per hour falls. On what may be called "the factor-price frontier" (shown as brown *ff*), landlords are seen to be better off at the high-rent Malthusian subsistence equilibrium *e* than they were in the earlier golden age at *a*. No wonder some landlords greeted with joy the introduction of the white potato, which enabled people to live on cheaper calories, and hence in effect lowered the old *ss* subsistence curve and raised equilibrium rents. And no wonder some self-centered landlords regarded the spreading of birth-control information as a threat to their own standards of living. One man's slavery is another man's comfort.[6]

## END OF THE LABOR THEORY OF VALUE

The simple labor theory of value, which said that the price ratios of goods can be predicted from labor costs alone independently of the utilities which bring out a demand for the goods, thus must be dropped to account for the facts of land scarcity. Costs of production now include rent as well as wage payments. Two goods, like food and clothing, may now have equal labor costs per unit; but if food requires more land cost per unit than clothing does, they will no longer sell on a one-to-one basis.

Worse than that from the standpoint of an advocate hankering for a labor theory of value, suppose that people in a capitalistic or socialistic state shift their demand toward producing more food and less clothing. This makes the price of food *rise* relative to that of clothing. Why? Because food requires more land per worker than clothing does. Hence, the fixed land becomes more scarce when people want more of the product that is "land-intensive," thereby bidding up rent at expense of the wage.

---

[6]The Ricardians actually exaggerated the conflict of class interest. While population growth might imply higher rent per acre, they were wrong to think it *had to* imply a larger *percentage share* of GNP going to land. Note in Column (5) of Table 37-1 that labor happens to continue to get 75 per cent of the total, even when the wage rate drops from *B* to *E* and the rent rises from *b* to *e*.

Historically, pure land rent has become a declining fraction of GNP and NNP. Edward Denison, in his study of American growth, estimates that land accounts for barely 3 per cent of product today as against 9 per cent before World War I. Colin Clark's estimates for various countries of the world also suggest that industrialized nations are able to substitute capital and labor for scarce land. E. Denison, *The Sources of Economic Growth in the United States* (Committee for Economic Development, New York, 1962); C. Clark, *Conditions of Economic Progress* (Macmillan, London, 1957, 3d ed.). Although modern science enables us to make nitrates and nylon out of air and of common products like coal and oil rather than having to pay high rents to scarce natural nitrate resources in Chile or to silkworm-cultivation facilities in Japan, natural resources still command high scarcity rents; they represent a generalization of the simpler classical concept of nature's gift of fixed land. Land is not included in the later capital statistics.

Under neither planned socialism nor market capitalism can we succeed in predicting commodity prices from labor requirements alone, taking no account of the pattern of tastes and demand and its effects on scarcity of nonlabor factors.[7]

What about labor's *right* to *all* the product? Labor is the only input that is human and can sweat, laugh, cry, and pray. True. Yet, even though dirt cannot sweat or cry, it does contribute toward the growing of potatoes and when scarce does need to be *economized* in the good society.

One who wants to make a logical case for labor's being "exploited" need not handicap himself by a simple labor theory of value. He may challenge the *title* to land of those who call themselves landlords and *their right* to rents. He may claim that only the peasants have a valid title to the land and to rent, or that only the state has valid title. Who receives rents is an ethical or legal problem. But whatever its solution, rational use of land does require that a rent cost be charged the consumers who buy its products and the factors that are best fitted to work with it. (Recall Chapter 27's earlier discussion of exploitation and the Appendix to Chapter 32 on efficient socialist pricing.)

Chapters 39 and 40 will return to problems of exploitation and racial discrimination, and Chapter 42 will do greater justice to the Marxian economic concepts.

## TECHNICAL ADVANCE AND CLASSICAL GROWTH THEORY

As mentioned, real wages have risen historically, not fallen. Population has not stabilized. Land rents per acre have risen surprisingly little and, relative to other factor-prices, have actually declined. It is evident that life has not consisted of a movement down an unchanged factor-price frontier or marginal-product curve. Inventions of science, of engineering, and of managerial practice have *shifted* the curves of Fig. 37-1 rightward and upward. The black lines of progress—*BB'B''* and *bb'b''*—show the actual course of history; the reader is invited to draw on his page 732 the shifted *dd* and factor-price frontiers that run through *B'* or *B''* and through *b'* or *b''*. Such shifts have more than won the race with diminishing returns, making the Malthusian equilibrium point of subsistence unrealistic in Western economies so far.

Not all inventions are even-handedly favorable to labor and to land. Thus, inventions which help to drain swamps or to grow more food on poor acres of land might help wages more than they help rents. Some economists would call these "land-saving inventions." In contrast, any inventions that tended to raise rents more than wages, thereby tending to increase landlords' share of GNP, might be called "labor-saving

---

[7]Footnote 5 has pointed out that, in the golden age of free land, society's production-possibility schedule was a straight line with slope determined by labor productivities alone. Now, with land scarce and more important in food than in clothing production, the production-possibility schedule is bowed out for the reasons explained in Chapter 2's discussion of the law of increasing (relative) cost. (Cf. also Appendix to Chapter 27, final question.) The slope of the *p-p frontier* that determines the competitive price ratio now depends on where people's demand leaves us. (It is thus shown that Ricardians erred in thinking they could "get rid of land as a complicating factor" by going out to "the external margin" of poor, no-rent land upon which output is so low that all its costs have to go to labor alone. Actually, *that external margin shifts when demand shifts!*)

inventions."[8] In between would be the case of inventions that raised both factor returns by the same percentage, leaving relative shares of GNP unchanged: these might be called "neutral inventions." In the history of the West, inventions have appeared to be land-saving on balance; but few inventions have been so land-saving as actually to lower rents *absolutely* along with lowering them relative to wages.

The ghost of Carlyle should be relieved to know that economics, after all, has not been a dismal science—in the advanced world.

## RICARDO-MARX-SOLOW[9] MODELS OF CAPITAL ACCUMULATION

So far we have stressed the classical preoccupation with scarce land. In the remainder of this chapter, we shall survey the more important model of capital and labor, pushing land to the side as being less important for the developed part of the world. We can now use exactly the same tools in a simplified two-factor model.

*Basic assumption of capital-labor model:* One production factor grows relative to the other. Now population will be regarded primarily as a noneconomic variable, being stationary (or growing slowly for sociological reasons). Accumulation will make capital the varying factor. In an oversimplified model where output is produced by a relatively fixed and a relatively varying factor, the law of diminishing returns sets in.

The return of the augmented factor falls; the return of the relatively scarce labor factor rises. In absence of technical change, a stationary state of equilibrium is approached.

Notions of capital   It is now capital,[10] written as $K$, that is the factor growing relative to labor, $L$. Capital goods consist of a great variety of things: machines of various kinds, plants and houses, tools, raw materials and goods in process (seed grain, growing wheat plants, harvested wheat, flour, dough, warm loaves, wrapped and delivered bread), and canned and frozen edibles.

Society can sum the market values of these physical goods to get total wealth or total capital value; but it cannot command a million dollars of electric generators to transmute themselves into a million dollars of oil-refining equipment. It is true, however, that as generators wear out, the resources which could have gone to replacing them can be shifted to turn out extra refining equipment; the financial counterpart of this physical alchemy is to have investors in the generator industry take the money funds accruing on account of depreciation there and transfer them over to finance extra investment in the equipment industry. Result: although the total balance sheet of money capital may show a practically unchanged total and although the national-income statistician shows only a cancellation of one kind of disinvestment against another kind of investment, still society has managed to change the physical composition of its capital stock without undergoing any change in current consumption of goods.

---

[8] The "green revolution" of new wheat and rice cultivation in recent years seems to have been more labor-saving than land-saving: the Asian peasants have not done so well as the owners who have access to irrigation and to the credit for purchase of fertilizer.

[9] In the mid-1950s, Robert Solow at MIT gave new life to the one-sector Ramsey-Clark neoclassical model of growth. T. Swan of Canberra and J. E. Meade of Cambridge analyzed similar adaptations of the classical Ricardo-Marx models, invoking criticism by Joan Robinson of Cambridge.

[10] Chapter 30 and Appendix discussed capital and intractable problems of measuring it.

To give the idealized or stylized story of development all the rope it needs, we shall oversimplify as all the statisticians and economic historians do: we shall work with an index number of real capital goods, *K*, supposing that its return is the rate of interest or profit.

**Effects of capital deepening**    What happens to per capita output when capital grows relative to labor—that is, when capital "deepens?" Recall what happened to output per acre when labor grew relative to land. Output grew less than proportionally to the growth in the varying factor (labor), and its factor-price (the wage) had to *fall*. A similar law of diminishing returns comes into operation in our oversimplified model whenever one factor (such as capital) grows faster than the other (such as labor) with all technical change absent:

1. Output will not grow in proportion to the growth in the capital stock.

2. The return to capital, the interest rate per annum—or what is the same thing if we rule out risk and technical change, the profit rate—will fall as capital deepens.

3. What happens to the wage rate now that each man works with more capital goods and with the more intricate capital goods that the economy can now afford in the environment of a lower interest and profit rate? Just as the rent earned by relatively scarce land rose in Fig. 37-1, here the competitive wage return to relatively scarce labor will rise, as men become worth more to capitalists and meet with spirited bidding up of their market wage rates. (NOTE: Competition, not altruism, is at work.)

4. Higher wage rates and lower interest rates do *not* necessarily imply a higher percentage *share* for labor at the expense of the percentage share of capitalists. Why not? Because the increase in capital relative to labor might offset (or even more than offset) the decline in the interest rate and the rise in the real wage.[11]

5. Finally, since output (per capita or total) grew less than in proportion to the increase in capital (per capita or total), the capital-output ratio would rise in the absence of technical change (e.g., from capital value being 3 times annual GNP up to $3\frac{1}{2}$ times).

Here is a final summary:

**Deepening of capital (unchanged technology):**
**capital/labor up; interest or profit rate down; wage rate up; capital/output up.**

## DEEPENING OF CAPITAL IN DIAGRAM FORM

Figure 37-2(a) and (b) are like Fig. 37-1(a) and (b); but now capital is the relatively growing factor. Capital's amount per capita is given on the horizontal axis of (a), and its interest or profit return goes on the vertical axes. And now labor is the relatively fixed factor, and its wage goes on the horizontal axis of (b) just the way land rent did in Fig. 37-1(b).

---

[11]EXAMPLE: Let capital double from $1 million to $2 million, while labor stays at 30 men; and let interest drop from 5 to 4 per cent, and the wage rise from $5,000 per year to $8,000. Total wage share then continues to be 3 times that of capital's, each having risen by 60 per cent from their initial respective shares of $150,000 and $50,000 per year.

**FIG. 37-2**

**Accumulation lifts real output and wage, and depresses interest or profit rate**

Adding more and a greater variety of capital goods to fixed labor will, in the absence of technical change, add less and less to total product, causing interest rate earned to fall along *dd* from B to E, which is the Ricardian equilibrium point at which saving will cease. Along *ff*, fall in interest rate from b to e must raise the real wage earnable from labor's higher productivity.

Historically, technical innovation has shifted *dd* and *ff* rightward just about fast enough to offset diminishing returns and to keep the interest and profit rate almost unchanged, as shown by horizontal arrows from B to B' and b to b'.

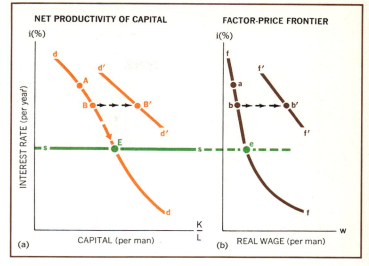

In the absence of technical change, capital accumulation takes us down the orange *dd* curve from A to B and perhaps ultimately to the Ricardian equilibrium point E at which people feel it no longer pays them to save any per cent of their incomes for enhanced future consumption. On the brown factor-price frontier *ff* in Fig. 37-2(b), society can successively be at *a;* or at *b* with the higher wage rate and lower interest rate that are implied by an augmented capital stock (more machines available of *every* kind per man); or at *e* with a still higher capital-output and capital-labor ratio. The earlier literary summary of the effects of capital deepening is verified by these graphs.

## TECHNICAL PROGRESS AND WAGES

Now let us reintroduce improving technology. This will shift the *dd* and *ff* curves outward, for example, to *d'd'* and *f'f'*. Instead of moving from B down to E, society may find that diminishing returns is offset; and the economy might in actual historical fact move from B to B', negating or concealing the Ricardo-Marx law of the declining rate of profit from capital deepening. Note in Fig. 37-2(b) that the real wage rate must definitely rise, with or without technical improvements, so long as the profit rate stays the same or falls.[12]

An alternative theory would ascribe the rise of wages under capitalism to (1) trade-union pressure, (2) government regulation of monopoly, and (3) interventions of a welfare and regulatory kind by democratic governments reacting to militant political pressures from the masses. This alternative hypothesis cannot be rejected as without substance, for we have seen throughout this book that government actions

---

[12] Indeed, we shall see later in the chapter that, unless a competitive industry's invention is so "labor-saving" as to raise the profit rate enormously, the invention must definitely boost the real wage rate. In real life, a monopolist's invention might not be so beneficent.

do have consequences for both good and evil. But the magnitude and pattern of the rise in real wages in this last century have been such as to cast doubt on union or political action as an important element in its explanation. Thus, America in the 1920s of Calvin Coolidge was run on the basis of limited government intervention: trade-unions were weak; monopoly was certainly not shrinking in that decade; yet real wages rose strongly. Similarly, Japan and West Germany have shown sharp growth in real wages linked with sharp growth in labor productivity, and this at times when government seemed pro-business rather than pro-labor.

With the advance of technology and the piling up of a larger stock of capital goods, it would take a veritable miracle of the Devil to keep real wages of men from being bid ever higher with each passing decade. Who fails to see that, fails to understand economic history as it actually happened. Economic theories that do not fit these facts have to be junked and replaced by others that do.

## THE APPROXIMATE FACTS OF MODERN DEVELOPMENT

Let us summarize our theoretical researches.

First we studied the crucial role of limited land and growing labor in economic progress. Then we passed from the labor-land world of Smith-Malthus to one that studied the role in economic growth of capital accumulation relative to labor. Last, but far from least, we stressed the factor of technological change and innovation. A look at the facts will now show why present-day economists think that scientific and engineering progress has been quantitatively the single most important factor for growth in the advanced countries.

Thanks to Simon Kuznets' Nobel-prize-winning work at the National Bureau of Economic Research,[13] to the works of others there, and to Robert Solow and Edward Denison, we can formulate certain general uniformities of economic development in the United States and the other advanced nations of the world. The ratio chart of Fig. 37-3 shows the great trends of economic development for America in this century. Similar findings apply to the leading nations abroad. Figure 37-3 is crucially important. Linger over it.

The top chart shows the growth since 1900 of labor, capital, and hence of real output. Population has more than doubled in 75 years of steady growth. (Taking into account shortening of the working week and changes in age distribution and in labor-force participation, the growth in total number of man-hours has been even more modest.) While labor has about doubled, the stock of physical capital has increased more than eightfold! Thus the substantial increase in capital per worker, the $K/L$ ratio, does represent a significant amount of "capital deepening."

What about the growth in output? Has output grown less than in proportion to capital, as in the model that ignored technical change? No. The fact that the $Q$ curve is not *in between* the two factor curves, but actually lies *up near* the capital curve

---

[13] S. Kuznets, *Capital in the American Economy* (Princeton University Press, Princeton, N.J., 1961), gives reference to pioneering National Bureau researchers, such as A. F. Burns, D. Creamer, S. Fabricant, R. W. Goldsmith, and J. Schmookler. See also J. W. Kendrick, *Productivity Trends in the United States* (Princeton University Press, Princeton, N.J., 1961), a pioneering Bureau study.

## FIG. 37-3
### Economic growth has displayed striking long-run regularities

**(a)**  Capital stock has grown faster than labor supply. Total output has nonetheless shown natural rate of growth in full pace with output.

**(b)**  Real wage rate has grown steadily, if anything overmatching growth in average labor productivity per man-hour. No pauperization or immiserization of the working class shows up in broad wage statistics.

**(c)**  Without technical invention and innovation, deepening of capital relative to labor would depress interest rate and raise capital-output ratio. But, in fact, technical change seems to have just about offset diminishing returns to capital accumulation. (Hence, static curves of Fig. 37-2 must have been shifting rightward. REMARK: If higher money interest rates were corrected for price inflation, trendless oscillation of interest and profit rates would be even more apparent—in defiance of any strong Law of Declining Rate of Profit.)

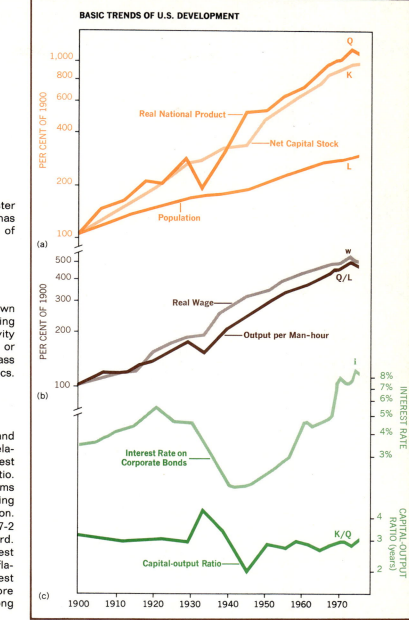

**BASIC TRENDS OF U.S. DEVELOPMENT**

(a) PER CENT OF 1900 — Q, K, Real National Product, Net Capital Stock, L, Population

(b) PER CENT OF 1900 — w, Q/L, Real Wage, Output per Man-hour

(c) i, Interest Rate on Corporate Bonds, INTEREST RATE (8%, 7%, 6%, 5%, 4%, 3%), K/Q, Capital-output Ratio, CAPITAL-OUTPUT RATIO (years) (4, 3, 2)

1900  1910  1920  1930  1940  1950  1960  1970

itself, shows that *there must have been technical change in actual history*. The close proximity of the output and capital curves shows that the capital-output ratio has not risen as in the simple deepening model; instead, as the lowest curve in the bottom chart shows, the capital-output ratio has remained remarkably close to 3 years (i.e., a balance-sheet calculation of current value of all capital goods would show it to be approximately equal to 3 years of total product).[14]

**Rising wages and trendless profit**    The real wage has indeed risen steadily, in accordance with what one would expect from the growth in capital tools cooperating with labor and from favorable technological trends. The interest rate—or, if we could get complete statistics, the rate of profit actually earned on more risky investments—does *not* show the decline that would be predicted from simple deepening of capital and diminishing returns. Interest rates and profit rates fluctuate much in business cycle and war, but display no strong trend upward or downward for the whole period. Either by coincidence, or as the result of some economic mechanism that needs study, technological change has just about offset diminishing returns.[15]

Output per man-hour is the brown curve shown in the middle chart of Fig. 37-3. As could be expected from the deepening of capital and from technological advance, $Q/L$ has risen steadily. Moreover—and this too represents a remarkable coincidence or the result of some economic mechanism needing study—the percentage growth in wage rates per hour has almost exactly matched the percentage growth in product per man-hour. This does not mean, as some Wall Street arithmetic has implied, that labor has captured *all* the fruits of productivity advance. It means, rather, that labor has kept about the *same share* of total product, with property also earning about the same relative share throughout the period. (A closer look at the middle chart suggests that there *might* have been a slow upward creep in the share of labor in GNP, with property's share dropping gently; but part of this might be the return to capital invested in education.)

## SIX BASIC TRENDS OF ECONOMIC DEVELOPMENT

These basic facts of economic history in the advanced nations can be summarized approximately by the following trends:

*Trend 1.* Population has grown, but at a much more modest rate than the capital stock, resulting in a "deepening of capital."

*Trend 2.* There has been a strong upward trend in real wage rates.

*Trend 3.* According to what is often called Bowley's Law, the share of wages and salaries relative to the total return to property has shown considerable constancy in the long run (but perhaps with slight signs of an edging upward of labor's share).

---

[14] Many charts show a stronger tendency for the capital-output ratio to decline in the last part of the period. Much of such a decline in $K/Q$ results from measuring the numerator so as to deflate out of it the relative rise that has taken place in capital-goods prices compared with other prices. In Fig. 37-3, the components of $K/Q$ are each measured in current dollars deflated by a *common* price index.

[15] Resist the temptation to think the law of diminishing returns is not operating: if, instead of being merely hidden, it were actually not operating at all, the real interest rate would have had to *rise* strongly as a result of technical change alone. (If we corrected interest rates for price changes—e.g., subtracting recent percentage price rises from recent high bond yields, as was suggested in earlier chapters—we would find the "real rate of interest or profit" to have been even more steady.)

*Trend 4.* Instead of observing a fall in the rate of interest or profit, we actually observe their oscillation in the business cycle but no strong upward or downward trend in this century (particularly if we deflate interest and profit rates of their price-change component, and deal with *real* rates).

*Trend 5.* Instead of observing a steady rise in the capital-output ratio as the deepening of capital invokes the law of diminishing returns, we find that the capital-output ratio has been approximately constant in this century.

*Trend 6.* The ratio of saving to output has oscillated in the business cycle—reaching about the same level at various high-employment phases of the cycle. Or taking into account the approximate constancy of the capital-output ratio, we can convert this approximate constancy of the ratio of investment to income into the following: national product has generally had a trend rate of growth at a roughly constant percentage rate per year.[16]

## ANALYZING THE LAWS OF MOTION OF THE MIXED ECONOMY

While these are only approximate truths and not like the unrepealable laws of physics, they portray fundamental facts about economic growth. How to explain them?

Trends 2 and 1—higher wage rates when capital deepens—fit nicely together with classical and neoclassical theories of production and distribution. Trend 3—Bowley's Law that the wage share is approximately constant—is an interesting coincidence that could consistently hold under *all* kinds of conditions only in a *statical* neoclassical model that possessed a special kind of production function relating $Q$ to $L$ and $K$ (what in Chapter 27 was called the "Cobb-Douglas function," for which relative factor shares are constant).

Trends 4 and 5, however, warn us that neoclassical theory cannot hold in *static* form! A steady profit rate and a steady capital-output ratio are incompatible with the more basic law of diminishing returns under deepening of capital. We are forced, therefore, to introduce *technical innovations* into our statical neoclassical analysis to explain these dynamic facts. And a good thing it is that we are told to introduce technical change, since we have much independent evidence of the importance of science and engineering in the modern era.

In terms of the analysis back in page 737's Fig. 37-2, we are forced to introduce an outward shift in the $dd$ and $ff$ curves there to account for all the trends. Thus, the eastward move in Fig. 37-2(a) from $B$ on $dd$ to $B'$ on $d'd'$, which corresponds to the eastward move in Fig. 37-2(b) from $b$ to $b'$, will be consistent with trends 1 to 6. The tendency toward diminishing returns has just been offset by the technical shift, with interest remaining at the same horizontal level and the wage rate rising just as much as output per head. The capital-output ratio, which cannot easily be read in Fig. 37-2, must stay constant if the interest return on capital is to constitute the same relative share as before.[17]

---

[16]EXAMPLE: Figure 37-3 shows $K/Q$ about 3 and the percentage growth of capital per annum almost $3\frac{1}{3}$ per cent per year. Only if net capital formation is about 10 per cent (equals $3\frac{1}{3} \times 3$) of output is this possible, as the next footnote and the Appendix make clear.

[17]As shown in the Appendix, trends 3, 4, and 5 cannot be independent, since arithmetically the constancy of any two of the three magnitudes ($iK/Q$, $i$, $K/Q$) implies the constancy of the third. (These basic trends can be rationalized by the hypothesis that invention has increased labor's efficiency by just enough to keep the ratio capital/labor-measured-in-efficiency-units constant. Hence, the reinterpreted model predicts constant $i$ and $K/Q$—as footnote 20 and the Appendix will elucidate.)

Professor Solow, utilizing his own methods of analysis and corroborating the independent findings of numerous scholars at the National Bureau of Economic Research and elsewhere, has come up with the following remarkable conclusion:

Scarcely half of the increase in America's productivity per capita and in real wages can be accounted for by the increase in capital itself. More than half of the increase in productivity is a "residual" that seems to be attributable to technical change—to scientific and engineering advance, to industrial improvements, and to "know-how" of management methods and educational training of labor.

This important finding needs careful interpretation.

First, although it is customary to measure and speak of the enhanced productivity of labor, there is no necessary implication that all the higher productivity (or most of it, or little of it) came from greater effort on the part of workers, or from more intensive conditions of sweat and strain; nor that it came from more effort and education, or from more initiative and incentives of the human labor force; nor, for that matter, from more energetic and clever executive management. The facts do not point to any simple interpretation.

Second, it is artificial to separate capital formation and technology completely. New techniques do tend to be *embodied* in new kinds of equipment. It is possible to imagine a stationary state—like the optimistic one of John Stuart Mill—in which there is no net saving and investment, but in which there is considerable technical progress as the depreciation charges of worn-out equipment finance their replacement by technically better equipment. Still, no one will deny that innovations can be introduced faster in a society which is performing *net* investment in addition to the gross investment corresponding to replacement. We all do learn from actually doing, and the society which gets to try out more new things will run that much ahead of the one which does little or no net saving.

## ARE INVENTIONS LABOR-SAVING OR CAPITAL-SAVING?

Any invention that wins its way under competition must raise the real wage rate or the interest rate or both.[18]

However, some inventions will by their nature have a tendency to increase the relative share of labor; others to increase the relative share of capital and property generally; and others to affect both factors in about the same degree. This suggests the convenience of the following definition:

*Definition:* An invention is called "labor-saving," "capital-saving," or "neutral," depending upon whether it tends to lower the relative share of labor, lower the relative share of property, or leave relative shares unchanged.

---

[18] In terms of Fig. 37-2(b)'s factor-price frontier, $ff$ must be shifted outward and upward or the invention will not succeed in the competitive market. As we'll see in Chapter 42, Karl Marx misunderstood this. One cannot validly promulgate the "law of the declining rate of profit [or interest rate]" alongside the "law of the immiserization of the working class [falling real wage rate]." Unless one invokes diminishing returns to land in the Malthus fashion—and Marx, who hated Malthus as an apologist for the rich and as a "plagiarist," paid insufficient attention to such phenomena—one has to give up one or both of the Marxian "laws" in a competitive model.

An extreme example of a labor-saving invention would be one that enabled un-manned machines to turn out robots that could do any of the manual and intellectual tasks of human labor. This would no doubt reduce the competitive wage drastically and could conceivably drop labor's share of NNP from its present level of about 75 to 80 per cent to below 50 per cent. An example of a capital-saving invention would be the case of a cheap computer that enabled firms to get along with much less inventory; or the invention of Kleenex tissue to replace durable handkerchiefs; or the invention of easily launched, wave-reflecting satellites that made ocean cables unnec-essary.[19] It is easy to specify innumerable examples of capital-saving or labor-saving innovations and of neutral innovations in between.

The steady rise in wage rates is thought by many economists to *induce* employers to come up with labor-saving inventions. This tendency is often offered to help explain the failure of the profit-and-interest rate to fall as capital is accumulated. Marx, a century ago, had used such an explanation to account for the success of capitalists in resisting a rise in wages and in creating an industrial reserve army of the un-employed. Sir John Hicks of Oxford has, in our day, advanced similar arguments of an inherent bias toward labor-saving innovation, and William Fellner of Yale has marshaled some evidence in favor of this thesis.

Whatever the ultimate merits of such arguments, we must recognize that *any* invention which lowers cost of production can benefit the first competitor who intro-duces it. Furthermore, since the relative share of wages in total costs has been approxi-mately constant for a century, any employer who is planning his research expenditures over the coming years will reasonably take this into account and will do well to spend now the same number of pennies on experimentation designed to save a dollar of future cost, whatever its source.[20]

We have seen that economic analysis can throw much light on the laws of motion of the mixed economy. And when we look at the 1975–1985 United States projections

---

[19] A capital-saving invention tends to shift downward Fig. 37-2(a)'s productivity curve of capital, twisting it toward the vertical and toward greater inelasticity, tending in all to reduce the fruits of sacrificing current consumption and accumulating capital. A neutral technical change would be one that shifts Fig. 37-2's curves generally outward and upward. Advanced treatises deal with various distinct definitions of what is meant by labor-saving; the discussion here is left general so as not to be inconsistent with either the definition associated with J. R. Hicks or R. F. Harrod.

[20] A theory of induced technical change can explain and unify all the six basic trends of economic development as follows: (1) Suppose any increase in capital relative to labor will tend to raise labor's relative share. (2) Suppose that effort devoted to making each laborer the new equivalent of more than one laborer will be induced when labor cost increases as the share of total costs (and that like efforts to "augment" capital's powers will now go down). (3) Finally, assume that a constant fraction of income is always saved and invested and that labor population grows at a constant slow rate. Then it will follow that the system will ultimately grow in "golden-age balance": (*a*) Capital and output will grow at the same high rate with a constant $K/Q$ ratio; (*b*) labor population will grow at a slower rate but, because of induced technological invention, "labor in effective or efficiency units" will grow at precisely the same rate as capital and output; (*c*) now with $Q$, $K$, and effective $L$ growing in balance, there will be no diminishing returns to capital and hence there will be a constant interest rate and constant relative labor share; (*d*) finally, the real wage will grow because each worker is having his effectiveness raised by the induced technical change. QED. Rigorous proof of this was presented by several authors in the mid-1960s without any reliance on Cobb-Douglas functions, as the Appendix will make clear.

by the Wharton School or other computer models, we see that these trends are still persistent.

Admittedly, growth theory is still at the frontier of economics, and the experts are not all agreed on the mechanisms of past and future paths of development. Some alternative theories are presented in the Appendix to this chapter. However, we are now armed to tackle in coming chapters the problems of growth in less developed economies, advanced economies, and collectivist systems like the Soviet Union.

## SUMMARY

1   Many writers have tried to read into economic history a linear progression through inevitable stages, such as primitive economy, feudalism, capitalism, and some form of communism. The actual facts have not agreeably stuck to such timetables; in particular, the mixed economies that dominate the Western world came into being without the permission of social prophets.

2   The classical models of Smith and Malthus describe economic development in terms of fixed land and growing population. A simple "labor theory of value" prevails so long as land is superabundant; and output develops steadily with population in this golden age where labor gets all the national product.

3   In the absence of technical change, increasing population ultimately exhausts the supply of free land. The resulting increase in population density invokes the law of diminishing returns: Fixity of land keeps output from growing proportionally to increased labor; with less and less of land to work with, each new man adds less and less extra product; the decline in labor's marginal-product means a decline in the competitively earned real wage. As each acre of land gets more and more labor to work with, its marginal-product and competitively earned rent go up. A fundamental factor-price frontier depicts how the rent rate must rise as the wage rate falls; but no one can predict what will happen to the *relative* shares of land and labor in national product.

4   The Malthusian equilibrium comes when the wage has fallen to the subsistence level, below which the supply of labor will not reproduce itself. However, in realistic fact, technical change has kept economic development going in the West by continually shifting the productivity curve of labor upward.

5   The Ricardo-Marx-Solow model stresses the deepening of capital, i.e., the process of accumulating capital goods of varied types faster than the growth in population and labor hours. In the absence of technical change, an increase in capital per capita will not be matched by a proportional increase in output per capita— because of diminishing returns. Hence, capital deepening lowers the interest rate (which is the same as the "profit-rate" if risk is ignored), raises the real wage along the factor-price frontier, and raises the capital-output ratio.

**6**  Historically, trends 1 and 2 on page 740—a rise in $K/L$ and in $w$—could be consistent with the *statical* model. Trend 3's approximate constancy of relative shares of labor and property—as measured by $wL/Q$ and $iK/Q$, where $Q = wL + iK$—is not mandatory in the statical model, but is consistent with a special technical case of it (Cobb-Douglas). However, trends 4 and 5—the failure of the interest and profit rate to fall and of the capital-output ratio to rise—show clearly that technical change *must* be brought into the analysis. (It is as if technical change acts to augment labor in efficiency units just enough to match capital's growth: in efficiency units there emerges no diminishing returns, no rising capital/output ratio, no falling rate of profit!) Trend 6—approximate constancy of the investment-income or saving ratio—taken together with the constancy of the capital-output ratio, arithmetically implies a constant percentage growth of output.

**7**  The facts suggest the hypothesis that capital accumulation is second to technical change in explaining rising productivity. But innovation and investment interact, as new techniques get embodied in new equipment and people learn by trying new investments. Increasing productivity can be expressed conveniently in terms of labor productivity—i.e., $Q/L$—but this does not necessarily imply anything about the reasons for the rise.

**8**  Inventions are defined as labor-saving, capital-saving, or neutral, depending upon whether they reduce labor's relative share of national product, reduce property's relative share, or leave shares unchanged. Experience with rising wage rates makes firms expect the trend to continue; whether or not they try for and succeed in making labor-saving inventions, firms will want to cut down on any cost items (labor, natural resources, capital costs).

Either by coincidence or cancellation of offsetting trends or as the result of economic mechanisms needing study,[21] the pace of invention has turned out to be about enough to offset the effect of diminishing returns to capital on the interest and profit rate; and innovations have not turned out to be so labor-saving or capital-saving as to change much the relative shares of labor and property.

## CONCEPTS FOR REVIEW

| | |
|---|---|
| stages of history | capital deepening, $K/L$ rise |
| Smithian golden age | capital-output ratio, $K/Q$ |
| labor theory of value | interest rate and profit rate |
| land scarcity and value | technical progress |
| Malthusian subsistence wage | labor-saving |
| factor-price frontier $ff$ | neutral |
| marginal-product $dd$ | capital-saving |
| diminishing returns | $Q$ growth from inventions, from |
| relative factor shares | more $K$ |

[21] Such as that described in footnote 20.

## QUESTIONS FOR DISCUSSION

1   Does the mixed economy fit any timetables of history? Was it foreseeable?

2   "If the democratic state subsidizes science and invention, controls the business cycle, and introduces sensible planning, we can expect growth that would astound the classical economists." Evaluate critically.

3   Draw the parallels between the models of Figs. 37-1 and 37-2: rising labor-output ratio and rising capital-output ratio; falling wage and falling interest rate; the two factor-price frontiers; technical shifts of *dd* and *ff* in both cases; land-saving or labor-saving and neutral innovations in both cases; relative factor shares; etc.

4   "Saving helps capitalists today, workers tomorrow." Assess this filter-down view.

5   "Without technical change and unemployment, persistent capital accumulation would ultimately mean euthanasia (death) of the capitalists." Explain by Fig. 37-2.

6   Since labor's share shows a slight uptrend and the capital-output ratio a slight downtrend, since the interest and profit rate fluctuates considerably, since the ratio of private net investment to private GNP shows fluctuation and, in recent years, perhaps some signs of an uptrend—in view of these facts, would you be much surprised if page 741's basic trends were to show future changes?

7   Give examples of labor-saving and capital-saving inventions.

8   "Had we saved less but spent more on experiments, we'd be richer." Assess.

## APPENDIX: Modern Discussions of Development Theory

Economics, not being a settled subject, is itself still undergoing development. While the broad facts of historical development discussed in the chapter are not in dispute, different interpretations of them are given by different authors. Some of the ideas associated with the names of the late Joseph A. Schumpeter, Sir Roy Harrod of Oxford, W. W. Leontief of Harvard, Professors Joan Robinson and Nicholas Kaldor of Cambridge University, and various American economists are sketched briefly in this Appendix.

While an elementary textbook cannot pretend to resolve advanced topics, today one would consider an introduction to physics old-fashioned if it did not somewhere give the reader a glance at fundamental issues on the frontiers of knowledge: atomic theory, elementary particles, generalized relativity, etc.

Similarly, many beginning students of economics will want to have a glimpse of the issues at the fron-

tier of current economic analysis. Without mastering every intricacy of this Appendix, the interested reader can capture the flavor of developing economic thought from it. In particular, many readers who are not concerned with the rest of the theories discussed in this Appendix may still want to turn to its final discussion (pages 754–756) of the fascinating and useful subject, input-output analysis of interindustry flows by Nobel-laureate W. W. Leontief.

### SCHUMPETERIAN INNOVATION

Joseph Schumpeter (1883–1950) of Vienna and Harvard was author of two economic classics:[1] *The*

[1] As can be seen by readers of his stimulating *Capitalism, Socialism and Democracy* (Harper & Row, New York, 1942), Schumpeter was more than an economist. Believing the

*Theory of Economic Development* (English ed., Harvard University Press, Cambridge, Mass., 1934) and the posthumous *History of Economic Analysis* (Oxford University Press, Fair Lawn, N.J., 1954).

Schumpeter emphasized the role of the innovator—i.e., the inventor, the developer, the promoter, the man who initiates and recognizes technical improvements and who succeeds in getting them introduced. Like Carlyle's faith in the role of the great man in history, Schumpeter's theory regards the innovator as the dynamic actor of capitalism, who rules profitably for a day, only to have his profits nibbled away by imitating competitors.

Figure 37-2(a) back on page 737 well represents Schumpeter's notion of what would happen if all innovations ceased. Competition and capital accumulation would quite quickly push society down the curve of diminishing returns *dd;* indeed, Schumpeter thought that the long-run *ss* horizontal line at which the supply of new saving will disappear would be at a zero rate of interest and profit, being properly drawn in Fig. 37-2(a) down on the horizontal axis itself. (His much-attacked theory of a zero interest rate in the innovationless stationary state can be replaced by a positive-interest-rate floor without much altering his theory of cyclical development.)

But now Schumpeter plays his trump card. Innovation is periodically shifting the *dd* curve upward and outward. The violin string is plucked by innovation; without innovation it dies down to stationariness, but then along comes a new innovation to pluck it back into dynamic motion again. So it is with the profit rate in economic life.

The profits due to innovation, we have seen, will be competed away by imitators, with labor and consumers soon benefiting from price reductions. The innovation-induced rise in interest rates will soon

coax out saving and capital formation, until the accumulation of the augmented capital stock leads to diminishing returns, a "profit squeeze," and minimal interest. But then along comes a new burst of innovations—e.g., railroads, electricity, automation, semiconductors—to pluck the system back into dynamic motion, and we are off on a new repetition of the process.

Ignoring Schumpeter's specific theories of the business cycle, we see that his theory of development is completely consistent with the first two trends of economic history: rising real wage rates, and capital increase outstripping population increase. Although his general theory does not specifically call for constant relative shares, a trendless profit rate, a constant capital-output ratio, or a trendless average propensity-to-consume-and-save, still, all or any of these could be quite consistent with Schumpeter's general schemata.

## UNEMPLOYMENT IN THE STATIONARY STATE?

Ricardo, Alfred Marshall, and Schumpeter had one thing in common with Lord Keynes of *The General Theory of Employment, Interest and Money.* They all thought that profit rates would be pushed to minimal levels in the absence of technical change. But Ricardo and company all thought that when this day of judgment came, the economy would be voluntarily consuming 100 per cent of its full-employment income; although positive investment would cease, people would then be spending enough on consumption to maintain full employment. (In terms of the diagrams of Part Two, in the Ricardian stationary state the $C + I + G$ curve would be intersecting the 45° line at the full-employment level, with $C + I + G$ actually equal there to $C + replacement + G$, because net investment ceases in the stationary state. For the remainder of this chapter we shall interpret $I$ as net investment rather than as gross investment; likewise for net saving.)

Keynes, on the other hand, feared that such minimal rates of interest and of profit on risky ventures might create a stationary state of stagnation with chronic unemployment:

People might still *want to save* at full employment, but no *matching real investment* would be forthcoming when the promised profit rate is too low to coax out risk taking. When the interest to be earned on short-term gilt-edge government bonds has become so low as to make people indifferent between

economic system to be itself essentially stable, Schumpeter advanced sociological and political reasons for his predicted decay of capitalism: he held that the very efficiency of capitalism will be its ruin, as intellectuals and the masses come to despise the market ideology and contrive to introduce hampering government interferences in the name of welfare. Unlike Marx, who thought capitalism would die of its own cancers, Schumpeter thought it would eventually commit suicide for psychosomatic reasons. The tremendous resurgence of the *mixed* economies in the 30 years since Schumpeter cheerfully gave his gloomy prediction is, apparently, a deviation from *his* timetable of history; but the disaffection of affluent college activists may be testimonial to his prophetic sociological insight.

hoarding much or little safe, idle money,[2] central bank policy can't do much to prevent stagnation.

This notion of a troublesome stationary state did not die with the 1930s. Prominent followers of Keynes at Cambridge University, such as Professors Joan Robinson and Lord Kahn have grave doubts concerning the possibility of a successful deepening of capital accompanied by full employment in a mixed economy. At the least, they would stress that it will never happen by itself in a country that confines itself to orthodox fiscal and monetary policies. At the most, they would harbor grave doubts that "managed capitalism" could, or would, pursue the unorthodox policies of monetary and fiscal expansion implied by a successful synthesis of neoclassical and post-Keynesian analysis.

Readers who go on to advanced economics can be referred to writings of these Cambridge authors.[3] Here, briefly, will be presented some of the points that need to be considered in doing justice to both sides of the argument as it bears on long-term economic development: no attempt will be made to identify ideas and writers meticulously.

## UNCHANGEABLE CAPITAL-OUTPUT RATIO?

The land-output and labor-output ratios were not constants in the first Smith-Malthus model of development. And the capital-output ratio in the Ricardo-Marx-Solow model of Fig. 37-2 was likewise not supposed to be a technical constant. In the absence of technical change, successful capital formation by society would enable output to grow; and the resulting phenomenon of diminishing returns would imply a *smoothly growing* capital-output ratio as capital deepening was taking place. On this view, *dynamic*

technical change has seemed historically to provide about the extra productivity needed to offset *statical* diminishing returns, keeping the measured capital-output ratio constant.

Many modern economists—Robert Eisner of Northwestern, the late Alvin Hansen of Harvard, Luigi Pasinetti of Cambridge, and others—hold that the capital-output ratio is very nearly a technical *constant,* and that any attempt to accumulate capital beyond the rate required by the annual growth in output will soon be unsuccessful. Profits or rents from equipment will fall off badly after any surge of capital investment like those of 1955–1957 and 1964–1972. Excess capacity will follow, and the resulting profit squeeze will kill off private investment, as it did in the sluggish years following 1973. Therefore, they argue, any long-term theory must utilize an *invariable* capital-output ratio like that shown in the historical data of Fig. 37-3.

## HARROD-DOMAR GROWTH MODELS

These concepts can be illuminated by some interesting models of balanced compound-interest (or "exponential") growth developed by Sir Roy Harrod in England and Professor E. Domar in America.[4] This theory has two aspects: the long-term "natural rate of growth;" the so-called "warranted rate of growth."

**The natural rate of growth**   The historical data of Fig. 37-3 can help explain Harrod's arithmetic; and, in turn, a simple Harrod-Domar model can give an oversimplified "explanation" of those historical trends.

Suppose hours of labor $L$ grow steadily at about 1 per cent per year.[5] And for extreme simplicity, assume that technical change is in effect making

---

[2] This floor on the profit-and-interest rate could help account for the historical constancy of the profit rate named in trend 4 (page 741), particularly if someone could supply reasons for a profit ceiling. With the profit rate allegedly running between two channels, its constancy would be removed from the realm of coincidence. (Recall also earlier discussion; page 352's "liquidity trap" or "depression pole," when elevated by riskiness, might provide such a profit floor.)

[3] J. Robinson, *Economic Philosophy* (Aldine, Chicago, 1962), Chap. 5; *Accumulation of Capital* (Macmillan, London, 1956); N. Kaldor, *Essays on Value and Distribution; On Economic Stability and Growth; On Economic Policy* (Duckworth, London, 1960).

[4] R. F. Harrod, *Towards a Dynamic Economics* (Macmillan, London, 1948); E. D. Domar, *Essays in the Theory of Economic Growth* (Oxford University Press, Fair Lawn, N.J., 1957). The same discussion of interacting accelerator-multiplier models in Chapter 14 is here applied to the trend of economic development rather than to the business-cycle deviations from that trend.

[5] Expansion of an industrial sector through the utilization of an unlimited supply of rural labor is associated with the name of Sir Arthur Lewis, an eminent development economist originally from Jamaica. Such diverse economists as the conservative Gustav Cassel of Sweden and the nonconservative Karl Marx had put forth similar Ricardian notions.

every man's efficiency as a laborer grow at another 2 per cent per year. Either because of more scientific methods of production or better education, it is as if 98 men can this year do what it took 100 to do last year; and this is repeated indefinitely. To coin a phrase, while *actual L* in its human man-hour units is growing at but 1 per cent per year, the number of "efficiency units of labor" *L\** is growing at 3 per cent per year because of the annual 2 per cent efficiency improvement. This leads to the concept of the natural rate of growth.

*Definition:* The *natural rate of growth* of a simplified Harrod system is the percentage growth per year of its labor supply expressed in "efficiency units" (which means natural labor units as augmented by the presumed increase in technical effectiveness of each man-hour); as a condition of *balanced* growth, output and capital must also be growing at this same natural rate per year.

With GNP (or *Q*) and with *L\** growing steadily at this natural rate of 3 per cent per year, the stock of capital *K* must also grow at the same natural rate of 3 per cent per year so as to keep in balanced pace. How much net investment is required each year to keep *K* growing at this natural rate of 3 per cent? Or, in other words, how much must people be steadily saving and investing out of their annual full-employment product to keep growth nicely balanced?

Evidently the needed saving-income, or saving-GNP, ratio depends on the numerical value of the capital-output ratio *K/Q* times the natural growth rate.[6]

We are now in a position to write down the arithmetic formula relating three historical things: the Harrod natural rate of growth of .03 per year, or in the general case *g* per year; the historical capital-output ratio of, say, $3\frac{1}{3}$, or in the general case *K/Q*;

the required saving-GNP ratio of .10, or in the general case *s*. We get

$$s = g \times \frac{K}{Q} \qquad \text{or} \qquad .10 = .03 \times 3\tfrac{1}{3}$$

This relationship determines the amount of voluntary saving *and* investment that is needed if the Harrod natural rate of growth is to be an *equilibrium state.*[7]

**Explaining the trends** Can this simplified Harrod-Domar model of balanced natural rate of growth account for all six of the basic trends listed on pages 740–741? Yes, as footnote 20 hinted. Let us check off the trends.

The model certainly gives a deepening of capital relative to man-hours of actual *L*, since *K* grows at 3 per cent and *L* only at 1 per cent. [However, in this simplified model, an observer who concentrates only on *L\**, labor in efficiency units, will see a con-stant (K/L)* with no "deepening" going on but merely an apparent "widening of capital" to keep *K* and *L\** balanced.]

Trend 2 is verified also. The wage rate rises— actually at 2 per cent per year. Why? Because each actual man (*L*, not *L\**) collects the marginal product of the increasing efficiency units *in him*, and these units work with their full quota of capital goods.

Trend 3 is verified and is no longer a coincidence. Because technical change was so nicely neutral as to make each man take on "the strength of ten," the balanced growth in *K* and *L\** means we are *dividing shares between the factors in precisely the same way as before*. (Recall that an observer of *L\** alone merely sees balanced *widening* of capital, not deepening; note that no Cobb-Douglas assumption therefore needs to be made.)

Trend 4's constancy of the interest rate is now precisely verified, being neither an approximation nor a coincidence. Each unit of *K*, being matched exactly by the same amount of *L\** as before, experiences no diminishing returns and has imputed to it the same competitive interest rate. (If degree of risk is the same, constancy of the interest rate means constancy of the somewhat higher profit rate.)

Trend 5 is of course verified, since the Harrod

---

[6]Thus, suppose *Q* is $1,000 billion per year, and that the capital stock is about $3\frac{1}{3}$ times as great, being $3,333 billion. Then, to add 3 per cent to *K* this year we must have net investment of $100 billion (equals .03 × $3.333 billion), which means that people must be saving and investing exactly 10 per cent (equals 3% × $3\frac{1}{3}$) of their incomes. [Check your understanding by showing that a 4 per cent natural growth rate would in this case require a $13\frac{1}{3}$ per cent (equals 4% × $3\frac{1}{3}$) saving ratio out of income; and that a 3 per cent natural growth rate with a *K/Q* ratio of only 2 would require only a 6 per cent saving-income ratio.]

[7]This is really the *I = S* schedule equality of Part Two. For in the case of the natural growth rate, *g = I/K* or *I = gK*; hence, *I/Q = S/Q = s = g(K/Q)*, the Harrod condition.

natural rate of balanced growth assumes from the beginning an unchanged $K/Q$ ratio. In terms of the Ricardo-Marx-Solow model, even if the capital-output ratio *could* smoothly change, it will not have to change at all in a situation where widening of $K$ to match $L^*$ means no diminishing returns and entails $Q$ growing in full proportion to $K$.

Trend 6's constancy of the saving-income ratio is verified from the basic Harrod formula for the natural rate of balanced growth at the same compound interest rate per year: $s =$ constant $g \times$ constant $K/Q$.

### Interdependence of trends

As mentioned in footnote 17, page 741, the six trends are not all logically independent. We could have saved time by checking any two of the three trends 3, 4, and 5, knowing that their correctness would arithmetically guarantee the correctness of the remaining trend. Here is why. If property always gets the same fraction of output, say, one-fourth, and if the profit rate stays constant, then the process of capitalization of an income stream discussed in Chapter 30 shows that the value of the capital stock must be a determinate multiple of output. [That is, $K$'s fractional share of $Q$ divided by the interest rate is equal to the capital-output ratio: $i(K/Q) \div i = K/Q$. Thus, if capital gets one-fourth of 1,000-billion-dollar $Q$, and this property return of $250 billion is capitalized by dividing it through by $i = .07\frac{1}{2} = \frac{3}{40}$, then the value of capital is seen to be determinate at $3,333 billion, or $3\frac{1}{3}$ times the value of output.]

### Harrod's warranted rate of growth

The natural rate of growth is designed to cope with long-term problems of economic development. A few words can be said about a related tool designed more to explain cyclical instability than long-term trend.[8]

What if society's *actual* saving fraction differs from that *needed* to keep the natural growth rate in nice balance? That is, suppose actual desired $S/Q = s_a$ at full employment is greater, or less, than $s$ given by $g(K/Q)$. Too high a schedule of saving, we saw in Part Two, will tend to lead to unemployment. Too low a saving schedule, relative to the investment schedule, was seen to produce an inflationary gap and tendency toward price inflation.

Very well. No longer is the natural growth rate $g$

---

[8] These next two sections may be skipped.

the one that the system will realize. Growth in balance has now become rather irrelevant. Still Harrod can ask this rather odd question:

*Starting from enough unemployed resources so that the natural growth rate of labor and other resources encounters no bottleneck or ceiling—starting from there, what rate of growth of output, W, if it could be achieved and maintained, would (through "the acceleration principle" of Chapter 14, page 262), lead to a large enough volume of investment to justify (via the multiplier analysis of Chapter 12) a continuance of its own growth rate W? The answering W is defined as the "warranted rate of growth."*

In short, to get $W$, reinterpret the old Harrod relation $s = g(K/Q)$; instead of taking $g$ as given in it, work the relation backward to solve for the growth rate of $Q$. Follow these steps: (1) Replace $s$ by the actual saving ratio $S/Q$ people insist on having namely, $s_a$. (2) Replace the $g$ specified by labor force and technological growth by the unknown warranted rate of growth $W$. (3) Provided that the capital-output ratio $K/Q$ is a hard constant, let it stand. (4) Solve for $W$ by removing $K/Q$ to the denominator under $S/Q$.

We go from the natural rate to the warranted rate thus: $s_a = W(K/Q)$ replaces $s = g(K/Q)$, and

$$W = \frac{s_a}{K/Q}$$

An example will help. With $g = .03$ and $K/Q = 3\frac{1}{3}$, Harrod needs $s = .10$ for his natural-growth process. But suppose people want to save $s_a = .13\frac{1}{3} > .10$. This overthrift would lead to unemployment. But suppose somehow Harrod could start a *faster* expansion, of $W$ per cent per year in $Q$, which can always get the labor it needs from the ranks of the unemployed. Then how fast must it expand to generate enough $I/Q$ to match $S/Q = s_a = .13\frac{1}{3}$? If every dollar of expanded $Q$ requires $K$ to expand by $3\frac{1}{3}$ dollars, our answer is $W = .13\frac{1}{3}/3\frac{1}{3} = .04$. $Q$ growth higher than $W = .04$ will generate $I/Q > .13\frac{1}{3}$, just as $Q$ growth less than .04 will generate $I/Q < .13\frac{1}{3}$.

The warranted rate is an odd concept. It does not tell you what will in fact happen, but only what would—if it came to happen by design or by luck—have certain self-warranting properties. Such a growth rate of output, $W$, if it could somehow be established and maintained, warrants a level of investment just big enough to match the voluntary saving that its own income growth entails.

**Cycles and instabilities**   Two observations should be made about cyclical instabilities involved in the warranted rate of growth.

1. Once all the unemployed are back at work, the natural rate of growth g must set a ceiling against which, alas, the faster warranted rate of growth must eventually collide. Thus W of 4 or 5 per cent per year and g of only 3 per cent per year ultimately means the Harrod warranted expansion will very soon hit full employment. As in Chapter 14 on business cycles, some writers[9] have constructed a theory of a collapse into recession based upon a bouncing back of the system from its collision with the natural-rate employment ceiling.

2. The warranted rate of growth, even if originally established, will not persist after being disturbed. In the Harrod model it is definitely unstable. To see this, note that if the actual growth rate temporarily *exceeds* $W = 4$ per cent, this new income will be generating in desired investment *more* than the $13\frac{1}{3}$ ($= 4\% \times 3\frac{1}{3}$) per cent ratio of desired saving—thereby accelerating its own growth *still faster* above W. (Show that a *less* than 4 per cent initial growth rate will similarly create a *deficiency* of intended investment relative to the $13\frac{1}{3}$ per cent intended saving, thereby *decelerating* its own growth still further below W.)

Just as an unmanned bicycle, which is unstable if disturbed from the vertical, can be converted into a stable system by a steadying and compensating human hand, so can a Harrod-Domar growth path that would be unstable under laissez faire be made stable by compensating monetary and fiscal policies in a mixed economy.

## NEOCLASSICAL DYNAMICS

The Ricardo-Marx-Solow model of smooth substitutability of labor for capital (i.e., of labor for a great variety of alternatively producible capital goods) has less need to work with Harrod-Domar concepts than those models which regard the capital-output ratio as a hard constant. However, it is useful to interpret

the Harrod-Domar concepts for a neoclassical model like Fig. 37-2.

By a simple "neoclassical growth model" is meant one in which the state uses monetary policies to make sure that thriftiness does not lead to unemployment and abortive thrift: by making equity and loan funds available at lower interest and profit rates (and possibly by unorthodox credit policies that provide guarantees against risks and uncertainties), such a managed system can contrive deepening of capital as described earlier.[10] Alternatively, this neoclassical model can be interpreted as picturing the technology of an efficiently run collectivist society that never faces macroeconomic problems of unemployment or of inflation due to lack of proper effective demand.

In such a society, where whatever is withheld from consumption goes into capital formation, *any* rate of growth is essentially a "warranted rate of growth." This is because there is (1) no dichotomy of saving-investment problem, and (2) no hard constant for the capital-output ratio.

Here is an idealized example. Add a new supply of L to a system that has a certain K and has previously been producing a certain Q. This new L can be put to work with the given K *as rapidly* as we like. There results a growth rate of Q that can be *as high* as the growth in L can produce. People can consume and invest out of the new output *as much or little* as they like. Depending on *whatever* amount of capital formation they decide on, there will result

---

[9] J. R. Hicks, *A Contribution to the Theory of the Trade Cycle* (Oxford University Press, Fair Lawn, N.J., 1950), gives a convenient summary of such nonlinear-cycle theories based on interacting accelerator-multiplier principles.

[10] This means that the variety of possible heterogeneous capital-goods processes is so great that any reduction of interest rate—even be it as little as from $i = .08$ to $i = .079$—will make it profitable to use some new pattern of known processes. For example, at .079 the machine tools may be made a little more durable. In consequence, the factor-price frontier of Fig. 37-2(b) will look fairly smooth to the naked eye, even though a microscope will show that it contains little line segments that meet in corners. When we introduce realistic uncertainties into the model, one is first tempted to think that minute changes in interest rate will have negligible effects. Actually, however, replacing certainty by probabilities smooths the small steps in a demand function into a continuous curve: a small change in $i$, long maintained, pushes some investment projects on the borderline of doubt into actual operation. See James E. Meade, *A Neoclassical Growth Model* (Oxford University Press, Fair Lawn, N.J., 1961), for alternative interpretations in terms of a flexible aggregate of capital.

a gradual accumulation of $K$ with the $K/L$ ratio able to move *in any way* without causing trouble.

All the above is in sharp contrast to a model with fixed capital-output ratio, which calls for a specific $W$ growth rate of $Q$. Contrast the Harrod case with the italicized words in the above paragraph!

**Three sources of growth**  Neoclassical output growth can be decomposed into three separate sources: growth in labor or $L$, growth in capital or $K$, and technical innovation itself. Momentarily ignoring technical change, note that a 1 per cent per year growth rate in $L$ together with a 1 per cent per year growth rate in $K$ is assumed to cause output to grow also at a 1 per cent per year rate. (Resist the temptation to add 1 per cent to 1 per cent and come out with 2 per cent; $L$ and $K$ cooperate in production, each needing the other.)

Suppose $L$ grows at 1 per cent per year and $K$ at 5 per cent. It is tempting, but wrong, to guess that $Q$ will then grow at 3 per cent, the simple average of 1 and 5. Why wrong? Because the two factors do not contribute equal shares to product: about three-fourths of all product goes to labor as wages and only one-fourth of $Q$ to property as its interest-profit share. This means $L$'s growth rate gets 3 times the weight of $K$'s; so, the correct answer is that $Q$ will grow at 2 per cent per year (= $\frac{3}{4}$ of 1% + $\frac{1}{4}$ of 5%).

Hence, output growth per year follows the law

$$\% \ Q \text{ growth} = \tfrac{3}{4}(\% \ L \text{ growth})$$
$$+ \tfrac{1}{4}(\% \ K \text{ growth})$$
$$+ \text{ T.C.}$$

where T.C. means technical changes that raise productivity by shifting the *dd* curve of Fig. 37-2; and where $\frac{3}{4}$ and $\frac{1}{4}$ would of course later be replaced by new fractions if the relative shares of the factors had later changed.

If we seek to explain *per capita* growth, matters are simpler still, since this enables us to get rid of $L$ as a separate growth source. Now, using the fact that capital gets one-fourth share of output, we have

$$\% \ \frac{Q}{L} \text{ growth} = \tfrac{1}{4}\left(\% \ \frac{K}{L} \text{ growth}\right) + \text{t.c.}$$

This relation shows clearly how deepening of capital would raise the capital-output ratio if there were no technical improvements being made: output per capita grows only one-fourth as fast as capital per capita, reflecting one aspect of diminishing returns.

This relation now explains the meaning of Solow's

conclusion—that more than half of the increased output recorded in historical statistics seems to be a residual attributable to scientific advance rather than to thrift and capital formation. This means that the second term in the above relation—t.c. for per capita technical change—appears, on statistical measurement, to have been definitely bigger than the first term representing the investment contribution. When Solow tries to allow for the fact that new techniques get embodied in new capital goods, the relative importance of the first term rises; but apparently it still remains below 50 per cent. (Although the primacy of technical change seems corroborated by German or Japanese statistics, the importance of the capital factor does seem greater in Britain, Canada, and Russia.)

## ALTERNATIVE THEORIES

**Repudiation of aggregate production functions**  Professors Joan Robinson and Nicholas Kaldor of Cambridge University are skeptical that "capital" can be usefully measured as an aggregate, which together with labor produces aggregate output. This is certainly a healthy skepticism. They are more skeptical that the marginal productivities calculated from such an alleged production function can be used to explain wage and profit rates and the relative shares in GNP of labor and property. They go further and doubt that economists can work with a detailed breakdown of numerous heterogeneous capital goods—machines of type A, B, C, . . .—to get quantitative results at all like the neoclassical case, in an actual realistic mixed economy of uncertainty and uneven growth.[11]

---

[11] Their works, cited earlier, can be contrasted by the advanced student in economics with the general neo-neoclassical viewpoint exposited in an advanced work like R. Dorfman, P. A. Samuelson, and R. M. Solow, *Linear Programming and Economic Analysis* (McGraw-Hill, New York, 1958). The latter makes the same supposition as was done here—that there are a great variety of alternative machines and processes known (or knowable) at any one time. If the interest rate changes even a little, say from .08 to .079 (as mentioned earlier), it will usually (but not inevitably!) pay to turn to a new blueprint that involves a slightly more durable machine. Hence, as already stated in footnote 10, the *ff* curve of Fig. 37-2(b) will look almost smooth to the naked eye, even though a microscope reveals it to consist of many short line segments that meet in corners. The simplified $K$ fable thus may give useful insight into a more realistic model, be it the U.S.S.R., the U.S.A., India, or China.

**Dissenting voices** Robinson and Kaldor by no means agree on what is to replace the aggregative analysis. Both incline, but in different degree, toward a macro-economic theory of income distribution with the following property:

Here is an economy with high property share and high growth. How wrong to think it is the thrift of the rich (or anybody else) which *causes* that fast growth. The causation runs the other way: fast growth produces high profits, rather than vice versa.[12]

This presumably wishes to assert something more than the familiar observation that when a country like Japan or West Germany experiences a miracle of productivity growth, people find it easiest to be thrifty out of the increase in income and to be slow in renegotiating real wage rates commensurate with the recent rises in marginal productivities. It is beyond controversy that such induced thrift does further speed up capital formation and tends (in neo-classical fashion) to speed up growth still further, but that is another story.[13] (Chapter 42 will explore further some ideological consequences of these doctrinal controversies.)

**Life-cycle saving and the wealth-income ratio** Professor Franco Modigliani, of MIT, has put forward an alternative theory that is quite at variance with those just above. Modigliani does not consider the constancy of the capital-output ratio a mere coincidence. He tries to explain it, not in terms of technological production nor induced innovation as in page 743's footnote 20, but in terms of people's psychological decisions about wealth, consuming, saving, and dis-saving. He puts the greatest stress on lifetime patterns of saving for old-age retirement.

Here is an example. An adult works for about 40 years and lives in retirement for 20. To keep his consumption standards somewhat equal all his life, he consumes less than his income during the working years; he gradually builds up his wealth to a maximum just before retirement; then he gradually uses up capital and pension rights by his retirement consumption; at death he leaves little wealth. [What keeps the saving rate from cancelling out to zero as the old dissave what the young save? In the life-cycle model, the positive natural rate of growth (a) of population, and (b) of per capita real income as a result of technical improvements in productivity.]

When population is growing at an even percentage rate, the age distribution remains constant over time. This steady increase in population, combined with confidently expected rising real income, causes the average level of wealth of the people of all ages to remain constant in ratio to total income. Except for the public-debt and land part of wealth, Modigliani has supplied a reason for $K/Q$ to be constant!

A test of Modigliani's theory, as against that of someone like Kaldor, who thinks that businessmen will somehow be led to make innovation and investment decisions in order to keep the $K/Q$ ratio from changing much, would be to perform the hypothetical experiment of juggling the public debt up or down and seeing whether the $K/Q$ ratio finally does change enough to keep the wealth-income ratio fairly constant. This experiment is not to be recommended, but it does remind us of Chapter 19's assertion that a public debt can make the present generation want to do more consuming and less saving for its old age.

## COMPENSATING FISCAL POLICY

Suppose it were true that monetary policy—because of balance-of-payments constraints, Hansen-like capital-output fixity, or other impotency—could make no effective change in private investment spending $I$. Then compensating fiscal policy would still lead to

---

[12] In long-run balanced growth, Robinson and Kaldor identify $i$ as $g/s_p$, where saving out of wages is negligible and $s_p$ is the average propensity of *property income* to be saved. This comes from matching the bracketed terms in the following identities: $I = (I/K)K = \{g\}K = I = S = \{s_p i\}K$. With the interest or profit rate known, if you believe in a constant capital-output ratio, $K/Q$, you can calculate property share in income as $i(K/Q)$. In effect, they say, "The share of property must somehow get spontaneously determined at just high enough a level to make the warranted rate $W$ come into equality with the given natural rate $g$." But they do not supply convincing reasons why it would do so.

[13] Kaldor also has a short-run theory of distribution: when $I$ drops exogenously in the short run, Kaldor denies that this produces multiplier drops in $Q$ and employment (as in Chapters 12 and 13); instead this depresses business demands, causing business to cut prices (relative to wages) until total profit, $iK$, has dropped enough to equate $s_p(iK)$ with lowered $I$. Mrs. Robinson disagrees with this new version of Say's Law and inevitable full employment, and most statistical analyses of profits in the mixed economy do too. (For more on Kaldor's 1955–1962 theories, cf. the 6th edition, 1964, of this book.)

results quite different from those given by laissez faire models of the simple Harrod-Kaldor type.

Whenever full-employment $s$ was out of line with $I/Q$, the government would run a budgetary surplus or deficit just big enough to alter the effective $s$ for society until it equaled $I/Q$. The effective "warranted rate of growth" could thereby be kept equal to any prescribed natural rate of full-employment growth.

Thus, in a year like 1972 when $I/Q$ tended to exceed full-employment $s$, the rational thing for the government to do was to create a large budgetary surplus: to raise tax rates and lower people's disposable incomes and personal saving, to cut down on government use of resources and on transfers, or to do both. This surplus is, in effect, government saving: call it $s_G$ and combine it with the private saving ratio $s_{pr}$ to get $s$ = average ($s_G$, $s_{pr}$) as big as is needed to equal $I/Q$ without demand-pull inflation.

During the sluggish years of the middle 1970s, the opposite fiscal policies would be designed to compensate: With $I/Q < s_{pr}$, a budget deficit creates government dissaving (or negative saving); then at full employment, $I/Q = s$, the average of $s_{pr}$ and the government *dis*saving ratio.

In summary, laissez faire Harrodian discrepancies can lose much of their terror and relevance in a properly managed mixed economy.

## THE EXPANDING UNIVERSE: A DIGRESSION

The late John von Neumann, a brilliant mathematician who helped build the hydrogen bomb and who founded the theory of games, described an economic model in which everything could be produced out of everything. If land and/or labor are no longer scarce limiting factors, then the law of diminishing returns no longer applies. All the fruits of production, above and beyond the costs of subsistence for horses, rabbits, looms, and comfortably living men, are plowed back into the system for growth of more horses, rabbits, looms, men.

In this system, which is like Smith's golden age except that it definitely involves capital goods, there is a maximal rate of balanced growth. And it turns out that such a growth rate—call it $g$ because of its resemblance to the Harrod natural rate of growth—is exactly equal to the interest rate $i$.

Because development theory, for countries like India and the United States, is preoccupied with the

concept of "balanced growth," the Neumann model is of considerable interest. It is particularly relevant to the case where an industrial sector in a poor country finds it can get an unlimited supply of laborers from the rural sector at the same wage cost in terms of subsistence; needing little land, the industrial sector can "take off" and grow at a constant Neumann-percentage rate per year, provided it can produce the capital goods needed to match the new labor or can be helped by imports from foreign lenders, aiders, or exporters.

If there is technical change, the system can advance at a rate even faster than the Neumann rate; indeed, if the system can, so to speak, manufacture new inventions that make labor grow in efficiency at a steady percentage rate, it will then appear to an observer to be capable of even faster Neumann growth.

A simple example of an expanding system would be the case of rabbits (or men) who produce 1.05 rabbits of output for each rabbit of input. The interest rate and the growth rate will obviously then be 5 per cent per period. Other examples are not so simple.

## LEONTIEF'S INTERINDUSTRY INPUT-OUTPUT

The important interindustry tableau of Wassily Leontief is a modern-day realization of the eighteenth-century dream of the physiocratic economist, Francois Quesnay, who first envisaged the *Tableau Économique,* or circular flow of economic life. A score of nations—such as France, Norway, Egypt, the United States, the United Kingdom, the Soviet Union, and India—have computed input-output tables as an amplification of their national-income data and as a possible aid in development planning.[14]

[14] For additional discussion of theory and applications see Wassily Leontief, *The Structure of the American Economy, 1919–1929* (Harvard University Press, Cambridge, Mass., 1941; 2d ed.: *1919–1939,* Oxford University Press, Fair Lawn, N.J., 1951): or Wassily Leontief, *Input-Output Economics* (Oxford University Press, Fair Lawn, N.J., 1966). As part of the price that Leontief has to pay to make Walras's general equilibrium empirically measurable, he is forced to make the technical assumption that all factor proportions—to each other and to total output—are technologically *fixed* or constant. (Back in Chapter 27's Appendix, page 555, we found reason to doubt that such an engineering assumption can be strictly realistic; but Leontief's clever statistical use of the fixed-coefficient case deserves notice here.)

**TABLE 37-2**

**The input-output tableau of Leontief X-rays the economy's structure**

Each industry appears twice, in a row and column: its row lists allocation of its total gross output as inputs for other industries and for final consumption; also, its column shows inputs needed to produce it.

The orange numbers show *gross* outputs, inclusive of amounts needed as intermediate inputs. To compute NNP without double counting, we add only the factor payments (or the "value added") of the green-shaded row; or alternatively, only the final-consumption flows of the shaded column. (Fill in the proper NNP in the indicated blank, and check it two ways.)

### COLD-WAR INTERINDUSTRY FLOWS

| | AGRICULTURE | MANUFACTURING | HOUSEHOLD FINAL CONSUMPTIONS | GROSS TOTALS |
|---|---|---|---|---|
| **AGRICULTURE** | | 800 | 400 | 1,200 |
| **MANUFACTURING** | 400 | | 1,200 | 1,600 |
| **HOUSEHOLD LABOR AND OTHER FACTORS** | 800 | 800 | —— | |
| **GROSS TOTALS** All numbers in billions. | 1,200 | 1,600 | | 2,800 |

Using agriculture and manufacturing as sample industries, Table 37-2 gives an oversimplified illustration of the table comprising several hundred industries that the government and Leontief have prepared for the American economy. Here is its general idea. Each industry is listed twice: in a *row* as an *output*; in a *column* as a needed *input*. In addition, the final consumption of households is treated as an extra column and their *labor* (or other primary factors of production supplied by households) as an extra row. These household figures are the numbers that enter into national income or net national product and are on the shaded part of the table. (Actually, Leontief also includes government, foreign trade, investment, and other details.)

The *gross* value of agricultural output is shown by the orange $1,200 (billion) twice: at its row's right as the sum of all the places where farm output went— $800 as input to manufacturing plus $400 directly consumed by households as food—and at its column's bottom as the sum of the $400 cost it paid for manufacturing inputs (chemical fertilizers, etc.) and the $800 cost it paid for labor input (and other household factors).

Give a similar interpretation of the orange $1,600 gross total for manufacturing.

The table also shows our old friend national income, or NNP (which will also be GNP if our example is simple enough to ignore depreciation). With no gov-

ernment or investment in the picture, NNP equals the sum of the third column's green final products; or alternatively NNP equals the sum of all factor-cost or values added shown in the third row's green wages. (NNP definitely does not include the *intermediate* purchases of one sector from another; the gross orange total of $2,800 definitely involves double counting. VERIFY: NNP = $1,600.)

This input-output table is more than a record of past history. How does Leontief or a planner hope to use it? *He hopes to use it to forecast the effects of changing consumption requirements.*

Thus, suppose Table 37-2 refers to a current cold-war situation where manufacturing employment and output have been swollen by military needs. (For dramatic effect we may think of peacetime goods, or "butter," as coming largely from the agricultural sector, and military goods, or "guns," as coming largely from the manufacturing sector.)

Now suppose "peace breaks out." What will have to be planned for the new deployment of labor and other inputs if full employment is still to be maintained? Suppose we now want to double agriculture's final consumption, from the old green $400 to new $800, exactly compensating by cutting the military manufacturing sector back from $1,200 to $800. Assuming fixed input-output coefficients, Leontief can solve linear equations for the new peacetime state

| PEACETIME INPUT-OUTPUT FLOWS | | | HOUSEHOLD FINAL CONSUMPTIONS | GROSS TOTALS |
|---|---|---|---|---|
| | AGRICULTURE | MANUFACTURING | | |
| AGRICULTURE | | 640 | 800 | 1,440 |
| MANUFACTURING | 480 | | 800 | 1,280 |
| HOUSEHOLD LABOR AND OTHER FACTORS | 960 | 640 | 1,600 | |
| GROSS TOTALS | 1,440 | 1,280 | | 2,720 |
| All numbers in billions. | | | | |

**TABLE 37-3**
**Input-output tableau helps nations plan**
End of cold war causes shift from guns to butter: agricultural final consumption goes up by $400 billion; manufacturing final consumption goes down same amount. Using fixed input-output coefficients from Table 37-2, Leontief calculates needed change in gross outputs shown here; and also resulting needed labor shifts, and intermediate input changes. Same techniques help in development planning.

and show that it must then be in the configuration given in Table 37-3.[15] Ten per cent of the workers, calculation shows, must be shifted from war work to

[15]All details aside, his key assumption is that $^{400}/_{1200} = ^{1}/_{3}$ of agriculture receipts will always be spent on manufacturing input, with the remaining $^{800}/_{1200} = ^{2}/_{3}$ always spent on labor input. Similarly, $^{800}/_{1600} = ^{1}/_{2}$ is the fraction that manufacturing will always spend on its needed agricultural input, the remainder $^{1}/_{2}$ being spent on needed labor input.

Table 37-2 is repeated here in abbreviated form to show how one derives the green fixed input-output coefficients

$$
\begin{array}{cc}
0 & 800 \\
400 & 0 \\
\hline
800 & 800 \\
1,200 & 1,600
\end{array}
\rightarrow
\begin{array}{cc}
0 & ^{1}/_{2} \\
^{1}/_{3} & 0 \\
\hline
^{2}/_{3} & ^{1}/_{2} \\
1 & 1
\end{array}
$$

needed for the transition to Table 37-3 or to any other situation envisaged by the planner. Now, if we call gross outputs of the two sectors $X_A$ and $X_M$ and their final-consumption amounts $C_A$ and $C_M$, Leontief must finally allocate the total Xs thus:

$$X_A = C_A + ^{1}/_{2} X_M \qquad X_M = C_M + ^{1}/_{3} X_A$$

For the peacetime tableau of Table 37-3, this means

$$X_A = 800 + ^{1}/_{2} X_M \qquad X_M = 800 + ^{1}/_{3} X_A$$

These can be solved simultaneously by simple algebra to give $X_A = 1,440$, $X_M = 1,280$, from which all of Table 37-3 can be filled in using the green fractions. Thus, we get the industries' labor requirements:

$$L_A = ^{2}/_{3} X_A = 960 \qquad L_M = ^{1}/_{2} X_M = 640$$

peace work. Similarly, Leontief's tableau scheme of input-output can help plan for any developmental change in final-consumption goods.

REMARK: To avoid simultaneous equations, Leontief can use a "multiplier" method. Each manufacture requires $^{1}/_{2}$ of agriculture as input, and each of these in turn requires $^{1}/_{3}$ of manufacture as its input; so indirectly each manufacture requires $^{1}/_{2} \times ^{1}/_{3} = ^{1}/_{6}$ of extra manufactures to produce itself. So $[1 + ^{1}/_{6} + (^{1}/_{6})^2 + \cdots]$ adds up to **1.2**, which is the needed expansion of new gross manufacture for each 1.0 expansion of consumption manufacture. Similarly, Leontief can calculate a multiplier for agriculture, showing how each billion-dollar change in its final consumption requires its own gross output to go up (coincidentally!) by **1.2** billion dollars. To compute what the shift of 400 billion dollars from guns to butter entails, Leontief must know how much gross agriculture and how much labor is needed to accommodate the 1.2 of manufacture that its own consumption expansion generated. The answer is not hard: The second column's green manufacturing input requirements give the answers—$^{1}/_{2}$ of 1.2, or **.6** in both cases. The reader should now be able to verify that when 1 new agriculture consumption entails 1.2 of its own gross output, the amounts needed for manufacturing and labor are $^{1}/_{3}(1.2) = $ **.4** and $^{2}/_{3}(1.2) = $ **.8**. Given the knowledge of this paragraph's green "own multipliers" and "cross multipliers"—the so-called "inverse matrix"—we perceive how Leontief is able to apply them to the **+400** consumption shift to agriculture and **−400** shift from manufacturing to get the changes needed to convert war Table 37-2 to peace Table 37-3. (Those who have been trained in algebra may wish to supplement this terse account by the final extra-credit problem.)

## SUMMARY TO APPENDIX

1  Schumpeter's stress on innovation, followed by competitive erosion of profit, is an important process of economic development.

2  If the capital-output ratio $(K/Q)$ is an inflexible constant, neoclassical deepening of capital cannot be engineered by expansionist monetary policy.

3  The Harrod-Domar concept of the "natural rate of growth" $g$ is determined by population growth and technical change. If $K$ and $Q$ are to grow at this balanced rate, the required fraction of income that has to be voluntarily saved is given by the Harrod condition, $s = g(K/Q)$. [The warranted rate of growth $W$ will be higher than the natural rate $g$ if the actual desired saving ratio $S/Q$ exceeds the $s$ needed by Harrod's condition. In the resulting balanced growth, we must have $W = s_a/(K/Q)$. Such a warranted rate would not be stably restored if departed from. And when $W > g$, a GNP expansion would ultimately run into a ceiling set by $g$. Fortunately, fiscal deficits or surpluses could be used to remove any discrepancy between $W$ and $g$.]

4  Where a neoclassical deepening of capital makes the $K/Q$ ratio an accommodating variable, the Harrod conditions lose their terrors. Whatever people's thrift dictates for their private full-employment $s$, a combination of monetary and fiscal policies can hope to induce the needed matching investment. Such fiscal and monetary policies can speed up capital formation and the technical changes embodied in, and stemming from, such new equipment. They can help the system grow faster than the natural growth of working population. They can stabilize the achievable rate of progress so that the system will be warranted in doing what comes naturally. But, even in a flexible neoclassical technology, laissez faire will not—in the absence of appropriate public monetary and fiscal policies—be led by an Invisible Hand to these ideal conditions.

5  The neoclassical model can parcel out the sources of $Q$ growth into growth from more $L$, from more $K$, and from technical change. The last residual factor interacts with $L$ through education and training and with $K$ through embodiment in new machines. Still, technical change seems to have been historically primary in advanced nations.

6  Robinson and Kaldor agree in their suspicion of aggregates of so-called "capital" and in their doubts about smooth deepening of capital under capitalism; both look to factors of dynamic growth for determination of profit shares. (Chapter 42 returns to this.)

7  It is intellectually unsatisfying to explain some constancy trends by appeal to "coincidence" or to fortuitous canceling out of diverse tendencies of diminishing returns and technical change. So one can applaud the attempts to find mechanisms (induced invention, lifetime saving, etc.) that bring the constancies about. However, if, like the present writer, you would not be much surprised to see $K/Q$ fall in the future or drift in either direction, the wage share gradually rise, or the rate of profit sag or soar, you must beware of "overexplanations." If a thing may actually be a coincidence, you are not saying much by calling it that. But to *explain away* a coincidence which truly *is only* a coincidence, is worse than a banality; it is a scientific sin.

8  Leontief's tableau of interindustry flows gives a useful picture of the relations lying behind aggregate NNP data. By positing fixed input-output coefficients, a planner can use the Leontief technique to program a shift from a war pattern of consumption to a peace pattern, or to achieve any other developmental target goal.

## CONCEPTS FOR REVIEW

innovation and deepening of capital
fixed versus variable $K/Q$ ratio
natural versus warranted growth
$s = g(K/Q)$, $W = s_a/(K/Q)$
neoclassical case vs. fixed $K/Q$

life-cycle saving
% $Q$ growth = % $L$ growth + $\cdots$
% $Q/L$ growth = % $K/L$ growth + t.c.
von Neumann model with $i = g$
input-output tableau

## QUESTIONS FOR DISCUSSION

1 Contrast unemployment notions of Keynes with those of Schumpeter and Ricardo.

2 Why is $g$ important for long trends? $W$ for business cycles? Reread Chapter 14's acceleration principle.

3 Explain to yourself the basic idea of the two-way Leontief tableau.

4 *Extra-credit problem* (*very challenging*): If you know matrix notation, you might be able to figure out the following summary of the Leontief input-output system, where $C$ is the column vector of final consumptions, $X$ the column vector of gross outputs, $a_{ij}$ the coefficients of production, $(L_j)$ the row vector of labor by industry, and $P$ the row vector of prices.

$$\begin{bmatrix} 0 & 800 & \vdots & \mathbf{400} \\ 400 & 0 & \vdots & \mathbf{1,200} \\ \cdots & \cdots & & \cdots \\ \mathbf{800} & \mathbf{800} & \vdots & 0 \\ \mathbf{1,200} & \mathbf{1,600} & \vdots & \mathbf{1,600} \end{bmatrix} = \begin{bmatrix} X_{11} & X_{12} & \vdots & \mathbf{C_1} \\ X_{21} & X_{22} & \vdots & \mathbf{C_2} \\ \cdots & \cdots & & \cdots \\ L_1 & L_2 & \vdots & 0 \\ X_1 & X_2 & \vdots & \sum_i C_i \end{bmatrix} ; \begin{bmatrix} a_{11} & a_{12} \\ a_{21} & a_{22} \\ a_{01} & a_{02} \end{bmatrix} = \begin{bmatrix} 0 & \frac{1}{2} \\ \frac{1}{3} & 0 \\ \frac{2}{3} & \frac{1}{2} \end{bmatrix} = \begin{bmatrix} X_{11}/X_1 & X_{12}/X_2 \\ X_{21}/X_1 & X_{22}/X_2 \\ L_1/X_1 & L_2/X_2 \end{bmatrix}$$

In matrix notation $\begin{bmatrix} a \\ \cdots \\ a_0 \end{bmatrix} = \begin{bmatrix} a_{ij} \\ \cdots \\ a_{0j} \end{bmatrix} = \begin{bmatrix} X_{ij}/X_j \\ \cdots \\ L_j/X_j \end{bmatrix}$, and the allocation of outputs satisfies

$$X = \begin{bmatrix} X_i \end{bmatrix} = \begin{bmatrix} \sum_j X_{ij} + C_i \end{bmatrix} = \begin{bmatrix} \sum_j a_{ij}X_j + C_i \end{bmatrix} = aX + C \quad ; \quad [I - a]X = C$$

$$X = [I - a]^{-1}C = \mathbf{A}C = \begin{bmatrix} 1.2 & .6 \\ .4 & 1.2 \end{bmatrix} \begin{bmatrix} C_1 \\ C_2 \end{bmatrix}$$

$$L = \sum_j L_j = \sum_j a_{0j}X_j = a_0X = a_0[I - a]^{-1}C = \mathbf{a_0 A}C = \mathbf{A_0}C = \sum_j \mathbf{A}_{0j}C_j$$

Because $X_{ij} \geq 0$ and $C_i > 0$, $I - a$ will be a nonsingular matrix and its inverse $[I - a]^{-1} = \mathbf{A}$ will have no negative elements (actually, they'll all be positive if each $C_i$ takes some of every $X_j$ and $L_j$ for its production, as will be the elements of the row vector $\mathbf{A_0}$ representing total labor requirements direct and indirect). If labor's wage is 1, and competitive prices are given by unit cost of production, the sum of wage plus material-input costs—then $P = 1 \cdot a_0 + Pa = a_0[I - a]^{-1} = \mathbf{A_0}$, the row vector of total labor requirements (direct labor plus indirect). In this case where output flows are measured in dollars, one can check the correctness of the operations by verifying that $\mathbf{A_0} = [1,1]$. If there is a positive interest or profit rate, $r$, we'd instead have $\mathbf{A_0} = a_0(1 + r)[I - a(1 + r)]^{-1}$

All the economic principles we have learned can now be brought to bear on perhaps one of the most challenging problems of the next quarter-century—the problem of underdeveloped economies.[1] There are almost 4 billion people in the world, and at this moment half of them are hungry—if not literally so, certainly malnourished. Only someone who has been pursuing beauty or health on a temporary diet of less than 1,500 calories per day will know how food can fill one's dreams and pervade every waking thought.

For conscience's sake, we are impelled to help. Besides, history teaches us that men do not always starve quietly.

## DEFINING UNDERDEVELOPMENT

Writers used to speak of "backward" nations, which naturally irritated the people of those lands. To avoid offense the United Nations sometimes uses the roundabout expression "developing" nations. Today most people adopt the expression "less developed" countries (LDCs). What is meant by the term? Alternative definitions are given. Most seem to involve the following:

A less developed country is simply one with real per capita income that is low relative to the present-day per capita incomes of such nations as Canada, the United States, Great Britain, and Western Europe generally. Optimistically, a less developed country is one regarded as being capable of substantial improvement in its income level.

Of course, every country is undeveloped in the sense that it is not yet perfect and hence is capable of being improved still further. Even

[1] Three useful anthologies on this subject are Theodore Morgan, George W. Betz, and N. K. Choudhry, *Readings in Economic Development* (Wadsworth Publishing Company, Belmont, Calif., 1963); A. N. Agarwala and S. P. Singh, *The Economics of Underdevelopment* (Oxford University Press, Fair Lawn, N.J., 1960); Bernard Okun and Richard W. Richardson, *Studies in Economic Development* (Holt, New York, 1961). Paul Baran, *The Political Economy of Growth* (Monthly Review Press, New York, 1957) stresses the role of colonial exploitation in the process.

## 38

# PROBLEMS OF ECONOMIC GROWTH AND DEVELOPMENT

I believe in materialism. I believe in all the proceeds of a healthy materialism, —good cooking, dry houses, dry feet, sewers, drain pipes, hot water, baths, electric lights, automobiles, good roads, bright streets, long vacations away from the village pump, new ideas, fast horses, swift conversation, theatres, operas, orchestras, bands,—I believe in them all for everybody. The man who dies without knowing these things may be as exquisite as a saint, and as rich as a poet; but it is in spite of, not because of, his deprivation.
FRANCIS HACKETT
*Ireland*

I almost envy China that she is still in the pre-automobile stage of walking, cycling, and breathing fresh air.
DR. PAUL DUDLEY WHITE

the so-called "advanced" countries were once less developed by most definitions and had to go through the process of development. Table 38-1 gives a picture of the relative stages of development of different countries.

About one-fifth of the world's population live in the highly developed group A with more than $3,500 per capita (in 1976 U.S. dollars); just over one-eighth live in the intermediate group B; about two-thirds live in the less developed group C.

About one-third of the world's population live in communist societies. The Soviet Union, Czechoslovakia, and East Germany now fall in the highly developed group A; but just barely. As for the rest of the communist countries, how are their people divided among the groups? Recalling the vast population of China, we are not surprised to find two-thirds of the communist population falling in the lowest group C. Little wonder, then, that economic development is a lively subject everywhere, in the East as well as in the West.

## CHARACTERISTICS OF UNDERDEVELOPED ECONOMIES

To bring out the contrasts between advanced and underdeveloped economies, imagine that you are a typical twenty-one-year-old in one of the underdeveloped countries, be it Haiti, India, Nigeria, Kenya, or Bangladesh.

You are poor: even after making generous allowance for the goods that you produce and consume, your annual income averages barely $300 per head, as against $7,000 per head of your fellow man in North America; perhaps you can find cold comfort in the thought that only 1 in 8 of the human race averages more than $2,000 per year. To each of your people who can read, there are three like you who are illiterate. Your life expectancy is little more than two-thirds that of the average man in the advanced country: already one or two of your brothers and sisters have died before reaching adulthood; and though your mother has had fewer children than her mother did, more of your brothers and sisters have lived to maturity, thanks to imported medical techniques—and you must compete with them for subsistence.

Most of your countrymen work on rural farms; few can be spared from food production for factories or service trades. You work with but one-sixtieth the horsepower of your prosperous North American fellow man. You know little of science, but much of folklore. Your methods and tools are primitive. Neither the discipline of markets nor the deliberations of planning commissions mean much to you. As a citizen in the poorer parts of Asia, Africa, or Latin America, you and your fellows together constitute 60 per cent of the world population, but you must divide among you only 12 per cent of world income. You brood over the fact that the United States, with 6 per cent of the people, enjoys over 25 per cent of world income; and that the other advanced noncommunist countries, with only 12 per cent of the world's population, consume 31 per cent of world income.

## URGENCY OF THE PROBLEM

There have always been differences between rich and poor. Why worry especially about the underdeveloped countries? Here are some reasons.

## COUNTRIES GROUPED BY LEVEL OF ECONOMIC DEVELOPMENT

**A. Highly developed**

Australia
Belgium
Canada
Czechoslovakia
Denmark
Finland
France
Germany (Democratic Republic)
Germany (Federal Republic)
Iceland
Israel
Italy
Japan
Kuwait
Luxembourg
Netherlands
New Zealand
Norway
Puerto Rico
Sweden
Switzerland
U.S.S.R.
United Kingdom
United States

**B. Intermediate**

Argentina
Austria
Bulgaria
Chile
Costa Rica
Cuba
Cyprus
Greece
Hong Kong
Hungary
Ireland
Jamaica
Lebanon
Libya
Malta
Mexico
Panama
Poland

Portugal
Romania
Saudi Arabia
Singapore
South Africa
Spain
Uruguay
Venezuela
Yugoslavia

**C. Less developed**

Africa:
Algeria
Angola
Cameroon
Chad
Congo
Dahomey
Ethiopia
Ghana
Guinea
Ivory Coast
Kenya
Liberia
Madagascar
Malawi
Mali
Mauritius
Morocco
Mozambique
Niger
Nigeria
Rwanda
Senegal
Sierra Leone
Somalia
Southern Rhodesia
Sudan
Tanzania
Togo
Tunisia
Uganda
United Arab Republic (Egypt)
Upper Volta
Zaire
Zambia

Americas:
Bolivia
Brazil
British West Indies
Colombia
Dominican Republic
Ecuador
El Salvador
Guatemala
Guyana
Haiti
Honduras
Nicaragua
Paraguay
Peru

Asia:
Afghanistan
Burma
Cambodia
China
Fiji
India
Indonesia
Iran
Iraq
Jordan
Korea (North)
Korea (South)
Jordan
Laos
Malaysia
Nepal
Pakistan
Philippines
Sri Lanka
Syria
Taiwan
Thailand
Turkey
Vietnam (North)
Vietnam (South)
Yemen

Europe:
Albania

**TABLE 38-1**

Most countries fall in the less developed category

(Sources: United Nations; Center for International Studies, MIT; updated to 1976 by author.)

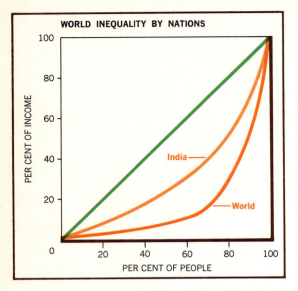

**WORLD INEQUALITY BY NATIONS**

PER CENT OF INCOME / PER CENT OF PEOPLE

India

World

**FIG. 38-1**
**Differentials of nations' living standards are great**
The poorest half of the nations receive only 8 per cent of the total world income. The tenth of the world who live in advanced communist countries enjoy about 18 per cent of the total; but the 25 per cent of the world who live in communist less developed countries receive only 5 per cent of world income, averaging only two-thirds the low per capita incomes of the other LDCs.

Contrast the inequality shown here with the Lorenz curve for India, and with that of Lorenz charts of Chapter 5 depicting inequality inside Sweden, the United States, or Sri Lanka. (Sources: World Bank; U.S. Department of State.)

**Widening differentials**   In contrast to the narrowing of income differentials within the advanced nations, the divergence between advanced and less developed countries is possibly now widening rather than narrowing. The United States and Western Europe have doubled their production per head since 1950. Many experts believe that living standards in India, Indonesia, and certain underdeveloped countries have not improved nearly that much since then and may even have deteriorated in some regions.

Figure 38-1 shows how unequal is the geographical distribution of real incomes. Contrast this Lorenz curve of inequality among nations with Figs. 5-2, 5-3, 5-4, and 9-1, which show less glaring inequality within a country, whether LDC or advanced.

Much of any widening gap between the richest and the less developed countries is due to the rapid real growth rates of the former; for, it is not the case that poor countries have generally been growing less rapidly than in their past, or for that matter, less rapidly than countries now rich did when they first began to develop. Figure 38-2 puts the trends of divergence into quantitative perspective.

**Ideological struggle**   In the modern ideological war between the free and the communist worlds, both sides regard the underdeveloped regions as being torn between following the pattern of the mixed economy or following the pattern of socialism. Revolutionaries naturally agitate in the "Third World," never failing to point out the poverty there, never failing to contrast it with our wealth, never failing to remind the people there of real and fancied evils of "colonialism." Cuba is a nearby example. Africa, Latin America, and Asia are cases in point.

Experience does not bear out the easy generalization, "Fill the stomachs of people, and they will refrain from going communist." Men in utter misery often seem incapable of revolting; and the great revolutions of the past (such as the French and Russian) have often taken place *at a time when some economic progress had already been achieved.*

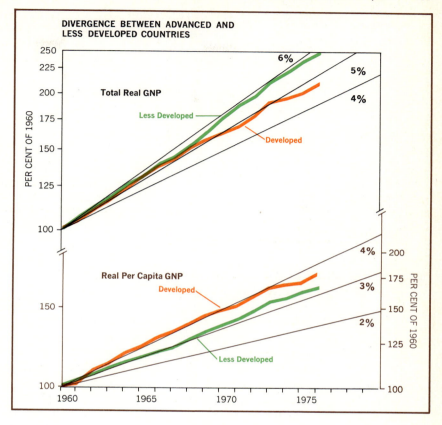

**FIG. 38-2**

Rich and poor economies both grow, but gap between them remains

Much of the growth of the LDCs, as shown in the upper panel with black left-hand ratio scale, is frittered away in burgeoning population growth. As a result, per capita income of LDCs (who need it most) cannot quite keep up with growth of post-Keynesian mixed economies. The picture is less sanguine for individual LDCs that have experienced chronically bad harvests, as in the case of Bangladesh and various sub-Saharan countries. (Source: Agency for International Development data on noncommunist economies, updated.)

Nonetheless, to turn our backs on the problem of development is to court future disaster. Harvard's distinguished economic historian Alexander Gerschenkron has drawn the following important lesson from history.[2]

The Soviet government can be properly described as a product of the country's economic backwardness. Had serfdom been abolished by Catherine the Great or . . . in 1825, the peasant discontent, the driving force and the earnest of success of the Russian Revolution, would never have assumed disastrous proportions, while the economic development of the country would have proceeded in a much more gradual fashion. . . . The delayed industrial revolution was responsible for a political revolution in the course of which the power fell in the hands of a dictatorial government to which in the long run the vast majority of the population was opposed. . . . The paramount lesson of the twentieth century is that the problems of backward nations are not exclusively their own. They are just as much problems of the advanced countries. It is not only Russia but the whole world that pays the price for the failure to emancipate the Russian peasants and to embark upon industrialization policies at an early time. Advanced countries cannot afford to ignore economic backwardness.

To reinforce this, tick off the advanced countries in Table 38-1. You cannot find a single democracy that had a successful revolution when its economy was strong.

[2]Alexander Gerschenkron, *Economic Backwardness in Historical Perspective*, (The Belknap Press, Harvard University Press, Cambridge, Mass., 1962), pp. 28–30.

**Great expectations and "demonstration effects"**   Within the underdeveloped countries, people are today acutely aware of their poverty and its contrasts with rich lands. They do not like it. What is more, they insist on doing something about it.

This was not always so: a century ago the Emperor of China sent a message to the Queen of England saying that his country neither needed nor desired economic improvement. Look at today's determined efforts in China and mark the contrast. In the ancient formula,

$$\text{Happiness} = \frac{\text{material consumption}}{\text{desire}}$$

it is easy for affluent Western observers to advocate Thoreau's counsel to hold down the denominator. In the poor countries, however, there is increasing insistence on increasing the numerator of material real income.

So nearly perfect are modern instruments of communication that people everywhere know about—and often envy—the comforts of modern Western life. No longer do they shrug their shoulders and accept their relative poverty as the divine will of Allah. Most important, this increased awareness comes at a time when the role of government is highly developed.

Today, when people want something done, they are likely to turn to government and to insist that programs be adopted toward the desired goal. They want to foreshorten history and get now what developed lands got late.

They want better health; land reform, the breaking up of landowners' holdings; better methods of land cultivation; industrialization; political rights as individuals. It is easy to see that men want these things for natural individualistic reasons. But economic welfare is not the only reason why men desire development. Modern peoples desire development also for reasons of *nationalism:* people want their country to be powerful, to be respected, and—let us face it—to be feared. Thus, the English and Dutch may have brought sanitation to their former colonies; they may have thereby increased people's life-spans and material well-being. But they at the same time set up exclusive clubs whose front doors were barred to the native citizenry. "Freedom from contempt" is one Asian's way of describing his goal.

## SUPERFICIAL THEORIES OF DEVELOPMENT

**Geography**   A look at Table 38-1 shows that all the advanced countries are in the temperate zones. Every tropical country is a poor one. Hence, the argument used to go, it is all a matter of *climate.*

This sweeping explanation will not fit the facts. The first civilizations were in regions of the Near East and Mediterranean (or, if you will, in the Mayan regions of Central America). Greece was in her glory when Germans and Saxons were hunting wild boar.

Certainly, climate is an important factor, but it is not all-important. It does help not to have tropical heat and erosion from jungle floods. It does help not to have arctic snows. But one of the consequences of modern technology is that fevers can be checked by DDT. The bitter Oslo or Oxford cold can be offset by heating; and the humid heat of Texas need no longer inhibit the pace of body and mind.

The geographical distribution of *natural resources*—topsoil, rainfall, dammable water for irrigation and power, oil and ore deposits—is important. But in a world where trade is increasingly possible, grave deficiencies in this respect can be at least partially offset, as the examples of Denmark, Japan, Rhode Island, and Israel have shown.

**Race**[3]  Throw a stone in the advanced countries and the skin you bruise is likely to be white. *Ergo*, the tale ran, prosperity is merely a matter of race.

No one has yet been able to find a causal link between a tendency toward albinism and productivity; the pioneers of Egyptian, Greek, Indian, and Roman cultures were generally not blond or tall. The most remarkable phenomenon of economic development in this last century and in this last decade has undoubtedly been the Japanese. Anthropologists cannot agree completely on how to classify *Homo sapiens* into Mongolian, Caucasian, and other categories.

A glance at history—at the Ethiopian and Berber cultures, at ancient China, primitive northwestern Europe, and flowering Near Eastern cultures—reveals that many factors have been dominant, and that the factor of race itself cannot be isolated as a discernible determinant of economic development. The Chinese at home were always said to lack entrepreneurship. Yet their descendants in Malaya and Southeast Asia, with the same genes in their cells, are accused of being too successful at the art of entrepreneurship.

**Custom and culture**  Victoria's England or Coolidge's America came as close as any culture ever has to being a business culture. In the 1920s a biography of Jesus in terms of accounting virtues could be a best-seller. Hence, some have leaped to the theory that people must behave like the *Homo economicus* of the classical textbooks if a nation is to prosper. (The Japanese have an apter expression: In reference to their industrial miracle of the last decades, they accuse themselves of being "economic animals.")

This view of *Homo economicus* is a caricature. It provides a truth, and hides a more important truth.

Material progress does depend on replacement of a belief in magic and superstition by discernment of and belief in the cause-and-effect relations of engineering and science. If it is a nation's tradition to abhor manual work or work in general; if its people emphasize the hereafter as against this world; if they despise material prosperity; if they discourage ordinary honesty in contractual dealings with strangers; if their way of life puts a great premium on current consumption rather than provision for the future; if their government officials are corrupt and inefficient; if classes battle over distribution or ideology—all such cultural traits are, of course, not particularly conducive to economic development.

But putting stress on these noneconomic factors does not solve the problem of *explanation*. It poses new problems. Why did the brains that might have gone into business in many countries go into science or the priesthood? Why did the anthropologists who stressed the unchangeable inertia of custom in Mexico go wrong in their predictions that penetration of the money psychology would be slow there?

We must not throw away seminal explanations merely because they turn out to be superficial and even wrong. But we must not overlook their superficialities and errors. Max Weber's

---

[3] See Chapter 39 for a more extensive analysis of the economics of racial discrimination.

celebrated emphasis on the "Protestant ethic" as both cause and effect of capitalistic development is a case in point. It did fit some facts: many of the advanced nations are Protestant. John Calvin and *some* Protestant theologians did break away from the Catholic Church's ancient edicts against interest. John D. Rockefeller, Sr., was both an avaricious profit maximizer and an ardent Baptist, who referred to his gains as "God's gold." Yet the "buts" that have to be applied to the Weber thesis are many and serious.

Northern Italy and Catholic Rhineland showed early development. You can find in eighteenth-century Japanese writings perfect passages of Weberian Protestantism. Jews, Chinese, and Basques have in many places played the role of the alienated stranger who pioneers in economic entrepreneurship. And if Weber seriously regards Benjamin Franklin—a prototype of the scientist, innovator, and business go-getter—as an other-worldly Protestant, biographers of that cynical deist tell us the name has lost all meaning. Modern statistical research on the Protestant and Catholic neighborhoods in German cities, on which Weber originally rested part of his case, shows that correct statistical tabulation even belies Weber's own findings.

Whether or not Weber in some subtle sense was right, think how badly a crude belief in his theory would have served for prediction 30 years ago: The economies that have shown the greatest miracles of growth since 1950 have been Japan, Taiwan, Korea, Singapore, Hong Kong, Puerto Rico, Mexico, Brazil, Thailand, Catholic France and Italy, largely Catholic West Germany, Israel, Austria, and atheistical Russia. Such predominantly Protestant countries as Canada, Britain, and the United States have done poorly in comparison.

All this proves nothing, because there is almost nothing to be proved.

## RECENT CONCEPTS TO DESCRIBE DEVELOPMENT

For decades now economists have been intensely interested in economic development. While they have developed no unified theory different from the basic growth models introduced in Chapter 37, they have added some special features to these models.

The following brief account represents a montage of the most important notions developed in the recent literature. It will pave the way for a systematic causal analysis in terms of the economic determinants of production: land and natural resources; labor (in quantity of man-hours and in quality of skills, training, and effort); capital formation (material and human); and finally, technological knowledge and innovation. The chapter ends with a brief discussion of modern development planning.

**Preconditions for growth**    Human history is long, and economic development is exceptional, being primarily the outcome of the last few centuries of Western history. During most of history, life was short, nasty, and brutish. A cruel Malthusian equilibrium prevailed in which deaths kept in balance with births.

In a few lucky places, warfare diminished. Superior production methods were applied to ample resources. A surplus over subsistence became possible. And usually wealth was so unequally divided among the aristocratic landowners and the bulk of the populace that the rich were able to abstain from consumption and to funnel savings into capital formation. Economic development could now take place.

**The take-off**    The more historians study the facts, the more gradual and evolutionary seems the process of growth. But revolution is always better drama and journalism than is evolution. So various economists like to use words such as "the take-off," "the spurt," and "the big push" to describe the period of accelerating growth. Thus, W. W. Rostow[4] develops stages of growth different from those of Marx and other writers described in the previous chapter. One of his stages is called the *take-off*, the obvious analogy being with an airplane, which can fly only after attaining a critical speed.

There is no purpose here in joining the search to find out when each country had its take-off: England in the eighteenth century, Japan in the late nineteenth, the Congo in the 1990s. Nor shall we divide a country's development in stages as Shakespeare divides man's life into various ages. Instead, we abandon strict chronology to stress the important economic *principles* that the take-off serves to dramatize.

**Increasing returns, social overhead capital, and externalities**   Chapter 37's models of growth proceeded for the most part in terms of the conventional economic principle of diminishing returns—referring to statical variations in labor applied to relatively fixed land, or to variations in the stock of capital goods applied to less rapidly expanding labor supply. Such a conventional model of production assumed that doubling all the factors together would, typically, exactly double total product—a principle referred to as "constant returns to scale" and serving as a background to the law of diminishing returns to a varying factor.

In dynamic economic development, however, the phenomenon of "*increasing returns*" is to be expected. Smith's *The Wealth of Nations* was in its day a manual of economic development. Smith stressed the advantage of *large-scale division of labor*. It is a case of the whole being bigger than the sum of its parts: If all factors together can be increased in size, product will grow *more* than proportionally. Each primitive region cannot develop the scale to achieve efficiency. A pile of enriched uranium suddenly goes active when it achieves a certain size. Similarly, the phenomenon of increasing returns can make it possible for dramatic spurts and accelerations to occur in economic development. (As we saw in Part Three, important areas of increasing returns cannot be left to the free play of competitive market forces; there is a case here for coordination to prevent monopoly and to channel it into optimal patterns.)

MIT's Paul Rosenstein-Rodan introduced, three decades ago, an important related phenomenon. He spoke of the crucial importance of "social overhead capital." To develop, a private economy must have public roads, a railroad, irrigation projects and dams, public health spraying against malarial mosquitoes, etc. All these involve bulky *indivisibilities* of the increasing-returns type. No small firm or family can profitably undertake them; nor can pioneering private enterprise hope to make a profit from them before the markets have been developed. They spread their benefits *socially*. Hence, it is argued, public, as well as private, responsibility is intrinsically involved in economic development from the beginning.

Another way of putting this, as in Chapters 8 and 24, is the following:

**Often there are strong "*external* economies" involved in development. A county agent adviser can simultaneously benefit all the farmers in his region. A railroad can benefit all industry. A multiple-purpose dam has similar externalities. It should be obvious that one**

---

[4] W. W. Rostow, *The Stages of Economic Growth: A Non-Communist Manifesto* (Cambridge University Press, New York, 1960). See Paul A. Samuelson, *Readings in Economics* (McGraw-Hill, New York, 1973, 7th ed.), for a strong critique of the Rostow theses by Simon Kuznets.

can find examples of externalities that do not involve increasing returns, and examples of increasing returns that are unrelated to social overhead capital or externalities. But it should be evident that there is often a strong interrelationship between these three notions—externalities, increasing returns, social overhead capital.

## BALANCED GROWTH AND INDUSTRIALIZATION

In the development literature, there has often been a fascination with *balanced* growth. One would not want the skull to grow more rapidly than the skin of one's head. It is similarly argued that growth in a shoe factory should be accompanied by growth in a stocking factory and in a brewery, if what people want at a higher standard of living is shoes, socks, and beer.

For the world as a whole, the budgetary laws of Engel (which were reviewed on page 209) will impose some limited balance on consumption growth. Food will grow, but it will not keep pace with luxury items. Indeed, despite the emphasis on balanced growth, Colin Clark and other writers have long noted an apparent tendency for development to proceed in three stages: *agricultural* dominance first; then *manufacturing* dominance; and finally, as we all become affluent, a shift toward *services*. Supply and demand spontaneously created these patterns in the old days of relatively free enterprise.

Is balanced growth inevitable or desirable for one region undergoing development? History suggests a negative answer:

America first developed by *specializing* in agricultural exports. Belgium early developed by specializing in glass and woolen production. The whole theory of comparative advantage, presented in Chapters 34 and 35, suggested that growth inside one single region does *not* best take place in balance.

This does remind us of an important issue, discussed on page 701, as to whether there is not an "infant-industry" and "young-economy" argument that can validly be used to criticize extreme specialization of a country along a few vulnerable lines of comparative advantage. If coffee demand and supply are volatile, and if *future* comparative advantage may lie in certain manufactures, a country like Brazil may be well advised to interfere with the market tendency to specialize in coffee production. But prudent diversification and truly balanced growth are by no means the same.

**Industrialization versus agriculture**   New Zealand, Denmark, Holland, Iowa, and Argentina are all regions where productivity in agriculture does not compare too unfavorably with productivity in industry. They are the exceptions. In most places, incomes in urban areas are almost double those in rural agriculture. And in affluent nations, large parts of total resources are devoted to manufacture. Hence, many nations jump to the conclusion: Industrialization is *cause* rather than *effect* of affluence.

One must be wary of making such an inference. As the saying goes, "Rich men smoke expensive cigars; but going out to buy an expensive cigar will not make you rich." Vanity seems to make each country want (1) an airline, and (2) a steel mill. Analysis of present and future comparative advantage suggests that for many nations these are ornamental luxuries.

It simply is not true that the greatest productivity advances of the last century have been in industry rather than agriculture. (Recall Chapter 21's discussion of agriculture.) If Bangladesh's five-year plan could increase the productivity of farming by 20 per cent, that would do more to release resources for production of comforts than would primary reliance on promoting industry.

The points made here are obvious. Yet they are often overlooked in political debate. But before leaving the subject, we should point to the germ of truth in the argument for pushing industrialization in order to speed development.

City and factory life tend to break up the cake of custom. People in close contact mutually stimulate each other. Hence, technical change is probably stimulated in the long run by subsidy to industrialization. Also, there is often much "disguised unemployment" in rural areas, in the sense that some members of each family could move to the city, or turn in off-harvest times to local industrial jobs, without causing much loss of farm product.

## CAPITAL NEEDS AND EFFICIENT RESOURCE ALLOCATION

To break out of a vicious circle of poverty and underdevelopment, capital formation is needed. But starving peasants cannot be expected to take much thought of the future. In past ages, inequality of landownership probably helped solve the problem of social thrift, but in a ruthless way. Collectivist economies like China, North Korea, and Russia have shown that, by command, they can impose the same ruthless abstention from current consumption.

Why cannot free economies do the same? Why cannot they use the fiscal measures discussed throughout this book to curb consumption and stimulate investment? An important reason lies in the realm of political science. Some of the developed countries are able to impose progressive income taxes and find that the taxes do get paid. In much of the world, this is probably not possible. Tax administration is primitive and inefficient. People simply will not cooperate. The problem is made worse where poverty is so great that public officials become corrupt.

As a substitute for taxation and coercion, many writers (such as Harvey Leibenstein) recommend that projects be favored which will produce incomes *for corporations and groups that can be counted on to do heavy investment*. They argue that this emphasis should be given even in some cases where there is an actual loss in current efficiency.

**Planning, with or without resource pricing**    After 1929, Soviet Russia established a first, second, and third Five-Year Plan. Most nations today, including those neutral between East and West, have similar development plans. These set up quantitative goals. Alternative goals are scrutinized for their realism and compatibility. Comparisons are made, and finally a compromise set of aggregate targets is worked out.

These targets may be specified in general terms or in quite detailed terms. Thus, India will take into account her growth in labor force; her growth in capital resources from internal sources; the amount of capital she can import from America or the Soviet Union. She will canvass her need for dams and electric power; for fertilizer, steel mills, and machinery; etc. In the end, priorities must be worked out lest the demands on the system become so great as to produce galloping inflation, or as to produce so much expenditure on imports that the country will run out of foreign exchange and have to either devalue or ration severely by austere import licensing.

Much of this planning will be in concrete physical terms. But much more has to be expressed in terms of rupees of *value*. More importantly, the planners will often find that the values quoted in the market place do not correspond to true national scarcities. Thus, in India people would starve if they were paid a zero wage; yet for many purposes labor is superabundant and ought to be regarded as almost a free factor of production. Capital goods, on the other hand, are truly scarce; charging 50 times as much for use of a tractor as for use of a man may be needed to do justice to the tractor's scarcity and superior productivity. Hence, some sophisticated planners (such as Jan Tinbergen, the noted Dutch economist and Nobel Laureate) advocate applying corrected "shadow prices," or "accounting prices," to labor, capital, and imported goods for the purpose of getting a more rational valuation and allocation of scarce resources. That way, growth can be maximized.

**Capital-output ratios and screening of investment projects**   Poor countries are long on labor, short on capital. They are advised, therefore, to economize on the use of heavily durable and intensely roundabout capital projects. Often they are advised to concentrate as much as they can on activities that have a low "capital-output ratio."

This advice is good. But it would be more accurate if expressed in terms of the investment concepts developed in Part Four. Each project should have calculated for it a percentage rate of return per annum: then a hydroelectric project that yields 20 per cent per annum ought to get done before a short-lived steam project that yields only 5 per cent per year—even if, to the superficial eye, the capital-output ratio of the steam plant seems smaller.[5]

We have described the general problem of underdevelopment and surveyed the concepts used in this field. Now we can turn to the constructive task of analyzing in detail the four economic fundamentals: (1) population, (2) natural resources, (3) capital formation, and (4) technology.

## POPULATION PROBLEMS

Mere growth in numbers does not necessarily mean development. Indeed, as writers since Malthus have warned, unbridled increase in numbers is likely to invoke the law of diminishing returns and to work against increases in per capita living standards. This can create problems. Thus we find many underdeveloped countries repeating the pattern of the eighteenth- and nineteenth-century economies: improved medical technology (e.g., sanitation and, in our day, cheap insecticides) first reduces the death rate; and with birth rates remaining high, population grows rapidly.

El Salvador, Java, and many other examples underline the twin lessons:

**First, much of the increase in output made possible by technological advance may be spent on duplication of numbers.**

[5] When experts shift from the capital-output ratio to the "marginal capital-output ratio," they can come out with the economists' correct yield procedures. Also, if capital will be less scarce 20 years from now—so that the correct interest rate society ought to use for its projects is 30 per cent this decade and 18 per cent next decade—a proper planning calculation will take this into account.

**Second, modern science, conquering disease faster than it promotes the food supply, may in the future keep people from dying from germs—only to threaten them with death from famine as they vie for insufficient food.**

The grave question being asked by demographers is this: Will birth rates fall in developing countries as they did in older countries? And before living standards do?

The Pill, loop, sterilization, rhythm techniques, and other birth-control devices do begin to cut down on the birth rate in poor countries once people come to want smaller families. When most of your offspring died in childhood, you needed many children to carry on your name and preserve your immortality. Once medical science lowers the death rate, people everywhere become more interested in preventing births of fourth and fifth children per family—eventually, perhaps, even third children.

**Improving human resources**   Since labor is an important factor of production, there is much constructive programming to be done in the manpower area. When planners draw up blueprints for hastening economic development, they write down the following specific manpower programs:

1. Control disease and push health and nutrition programs—both to make people happier and to make them more productive workers. Accordingly, do not look on hospitals and sewerage projects as luxuries but as vitally needed social overhead capital.

2. Educated people make more productive workers. Therefore, budget for schools and other programs to reduce illiteracy. Beyond reading and writing, train people in new techniques of agriculture and industry. Send your best minds abroad to bring back knowledge of engineering and business. (But beware that they do not get drained off to the advanced nations!)

**Disguised unemployment**   One important condition for promoting development is the better utilization of manpower. In poor countries, particularly rural ones, often a large part of the manpower pool does almost nothing because there is nothing for it to do. Such people may not be counted in the census of unemployment, but they can scarcely be called employed; they live with their kinfolk, and when a boom or a development plan comes along, sweeping them into productive city jobs, there is not much reduction in the product back on the farm. The same phenomenon of disguised unemployment is met in advanced countries, both in the subsistence farming regions and in the city streets, where men eke out a bare existence doing door-to-door selling or begging and hustling whenever productive jobs are unavailable.

For a satisfactory solution to this underemployment and unemployment problem, governments sometimes find it desirable, along with manpower programs, to pursue expansionary fiscal and monetary policies like those in the advanced countries—even though these methods raise problems of inflation and of deficits in the balance of international payments.

## NATURAL RESOURCES

Poor countries typically have been poorly endowed by nature. And such land and minerals as they do possess must be divided among dense populations. The romantic notion of overlooked geographical areas, rich in resources, has largely been exploded by geographers. Generally, people have *already* settled in the most productive regions.

True, geologists are still seeking and finding new hidden resources; and there are authenticated cases where control of malaria by DDT has reclaimed from the jungle hundreds of square miles of fertile Asian land. Balanced against these cheerful considerations is the fact that many less developed countries are rapidly depleting their mines, their topsoil, and their irreplaceable natural resources.

Moreover, as was noted, many of the present-day resources of tropical countries are becoming obsolete in competition with scientific creation of *synthetic* substitutes from cheap substances found in abundance within the advanced countries. Thus nylon harmed the silk industry and impoverished millions; if synthetic rubber were to replace natural rubber completely, the Malaysian peninsula would find itself even harder hit.

Economic geographers are agreed that further development must now largely come from discovery and better use of existing resources. Gone are the opportunities of a Columbus; and half-closing is the open door beckoning the poor of the older regions, begging them to migrate to the fertile prairies of North and South America or to the empty regions of Australia and New Zealand.

Of course, the quip still holds: "There's nothing wrong with any poor country that discovery of oil can't cure." The fact that primitive Kuwait falls, in Table 38-1, in the most prosperous category illustrates the point. Iran, the Mideast generally, Indonesia, Nigeria, Venezuela, and now Alaska, are cases where oil helps development.

**Land reform** Even without creating or finding new land, nations can make better use of the land they do have. The medieval village was divided into strips of land one could hardly turn around on, and each man might have to live off the produce of two or three such strips, frequently distant from one another. The same is still true in many parts of the world. It took from the thirteenth to the eighteenth century for the painful, and bitterly resented, *enclosure* movement in England to break up the common lands and to gather together into efficient, larger-scale plots the land of the country. In the process, many peasants were dispossessed and had to go to the city slums. The ruthless, and not altogether successful, "collectivization" of Russian agriculture in the 1920s provides an analogous case; China's collectivization program has encountered some similar difficulties. The displacement of dust-bowl farmers during the 1930s by the tractor has been dramatically portrayed in John Steinbeck's best-seller *The Grapes of Wrath*. In many parts of the world, this same painful process of consolidating too small holdings is yet to be carried out.

At the other extreme, we see in many underdeveloped countries landholding of huge estates too large for efficiency. The tenant farmer has no incentive to improve the property, knowing that he can be dispossessed at any time and having learned from bitter experience that little of the fruit of his initiative will ever accrue to him. The landlords in turn have no incentive to improve the property, never knowing whether an irresponsible tenant will dissipate the costly resources placed at his disposal.[6]

As Communists well know, the situation is explosive, and agitation for land reform signifies a ground swell of public sentiment not long to be denied. More than one agricultural economist has linked productivity with land reform.

---

[6] We saw on page 571, Chapter 28, how inefficient systems of land tenancy can put society inside its production-possibility frontier.

**Successful reform that puts land in the hands of owners who can count on the fruits of their own enterprise has, many times, literally "turned sand into gold."**

Anthropologists in Central America and elsewhere have noted to their surprise that peasant production management is often shrewd and rational, defying the inertia of custom and reacting to monetary incentives. But it is quite wrong to believe that tenant farming has never succeeded in making substantial productivity advance or that plantation culture must always be inefficient. So it is not all a one-sided story.

The problems of natural-resource development merge with the problem of improved technology and with the problem of improved capital-goods capacity for utilizing and discovering natural resources.

## CAPITAL FORMATION

The fingers and brains of men in the underdeveloped countries are much like the fingers and brains of their more prosperous brethren; but men in the advanced nations work with a plentiful supply of capital goods built up over the years. To pile up net capital formation requires, as we have earlier seen, a sacrifice of current consumption. But there's the rub: underdeveloped countries are already so poor as to be often near the minimum of subsistence; they claim that they cannot—in fact, they generally do not—save a very large share of their current national incomes.

Thus, in the advanced nations, from 10 to 20 per cent of income may go into capital formation; but in the less developed nations, the rate of saving and investment may be less than 5 per cent.[7] Merely to provide for rapidly growing population, the primitive tools and housing now enjoyed can use up most of this saving. What is left, then, for development?

**Until we learned how to prevent mass unemployment, many economists worried about *oversaving* in *advanced* countries. But for *underdeveloped* countries the problem is often the classical one of *undersaving:* more precisely, the problem is the urgency of current consumption which competes for scarce resources—leading to underinvestment in productive instruments capable of increasing the nation's rate of economic progress.**

**Qualitative distortion of investment**   There is a further problem. Not only are saving and investment *quantitatively* low in these countries; equally serious is the fact that the *qualitative composition of investment* is often bad from the standpoint of national development. Thus, too much of the limited saving of India goes into hoarding of gold and jewelry, imported legally or illegally and using up scarce foreign exchange.

Many developing countries, like Brazil or Argentina, suffer from chronic inflation; hence, there is a natural tendency for people to invest in real estate and in hoarding of inventory. When you can make 20 per cent on your money by hoarding goods, why seek an additional and problematical few per cent from manufacturing? Thus, no less than 55 per cent of Brazil's 1947 investment was in the form of construction. Observers are also struck with the fact that, in many of the poorest regions of the world, *luxury* apartment dwellings seem to mushroom while industry languishes.

---

[7] In countries going through civil disorders—like Uganda or Chile—net saving could be negative. When colonial shackles are first thrown off, a decline in income—hopefully temporary—often ensues.

Still another qualitative dissipation of the limited saving in an underdeveloped country comes from the frequent tendency of the wealthy to pile up their savings *abroad,* legally and illegally, making them unavailable for internal development.

**Capital from abroad**    If there are so many obstacles to domestic-financed capital formation, why not rely more heavily on foreign sources? After all, did not England in the nineteenth century invest heavily in the United States, Canada, Australia, and Latin America? Did not France before 1914 invest heavily in Czarist Russia and Egypt? And did not Germany invest heavily in Eastern Europe? Does not economic theory tell us that a rich country which has used up all its own high-interest investment projects can benefit itself and at the same time benefit a poor country if only it will shift investment to the high-interest projects not yet exploited abroad?

Actually, prior to 1914, economic development did proceed in this natural fashion. Britain in her heyday saved about 15 per cent of her GNP and invested fully half this amount abroad! If the United States were to match these percentages today, *every year* we should have to lend and invest privately abroad almost $100 billion, or many, many times the combined Marshall Plan and foreign-aid programs of the federal government, Export-Import Bank, World Bank, and all the rest.

For many reasons, we moderns cannot expect such great amounts of foreign investment. After all, was the pre-World War I pattern so natural, or was it perhaps the special result of fortuitous historical coincidences?

Thus, loans from Europe to the New World typically *went together with migration* of European peoples to those same new lands: Englishmen went along with their money, so to speak, to the American colonies, Canada, Australia, and other dominions. And notice that the same pattern of laws and customs prevailed in the capital-importing countries as in the capital-investing country.

Remember, too, that this antebellum world was an unbelievably cosmopolitan one. You could travel everywhere with no passport. You could migrate freely from country to country. You could expect low tariffs and no trade quotas. You knew the international gold standard would let you transfer capital from place to place at your slightest whim. You knew your property was safe abroad from government confiscation: back in those days, few dreamed of questioning the sanctity of private property, and those nationalistic countries which did raise such questions could be easily intimidated by dispatch of battleships for off-coast maneuvers. Finally, you could buy up—literally!—dictatorial governments in many backward countries and bribe them into giving you extremely favorable mining and other concessions.

If this sounds like an investor's paradise, be reminded that the historical facts were not really quite so rosy. Foreign investments often did go bankrupt, there being insufficient commercial demand for the railroads built across the plains of the New World. Also, the people in the countries importing capital do not seem, from their historical utterances, to have been all that happy over this investor's paradise.

Still, the system did function. And often it did confer *mutual benefits* on both the advanced and backward areas. After dividends went abroad, a net increment of product due to the imported capital was left at home in the form of higher real wages.

Now all this is ancient history. That antebellum world is gone. Never was nationalism stronger than today. Never have borrower and lender been so much in agreement: the less developed countries are agreed not to sell to foreigners long-term rights in the development of their countries, no matter how advantageous the price; the developed countries are agreed it would be rash to buy bonds and stocks from backward countries in the old pattern.[8]

This does not mean we must rule out substantial foreign capital investment programs. But to be realistic, we must search out new instrumentalities for carrying them out. Often these will involve agreements between governments or various government guarantees of private ventures. Always foreign investment will have to take into account the rising tide of nationalism. Local management must be trained to take over ultimately; local sharing in ownership of branch plants is a modern necessity.

Along with import of capital from abroad that comes from private investors interested in a profit return, there is also the possibility of foreign-aid programs from the advanced countries and development loans from the World Bank and various United Nations agencies. (Chapter 36 on international trade discussed these channels.) For the 1970s the goal has been set up that each prosperous nation devote 1 per cent of its GNP to this important purpose. But almost none have lived up to this noble target. (The United States official assistance is now below $\frac{1}{2}$ of 1 per cent of GNP, less than that for Australia, Portugal, France, and Sweden.)

## TECHNOLOGICAL CHANGE AND INNOVATIONS

In addition to the fundamental factors of population, natural resources, and capital formation, there is the vitally important fourth factor of technology. Here we can strike a cautiously optimistic note. Here the underdeveloped countries have one possible advantage. They can hope to benefit *by copying the more advanced technology of the developed nations.*

**Imitating technology**   The new lands need not develop still unborn Newtons to discover the law of gravity: they can read about that law in any book. They need not go through the slow, meandering climb of the Industrial Revolution: they can find in any machine catalogue wonders undreamed of by the great inventors of the past.

Japan, Germany, and Russia clearly illustrate all this in their historical developments. Japan joined the industrial race late: at the end of the nineteenth century she sent her students abroad and began to copy Western technology. Her government took an active and creative role in stimulating the pace of development, building railroads and utilities, and taxing heavily the newly created increments of land value resulting from the improvements in agriculture. A few energetic, wealthy families were permitted to develop vast industrial empires in cooperation with the Emperor's bureaucracy, while at the same time the general population was made to work, and work hard, in order to earn its living. Without relying on net foreign capital imports, Japan in a few decades moved into the front rank, both militarily and industrially.

---

[8] Even in friendly Canada, citizens have resented the vast post-World War II investment by large United States corporations, and penalties have been introduced in the 1970s. New investment codes, limiting foreigners' rights, are being formulated in Latin America and elsewhere.

Only after the Revolution of 1848 did Germany really accelerate her industrialization. Through government aid to her universities, German scientists soon became preeminent in mathematics, physics, chemistry, and engineering. A century ago, most American professors of these subjects—and of history, economics, and philology, too—went to Germany for their postgraduate degrees. German prowess in organic chemistry, optics, glass manufacture, and electrical equipment was unsurpassed until the two world wars set her back. Russia, too, illustrates the possibility of fast development through technological imitation of Western techniques and practices.

Finally, the case of the United States itself provides an optimistic example to the rest of the world. Until Hitler made us a present, in the 1930s, of many of the best Continental scientists of all faiths, we could not honestly boast of having quite reached the very front rank in the field of pure science. Yet, for a century our applied technology had admittedly been outstanding. Examine one by one the key inventions involved in the automobile. Where did they originate? Mostly abroad. Nevertheless, Henry Ford and General Motors long outproduced the rest of the world. "Yankee ingenuity" is a phrase that *explains* nothing; but it does refer to a real phenomenon (and one now subject to erosion).

**Interplay of technology and capital**  It is all very well to speak of underdeveloped countries copying advanced technology. But have we not overlooked something important? Is not advanced technology embodied in the form of complex capital goods? And have we not already seen that those countries are short of capital? So how can we expect them to copy superior technology?

Certainly there is much truth in these suggestions. Technological change and capital investment do go hand in hand; often they are inseparable. All the same, we are right to treat them as analytically distinct—albeit related—processes. Here is an example:

Farming is inefficient in many backward countries. You see peasants breaking up the soil by the same primitive methods their ancestors were using back in the time of David and Solomon. Perhaps an ingenious light plow—something simple that would cost no more than a dollar and would pay for itself in the first month—can be found that will both lessen the total amount of capital needed and greatly increase output. This shows how technological innovation can often be capital-*saving* rather than capital-*using*.

Moreover, even in the poorest countries, some gross capital formation is always going on as things are wearing out and are being replaced. Why replace them with the same thing? Why let much of the economy's capital go into mere *duplicative projects?* Surely, it is much better to embody the newly available investment funds in the form of more efficient technological implements. Thus, we see how the interrelated factors of capital formation and technology can be mutually reinforcing.

**Entrepreneurship and innovation**  Does this sound like an easy task for an underdeveloped economy? All that it must do to telescope into a few years the scores of years it took us to develop is the following: Go abroad and copy more efficient methods; bring them back and put them into effect at home; then sit back and wait for the extra product to roll in.

Of course, it does not work quite this way. People in the underdeveloped countries know this from bitter experience. Yet the same illusion keeps cropping up among the people in the so-called "advanced" countries. Too often we think we can send a few technical experts on a short junket to a poor country; after surveying the field for a month or so, they can write up their recommendations for improvement, and then the neatly typed report they leave behind can be "implemented." In this way, development will be solved.

Occasionally, in connection with particular technological processes, experts have indeed been able to work wonders in this facile way; thus, an American expert on leather tanning was sent out to Libya to advise on some of its difficulties, and in a short time he did diagnose the chemical troubles and come up with an effective cure.

**Technologists soon discover, however, that this sort of quick miracle is exactly what cannot be accomplished in connection with the *development of a whole economy*. Indeed, the typical pattern is one of complete disillusionment: after spending several months surveying an underdeveloped country, the expert is thoroughly impressed with the thousands of cultural and economic barriers to progress, so much so that he comes back with a hopeless feeling of defeat. This thoroughly pessimistic conclusion is probably just as wrong in its way as was the opposite optimistic illusion.**

Experience shows development is truly a hard and slow process—but not an impossible one. To hasten its evolution, spontaneous entrepreneurship and innovation must develop among the peoples directly involved. Remember, many cultures begin with a contempt for dirty, hard work—a contempt they often inherit from the colonial elite who used to rule over them. Often, too, they have a contempt for business—for money-grubbing and production. Gradually, they must develop for themselves, *within their own mixed cultural pattern,* a creative group of producers alert to trying out new ways, alert to consumer wants, responsive to pecuniary risk taking and rewards.

Why place the emphasis on creative innovation? Because it is by no means a cut-and-dried task to adapt advanced foreign technology to an underdeveloped country's own use. Remember, the advanced technology was itself developed to meet the special conditions of the advanced countries. What are these conditions? High money wage rates; laborers scarce in number but replete with industrial skills; plentiful capital inherited from the past; mass production; and so forth. These conditions do not prevail in less developed lands.

Time and time again, experience has shown us how easy it is to obtain a foreign loan to put up a model factory in Turkey or Burma. Often it is imported piece by piece from abroad and embodies the latest wrinkles of Western technology. Yet, with what result? With high production and sales in excess of costs, yielding a comfortable profit that can be plowed back into further industrialization? Only too rarely! Often such grandiose imported projects turn out to be extremely unprofitable. The factory that is an optimal investment for New York may in Ankara or Rangoon be a fiasco.

This task of creative innovation is not one for undiluted rugged individualism. The government can do much to set up extension services in each region for consulting with farmers on the best seeds, methods of cultivation, and implements. By sponsoring vocational schools and training courses in machine methods—and in bookkeeping, too—the government itself can innovate creatively. Somewhere between complete laissez faire and totalitarianism each developing nation has to work out its own destiny.

## FIVE-YEAR PLANS: HOW TO GET FROM HERE TO THERE

The advanced nations did not develop by means of a formal plan. Historically, England and the United States grew primarily in a spontaneous and unselfconscious fashion. And in a degree the same holds for the nations late to become industrialized, such as Japan at the end of the nineteenth century. On the other hand, as we've seen, the Soviet Union introduced successive five-year plans from the late 1920s onward.

Today all over the underdeveloped world, planning is a fashionable word. No country is too small or backward to have its five- or ten-year plan. Sometimes these are merely fancily worded documents with little relationship to actual reality and performance. But sometimes they are carefully executed analyses which spell out in considerable detail programs for macroeconomic and microeconomic development. Here is a closer look at some of the elements involved in a good plan.

1. The plan is based upon the *initial resources* of the country, presupposing a careful inventory of present and future availability of manpower and domestic resources.

2. The plan sets up feasible *targets* or *goals* for the terminal date.

3. The plan sets out the *feasible policies* that permit achievement of the terminal goals from the initial resources, taking into account the intermediate economic resources that can be imported from abroad (through loans or gifts) and that can be produced at home out of the initial resources by the mechanism of domestic investment.

**Degrees of planning**   At the least, a plan will involve careful computation of the macroaggregates of gross national product: balance of saving and investment; allocation of resources between public and private sectors, between one region and another, between city and countryside. A good plan will not be so ambitious as to lead to inefficient galloping inflation, or so unambitious as to lead to stagnation and underemployment. Along with macroeconomic fiscal and monetary policies, it will take care that the resulting import demand does not exceed the available supply of foreign exchange, whether this is accomplished by the pricing system or by rationing. An ideal plan will provide for social overhead capital projects and be alert to the problems of externalities and indivisibilities.

Some plans will involve, at the microeconomic levels, no more than "indicative planning," merely keeping diverse industries acquainted with what is going to happen to the aggregates and to their own share of the total, but leaving to their pursuit of profit the resulting response. Other plans will involve detailed allocation of inputs among different output uses, taking care to check the balance between inputs and outputs. They may or may not use the input-output techniques of general equilibrium developed by W. W. Leontief, which give a detailed view of interindustry flows (as in Chapter 37's Appendix). The plan may or may not use the modern techniques of linear and nonlinear programming, in a form suitable for the giant computer.

Often the plan will make mistakes. A crop failure due to bad weather may throw it out of kilter. Overambitious targets may produce foreign exchange shortages and rampant inflation. Sometimes the subsequent five-year plan will learn from the mistakes of its predecessors. Sometimes a situation goes from bad to worse.

A cynic can find in the annals of the 1960s and 1970s countless examples of governmental and private bungling. But an optimist, looking at "miracles" of development in Thailand, Taiwan, Korea, Puerto Rico, Brazil, Singapore, Mexico, Israel, and El

Salvador, can face the rest of the century with some confidence in the ability of nations to accelerate their own economic development—particularly if given some helping aid.

## SUMMARY

1  Most of the world consists of less developed countries: countries with low per capita incomes relative to the most advanced economies; countries capable of improvement but now lagging behind the growth rates of the advanced nations. The increasing political self-consciousness of such countries, plus the eagerness of the communist ideology to help them "skip the capitalistic stage of development," reinforces self-interest in finding new sources of mutually advantageous aid and trade—not new objects for imperialistic make-work programs. All this and altruism, too, make the development problem of major interest.

2  Geography and climate, race and custom, religion and business attitudes, class conflicts and colonialism—each affects economic development, but none does so in a simple and invariable way.

3  The phenomena of increasing returns, externalities, and social overhead capital provide some substance to notions of "take-offs," "spurts," and "big pushes." They suggest a scope for supplementation of competitive market forces. But they do not at all necessarily lead to any simple concept of "balanced growth."

4  The key to development lies in four fundamental factors: population, natural resources, capital formation (domestic or imported), and technology. *Population* causes sociological problems of explosive growth as death rates fall before birth rates fall; the Malthusian devil of diminishing returns stalks less developed realms. On the constructive agenda, improving the population's health, education, and technical training has high priority. The pool of "disguised unemployment" provides an important manpower source for extra product; the "brain drain" of talented men to developed countries provides an important threat to human capital of the LDCs.

5  Even in densely populated areas, discovery and better utilization of *natural resources* can help offset the law of diminishing returns. Land reform raises real problems of transition. The process of capital formation—investing in soil conservation, irrigation, drainage, and so forth—interacts with the natural-resource category, just as it does with population—through investing in people.

6  Rates of productive *capital formation* in less developed countries are low because of (*a*) poverty, (*b*) lack of a bourgeois ethic stressing frugality and acquisitiveness, (*c*) qualitative distortion of saving outlets toward unproductive hoarding of precious objects and inventory and toward luxury real estate or outlets abroad, (*d*) emulation of consumption standards of advanced nations, and (*e*) nationalistic barriers to importing capital on terms acceptable to investors in the advanced countries and to multinational corporations.

**7**  *Technological change* interacts with, and is embodied in, new capital goods. Nevertheless, it is a distinct process, and one which offers much hope to underdeveloped nations inasmuch as they can copy from advanced nations. The experience of Japan, Russia, and the United States shows that the process of adapting to one's own uses the methods developed elsewhere is not easy. It takes a degree of *entrepreneurship* and innovation. One task of development is to spur internal growth of the scarce entrepreneurial and commercial spirit.

**8**  Five-year plans, to achieve feasible *targets* out of *initial conditions* by optimal macroeconomic-microeconomic *intermediate programs,* occur widely.

## CONCEPTS FOR REVIEW

characteristics of LDCs
"take-off," "spurt," etc.
increasing returns, externalities, social overhead capital
capital-output ratio
balanced growth, diversification
disguised unemployment
planning, accounting "shadow prices"
capital and technology
population and natural resources

medical innovations outstripping food
inequality, poverty, emulation, foreign lending and aid—as affecting capital formation
entrepreneurship and innovation
inflation and development
tenancy and land reform
public and private responsibility
five-year plans: initial states, goals, programs

## QUESTIONS FOR DISCUSSION

**1**  Would you expect everyone to agree with the praise of material well-being expressed in the chapter's first quotation? With Dr. White's quotation?

**2**  Bertrand Russell was one of the greatest contemporary philosophers, logicians, and writers; yet the following words of his are agreed by competent historians to be incautious in asserting that the Industrial Revolution *worsened* living standards generally. "The industrial revolution caused unspeakable misery both in England and in America. I do not think any student of economic history can doubt that the average happiness in England in the early nineteenth century was lower than it had been a hundred years earlier; and this was due almost entirely to scientific technique." Without good 1720–1820 GNP statistics, how can he know?

**3**  Formulate your views on geography, race, culture, and development.

**4**  List the principal contrasts between life in America and in a typical LDC.

**5**  Delineate factors important in development; fit each into the outline involving the four main factors: population, . . . .

**6**  Is it fair for the advanced countries, in the interest of conserving bird life to deprive poor countries of the DDT that prevents early death from malaria?

Most of the world is nonwhite. But the white minority do control most of the economic power, and do enjoy a disproportionately high standard of living. Within the most advanced economic society, the United States, the one in nine citizens who is black has long had to do with a measurably lower level of income and wealth. Along with these economic disadvantages have gone political and sociological deprivations that the modern conscience can no longer ignore.

Other minorities have also suffered from discrimination and lack of ordinary privilege. Americans of Mexican origin receive less-than-average incomes and have been the victims of prejudice in the Southwest and elsewhere. In recent decades our Eastern cities have been the mecca for a host of migrants from Puerto Rico, and for them the American melting pot has been slow to assimilate. The first inhabitants of this continent, the American Indians, have yet to receive their full share of the economic and social opportunities we boast of in our Fourth of July orations.

Half the population is female. How is it that a woman who has the same amount of schooling as a man, who also has two eyes and hands, the same tested IQ and aptitude scores, the same parental background, nonetheless ends up getting paid for full-time work an average of only 70 per cent of what a man of similar abilities gets?

## IMMIGRATION AND THE MELTING POT

Sometimes it is argued that such discrimination is nothing new or permanent. Three hundred years ago the settlers from Britain became the dominant elite. Anthropologists observe that every in-group is somewhat hostile to the outsider. Hence, when the potato famine of the 1840s sent hundreds of thousands of Irishmen to our shores, there was naturally resentment of these newcomers, particularly since they were often illiterate farmers. (Boston Brahmins are reminded of what is historical fact, that many of *their* first American ancestors signed their mark because they could not yet sign their names.)

I have a dream . . . I've been to the mountain top . . . I've seen the promised land.
MARTIN LUTHER KING, JR.

If a careful calculation of the GNP were made over the last 10,000 years, in most places and times it would probably be true that women produced more than half of the real GNP.
ALVIN H. HANSEN

781

As the tale goes, then came the Germans. Their strange language made them the butt of local humor: "No dogs or Germans need apply" was a frequent sign in lodging houses and in notices concerning job opportunities. But in time, as the society pages of Milwaukee and St. Louis newspapers will confirm, the children of German immigrants became part of the ruling elite. When you read Sinclair Lewis's novels about life on the main streets of Minnesota, you are reminded of how the Scandinavians were regarded as boorish "Norskies," whereas today to have the name of Andersen or Olson is a positive advantage in the search for elective office. And so it has been with respect to the turn-of-the-century tide of immigration from Eastern and Southern Europe. A few Jews from Holland and Germany came to this land early and prospered as merchants and investment bankers; a subsequent mass migration from Russia led, at first, to sweatshop conditions within a stone's throw of the Ellis Island point of entry; but gradually, through the workings of the marvelous American melting pot, their grandchildren have come to occupy comfortable homes in Westchester or Los Angeles County. In the same way, the descendants of the Italian immigrants who crowded into Boston's North End 60 years ago are now found throughout the greater Boston or San Francisco area. So runs the familiar argument.

Of course, there is a measure of truth in this romanticized view of American history. But only a naïve sentimentalist would believe that this view of *discrimination as only temporary* applies here, or anywhere else. Nowhere is there a classless society free of prejudice and in which the laws of supply and demand operate in an even-handed way. It is the kernels of truth in the tales of successful integration of immigrant groups into the mainstream of American life which point up ironically the problems of Black Americans, Spanish-surname Americans, and American Indians. The Sioux did not arrive in this country yesterday. And it has been more than 100 years since slavery was abolished.

Obviously the ancient timetable of gradual immigrant assimilation is not the relevant pattern for the student of the economics of race. Instead of complacency, new initiatives are required.

## ECONOMICS OF SLAVERY

Little has been told in our history books about the black civilizations and cultures that were flourishing in Africa when the noble Teuton was still cowering over his primitive campfires in Northern Europe. We do know how the profit motive led to the slave trade: pursuing maximum profit—equating marginal revenues and costs, so to speak—merchants used bribery and force to abduct Africans in order to export and sell them in the New World. So long as a plentiful supply of replacement imports could be counted on, each slave was regarded as an exhaustible resource. Just as a vein of copper can be worked to depletion, a slave could be worked to death without regard for natural reproduction or old-age incapacity. (The Spaniards had already found in South America that the native Indian population would not fruitfully produce and reproduce while in captivity; instead they died out rapidly from disease and overwork.)

When conscience led to legal abolition of slave importation, around 1800, economics adjusted.[1] The newer farmlands of the Mississippi afforded a high marginal-product to the slaveowners. The older, depleted soils of the tidewater and border regions could no longer make such good economic use of slave manpower. Hence, the Invisible Hand of competition caused the tidewater regions to specialize in the production and reproduction of slaves, for sale to the fertile lands westward.

**Spontaneous decay of slavery?**    Among historians, most of whom knew little economics, a myth later grew up that slavery in the decades before the Civil War was *becoming economically unprofitable.* According to the myth, if Lincoln could have been a little more patient, the South's peculiar institution would have collapsed of its own weight. Economists, such as John Meyer and Alfred Conrad, have convincingly utilized econometric analysis to show how unfounded this idea was. Quotations for slaves in the auction markets of Savannah and Charleston, taken in conjunction with the costs of food and of child-rearing in the tidewater, show that as high a competitive profit could be earned from the production of slaves as from the production of tobacco or cotton. (The intersection of *ss* supply and *dd* demand curves showed no signs of moving toward the vertical axis of zero slavery!)

The tools of economic analysis tell us that labor productivity was rising mightily in the years before and after the Civil War. Why, then, should technological innovations have downgraded the marginal productivity of black hands and minds? If Swedes and Poles and Welshmen were needed for productive jobs in the northern mines and prairies of a century ago, and if supply and demand bid up their wages to far beyond levels in Europe and far beyond subsistence levels of reproduction, how could anyone but an economic illiterate have believed in the economic decay of slavery? Researches by recent economic historians show it to be a myth that the slaves were lazy and unproductive economic producers.

## THE REVOLUTION DELAYED

After an abortive period of Reconstruction, Jim Crow legislation restored the black population to a caste system of peonage. The economic concept of "noncompeting groups" became applicable with a vengeance. Most of the well-paying jobs were simply unavailable to blacks (and, deprived of education, they could hardly have qualified for them). The existing supply of black workers had to be auctioned off along the demand schedules for the low-skill jobs that were open to them. Figure 39-1 on page 784 shows the economics of discriminatory exclusion, whether it be in Jim Crow America, or for that matter in the insurance and banking industries that still discriminate strongly in favor of native white Protestants of Anglo-Saxon origin.

Supply and demand for some favored employment is shown in Fig. 39-1(a). The supply of privileged white labor is shown by SS. The demand curve for their labor, derived from their productive worth at the margin to the employers producing the important goods in industries from which blacks are excluded, is shown as *DD*. Equi-

---

[1] Illegal importation of slaves continued well into the last century, as pursuit of profit led to the same flouting of law that one sees in connection with traffic in narcotics. For that matter, illegal slavery is still a problem in some lands, as United Nations commissions well know.

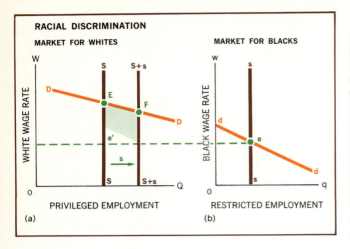

**RACIAL DISCRIMINATION**

MARKET FOR WHITES

MARKET FOR BLACKS

**FIG. 39-1**
**Discrimination exploits blacks, lowers GNP**
Blacks, excluded from good employment in (*a*), must work in inferior jobs (say, menial domestic service) in (*b*). So whites get high wage at *E*; blacks get low wage, in (*b*) at e. When discrimination ends, blacks go to (*a*) as shown by green arrow of shifted supply there. New equilibrium with equal wages for all comes at *F*, where *SS* + *ss* intersects demand. Gain in black wages is not at the expense of an equal fall in white wages (which fall but little). Ending discrimination increases total product, so gainers (including now-better-off white capitalists!) always gain more than losers lose—as shown by the shaded area under *EF*.

librium is at the high white wage shown at *E*. Meantime, Fig. 39-1(b) shows what is happening on the plantation or in the ghetto industry. Working with inferior tools and being permitted to produce only certain limited goods that are not particularly desired by society, the demand curve for occupations open to blacks is shown as *dd*. Their supply *ss* intersects *dd* at the low equilibrium *e*, where *their* market is just cleared. Note the discrepancy between the two equilibria.

*Exclusion has discriminated against the earning power of the black workers.* They are much worse off than the white workers. Such is the remorseless verdict of supply and demand if discrimination can be enforced by custom, law, or union collusion.

What would be the ideal situation in terms of both human equity and economic efficiency? If we let the *ss* supply of Fig. 39-1(b) be added to the *SS* supply of Fig. 39-1(a), we would have the new thin *S* + *s* curve of nondiscriminatory supply. Now at little expense to white wages, we would see a big increase of black wages. Where would the extra wage income come from? It would *not* come primarily from an exaction by the blacks from the whites. For the white workers receive pretty much the same wage as before, their only diminution coming from the weak operation of the law of diminishing returns, as shown by the slight drop along *DD*. *The extra income for the blacks comes from the extra GNP that their higher productivity in their new employment brings compared with lower productivity enforced by discrimination.*

Instead of sweeping the kitchen floor with an old broom, so to speak, now a black worker draws good pay working a modern computer-billing machine. Instead of cutting another ghetto resident's hair, the urban black now can hope to practice group-health medical care in the inner city, or launch his own data-processing business. That is the implication of Fig. 39-1 *after* discrimination has vanished and the educational disadvantages that go with it have disappeared.[2]

---

[2]For emphasis, Fig. 39-1 is drawn with *dd* shown as below *DD* from the beginning, implying that after discrimination is removed all menial work disappears. It would be more realistic to redraw *dd* so that it begins upward on the left asymptotically toward the vertical *W* axis. Then new nondiscriminatory equilibrium comes on a new third diagram, at intersection of horizontally-added *SS* and *ss* with horizontally-added *DD* and *dd* at an equilibrium just above *F* (but at a common wage

## CHANGES IN ATTITUDES

That day of nondiscrimination has not remotely arrived. By custom, it used to be rare for blacks to be given supervisory jobs in which they give orders to whites. And in many industries, white workers said they would not countenance working alongside black workers. Slowly, by the force of laws against discrimination, by education, and by militant protest, this pattern of segregation has been loosening up a little. Progress is slow, but things are changing. Both in the South and in the North, the good jobs are said to be, in principle, now open to all races. Indeed, the phenomenon of "tokenism" has begun to develop: large corporations vie for a presentable black Harvard Business School graduate in order to be able to boast of an assistant vice-president who is a Black American.

Do the facts bear out a gradual improvement in the relative status of nonwhites as a whole? Yes, slightly. In the stagnant 1950s, nonwhite family incomes averaged about half those of white families. In the 15 years after 1961, this fraction climbed from one-half to about three-fifths. Progress? Yes, slow progress. But note that some of the improvement came from the swing of the business cycle from recessionary stagnation to brisker growth. Fortunately, in the years of relative stagnation in the 1970s, blacks seem not to have lost all the gains won in the 1960s. As usual in recessions, their incomes have fallen the most, but they have not lost their beachheads in better occupations.

## IMPROVING EDUCATIONAL OPPORTUNITY

Illiterates—white or nonwhite—get low pay, have to do dirty work, and suffer much unemployment. To a degree, the same is true of those who dropped out of school after 8 years. And of course, college-trained people tend to draw higher salaries than high school graduates.

Since nonwhites receive less schooling than whites, this gives rise to racial differentials in income *beyond* those attributable to on-the-job discrimination. If Southern-rural and ghetto-urban schooling is of lower quality than that out in the white suburbs, the differentials become all the greater. Finally, if a black child comes from a home where no father is present, where no books line the shelves, and where the mother is hard-pressed to care for many children on a limited relief check, then, already at the age of six, the beginning student is under a handicap with respect to learning performance and educational achievement. From ages six to fourteen, the disparities in reading ability or arithmetical and verbal skills become all the greater—particularly if white teachers are relying on middle-class modes of instruction and tests of accomplishment. (A so-called "IQ test," which purports to measure "native general intelligence," is easier for a white if it uses familiar concepts like a bank check than if it were to ask "How long do you cook chitlings?")[3]

---

lower than *E*). See Gary Becker, *Economics of Discrimination* (University of Chicago Press, Chicago, 1957) for further economic analysis of the economic costs that result if people insist on indulging their prejudices against hiring or working with blacks, Puerto Ricans, Chicanos, and women.

[3] It costs money to improve teaching and learning. The Coleman Report of 1966 tended to show statistically that more money spent on schooling to compensate for nonwhite disadvantage from preschool ages would improve things but little. (See James S. Coleman et al., *Equality of Educational Opportunity*, U.S. Government Printing Office, Washington, 1966.) More controversially, an article by Arthur Jensen in the Winter, 1969, *Harvard Educational Review* alleged that the average 15

Gradually, leading universities are recruiting black students. By law, public schools are becoming a bit less segregated; at the same time it is whites who can run, and do run, out of the inner cities. The mere fact that nonwhites tend to be poor, and the poor tend to live together, leads to de facto segregation without any need for deliberate discrimination. Still, we can hope for nonwhites of the next generation to improve somewhat in opportunity and in relative economic status.

## PROFESSIONAL AND ENTREPRENEURIAL OPPORTUNITY: "BLACK CAPITALISM"

In the past, few nonwhites became engineers or vice-presidents of large corporations. A very few did become doctors, dentists, and lawyers—catering primarily to the "protected market" of black clients. Many more, particularly women, became teachers—again largely teaching black pupils.

Of course there have always been a few black millionaires from banks or insurance companies catering to black customers. But a census of nonwhite businesses still shows a rather dismal picture: barber and hairdressing shops, laundries and dry cleaners, small restaurants and grocery stores—these, and real-estate operations in the ghetto, cover much of historic black capitalism.

What about the future? Can private enterprise *spontaneously* close the gap between the races in incomes and standards of life? Few believe this. Capital is scarce in the ghetto; credit is dear and hard to get. Risks are great, with bankruptcy and failures frequent. Because of riot and theft risk, insurance is many times more expensive and often simply unobtainable without government subsidy. Since inventories must be kept to a minimum to reduce risk, customer choice is limited. Because ghetto dwellers are poor, credit must often be granted (particularly to customers of one's own race), and the price charged must be raised in order to cover risk of default.

**Slums as underdeveloped areas**   Many of the tools of Chapter 38 on economic development can be applied to understand the problems of the ghetto. It can be regarded as an underdeveloped area, but one operating with the great disadvantage of having to be contiguous to and compete with the most developed economy in the world. Just as the Malay peasants resent the Chinese entrepreneurs and the Kenyan natives resent the poor Indian traders in their midst, ghetto dwellers naturally resent the white merchants who run small stores in the inner city. These merchants tend to be regarded as "exploiters" who return at night to their comfortable suburban homes loaded with surplus value garnered from the poor.[4] Actual statistics on rate of return of such small-scale white businesses suggest that their rate of profitability is low relative to the labor and resources required. When they can, the sons of white merchants leave

---

per cent shortfall of black IQs in comparison with whites was substantially due to genetic factors and, hence, that it would be better to give nonwhites vocational and rote (rather than analytical) instruction. However, critics in great number have concluded that Jensen was *not able* to control properly for the differences in environment (nongenetic) factors, which operate to handicap nonwhites in preschool years.

[4] This helps explain the occurrence of some black anti-Semitism. However, careful studies in New York by Columbia researchers show that merchants are regarded as white exploiters, and suggest that if as many of them were Italians or Irish as are now Jews, there would presumably arise anti-Italian and anti-Irish sentiment in the ghetto. Other surveys also report less latent anti-Semitism among blacks than among various other urban white groups.

the ghetto for more profitable pastures elsewhere. And the slumlord is more likely to be a low-middle-class capitalist than a tycoon of high finance. (Some slum tenements are actually being abandoned by their owners as not netting their taxes.)

Can salvation come by replacing the small-scale white "exploiters" by a new group of small-scale black "exploiters"? There is in any case little likelihood of such a spontaneous flowering of black capitalism. Before the French revolution, Marie Antoinette said, "Let them eat cake." It is as irrelevant and cruel today to quote to the 11 per cent black population Ben Franklin's adage, "Keep thy shop and thy shop will keep thee."

**Subsidized black capitalism**    If the ghetto is like an underdeveloped country, why not rely on all the devices that have been suggested to stimulate economic development? As Chapter 38 discussed, these include import of capital from the more developed economies, and also foreign aid in the form of welfare transfers or gifts of capital. Transmission of knowledge, skills, and business-management methods is also indicated along the lines of the international Point Four programs. And just as the best students are sent from Asia to the United States for higher education, so one can hope that some of the talented youth from the inner city will return, after their years in the Ivy League and the Yale Law School, to work on urban and race problems. Domestically, as well as internationally, one must worry about a "brain drain" of the best black talents away from the sector most in need of development.

Specific programs could involve government subsidies (a) to bring industry to the ghetto and inner city itself, (b) to provide cheaper risk capital and lower insurance rates for black enterprise, and (c) to help develop basic business skills that can serve whites as well as blacks. Although Washington pays lip service to such measures, by 1973 comparatively little had yet been accomplished along these lines. More could be done by the use of the tax system to give special tax subsidies to activities that add to ghetto employment. Or, since transportation from the inner ghetto to factories on the city perimeter is often unavailable, and since the unemployed are unlikely to have cars, subsidies to commuter-bus services make sense.

Andrew F. Brimmer, an eminent black economist, one-time Governor of the Federal Reserve Board in Washington, now professor at the Harvard Business School and director on many corporate boards, has cautioned against false hopes.

. . . my purpose today is not to demean small businesses [serving ghetto customers] which I feel do offer modest opportunities for some potential Negro enterprises. . . . I am personally convinced that the most promising path of economic opportunity for Negroes lies in full participation in an integrated national economy. This holds for Negroes who want to be businessmen as well as for everyone else.[5]

---

[5]Sir Arthur Lewis, who was born in the black community of the West Indies and is one of the leading economists in the world, has observed: "The black problem is that while we are 11 per cent of the population, we have only 2 per cent of the jobs at the top, 4 per cent of the jobs in the middle, and are forced into 16 per cent of the jobs at the bottom. . . . The measure of whether we are winning our battle is in how many of us rise to the middle and the top. . . . Let the clever young black go to a university to study engineering, medicine, chemistry, economics, law, agriculture, and other subjects which are going to be of value to him and his people. And let the clever white go to college to read black novels, to learn Swahili, and to record the exploits of Negro heroes of the past: they are the ones to whom this will come as an eye-opener."

Thirty years ago, the percentage of black youth unemployment was *less* than that of whites! Few know this remarkable fact—remarkable because today we know ghetto youth unemployment to be double and triple that of white.

Many partial explanations may be given for this: (*a*) World War II was favorable to black employment, and that war is ever farther away; (*b*) there has more recently been a mass migration of blacks from the rural South to the ghettos, and quick absorption could be expected to be difficult; (*c*) because of the post–World War II baby boom, there has been a plethora of young people of all races, a condition which makes for generally lower wages and more unemployment; (*d*) since more young people are in college and school today, those who are not may be of lower average quality than used to be the case, and unemployment for people of lower skills has always been greater; and (*e*) finally, critics of the minimum-wage laws have long claimed that such laws hurt precisely those classes they purport to help: if a man or woman is not worth $2.30 per hour to some employer, even if he is worth $2 and is desperate for a job, he is condemned to complete unemployment.[6]

If the cure for lack of skill is further training, this suggests that more resources must be provided by government to improve manpower-training programs. Public policy can work on the demand side as well as the supply. If employers realize that getting government contracts depends on hiring blacks as well as whites, their self-interest will serve to make job opportunity more equitable. And, on a more cheerful note, some of the difficulties noted would seem to be of a transitional character. When militancy has paid off so that it is no longer necessary to insist on one's rights at every turn, the supply of labor and its marginal-product can cease to show the effects of a sociological revolution in process of taking place.

### ECONOMICS OF GHETTO HOUSING

Job disadvantages of minorities are exacerbated by geographical patterns of racial segregation. The environmental disadvantages of slum living and segregated schools, as we have seen, have a cumulative impact in handicapping the economic status of the nonwhite population. Blacks do not choose to live in smog and congestion in preference to suburban greenlands. Because of historic patterns of segregation, they face limited choice. Traditionally, racial covenants in real-estate deeds were used to keep neighborhoods restricted against minority occupation. After the courts had struck down such covenants, tacit discrimination by real-estate agencies and landlords pretty much continued the old pattern.

In the beginning, bigotry was shameless. Later, it became somewhat shamefaced. More and more people began to say: "*I* am not bigoted. But *others* are. And it is a well-known fact that property values go to pieces when Negroes get a toehold in a white neighborhood."

This becomes, then, what the Columbia sociologist Robert K. Merton calls a "self-fulfilling prophecy." If people believe in it and act on it, even if originally it were false, it may become true.

---

[6]See, for example, Milton Friedman's strong criticism of the minimum wage, in P. A. Samuelson, *Readings, op. cit.,* and some counterarguments there.

**FIG. 39-2**

**Discrimination raises rents to blacks**

Orange demand curves are drawn to be the same per capita, the more numerous whites having the more extended *DD*. But suppose, under segregation, blacks are given only half their per capita share of space. Then their *dd* intersects their allotted *ss* at high *e* rentals. Whites' *DD* intersects their unfairly swollen *SS* at low-level *E*. The green arrow on the left measures the gap due to discrimination. (Though slumlords gain, in this straight-line case the landlords as a class actually lose!)

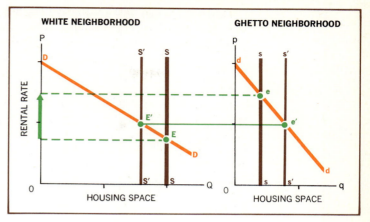

However, turn to the economic facts about race and real estate. If you tabulate bills of sale in two similar communities—one that has had blacks move into it and another that has not had such in-movements—what would such a controlled experiment show? That is the relevant question, because it is obvious that many inner-city neighborhoods which are in economic decay will have falling prices anyway, without regard to race; and it is also well known that the black community tends to be confined to decaying neighborhoods which only poor people can afford.

A careful study of *matched* city neighborhoods, carried out under the auspices of the University of California[7] researchers and covering such diverse cities as Oakland and Detroit, Chicago and Portland, reveals:

*It is largely a myth that desegregation of a neighborhood is harmful to* ultimate *real-estate values. "Block busting," so-called, in fact if anything, ultimately* raises *property values (as the block buster who spreads false rumors knows well).*

And why not, when you come to think about it? Precisely because the black buyer and renter is discriminated against, his demand bids up the prices of those properties which may be available to him. Figure 39-2 illustrates the economics of housing discrimination in a fashion reminiscent of Fig. 39-1's analysis of job discrimination. When the real-estate market is split into two parts, and if the blacks are allotted less than their per capita share, the auction market bids up the rentals that can be exacted from them. After the barriers have been eliminated, rentals for similar accommodations become equalized—resulting in both a more equitable and a more efficient equilibrium.

## ECONOMIC DISADVANTAGES OF WOMEN

No discussion of discrimination would be complete without analysis of the inferior position given to women. We saw in Chapter 5's discussion of inequality of income

[7]L. Laurenti, *Property Value and Race: Studies in Seven Cities* (University of California Press for Commission on Race and Housing, Berkeley and Los Angeles, 1960).

distribution that women's earnings turn out to average only about two-thirds of men's.

Thus, female *college* graduates of the past enjoyed earning opportunities, over a lifetime, fully as unfavorable as male *high school* graduates. Although white males, for the most part, receive increases in annual earnings as they grow older, the census shows that women in their late twenties earn as much on the average as women of older ages.

How can it be that there are relatively more honors graduates among the Radcliffe fraction of Harvard students than among the males—and yet, when the twenty-fifth reunion of the class compiles frequency distributions of full-time earnings, the men *begin* where the women *leave off* in the salary scale? Little wonder, then, that school teaching and library jobs are considered to be high-paying for a woman and quite low-paying for a similarly qualified man. If you examine the organization charts of large corporations, banks, insurance companies, how is it that there are so many male mediocrities among the vice-presidents, and so few women with rank above that of assistant vice-president (and then usually for female personnel administration)?

There is no need to belabor these facts, which are all too well known by everyone. Even after you exclude from comparison those women who genuinely want to be mothers and wives in the home, and confine your attention to those women who have made a career their principal lifetime goal, there remain differences in economic position that no psychologist has yet been able to relate to objective differences.

**Clichés**   Of course, in any society where discrimination has long prevailed, there will be no shortage of myths to explain and justify the differentials. Here are examples.

Women are built by nature to tend babies in the home. They are emotional. They have monthly ups and downs. They cannot carry heavy weights. They lack self-confidence. Men will not work under a woman. Man-to-man talk will be inhibited by the presence of women. Even women prefer a male physician to a female one. Women lack imagination and real creativity. If you mix men and women on the job, they will carry on to the detriment of efficiency and good morals. By the time you have trained a woman, she'll get married and leave you; or have a baby; or alternatively, you won't be able ever to get rid of a woman once you've hired her. If a woman does turn out to be a superlative economic performer, she's not feminine, she's harsh and aggressive, with a chip on her shoulder against men and the world (and she's killing her chances of getting married). Women workers, seeking pin money, take bread from the mouths of family breadwinners. . . .

**Vicious circles**   This list of clichés could be multiplied. And, as every social psychologist knows, discrimination feeds on itself and induces certain self-fulfilling prophecies. If long downtrodden, members of every minority group will begin to show self-hates, shrillness, and doubts that mirror those of the dominant society around them. Many of both sexes who have an impulse to break away from the prevailing pattern will meet the rebuff, "I am not myself prejudiced; but because my customers (or employees) are, I must in fact discriminate." Improvement in such situations seems maddeningly slow—to all but historians.

## CHANGING OCCUPATIONAL AND INDUSTRIAL PATTERNS BY SEX

In turning to economic analysis, historical perspective is useful. From the dawn of recorded history, we find that women have played an important role in producing the GNP. Among human societies, as among animal species, there have been many alternative patterns of specialization with respect to hunting, foraging, herding, planting, and sowing. Only in the art of warfare have men shown any unique talent—and that claim could be disputed. Indeed, in many societies that anthropologists have studied, it has been women who have produced virtually all of the GNP, men filling at best the role of an attractive nuisance. Particularly in self-sufficient agriculture, whether of Old World peasantry or New World frontier, it has been quite impossible to differentiate between the cooperative roles of men and women in producing the GNP. Patterns of dominance, as between patriarchal and matriarchal systems, have shown no close relation to economic organization and performance.

By the nineteenth century, and with Victorian England serving as a paradigm, there grew up the caricature of the lady incapable of performing economic functions outside the home. As Thorstein Veblen wryly observed in his *Theory of the Leisure Class,* status in an affluent society was proved by the uselessness of your chattels except for display. A fair skin, never sullied by exposure to the sun, played much the same role as did the binding of feet of Chinese girl-babies: your wife, your slave, your concubine, manifestly could do no useful work—what a rich gentleman you must then be.

**New trends**    As the Industrial Revolution developed, as methods of birth control released years of a woman's life from the bearing and nurturing of infants, there was a decaying of the Victorian pattern (which in any case had only prevailed among the bourgeoisie and gentry, who always relied on lower-class women to serve as wet nurses, cooks, maids, mill hands, and prostitutes). One of the strongest trends recorded in the statistics is the increased participation by women in the labor force for pay—the words "for pay" remind us that unpaid work in the home is one of the hardest kinds of work.

Many women are gainfully employed all their lives, from school to old-age retirement. Many work for some years after schooling, then drop out a few years for marriage and child bearing, returning to the job market once their youngest child passes beyond infancy. But a recent phenomenon is the increasing proportion of mothers who return to work even while their children are still babies or who never leave working.[8]

America, which thinks of itself as advanced, is in some ways a laggard in the emancipation of women. India, Sri Lanka, Argentina, and Israel have had women heads of government. In Russia, most physicians by far are women. Travelers to Japan, Russia, and China are surprised to see women doing heavy work on the roads. Not only do women live longer than men, they also seem more capable of sustained acts of responsible effort than the so-called stronger sex.

## ECONOMIC ANALYSIS OF SEX DISCRIMINATION: A TECHNICAL DIGRESSION

Figure 39-3 can illustrate both the fact and the tragedy of sex discrimination. We assume equal numbers of men and women, as shown by the lower orange bracket for men being equal in length to the brown bracket for women. We assume three identical

---

[8]No wonder there is a demand for day-care centers. Unfortunately, such a demand has not been easy to meet. If a child is to be given the individual, professional, and loving care that middle-class mothers have insisted on in the past, no obvious pattern of organization has been found that will bring the cost per mother down to a great deal less than the working mother can earn at work. Experts who turn their attention to the analysis of corporations, cooperatives, trade-unions, and factories, should begin to focus on this quantitatively important economic problem.

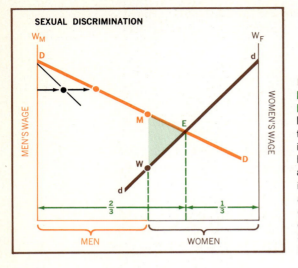

**SEXUAL DISCRIMINATION**

**FIG. 39-3**

**Discrimination hurts women's wage, raises male wage, but definitely lowers total economic product**

Male half of population monopolizes two of three industries, enjoys generous orange $DD$ demand. Female half is confined to one of three industries, with rapidly falling brown $dd$ (measured right to left!). Supply of men is auctioned for high wage at orange $M$. Women get discriminatory low wage at brown $W$. If discrimination ceases, men and women work equally in every industry. Equilibrium comes at $E$ with equal wage rates for both sexes and every industry having some fraction of work force. Shaded area $MEW$ measures gain in GNP from eliminating irrational discrimination.

industries, whose $dd$ curves for labor could be filled as well by men or women workers, their abilities being identical for the jobs.

But now suppose that, for reasons solely of irrational prejudice and bigotry, two industries are reserved for men. Women are crowded into the third industry. The orange line $ME$ shows the $DD$ curve of marginal-product for the two choice male industries. The brown line $EW$ shows demand of the "ghetto" female industry (measured right to left). NOTE: $EW$ has a slope that falls off twice as rapidly as $ME$'s slope. Why? Because men can spread over *two* industries and thus slow down the workings of the law of diminishing returns. ($ME$ came from adding horizontally two $EW$ lines.)

Where is the bigotry equilibrium? At $W$ for females, where they get only 40 per cent of the wage that the males get at $M!$

Where should it be if irrational bigotry were removed? At $E$, where one-third of the women work in each industry along with one-third of the men, each getting and deserving equal pay.

Who is exploited? Women, of course. Who is the exploiter? In a sense, men—who are climbing, so to speak, on the shoulders of the downtrodden women.[9] But that is not the whole story.

Total GNP (or Net Economic Welfare) is down. The shaded triangular area, $MEW$,

---

[9] Also, in this straight-line case, employers as a whole are getting lower profits: ghetto employers happen to gain from discrimination less than employers in the two other industries lose. The present diagram is analytically a variant of those used to analyze discrimination in Figs. 39-1 and 39-2. It can be used to illuminate other kinds of discrimination—against Jews, Catholics, homosexuals, Chinese, Basques, Indians, etc. (The reader is warned that some of the conclusions of the straight-line case—e.g., that discrimination hurts total profits or total landlord rents—need not hold in general. But the basic conclusion, that those discriminated against lose more than the rest of the community gains, does hold: A triangle, like $MEW$, of deadweight economic loss always occurs.) Most important—but, alas, far from obvious—is the fact that society as a whole is losing.

is a measure of the loss in total output or social satisfaction from irrational discrimination. Humanity as a whole loses. That is, the males fail to get as much economic benefit from exploitation as the females lose!

The moral of this diagram must be obvious.

## QUALIFICATIONS AND CHALLENGES

One should not leave this subject with the notion that all differentials between racial, ethnic, or sexual groups are based upon discrimination. If that were so, the outlook for equality would be a more cheery one. No mere banishing of prejudice and bigotry will be able to provide miraculous uniformity of opportunity and incomes.

Many in minority groups do have poorer education. Economists know that investment in human capital is necessary if higher incomes are to be earned. Therefore, so long as employers can rationally count on women not to stay as long in their employment, they will withhold the on-job training that could be conducive to higher lifetime earnings and status.

We cannot take it for granted that all people want to be equally zealous in seeking higher earnings. Some prefer to follow the drumbeat of the counterculture, seeking richness of inner experience in preference to that of the marketplace.

But to the degree that there remains a gap between society's ethical professions and its actual practices, economic analysis demonstrates that great gains can be expected from removal of irrational discriminations.

## SUMMARY

1 By accident of history, the minority of white males in the world have enjoyed the greatest affluence. Naked exploitation under slavery was not a self-curing process. And a century *after* slavery, inequality of opportunity and economic racial discrimination can be shown, by the tools of competitive supply and demand, to lead to irrational loss of income by the underprivileged classes.

2 Economic progress of the nonwhite population has been slow. The analogy with earlier immigrant groups does not stand up to the facts of history. So long as substantial differences in educational and other opportunities remain, Black Americans, Puerto Ricans, Mexican-Americans, and American Indians will inherit poverty from the environment itself. *Spontaneous* black capitalism seems as yet an empty promise. Compensatory spending to offset inequalities of environment seems indicated, and the needed costs should not be underestimated.

3 Segregated housing leads de facto to educational and other discriminations. Again, the tools of supply and demand show that segregation leads to higher rents for those discriminated against, so that partially black neighborhoods find their real-estate values rising relative to what they'd otherwise have been—in contrast to usual myths. The vicious circle of handicaps in education, residential location, income, and opportunity can be broken only by vigorous social action.

4  Discrimination by sex can be analyzed by the same economic tools as discrimination by race, nationality, or political belief. Liberation of women, aside from being desirable and equitable for its own sake, provides also an enhancement of economic well-being through more efficient use of economic resources. One half of the population can hardly be regarded as an exploitable minority.

## CONCEPTS FOR REVIEW

transient and lasting discrimination

wage differentials in divided markets

black capitalism

rent differentials in divided markets

self-fulfilling vicious circles

economics of discrimination by sex

## QUESTIONS FOR DISCUSSION

1  What are comparative world numbers of white, brown, black, and yellow peoples? How are real per capita GNPs distributed geographically among them?

2  Discuss slavery as an economic problem, in actual history and as myth. Has there been any lessening in racial discrimination? Sketch changes you think are needed in the future. Even if all discrimination ceased in the future, show what reparations in the form of compensatory educational expenditures would be needed to remove inequalities of opportunity inherited from the past. Give pros and cons of integration, separatism, and militant black power. Of spontaneous versus subsidized black capitalism. Would college blacks today agree with the Brimmer and Lewis quotations given in the chapter?

3  Describe the overlap in analysis between segregated housing and segregated economic opportunity. Between race and urban problems.

4  Can there be "reverse discrimination," in which, say, white, male Protestants are displaced by quotas that favor minorities possessed of lower objective qualifications? Is this defensible in the long run? What about the short run?

5  In connection with the previous question's topic of reverse discrimination, can you see how the tools of Figs. 39-1 or 39-3 could be applied to demonstrate resulting economic inefficiency and deadweight loss? (HINT: In Fig. 39-3, give women two out of three industries.)

Humanity does not live by GNP alone. Better a smaller social pie divided *equitably* among the populace, many ethical observers will say, than a larger one devoted to the vulgar objects of material display. Why seek what William James called the Bitch-Goddess of success, if the price of that striving is despoliation of man's environment and in the end the nonattainment of happiness and serenity?

The issues raised in this chapter go beyond the technicalities of narrow economic analysis. Yet they are issues that have come to the forefront of debate all over the world: not only in the affluent society of North America and Europe, but also in the Soviet Union and other societies for whom affluence is just ahead.

Is there a clash between the *quantity* and the *quality* of economic life? A clash between economic "efficiency" and ethical "equity"? A clash between "security" and "growth"? Indeed, is growth still possible? Still desirable if possible? Finally, does economics have anything to say about non-material ends—about love and altruism, and about law and justice; about how people make their most important choices of life and death, of marriage and parenthood, and how we spend our most precious resource, time?

None of these vital matters *used* to enter the economics textbooks. Today and tomorrow much of the energies of the economics profession are to be absorbed by the study of the *quality of life*.

## ANALYSIS IN THE SERVICE OF CONTROVERSY

All of the present issues involve value judgments. They involve strong differences in tastes and convictions. Even though they go beyond economics, there is much that economic analysis can contribute to the elucidation of the issues. Thus, until you know the costs of alleviating inequality and poverty, how can you *rationally* determine how far to carry your campaign in that direction? And even if you believe that the ends justify the means, how in a complicated subject like economics can you be sure that the means are not calculated to produce exactly the *opposite* effect to the one you desire?

# 40

# THE QUALITY OF LIFE: POVERTY AND INEQUALITY, ECOLOGY AND GROWTH, LOVE AND JUSTICE

Ill fares the land,
    to hastening ills a prey,
Where wealth accumulates,
    and men decay.
OLIVER GOLDSMITH
*The Deserted Village*

795

Will banning DDT save birds and kill Asians? Will banning phosphates in detergents lead to even worse water pollution from substitutes?

Will a very high minimum wage add to the well-being of the poorer workers? Or will the poor be the prime victims of this well-intentioned measure?

Will putting a low interest ceiling on small loans to consumers—say, 8 per cent per annum, which to many will not seem very low—help the needy and unlucky? Or will it play right into the hands of the lobbyists for the loan sharks?

Many a social revolution—in the Middle East, in Latin America, in Africa—has sought to help the workers and peasants, but during the transition has resulted in a lower standard of life for all the population.

Many a technical improvement—for example, the famous "green revolution" of hybrid grains in Asia—has increased the total GNP, while at the same time widening the spread between rich and poor.

The problems of social reform are not easy. If they were, many of those improvements which command a consensus among people of goodwill would have been made long ago. On the other hand, economic analysis can reveal how specious are many of the arguments for maintenance of the status quo. Despite what your grandfather's economic textbook used to say, a rich country can afford a large measure of redistributive taxation. The Roman Empire did not really fall, or even decline, because of an unbalanced budget or from planning by bungling bureaucrats.

In short, careful economic analysis is the indispensable handmaiden both of those who seek social reforms, as well as of those who wish to preserve and conserve the inherited order.

### SINCE EDEN: INEQUALITY

Chapter 5 has already summarized the important facts about poverty and income inequality. Under laissez faire, income and wealth get distributed far from equally. The mixed economy has somewhat modified the inequality of distribution that was characteristic of the laissez faire regime, but the Lorenz curves of Figs. 5-3 and 9-1 show how considerable are the variations in economic well-being that still remain.

Chapter 5 also demonstrated how, in a growing economy, the numbers shrink of those who fall below any fixed, absolute standard of poverty. *As the whole nation becomes more affluent, our standards rise for what we deem to constitute the minimum needed for a decent life.* We shall always have a lowest 20 per cent of the population with us. But in some decades of successful development, a society will do better than in others in improving the lot of those at the bottom of the income pyramid.

Thus the period of the 1920s was one of great advance in American GNP. But they were years in which there was probably a deterioration in the quality of American life as measured by the degree of income inequality. Ironically, it was the war decade of the 1940s that raised the average income and reduced the dispersion around that average.

Some ask:

Why worry about the disparities of income within the United States when poverty here is as nothing in comparison with that abroad? A family on welfare lives better in Cleveland than a workingman in Volgograd, and infinitely better than a peasant in India. Hunger in America still exists in some rural and ghetto pockets; but it represents largely malnutrition and *isolated* hunger, not the widespread famine that has characterized all history and still characterizes large parts of the globe.

Informed humanitarians often answer much like the following:

An affluent society can afford to provide a decent minimum for all its members. The fact that India is too poor to ensure good food and housing for most of her people may be an argument for a larger measure of our foreign aid; but it is not a valid reason for our countenancing at home the glaring disparities that the market solution provides to the basic problems of What, How, and For Whom.

## INEVITABLE LAWS OF THE DISMAL SCIENCE?

We've already met the view of Pareto that "Essentially nothing can be done about inequality. The basic forces determining inequality are too strong and persistent to be affected by state intervention."

In this matter Pareto was essentially following in the tradition of most of the classical economists. The Reverend Malthus, Stockbroker Ricardo, and their popularizing disciples all thought that economics was the dismal science of unalterable distribution of income. The wages of labor, the rent of land, the profit of capital were determined by Economic Law, and not by Political Power. If labor unions or reform political parties tried to use the state to modify these facts of life, they would be ineffective in the end. All that they would accomplish in the attempt would be *to contrive a smaller social pie,* which would probably still get distributed in about the same way. Vexation and violence in trying to alter this would merely produce economic chaos and class warfare.

## THE WELFARE STATE

Ricardo and the young Marx turn out to have been wrong about the laws of motion of *politics,* as well as of economics. As every schoolboy now knows, the century since 1880 has been the century of state intervention in economic life. Gladstone and Disraeli in England and Bismarck in Germany began in Europe of the last century what Franklin Roosevelt and the Great Depression accelerated in America of this century—namely, the modern welfare state or the mixed economy.

**Voting class-interests**    In retrospect there is nothing mysterious about this political process of using the state to change the distribution of income. The founding fathers of our Republic—particularly such Federalists as John Adams, James Madison, and Alexander Hamilton—were strong believers in the class struggle before Karl Marx was born. They feared that the rights of property would be infringed if votes were given to all. Since the poor outnumber the rich, under universal suffrage the lower elements would legislate against the established wealthy. And that is why our Constitution provided checks and balances of limited government. That is why the suffrage was severely limited in the first half-century after the American Revolution.

The same debate went on in Europe in the middle of the last century. Whigs like

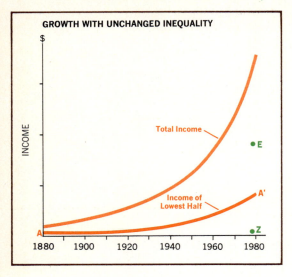

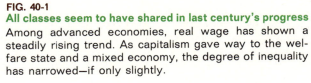

**FIG. 40-1**
**All classes seem to have shared in last century's progress**
Among advanced economies, real wage has shown a steadily rising trend. As capitalism gave way to the welfare state and a mixed economy, the degree of inequality has narrowed—if only slightly.

the historian Macaulay, although by no means reactionary in their own day, warned against universal suffrage:

Give votes to all and you must expect the instinct of self-interest—that *same* self-interest which Adam Smith counted on to work in the economic sphere of laissez faire—to lead to state interference with the inequality of incomes and property. [And, despite the prophecy by the revolutionaries of those days that the privileged classes would *never* yield to the proletariat the right to vote, in country after country conscience and agitation led to widening of suffrage.]

Conservative, liberal, and radical parties may win and lose future elections, but the apparatus of the welfare state persists: in Protestant Norway and Catholic Italy; in outlying Australia and the home counties of England; in free enterprise Switzerland and planned Sweden; in America, the early prototype of Smith's utopia.

**A century's progress**  Figure 40-1 provides a simplified summary of the laws of motion of economic and political development of the last century. The point A on the low curve shows that the lowest half of the population got much less than half of the total social product in 1880. By 1976 the total of GNP had grown mightily. If Pareto were right about the inevitability of the same relative share of product, the new division would be at A'. Real wages would have risen mightily—along with real incomes from property. But if the cruder forms of Marxism had been right, the system would have deteriorated to Z, with the poor reaching complete immiserization (and with a bloody revolution no doubt unavoidable).

Actually, we have no accurate statistics of Lorenz curves for a century ago. What economic historians, such as Colin Clark and Simon Kuznets, do know is that *there has been some slight reduction of Lorenz-curve inequality in modern, as compared with less developed, nations, and in welfare states such as Sweden or Israel as compared with free enterprise societies such as Hong Kong.* So the best guess is to suppose a

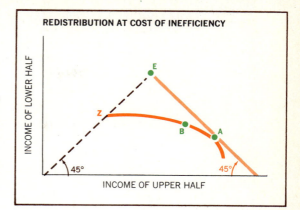

REDISTRIBUTION AT COST OF INEFFICIENCY

INCOME OF LOWER HALF

INCOME OF UPPER HALF

**FIG. 40-2**

**Redistributing social pie of GNP may reduce its total**

The point *A* marks the outcome of laissez faire, prior to redistributive taxation. The green point *E* marks same GNP with complete equality. Often, though, the attempt to redistribute income will create disincentives and resulting deadweight inefficiency. So, instead of being able to move from *A* to *E*, feasibility says we in fact will be moving along *ABZ*. The challenge is to develop tax and other programs that will minimize deadweight-loss gap between *AE* and *ABZ*.

country like the United States or England or Japan is now at a point just above *A'*. The welfare state, through redistributive taxation and through educational opportunity designed to lessen inequality of advantage, has moved the system a bit toward greater equality. But note that the system is still a long way from the point *E* where both halves of the population get the same share of the total social product.

Is this a good or a bad thing? Apologists for the system say, "It is great; look at the doughnut and how it has grown." Critics of the system say, "It is not nearly enough; look at the hole in the doughnut."

There is available an agreed-upon record of facts about real wage trends in the last century. Real wages have risen steadily and strongly in the last century. These laws of motion of capitalism and of the mixed system are, as Chapter 37's analysis of technical change delineates, in line with what we should expect from the dynamic forces of supply and demand. Ford workers get real wages ten times what their great-grandfathers got because their present-day productivity enables that wage to be paid. Even in the economic academies of Eastern Europe it is now agreed that the mixed economies of Western Europe and North America are likely in 1999 to have real wages some 30 to 60 per cent higher than those prevailing in the 1970s.

But these days, good is not good enough. Why be satisfied with existing relative inequalities? Why permit any hunger in the affluent society? Why not an all-out war on poverty? So declare critics of the existing order in increasing numbers.

Philosophers have joined in the debate. Harvard's John Rawls, in his influential 1971 *A Theory of Justice* (Harvard University Press, Cambridge, Mass.), has argued in the following vein. People, so to speak, come together to form a fair society; each does not know how he will fare in it; but all can agree that the natural rights of any one person can be infringed only if that is necessary to raise the welfare of the worst-off persons. Even if one doubts the relevance of hypothetical social compacts, and wishes to qualify Rawls' extreme "minimax" principle, the mere discussion of fairness and justice brings the problem of "inequality" to the fore.

## EQUITY VERSUS EFFICIENCY

Even without the gift of prophecy, one can bet that the welfare state will long be with us. When a Ford or Eisenhower comes into office, he consolidates rather than liquidates the economic reforms of his predecessors. The same pattern was seen abroad when socialist governments in Norway, Australia, or Britain were replaced by more conservative parties. The question naturally arises therefore: Why not go all or much of the way toward equality of incomes? Why wait until 1999 to do what can be done *today* by a determined electorate?

**Deadweight burdens**    Figure 40-2 illustrates the opportunities and difficulties. How can one go from the present point A to the equality point E? If we make income taxes more steeply progressive, decisions to invest in risky ventures and to work hard at one's profession will be profoundly affected. If we freeze prices and rents or put floors on wages, we alter production and employment. Conservatives no doubt exaggerate the problems of distortion, but only romantics deny their reality.

Schematically, the heavy ABZ curve bends inward as a result of the deadweight cost, or burden, that is inevitably associated with strong state interference with the workings of the market mechanism.[1] Indeed, experience has shown that in some cases the distortions due to interference can become so great that the attempt to help one social class at the expense of another can end hurting them all. (Thus the 1948 decision by Ludwig Erhard to end the rationing and price controls that were stifling the West German economy led to a dramatic movement—like that from B or inside A northeast to the *p-p frontier*—which much improved the lot of just about every income class.)

**Argument and counterargument**    Intentionally, Fig. 40-2 presents a gloomily realistic picture of some of the difficulties. How might one react? First, some may say that the effort is still worth the cost, that greater equality is more important than greater affluence and is worth its cost. (And still others may demur, or reduce their aspirations.)

Second, one can mobilize the tools of economics to minimize the costs and distortions. Let the reader pencil in a new curve to lie between the solid ABZ and light AE. By skillful design of programs against poverty and inequality, the deadweight burden can definitely be lessened and society may move on such a new and better curve. Thus, the subsidy of low-income housing may be a more efficient long-run solution to our urban problems than freezing rents by direct controls.

## CAUSES OF INEQUALITY

To alleviate inequality one must first diagnose its principal causes. Here are some of the important factors involved.

**Differences in property wealth**    The greatest disparities in income are due to differences in *wealth ownership*. After the father of William Randolph Hearst discovered a mountain of silver, his children and grandchildren automatically moved to the top of the pyramid of wealth and power. The history of great fortunes—associated with names read on plaques of college buildings: Mellons, Rockefellers—shows that differences in personal abilities are dwarfed by differences in property owned.

---

[1] Experience and analysis show that even once-and-for-all confiscation can result in subsequent slower growth, unless the new order provides for efficient operation, maintenance, and growth of the capital which has changed ownership. *Capital will not automatically maintain itself, or be replaced, or be augmented along the most efficient lines without public or private entrepreneurship.*

Many of these differences in wealth were associated with plain luck in *discovery of natural resources*. Some were due in part to astuteness of exploration and productive innovation. Indeed, the new multimillionaire today is often someone like Edwin Land, who as a dropout from Harvard in the 1930s persevered in his research on polarizing materials, ending up with several hundreds of millions of wealth in Polaroid stock. The *Wall Street Journal* and the London *Financial Times* are replete with similar stories of wealth in one generation due to innovational skill or luck. Since there are loopholes in the tax law favoring capital gains, it is simply not true that today's mixed economy prevents one from becoming a multimillionaire.

**Differences in personal ability**   Some abilities may be *inherited:* within every family there are evident differences in physical and mental abilities; and between families one expects, from the Mendelian theory of genetics, that there will be some dispersion. Students tend to think of intelligence or IQ as the important variable; but when it comes to making money, such traits as energy, ambition, canniness, and flair can be just as important. (As Mark Twain said, "You don't have to be smart to make money. But you *do* have to know how to make money!")

While differences in inherited ability play some role, the common man if anything exaggerates them in comparison with the trained biologist and social psychologist. We all inherit from our environment as well as from our parents' genes. By the age of one, the affluent child of attentive parents already has a leg up in the race for economic status and success. By the time of going to first grade in the suburbs, she or he already has an increased lead over the slum or rural six-year-old. And for the next 12 to 20 years, the scales are increasingly tipped toward them who already have.

**Differences in education, training, and opportunity**   An important factor working for reduced inequality in the last centuries has been the provision of public education. Here is the socialism that subverted the ancient order of privilege, in which there used to be an infinite gulf between the educated upper classes and the illiterate masses.

The provision of schooling for all the population has begun to emancipate women from the ancient domination of male chauvinists. (Indeed, Nora of Ibsen's *A Doll's House* could not have declared her independence if careers were still closed to women; even today, equality of career opportunity between the sexes is all too rare.)

**Class barriers to opportunity**   We saw in the previous chapter's discussion of the economics of race how important the economic role of education and opportunity is. Modern economists have analyzed the problem of putting capital into people through education and training, in much the same way that one puts money capital into plant or equipment. To finish high school or medical school requires an investment that in the past those born poor simply could not afford. At the turn of this century, few but the affluent gentry sang the Whiffenpoof song at Yale; and even the state universities of the Middle West were the province of the privileged.

In a meritocracy, opportunities to pursue advanced education and training will be somewhat divorced from parental affluence. By fellowships and living allowances from the state and by partially repayable loans, those with the ability to benefit from education will be granted the opportunity. Nor will this be confined to professional training and advanced education: GNP is as much enhanced when several Appalachian high school dropouts are trained to program a computer or run a modern filing machine as when similar dollars are spent on training a lawyer or a doctor. On-the-job training in welding, steam-fitting, plumbing, and other vocational pursuits will involve great social payoff and also contribute toward the good society.

Graduates of Groton, Yale, and the Harvard Law or Business School show high earnings, as do Eton and Oxford graduates. Much of this may be the result of superior training and of selection standards that stress high personal ability. But, historically, part has represented differences in opportunity. The executive suites used to be full of Ivy League graduates with no particular superiority over Big Ten graduates. As more objective standards become relevant for recruitment and promotion in an open society, the boardrooms of business and Cabinet offices of government will see more chaps (and, it is hoped, lasses) who aren't Episcopalian, whose eyes aren't blue, and whose mates don't belong to the Sons or Daughters of the American Revolution.

Although public expenditure on education has been an important historical influence making for a more open society, it is, alas, not the case that all such expenditures work toward reducing inequality. For there is a great deal of evidence that much of state expenditure on higher education goes to *subsidize the middle classes* rather than the urban and rural poor. Calculations made for California, where college attendance is more widespread than anywhere else in the world, show that the families of students at state universities (and at community colleges, too) have incomes well above the median of the population at large. The same relative scarcity of children of working-class families at state universities is found in Europe and in the LDCs.

**Difference in age and health**    Even if people were all born alike and subject to pretty much the same environment, some will suffer the vicissitudes of bad health. Cardiac disaster can strike anywhere. Neurosis and psychosis are not ailments that you can choose to have or not have. Alcohol and drugs take their toll in every stratum of society. And no one stays young and vigorous forever. Under laissez faire it has always been the aged who have been most subject to economic want.

**The successful attainment of high employment has done more than any other single program to banish economic want and mitigate economic inequality. Differences in unemployment experienced have always been the single greatest cause of *economic variance within the working classes themselves*.**

Moreover, if an observer were to follow a social welfare worker on her rounds in any typical week in the 1970s, he would find that every one of the health and personality problems encountered is exacerbated by the absence of money.

An alcoholic can be desperately unhappy. But if he is of independent means, his children need not go hungry on that account and his dependence upon a steady job is vitally lessened. In a lower-middle-class family, the onset of mental illness of a mother is a financial disaster in a way that is not true at the top of the income pyramid.

What inherited property has always provided for the privileged few, the modern welfare state in limited measure provides for the bulk of the populace. As we shall see, through *direct* public services and through *transfer*-payment programs, the modern mixed economy is in effect a gigantic *system of mutual insurance* against the worst economic disasters of life. "There but for the grace of God go I," each one of us thinks when he sees disaster strike some neighbor. And realizing we are all in the same boat, we troop to the polls every four years and vote upon ourselves the costs of the mutual-benefit programs that we call social security, Medicaid, and welfare.

## DIRECT PROGRAMS FOR POVERTY AND INEQUALITY

Governments have always had some responsibility for the poor. Thus Elizabethan poor farms and Victorian orphanages have formed the targets of great novels of the past.

**Private charity**  Years ago, private charity had to play a significant if inadequate role: hand-me-downs for the poor, church missions and soup kitchens, handouts for beggars, and free medical clinics were part of the conscience money that the lucky paid to the unlucky.[2] Moreover, in an earlier time, the extended family system meant that each working generation took care of its parents in retirement: the institution of the baby-sitter was little known because there was always a resident maiden aunt or grandmother. After you had settled in New York or Detroit, your cousins from Ireland, Poland, or Alabama could move in with you. Privacy was only a privilege for the middle class.

Private charity was never adequate (even though the situation would often have been frightful without it). Today, it is quite eclipsed in relative importance by the welfare functions of the state, of which the following are only a sample.

**Hospitals and medical insurance**  Help *in kind* was the primary form that public assistance originally took. Not very long ago, it was said, "Only the very rich and the very poor can afford adequate medical care." But that was of course an exaggeration except as applied to those who happened to be near a teaching hospital located in a slum, and who were not deterred by a demeaning means test from providing their bodies for medical experimentation and demonstration. As mentioned, poor farms and mental institutions are among the oldest of public agencies.

An argument still goes on in the modern welfare state. One school says, "Give people money and let them buy health services and the foods they need." The other school says, "If you give money for milk to the poor, they will spend it on beer. Your dollar goes farther in alleviating the rickets of malnourishment and the ravages of disease if you provide the services in kind. The dollar that a man earns may be *his* to spend, but the dollar that society makes available to him to meet particular deficiencies is a dollar that society has the right *paternalistically* to channel directly to its targets."

Neither side wins the argument. Whether in Sweden or America, whether at the national or local level of government, both forms of aid coexist. Without the vast expansion of social medicine, the health-care industry would not today be showing its strong *growth* trend.

**Food allotments**  After America rediscovered in the 1960s that there were indeed still many children and adults subject to hunger in this most affluent of societies, Presidents Kennedy, Johnson, and Nixon instituted a vast expansion of the food-stamp program. Under this program, families that qualify by virtue of their low incomes receive stamps that permit them to get allotments of food at fractional or even zero cost. Since the Department of Agriculture already often supports farm prices by the many loan and storage schemes described in Chapter 21, it seems only logical to have some of any unwanted market surplus go into the stomachs of hungry Americans as well as into the stomachs of hungry peoples from the less developed parts of the world.

[2] See George Orwell, *Down and Out in Paris and London* (Berkley Publications, New York, 1966), for a moving account of what life was like among the derelicts of the 1930s.

**Welfare assistance**   In every county and city there exists some apparatus for help to the destitute. These programs involve some element of direct aid at the same time that they often involve some element of transfer of abstract purchasing power. Thus, in a Northern city a welfare mother with three young children may be receiving a check of $400 per month. Some of this she may be free to spend as she wishes; but some is under the supervision of the welfare worker assigned to her case, who lays down guidelines of how much can go for clothing, house furnishings, and so forth.

Because the minimum standards insisted upon by modern society have risen significantly, the cost of welfare programs has burgeoned in recent decades. Consequently there is great unease among the tax-paying citizenry over such programs. Thus a Gallup-like poll in 1976 would show that half the public think that welfare assistance is shot through with gross abuses. Anecdotes are told of mothers who spend hundreds of dollars fixing their teeth or buying color television sets with funds that ought to go for vitamin A drops for the baby. Illegitimate births among mothers on relief are not greeted with the same tolerance as are similar blessed events among debutantes.

Among informed professionals in the area of welfare and social psychology, there is a similar feeling of disquiet with the present apparatus of welfare assistance. It is indeed costly. And often inefficient. It puts a heavy psychological tax upon the recipients, and in some cases helps to create a caste of poor who must be taken care of in the same way that their parents were taken care of. A higher standard of sexual and other conduct is often demanded of those on relief than the critics themselves can, with all their advantages, live up to. Thus, in some states the father of a family on relief may find that the noblest thing he can do to enhance the well-being of his loved ones is to leave home and disappear. Only then can his wife and children continue to get the aid they so much need. (And lest he return at night, the social-service caseworker is often supposed to initiate the odious practice of surprise bed checks.)

**Welfare payments and economic inefficiency**   If a welfare father were to be offered a job that paid him several hundred dollars, taking that job might in many states cost him several thousand dollars in the form of lost relief payments. Even a steady job at a minimum wage might represent a net loss to him in terms of what is left over after *deductions* from his welfare allotments.

Economically, the traditional system of welfare payments geared to need and earnings involves massive hidden costs in terms of *disincentive* effects. Literally billions of dollars of lost national product stems from the disincentive structure of existing relief systems.

The financial plight of New York City in the mid-1970s is indicative of the load on localities that welfare assistance programs still involve.

## THE NEGATIVE INCOME TAX

Contemplating the great economic inefficiency of existing welfare programs to mitigate poverty and inequality, economists of quite varied political persuasions have come to agreement on the need for a basic reform in the modern welfare state. Liberals like James Tobin of Yale and conservatives like Milton Friedman of Chicago agree that it will be both cheaper and more humane to replace or supplement the mess that we call welfare assistance by a federal program that utilizes the efficient apparatus of the tax structure to attune incomes with needs.

Here is an idea whose time has almost come. Most economists have for some time favored what may be called the negative income tax. Indeed, almost everything is good about the negative income tax except its name—which sounds so negative. So call it, if you like, the "incentive-guaranteed-income" plan.

**How it works**   The basic notion is simple. When I make $12,000 a year, I pay positive income taxes (as seen back in Chapter 9). When I earn an extra thousand dollars, I do pay extra taxes, but only in fractional amounts so that I am strongly motivated to earn more in order to have more.

Now consider a family below some defined poverty level—say, $6,000, in a typical year in the mid-1970s, for a couple with two children. Below that level they are deemed to have no capacity to pay any taxes; and indeed, under current philosophies of equity and ability to pay, our democracy feels that they should receive government aids. In short, these aids constitute a tax in reverse—a *negative* income tax.

But here is where incentives come in. It is a common mistake to think that only the unemployed are poor, or that only fatherless families are poor. Statistics show that much of poverty is among the *working* poor—people who simply cannot earn in the marketplace what is today considered a minimum-needed income. They, and their children, are deemed to merit government help.

Yet how can these aids be given them so as not to deter their efforts and incentives? Here is where the negative income tax provides a great improvement over those welfare programs that deprive people of all assistance the moment they get even a poor job. (And, of course, those on assistance know this very well and are thus deterred from trying to improve their position.) Just as the positive income tax is geared between $12,000 and $13,000 to leave people with an incentive to better themselves, the formula for the negative income tax is gauged to leave the poor with more income after they have used their own efforts to raise their private earnings by a thousand dollars, or even by a dollar. Even when their total tax is negative, their marginal tax rate is always a positive fraction less than unity. (Table 40-1 will show this.)

**Possible formula**   Table 40-1 illustrates how a typical negative income tax might work. What is shown there for a family with two children could be easily modified in the

**TABLE 40-1**
**Negative income tax sets minimum-income standards, preserving incentives and administrative efficiency**

Above an exemption level, determined by some agreed-on definition of the poverty line, people naturally expect to pay positive taxes that rise with their incomes. It is therefore logical that *below* the poverty line, they should receive transfer income—in effect, negative taxes. Note in the third column that incentives are maintained: it always pays in keep-home spendable income to make the effort to increase one's earnings.

| PRIVATE EARNINGS | ALGEBRAIC TAX (+ if tax; − if aid received) | AFTER-TAX INCOME |
|---|---|---|
| POSSIBLE FORMULA FOR NEGATIVE INCOME TAX | | |
| $   0 | −$3,000 | $3,000 |
| 2,000 | − 2,000 | 4,000 |
| 4,000 | − 1,000 | 5,000 |
| 5,000 | − 500 | 5,500 |
| **6,000** | **0** | **6,000** |
| 7,000 | + 500 | 6,500 |

case of more or fewer family members. And of course, as the country grows richer and can afford to be more generous, the formula could be changed to begin at a higher level and to define a poverty level that is higher both in dollar terms and perhaps in terms of dollars of constant purchasing power.

The paramount advantages of the negative income tax are many.

1. It can replace much of present welfare assistance that destroys incentives.
2. It can help to equalize minimum levels of well-being regionally.
3. It is less demeaning to the poor.
4. It can be simply administered by the Internal Revenue Service.[3]

## THE NEW MICROECONOMICS

It used to be thought that economics deals only with goods and services that lend themselves to the measuring rod of money and market pricing: to corn, cloth, skilled personhours, and quarts of fertilizers. Then, as in Chapter 32's bird's-eye view of pricing even in a perfectly planned society, economists learned how to describe the problems of WHAT, HOW, and FOR WHOM in non-market as well as in market societies.

"But," it still was said, "the best things in life are free—or if not free, at least not subject to the calculus of economic dollars and cents and marginal utility. What is the price of mother love? Providence gives us but 24 hours a day, and three score and ten years of life. What does economics have to say on such fundamental matters as time, love, marriage, parenthood, crime, and justice?"

In the nineteenth century, moralists like Thomas Carlyle and John Ruskin declaimed against the acquisitive society. The poet Wordsworth expressed a common sentiment:

Give all thou canst; high Heaven rejects the lore
Of nicely-calculated less or more.

And as a society becomes more comfortably situated, the more can it afford to indulge this distaste for a purely pecuniary motivation based on self-interest. These days a new frontier in the study of political economy has to do with precisely these important non-material aspects of existence.

**Economics of time**   Chapter 22 discussed how a canny consumer allocates his limited income between goods such as food and clothing until their respective marginal utilities are the same for each last dollar spent on them. To make this plausible, we gave the example there of how a student spends his limited time available for studying different courses: you reach optimal equilibrium only when the last minute spent on improving your understanding and grade in English bring you the same marginal gain as the last minute spent on the study of history.

Chicago's Gary Becker has pointed out that all of us are involved in *economizing on time*. If we are retired and have a low pension income, we spend much time in shopping for bargains; and we find it rational to buy food that is underprocessed, utilizing our inexpensive leisure time to do the preparations ourselves. By contrast,

[3] For more on the negative income tax, see the readings by James Tobin and others in P. A. Samuelson, *Readings in Economics* (McGraw-Hill, New York, 1973, 7th ed.).

if you are a high-paid career woman, you rationally conserve time by shopping in an expensive store with many salespersons; you may order your groceries delivered by phone, paying for the special privileges; your table napkins are disposable, and your corn flakes come in a single-serving aluminum-foil container that is very expensive indeed. You do all this, not by miscalculation, but as a matter of rational calculation and adjustment to competitive conditions. The reader can think of innumerable similar examples of the rational allocation of time: e.g., the use of automatic durable equipment in an age where personal servants have become expensive and hard to get.

These are not excursions outside of conventional economics. They are among the many overdue applications of economic decisionmaking to areas not conventionally dealt with in economics.[4]

**Human capital**    We saw back in Chapter 5's discussion of occupational differences in training and earnings that the capital of a nation is not merely embodied in its machines and bricks. Human skills, achieved by education and on-the-job training, also constitute the productive capital of a country. Analyzing human capital is as much a part of modern economics as analyzing any other form of capital formation. The fact that the fate of human beings is involved does not affect its susceptibility to the principles of economics.

Juries in workmen's compensation and accident cases have to arrive at the "present discounted value" of a person's services. Students in deciding how far to carry their schooling need to make similar implicit calculations: to go to medical school means deferring earnings for a long time, means paying out much in tuition, and foregoing many of life's current pleasures; on the benefit side, to put against these costs, are the incremental future earnings that a trained physician can expect to receive. Economic analysis is required in order to synthesize these quantifiable and intangible matters into a final optimal decision.

The problem for economic analysis of human capital decisions is a never-ending one. Thus, the demonstration that college training was very much worthwhile in the 1950s may need to be modified downward in the later 1970s when there threatens to be an oversupply of trained teachers and professionals. The time may come when many young persons will be better off to quit college early, go to work and invest their time and surplus earnings in bonds and stocks rather than in their own further training.

**Economic theories of population**    The birth rate has been falling since 1960. Economists now think they may be able to throw light on the process by which people decide to have fewer children. The decision to see a movie is hardly comparable to the decision

[4]Thorstein Veblen wrote at the beginning of the century on *The Theory of the Leisure Class,* showing how affluence is used to advertise itself by having one's wives and daughters appear to be helpless and cared for. Staffan Linder Burenstam of Stockholm has written in our time on *The Harried Leisure Class* (Columbia University Press, New York, 1970), pointing out that although we have more goods and services than ever before, we still have only the same hours of the day to enjoy them in: often in modern life, people are too busy to have fun, to find time for love and enjoyment with one's own family.

to have a first, or even a third child. But the decision to buy a durable good, such as a house or a car, lends itself to the same apparatus of analysis as the decision to have a first child in, say the third year of marriage and while both spouses are still in their middle twenties.

Can the indifference curves of Chapter 22's Appendix and the marginal utility apparatus of the main chapter throw useful light on the tendency of affluent families today to have fewer children? Many economists and demographers have thought so. They argue much like this: with more income people usually want more economic goods. Other things equal, they would want more children. But other things are not equal. With incomes high, mother and father lose much in interrupting careers. If parents are affluent, they wish to give greater quality to their upbringing of children: the parents have limited and valuable time; 1, 2, or possibly 3 children can be given that intensive parental care which a larger family could not receive. Moreover, in the city children are not the economic asset that they used to be on the farm. With modern health care much improved, one does not need to have six children in order to have two survive to be adults, to carry on one's name and to provide for their parents in old age. The modern social security system takes care of the elderly, and somewhat shifts the decision making against the larger family.

Is it calloused and demeaning to let rational considerations of marginal advantage and disadvantage enter into the sacred decisions of life and death? Some think it so. But many scholars with a keen sense of the importance of family life have thought it useful to marshal every possible descriptive mechanism to the understanding of actual human and social behavior. "Sociology is too important to leave only to the sociologists," is then a Clemenceau-like dictum. Thus, Penn's Richard Easterlin has put forth an ambitious hypothesis to explain the ups and downs of the babyboom in terms like this:

The young couples marrying in the middle and late 1940s were well off compared to their parents—in part because there were so few of marriageable age in 1950. Therefore, they produced so many babies right after the war that, twenty years later, the supply of young people was great relative to demand for them. So they were badly off and insecure compared to their parents. So they have been having fewer children. You can see how the cycle might come back once again in the future toward more children. And you can see why Professor Easterlin explains the falloff in number of children in any farm region after it becomes settled and parents can no longer look to a rising tide of land value and opportunity for numerous offspring.

The test to be applied to economists' analysis of population is pragmatically whether they do help to make good predictions and good explanations of real world phenomena.

**Economics of law**  Even the law schools are finding themselves invaded by the economists.[5] Is no-fault insurance a good or bad thing? Is it better *to pass an ordinance prohibiting* a factory from issuing smoke in a certain zone? Or better rather *to tax*

[5] See Richard A. Posner, *Economic Analysis of Law* (Little, Brown, Boston, 1973) for an example of an influential textbook that has attempted to bring into the legal curriculum some of the methods of economics.

*the factory for any effluents* it does spit out into the atmosphere? Or perhaps better still to let all whose persons or property are harmed by the smoke emitted *have the right to sue* the business for the tort committed against them?

Each such issue is one that lends itself to economic analysis of the incidence of each alternative procedure. Other legal issues that economics can throw light on may even involve life and death. Thus, when the drug thalidomide was first put on the market as a sleeping remedy, it was not realized that a pregnant woman who takes it might give birth to deformed offspring. Here and abroad pharmaceutical companies were sued for having caused such defects. And regulations were promulgated withdrawing thalidomide from production and sale. All this seems straightforward.

Economists and statisticians have pointed out, however, that the problem is more complicated than judges and legislatures have realized. When you tighten up the regulation of new drugs, you may prevent from happening the error of permitting sale of a harmful drug. But in avoiding one kind of error, you may increase the incidence of another kind of error: tight drug regulation delays the time when some new good drug can come into use, thereby causing some people to die or be sick who would be well in the absence of tight regulation. Strict rules on drugs may also discourage firms from investing in experimentation and development of sorely needed new drugs, for the reason that the firm fears its liability in the regime of strict regulation.

The moral is not that economic analysis teaches us to be soft in our regulation of drugs. The true moral is that it tells us that we must weight the two kinds of errors that are inseparably involved in any experimental improvements in the art of medicine. One must by intelligent calculation of the ineluctable risks compromise at some approximation to a golden mean. Every boon to humanity has had allergic reactions on some subset of the populace; there can be no total avoidance of risk. On the other hand to let any firm that can make a fast buck selling what the populace and physicians may not realize is a harmful preparation would represent a perverse condition of laissez faire not calculated to realize the *summum bonum*.

Even crime and punishment are susceptible to economic analysis. Does crime pay? If there were no police and courts and never any punishments or deterrents to crime, more people would find themselves rewarded for engaging in illegal activity. On the other hand, if strong locks are employed, private and public watchmen maintain a vigilant guard, if apprehension is likely, if trial is swift and the jury and judge can be presumed to be quite accurate in distinguishing between the truly guilty and the innocent, that part of crime which is undertaken in the hope of reward may be reduced in total amount.

**Economics of love and altruism**   That part of economics which deals with ethical rights and wrongs, so-called welfare economics, has a good deal to say about such subjects as charity and selfishness. It is a tired and rather empty truism often attributed to economics that "There is no such thing as a free lunch." This has a germ of truth in it when attention is being called to the fact that you can't build a city hall without using up resources that might have been usefully employed elsewhere; and it gives a salutary reminder that people on the street don't usually hand you one hundred dollar bills. But if the no-free-lunch doctrine is interpreted to mean that everybody acts perfectly selfishly and that the only way to run a society is by a laissez faire market system, then it is not a scientific proposition that can be defended or attacked by economic science.

Every person alive was a helpless baby once. Had lunches not been free during the first decade of life, human beings would be extinct. An old and mistaken version of Darwinian evolution put complete stress on selfishness in the struggle for survival. Modern Darwinians, such as Harvard's Edward O. Wilson in his 1975 textbook on *Sociobiology* has redressed the balance in his insistence on the survival value in evolution of reciprocal altruism: a parent will die to save a child, and such unselfish behavior enables that parent's genes to survive. Close-knit families are modes of mutual reinsurance that also have survival value as well as utility. Cohesive societies, in which the different voters provide for comprehensive social insurance on the sensible ground that any person might find himself in unemployment, poverty, ill-health and old-age dependency, these tend to prevail in the long run over societies composed of selfish loners, who put sand in sugar if they can foist this on the competitive marketplace and who are only self-regarding in their lifetime actions.

*Love*, not in the Greek sense of *eros* (which is another story), but in the sense of *agape*, concern for other humans, is after all good business and good economics. Still, when the late Sir Dennis Robertson of Cambridge spoke at Columbia's bicentennial, he picked for his topic the title, "What is it that economists economize?" He surprised his audience by insisting that it is "love" that society must economize, for the reason that it is so important and there is so limited an amount of it. Society must for the most part rely on the market and on the laws so as not to use up the limited ration of civic goodwill on once-and-for-all and ephemeral social needs.

## THE POLLUTED ENVIRONMENT

One sees in today's cities in exaggerated degree a problem common to all modern life, namely, contamination of the general environment. The smog in Los Angeles is the sign in the skies of what is impending for cities elsewhere. Really clear days in New York, Paris, or Tokyo are almost completely a thing of the past.

Mark Twain said, "Man is the only species that feels shame—or has reason to." Certainly man is the only animal who has managed to pollute the atmosphere itself. Sulfur dioxide and particulates contaminate the air of every city. The climate of the world changes as a result of what the Industrial Revolution has done to the concentration of carbon dioxide in the atmosphere. Some scientists believe that the irreversible accumulation of lead in the air we breathe will soon become a problem everywhere. Strontium 90 and radioactive trace elements have been the consequence of atomic testing; and the threat of the ultimate-doomsday cobalt bomb that can end all human life is more than an old-wives' bogey tale. Even noise pollutes the city.

**External diseconomies**    Here is a case of what we have met earlier under the heading of an "external diseconomy." The most pessimistic diagnosis of all is that ultimately the automobile is the prime cause of smog. Factories can be made to have high chimneys and to burn sulfur-free fuels. Strip mining of coal, which despoils the scenery, can be forbidden unless the topography is restored. Thermal contamination of rivers can be controlled by zoning ordinances and costly cooling towers. But to deprive each commuter of his natural right of driving to work each day in a box full of air is apparently more than any modern electorate will stand.

If the consumer will not willingly pay for the extra devices needed to limit air pollution, how can one expect the auto manufacturers to solve the problem? That is like expecting the cigarette companies to commit suicide voluntarily.

Is reliance on spontaneous business efforts futile in the solution of a problem like this? Experience gives a pessimistic answer. There has been one case, though, that offers a glimmer of hope. Detergents poured into our sewage systems were found to continue to foam and to contaminate the very water table into which all rivers and underground streams flow. Conservationists gave a great outcry. And, in this story with a happy ending, the trade association of the industry did sponsor chemical research that did come up with a complete solution to the problem. By industry self-regulation, every firm in the industry has adopted the new formulas, and we have heard nothing of this problem for many years. (But then along came the phosphate problem!)

Would that the contamination of wildlife by DDT, of which the late Rachel Carson wrote so eloquently, would as nicely disappear as a problem. Or that the perfect electric battery, or more plausibly a steam engine, could be developed to reverse the smog and carbon-monoxide effects of the internal-combustion engine.

## GOVERNMENT LAWS, TAXES, AND PLANNING

Since no one profit maker has the incentive, or indeed the power, to solve problems involving "externalities," here is a clear case for some kind of public intervention. Thus, the threat of the California Legislature to ban all internal-combustion engines by 1975 may be an example of the action needed to galvanize Detroit into action. Or a heavy tax on fume-emitting vehicles or factories might be in order. Furthermore, the consumer has an important role to play. He must not curse Consolidated Edison for burning fuel oil with a heavy sulfur content, and then complain if there is added onto his utilities bill an extra charge to cover the removal of sulfur or finance the purchase of more expensive, sweeter fuels.

Examples of needed rules of the road are endless. Lake Erie is dead, killed by the sewage and fertilizers that have been allowed to pour into it. Not only must the cost of producing in the regions bordering on it be increased by the amount needed to decontaminate industrial and other wastes, but in addition, each farmer cannot be allowed to use the chemical fertilizers *he* deems best—since the residue of them flows into the brooks that empty into the rivers that empty into Lake Erie. Nor can farmers and firms be allowed to dig all the artesian wells they please, since the water table underlying much of the country can become dangerously low from unrestrained use.

## THE ENERGY CRISIS

Rich deposits of fossil fuels laid down over millions of years have been plundered in the last century in order to provide the advanced nations with the affluent life. Irreplaceable concentrations of copper and iron ores, of other metals and of timber have been the first to be used up, forcing recourse to lower grade sources of needed raw materials. Futurologists began to warn public opinion that the pace of growth cannot be maintained, but few listened.

Then, more or less fortuitously, along came the post-1973 quadrupling of the price of oil by the exporting countries, the OPEC cartel. Suddenly people became conscious of the true need to economize on what has been an extravagant squandering of scarce and irreplaceable energy sources. For the first time in decades, the real standard of earnings ceased to grow in the mid-1970s as a higher price has to be paid for oil and its substitutes, and at the same time had to be paid for foodstuffs as world inventories of grain were depleted by several years of harvest failure in Asia, Europe, and North America.

Part of this shortfall of growth represented a massive transfer of one and one-half percent of world real GNP to the Persian Gulf and other oil producing countries; part represented a shift of income to commercial producers of agricultural goods much in demand; part represented the deadweight loss of poor harvest, possibly associated with a cycle of bad weather. The Third World of LDCs was quite hard hit in its food production since fertilizer and irrigation are both heavily dependent upon energy sources.

Adjustments to the new scarcity of energy took many forms. In the short run, reliance was placed on patriotic slogans and on long lines at gasoline stations. Families voluntarily curtailed their Sunday driving, lowered their thermostats, and sought to form car pools. In the longer run, reliance has had to be placed increasingly on higher real prices for each form of energy. With gasoline more expensive, lighter and more efficient autos become desired. Architects stop building structures with poor insulation and begin to design from the standpoint of economizing on heating, air conditioning, and lighting.

With oil more expensive, greater reliance is had on coal—which in turn becomes more expensive. At higher oil prices, old wells can be dug deeper, and it pays to explore in new places at home for domestic oil. One can begin to talk about unconventional energy sources: Western stripmining of coal; oil from shale; oil from tar sands; energy from the winds; solar energy utilization; increased reliance on atomic energy by means of fission; and increased development of future processes for achieving energy through a controlled fusion reaction.

Even ecological and safety standards are put under attack by the new scarcity of energy. Auto emission standards, which sacrifice efficiency of gas mileage in the combustion engine, are often relaxed. Electric plants are given permission to burn higher-sulfur oil and coal, even if that presents some threat to the purity of the atmosphere. The danger of a nuclear malfunction in fission-generating stations may tend to be ignored under the pressure of making the country less dependent on oil imports. Ocean drilling off populous coasts may be instituted under the goad of energy shortage.

The distribution of well-being within a country is affected, as between the urban and rural poor and those who have some ownership in the energy sources now gone up in value. Regions heavily dependent on imports, like the U.S. East Coast, are relatively harmed. Programs to tax the windfall gains of the large oil companies meet with the political objection that higher prices are needed in order to coax out a larger supply and undermine the monopoly position of the OPEC cartel.

**Policy choices** Decontrolling energy prices gradually can help to limit the distress and unrest involved. A government program to tax some part of windfall rents, as in the case of Henry George's taxation of pure land rent, can be compatible with maintenance of some incentive to exploit new supplies of oil. Government subsidy to the importing and storing of oil in times when its world price is relatively low makes good sense, and helps to protect against the likelihood and the virulence of any future oil boycott brought about for power-politics as well as economic-profits reasons.

More controversial is the notion that one should fight the fire of monopoly or oligopoly with the fire of a consumer cartel (what economists call a *monopsony* or monopoly power on the part of buyers). Having the American Secretary of State sit down at international conferences and bargain with the OPEC cartel has its dangers, if what is implied is our agreeing to oil-price floors that will be respected, while they are agreeing to oil-price ceilings that run the risk of not being worth the paper they are written on.

It was Marie Antoinette who earned fame by her fatuous remark about the poor: "Let them eat cake." There is something of the same wry irrelevance in the advice often heard today for the non-oil countries that produce raw materials for export. "Let them form a successful OPEC cartel to sell *their* staples at a better price." It is not all that easy, as history shows, to form and maintain a successful cartel. The conditions for oil are not necessarily matched where cotton, cocoa, sugar, coffee, bauxite, and other staples are concerned.

The crisis in energy is perhaps an omen of a bigger crisis yet to come, some will argue. Isn't the world facing definite limits to growth that modern economics must become alert to?

## HARD CHOICES AND THE ECOLOGY OF NATURE

Our more-than-trillion-dollar GNP, we have seen in discussion of NEW (Net Economic Welfare, as defined in Fig. 1-1 and Fig. 10-4), is in part an illusion. When we finally pay our way in terms of conservation and in preserving the environment, perhaps we shall have less than before left for ordinary GNP growth. Nor is it a question of *affording* the taxes to finance these expensive government programs. In a real sense we cannot afford *not* to have them.

And, as in all cases of public interest, there will be conflicts of interest. Shall Dade County be allowed to build a jet airport near the Everglades National Park if that threatens wildlife there? Shall the Disney Corporation be allowed to develop a winter skiing and recreation facility deep in the Sierras if that means disturbing the historic serenity of nature? Or to take a smaller example that points up the dilemma: Shall a small town near Boston, like Lincoln, Massachusetts, be permitted to remain an island of rural serenity if, by its remaining so, the teeming masses of Boston have their recreational activities limited, and are forced to huddle on the hot pavements and crowd a few adjacent beaches?

There can be no simple scientific resolution of these conflicts. The living, and those who will live, have their rights as against the historic past. But woe to a culture that destroys all its architectural glories and turns over its rural countryside to fried-chicken and hot-dog stands.

Modern economics teaches us that the curse of overpopulation is not simply that of Malthusian food shortage due to diminishing returns. It involves also the loss of privacy and uncrowded, pure living space. Modern technology has not solved all our economic problems and repealed the laws of scarcity. On the contrary, for the rest of the century, the social agenda will be filled with these programs of the highest human priority.

## ZERO POPULATION GROWTH? ZERO ECONOMIC GROWTH?

Public opinion in the advanced world is rapidly shifting away from worship of mere growth as such. ZPG (Zero Population Growth) and even ZEG (Zero Economic Growth) are increasingly popular movements. Rachel Carson, Paul Ehrlich, Barry Commoner, and other natural scientists have warned that civilized life must be put on a self-sustaining, closed-system basis, lest ecological disaster overtake humanity.

The good forester plants trees as he chops trees down. The good farmer restores the soil's nutrients in a maintainable cycle. The miner must be made to restore the topsoil his stripmining has desecrated. Similarly, the modern economy must purify the streams it has fouled, the atmosphere it has polluted. Fortunately, as René Dubos notes, nature has great recuperative powers if given a chance: Lake Washington in metropolitan Seattle, not long ago one of America's most polluted lakes, began to purify itself once further sewage and fertilizer effluents were banned.

Jay Forrester's *World Dynamics* (1971), and the kindred analysis in the MIT Club of Rome study, by Dennis Meadows and co-authors, *The Limits to Growth* (1972), have excited much attention—most of it favorable with the lay public, much of it critical with the economics profession. Figure 40-3 illustrates two typical computer printouts illustrative of the Forrester-Meadows methodology and recommendations.

Here we have Malthus all over again: but now the simple geometric and arithmetic progressions have become respectively exponential differential equations of biological growth running head on against assumed-to-be-constant limits on total resources. "The computer that cried wolf," is how Carl Kaysen, Director of the Institute of Advanced Studies in Princeton, put it. Less objective critics, using the lingo of the programmers, have dismissed it as a case of GIGO ("garbage in, garbage out"—inadequate premises leading to misleading deductions). To dismiss such investigations without fair and constructive analysis of their content is to miss the point of their undoubted appeal to the modern mind.

In Fig. 40-3(a) on the left, we see the alleged increase in pollution, exhaustion of natural resources, and inevitable decline in future per capita real incomes. This exactly parallels Malthus's first 1798 edition in which he argued that contemporary trends could not be avoided. Then, in Fig. 40-3(b) on the right, we see, as in later editions of Malthus, how humanity can avoid its fate once it undertakes drastic measures: abolishes all population growth immediately; abolishes all net capital formation and production growth; concentrates on food and services and recycling of resources.

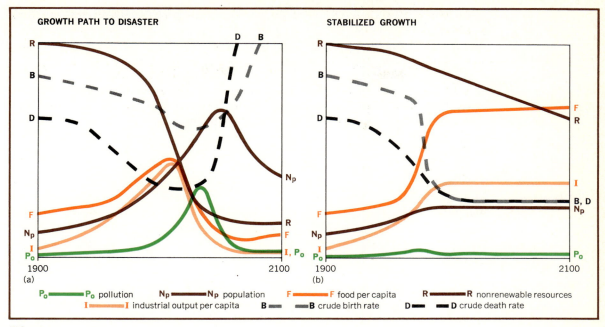

**FIG. 40-3**

**Where, between the poles of complacency and hysteria, do these computer printouts fall?**
**(a)**  High birth rates (*BB* in gray) lead inexorably to brown *RR* curve of declining resources, and to worsening pollution ($P_o P_o$ in green). RESULT: Imminent decline in available food per capita (*FF* in orange); and decline in industrial output (*II* in screened orange).
**(b)**  Disaster is averted on right by immediate ZPG and ZEG (Zero Population and Economic Growth). Shift is to recycling and to services that don't use up resources. If people of the poor countries by the billions are to share equitably in stabilized world output, U.S. standard of living must halve and halve again! What mixture of pseudoscience and common sense do studies like this one by the Club of Rome represent? [Source: Meadows et al., *The Limits to Growth* (1972). Scale in original purposely left vague to indicate lack of precision of forecast.]

Sometimes to sell you must oversell. An antidote to complacency can be provided by hysteria. Few who have looked into the equations and sources of the Forrester-Meadows Club of Rome works can agree that these have realistically captured the likely pattern of the future. Not only have they conceptual flaws and factual inaccuracies, but in addition, they ignore almost completely what scarcity will do to changing relative prices, and what these differential price changes will do to encourage substitutions and to relieve the shortages. Yet they do point to some impending problems.

**Conflicts of Interest**   To those who happen not to live in lucky regions like North America and Western Europe, freezing real incomes at their present levels would be intolerable. Nor is it convincing to claim that Americans and Europeans will give up half or more of their present real incomes so that poor people elsewhere can be raised to a tolerable minimum of life. No one believes that this will happen of its own accord.

Indeed, at international conferences, the less developed nations regard pollution concern as the luxury of the well-to-do. As has already been mentioned, they still want to develop the industry that will pollute.

A dramatic example is the complaint by Sweden that the Russians are prone to pollute the Baltic. Although it would be naïve to think that socialism cures pollution, it is no less absurd to think that it promotes pollution. It is because Russia has a lower per capita income than Sweden that she does not feel she can afford the same programs that the latter can. To prove that the system of government socialism is not the important thing, mention should be made that the Swedes complain with reason about Finland, also a poorer country.

Robert Heilbroner has put the matter dramatically:[6]

[In] our Spaceship Earth . . . sustained life requires that a meticulous balance be maintained between the life-support capability of the vehicle and the demands made by the inhabitants of the craft. . . . [W]e are well past that capacity, provided that the level of resource intake and waste output represented by the average American or European is taken as a standard to be achieved by all humanity. To put it bluntly, *if we take as the price of a first-class ticket the resource requirements of those passengers who travel in the Northern Hemisphere of the Spaceship, we have now reached a point at which the steerage is condemned to live forever . . . at a second-class level;* or at which a considerable change in living habits must be imposed on first class if the ship is ever to be converted to a one-class cruise.

Back to the simple life? Biologists such as Barry Commoner and economists such as Nicholas Georgescu-Roegen are beginning to rethink the wisdom of a return to a simpler (but still comfortable) style of life in which one depends on the renewable flow of energy from the sun rather than on depletable fossil deposits of past sunshine. One walks more and rides less. One grows trees as a crop. Most important, one leaves the environment as one found it: ashes to the same ashes; dust to the same dust.

## WHEN SCARCITY ENDS?

Galbraith was premature in proclaiming the end of scarcity. But actually, John Maynard Keynes had anticipated Galbraith by almost 30 years. In 1930 Keynes made the following prophecy with respect to the future.[7]

[S]uppose that a hundred years hence we are all of us . . . eight times better off . . . than we are today. . . . Assuming no important wars and no important increase in population, the *economic problem* may be solved. . . . This means that the economic problem is not—if we look into the future—*the permanent problem of the human race.*

Why, you may ask, is this so startling? It is startling because—if instead of looking into

---

[6] R. L. Heilbroner, "Ecological Armageddon," *The New York Review of Books,* April 23, 1970. Allen V. Kneese of Resources for the Future has pointed out how these environmental external diseconomies necessitate taxes, penalties, zoning and land-use restrictions, and quantitative planning. And Walter Heller has reminded us that costs and benefits must be brought into optimal balance: to make the Hudson River clear enough for swimming may well be an uneconomic operation from humanity's viewpoint. Likewise, keeping peregrine falcons from becoming extinct at the cost of millions of deaths in Asia from post-DDT revivals of malaria could be an unspeakable tragedy.

[7] J. M. Keynes, "Economic Possibilities for Our Grandchildren," reprinted in his *Essays in Persuasion* (Macmillan, London, 1933) and also in P. A. Samuelson, *Readings, op. cit.*

the future, we look into the past—we find that the economic problem, the struggle for subsistence, always has been hitherto the primary, most pressing problem of the human race—not only of the human race, but of the whole of the biological kingdom from the beginnings of life in its most primitive forms.

Thus we have been expressly evolved by nature—with all our impulses and deepest instincts—for the purpose of solving the economic problem. If the economic problem is solved, mankind will be deprived of its traditional purpose. . . . I think with dread of the readjustment of the habits and instincts of the ordinary man, bred into him for countless generations, which he may be asked to discard within a few decades.

To use the language of today—must we not expect a general "nervous breakdown"? . . . Thus for the first time since his creation man will be faced with his real, his permanent problem—how to use his freedom from pressing economic cares, how to occupy the leisure, which science and compound interest will have won for him, to live wisely and agreeably and well. . . .

There are changes in other spheres too which we must expect to come. When the accumulation of wealth is no longer of high social importance, there will be great changes in the code of morals. We shall be able to rid ourselves of many of the pseudo-moral principles which have hag-ridden us for two hundred years, by which we have exalted some of the most distasteful of human qualities into the position of the highest virtues. . . . The love of money as a possession—as distinguished from the love of money as a means to the enjoyments and realities of life—will be recognized for what it is, a somewhat disgusting morbidity, one of those semi-criminal, semi-pathological propensities which one hands over with a shudder to the specialists in mental disease.

But beware! the time for all this is not yet. For at least another hundred years we must pretend to ourselves and to every one that fair is foul and foul is fair; for foul is useful and fair is not. Avarice and usury and precaution must be our gods for a little longer still.

. . . in making preparations for our destiny . . . let us not overestimate the importance of the economic problem. . . . It should be a matter for specialists—like dentistry. If economists could manage to get themselves thought of as humble, competent people, on a level with dentists, that would be splendid!

## SUMMARY

1    Where economic inequality serves no economic purpose, ethical observers criticize its existence. And even where it does serve a function, such observers are willing to pay a considerable price in terms of inefficiency for alleviating it. Now that a measure of affluence, above and beyond the minimum of subsistence, is available, the citizenry insists upon certain minimum living standards for all.

2    The view, associated with Pareto, that inequality is a universal constant, unchangeable by policy, is not consonant with historical experience. In the advanced countries, Lorenz curves of inequality show less disparity of living standards than they do in the less developed regions. Coupling Smithian self-interest with universal suffrage has led, as the founding fathers predicted, to the modern welfare state with its multifarious social security programs of *mutual reinsurance*.

3    The major causes of inequality involve differences in (*a*) property ownership, (*b*) personal ability (attributable to both environment and heredity, (*c*) education, training, and opportunity, and (*d*) age and health. Decaying, but still with us in some degree, is the belief that it is the fault of the poor themselves if they are poor; and that private charity can handle the cases of greatest distress.

4    For centuries, public policy has provided asylums and hospitals, poor farms and old-people's homes, and various forms of ad hoc relief in times of famine and depression. But only in modern times has broad cradle-to-grave social security and medical care become common among the mixed economies abroad. The battle against poverty continues with some form of the negative income tax still ahead.

5    The "new microeconomics" brings into political economy study of basic non-material facets of life: the economics of time and of human capital; use of tools of marginal utility and choice for crucial decisions on family size and population determinants; the analysis of law and crime; the study of altruism and community as factors in social organization and Darwinian survival. Modern economics transcends the mere dollar sign.

6    Quadrupling of the price of oil by the OPEC cartel has altered world distribution of real GNP. Lavish use of energy gives way, under pressure of higher prices, to economizing, recourse to alternative energy sources—domestic wells, coal, nuclear energy, and to such unconventional sources as oil-shale, oil-tars, wind, and solar. Contingent on future control of nuclear-fusion processes, a reversion to more self-sustaining modes of life provides one way to slow down the exhaustion of limited natural resources.

7    Zero Population and Zero Economic Growth are understandable reactions to life on crowded Spaceship Earth. Smog and air pollution that can change even the climate, water pollution from sewage, industrial wastes, fertilizers, and detergents, and even from the heat thrown off by nuclear and nonnuclear power plants—these have made a wasteland of our earthly inheritance. Such "economic externalities and diseconomies" cannot be expected to be set aright by market competition and the pursuit of profit. They call for government zoning ordinances, fiats and prohibitions, planning and coordination, subsidies and penalties of taxation. Calculations of NEW show that we are not so affluent as our statistics of GNP would indicate.

## CONCEPTS FOR REVIEW

Pareto's laws
Lorenz measures of inequality
New microeconomics:
     time, human capital, population economics, altruism
energy crisis

negative income tax:
disturbed ecology and
     environmental pollution
ZEG and ZPG
externalities and intervention

## QUESTIONS FOR DISCUSSION

1 From 1945 to 1976, inequality of incomes in the United States didn't change much. Is this an indictment of the system, in your view? Or a symptom of the difficulty of a program for changing matters quickly in this sphere?

2 Is equality of opportunity enough? Can persons of different abilities enjoy equal opportunity? Do you agree with the Rawls' notion that people gather to form a social compact designed to protect and improve the lot of the least-advantaged?

3 "If economists must apply their demand-decision theory to marriage and family decisions, let them stress the same role of fashion involved in demand for clothing. Suddenly in one decade early marriage and large families are in; another decade and they are out." Agree or disagree.

4 If lawmakers can't agree on whether capital punishment lessens murders, how far will economists get in trying to determine whether "crime doesn't pay"?

5 To install solar heating in Atlanta cost in 1976 twenty-years' heating payments in advance. Windmill-generated power involved a Vermont farmer 1976 startup cost of $8,000. With interest rates above 5%, does this suggest that solar heating and windmill-generated power are still pretty academic?

6 Banning of soft coal for city heating has actually improved the atmosphere of London and some other cities. Can you find other examples of progress? Of decay?

7 Look up "external diseconomies" in the Index and trace the pervasive influence in modern economics of this vital concept.

8 Evaluate Club of Rome and Forrester doomsday models. Will Americans ever willingly give up two-thirds of their living standards in a stabilized world-GNP?

9 How realistic is a return to the simple full-recycling life?

# 41

## FULL EMPLOYMENT AND PRICE STABILITY IN THE MIXED ECONOMY

No jury of expert economists can agree on a satisfactory solution for the modern disease of "stagflation": many of the proffered cures may be as bad as the disease itself. That is why one can say that some young economist can win for herself or himself a Nobel Prize on the basis of an empirical or theoretical breakthough that will help the mixed economy cope better with this present-day scourge.

PAUL A. SAMUELSON

Modern macroeconomics has come a long way since before the age of Keynes. We have seen in Part Two how fiscal and monetary policy are today able to prevent the great depressions of the past. No longer is the world at the mercy of the happenstance of gold discoveries that may lead in one epoch to galloping inflation and in another to chronic shortage of domestic and international liquidity.

In this chapter we shall see that there are ancient problems that are solvable and have been solved. (For example, however true it might have been in the turn-of-the-century era of Lenin and Rosa Luxemburg, it is definitely no longer the case in the age after Keynes that prosperity of a mixed economy has to depend on cold-war expenditure.)

But there are also important problems yet unsolved. Economics still has its work cut out for it to come up with a solution to "stagflation"—stagnation of production and employment along with creeping price inflation. Experts do not yet know how to agree on an "incomes policy" that will permit us to have *simultaneously* the full employment and price stability that our monetary and fiscal policies are able to create the purchasing power for.

### PROSPERITY AND WAR EXPENDITURES

Let us dispose briefly of an easy problem, in order to make way for the hard problems.

"Capitalism is prosperous only in wartime. Only then are there plenty of jobs. In normal peacetime the unequal distribution of income will always give too much to rich hoarders, too little to the consuming masses. So, even in peacetime, capitalism will contrive cold-war expenditures. And it will try to hold up sagging profit levels and markets at home by finding imperialistic ventures for foreign investment abroad. The underdeveloped world will, temporarily, provide capitalism with the markets it needs to stave off slump." Thus goes the argument that used to be propounded 70 years ago.

Today, not even the experts in the Kremlin believe such arguments are any longer valid. Electorates have eaten of the tree of knowledge concerning fiscal and monetary policy, and there is no turning back to the pre-Keynes age. If all it takes, to keep a nation's banking system from having runs on it that shut its doors, is the printing of little bits of currency paper, you may be sure that populist democracy will insist that such currency be issued. Central-bank open-market operations, to finance huge budgetary deficits, can always avert permanently the stagnation of purchasing power that worried Rosa Luxemburg and V. I. Lenin so much just before World War I.

Turn back to Chapter 18. See, in Fig. 18-1, page 336, how monetary policy can stimulate $C + I + G$ to the total needed for full employment. And review Figs. 18-2 and 18-3, where it is shown how budgetary deficits—lowering of tax rates and/or increasing of $G$ in $C + I + G$—can serve to offset even the gravest cases of automation and labor-saving technical change.

**Correct multiplier analysis**    Anyone who understands macroeconomic analysis can realize that there is nothing that spending money in Indochina or the Mideast can succeed in accomplishing which cannot be accomplished as well or better by spending on useful projects at home. Does building missiles and warheads create jobs and secondary chains of multiplied respending? Then so too will building new factories, better roads, and schools, cleaning up our rivers, and providing minimum income-supplements for our aged and handicapped. Aside from the primary and secondary money spending, we also get the lasting benefits of clean rivers, productive schools and plants, and higher living standards. In terms of economic mechanics and social priorities, you should be able to realize which of the following should win hands down: (1) a manned bomber squadron that never even leaves its base, or (2) a hospital for the alleviation of suffering and prolongation of life.

To test your understanding of all this, draw two diagrams. In the first, let "peace break out" and shift down $G$ and $C + I + G$. For the moment, unemployment may grow. But now show how expansionary budget policy will shift up $CC$ and $G$ expenditure; and show how monetary expansion will shift up $II$. In short, draw in a new, higher $C' + I' + G'$ schedule that intersects the $FF$ full-employment level exactly as in Fig. 18-3(b), on page 344.

*Conclusion:* **The modern mixed economy can afford peace in the post-Keynesian age. The two miracle nations in the years since 1950 have been Japan and Germany—defeated nations forbidden by treaty to waste their sustenance on military expenditures! This demonstrates that every mixed economy has the macroeconomic knowledge *to create at home* without war whatever purchasing power it needs for full employment. And electorates do put pressure on governments—whether Republican or Democratic, Conservative or Labour—to use these known fiscal and monetary tools.**

**Political qualification?**    One question used to be asked after these economic principles became understood. "Politically, will there be as much urgency to spend what is needed for useful, peacetime full-employment programs as there is urgency and willingness to spend for hot- and cold-war purposes?"

It was proper to ask this question back in the 1950s. But as has already been said, experience since then has shown that modern electorates have become very sensitive to levels of unemployment that would have been considered moderate back in the good old days. And they do put effective pressure at the polls on their governments.

Yet, alas, there still does prevail in the United States and (in lesser degree) abroad a problem of unemployment. But the unemployment problem that plagues America and Western Europe in the 1970s is not of the sort that can be validly traced to *inability to create purchasing power*. Rather, we shall see that the *new problem of cost-push (or sellers') inflation* throws up perplexing dilemmas of "stagflation"—unemployment and inflation at the same time.

## THE OPEN QUESTION

There is a specter that haunts the mixed economy everywhere. Can a nation simultaneously enjoy the blessings of full employment and price stability? Or is there a fundamental dilemma of choice between high employment and reasonable price stability? Must full employment lead to creeping inflation? And to accelerating inflation? Is there no way to fight inflation in a modern mixed economy other than to engineer deliberate unemployment and a contrived slowdown to cool off the economy?

Put another way: Is there need for a new thing called an "incomes policy" to reinforce and back up macroeconomic fiscal and monetary policies? And if there is such a need, where is the ideal incomes policy to be found? In direct *price-wage controls* by government? In voluntary Presidential *wage-price guideposts* or guidelines? Or is the goal of an incomes policy a snare and a delusion?

**What science doesn't know**   Questions, questions, questions. For the most part, the chapters of a modern economics textbook speak with crisp decisiveness: that thing is true; this thing is false; these matters are still subject to some dispute; etc. But the first duty of any discipline is to tell the truth. If, in the present state of medical knowledge, certain kinds of cancer cannot be cured or even checked, it is the duty of the good physician to face up to this fact, to profess the limits of scientific knowledge and therapy.

So it is the duty of modern political economy to record a simple truth. In the current state of knowledge about the modern mixed economy, no jury of competent economists can reach broad agreement on how to recommend a feasible and optimal incomes policy.

**Poles of thought**   A minority of the jury (primarily Chicago School Libertarians) will *deny that any incomes policy is needed,* deny that any problem exists; or will insist that if such a problem does perhaps truly exist, no incomes policy is going to do anything but make it worse.

Another minority (primarily admirers of John Kenneth Galbraith) have an equally simple position. "In time of war, we controlled prices and wages by imposed ceilings and commands. Peace is no different from war. The only solution for the creeping wage inflation and its concomitant inflation of oligopolistically administered prices is *permanent* wage-price controls."

Minorities on a jury do not make for an agreed decision. The bulk of economic experts, and this remark applies as well to Western Europe as to North America, admit to the complexity of the problem. As they study the years after 1965, they feel forced to recognize the existence of a *new* kind of inflation: "cost-push (or sellers') inflation" that differs in important degree from old-fashioned "demand-pull (or demanders') inflation." New diseases require new remedies—if we can find them.

Whatever view wins out among informed juries of the future, analytical study of the patterns of experience is essential.

## DEMAND-PULL INFLATION

We saw in Part Two how monetary and fiscal policy can stimulate the economy to the point of full employment and beyond. If the total of consumption-plus-investment-plus-government spending exceeds the value of what the economy can produce at full employment, demand dollars will beat against the limited supply of producible goods and services and will bid up their prices. Since labor is a service and since at such times the labor market has become very tight, the bidding up of wages is also part of the process.

But the direction of causation is clear-cut. It proceeds *from* demand *to* inflation.

Thus, if the 1922 German central bank prints off trillions and trillions of paper marks and these come into the market place in search of bread or housing, it is no wonder that the German price level rises trillionfold. This is demand-pull inflation with a vengeance. But the matter would not be essentially different if there were an 1849 gold discovery in California. Or if the World War I Federal Reserve System created new currency and bank deposits in large enough amounts to bring the system past the point of full-employment spending.

It is important to emphasize that monetarists, who think that $M$ change in an $MV \equiv PQ$ Quantity Equation is the only good clue to explain macroeconomics, agree with post-Keynesians in their diagnosis of *what* demand-pull inflation is. Although the post-Keynesians prefer to use a $C + I + G$ approach, both models agree that it is "too much money spending beating against a limited supply of goods producible at full employment" that constitutes the essence of demand-pull inflation.

**Curing demand-pull inflation**  If only the world of the last part of the twentieth century were more like that of a century ago with its simple demand-pull inflation! Knowledge of modern macroeconomics would then make cure of inflation fairly simple. Brushing aside some short-run problems of forecasting changes in total demand, economists are agreed on the general direction in which macroeconomic policy has to work to wipe out an inflationary gap of the demand-pull type.

To recapitulate briefly, both $C + I + G$ or its equivalent $MV$, can be brought down by (*a*) *monetary policy* (reducing the level or rate of growth of the money supply by Federal Reserve open-market sales, and by reinforcing discount and reserve-requirement increases), and/or by (*b*) *fiscal policy* (reducing government expenditure, increasing tax rates, increasing budget surpluses and reducing budget deficits). The art of dealing with demand-pull inflation is to apply the *proper dosage* of monetary and fiscal policy—fighting unemployment by enough expansion to lead the system to the lip of the cup of full employment, yet with enough moderation so that the flow of purchasing power does not spill over that lip in price inflation; fighting an inflationary gap by cutting back by just enough to bring the system back to a reasonably recognizable full-employment level, without causing an overshoot into recession and depression unemployment.

Admittedly, no one can read the future perfectly. Hence, macroeconomic dosage could not be expected to be exactly perfect in every short run. But *there would be no excuses for chronic slumps or chronic eras of inflation in the simple demand-pull world*. It is time to leave that paradise for the cold real world of the present.

## A NEW KIND OF INFLATION?

No country in the world has been simultaneously enjoying (*a*) full employment, (*b*) free markets, and (*c*) stable price levels. A glance back at page 271's chart of the price level will remind us that we live in a one-way era of creeping inflation. The same story is told in Germany and Japan, Sweden and Switzerland, Italy and France, in all the mixed economies of the world.[1]

What differentiates modern inflation from that of the past is this: Prices and wages begin to rise *before* any identifiable point of full employment; *before* tight labor markets and full-capacity utilization is reached.

Under modern cost-push (or sellers') inflation, a mixed economy may experience "stagflation"—stagnation of growth and employment at the same time that prices are rising!

Clearly, no sophisticated wielding of the tools of $C + I + G$ or of $MV$ is going to be able to cure the new disease by administering the simple monetary-fiscal policy mix appropriate to demand-pull inflation.

For, *when we apply the monetary and fiscal brakes, at the same time that we limit the rate of cost-push inflation we shall kill off the golden goose of prosperity.* Many will regard the remedy as worse than the disease.

**Structural elements**   Indeed, this throws a new light on the reasons that underlie "excessive expansion of monetary and fiscal policy." It is not that central bankers and parliaments have suddenly lost their senses, creating excess purchasing power like drunken sailors. Nor that they have less economic knowledge than their predecessors did. It is rather that the mixed economy, under the prodding of populist democracy, gets itself into a *structural bind*.

If macroeconomic policy is not expansionist enough to match the push of wages and costs, then the result will be slow growth and mass unemployment. The electorate will soon replace any central bankers or heads of state who practice the simple nineteenth-century virtues of fixed money supply with balanced budgets.

## COST-PUSH, OR SELLERS', INFLATION

The growth of cost-push inflation has been a gradual evolution. At the end of World War II, Lord Beveridge, the father of the British social security system, foresaw the dilemma between full employment, stable prices, and free markets.

---

[1]A glance at Latin America shows that galloping inflation, with chronic price rises of 20, 50, 70, and even 200 per cent per year, long prevailed in Chile, Argentina, Brazil, and elsewhere.

**Union push only?**  Businessmen naturally point to increases in wage costs as the reason for their having to raise prices. Often public opinion puts the blame on union leaders who force rises in money wage rates that exceed any rises in labor productivity. Inevitably, unless profit margins can be squeezed indefinitely, such wage costs must be accompanied by price rises. So it is argued.

This view of union leaders as the clear-cut villains of the drama has generally failed to fit the complex historical facts.[2] First, experts on organized labor pointed out that the rank and file are usually even more militant than their leaders. When a leader runs behind his constituency, he gets thrown out of office—as with the head of the steelworkers. Second, the immediate post-1945 inflation was pretty much of the traditional demand-pull type, being attributable to the wartime buildup of liquidity and unsatisfied consumption and investment needs. A number of historical studies have shown that often it was nonunion wage rates that rose first and most, because of the lags involved in collective bargaining; it was as accurate to say that unions *slowed up* inflation as that they made it accelerate.

But most important was the fact that the large corporations who bargain with unions have been able to pass on the wage increases to the consumer and to pretty much maintain profit margins.

**Administered price-wage push**  Even in periods of excess capacity, the price index continues to advance. Therefore some experts began to wonder whether this was not often a case of *price-push* as well as "wage-push." Nor did it seem to take many strikes to get wage increases along with the price increases. The wage-push happened *outside* the unionized industries, too. In the unionized sectors some observers said:

In pushing for higher wages, labor is pushing against an open door. The employers do not fight the increases the way they used to. They act as if they think the Treasury and the Fed will keep aggregate demand high enough to buy the higher-cost output; so they grant the wage increases, and this sends up costs of production, which sends up the prices that firms charge for their goods. The result is a new kind of inflation. When the Fed and Treasury try to handle it by the usual weapons that affect demand, they create unemployment and a recession as in 1957–1958, 1960–1961, 1969–1970, and most particularly in the serious 1973–1975 worldwide recession. From 1958 to 1963, wholesale prices were stable, but it seemed to require unemployment of more than 5 per cent to make this so.

Explanatory emphasis has shifted away from exclusive reliance on wage-push to more general cost-push. Thus, the Joint Economic Committee of Congress reported research suggesting that the increase in steel prices during the 1950s was by itself responsible for a significant fraction of the increase in the wholesale price index. But the committee also found that profit margins stayed up in this administered-price industry, along with wage increases, and blamed nonlabor pressures as well as labor costs.

---

[2]Professor Milton Friedman, the leading skeptic concerning union wage pressure as the cause of price inflation, believes that this view may have had some merit only in the 1933–1934 NRA days, when government also intervened.

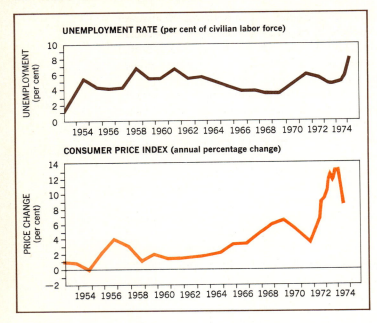

UNEMPLOYMENT RATE (per cent of civilian labor force)

CONSUMER PRICE INDEX (annual percentage change)

**FIG. 41-1**
**"Cost-push (or sellers')" inflation differs from demand-pull kind**
Since the mid-1950s, prices have tended to rise even at times of slack labor markets and gaps from full employment. Particularly after the 1965 escalation of the Vietnam war, wages and prices crept upward. By 1972–1974, the whole world was moving into "2-digit accelerating inflation." The worst recession of the post–World-War-II epoch was deliberately contrived to fight this inflation. Even though the recession got out of hand in its virulence, and did succeed in bringing down the rate of inflation, its reward-benefit ratio—i.e., degree of inflation abatement per unemployment suffering—seemed lower than in earlier times.

**Sellers' inflation**   A. P. Lerner broadened the whole concept to that of *sellers' inflation:*

**If all sellers, whether of labor or of property services or of goods, negotiate and determine their prices to try to get among them all *more* than 100 per cent of the total national product, then the result cannot help but be a frustrating upward push of the price level—a case of sellers' inflation.**

Figure 41-1 shows that low unemployment rates—as in the 1972–1973 boom, when the average rate dropped to 4½ per cent or 1968's 3⅓ per cent tightness—are associated with a quickening of price inflation. It also shows the stagflation that ensued in subsequent years when the Nixon and Ford Administrations attempted to cool off the economy by introducing some slack in industrial capacity and the labor market. By 1975 unemployment rose in the U.S. to over 9 per cent of the labor force. Industry after industry operated at only 70 per cent of rated capacity. Yet inflation was not brought to an end, but rather was only slowed down somewhat from its previous 2-digit per year rate.

## WORLDWIDE INFLATION AND RECESSION IN THE 1970s

Before World War II there tended to be one unified, synchronous business cycle all over the world. The years 1929–1932 brought depression to North America and Europe at the same time and did not spare the remotest corner of the world. So economic historians had found it always to be.

First, England and France were industrialized and became subject to recurrent business fluctuations. As each new country swung into the industrial orbit—Germany prior to 1850, Japan after the Meiji restoration in the last half of the nineteenth century—one began to see its statistical indicators take on the common international rhythm. Even the non-industrialized regions felt the common pulse: the price accorded their raw material exports dropped in recession relative to the industrial goods they must import from the developed nations.

After World War II, it looked as if the common international cycle had been broken. A country could utilize its own Keynesian fiscal and monetary policies to determine its own fate. When the U.S. had a recession in 1953, Western Europe remained buoyant. When the Common Market countries began to run into slack times, Canada and the United States continued to enjoy prosperous business conditions.

Economists who had lived through both regimes preferred the diversification of the new postwar pattern. But just as some analysts were becoming rather complacent, there seemed to be a reversion back to the prewar lockstep.

Thus, in 1972 and early 1973, all over the world there was one exuberant boom. At one and the same time the production index was booming in Europe, Asia, Australasia, and the Americas. Japan and other nations were in the market competing for the scarce supplies of meat and of various raw materials. Countries like Indonesia and New Zealand found that there was brisk demand for whatever they had to sell: lumber, tin, natural gas, lamb, wool, oil, and so forth.

Then after the spring of 1973, and increasingly into 1974, the tide turned. All began to feel the pinch simultaneously. A country like Japan, which had felt recession in the last quarter-century only in the sense of slowing down from a 10 per cent annual rate of real growth to 4 per cent, suddenly found itself in 1974–1975 in an absolute decline.

**Exogenous inflation factors**   Harvests were intermittently bad throughout the 1970s. Corn fungus hit the Mississippi Valley. The Russians experienced a lack of snow cover for their wheat crop two years running, and had to come into the U.S. market for heavy 1972 and 1975 wheat purchases. This sent grain prices soaring. A drought in China and elsewhere in Asia cut down on the rice and grain crops there. The monsoons of India, upon which crops so much depend, were disappointing. The Sub-Sahara wilted from lack of rain.

As a result of these exogenous supply factors, inflationary pressure resulted at the same time in most parts of the world. This tends to raise $P$ in the equation $MV = PQ$. Fossil classical economists, who like Rip Van Winkle lived on into the modern era, completely misunderstood what was happening around them. To them, $P$ inflation is always and simply a question of what is happening to $M$. For this to have been still true, it would have had to be the case that as exogenous factors of supply raised the prices of food, fiber, metals, and energy generally, *other prices in the overall price level should have fallen in an offsetting way*—so as to keep the average $P$ unchanged. Most importantly, among the other prices that would have had to fall flexibly would have been the money wage level, $W$.

No matter how hard Rip Van Winkle looks around, he cannot today find a single mixed economy in which $W$ falls flexibly downward, even in the limited degree that it used to do during the great depressions of the 1930s and earlier decades.

If $P$ rises, what must give in the $MV = PQ$ identity? Or in the $C + I + G = PQ$ identity? Unless the Federal Reserve Bank, and the Central Banks generally in each country, permit the $M$ to rise in an offsetting way, exogenous forces tending to raise the average of the price level must induce a recessionary decline in $Q$. The fall in output is what we mean by recessionary stagnation; even its failure to grow must result, in a world of productivity increase and labor-force growth, in a rise in the unemployment rate.

The Federal Reserve is not a fourth branch of government, along with the Executive, Legislative and Judicial branches. No Central Bank rules as an absolute monarch, immune from the pressures of populist democracy or despotic dictatorship. The result is that $M$ is deliberately engineered to rise at rates not compatible with long-run price stability!

NOTE: there is *no erroneous forecasting* involved in this. Rather it is the working out of the contradictions that are involved in the increasing wage and price rigidities of the mixed economy.

We must survey the economics of price and wage rigidities that are at the heart of inflation dilemmas in the last quarter of the twentieth century.

## MICROFOUNDATIONS OF UNEMPLOYMENT AND INFLATION

In a perfect competitive market, price is always determined by the intersection of a supply and a demand schedule. There can be no overproduction or unemployment: The price or wage simply falls until the market is cleared. Recall Chapter 4's primer on supply and demand (or Chapter 20's development of that analysis). Again, Chapter 32's bird's-eye view of abstract *general equilibrium theory* generalized to any number of goods and factors this notion of *a perfect market clearing mechanism*. Leon Walras, the pioneer in mathematical economics, worked out a century ago the simplest model in which unemployment and overproduction is impossible in a system where all prices and wages float in order to reach simultaneous-equation solutions for all the relative prices and wages that will clear all markets. In such an abstract microeconomic model, the kind of unemployment that Keynes wrote about in his 1936 General Theory, and which the world was then experiencing in the Great Depression and which it continues in a degree to experience, such unemployment would be simply impossible.

Keynes' great breakthrough was to let the facts oust a beautiful but somewhat irrelevant theory. He could not present an elegant theory of price and wage rigidity that would explain exactly how unemployment and job vacancies are possible. So he simply assumed in an unexplained way that pricing would be such as to permit of a mismatch between job seekers and jobs, between the goods that firms want to sell and what they succeed in finding customers for.

Only in the last decade or so have economists devoted a great deal of time to the problem of imperfect information about job opportunities. Workers simply don't know whether if they accept this low-paying job, they will be depriving themselves of a better job that might be about to turn up. Even if a worker would like to get back to work for General Motors, there is no way that he can auction himself off on the market, offering to take less than the lucky ones who have kept their jobs, and thereby effectively managing to avoid his own unemployment. A bushel of graded wheat can always get itself sold on the Chicago Board of Trade. The price falls there to clear the market. Workers are not wheat. No two workers are alike. In the short run employers tend to name a wage scale at which they will hire a limited number of workers: Wage rates in a Chicago or Hanover, New Hampshire labor market do not float up or down so as to provide a perfect match of jobs and people.

The same is true, when you think about it, of the supply and demand for apartments. No two flats are exactly alike. No auction mechanism guarantees zero vacancies. It is even rational for some landlords to hold up their rental rates and accept several months of vacancy and no rental income, rather than cut the rate immediately; in the end there may come into view a tenant who will be willing to pay the higher rent.

The problem of search, information, and imperfect price adjustment is all the more complicated when human labor is involved. What you get in the way of Chapter 28's marginal product from a worker depends in part on what wage you pay him. If you cut his wage and he must still work for you, you do not necessarily thereby bring down your production costs and raise your profits. His morale may suffer and the product that emerges from his work may now be lower.[3] All these considerations are crucial in understanding the complexities of the so-called Phillips curve problem.

### THE PHILLIPS-CURVE TRADEOFF: FULL EMPLOYMENT OR PRICE STABILITY?

To understand conventional "demand-pull" inflation is easy in an idealized model where wages cannot rise so long as there is still one unemployed worker to keep down the wage rate. And in the same idealized model of demand-pull where goods are all auctioned off in perfectly competitive markets, there could be no general price rises so long as there is spare capacity available to produce more output at (marginal) costs no higher than the ruling prices.

**Simple demand-pull**   In such a model, begin with full employment, where the macro-economic managers have created just enough $C + I + G = MV$ spending to absorb all the full-employment output. If the managers now raise total spending by, say, 10 per cent, there will be more dollars of spending coming on the demand markets than can be supplied with goods at the previous equilibrium prices. We have engineered one of Chapter 13's so-called "inflationary gaps." Prices will then generally rise— ultimately by the 10 per cent needed to match the added $C + I + G$ spending. At the higher prices, employers will scramble to get more workers, bidding up wages ultimately also by 10 per cent (and thus leaving profits also higher by 10 per cent, but with all real or deflated wages being exactly the same as before).

In this first simplified model, demand has *pulled up* prices and wages.[4] Hence the repeated use of the name "demand-pull."

---

[3]The formula of Chapter 27, p. 544, "Wage Equals Marginal-Product of Labor," no longer applies in its simplest form. Readers of intermediate books on economics will find references there to writers on the new microfoundations of employment theory such as E. S. Phelps, A. A. Alchian, A. Leijon-hufvud, Robert E. Hall, and many others.

[4]Note that money wage rates have risen by 10 per cent more than productivity (which in our simple example has actually not changed at all) is rising. But that fact tells us nothing about the direction

**Simple cost-push**   Now become more realistic. Drop the notion that labor gets auctioned off at a flexible wage rate. Go to the other extreme. Suppose that by union power or by the strong pressure of custom in the nonunionized areas, wage rates always rise by 8 per cent per year regardless of the amount of unemployment. And, since we are not trying to be entirely realistic, suppose that labor productivity always rises by exactly 3 per cent per year. Then, if the employers can always administer their prices so as to keep the share of profit (or property return) unchanged—say, near the conventional one-fourth level—how will prices all rise?

By arithmetic, we find that prices must rise by 5 per cent per year—which is the 8 per cent wage rise minus the 3 per cent productivity rise. The real wage rate also rises by only the 3 per cent productivity rise—since the 8 per cent money-wage rise has the 5 per cent of price rise deflated out of it. The total *real* return to property owners has also risen by the 3 per cent change in average labor productivity—because the relative wage share stays at three-fourths.

Note that nothing at all has been said thus far about demand, about $C + I + G$ or $MV$ total spending. In this extreme cost-push model, demand has nothing to do with prices—which get set exclusively by wages and productivity. Prices rise at 5 per cent per year whether there is peace or war, recession or prosperity, tight or loose Federal Reserve and fiscal policy, a Chapter 13 inflationary or deflationary gap. What, then, is the role of demand in this paradoxical extreme model of simple cost-push?

Under extreme cost-push, demand has *no* effect on prices, $P$. It becomes completely a theory of output, $Q$, if $P$ is determined elsewhere. Demand can still determine how total $PQ$ = GNP behaves at all times; for these are simply other names for total $C + I + G$ or $MV$ spending (as we saw in Chapter 15's tautological "equation of exchange"). With $P$ in $PQ$ given, demand has only $Q$ to determine.

**Policy dilemma**   Let us examine the problems now created for the macroeconomic managers of fiscal and monetary policy.

If we began at full employment and money wage rates go up by 8 per cent instead of the 3 per cent of productivity growth, unless the macro managers engineer an increase in aggregate demand of 8 per cent—big enough to match the wage increase, which means big enough to finance the 5 per cent increase in $P$ and the 3 per cent increase in $Q$—full employment will ebb away. (Perhaps the union leaders and oligopolists were counting on the managers to create the needed increase in demand.)

Thus, suppose the macro managers wrongly think they are facing old-fashioned demand-pull inflation when actually they are facing simple cost-push. Logically, they might decide to hold total GNP demand constant. What will happen? Output and employment will drop by 8 per cent a year! First 1 man out of 12 will be unemployed;

---

of causation (which we know in this case definitely *not* to have been from wages as cause to prices as effect). Whenever prices are rising and the relative sharing of profits-to-wages is constant, as a matter of mere arithmetic, money wage rates must be outstripping average labor productivity by the amount of the price rise, with real wages merely matching the productivity rise. But, contrary to the confused arithmetic of conservative financial columnists, when real wages are thus advancing in line with average labor productivity, that does not mean that labor is "appropriating" or absorbing *all* the fruits of technological progress (which admittedly may have come from better machines and management methods as well as from greater worker effort or skill). It merely means that profit receivers and labor *share* in progress on same terms as before—say, at the usual $(\frac{1}{4}, \frac{3}{4})$ fractions.

then 2; . . .; and if the irresistible force of cost-push meets the immovable object of macroeconomic policy, in the end the system will run down to literally nothing, with the last starving man losing his job and dying out. This is not a very tenable outcome, so no doubt the macro managers will drop their stubbornness and will create enough money spending to countenance the creeping inflation *indefinitely*.

**Neither simple pole**    It is too bad that the simple demand-pull model is not realistic, for under it the job of the macro managers would be the easy one of turning on or off the faucets of fiscal and monetary policy to keep employment just full. Yet it is fortunate that the nightmare of *simple* cost-push is also not realistic, for in it there is simply no control of inflation or influence that the macro managers can contrive.

**The real world is somewhere between the two extremes. The amount of unemployment does in some degree hold down the excess of money wage increase over productivity increase. Budget surpluses and open-market sales—all the weapons in Part Two's macro arsenal to control $C + I + G$ or $MV$ total spending—can now have some effect on price and wage inflation (but, alas, at the same time an effect on output).**

Thus, when the Vietnam war caused a rise in spending that was not offset by determined tight-enough budgetary and Federal Reserve policy, there was a quickening in the rate of price inflation; from 1965 to 1968, we had mostly demand-pull inflation; and it was nonunion wages that rose first and fastest. But demand-pull for three years led inevitably to cost-push in subsequent years 1969 through 1971, and again in 1974–1975.

In some ways the macro managers are thrown into the most perplexing of all possible worlds. They are neither in the easy world of simple demand-pull nor the hopeless world of simple cost-push where they can do nothing about the rate of inflation. They are in the difficult world where the attempt to bring a 10 per cent rate of inflation down to 3 per cent may, at least in the short run, necessitate a retardation of real growth like that of 1969–1971 or 1974–1975, with rising unemployment, ghetto unrest, and all the wastes of a growing gap between our achieved and potential GNP.

**The Phillips curve**    The late A. W. Phillips, formerly of the London School of Economics and the Australian National University, made a pioneering attempt to quantify the tradeoff relationship between unemployment and price-wage rises. Figure 41-2 pictures the typical downward-sloping Phillips curve, in which as you move leftward to reduce unemployment, then the rate of price and wage creep along the curve becomes higher.

On the diagram's horizontal axis is the percentage of unemployment. On the black left-hand vertical scale is the algebraic percentage change per annum in average prices; on the right-hand orange scale is the accompanying percentage change in money wage rates per hour. These two scales differ only by the postulated amount of productivity increase per year (so that the price change of 5 per cent per year would correspond to a wage change of 8 per cent per year if productivity grew by 3 per cent per year and its fruits were shared in the same old proportions by labor and nonlabor).[5]

Be it noted that the $MV$ and $C + I + G$ approaches to aggregate dollar spending are still applicable *offstage*, but one needs the information of the Phillips curve to

---

[5] A higher rate of productivity growth will show itself in an equal downward shift of the orange curve and scale. Thus, with productivity growing at 6 per cent per year, an 8 per cent wage increase would correspond to only a 2 per cent annual price rise. A profit squeeze could be similarly shown.

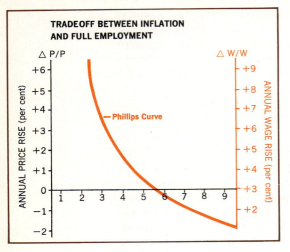

**TRADEOFF BETWEEN INFLATION AND FULL EMPLOYMENT**

**FIG. 41-2**

**The Phillips curve depicts the crucial tradeoff between degree of unemployment and wage-price creep**

Orange wage-change scale on right-hand vertical axis is higher than black left-hand price-change scale by assumed 3 per cent rate of average productivity growth. The greater is unemployment on the horizontal axis, the lower is rate of price inflation. In recent decades, the U.S. Phillips curve seems to have twisted higher to the right. This means more unemployment is needed to hold inflation down now than used to be the case (or than may be the case in, say, Germany).

translate the resulting product $P \times Q$ into its separate components. In simple demand-pull,[6] the Phillips curve would be a vertical line at the minimal unemployment level: $Q$ would then always correspond to full employment, and $P$ would float in free labor markets to whatever level total money spending would determine. In simple cost-push the Phillips curve is a horizontal line, with no level of unemployment leading to price stability. By contrast, the real-life curve slopes downward somewhere in between.

**The Phillips curve depicts the tradeoff between unemployment and price-wage inflation in each short run.**

[6]Note the difference between the realistic Phillips curve and the way it would look in the cases

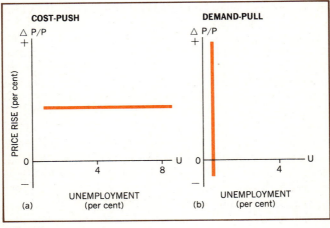

**FIG. 41-3**

of simple demand-pull and simple cost-push. In simple cost-push, Fig. 41-3(a) shows the curve to be completely horizontal with no tradeoff possible. Figure 41-3(b) shows the curve becoming completely vertical in simple demand-pull, with no tradeoff being necessary. [Actually, in Fig. 41-3(a), if the macro managers insisted on boosting demand faster than the indicated wage rise, they would push the system to such minimal unemployment as to cause a frantic bidding up by employers of the market wage rate *above* the wage administered by the unions; and this gives rise to what in Scandinavia has been called the "wage drift," in which wages always run ahead of the minima set by collective bargaining. This means the horizontal curve really ceases to be horizontal when you move near to the vertical axis.]

The Phillips curve is a dramatic way of describing the dilemma for macro policy, even though it does not go beyond description to give us "explanation." Thus, the problem is posed: How can a mixed economy supplement monetary and fiscal macro policy by an incomes policy *designed to give itself a better Phillips curve?* Better in what sense? Better in the sense that it will permit us to enjoy a lower minimum level of unemployment at which the system can avoid undue price inflation.

**Longer run**   Before grappling with the hard problems of policy, we should reemphasize that economics is not an exact science. The data will not really fit any one two-variable Phillips curve perfectly. More important still is the fact that the measured Phillips curves represent *short-term* relationships that will definitely shift in the longer run.

Thus, if Eisenhower runs a slack economy for many years of the fifties, that may kill off inflationary expectations and slow down wage demands. In short, much unemployment, long maintained, may gradually *shift* the short-term Phillips curve leftward. Then, when a Kennedy comes along, he may be lucky enough to cash in on the Eisenhower "investment in sadism" by being able to engineer in the 1960s a long growth in $C + I + G$ before prices and wages misbehave badly.

By the same reasoning, after more than 100 months of uninterrupted expansion, and particularly as the result of Vietnam spending, continued low unemployment may shift the short-term Phillips curve rightward, making the policy problems of the 1970s that much harder. A vicious circle follows: As people fear and expect price inflation, they shift upward their effective Phillips curves and bring on stagflation—unemployment and inflation. And years of retardation, as in the early 1970s, may be needed before inflationary momentum is overcome.

## WANTED: AN INCOMES POLICY

Now turn from analysis to the pressing problems of policy for the mixed economy. Not only has the United States not learned how to avoid having to make compromises between price stability and full employment, but neither have the other leading nations. How to resolve the dilemma of tradeoff between inflation and unemployment, review of experience shows, is still an open question in Switzerland and Sweden, Germany and Japan, Holland and Italy, France and Britain.

1. *Stop-go driving* of the British economy has proved ineffective in controlling inflation; and it has exacted a cruel price in terms of productivity and living standards.

2. *Peacetime wage-price controls* have been extensively used in Scandinavia, the Netherlands, and elsewhere. Although in the short run they have sometimes been effective—Finland in 1967–1971 being a notable case, and America in 1971–1973 perhaps another—in the longer run such controls have either blown up or have been allowed to become ineffective by attrition.

3. *Quasi-governmental wage-price guideposts* proved better than nothing in the Netherlands, and also in the United States during the Kennedy-Johnson years. But with time they tended to become ineffective and inequitable, particularly when not ac-

companied by fiscal and monetary policy successful in keeping down excessive demand-pull spending. Nixon's Phase III revived voluntary guidelines in 1973.

4. *Government to get tough with unions,* has frequently been urged by employers. Such talk is easy. But in practice, as the United Kingdom's Heath government learned in the early 1970s, this often serves only to exacerbate class conflicts, encourage strikes and slowdowns, and make for recalcitrant union demands.

5. *Collective bargaining to take place between one vast association of employers and one vast association of all unions? And with the government sitting in as a referee?* Something like this has long been in effect in Scandinavia and the Netherlands. But after initial years of success, there finally resulted wage blowoffs of 10 per cent a year and more, and steadily creeping domestic price levels.[7]

Moreover, if a heterogeneous country like the United States is concerned, who in American life could possibly speak for all of American labor, to say nothing of all of American industry? President George Meany of the AFL-CIO? He is only the head of a federation set up for public relations and government-lobbying purposes. Meany cannot compel a national union or a local union to make one wage settlement rather than another. On the employers' side, neither the National Association of Manufacturers (NAM) nor the United States Chamber of Commerce could negotiate for any industry, much less all industry. Within particular industries, say the auto industry, no one committee can bind Ford, GM, and Chrysler to wage agreements.

**Open inflation?**   All the above cures for creeping inflation have been advocated, and in every possible combination. In despair, some economists ask:

What's so bad about creeping inflation anyway? It is better than mass unemployment and excess industrial capacity. Moreover, by various sliding scales in wage contracts, and government bonds of *guaranteed real purchasing power,* the human burdens of unanticipated inflation can be substantially reduced.

Undoubtedly such a solution is better than a masochistic throttling down of the economy that puts the burden for fighting inflation on the marginal workers who can least afford to bear that burden—young workers, minority workers, female workers, unskilled workers.

But will the rate of inflation accelerate once you stop fighting it? Skeptics warn:

The system does not really have a permanent choice between less-unemployment-cum-more-price-inflation and more-unemployment-cum-less-price-inflation. It has a choice only between less unemployment *now* at the cost of more unemployment *later.* It all comes out in the

---

[7] Lloyd Ulman and J. Flanagan, in *Wage Restraint; A Study of Incomes Policies in Western Europe* (University of California Press, Berkeley, 1971), give the rather pessimistic summary: "Incomes policy, to generalize from the experience of the [seven] countries studied in this account, has not been very successful. . . . [A]ccumulation of experience . . . suggests that in none of the variations so far turned up has incomes policy succeeded in its fundamental objective, as stated, of making full employment consistent with a reasonable degree of price stability." However, it should be noted that although the domestic price levels have grown more rapidly abroad than here, this has taken place *at lower average levels of unemployment there.* (Also, a dual price system—more stable export prices along with rising domestic prices—has been maintained in many foreign countries.)

long-run wash![8] There is a law of conservation of unemployment in any economy: If you get rid of unemployment now, you will only get the same amount later. [See footnote 8's Fig. 41-4(b).]

No conclusive evidence establishing so definite a view has yet been forthcoming. And, even if this pessimistic view were to have an element of truth, no doubt many would argue that, in an uncertain world, it is better to grasp the lower unemployment that can be had at hand than wait for the lower unemployment that, so to speak, can be found only in some future bush.

Still, extensive studies of mixed economies justify the following observation.

**Keeping unemployment in a mixed economy down below some critical region does result in a *tendency* for the rate of creeping inflation to become a canter or even a gallop. To avoid accelerating inflation, one must find new tools of incomes policy to *shift* Phillips-curve tradeoffs, short-run and long-run, and not merely turn on the steam of fiscal and monetary policy to move the system along unchanged Phillips curves that look temporarily appealing.**

[8]Some try to define a long-run Phillips curve from the systematic shiftings of the short-run curves (in much the same way that Fig. 20-5 was able to depict long-run Marshallian supply curves from systematically shifting short-run supply curves). The long-run Phillips curve tends to be twisted clockwise, as in Fig. 41-4(a). There is even one strong theory, suggested by W. Fellner and H. Wallich of Yale, M. Friedman of Chicago, and E. Phelps of Columbia, which in effect says: "The Phillips tradeoff is based only on the *illusion* of *unanticipated* price-wage inflation. Once the system settles down to any constant rate of price-wage inflation, people will come to learn the fact and to expect it in the future. So you will then have just as much excess wage pressure over that constant rate as you had when prices were stable. There is really a 'natural rate of unemployment,' defined by a vertical long-run Phillips curve as shown in Fig. 41-4(b). If you temporarily bring unemployment below the natural rate, your short-term curves will twist upward indefinitely and your price rise will accelerate; if you temporarily bring unemployment above the natural rate (the Nixon rather than Kennedy pattern), the short-term curves will there twist downward indefinitely and your price rise will decelerate. In order for people to be adjusted to the rate of price change so that it will not be accelerating or decelerating, you have to be *on the long-run vertical line*." These writers conclude: "Since you will be stuck with the natural rate of unemployment in the long run anyway, the macro managers should keep demand growing at only the rate of real growth of the system—say, 3 to 4 per cent per year so that $P$s will be steady. To reduce unemployment's natural rate, policies other than macro fiscal and monetary measures are needed—such as repealing minimum-wage laws or restrictive union practices." Critics of these writers say that by the time *their* proposed equilibrium is reached, the system may well have been torn apart by voter revolt, urban riots, and unemployment-induced hardships and dissatisfactions. And besides, the data of experience are not yet available to judge whether Fig. 41-4(a) or 41-4(b) is the more realistic.

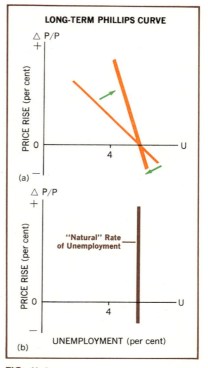

FIG. 41-4

## REDUCING STRUCTURAL UNEMPLOYMENT FOR BETTER PHILLIPS CURVES

Agreement will be found among labor-market experts on the following programs to lower the sustainable rate of unemployment.

1. *Manpower training programs and improved labor-market mechanisms* so that the unskilled can qualify for jobs available, and those with obsolete skills can retread themselves. Better communication concerning job vacancies and regional relocation programs, both for workers and for industries, could also help.

2. *Reduction of discrimination* against particular classes in the labor force on the side of employers and co-workers, and *increased realism* on the side of would-be workers concerning the remunerations and qualifications relevant to viable employment opportunities. In particular, some flexibility in minimum wage rates for the young and handicapped, if such can be found without undermining competitive standard rates, would help improve the Phillips curve and bring down high unemployment rates.

Subject to more controversy, but still increasingly favored by many economists, is a program *to make the government the employer of last resort* for job seekers.

## THE HUMANE ECONOMY

Thoughtful economists increasingly are impressed with a fundamental diagnosis of what lies at the base of the whole problem of stagflation. They fervently hope their diagnosis is wrong, because it is so fundamental as to go to the very heart of the mixed economy, the modern welfare state.

**The root cause of the increasing bias toward rising prices rather than stable prices lies in the fact that we no longer run the cruel economy that was taken for granted in the days of unbridled laissez faire.**

Capitalism was often an efficient system. But it was a system in which he who would not work had to starve. Little children had the bowlegs of rickets because their fathers were drunkards, or neurotics, or had deserted their families, or were simply unlucky in the struggle for jobs when total unemployment was large. The system made unemployment so uncomfortable that people would walk a dozen miles per day to earn a pittance if necessary.

Today we will not tolerate such limits of cruelty. Today we have unemployment compensation, severance pay, public service employment, welfare-assistance support if not yet a negative income tax. Few would be willing to turn the clock back to the old ruthless regime of pure capitalism. Yet, one must be prepared to recognize that, along with the humane advantages of the new order, there may come new laws of behavior of price and wage flexibility. *Larger and larger amounts of unemployment are needed today to have the same wage and price restraining effect as in the past.* And so, in a vicious circle, the modern mixed economy finds itself having larger and larger amounts of unemployment.

What is the moral? Start being cruel? Refuse to recognize that each new reform has, along with its benefits, some costs? Neither of these alternatives is really open to one. The moral, I would think, is to persevere in trying to find structural reforms that will retain and augment humanitarianism while at the same time hoping to encourage the system to behave more like the market-clearing mechanism that experience shows is conducive to both efficiency and stability.

The task of political economy is never done.

## SUMMARY

1  Back in the days of laissez faire, when Queen Victoria reigned from Windsor Castle and William McKinley dozed in the White House, there may have been some validity to the fear that capitalism would intermittently suffer from underconsumption and shortage of overall purchasing power. The view of Lenin and Luxemburg that capitalism's inadequacies of markets could be cured only by desperate imperialistic foreign investments and warlike expenditures may then have had some occasional truth in it. But whatever their merits then, in the age *after* Keynes, every mixed economy has the effective knowledge and ability to utilize monetary and fiscal policies to create—by useful peacetime expenditures—a sufficiency of overall purchasing power. $M$ creation and fiscal deficits have succeeded all over the globe in banishing fear of chronic depression. The problem remaining is of a new kind—cost-push inflation and stagflation.

2  The distinction between demand-pull inflation ("demanders' inflation") and cost-push "stagflation" ("sellers' inflation") is crucial. Old-fashioned demand-pull inflation can be controlled by proper dosage of monetary and fiscal policy—central-bank or Federal Reserve policy and budgetary spending-taxing policies.

3  In modern cost-push inflation, prices and wages do not float to clear all markets. They begin to creep upward *even before* employment is full and industrial capacity fully utilized. To clamp down on monetary and fiscal policy to fight such inflation will only result in unemployment and stagnation. But not to act is to accept creeping inflation that may accelerate into a canter or gallop.

4  The Phillips curve relates the tradeoff between price inflation and the degree of unemployment in the system—by its position in the short run, and also by its induced shiftings in the longer run. Thus, suppose that at unemployment levels below 5 per cent, money wage rates always rise 4 per cent faster than the 3 per cent productivity growth of the system; then the price level will creep forward at 4 per cent as corporations pass on the cost increases and maintain their profit margins. We have a case of sellers' inflation.

5  An "incomes policy" is needed to supplement fiscal and monetary policy—in order *to give the mixed economy a better Phillips curve*. But it remains an unsolved problem of modern economics to get experts to agree on an incomes policy: benign neglect, governmental guideposts (voluntary or quasi-voluntary), direct wage-price controls, centralized collective bargaining, stop-go driving of the economy to cool it down, manpower and retraining programs to lower the natural level and range of structural unemployment—all these are studied to retain the humane qualities of the modern order while achieving efficiency and stability.

# CONCEPTS FOR REVIEW

peace and prosperity or
   antislump imperialism
post-Keynes macroeconomics
   monetary policy (Federal $M$
   supply and interest policy)
   fiscal policy (taxes and $G$
   in $C + I + G$)
floating $P$ to clear markets
synchronous or independent cycles

exogenous price forces
stagflation (inflation-cum-stagnation)
cost-push (sellers') inflation
   versus demand-pull inflation
Phillips-curve tradeoff dilemma
incomes-policy debate: guideposts
   and price-wage controls
improved labor-market structure
humaneness cum flexibility

# QUESTIONS FOR DISCUSSION

1   Can modern capitalism "afford peace?"

2   "Colonial America, like the Confederacy, lacked taxing capacity. So the Revolutionary and the Civil Wars had to be financed by demand-pull inflation." Explain.

3   "Unemployment is high in the construction industries in 1976, but wage rates are rising in many regions by 10 per cent per year." Show that this is cost-push (sellers') inflation rather than demand-pull in a labor-auction market.

4   Describe an auction world in which all prices and wages float to clear *all* markets. (*a*) Would macropolicy be easier in such a world? Why? (*b*) What would be effects of $I$ or $G$ fluctuations in such a world? Of $M$ fluctuations on $MV = PQ$ in such a world?

5   What is a Phillips curve? What is on its horizontal axis? On its vertical axis, or better, axes? Why is it good to get the curve shifted to the left and down? Why might low unemployment now cause it to rotate clockwise (as in footnote 8, p. 835)?

6   Explain what is meant by "incomes policy." Debate the alternative proposals.

7   Can mere science in political economy provide the same answer on the degree to which we should compromise between the evils of unemployment and of inflation for (*a*) Congresswoman Shirley Chisholm, who represents slum dwellers in Brooklyn, and (*b*) the Congressman for the elderly in Florida.

8   Will the 1984 price index be lower or higher than now? Defend your view.

9   "Cost-push inflation due to $W$-$P$ rigidity and bad Phillips curve tradeoffs is *not* inconsistent with $C + I + G \equiv MV = PQ$ Keynesianism or monetarism. Why not? Because bad behavior of $P$ would result in unemployment and low $Q$ if the electorate did not insist on expansionary macropolicies to expand $G$ and $M$, whatever the consequences for future $P$ trends." Explain.

42

Up 'til now the philosophers have only interpreted the world in various ways. The point, though, is to *change* it!
KARL MARX
*Theses on Feuerbach* (1845)

Political economy is about the economic system, not about economists. To fail to realize this is to make the mistake Edward Gibbon was accused of when writing the *Decline and Fall of the Roman Empire:* namely, that sometimes Gibbon was unable to distinguish between himself and the Roman Empire.

At the end of a long book, though, we may perhaps indulge ourselves with a brief excursion into the history and present status of economics as a scholarly discipline and as a chapter in the intellectual history of mankind. We can do this with a better conscience in light of the fact that such a survey of the ivory tower will enable us to understand better the real economic events outside its windows.

For, as we saw in the opening chapter, there is an irreducible subjectivity inherent in every objective science. How we are able to perceive the economic system must depend crucially on the quality of the spectacles through which we look at it. Once a student of economics knows how the theories he now fervently believes in grew out of the past, he may be better prepared for the modifications that they will assuredly undergo in the future.[1]

## PREHISTORY OF ECONOMICS

Like a baby, political economy was taking shape even before it was born. The family tree of economics, shown on the back flyleaf can, with pardonable exaggeration, declare political economy to be but two centuries old; *The Wealth of Nations* (1776) of Adam Smith (1723–1790) can be taken as providing its birthday.

---

[1]Good introductions to the history of political economy are Robert L. Heilbroner, *The Worldly Philosophers* (Simon and Schuster, Inc., New York, 1953), or Eric Roll, *A History of Economic Thought* (Prentice-Hall, Englewood Cliffs, N.J., 1972). The standard advanced reference is the posthumous classic, Joseph A. Schumpeter, *History of Economic Analysis* (Oxford University Press, New York, 1957).

839

From its earliest beginnings, political economy was concerned with policy. Thus, both Testaments of the Bible warn against interest or usury, as do Aristotle and St. Thomas Aquinas. The predecessors of Adam Smith, the Mercantilists, were advisers to the prince, in their orientation not unlike the modern Council of Economic Advisers or the economists of the Bank of England. When the Mercantilists favored protective tariffs, it was in the sincere belief, however misguided, that these would add to the nation's prosperity.

The expression "the greatest good for the greatest number" appears and reappears long before Jeremy Bentham (1748–1832) subjected every institution in England to ruthless scrutiny in terms of its social utility; the expression was already in Machiavelli and other early writers. Adam Smith's contemporaries on the continent, the Physiocrats, who believed in a circular flow of economic life based on the primacy of land, were men of the Enlightenment, *philosophes* hopeful to reform the *ancien régime* of prerevolutionary France.

People babbled prose long before there were English teachers. The first contributors to economic analysis were certainly not professional economists. Copernicus, the astronomer, enunciated the Quantity Theory of Money and Prices—just as did John Locke, the philosopher. (Locke also formulated the labor theory of value.) David Hume (1711–1776) earned his living as a philosopher and historian; only in passing did he make his great contribution to the understanding of the automatic regulation of the gold standard by the corrective flow of specie, with resulting effects on price levels that served to correct the imbalance of trade. (Hume also formulated the theory of land rent and recognized inflation's stimulus to business activity.) John Law, one of the first to try to bring on prosperity by priming the pump of money creation, was a Scottish adventurer moved to France—as much rogue and confidence man as scholar. Richard Cantillon was an international merchant, one of the many early writers who was not without a commercial interest in the doctrines he was espousing.

## CLASSICAL ECONOMICS: SMITH THE PROPHET OF LAISSEZ FAIRE

Not only were the earliest economists interested in policy; they were even too crudely eager to interfere. It is Adam Smith's greatest contribution that he glimpsed in the social world of economics what Isaac Newton (1642–1727) had recognized in the physical world of the heavens: a self-regulating *natural order*. Smith's message said:

You think you are helping the economic system by your well-meaning laws and interferences. You are not. Let be. The oil of self-interest will keep the gears working in almost miraculous fashion. No one need plan. No sovereign need rule. The market will answer all things.

Adam Smith was far from being a cold geometer. He was not merely stating the syllogism of the Invisible Hand in the fashion of a high school teacher stating the Pythagorean theorem, when he enunciated his famous words:

. . . every individual . . . neither intends to promote the public interest . . . he intends only his own gain, and he is in this, as in many other cases, led by an invisible hand to promote an end which was no part of his intention. [*The Wealth of Nations*, Book IV, Chap. II]

Smith never did *prove* the truth of this. Indeed, as late as the time when the present writer was an undergraduate, no one yet knew how to prove—or even state properly!—the kernel of truth in Smith's doctrine of the Invisible Hand. *What Smith did do in his great book was to enumerate empirically countless cases of follies by government.* He raided all ancient and contemporary history for telling illustrations of the harms from well-meaning governmental regulations.

His book is a masterpiece. It has magisterial style. It is a veritable handbook that could as well be entitled: *How to Make the GNP Grow.* And withal, it lays the foundations for the general equilibrium of supply and demand.

**Spirit of the Bourgeois Age**    But, of course, its many excellences cannot explain why *The Wealth of Nations* had so dramatic an impact on the century to follow. In a real sense, the rising bourgeois class needed a spokesman for their interests. Smith provided them with the ideology that served their purpose. Equally important, his ideology of laissez faire fed their self-esteem and moral needs. By minding his shop, the merchant of Manchester could know he was both doing God's will and helping the King's realm.

None of this is to imply that Smith was a flunky to the establishment. Actually, he had a healthy distrust of businessmen (saying, for example, "People of the same trade seldom meet together, even for merriment and diversion, but the conversation ends in a conspiracy against the public, or in some contrivance to raise prices"). Smith was definitely for the common man. But he was convinced, as so many economists have been since, that the road to hell is paved with good intentions. The attempt by government to keep masters from conspiring in monopolies would probably, he thought, make a bad situation worse rather than better. Smith's very eclecticism and pragmatism added to the persuasiveness of his *Weltanschauung*.

## CLASSICAL ECONOMICS: AUTUMN FOR MALTHUS AND RICARDO

In the half-century after *The Wealth of Nations*, the law of diminishing returns was discovered. Ironically, just as the Industrial Revolution was offsetting for the Western world the dire workings of that dismal law, the Reverend T. R. Malthus (1766–1834) enunciated the theory that growth of population is bound always to reduce workers' wages to the margin of bare subsistence.

The key figure of the age, however, is not so much Malthus as David Ricardo (1772–1823). To few writers is there given the luck of a Robert Frost, who appeals both to the lowbrow and the high. David Ricardo is one of those lucky few. The classical, neoclassical, and post-Keynesian scholars all trace their ancestry through his family line. And so too do the writers of Marxian socialism. We shall see that Karl Marx had little use for the vulgar bourgeois economists of the classical school. Ricardo, however, is a charmed exception, the master from whom Marx thought truth could be developed.

David Ricardo never went to college. Born to an affluent family of Spanish-Dutch Jews who had migrated to England, he was cut off by his father with £800 for having married outside his faith. Within 12 years, he retired from being a stockbroker with a nest egg in the millions. When already established and affluent, he chanced to read Adam Smith. Fascinated, Ricardo believed that there were basic errors in Smith's analysis and also gaps in his macroeconomic writings. But for the insistent advice of James Mill, father of the precocious John Stuart Mill (1806–1873), Ricardo would have been no more than a pamphlet writer and Member of Parliament for a rotten borough. But the elder Mill browbeat Ricardo into writing his *Principles of Political Economy and Taxation* (1817), and Ricardo's fame was made.[2]

Such is the subtlety of Ricardo's logic and the obscurity of his style that he stands in some danger of being overrated, both in comparison with Smith and Keynes, and with such contemporaries as Malthus, J. S. Mill, and such later writers as Jevons, Walras, Marshall, and Wicksell. George J. Stigler, who is if anything partial to Ricardian economics, has justly observed that Ricardo's logic "was severe in its simplifications rather than superlative in its rigor."

The vices as well as the virtues of classical economics stand out in Ricardo. He maintained an overly simple, and empty, version of Say's Law, according to which supply always creates its own demand and no problem of over- or under-saving is ever conceivable. He stated results valid for the long run as if they were valid for the short. He vacillated in blowing hot and cold over the labor theory of value. His example encouraged lesser economists to try to make economics a nonempirical, purely deductive science. Many will agree with Jevons and Keynes that David Ricardo shunted economics onto the wrong track.

**Stagnant wage predictions and class oppositions** From 1820 to 1870, full half a century, Ricardo kept economists and statesmen hypnotized. Like Malthus, he bet on the wrong horse of diminishing returns, just when the Industrial Revolution was bypassing and offsetting that law. In the century that was to come, when the landowner was in fact withering away in importance (recall Part Four's quoted findings of Denison that land rent has dropped to less than 5 per cent of modern GNP!), Ricardo's vision was that rents would rise and unaugmentable land form the bottleneck to economic growth.

This autumn view of the economy—inevitably on its way to a rendezvous with poverty for most people—was what the man in the street and the men of the world took from Ricardo. Equally important:

**To Ricardo the most important thing in economics was the *laws of distribution* of the national product among the great classes of society: wages for workers, profits for capitalists, and rents for landowners. With a total social pie limited in its growth, what went to one social class had to be taken away from another.**

No wonder the capitalists liked Ricardo. They could glean texts from him to prove that trade-unions and reforms can accomplish little for the masses. No wonder the socialists liked Ricardo. They found in him the demonstration that capitalism would have to be destroyed if workers were to get their right to the whole product. Ironically, that same self-interest that Smith and Ricardo presupposed was, in the twentieth century, to lead the proletariat, as if by "an Invisible Hand," to the ballot box—to wrest for themselves through government action a larger share of the GNP.

---

[2] One of the great feats of scholarship of our times is the many-volume edition by Piero Sraffa, for the Royal Economic Society, of *The Works and Correspondence of David Ricardo* (Cambridge University Press, Cambridge, England, 1953).

**Decadence**   Thomas Kuhn, in his history of the physical sciences, *The Structure of Scientific Revolutions* (University of Chicago Press, Chicago, 1962, 1970), analyzes how science progresses discontinuously. An old school dies. A new school is born. It has new models and theories—new "paradigms," in Kuhn's terminology. The new school explains a wide range of facts to its satisfaction.

But schools, like people, are subject to hardening of the arteries. Students learn the embalmed truth from their teachers and sacred textbooks. The travail in which the new ideas were born is lost to view. The imperfections in the orthodox doctrines are glossed over as unimportant, if indeed they even continue to be noticed.

Decadence if not senility had set in. Thus, John Stuart Mill, himself important in areas other than technical economics (and underrated within that area of economics), could write in his middle-of-the-nineteenth-century classic, *Principles of Political Economy:* "Happily, there is nothing in the laws of Value which remains for the present and any future writer to clear up . . . ."

The time had come for new blood.

## NEOCLASSICAL ECONOMICS

Just a century ago the tree of economics bifurcated. One branch led through neo-classical economics and Keynesian economics to the present-day era of post-Keynesian mainstream economics. The other branch stemmed from Marx's *Das Kapital* (1867, 1885, 1894) and from his rediscovered earlier writings in economics.

Classical writers had emphasized cost, to the neglect of utility and demand. It was as if they had been working with horizontal *ss* curves and neglecting all *dd* curves. Around 1870, three men simultaneously and independently laid the foundations for a more symmetric, general-equilibrium analysis that could synthesize both utility and disutility elements: W. Stanley Jevons (1835–1882) in England; Carl Menger (1840–1921) in Austria; and Leon Walras (1834–1910), a Frenchman unable to get a professorial chair except in Lausanne, Switzerland.

**Utility, marginalism, general equilibrium**   The neoclassical revolution was important not merely because it discovered how to analyze demand and utility preferences. In addition, it generalized the marginal notions present in primitive form in Ricardo's theory of rent. Finally, particularly in the deep mathematical analysis of Leon Walras, the analysis of general equilibrium was achieved.

The late Joseph Schumpeter (1883–1950) used to say that of all great economists, surely Walras was the greatest, since it was he who discovered general equilibrium. It was Lagrange, "the Shakespeare of mathematics," who said: "Of all scientists Newton was surely the greatest. For it was he who discovered the system of the world. And, alas, there is but one system of the world to be discovered." Schumpeter apparently felt that Walras was also lucky as well as great, since there is only one system of general economic equilibrium to be discovered.

**Policy concerns**   As political economy became more "scientific," it never lost its interest in policy. Most of the great economists tell us in their autobiographies that they became economists in order to do good. Still, it is true that after a man has been a professor of economics for a lifetime, he tends to become more cautious in his belief that this measure or that will end up fulfilling its promise to improve the common lot. With age comes a preoccupation with "feasibility." It is perhaps this, more than the tendency to become reactionary as one gains honors and comfortable position in the class structure, that explains the cooling off of the socialistic ardors of the English Alfred Marshall (1842–1924) or the American John Bates Clark (1847–1938).

An even more interesting case is that of the great Scandinavian economist, Knut Wicksell (1851–1926). Wicksell failed to win an academic chair until he was almost fifty. He was a premature counterculture bohemian who would not in principle agree to the sacrament of marriage with his wife. In the end, even though he thought it meant he would not get the chair his family finances so desperately needed, Wicksell could not bring himself to address the King of Sweden formally as "Your Majesty." Fortunately, "Dear Sir" got him the job.

Wicksell believed in birth control, heresy in the 1870s. He disbelieved, publicly, in the Virgin Birth and wrote a book from jail after a blasphemy conviction. When the Czar's army stood on the Swedish borders, Wicksell advised his countrymen to dismantle their army. Though he never hesitated to speak out in behalf of unpopular causes, Wicksell's recommendations to reform society were essentially an anticipation of the Swedish welfare state, with its income redistribution and transfer benefits. His was a calculated rejection of traditional socialism as an unpromising path to the better society.

**Monopolistic-competition paradigm**    What is today called microeconomics was increasingly developed by the neoclassical writers. Belatedly, by the early 1930s, the turn-of-the-century burgeoning of monopolies and imperfect competition became absorbed within the paradigm of neoclassical economics.[3] Particularly in America, and to a degree in Germany, empirical studies of patterns of competition and industrial organization flourished. Labor markets and union activity were studied intensively.

**Mathematical economics and econometrics**    Jevons, Walras, and Vilfredo Pareto (1848–1923) had already introduced mathematics into economics. But after 1930, this activity underwent a rebirth.[4]

Econometric measurement, involving the tools of modern probability and statistics and special techniques appropriate to a nonexperimental domain like economics, represents a prominent feature of our times. Also, quantitative measurement came to give economic history a new focus. National-income growth was studied by such masters as Simon Kuznets, Colin Clark, and Edward Denison. Economic historians ("cliometricians") studying the economics of slavery and of the revolution in railroad transportation utilized the most sophisticated tools of the economic analyst.

[3] E. H. Chamberlin, *The Theory of Monopolistic Competition* (Harvard University Press, Cambridge, Mass., 1933, 1962), and Joan Robinson, *The Economics of Imperfect Competition* (Macmillan, London, 1933), are the standard references. But both writers built on earlier work of Cournot (1838), J. M. Clark (1923), Sraffa (1926), and many other contemporary writers.

[4] Writers from many countries led the wave: Ragnar Frisch, Trygve Haavelmo, and Leif Johansen from Norway; Jan Tinbergen and Henri Theil from Holland; J. R. Hicks and R. G. D. Allen from England; M. Allais and E. Malinvaud from France; migrants to America such as J. von Neumann, T. Koopmans, J. Marshack, L. Hurwicz, and G. Debreu; American-trained economists such as Harold Hotelling, the present author, K. J. Arrow, R. M. Solow, R. Radner, H. Scarf, H. Kuhn, D. Gale, and J. Tobin. The present list could be doubled and redoubled in length, going back to the 1838 classic of A. A. Cournot and including the turn-of-the-century writers F. Y. Edgeworth, Philip Wicksteed, L. von Bortkiewicz, G. Cassel, and others.

## THE KEYNESIAN REVOLUTION

In the years after World War I, political economy made great strides in describing and analyzing the economic world of both less developed and developed regions. One thing, however, had long been lacking. Although Wesley Mitchell, Alvin Hansen, and many Continental writers, such as Arthur Spiethoff, had gone far in describing the business cycle, neoclassical economics was handicapped in that it lacked a developed macroeconomics to match its almost overdeveloped microeconomics.

Finally, with the Great Depression came the breakthrough of the *General Theory of Employment, Interest and Money* (Macmillan, London, 1936) by John Maynard Keynes. Economics could never be the same again. The simple-minded belief in Say's Law was banished. Even the neoclassical theories of money and the price level, which had already been developed by Marshall, Wicksell, and Yale's Irving Fisher (1867–1947), were capable of being given a more fruitful restatement in terms of the Keynesian concepts. Ironically, even the theory of full employment was capable of being demonstrated more validly in terms of the Keynesian innovations—as the pre-Keynesian, A. C. Pigou (1877–1959), handsomely conceded.

A Thomas Kuhn who applied himself to the study of economic thought would realize that it takes a generation for new ideas to become part of the conventional wisdom. Once again it was a case where, funeral by funeral, science progressed.

## MAINSTREAM ECONOMICS

The whole of this book has been devoted to modern post-Keynesian political economy—the mainstream economics that prevails in America and Scandinavia, in England and Holland; and that is coming to prevail increasingly in Japan, France, Germany, Italy, and most of the Western world. The fruits of post-Keynesian economics have been the better working of the mixed economy. The era since World War II has witnessed a world growth in output and living standards unmatched in recorded history (but also increasingly marred by "stagflation").

The purpose here, however, is not to glorify past achievements. As Chapter 41 demonstrated, the millennium has not even remotely arrived for the mixed economy. We still do not know how to find that perfect incomes policy which will spare us the need to choose between the alternatives of full employment and price stability.

What we need to do at this point is to render justice to the *critiques* of conventional political economy that have prevailed in the past, that prevail now, and that will undoubtedly continue to flourish in the future. For, as Kuhn reminds us, a discipline that does not stay young, alive, and open will find itself elbowed out by the competition of fresh paradigms and preoccupations. Just as civilization did not evolve merely in order to reach the permanent state of the post-New Deal political system, neither is political economy a drama in a finite number of acts that culminates in the new economics of Kennedy's Camelot or Scandinavia's bureaucracies.

## ROMANTIC AND NATIONALISTIC REJECTIONS OF CLASSICAL ECONOMICS

America, young in the nineteenth century and vigorously growing, could not accept the autumnal scenario of Ricardian economics. One had only to look around to see economic progress, both in scale and standards of life. Henry C. Carey (1793–1879) rejected diminishing returns. Accepting a naïve labor theory of value, he deduced that technological change would set into motion the law of *increasing* real wage. Later, social Darwinism was to prevail in America, according to which ruthless laissez faire competition would lead to rugged growth and not to Malthusian subsistence.

Goethe's Germany, still a backwater of Europe and lagging behind cosmopolitan France and England, could also not accept the gloomy timetable of classical economics. Wagnerian-like notions of race and folk combined with Hegelian notions of historical stages to form a repudiation of classical economics and the Newtonian synthesis of the Enlightenment. Friedrich List (1789–1846), though founder of the nationalist school of German economic romanticism, spent his formative years in America. It was there that he developed his notions of protective tariffs to speed economic development and ensure organic diversity, even though his *National System of Political Economy* (1841) was later published in Germany.

**German Historical School**   The Hegelian *Zeitgeist* culminated, as we shall see, in Marxian economics on the one hand. But on the other hand, it led to the German Historical School composed of scholars who professed to be rejecting all economic theory in favor of letting the multivarious facts tell their own organic story. By the latter part of the nineteenth century, this school was associated with the *Kathedersozialisten* ("socialists of the chair") who believed in the star of the Prussian state and its fruitful interferences with the market.

We shall see that the Historical School had a strong influence on American critics of classical and neoclassical economics. But with the collapse of the German Empire in World War I and the exhaustion of its own creative energies in scholarly innovation, the Historical School simply ran out of steam.

## INSTITUTIONAL ECONOMICS AND VEBLEN

In view of the fact that so many Americans received their advanced training a century ago in the graduate schools of Germany,[5] it was no wonder that the Historical School took root here, this time under the new name of "Institutionalism" (*c.* 1890–1935). Richard T. Ely (1854–1943), in founding the American Economic Association in the 1880s, stated what was then heretical doctrine—that the state has a positive role to play in economic life![6] At the University of Wisconsin, he and John R. Commons created a new kind of factual, policy-oriented economics that put the talents of the university into the services of the progressive LaFollette state government, and that eventually helped launch the nation's unemployment and social security systems of the Roosevelt New Deal era.

[5] It is interesting that Americans were then less influenced by the Austrian School of Menger, E. Böhm-Bawerk (1851–1914), and F. von Wieser (1851–1926), which was much more deductive, conservative, and neoclassical. Among the subsequent Austrians are Schumpeter, Ludwig von Mises, Friederich Hayek, Gottfried Haberler, and Fritz Machlup.

[6] The television dramatizations growing out of John F. Kennedy's book *Profiles in Courage* included an incident of the 1890s in which Ely came under attack at the University of Wisconsin for being a "socialist." It says something about academic freedom of the time that, in the trial that finally won him acquittal, Ely denied that he was a socialist but agreed that if it could be proved that he was, the finding would be just cause for dismissal from the state university.

**Veblen**   Thorstein Veblen (1857–1929), sometimes called the American Marx and certainly our greatest iconoclast prior to John Kenneth Galbraith, sided with the Institutionalists in rejecting neoclassical economics. Titles of Veblen's books give some flavor of the thought of this bohemian son of Norwegian homesteaders on the Wisconsin and Minnesota frontier: *The Theory of the Leisure Class* (1899), *The Theory of Business Enterprise* (1904), *The Instinct of Workmanship* (1914), *Imperial Germany and the Industrial Revolution* (1915), *The Higher Learning in America* (1918), *The Engineers and the Price System* (1921), *Absentee Ownership* (1923).

Although Veblen and the Institutionalists had some followers in American academic life—as, for example, Wesley Clair Mitchell, the founder of the National Bureau of Economic Research and theory-eschewing taxonomist of business cycles—40 years ago Institutionalism withered away as an effective counterforce in economics. Who can explain it when a movement turns sterile? Perhaps it was the case that mainstream American economics had always been more pragmatic and empirical than Austrian or English or French economics; it was therefore able, so to speak, to absorb and take over with superior analytical and econometric tools the descriptive tasks and policy formulations of the Institutionalists.

This completes our historical sketch of classical, neoclassical, and Keynesian economics. And of the unsuccessful revolts against it by romantic, nationalistic, historical, and institutionalist schools of thought. For the rest of this chapter, the time has come to survey briefly the vigorous and still lively schools that are critical of mainstream economics of the post-Keynes age. Because any literate person should have some glimmering of acquaintanceship with the economics and thought of Karl Marx, the ideological hero of a billion people over the globe, most of the technical analysis of his economics has been placed in a self-contained appendix.

## CONSERVATIVE COUNTERATTACKS AGAINST MAINSTREAM ECONOMICS

What is recognizable as a modern economic consensus is now increasingly under attack from several directions.[7] First there is simply the rejection by the conservative interests. Although in terms of *realpolitik* it may be the most potent and long-lasting of the oppositions, this historic rejection lacks intellectual interest. Either you feel it or you don't, and there is not much intellectual arguing that can be done.

**Chicago School Libertarianism**   Roughly speaking, working our way from right to left, we have the second assault against the new economics from within the profession of economics by Libertarians—the apostles of laissez faire. Names like Frank Knight (1885–1972), Henry C. Simons, Friedrich Hayek, and Milton Friedman are associated with this general school.[8] Their function in reminding us of what it is that market

---

[7] The next few sections have been adapted from P. A. Samuelson, "Liberalism at Bay," Gerhard Colm Memorial Lecture, New School for Social Research, *Social Research* (Spring 1972), pp. 16–31.

[8] Among the lay public, under the banner of Ayn Rand and avowed self-interest, there is a new radical right that is allied with the academic movement of the Chicago School. It is curious, and upon reflection perhaps not surprising, that there is a tendency for the radical left and the radical right to join in their attack on the conventional economics. This is not merely a matter of tactics, like that involved in the Weimar Republic just before Hitler's successful rise to power. Rather, it

pricing accomplishes, and what are some of the penalties to society from disregarding these lessons, is an important one.

Thus, there are indeed grave deficiencies in present systems of rent control. Again, 20 years ago, Friedman's was a lone voice crying in the wilderness that the pegged exchange-rate system of Bretton Woods was fatally flawed at its core in a world where countries will not inflate and deflate according to the old dictates of the automatic gold standard.

People of all political persuasions should read Friedman's *Capitalism and Freedom*.[9] It is a rigorously logical, careful, often persuasive elucidation of an important point of view. *Before you read it, you may ask:*

Can a man today seriously be against social security? Against flood relief? Farm legislation? Pure food and drug regulation? Compulsory licensing and qualifying of doctors? and of auto drivers? Be against foreign aid? Public utility and SEC regulation?

Against the post office monopoly? Minimum wages? The draft? Price and wage controls? Anticyclical fiscal and monetary policies? Auto-safety standards? Compulsory and free public schooling? Prohibition of heroin sales? Stricter federal and state housing standards for migrant workers? Maximum interest-rate ceilings on usurious lenders? Truth-in-lending laws? Government planning? Can a man of good will oppose Pope Paul VI's encyclical naming central economic planning as the key to economic development?

If you read Professor Friedman's works, or collections of his *Newsweek* columns, you will find every one of these provocative negations cogently defended. Although one may, on reflection, agree with many or few of the positions advocated, it has been well said: "If Milton Friedman had never existed, it would have been necessary to invent him."

### GALBRAITHIAN CRITIQUE

A third challenge to the new economics comes from J. K. Galbraith. By now even high school students are familiar with his works *The Affluent Society* (1957), *The New Industrial State* (1967), *Economics and the Public Purpose* (1973), and *Money* (1975).[10]

Fifteen years ago in a presidential address to the brethren within the economists' guild, I had to say that the noneconomists take Galbraith too seriously, but that we in the profession do not take him seriously enough. It is premature to evaluate what it is about Galbraith that differs from the new economics *and* is also likely to be deemed valid in the future. But this much can be said.

---

is a fact that radical libertarianism is a form of anarchism, except for its market worship, not all that different from the antibureaucratic anarchism of the New Left.

[9]The University of Chicago Press, Chicago, 1962, hardcover and paperback. See also M. Friedman, *An Economist's Protest* (Thomas Horton & Co., Glen Ridge, N.J., 1972) a collection of his *Newsweek* columns. Reference was made in Chap. 17 to his monetarist position in opposition to post-Keynesian macroeconomics, an issue within the economics family, so to speak.

[10]Galbraith, originally an Ontario Scot, began as an agricultural economist. After achieving early fame as an impudent price controller at the wartime OPA, he became editor, philosopher, political speechwriter, politician, braintruster, novelist, art connoisseur, ambassador (to India for John F. Kennedy), memoirist, jet setter, and skier. He has been an important adviser to Adlai Stevenson, John F. Kennedy, and George McGovern. In addition to the cited books, a fourth work, *American Capitalism, The Concept of Countervailing Power* (Houghton Mifflin, Boston, 1956), signaled his emancipation from a successful professional career in mainstream economics. The flavor of his catholic interests is indicated by other titles: *A Theory of Price Control; Economics and the Art of Controversy; The Great Crash, 1929; Economic Development; The Scotch; Ambassador's Journal.*

**Scholar as artist**   Many academics consider it a crime, a misdemeanor if not a felony, to write too well: to do so, they complain, is to puff up the importance of one's ideas beyond their genuine worth. Hence, Galbraith is automatically suspect: anyone who sells so well must automatically be shallow!

Then too, as with Marx, learned men say Galbraith's ideas are not original. *The Affluent Society* is derivative even in title from R. H. Tawney's *The Acquisitive Society;* the "technostructure" is merely another name for the bureaucrats of James Burnham's managerial revolution; the manipulation of consumers' tastes by advertising is warmed-over Ruskin; emphasis on the public sector's needs is Alvin Hansen popularized; corporate autonomy is merely Berle-Means 40 years later; the glorification of bigness in corporations is Schumpeterian; the military-industrial complex stems from Eisenhower's valedictory warning.

This is to miss the point. In technology, it is not the inventor who is the innovator. And, in the history of ideas, the thinker who creates a new synthesis and speaks in telling fashion to a new age is the man who counts.

**Iconoclast**   Galbraith in a sense has no disciples. There are few testable, researchable propositions in his writings that could serve for the purpose of Ph.D. theses or articles in learned journals. How can a jury prove his attitudes and insights right or wrong?

But Galbraith does provide a ware that is in great effective demand: a critique in viewpoint against the prevailing orthodoxy in economics—against the "conventional wisdom," in his phrase, the "received learning," in Veblen's. His criticism cannot itself kill. But it acts like a virus, softening the way for more deadly critiques on the part of the New Left and its professional radical economists.[11]

## THE NEW LEFT AND RADICAL ECONOMICS

Just as it is premature to give a textbook evaluation of Galbraith's lasting impact, it is premature to pass judgment on the lasting importance of the critique on mainstream economics—on the so-called new economics of post-Keynesian eclecticism—now being worked out by the new school whose adherents proudly style themselves "radical economists," and who number at least a tenth of U.S. economists.

**Attack**   To give the flavor of this critique, here are the words of one of its most prominent members, John G. Gurley of Stanford, who, together with Edward Shaw,

---

[11] For controversy between Galbraith, Robert Solow, and other economists, see P. A. Samuelson, *Readings in Economics* (McGraw-Hill, New York, 1973), 7th ed. Robert Fitch, a spokesman for radical economics, argues there that it is a superficial error to think Galbraith is radical rather than reactionary, that Galbraith is naïve in his view that a Henry Ford II (or, for that matter, a GM board) can be dictated to by computer-expert technocrats. The jury has not sustained Galbraith's view that modern corporations, run by their technostructure, are absolute monarchs that make their own markets. But, in light of Chap. 41's demonstration that the mixed economy has not found an incomes policy to conquer cost-push inflation, Galbraith's advocacy of permanent peacetime price-wage controls is intermittently influential. A topic for advanced texts is the Galbraith-Baumol-Marris hypothesis that "maximum growth," not "maximum profit," motivates corporate behavior.

earlier did work in monetary analysis that established his eminence and competence as a mainstream economist, but who in recent years has become both an expert on China and an eloquent advocate of radical economics.[12]

. . . [This is a] time when the assumptions and methods of economics are being challenged, almost as never before, by a growing number of our younger economists, and indeed by many older ones, too. Some of the attacks have reflected dissatisfaction with the many trivial problems that economists seem to spend so much of their time on. Still others have questioned the economic goals so widely-accepted by economists, especially that of ever-increasing GNP, and a few have examined this issue within the wider framework of ecological systems.

Many of the attacks on present-day economics have taken the form of radical analyses of U.S. imperialism—of how the United States profits from its leading role in the hierarchical structure of rich and poor countries that make up the international capitalist system. Other radical analyses have examined how certain groups in the United States itself profit from the maintenance of a hierarchical class structure which produces both wealth and poverty, both privilege and oppression. These analyses, which generally conclude that capitalism is largely responsible for such social and economic disparities, accordingly deny that capitalist society is able (i.e., willing) to solve these problems.

All of these studies may be said to deal with various aspects of wealth and poverty—that is, with the broad social, economic, and political determinants of income and wealth distribution—both domestically and internationally. All of them strike at the very heart of conventional economics, and many of them come from young economists associated with the Union for Radical Economics.

[Standard economists] have disregarded all of this literature of dissent and of challenge to the basic tenets of present-day economics. As a result, an innocent reader . . . would never know of the deep rethinking that is now going on by many members of our profession. In fact, he would gain quite the opposite impression from his reading—namely, that all is well with economics; that there is almost unanimous agreement on the fundamentals of the discipline; that economists are superbly prepared to solve what these authors call—incredible as it may seem—"newly-emerging problems" like poverty and "hot subjects" like urban decay. The dominant tone . . . is one of great self-satisfaction and self-confidence.

I write . . . to say that such a tone is unwarranted.

**Reaction**   Attack naturally evokes defense. Robert Solow of MIT argued in reply:

Radical economics may conceivably be the wave of the future, but I do not think it is the wave of the present. In fact, to face the issue head on, I think that radical economics as it is practiced contains more cant, not less cant; more role-playing, not less role-playing; less facing of the facts, not more facing of the facts, than conventional economics. In short, we neglected radical economics because it is negligible.

[12]This quotation, and the reply by Robert Solow, are taken from "The State of Economics," *The American Economic Review,* vol. LXI (May, 1971, Papers and Proceedings), pp. 43–68. See also P. A. Samuelson, *Readings, op. cit.,* and Paul M. Sweezy, "Toward a Critique of Economics," *Review of Radical Political Economics,* Spring 1970, where orthodox economics is criticized for unrealistically taking ". . . the existing social system for granted . . . [for searching] for harmonies of interest . . . tendencies toward equilibrium . . . [concerning] itself with smaller and decreasingly significant questions . . . elaborating and refining its techniques." See also R. C. Edwards, M. Reich, T. E. Weisskopf, *The Capitalist System* (Prentice-Hall, Englewood Cliffs, N.J., 1972), for readings by Paul Baran, Paul Sweezy, Stephen Hymer, Samuel Bowles, Herbert Gintis, James O'Connor, André Gorz, Arthur MacEwan, Harry Magdoff, and others.

First I want to say that I think radical economists have corrupted Thomas Kuhn's notion of a scientific paradigm, which they treat as a mere license for loose thinking. If you look at Kuhn's examples—all from natural science, of course—you will see that they represent well developed models or frameworks for thought. Some of his examples are Newtonian dynamics, Copernican astronomy, Ptolemaic astronomy. . . . In this sense, neoclassical economics is pretty clearly a scientific paradigm. It may be a bad one, or a worn-out one, or it may have served to advance the interests of the capitalist class, but it is the sort of thing Kuhn means. As far as I can see, radical political economics is no such thing. It is more a matter of posture and rhetoric than of scientific framework at all. . . . [I]n Kuhn's language . . . a scientific paradigm is to provide a framework for "normal science." But there is little evidence that radical political economics is capable of generating a line of normal science, or even that it wants to.

Here are some examples of what I mean. Professor Gurley says: "As radical economists see it, the shares of national income going to workers and to property owners are largely determined by the relative power of the two groups, although relative factor supplies set limits within which the power exerts itself." Am I to presume from this that there are studies of time series that show that short-run fluctuations in distributive shares reflect short-run fluctuations in the distribution of power in society? This would mean that workers are more powerful when there is a lot of unemployment than they are when there is very little, because the share of wages is highest when the economy is depressed. Or has it been found in many countries that the direction of long-run change in distributive shares corresponds to the long-run trend in the independently measured distribution of power in society? Or are there perhaps cross-section studies among industries showing that the share of wages in value added is highest in industries where the power of the workers is highest, and lowest where the social power of capitalists is highest? Or is it demonstrable that international differences in functional income distribution correspond more or less closely to international differences in the relative power of workers and property owners?

## NEW LEFT THOUGHT

The radical economists are now still doing the research on which they would have the future judge them. For a thoughtful survey of the noneconomist New Left, which is undoubtedly an important movement in modern thought, the reader may be referred to a modern de Tocqueville from Sweden. Assar Lindbeck developed, during a visiting professorship to America in the late 1960s, his paperback *The Political Economy of the New Left—An Outsider's View* (Harper & Row, New York, 1971). He points out there that an economist from Hungary or anywhere in Eastern Europe would be struck by the fact that often the New Left manages to be critical *both of the market and of the bureaucracy,* with a sentimental hankering for the utopian self-sufficient *kibbutz,* a case of the *rentier* life of the elite university student body wishfully projected as a model for the world. By implication he deplores such naïve sentimentalism.[13]

The difference between the Old Left and the New Left should not be exaggerated. In the Pantheon of their saints and heroes, beginning with Marx, Engels, and Lenin, the name of Stalin has been replaced by Mao. And along with names like Gramsci, Baran, Sweezy, and Mandel, the new names of Marcuse, Fromm, and Paul Goodman

[13]For a response to Lindbeck's analysis, see the 1972 replies by Paul Sweezy, Stephen Hymer, and others reproduced in P. A. Samuelson, *Readings, op. cit.*

have been added. But it is still the tradition of Marx that counts—not merely the mature Marx, but the young Marx too.

Our chapter concludes with a general overview of Karl Marx, leaving to the Appendix his technical economics.[14]

## BIOGRAPHY OF KARL MARX

Karl Marx (1818–1883) was born the year after Ricardo published his *Principles*. Just as Newton was born the year Galileo died, Marx died the year Keynes and Schumpeter were born. On the surface, Marx lived an uneventful life of study, much of it in London exile at the library of the British Museum. But his influence lives on in Moscow and Peking; in Outer Mongolia and Cambridge, Massachusetts; in Havana and Peoria.

**Early life**  Descended from a long line of rabbis, Marx's father converted to Lutheranism in order to pursue his career as a lawyer in the years of post-Napoleonic reaction. Karl was always an outsider, even in the Prussian Rhineland where Catholics heavily outnumbered the few bourgeois Protestants. After the usual bright boy's triumphs in school, Marx went on to university study at Bonn and Berlin—first at law, until the charms of philosophy killed all career interests. Hegel's philosophy was then mesmerizing Germany. After an initial resistance, Marx succumbed to Hegelianism, but with his own replacing of mind over matter by matter over mind, and his replacing of the absolute Prussian monarchy as the culmination of history by the ultimate state of communism as a culmination.

When a professorial career was closed to Marx because of his alien nature and radical ideas, he turned to journalism. Each radical paper he edited succumbed to bankruptcy or the Prussian censor. Exile to Paris and Brussels, and ultimately to London, followed. His aristocratic childhood sweetheart, Jenny von Westphalen, stood by him as wife and companion through thick and thin. That the life of a penniless radical scholar did not involve more of the thin was due solely to the friendship of Friedrich Engels, his lifelong collaborator and financial angel.

**Engels and Marx**  Throughout all the annals of science and revolution there cannot be a more remarkable friendship than that of Marx and Engels. Together they wrote the *Communist Manifesto* (1848) and much else. After Marx died with two of his three volumes of *Das Kapital* unfinished, Engels edited the uncompleted notes and manuscripts, even though he was himself by then old and going blind.

Engels was an important intellect in his own right, and we must not take him at

---

[14]One important school critical of mainstream economics must not be ignored. Joan Robinson, Nicholas Kaldor, Piero Sraffa, and Luigi Pasinetti—the so-called Italo-Cantabridgian school (which, in fact, has able supporters all over the world, including India)—have rejected marginal-productivity doctrines of distribution (*a*) as mere apologetics for the status quo of capitalist society, and (*b*) as foundering on the analytical and empirical inadequacies of production functions that assume continuous variability of input combinations and illegitimately employ abstract aggregates of capital whose net productivity is alleged to be the interest rate. The chapter's appendix will revert to this scientific critique. Reference was already made in Chap. 27 to Kaldor's alternative macroeconomic model of distribution, and in Chapters 30 and 37 to the phenomenon of "reswitching" that is incompatible with the *simpliste* parables of thrift and its productivity fruits.

his own modest evaluation when he wrote: "Marx was a genius . . . the rest of us were talented at best." But this modesty vis à vis Marx undoubtedly made possible a lifetime friendship with that truculent and most difficult of men.

**Personality inessentials** It is the ideas and writings of Marx that constitute his importance in the history of thought and political development of the modern world. Next to these ideas, facts of his personality—such as that he was often deemed imperious, quarreling with Proudhon, Lassalle, Bakunin, and other stalwarts in the revolutionary movement—are as naught. It is enough that Isaiah Berlin could say, at the beginning of his readable little biography, *Karl Marx* (Oxford University Press, London, 1939, 1948): "No thinker in the nineteenth century has had so direct, deliberate, and powerful an influence on mankind as Karl Marx." That is all that counts. And that is what warrants our giving him a fair hearing and rendering him even-handed justice.

## MARX'S SCHEMATA

Engels aptly characterized Karl Marx's system as a combination of German Hegelian philosophy, French socialism, and English political economy. It is with the latter that we must be concerned here—his belief *to have deduced scientifically the inescapable transition from capitalism to socialism.* But this is not to deny that economics may in the end be deemed by posterity to be the least-lasting part of Marx's thought.

**Prophecies** Each generation must recreate its predecessors. It used to be thought that Marx's great achievement was the more-than-a-million-word *Das Kapital*, which *scientifically* foretold *the laws of motion of capitalism* unto its inevitable death.

The law of the falling rate of profit. The law of immiserization and pauperization of the working class. The ever-growing inequality under capitalism, and gradual emergence of class consciousness on the part of the downtrodden proletariat. The necessity toward larger and larger scales of production, culminating in the demise of competition and formation of monopoly capitalism. Intensifying business cycles and crises as the masses suffer from underconsumption and lack of purchasing power, until the final cataclysmic depression sounds the death knell of the system. The desperate attempts to stave off the day of doom by imperialistic ventures in colonial exploitation, dynastic wars, and foreign investment.

Finally, the ultimate unavoidable day when, like overripe fruit ready to fall off the tree, capitalism has become so trustified in one big combine that the workers can take over in a sudden, necessarily violent revolution.

Such is the vulgar view of what Marxism was all about. When you read biographies of members of the Old Left, to say nothing of the New, you will find that scarce one in ten believers ever got past the first few chapters of Volume I. They need to read just enough to be able to take on faith that Spinoza-like proofs of the decline of capitalism have assured the scientific certainty of socialism.

## CRISIS IN MARXISM

In 1900, a third of a century after the 1867 publication of *Capital*, even the most fervent Marxist had to face up to the fact that the absolute real wage was rising in the western world, not falling. And following Keynes' 1936 *General Theory,* the swelling of the reserve army of the unemployed and worsening of the business cycle became patently contradicted. What to do? Here were some of the patterns followed.

1. Ignore the facts. Deny them. At least gloss over them.[15]

2. Like Eduard Bernstein, revise your Marxism into a Fabian-like evolutionary socialism of the Bernard Shaw and Webbs type. Pin your faith in trade-unions, and in winning Parliament over gradually so that prolabor legislation can be assured.

3. Like Lenin, admit that a privileged stratum of workers can themselves become bourgeois and share in the exploiter's swag. But affirm that these renegades to the proletariat are simply living off the exploitation of colonies outside the metropolitan centers of Europe and North America. Affirm that the prosperity is bound to falter in the future; and that the proletariat need to be led by a revolutionary elite.

4. Reexamine and reformulate the arguments in Marx. Discover that he may not really have meant to predict falling real wages under capitalism. And elevate your requirements for tolerable economic performance of the mixed economy.

## THE NEW LEFT AND THE YOUNG MARX

Today the focus has understandably shifted away from *Capital* as the capstone and culmination of Marx's writing. Instead there is a new interest in, to use a common phrase, *Marx before he was a Marxist*—the Young Marx of 1844 and the years before the *Communist Manifesto.* Further, the discovery of his 1857 notes for a monumental work that was to contain *Capital* in only one corner, the so-called *Grundrisse,* suggests to the modern age that it was wrong to think of Karl Marx as having outgrown his Hegelian garments.

**Alienation**    Thus consider the important notion of *alienation* that appeals so resonantly to our own age. Long before Marx's sojourn in the British Museum mastering Ricardo and the theories of surplus value, his Hegelian critiques had alerted him to the fact

---

[15] There are few admirers of Marx who have the unflinching candor of Joan Robinson, whose *Essay on Marxism* (Macmillan, London, 1942, 1964) provides perhaps the best short introduction to the economics of the mature Marx. A less unflinching introduction that might be read at the same time as an antidote is Paul Sweezy's *The Theory of Capitalist Development* (Oxford University Press, New York, 1943). On the false forecast of immiserization of labor, Professor Robinson says, "This error, like Jesus's belief that the world was shortly coming to an end, is so central to the whole doctrine that it is hard to see how it could have been put afloat without it. . . . 'You have nothing to lose but the prospect of a suburban home and a motor car' would not have been much of a slogan for a revolutionary movement." As I had to remark on the Centennial of *Capital,* "With friends like this, one has hardly need for an enemy." Jokes aside, it is quite mistaken to charge Marx with opportunism in this. Rightly or wrongly, Marx believed that he had *deduced by cogent and innovative economic reasoning* what he was forecasting as the laws of motion of capitalism. This chapter's Appendix gives a brief overview of Marx's economic innovations. Only after one has fairly studied Marx's syllogisms can it be realized that the miscarriage of his prediction was not merely a case of bad luck (who expects prediction over a century to be immune from bad luck?). The internal logic of Marx's economics was flawed at the core: *There is no way to infer from the new concepts of surplus value* whether the reserve army of the unemployed would equal 1 or 50 per cent of the British or American labor forces of 1867 or 1967, and whether the capitalistic real wage would be changing at an average annual rate of −5 per cent, +3 per cent, 0 per cent or anything else.

that the worker under advanced capitalism becomes an alienated cog in the machine. And, as we reread *Capital* carefully from this view, we see that Marx never abandoned the concept of alienation.

Herbert Marcuse, Erich Fromm, or Charles Reich feel no need to deny that wages are higher in 1976 America than in 1776 or 1876; and higher than in India, or Leningrad, or Peking, or Havana. The worker may not be pauperized in the sense of lacking TVs, autos, or even penicillin. But, it is argued, his spirit is pauperized as he tends the monotonous assembly line and submits to the discipline of the foreman and the regular working week. Advertising debases his tastes. The press brainwashes him into voting for wasteful military expenditures that kill his neighbors overseas, and for programs that corrupt his government in the interests of the giant corporations. So clever is the system of repression that, in Marcuse's words, it represses the worker *by tolerance!*

**Egalitarian aspirations**   In cold economic terms, grant that real wages rise.

But, ask critics, do they rise by as much as real GNP rises, so that the relative share of property is kept from being a larger fraction?

Or if, after counting in business-expense accounts and lightly taxed capital gains, it should still be the case that labor's share in the growing GNP of the mixed economy is *not* a declining fraction, nonetheless critics ask how there can be an ethical warrant for the evident continuation of unequal wealth and opportunity. "Nothing short of 100 per cent for labor of that which is rightfully labor's in a good society"—this is stipulated as the irreducible ultimate goal. Only after a rational planned society is introduced, it is argued, can the wastes of cost-push inflation and stagnation be solved. And the evils of wasteful advertising be purged.

Moreover, when we turn to the Third World, socialists claim that only under communism can development take place quickly. Forced saving by the state can do what voluntary saving by the impoverished peoples can never do spontaneously. To fail to understand these aspirations is to miss the point of "the system's" critics.

## THE CLASS STRUGGLE AND DYNAMICS OF SOCIAL LIFE

The appendix can be read by those who want to savor the flavor of traditional, mature Marxian economics. Before leaving Karl Marx, let us note that he was always more than a political economist. He was as much a philosopher, historian, sociologist, and revolutionist. And make no mistake. He was a learned man. To denigrate Marx, scholars sometimes point out that not all his ideas were completely original with him.[16] Of course not. Ideas never are virginally new. As Whitehead said, every great idea was originated by someone who was not the first to discover it. How Marx synthesized, shaped, and promoted his ideas is what matters. And how they were received!

---

[16] As Berlin observes, "What is original is not any one component element, but the central hypothesis by which each is connected with the other." Little matter then that Spinoza and Feuerbach earlier had historical materialism; Saint-Simon and Guizot, the class struggle; Sismondi, economic crises; Moses Hess and Babeuf, the rise of the proletariat; Fourier and such post-Ricardians as Bray, Thompson, and Hodgkinson, the notions of exploitation and surplus value.

**Class interests and ideology**   The economic interpretation of history by Marx and Engels may perhaps rank among man's greatest achievements. To think that our ideology shapes our behavior is to stop short of being interesting. What shapes our ideology? The businessman votes conservative. The union leader votes for minimum-wage and unemployment-compensation legislation. The superstructure of opinion is not shaped by hairsplitting logical analysis. The superstructure of beliefs, laws, and ideologies is reflective of *the material conditions of life and the material interests of the class*.

Here we have Adam Smith's self-interest generalized away from the mundane dollar voting of the marketplace to the ballot voting of the elections and the bullet voting of the barricades. Once our eyes have been opened, can we be really surprised at the threat of a military-industrial complex? And how can we fail to realize that universal suffrage in one decade must assuredly lead to redistributive taxation in the following half-century?

The calculus of power and the calculus of dollars are not so different after all. The von Neumann game-theoretic concepts of coalition and rivalry are seen to be as applicable to the class struggle and its codes of theology as to the analysis of oligopolists selling steel in rival markets.

In conclusion, the reader of Marx can never fall into the fallacy of Whig history—fancying that the capitalism of Macaulay's time is the culmination of all evolution, or that the welfare state of the late 1970s is here to stay unchanged, or even that the ultimate triumph of the victorious proletariat and peasantry must inevitably bring an end to the history of the class struggle.[17]

"This too will pass away." That is Karl Marx's ultimate thesis.

[17]Only a supersophisticated Marxist could have coined the wry joke that went the rounds in Poland and Czechoslovakia a decade ago: "Under capitalism, it's a case of man exploiting man. Under socialism, it's a case of vice versa."

## SUMMARY

1   Political economy as a discipline begins with the classical economists: Adam Smith, the critic of government interferences with beneficent and orderly laissez faire; Malthus and Ricardo, the gloomy prophets of diminishing returns and the struggle over distribution of the limited social income among the wage workers, land-owners, and profit-seeking capitalists.

2   Flagging classicism gave way a century ago to neoclassical economics: general-equilibrium analysis of utility as well as disutility; marginalism extended beyond Ricardian rent analysis to all factors of production; econometric measurement involving increasingly sophisticated tools of mathematics and statistics; the monopolistic and imperfect-competition revolution to displace perfect competition's theoretical monopoly.

3   The Keynesian revolution added to the developing microeconomics of neoclassical economics an overdue, elaborated macroeconomics that eventually synthesized

fiscal and monetary analysis, cyclical trends in unemployment and inflation. (But recall the unsolved problem of an incomes policy to cure stagflation in the mixed economy.)

4 Romantic, nationalistic, and antitheoretical rejections of mainstream economics inevitably arose: in Germany, List and the Historical School; in America, the World War I era of Institutionalist Economics and Thorstein Veblen.

5 The most important counterweight to mainstream economics has come from the right and the left: from conservative self-interest and the reasoned libertarianism of the Austrian and Chicago schools (Hayek, Knight, Friedman); from Galbraithian iconoclasm concerning autonomous corporations and technostructure in the affluent industrial state; from the Old and New Left, and the new school of radical economists.

6 Globally, the Marxian offshoot from Ricardian classicism has played a pivotal role in intellectual and political history. Scientific socialism predicts with Hegelian certainty the laws of motion of capitalism: exploitation and pauperization, class struggle and class-conditioned ideology, imperialism, cyclical crises, proletarian victory. Gradual attrition of mature *Das Kapital* Marxism has shifted the limelight to earlier works, particularly those of the Young Marx, the left-Hegelian exponent of alienation.

## CONCEPTS FOR REVIEW

pre-Smith amateurs: philosophers, merchants, Mercantilists, Physiocrats
Adam Smith's Invisible Hand
Ricardian diminishing returns, class oppositions
neoclassical economics
the Keynesian revolution

Historical School and Institutionalists, Veblen
Chicago School Libertarianism
Galbraith's world: autonomous firms and technostructure
New Left and radical economics
Marxian laws of motion and general *Weltanschauung*

## QUESTIONS FOR DISCUSSION

1 Now that you've studied economics, how have your economic views changed?

2 Pencil in, on the back flyleaf's family tree of political economy, the romantics, Historical School, and Institutionalists. Also the living schools now putting mainstream economics into question.

3 Which parts of a modern economics textbook would be received badly in Moscow, Havana, or Peking? In Santiago, Nairobi, or Delhi? Which well received?

4 If many of Marxians' most confident predictions failed to materialize, does that discredit them? Why not? Why? Is Kuhnian science just another name for each generation's peculiar prejudices?

# APPENDIX: Rudiments of Marxian Economics

In his mature three-volume work, *Capital* (1867, 1885, 1894),[1] Marx tried (*a*) to lay bare the nature of *exploitation* of labor by capitalists, and (*b*) to reveal the *laws of motion* of developing and dying capitalism. The notions that he considered to be crucial centered in his concept of "surplus value."

Space permits us here to go only to what Marx, Engels, and Lenin thought was the heartland of Marx's theoretical contribution to economics—his belief that he had demonstrated by his new tool of surplus value the exploitation of labor by capital. As Marx put it:

Now suppose that the average amount of the daily necessaries of a labouring man *require six hours of average labour* for their production. But our man is a wages labourer. He must, therefore, sell his labouring power to a capitalist [who will], therefore, make him work, say, daily *twelve* hours . . . he will therefore, have to work *six other hours,* which I shall call hours of surplus labour, which surplus labour will realize itself in a *surplus value* . . . .[2]

If valid, this would seem to be a grave indictment of capitalism. Engels, recognizing that here is the essence of Marx's economic innovation, went on to observe in 1891, "with every new . . . invention, this surplus of its [labour's] daily product over its daily cost increases." So important did Marxists consider this surplus value of Marx to be, that Lenin, on the eve of World War I, summed up the economic component of Marxism in similar words:

The worker spends one part of the day covering the cost of maintaining himself and his family (wages), while the other part of the day he works without remuneration, creating for the capitalist *surplus value,* the source of profit, the source of wealth of the capitalist class.

Marx sought to find in labor a common denominator in which to express values. The modern view is that it is enough, in explaining relative values or relative prices of two goods—say, deer and beavers, in Adam

Smith's famous example—to assert, "Supply (as determined by the difficulties of production) interacts with demand (as determined by tastes and wealth) to determine the exchange or price ratios that we observe in the market."

But remember that Marx was a nineteenth-century German philosopher: he thought there was a need for an *absolute* measure of value by which to make commensurable the incommensurabilities of deer and beaver.

"Socially necessary labour," he argued, provided the solution to the absolute standard.[3] David Ricardo, and Adam Smith even earlier, thus provided the springboard for Marx's development of "classical economics," as shown in the family-tree chart on the back flyleaf of this book.

As Smith put the labor theory of value in a dawn-of-history Eden:

In that early and rude state of society which precedes both the accumulation of stock [i.e., the need for capital goods] and the appropriation of land, . . . the quantity of labour necessary for acquiring different objects seems to be the only circumstance which can afford any rule for exchanging them one for another. If . . . it usually costs twice the labour to kill a beaver which it does to kill a deer, one beaver should naturally exchange for or be worth two deer.[4]

**Undiluted labor theory of value**   Replace hunting by more realistic examples of coal and corn. Let it take 4 hours of a 12-hour day to produce 1 coal. Let it take 4 hours to produce 1 corn. Then the "socially necessary" labor costs are 4 and 4 respectively.

And, if there are to be any exchanges at all, competition will set the exchange ratio at "1 coal equals 1 corn":

$$\text{Labor Value}_{corn}/\text{Labor Value}_{coal} = 4 \text{ hr}/4 \text{ hr} = 1$$

**Direct and indirect labor**   Now complicate the story a bit. Let coal be produced by 4 direct labor as be-

---

[1] There are many convenient editions, particularly of Vol. I, the only one completed before Marx's death in 1883.

[2] K. Marx, *Wages, Prices and Profit* (1865), Sec. VIII, as reproduced in K. Marx and F. Engels, *Selected Works* (International Publishers, New York, 1968). The Engels and Lenin quotes are from the same work.

[3] Joan Robinson of Cambridge, a brilliant critic of capitalism and an admirer of Marx, has said: ". . . no point of substance in Marx's arguments depends upon the labour theory of value." See *An Essay on Marxian Economics* (Macmillan, London, 1942, 1964), p. 22.

[4] A. Smith, *The Wealth of Nations* (1776), Book I, Chap. VI.

fore. But now suppose each 1 of corn requires 1 of coal as raw material, along with 4 of direct labor.

How will total labor costs now be reckoned? Clearly,

$$\text{Labor Value}_{\text{corn}}/\text{Labor Value}_{\text{coal}} = (4 \text{ hr} + 4 \text{ hr})/4 \text{ hr}$$
$$= 8/4 = 2$$

We now have 4 hours direct (or "live") labor in a unit of coal or corn. But in corn we additionally have 4 hours of indirect (or "dead") labor—namely, the 4 hours needed at the earlier stage to produce the coal raw material needed to produce corn.

**In a regime of undiluted labor values, all goods have competitive values equal to their socially necessary total labor contents (direct plus indirect).[5]**

**Variable capital and constant capital**  Marx gave new names to live and dead labor. The direct labor costs—outlays for payrolls advanced to workers to spend now before the goods they work on are complete—he called "variable capital" and wrote as $v$: $v_{\text{coal}}$ and $v_{\text{corn}}$, or $v_1$, $v_2$, and $v_i$, ... for the 1, 2, ..., $i$, ... industries or departments.

Marx gave the name "constant capital" to dead labor—i.e., to outlays for raw materials produced by labor in *earlier* stages and that are now needed for live labor to work with in this stage. He writes constant capital as $c$: $c_1$, $c_2$, ..., $c_i$, ....[6]

Here is how Marx writes undiluted labor values for coal and corn:

$$\text{Labor Value}_1 = c_1 + v_1 = 0 \text{ hr} + 4 \text{ hr} = 4 \text{ hr}$$
$$\text{Labor Value}_2 = c_2 + v_2 = 4 \text{ hr (coal)} + 4 \text{ hr} = 8 \text{ hr}$$

NOTE: There is no exploitation in the Eden of the undiluted labor theory of value. Labor gets *all* the product. There is no profit, no interest, no rent, no

markup over competitive labor costs, no surplus, no surplus value.

Marx writes any markup or "surplus" tacked on to $c + v$ as $s$: for example, $s_1$ for coal, $s_2$ for corn, ..., $s_i$ for industry $i$. Hence in our rude Eden, we have $s_1 = 0$, $s_2 = 0$, ..., $s_i = 0$, and

$$c_i + v_i + s_i = c_i + v_i + 0 \qquad \text{everywhere}$$

Each laborer, if he works 12 hours a day, works only for himself, none for an exploiting capitalist. (Thus, the minimum of subsistence he enjoys in real wages may be a very comfortable minimum indeed: he can consume $1\frac{1}{2}$ of corn every day, working 6 direct hours for it in the corn industry, and 6 indirect hours for it in the coal industry. Perhaps without this comfortable daily ration of $1\frac{1}{2}$ corn, workers will not have enough children to reproduce the labor supply.)

## SURPLUS VALUE AND EXPLOITATION

Now leave Eden. Workers need corn for survival and reproduction. But they can't wait for the harvest to get the subsistence they need now if they are to perform work. And they can't produce corn unless some capitalist provides them with the coal needed (along with their direct labor) to produce the corn-industry output.

In short, a small group of thrifty or lucky capitalists, who happen to own "capital" (coal raw materials, and last season's corn to advance as food), can now garner a surplus—a profit, an interest rate, or as Marx would prefer to say, a surplus value.

**Markup on live labor only**  Here Marx rejects the bourgeois economics of Smith and Ricardo. In Volume I, Marx posits that *the surplus or markup, s, is on direct labor only*. (Remember man is the measure of all things, not fetishistic commodities!)

POSTULATE: In a Marxian regime of "values," each $s_i$ is marked up the same percentage on each variable capital, $v_i$—not on each total capital ($c_i + v_i$). This uniform ratio of $s_i$ to $v_i$ is called the "rate of surplus value" ("mehrwert" in German). We write it as $m$, which is the common value of all industry $m$'s: $m_1$, $m_2$, ..., $m_i$ .... It is simply

$$m = m_1 = m_2 = \ldots = m_i = \ldots$$
$$s_1 = mv_1, \; s_2 = mv_2, \ldots, \; s_i = mv_i, \ldots$$

An example will help. Suppose the rate of surplus value is 200%: $m = 2.00$. We each work 4 hours a day

---

[5]Marx, for simplicity, assumed all labor was homogeneous. Or, if, say, women are twice as productive as men in both departments or industries, he'd reckon each woman-hour as 2 lowest-common-denominator man-hours. There is no harm in this simplification, provided we realize it won't work in cases where women are three times as productive as men in welding, twice as productive in mining, and three-fourths as productive in distilling. Then general-equilibrium methods are mandatory. Like Marx, we at first ignore land.

[6]More complicated examples would involve use of machines—e.g., plows—as well as raw materials to produce corn. Then $c_2$ would also include the used-up amount of plows, its "depreciation," in producing 1 corn.

for ourselves, 8 hours for the capitalists. Now our Values Tableau begins with coal's row:

$$c_1 + v_1 + s_1 = c_1 + v_1 + mv_1$$
$$= 0 + 4 + 2.00(4)$$
$$= 12 \text{ for each coal's ''value''}$$

How do we complete the corn row in the Values Tableau? Clearly, we must add the coal raw-material cost to corn's direct labor and the latter's marked-up surplus to get

$$c_2 + v_2 + s_2 = c_2 + v_2 + mv_2$$
$$= 12(1) + 4 + 2.00(4)$$
$$= 24 \text{ for each corn's value}$$

NOTE: We still do have corn double coal's value

$$\text{Value}_{corn}/\text{Value}_{coal} = 24/12 = 2$$

But now both the numerator of 24 and the denominator of 12 have ended up tripled because of the 200% surplus-value markup.[7]

Before, with $m = 0$ and no surplus value, 12 hours bought a worker $1\frac{1}{2}$ of corn. Now he gets only one-third as much—namely (12 hr of the day)/(24 hr cost of corn) $= \frac{1}{2}$ corn subsistence per day.

**Minimum-of-subsistence exploitative wage**  Evidently the higher the rate of surplus value, $m$, that the capitalist can exact, the lower the worker's real wage. What sets the limit on surplus value?

According to simplest Marx, just as corn and coal have their cost of reproduction, so too does labor power. Labor power will get only its cost of (re)production, not the total of what it can produce.

**The minimum real wage at which labor can be recruited from the reserve army of the unemployed, and be kept reproducing itself—that minimum-subsistence level will determine the exploitative rate of surplus value $m$.**

Our previous example applies. Suppose it takes $\frac{1}{2}$ corn per day to keep a worker alive and reproducing

himself. We should be able to deduce that the rate of surplus value is 200%, $m = 2.00$, and each worker works 8 hours a day for the exploiting capitalist and only 4 hours a day for his own subsistence.

Recall that this gives rise to Volume I's Tableau

$$c_1 + v_1 + mv_1 = 0 + 4 + 2.00(4) = 12$$
$$c_2 + v_2 + mv_2 = 1(12) + 4 + 2.00(4) = 24$$

The laborer must pay 24 hours to buy 1 corn. He has, of course, only 12 hours in the day. Hence, we verify he gets his needed minimum-subsistence ration of

$$\tfrac{1}{2} \text{ corn} = \frac{12 \text{ hr of the day}}{24 \text{ hr for corn}} = \tfrac{1}{2} \text{ corn} \qquad \text{QED}$$

**Contradiction?**  Marx knew bourgeois economists would object to his making rates of surplus value the same in all industries. They could be expected to contend:

"Why should the coal and corn industries, just because they have equal outlays *on labor*, be satisfied with the same total profit? The corn profits are too low, when they are related (as they should be) to the much larger $(c_2 + v_2)$ outlay. The coal profits are relatively too high when they are related to the no-larger $c_1 + v_1 = 0 + v_1$.

"Competition will in fact equalize the profit rates, $s_i/(c_i + v_i)$ in all industries, not $s_i/v_i$ alone. We should put equal rates of profit, $\pi$("pi," for profit),

$$\pi = s_1/(c_1 + v_1) = s_2/(c_2 + v_2)$$

in the place of equal rates of surplus value."

How would Marx reply? In effect he would say:

"I agree that equal rates of surplus value imply unequal rates of profit: the more labor-intensive industries will be getting higher rates of profit." (What is the same thing, "equal rates of profit" imply "unequal rates of surplus value.")[8]

Marx might continue: "Wait until my Volume III is published, when I shall reveal how to replace my 'Values' Tableau based on equal rates of surplus value by a 'Prices' Tableau based on equal rates of profit."

---

[7]This takes place uniformly at every stage of production. Each industry's direct-labor "value-added" is marked up by the same percentage: so, by the careful value-added reckoning like that for Table 10-2's loaf of bread, we realize all final goods—coal or corn or . . .—must be increased equally in value relative to an hour's wage. In consequence of the 200 per cent of markup, real wages have been exploited down to one-third their Eden level!

[8]Marx points out one case in which there would be no contradiction between equal rates of profit and equal rates of surplus value. If the "organic compositions of capital" were the same in all industries, as measured by *equal* indirect-labor-intensities, $c_i/v_i$, then both methods will agree. Much of Marx would go through smoothly, if we would agree to this harmless (albeit unrealistic) simplification.

**Equal-profit-rate regime**   We can now write down for our coal-corn example the Volume III bourgeois alternative. Since $\pi$ is earned on $c + v$, the base that is larger than $v$ alone, the profit rate must be smaller than the 200% level for surplus value.

Our example will work out to the same subsistence-exploitative wage of $\frac{1}{2}$ corn per 12-hour day, if we make the lucky guess of a 100% profit rate, $\pi = 1.00$. Now the price of coal can be written down in terms of $C_1 + V_1$ (where, be it noticed, we are better advised to use capital letters for the bourgeois "prices" regime to keep it separate from the Volume I "values" regime with its $c_1 + v_1$ small letters.) The Prices Tableau begins with

$$(C_1 + V_1) + S_1 = (C_1 + V_1) + \pi(C_1 + V_1)$$
$$= (0 + 4) + 1.00(0 + 4) = 8$$

for the *price* of coal.

Now for the price of corn in the Prices Tableau:

$$(C_2 + V_2) + S_2 = (C_2 + V_2) + \pi(C_2 + V_2)$$
$$= [1(8) + 4] + 1.00(8 + 4) = 24$$

for the *price* of corn. (NOTE: Again workers are getting their subsistence of only $\frac{1}{2}$ corn per day, derived from (12 hr per day)/(24 hr cost of corn) $= \frac{1}{2}$.

**"Explaining" exploitation**   Which formulation is better? "Values" or "Prices"? Bourgeois economists have answered, "Prices." Marxians would not agree.

But a month in any good library will convince any scholar that Marxians have not all agreed on *why* surplus-value concepts are better. And remember that Marx died before he had completed Volumes II and III for publication. So Engels, old and handicapped by vision problems and political demands on his time, had to edit these unfinished manuscripts for publication.

Since this is an appendix that attempts to present Marx's concepts sympathetically, leaving to advanced books pro-and-con evaluations, let us simply provide one line of defense and exposition.

1. Surplus value provides a *simpler* way to explain exploitation to beginners. It focuses on human labor as being directly exploited. (And, note, its *algebra* is much simpler for nineteenth-century readers—since solving for $\pi = 1.0$ can be shown to be equivalent to solving for the root of a quadratic polynomial.)

2. Marxians claim that the *microeconomic* parceling out of surpluses as between industries, around a determined average level, may indeed be compelled by ruthless competition to follow the pre-*Capital* bourgeois rules of equal profit (equal $\pi$ as against equal industrial $m$'s of surplus value). But that *average level* of profit exploitation, and how it grows under capitalism, Marxians believe can be most simply determined *macroeconomically* by the concept of surplus-value markups on exploited direct labor.

What to think? If we agree with the first point, that surplus value is an easier approximation to explain, then perhaps we need not worry if the second point of defense turns out to be deemed unnecessary by a jury a hundred years from now made up of Marxians and non-Marxians alike.[9]

## LABOR-SAVING INVENTION AND THE RESERVE ARMY OF THE UNEMPLOYED

Enough of the flavor of Marx's $c + v + s$ concepts has been sketched. Let us mention some of the key trends that Marxians contemplate as the laws of motion of capitalism.

1. Capitalists have an urge to accumulate, the way a cancer cell has an urge to grow. In self-defense, as monopolies require an ever-larger scale of production to survive, capitalists are forced to accumulate. "Accumulate! Accumulate! Accumulate! That is [the Law of] Moses and the Prophets," observed Marx.

2. Accumulation tends to erode the rate of profit (and threatens to raise real wages). Therefore, labor-saving invention of machinery will be introduced to keep profits up and prevent wages from rising unduly.

RESULT: Recruits to the "reserve army of the unemployed," depressed wages, and misery.

---

[9] The 8 and 8 of surpluses in the coal-corn Values Tableau, Marx himself would have related, in Vol. III, Book III, Chap. IX, to the *total* $(c + v)$ of $(0 + 4)$ plus $(12 + 4)$ to get an *average* profit rate of 16/20 instead of the correct $\pi = 1.00$. But he realized that his proposed solution to the "transformation (from 'values' to 'prices') problem" was not quite right, since in a prices regime he should be using for corn's coal its $C_2$ and not its $c_2$ taken over from the values regime. However, many Marxians (Sweezy, Dobb, Winternitz, Johansen) and non-Marxians (Bortkiewicz, Seton-Morishima, Samuelson, . . .) have shown how his transformation procedure can be given the small needed correction, as done here. The present author has reviewed this matter in the *Journal of Economic Literature* for 1971.

3. These are not very cheerful laws of motion of capitalism. Therefore, after a stage of increased monopoly and intensified business cycles, the working class finally engineers a more-or-less violent revolution. "The expropriators are expropriated!"

4. As the twentieth century developed, Marxian writers like Rosa Luxemburg and V. I. Lenin added the view that mature capitalist countries will engage in *imperialistic exploitation* of colonial peoples. Capitalism's prosperity will depend on exploiting oil, bauxite, iron ore, uranium, and other natural resources. To keep up purchasing power at home and avoid mass unemployment, and to stave off falling rates of profit from accumulation at home, mature capitalist nations will indulge in much foreign investment and cold-war expenditures. So it is argued.

**Modern reality**    Enough has been said already in connection with Fig. 37-3, page 739, on what the actual trends of the advanced world have been: rising real wage trends; constant or gently rising wage share in GNP; profit rates of no clear long-run tendency; compound-interest growth in population; and still-higher growth rate in real GNP and matching capital stock. These are what Kaldor calls the "stylized facts" that have to be explained. And they are definitely at variance with vulgar Marxists' predicted trends under capitalism.

Also, in the age after Keynes, there is no need to belabor the fact that fiscal policy (deficits, if necessary) and central-bank money creation rob the Luxemburg-Lenin thesis of imperialism-to-stave-off-unemployment of whatever merit it may well have had in the early-century era of William Howard Taft and King Edward VII.

**Logical non sequiturs**    As mentioned in footnote 13 of the main part of this chapter, Karl Marx was not merely unlucky in his predicted factual laws of motion of capitalist development. The purported laws—as, e.g., the law of the declining rate of profit and the immiserization of the workers—are not cogently derivable from Marx's own conceptual schema. The level of the rate of surplus value, $m$, and the implied real wage (in this case, $\frac{1}{2}$ corn per day)—as well as their changes through time, are simply not deducible from within the Marx system. Here is why.

Unlike Malthus, Marx does not put much stock in a physiological minimum-subsistence wage. He is

reduced to appealing to the *deus ex machina* of a "reserve army of the unemployed" (for which he supplies *no theory* of determinate size and calculable incidence on the real wage level); and to the *deus ex machina* of whatever degree of labor-saving technical invention he needs to paint a sufficiently gloomy scenario of capitalistic development. Or, to put the same point in a different way, a Karl Marx brought back to life in J. B. Clark's era could have as easily assumed the case for immiserization by *merely postulating sufficient labor-saving technical change* in a Clark-Solow production function of aggregative type. Or, if brought to life in the post-1960 Sraffian era, Marx, eschewing surplus-value concepts, could have simply postulated low wages and high profits, again with no need or benefit from equalized-rate-of-surplus-value concepts.

## REJECTION OF MARGINAL-PRODUCTIVITY DISTRIBUTION THEORY

To question the fruitfulness in 1976 of 1867 Marxian concepts is not at all thereby to prove that everything is for the best in a bourgeois world where wages, rents, and interest are alleged to be determined by global marginal-productivity theory. Notice must be taken of Joan Robinson's critique of mainstream economics' theory of distribution.

Our coal-corn example can illustrate the point she and Sraffa have stressed.

"Each different profit or interest rate will give rise to a different real wage. So long as labor and coal *cannot* be smoothly substituted for each other along equal-corn-product contours like those in Fig. 27-3, economists lack an effective equation to determine the steady-state profit rate and the corn real wage. (How much more they lack a defensible theory of distribution in non-steady states!)" This, critics say.

**Alternative theories**    Professor Robinson, along with Kalecki and Kaldor, has suggested possible alternatives to marginal productivity. Thus, suppose labor grows at a compound rate of $g$ per period. And suppose that $\sigma_s$ is the fraction of profit income saved, with all of wages being consumed. Then in long-run balanced-growth equilibrium, we must have the following equation for the profit rate, $\pi$:

$$\pi = g/\sigma_s$$

For example, $20\% = 4\%/.2$.

Once $\pi$ is known, the corn real wage can be worked out from the profit-wage factor-price trade-off.[10]

### Wage determination by power?
Since the publication of Keynes' *General Theory* (1936), economists have realized that for workers to insist upon getting higher money wages need not mean their getting any higher real wages. Those who reject neoclassical marginal-productivity theories in favor of one or another macro theory of distribution (e.g., that of Kaldor-Kalecki) may still claim—as Böhm-Bawerk did by inference in a famous essay of 70 years ago entitled *Economic Law or Power?*—that capitalism will successfully resist any quick lowering of the share in GNP of profits.

We saw in the previous chapter the dynamics of never-ending cost-push inflation. We shall see, in next chapter's discussion of the economics of fascism, that strong-arm governments that are tough on unions and intellectuals can sometimes produce short-run, so-called "miracle" sprints of real growth—even with near-term real-wage growth. (Brazil's strong regime is a cited instance in the 1970s.)

Further research is needed if the alleged inadequacies of Marxian, neoclassical, and macroeconomic versions of distribution are not to leave economists with a vacuum where a theory of economic distribution should be. The actual real world will not know or care whether economists have "explained" distribution. But serious economists should care.

---

[10]To strengthen the case against the notion that thrift *always* increases some capital-output ratio and lowers the interest or profit rate, as in the simplest neoclassical parables, we may notice Chapter 30's possibility of "reswitching," page 617. Suppose that we can produce 1 coal by 4 labor invested for 1 year (two 6-month periods). This agrees with our Tableau's technology. But suppose we can alternatively produce 1 coal by the combination of 24/7 labor invested for 6 months (one 6-month period) and 8/7 labor invested for 18 months (three 6-month periods). Then, at very high profit rates and very low profit rates, above 100% per 6-month period and below 50% per 6-month period, competition will switch from, and then switch back to, the 4 labor method. But in between it will pick the "$^{24}/_7$ and $^8/_7$" method. How can the neoclassical parable explain the fact that reducing the interest rate first lowers the system's consumable GNP before restoring it to where it began? Clearly the usual neoclassical parable is oversimple.

### STEADY AND EXPANDED REPRODUCTION
Whatever the ultimate failure of mature Marxian analysis to explain the dynamics of the real wage under competitive capitalism, economists of all schools can agree that Karl Marx did make one stellar analytical contribution to what today we call von Neumann-Leontief input-output growth models.

### Steady reproduction
Our coal-corn example can serve nicely. But to be the more faithful to Marx's text, we add a third department or industry that produces a purely luxury good—say, valet services, with 1 labor hour needed for each unit of good 3.

Since this is to be a model of the steady state, we assume that capitalists save nothing, $\sigma_s = 0$, spending all their profits on luxury valet services. Workers spend all their wages on their minimum-subsistence corn. Since there is no net capital formation, all the coal produced is fed back into the system as raw material.

The stage is set. Here are the physical facts.

One-third of labor will work to produce workers' subsistence. So let our economy be forever endowed with, say, 100 labor days, or 1,200 labor hours. Then half the 400 hours that serve the workers goes for live labor in the corn industry, the other half going as dead labor to the coal industry to produce the 50 of coal needed for the 50 of corn subsistence. The other 800 hours is at the exploiting capitalists' disposal and goes to the third luxury department to produce 800 valet services.

Stationary equilibrium is maintained forever: The workers get their subsistence; the capitalists are doing zero net saving; exploitation proceeds to the end of time at a steady rate.

How would the "Values" and "Prices" Tableaux look? We can begin with either. That is, we can work with a 100% bourgeois profit rate, $\pi = 1.00$, and "prices" of coal, corn, valet service that are (8, 24, 2). Or we can work with a 200% rate of surplus value, and have "values" per unit of the three respective goods at (12, 24, 3).

Toss a coin, heads rather than tails wins, so the Values Tableau is to come first—on the left as (a) in next page's Table 42-1. (NOTE: Marx's notation reads "$400v_1$" as "400 of $v_1$," not as the mathematician's "400 *times* $v_1$." And likewise in all the Tableaux.)

The color coding makes it obvious that the orange

| TABLEAUX OF STEADY REPRODUCTION ($\sigma_s = 0$) | | |
|---|---|---|
| VALUES ($m = 2.00$) | | PRICES ($\pi = 1.00$) |

$$0c_1 + 200v_1 + 2.00(200)s_1 = \phantom{0}600 = 12(50)$$
$$12(50)c_2 + 200v_2 + 2.00(200)s_2 = 1{,}200 = 24(50)$$
$$0c_3 + 800v_3 + 2.00(800)s_3 = 2{,}400 = 3(800)$$

(a)

$$0C_1 + 200V_1 + 1.00(\phantom{0}0 + 200)S_1 = \phantom{00}400 = 8(50)$$
$$8(50)C_2 + 200V_2 + 1.00(400 + 200)S_2 = 1{,}200 = 24(50)$$
$$0C_3 + 800V_3 + 1.00(\phantom{0}0 + 800)S_3 = 1{,}600 = 2(800)$$

(b)

TABLE 42-1

sum of wages does equal the orange total of consumption corn. The green sum of surpluses does equal the green total of luxury goods. The brown sum of constant capitals does equal the brown total of coal raw material produced.

Now essentially the same physical story, but of course with changed pricing and valuations of the components, is shown by the bourgeois model—as (b) on the right of Table 42-1.

What is to be stressed is that the same physical totals are involved in the alternative models: the same valet services, the same subsistence corn, the same technological coal. The orange numbers agree because our convention is to use labor hours as our units in both cases; also, because in either model it takes $\frac{1}{2}$ of corn as subsistence to live each 12-hour day; and only when 1 corn costs 24 in both Tableaux, will we correctly depict the rock-bottom exploitative wage.

**Expanded reproduction**   Now go to the other extreme for exaggerated emphasis. Let capitalists save *all* their incomes, instead of none of their incomes as in the state of steady reproduction. Provided the system's labor grows at 100% per period (to match the von Neumann-like 100% profit rate), Marx can show that balanced-growth equilibrium could prevail forever.[11]

Here are the new physical facts.

As before, at the beginning when, say, each 100 man-days (or 1,200 hours) are available, we must still have at hand $\frac{1}{2}$ corn per man or 50 in all for minimum subsistence of the 100 men.

But since the system will next period be of twice

[11]*Capital*, Vol. II, Book II, Part III; Vol. III, Part VII, Chap. XLIX. The reader will note how much Leontief's input-output analysis of Chapter 37's Appendix, Table 37-2 on page 755, was anticipated by Marx a century ago.

the present size in *all* respects, we must be "planning" to produce now *twice* 50 corn for next period's subsistence. ("Planning" is in quotes because market forces might be the operative mechanism rather than bureaucracy or a computer.)

To produce this next harvest of 100 corn, we must now allocate 400 of our as-yet-only 1,200 hours to corn industry 2. Also, we must now allocate to corn production the needed 100 of coal raw material.

How much valet services are produced? None, if capitalists literally save all. The whole of their surpluses are invested in the growth of coal and corn inventories.

Exactly how much coal is scheduled for production now? To meet next period's doubled raw-material requirement, we must now allocate 800 hours to industry 1 to produce 200 coal. The stage is set.

Toss a coin once again. This time the Prices Tableau is to come first—as Table 42-2(a) on the next page.

Now the color coding is no longer quite so simple. Orange corn end-of-period consumption-output measured as 2,400 on the right is *twice* the total of orange wages on the left. Why? Because the system is *doubling* every period! Similarly, brown coal-output on the right must be double the total of brown coal-inputs on the left; that is why **200/2** always appears at the beginning of row 2.[12]

In leaving these Tableaux of reproduction, we may

[12]The sum of the green surpluses no longer equals the (zero!) total of luxury production. It could be shown that, with $\sigma_s = 1$, the total of surpluses equals net capital formation: the $\frac{200}{2}$ increment of coal and the $\frac{100}{2}$ increment of corn from this period to the next. The reader is invited to double all the numbers in Table 42-2, and contemplate next period's Tableaux. He will then verify that the total of the green surpluses in the first period does equal the jump *between* the periods in the coal and corn totals. Likewise for all the doubling and redoubling Tableaux in the future.

mention that Marxians can use them to disprove the contention of Rodbertus and Luxemburg that a limited-consumption system *must* ultimately run short of purchasing power. Marx sensed early what Harrod proved in our day: If a model grows fast enough, it can perform a self-warranted natural growth as indicated by the accelerator-multiplier model. (But, of course, it is not guaranteed without macroeconomic policy to stay on such a growth path.)

## SECULARIZING MARXIAN ECONOMICS

"Religion is the opiate of the people." This well-known aphorism of Karl Marx was inverted by Raymond Aron to become, "Marxism is the opiate of the intellectuals." With less wit, one can make the serious point: In economics, too often, "Marxism is the opiate of the Marxists."

Opiate in what sense? If you look up Marx's original quotation, you will probably be surprised to see that he meant there—not that religion is the elixir fobbed off by the ruling classes to dull the resentments and pains of the proletariat but that religion is an opiate in the sense of a comfort to wretched people.

Marx's Hegelian view of an inevitable revolution, soon to come, has similarly served as a comfort to Marxians, as well as serving as an analgesic to make the pain of hope long deferred more bearable.

Unfortunately, there is still a third connotation of the word "opiate"—namely, something that dulls the power to reason. And as one reviews the analyses made by Marxists in Eastern Europe, Asia, and the West, one has to recognize that until recently the use of Marxian categories did all too often addle the wits of those hoping to understand the realistic laws of motion of Western systems.

**Epicycles** If a religion—nay, if any Kuhnian system of paradigms—is to be adhered to in an epoch of change, it must develop certain flexibility to accommodate itself to transparent contradiction.

"To save the appearances," Ptolemaic astronomy could always add a new epicycle to allow for newly observed aberrations. Classical Marxism has survived by adaptation to the changing environment. Some well-known instances of dialectical reformulation may be mentioned.

1. The proletarian revolution is Hegelianly inevitable. But, the point is, one can hurry it along by political action.

2. The revolution is to take place first in the most advanced countries that have already gone through their bourgeois revolution and stage of decaying capitalism. But, Czarist Russia may be able to skip a revolution and the bourgeois stage. (Edmund Wilson even argued that Stalin's bureaucrats were, so to speak, Russia's bourgeoisie!)

3. The industrial proletariat is the revolutionary proletariat. But, in 1917 Russia, 1960 Cuba, and Mao's 1976 China, the peasantry may constitute the true proletariat.

4. The revolution must necessarily be violent. But, as Marx and Engels came to think late in life as they observed Victorian England, it could possibly be nonviolent, evolutionary, and (shades of ameliorist Samuel Gompers) trade-union and political action might better the workers' lot under late capitalism.

5. Immiserization and pauperization of the working classes are corollaries of the ineluctable laws of motion of capitalism. But, when one examines closely the texts of Marx, it may be that all the master meant is that (a) workers' relative share of GNP goes down; or that (b) this share fails to rise as fast as

| TABLEAUX OF EXPANDED REPRODUCTION ($\sigma_s = 1$) | |
|---|---|
| **PRICES ($\pi = 1.00$)** | **VALUES ($m = 2.00$)** |
| $0C_1 + 800V_1 + 1.00(\ 0 + 800)S_1 = 1,600 = 8(200)$ | $0c_1 + 800v_1 + 2.00(800)s_1 = 2,400 = 12(200)$ |
| $8\left(\dfrac{200}{2}\right)C_2 + 400V_2 + 1.00(800 + 400)S_2 = 2,400 = 24(100)$ | $12\left(\dfrac{200}{2}\right)c_2 + 400v_2 + 2.00(400)s_2 = 2,400 = 24(100)$ |
| $0C_3 +\ \ 0V_3 + 1.00(\ 0 +\ \ 0)S_3 =\ \ \ \ 0 = 2(0)$ | $0c_3 +\ \ 0v_3 + 2.00(\ \ 0)s_3 =\ \ \ \ 0 = 3(0)$ |
| (a) | (b) |

**TABLE 42-2**

their legitimate expectations or those of an egalitarian; or even merely that (c) workers under modern capitalism will feel increasingly "alienated."

One could go on, not in any sense of superior outside criticism, but because every one of these issues has played a central role *inside* the circle of discussion by the best-informed Marxists of each generation. And make no mistake. It is better to add an epicycle to explain the planet Uranus, than, ostrich-like, to deny its existence! Nonetheless, scientific cake that you are able at the same time to have and eat may not be worth having or eating.

In conclusion, Marxism may be too valuable to leave to the Marxists. It provides a critical prism through which mainstream economists can—to their own benefit—pass their analyses for unsparing audit.

## CONCEPTS FOR REVIEW

direct (live) and indirect (dead) labor
variable capital, $v_i$; constant capital, $c_i$
rates of surplus value: $s_1/v_1$, $s_2/v_2$, $m$
rates of profit, $S_1/(C_1 + V_1)$, $S_2/(C_2 + V_2)$, $\pi$
"Values": $c_i + v_i + s_i = c_i + v_i + mv_i$
"Prices": $(C_i + V_i) + S_i = (C_i + V_i) + \pi(C_i + V_i)$

exploitative subsistence wage
alleged laws of motion of wage and profit rates
critique of marginal productivity, reswitching,
    macroeconomic alternatives, power vs. law
steady reproduction Tableaux
expanded reproduction Tableaux

## 43 ALTERNATIVE ECONOMIC SYSTEMS

*Your old men shall dream dreams, your young men shall see visions.*
*Old Testament*

### THE CRISIS OF CAPITALISM?

After World War I, new governments were set up all over Europe. By 1925 an impartial observer might have said that the future of the capitalistic way of life appeared serene and assured.

Yet, within barely ten years, country after country succumbed to dictatorship; totalitarian fascist governments covered the map of Europe. The depression decade of the 1930s finally ended in a great world war.

After World War II, the outlook had changed. The world was divided into great blocs. The mixed economies of North America, Western Europe, Japan, and Australasia formed one common pattern. The great communist powers, the Soviet Union, China, and the other socialist countries of Eastern Europe, formed another common pattern. Finally, in Africa, Asia, and Latin America, there were the less developed nations, throwing off their colonial shackles and choosing coolly between the rival ideologies of the great powers.

Within the advanced countries themselves, the scene was drastically changed from the Victorian days of laissez faire capitalism. Almost unconsciously, undiluted capitalism had been evolving into a *mixed economy* with both private and public initiative and control. The clock of history sometimes evolves so slowly that its moving hands are never *seen* to move. After the New Deal, American economic life was never again the same. We had converged with Western Europe to the mixed economy.

Every news dispatch reminds us that the mixed-economy way of life is on trial. Not only must it perform adequately, but more than that, it must perform superlatively. Vitally important is the image that a society has of itself—particularly in the minds of its own youth. And a quarter of a century ago, a failure of nerve was becoming evident in the West.

## THE NEW LOOK

Little wonder, then, that profound social philosophers, like Harvard's Joseph Schumpeter, thought they could foretell in the years after 1945 the displacement of capitalism by socialism. Even profound philosophers can turn out to be quite wrong. Following World War II, gradually the "New Economics" of the modern mixed economy, trumpeted in advance by no ideology, began to take over. If Keynes could have come back from the grave, he might have said: "I have seen the present. And it works!"[1]

In West Germany there was a miracle of recovery and development. The same thing happened in the Netherlands, France, Italy, and the Common Market countries of Europe generally. Japan, by a mixture of private initiative and state planning, embarked on a sprint hardly ever before equaled in history. Israel—helped, to be sure, by gifts and loans from abroad—had her miracle decades. Even ancient problem economies, like Greece, Austria, and Brazil, were able to find in the mixed economy a path to rapid and sustained economic growth. Taiwan, Mexico, Thailand, and Korea all sprinted forward.

Something new has been born under the sun. The prophesied timetable of inevitability—savagery to feudalism, feudalism to capitalism, capitalism to socialism, socialism to communism—has for the moment taken on the appearance of a fable.

But fables and legends and aspirations have a hold on the minds of men. It is therefore worth reviewing, if only briefly, the traditional forms of alternative economic systems. These are of interest for their own sakes. They are also of interest as part of the intellectual history of the human race. And not least, they are of interest in disabusing our minds of the tyranny of certain facile generalizations which, like most facile generalizations, simply will not stand up to the hard facts of actual experience.

**Political freedoms inseparable from economic freedoms?**   Thus, is it true that without free markets for goods and services, democratic freedoms and political civil rights cannot prevail? Many economic libertarians argue this: that *personal* liberties and *property* liberties are one and inseparable. But are they right?

At the other extreme, many advocates of socialism argue that "political democracy" is but a sham if the state does not get rid of "production for profit" and replace it by "production for use" and guarantee "fair shares" all around. But are they right?

And in particular, is the argument correct in the learned and persuasive book *The Road to Serfdom* (1945), by Friedrich Hayek (of Austria, England, the United States, and Germany), that each step away from the market system and toward the social reforms of the welfare state is *inevitably* a journey that must end in a totalitarian state with neither efficiency nor liberty? The opposing view, held by such evolutionists as Roosevelt, Churchill, and Nehru, is that gradual reforms are the only way to prevent a cataclysmic descent through revolution into a communist dictatorship. If the evolutionists are right, Hayek is quite wrong—as Fig. 43-2 will later investigate.

Let us review the troops.

[1] This echoes the words of Lincoln Steffens when he visited Russia after the 1917 revolution: "I have seen the future. And it works!"

## A BOUQUET OF ISMS

Men have always had visions of a more perfect society: Plato's Republic, Sir Thomas More's Utopia, Marx's Dictatorship of the Proletariat, and so on without number. It is easy to look at concrete present-day imperfections and then to contrast them with the ideal features of a vaguely defined utopia. Beyond agreeing that the present order has faults, different schools of reform often have little in common.

At the one extreme are the anarchists, who believe in no government at all; at the other, the apologists for an all-powerful, collectivized, totalitarian, communistic social order, where the first person singular is all but replaced by the first person plural. Within the field of socialism itself, we find subdivisions: Christian socialism, state and Marxian socialism, guild socialism, Fabian (evolutionary) socialism, and many others.

In the popular mind, socialists are characters who meet in a cellar lit by a candle thrust in an empty wine bottle to plot a bloody revolution, or at least to brew bombs sent in laundry parcels to government officials and capitalists. Or the term "socialist" is often used as a disparaging stereotype to discredit anyone who believes in social security, progressive taxation, bank-deposit insurance, pollution-control, or free love.

Whatever the strength of radical parties abroad, in America no third party has yet been able to develop in any strength.[2] The American Socialist party runs a candidate for the presidency—along with the Prohibition and Conservative parties—but gains only a negligible fraction of the vote. The American Communist party never could gain a sizable vote, either under its own name or in camouflage.

If we look at Europe, we find the names of almost all the parties have the word "socialism" in them. But this does not mean much: a party such as France's Radical Socialists turns out to be anything but radical, being one of the conservative parties. Even Hitler's fascistic party took the name of "National Socialism."

Often, however, the leading European reform parties can be characterized as "social democrats." For example, the Labor party in Britain, the German Social Democratic party, the ruling parties in much of Scandinavia—all these claim to be in favor of gradual, nonrevolutionary extension of socialism by peaceful and democratic methods.

It is clear, therefore, that we do not have to master all the thousand and one different "isms" in order to understand the world today. It is enough to understand something of (*a*) relative laissez faire, from which the mixed economy evolved; (*b*) socialism; (*c*) communism; and (*d*) fascism.

There is no hard-and-fast boundary between these; it is a matter of degree. Moreover, we cannot even range them along a line, with fascism at the extreme right wing and communism at the extreme left wing. In some ways—although neither would admit it—communism and fascism have much in common. Anarchism of the New Left unites with Herbert Spencer's libertarianism in its contempt for the liberal state. Labor Syndicalists favor the violent methods of Fascists.

---

[2] Theodore Roosevelt's 1912 Bull Moose party was primarily an offshoot of the Republican party. Old Bob La Follette's 1924 Progressive party was the most successful third party, yet was able to carry only his state, Wisconsin. Henry Wallace's 1948 Progressive party was an utter failure. George Wallace, catering to regionalism, racial backlash, and antiestablishment discontents and conservatism, had to pin his hopes for influence on an Electoral College stalemate and on increasing the bargaining power of the petty bourgeoisie and the privileged workers who fear loss of status.

Capitalism, in the sense of undiluted laissez faire, died before Queen Victoria died. And most of this book has been concerned with describing the mixed economy which buried it. So we may turn briefly to the others.

## FASCISM

This is easier to characterize politically than economically. Be it in Hitler's Germany, Mussolini's Italy, Franco's Spain, Salazar's Portugal, Perón's Argentina, the Greek, Pakistani, Brazilian, or Chilean juntas, fascism was usually characterized by a one-man dictatorship, by one political party with all others abolished, by the disappearance of civil liberties of the type granted in our Bill of Rights. Fascistic movements are always highly nationalistic, sometimes with emphasis placed on a vaguely defined "master race" which exploits minority groups. In the words of Mussolini, fascists are urged to "live dangerously"—to value war and national power as ends in themselves. The individual is to be secondary to the state.

On the economic side, Mussolini's fascism happened to toy with the notion of a "syndicalist," or "corporate," state; each industry and group of workers was organized in a syndicate, and these were to meet and bargain and plan how the economy should be run. However, outside of its socialist manifestation in Yugoslavia, this syndicalism has never come to much and has not been especially characteristic of other fascist regimes. Almost all of them are against free and militant trade-unionism; almost all give the central government great regulatory power over every sphere of economic life. Some work hand in glove with religious authorities; others are antichurch. The fascist mentality tends to be intolerant of opposition, romantic and antirational, often with an especial appeal to youth. Usually, capitalists and the lower middle classes contribute to the *initial* strength of fascist movements; but later, when the fascist movement begins to take on—as they sometimes do—revolutionary aspects, the capitalists may regret the Frankenstein's monster that they helped to create.

Their only consolation lies in the fact that one of the earmarks of a fascist regime is opposition to communism. Generally, fascism sails into power by exaggerating the immediate likelihood of a Marxist revolution, and after it has come into power, the threat of communism is used as an excuse for the suppression of democratic processes.

Fascism is the great spoiler. It thrives on the breakdown of markets and of democratic processes. Often its leaders are revolutionaries turned reactionary. Its followers are military officers, dispossessed farmers and small merchants, groups who are losing economic and social status or who resent newly rising groups—big business, blacks, foreigners, the poor living on governmental welfare assistance, etc. Big business itself chimes in, both to hedge its bets and in fear of a communist takeover.

**Order and economic efficiency?**  We have seen that many economies may be subject to the disorder of creeping inflation. Full employment and price stability are then apparently incompatible goals. Undoubtedly, the struggle by union workers to raise their hourly wage rate has for its goal improving labor's share of the total pie of GNP. But, in fact, higher hourly wages lead to higher prices as corporations fight back to preserve property's share in the pie of GNP. Real wages are seen not to be capable of being raised much, if at all, by the bootstrap operation of militant collective bargaining, slowdowns, strikes, sitdown strikes, general strikes, and so forth.

Lenin is often quoted (by Keynes, for one) as having once said: "We shall contrive the death of capitalism by debauching its currency." There is no evidence he ever wrote this; at least no one has been able to locate the quotation. But his alleged aphorism can be improved on, in the following form.

"The best way to ruin a mixed economy—to kill off its full-employment progress and exacerbate its class struggles—is to contrive (as was done in Peron's Argentina) a 40 per cent overnight increase in wage rates. The result will be structural inflation, lockouts, strikes, breakdowns, bankruptcies, and public unrest."

When a populistic mixed economy is running badly, experiencing both inflation and unemployment at the same time, will there then emerge a demand for a fascist takeover—to restore "orderly conditions and promote economic growth"? Alas, the answer too often is, Yes.

Dictatorial regimes, or states run with an iron hand, do witness an occasional economic success—in the short run. Thus, in the 1970s, the Brazilian military regime may have been hard on professors, intellectuals, and a free press. But, as people used to say in Mussolini's time, "At least the trains run on time. . . ." And, when one looks in the U.N. *Statistical Year Book,* one finds that Brazil was in those same years the veritable Japan of Latin America, averaging annual rates of real GNP growth of 10 per cent per year.

Benevolent despotisms, history demonstrates, rarely remain benevolent, and almost never even stay efficient. Mussolini failed to deliver what his speeches promised. Hitler's Germany, we now know from captured records, was a poorly run economy. If one Pakistan dictator seems for a time to make the agricultural sector grow, the next dictator plunges the country into dismembering warfare!

The blueprint of fascism, in blunt fact, rarely works out well in real life even in its own terms. Which is not to deny that social disorder kills off economic progress.

## SOCIALISM

In defining fascism, we were able to point to Nazi Germany or fascist Italy. Socialism cannot be so easily described. Of course, we can describe the Swedish socialist government or the British Labour party's program, but these do not present such dramatic contrasts with our system. They represent a middle way more like our own "mixed system" than that of Soviet Russia or China.

There are a few common elements that seem to characterize socialist philosophy:

1. *Government ownership of productive resources.* The role of private property is gradually to be lessened as key industries such as railroads, coal, and even steel are gradually nationalized. Unearned profits from increases in land value are also limited. (In West Germany and the United Kingdom, enthusiasm for nationalization has ebbed.)

2. *Planning.* Instead of permitting the free play of profit motives as in a laissez faire market economy, coordinated planning is to be introduced. Sometimes the program of "production for use rather than profit" is advocated; advertising expenditure on gadgets is to be reduced; workers and professional people are to develop

instincts of craftsmanship and social service so that they will be guided by motives other than those of our "acquisitive society."

3. *Redistribution of income.* Inherited wealth and swollen incomes are to be reduced by militant use of government taxing powers. Social security benefits, free medical care, and cradle-to-grave welfare services collectively provided are to increase the well-being of the less-privileged classes and guarantee minimum standards of living.

4. *Peaceful and democratic evolution.* Socialism, as distinct from communism, often advocates the *peaceful and gradual extension* of government ownership—revolution by *ballot* rather than by *bullet*. This aim is often more than a tactical move—rather, a deep philosophical tenet of faith.

**British socialism**   A brief look at British socialism will point up the modern issues. Just when Adam Smith's classical economics had won the day from its mercantilistic and feudal predecessors, English intellectual opinion began to move beyond laissez faire and toward socialism. A key case is that of John Stuart Mill, who was brought up by an eighteenth-century exponent of utilitarian individualism (his father, James Mill), but who had by the last half of the nineteenth century turned to a kind of socialism. Then, early in the twentieth century, university and night-school intellectuals were won to the Fabian doctrines of the *inevitability of gradualism.* And these socialist views of Bernard Shaw and Beatrice and Sidney Webb became pretty much the views of the trade-union movement.

All this was hidden until World War I. After that war, the Liberal party was ground away between the millstones of the Conservative and Labour parties. Only after World War II did Labour really come into power. Its early goals included (*a*) vast extension of welfare services by the state—in which Conservative governments in large degree have acquiesced; (*b*) heavy redistributive income and estates taxation—in which to a degree the Conservatives also acquiesce; (*c*) extensive centralized planning, including stringent regulation of land use and zoning; and finally (*d*) initially a fairly sweeping program of nationalization, beginning with coal, power, and railroads and, in the doctrines of the left wing of the party, reaching beyond steel to many branches of wholesaling and distribution, engineering, ordnance, and the largest corporations.

In the mid-1970s, the Labour party finds itself quite divided and doubtful on how far to carry traditional socialism. This shows itself in debates over the extent to which nationalization should be pressed and the degree to which reliance should be placed on market mechanisms. At the intellectual level, now that so many of the goals set up years ago in *Fabian Essays* have been realized, there is much soul searching going on; and challenging new Fabian essays are hard to write. Is "mere New Dealism designed to make capitalism work well" adequate? And can the mixed economy command the idealistic enthusiasm that more sweeping reforms were historically able to fire? Has the improvement of living standards pushed the militant poor up into the contented middle classes? Has making society more fluid tended to drain off the bright son of poor parents to Oxbridge and the Establishment, alienating him from the radical trade-union tradition? Has the search for equality been at the expense of material progress?

Nor is this quandary unique to Britain. In Sweden, Norway, Denmark, Australia, and New Zealand, the so-called "middle way" of moderate labor socialism has now been in, or knocking on the door of, power for half a century. Yet every one of these economies begins to look more and more like what the United States itself has become after five decades of administration by Roosevelt, Truman, Eisenhower, Kennedy, Johnson, Nixon, and Ford. With some exaggeration, John Kenneth Galbraith and Jan Tinbergen can point to a convergence, all over the globe, to a single modern industrial state—not capitalism, not socialism, but a mixed economy.

**French "indicative planning"**  Ideologically rather removed from traditional socialism is the development in France of planning by the state. Both before and after de Gaulle, many important industries are owned and run by the French government: railroads, electricity, and mines, for example. The tools of economics—marginal-cost pricing of power, benefit-cost analysis of the worthwhile program of investments in these state industries—deserve much of the credit for the remarkable rate of real growth in France during the 1950–1975 period. But that is not all.

Even private industry is brought into a comprehensive national plan. This involves, however, one important difference from the traditional planning of socialist societies. In the French mixed economy, participation in *Le Plan* is *mostly voluntary*. (But, as everywhere these days, what firm dares get the authorities too angry at it—particularly when permission to go to the capital markets often is controlled by government?)

Representatives of different industries sit down together in committees, presided over by civil servants who serve the plan. Businessmen are given quantitative information on realizable national goals for the years ahead; and they respond with information on what these goals will mean for their own industries. In turn, these replies are made the basis for a *recalculation* of the aggregates and details of the plan.

In the end, each industry learns that it can count on an expanding market. And as business firms in those industries proceed to meet these indicated goals, they do generate the production, income, and demand called for by the plan.

How has it all worked out? Tolerably well if we can judge by results. In the late 1960s, many an English reformer would have traded some of the "pie in the sky" of traditional socialism for some pragmatic fruits of indicative planning. A National Economic Development Council ("NEDDY") was set up to imitate the French methods, and Wilson's Labour government set up a Ministry of Economic Affairs to promote such programs—but with little success.

Similarity must not conceal diversity. In Egypt, Burma, Ghana, and many other countries recently released from colonialism, there has been widespread nationalization of industry. But, as yet, there have been few cases where the result has been a rapid rate of real economic growth. Similarly, economies like Argentina, despite resources and technology that many a poor country would envy, stagnated under state controls introduced by dictator Perón. The dismal records in the 1950s of Ghana under Nkrumah and Indonesia under Sukarno show that the slogans of socialism under a great national leader will not themselves suffice to solve the economic problem of WHAT, HOW, and FOR WHOM. To take but three examples, Nkrumah, Sukarno, and Perón give one new respect for Mao—and for Adam Smith too!

### MARXIAN COMMUNISM AND SOVIET RUSSIA: HISTORY

Marxian communism represents a departure both from earlier utopian socialist movements and also from evolutionistic socialist movements of the last century. In the previous chapter, we surveyed the chief theoretical doctrines of Marx and his successors. Let us review how these ideas worked themselves out.

In 1917, the big moment came. Czarist Russia was knocked out of the war by the Germans. Lenin, a follower of Marx, was transported in a sealed railroad car across Germany and into Russia. Aided by Trotsky, a one-time New Yorker, Lenin's Bolsheviks snatched power from the moderate Kerenski regime that had overthrown the monarchy. Preaching peace and promising land for the peasants and a dictatorship of the proletariat, the followers of the Red hammer and sickle gained adherents in the navy and army and forcibly took power.

There followed what John Reed of Harvard (later buried in the Kremlin) called "ten days that shook the world." The meeting of the democratic Constituent Assembly, only few of whose elected representatives were pro-Bolshevik, was forbidden. An army was organized and trained by Trotsky, and successive towns were won over to the revolutionary forces—often by strategic capture of the water and power supplies alone. Then followed a great civil war between the Red and White armies, the latter aided by Poland and Western powers. In the end, the officers of the White army ended up chiefly in Paris, driving taxicabs and drinking vodka to the memory of Czar Nicholas.

**The revolution achieved**    The world expected a Russian collapse; but the communist regime persisted—not without experiencing horrible famines, in which literally millions perished. Aristocrats and bourgeoisie were ruthlessly purged and liquidated. The Communist party was the only political party permitted; only a fraction of the population could belong to this elite group; it elected the members of local "soviets" of factories and farms. These elected representatives to still higher soviets, until, at the very top, over all the federated Union Republics, stood the Council of People's Commissars of the Supreme Soviet of the U.S.S.R. (Union of Soviet Socialist Republics).

The Soviet leaders had no blueprint to guide them. Marx had confined himself largely to the *faults* of capitalism and had revealed very little about what the promised land was to be like. It was not even on the timetable that backward Russia, which had hardly emerged from feudalism into capitalism, should experience its revolution before the downfall of the top-heavy industrialized nations. During the 1920s, Lenin compromised with capitalistic enterprise in the NEP (New Economic Policy). But in 1928–1929, the first Five-Year Plan for industrialization of manufacturing and collectivization of agriculture was drafted. This was followed by later Five-Year Plans.

Because of the rapid pace of capital formation, war preparedness, and the state of Russian technology, consumption was severely rationed throughout these years. Workers had ration cards that were honored at specific stores, but money continued to be used. Excess money income could be spent only upon special goods at higher prices than on the basic ration. Real and money wages differed among occupations, with piece rates and incentive pay for high productivity becoming ever more dominant.

**Stalinism**    Stalin, one of Lenin's many lieutenants, finally won out in the struggle for power after Lenin's death in the early 1920s. Trotsky and other old-line revolutionaries were accused of plotting with foreign powers against the Soviet Union, and in the middle 1930s a tremendous purge of generals and officials culminated in the sensational Moscow trials—sensational because defendants vied with one another in avowing their own guilt. After the Chamberlain-Hitler appeasement pact, Nazi Germany and Soviet Russia in 1939 signed a nonaggression pact, which lasted until Hitler—flushed with his victory over Poland and France and lusting for the farmlands of the Ukraine—attacked the Soviet Union.

With fanatical patriotism and aided by the United States lend-lease, the Russians traded their blood for the Germans' blood, until few Germans were left in the U.S.S.R. After the defeat of the Axis, the comradeship with the West flickered out, and the world stood in the cold-war shadow of the hydrogen bomb, with the Soviet Union trying to spread its influence over Europe and Asia, with the Atlantic nations and us bent on stopping it on the one hand, and China threatening it on the other.

In the postwar period, Stalin's one-man rule became more and more paranoid, and his death in 1953 brought in the inevitable revulsion toward his regime. What seemed to be a thaw set in under the rule of Khrushchev, and sprigs of criticism began to push up their sprouts. But the Poles, Hungarians, and Leningrad students learned that winter was not quite over. Peaceful coexistence and détente became the 1970s official line, and was continued after Khrushchev's replacement by the committee rule of Brezhnev. Faced by the rivalry of China, the Soviet Union was in no mood to tolerate a free press and electorate in Czechoslovakia, much less dissident intellectuals and ethnic militants at home.

## DIVERSITY ON THE LEFT: YUGOSLAVIA

Let's turn from history to present-day reality. Reserving the Soviet economy for later, let's look at two polar patterns: decentralized Yugoslavia, centralized China.

**Yugoslav decentralization**   The communist resistance-movement came to power under Tito after World War II. From 1945 to 1950 a program of planned development along conventional Stalinist lines worked out badly—both in terms of planning goals and in comparison with post-World War I similar years. Following the political break with the Russian COMINFORM in 1948, Yugoslavia undertook a new "separate path to socialism" involving "decentralization and popular participation." The experiment has excited much interest abroad, both for its own sake as an example of "participatory democracy" and as the only instance of a successful retreat from Soviet dominance.

In essence, Titoism has involved a return to greater dependence on market pricing, on profitability criteria and incentives. It has not meant abandonment of socialism and one-party control, nor of central planning. But it has meant that a factory may be run by its own workers in many sectors of the economy. Here is a sample case.

Twenty to one hundred workers in a factory form a workers' council. Nominally they elect their own managers. (They may even advertise for a trained executive!) They "borrow" their capital from the central pool. (Sometimes capital is "auctioned" off to the highest bidder.) *The firm can decide to produce what it thinks will sell.* It may import raw materials from abroad, sometimes even on foreign credit. It can cut costs in the hope that, after it has paid its income and land taxes, what is left over can go to the workers as bonus income or be plowed back into the enterprise.

How have things worked out? From 1950 to 1976 progress has been uneven with oscillations between centralization and decentralization. But the system has been viable, and growth under it has surpassed that of the earlier Stalinist period. Even if the cynicism expressed by insiders concerning the amount of power the workers themselves exercise is justified, this system of syndicalist structure presumably offers some counter-vailing influence to the power of the bureaucrats, those whom Milovan Djilas has called "the new class." The crucial test comes with Tito's death.

## MAOIST CHINA

China is as far to the left of the U.S.S.R. as Yugoslavia is to the right. China and the U.S.S.R. each claim that the other has deviated from the legitimate Marx-Lenin line of communist development. (See the back flyleaf for the bifurcated genealogy.)

China has a special interest to the rest of the world because of its vast size and population. The fact of its historical poverty adds interest: If a dictatorship, not of the proletariat but of the peasantry, can succeed in ending poverty in so poor a region, there are many other places in the world that will wish to explore the same patterns. The Soviet Union, for the first time since the days of Lenin, faces a serious ideological challenge as the leader and spearhead of socialism.

Cuban experiments that require professors and white-collar people generally to cut sugar cane have their counterpart in the Chinese insistence that all people share the experience of manual labor. More dramatic than ping pong or acupuncture is the apparent transformation of the traditional Chinese way of life. Venereal disease, according to Paul Dudley White, the eminent heart specialist who took care of President Eisenhower, has been eradicated in China. The filth and cursing in the streets, so familiar to old China hands, seems miraculously gone. No wonder that those with a belief in regeneration of human nature—who, like the Webbs, used to see miracles in Soviet life until the truth about Stalinism belatedly seeped out—should look with noble hopes toward the Chinese experiment.

As the inevitable succession to Mao takes form, China moves toward closer rapprochement with the rest of the world. The visit to Peking of President Nixon signaled a new epoch, in which admittance to the U.N. of the People's Republic of China provided an opening symbol. New political and economic relations with Japan continued the trend. But what are the facts on the Chinese economy?

In 1960 a fair-minded observer of mainland China, India, and Pakistan might have expected China to show by far the greatest rate of real growth in the following dozen years. Under Chairman Mao, the populace was mobilized for collective effort and sacrifice. It was even expected that steel could be produced in thousands of backyard furnaces. A "great leap forward" seemed to be in the offing.

Looking back from 1976, we see that reality fell a bit short of these expectations. India, under democracy, made uneven progress—depending on monsoon weather conditions and foreign aid. Pakistan, under military dictatorship and by dint of massive foreign aid to agriculture, was able to increase fertilizer and food production—until repression led to partition. China was notably successful in producing a uranium bomb, and then, later, a hydrogen bomb. But the intervening emphasis on ideological sound-ness and hostility toward technical experts led to a surprising degree of economic stagnation. Unlike the Russian statistics, which turned out under careful audit to have some tolerable relation to reality, the initial Chinese claims for production increases turned out, in subsequent careful examination and cross-checking, to be grossly inflated. The opinion of two Cornell experts alleges a more sobering tale:[3]

The national product fell by roughly 15 per cent from 1958 to 1961. . . . Only by 1965 did the economy finally regain the 1958 level. . . . The Great Proletarian Cultural Revolution . . . led to a loss of 400,000 specialists. . . . Economism—i.e., efficiency, became one of the worst epithets. . . . Revolutionary mass enthusiasm replaced trained management. . . .

As against this pessimistic appraisal, here is the summary by Professor John Gurley of Stanford, a sympathetic student of Chinese economics. This appraisal was made before Gurley's 1972 trip to China, which seemed to fulfill his optimistic expectations.[4]

. . . the Chinese people over the past two decades have made very remarkable economic advances (though not steadily) on almost all fronts. The basic, overriding economic fact about China is that for twenty years she has fed, clothed, and housed everyone, has kept them healthy, and has educated most. Millions have *not* starved; sidewalks and streets have *not* been covered with multitudes of sleeping, begging, hungry, and illiterate human beings; millions are *not* disease-ridden. . . . In this respect, China has outperformed every underdeveloped country in the world . . . . China's gains in the medical and public health fields are perhaps the most impressive of all.

A. G. Ashbrook, a U.S. government expert not expected to be soft on China, sums up the 1975 outlook thus:[5]

. . . the economy of the People's Republic of China has proved an effective mechanism for supplying the minimum needs of the population, modernizing the industrial sector, and supporting a formidable defense establishment. . . . With its floor under consumption, its purposeful investment program, its control over migration to urban areas, and its hard-driving leadership, China has easily outdistanced other LDCs.

Clearly, as the criticisms of the bureaucratic regime of the U.S.S.R. by Nobel prize winners Solzhenitsyn and Sakharov lessen its appeal to radicals elsewhere, it is not surprising that China tends to serve as a model for leftist movements around the world, the first successful ideological competitor to post-Lenin Russia.

## THE SOVIET ECONOMY

We now turn for a look in depth at the single most important socialist economy—that of the U.S.S.R. How does the Soviet Union get the three basic problems decided: WHAT shall be produced, How, and FOR WHOM?

In broad outline,[6] the picture is this: *The state owns almost all factors of production:*

[3] Letter to *New York Times*, June 17, 1969, by Professors Walter Galenson and Ta-Chung Liu.
[4] This quotation is taken from John G. Gurley, "Capitalist and Maoist Economic Development," *Monthly Review* (February, 1971), pp. 15–35, particularly pp. 26–27.
[5] A. G. Ashbrook, Jr., "China: Economic Overview, 1975," in Joint Economic Committee, *Compendium on China*, July 10, 1975.
[6] F. D. Holzman, *Readings in the Soviet Economy* (Rand McNally, Chicago, 1962), is a useful reference. See also, in P. A. Samuelson, *Readings in Economics* (McGraw-Hill, New York, 1973, 7th ed.), discussion by expert Abram Bergson of Harvard.

factories, mines, and land. Workers generally earn their living *by wages;* they do have considerable choice of occupation, but a Soviet citizen does not have unlimited right to seek employment in any region and industry that happens to capture his fancy.

**WHAT**  A political decision is made that defense and capital formation are to be pushed hard; what is left over is permitted to go to consumers' goods. While a Russian can indicate his preferences among different goods by the way he spends his income, any resulting shortages or gluts have been permitted only recently to result in the bidding up or down of consumer goods prices, thereby automatically producing the positive or negative returns that serve to rechannel resources. So long as goods were very scarce, central planners could decide that people would want so much of food, so much of shoes, and so much of various other necessities of life. Any and all of these were eagerly bought as they became available; if the local store or commissary had shoes not exactly your size, you were glad to take them a little large rather than do without.

Now that some of the comforts—and even luxuries—of life are beginning to become available, it is no longer enough to think of giving people merely what they "need". Centralized planning has become a little more difficult. These days, certain goods will not get bought at all, and the planners have come to learn that they must cut back on them. Even advertising and selling have reared their heads in Russia! It is harder to learn what people want than what they do *not* want, and marketing surveys are still in their infancy. The Soviet commissars are not yet experienced in determining what people would want most *if* they had the choice; but they do find it useful to watch what Americans and others abroad like to consume and then later introduce such products. Thus, that rare comrade who gets a car will find it resembling our cars of the past; and experts tell us this imitative pattern, which is not at all irrational (since it assumes that what one human being will like, so will another), is becoming more common.

With respect to capital goods and military expenditure, *direct state decisions* are made. Industrialization is pushed hard: electrification, transportation, mining development, a big push in chemicals and fertilizers, collectivization of agriculture and crop patterns—*such matters are broadly determined by conscious political decision.*

**How**  Private enterprise is negligible in importance. Instead, the typical Soviet factory will be a state-owned *enterprise.*

Just as the president of General Motors owns little of its total stock, the manager or head of this state-owned enterprise has no ownership of its capital; but he does get better-than-average pay for his work, plus various travel expenses, auto transport, and other special privileges. This member of the Galbraithian "technostructure" may even get bonuses, and his chance of promotion to a bigger enterprise will depend upon how well his enterprise meets its quota. He gives orders much like any boss and expects his subordinates to obey them, just as he obeys orders from above. (To avoid penalties for failing to meet his quota, he may hoard steel and other materials rather than give them to some other enterprise; and many cases have been observed where bureaucrats will contrive to make it appear that their plant has been very productive, even if that means they must conceal its true potential efficiency. EXAMPLES: Enterprises may malinger so as to get a low quota that can be easily achieved or surpassed. Stories have been well told of a transportation enterprise which moved carloads of water back and forth in order to be able to say it had accomplished the target of so many physical ton-miles.)

In recent years, meaningless physical quotas are beginning to be replaced by "profitability" criteria of performance that do involve *economic valuation* of diverse goods—a modest step in the direction of Western pricing methods and mathematical programming.

The decision of how to combine various productive factors—land and labor, degree of mechanization—appears to depend on a mixture of purely technical considerations and adaptations to the scarcities of various economic resources. A continual process of trial and error goes on. The observer finds operations curiously uneven: on the one hand, he may see a military ballistic plant which has achieved a precision of ball bearings and gyroscopes rivaling the best in the world; on the other hand, he may find things being done in an almost unbelievably primitive way, with the quality of output practically worthless. (EXAMPLE: A Soviet farmwoman may still be assigned 1 cow to take care of; on a mechanized Wisconsin dairy farm, a man and a wife may take care of 50 cows, in addition to performing countless other daily chores. Private allotments of land on the collective farms often have much higher, not lower, productivity than the collectivized sectors.)

All Soviet economic life is a pyramid tapering upward. Above the individual enterprises in an industry and region will be a regional economic council. Above the regional councils will be a council of ministers; alongside the ministries will be the planners of the Gosplan. Experts tell us it is quite misleading to concentrate on the organizational charts of the process, for *there is a constantly changing mixture of centralization and decentralizing:* commands, delegated responsibility, and initiative; carrots of reward and kicks or imprisonments as penalties.

Some things are very much the same everywhere. The head of an enterprise will, almost certainly, be a member of the Communist party. A successful bureaucrat there is something like a successful "organization man" here: he must be obedient but resourceful, both obsequious and arrogant, energetic and nonsentimental. The point is not that the worst types get ahead. The point is that ability does count, on the average; but mere technical ability without the skill of getting along with people is not enough either in Detroit or in Volgograd. Padding of expense accounts and contriving to hold business meetings near popular Black Sea resorts or spas in the Caucasus Mountains are complained of regularly in the Soviet press.

Experts also tell us that it is naïve to think that there is an elaborate formalized structure of planning, so that one could write a treatise on pure communistic economics that would equal in length a treatise on the general equilibrium of competitive markets.

FOR WHOM   To a considerable degree the Russian economy works for the security of the state and for the future. How much the present generation of Russians consume of private goods is *not* primarily determined by *their day-to-day* spending and working decisions. True, they do earn wages (and a small amount of interest or lottery winnings on government bonds is also permitted). Moreover, wages are by no means equal, and certainly not higher for the needy and handicapped than for the energetic and educated. Skilled workers get much more than unskilled. Free trade-unions as we know them do not exist, but woe to the manager who gets all the workers against him. Piece rates and incentive systems are frequently used, and there is much exhortation toward working hard for the fatherland and for the "brotherhood of man." (Soviet novels often have for their plots the tale of how a good boy and girl foil the malingering of antisocial culprits and, by use of a virtuous tractor, overcome the recalcitrance of the stubborn soil. Boy meets girl here as everywhere, but the durable goods are much in evidence.)

Social classes as Marx and Engels knew them in 1848 may not exist in the Soviet Union. But there is a definite pattern of social and political stratification. A poor boy who is bright may become a physicist and live well. It is important for him to rank high in the exams that select the few who can go to college. (His way at the university is completely paid for, just as the comrade who puts the shot in the Olympics is paid to pursue that occupation.) After graduation he hopes to score well enough to be able to pursue the study of physics in Moscow, rather than be sent out as a technician and engineer to the Ural Mountains or some other distant post. As a well-paid professor he can look down on all but the top bureaucrats: he may have a car, a cottage in the country, and finely equipped laboratories. Of course, he cannot take it with him, but he can at least hope to give his son a good start in the stiff educational competition.

There are various economic devices by which the system ensures that it gets the For Whom it desires—heavy emphasis on *industrialization* and military *security*.

For one thing, goods at every stage of production are subject to heavy taxation (the so-called "turnover tax," which contrasts with a tax on true value added). The resulting elevation of prices in relation to wages paid out ensures that the public will be able to consume only a part of all that it can produce, in quite the same way as our economy uses taxes to siphon resources away from private and into public channels. Macroeconomic equilibrium is needed there as here!

Another device is to set a much higher markup over costs for consumers' goods, ensuring that they generally are priced much higher in relation to some set of true economic costs than are military and capital goods. As a third device, certain consumers' goods, such as comfortable housing, are just not purchasable at any price for any but the few lucky persons of peculiar economic and political status.

By all such methods the Soviet authorities fight the battle against the price inflation that would otherwise burst out as workers try to spend their incomes on the limited supply of consumers' goods. To one who has studied modern economics, it is evident that these are devices by which their society determines For Whom goods will be produced in accordance with *social* decision making.

### NEW TRENDS IN EASTERN EUROPEAN ECONOMICS?

Communist economics is in a state of flux. In recent years, intense debates have broken out in Poland, Hungary, Czechoslovakia, and within Russia itself. These concern the use of some kind of pricing and profitability criteria that begin to approach a little the analytical tools of Western economics. Nineteenth-century Marxian concepts seem to be reserved for ideological training of the young and for alleged explanation and denouncement of capitalistic economies.

Among the high-level planners themselves, few words are squandered on such subjects. Instead, as in the much-debated writings of E. Liberman, there are attempts to get away from setting of crude quantitative goals expressed in physical units. There is to be emphasis on quality and on weighting items by their importance, setting for the plant manager the goal of maximizing something like a *profitability* magnitude. The hope is to get him to try new products and methods and to economize on input requirements, rather than to concentrate on establishing a low quota for his plant. Pilot experiments with markets are being planned.

Mathematical methods, such as the input-output analysis associated with W. W. Leontief of Harvard, have been released from Stalin's ban, and are debated as a possible tool for helping the planners allocate their available resources. More advanced methods, known in the West as linear and general mathematical programming, have been developed by eminent Soviet mathematicians (Kantorowich, Pontryagin, . . .); rates of discount, rather like the interest rates used in mixed economies to screen out less important capital projects, have been proposed in considerable variety.

Although it cannot be said that planners anywhere in the world rely primarily on the socialist game of a pricing system as described in Chapter 32's Appendix, there seems increasingly to be a pragmatic mixture of physical accounting and economic planning. And, remember, the pendulum oscillates between epochs of decentralization and of centralization.

It is a vulgar mistake to think that most people in Eastern Europe are miserable. Although it is undoubtedly true that few citizens of the West would trade their degree of economic comfort and political freedom for life in the Soviet, it is also true that a Soviet citizen thinks that he is living in a paradise in comparison with life in China or in earlier times. Remember that life under the Czars was no bed of roses for most classes; and to the eye of the traveler from impoverished Asia and Africa, the rising degree of Russian affluence must seem impressive.

## COMPARATIVE ECONOMIC GROWTH: THE FUTURE

Today we know many facts about the Russian system. Teams of our economic experts pore over U.S.S.R. statistics, and while they often find the data incomplete and occasionally deliberately misleading, the experts are largely in agreement that it is possible to make an objective appraisal of the approximate dimensions of the Russian economy. No longer is there any excuse for the extreme views that the Soviets are so hopelessly inefficient that they cannot keep even one Model T Ford in good repair, or that they are giants 7 feet tall who will soon outstrip everyone else in productivity.[7]

**Present status**    The basic facts, as audited by numerous independent scholars here and abroad, seem to be these: In the late 1970s the Soviet gross national product is between one-half and three-fourths of ours in size, depending on whether one makes

---

[7]Quite aside from a rash of bad grain harvests in the mid-1970s, agricultural performance still seems to be remarkably bad on the Russian collective and state farms. These appear to be much too large for efficiency, averaging 7,000 and 22,000 acres of sown land, in contrast to the 400-acre average of our efficient commercial farms. Uniform rules, ill-informed and subject to swings of fad and fashion, get imposed on everybody in a region. Supplies of tractor equipment, spare parts, fertilizers, and fungicides are quite limited, and optimal use is not made of them by the rural populace, who have little incentive to be efficient. Despite unfavorable weather, much-improved efficiency would seem technically feasible in the future.

this difficult comparison by using dollar price weights or ruble price weights.[8] By splitting the difference for the purpose of a rough approximate calculation, one can give a reasonable estimate:

**In the late 1970s, U.S.S.R. real GNP is about three-fifths United States real GNP, slightly up from the one-half of the early 1960s.**

Since the Soviet Union's population is larger than the American and since she devotes a smaller fraction of her GNP to consumption, it follows that her real consumption per capita is an even smaller fraction of ours—perhaps about 48 per cent. This conclusion of experts is confirmed by casual observation of visitors to Russia.

**Likely future**    But the issue that dominates debate is not the comparative strengths of the two economies now, but rather whether one is growing so much faster than the other as to be able to narrow or close the gap in the decades ahead. This led a decade ago to the great game of what used to be called "growthmanship." While it would be idle to deny that a great deal of nonsense has been talked and written about this subject and while the experts are the first to admit that their estimates are only approximations, there is a nucleus of objective economic fact that is deserving of impartial analysis.

Depending upon what years have been selected for comparison, one can say that America's real GNP grows at a long-term rate of about 4 per cent per year or a bit less. Although there is often talk of a 6 per cent growth rate as a goal for the United States, a careful canvass of economic experts of all shades of political opinion will suggest that most do not really think this likely in the decades ahead. Figure 43-1 therefore extrapolated from 1976 a range of U.S. growth rates, varying from the reasonably optimistic to the reasonably pessimistic.

Estimates for the Soviet Union are more difficult to make. All seem to agree that her post-World War II growth rates started out considerably greater than ours as a percentage per year,[9] even though they have not surpassed the performance of such mixed economies as West Germany and Japan. Furthermore, many experts believe that it is easier for an economy that starts out from a lower level of productivity to show high initial percentage improvement. (After all, to go from zero to any positive level is an infinite jump.) They suspect that, as the Soviet Union reaches stages of development more comparable with ours and places greater emphasis on services, she is likely to show a retardation in her rate of growth and may lose the advantage of

---

[8]There is a technical index-number problem involved that need only be indicated. Here luxuries are fairly plentiful compared with necessities; the opposite is the case there, as can be illustrated by the fact that the ratio of auto prices to rye-bread price will there be many times the price ratio here. Result: If we calculate real GNPs for both places using *their* ruble price ratios, our numerous autos will show up with terrific weight, and their GNP will be little more than one-third ours. By the same token, reckoned in dollar prices, their GNP will become considerably more than half ours.

[9]In the last dozen years both growth records were comparable. And it should be pointed out that, if our GNP is twice that of Russia, then to equal our *absolute* rate of growth, her percentage rate would now have to be twice ours. Expert testimony before Congress and elsewhere estimates the following percentage annual growth rates for the Soviet Union: 1950–1958, 6.8; 1955–1960, $6\frac{1}{2}$; 1958–1963, 4; 1963–1964, 3; 1964–1970, $5\frac{1}{2}$; 1970–1976, 4–6.

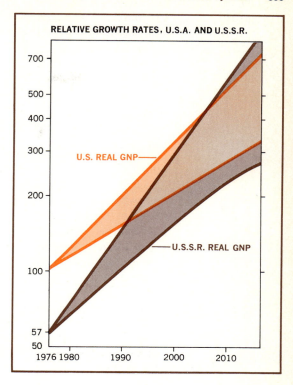

RELATIVE GROWTH RATES, U.S.A. AND U.S.S.R.

U.S. REAL GNP

U.S.S.R. REAL GNP

**FIG. 43-1**
Sizable gaps can narrow in future decades,
but discontinuous change is hardly likely
The range of estimates shown here can make no claim
to nice accuracy, but they do represent the spread of best
expert opinion. (NOTE: All indices have a base for U.S. real
GNP of 1976 = 100, and a base for U.S.S.R. real GNP of
1976 = 57.)

imitation of more advanced technologies. So they caution against blindly extrapolating the data of the recent past into the future.

Although there is much that is persuasive in such arguments, there is also the fact that they may provide temptingly optimistic rationalizations to patriots who are wishful that America can stay forever ahead. Moreover, the cases of Germany and other nations that are ahead of the Soviet Union in productivity, and yet seem to have hit a new rate of advance, warn us that such arguments of inevitable senility can, at least for a while, go into reverse. And although Marxians have in the past argued as if society were like a child, sure to go through certain inevitable stages of development, modern scholars know better than to be dogmatic about pronouncing on the *necessary* timeshape of industrial development. Consequently, in Fig. 43-1 the extrapolation for the Soviet Union shows a spread that can encompass both optimistic and pessimistic views.

It will be evident that the Soviet Union is unlikely to overtake our real GNP for a long time to come, and our per capita welfare level for a still longer time to come.

The gap between Western and Eastern living standards may narrow in the future as it has between regions of the affluent West. But economic history suggests that *continual evolution*, rather than discontinuous jumps, is the more probable pattern.

In concluding any comparison of the growth patterns of the two systems, the economist ought to state two cautions:

**Coexistence**    War strength today cannot be measured by real GNP alone. Military analysts estimate that the U.S.S.R. now mounts about the same military effort as does the United States. Her real GNP may be near half ours, but she devotes a larger fraction of the total to security purposes. Furthermore, both parties have innumerable nuclear bombs, and the U.S. and the U.S.S.R. enjoy a parity in the missile and warhead area. Therefore, it is not the case that the United States, even by considerably increasing the fraction of her GNP spent on defense, could thereby gain decisive military advantage. Hence, for those concerned with the power struggle, any retained superiority in real GNP is not a sufficient condition for complacency or belligerence.

Recall, too, the fact that the two systems are on trial in the eyes of many uncommitted underdeveloped nations. Even if the United States stays well ahead of the U.S.S.R., were we to stagnate and she to show a vastly more rapid percentage rate of growth, that might tempt neutrals to imitate in the years ahead the totalitarian pattern of "full speed ahead"—limitation on democratic and personal freedom, and collectivist decision to cut down ruthlessly on current consumption in order to enlarge capital formation and development.

## A FINAL VIEW: BUSINESS AND HUMAN FREEDOMS

We have studied the tools of economic analysis to understand how an economy works. Most of our chapters have been devoted to the mixed economy—not to the laissez faire dreamworld that never existed or to the utopia still unborn. And as that mixed economy changes, the tools to analyze it and its alternatives are ever in need of improvement.

There is a temptation for those living in the most prosperous part of the world to succumb to complacency, both about themselves and about their mixed economy. And indeed in our discussions of national-income determination, of microeconomic pricing, of growth and stabilization policies of the New Economics, there has appeared to be tremendous progress in comparison with even so recent a date as 1929.

**Aspirations**    But at the same time, objective analysis of things as they are shows there do remain many features of economic life which the concerned younger generation find ethically troublesome. What matters it to them that monopoly be less prevalent in 1980 than in 1900—if it still is too much prevalent, and if no great diminution has taken place since 1945? What to them that the poor are less numerous and less poor than they used to be—if still there persist stubborn inequalities of economic opportunity, and no strong reductions in inequality of income since 1945? In their eyes, how can a system be deemed satisfactory which still countenances discrimination by race, sex, religion, and ethnic affiliation? True, our modern economic world is better in many ways than the past. But more is now expected of it.

This raises unanswerable questions concerning the rate of improvement of the system. This has been a century of change in the mixed economy. But how fast is fast enough? How fast is too fast? You cannot expect a hungry mother in Appalachia to give the same answer to this question as a self-made tycoon. The role of value judgment can never be usurped by so-called "neutral science."

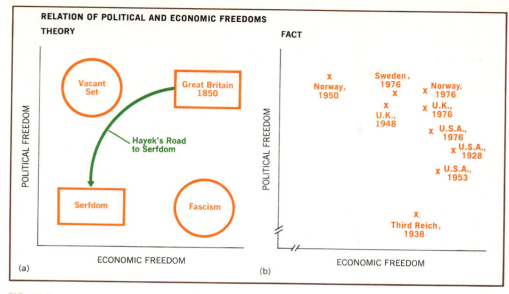

**FIG. 43-2**

**History and current experience question that economic reform must lead to serfdom**
The libertarian thesis of Hayek alleges—as in (a) on the left—that government modification of market laissez faire must lead *inevitably* to political serfdom. But confronting this hypothesis with the facts—as marshaled in (b) on the right—do we find it validated?

**Political and economic freedoms**   Beyond the internal questions of technical economics, there emerge basic political questions concerning the relationships between (a) *personal* freedoms—civil liberties and individual rights—and (b) *business or market* freedoms—property rights, freedom from price ceilings and floors, rationing, etc.

Almost always those who wish to reform the workings of the system wish to turn to government for new programs and measures. Those concerned to conserve what they regard as valuable in our society counter them with the arguments: "In seeking *a better division* of the pie, you will *reduce the size* of the pie by creating distorting inefficiencies. But more important, *personal and property freedoms are one and inseparable.* Only in the Herbert Spencer laissez faire society that you find so repellent will men be free to speak their minds and choose their rulers."

Here at the end of the book, after the major task of analyzing the economic world has been surveyed, perhaps an author can relax the rigor of analysis and speculate about what has not yet been capable of scientific agreement.

*What are the presumed relationships, suggested by experience and plausible reflection, between the state of individual freedoms and the interventions by government in the mixed economy?*

Figure 43-2 suggests an eclectic alternative to the despairing extreme of a Hayek who says, Economic reform is the road to serfdom. And perhaps suggests an alternative to the extreme of those who, like Sidney and Beatrice Webb, argued: Political democracy is nothing without the economic democracy that comes only with collective ownership of the means of production.

Speaking for myself, I venture to read in the face of history the more optimistic message: One can try to have the best of both worlds—programmed improvement of the workings of the market economy along with those best things of life that aren't measured in gross national product—freedom to do one's own thing, freedom to criticize, and freedom to change.

## CONCEPTS FOR REVIEW

laissez faire, mixed economy
anarchism, fascism, socialism, communism
nationalization of industry
indicative planning, French style
centralized planning, Soviet style
Yugoslavian hybrid

Maoist pattern in China
centralization and decentralization of planning
new U.S.S.R. pricing and profitability trends
comparative growth rates
economic freedoms, democracy

## QUESTIONS FOR DISCUSSION

1   Make a list of a number of "isms," describing each and its history.

2   Describe your own vision of Utopia. Does it differ from the present?

3   Compare and contrast fascism and communism. What is the relation of socialism and capitalism to each? To laissez faire and the mixed economy?

4   "The Russians claim they have 'industrial democracy.' This is clearly a different commodity from our political democracy. Even defenders of the Soviet Union will admit that expressions of opinion against the government or Communist party will not be tolerated. Free press—in our sense—is forbidden. Even if a majority of the Russian people were to prefer their form of government, no one should blind himself to its great differences from our own concepts of democracy and freedom." Discuss as objectively as you can.

5   Outline WHAT, HOW, and FOR WHOM in Russia.

6   What economic policies in the free world might predispose developing countries, like Ghana, Egypt, India, and Indonesia, to eschew totalitarian paths?

7   The U.S.S.R. is showing new interest in *input-output* and *linear programming* techniques. Review page 754's discussion of Leontief, and the sampling of linear programming on page 40.

8   Describe the problems of comparing growth rates in the United States and the U.S.S.R., in India and China, North and South Korea, East and West Germany.

9   Would you rather be born a 1978 baby in an India-like or a China-like economy? Contrast life expectancy and inequality in the old and the new China. Must the price of uniformity and collective control be paid?

# INDEX